THE ARLINGTON READER

Contexts and Connections

Second Edition

Lynn Z. Bloom
University of Connecticut

Louise Z. Smith
University of Massachusetts—Boston

Bedford/St. Martin's

Boston ◆ New York

For Bedford/St. Martin's

Developmental Editor: John Sullivan
Editorial Assistant: Alicia Mae Young
Production Supervisor: Andrew Ensor
Marketing Manager: Karita dos Santos
Project Management: Books By Design
Text Design: Jean Hammond
Photo Research: Naomi Kornhauser
Cover Design: Stephen Gleason
Cover Art: *Piazza del Duomo*, by Oliver Beran. Oil on canvas, 40 × 81 cm.
Composition: Achorn International, Inc.
Printing and Binding: RR Donnelley & Sons Company

President: Joan E. Feinberg
Editorial Director: Denise B. Wydra
Editor in Chief: Karen S. Henry
Director of Marketing: Karen Melton Soeltz
Director of Editing, Design, and Production: Marcia Cohen
Manager, Publishing Services: Emily Berleth

Library of Congress Control Number: 2007925239

For information, write: Bedford/St. Martin's, 75 Arlington Street, Boston, MA 02116   (617-399-4000)

ISBN-10: 0-312-44884-8
ISBN-13: 978-0-312-44884-4

Preface for Instructors

WHY THIS BOOK?

This new edition of *The Arlington Reader* presents a mix of class-tested and cutting-edge essays and graphic images designed not only to encourage discussion but also to provoke and address controversy. We hope to engage first-year composition students with topics that matter to them and to the world.

If the changes between the original *Arlington Reader* and this revision could be conveyed through a pair of images, you'd see the original as a spacious room with handsome furniture arranged in conversational clusters. The decor looks solid, substantial, classic. In the second edition some of the furniture has been moved out to make room for equally well-designed, more contemporary pieces. The atmosphere is enlivened with more graphics—photographs, cartoons, graphic essays—and the conversations and commentaries are more edgy.

The revisions to *The Arlington Reader* are based on our extensive experience as researchers, writing teachers, and discriminating readers of contemporary writing. This blend of wide reading, theory, research, and practical expertise governs the book's philosophy and pedagogy. *The Arlington Reader* aims to

- teach students how to read, write, and think critically at the college level.
- respond actively to written texts and illustrations, with reflection, critique, dialogue, and debate.
- enable students to read selected essays in their original cultural and intellectual contexts rather than as bodies of words floating free of time and place.
- differentiate and make connections among important ideas.
- introduce students to a wide range of excellent modern and contemporary prose writers and major thinkers whose works are central to a liberal education.
- acquaint students with what professionals in various disciplines think, value, and argue about as critically important in our contemporary world.
- help newcomers to American culture respect their own traditions and values while they are learning new ones.
- enable all students, irrespective of birth and background, to share in America's ever-changing multicultural values and viewpoints.

CRITERIA FOR INCLUSION IN *THE ARLINGTON READER*

For an essay to swim from the vast pool of essays being published every year in magazines, newspapers, and professional journals into a long life as a textbook favorite, teachers around the country have had to love it. They must find it relevant, exciting, well written, teachable—and of value to their students. Lynn Bloom's five years of research on the essay canon has identified the major essayists of the past fifty years, those whose essays have been the most widely reprinted in American college textbooks. This *teaching* canon is distinct from a *critical* canon, and it is unique. Although other literary canons—of works by novelists, poets, playwrights—are determined by editors, reviewers, and critics, the essay canon is the only one determined by teachers and, indirectly, by their students. It is not only the most democratic canon, but the one with the most real-world orientation, for the works in it may, indeed, constitute the core of a liberal education for many students nationwide. We include in each chapter several essays drawn from this canon, contextualized with additional materials. You will recognize the authors of long-standing reputation, among them Joan Didion, N. Scott Momaday, E. B. White, Richard Rodriguez, George Orwell, Maxine Hong Kingston, and Martin Luther King Jr.

To be included in *The Arlington Reader*, an essay must first and foremost be teachable; it must contribute to the intellectual, political, and rhetorical balance of the whole book; and it must serve as a good illustration of professional or literary writing, in substance and in style.

An essay's *teachability* is determined in part by its *accessibility*. How much do teachers have to know or learn in order to teach the work? Will students understand its concepts and vocabulary, with or without much explanation in class? Is it intellectually appropriate for them? Is it too technical, too allusive, too arty for students to stick with it? Is the essay short enough to be discussed in one or two class periods?

An essay's *balance with the rest of the book* is reflected in the ways that its topic, point of view, and moral and ethical stance contribute to the kinds of dialogue, debate, and critical thinking *The Arlington Reader* hopes to engender. Will it enlarge the students' understanding of the world or of a particular issue? Does the essay represent views and values that students should consider, confront, and either challenge or adopt? Does the author's reputation, stand on issues, ethnicity, or gender contribute to the anthology's balanced perspective?

An essay's *aesthetic qualities* are related to form and style. Is its *form* a good example of narration or description or definition or comparison and contrast and the rest? Are these rhetorical patterns woven into an argument in a compelling way? (since, it could be argued, every text is some kind of argument). Is the essay clearly organized? Is its *style* rich in sentence rhythms, vocabulary, figurative language, tone, even wit? Does the author "make it new," enabling readers to see the subject afresh?

FEATURES

Readings. *The Arlington Reader* includes a mix of class-tested and contemporary essays that instructors will enjoy teaching and students will enjoy reading. Numerous *classic authors*, spanning the centuries but primarily from the twentieth and twenty-first centuries, provide continuity and intellectual solidity in this collection of significant writing. Among them are Jonathan Swift, Charles Darwin, Henry David Thoreau, Stephen Jay Gould, Alice Walker, Martin Luther King Jr., and Annie Dillard. Distinguished *fresh voices* include authors from a variety of disciplines: Karen Armstrong (theology), Kenji Yoshino (law), Stephanie Coontz (sociology), Eric Liu (public affairs), Bill McKibben (science), and Elaine Scarry (English) bring contemporary perspectives to ideas debated in classic essays. *The Arlington Reader* also includes many women and multicultural authors, among them Sherman Alexie, Gloria Anzaldúa, Gloria Naylor, Leslie Silko, Alice Walker, and Amy Tan, who bring alternative views and contemporary voices to the classroom.

Reflecting the needs of today's instructors and the interests of today's students, *The Arlington Reader* offers essays that are excellent models of good writing in style and technique and that illustrate one or more significant rhetorical concerns such as argument, comparison and contrast, and narrative. The essays range from three to fifteen pages long, so they're brief enough to be taught in one or two class periods but substantial enough to elicit serious discussion and writing.

Thematic orientation. Nine thematic chapters address important areas of intellectual inquiry and controversy, intended to appeal to contemporary student writers. The chapters include (1) Writing, Reading, and Speaking; (2) Identity; (3) Relationships; (4) Education; (5) History; (6) Society and Politics; (7) Science and Technology; (8) Ethics; and (9) The World in the Future. The chapters are broad and flexible enough to encompass a variety of topics, and the range of disciplines allows students to work across a number of academic subject areas. An alternative *Rhetorical Table of Contents* allows this book to be easily adapted to individual instructors' needs.

Distinctive contextual materials. Throughout *The Arlington Reader*, contextual materials reveal authors' and readers' changing understandings of the essays. In each chapter, one or two classic, often-taught pieces are followed by a five- to ten-page cluster of related materials that allows instructors and students alike to understand these time-tested selections in greater depth. For instance, the context for George Orwell's classic "Shooting an Elephant" includes a photo of the author in 1923; an excerpt from Kipling's "The White Man's Burden," reinforced by historian John Kaye's enumeration of differences between Eastern and Western culture; Alok Rai's Marxist interpretation of Orwell; extracts of reviews from Stephen Spender, Christopher Sykes, and Edmund Wilson; and Robert Pearce's explanation of "why historians admire Orwell." Contextual materials add depth, freshness, and new perspectives to essays, and students see the sources, motives, and circumstances of an important piece of writing. These correlated readings also enable teachers to encourage student dialogues with the works they read, and to experiment with various forms of writing, gaining "textual power" as Robert Scholes recommends, by creating "a text in response to a text."

Photographs. Each chapter contains two or more photographs, many by well-known photographers; supplemented, at times, by cartoons and graphic essays.

The accompanying commentary is designed to help students learn to analyze images with the thoughtful, critical attention that leads to new insights. For example, in looking at Dorothea Lange's "Migrant Mother," the photograph that gave a human face to America's Great Depression in the 1930s, students are encouraged to consider humanitarian issues on a large as well as individual scale and to consult the Smithsonian Web site to see Lange's additional photographs of destitute Florence Owens Thompson and her seven hungry children.

Apparatus. Informative yet unobtrusive editorial commentary helps students move from critical reading to thoughtful writing and revising.

- *A unique two-part introduction* contains advice on critical reading to help students fully engage with the selections as well as advice on writing essays in a variety of genres. It guides students through the process of turning analytical reading into thoughtful writing.
- *Headnotes* supply a substantial biographical note about the author of each essay and provide historical, cultural, and rhetorical contexts for essays.
- *Reading and discussion questions* follow each essay, "Linked Readings" section, and "Brief Takes" section. They include open-ended suggestions for discussion, interpretation, commentary, or dissent in which the readers and writers using *The Arlington Reader* will have the last words. These questions help students to read, think, and write about the essay's content, style, and rhetorical strategies and to make connections with other readings in the book and with issues outside the text, as well.

Thorough and practical instructor's manual. *Resources for Teaching* THE ARLINGTON READER includes four suggested syllabi and commentary on each of the readings, offering practical classroom advice that serves the needs of novice and experienced instructors alike.

Companion Web site. Located at bedfordstmartins.com/arlington, it offers links to thematically related pieces and references *Re:Writing* (at bedfordstmartins.com/rewriting), the largest, most comprehensive collection of free resources for the writing class, with plagiarism tutorials, model documents, style and grammar exercises, visual analysis activities, research guides, bibliography tools, and much more.

NEW TO THIS EDITION

Edgier readings deal with current, controversial topics. In response to readers who asked for more contemporary pieces, including material on popular culture, we've added fifty-six readings calculated to provoke good discussion and good writing. For instance, a new section of Chapter 8, "Ethics," is concerned with issues of academic integrity. Research is addressed by Wendy Simonds's "Talking with Strangers." Potential pitfalls are considered in Kelly Ritter's discussions of "The Economics of Authorship: Online Paper Mills . . ." and G. Anthony Gorry's essay "Steal This MP3 File: What Is Theft?" The discussion continues in Michael

J. Bugeja's "Facing the Facebook." Other new pieces include Anna Quindlen on the ties of motherhood, Sara Ivry on entrance examinations, and Nicholas Sambanis on the state of things in Iraq.

Two new chapters explore relationships and the future. Chapter 3 addresses "Relationships and Life Choices: Where We Live and What We Live For." A new set of linked readings in Chapter 3 looks at contemporary families. It brings together Stephanie Coontz, whose "Blaming the Family for Economic Decline" examines the forces behind some disturbing trends, with Kate Zernike, who asks, "Why Are There So Many Single Americans?" David Brooks follows with an analysis of falling marriage rates in "The Elusive Altar," and Judith Wallerstein then looks at "The Legacy of Divorce." Chapter 9 explores "The Twenty-First-Century World: Issues of Ecology, War and Peace, Spirituality," addressing issues such as global climate change, human rights, and the inevitability—or not—of war.

"Linked Readings" present various views of one broad theme. In addition to the contextualized essays and related readings, each chapter has clusters of two or three selections, accompanied by resonant photographs, cartoons, or short quotations to extend the connections students can make among the materials. For example, Chapter 9, "The Twenty-First-Century World," includes Margaret Mead's assertion that "Warfare Is Only an Invention—Not a Biological Necessity," followed by a photograph of an Iraqi mother carrying her child through a rubble-strewn street while U.S. soldiers, armed and helmeted, and heavy military trucks go about the business of war. This is juxtaposed with Abraham Lincoln's "Gettysburg Address," Pope John XXIII's "Disarmament," and speeches by two Nobel Peace Prize recipients, Rigoberta Menchú and the fourteenth Dalai Lama. Students can therefore respond to a multinational, multicultural commentary on the fate of their world.

"Brief Takes" contain short selections on one theme and genre. Each chapter offers four to eight brief pieces on a single topic. For instance, in Chapter 1 "Brief Takes on Writing: How to Do It" addresses writing processes with eight short pieces of advice. Selections in each "Brief Takes" section range from a paragraph to a page or two and together provide enough material for one class, so instructors can get students talking and writing right away.

Visual essays present expanded dimensions. In addition to many more photographs, this edition of *The Arlington Reader* includes visual essays in the form of *cartoons*, such as Roz Chast's "The I.M.s of Romeo and Juliet," and *diagrams*, such as Henry Groskinsky, "Replaceable You." *Graphic essays* by Scott McCloud ("Reading the Comics"), Art Spiegelman ("Mein Kampf" and part of "Maus"), and Lynda Barry ("Hate") are a new and significant aspect of this edition; their detailed drawings represent complex and critical social messages that cannot be ignored.

A compact book presents an abundance of material. In response to users' requests, we've reduced the length of *The Arlington Reader*, yet we've added dimensions without sacrificing character and quality—it still includes abundant material for a wide range of classroom uses.

ACKNOWLEDGMENTS

We thank the following reviewers: Christopher Anderson, Texas State University; Pamela Joan Bentley, Northern New Mexico Community College; Emily Blair, Solano Community College; Debbie Cunningham, Adams State College; Lauren Dixon, Texas State University; Jessica Enoch, University of New Hampshire; Joshua P. Fenton, University of California–Riverside; Rebecca Fisher, Holyoke Community College; Katherine Gillen, University of New Hampshire; Donna L. Halper, University of Massachusetts; Amanda Hollis, Wake Technical Community College; Daniel Michael Keleher, Kennesaw State University; Lisa Drnec Kerr, Western New England College; Patricia Kimbrell, Houston Community College; Maxim J. Losi, Rider University; Jaime Armin Mejía, Texas State University; Thomas F. O'Connell, Cape Cod Community College; Amy Sattler, University of New Hampshire; Dawn Skorczewski, Emerson College; Michael Smith, James Madison University; Patricia Valdata, Neumann College; and Patrick Vecchio, St. Bonaventure University. We are also grateful to the reviewers who chose to remain anonymous.

In the first edition, Chuck Christensen, Joan Feinberg, and Nancy Perry were instrumental in the conception and evolution of *The Arlington Reader* from a canonical list to a finished book. Ning Yu brought his multicultural, Asian American scholar's perspective to a number of the headnotes and study questions and to the instructor's manual. Mark Gallaher and Matthew Simpson scrutinized our headnotes and questions and wrote some new ones, as did Matthew for the new edition. Kathrine Adeylott, crack researcher, was able to find everything we needed via the Web and in libraries; Susan Doheny found a number of pieces of art under a tight deadline; and Alice Lundoff expertly tracked down many obscure images. As always, George W. Smith gave quiet encouragement.

For this second edition, Denise M. Lovett, a novelist of distinction, has made significant revisions to the apparatus, as well as preparing the new material for the instructor's guide. Sandy Schechter and Sue Brekka oversaw text permissions and Naomi Kornhauser cleared permissions for art. Lori Corsini-Nelson helped with manuscript preparation. Emily Berleth and Herb Nolan supervised the book's production. Jennifer Lyford and Alicia Young handled innumerable details with good humor and patience. On this edition, as well as the first, John Sullivan coordinated the entire project, keeping track of thousands of details great and small, and keeping the work on target and on time with grace, good answers, and good will.

Our students over the years have been emphatic about what works and what doesn't; their experiences reverberate throughout *The Arlington Reader*. Martin Bloom, philosopher and social psychologist, has contributed his expertise and a parodist's intolerance of the banal and trivial, an attitude he shares with our students.

Contents

Preface for Instructors   iii

Introduction: Reading and Writing in Context   1

Reading in Context   1

Writing in Context   7

1   Writing, Reading, and Speaking: Words That Make Us Human   27

David Hanover, *The Work of Writing* [photograph]   27

Stephen King, *Write or Die*   28

"Write with the door closed, rewrite with the door open. Your stuff starts out being just for you, in other words, but then it goes out."

John F. Kennedy, *The Purpose of Poetry*   30

"When power leads man toward arrogance, poetry reminds him of his limitations."

Eudora Welty, *Listening*   33

"Ever since I was first read to, then started reading to myself, there has never been a line read that I didn't hear. As my eyes followed the sentence, a voice was saying it silently to me."

LINKED READINGS: OUR MOTHERS' VOICES

Amy Tan, *Mother Tongue*   38

"Language is the tool of my trade. And I use them all—all the Englishes I grew up with."

Amy Borkowsky, *Amy's Answering Machine*   42

"I think it's always easier to laugh at someone else's mother."

Marjorie Agosín, *Always Living in Spanish*   44

"How does one name the unfamiliar? How can one be another or live in a foreign language? These are the dilemmas of one who writes in Spanish and lives in translation."

Sherman Alexie, *The Joy of Reading and Writing: Superman and Me* 47

"I refused to fail. I was smart. I was arrogant. I was lucky. I read books late into the night. . . . I was trying to save my life."

LINKED READINGS: WHY READ?

Gloria Naylor, *The Love of Books* 51

"I felt trapped within my home and trapped within school, and it was through the pages of books that I was released into other worlds."

Richard Wright, from *Fighting Words* 57

". . . The impulse to dream had been slowly beaten out of me by experience. Now it surged up again and I hungered for books, new ways of looking and seeing."

Anne Fadiman, *Marrying Libraries* 60

"We . . . invested in our books the kind of emotion most people reserve for their old love letters."

LINKED READINGS: UNDERSTANDING TEXT AND CONTEXT

Scott McCloud, *Reading the Comics* [graphic essay] 62

"Every act committed to paper by the comics artist is *aided* and *abetted* by a *silent accomplice. . . . The Reader.*"

Deborah Franklin, *"Informed Consent"—What Information? What Consent?* 64

"If doctors' overreliance on consent forms is bad for patients who can read well, it is a disaster for the 21 percent . . . who read at a sixth-grade level or below, and for an additional 27 percent who . . . lack the proficiency needed to navigate the health care system easily."

Georgina Kleege, *Up Close, In Touch* 65

"I did not consciously work to conceal my blindness from my friends, but it was just often easier to pretend that I saw what they did."

Joan Didion, *On Keeping a Notebook* 73

"The impulse to write things down is a peculiarly compulsive one. . . ."

CONTEXTS for *On Keeping a Notebook* 79

Joan Didion, *Why I Write* 79 • Tom Wolfe, *The New Journalism* 81 • Joan Didion, *Last Words* 83 • *Interview (1999)* 84 • Wendy Bishop, *Revision is a Recursive Process* 85 • Katherine Anne Porter, *You Do Not Create a Style. You Work . . .* 86

Garrison Keillor, *The Anthem: If Famous Poets Had Written "The Star-Spangled Banner"* 88

"It was beautiful/So free/And so brave."

Dennis Baron, *The New Technologies of the Word* 92

"Three new written genres have emerged: email, the web page, and instant messaging now form a significant slice of writing practice" worldwide.

Roz Chast, *The I.M.s of Romeo and Juliet* [cartoon]   102

BRIEF TAKES ON WRITING: HOW TO DO IT   104

Roger Rosenblatt, *Never Correct Anybody's English* 104 • James Thurber, *Telling Stories* 104 • Rita Mae Brown, *Kissing Off Ma Bell* 105 • Ernest Hemingway, *Write Every Morning* 105 • Peter Elbow, *Freewriting* 106 • Anne Lamott, *Getting Started* 107 • Donald M. Murray, *Creating a Design* 108 • Jane Kenyon, *Have Good Sentences in Your Ears* 108

2   Identity With Attitude: Who We Are and How We Got That Way   110

Franz Boaz and George Hunt, *An Authentic Indian* [photograph]   110

John Henley, *The Graduates* [photograph]   111

Eric Liu, *Notes of a Native Speaker* 112

"The typical Asian I imagined, and the atypical Asian I imagined myself to be, were identical in this sense: neither was as much a creature of free will as a human being ought to be."

LINKED READINGS: RACE AND IDENTITY

James Baldwin, *Stranger in the Village* 118

"This world is white no longer, and it will never be white again."

W. E. B. Du Bois, *The "Veil" of Self-Consciousness* 127

"It is a peculiar sensation, this double-consciousness, this sense of always looking at one's self through the eyes of others, of measuring one's soul by the tape of a world that looks on in amused contempt and pity."

Esmeralda Santiago, *Jíbara* 129

"I wanted to be a *jíbara* more than anything world, but Mami said I couldn't because I was born in the city . . . If we were not *jíbaros*, why did we live like them?"

Bobbie Ann Mason, *Being Country* 135

"I felt inferior to people in town because we grew our food and made our clothes, while they bought whatever they needed. Although we were self-sufficient and resourceful and held clear title to our land, we lived in a state of psychological poverty."

Art Spiegelman, *Mein Kampf (My Struggle)* [graphic essay]   139
"It's all a matter of record: I made a comic book about it . . . you know . . . the one with Jewish mice and Nazi cats. . . . You've gotta boil everything down to its essence in comix. . . ."

Sherman Alexie, *What Sacagawea Means to Me*   142
"The Lewis and Clark Expedition was exactly the kind of multicultural, trigenerational, bigendered, animal-friendly, government-supported, partly French-Canadian project that should rightly be celebrated by liberals and castigated by conservatives."

N. Scott Momaday, *The Way to Rainy Mountain*   145
"Although my grandmother lived out her long life in the shadow of Rainy Mountain, the immense landscape of the continental interior lay like memory in her blood."

CONTEXTS for *The Way to Rainy Mountain*   151
Rainy Mountain [photograph] 151 • N. Scott Momaday, *East of My Grandmother's House* 152 • *I Invented History* 152 • *Disturbing the Spirits* 153 • *The Native Voice* 154 • *The Whole Journey* 155 • *Three Voices* 156 • Paula Gunn Allen, *Voice of the Turtle: American Indian Literature, 1900–1970* 156 • *Portrait of N. Scott Momaday* [photograph] 157

Gloria Anzaldúa, From *Beyond Traditional Notions of Identity*   159
"Today we need to move beyond separate and easy identifications, creating bridges that cross race and other classifications among different groups via intergenerational dialogue."

Thomas Jefferson, *George Washington*   161
"Never did nature and fortune combine more perfectly to make a man great. . . ."

Paul Starobin, *Misfit America*   164
American culture contains a unique and "striking combination of deep religious faith and nearly libertarian social permissiveness. These qualities don't rub elbows easily. . . ."

Deirdre N. McCloskey, *Yes, Ma'am*   173
"It's hard to pass. . . . You'll be surprised at how many gender clues there are and how easy it is to get them wrong."

BRIEF TAKES ON CREATIVITY: INTERVIEWS   180
Alice Walker, *Eudora Welty: An Interview* 180 • Kenneth A. Brown, *Steve Wozniak: Inventing the PC* 181 • Dave Roberts, *An Interview with Accidental Movie Star Al Gore* 183 • Frances Mayes, *Interview: On Writing Under the Tuscan Sun* 184 • Calvin Trillin, *Writing about Family* 185

3 Relationships and Life Choices: Where We Live and What We Live For   187

LINKED READINGS: THOREAU'S CHOICES

Henry David Thoreau, *Where I Lived and What I Lived For*   187
"I went to the woods because I wished to live deliberately, to front only the essential facts of life, and see if I could not learn what it had to teach, and not, when I came to die, discover that I had not lived."

Henry David Thoreau, from *Civil Disobedience*   192
"It is not desirable to cultivate a respect for the law, so much as for the right. The only obligation which I have a right to assume is to do at any time what I think is right."

E. B. White, *Once More to the Lake*   194
"I began to sustain the illusion that [my stepson] was I; and therefore, by simple transposition, that I was my father. . . . I seemed to be living a dual existence."

CONTEXTS for *Once More to the Lake*   199
E. B. White at Belgrade Lake [photograph] 199 • Brian Doyle, *Joyas Voladoras* 200 • Chang-Rae Lee, *Coming Home Again* 200 • Scott Russell Sanders, *The Inheritance of Tools* 202

LINKED READINGS: LOST PARENTS

Scott Russell Sanders, *Under the Influence: Paying the Price of My Father's Booze*   209
"I did not cause my father's illness, nor could I have cured it. Yet for all this grownup knowledge, I am still ten years old, my own son's age, and as that boy I struggle in guilt and confusion to save my father from pain."

Anna Quindlen, *Anniversary*   219
"No matter what others may see, or she herself thinks, we believe down to our bones that our mother's greatest calling was us; with that fulcrum to our lives gone, we become adults overnight."

David Sedaris, *Old Faithful*   222
"I needed a boyfriend as conventional as I was, and luckily I found one. . . ."

LINKED READINGS: FAMILIES, TOGETHER AND APART

Stephanie Coontz, *Blaming the Family for Economic Decline*   228
"The fallback position for those in denial about the socioeconomic transformation we are experiencing is to admit that many families are in economic stress but to blame their plight on divorce and unwed motherhood."

Kate Zernike, *Why Are There So Many Single Americans?* 233

". . . Someone who is educated is more likely to marry someone who is educated, and someone who is not educated is more likely to marry someone who is not educated."

David Brooks, *The Elusive Altar* 236

". . . The fact that many more people are getting divorced or never marrying at all is not such good news."

Judith Wallerstein, *The Legacy of Divorce* 238

"What are the consequences for all of us when 25 percent of people today between the ages of eighteen and forty-four have parents who divorced? What does it mean to a society when people wonder aloud if the family is about to disappear?"

Walker Evans, *Ford River Rouge Plant, Michigan, 1947* [photograph] 242

Barbara Ehrenreich, *Serving in Florida* 243

"Managers can sit—for hours at a time if they want—but it's their job to see that no one else ever does, even when there's nothing to do, and this is why, for servers, slow times can be as exhausting as rushes."

LINKED READINGS: COMING TO AN UNDERSTANDING

Malcolm Gladwell, *The Physical Genius* 251

"When psychologists study people who are expert at motor tasks, they find that almost all of them use their imagination in a very particular and sophisticated way."

Perri Klass, *The One-in-a-Thousand Illness You Can't Afford to Miss* 260

". . . To treat it, you need to diagnose it . . . and to diagnose it, you need to think about it."

Nancy Andreasen, *The Creative Mind* 262

". . . Openness to new experience often permits creative people to observe things that others cannot, because they do not wear the blinders of conventionality when they look around them."

Evan Eisenberg, *Dialogue Boxes You Should Have Read More Carefully* [graphic essay] 264

"Are you sure you want to restart your computer now? If you do, all open applications will be closed and the Windows operating system will be bundled with the genetic code of your future offspring."

BRIEF TAKES ON TRAVEL: REPORTS FROM OTHER PLACES 267

Kyoko Mori, *Date Stamp* 267 • Paul Theroux, *Every Trip Is Unique* 267 • Mark Twain, *Learning the River* 268 • E. Annie Proulx, *Travel Is . . . an*

Unnerving Experience 269 • Ryszard Kapuscinski, *The Truck: Hitchhiking through Hell* 271 • Mary Morris, *My First Night Alone in Mexico* 272

4 Education and the American Character: Issues of Economics, Politics, and Culture 273

Jonathan Kozol, *The Human Cost of an Illiterate Society* 273
"What do I do if one of my kids starts choking? I go running to the phone . . . I can't look up the hospital phone number."

Shirley Brice Heath, *Literate Traditions* 280
"Jointly or in group affairs, the children of Trackton read to learn before they go to school to *learn to read.*"

LINKED READINGS: NATIVE AMERICAN PERSPECTIVES

Leslie Marmon Silko, *Language and Literature from a Pueblo Indian Perspective* 287
"The stories are always bringing us together, keeping this whole together, keeping this family together, keeping this clan together."

Zitkala-Sa, From *The School Days of an Indian Girl* 292
"I was . . . neither a wild Indian nor a tame one. This deplorable situation was the effect of my brief course in the East, four years in a boarding school run by whites."

Stephanie Maze, *Literacy in Progress* [photograph] 297

Richard Rodriguez, *Aria: A Memoir of a Bilingual Childhood* 298
"I was a bilingual child, but of a certain kind: 'socially disadvantaged,' the son of working-class parents, both Mexican immigrants."

CONTEXTS for *Aria: A Memoir of a Bilingual Childhood* 307
Rodriguez at Eighteen [photograph] 307 • Richard Rodriguez, *Interview Excerpt* 308 • *Slouching towards Los Angeles* 308 • *Rodriguez as a Mask* [photograph] 309 • Octavio Paz, *The Labyrinth of Solitude* 310 • José Antonio Villarreal, *Pocho* 311 • Richard Hoggart, *The Uses of Literacy* 312 • Paul Zweig, *The Child of Two Cultures* 314 • Richard Rodriguez, *Interview (1999)* 315

Natalie Behring, *The Entrance Exam* [photograph] 318

Plato, *The Allegory of the Cave* 319
"In the world of knowledge, the last thing to be perceived and only with great difficulty is the essential Form of Goodness. . . . Without having had a vision of this Form no one can act with wisdom, either in his own life or in matters of state."

LINKED READINGS: MEASURING INTELLIGENCE

Howard Gardner, *Who Owns Intelligence?* 322
"All human beings possess at least eight intelligences: linguistic and logical-mathematical . . . , musical, spatial, bodily-kinesthetic, naturalist, interpersonal, and intrapersonal."

Sara Ivry, *Entrance Exams, Deconstructed* 335
"The best way to develop your range of vocabulary is by reading. If you're a big reader, you're going to tend to be a better writer as well."

American Institutes for Research, *American College Grads — Barely Literate, and Beyond* 337
"More than 75 percent of students at 2-year colleges and more than 50 percent of students at 4-year colleges do not score at the proficient level of literacy."

BRIEF TAKES ON THE UPRIGHT LIFE: GOOD ADVICE   339
Benjamin Franklin, *Arriving at Moral Perfection* 339 • Ben Stein, *Birds and Bees? No, Let's Talk About Dollars and Cents* 341 • Theodore Roosevelt, *What College Graduates Owe America* 343 • Jackie Spinner, *The Only Thing You Should Be Advocating Is the Truth* 344 • Jacob Neusner, *The Speech the Graduates Didn't Hear* 346 • David Sedaris, *What I Learned/And What I Said at Princeton* 348 • Anonymous, *How Many Virginia University Students Does It Take to Change a Lightbulb?* 349

5   History: What Really Happened? How Do We Know or Decide What It Means?   351

Dorothea Lange, *Migrant Mother* [photograph]   351

Alice Walker, *In Search of Our Mothers' Gardens* 352
"How was the creativity of the Black woman kept alive, year after year and century after century, when for most of the years Black people have been in America, it was a punishable crime for a Black person to read and write."

CONTEXTS for *In Search of Our Mothers' Gardens*   360
James Baldwin, *Autobiographical Notes* 360 • Amiri Baraka, *The Myth of Negro Literature* 361 • Daniel Patrick Moynihan, *The Negro Family: The Case for National Action* 362 • Alice Walker, *Looking to the Side, and Back* 364 • *My Grandmother Takes in Washing* [poster] 366 • Alice Walker, *Interview (1983)* 367 • Toni Morrison, *The Pain of Being Black* 368

Thomas Jefferson, *The Declaration of Independence* 369

"We hold these truths to be self-evident, that all men are created equal, that they are endowed by their Creator with certain unalienable Rights, that among these are Life, Liberty, and the pursuit of Happiness."

Sojourner Truth, *Ain't I a Woman?* 373

"I could work as much and eat as much as a man—when I could get it—and bear the lash as well! Ain't I a woman? I have borne thirteen children, and seen them most all sold off to slavery. . . . Ain't I a woman?"

Elizabeth Cady Stanton, *Declaration of Sentiments* 375

"We hold these truths to be self-evident: that all men and women are created equal . . . "

George Orwell, *Shooting an Elephant* 378

"It was a tiny incident in itself, but it gave me a better glimpse of . . . the real motives for which despotic governments act."

CONTEXTS for *Shooting an Elephant* 384

Blair in 1923 [photograph] 384 • Rudyard Kipling, *The White Man's Burden* 384 • John Kaye, *History of the Indian Mutiny of 1857–8* 385 • Alok Rai, *Orwell and the Politics of Despair* 386 • Stephen Spender (1950) 386 • Christopher Sykes (1950) 387 • Edmund Wilson (1951) 388 • Robert Pearce, *Orwell Now* 388

Linda Simon, *The Naked Source* 390

"What students really need to learn, more than 'history,' is a sense of the historical method of inquiry . . . they need to practice, themselves, confronting sources, making judgments, and defending conclusions."

Will Counts, *Central High School, Little Rock, Arkansas, September 4, 1957* [photograph] 396

LINKED READINGS: DIFFICULT IMAGES

Susan Sontag, *Looking at the Unbearable* 397

The eighty-two prints in Goya's *Disasters of War* "are meant . . . to awaken, shock, rend."

Francisco Goya, from *The Disasters of War* [paintings] 400

H. Bruce Franklin, *From Realism to Virtual Reality: Images of American Wars* 402

"The logic of this comic-book militarism, put into practice for each of America's wars since Vietnam, is inescapable: photographers must be allowed to image for the public only what the military deems suitable."

BRIEF TAKES ON WAR AND PEACE: DIARIES AND MEMOIRS   414
Walt Whitman, *A Night Battle* 414 • Mary Chesnut, *Slavery a Curse to Any Land* 415 • Anne Frank, *We Live in a Paradise Compared to the Jews Who Aren't in Hiding* 416 • Art Spiegelman, from *Maus* [graphic essay] 418

6   Society and Politics: Human Rights, Social Class   420

Maxine Hong Kingston, *No Name Woman*   420
"Chinese-Americans, when you try to understand what things in you are Chinese, how do you separate what is peculiar to childhood, to poverty, insanities, one family . . . from what is Chinese? What is Chinese tradition and what is the movies?"

CONTEXTS for *No Name Woman* 429
Maxine Hong Kingston, *Interview (1982)* 429 • *Maxine Hong Kingston* [photograph] 430 • Sara Blackburn, *Review of* The Woman Warrior 431 • Maxine Hong Kingston, *Interview (1998)* 431 • *Interview (1982)* 433 • Frank Chin, *Come All Ye Asian American Writers of the Real and the Fake* 434 • Maxine Hong Kingston, *Imagined Life* 435 • Paula Rabinowitz, *Eccentric Memories: A Conversation with Maxine Hong Kingston* 436

Lynda Barry, *Hate* [graphic essay]   438
The substitute teacher "was the first person to explain the difference between the kind of hate that has destructive intent and the kind that's a response to something destructive."

Harriet Jacobs, *The Slaves' New Year's Day*   449
"But to the slave mother New Year's day comes laden with peculiar sorrows. She sits on her cold cabin floor, watching the children who may all be torn from her the next morning; and often does she wish that she and they might die before the day dawns."

Frederick Douglass, *Resurrection*   452
"You have seen how a man was made a slave; you shall see how a slave was made a man."

Kenji Yoshino, *The Pressure to Cover*   456
"Covering"—playing down a "disfavored trait so as to blend into the mainstream"—is the "civil rights issue of our time."

Bob Daemmrich, *Nobody Knows I'm Gay* [photograph]   468

Jonathan Swift, *A Modest Proposal*   469

"I have been assured . . . that a young healthy child well nursed is at a year old a most delicious, nourishing, and wholesome food, whether stewed, roasted, baked, or broiled. . . ."

Wole Soyinka, *Every Dictator's Nightmare*   475

"There is . . . a nobler idea . . . that has now begun to flourish: the idea that certain fundamental rights are inherent to all humanity."

Richard A. Posner, *Security versus Civil Liberties*   480

In the presence of threats "from international terrorism . . . our civil liberties . . . should be curtailed, to the extent that the benefits in greater security outweigh the costs in reduced liberty."

Elaine Scarry, *Acts of Resistance*   484

"The objective of the Patriot Act becomes even clearer if it is understood concretely as making the population *visible* and the Justice Department *invisible*. The Act inverts the constitutional requirement that people's lives be private and the work of government official be public."

Mary Ellen Mark, *The Damm Family in Their Car, Los Angeles, 1987* [photograph]   491

BRIEF TAKES FROM INSIDERS: CODES, CONVERSATIONS, CONVENTIONS   492

Richard Rodriguez, *Family Values* 492 • Cathy Davidson, *Laughing in English* 493 • Henry Louis Gates Jr., *Signifying* 494 • Beth Kephart, *Playing for Keeps* 496 • Robert Coles, *Two Languages, One Soul* 496

7   Science and Technology: Discovery, Invention, and Controversy   498

Ellen Goodman, *Cure or Quest for Perfection?*   498

"Using clusters of cells to cure suffering of existing humans passes the moral threshold test."

Bill McKibben, *Designer Genes*   500

"Suppose parents could add thirty points to their child's IQ? Wouldn't you want to do it? . . . Deciding not to soup them up . . . well, it could come to seem like child abuse."

Henry Groskinsky, *Replaceable You* [photograph]   511

Stephen Jay Gould, *Evolution as Fact and Theory*   512

"Well, evolution is a theory. It is also a fact. And facts and theories are different things, not rungs in a hierarchy of increasing certainty. Facts are the world's data. Theories are structures of ideas that explain and interpret facts. Facts do not go away when scientists debate rival theories to explain them. Einstein's theory of gravitation replaced Newton's, but apples did not suspend themselves in mid-air pending the outcome."

CONTEXTS for *Evolution as Fact and Theory*   518

Thomas Henry Huxley, *Evolution and Ethics* 518 • Phillip E. Johnson, *The Unraveling of Scientific Materialism* 520 • James Gleick, *Stephen Jay Gould: Breaking Tradition with Darwin* 523

Charles Darwin, *Understanding Natural Selection*   525

"Natural selection is daily and hourly scrutinizing, throughout the world, every variation, even the slightest; rejecting that which is bad, preserving and adding up all that is good; silently and insensibly working . . . at the improvement of each organic being in relation to its organic and inorganic conditions of life."

Edward O. Wilson, *Microbes 3, Humans 2*   530

"I am unwilling to give up entirely the quest for successful species. So let me use subjective, human-oriented criteria to pin some gold medals on members of the world's fauna and flora."

Stanley Fish, *Academic Cross-Dressing: How Intelligent Design Gets Its Arguments from the Left*   532

"Intelligent Designers and Holocaust deniers . . . play the same shell game; they both say: Look here, in the highest reaches of speculation about inquiry in general, and not there, in the places where the particular, nitty-gritty work of inquiry is actually being done."

Natalie Angier, *Men, Women, Sex, And Darwin*   538

"It needn't be argued that men and women are exactly the same, or that humans are meta-evolutionary beings, removed from nature and slaves to culture, to reject the perpetually regurgitated model of the coy female and the ardent male."

LINKED READINGS: BAD SCIENCE   548

Norimitsu Onishi, *In a Country That Craved Respect, Stem Cell Scientist Rode a Wave of Korean Pride*   548

The "spectacular rise and fall" of Korean stem cell scientist Dr. Hwang Woo Suk, perpetrator of "one of the biggest scientific frauds in recent history, took place in the crucible of a country whose deep-rooted insecurities had been tempered by a . . . yearning for international recognition."

Robert L. Park, *The Seven Warning Signs of Bogus Science*   551

"Spotting voodoo science is a skill that every citizen should develop."

David Dobbs, *Trial and Error*   555

"Peer review was meant to ensure candid evaluations and elevate merit over personal connections. But its anonymity allows reviewers to do sloppy work, steal ideas or delay competitors' publication by asking for elaborate revisions (it happens) without fearing exposure. And it catches error and fraud no better than good editors do."

BRIEF TAKES ON TECHNOLOGY: WRITING HUMOR   559

James Thurber, *The Wild-Eyed Edison's Dangerous Experiments* 559 • Erma Bombeck, *Technology's Coming . . . Technology's Coming* 560 • Bailey White, *Flying Saucer* 561 • Fran Lebowitz, *The Sound of Music: Enough Already* 562 • Umberto Eco, *Ideal Operating Instructions* 563

8   Ethics: Principles and Actions   565

Martin Luther King Jr., *Letter from Birmingham Jail*   565

"An individual who breaks a law that conscience tells him is unjust, and who willingly accepts the penalty of imprisonment in order to arouse the conscience of the community over its injustice, is in reality expressing the very highest respect for the law."

CONTEXTS for *Letter from Birmingham Jail*   578

Brooks Hays, *A Southern Moderate Speaks* 579 • *Eight Clergymen's Statement* 580 • *King and Abernathy Under Arrest* [photograph] 581 • King and Abernathy [photograph] 582 • *Two Christians' Responses to King's Views* 582 • T. Olin Binkley, *Southern Baptist Seminaries* 583 • Will Herberg, *A Religious "Right" to Violate the Law?* 583 • Martin Luther King Jr., *Boycotts Will Be Used* 586 • *Martin Luther King Defines "Black Power"* 586

Leonard Freed, *Martin Luther King Jr. after Receiving the Nobel Peace Prize, Baltimore 1963* [photograph]   589

John Donne, *Meditation*   590

"No man is an island, entire of itself; every man is a piece of the continent, a part of the main."

Jeffrey Wattles, *The Golden Rule—One or Many, Gold or Glitter?*   592

"The golden rule, happily, has more than a single sense. It is not a static, one-dimensional proposition with a single meaning to be accepted or rejected . . . but is a symbol of a process of growth on emotional, intellectual, and spiritual levels."

Anna Quindlen, *Uncle Sam and Aunt Samantha* 598
"Only men are required to register for the military draft that would be used in the event of a national-security crisis."

Peter Singer, *The Singer Solution to World Poverty* 601
"I'm saying that you shouldn't buy that new car, take that cruise, redecorate the house or get that pricey new suit. After all, a $1,000 suit could save five children's lives."

George F. Will, *Life and Death at Princeton* 607
Singer's utilitarianism notwithstanding, "there is heightened receptivity to philosophies that recognize that dependence on others is a universal and permanent fact of every life, throughout life."

Wendy Simonds, *Talking with Strangers: A Researcher's Tale* 611
"I continually struggle with the research process and feel uncomfortable in my roles as interrogator and observer. Am I more than an intruder, a voyeur, a manipulator? I hope I am."

Kelly Ritter, *The Economics of Authorship: Online Paper Mills, Student Writers, and First-Year Composition* 615
"What is the complicated relationship . . . between student authors and consumer culture that dictates the role that writing plays in one's college career?"

G. Anthony Gorry, *Steal This MP3 File: What Is Theft?* 622
"What should we make of the typical admonition on compact-disc covers that unauthorized duplication is illegal? Sure the MP3 file was a duplication of the original. To what extent is copying stealing?"

Michael J. Bugeja, *Facing the Facebook* 626
"Facebook . . . is a Janus-faced symbol of the online habits of students and the traditional objective of higher education, one of which is to inspire critical thinking in learners rather than multitasking. . . . The situation will only get worse as freshmen enter . . . equipped with gaming devices, cell phones, iPods, and other portable technologies."

Frank Gannon, *Pre-approved for Platinum* 631
"Dear Occupant: You've been pre-approved!"

BRIEF TAKES ON ETHICAL CODES: PRESCRIPTIONS FOR THE GOOD LIFE 634
Confucius, from *The Analects* 634 • *The Ten Commandments* 636 • *Fundamentals of Islam* 636 • Society of Professional Journalists *Code of Ethics* 638

9   The Twenty-First-Century World: Issues of Ecology, War and Peace, Spirituality   641

Annie Dillard, *Heaven and Earth in Jest*   641
"In the Koran, Allah asks, 'The heaven and the earth and all in between, thinkest thou that I made them *in jest?*' It's a good question. What do we think of the created universe, spanning an unthinkable void with an unthinkable profusion of forms?"

CONTEXTS for *Heaven and Earth in Jest*   649
Henry David Thoreau, from *Journal* 649 • From the Koran, *Al-Mu'Menoon ("The Believers"), Verses 112–116* 651 • Blaise Pascal, from *Pensées* 652 • Nikos Kazantzakis, *Report to Greco* 652 • Wendell Berry, *A Secular Pilgrimage* 653

Keith Carter, *Fireflies* [photograph]   655

Terry Tempest Williams, *The Clan of One-Breasted Women*   656
"I belong to a Clan of One-Breasted Women. My mother, my grandmothers, and six aunts have all had mastectomies. Seven are dead. The two who survive have just completed rounds of chemotherapy and radiation."

Rachel Carson, *The Obligation to Endure*   663
"We allow the chemical death rain to fall as though there were no alternative, whereas in fact there are many, and our ingenuity could soon discover many more if given opportunity."

LINKED READINGS: GEOGRAPHY AND ECOLOGY   669

Barry Lopez, *The American Geographies*   669
"As Americans, we profess a sincere and fierce love for the American landscape, for our rolling prairies, free-flowing rivers, and 'purple mountains' majesty'; but it is hard to imagine, actually, where this particular landscape is."

Sandra Postel, *Troubled Waters*   675
"The tragedy of the Aral Sea is by no means unique. Around the world countless rivers, lakes, and wetlands are succumbing to dams, river diversions, rampant pollution, and other pressures."

Kim Warp, *Rising Sea Levels—An Alternative Theory* [cartoon]   677

William E. Rees, *Life in the Lap of Luxury as Ecosystems Collapse*   678
"We are accustomed to expecting a future of more and bigger, of freewheeling technological mastery over the natural world. But that road leads inevitably to a dead end."

Margaret Mead, *Warfare Is Only an Invention—Not a Biological Necessity*   682

Warfare "is not inevitable . . . it is due to historical accident. . . . " It is "a defective social institution."

Jim MacMillan, *Family and Soldiers in Iraq* [photograph]   689

Abraham Lincoln, *The Gettysburg Address*   690

"The government of the people, by the people, for the people, shall not perish from the earth."

Pope John XXIII, *Disarmament*   691

"Nothing is lost by peace; everything may be lost by war."

LINKED READINGS: NOBEL PEACE PRIZE ACCEPTANCE SPEECHES   694

Rigoberta Menchú, *Five Hundred Years of Major Oppression*   694

"Who can predict what other great scientific conquests and developments those [Mayan] people could have achieved, if they had not been conquered in blood and fire, and subjected to an ethnocide that affected nearly 50 million people in the course of 500 years."

The Dalai Lama (Tenzin Gyatso), *Inner Peace and Human Rights*   697

"Peace . . . starts with each one of us. When we have inner peace, we can be at peace with those around us. When our community is in a state of peace, it can share that peace with neighboring communities."

Karen Armstrong, *Does God Have a Future?*   702

"All religions change and develop. If they do not, they will become obsolete." Consequently, "each generation has to create its own imaginative concept of God."

David Owen, *Your Three Wishes: F.A.Q.*   713

"Do my wishes have an expiration date?"

Rhetorical Index   725

Index of Titles and Authors   737

Introduction:
Reading and Writing in Context

READING IN CONTEXT

For each chapter's context essay, *The Arlington Reader* provides Context readings. You can think of the Contexts as a room with many groups of people in conversation, each group discussing a series of questions and answers. Someone entering the room listens for a while to the conversations, identifies the question others are talking about (anywhere from "Which film will win the Academy Award for Best Picture?" to "How can the United States foster peace in the Middle East?"), finds something relevant to say about it, and thus evokes others' answers. Likewise, every piece of writing enters into conversation with others; it has its say and is answered by later writing. Every text—from a grocery list to a political speech to a sonnet—answers a question even as it raises other questions. Interpretation depends on readers' answers to questions the text is raising, sometimes many answers to many questions. The contextualized essays, widely reprinted and often beloved, remain central because they raise a multitude of fundamental questions ("What is the meaning of truth, beauty, justice, life itself?") even as they provide a wealth of answers that many generations of readers find useful. Writers work not in a vacuum but in a world of words—other people's speaking and writing as well as their own. Therefore, writers always have other texts (their questions and answers) in mind when they sit down to write a new piece, and they expect some of their readers to have some of those texts in mind, too.

Sometimes writers explicitly signal such expectations. For instance, Richard Rodriguez opens the prologue to his *Hunger of Memory* (see "Aria" p. 298) with "I have taken Caliban's advice. I have stolen their books. I will have some run of this isle." In one stroke, Rodriguez tells readers that he expects us to share his knowledge of at least some of the following things about Caliban.

- He is the character in *The Tempest* whom Shakespeare describes as "savage and deformed."
- He lives alone on his island until Prospero, the highly educated Duke of Milan, arrives, enslaves him, and teaches him to talk.

1

- He represents "natural man" to some people.
- He represents native peoples oppressed by imperialism to others.

This sort of reference, in which a word or phrase calls forth a whole cluster of information and associations in the readers whom a writer imagines addressing, is called *allusion*. Some readers will recognize Caliban, and others won't. That is how writers establish solidarity with some readers and, just as important, how they set themselves apart from others. Even if we don't recognize Caliban, Rodriguez expects that as we read we will pick up enough clues from other things he says about Caliban to keep us going as we seek and construct meaning. As we read the "Aria," we'll gradually understand what Caliban's having "stolen their books" has to do with Rodriguez.

Most of the time, however, writers are much less explicit about which works they assume readers already know or know about. Neither in "Why I Write" (p. 79) nor in "On Keeping a Notebook" (p. 73) does Joan Didion explicitly mention the kind of reporting that she helped to invent—and that these two essays illustrate: the 1960s' New Journalism. Yet works by Didion and other New Journalists (such as Tom Wolfe, p. 81) form the contemporary context that helps us understand "On Keeping a Notebook" much better than if we read it simply as a statement of Didion's personal interests. By reading her essays on other writers, reviews of her books, and other texts (including ads, films, and news reports) that were part of the conversation she was participating in, we can infer the contemporary context of her works. By inferring, we can imaginatively enter her world to some extent, though never entirely: as readers, each of us always has to stand in our own historical and cultural moment. There is no such thing as a static reader, a timeless and universal being whose reaction to a text is always predictably the same. As time ceaselessly moves on, our readings of necessity change to accommodate whatever is relevant at the time in the world, in our own lives.

Besides paying attention to earlier contexts (like *The Tempest* for Rodriguez) and to contemporary contexts (like the New Journalism for Didion), we also need to look at the ways people who read a text long after it was written view it. As you already know, a work becomes canonical when generations of readers have found it useful. However, later readers don't all use it the same way. For example, 1940s readers used E. B. White's "Once More to the Lake" (p. 194) to find pleasure in its elegant, gently witty style and to find comfort during wartime in its portrayal of a prewar world (the Nazis had occupied Paris since June 1940 and by June 1941 had widened World War II by invading the Soviet Union). In fact, some readers even thought that White's essay encapsulated the very way of life that American G.I.s were fighting to protect and yearning to come home to. In the postwar period—indeed, throughout the rest of the twentieth century—this essay has maintained its role as a model of style for college writers. But readers also found new uses for it. In the 1980s, some used the essay to examine mythic and psychoanalytic elements in a father's confronting his own mortality through his son's unawareness of death. In the 1990s, some used the essay to represent white, male, middle-class complacency about differences in race, gender, and class. They criticized White for not addressing issues he could not have anticipated when he was writing half a century earlier. As "multiculturalism" and "diversity" increasingly displaced "style" in college composition courses, "Once More to the Lake" began to disappear from composition textbooks. Some day it may return, however, if readers find other relevant meanings, as happened when people stopped reading Louisa May Alcott's *Little Women* (1868) entirely as a children's classic and began using it to document feminist arguments about gender roles and women's education.

A multitude of other readings from many perspectives, far too many to represent in this book, forms the contexts for each of *The Arlington Reader*'s nine contextualized essays. (Moreover, as you realize by now, *every* piece of writing has its contexts.) Each writing in the context cluster focuses on the theme, topic, or background of the lead essay.

Reading Interpretively

How else would you read?

If that was your first reaction to our heading, then you're already doing it. That is, a voice in your head is already conversing with the voice on the page, asking, "What does 'interpretively' say that 'reading' doesn't already say?" or "Is there some kind of 'reading' that's not 'interpretive'?" As you talk back — reacting, questioning, and constructing responses — you are creating meaning. That's interpretation: a creative conversation between the voice on the page and the voice in your head. Just as we all sometimes tune out of conversations, so we sometimes find ourselves passing our eyes along the page while our minds are somewhere else. At these times, we are not reading interpretively. Then we have to backtrack to where we began just going through the motions. We pick up the dropped threads of attention and move forward, back-stepping to fit new passages into what we already read and reminding ourselves of how we got to where we are now, looking for repetitions and variations, listening to personal associations, considering how we might put this piece to use. Not simply *on* or *off*, interpretation involves acts of mind — feeling, reasoning, remembering, predicting, associating, applying — that overlap and tumble and zigzag, each from moment to moment playing greater or lesser roles in the conversation.

Readers call on all these activities to answer *interpretive questions* — that is, questions to which reasonably well-informed readers of a text might give differing answers. Interpretive questions call on more than simple recall. "What is Maxine Hong Kingston's ethnicity?" is not an interpretive question, but a matter of fact. What reader of "No Name Woman" (p. 420) would reply with anything but "Chinese American"? In contrast, "How does ethnicity affect Kingston's family relationships?" is an interpretive question: Well-informed readers would give different answers depending on which aspects of her memoir they found most significant or vivid or lasting or ambivalent. And so on.

General Strategies for Interpretive Reading

Why Are You Reading? For fun? The fun results from interpretation you're already doing, so go for it! To satisfy a college assignment (which also could be fun)? Then keep in mind what the assignment asks you to do. Are you merely supposed to know what the piece is about? If so, then reading the introduction may suffice. To summarize? Then you can skim the introduction, conclusion, and paragraph beginnings and get the gist. Are you supposed to recall detailed information from an economics or biology textbook? Does this piece march along, posing a question, marshaling arguments and evidence, and advocating a belief or action? Are you supposed to explain why you agree or disagree? Or does the piece circle around an idea or experience, looking at it in various ways without even trying to reach a definitive conclusion? Are you supposed to relate it to your personal experience? To other things you have read? Each of these purposes requires a somewhat different kind of reading.

How Does It Relate to You? What is the title? What do you already know about the subject, and how do you know it? What are your related experiences, opinions, and feelings? How does it fit in with lectures, discussions, and other readings in your course? What do you know about the author's qualifications to write on this subject? What are you required to do with it? Pass an exam? Follow its directions? Write a personal essay? Incorporate it with other texts in a long paper?

How Does the Format Help You? The editors of some textbooks, such as those for biology and economics, employ typographical features—such as centered and left-justified headings, different type fonts, and colors—that highlight the main ideas and show how each part relates to the other parts. The headings, for instance, make up a rough outline; all of the elements can suggest what questions to keep in mind as you're reading and what information to acquire for the exam.

If the reading at hand doesn't have many headings or other special features, like most of the selections in this book, then the marks you make—commenting in the margins, for example, or circling key words—gradually create the picture, showing what you noticed and what you'll come back to later. No two readers' marks will be quite the same, and yours won't be the same next month or next year as they are today. Thus, no two readers will create the same picture of a text, and you won't create the same picture twice. But what's important is that you do create a picture, that it is *your* picture, and that you will risk setting it beside another picture. The only way to become an active learner and an interpretive reader, not just a parrot of others' learning, is to start marking up what you're reading—one of the best reasons for reading a work in hard copy. In a few moments, we'll say more about how to make the marks of creative reading.

What Are You Marking—and Why? Let's assume you *are* marking your texts. Readers who aren't doing so fail to get the most out of what they read. In class, you refer to your marks and quickly spot passages that raise interesting questions, support or challenge a view that is emerging from class discussion, or open up a whole new approach. Meanwhile, readers who don't mark are flipping pages, knowing they saw just the right thing—but where? By the time they've found it, the discussion has moved on to something else. At exam and paper-writing time, you're reviewing your marks, while they're spending time rereading everything— or not. So, the question is not whether to mark, but how.

Marking a book you own multiplies both its value and the efficiency of your reading time. Marking does not deface a book, as some believe (inheriting attitudes from the days of costly clothbound books), unless it's a library volume whose readers should not be obliged to work with—or around—your interpretations. Artist Chuck Close observes of his time in Yale's School of Art, "You could always tell who Richard [Serra] had been studying when you'd go to the library and find a book all stuck together with paint." Rather, marking honors a book with your active engagement, bringing you more nearly face-to-face with the writers' voices on the page. If your book is new, you haven't yet left any traces of your conversations with the author(s). If you lost it the same day you bought it, you'd lose money. But if you lost it in a few months, after your markings have made many parts of the book *really* yours, that would cost far more—months of your own thinking, responding, generating new ideas. So mark up this book as you wish; you can even use Post-Its to comment on key spots.

When to mark? Active, independent-minded readers mark while reading and afterward. That way, they are making their own observations, picking up names and definitions, noticing patterns, forming questions: all the things strong readers do. More timid readers, fearing that they won't notice or question the "right" things, may postpone marking until class discussion, when other readers (and the instructor) call attention to passages which then, *ipso facto,* become the "right" ones. Unfortunately, those less confident readers are merely recording other people's readings, and—like auditing an aerobics class—that doesn't strengthen the body of their own ideas. Instead, they should stop worrying about whether they're reading "right" and instead ask, "What do I *notice*? What meanings can I *make* of that?" There's only one wrong answer to those questions: "nothing." When you mark up your reading before class, then you're all set to ask questions, offer evidence, and contrast your reaction with someone else's: then *your* reading becomes the "right" stuff.

What to write? The traces previous owners have left in your used books can help answer that. You may have wondered:

- "Why did you color almost this whole page with a green highlighter?"
- "Why did you underline this phrase and write 'Ha!'?"
- "Why did you write 'steers ~ shoes'?"

The reader with the green highlighter meant to emphasize important things but then drowned emphasis in overuse. Or else the reader tuned out, highlighting away while thinking of other things, later writing "Ha!" Although this is a strong response, was it delight? Skepticism? Sarcasm?—then "steers ~ shoes" beside paragraph 10 of Annie Dillard's "Heaven and Earth in Jest" (p. 641). When you read this, you share the commentator's understanding that steers themselves are just as much manufactured goods as the shoes their hides will furnish. (The reader borrowed ~ from geometry, where it means "similar.") When you write a phrase or sentence in the margin, that's the best kind of marking: Later, you'll know not only what got your attention but also why: *what you made of it.*

Noticing the Structure. The headings in a biology or economics book show a chapter's structure at a glance. A text without headings often puts a paragraph's main idea at or near the beginning, and it uses transitions to show its structure. A writer who promises to explain three steps or kinds or reasons may enumerate them with transitions like *first* (or *in the first place), second,* and *third,* or *to begin with, next,* and *finally.* You would write in the margin, "three reasons for . . ." followed by paragraphs numbered 1, 2, 3, plus a phrase or sentence to label each (like "steers ~ shoes"). To signal that a new paragraph is adding something similar to what was just said, you would use transitions such as *and, in addition, likewise,* and *moreover.* In contrast, transitions like *but, however, in contrast,* and *whereas* to signal a subtraction as it were, a different, if not opposite, direction in thinking. *Because, as a result, thus, so,* and *therefore* signal cause-and-effect thinking.

More speculative, meandering pieces often send more subtle connective signals, linking paragraphs by repeating a name or key word, by using a pronoun (*it, he, they*) to refer to a term (*antecedent*) in the previous paragraph's last sentence, or by using comparative terms like *more* and *less*. Thus, repetitions such as these signal a more "meandering" paragraph, in contrast to the more tightly logical writing described in the preceding paragraph. Sometimes even the repetition of an image, or variations of a sound or an image (say, a lighthouse beam in one paragraph, headlights in the next), is enough to link thought to thought.

Paragraph middles often include colorful details or anecdotes that exemplify or illustrate the paragraph's main point. Likewise, a section of several paragraphs often includes some that give examples and illustrations. In fact, everything we've said about paragraph structure applies to sections of essays. Sometimes writers call attention to their illustrations with *for example,* but not always. So don't mistake these details for main ideas; that is, keep your attention on what the illustration illustrates. Keep asking, "Why are you telling me this?"

Noticing Surprises. Suppose while reading through a series of long, winding, complicated sentences you are suddenly hit with a short one. *Pow!*—a fragment. These sentences are using formal, even esoteric, language, but then the writer says, "*Pow!*" You are reading about Homeric heroes, but then you see Michael

Jordan's name. You may notice that the meaning of a key term changes little by little each time the writer uses it. Or, to take an example from Martin Luther King's "Letter from Birmingham Jail" (p. 565) you are reading one sentence many lines long that builds and builds through ten situations each beginning with "when" and leading up to a thunderclap: "then you will understand" (paragraph 14). These surprising changes—respectively, in *syntax* (word order), *register* (the degree of formality in word choice), *domain* (the area referred to, in this case classical literature or modern U.S. pro sports), *definition*, and *rhythm*—create emphases. You can legitimately ask (but seldom answer with certainty), "Why are you telling me this *this* way?" You can describe with certainty how such surprises affect you as a reader.

Using What You've Read. You may ask of your reading, almost automatically, "What does this have to do with my experience?" You may also ask what assumptions a writer expects you to share. For example, what must you assume about the role of art institutions in defining what constitutes "art" in order to share Alice Walker's views of the quilt in the Smithsonian, of blues singers, and of her mother's garden (p. 180)? What must you assume or learn about cultural meanings of silence among Mexican men in order to understand the silence of Richard Rodriguez's father (p. 298)? Another important question you may ask is, "What must I do, or not do, if I accept what this writer is saying?" What must you teach your child if you accept N. Scott Momaday's (p. 145) or E. B. White's (p. 194) view of parenthood? In asking "How can I use this essay?" you enter the stream of conversation among the generations of readers who constitute its contexts. Welcome (again)!

WRITING IN CONTEXT

How do I know what I think until I see what I've said?
—E. M. FORSTER

Imagine your entire life—past, present, and maybe even future—being projected before you on a large computer screen. You can see any part of it by zooming in for a close-up of any thought, experience, belief, or understanding you've ever had. The close-up can help you review anything you've ever known, wondered about, or investigated—with or without answers. Or, you can zoom out to get enlarged views of the world you've been living in—people and places you know or have read about at home and abroad; theories, philosophies, and political systems—not only in your own community, state, or country but around the world.

As a writer, you can draw on your whole life, everything you've experienced or imagined, thought or read about, and bring it to bear on the work at hand. When you begin to bring your vast background into the foreground of your consciousness, you'll be surprised to find that the sharpened focus reveals how much more you know than you thought you knew. Vague and fuzzy ideas can gain new clarity—and your job as a writer is to expand and translate these ideas into prose others can understand. *The Arlington Reader* aims to enlarge the context, the universe of your reading, and the ways and means to translate that reading into writing.

Writing in College

A writing course for first-year college students is a common requirement in the United States. Because good writing is essential to learning and communicating throughout your college experience—and indeed, throughout the rest of your life—writing courses are designed to help you not only learn to write but also write to learn, in ways that are effective, efficient, and enjoyable. No matter what your career plan, even as a stockbroker or a Web designer, your life is inescapably bound up in writing, as it is in reading. If you use a computer (and who doesn't?), you're awash in e-mail, instant messaging, chat rooms, and reading—and responding to—material on an exuberant explosion of Web sites. You write notes, in longhand or electronically; make lists to put your day—or your life— in order; give advice and directions; complain, criticize—and say "thank you"; tell stories or jokes (and sometimes write them down); explain processes—how things work (or don't), the nature of a natural or scientific phenomenon; inter-pret maps, diagrams, charts; take a stand through a letter to the editor or your legislator, or an op-ed piece for the school paper; or write privately to yourself in a journal or to friends—and thus revisit the significance of notes, messages, and, yes, love letters and letters to the world. You may already have been writing for work—memos, instructions, reports, project proposals, research designs, prod-uct manuals. Or you've written for more personal reasons (perhaps a combina-tion of work and play) to convey a record of your experience, your family, or your culture, or as a witness to events of historical or political significance (on and beyond September 11, 2001). *The Arlington Reader* provides readings that will help expand your vision of the world and of the ways to become a meaning-ful part of it through your writing.

    In college, much of your writing necessarily has an academic focus. You write to understand the dimensions of a particular subject or field: what its key terms and concepts are; its scope, dimensions, major issues, points of agreement and controversy, changes and developments. You're learning the language, gen-eral and specific, and one or more ways of looking at an issue or the field it's embedded in. To make the subject your own, you need to understand it well enough to take into account the perspectives of others, explain them in your own language, weigh the evidence, and come to your own informed opinions. As you gather information and evidence for your papers, you may also become a sophisticated user of Internet and library information sources and of ways to evaluate their utility and worth. To be able to do all these things is to write with the authority you'll be developing throughout your college career and the rest of your life. The information on the following pages is designed to help you write with authority, power, and pleasure; the checklists throughout highlight the issues addressed.

Learning to Write with Ease, Effectiveness, and Efficiency

The Best Place. You'll write better if you have an agreeable place to work—a comfortable chair, good light, space free from distractions where you can leave your equipment out, ready for use. If your computer has access to a dictionary, encyclopedia, and the Internet (and music!), you may have most of what you need readily at hand, including many specialized books and journals available through your college's Internet subscription; if it's a laptop and your home or dorm room is noisy, you can easily move to a quieter spot.

The Best Time, Schedule, and Frame of Mind. The best time for writing is when you're most alert. If you haven't discovered when this is, try writing at different times of the day or night to discover a predictable pattern—that is, the time when you get the most done with the greatest pleasure. Try to build your schedule around this optimum time, even if it means getting up early or staying up late to capture the best stretch of time. A half hour or more of quality time adds up. Then, when you're away from your desk—reading, walking, sleeping—your ideas will continue to percolate. You also need to determine a writing schedule, perhaps with your teacher's help, that will allow adequate time for investigating your subject, drafting your paper, and revising and editing your work. If you start the process early and schedule your work in blocks, even short ones, over a period of days you'll avoid last-minute panic and unrealistic all-nighters.

Ask yourself these questions:

- When and where do I do my best writing? How can I (re)arrange my schedule and my space to get my work done efficiently?
- What else will help me enjoy the process? Food? Music? Exercise? Working on the assignment with a friend or trusted reader to help talk it over?
- After you've finished one paper, ask What worked best for me? What will I change the next time?

Audience. The purpose(s) of your writing is (are) intimately related to the audience you're writing for. Although your immediate readers are your teacher and fellow students, it's useful to think of a target group of readers beyond your classroom—strangers who may become friends, even converts to your point of view. Because your assignments and reasons for writing will vary, you are likely to be writing different papers for different audiences—an op-ed article for newspaper readers, a how-to essay for fellow cooks, a research report for a biology class or lab job, a term paper for a course but also for readers in the professional field, a résumé and application letter for prospective employers. Although you can reasonably expect your readers to have common sense and share a fund of common knowledge, your sense of audience will help you decide whether to write in a manner general or specific, simple or complicated; what language to use; which terms to define; and how much background information to provide.

Audience Checklist

- Do I have a specific group or groups of readers in mind—my family, parents of teenagers, churchgoers, legislators, or scientists?
- What aspects of their age range, ethnicity or nationality, gender, and levels of education and income do I need to consider?
- What opinions and values do they probably share that are relevant to my topic? Are they likely to agree with one another? With me?
- Do they know more, or less, than I do about the subject? What do I need to learn in order to address this audience?
- How simple or technical should my language be? What terms or concepts will I need to define, explain, or illustrate?
- What do I want to accomplish in writing this? To teach my readers something? Convince them of my point of view? Move them to action—or to tears? Entertain them?

Developing an Effective Writing Process

College writing is as varied as college writers and the disciplines they write in. And just as there is a wide range of essays in *The Arlington Reader,* there is a wide range of ways to write them (pp. 16–26). The information and checklists that follow apply to college writing in general; your instructor can suggest adaptations to specific assignments. For clarity, this discussion presents the writing process as a sequence of stages—inventing and planning, drafting, revising, and editing. However, in reality, while you're working on a paper, the process may resemble a series of loops rather than a straight line. The process of writing stimulates new ideas, new ways of handling what you've already written—a process ideally adapted to writing on a computer, where you can easily add, delete, and move material without destroying the parts you want to save and build on. Moreover, the process of writing different types of papers can vary considerably. If you're writing a lab report, you can slot the information discovered in the lab into a prescribed format; writing an argument can involve a lot more variation (p. 17).

Writing Assignments

Most writing assignments allow some latitude of topic and perhaps of form and style. Once you know the purpose of the assignment, you can begin exploring relevant topics. The stronger your interest in a particular topic—human rights, international terrorism, creativity—the more incentive you'll have to write about it. Because of your interest, you may already know enough about the subject to think of different ways of looking at it. Thus you could imagine a series of questions, such as "How can international terrorism be prevented?", "What's the best way to do this?" and "What preventive measures can the United States take?" Be sure to capture these questions in writing so that they won't escape you later on. When you arrive at an appealing topic, find an angle of vision that allows you to narrow your focus and make the topic manageable to write about in the time allotted to do so. For example, you could ask "What measures can the United States take to prevent international terrorism without curtailing the civil liberties guaranteed under the Constitution?" You could further restrict the topic to a single type of terrorism (say, airline hijacking) and a single civil liberty (such as freedom of the press).

Writing Assignment Checklist
- What is the purpose of the assignment?
- How can I find a subject and focus that mean a great deal to me? (The more you care about your writing, the better it's likely to be.)
- What kind of a paper am I going to write? What key words (words that identify main or key concepts, such as *explain, analyze, define,* and *argue*) or other instructions indicate this?
- What steps do I have to go through to write it? (When in doubt, ask the instructor.)
- Is this a major or minor assignment? How much time should I expect to spend on it, and over what period of time? One week? Two weeks? A month?

Invention: Developing Your Ideas

When you begin a paper, it's a good idea to take an inventory of what you already know about your subject—from your participation in a job or activity, from the people and places you know, and from your reading and life experiences. Talk to friends, relatives, and specialists—perhaps by means of interviews or a listserv. As you list your areas of knowledge, the gaps will also show up, and you can focus your reading and Internet and library searches on the sorts of information you need to find out. Unless you're writing a research paper, two or three reliable, up-to-date sources (books, research articles, or Web sites) are probably enough. Beware of sources such as Wikipedia that are not always reliable. Don't forget the value of facts and figures, illustrations, maps, graphs, and charts. But be selective; if you discover as you write that you need more information, you can always include more later. Keeping your limited focus in mind, resist the impulse to download everything you can find on the Internet or to quote long blocks in your paper. Be sure to indicate where you found the items you're likely to use; that way you can locate them again and acknowledge the sources as your paper develops.

Invention Checklist
- What are the main points, crucial information, and essential definitions in each of my sources? Where do they agree or disagree with other sources?
- What clusters of ideas are emerging as I investigate the subject? What's missing? List the major ideas, by key words or phrases.
- Where do I agree and disagree with my sources? Why?
- Do the ideas cluster around a central point that identifies a subject and my attitude toward it? Could this be my trial thesis? Is it interesting to me? To my audience? Is it worth writing about?

- What arrangements of my list of ideas are possible? Which one do I like best for its logic? Organization? Dialogue among sources? Sense of play?
- What is the visible structure or skeleton of my preferred arrangement? Where do the major elements—those in the most prominent places, occupying the most space—and the minor ones fall?
- Do I need to make a more formal outline? Will the longer sentences and greater detail help me develop my ideas?

Drafting

Now it's time to start writing. To get started, you might want to dash off a focused freewriting on your general topic, or a "zero draft"—a throwaway version that roughs out some of the ideas you've found. Let a trial thesis emerge, and post it where you can see it as you write; if you get off the track, you can either change the thesis to fit what you're saying or tailor your discussion to fit the thesis. Trust your taste and intuition (what looks as if it will work best?) to decide what to include, what to emphasize, and what to omit. Your common sense can help you counteract myths that produce writer's block if you take as your motto, "I'm going to do the best I can in the time I have to work on this paper." Your writing does not have to be perfect right from the outset. Or ever. Your early draft may be enough for one day's work, but let the ideas steep so that when you return you'll have something to build on.

When you revisit your paper you'll have two main tasks: to develop the material you started with and to find a design—or pattern of organization—that best fits the type of paper you're writing. Your paper will begin to grow before your eyes as you write short sections—on a single word, concept, or subsection of the larger paper. When you get enough pieces, separate or loosely related, you can begin to put them together, clustering each around a central concept embedded in a key word or phrase. Your key words should emphasize the main points and signal the major divisions, clues to your paper's emerging structure and rhetorical type (for instance, exposition, narration, description, argument—see p. 16). If you see an essay in this book of the rhetorical type that does what you'd like to do, you can use it as a model or select those parts that apply. The Rhetorical Index (pp. 725–735) identifies specific selection titles under their rhetorical headings.

When drafting, you don't have to begin at the beginning and march through to the end. If a workable introduction doesn't emerge after a few minutes, move on to another section—what you know or like best—and write that first. That should lead to another section and then another. You can even write the introduction last. If you decide not to write the whole paper in a single sitting, try to draft a section—say, one or two pages—before you take a break. Writing on a computer makes it easy to move the parts around and reassemble them when you're through. But save—don't discard—the false starts and paragraphs you decided to omit; you might like them better later, or you might decide to use them in some other piece of writing.

Thoughtful responses to your writing—from yourself, a writing group, your instructor—can be particularly valuable after you've completed your first draft. Set it aside for at least a day to gain perspective, then be especially tough-minded. It's easy to be seduced by the crisp appearance of a paper fresh from your printer, but don't be fooled by that pretty face. Ask the following questions instead—of yourself, your peer group, your instructor, or all three. The checklist can also be used to guide peer-group discussions.

Drafting Checklist

- What's the "heart"—the center of gravity—of my material? Does my draft concentrate on this?
- What works best in this draft? Why?
- How can the rest of the paper be changed to come up to this standard?

You could stop right there, and the discussion would be profitable. Or you could continue with the following questions:

- What don't my readers (or I) understand that needs to be explained? Where do I need to add information, illustrations (in words or images), or more analysis?
- What bores or annoys me, or my readers, in this draft? Do I need to delete warm-up attempts or other material that's off the point?

Re-vision and Revision

Revision is central to the writing process. It doesn't occur only when you've finished drafting; you may be revising continually as you compose to make what emerges on paper more closely match what's going on in your mind. This is particularly true if you get new ideas as you write and see your subject from new angles. Although the specifics of how and what you revise depend on what you did in the earlier draft(s), be prepared, if necessary, to make big changes. You may need to frame a new thesis or drastically revise your current one. You may need to reorganize your work according to a different format or arrangement. You may need more information or more material from more reliable and up-to-date sources in order to write with greater authority. In revision, rewrite to enhance the strongest aspects of your writing, and discard irrelevant material and the weakest sections. If, however, you've hit a home run with an early draft, you can concentrate on matters of style, usage, and documentation as you do the final edit.

Revision Checklist

- If my paper has an explicit thesis, does it reflect what I am really trying to say? Do I need to change the thesis to make it fit my subject better? (Some papers—such as one concentrating on telling a story, a character sketch, or an extended description—won't necessarily have an unexplicit thesis, though one may be implicit.)
- Is each major point developed sufficiently to make it compelling? (One clue: Is the paper long enough to do the job I set out to do?)

- Do comparable points receive equal development and emphasis?
- What pattern of organization best fits my material?
- Do the section and paragraph headings (if any) and breaks reflect my emphasis? Do transitional words or phrases signal where the essay has been—and where it's going?
- What proportion of the work does my introduction occupy? (If it takes up more than 20 percent, it's probably too long.) Does it encourage readers to continue? Does it contain key words and concepts that signal what follows?
- Does the conclusion follow logically or otherwise appropriately from what precedes it?

Style and Editing

"Style is organic to the person doing the writing," says writer William Zinsser (*On Writing Well*, New York: Harper, 1998), "as much a part of him as his hair, or, if he is bald, his lack of it. Trying to add style is like adding a toupee." All writing, like all writers, has some sort of intrinsic style, whether it's dull and boring, clear and straightforward, or lively and engaging. Yet while you're in the early or middle stages of drafting and revising a paper, it's uneconomical to spend much effort on the length and rhythm of your sentences, on the variety and felicity of your words, or even on spelling and grammatical correctness. There's no point in polishing parts of a paper that may ultimately be cut out. But after you've settled on the content, you'll need to pay attention to these matters of style. They make the difference between a casual paper and one dressed to go on a job interview, where you know you'll be judged, in part, on your language, appearance, polish, ease—and character.

The style you write in should suit you, your subject, and the type of essay you're writing. Your style—like the writer it portrays—should be appealing to your readers, attracting them to your subject, your point of view, and your character and credibility that inevitably emerge through your writing. Don't be afraid to let your humanity show through. If you find your subject fascinating, exciting, or enraging, you'll have an incentive to write with compelling conviction—and metaphor and symbol, wit and humor, when they fit. You'll want to avoid clichés (often the first figurative language that comes to mind, such as "pretty as a picture")—stale language that clogs your writing like hair plugging a drain.

In most papers for a first-year composition course or an audience of nonspecialists, you'll probably aim for a slightly more formal version of the language you use in conversation—a middle range that's neither slangy nor stuffy but that allows you to write in the first person and to use contractions. If you're writing on technical issues you'll need some technical vocabulary. Thus, in a paper on a legal issue, *domicile* might well be one of your words, along with *habeas corpus* and other legal terms for which there is no exact English equivalent. Likewise, your sentences and paragraphs will probably land in the middle range. This means that although your sentences can range from short to very long, they'll average out to between fifteen words (slightly longer than sentences in newspaper editorials) and twenty-five to thirty words (the average for professional academic writing). For easy reading, newspapers often put breaks at every column inch, but your paragraphs will be somewhat longer than these. In academic writing, paragraph breaks are dictated not by the eye but by the amount of development required for the ideas you're expressing. In fact, the appearance of a lot of short paragraphs (except in dialogue) in your essay may signal that your ideas need greater elaboration.

The best way to tell how your writing sounds is to read it aloud—to yourself or, better yet, to someone from your target group of readers. Go with the flow. If you have to pause (even gasp!) for breath as you read a sentence, consider breaking it up or using more punctuation. If you have a lot of short, choppy sentences, combine some. Repetition may be necessary for emphasis, as in Caesar's boast: "I came, I saw, I conquered." Nevertheless, if you're repeating yourself— too many words or too many of the same words that drone on and on—vary your vocabulary (synonyms abound in your dictionary and spell-check) and cut out the excess. But beware: Don't use spell-check or dictionary words unless you're familiar with them or can see them used in context, for not all synonyms are equivalent. How would Caesar's boast sound as "I came, I saw, I trounced"? Or "thrashed"? Or "subdued"? "Steamrolled" would, of course, be impossible, even if your dictionary allows it.

Style and Editing Checklist
Title and Thesis

- Is the title specific? Accurate? Witty, provocative, or otherwise appealing?
- Is my thesis (overt or implied) clear? (Not every paper needs an explicitly stated thesis. The central point or emphasis of character sketches, descriptions, and satires, for instance, may be implied.) Does everything in the paper have relevance to this?

Words

- Do I use strong, emphatic, active verbs ("My research team wrote the report" rather than "The report was written by my research team")? Have I used the passive voice to imply passivity ("The World Trade Center was destroyed . . .")?
- Are verb tenses congruent? If there are shifts between present and past tenses, are they intentional?
- Are pronoun references clear? (If I say *it* or *that*, will readers know what I'm referring to?)
- Is my vocabulary appropriate to the subject, the audience, and the paper's degree of technicality?
- Have I omitted vague words and unnecessary repetitions—have I?
- Have I defined key concepts and words used in specialized or unfamiliar ways?

Sentences

- Do my sentences have an emphasis and variety that reinforce their meaning?
- Does the paper contain sentence fragments? Can these phrases—punctuated with a period but lacking a subject or verb—really stand alone, or should they be incorporated into other sentences?
- Have I treated comparable concepts and grammatical structures in parallel ways ("I came, I saw, I conquered")?

Spelling, Mechanics, and Citations

- Have I acknowledged sources—including Web links—accurately and completely (with sufficient information to send readers to the exact spot)? Are they in the appropriate note and citation form?
- Have I integrated quotations, paraphrases, and summaries smoothly into my own text?
- Have I checked all spelling and issues of grammar and usage that gave me trouble in this paper? (Use a reliable handbook to double-check your spell- and grammar-checks.)

Finally . . .

- Is there anything I should have done on this paper that I haven't yet done? If so, why not do it now, rather than face another revision?

Writing in a Universe of Nonfiction

This section illustrates some of the common types of writing you'll find in *The Arlington Reader,* various forms of short nonfiction prose that you'll be reading and responding to. It identifies the general characteristics of each rhetorical type as well as strategies for talking or writing about a specific piece or the type it represents. You can use these illustrations (listed below in alphabetical order) for ideas and as examples of types of writing—in class discussion in person or online, in writing groups, or on your own.

Although this discussion highlights characteristics of each rhetorical type of writing (for example, definition or description), in the real world, most writing is a hybrid of forms, perhaps with one type dominating. For instance, E. B. White's "Once More to the Lake" (p. 194) is a *personal essay* that develops and interprets ideas in relation to the author's experience, *narrating* the story of a father's return to a summer camp in Maine with his young son. It also includes *comparison and contrast* (between past and present, father—now and earlier—and son), *description* of the setting, *explanation* in the form of *process analysis* (how they spent their summer vacation), and *illustration* (of an idyllic summer), which also serves as a *definition* of a loving father–son relationship. The entire piece can also be read as a historical document; or as an *implied argument* in favor of both rural vacations and parents and children spending long, lazy times together. When you're writing, don't worry about trying to separate out the types or even about identifying them.

No matter what you're concentrating on—say, an argument—other types will simply emerge as you write and become absorbed in your main focus.

Analysis. *Analysis* involves dividing something into its component parts and scrutinizing each part for its intrinsic merit and its relationship to the whole. It's usually easier to understand the subject in smaller parts than it is to try to make sense of a complicated whole all at once. Consequently, when you're reading printed material—whether it's an essay, a novel, a poem, a play, a textbook chapter, or a Web site—it's useful to consider the elements in the following list. You can use the same questions—and answers—to govern your analytic writing about essays, fiction, and other forms of literature when you're writing criticism or a review.

Analysis Checklist
- What is the writer's purpose or multiple purposes? Do these reinforce one another, or do they conflict?
- What's the thesis, or main point, and significant subpoints? Are they presented logically? Accurately? Where do we agree, and where will I (or others) dispute the author?
- What evidence does the writer use to support these claims? Are they logical? Appropriate?
- Who is the intended audience—primary (the immediate readers, such as teachers and fellow students) and secondary (others who might read the paper, such as newspaper readers of a letter to the editor initially written for class)? What knowledge—and biases—does each bring to the subject? What do they need to know? What biases have to be cultivated (such as understanding another culture) or overcome (male chauvinism, for instance)?
- How does the writer's purpose and imagined audience influence the choice of language, organization (what comes first, in the middle, last—and why?), illustrations, and tone?
- In what context—time, place, culture—and with what political, economic, and social issues in mind was this work written? What significant changes have occurred between the original context and the context in which you are now reading this?

Argument. *Argument* dominates academic writing—indeed, any writing in which the author is doing what Joan Didion says all writers do: "Listen to me, see it my way, change your mind." An argument seeks to convince readers of the truth or merits of an idea and often hopes to discredit alternative views. An argument may be a call to action—even revolution (the Declaration of Independence, p. 369)—intended to change readers' minds or behavior, to right a wrong, or to effect reform.

   Direct arguments require evidence, good reasons, and a logical way to dispel disagreements. Scientific papers, critical articles, position papers, and many other types of academic writing are based on considerations such as the following.

- At the outset, do I expect my readers to agree with my position? To be neutral? To oppose my point of view? Given this starting point, what do I need to do to ensure their agreement?
- What is my strongest (and perhaps most controversial) point? If the audience agrees with this point, the discussion belongs at the beginning. But if the audience is hostile, it's better to identify points of agreement and lead up to the major controversy gradually—near the end. Usually the most controversial points warrant the most detailed discussion.
- What are my best sources of evidence? Personal experience—my own or that of others? Judgment from experts in the field? Scientific evidence, statistical data, historical records, or case histories?
- How can I evaluate the evidence? (Just because something appears on a Web site or in print doesn't make it reliable.) For starters, it should be authoritative, up-to-date, taken from a reputable source, and representative enough to permit generalizations.
- Even if I can't convince my readers, what language and tone will best compel their thoughtful attention to my point of view? Sincere or sarcastic? Cool or passionate? Angry or conciliatory? Something else? What can I do to make sure they'll hear me out and not stop paying attention partway through? (Here's a good place to ask your writing group for suggestions.)

Indirect arguments promote their case through ethics—trust in the writer and the writer's values—and appeals to emotion as well as facts. Implied or indirect arguments are present in many varieties of writing, including personal writing, eyewitness accounts, stories, character sketches, case histories (such as accounts of "poster children"), and satires (Jonathan Swift's "A Modest Proposal," p. 469). Indirect arguments, through means such as these, are often incorporated into direct arguments as well; the more extensively that ethical and emotional appeals are used, the more likely the argument is to be made through indirect rather than direct means. The essence of an emotional appeal is passion ("I have a dream"; "We shall overcome"). Yet because academic culture prefers understatement to overkill, it's better to present revealing facts and telling narratives and to let your readers interpret these for themselves—as Lynda Barry does in "Hate" (p. 438)—rather than harangue them. If you can put them in your shoes, they're likely to walk your walk.

Argument Checklist

- How can I best convince my readers that my judgment and character are sound (judgment and character together equal *authorial ethos*) and qualify me to make my case? ("I am a genius" won't work.)
- To reinforce my ethical appeals and authorial ethos, what's the best evidence I can use? Examples from my own life? Others' experiences? References to literature, statistics, and scientific research?
- How can I be sure my readers will react the way I want them to (with sympathy, anger, or resolve to change things)? Can I trust my examples to speak for

themselves? What language and details will reinforce the examples without being preachy? (Test the reactions of people unfamiliar with your examples. Do they get the point? Are they moved?)

Definition.   *Definitions* essentially answer the question "What is *X*?" They identify something as a member of a class (sports cars) and then specify what distinguishes it from all other members of that class (Mazda Miata). Any definition of a class must include all of its members. *Negative definitions* explain what is excluded from a given class and why (why the Volkswagen Passat 3.6 is not a sports car). Definitions are necessary in much academic writing, either to explain unfamiliar terms or to tell readers how you're interpreting a controversial or ambiguous term used in an argument that follows. Many definitions reflect cultural and other biases; what connotations do "rural area," "small town," and "big city" (and is that the same as "teeming metropolis"?) have for you? Definitions can employ a variety of techniques, such as analogy, comparison and contrast, and division and classification.

Definition Checklist

- *Explanatory definitions* interpret things according to their purpose: What is *X* for? What does *X* do?
- *Descriptive definitions* focus on individuality—for instance, a person's ("George Washington," p. 161) or a group's ("Notes of a Native Speaker," p. 112).
- *Essential or existential definitions* ask: What is the essence or fundamental nature of *X* (an abstraction such as truth, beauty, or play)? Or what does it mean to be *X* (Georgina Kleege on blindness, p. 65) or to live as an *X* or in a state of *X*?
- *Logical definitions,* common in scientific and philosophical writing, identify the term as a member of a more general class (for example, intelligence), and then specify the features that make it different from all other members of that class (as Howard Gardner does with different kinds of intelligence—such as emotional and artistic—in "Who Owns Intelligence?," p. 322).
- *Process definitions,* often used in how-to-do-it and scientific writing, consider such questions as: How is *X* produced? How does it work? What does it do or not do? With what effects?

Description.   *Description* aims to bring a scene, an event, or a person to life by conveying a sensory impression, by creating a mood, or both. It re-creates a particular context. Drawing heavily on sensory information, description tells how a subject looks, sounds, smells, tastes, acts, and feels, as in N. Scott Momaday's "The Way to Rainy Mountain," (p. 145). Although it's tempting to think of description as a series of snapshots in adventure pieces (George Orwell's "Shooting an Elephant," p. 378) or snapshot-like travel accounts, description is really much broader than that; Orwell, for instance, is presenting a political and ethical argument. Details about how people live—their characteristic behavior, values, companions, possessions, beliefs, fears—can present vivid portraits, as Barbara

Ehrenreich does in anatomizing a waitress's life in "Serving in America." Nonsensory details help describe an abstraction, such as a psychological moment or state of mind—for instance, happiness or terror. Images and analogies ("My love is like a red, red rose") also help. You are never a neutral observer; everything you decide to include or omit reveals your attitude toward the subject and will influence your readers.

Description Checklist

- From what perspective do I want to present this information? Distant? Close up? As a series of snapshots or vignettes? With admiration or as a critique?
- How will I organize my description? (See "Lists," p. 22.)
- Have I let the heavy-duty words—nouns and verbs—bear the weight of the description and thereby avoided piles of adjectives that would bury the subject?

Editorials and Op-Eds.   The placement of these short "think pieces" on a newspaper's editorial pages tells readers they can expect expressions of opinion—commentary, discussion, argument, reflection—often in dialogue with other pieces on the same pages or in previous issues of the paper. Although these brief essays (of between five hundred and eight hundred words) often address current events, the best convey the columnist's distinctive style, quality of mind, and point of view in memorable writing that transcends time (see the essays by Anna Quindlen (p. 598), Peter Singer (p. 601), and George Will (p. 607)). For suggestions on how to write these essays, pick the type that best fits what you want to say (such as analysis, argument, definition, or satire) and consult that category.

Exposition.   As its name indicates, *exposition* exposes information through explaining, defining, or otherwise interpreting its subject. This broad term encompasses most of the essays in this book. Expository writing, the all-purpose utility vehicle of academia, includes most research reports, critical analyses, literature reviews, case histories, exam answers (which you can think of as mini-essays), and term papers. Expository writing can incorporate many techniques used in other sorts of writing as well: definition, illustration, comparison and contrast, cause and effect, division and classification, and analogy. For suggestions on writing, see the other categories.

Parody and Satire.   *Parody* and *satire* make fun of their subject, exaggerating or otherwise distorting the subject, values, style, language, characters (who, in a satire, correspond directly to people in real life), or other features of an author, work, or prevailing philosophy. Satire is always critical of the people or groups it's attacking, aiming for improvement and reform (see Swift's "A Modest Proposal," p. 469). In Art Spiegelman's "Mein Kampf" (p. 139) and "Maus" (p. 418), satire is visual as well as verbal. Whereas satire may be comical or bitter, parody always aims to make people laugh (see "Nonfiction Types: Writing Humor,"

p. 559). For either type to succeed, readers must recognize the correspondence between the target and the wit of the writer's presentation. You're not trying to win
hearts and minds through sweet reason; satire and parody allow enough latitude
for you to gross out your readers (as Swift does in treating cannibalism of infants
with pseudo-seriousness) and still expect them to stick with you to the end.

Parody and Satire Checklist

- What annoys, provokes, angers, or strikes me as sufficiently ridiculous (or
  boring) to be a fit subject for satire or parody?
- Will my readers recognize the subject, even after my distortions?
- What can I do to ensure that my readers will take my side, directing their
  own laughter or scorn at the object of my witty imitation (or attack)? Have I
  checked out my peers' reactions to the features I'm exaggerating: the subject's typical manner of speech (typical vocabulary, expressions, sentence
  patterns, jargon), gestures, behavior, dress, mental or moral qualities, activities, and so on?
- Is my piece short? Satire and parody depend on a fast pace; prolong the
  humor and the punch loses its fizz.

Interviews.   Encouraging people to talk about themselves in *interviews* is a fairly
simple way to do original research. Almost anyone—expert or amateur, friend
or stranger—can be informative or engaging to an interviewer with a lively curiosity and a sympathetic ear. Take notes—quoting in particular proper names,
key words, colorful language—even if you're taping at the same time. That will
eliminate the need, and the time, to make a long transcript. When you write up
what you've heard, you can highlight the key words and group similar ideas by
topic. Your write-up will probably salvage the most quotable 10 percent of the
interview's "pure gold," as interviewer Studs Terkel calls it.

Interview Checklist

- Set up the appointment in advance, identifying who you are and why you'd
  like to talk with this person.
- Keep your purpose in mind. Do you want to focus on the subject's entire life or
  just part of it? Obtain information about something the subject knows (how to
  write well), can do (how to sculpt in stone or wood), has invented (Apple computers), or has experienced, such as a historical period (the 1970s), a significant
  event (September 11), or an unusual opportunity (Peace Corps service).
- Do your homework. Learn enough about your topic beforehand so that you
  won't waste time on the trivial or the obvious.
- Begin with low-key, factual questions, and then move gradually toward more
  complicated ones about issues and matters of opinion. Prepare a number of
  open-ended questions that can't be answered with a laconic "yes" or "no."
- Talk as little as necessary, and keep the focus on the person you're interviewing, not on yourself.

- Write up and amplify your notes as soon as possible, while the interview is still fresh in your mind.

Lists.   A *list* may start out as a random assemblage of notes jotted down as you try to decide your next paper topic. Yet as you move the items around you'll discover that each list has its own logic and that each reconfiguration of the items embeds new possibilities. You can also group like items and move the groups around—as you might in making a grocery list, which you would ultimately arrange to match your circuit through the grocery store—fruits, vegetables, meat, baking ingredients, dairy. If you add numbers, a list can be the basis of an outline; if you draw in connections, a list can become a diagram in linear or cluster form. Lists can metamorphose into no-nonsense statements of commandments or rules (see "Brief Takes on Ethical Codes," p. 634). Common patterns of organization are listed below. Each pattern can also be reversed.

- From farthest away in space or time to nearest. (Common in historical accounts. Travel writing usually reverses this, starting at home and moving away.)
- Most important, urgent, or necessary to least important, urgent, or necessary. (A common pattern in argument.)
- Points of agreement (in order of importance), followed by points of disagreement.
- Most intimate (human relationship) to most distant.
- Highly dominant (largest, strongest, loudest) to least conspicuous (smallest, weakest, softest).
- Most to least familiar or interesting.
- Most to least ethical, political, social, or costly in terms of resources or consequences.

Narration.   "We tell ourselves stories in order to live," says Joan Didion. Indeed, *narratives* form the basis of stories both true and fictional—autobiography and many personal essays; history; newspaper accounts of breaking events, from sports to murder to terrorism-in-progress; accounts of travel and adventure; short stories and novels; jokes, fables, and other cautionary tales. Narratives recount the action of an event or series of interrelated events, often in a chronological sequence—how to get from there to here, sometimes with flashbacks or flash-forwards that anticipate the ending. For shifts between past, more remote past, and present see E. B. White, "Once More to the Lake," (p. 194). Essential questions to ask include the following:

Narration Checklist

- Why am I telling this story—for its own sake, to convey information, or to make a larger point about its subject? What does it mean to me? To my readers?
- What background information will I need to supply for readers who haven't been there; haven't done that; or don't know the people, the history, or the culture they represent?

Narratives answer some or all of the journalist's basic questions—which are also fundamental to analyzing a *process* and explaining a *cause-and-effect* relationship:

- *Who* participated? What were their motives?
- *What* happened?
- *Why* did this event or phenomenon happen?
- *When* did it happen? Would it make sense—or good drama—to discuss this in flashbacks?
- *Where* did it happen? Should I describe the scene?
- *How* did it happen? Under what circumstances?

Writing about People.   "I like man, but not men," said essayist Ralph Waldo Emerson, perhaps anticipating Mark Twain's observation that "Man is the only animal that blushes. Or needs to." People write about people (including themselves) more than any other subject. People are the focus of portraits (individual or group), character sketches, interviews, personal narratives, and human-interest vignettes; all of these can be freestanding or incorporated into longer essays or works of history, social analysis, scientific discovery—writing of all sorts on virtually any subject. Writers focus on human subjects because they're intrinsically fascinating, antagonizing, repellent, problem-causing and problem-solving, inspiring, and evocative of a host of other reactions, as the contents of the entire *Arlington Reader* reveal. We will take a close look at particular people and cultures in Chapter 2, "Identity with Attitude: Who We Are and How We Got That Way." Even when the focus is on a topic other than specific people (such as science or social issues), it's humans who are interpreting it, and it's writing that will help determine how people will understand the subject years, even centuries, later—as essays in Chapter 5 by Linda Simon (p. 390) and H. Bruce Franklin (p. 402) reveal (not by chance is this chapter titled "History: What Really Happened? How do we know or decide what it means?"). So varied are writings about people, interpreted globally, that all the suggestions in this list are applicable in some circumstances. If you're concentrating on an individual, consider the following questions.

Writing about People Checklist

- Do I know this person well enough to write about him or her? From personal acquaintance or experience (say, watching the subject's public performance on stage, TV, film, or in the news)?
- Do I have a reliable sense of the subject's inner as well as outer selves? From what sources have I gotten information (beware of press releases and other biased news sources)? How do I decide among conflicting sources?
- What am I emphasizing—character or personality, philosophy, values, roles or relationships, decisions or actions, contributions or failings, or some combination?
- Can I convey the actual or potential long-term significance of whatever aspects of the subject I'm concentrating on?

Writing about Places.   Places don't proclaim their significance, people do—in the course of interpreting Indian pueblos, Walden Pond, and toxic-waste dumps. Scientists write about the *natural world,* including matters of ecology (Rachel Carson, p. 663), natural history (Terry Tempest Williams, p. 656), and the physical sciences (Stephen Jay Gould, p. 512), whereas other writers find spiritual inspiration in the same settings (Henry David Thoreau, p. 187; Leslie Marmon Silko, p. 287). Social analysts interpret places as the sites of social or political history (N. Scott Momaday, p. 145) or criticism (George Orwell, p. 378). Roving correspondents and people on the move write about places as contexts for adventure and exploration—the more grungy or harrowing, the better the story. Aim for understatement; let telling details, vignettes, and dialogue demonstrate the significance of the place rather than belabor your interpretations. For writing, the suggestions under "Description," "Lists," and "Narration" earlier in this chapter will help you avoid predictable, postcard-pretty shots. Also consider the following questions.

Writing about Places Checklist

- Do I have original observations about this place or an unusual perspective to view it from? What can I include to keep my commentary about a familiar place fresh to readers who already know it well?
- Should I use photographs or other illustrations? It's your call as to whether they will stimulate or stunt your readers' imaginative understanding.
- What kind of character do I (as participant-author) appear to be in this writing? Authoritative scientist? Humble wayfaring sojourner? Stranger in a strange land? Cool adventurer?

Writing about Processes.   Accounts of how things are done, accomplished, made, or played or performed abound in a wide variety of writings. How-to-do (or not do) it, steps to success, recipes, plans, and rules all interpret processes for individuals, disciplines, and whole societies to get things done. They focus on attaining a maximum of success with a minimum of struggle. Those in *The Arlington Reader* concern writing and other forms of creative processes (Chapter 1), ethics (Chapter 8), decision making and policy making (Chapter 6), and work and play (throughout the book as in Chapters 8 and 9). Analyses of how things work and develop in nature abound in science writing (Chapter 7). Most process writings follow a logical sequence from the beginning of the process to the end, dividing the process into steps according to what has to be done first, second, third, and so on. Dr. Spock's advice on bringing up children—"Trust yourself. You know more than you think you do."—offers a good beginning: Take stock of what you (and your readers) know, and build from there. The more complicated the process—like rearing a child—the more varied the explanation of how to do it may be, though what you emphasize and in how much detail, and what you can skip, depend on how much your readers already know and can tolerate. Both amateurs and experts may want to know a lot more about the process at hand, but whereas novices need the basics, experts may crave the esoteric.

Writing about Processes Checklist

- Is my knowledge of the process derived from intimate knowledge? Mine or someone else's? Is it up-to-date?
- Why have I chosen this particular means to an end? Am I aware of other ways (worse? better?) to do it?
- Will a typical reader be able to follow my directions successfully and with relative ease? If a test audience gets confused, what do I need to provide to untangle the process? More information? Specific details? Diagrams or photographs? Citations of books or links to relevant Web sites?

Research Reports.   *Research reports* may take a variety of forms, particularly in the humanities. In the physical or social sciences; engineering, computer science, or other technology; and business or industry, each context for writing (lab, journal, subspecialty) may have its own form. Nevertheless, the following model represents a common format employed in scientific papers and lab reports: (1) Statement of the problem, incorporating the proposition(s) to be tested and definitions of key terms; (2) review of major research articles and books on the topic to be investigated, to provide an intellectual and sometimes methodological context into which the current research fits; (3) step-by-step description of the research design, method, equipment, procedure (see "Writing about Processes," above), and ways of measuring the results; (4) statement of research results, often combined with (5) analysis of these. The results/analysis section is often (but not always) the longest; many of the pieces in Chapter 7, "Science and Technology," deal with the results of "Discovery, Invention, and Controversy." (6) Conclusion and suggestions for additional research. When you're writing, ask yourself, your instructor, and your peer group whatever questions pertain from the following list.

Research Report Checklist

- Do I have enough information on hand (say, from lab investigation or others' research) to write about this subject? Is my information up-to-date? State of the art?
- Am I writing for specialists who know more than I do about the subject? For a general audience, who may know less? In either case, how will I adapt my material—definitions, references to others' work, explanations of my process—to my readers' level of understanding and interest? What will they take for granted that I don't need to elaborate on at all?
- Is my writing organized clearly, according to the logical (and expected) pattern of a process, a research sequence, or the development of a phenomenon over time?
- Do I need to use supporting illustrations, such as facts, figures, case histories, graphs, statistics, maps, or photographs? (See "Visible You.")
- Does my writing embed extended definition, explanation, or narrative? Does it argue for my view of the subject—and oppose other interpretations? Or some combination of these?

Writer's Notebook or Journal.   Keeping a *writer's notebook* or *journal* can be a good way to jump-start your writing. Whether you write with pencil, pen, or word processor, you can freewrite—following an idea or key word to see where it leads, perhaps as a response to a writing assignment. You can doodle, make lists, draw pictures, or paste in citations or articles. You're not providing a record of your daily life; you're including material that you might want to write about someday (see "Brief Takes on War and Peace: Diaries and Memoirs," on p. 414). What's in the notebook is private, intended only for yourself, so you may not have to elaborate on fragmentary notes or ideas—just put in enough to jog your memory when you revisit the scene. It's helpful to date each entry, or even identify it by topic, so that you can find it easily if you want to consult it when you're writing a paper. Your entries might include some of the following:

Writer's Notebook Checklist

- Reactions to your reading, or provocative quotations from it. Be sure to identify your sources for return visits.
- Commentary on notable, puzzling, or problematic events—current or past; local (college, hometown), national, or international.
- Good (or even bad) ideas—your own or those of others.
- Problems or puzzles—of an academic or human nature—to solve.
- Sketches of people who are intrinsically memorable or associated with interesting events, professions, activities, or lifestyles.
- Photographs, drawings, maps, diagrams, graphs, or charts.
- Jokes; cartoons; funny, weird, or unusual names of people, places, pets, or businesses.
- Titles of or key words from articles, books, films, songs or albums, or TV shows.
- Internet sites.

CHAPTER 1

Writing, Reading, Speaking: Words That Make Us Human

DAVID HANOVER

The Work of Writing

QUESTIONS FOR DISCUSSION AND WRITING

1. The man in this photograph is using his laptop while holding a pencil in his mouth. How do these two writing technologies work together? How does the photograph depict the writing product and process? Does the photograph suggest that the man is writing, as Stephen King discusses (p. 30), "with the door closed" or rewriting "with the door open"? Explain your interpretation.

2. The photograph portrays writing as a mobile and informal activity. People can write either by hand or electronically and in a variety of environments. What is your ideal writing environment?

3. Describe the composition of this photograph, including light and tone, and the personal items surrounding the subject and how they contribute to the image's meaning. What does the photograph suggest about literacy and technological skill?

STEPHEN KING

Write or Die

One of the most popular and prolific authors of our time, Stephen King (also writing as Richard Bachman and John Swithen) began writing because he loved reading; the range of authors whom he cites as models includes H. P. Lovecraft, Ernest Hemingway, Elmore Leonard, Joyce Carol Oates, Graham Greene, and T. S. Eliot. Born in 1947, King began submitting stories to magazines and collecting rejection slips when he was twelve. He published his first story at age nineteen. Growing up in rural Maine, he helped his mother support the family with a number of tough jobs, including janitor, mill hand, and laundry laborer. After graduating from the University of Maine (B.A., 1970), King taught high school English while working on his extremely popular first novel, Carrie *(1974). A rush of best-sellers followed:* Salem's Lot *(1975),* The Shining *(1977),* The Stand *(1978),* The Dead Zone *(1979),* Firestarter *(1980), and* Cujo *(1981). After his novella "The Body" (from the collection* Different Seasons, *1982) was turned into the coming-of-age film* Stand by Me, *King's reputation grew beyond his core fans of horror, fantasy, and science fiction.*

On Writing: A Memoir of the Craft *(2000) is part autobiography, part writing manual. "Write or Die," an excerpt from* On Writing, *discusses two key influences on his writing—a guidance counselor at the end of his rope with the young King and a ruthlessly honest newspaper editor.*

Hardly a week after being sprung from detention hall, I was once more invited to step down to the principal's office. I went with a sinking heart, wondering what new shit I'd stepped in.

It wasn't Mr. Higgins who wanted to see me, at least; this time the school guidance counselor had issued the summons. There had been discussions about me, he said, and how to turn my "restless pen" into more constructive channels. He had enquired of John Gould, editor of Lisbon's weekly newspaper, and had discovered Gould had an opening for a sports reporter. While the school couldn't *insist* that I take this job, everyone in the front office felt it would be a good idea. *Do it or die*, the G.C.'s eyes suggested. Maybe that was just paranoia, but even now, almost forty years later, I don't think so.

I groaned inside. I was shut of *Dave's Rag*, almost shut of *The Drum*, and now here was the Lisbon *Weekly Enterprise*. Instead of being haunted by waters, like Norman Maclean in *A River Runs Through It*, I was as a teenager haunted by newspapers. Still, what could I do? I rechecked the look in the guidance counselor's eyes and said I would be delighted to interview for the job.

Gould—not the well-known New England humorist or the novelist who wrote *The Greenleaf Fires* but a relation of both, I think—greeted me warily but with some interest. We would try each other out, he said, if that suited me.

Now that I was away from the administrative offices of Lisbon High, I felt able to muster a little honesty. I told Mr. Gould that I didn't know much about sports. Gould said, "These are games people understand when they're watching them drunk in bars. You'll learn if you try."

He gave me a huge roll of yellow paper on which to type my copy—I think I still have it somewhere—and promised me a wage of half a cent a word. It was the first time someone had promised me wages for writing.

The first two pieces I turned in had to do with a basketball game in which an LHS player broke the school scoring record. One was a straight piece of reporting. The other was a sidebar about Robert Ransom's record-breaking performance. I brought both to Gould the day after the game so he'd have them for Friday, which was when the paper came out. He read the game piece, made two minor corrections, and spiked it. Then he started in on the feature piece with a large black pen.

I took my fair share of English Lit classes in my two remaining years at Lisbon, and my fair share of composition, fiction, and poetry classes in college, but John Gould taught me more than any of them, and in no more than ten minutes. I wish I still had the piece—it deserves to be framed, editorial corrections and all—but I can remember pretty well how it went and how it looked after Gould had combed through it with that black pen of his. Here's an example:

Last night, in the ~~well-loved~~ gymnasium of Lisbon High School, partisans and Jay Hills fans alike were stunned by an athletic performance unequalled in school history. Bob Ransom, ~~known as "Bullet" Bob for both his size and accuracy,~~ scored thirty-seven points. Yes, you heard me right. ~~Plus~~ he did it with grace, speed . . . and with an odd courtesy as well, committing only two personal fouls in his ~~knight-like~~ quest for a record which has eluded Lisbon ~~thinclads~~ players since ~~the years of Korea~~ 1953 . . .

Gould stopped at "the years of Korea" and looked up at me. "What year was the last record made?" he asked.

Luckily, I had my notes. "1953," I said. Gould grunted and went back to 10 work. When he finished marking my copy in the manner indicated above, he looked up and saw something on my face. I think he must have mistaken it for horror. It wasn't; it was pure revelation. Why, I wondered, didn't English teachers ever do this? It was like the Visible Man Old Raw Diehl had on his desk in the biology room.

"I only took out the bad parts, you know," Gould said. "Most of it's pretty good."

"I know," I said, meaning both things: yes, most of it was good—okay anyway, serviceable—and yes, he had only taken out the bad parts. "I won't do it again."

He laughed. "If that's true, you'll never have to work for a living. You can do this instead. Do I have to explain any of these marks?"

"No," I said.

"When you write a story, you're telling yourself the story," he said. "When 15 you rewrite, your main job is taking out all the things that are *not* the story."

Gould said something else that was interesting on the day I turned in my first two pieces: write with the door closed, rewrite with the door open. Your stuff starts out being just for you, in other words, but then it goes out. Once you know what the story is and get it right—as right as you can, anyway—it belongs to anyone who wants to read it. Or criticize it. If you're very lucky (this is my idea, not John Gould's, but I believe he would have subscribed to the notion), more will want to do the former than the latter. . . .

QUESTIONS FOR DISCUSSION AND WRITING

1. Why do you suppose King initially regarded writing for a newspaper as a punishment rather than an opportunity?

2. How does King's reproduction of Gould's editing illustrate his advice to the young writer? Explain Gould's distinction between writing "with the door closed" and rewriting "with the door open" (paragraph 16). Why are both important?

JOHN F. KENNEDY

The Purpose of Poetry

President John F. Kennedy (1917–1963) brought a genuine appreciation for literature, the arts, and intellectual life to the White House. The first Roman Catholic and the youngest man ever to be elected president, he held office for only 1,037 days be-

fore his tragic assassination in Dallas, Texas, on November 22, 1963. But his term in office was nothing if not eventful. While he and other Western leaders were confronting the Soviet Union, bringing the world close to total nuclear war, Kennedy championed civil rights and committed the nation to landing an American on the moon. Wherever they traveled, the president and first lady Jacqueline Kennedy won hearts and minds with their charisma and elegant style, and many young Americans were drawn to the president's idealism and his innovative programs such as the Peace Corps.

At his inauguration, Kennedy demonstrated his love for poetry when he invited Robert Frost to the podium to read his poem for the occasion; "Dedication" spoke of "a golden age of poetry and power." However, the sun's glare on the snow-covered ground prevented the aged poet from reading his manuscript, so instead Frost recited a poem from memory—"The Gift Outright." Two years later, after Frost's death, Kennedy repaid the compliment in a speech at Amherst College, "The Purpose of Poetry" (Atlantic, 1964; rpt. Jan.–Feb. 2006). Here Kennedy takes up Frost's theme of "poetry and power" with an extended meditation on the role of the artist in modern society.

A nation reveals itself not only by the men it produces but also by the men it honors, the men it remembers . . .

The men who create power make an indispensable contribution to the nation's greatness, but the men who question power make a contribution just as indispensable, especially when that questioning is disinterested, for they determine whether we use power or power uses us . . .

When power leads man toward arrogance, poetry reminds him of his limitations. When power narrows the areas of man's concern, poetry reminds him of the richness and diversity of his existence. When power corrupts, poetry cleanses, for art establishes the basic human truths which must serve as the touchstones of our judgment. The artist, however faithful to his personal vision of reality, becomes the last champion of the individual mind and sensibility against an intrusive society and an officious state. The great artist is thus a solitary figure. He has, as Frost said, "a lover's quarrel with the world." In pursuing his perceptions of reality he must often sail against the currents of his time . . .

If sometimes our great artists have been the most critical of our society, it is because their sensitivity and their concern for justice, which must motivate any true artist, make them aware that our nation falls short of its highest potential.

I see little of more importance to the future of our country and our civilization 5 than full recognition of the place of the artist. If art is to nourish the roots of our culture, society must set the artist free to follow his vision wherever it takes him . . .

In free society art is not a weapon, and it does not belong to the sphere of polemics and ideology. Artists are not engineers of the soul. It may be different elsewhere. But in a democratic society the highest duty of the writer, the composer, the artist, is to remain true to himself and to let the chips fall where they may. In serving his vision of the truth, the artist best serves his nation . . .

I look forward to a great future for America—a future in which our country will match its military strength with our moral strength, its wealth with our wisdom, its power with our purpose.

I look forward to an America which will not be afraid of grace and beauty, which will protect the beauty of our natural environment, which will preserve the great old American houses and squares and parks of our national past, and which will build handsome and balanced cities for our future.

I look forward to an America which will reward achievement in the arts as we reward achievement in business or statecraft.

I look forward to an America which will steadily raise the standards of artistic accomplishment and which will steadily enlarge cultural opportunities for all of our citizens.   10

And I look forward to an America which commands respect throughout the world, not only for its strength but for its civilization as well.

And I look forward to a world which will be safe, not only for democracy and diversity but also for personal distinction.

QUESTIONS FOR DISCUSSION AND WRITING

1. In John F. Kennedy's inaugural speech (January 20, 1961), he famously exclaimed "ask not what your country can do for you; ask what you can do for your country." Notice that throughout "The Purpose of Poetry" the nation, the country, and America are referred to repeatedly. What is the overall effect of these references? To what extent does Kennedy's emphasis on this central concept help him persuade the listener to accept his point of view?

2. One of the central claims in Kennedy's argument emerges in his title and is developed in paragraph 3: poetry and power are diametrical opposites. But are poetry and power really such different spheres as Kennedy makes them out to be? In what ways might poetry and power be intertwined? Could Kennedy's claims be reversed, perhaps? For example, could poetry lead people toward arrogance but power remind them of their limitations? In what way might poetry narrow the areas of people's concerns, just as power does? With a partner, choose a theme (poetry or power) and collaborate on an essay in which you analyze Kennedy's polarization of poetry and power and discuss your conclusions.

3. The question of artistic freedom looms large in "The Purpose of Poetry." For Kennedy, the artist "in pursuing his perceptions of reality . . . must often sail against the currents of his time" (paragraph 3). Kennedy advocates creating room for artists to criticize society, since they do so out of "sensitivity" and a "concern for justice" (paragraph 4). Individually or with a partner, do some research on an artist or writer, living or dead, whose work criticizes some aspect of society. Write a paper based on your research exploring the following issues: to what extent was this artist driven by a particular sensitivity or a concern for jus-

tice? In what way, if any, did the artist meet with criticism, censorship, or repression because of his or her work? To what extent has this artist's work succeeded in making others more aware of certain issues or concerned with justice?

4. As a class, make a scorecard of American achievement based on Kennedy's vision for the nation in paragraphs 7 through 12. Discuss how far our nation has progressed toward achieving the goals that Kennedy set for it. For example, how good a job are we doing at matching our military strength with our moral strength? How well are we protecting the beauty of our natural environment, preserving great architecture and parks, and building handsome and balanced cities? How well do we reward achievement in the arts compared to achievement in business? To what extent are we raising the standards of artistic accomplishment and enlarging cultural opportunities for all citizens? To what extent do we command respect throughout the world for our civilization, as well as our strength?

EUDORA WELTY

Listening

Born in Jackson, Mississippi, Eudora Welty (1909–2001) devoted most of her life to reading, writing, and gardening in the house her parents built in the 1920s. Her one extended departure from the South took her to the University of Wisconsin (B.A., 1929) and then to Columbia University in New York. She soon returned, however, traveling through "Depression-worn" Mississippi towns as a part-time journalist and photographer for the Works Progress Administration. Her fiction—short stories such as "Why I Live at the P.O." and "Death of a Traveling Salesman" as well as novels such as Delta Wedding *(1946),* The Ponder Heart *(1952), and* The Optimist's Daughter *(1972)—reflects the rural and small-town southern life she came to know during the first half of the twentieth century. Her work has received a Pulitzer Prize (1972) and numerous other awards, including the Presidential Medal of Freedom. Welty died in Jackson on July 23, 2001.*

Welty's experience of language largely involved listening—even to the words she read. Welty reflects on her own literary skill in her autobiographical account of her development as a writer, One Writer's Beginnings *(1983). An excerpt from the chapter entitled "Listening" follows, taking as its motif Welty's observation that "Ever since I was first read to, then started reading to myself, there has never been a line read that I didn't hear."*

I learned from the age of two or three that any room in our house, at any time of day, was there to read in, or to be read to. My mother read to me. She'd read to me in the big bedroom in the mornings, when we were in her rocker together, which ticked in rhythm as we rocked, as though we had a cricket accompanying the story. She'd read to me in the diningroom on winter afternoons in front of the coal fire, with our cuckoo clock ending the story with "Cuckoo," and at night when I'd got in my own bed. I must have given her no peace. Sometimes she read to me in the kitchen while she sat churning, and the churning sobbed along with *any* story. It was my ambition to have her read to me while I churned; once she granted my wish, but she read off my story before I brought her butter. She was an expressive reader. When she was reading "Puss in Boots," for instance, it was impossible not to know that she distrusted *all* cats.

It had been startling and disappointing to me to find out that story books had been written by *people*, that books were not natural wonders, coming up of themselves like grass. Yet regardless of where they came from, I cannot remember a time when I was not in love with them—with the books themselves, cover and binding and the paper they were printed on, with their smell and their weight and with their possession in my arms, captured and carried off to myself. Still illiterate, I was ready for them, committed to all the reading I could give them.

Neither of my parents had come from homes that could afford to buy many books, but though it must have been something of a strain on his salary, as the youngest officer in a young insurance company, my father was all the while carefully selecting and ordering away for what he and Mother thought we children should grow up with. They bought first for the future.

Besides the bookcase in the livingroom, which was always called "the library," there were the encyclopedia tables and dictionary stand under windows in our diningroom. Here to help us grow up arguing around the diningroom table were the Unabridged Webster, the Columbia Encyclopedia, Compton's Pictured Encyclopedia, the Lincoln Library of Information, and later the Book of Knowledge. And the year we moved into our new house, there was room to celebrate it with the new 1925 edition of the Britannica, which my father, his face always deliberately turned toward the future, was of course disposed to think better than any previous edition.

In "the library," inside the mission-style bookcase with its three diamond-latticed glass doors, with my father's Morris chair and the glass-shaded lamp on its table beside it, were books I could soon begin on—and I did, reading them all alike and as they came, straight down their rows, top shelf to bottom. There was the set of Stoddard's Lectures, in all its late nineteenth-century vocabulary and vignettes of peasant life and quaint beliefs and customs, with matching halftone illustrations: Vesuvius erupting, Venice by moonlight, gypsies glimpsed by their campfires. I didn't know then the clue they were to my father's longing to see the rest of the world. I read straight through his other love-from-afar: the Victrola Book of the Opera, with opera after opera in synopsis, with portraits in costume of Melba, Caruso, Galli-Curci, and Geraldine Farrar, some of whose voices we could listen to on our Red Seal records.

My mother read secondarily for information; she sank as a hedonist into novels. She read Dickens in the spirit in which she would have eloped with him.

5

The novels of her girlhood that had stayed on in her imagination, besides those of Dickens and Scott and Robert Louis Stevenson, were *Jane Eyre, Trilby, The Woman in White, Green Mansions, King Solomon's Mines.* Marie Corelli's name would crop up but I understood she had gone out of favor with my mother, who had only kept *Ardath* out of loyalty. In time she absorbed herself in Galsworthy, Edith Wharton, above all in Thomas Mann of the *Joseph* volumes.

St. Elmo was not in our house; I saw it often in other houses. This wildly popular Southern novel is where all the Edna Earles in our population started coming from. They're all named for the heroine, who succeeded in bringing a dissolute, sinning roué and atheist of a lover (St. Elmo) to his knees. My mother was able to forgo it. But she remembered the classic advice given to rose growers on how to water their bushes long enough: "Take a chair and *St. Elmo.*"

To both my parents I owe my early acquaintance with a beloved Mark Twain. There was a full set of Mark Twain and a short set of Ring Lardner in our bookcase, and those were the volumes that in time united us all, parents and children.

Reading everything that stood before me was how I came upon a worn old book without a back that had belonged to my father as a child. It was called *Sanford and Merton.* Is there anyone left who recognizes it, I wonder? It is the famous moral tale written by Thomas Day in the 1780s, but of him no mention is made on the title page of this book; here it is *Sanford and Merton in Words of One Syllable* by Mary Godolphin. Here are the rich boy and the poor boy and Mr. Barlow, their teacher and interlocutor, in long discourses alternating with dramatic scenes—danger and rescue allotted to the rich and the poor respectively. It may have only words of one syllable, but one of them is "quoth." It ends with not one but two morals, both engraved on rings: "Do what you ought, come what may," and "If we would be great, we must first learn to be good."

This book was lacking its front cover, the back held on by strips of pasted paper, now turned golden, in several layers, and the pages stained, flecked, and tattered around the edges; its garish illustrations had come unattached but were preserved, laid in. I had the feeling even in my heedless childhood that this was the only book my father as a little boy had had of his own. He had held onto it, and might have gone to sleep on its coverless face: he had lost his mother when he was seven. My father had never made any mention to his own children of the book, but he had brought it along with him from Ohio to our house and shelved it in our bookcase.

My mother had brought from West Virginia that set of Dickens; those books looked sad, too—they had been through fire and water before I was born, she told me, and there they were, lined up—as I later realized, waiting for *me.*

I was presented, from as early as I can remember, with books of my own, which appeared on my birthday and Christmas morning. Indeed, my parents could not give me books enough. They must have sacrificed to give me on my sixth or seventh birthday—it was after I became a reader for myself—the ten-volume set of *Our Wonder World.* These were beautifully made, heavy books I would lie down with on the floor in front of the diningroom hearth, and more often than the rest volume 5, *Every Child's Story Book*, was under my eyes. There were the fairy tales—Grimm, Andersen, the English, the French, "Ali Baba and the Forty Thieves"; and there was Aesop and Reynard the Fox; there were the myths and legends, Robin Hood, King Arthur, and St. George and the Dragon, even the history of Joan of Arc; a whack of *Pilgrim's Progress* and a long piece of *Gulliver*. They all carried their classic illustrations. I located myself in these pages and could go straight to the stories and pictures I loved; very often "The Yellow Dwarf" was first choice, with Walter Crane's Yellow Dwarf in full color making his terrifying appearance flanked by turkeys. Now that volume is as worn and backless and hanging apart as my father's poor *Sanford and Merton*. The precious page with Edward Lear's "Jumblies" on it has been in danger of slipping out for all these years. One measure of my love for Our Wonder World was that for a long time I wondered if I would go through fire and water for it as my mother had done for Charles Dickens; and the only comfort was to think I could ask my mother to do it for me.

I believe I'm the only child I know of who grew up with this treasure in the house. I used to ask others, "Did you have Our Wonder World?" I'd have to tell them the Book of Knowledge could not hold a candle to it.

I live in gratitude to my parents for initiating me—and as early as I begged for it, without keeping me waiting—into knowledge of the word, into reading and spelling, by way of the alphabet. They taught it to me at home in time for me to begin to read before starting to school. I believe the alphabet is no longer considered an essential piece of equipment for traveling through life. In my day it was the keystone to knowledge. You learned the alphabet as you learned to count to ten, as you learned "Now I lay me" and the Lord's Prayer and your father's and mother's name and address and telephone number, all in case you were lost.

My love for the alphabet, which endures, grew out of reciting it but, before 15 that, out of seeing the letters on the page. In my own story books, before I could read them for myself, I fell in love with various winding, enchanted-looking initials drawn by Walter Crane at the heads of fairy tales. In "Once upon a time," an "O" had a rabbit running it as a treadmill, his feet upon flowers. When the day came, years later, for me to see the Book of Kells, all the wizardry of letter, initial, and word swept over me a thousand times over, and the illumination, the gold, seemed a part of the word's beauty and holiness that had been there from the start.

My mother always sang to her children. Her voice came out just a little bit in the minor key. "Wee Willie Winkie's" song was wonderfully sad when she sang the lullabies.

"Oh, but now there's a record. She could have her own record to listen to," my father would have said. For there came a Victrola record of "Bobby Shafftoe" and "Rock-a-Bye Baby," all of Mother's lullabies, which could be played to take her place. Soon I was able to play her my own lullabies all day long.

Our Victrola stood in the diningroom. I was allowed to climb onto the seat of a diningroom chair to wind it, start the record turning, and set the needle playing.

In a second I'd jumped to the floor, to spin or march around the table as the music called for—now there were all the other records I could play too. I skinned back onto the chair just in time to lift the needle at the end, stop the record and turn it over, then change the needle. That brass receptacle with a hole in the lid gave off a metallic smell like human sweat, from all the hot needles that were fed it. Winding up, dancing, being cocked to start and stop the record, was of course all in one the act of *listening*—to "Overture to *Daughter of the Regiment*," "Selections from *The Fortune Teller*," "Kiss Me Again," "Gypsy Dance from *Carmen*," "Stars and Stripes Forever," "When the Midnight Choo-Choo Leaves for Alabam," or whatever came next. Movement must be at the very heart of listening.

Ever since I was first read to, then started reading to myself, there has never been a line read that I didn't *hear*. As my eyes followed the sentence, a voice was saying it silently to me. It isn't my mother's voice, or the voice of any person I can identify, certainly not my own. It is human, but inward, and it is inwardly that I listen to it. It is to me the voice of the story or the poem itself. The cadence, whatever it is that asks you to believe, the feeling that resides in the printed word, reaches me through the reader-voice. I have supposed, but never found out, that this is the case with all readers—to read as listeners—and with all writers, to write as listeners. It may be part of the desire to write. The sound of what falls on the page begins the process of testing it for truth, for me. Whether I am right to trust so far I don't know. By now I don't know whether I could do either one, reading or writing, without the other.

My own words, when I am at work on a story, I hear too as they go, in the same voice that I hear when I read in books. When I write and the sound of it comes back to my ears, then I act to make my changes. I have always trusted this voice. 20

QUESTIONS FOR DISCUSSION AND WRITING

1. What connections does Welty make among listening, reading, and writing? Explain why Welty devotes so much space to her childhood *reading* in her essay on "Listening." Why are the people, places, and objects around which her reading took place so important?

2. With a partner, take turns reading aloud sentences or paragraphs from this essay or another essay of your choice. Notice where the emphasis in each sentence falls, where you have to pause for breath, the characteristic sounds of the words and cadence of the sentences. Repeat words, phrases, and whole sentences to understand their feeling and their meaning. Then try the same with your own writing and your partner's. What does your experience of close listening teach you about writing? What strikes you when you listen that you didn't notice when you read these silently?

3. Compare Welty's experiences as one who loves reading and books with Gloria Naylor's in "The Love of Books" (p. 51). Not every avid reader becomes a writer. What enabled these people to move from childhood reading to careers as writers?

AMY TAN

Mother Tongue

Amy Tan's first novel, The Joy Luck Club *(1989), an integrated suite of stories about mothers and daughters, was a finalist for the National Book Award. Tan earned a bachelor's degree in English (1973) and a master's degree in linguistics (1974) at San Jose State University. After working as a child language development specialist and a freelance speechwriter, she began to write fiction. Tan's second novel,* The Kitchen God's Wife *(1991), is based on her mother's life in China before she immigrated to the United States after World War II. Her third book,* The Hundred Secret Senses *(1995), examines marriage and the meanings of motherhood and sisterhood in two cultures.* The Bonesetter's Daughter *(2001) returns to the complex relationship of Chinese mothers and their American-born daughters.*

In "Mother Tongue," first published in the Threepenny Review *(Fall 1990), Tan discusses "all the Englishes I grew up with"—the "simple" English "I spoke to my mother," the "broken" English "she used with me," her "'watered down'" translation of her mother's Chinese, and "her internal language," or what Tan "imagined to be her translation of her Chinese if she could speak in perfect English."*

I am not a scholar of English or literature. I cannot give you much more than personal opinions on the English language and its variations in this country or others.

I am a writer. And by that definition, I am someone who has always loved language. I am fascinated by language in daily life. I spend a great deal of my time thinking about the power of language—the way it can evoke an emotion, a visual image, a complex idea, or a simple truth. Language is the tool of my trade. And I use them all—all the Englishes I grew up with.

Recently, I was made keenly aware of the different Englishes I do use. I was giving a talk to a large group of people, the same talk I had already given to half a dozen other groups. The nature of the talk was about my writing, my life, and my book, *The Joy Luck Club*. The talk was going along well enough, until I remembered one major difference that made the whole talk sound wrong. My mother was in the room. And it was perhaps the first time she had heard me give a lengthy speech, using the kind of English I have never used with her. I was saying things like, "The intersection of memory upon imagination" and "There is an aspect of my fiction that relates to thus-and-thus"—a speech filled with carefully wrought grammatical phrases, burdened, it suddenly seemed to me, with nominalized forms, past perfect tenses, conditional phrases, all the forms of standard English that I had learned in school and through books, the forms of English I did not use at home with my mother.

Just last week, I was walking down the street with my mother, and I again found myself conscious of the English I was using, the English I do use with her. We were talking about the price of new and used furniture and I heard myself saying this: "Not waste money that way." My husband was with us as well, and he didn't notice any switch in my English. And then I realized why. It's because over the twenty years we've been together I've often used that same kind of English with him, and sometimes he even uses it with me. It has become our language of intimacy, a different sort of English that relates to family talk, the language I grew up with.

So you'll have some idea of what this family talk I heard sounds like, I'll 5 quote what my mother said during a recent conversation which I videotaped and then transcribed. During this conversation, my mother was talking about a political gangster in Shanghai who had the same last name as her family's, Du, and how the gangster in his early years wanted to be adopted by her family, which was rich by comparison. Later, the gangster became more powerful, far richer than my mother's family, and one day showed up at my mother's wedding to pay his respects. Here's what she said in part:

"Du Yusong having business like fruit stand. Like off the street kind. He is Du like Du Zong—but not Tsung-ming Island people. The local people call putong, the river east side, he belong to that side local people. That man want to ask Du Zong father take him in like become own family. Du Zong father wasn't look down on him, but didn't take seriously, until that man big like become a mafia. Now important person, very hard to inviting him. Chinese way, came only to show respect, don't stay for dinner. Respect for making big celebration, he shows up. Mean give lots of respect. Chinese custom. Chinese social life that way. If too important won't have to stay too long. He come to my wedding. I didn't see, I heard it. I gone to boy's side, they have YMCA dinner. Chinese age I was nineteen."

You should know that my mother's expressive command of English belies how much she actually understands. She reads the *Forbes* report, listens to *Wall Street Week,* converses daily with her stockbroker, reads all of Shirley MacLaine's books with ease—all kinds of things I can't begin to understand. Yet some of my friends tell me they understand 50 percent of what my mother says. Some say they understand 80 to 90 percent. Some say they understand none of it, as if she were speaking pure Chinese. But to me, my mother's English is perfectly clear, perfectly natural. It's my mother tongue. Her language, as I hear it, is vivid, direct, full of observation and imagery. That was the language that helped shape the way I saw things, expressed things, made sense of the world.

Lately, I've been giving more thought to the kind of English my mother speaks. Like others, I have described it to people as "broken" or "fractured" English. But I wince when I say that. It has always bothered me that I can think of no way to describe it other than "broken," as if it were damaged and needed to be fixed, as if it lacked a certain wholeness and soundness. I've heard other terms used, "limited English," for example. But they seem just as bad, as if everything is limited, including people's perceptions of the limited English speaker.

I know this for a fact, because when I was growing up, my mother's "limited" English limited *my* perception of her. I was ashamed of her English. I believed that her English reflected the quality of what she had to say. That is, because she expressed them imperfectly her thoughts were imperfect. And I had plenty of empirical evidence to support me: the fact that people in department stores, at banks, and at restaurants did not take her seriously, did not give her good service, pretended not to understand her, or even acted as if they did not hear her.

My mother has long realized the limitations of her English as well. When I   10
was fifteen, she used to have me call people on the phone to pretend I was she. In this guise, I was forced to ask for information or even to complain and yell at people who had been rude to her. One time it was a call to her stockbroker in New York. She had cashed out her small portfolio and it just happened we were going to go to New York the next week, our very first trip outside California. I had to get on the phone and say in an adolescent voice that was not very convincing, "This is Mrs. Tan."

And my mother was standing in the back whispering loudly, "Why he don't send me check, already two weeks late. So mad he lie to me, losing me money."

And then I said in perfect English, "Yes, I'm getting rather concerned. You had agreed to send the check two weeks ago, but it hasn't arrived."

Then she began to talk more loudly. "What he want, I come to New York tell him front of his boss, you cheating me?" And I was trying to calm her down, make her be quiet, while telling the stockbroker, "I can't tolerate any more excuses. If I don't receive the check immediately, I am going to have to speak to your manager when I'm in New York next week." And sure enough, the following week there we were in front of this astonished stockbroker, and I was sitting there red-faced and quiet, and my mother, the real Mrs. Tan, was shouting at his boss in her impeccable broken English.

We used a similar routine just five days ago, for a situation that was far less humorous. My mother had gone to the hospital for an appointment, to find out about a benign brain tumor a CAT scan had revealed a month ago. She said she had spoken very good English, her best English, no mistakes. Still, she said, the hospital did not apologize when they said they had lost the CAT scan and she had come for nothing. She said they did not seem to have any sympathy when she told them she was anxious to know the exact diagnosis, since her husband and son had both died of brain tumors. She said they would not give her any more information until the next time and she would have to make another appointment for that. So she said she would not leave until the doctor called her daughter. She wouldn't budge. And when the doctor finally called her daughter, me, who spoke in perfect English — lo and behold — we had assurances the CAT scan would be found, promises that a conference call on Monday would be held, and apologies for any suffering my mother had gone through for a most regrettable mistake.

I think my mother's English almost had an effect on limiting my possibilities   15
in life as well. Sociologists and linguists probably will tell you that a person's de-

veloping language skills are more influenced by peers. But I do think that the language spoken in the family, especially in immigrant families which are more insular, plays a large role in shaping the language of the child. And I believe that it affected my results on achievement tests, IQ tests, and the SAT. While my English skills were never judged as poor, compared to math, English could not be considered my strong suit. In grade school I did moderately well, getting perhaps B's, sometimes B-pluses, in English and scoring perhaps in the sixtieth or seventieth percentile on achievement tests. But those scores were not good enough to override the opinion that my true abilities lay in math and science, because in those areas I achieved A's and scored in the ninetieth percentile or higher.

This was understandable. Math is precise; there is only one correct answer. Whereas, for me at least, the answers on English tests were always a judgment call, a matter of opinion and personal experience. Those tests were constructed around items like fill-in-the-blank sentence completion, such as, "Even though Tom was _____, Mary thought he was _____." And the correct answer always seemed to be the most bland combinations of thoughts, for example "Even though Tom was shy, Mary thought he was charming," with the grammatical structure "even though" limiting the correct answer to some sort of semantic opposites, so you wouldn't get answers like, "Even though Tom was foolish, Mary thought he was ridiculous." Well, according to my mother, there were very few limitations as to what Tom could have been and what Mary might have thought of him. So I never did well on tests like that.

The same was true with word analogies, pairs of words in which you were supposed to find some sort of logical, semantic relationship — for example, "*Sunset* is to *nightfall* as _____ is to _____." And here you would be presented with a list of four possible pairs, one of which showed the same kind of relationship: *red* is to *spotlight, bus* is to *arrival, chills* is to *fever, yawn* is to *boring.* Well, I could never think that way. I knew what the tests were asking, but I could not block out of my mind the images already created by the first pair, "*sunset* is to *nightfall*" — and I would see a burst of colors against a darkening sky, the moon rising, the lowering of a curtain of stars. And all the other pairs of words — red, bus, spotlight, boring — just threw up a mass of confusing images, making it impossible for me to sort out something as logical as saying: "A sunset precedes nightfall" is the same as "a chill precedes a fever." The only way I would have gotten that answer right would have been to imagine an associative situation, for example, my being disobedient and staying out past sunset, catching a chill at night, which turns into feverish pneumonia as punishment, which indeed did happen to me.

I have been thinking about all this lately, about my mother's English, about achievement tests. Because lately I've been asked, as a writer, why there are not more Asian Americans represented in American literature. Why are there few Asian Americans enrolled in creative writing programs? Why do so many Chinese students go into engineering? Well, these are broad sociological questions I can't begin to answer. But I have noticed in surveys — in fact, just last week — that Asian students, as a whole, always do significantly better on math achievement tests than in English. And this makes me think that there are other Asian American students whose English spoken in the home might also be described as "broken" or "limited." And perhaps they also have teachers who are steering them away from writing and into math and science, which is what happened to me.

Fortunately, I happen to be rebellious in nature and enjoy the challenge of disproving assumptions made about me. I became an English major my first year in college, after being enrolled as pre-med. I started writing nonfiction as a freelancer the week after I was told by my former boss that writing was my worst skill and I should hone my talents toward account management.

But it wasn't until 1985 that I finally began to write fiction. And at first I   20 wrote using what I thought to be wittily crafted sentences, sentences that would finally prove I had mastery over the English language. Here's an example from the first draft of a story that later made its way into *The Joy Luck Club,* but without this line: "That was my mental quandary in its nascent state." A terrible line, which I can barely pronounce.

Fortunately, for reasons I won't get into today, I later decided I should envision a reader for the stories I would write. And the reader I decided upon was my mother, because these were stories about mothers. So with this reader in mind— and in fact she did read my early drafts—I began to write stories using all the Englishes I grew up with: the English I spoke to my mother, which for lack of a better term might be described as "simple"; the English she used with me, which for lack of a better term might be described as "broken"; my translation of her Chinese, which could certainly be described as "watered down"; and what I imagined to be her translation of her Chinese if she could speak in perfect English, her internal language, and for that I sought to preserve the essence, but neither an English nor a Chinese structure. I wanted to capture what language ability tests can never reveal: her intent, her passion, her imagery, the rhythms of her speech, and the nature of her thoughts.

Apart from what any critic had to say about my writing, I knew I had succeeded where it counted when my mother finished reading my book and gave me her verdict: "So easy to read."

AMY BORKOWSKY

Amy's Answering Machine

Amy Borkowsky works by day as creative director for a Manhattan advertising agency, by night as a comedian. She explains, "Residing almost 1000 miles away from her mother, Amy enjoys sitting too close to the TV, talking to strangers, and leaving the house without a sweater." Her mother, a former office manager, has "appointed herself to the position of Manager of Amy's Entire Life."

BOB EDWARDS, HOST: Amy Borkowsky is a stand-up comic who lives in New York.

(Soundbite of answering machine message)

(Soundbite of beep)

AMY'S MOTHER: Hi, Amila. It's me, honey. Maybe I could come up for a little while, like for a few months maybe?

EDWARDS: For more than 10 years, Amy Borkowsky has been collecting phone 5 messages from her mother, whom she identifies only as "Mom." The funniest and warmest of those messages have been compiled in a CD and a book titled "Amy's Answering Machine." [2002]...

(Soundbite of answering machine message)

(Soundbite of beep)

AMY'S MOTHER: Amila, I hope you're on your way home. I just heard on the weather; there's a big storm headed for New York. On the weather map, they had snowflakes the size of bagels. So if you have to go out, wrap a scarf around your face to protect it because, you know, there was that man who climbed Mt. Everest and lost his entire nose. OK, honey? Bye-bye.

EDWARDS: She's always been like this, right?

MS. BORKOWSKY: Oh, yes. My mother has always been overprotective. The differ- 10 ence is, it's appropriate when you're like two years old and your mother's asking you if you need to go potty. That's appropriate. But once you, like, hit 30, it's really not necessary.

(Soundbite of answering machine message)

(Soundbite of beep)

AMY'S MOTHER: Hi, Amila. I just was watching the news, and I heard about that little girl who was alone in an apartment for nine days without food. Honey, please, be sure you have what to eat in the fridge, 'cause last time you came to visit, you looked like Olive Oyl. OK, honey. Bye-bye.

EDWARDS: When did you realize she was funny?

MS. BORKOWSKY: I'm still waiting to realize that. Other people seem to get a kick 15 out of her. I think it's always easier to laugh at somebody else's mother.

EDWARDS: Well, this had to be exasperating once.

MS. BORKOWSKY: Oh, yeah. Now I'm torn, because part of me, of course, is still frustrated, and another part of me thinks, 'OK. Here comes volume two.'

(Soundbite of answering machine message)

(Soundbite of beep)

AMY'S MOTHER: Yeah, Amila, hi, it's me. I meant to tell you so you don't set off the metal detector at the airport, make sure you don't wear an underwire bra. A lady on the bus said it happened to a woman she knew, and she claims they frisked her for four hours. Even if she's exaggerating and it was only two, that's a long time to have a stranger surveying your land. So just for one day, you may even want to consider going braless. Love you. Bye.

MS. BORKOWSKY: That actually happened. I was going to a fund-raiser in, I think it 20 was Omaha, and the alarm went off. And they asked me—the guy said, 'Are you wearing an underwire bra?' And actually, I was, so sometimes she's right, as much as I hate to admit it.

QUESTIONS FOR DISCUSSION AND WRITING

1. What connections does Tan make throughout the essay between speaking and writing? In which English has Tan written "Mother Tongue"? Why?

2. How do the "Englishes" spoken by Tan and her mother help them communicate their personalities, intelligence, and relationship with one another? Compare and contrast Tan's and Borkowsky's mothers as they appear in their daughters' loving, amusing re-creations of their "mother tongue."

3. What differences are there between language used for family or home and language for public use?

4. With family, friends, teammates, or colleagues at school or work, tape (video or audio) a conversation that involves more than one "language"—formal, informal, slang, specialized for the task at hand, or bilingual. Then analyze the tape and write a paper identifying the conspicuous features of the languages involved. How do the speakers know which language(s) to use under what circumstances?

5. Present to an audience of college-educated Americans an argument for or against the necessity of speaking (or writing) in standard English. (What, in your estimation, are the conspicuous features of standard English?) Are there times and places where you'd allow for exceptions?

MARJORIE AGOSÍN

Always Living in Spanish

Writer and human rights activist Marjorie Agosín was born in 1955 into a Jewish family that resided in Chile, having left Europe under the shadow of the Holocaust. At the age of sixteen, Agosín was uprooted from her girlhood in Santiago de Chile

when the Socialist government of Salvador Allende was overthrown. Her family im-
migrated to the United States, where she attended the University of Georgia (B.A.,
1976) and earned advanced degrees at Indiana University (M.A., 1977; Ph.D.,
1982). Currently a professor of Spanish at Wellesley College, Agosín is the author of
several volumes of poetry and autobiography, including Dear Anne Frank, *which*
was published in an English edition in 1998. She has also published literary criticism
and nonfiction about women and other groups targeted for discrimination in third-
world countries, including Invisible Dreamer: Memory, Judaism, and Human
Rights *(2001). Among her numerous literary honors is the Latino Literature Prize*
for Poetry (1995) for Toward the Splendid City *(1994).*

"Always Living in Spanish" explores the link between language and identity,
from the personal to the ethnic to the geographic versions of the self. Each of Agosín's
languages evokes a different set of images and feelings; writing in her native Spanish
connects her to her formative experiences.

In the evenings in the northern hemisphere, I repeat the ancient ritual that I observed as a child in the southern hemisphere: going out while the night is still
warm and trying to recognize the stars as it begins to grow dark silently. In the
sky of my country, Chile, that long and wide stretch of land that the poets blessed
and dictators abused, I could easily name the stars: the three Marias, the Southern Cross, and the three Lilies, names of beloved and courageous women.

But here in the United States, where I have lived since I was a young girl, the
solitude of exile makes me feel that so little is mine, that not even the sky has the
same constellations, the trees and the fauna the same names or sounds, or the rubbish the same smell. How does one recover the familiar? How does one name the
unfamiliar? How can one be another or live in a foreign language? These are the
dilemmas of one who writes in Spanish and lives in translation.

Since my earliest childhood in Chile I lived with the tempos and the melodies
of a multiplicity of tongues: German, Yiddish, Russian, Turkish, and many Latin
songs. Because everyone was from somewhere else, my relatives laughed, sang,
and fought in a Babylon of languages. Spanish was reserved for matters of extreme
seriousness, for commercial transactions, or for illnesses, but everyone's mother
tongue was always associated with the memory of spaces inhabited in the past: the
shtetl, the flowering and vast Vienna avenues, the minarets of Turkey, and the
Ladino whispers of Toledo. When my paternal grandmother sang old songs in
Turkish, her voice and body assumed the passion of one who was there in the city
of Istanbul, gazing by turns toward the west and the east.

Destiny and the always ambiguous nature of history continued my family's
enforced migration, and because of it I, too, became one who had to live and speak
in translation. The disappearances, torture, and clandestine deaths in my country
in the early seventies drove us to the United States, that other America that looked
with suspicion at those who did not speak English and especially those who came
from the supposedly uncivilized regions of Latin America. I had left a dangerous
place that was my home, only to arrive in a dangerous place that was not: a high

school in the small town of Athens, Georgia, where my poor English and my accent were the cause of ridicule and insult. The only way I could recover my usurped country and my Chilean childhood was by continuing to write in Spanish, the same way my grandparents had sung in their own tongues in diasporic sites.

The new and learned English language did not fit with the visceral emotions and themes that my poetry contained, but by writing in Spanish I could recover fragrances, spoken rhythms, and the passion of my own identity. Daily I felt the need to translate myself for the strangers living all around me, to tell them why we were in Georgia, why we are different, why we had fled, why my accent was so thick, and why I did not look Hispanic. Only at night, writing poems in Spanish, could I return to my senses, and soothe my own sorrow over what I had left behind. 5

This is how I became a Chilean poet who wrote in Spanish and lived in the southern United States. And then, one day, a poem of mine was translated and published in the English language. Finally, for the first time since I had left Chile, I felt I didn't have to explain myself. My poem, expressed in another language, spoke for itself . . . and for me.

Sometimes the austere sounds of English help me bear the solitude of knowing that I am foreign and so far away from those about whom I write. I must admit I would like more opportunities to read in Spanish to people whose language and culture is also mine, to join in our common heritage and in the feast of our sounds. I would also like readers of English to understand the beauty of the spoken word in Spanish, that constant flow of oxytonic and paroxytonic syllables (*Vérde qué té quiéro vérde*),[1] the joy of writing—of dancing—in another language. I believe that many exiles share the unresolvable torment of not being able to live in the language of their childhood.

I miss that undulating and sensuous language of mine, those baroque descriptions, the sense of being and feeling that Spanish gives me. It is perhaps for this reason that I have chosen and will always choose to write in Spanish. Nothing else from my childhood world remains. My country seems to be frozen in gestures of silence and oblivion. My relatives have died, and I have grown up not knowing a young generation of cousins and nieces and nephews. Many of my friends were disappeared, others were tortured, and the most fortunate, like me, became guardians of memory. For us, to write in Spanish is to always be in active pursuit of memory. I seek to recapture a world lost to me on that sorrowful afternoon when the blue electric sky and the Andean cordillera bade me farewell. On that, my last Chilean day, I carried under my arm my innocence recorded in a little blue notebook I kept even then. Gradually that diary filled with memoranda, poems written in free verse, descriptions of dreams and of the thresholds of my house surrounded by cherry trees and gardenias. To write in Spanish is for me a

---

[1]Oxytonic places the main stress on a word's last or only syllable. Paroxytonic stress occurs on a word's next to last syllable. *Vérde qué té quiéro vérde* "Green how I want you green" is the opening line of a poem by Federico García Lorca that illustrates this stress pattern.

gesture of survival. And because of translation, my memory has now become a part of the memory of many others.

Translators are not traitors, as the proverb says, but rather splendid friends in this great human community of language.

QUESTIONS FOR DISCUSSION AND WRITING

1. How many sources of identity does Agosín mention in this essay? Consider dimensions of the self such as languages, locations, time periods, and ethnicity. Do you think her struggle to reconnect or stay connected to these parts of herself is atypical, or does everyone experience this struggle? Give examples to support your answers.

2. This essay expresses Agosín's feelings about her native Spanish and her feelings about English. What is the main difference between the two languages for her? What different feelings and ideas does each language evoke? Can Agosín's writing in English—for an English-speaking audience—adequately convey her feelings and thoughts about writing in Spanish? Or can only Spanish do justice to this subject? What does Agosín say to evoke a sympathetic understanding from even monolingual readers?

3. If you speak a second language—fluently or as a beginner—have you noticed that you associate different feelings, thoughts, or parts of your identity with that language? Write about the sensual, geographic, ethnic, or life-history aspects of your "first" compared with your "second" language. Alternatively, you could discuss within your family or circle of friends how various forms of language such as slang, sarcasm, or acronyms (used in text messaging) shape and express identity.

4. Write about the problem of being expected to function in a culture different from the one you grew up in—one of the central issues in Agosín's essay. Discuss how you, or someone you know, dealt with being placed in an unfamiliar environment—perhaps through emigration or a move, extended travel, a new job, or study abroad—where differences of language or culture presented a major challenge. In what ways did this experience compare to the experiences that Agosín describes, such as longing for the familiar or trying to reconnect with one's past? Draw some general conclusions about the way people cope with "living 'in translation'" (paragraph 2).

SHERMAN ALEXIE

The Joy of Reading and Writing:
Superman and Me

For author Sherman Alexie, Native American identity is a challenge to be met with imaginative writing. In over a dozen novels and collections of stories and poems, Alexie uses stories to deal with the tragic depression, stultifying normalcy, and quirky comedy of Indian life on and off the reservation. Unlike some authors, however, Alexie is impatient with mythical stereotypes. As he wryly informed a Cineaste *magazine interviewer, "I've never seen an Indian turn into a deer. I mean, I know thousands of Indians, I've been an Indian my whole life, and I've yet to see an Indian turn into an animal!" A descendent of Spokane and Coeur d'Alene tribal ancestors, Alexie was born in 1966 on the Spokane Indian Reservation in Wellpinit, Washington. He attended Gonzaga University and finished his degree at Washington State University (B.A., 1991). A year after graduation his first book,* The Business of Fancydancing: Stories and Poems, *appeared. Other work includes the screenplay for the film* Smoke Signals *(1998), based on his story collection* The Lone Ranger and Tonto Fistfight in Heaven *(1993). His story collection* Ten Little Indians *appeared in 2003.*

"The Joy of Reading and Writing: Superman and Me" (first published in The Most Wonderful Books, *1997) discloses the excitement, stimulation, and power that being immersed in books, literally and figuratively, can convey to readers, novice and sophisticated alike. As a child, Alexie understood their many messages, which together meant "I refused to fail."*

I learned to read with a *Superman* comic book. Simple enough, I suppose. I cannot recall which particular *Superman* comic book I read, nor can I remember which villain he fought in that issue. I cannot remember the plot, nor the means by which I obtained the comic book. What I can remember is this: I was three years old, a Spokane Indian boy living with his family on the Spokane Indian Reservation in eastern Washington state. We were poor by most standards, but one of my parents usually managed to find some minimum-wage job or another, which made us middle-class by reservation standards. I had a brother and three sisters. We lived on a combination of irregular paychecks, hope, fear, and government surplus food.

My father, who is one of the few Indians who went to Catholic school on purpose, was an avid reader of westerns, spy thrillers, murder mysteries, gangster epics, basketball player biographies, and anything else he could find. He bought his books by the pound at Dutch's Pawn Shop, Goodwill, Salvation Army, and Value Village. When he had extra money, he bought new novels at supermarkets, convenience stores, and hospital gift shops. Our house was filled with books. They were stacked in crazy piles in the bathroom, bedrooms, and living room. In a fit of unemployment-inspired creative energy, my father built a set of bookshelves and soon filled them with a random assortment of books about the Kennedy assassination, Watergate, the Vietnam War, and the entire twenty-three-book series of the Apache westerns. My father loved books, and since I loved my father with an aching devotion, I decided to love books as well.

I can remember picking up my father's books before I could read. The words themselves were mostly foreign, but I still remember the exact moment when I first understood, with a sudden clarity, the purpose of a paragraph. I didn't have the vocabulary to say "paragraph," but I realized that a paragraph was a fence that held words. The words inside a paragraph worked together for a common purpose. They had some specific reason for being inside the same fence. This knowledge delighted me. I began to think of everything in terms of paragraphs. Our reservation was a small paragraph within the United States. My family's house was a paragraph, distinct from the other paragraphs of the LeBrets to the north, the Fords to our south, and the Tribal School to the west. Inside our house, each family member existed as a separate paragraph but still had genetics and common experiences to link us. Now, using this logic, I can see my changed family as an essay of seven paragraphs: mother, father, older brother, the deceased sister, my younger twin sisters, and our adopted little brother.

At the same time I was seeing the world in paragraphs, I also picked up the *Superman* comic book. Each panel, complete with picture, dialogue, and narrative, was a three-dimensional paragraph. In one panel, Superman breaks through a door. His suit is red, blue, and yellow. The brown door shatters into many pieces. I look at the narrative above the picture. I cannot read the words, but I assume it tells me that "Superman is breaking down the door." Aloud, I pretend to read the words and say, "Superman is breaking down the door." Words, dialogue, also float out of Superman's mouth. Because he is breaking down the door, I assume he says, "I am breaking down the door." Once again, I pretend to read the words and say aloud, "I am breaking down the door." In this way, I learned to read.

This might be an interesting story all by itself. A little Indian boy teaches himself to read at an early age and advances quickly. He reads *Grapes of Wrath* in kindergarten when other children are struggling through Dick and Jane. If he'd been anything but an Indian boy living on the reservation, he might have been called a prodigy. But he is an Indian boy living on the reservation and is simply an oddity. He grows into a man who often speaks of his childhood in the third-person, as if it will somehow dull the pain and make him sound more modest about his talents.

A smart Indian is a dangerous person, widely feared and ridiculed by Indians and non-Indians alike. I fought with my classmates on a daily basis. They wanted me to stay quiet when the non-Indian teacher asked for answers, for volunteers, for help. We were Indian children who were expected to be stupid. Most lived up to those expectations inside the classroom but subverted them on the outside. They struggled with basic reading in school but could remember how to sing a few dozen powwow songs. They were monosyllabic in front of their non-Indian teachers but could tell complicated stories and jokes at the dinner table. They submissively ducked their heads when confronted by a non-Indian adult but would slug it out with the Indian bully who was ten years older. As Indian children, we were expected to fail in the non-Indian world. Those who failed were ceremonially accepted by other Indians and appropriately pitied by non-Indians.

I refused to fail. I was smart. I was arrogant. I was lucky. I read books late into the night, until I could barely keep my eyes open. I read books at recess, then during lunch, and in the few minutes left after I had finished my classroom assignments. I read books in the car when my family traveled to powwows or basketball games. In shopping malls, I ran to the bookstores and read bits and pieces of as many books as I could. I read the books my father brought home from the pawnshops and secondhand. I read the books I borrowed from the library. I read the backs of cereal boxes. I read the newspaper. I read the bulletins posted on the walls of the school, the clinic, the tribal offices, the post office. I read junk mail. I read auto-repair manuals. I read magazines. I read anything that had words and paragraphs. I read with equal parts joy and desperation. I loved those books, but I also knew that love had only one purpose. I was trying to save my life.

Despite all the books I read, I am still surprised I became a writer. I was going to be a pediatrician. These days, I write novels, short stories, and poems. I visit schools and teach creative writing to Indian kids. In all my years in the reservation school system, I was never taught how to write poetry, short stories, or novels. I was certainly never taught that Indians wrote poetry, short stories, and novels. Writing was something beyond Indians. I cannot recall a single time that a guest teacher visited the reservation. There must have been visiting teachers. Who were they? Where are they now? Do they exist? I visit the schools as often as possible. The Indian kids crowd the classroom. Many are writing their own poems, short stories, and novels. They have read my books. They have read many other books. They look at me with bright eyes and arrogant wonder. They are trying to save their lives. Then there are the sullen and already defeated Indian kids who sit in the back rows and ignore me with theatrical precision. The pages of their notebooks are empty. They carry neither pencil nor pen. They stare out the window. They refuse and resist. "Books," I say to them. "Books," I say. I throw my weight against their locked doors. The door holds. I am smart. I am arrogant. I am lucky. I am trying to save our lives.

QUESTIONS FOR DISCUSSION AND WRITING

1. Elaborate—in discussion or in a paper—on Alexie's observations that "A smart Indian is a dangerous person" and "I refused to fail. I was smart. I was lucky. I read books late into the night" (paragraphs 6 and 7). Why is a "smart Indian . . . widely feared and ridiculed by Indians and non-Indians alike" (paragraph 6)? What threats does an independent-minded Indian (or anyone) pose to complacent or powerful people or to society in general?

2. Compare and contrast Welty's "Listening" (p. 33), Naylor's "The Love of Books" (p. 51), and Alexie's "Superman and Me" (p. 47). Using the Questions for Discussion and writing following Welty (p. 37), examine the connections each makes between the acts of reading and writing.

3. Write a paper, either individually or with a partner, on reading as a source of empowerment for the reader. Draw on your experiences as a reader, as well as those of Alexie, Welty, and Naylor.

GLORIA NAYLOR

The Love of Books

Naylor's parents, from Mississippi sharecropper families, worked twelve hours a day in the fields, "from can't see to can't see," says their daughter. Her mother, an avid reader denied access to the public library, vowed to live in the North where her children would have the freedom to learn. Naylor (b. 1950) was raised in Brooklyn, although hers was "a southern home, with southern food, southern language, southern values, [and] southern codes of behavior." She majored in English at Brooklyn College (B.A., 1981) and earned a master's degree in Afro-American Studies from Yale in 1983. Inspired by Zora Neale Hurston, Alice Walker, and Toni Morrison, Naylor's first novel, The Women of Brewster Place, *won the American Book Award in 1983. She has since published four more novels,* Linden Hills *(1985),* Mama Day *(1988),* Bailey's Cafe *(1992), and* The Men of Brewster Place *(1998), and* 1996 *(2005), a fictionalized memoir.*

In "The Love of Books," first published in The Writing Life *(1995), a collection of essays by winners of the National Book Award, Naylor responds to the question "Why do I write?" Her answer, embedded in the autobiography of a black girl learning to read and a black woman learning to write, extends to encompass a race and a worldwide culture: "By learning there was this heritage of writers behind me, specifically black female writers, when I looked in the mirror there was the image I desperately needed to see. . . . [It] did not say that black was beautiful, it did not say that black was ugly. It said simply: you are."*

Any life amounts to "organized chaos": biologically we are more space than matter and that matter consists of careening atoms always in flux; psychologically we are minute electrical charges, running from the brain to the spinal cord, the organs, the hormonal systems. Sitting apart from that is a consciousness that orders, to our specific preferences, any given reality at any given time. A long way of saying: our lives are what we make them. And definitely our "writing lives," which is miming life in both its execution and its product. And so to make sense of the senseless, writers reach for metaphors to explain—to themselves and others—exactly what it is that they do. Those metaphors and the resultant explanations are value-laden; they spring from our specific culture and our personal politics.

Why do I write? The truth, the unvarnished truth, is that I haven't a clue. The answer to that question lies hidden in the same box that holds the origin of human creativity, our imperative need as a species to communicate, and to be touched. Many minds for many years have busied themselves trying to unlock that box, and writers, for the most part, are quite happy to allow the literary critics, anthropologists, psychologists, and biologists to argue interdiscipline and intradiscipline while they stay out of the fray. And when writers are invited in, they'll reach for some shorthand, some metaphor, to throw quickly into the ring so they can get back to doing—for whatever reason—what they do best.

I normally reach for a poem called "The Unclaimed," by Nikky Finney, a young African-American woman who evokes the spirit of all the women in her past "whose names do not ripple in neon lights or whose distinctiveness has yet to be embedded on printed paper." These women, the poet tells us, were never allowed time to pamper themselves in front of mirrors or even time to cry. They were women who sang over stovetops and washtubs; scribbled poems on bits of paper and dinner napkins—women who acted out the drama of their lives unsung and forgotten. And so she concludes:

> for all that you were
> for all that you always wanted to be
> each time i sign my name
> know that it is for a thousand like you
> who could not hold a pen
> but who instead held me
> and rocked me gently
> to the creative rhythms
> i now live by

I elect to trace the untraceable, my passionate love of books and my affair with the written word, back to my mother, who was also an avid lover of books. She and my father were from sharecropping families and grew up in the 1930s in Mississippi. She was not allowed to use the public libraries; and purchasing books was out of the question for her. What many young people tend to forget today, in the age of excessiveness and of almost ingrained waste that we have in consumerist America, is that books were once a luxury for people until the advent of the ten-cent novel which ultimately evolved into the paperback. Most people, especially working-class and poor people, were not able to buy books so they depended on the public libraries. That was why Ben Franklin instituted the free lending library, hoping to give the children of the working class at least a competitive edge with the children of the upper classes, who could afford to have books.

My mother was one of eight children and her family worked collectively on a ⁵ farm from Monday to Friday to bring in the requisite crop—for them it was cotton. Since this was in the South, in the Bible Belt, it meant that Sunday was spent in church—all day. Saturday was then the only free time my mother had. So while her sisters and brothers went off to town to spend their time, she would hire herself out in someone else's field on her free Saturdays. For that labor, she received fifty cents—a day but it was her fifty cents. At the end of the month she had two dollars and she would take that two dollars and send away to book clubs. And that's how she got her reading material.

She made a vow to herself that she would never raise a child in the South. It is ironic that when my parents, in 1949, moved north to New York City, they left behind a region that would eventually become a place much more conducive for African-Americans to hold power than the place to which they fled. But who was to know the future? My mother only knew her past. And her history spoke loud and clear: if you were poor, and if you were black in Tunica County, you were not going to read. She always told my sisters and me that she was not ashamed of her background—it was no sin to be poor. But the greatest sin is to keep people from learning to dream. And my mother believed that books taught the young how to dream. She knew, of course, that she would not be eradicating racism from her life by moving, as Malcolm X said, "from down South to up South." But she was aware that, in New York City at least, her tax dollars would go to support public institutions that would be open to her children.

Because we grew up without much money and a whole lot of dreams, we spent a great deal of time in the public libraries. The law in New York was that a child had to be able to write their name in order to get a juvenile library card. But before my sisters and I had even attained the age of literacy, my mother would take us on these pilgrimages to the library. They live in my mind as small dark rooms with heavy wood bookcases and the heavy desks of the librarian, who looked like Olive Oyl. My mother would say, "Do you see all these books? Once you can write your name, all of these books will be yours. For two weeks. But yours."

I had to get much older to understand why she took us on those pilgrimages. While indeed it was to educate us, I think it was also to heal some place within herself. For me it made the library a place that was quite familiar, a place that was even welcoming. I was eager to be able to qualify to enter those doors. I was eager to discover whatever mystery was within the ink upon that paper, because also within me—and this had to be genetic—was a fascination with the written word. I used to love the feel and the heft of a book. In those days, they were made with a certain kind of glue and when you broke the binding you could smell that special glue. I'm not saying I was getting high off that glue. There was just this wonderful, earthy smell to it.

My mother didn't know then and, of course, at four and five I didn't know that I was on my way to being a very shy and very repressed adolescent. Books were to be my only avenue out of the walls my emotions built around me in those years. I felt trapped within my home and trapped within school, and it was through the pages of books that I was released into other worlds. I literally read my way from the A's to the Z's in the children's section of the library. I can still see that two-shelf row of books, and it ran the whole length of the room. Louisa May Alcott's, I recall, was the first set of books—*Little Women,* and *Little Men,* and *Jo's Boys,* and *Under the Umbrella*—she wrote a whole slew of books following those young women from adolescence into adulthood. I can remember reading all the way through to the last author because there was another set of books by Laura Ingalls Wilder—*Little House on the Prairie, Little House in the Big Woods,*

Those Happy Golden Years. Once again following a young girl in her coming-of-age from adolescence all the way into adulthood and marriage. It was the world through which I lived.

I don't believe this would have been enough to have created a writer, although most writers first begin as avid readers. But a writer needs something else —a conscious connection between the validity of their personal experiences and the page. My shyness kept me from communicating verbally, to the point that my teachers thought perhaps I was slow. The theory of education in those years—the fifties and early sixties—held that a well-rounded child participated in class. That meant raising your hand, which for a child like me meant to break out in a cold sweat. The idea that I had to step forth and give voice to something was a nightmare.

My mother, seeing that I was not a talker and understanding that indeed I was, of the three girls, perhaps her most gifted child (the teachers came to understand that later as well because I always excelled in the written tests), went out to Woolworth's and bought me one of those white plastic diaries. I think they went for something like ninety-nine cents in those days, and stamped on it in gold leaf was "One Year Diary"—the kind with the cheap lock your sister could open with a bobby pin. My mother said, "You know, Gloria, I'll bet there are a lot of things going on in the world you don't understand and I'm sure there are even things going on in here in our home that might be troubling you, but since you can't seem to talk to your father and me about these things, why don't you write them down in here." She threw the book on the bed and was wise enough to leave the room, and not belabor the point. I picked up the diary and I did just that, I proceeded to write down all the things that I could not say.

From the age of twelve I made the vital connection between inarticulate feeling and the written word. Whatever went into those original pages are not eternal keepsakes, they are not classic thoughts, but they were my feelings, it was my pain, and the pain was real to me at twelve years old. And we wonder about the rise in teenage suicides. It is because adults resist believing that whatever the demons are, if they're twelve-year-old, thirteen-year-old, fourteen-year-old demons, they are *real.* I know; I had them.

Through the luck of the draw of having a very wise and perceptive mother who happened to match what I needed with the gift of that diary, my life was saved. Because those feelings were going to come out. I was going to speak one day. But the horrifying question is, In what language would those feelings have been expressed? I paraphrase Toni Morrison in *Sula:* An artist without an art form is a dangerous thing. It is probably one of the most dangerous things on this earth. And being a female in the 1960s, I would have, I think, directed that destruction inward as opposed to outward. But instead, I filled up that diary, and then proceeded to fill up the spare pages in my loose-leaf notebook at the end of the school year with my ramblings that slowly turned into poems. The poems slowly evolved into *Twilight Zone*–type short stories—I have always been enamored somehow with the mystical and the idea of alternative realities, and began writing supernatural stories even as an adolescent.

But it took until I was twenty-seven years old for me to believe that I had the faintest chance of being a writer. I went through my adolescence and young adulthood being told that black people did not write books. How did this come about? I was a kid who read to the tune of a book a day, who had been "discovered" by her middle-school teachers, who plied me with extra reading, which I would take home on the weekends. In those hundreds of texts that I read, there was nothing about black Americans or by black Americans. Those authors weren't on the shelves in the public libraries in New York City, and they definitely weren't on my standard junior high school or high school curriculum. If black people had written books, would I not have read them? Would I not have been taught them? If Gwendolyn Brooks had indeed won the Pulitzer Prize the year she did, 1950 (ironically the year I was born), should she not qualify as a talented enough American writer to be on my syllabus?

We do not have to say to our children, "You are nothing." We don't have to 15 stand up in an auditorium, on a parade ground, and blatantly shout out to them, "You have nothing to give." We have done this much more effectively, through silence, through what they do *not* see, through what is *not* there when we parade before them what we declare is worthy. It is a very effective message. It was the one that I received. And I received it from well-meaning people, who thought I was bright, I had a future, I had promise. It took the unrest in the sixties and the kids then in their late teens and early twenties, who were willing to put their careers on the line, their lives on the line—and some lost them at Jackson and Kent State—in order to give birth to the educational institutions that began to exist in the mid seventies. Ones which taught what America really was, that provided an education that edified and represented the entire citizenry. This was the gift that they gave me. And so by the time I entered Brooklyn College, once again an institution supported by public funds, there was an Africana Studies Department, a Women's Studies Program, Chicano Studies (as they were called in those years), Asian Studies. And I then was able to encounter the works of Ralph Ellison, Toni Morrison, Nikki Giovanni, James Baldwin, Richard Wright, Zora Neale Hurston . . . the list goes on and on. We're not talking about people who deserved a Black Literature Day or a Black Literature Hour in our curriculums. These are names that will be here in the year 3000, because they have helped to define not only American literature, but world literature. I owe those young people who spilled their blood in the sixties a huge debt of gratitude, because by learning that there was this heritage of writers behind me, and specifically black female writers, when I looked in the mirror there was the image I desperately needed to see. What I had seen previously was no image. Slowly, by completing my diet with these books, an outline was filled in. And that outline did not say that black was beautiful, it did not say that black was ugly. It said simply: you are. You exist. It reverberated enough to give me the courage to pick up the pen. And it's what finally validated me.

My first novel, *The Women of Brewster Place*, literally began that very semester at Brooklyn College when I discovered that there was a whole history of black writing in America; and that I had foremothers and forefathers who stood behind me with the ghosts of their excellence. And I was determined that if I had only one novel in me, I was going to write about what I had not had, in those twenty-some odd years of literacy, the privilege to read about. I was going to write all about me. And I knew that if I just chose one female character, one protagonist, she could not do justice to the diversity of the black female experience in America. One woman couldn't do it all. So I hit upon the structure of having different chapters devoted to the lives of different women. I can remember making a mental list of how they would differ. They were to vary, beginning with something as superficial as their skin colors. I know it's not currently in vogue but I do like the word "colored." Because when I look around, that's what I see—colored people—pink on up in the European American; then moving from alabaster to ebony in the black female. We also range from being devotedly religious to almost irreligious. We are young and old. We are political, nonpolitical. We even differ in our sexual preferences. So on this dead-end street, I had hoped to create a whole panorama of what it meant to be black and female in America. To claim and to validate as many lives as I possibly could. To give them each the dignity that I felt they each deserved. To this day I still call that book—which is now fifteen years old—my love letter to the black woman in America. But it first began as a love letter to myself. And by beginning with what was indeed a very visceral and personal statement it had reverberated and touched women all over the world. I have received letters from as far away as Japan, from Korean women who inform me that they are a minority within that society. They saw their own grandparents and aunts on that dead-end street.

Every writer must articulate from the specific. They must reach down where they stand, because there is nothing else from which to draw. Therefore were I to go along with the traditional view that the Western literature began with Homer (a good argument to the contrary is the subject of another essay)—Homer didn't write about the Romans, nor the Phoenicians, nor about the Huns. He wrote about the Greeks because that's what he was. Shakespeare wrote about Elizabethan Englishmen. He put them in the Caribbean, he put them in Denmark, he put them in Verona—but they were all Elizabethan Englishmen. Joyce wrote about the Irish; Philip Roth writes about the Jews, Maxine Hong Kingston about Chinese-Americans. You write where you are. It's the only thing you have to give. And if you are fortunate enough, there is a spark that will somehow ignite a work so that it touches almost anyone who reads it, although it is about a very specific people at a very specific time. And so that's what I attempt to do with my work—to reach down where I am and to articulate those lives. I could spend my entire life, what I have left of a natural life span, writing only about the Brewster Places in America and never exhaust that which is universal to it.

What I plan to do though with the rest of my life is indeed to communicate with images. They will not always be written images. I love working for the stage.

I will write for film. I will always have stories to tell. They may not be good stories, they may not be bad stories. But I would like to believe that I will always tell honest stories and that to the lives that come to me I will somehow do them justice.

RICHARD WRIGHT

From *Fighting Words*

Wright, son of sharecroppers, was born in Mississippi in 1908. He grew up in a household impoverished in body, soul, and spirit and dominated by a fundamentalist grandmother who forbade reading anything but the Bible. His autobiography, Black Boy *(1945), chronicles the discrimination, despair, and anger that impelled Wright to move to Chicago, and, ultimately, to Paris, where he lived until his death in 1960. His internationally distinguished reputation puts him in the ranks of the celebrated authors he cites in paragraph 45 of "Fighting Words."*

I stood at a counter [in the bank lobby] and picked up the Memphis *Commercial Appeal* and began my free reading of the press. I came finally to the editorial page and saw an article dealing with one H. L. Mencken. I knew by hearsay that he was the editor of the *American Mercury*, but aside from that I knew nothing about him. The article was a furious denunciation of Mencken, concluding with one, hot, short sentence: Mencken is a fool.

I wondered what on earth this Mencken had done to call down upon him the scorn of the South. . . . Undoubtedly he must be advocating ideas that the South did not like. Were there, then, people other than Negroes who criticized the South? . . .

Now, how could I find out about this Mencken? There was a huge library near the riverfront, but I knew that Negroes were not allowed to patronize its shelves any more than they were the parks and playgrounds of the city. I had gone into the library several times to get books for the white men on the job. Which of them would now help me to get books? And how could I read them without causing concern to the white men with whom I worked? . . .

One morning I paused before the [desk of a] Catholic fellow [who was hated by white Southerners].

"I want to ask you a favor," I whispered to him.

"What is it?"

"I want to read. I can't get books from the library. I wonder if you'd let me use your card?"

He looked at me suspiciously.

"My card is full most of the time," he said.

5

"I see," I said and waited, posing my question silently.   10

"You're not trying to get me into trouble, are you, boy?" he asked, staring at
me.

"Oh, no, sir."

"What book do you want?"

"A book by H. L. Mencken."

"Which one?"   15

"I don't know. Has he written more than one?"

"He has written several."

"I didn't know that."

"What makes you want to read Mencken?"

"Oh, I just saw his name in the newspaper," I said.   20

"It's good of you to want to read," he said. "But you ought to read the right
things."

I said nothing. Would he want to supervise my reading?

"Let me think," he said. "I'll figure out something."

I turned from him and he called me back. He stared at me quizzically.

"Richard, don't mention this to the other white men," he said.   25

"I understand," I said. "I won't say a word."

A few days later he called me to him.

"I've got a card in my wife's name," he said. "Here's mine."

"Thank you, sir."

"Do you think you can manage it?"   30

"I'll manage fine," I said.

"If they suspect you, you'll get in trouble," he said.

"I'll write the same kind of notes to the library that you wrote when you sent
me for books," I told him. "I'll sign your name."

He laughed.

"Go ahead. Let me see what you get," he said.   35

That afternoon I addressed myself to forging a note. Now, what were the
names of books written by H. L. Mencken? I did not know any of them. I finally
wrote what I thought would be a foolproof note: *Dear Madam: Will you please let
this nigger boy*—I used the word "nigger" to make the librarian feel that I could
not possibly be the author of the note—*have some books by H. L. Mencken?* I
forged the white man's name.

I entered the library as I had always done when on errands for whites, but I
felt that I would somehow slip up and betray myself. I doffed my hat, stood a re-
spectful distance from the desk, looked as unbookish as possible, and waited for
the white patrons to be taken care of. When the desk was clear of people, I still
waited. The white librarian looked at me.

"What do you want, boy?"

As though I did not possess the power of speech, I stepped forward and simply handed her the forged note, not parting my lips.

"What books by Mencken does he want?" she asked.   40

"I don't know, ma'am," I said, avoiding her eyes. . . .

"You're not using these books, are you?" she asked pointedly.

"Oh, no, ma'am. I can't read." . . .

I said nothing. She stamped the card and handed me the books.

That night in my rented room . . . I opened *A Book of Prefaces* and began to   45
read. I was jarred and shocked by the style, the clear, clean, sweeping sentences. . . .
Yes, this man was fighting, fighting with words. He was using words as a weapon,
using them as one would use a club. Could words be weapons? Well, yes, for here
they were. Then, maybe, perhaps, I could use them as a weapon? No. It frightened me. I read on and what amazed me was not what he said, but how on earth
anybody had the courage to say it.

Occasionally I glanced up to reassure myself that I was alone in the room.
Who were these men about whom Mencken was talking so passionately? Who
was Anatole France? Joseph Conrad? Sinclair Lewis, Sherwood Anderson, Dosto-
evski, George Moore, Gustave Flaubert, Maupassant, Tolstoy, Frank Harris,
Mark Twain, Thomas Hardy, Arnold Bennett, Stephen Crane, Zola, Norris,
Gorky, Bergson, Ibsen, Balzac, Bernard Shaw, Dumas, Poe, Thomas Mann, O.
Henry, Dreiser, H. G. Wells, Gogol, T. S. Eliot, Gide, Baudelaire, Edgar Lee Masters, Stendhal, Turgenev, Huneker, Nietzsche, and scores of others? Were these
men real? Did they exist or had they existed? . . . I concluded the book with the
conviction that I had somehow overlooked something terribly important in life. I
had once tried to write, had once reveled in feeling, had let my crude imagination
roam, but the impulse to dream had been slowly beaten out of me by experience.
Now it surged up again and I hungered for books, new ways of looking and seeing. It was not a matter of believing or disbelieving what I read, but of feeling
something new, of being affected by something that made the look of the world
different.

QUESTIONS FOR DISCUSSION AND WRITING

1. Judging from your own life history and what Naylor says about the "conscious
   connection between the validity of [writers'] personal experiences and the page"
   (paragraph 10), as well as the experiences of Wright (p. 57), why do you suppose
   that some people who love to read become writers, while many do not?

2. How can a literary work that is "about very specific people at a very specific
   time" have relevance for "almost anyone who reads it" (Naylor, paragraph 17)?

3. Writing as an instrumental medium—producing, for instance, directions, operators' manuals, records of meetings, contracts and other legal documents—
   forms the foundation of many transactions and professions, including advertising, the law, and many aspects of engineering and computer programming. In
   contrast, Welty, Naylor, Alexie, Richard Wright and other creative writers view
   writing as a means of exploring oneself, one's gender, and one's culture, and as a
   form of storytelling that provides insight as well as entertainment. Write a brief

paper in two parts, perhaps defining a favorite topic (work, love, ethics) or explaining how to do something you enjoy doing. One part should reflect an instrumental approach to the subject; the other should be a narrative disclosing your passion for the subject and/or the process.

ANNE FADIMAN

Marrying Libraries

Fadiman (b. 1953) was born into the library-loving family of Clifton Fadiman, noted editor and anthologist. As editor of Civilization *and* The American Scholar, *she has nurtured a decade of distinguished nonfiction writers, contributing to the genre herself with* The Spirit Catches You and You Fall Down: A Hmong Child, Her American Doctors, and the Collision of Two Cultures *(1997) and* Ex Libris: Confessions of a Common Reader *(1998), from which "Marrying Libraries" is taken.*

A few months ago, my husband and I decided to mix our books together. We had known each other for ten years, lived together for six, been married for five. Our mismatched coffee mugs cohabited amicably; we wore each other's T-shirts and, in a pinch, socks; and our record collections had long ago miscegenated without incident, my Josquin Desprez motets cozying up to George's *Worst of Jefferson Airplane*, to the enrichment, we believed, of both. But our libraries had remained separate, mine mostly at the north end of our loft, his at the south. We agreed that it made no sense for my *Billy Budd* to languish forty feet from his *Moby-Dick*, yet neither of us had lifted a finger to bring them together.

We had been married in this loft, in full view of our mutually quarantined Melvilles. Promising to love each other for richer or for poorer, in sickness and in health — even promising to forsake all others — had been no problem, but it was a good thing the *Book of Common Prayer* didn't say anything about marrying our libraries and throwing out the duplicates. That would have been a far more solemn vow, one that would probably have caused the wedding to grind to a mortifying halt. We were both writers, and we both invested in our books the kind of emotion most people reserve for their old love letters. Sharing a bed and a future was child's play compared to sharing my copy of *The Complete Poems of W. B. Yeats*, from which I had once read "Under Ben Bulben" aloud while standing at Yeats's grave in the Drumcliff churchyard, or George's copy of *T. S. Eliot's Selected Poems*, given to him in the ninth grade by his best friend, Rob Farnsworth, who inscribed it "Best Wishes from Gerry Cheevers." (Gerry Cheevers, one of Rob's nicknames, was the goalie of the Boston Bruins, and the inscription is probably unique, linking T. S. Eliot and ice hockey for the first time in history.)

Our reluctance to conjugate our Melvilles was also fueled by some essential differences in our characters. George is a lumper. I am a splitter. His books commingled democratically, united under the all-inclusive flag of Literature. Some were vertical, some horizontal, and some actually placed *behind* others. Mine were balkanized by nationality and subject matter. Like most people with a high tolerance for clutter, George maintains a basic trust in three-dimensional objects. If he wants something, he believes it will present itself, and therefore it usually does. I, on the other hand, believe that books, maps, scissors, and Scotch tape dispensers are all unreliable vagrants, likely to take off for parts unknown unless strictly confined to quarters. My books, therefore, have always been rigidly regimented.

After five years of marriage and a child, George and I finally resolved that we were ready for the more profound intimacy of library consolidation. It was unclear, however, how we were to find a meeting point between his English-garden approach and my French-garden one. At least in the short run, I prevailed, on the theory that he could find his books if they were arranged like mine but I could never find mine if they were arranged like his. We agreed to sort by topic—History, Psychology, Nature, Travel, and so on. Literature would be subdivided by nationality. (If George found this plan excessively finicky, at least he granted that it was a damn sight better than the system some friends of ours had told us about. Some friends of *theirs* had rented their house for several months to an interior decorator. When they returned, they discovered that their entire library had been reorganized by color and size. Shortly thereafter, the decorator met with a fatal automobile accident. I confess that when this story was told, everyone around the dinner table concurred that justice had been served.) . . .

We each owned copies of about fifty books in common. We decided that hardbacks would prevail over paperbacks unless the paperbacks contained marginalia. We kept my *Middlemarch*, read at eighteen, in which were registered my nascent attempts at literary criticism (page 37: "Grrr"; page 261: "Bullshit"; page 294: "Yccch"); George's *Magic Mountain*; my *War and Peace. Women in Love* generated the most agonizing discussion. George had read it at sixteen. He insisted that whenever he reread it, no edition other than his original Bantam paperback, with its psychedelic cover of one nude and one seminude woman, would possibly do. I had read it at eighteen. I kept no diary that year, but I had no need of one to remind me that that was the year I lost my virginity. It was all too apparent from the comments I wrote in my Viking edition (page 18: "Violence substitute for sex"; page 154: "Sexual pain"; page 159: "Sexual power"; page 158: "Sex"). What could we do but throw in the towel and keep both copies?

After a final, post-midnight push, we were done. Our duplicates, plus another hundred or so painful culls, were neatly stacked, ready to be carted off to Goodwill. Sweating and panting beneath our triumphantly united Melvilles, we kissed.

SCOTT McCLOUD

Reading the Comics

Scott McCloud (b. 1960) is a cartoonist (Zot! 1984). Since the publication of Understanding Comics: The Invisible Art *in 1993 (itself written as a comic), he is also an internationally acknowledged theorist of comics as an artistic and literary form.*

THE CLOSURE OF *ELECTRONIC* MEDIA IS *CONTINUOUS*, LARGELY *INVOLUNTARY* AND *VIRTUALLY IMPERCEPTIBLE.*

BUT CLOSURE IN **COMICS** IS *FAR* FROM CONTINUOUS AND *ANYTHING* BUT *INVOLUNTARY!*

NOW YOU *DIE* !!

NO! NO!

EEYAA!!

EVERY ACT COMMITTED TO PAPER BY THE COMICS ARTIST IS *AIDED* AND *ABETTED* BY A *SILENT* ACCOMPLICE.

AN *EQUAL PARTNER IN CRIME* KNOWN AS *THE READER.*

I MAY HAVE DRAWN AN *AXE* BEING *RAISED* IN THIS EXAMPLE, BUT I'M NOT THE ONE WHO LET IT *DROP* OR DECIDED HOW *HARD* THE BLOW, OR *WHO* SCREAMED, OR *WHY.*

NOW YOU *DIE* !!

NO! NO!

EEYAA!!

THAT, DEAR READER, WAS *YOUR SPECIAL CRIME,* EACH OF YOU COMMITTING IT IN YOUR OWN *STYLE.*

ALL OF YOU *PARTICIPATED* IN THE MURDER. ALL OF YOU *HELD THE AXE* AND *CHOSE YOUR SPOT.*

DEBORAH FRANKLIN

"Informed Consent"—What Information?
What Consent?

Deborah Franklin is a San Francisco–based writer who focuses on science and medicine; she has published regularly in Health *and* Fortune. *Here she defines "informed consent" and argues that signing such a form should be a thoughtful and questioning, rather than automatic, act. Our lives could depend on this.*

"Getting truly informed consent means you have explained what the procedure is, and the risks, benefits and alternatives," [pulmonary and critical care specialist] Dr. [Constantine] Manthous said. "Then you ask the patient to replay it: 'Could you tell me in your own words so that I can make sure you've got it?' Only then should you be giving them a piece of paper to sign."

Dr. Dean Schillinger, a health literacy specialist at the University of California, San Francisco, urges doctors to take the discussion a step further. "You want to say something like, 'I don't know much about your particular concerns, but what keeps you up at night about this procedure?'" he said, adding, "That's when you'll start to hear the worries about sexual dysfunction and the like."

Dr. Clarence Braddock III, an internist and bioethicist at Stanford who is also looking for ways to improve the process, says it doesn't help that the language of the written permission slips is usually either too broad or amounts to a lawyer-driven list of everything that could possibly go wrong.

In practice, the relative risks and benefits can be very different for each patient depending on age, health and other factors. These differences can readily be spelled out in a conversation, but not in a one-size-fits-all form, Dr. Braddock said. . . .

If doctors' overreliance on consent forms is bad for patients who can read well, it is a disaster for the 21 percent of adults in the United States who read at a sixth-grade level or below, and for an additional 27 percent who, according to the National Adult Literacy Survey, lack the proficiency needed to navigate the health care system easily.

Unless they pay close attention, doctors may miss the signs that a patient is a poor reader, said Toni Cordell, a literacy advocate who graduated from high school reading at a fifth-grade level. "We're often ashamed, and we get really good at hiding it," she said.

At the University of Michigan, Dr. Alan Tait has been working with colleagues in the department of anesthesiology to develop an improved consent form aimed at parents with low literacy skills whose children are facing surgery.

"Using simpler, friendlier language is just the first step," Dr. Tait said. The form in one experimental survey of 305 parents was vastly preferred by those who read well in addition to those with low literacy skills. It also used a larger typeface, shorter paragraphs, illustrations and bulleted points to help clarify the message.

Elsewhere, health literacy specialists are working on audio or video consent forms—interactive audiotapes or DVDs that can be navigated at a patient's own pace via a telephone keypad, a touch-screen kiosk or an inexpensive DVD player.

Most rely on live-action vignettes and colorful images instead of dense 10 blocks of text to explain complicated concepts like the risks and benefits of different types of blood pressure medicines or asthma inhalers or the ins and outs of glucose monitors used for diabetes.

The new forms, aids and devices may eventually supplement or even replace some existing forms. But none can or should be expected to replace the bond of trust between doctor and patient that is crucial to good care and is forged only during the give and take of a good conversation.

QUESTIONS FOR DISCUSSION AND WRITING

1. Read the words and images in McCloud's first three panels to explain how he arrives at his definition of comics in the fourth: "Comics **is** closure!" How does the reader participate in making meaning and attaining closure (panels 5–9)? Look at any of the illustrations in *The Arlington Reader*, such as "The Entrance Exam" (p. 318), "Migrant Mother" (p. 351) or "The Damm Family in Their Car" (p. 491), and "read" them to provide a satisfactory interpretation for yourself before examining the accompanying commentaries. Did your reading provide satisfying "closure"? Why or why not?

2. Franklin's discussion of "informed consent" encourages doctors to explain the implications of medical procedures to their patients and to use simple, nonmedical language to make sure patients understand exactly what they're agreeing to. Think of an example of your own or your family's experience with "informed consent." Was it truly informed? Did you understand what you were consenting to? In what ways is the relationship between doctor and patient similar to that of cartoonist and reader as explained by Scott McCloud?

GEORGINA KLEEGE

Up Close, In Touch

*Legally blind by the age of eleven, Georgina Kleege (b. 1956) nevertheless kept up with her schoolwork and attended Yale University (B.A. in English, 1979). She is a novelist (*Home for the Summer, *1989), and translator (*Sitt Marie Rose *by Lebanese writer Etel Adnan); her articles have appeared in publications as varied as* Redbook, The Yale Review, *and* Disability Studies Quarterly.

In Sight Unseen (1999), Kleege explores the dimensions of a world limited to peripheral vision—not to evoke pity but to understand and embrace her experience. As Kleege explains in the introduction, "Writing this book made me blind. By this I do not mean that the physical exertion of writing led to a deterioration of my eyesight" but that "today I am likely to identify myself as blind; five or six years ago I would have been more likely to use less precise phrases, such as 'visually impaired' or 'partially sighted.'" Overcoming this resistance helped Kleege take steps to improve her situation, by learning braille, for example.

In "Up Close, In Touch," a chapter from Sight Unseen, Kleege portrays her daily struggle to read. As she details the techniques she has employed over the years— holding a book two inches from her face, reading thirty-six-point type on her computer screen, using reading machines—a picture of determination and devotion emerges.

There is pain above my right eye, between my eyebrow and the tear duct. It is a dull, constant pain, an ache rather than a throb, not excruciating by any means. If I continue writing as I am, my nose skimming the page, my eye peering through a heavy magnifying lens, the pain will deepen and spread, migrating to my forehead and the other eye. My neck and shoulders will start to ache too, since I am in a rather cramped position. But that pain is only muscular. I can relieve it by stretching and shifting my posture.

The pain around my eye may be muscular too. Muscles squeeze the lens tight for close focus. The standard remedy for this kind of eyestrain is to look at a distant object. The muscles that compress the lens, making it thick for reading and writing, will relax for distance vision. But when I look up, the image through the window seems chaotic. There is a shifting scintillation of light and color. It is a windy day, and tree limbs shift with each gust. Sunlight is reflecting off the smooth surface of leaves. On top of this, there is the ever-present quivering motion that comes from my marred central vision. But today my vision seems worse than usual. For some reason my brain will not resolve what I see into anything meaningful. If I had not just been writing, my brain would be able to sort out the different aspects of the image and perceive a comprehensible impression—not what a sighted person would see, naturally, but familiar enough for me to say, "That's part of the tree. That's part of the neighbor's house." But now, because (as I surmise) I've had my eyes clenched in extreme close focus, they seem unable to shift back, so everything appears blurry and indistinct. In fact, I have trouble seeing beyond the window itself. The verticals and horizontals of the frame and panes shimmy wildly. Outside the window, the wind blows harder, and I feel a little seasick as the motion increases.

But if I work at it, concentrating on a known, stable object—the white trim along my neighbor's roofline—I can feel my focus shift. The chaos resolves into recognizable (to me, anyway) shapes. I can distinguish different objects from one another, light from shadow, inside from outside. . . .

There is urgency now. I should stop, or at least move to the computer since I can type without focusing. Or I could just close my eyes, but even then I feel the same tautness inside. Besides, I want to finish this thought, commit this idea to paper while it's still fresh. I bargain with the pain: I'll stop, I promise, just let me get to the end of the paragraph. Another minute, another sentence, one more word.

I bring this on myself. The damage to my maculas impairs my ability to per- 5 ceive detail, such as the letters in the words I am writing. To read them at all I must bring my eye very close to the page. I augment the physical proximity with a magnifying lens. I used to use handheld magnifiers, but now I wear eyeglass frames with a magnifying lens mounted on the right side. The lens enlarges everything six times normal size. This magnification means that my blind spot, which obliterates whatever is directly before my eyes, affects a smaller portion of the enlarged word. So if I stare at the middle of a word (the *dd* in "middle," for instance) I can see the *m* at the beginning and the *e,* even the *le* at the end. It looks like *m———le.* As I move my eye to the right while my pen tip begins the next word, my blind spot erases the end of the word: *mid———.*

I use only my right eye when I read and wear no lens over the left. I used to wear a patch over that side of my glasses, but I discovered that I didn't need it. My left retina is more degenerated than my right, so as my pen travels across the page, everything to the left of it fades to blankness—my blind spot erases what I've just written. Occasionally my left eye still seems to think that it should be doing something. Sometimes there's an odd muscular twitch, or I feel my eye drift out of alignment, giving me double vision, ghost lines of writing veering off at crazy angles. If it gets bad, I hold the lid closed with a finger.

Of course, I don't have to write this way. When I type I don't have to focus my eyes on anything. And the computer allows me even more magnification. At the moment I'm typing at 36 point. This *L* is about half an inch tall. To read what I've just written, I still must get very close, about two inches from the screen, and to proofread it (to be sure there are two *e*'s in screen) I put on my glasses and move in closer, my nose brushing the screen. Now my blind spot effaces only parts of letters, everything below or above the median line. . . .

Oddly, even with all this magnification, I find it necessary to be very close to the text when I read. It feels unnatural to read from a distance. There are aids that would force me to back away from the text. I could, for instance, get a pair of eyeglasses with miniature telescopes mounted in the lenses. These would be set to allow me to stand at a podium and read a text without holding it up in front of my face. The problem would be that glasses set for that distance and that angle of vision would not work if I wanted to read a book while lying on the couch. The solution then would be several pairs of glasses, and for the time being I'm unconvinced that the advantages outweigh the inconvenience and expense.

The fact is, reading close is such an old habit I'm not sure that I can shake it this late in life, or even that I should. Contrary to popular belief, reading from a closer than average distance does not necessarily damage the eyes. Eyestrain won't make you nearsighted or farsighted; it may simply indicate to your eye doctor that you have developed one of these, or some other condition. Changes in the curvature of the cornea or the shape of the lens or the eyeball occur genetically or as a result of the body's aging process, not as a side effect of reading habits. Besides, the notion of a correct distance for reading is only a measure of what's average. If your visual acuity measures 20/20, it means when you stand 20 feet from the eye chart, you can read what the average person reads from that distance. When George Snellen created his familiar eye chart in the middle of the nineteenth century, he chose twenty feet as the base unit for no better reason than it was the length of the typical classroom of his day. And perhaps the catchy ring of the phrase "20/20" was irresistible.

Thus, though my up-close reading posture deviates from convention, it 10 probably won't make my eyesight any worse. So it shouldn't matter. Except for the pain. The reason reading becomes painful to me is that my eyes are focusing at the maximum for prolonged periods of time. The angle at which the light enters the eye tells the brain how far the object of interest is from the eyes, and the brain automatically adjusts the muscles that control the lenses to refract the light onto the retina. My lenses and the muscles that contract and relax them are more or less normal. They do what they're told, oblivious to the defect in the retinas behind them. With my head pressed close to the computer screen this way, the focusing muscles receive the instruction to focus as if for extremely close reading — the fine print at the bottom of a contract, the ingredients list on a medication label, the *Oxford English Dictionary*. The pain I feel is the same as a sighted person feels when reading a dictionary for a long time.

When I first heard the expression "close reading" as an English major in college, I felt a tremendous sense of affirmation. This was the Yale English department, where close reading was something like a religion, and hearing the phrase made me feel that I belonged. I always read close. I always read every word, every syllable, every letter. So the literary practice, to read every word, to dwell on them, to contemplate not only their meanings but connotations, resonances, and history, came very naturally to me. Close reading presupposes that the text is worth taking time over. Close reading is a task of discovery, recovery, uncovering, detection, dissection—struggle. Sometimes close reading is even painful. Since all print is fine print to me, I must always read it closely. Fine print is not only the part that gives you headaches but also the part that only the truly patient, diligent, and discerning reader can decipher. I felt physically well-suited, if not predestined, to be a close reader.

Around this time I met my husband, Nick. He recalls that the first time he saw me I was reading in the library. The book was in French, and he could tell (his vision is normal) that it was not a textbook but a recently published novel. It was my unusual posture that attracted his attention. My nose was scraping across the page, the covers of the book folded around my face. He thought, "If reading is that difficult, it must really matter to her." Was this love at first sight? Not exactly. But Nick's first glimpse of me revealed something fundamental about who I was. As an aspiring writer and student of literature, reading was not only the way I spent most of my time but the central activity of my life. Reading mattered more than anything. And he probably recognized a kinship, a shared passion, or at least our common education. As a graduate student in the same department he perhaps saw in me the physical embodiment of close reading.

But the literary scholar who can dwell for hours on a single passage can also skim junk mail, scan the box scores for a particular team, and speed-read a pile of student midterms. Competence in reading involves more than holding the text at a distance that does not lead to eyestrain. Efficient reading means that the eyes move across and down the page in an orderly way, with a minimum of regressive or backward movements. The eye of a normally sighted, competent reader does not track along the line but moves in short jumps, or saccades, fixating briefly on small groups of characters before jumping to a new location. During the microsecond that the eye fixates on a single word or group of words, the brain processes the characters whose images fall on the center area of the retina, which is most sensitive to detail. At the same time, peripheral areas of the retina give a general preview of what's coming. Your peripheral vision can make broad, general distinctions about the size and shape of the words that follow the one in your central vision. You combine this general preview with your knowledge of the language you're reading, and the context of what you're reading, make an educated guess about what's next, and jump ahead. The most proficient readers can both process a large number of characters at each fixation and jump over a large number of characters with each saccade. And they rarely need to look back to verify what they've just read.

When I read, I keep my eyes staring straight ahead and move either the text or my head. Since I am always reading magnified text, my eye can process only about three characters at each fixation, while yours may process as many as a dozen at a time. And while my eye moves forward a character or two at a time, your eye may leapfrog fourteen or fifteen characters in a single saccade. Since I have next to no central vision, I rely on my peripheral vision to give me the general features of the letters and words. But the information is vague. The cells on the periphery are not sensitive to detail in the way cells at the center are. I can distinguish tall letters from short ones and straight lines from curves, but I lack the kind of cells that can definitively discern the orientation of these features relative to each other. An *a* could be an *o*, which could be a *c*, which could be an *e*. It's all too easy to confuse an *r* with a *t* or even an *f*. I regularly reverse or invert some letters—*b* and *d*, *p* and *q*. My tendency toward double vision makes minims multiply. I suspect every *n* might be an *m*, every *u* a *w*.

Thus, my problem with reading is not simply that my oversized blind spot   15
erases every character as I look at it. I also lack the visual equipment to allow me to make definitive judgments. As I stare at a word, it changes. I move my gaze around each letter, and it seems to reconfigure before my eyes. In quick succession a series of alternatives present themselves. The word "road" could easily be "toad," which could be "tool." "Wood" could be "weed" or perhaps "ward," or even "word." . . .

Still, what I do is child's play compared to your fluency. I read so slowly, with such difficulty and inaccuracy, that I can hardly claim to read at all. Fortunately, there are other ways to read—books on tape, for instance, which I began to rely on in my early twenties, and braille, which I have learned in the past few years.

Like most of the truly important inventions in human history, the braille code is elegantly simple. The braille cell is made up of six raised dots, arranged like the six in dominos, two vertical columns of three. All the letters of the alphabet, plus special symbols for certain common words, consist of from one to all six of these dots. Each character is the right size to fit even a child's fingertip, so the reader moves the finger smoothly from left to right. The braille alphabet is easy to memorize, and it's hard to mistake one letter for another.

When I learned all the letters of the alphabet I read this: "Congratulations! You have now mastered the entire braille alphabet." I was startled, then enthralled. I read it again. For the first time in decades I felt in absolute and stable contact with the text. This had nothing to do with the precarious guesswork I'd called reading since I lost my visual acuity. This was certain, unequivocal. I touched the words. Meaning flowed into my brain. Suddenly, my mind rushed ahead to imagine the thousands of texts I wanted to read and reread in this way. I moved on to study Braille II, the system of contractions and special signs that makes braille less cumbersome. I found the contractions so intuitive, so akin to the personal shorthands that people use taking notes, it hardly required memorization. Frequently, the initial letter or letters are used to stand for the whole word, so *p* stands for people, *ab* for about, and *imm* for immediate. Other contractions omit the vowels: *grt* means great, *rcv* means receive. Braille readers, like sighted readers, don't read every letter. This is not to say that reading braille is perfectly analogous to reading print. The finger does not saccade as the eye does, and it's necessary to stay in touch with the text. Still, proficient braille readers can skim text in much the way sighted readers do, reading only the first sentences of paragraphs or only the central three or four words of each line. As I read I found that context allowed me to speed up, my finger barely grazing articles, prepositions, and conjunctions. As soon as I could identify a word from the first few letters, my finger glided rapidly over the rest and on to the next word.

In the beginning, I found myself leaning close to the page, as I would with print. But soon I leaned back, way back, the book pushed away from me, my forearms stretched out comfortably on the table. This became a source of pleasure in itself, because reading had always been up-close and closed-in. When I read visually, my nose brushing the page, or aurally, a recorded voice in my ears, I am sometimes oppressed by claustrophobia. Now I felt refreshed by the space around me. I stretched out on the couch, the book on my lap. I leaned my head back. I closed my eyes. The muscles of my lips and tongue twitched, whispering. My progress was slow but steady. My brain did not backtrack as it would reading print. I recognized each letter or contraction, then it stood still, steadfast, unwavering. The frantic uncertainty of reading print was gone. And there was no pain. The anxiety that another word would be one too many, the nausea and dizziness creeping toward the surface of consciousness—none of this now. Occasionally my wrist cramped, and I learned that I was pressing too hard. My touch became lighter, more fleeting, and the pain went away. I was serene, floating. A tranquil faith sustained me letter by letter, word by word.

Why did I wait so long to learn this? If braille is such a pleasure, and if it seems to hold out the possibility that I can read fluently and without pain, why didn't I learn it sooner? After all, when I lost my visual acuity in the mid-sixties, the sight-enhancing technologies available today were not yet invented. And surely as a child of eleven I would have picked it up quickly. I was in school; braille could have been a part of my regular curriculum. Learning it as an adult, I often had to juggle to fit practice time into my schedule.

In fact, when I lost my sight, my mother made inquiries about braille instruction for me. We were told that I had too much sight. The inference was that only the totally blind could become proficient at braille. A person with any sight at all would be tempted to cheat, to read the pattern of raised dots visually rather than through touch. It was an odd thing to say, since many sighted people have learned braille, teachers and family members of blind children, for instance, not to mention sighted braille transcribers. In fact, though Louis Braille was blind, his writing system was a modification of a system designed by a sighted French artillery officer, Captain Charles Barbier de la Serre. Barbier's code was originally intended as a method of night writing so that officers at the front could write and read messages without signaling their location to the enemy by showing a light.

But I didn't know this then. As it turns out, I cannot see braille. When I stare at a page of braille it looks blank at first. I move my gaze around it and detect a few speckles of shadow. These seem to shiver and shake, to move and multiply. It takes a lot of magnification and a good deal of effort for me to make out any pattern there.

But at the time, no one so much as showed me a page of braille. My mother may have been too quick to accept that person's advice. Or perhaps she did not describe my condition adequately. She tended to shy away from the ugly words "blindness" and "macular degeneration" and use the more neutral "vision problem" instead. Like many parents of newly blind children, she was eager for good news. This made it easy to translate "cannot learn braille" into "does not need braille," which was reassuring. If I did not need braille then my vision must not be "that bad." And for my part, I accepted this misinformation without question. I was eleven. I didn't want to be blind. The only blind person I'd ever seen was a beggar in the subway. And I had faith that adults generally looked out for my best interests and that experts knew what they were talking about. Besides, they were only reinforcing my uncertainty about my new status as blind. How could I be blind if I still saw as much as I did? It made me feel ashamed for even asking. They seemed to be saying that asking for braille was like wanting a wheelchair for a skinned knee. I had sight, so I should use it to read print, because that's how sighted people do it. If it was difficult, I must simply try harder. If it hurt, it must be the kind of discomfort that leads to some ultimate good.

I was only too eager to oblige. Being a good student and a good girl were defining principles of my identity. From the beginning I'd found being good in school to be the best way for me to earn attention and praise. Being good in school meant making it look easy. When something was hard, you simply had to try harder. I had also been studying ballet from the age of about five and had absorbed a different version of the same idea. If it hurt to extend your leg on the barre, you simply had to keep at it. Contributing to this was the fact that my mother was not particularly patient about any form of illness or injury. When I was nine I broke my wrist twice in the space of about six months. The second time, I remember feeling that my mother was angry at me, though probably she was angry at the adults who were supposed to be supervising me when I broke it. In any case, I was not inclined to complain about the pain of the fracture or the inconvenience of the cast.

Generally speaking, I was not much of a complainer. To my parents' credit, I   25
was raised with an acute sense of all that I had which others did not. I grew up in New York City, in the neighborhood now called the East Village. Though my apartment building was solidly middle-class and my school was private, poverty was only a few blocks away. And it was the 1960s. In the left-leaning artistic circles of my parents and their friends, to ignore the economic and social inequities all around us was to be part of the problem. Good liberals do not complain about the petty annoyances in their lives when there is true suffering in the world.

Driven to excel, and socialized not to complain, I dealt with my lost sight accordingly. Since macular degeneration had no cure or treatment, complaining about it would only make me more troublesome and less lovable. Offered no means of coping with my condition (the word "blindness" was to be avoided), I did everything I could to conceal it. And because reading was my one regular activity in which my defect was most visible, I avoided drawing attention to it. I never said, "I can't read that." I never talked about the pain. At school, I learned to listen very carefully, conscious that my teachers tended to repeat whatever the textbook said and read aloud whatever they wrote on the board. I dreaded reading aloud myself, since my halting delivery and frequent errors would reveal my defect. So I would memorize passages from assignments in advance, then volunteer to "read" aloud what I had learned by heart. I did my homework with a magnifying glass but did not bring it to school. I remember once doing homework at a friend's house. We were reading *David Copperfield,* and I was ashamed when she finished the assignment long before I was a third of the way through. It was bad enough that reading the way I did left me with ink on my nose. Now this? So I closed my book, pretending that I was done too, and finished the reading later.

All this was denial, of course. When my eye doctor first pronounced me "blind," he failed to detach the word from the tangle of prejudice and fear that I had internalized without question or understanding. And what made me blind anyway? A mere technicality based on a notion of a correct distance for reading. Because my acuity dipped below the arbitrarily chosen 20/200 line of legal blindness, all I had to do to stave off the horror was to hide, disguise, or downplay my difficulties. With this mind-set, reading braille was out of the question.

I was not alone in this denial. The adults around me did not observe my struggle and never suggested that I might do well to look into braille. People see what they want to see, and they wanted me to be the child I had been before or, at worst, a child only mildly inconvenienced by an incurable and imprecisely defined visual impairment. If I had been reading braille they would have been obliged to see me as blind. . . .

The thing about denial is that it doesn't feel like denial while it's going on. I do not remember feeling unusual or unfairly afflicted while I was in school. I needed more time to do homework than anyone else, but I accepted this and watched less TV. In eighth grade I was surprised to discover that everyone else did not take aspirin two or three times a day as I did, but this did not seem something to worry about. I worried about the same things my friends did—friendships, boys, our changing bodies. I did not consciously work to conceal my blindness from my friends, but it was just often easier to pretend that I saw what they did. . . .

QUESTIONS FOR DISCUSSION AND WRITING

1. Kleege describes how painful it is for her to write in longhand. Why do you suppose she persists in writing longhand rather than typing, which causes less strain to her eyes?

2. What connection does Kleege make between "reading close," which she must do in order to see, and "close reading" of literary texts? What does this suggest about Kleege's feelings about reading?

3. Consider the differences between Kleege's difficulty with reading and the reading of sighted people—for example, that sighted readers preview what is coming next in a way that Kleege cannot. What can you learn about your own methods of reading from Kleege's description of her reading versus that of sighted readers?

4. Why did Kleege not learn braille until so late in life? What does her and her parents' "denial" of her blindness suggest about attitudes toward disabilities? Do you think these attitudes have changed since Kleege was growing up in the 1960s?

5. Write an essay in which you describe how you would cope with a disability—imagined or real—that inhibited your ability to read and write.

JOAN DIDION

On Keeping a Notebook

Born in 1934 and reared on a ranch near Sacramento, California, Didion graduated from the University of California, Berkeley (1956). Winning Vogue's *Prix de Paris writing contest enabled her to start near the top, working in New York as a* Vogue *copywriter and editor for the next eight years. In 1964 she married John Gregory Dunne and moved to Los Angeles, where the couple, both novelists and nonfiction writers, began a long career of collaborating on screenplays until his death in 2003.*

Among their films are Panic in Needle Park *(1973) and* A Star Is Born *(1976). Their screenplay for* Up Close and Personal *(1996) took eight years, twenty-seven drafts, and three hundred additional revisions. "We were each the person the other trusted," Didion explains in* The Year of Magical Thinking *(2005), a meditation on "marriage and children and memory" prompted by Dunne's death in December 2003 and interwoven with their daughter Quintana's mysterious, mortal illness.*

Didion's novels, including A Book of Common Prayer *(1977) and* Democracy *(1984), have been praised for their elegant prose and distinctive voice—precise, controlled, and concise. These qualities also characterize her essays, particularly those collected in* Slouching Towards Bethlehem *(1968) and* The White Album *(1979). Many are cynical commentaries on the erosion of traditional American pioneer values expressed in strong family and social structures. In "On Keeping a Notebook" (Holiday, 1966), Didion discusses what a notebook means for someone who writes, or wants to—not to provide "an accurate factual record of what I have been doing or thinking" but a way to demonstrate "how it felt to me." Thus the notebook collects an "indiscriminate and erratic assemblage" of facts, names, events, oddities, all filtered through the writer's consciousness and imagination, the "images that shimmer around the edges" (as she explains in "Why I Write," page 79)—"You just lie low and let them develop."*

"'That woman Estelle,'" the note reads, "'is partly the reason why George Sharp and I are separated today.' *Dirty crepe-de-Chine wrapper, hotel bar, Wilmington RR, 9:45 a.m. August Monday morning.*"

Since the note is in my notebook, it presumably has some meaning to me. I study it for a long while. At first I have only the most general notion of what I was doing on an August Monday morning in the bar of the hotel across from the Pennsylvania Railroad station in Wilmington, Delaware (waiting for a train? missing one? 1960? 1961? why Wilmington?), but I do remember being there. The woman in the dirty crepe-de-Chine wrapper had come down from her room for a beer, and the bartender had heard before the reason why George Sharp and she were separated today. "Sure," he said, and went on mopping the floor. "You told me." At the other end of the bar is a girl. She is talking, pointedly, not to the man beside her but to a cat lying in the triangle of sunlight cast through the open door. She is wearing a plaid silk dress from Peck & Peck, and the hem is coming down.

Here is what it is: the girl has been on the Eastern Shore, and now she is going back to the city, leaving the man beside her, and all she can see ahead are the viscous summer sidewalks and the 3 a.m. long-distance calls that will make her lie awake and then sleep drugged through all the steaming mornings left in August (1960? 1961?). Because she must go directly from the train to lunch in New York, she wishes that she had a safety pin for the hem of the plaid silk dress, and she also wishes that she could forget about the hem and the lunch and stay in the cool bar that smells of disinfectant and malt and make friends with the woman in the crepe-de-Chine wrapper. She is afflicted by a little self-pity, and she wants to compare Estelles. That is what that was all about.

Why did I write it down? In order to remember, of course, but exactly what was it I wanted to remember? How much of it actually happened? Did any of it? Why do I keep a notebook at all? It is easy to deceive oneself on all those scores. The impulse to write things down is a peculiarly compulsive one, inexplicable to those who do not share it, useful only accidentally, only secondarily, in the way that any compulsion tries to justify itself. I suppose that it begins or does not begin in the cradle. Although I have felt compelled to write things down since I was five years old, I doubt that my daughter ever will, for she is a singularly blessed and accepting child, delighted with life exactly as life presents itself to her, unafraid to go to sleep and unafraid to wake up. Keepers of private notebooks are a different breed altogether, lonely and resistant rearrangers of things, anxious malcontents, children afflicted apparently at birth with some presentiment of loss.

My first notebook was a Big Five tablet, given to me by my mother with the 5 sensible suggestion that I stop whining and learn to amuse myself by writing down my thoughts. She returned the tablet to me a few years ago; the first entry is an account of a woman who believed herself to be freezing to death in the Arctic night, only to find, when day broke, that she had stumbled onto the Sahara Desert, where she would die of the heat before lunch. I have no idea what turn of a five-year-old's mind could have prompted so insistently "ironic" and exotic a story, but it does reveal a certain predilection for the extreme which has dogged me into adult life; perhaps if I were analytically inclined I would find it a truer story than any I might have told about Donald Johnson's birthday party or the day my cousin Brenda put Kitty Litter in the aquarium.

So the point of my keeping a notebook has never been, nor is it now, to have an accurate factual record of what I have been doing or thinking. That would be a different impulse entirely, an instinct for reality which I sometimes envy but do not possess. At no point have I ever been able successfully to keep a diary; my approach to daily life ranges from the grossly negligent to the merely absent, and on those few occasions when I have tried dutifully to record a day's events, boredom has so overcome me that the results are mysterious at best. What is this business about "shopping, typing piece, dinner with E, depressed"? Shopping for what? Typing what piece? Who is E? Was this "E" depressed, or was I depressed? Who cares?

In fact I have abandoned altogether that kind of pointless entry; instead I tell what some would call lies. "That's simply not true," the members of my family frequently tell me when they come up against my memory of a shared event. "The party was *not* for you, the spider was *not* a black widow, *it wasn't that way at all.*" Very likely they are right, for not only have I always had trouble distinguishing between what happened and what merely might have happened, but I remain unconvinced that the distinction, for my purposes, matters. The cracked crab that I recall having for lunch the day my father came home from Detroit in 1945 must certainly be embroidery, worked into the day's pattern, to lend verisimilitude; I was ten years old and would not now remember the cracked crab. The day's events did not turn on cracked crab. And yet it is precisely that fictitious crab that makes me see the afternoon all over again, a home movie run all too often, the father bearing gifts, the child weeping, an exercise in family love and guilt. Or that is what it was to me. Similarly, perhaps it never did snow that August in Vermont; perhaps there never were flurries in the night wind, and maybe no one else felt the ground hardening and summer already dead even as we pretended to bask in it, but that was how it felt to me, and it might as well have snowed, could have snowed, did snow.

How it felt to me: that is getting closer to the truth about a notebook. I sometimes delude myself about why I keep a notebook, imagine that some thrifty virtue derives from preserving everything observed. See enough and write it down, I tell myself, and then some morning when the world seems drained of wonder, some day when I am only going through the motions of doing what I am supposed to do, which is write—on that bankrupt morning I will simply open my notebook and there it will all be, a forgotten account with accumulated interest, paid passage back to the world out there: dialogue overhead in hotels and elevators and at the hatcheck counter in Pavillon (one middle-aged man shows his hat check to another and says, "That's my old football number"); impressions of Bettina Aptheker and Benjamin Sonnenberg and Teddy ("Mr. Acapulco") Stauffer; careful *aperçus* about tennis bums and failed fashion models and Greek shipping heiresses, one of whom taught me a significant lesson (a lesson I could have learned from F. Scott Fitzgerald, but perhaps we all must meet the very rich for ourselves) by asking, when I arrived to interview her in her orchid-filled sitting room on the second day of a paralyzing New York blizzard, whether it was snowing outside.

I imagine, in other words, that the notebook is about other people. But of course it is not. I have no real business with what one stranger said to another at the hat check counter in Pavillon; in fact I suspect that the line "That's my old football number" touched not my own imagination at all, but merely some memory of something once read, probably "The Eighty-Yard Run." Nor is my concern with a woman in a dirty crepe-de-Chine wrapper in a Wilmington bar. My stake is always, of course, in the unmentioned girl in the plaid silk dress. *Remember what it was to be me:* that is always the point.

It is a difficult point to admit. We are brought up in the ethic that others, any others, all others, are by definition more interesting than ourselves; taught to be diffident, just this side of self-effacing. ("You're the least important person in the room and don't forget it," Jessica Mitford's governess would hiss in her ear on the advent of any social occasion; I copied that into my notebook because it is only recently that I have been able to enter a room without hearing some such phrase in my inner ear.) Only the very young and the very old may recount their dreams at breakfast, dwell upon self, interrupt with memories of beach picnics and favorite Liberty lawn dresses and the rainbow trout in a creek near Colorado Springs. The rest of us are expected, rightly, to affect absorption in other people's favorite dresses, other people's trout.

And so we do. But our notebooks give us away, for however dutifully we record what we see around us, the common denominator of all we see is always, transparently, shamelessly, the implacable "I." We are not talking here about the kind of notebook that is patently for public consumption, a structural conceit for binding together a series of graceful *pensées*; we are talking about something private, about bits of the mind's string too short to use, an indiscriminate and erratic assemblage with meaning only for its maker.

And sometimes even the maker has difficulty with the meaning. There does not seem to be, for example, any point in my knowing for the rest of my life that, during 1964, 720 tons of soot fell on every square mile of New York City, yet there it is in my notebook, labeled "FACT." Nor do I really need to remember that Ambrose Bierce liked to spell Leland Stanford's name "£eland $tanford" or that "smart women almost always wear black in Cuba," a fashion hint without much potential for practical application. And does not the relevance of these notes seem marginal at best?:

> In the basement museum of the Inyo County Courthouse in Independence, California, sign pinned to a mandarin coat: "This MANDARIN COAT was often worn by Mrs. Minnie S. Brooks when giving lectures on her TEAPOT COLLECTION."
> Redhead getting out of car in front of Beverly Wilshire Hotel, chinchilla stole, Vuitton bags with tags reading:
>
> MRS LOU FOX
> HOTEL SAHARA
> VEGAS

Well, perhaps not entirely marginal. As a matter of fact, Mrs. Minnie S. Brooks and her MANDARIN COAT pull me back into my own childhood, for although I never knew Mrs. Brooks and did not visit Inyo County until I was thirty, I grew up in just such a world, in houses cluttered with Indian relics and bits of gold ore and ambergris and the souvenirs my Aunt Mercy Farnsworth brought back from the Orient. It is a long way from that world to Mrs. Lou Fox's world, where we all live now, and is it not just as well to remember that? Might not Mrs. Minnie S. Brooks help me to remember what I am? Might not Mrs. Lou Fox help me to remember what I am not?

But sometimes the point is harder to discern. What exactly did I have in mind when I noted down that it cost the father of someone I know $650 a month to light the place on the Hudson in which he lived before the Crash? What use was I planning to make of this line by Jimmy Hoffa: "I may have my faults, but being wrong ain't one of them"? And although I think it interesting to know where the girls who travel with the Syndicate have their hair done when they find themselves on the West Coast, will I ever make suitable use of it? Might I not be better off just passing it on to John O'Hara? What is a recipe for sauerkraut doing in my notebook? What kind of magpie keeps this notebook? *He was born the night the Titanic went down.*" That seems a nice enough line, and I even recall who said it, but is it not really a better line in life than it could ever be in fiction?

But of course that is exactly it: not that I should ever use the line, but that I should remember the woman who said it and the afternoon I heard it. We were on her terrace by the sea, and we were finishing the wine left from lunch, trying to get what sun there was, a California winter sun. The woman whose husband was born the night the *Titanic* went down wanted to rent her house, wanted to go back to her children in Paris. I remember wishing that I could afford the house, which cost $1,000 a month. "Someday you will," she said lazily. "Someday it all comes." There in the sun on her terrace it seemed easy to believe in someday, but later I had a low-grade afternoon hangover and ran over a black snake on the way to the supermarket and was flooded with inexplicable fear when I heard the checkout clerk explaining to the man ahead of me why she was finally divorcing her husband. "He left me no choice," she said over and over as she punched the register. "He has a little seven-month-old baby by her, he left me no choice." I would like to believe that my dread then was for the human condition, but of course it was for me, because I wanted a baby and did not then have one and because I wanted to own the house that cost $1,000 a month to rent and because I had a hangover.

It all comes back. Perhaps it is difficult to see the value in having one's self back in that kind of mood, but I do see it; I think we are well advised to keep on nodding terms with the people we used to be whether we find them attractive company or not. Otherwise they turn up unannounced and surprise us, come hammering on the mind's door at 4 a.m. of a bad night and demand to know who deserted them, who betrayed them, who is going to make amends. We forget all too soon the things we thought we could never forget. We forget the loves and the betrayals alike, forget what we whispered and what we screamed, forget who we were. I have already lost touch with a couple of people I used to be; one of them, a seventeen-year-old, presents little threat, although it would be of some interest to me to know again what it feels like to sit on a river levee drinking vodka-and-orange-juice and listening to Les Paul and Mary Ford and their echoes sing "How High the Moon" on the car radio. (You see I still have the scenes, but I no longer perceive myself among those present, no longer could even improvise the dialogue.) The other one, a twenty-three-year-old, bothers me more. She was always a good deal of trouble, and I suspect she will reappear when I least want to see her, skirts too long, shy to the point of aggravation, always the injured party, full of recriminations and little hurts and stories I do not want to hear again, at once saddening me and angering me with her vulnerability and ignorance, an apparition all the more insistent for being so long banished.

It is a good idea, then, to keep in touch, and I suppose that keeping in touch is what notebooks are all about. And we are all on our own when it comes to keeping those lines open to ourselves: your notebook will never help me, nor mine you. *"So what's new in the whiskey business?"* What could that possibly mean to you? To me it means a blonde in a Pucci bathing suit sitting with a couple of fat men by the pool at the Beverly Hills Hotel. Another man approaches, and they all regard one another in silence for a while. "So what's new in the whiskey business?" one of the fat men finally says by way of welcome, and the blonde stands up, arches one foot and dips it in the pool, looking all the while at the cabaña where Baby Pignatari is talking on the telephone. That is all there is to that, except that several years later I saw the blonde coming out of Saks Fifth Avenue in New York with her California complexion and a voluminous mink coat. In the harsh wind that day she looked old and irrevocably tired to me, and even the skins in the mink coat were not worked the way they were doing them that year, not the way she would have wanted them done, and there is the point of the story. For a while after that I did not like to look in the mirror, and my eyes would skim the newspapers and pick out only the deaths, the cancer victims, the premature coronaries, the suicides, and I stopped riding the Lexington Avenue IRT because I noticed for the first time that all the strangers I had seen for years— the man with the seeing-eye dog, the spinster who read the classified pages every day, the fat girl who always got off with me at Grand Central—looked older than they once had.

It all comes back. Even that recipe for sauerkraut: even that brings it back. I was on Fire Island when I first made that sauerkraut, and it was raining, and we drank a lot of bourbon and ate the sauerkraut and went to bed at ten, and I listened to the rain and the Atlantic and felt safe. I made the sauerkraut again last night and it did not make me feel any safer, but that is, as they say, another story.

CONTEXTS FOR "ON KEEPING A NOTEBOOK"

JOAN DIDION

Why I Write

In "Why I Write," first published in the New York Times Book Review *(1976), Didion confesses that she "stole the title" from George Orwell's manifesto, in which he identifies the writer's purposes as egotistical, historical, aesthetic, and political. Didion's own writings reflect these, as well. In "Why I Write" she concentrates on the aesthetic and the spiritual, trying to make each word and sentence represent precisely each "physical fact" in "the pictures in [her] mind."*

From Joan Didion, "Why I Write," *New York Times Book Review*, December 5, 1976.

Of course I stole the title for this talk from George Orwell. One reason I stole it was that I like the sound of the words: *Why I Write.* There you have three short unambiguous words that share a sound, and the sound they share is this:

I

I

I

In many ways writing is the act of saying *I*, of imposing oneself upon other people, of saying *listen to me, see it my way, change your mind.* It's an aggressive, even a hostile act. You can disguise its aggressiveness all you want with veils of subordinate clauses and qualifiers and tentative subjunctives, with ellipses and evasions—with the whole manner of intimating rather than claiming, of alluding rather than stating—but there's no getting around the fact that setting words on paper is the tactic of a secret bully, an invasion, an imposition of the writer's sensibility on the reader's most private space.

I stole the title not only because the words sounded right but because they seemed to sum up, in a no-nonsense way, all I have to tell you. Like many writers I have only this one "subject," this one "area": the act of writing. I can bring you no reports from any other front. I may have other interests: I am "interested," for example, in marine biology, but I don't flatter myself that you would come out to hear me talk about it. I am not a scholar. I am not in the least an intellectual, which is not to say that when I hear the word "intellectual" I reach for my gun, but only to say that I do not think in abstracts. During the years when I was an undergraduate at Berkeley I tried, with a kind of hopeless late-adolescent energy, to buy some temporary visa into the world of ideas, to forge for myself a mind that could deal with the abstract.

In short I tried to think. I failed. My attention veered inexorably back to the specific, to the tangible, to what was generally considered, by everyone I knew then and for that matter have known since, the peripheral. I would try to contemplate the Hegelian dialectic and would find myself concentrating instead on a flowering pear tree outside my window and the particular way the petals fell on my floor. I would try to read linguistic theory and would find myself wondering instead if the lights were on in the bevatron up the hill. When I say that I was wondering if the lights were on in the bevatron you might immediately suspect, if you deal in ideas at all, that I was registering the bevatron as a political symbol, thinking in shorthand about the military-industrial complex and its role in the university community, but you would be wrong. I was only wondering if the lights were on in the bevatron, and how they looked. A physical fact.

Why have the night lights in the bevatron burned in my mind for twenty years? 5
What is going on in these pictures in my mind?

When I talk about pictures in my mind I am talking, quite specifically, about images that shimmer around the edges. There used to be an illustration in every elementary psychology book showing a cat drawn by a patient in varying stages of schizophrenia. This cat had a shimmer around it. You could see the molecular structure breaking down at the very edges of the cat: the cat became the background and the background the cat, everything interacting, exchanging ions. People on hallucinogens describe the same perception of objects. I'm not a schizophrenic, nor do I take hallucinogens, but certain images do shimmer for me. Look hard enough, and you can't miss the shimmer. It's there. You can't think too much about these pictures that shimmer. You just lie low and let them develop. You stay quiet. You don't talk to many people and you keep your nervous system from shorting out and you try to locate the cat in the shimmer, the grammar in the picture.

Just as I meant "shimmer" literally I mean "grammar" literally. Grammar is a piano I play by ear, since I seem to have been out of school the year the rules were mentioned. All I know about grammar is its infinite power. To shift the structure of a sentence alters the meaning of that sentence, as definitely and inflexibly as the position of a camera alters the meaning of the object photographed. Many people know about camera angles now, but not so many know about sentences. The arrangement of the words matters, and the arrangement you want can be found in the picture in your mind. The picture dictates the arrangement. The picture dictates whether this will be a sentence with or without clauses, a sentence that ends hard or a dying-fall sentence, long or short, active or passive. The picture tells you how to arrange the words and the arrangement of the words tells you, or tells me, what's going on in the picture. *Nota bene:*

It tells you.

You don't tell it.

TOM WOLFE

The New Journalism

To use writing as a way to "remember how it was to be me"—the purpose Didion identifies in "On Keeping a Notebook"—inspired the New Journalists of the 1960s. Didion, Truman Capote (In Cold Blood, *1966), George Plimpton* (Paper Lion, *1966), Hunter Thompson* (Hell's Angels, *1967), Norman Mailer* (Armies of the Night, *1968), and others abandoned traditional "objective," "voiceless" reportage and instead immersed themselves in events and in the language people actually spoke. By representing their own physical and emotional experiences of events, the New Journalists produced feature articles that sounded like novels. Tom Wolfe, in such books as* Kandy-Kolored Tangerine-Flake Streamline Baby *(1965),* The Electric Kool-Aid Acid Test *(1968), and* The Right Stuff *(1979), revitalized "objective" reporting with New Journalism's "personality, energy, drive, bravura . . . style, in a word." In*

From Tom Wolfe, *The New Journalism*, ed. Tom Wolfe and E. W. Johnson (New York: Harper, 1973).

this excerpt from Wolfe's The New Journalism *(1973), he identifies four novelistic elements of that art form: scene-by-scene construction; fully recorded dialogue; the witnessing of each scene through the eyes of an individual character, whom the journalist interviews; and the inclusion of objects, gestures, and styles through which people express their "status life," or "position in the world."*

If you follow the progress of the New Journalism closely through the 1960s, you see an interesting thing happening. You see journalists learning the techniques of realism—particularly of the sort found in Fielding, Smollett, Balzac, Dickens and Gogol—from scratch. By trial and error, by "instinct" rather than theory, journalists began to discover the devices that gave the realistic novel its unique power, variously known as its "immediacy," its "concrete reality," its "emotional involvement," its "gripping" or "absorbing" quality.

This extraordinary power was derived mainly from just four devices, they discovered. The basic one was scene-by-scene construction, telling the story by moving from scene to scene and resorting as little as possible to sheer historical narrative. Hence the sometimes extraordinary feats of reporting that the new journalists undertook: so that they could actually witness the scenes in other people's lives as they took place—and record the dialogue in full, which was device No. 2. Magazine writers, like the early novelists, learned by trial and error something that has since been demonstrated in academic studies: namely, that realistic dialogue involves the reader more completely than any other single device. It also establishes and defines character more quickly and effectively than any other single device. (Dickens has a way of fixing a character in your mind so that you have the feeling he has described every inch of his appearance—only to go back and discover that he actually took care of the physical description in two or three sentences; the rest he has accomplished with dialogue.) Journalists were working on dialogue of the fullest, most completely revealing sort in the very moment when novelists were cutting back, using dialogue in more and more cryptic, fey and curiously abstract ways.

The third device was the so-called "third-person point of view," the technique of presenting every scene to the reader through the eyes of a particular character, giving the reader the feeling of being inside the character's mind and experiencing the emotional reality of the scene as he experiences it. Journalists had often used the first-person point of view—"I was there"—just as autobiographers, memoirists and novelists had. This is very limiting for the journalist, however, since he can bring the reader inside the mind of only one character—himself—a point of view that often proves irrelevant to the story and irritating to the reader. Yet how could a journalist, writing nonfiction, accurately penetrate the thoughts of another person?

The answer proved to be marvelously simple: interview him about his thoughts and emotions, along with everything else. This was what I had done in *The Electric Kool-Aid Acid Test*, what John Sack did in *M* and what Gay Talese did in *Honor Thy Father*.

The fourth device has always been the least understood. This is the recording 5
of everyday gestures, habits, manners, customs, styles of furniture, clothing, deco-
ration, styles of traveling, eating, keeping house, modes of behaving toward children, servants, superiors, inferiors, peers, plus the various looks, glances, poses,
styles of walking and other symbolic details that might exist within a scene. Symbolic of what? Symbolic, generally, of people's *status life,* using that term in the
broad sense of the entire pattern of behavior and possessions through which people express their position in the world or what they think it is or what they hope it
to be. The recording of such details is not mere embroidery in prose. It lies as close
to the center of the power of realism as any other device in literature.

JOAN DIDION

Last Words

*Here Didion describes how, by studying Hemingway's stripped-down sentences, she
learned to style her own. For Didion, as for Hemingway and Orwell (see Chapter 5),
words are "the manifest expression of personal honor."*

In the late summer of that year we lived in a house in a village that looked
across the river and the plain to the mountains. In the bed of the river there
were pebbles and boulders, dry and white in the sun, and the water was
clear and swiftly moving and blue in the channels. Troops went by the
house and down the road and the dust they raised powdered the leaves of
the trees. The trunks of the trees too were dusty and the leaves fell early that
year and we saw the troops marching along the road and the dust rising and
leaves, stirred by the breeze, falling and the soldiers marching and afterward
the road bare and white except for the leaves.

So goes the famous first paragraph of Ernest Hemingway's *A Farewell to Arms,*
which I was moved to reread by the recent announcement that what was said to
be Hemingway's last novel would be published posthumously next year. That
paragraph, which was published in 1929, bears examination: four deceptively
simple sentences, one hundred and twenty-six words, the arrangement of which
remains as mysterious and thrilling to me now as it did when I first read them, at
twelve or thirteen, and imagined that if I studied them closely enough and practiced hard enough I might one day arrange one hundred and twenty-six such
words myself. Only one of the words has three syllables. Twenty-two have two.
The other hundred and three have one. Twenty-four of the words are "the," fifteen are "and." There are four commas. The liturgical cadence of the paragraph

From Joan Didion, "Last Words," *The New Yorker,* November 9, 1998, 74–80.

derives in part from the placement of the commas (their presence in the second and fourth sentences, their absence in the first and third), but also from that repetition of "the" and of "and," creating a rhythm so pronounced that the omission of "the" before the word "leaves" in the fourth sentence ("and we saw the troops marching along the road and the dust rising and leaves, stirred by the breeze, falling") casts exactly what it was meant to cast, a chill, a premonition, a foreshadowing of the story to come, the awareness that the author has already shifted his attention from late summer to a darker season. The power of the paragraph, offering as it does the illusion but not the fact of specificity, derives precisely from this kind of deliberate omission, from the tension of withheld information. In the late summer of *what* year? *What* river, *what* mountains, *what* troops?

The peculiarity of being a writer is that the entire enterprise involves the mortal humiliation of seeing one's own words in print. The risk of publication is the grave fact of the life, and, even among writers less inclined than Hemingway to construe words as the manifest expression of personal honor, the notion that words one has not risked publishing should be open to "continuing investigation" by "serious students of literature" could not be calculated to kindle enthusiasm.

JOAN DIDION

Interview (1999)

Joan Didion's writing itself hinges on the main thrust of her writing process: to keep on writing. Like professional writers of poems, plays, fiction, and nonfiction, student writers also need purposes and persistence.

LBF: What advice would you give to beginning writers?

JD: The most important and hardest thing for any writer to learn is the discipline of sitting down and writing even when you have to spend three days writing bad stuff before the fourth day, when you write something better. If you've been away from what you've been working on even for a day and a half, you have to put in those three days of bad writing to get to the fourth, or you lose the thread, you lose the rhythm. When you are a young writer, those three days are so unpleasant that you tend to think, "I'll go away until the mood strikes me." Well, you're out of the mood because you're not sitting there, because you haven't had that period of trying to push through till the fourth day when the rhythm comes.

From Lewis Burke Frumkes, "A Conversation with Joan Didion," *The Writer*, March 1999, 14–15.

WENDY BISHOP

Revision Is a Recursive Process

Wendy Bishop (1963–2003) was born in Japan, grew up in Ventura, California, and elsewhere, and earned a Ph.D. in English at Indiana University of Pennsylvania. She was distinguished as a teacher at Florida State University, a writer, and a professional leader by the grace and personal style of her prolific writing of poetry and textbooks, including Thirteen Ways of Looking for a Poem *(1999) and* Metro: Journeys in Writing Creatively *(2004). "Revision Is a Recursive Process" was first published in* Working Words: The Process of Creative Writing *(1992). This is practical advice from a writer who understands the process of writing as a fluid, informal series of stages where the writer can maintain a shifting focus between the whole piece and its components. Thus she recommends beginning with general ideas and the "big picture" and moving later to smaller and smaller concerns, such as paragraphs and individual words (spelling and grammar come last!), but always with the option of revisiting and changing any aspect at any time.*

Many of us begin to revise before we put words to paper—as we take a walk we raise and then reject or accept various "openings" or "developments"—but most of us start revision work in earnest once we have a draft. . . . I draw a somewhat artificial distinction between early and late revision, and I separate both those ways of looking at your writing from the process of editing—that is, preparing a *final draft* for submission to a teacher or editor. . . . Following is what a writer's fullest possible revision process might look like. Although I've described a sequence here, revision is actually always recursive; at any time, you may stop and redraft, add, delete, rethink a piece, and so on. To get to the finished product you want, however, it is useful to focus on certain aspects of revision at particular times.

Early Revision

- Concerned with developing your ideas
- Concerned with making initial decisions about what form will best convey those ideas
- Concerned with trying out options
- Concerned with the "big picture"
- *Not* too concerned with fine details, mechanics, spelling, punctuation, final word choice, and so on
- *Not* concerned with perfection

In early revision, you explore your first conceptualization of your work. Early revision may take place across several drafts.

From Wendy Bishop, *Working Words: The Process of Creative Writing* (New York: McGraw-Hill, 1992).

Late Revision

- Concerned with finalizing your ideas
- Concerned with fitting those ideas to the form you have chosen
- Concerned with smaller options, particularly at the paragraph, sentence, or word level
- Concerned with the "smaller picture"
- Concerned with the final effect on the intended reader; will he or she understand/enjoy this?
- *Not* overly concerned with the finest of details, mechanics, spelling, punctuation, and so on
- *Not* yet concerned with perfection

In late revision, you finalize your original conception for a piece. Late revision, depending on the circumstances of drafting (particularly, what is your deadline?), may take place during drafts two through fifty, or more.

Editing

- Concerned with perfection, with surface-level clarity, with "getting the last draft right"
- Concerned with detail and mechanics—getting dark type from the typewriter ribbon or printer, setting standard margins, having a title, including your name, proofreading for spelling errors, checking for *unintentional* punctuation and/or grammar errors

KATHERINE ANNE PORTER
You Do Not Create a Style. You Work . . .

Katherine Anne Porter (1890–1981) was born in Indian Creek, Texas. She concealed in later life the poverty that caused her to receive little formal education and to make an early, abusive, and brief marriage. Her writing career began as a journalist during the two years spent in a tuberculosis sanatorium. After recovery, in the 1920s she lived alternately in New York City and Mexico, the site of some of her best essays and short stories collected in Flowering Judas *(1930). Her short novel* Pale Horse, Pale Rider *(1938) was based on her near-fatal bout of influenza in 1919.* Ship of Fools *(1962), Porter's only full-length novel, brought her financial and popular success. This excerpt from a* Paris Review *interview (1963) reveals Porter's understanding that style is integral to the writer, just as symbols are integral to the work.*

Katherine Anne Porter, "You Do Not Create a Style. You Work . . . ." Excerpt from *The Paris Review*, Winter–Spring, 1963.

INTERVIEWER: You are frequently spoken of as a stylist. Do you think a style can be cultivated, or at least refined?

PORTER: I've been called a stylist until I really could tear my hair out. And I simply don't believe in style. The style is you. Oh, you can cultivate a style, I suppose, if you like. But I should say it remains a cultivated style. It remains artificial and imposed, and I don't think it deceives anyone. A cultivated style would be like a mask. Everybody knows it's a mask, and sooner or later you must show yourself—or at least, you show yourself as someone who could not afford to show himself, and so created something to hide behind. Style is the man, Aristotle said it first, as far as I know, and everybody has said it since, because it is one of those unarguable truths. You do not create a style. You work, and develop yourself; your style is an emanation from your own being. Symbolism is the same way. I never consciously took or adopted a symbol in my life. I certainly did not say, "This blooming tree upon which Judas is supposed to have hanged himself is going to be the center of my story." I named "Flowering Judas" after it was written, because when reading back over it I suddenly saw the whole symbolic plan and pattern of which I was totally unconscious while I was writing. There's a pox of symbolist theory going the rounds these days in American colleges in the writing courses. Miss Mary McCarthy, who is one of the wittiest and most acute and in some ways the worst-tempered woman in American letters, tells about a little girl who came to her with a story. Now Miss McCarthy is an extremely good critic, and she found this to be a good story, and she told the girl that it was—that she considered it a finished work, and that she could with a clear conscience go on to something else. And the little girl said, "But Miss McCarthy, my writing teacher said, 'Yes, it's a good piece of work, but now we must go back and put in the symbols!'" I think that's an amusing story, and it makes my blood run cold.

QUESTIONS FOR DISCUSSION AND WRITING

1. Make a list of all the ways you use writing and another list of all the ways people in your household use writing. Include everything from notes on the fridge to love letters to legal documents. Compare your lists with those of others in your class. What is distinctive about your lists? What factors do you think might account for the differences in the composition and style of your and your peers' lists?

2. In her 1999 interview, Didion advises beginning writers to learn "the discipline of sitting down and writing" (paragraph 2). What methods help you keep writing even when you write "bad stuff" (paragraph 2)?

3. In "Why I Write," Didion uses repetition to emphasize the "aggressiveness" of the act of writing (paragraph 5). What phrases does she repeat? What is the effect on you as a reader? How do these differ from or resemble the effect she feels as a reader of Hemingway (see "Last Words," p. 83).

4. Observe an ordinary event—people taking seats on a bus, sharing a meal, waiting in an office. Write "just the facts" you see objectively, withholding your attitudes and judgments. Then rewrite the account from your perspective, adding and changing language in order to express your eyewitness experience. What does this exercise suggest about telling the truth and telling lies, one of Didion's major concerns in "On Keeping a Notebook"? How does this revision reflect your personal style?

5. In the excerpt from "The New Journalism" (p. 81), Tom Wolfe explains that some writers use details to let readers know their "*status life*," or "position in the world" (paragraph 5). What details and word choices does Didion use to express her "status life"? What other stylistic gestures do other writers in Chapter 2 use to embody their "status lives"?

6. For what purposes do you revise your writing? Examine Bishop's method for early and late revision and for editing. Explain how revising a paper by following Bishop's suggestions helps you, in Katherine Anne Poster's words, to "develop yourself" and to define a style that is "an emanation from your own being" (paragraph 2).

7. For what purposes do you revise your writing? Examine Bishop's suggestions carefully for early and late revision and for editing. Try to follow these with every paper you write. You should find that they help you to write more easily and efficiently and that they save you considerable time.

GARRISON KEILLOR

The Anthem: If Famous Poets Had Written "The Star-Spangled Banner"

Keillor (b. 1942 in Anoka, Minnesota) launched his radio show, "A Prairie Home Companion," in 1974 to have "something funny to do with my friends." In the ensuing decades his weekly broadcasts from the imaginary Minnesota town of Lake Wobegon have grown to reach a National Public Radio audience of millions. In the process, Keillor transformed an old-fashioned pretelevision live radio format into a modern vehicle for humor, live music, small-town quirkiness, and arcane wisdom incorporated in his weekly monologues. Keillor's self-deprecating wit derives from his strict Lutheran upbringing, education (B.A., University of Minnesota, 1966), and love of literature—to which he has contributed a dozen books, including Lake Wobegon Days *(1985) and* Love Me *(2003), as well as articles in the* New Yorker.*

In "The Anthem," Keillor applies his wit to literary satire, as he reworks our national song in the idiom of famous American poets ranging from Walt Whitman to Emily Dickinson to Billy Collins (U.S. Poet Laureate, 2001).

Here on the shore of Baltimore observing the barrage of rockets and bombs
   from the man o' war,
The gunnery mates stripp'd to the waist and glistening with sweat,

Shouting each to the other and working together in close drill,
Ramming the powder charge and then the enormous projectile,
Each of them a man like myself and possessed of secret longings,
Each of them comely and well-appointed,
Especially the tall one on the left with black curls and taut abdominal muscles,
Who looks so long and lovingly at me, a stranger in big boots,
And I return his gaze—O aficionado, come, take my hand—
Leave your cannonading and we shall travel the open road
Where there are no banners except of affection and the love of dear comrades.

—*Walt Whitman*

The Banner—that we watched in Air
So Proudly as it Gleamed
Was Proven by the Rocket Glare
Or so to us it Seemed—

And so we waited for the Dawn
To see if it still flew
Or if—in Tatters—it is Gone—
As happened once—with You.

I woke up—at the Matin Bell—
A vast and empty Bed—
The Pillow bore—the slightest smell
Of Oil—from your Head.

A fleeting Phantasy—perhaps—
The Ghost of—Not To Be—
And Postmen—in their Crimson Caps—
Aim their Artillery.

—*Emily Dickinson*

Whose flag this is I think I know
His house is being bombed now though
He will not see that I have come
To watch the twilight's ebbing glow.

My little horse must think it dumb,
The cannons' pandemonium,
The rockets bursting in the air,
The sound of bugle, fife, and drum,

He turns and shakes his derrière
To show me that he doesn't care
Who takes this battle flag or why,
When in the redness of the glare

I see the banner flying high
Through the tumult in the sky
And, knowing all is now okay,
We walk away, my horse and I.

The flag is lovely, hip hooray,
But I have things to do today,
Some here and others far away,
Before I stop to hit the hay.

—*Robert Frost*

She being brand
New he threw
A flag over h
Er & began
The bombard
Ment & was soon
Rocketing
A (long) & feeling
Braveandfreeand(proudly)perilous
Can you see? Said he
Oui oui, said she
And it was love and it was
Spring and roses and it was
Dawn &
He
B
U
R
S
T
Into song.

—*e. e. cummings*

This is just to say
I have taken
The flag
That was
Flying

And which
You probably expected
To see
This morning

Forgive me
It was beautiful
So free
And so brave

—*William Carlos Williams*

Up in the night to piss
Saw the flag
Stripes & stars
Reflected in the stream
& in the morning
Still there

—*Gary Snyder*

On the ship, I sit and wait for the dawn
In the midst of the bombs and rockets and so forth,
A prisoner of these British marines who might shoot me,
You never know in a situation like this.

Like so many great moments in history,
You come upon it without meaning to.
You're a lawyer who goes to negotiate for the release of a prisoner
And voilà you become one yourself.

There is this incredibly perilous fight going on
And I suppose a person should be thinking about freedom
Or bravery but I must admit
I would give anything for a cup of coffee right now.

Like a Starbucks made by a girl in a striped blouse,
A latte streaming and gleaming.
But that seems less likely at the moment
Than Betsy Ross doing a striptease, stripe by stripe.

The graceful arc of the rockets, like Don
Larsen's curve ball for the Bronx Bombers.
He was a hero and then suddenly he was gone.
I wonder what's going to happen to that flag.

Somebody could write a poem about this,
Something to mark this whole thing that's going on,
But if they did, probably they shouldn't include
The coffee and the part about Betsy dropping the flag.

—*Billy Collins*

QUESTIONS FOR DISCUSSION AND WRITING

1. Although a humorous piece doesn't *have* to be explained, explaining humor is a great way to challenge one's analytical skills. In a discussion or an expository essay, take any of the "anthems" in Garrison Keillor's piece and explain how it works to create humor or satire. After doing some biographical research on your chosen poet, and with one or two of his or her poems in hand, answer the following questions. What does Keillor's parody tell us about the style and life of the poet in question? How does it comment upon our national anthem and our nation? To what extent do you sympathize with Keillor's sense of humor? How would you characterize the tone of Keillor's parody?

2. Write your own version of "The Star-Spangled Banner" in the style of one of your favorite poets or songwriters. Then write a short explanation of how your version comments upon both the anthem and your chosen author. Alternatively, parody another classic piece of American music or oratory, such as Lincoln's "Gettysburg Address."

DENNIS BARON

The New Technologies of the Word

Dennis Baron, Professor of English and Linguistics at the University of Illinois–Urbana, studies language and society. As he explains, "I am interested in a variety of topics dealing with the history of the English language, literacy, the question of sexism and language, attitudes toward language use, the movement to make English the official language of the United States, attempts to change language, and the effects of technology on our ways of reading and writing." Born (1944) in New York City, Baron attended Brandeis University (B.A., 1965) and earned a Ph.D. at the University of Michigan in 1971. His publications include Grammar and Gender *(1986) and* The English-Only Question: An Official Language for Americans? *(1990). His* Guide to Home Language Repair *(1994) is a lively handbook on real-world grammar and usage. Baron also publishes articles in the* New York Times, *the* Chronicle of Higher Education, *and a variety of professional journals.*

"The New Technologies of the Word" examines the way new communication methods spawned by computers and cell phones—currrently 1.5 billion in use worldwide—influence not only writing but a myriad of other behaviors. In particular, Baron argues that e-mail and cell phones produce new modes of communication, and "watching these new genres arise and evolve is like being present at the birth of stars." Indeed, with Wi-Fi and fiber optics promising broadband speeds 100 times faster than the current digital subscriber lines or cable, Baron's discussion of technological advances may require daily updating!

I am going to talk specifically about how electronic technologies are introducing major changes in the practice of American English: the computer has altered the ways we write and read significantly in the past 20 years, and the cell phone is changing spoken interaction in ways that continue to evolve. Both technologies are reconfiguring our notions of public and private language, and both are calling our attention increasingly to what is being called the "digital divide" between haves and have nots—and that is what brings us back to language policy both on the national and the global scale.

I think that the new technologies of the word, as I call them, are reinforcing two trends that we may all be observing in what is going on with English around the world. One is the continued spread of English as a world language (with the caveat so nicely articulated by [scholars] many years ago that world languages, like world empires, come and go). But this accent on global English is balanced by what I see as a new emphasis on the local: both local varieties of English set against the umbrella of World Englishes. And also a renewed emphasis on local languages and varieties in tandem with and in resistance to dominant world and national languages. The new technologies of the word are the tools of the globalizers, working for standardization. But what they produce after their initial spread is often a surprising reinforcement of the local.

Not so long ago the claim was going unquestioned that English was the language of the World Wide Web, and that the web itself embodied a kind of digital imperialism increasing the domination by English of the communication pathways. After all, it was argued, computers were limited in their ability to represent non-Roman alphabets, and anyway it was felt that everyone who had anything important to say was saying it in English. How could we be so naïve—and so colonialist—in what we envision as an increasingly postcolonial world? In any case it has become clear that many languages are now claiming their own space in a cyberspace that is perfectly able to stretch to fit them, and that the effects of technology on language practice apply not just to speakers and writers of English, but to users of any language. What is true across languages is true as well within them: the standard language imposed top down by governments, schools, and cultural norms is everywhere met by the infinite variety of local forms and practices. The computer can transmit norms downward from the top, but it can also empower individuals "at the bottom" as it were to take control of authorship: nowadays you don't have to seize the radio stations and the mimeograph machines to support the revolution. Instead, in this age of digital reproduction, you can simply fire up your PC and send your manifesto into cyberspace.

TECHNOLOGY

Language, both written and spoken, depends heavily on technology for its transmission. I would argue that speech itself is a technology, as is writing. And the means we use to transmit speech and writing are technological as well.

Today we tend to think of technology as referring primarily to computers, 5
and when I speak of the new technologies of the word I too will consider the impact of digital technology on our communication practices. But we shouldn't lose
sight of the fact that there are other technologies—old technologies of the word,
if you will—that remain even today more prevalent than computers—that mediate our communication.

For example, there's the humble wood pencil [hold up pencil], which as
Henry Petroski [author of *The Pencil*, 2002] has shown, is a complex technology. True it has no electronics, nor any moving parts, and it costs only a few
cents to manufacture and purchase in this age of mechanical reproduction. But
a pencil is complex enough that you could not easily replicate one in a home
workshop, and even if you could master the technologies of woodworking,
chemistry, mineralogy, painting and engineering necessary to make a do-it-
yourself pencil, the materials would cost you something on the order of $50, not
a few cents per unit. . . .

[Henry David] Thoreau . . . was an engineer and entrepreneur who took a
marginal [family] business which churned out a cheap, low-quality product
and turned it profitable. Thoreau may have written idealistically, but he spent
six months in the Harvard College library researching European pencil technology in an effort to make the Thoreau pencil better and more expensive than
any import. And the man who invented civil disobedience, refusing to pay
taxes being used to finance an unjust war, used his marketing skills to sell his
pencils. . . .

NOSTALGIA FOR THE OLD WAYS

Socrates warned that the new technology of writing would work to the detriment
of the old technology of memory. We remember this, of course, because Plato
wrote it down. One of the common complaints we hear today is that computers
signal the death of handwriting. Penmanship, as it was once called in American
schools, is no longer practiced with any rigor, except by those few diehards who
want to bring back the fountain pen.

Perhaps copying all the letters in a big round hand, as the Ruler of the
Queen's Navee did to gain advancement, is a lost art for most of us, but standardized handwriting was a literacy technology just as computer writing is today.
From a purely practical standpoint, uniform script was once enforced for scribes
and clerks to ensure legibility in documents destined to have multiple readers.
Indeed, a copperplate-perfect handwriting in the nineteenth century was a class
marker. The rich didn't need a nice round hand, for they didn't work in offices
and could afford to allow their handwriting to express their individuality. Once
the press freed us from a dependence on hand-copied manuscripts, and the typewriter liberated the office from the tyranny of the inkwell, it was inevitable that
handwriting would become a lost art, revived from time to time by people who
feel trapped in the present.

THE BIRTH OF GENRES

OK, enough about the old technologies of the word. Let's take a look at the new. 10
In the last decade or two, three new written genres have emerged: email, the web
page, and instant messaging now form a significant slice of writing practice in the
United States and at least email and the web page are gaining importance around
the globe as well. In addition, the mobile phone is now a major factor influencing
spoken communication. Watching these new genres arise and evolve is like being
present at the birth of stars: we have the unusual opportunity to observe these
linguistic genres spin off from older ways of doing things with words, starting out
as one sort of communication practice and winding up as something completely
different, developing their own conventions of style and usage, of appropriateness and correctness, of grammaticality and acceptability. . . .

Email started out in the emerging computer companies of the 1960s and
1970s for in-house electronic memos. In addition, programmers sent email to
one another to pass the time while their programs were compiling—much as
telegraphers in the early days of electronic communication sent personal messages to one another, and played games, while they waited for paying customers.
The first email users were techies, and the mainframe computer systems they
sent their email on were not user-friendly. Those computers were designed for
number-crunching, not word-processing. Even programmers didn't program on
the machines: they wrote out their code on pads of paper—and they probably
used no. 2 pencils to write with. Line editors were cumbersome to work with, and
initially computer keyboards only allowed working in one case, upper or lower.

This technology was so unforgiving that only a few diehards saw the possibilities that computers offered writers. Many of the early computer writers were a
ragged and persistent gang, and as a result, in the early days of email, a frontier
mystique developed around computer writing: it wasn't something for the faint
of heart. Because correcting text was so difficult, and perhaps also because programmers wanted to give the impression that they had more important things to
do than submit to the niceties of writing conventional prose, emailers were law-
less—at least when it came to observing the laws of spelling, grammar, and usage
that constrain writers using conventional technologies. They typed their email
quickly, without concern for form or style: it was their version of shooting from
the hip. They wore incorrectness as a badge of authority. They keyed their messages in lower case. They rejected linguistic conventionality and wrapped themselves in the mantle of Thoreau.

But as it is with all communication, an initially chaotic system began to self-
organize. Plus, the early chaos of email may have been more myth than reality.
Anecdotal evidence supports a claim that there was plenty of concern for linguistic correctness when computer writing was young. And even those writers of
emails who openly derided the schoolmarm approach to grammar developed
conventions early on. For one thing, writers were using computers to send conventional messages—memos, reports, notices of meetings—at the same time
that what I will call the "desperado email" was emerging. . . .

As with the early days of writing itself, digital literacy was limited to a class of scribes, or programmers, who had mastered the steep learning curve of the technology and who could, if necessary, mediate the literacy technology for the uninitiated. For digital writing to spread beyond this small group of adepts a number of things had to happen: the practice had to become easier to learn (both the hardware and the software needed to be made more writer-friendly); and computers had to become less expensive if more people were to have access to them.

In fact both of these things started to happen, first with the success of the personal computer in the early 1980s. Then in the later 1980s, graphical user interfaces and black-on-white screens allowed for text display approximating an actual typed or printed document. This, combined with significantly lower costs, led more people both to be able to afford the machine and to see that it could allow them to produce the kinds of documents they were already used to producing.

As more people adopted the technology, they brought with them their conventional concerns. The new converts to digital writing, like typists and pen-men before them, wanted to know how to do it right: how to write a business letter; how to write a report; how to write a personal letter, and they brought their concern for this medieval *ars dictaminis*, as updated for the modern office, to the newly emerging genres of email and newsgroups. The electronic frontier was suddenly becoming settled and urbanized, and there arose a sometimes not-so-subtle distinction between newcomers and old-timers. The old-timers clung to their lawlessness as a badge of authority. They were there first, after all: they invented the wheel. Newcomers asked silly questions like, "Should an email have a greeting?" And newcomers to the discourse show an inordinate fondness for spell-checking.

Soon manuals on correct electronic communication, or netiquette, began to surface. There are numerous on-line lists of do's and don'ts for email. . . . One sure sign that conventionality has come into play once and for all, that the electronic frontier is finally becoming civilized, is the appearance of chapters on electronic communication in every major college writing textbook.

THE CHARGE AGAINST EMAIL

While it is heralded by its proponents as the best thing since sliced bread, technology also seems often to generate suspicion. Critics of email view it as a leading force in the inevitable decline and fall of the English language.

Located somewhere between the traditional letter and the phone call, email continues to carve out its own communication space. True, there are junk emails that replicate conventional technology's junk mail. And there are email confidence schemes that are as intrusive as the soliciting phone calls timed to coincide with dinner. Email seems private but is in fact very public: it is discoverable in court, and if you use email at work, it is the property of your employer, who may spy on your email as well as your phone calls at will.

But the main charge against email is that it is too informal. By 'too informal'   20
critics tend to mean that, despite the prevalence of usage guides, emailers do not
evince enough concern for spelling and usage. They use too many shortcuts:
acronyms like IMHO or BTW, and emoticons. There's too much slang. In short,
the language of Shakespeare, Addison and Steele, and Hemingway gets no respect
from emailers. And emoticons have become our newest punctuation marks.

Of course emails vary in their degree of formality, and in their observance
of stylistic niceties, the way any text may. The speed of email, compared to the
post office, may take some getting used to. And so perhaps the most common
complaint of emailers themselves doesn't concern error or slang, it's the experience many of us have had of sending off an email before we are really ready. It
may be an angry email, or an incomplete one. Or we may have sent it to the
wrong recipient. . . .

Nonetheless email has made inroads in our communication practice. Once
you start down the email path, there's no going back. See what happens when the
computers go down in an office. People don't immediately switch over to the
phone, or walk down the corridor for a chat. Initially, at least, they sit around
staring at their screens, wondering how they're going to get anything done today.

INSTANT MESSAGING

Instant messaging [IM] is an even newer genre than email, popular with college
students as well as the teen and pre-teen set. It differs from email in that it is a
real-time exchange, a digital conversation among two or more selected participants, the so-called "buddy list," that seems to thrive on short turns, rapid
turn-taking, with participants dropping in and out of the conversation with
regularity. . . .

From what I can tell by looking at transcripts of IM sessions among the
seventh-grade set, IM is mostly phatic communication. "I'm here. Are you there?"
"I'm here." "Silly joke, silly joke." "Acronym, acronym." "G2G." "TTFN." If Monty
Python were still going strong, they'd surely do an IM skit. . . .

IM is more than a written conference call, with images and sounds to ac-   25
company its staccato exchanges. It is already thriving beyond the teen set in offices everywhere: it provides an easier switch than email does between onscreen
work and chatting with a friend, since the IM screen can remain open alongside
the spreadsheet or word processing document. It seems safe to predict that IM
will develop more fully just as email has done, and that it too, while remaining
reasonably informal, will develop rules and conventions of the kind every speech
community seems to form.

CELL PHONES

IM, even when only two buddies converse, seems to be private discourse carried
on in a public electronic space. Both email and Instant Messaging are skewing

our ideas of public and private language. But cell phones warp the contexts of public and private even more noticeably. Consider these scenarios:

- In a crowded gate area at O'Hare Airport in Chicago, a man who looks like he's been sleeping in his clothes marches up and down amidst the clumps of weary passengers huddled with their luggage. There's a scowl on his face and his arms saw the air as he talks loudly and angrily to himself. Terrorist? Psychotic off his meds? Neither, actually: he's a frustrated business traveler talking on his hands-free cell phone, squeezing in some work while he waits for his long-delayed flight to board. . . .

- It's the first day of my "Literacy and Technology" class at the University of Illinois, and just as I begin my soliloquy on how the new technologies are changing the ways we communicate, a tinkling melody emanates from a backpack. Without any embarrassment, a student digs out her phone, answers the call, carries on a short conversation, then hangs up. I say, pointedly, "As I was saying . . . ," though only some of the students see the irony: what just happened was exactly the point I was trying to make, that mobile telephony changes conditions for more people than just the caller and the called. Subsequent in-class phone calls are less well-timed to coincide with the syllabus. Despite my requests that students turn their phones off before coming into the room — requests there was no need to make only a semester earlier — it takes the class a while to get into the habit. Then one day my own phone rings while I am teaching. I answer the call, have a short, embarrassed conversation while the class giggles and strains to hear what I am whispering, then go back to teaching. We have no more interruptions that semester, but I notice that students now turn their phones back on even before they close their books and stow them away — the traditional signal to the instructor that my fifty minutes is up. . . .

Cell phones have come a long way in a few short years. In 1994, . . . perhaps 10 million Americans had cell phones. Today more than 100 million Americans have them[1] and some people are giving up their land phones entirely. They are changing both the nature of telephone interaction and the way people behave in public. . . .

More and more I see people walking together in an animated group, but each person is talking on a phone to someone else. At least I presume they're talking to someone else. There is, after all, that scene in the movie "Clueless" where Cher strolls alongside her best friend, Dionne, and they are chattering to one another on their cell phones.

Before cell phones, people in a group could talk to one another face to face, and people alone could give full attention to their immediate surroundings: looking at the scenery, driving the car, perusing the menu, observing the *comédie hu-*

---

[1] But see Baron headnote.

maine. Now the cell phone connects us across space, freeing us from our local context just as the land phone did when it first came on the scene.

Cell phones used in public can create an instant audience, albeit a sometimes 30 unwilling one. This morning at the local coffee bar, a woman came in already talking loudly on her phone, and while she was ordering her latte she took a second call and switched deftly between her two callers and the barista, at times involving all three in what seemed to be a single conversation. But the rest of us in the coffee line were also auditors, for talking on a cell phone seems to bring out an emotive voice. People bare half a conversation to an audience of strangers, a conversation that is sometimes uncomfortably personal for those within earshot, though it is even more often boring (who cares what your mother ate for lunch?) or simply distracting (I can't hear the person I'm with because the cell phone talker is so loud). . . .

When telephones first came on the scene, in the 1880s, whispering was not an option. Neither was privacy. Phones were rare, and when households or businesses got their first phones, they were placed in a central location: a first-floor hallway or a front desk or counter. Speaking on the telephone meant there was no place to hide, and it took some time before extensions became available that allowed callers to retreat into bedrooms or back offices, or phone cords became long enough for teenagers to haul the phone into a closet or bathroom for privacy. Not only bystanders listened in to phone calls. Telephone operators were required to check in on conversations to determine whether the line was still in use, since the connection was not automatically broken when a caller hung up the phone. But soon enough operators took on the role of conversation monitors, occasionally threatening to suspend the phone privileges of callers who used vulgar language and profanity. Privacy was further compromised in rural areas by party lines, where members of other households on the same phone line could eavesdrop.

Early telephone technology was poor by today's standards, too. Voice reproduction was so unnatural, and line noise so common, that in many cases speakers had to shout or speak very loudly in order to be heard. And speakers shouted as well in response to the room noise that occasionally made it hard for them to hear their callers. This same attempt to overcome background noise from traffic, machinery, and other talkers nearby, may lie behind the tendency of cell phone users to speak more loudly on the phone than they would to someone who is right next to them.

CONCLUSIONS

New technologies of communication often get their big break by duplicating older ones. When writing emerged in the ancient Mediterranean as an inventory device, it was useful to merchants. But once someone realized that writing could duplicate speech, there was no turning back. Cabinet makers invented the wood pencil in the sixteenth century to mark measurements in wood without gouging the wood. Once someone realized they were perfect portable writing and drawing instruments, freeing writers from their dependence on the inkwell, pencils became the first laptops. Computers began life as number crunchers (the name *computer* was first used to refer to human beings doing repetitive computations). They still crunch numbers, it's true, but most of us now depend on our computers as writing tools, not calculators.

Our communication practices have been permanently altered by electronic technologies, and that should surprise no one, nor should it be the cause of lamentation. The computer allows more people to become authors, if by authors we mean any writer who sends a creation out into the world of readers. By doing that, the computer allows more authorial languages to claim public space and authority they might not otherwise have had.

But at the same time, as authorship and linguistic prominence shift from older technologies to the computer, this democratization of the public word reinforces the divide between those who have computers and those who don't, and it further distances those who have literacy from those who don't.

But even as we worry about access to computers, equating that, perhaps mistakenly, with access to literacy, the technology is moving in new ways that may cause us once again to rethink what we mean by literacy, and to re-evaluate the interactions of language practice and technology. Already mobile phones are becoming more computer-like, and there is some chance that computers will become more like telephones. If the next big development in the digital world is the perfection of speech-to-text software, then writers will no longer key in their texts, they'll speak them, and their words will magically appear on screen.

If this actually works, and it's probably still a long time coming, it will signal a change in writing practice: we will all be dictating our text to our computers. More important, it will mark a change in our thinking about literacy. Computers can already turn text to speech efficiently enough to eliminate our dependence on the visual processing of text. Link speech to text with text to speech and you eliminate the middle terms: writing and reading could conceivably be reconfigured in such a way that they become an invisible part of the communication.

At the very least, this will cause traditionalists to lament the decline in the keyboarding skills of the young. But in fact the implications of speech to text for reconfiguring literacy are staggering. However there's no need to see the library going the way of the 8-track tape, or the quill pen. Even though my cell phone can receive email messages, for now speech to text still belongs in the realm of science fiction, like cold fusion or, dare I say, machine translation?

QUESTIONS FOR DISCUSSION AND WRITING

1. Baron begins his discussion of technology with the pencil, manufactured (and used) by Henry David Thoreau, and the importance of handwriting in America in the nineteenth and twentieth centuries (paragraphs 6–10). What, if anything,

do you write by hand? Under what circumstances? Were you taught penmanship in school? When did you learn to use a computer or other electronic communication device(s)? Did you teach yourself or learn by trial and error? Note that Baron skips completely over typewriters, the mainstay of American offices throughout most of the twentieth century. Why?

2. Based on the examples that Baron supplies (paragraph 26), do you agree that electronic technologies such as e-mail, cell phones, message boards, and blogs are causing "major changes in the practice of American English"? (paragraph 1). How are these changes creating written or unwritten guidelines for using e-mail, cell phones, and instant messaging? What is the basis of rules such as those imposed by Internet discussion lists on behaviors such as "flaming" and "spamming," by colleges and high schools on in-class cell phone use, and by some states on using a cell phone while driving? To what extent are these rules justified as matters of privacy, etiquette, safety, or ethics?

3. Baron writes about the way the World Wide Web and language affect each other, arguing that the Web could be both an agent of language "imperialism" and a way to empower individuals "at the bottom" to "take control of authorship" (paragraph 3). By yourself or with a group, write a paper about language "imperialism" or language liberation involving the Web, using research and your own experience. Focus on a case in which individuals, or relatively powerless groups, used the Internet to gain power or a case in which institutions or governments used the Internet to dominate others.

ROZ CHAST

The I.M.s of Romeo and Juliet

QUESTIONS FOR DISCUSSION AND WRITING

1. What characteristics of instant messaging does this dialogue between Romeo and Juliet illustrate? How do these messages depart from standard English? Is this real writing or a form of shorthand or code?

2. Are Romeo and Juliet typical American teenagers? What electronic equipment, clothing, books, and food reinforce your opinion? Why are these strewn so messily on the floor?

3. Do readers need to be familiar with Shakespeare's *Romeo and Juliet* to understand the humor of "The I.M.s of Romeo and Juliet"? To provide "closure" (see McCloud, p. 62)? In either case, why or why not?

BRIEF TAKES ON WRITING: HOW TO DO IT

If you've ever stared at a blank sheet of paper under pressure—and if you haven't, you probably will at some point—you may have wondered how professional writers do their work. Hemingway advises us to develop the habit of writing at a certain time of day every day: "Write every morning." A lot of writing goes on when we're not sitting at a desk but going about other tasks—driving, running, cooking—even, as Thurber tells us, at parties. Elbow shows how we can free ourselves to write, and Murray offers a way to keep track of where we are. Writing is, for Lamott, at heart a matter of work and time and effort. "So," she says, "you might as well get started."

ROGER ROSENBLATT

Never Correct Anybody's English

Roger Rosenblatt is an essayist, author, commentator, and journalist.

Never correct anybody's English. Oh-so-educated you know when to use she and him and that everyone takes the singular verb. Whoopie for you! Keep that knowledge to yourself. Nobody wants to have his English corrected, and to prove it, he will say: "Oh, thank you. I never get that right! Ha ha." Then he will kill you. Between you and I, it's safer for everyone to keep their mouth shut. . . .

JAMES THURBER

Telling Stories

James Thurber is best known for his cartoons and short stories. He also wrote an autobiography, fiction, children's fantasy, and commentary.

INTERVIEWERS: Does it bother you to talk about the stories on which you're working? It bothers many writers, though it would seem that particularly the humorous story is polished through retelling.

THURBER: Oh, yes. I often tell them at parties and places. And I write them there too.

INTERVIEWERS: You write them?

THURBER: I never quite know when I'm not writing. Sometimes my wife comes up to me at a party and says, "Dammit, Thurber, stop writing." She usually catches me in the middle of a paragraph. Or my daughter will look up from the dinner table and ask, "Is he sick?" "No," my wife says, "he's writing something." I have to do it that way on account of my eyes. I still write occasionally—in the proper sense of the word—using black crayon on yellow paper and getting perhaps twenty words to the page. My usual method, though, is to spend the mornings turning over the text in my mind. Then in the afternoon, between two and five, I call in a secretary and dictate to her. I can do about two thousand words. It took me about ten years to learn.

RITA MAE BROWN

Kissing Off Ma Bell

*Rita Mae Brown is a poet and novelist (*Rubyfruit Jungle, *1973, among many others).*

Have you ever heard of *The Collected Phone Calls of Gertrude Stein*? Writers should learn to write letters and save the telephone for business. Charles Jerry Hannah, a writer, used to bedevil his students with the idea of writing letters. He was right. Any excuse to get you to the typewriter, computer, or pen will begin oiling your brain. The more you write, the better you'll get. You might want to write a letter to a friend before you begin your day's work. I give an exercise in class in which you've got fifteen minutes to write a letter to a public or historical figure. The person may be living or dead. All I care about is that the rest of the class will know who it is. Then we read the letters.

A letter is halfway to first-person narrative but it's in the author's voice.

ERNEST HEMINGWAY

Write Every Morning

Ernest Hemingway was one of the twentieth century's most influential writers. He is probably best known for his novella "The Old Man and the Sea" (1952) and the novel The Sun Also Rises *(1926). He received the Nobel Prize for Literature in 1954.*

INTERVIEWER: Are these hours during the actual process of writing pleasurable?
HEMINGWAY: Very.
INTERVIEWER: Could you say something of this process? When do you work? Do you keep to a strict schedule?
HEMINGWAY: When I am working on a book or a story I write every morning as soon after first light as possible. There is no one to disturb you and it is cool or cold and you come to your work and warm as you write. You read what you have written and, as you always stop when you know what is going to

happen next, you go on from there. You write until you come to a place where you still have your juice and know what will happen next and you stop and try to live through until the next day when you hit it again. You have started at six in the morning, say, and may go on until noon or be through before that. When you stop you are as empty, and at the same time never empty but filling, as when you have made love to someone you love. Nothing can hurt you, nothing can happen, nothing means anything until the next day when you do it again. It is the wait until the next day that is hard to get through.

PETER ELBOW

Freewriting

Author of six books, including Writing with Power *(1981), Peter Elbow has taught English at the University of Massachusetts at Amherst, the Massachusetts Institute of Technology, and the State University of New York at Stony Brook, where he also directed the Writing Program.*

The most effective way I know to improve your writing is to do freewriting exercises regularly. At least three times a week. They are sometimes called "automatic writing," "babbling," or "jabbering" exercises. The idea is simply to write for ten minutes (later on, perhaps fifteen or twenty). Don't stop for anything. Go quickly without rushing. Never stop to look back, to cross something out, to wonder how to spell something, to wonder what word or thought to use, or to think about what you are doing. If you can't think of a word or a spelling, just use a squiggle or else write, "I can't think of it." Just put down something. The easiest thing is just to put down whatever is in your mind. If you get stuck it's fine to write "I can't think what to say, I can't think what to say" as many times as you want; or to repeat the last word you wrote over and over again; or anything else. The only requirement is that you *never* stop.

What happens to a freewriting exercise is important. It must be a piece of writing which, even if someone reads it, doesn't send any ripples back to you. It is like writing something and putting it in a bottle in the sea. The teacherless class helps your writing by providing maximum feedback. Freewritings help you by providing no feedback at all. When I assign one, I invite the writer to let me read it. But I also tell him to keep it if he prefers. I read it quickly and make no comments at all and I do not speak with him about it. The main thing is that a freewriting must never be evaluated in any way; in fact there must be no discussion or comment at all.

ANNE LAMOTT
Getting Started

Anne Lamott is the author of six novels as well as four best-selling books of nonfiction, including Traveling Mercies *(1999), a collection of autobiographical essays on faith. She has been honored with a Guggenheim Fellowship.*

"But how?" my students ask. "How do you actually do it?"

You sit down, I say. You try to sit down at approximately the same time every day. This is how you train your unconscious to kick in for you creatively. So you sit down at, say, nine every morning, or ten every night. You put a piece of paper in the typewriter, or you turn on your computer and bring up the right file, and then you stare at it for an hour or so. You begin rocking, just a little at first, and then like a huge autistic child. You look at the ceiling, and over at the clock, yawn, and stare at the paper again. Then, with your fingers poised on the keyboard, you squint at an image that is forming in your mind—a scene, a locale, a character, whatever— and you try to quiet your mind so you can hear what that landscape or character has to say above the other voices in your mind. The other voices are banshees and drunken monkeys. They are the voices of anxiety, judgment, doom, guilt. Also, severe hypochondria. There may be a Nurse Ratched–like listing of things that must be done right this moment: foods that must come out of the freezer, appointments that must be canceled or made, hairs that must be tweezed. But you hold an imaginary gun to your head and make yourself stay at the desk. There is a vague pain at the base of your neck. It crosses your mind that you have meningitis. Then the phone rings and you look up at the ceiling with fury, summon every ounce of noblesse oblige, and answer the call politely, with maybe just the merest hint of irritation. The caller asks if you're working, and you say yeah, because you are.

Yet somehow in the face of all this, you clear a space for the writing voice, hacking away at the others with machetes, and you begin to compose sentences. You begin to string words together like beads to tell a story. You are desperate to communicate, to edify or entertain, to preserve moments of grace or joy or transcendence, to make real or imagined events come alive. But you cannot will this to happen. It is a matter of persistence and faith and hard work. So you might as well just go ahead and get started.

DONALD M. MURRAY
Creating a Design

For two decades, poet and Pulitzer Prize–winner Donald M. Murray wrote a column for The Boston Globe.

The writer usually finds it helps to chart what he has to write, to be able to see the structure on the page. He may create a formal "Harvard" outline in which each point is in a complete sentence. It is more likely, however, that he doesn't follow the rules of Roman numerals and Arabic numbers, of capital letters and small letters, but draws what he has to say in a circle or a square, develops it in a chart form, or scribbles it very informally, putting ideas down in random patterns and then drawing lines between ideas. The important thing is that he sees the design. He is not trying to win a contest by the clarity of his design. No one has to see or understand his design but himself. But he must have, in his mind's eye or on paper, an idea of where he is to begin and where he is to end.

The amateur driver may just go out for a drive, having no idea where he is headed or where he will end up. It is fun, and amateur writing is fun. But the professional writer has a clear idea of where he is going. He doesn't start out with a gallon of gas to drive from Los Angeles to Chicago. He doesn't leave Philadelphia to go to Chicago and wander through Miami on the way. The writer knows where he is going and how he wants to get there.

The writer understands that writing is a process, not a rigid procedure. He constantly rediscovers his subject. He gets to know his audience better and sees what they need to know. When he gathers facts, the facts will change, refine or perhaps even destroy his subject. When he creates a design of what he has to say, his outline may show him he needs to expand or limit the subject. He may discover he cannot speak to the people he wanted to speak to, and he must find a new audience. Sometimes he will give up what he has to say and start on a new subject. He must be open to these changes, for writing is a continuing state of discovery. He is doing something, building something, creating something, and it will change under his hands. That is part of the terror and the excitement of writing.

JANE KENYON
Have Good Sentences in Your Ears

At the time of her death in 1995 Jane Kenyon was the poet laureate of New Hampshire. She is the author of five books of poetry, including Otherwise: New & Selected Poems *(1996).*

Be a good steward of your gifts. Protect your time. Feed your inner life. Avoid too much noise. Read good books, have good sentences in your ears. Be by yourself as often as you can. Walk. Take the phone off the hook. Work regular hours.

CHAPTER 2

Identity with Attitude: Who We Are and How We Got That Way

FRANZ BOAZ AND GEORGE HUNT

An Authentic Indian

JOHN HENLEY
The Graduates

QUESTIONS FOR DISCUSSION AND WRITING

1. The first photograph shows anthropologist Franz Boaz (*left*) and photographer George Hunt (*right*) creating an artificial backdrop to make their Kwakiutl Native Peoples subject appear more "authentic" than she would look if posed against the real-life background of picket fence or columned building. What does this staging say about the construction and reading of ethnicity? How does this photograph serve as a visual metaphor for Alexie's "What Sacagawea Means to Me" (p. 142)? Might it also have relevance for Momaday's "Way to Rainy Mountain" (p. 145)?

2. Compare the first image with John Henley's photograph of university graduates. How many ethnicities do these graduates appear to represent (remember, you are only seeing their faces and a few hands)? What does the background signify? What messages does this photograph send? Might this photograph be as staged as that of the Kwakiutl woman? Does your recognition of this possibility, even likelihood, affect how you interpret either or both pictures?

ERIC LIU

Notes of a Native Speaker

Eric Liu was born in Poughkeepsie, New York, in 1968. "My own assimilation began long before I was born," writes Liu, whose parents came to the United States from Taiwan in the late 1950s. His father was an IBM executive, and his mother worked as a computer programer. Liu and his sister grew up with the photos and pilot stories of their grandfather, a general in the Nationalist Chinese air force during World War II. "Shadow-dancing" with his identity as a "Renaissance boy" or an "Asian overachiever," Liu graduated summa cum laude with a bachelor's degree in history from Yale (1990). He interned with Senator Daniel Patrick Moynihan one summer and spent two other summers in Marine Officer Candidate School in Quantico, Virginia. At age twenty-five, Liu became President Bill Clinton's youngest speechwriter. He attended Harvard Law School and then, in 2000, returned to the White House as deputy domestic policy adviser. He is a political commentator on CNN and CNBC.

The title of Liu's memoir, The Accidental Asian: Notes of a Native Speaker *(1998), is a multiracial reference to Anne Tyler's* The Accidental Tourist *(1985), James Baldwin's essay "Notes of a Native Son" (1955), and Richard Wright's* Native Son *(1940). Although Liu grew up speaking a mixture of English and Mandarin, English is his native language. Refusing to look at ten million Americans of Asian descent as an ethnic group, Liu focuses on the diversity of Asian American heritage and downplays race.*

Here are some of the ways you could say I am "white":

> I listen to National Public Radio.
> I wear khaki Dockers.
> I own brown suede bucks.
> I eat gourmet greens.
> I have few close friends "of color."
> I married a white woman.
> I am a child of the suburbs.
> I furnish my condo à la Crate & Barrel.
> I vacation in charming bed-and-breakfasts.
> I have never once been the victim of blatant discrimination.
> I am a member of several exclusive institutions.
> I have been in the inner sanctums of political power.
> I have been there as something other than an attendant.
> I have the ambition to return.
> I am a producer of the culture.
> I expect my voice to be heard.
> I speak flawless, unaccented English.

I subscribe to *Foreign Affairs.*
I do not mind when editorialists write in the first person plural.
I do not mind how white television casts are.
I am not too ethnic.
I am wary of minority militants.
I consider myself neither in exile nor in opposition.
I am considered "a credit to my race."

I never asked to be white. I am not literally white. That is, I do not have white skin or white ancestors. I have yellow skin and yellow ancestors, hundreds of generations of them. But like so many other Asian Americans of the second generation, I find myself now the bearer of a strange new status: white, by acclamation. Thus it is that I have been described as an "honorary white," by other whites, and as a "banana," by other Asians. Both the honorific and the epithet take as a given this idea: to the extent that I have moved away from the periphery and toward the center of American life, I have become white inside. *Some are born white, others achieve whiteness, still others have whiteness thrust upon them.* This, supposedly, is what it means to assimilate.

There was a time when assimilation did quite strictly mean whitening. In fact, well into the first half of this century, mimicry of the stylized standards of the WASP gentry was the proper, dominant, perhaps even sole method of ensuring that your origins would not be held against you. You "made it" in society not only by putting on airs of anglitude, but also by assiduously bleaching out the marks of a darker, dirtier past. And this bargain, stifling as it was, was open to European immigrants almost exclusively; to blacks, only on the passing occasion; to Asians, hardly at all.

Times have changed, and I suppose you could call it progress that a China-man, too, may now aspire to whiteness. But precisely because the times have changed, that aspiration—and the *imputation* of the aspiration—now seems astonishingly outmoded. The meaning of "American" has undergone a revolution in the twenty-nine years I have been alive, a revolution of color, class, and culture. Yet the vocabulary of "assimilation" has remained fixed all this time: fixed in whiteness, which is still our metonym for power; and fixed in shame, which is what the colored are expected to feel for embracing the power.

I have assimilated. I am of the mainstream. In many ways I fit the psychological profile of the so-called banana: imitative, impressionable, rootless, eager to please. As I will admit in this essay, I have at times gone to great lengths to downplay my difference, the better to penetrate the "establishment" of the moment. Yet I'm not sure that what I did was so cut-and-dried as "becoming white." I plead guilty to the charges above: achieving, learning the ways of the upper middle class, distancing myself from radicals of any hue. But having confessed, I still do not know my crime.

To be an accused banana is to stand at the ill-fated intersection of class 5 and race. And because class is the only thing Americans have more trouble talking about than race, a minority's climb up the social ladder is often will-fully misnamed and wrongly portrayed. There is usually, in the portrayal, a strong whiff of betrayal: the assimilist is a traitor to his kind, to his class, to his own family. He cannot gain the world without losing his soul. To be sure, something *is* lost in any migration, whether from place to place or from class to class. But something is gained as well. And the result is always more compli-cated than the monochrome language of "whiteness" and "authenticity" would suggest. . . .

I recently dug up a photograph of myself from freshman year of college that made me smile. I have on the wrong shoes, the wrong socks, the wrong checkered shirt tucked the wrong way into the wrong slacks. I look like what I was: a boy sprung from a middlebrow burg who affected a secondhand preppiness. I look nervous. Compare that image to one from my senior-class dinner: now I am attired in a gray tweed jacket with a green plaid bow tie and a sensible button-down shirt, all pur-chased at the Yale Co-op. I look confident, and more than a bit contrived.

What happened in between those two photographs is that I experienced, then overcame, what the poet Meena Alexander has called "the shock of arrival." When I was deposited at the wrought-iron gates of my residential college as a freshman, I felt more like an outsider than I'd thought possible. It wasn't just that I was a small Chinese boy standing at a grand WASP temple; nor simply that I was a hayseed neophyte puzzled by the refinements of college style. It was *both*: color and class were all twisted together in a double helix of felt inadequacy.

For a while I coped with the shock by retreating to a group of my own kind—not fellow Asians, but fellow marginal public-school grads who resented the rah-rah Yalies to whom everything came so effortlessly. Aligning myself this way was bearable—I was hiding, but at least I could place myself in a long tradi-tion of underdog exiles at Yale. Aligning myself by race, on the other hand, would have seemed too inhibiting.

I know this doesn't make much sense. I know also that college, in the multi-cultural era, is supposed to be where the deracinated minority youth discovers the "person of color" inside. To a point, I did. I studied Chinese, took an Asian American history course, a seminar on race politics. But ultimately, college was where the unconscious habits of my adolescent assimilation hardened into self-conscious strategy.

I still remember the moment, in the first week of school, when I came upon   10
a table in Yale Station set up by the Asian American Student Association. The up-perclassman staffing the table was pleasant enough. He certainly did not strike me as a fanatic. Yet, for some reason, I flashed immediately to a scene I'd witnessed days earlier, on the corner outside. Several Lubavitcher Jews, dressed in black, their faces bracketed by dangling side curls, were looking for fellow travelers at this busy crossroads. Their method was crude but memorable. As any vaguely Jewish-looking male walked past, the zealots would quickly approach, extend a pamphlet, and ask, "Excuse me, sir, are you Jewish?" Since most were not, and

since those who were weren't about to stop, the result was a frantic, nervous, almost comical buzz all about the corner: Excuse me, are you Jewish? Are you Jewish? Excuse me. Are you Jewish?

I looked now at the clean-cut Korean boy at the AASA table (I think I can distinguish among Asian ethnicities as readily as those Hasidim thought they could tell Gentile from Jew), and though he had merely offered an introductory hello and was now smiling mutely at me, in the back of my mind I heard only this: *Excuse me, are you Asian? Are you Asian? Excuse me. Are you Asian?* I took one of the flyers on the table, even put my name on a mailing list, so as not to appear impolite. But I had already resolved not to be active in any Asians-only group. I thought then: I would never *choose* to be so pigeonholed.

This allergic sensitivity to "pigeonholing" is one of the unhappy hallmarks of the banana mentality. What does the banana fear? That is, what did *I* fear? The possibility of being mistaken for someone more Chinese. The possibility of being known only, or even primarily, for being Asian. The possibility of being written off by whites as a self-segregating ethnic clumper. These were the threats—unseen and, frankly, unsubstantiated—that I felt I should keep at bay.

I didn't avoid making Asian friends in college or working with Asian classmates; I simply never went out of my way to do so. This distinction seemed important—it marked, to my mind, the difference between self-hate and self-respect. That the two should have been so proximate in the first place never struck me as odd, or telling. Nor did it ever occur to me that the reasons I gave myself for dissociating from Asians as a group—that I didn't want to be part of a clique, that I didn't want to get absorbed and lose my individuality—were the very developments that marked my own assimilation. I simply hewed to my ideology of race neutrality and self-reliance. I didn't need that crutch, I told myself nervously, that crutch of racial affinity. What's more, I was vaguely insulted by the presumption that I might.

But again: Who was making the presumption? Who more than I was taking the mere existence of Korean volleyball leagues or Taiwanese social sets or pan-Asian student clubs to mean that *all* people of Asian descent, myself included, needed such quasi-kinship groups? And who more than I interpreted this need as infirmity, as a failure to fit in? I resented the faintly sneering way that some whites regarded Asians as an undifferentiated mass. But whose sneer, really, did I resent more than my own?

I was keenly aware of the unflattering mythologies that attach to Asian Americans: that we are indelibly foreign, exotic, math and science geeks, numbers people rather than people people, followers and not leaders, physically frail but devious and sneaky, unknowable and potentially treacherous. These stereotypes of Asian otherness and inferiority were like immense blocks of ice sitting before me, challenging me to chip away at them. And I did, tirelessly. All the while, though, I was oblivious to rumors of my *own* otherness and inferiority, rumors that rose off those blocks like a fog, wafting into my consciousness and chilling my sense of self.

As I had done in high school, I combated the stereotypes in part by trying to disprove them. If Asians were reputed to be math and science geeks, I would be a student of history and politics. If Asians were supposed to be feeble subalterns, I'd lift weights and go to Marine officer candidate school. If Asians were alien, I'd be ardently patriotic. If Asians were shy and retiring, I'd try to be exuberant and jocular. If they were narrow-minded specialists, I'd be a well-rounded generalist. If they were perpetual outsiders, I'd join every establishment outfit I could and show that I, too, could run with the swift.

I overstate, of course. It wasn't that I chose to do all these things with no other purpose than to cut against a supposed convention. I was neither so Pavlovian nor so calculating that I would simply remake myself into the opposite of what people expected. I actually *liked* history, and wasn't especially good at math. As the grandson of a military officer, I *wanted* to see what officer candidates school would be like, and I enjoyed it, at least once I'd finished. I am *by nature* enthusiastic and allegiant, a joiner, and a bit of a jingo.

At the same time, I was often aware, sometimes even hopeful, that others might think me "exceptional" for my race. I derived satisfaction from being the "atypical" Asian, the only Chinese face at OCS or in this club or that.

The irony is that in working so duteously to defy stereotype, I became a slave to it. For to act self-consciously against Asian "tendencies" is not to break loose from the cage of myth and legend; it is to turn the very key that locks you inside. What spontaneity is there when the value of every act is measured, at least in part, by its power to refute a presumption about why you act? The *typical Asian* I imagined, and the *atypical Asian* I imagined myself to be, were identical in this sense: neither was as much a creature of free will as a human being ought to be.

Let me say it plainly, then: I am not proud to have had this mentality. I be- 20 lieve I have outgrown it. And I expose it now not to justify it but to detoxify it, to prevent its further spread.

Yet it would be misleading, I think, to suggest that my education centered solely on the discomfort caused by race. The fact is, when I first got to college I felt deficient compared with people of *every* color. Part of why I believed it so necessary to achieve was that I lacked the connections, the wealth, the experience, the sophistication that so many of my classmates seemed to have. I didn't get the jokes or the intellectual references. I didn't have the canny attitude. So in addition to all my coursework, I began to puzzle over this, the culture of the influential class.

Over time, I suppose, I learned the culture. My interests and vocabulary became ever more worldly. I made my way onto what Calvin Trillin once described as the "magic escalator" of a Yale education. Extracurriculars opened the door to an alumni internship, which brought me to Capitol Hill, which led to a job and a life in Washington after commencement. Gradually, very gradually, I found that I was not so much of an outsider anymore. I found that by almost any standard, but particularly by the standards of my younger self, I was actually beginning to "make it."

It has taken me until now, however, to appraise the thoughts and acts of that younger self. I can see now that the straitening path I took was not the only or even the best path. For while it may be possible to transcend race, *it is not always necessary to try.* And while racial identity is sometimes a shackle, it is not *only* a shackle. I could have spared myself a great deal of heartache had I understood this earlier, that the choice of race is not simply "embrace or efface."

I wonder sometimes how I would have turned out had I been, from the start, more comfortable in my own skin. What did I miss by distancing myself from race? What friendships did I forgo, what self-knowledge did I defer? Had certain accidents of privilege been accidents of privation or exclusion, I might well have developed a different view of the world. But I do not know just how my view would have differed.

What I know is that through all those years of shadow-dancing with my   25 identity, something happened, something that had only partially to do with color. By the time I left Yale I was no longer the scared boy of that freshman photo. I had become more sure of myself and of my place—sure enough, indeed, to perceive the folly of my fears. And in the years since, I have assumed a sense of expectation, of access and *belonging,* that my younger self could scarcely have imagined. All this happened incrementally. There was no clear tipping point, no obvious moment of mutation. The shock of arrival, it would seem, is simply that I arrived.

QUESTIONS FOR DISCUSSION AND WRITING

1. In the opening paragraph, how does Liu intend for his list to portray the essence of "whiteness"? Explain why this list is an effective definition of whiteness—or why it fails to define whiteness—for you.

2. Liu says "college was where the unconscious habits of my . . . assimilation hardened into self-conscious strategy" (paragraph 9). Describe the strategy of assimilation that he developed. What did it consist of? What stages did it go through? What did it accomplish for him?

3. Considering the focus on self-definition in this essay, do you find that it celebrates self-centeredness? Does Liu say too much about himself and not enough about others? What does he gain and what does he lose by focusing on himself? Write an essay in which you either defend or criticize Liu's focus on himself. Include references to yourself, if they fit.

4. Have you ever felt that you had to assimilate yourself into a group? Write about your experience of assimilation, stressing any stages that you went through and explaining the positive or negative aspects of the process. Or, write about someone else's assimilation into a group. Does the desire to assimilate ever justify deception, withholding information, or other forms of manipulating evidence or other people?

JAMES BALDWIN
Stranger in the Village

Through his fiction, James Baldwin (1924–1987) undertook to arouse the conscience of America during a time of social strife and racial polarization. Born in Harlem, he supplemented his education with intensive and obsessive reading. Baldwin's work would draw extensively on his Harlem youth—especially his struggle with a stepfather who called him ugly and refused to recognize his talent. Editing school newspapers, writing stories, and publishing articles, Baldwin entered literary circles but, disgusted by racial encounters and an unsatisfactory personal life, moved to Paris in 1948. During a sojourn in Switzerland he completed his first novel, Go Tell It on the Mountain *(1953). The novels that followed center on family relations, homosexual love, and race; the best known are* Giovanni's Room *(1956) and* Another Country *(1962). Two of his plays,* The Amen Corner *(1955) and* Blues for Mister Charlie *(1964), have been produced on Broadway. Baldwin's two best-selling essay collections,* Notes of a Native Son *(1955) and* The Fire Next Time *(1963), give voice to the urgent emotional and spiritual dangers of racism. Essayist Phillip Lopate calls Baldwin "the greatest American essayist in the second half of the twentieth century." Baldwin retained his U.S. citizenship but lived primarily in France until his death, returning to the United States several times to lend his support to civil rights marches with Martin Luther King, Jr., Stokely Carmichael, and Malcolm X.*

In "Stranger in the Village," from Notes of a Native Son *(1955), Baldwin's account of his experience as the only black person living in a Swiss village, leads into a meditation on blackness, whiteness, and the unique challenge of an American identity.*

From all available evidence no black man had ever set foot in this tiny Swiss village before I came. I was told before arriving that I would probably be a "sight" for the village; I took this to mean that people of my complexion were rarely seen in Switzerland, and also that city people are always something of a "sight" outside of the city. It did not occur to me—possibly because I am an American—that there could be people anywhere who had never seen a Negro.

It is a fact that cannot be explained on the basis of the inaccessibility of the village. The village is very high, but it is only four hours from Milan and three hours from Lausanne. It is true that it is virtually unknown. Few people making plans for a holiday would elect to come here. On the other hand, the villagers are able, presumably, to come and go as they please—which they do: to another town at the foot of the mountain, with a population of approximately five thousand, the nearest place to see a movie or go to the bank. In the village there is no movie house, no bank, no library, no theater; very few radios, one jeep, one station wagon; and at the moment, one typewriter, mine, an invention which the woman next door to me here had never seen. There are about six hundred people living here, all Catholic—I conclude this from the fact that the Catholic church is open all year round, whereas the Protestant chapel, set off on a hill a little removed from the village, is open only in the summertime when the tourists arrive. There are four or five hotels, all closed now, and four or five *bistros*, of which, however, only two do any business during the winter. These two do not do a great deal, for life in the village seems to end around nine or ten o'clock. There are a few stores, butcher, baker, *épicerie*, a hardware store, and a money-changer—who cannot change travelers' checks, but must send them down to the bank, an operation which takes two or three days. There is something called the *Ballet Haus*, closed in the winter and used for God knows what, certainly not ballet, during the summer. There seems to be only one schoolhouse in the village, and this for the quite young children; I suppose this to mean that their older brothers and sisters at some point descend from these mountains in order to complete their education—possibly, again, to the town just below. The landscape is absolutely forbidding, mountains towering on all four sides, ice and snow as far as the eye can reach. In this white wilderness, men and women and children move all day, carrying washing, wood, buckets of milk or water, sometimes skiing on Sunday afternoons. All week long boys and young men are to be seen shoveling snow off the rooftops, or dragging wood down from the forest in sleds.

The village's only real attraction, which explains the tourist season, is the hot spring water. A disquietingly high proportion of these tourists are cripples, or semi-cripples, who come year after year—from other parts of Switzerland, usually—to take the waters. This lends the village, at the height of the season, a rather terrifying air of sanctity, as though it were a lesser Lourdes. There is often something beautiful, there is always something awful, in the spectacle of a person who has lost one of his faculties, a faculty he never questioned until it was gone, and who struggles to recover it. Yet people remain people, on crutches or indeed on deathbeds; and wherever I passed, the first summer I was here, among the native villagers or among the lame, a wind passed with me—of astonishment, curiosity, amusement, and outrage. That first summer I stayed two weeks and never intended to return. But I did return in the winter, to work; the village offers, obviously, no distractions whatever and has the further advantage of being extremely cheap. Now it is winter again, a year later, and I am here again. Everyone in the village knows my name, though they scarcely ever use it, knows that I come from America—though, this, apparently, they will never really believe: black men come from Africa—and everyone knows that I am the friend of the son of a woman who was born here, and that I am staying in their chalet. But I remain as much a stranger today as I was the first day I arrived, and the children shout *Neger! Neger!* as I walk along the streets.

It must be admitted that in the beginning I was far too shocked to have any real reaction. In so far as I reacted at all, I reacted by trying to be pleasant—it being a great part of the American Negro's education (long before he goes to school) that he must make people "like" him. This smile-and-the-world-smiles-with-you routine worked about as well in this situation as it had in the situation for which it was designed, which is to say that it did not work at all. No one, after all, can be liked whose human weight and complexity cannot be, or has not been, admitted. My smile was simply another unheard-of phenomenon which allowed them to see my teeth—they did not, really, see my smile and I began to think that, should I take to snarling, no one would notice any difference. All of the physical characteristics of the Negro which had caused me, in America, a very different and almost forgotten pain were nothing less than miraculous—or infernal—in the eyes of the village people. Some thought my hair was the color of tar, that it had the texture of wire, or the texture of cotton. It was jocularly suggested that I might let it all grow long and make myself a winter coat. If I sat in the sun for more than five minutes some daring creature was certain to come along and gingerly put his fingers on my hair, as though he were afraid of an electric shock, or put his hand on my hand, astonished that the color did not rub off. In all of this, in which it must be conceded there was the charm of genuine wonder and in which there were certainly no element of intentional unkindness, there was yet no suggestion that I was human: I was simply a living wonder.

I knew that they did not mean to be unkind, and I know it now; it is neces-   5
sary, nevertheless, for me to repeat this to myself each time that I walk out of the chalet. The children who shout *Neger!* have no way of knowing the echoes this sound raises in me. They are brimming with good humor and the more daring swell with pride when I stop to speak with them. Just the same, there are days when I cannot pause and smile, when I have no heart to play with them; when, indeed, I mutter sourly to myself, exactly as I muttered on the streets of a city these children have never seen, when I was no bigger than these children are now: *Your* mother *was a nigger.* Joyce is right about history being a nightmare—but it may be the nightmare from which no one *can* awaken. People are trapped in history and history is trapped in them.

There is a custom in the village—I am told it is repeated in many villages—of "buying" African natives for the purpose of converting them to Christianity. There stands in the church all year round a small box with a slot for money, decorated with a black figurine, and into this box the villagers drop their francs. During the *carnaval* which precedes Lent, two village children have their faces blackened—out of which bloodless darkness their blue eyes shine like ice—and fantastic horsehair wigs are placed on their blond heads; thus disguised, they solicit among the villagers for money for the missionaries in Africa. Between the box in the church and the blackened children, the village "bought" last year six or eight African natives. This was reported to me with pride by the wife of one of the *bistro* owners and I was careful to express astonishment and pleasure at the solicitude shown by the village for the souls of black folks. The *bistro* owner's wife beamed with a pleasure far more genuine than my own and seemed to feel that I might now breathe more easily concerning the souls of at least six of my kinsmen.

I tried not to think of these so lately baptized kinsmen, of the price paid for them, or the peculiar price they themselves would pay, and said nothing about my father, who having taken his own conversion too literally never, at bottom, forgave the white world (which he described as heathen) for having saddled him with a Christ in whom, to judge at least from their treatment of him, they themselves no longer believed. I thought of white men arriving for the first time in an African village, strangers there, as I am a stranger here, and tried to imagine the astounded populace touching their hair and marveling at the color of their skin. But there is a great difference between being the first white man to be seen by Africans and being the first black man to be seen by whites. The white man takes the astonishment as tribute, for he arrives to conquer and to convert the natives, whose inferiority in relation to himself is not even to be questioned; whereas I, without a thought of conquest, find myself among a people whose culture controls me, has even, in a sense, created me, people who have cost me more in anguish and rage than they will ever know, who yet do not even know of my existence. The astonishment with which I might have greeted them, should they have stumbled into my African village a few hundred years ago, might have rejoiced their hearts. But the astonishment with which they greet me today can only poison mine.

And this is so despite everything I may do to feel differently, despite my friendly conversations with the *bistro* owner's wife, despite their three-year-old son who has at last become my friend, despite the *saluts* and *bonsoirs*[1] which I exchange with people as I walk, despite the fact that I know that no individual can be taken to task for what history is doing, or has done. I say that the culture of these people controls me—but they can scarcely be held responsible for European culture. America comes out of Europe, but these people have never seen America, nor have most of them seen more of Europe than the hamlet at the foot of their mountain. Yet they move with an authority which I shall never have; and they regard me, quite rightly, not only as a stranger in their village but as a suspect latecomer, bearing no credentials, to everything they have—however unconsciously—inherited.

For this village, even were it incomparably more remote and incredibly more primitive, is the West, the West onto which I have been so strangely grafted. These people cannot be, from the point of view of power, strangers anywhere in the world; they have made the modern world, in effect, even if they do not know it. The most illiterate among them is related, in a way that I am not, to Dante, Shakespeare, Michelangelo, Aeschylus, Da Vinci, Rembrandt, and Racine; the cathedral at Chartres says something to them which it cannot say to me, as indeed would New York's Empire State Building, should anyone here ever see it. Out of their hymns and dances come Beethoven and Bach. Go back a few centuries and they are in their full glory—but I am in Africa, watching the conquerors arrive.

---

[1] "Hellos" and "good evenings."

The rage of the disesteemed is personally fruitless, but it is also absolutely in-   10
evitable; this rage, so generally discounted, so little understood even among the
people whose daily bread it is, is one of the things that makes history. Rage can
only with difficulty, and never entirely, be brought under the domination of the
intelligence and is therefore not susceptible to any arguments whatever. This is a
fact which ordinary representatives of the *Herrenvolk*,[2] having never felt this rage
and being unable to imagine, quite fail to understand. Also, rage cannot be hidden, it can only be dissembled. This dissembling deludes the thoughtless, and
strengthens rage and adds, to rage, contempt. There are, no doubt, as many ways
of coping with the resulting complex of tensions as there are black men in the
world, but no black man can hope ever to be entirely liberated from this internal
warfare—rage, dissembling, and contempt having inevitably accompanied his
first realization of the power of white men. What is crucial here is that, since
white men represent in the black man's world so heavy a weight, white men have
for black men a reality which is far from being reciprocal; and hence all black
men have toward all white men an attitude which is designed, really, either to rob
the white man of the jewel of his naïveté, or else to make it cost him dear.

The black man insists, by whatever means he finds at his disposal, that the
white man cease to regard him as an exotic rarity and recognize him as a human
being. This is a very charged and difficult moment, for there is a great deal of
will power involved in the white man's naïveté. Most people are not naturally
reflective any more than they are naturally malicious, and the white man prefers
to keep the black man at a certain human remove because it is easier for him
thus to preserve his simplicity and avoid being called to account for crimes committed by his forefathers, or his neighbors. He is inescapably aware, nevertheless, that he is in a better position in the world than black men are, nor can he
quite put to death the suspicion that he is hated by black men therefore. He does
not wish to be hated, neither does he wish to change places, and at this point in
his uneasiness he can scarcely avoid having recourse to those legends which
white men have created about black men, the most usual effect of which is that
the white man finds himself enmeshed, so to speak, in his own language which
describes hell, as well as the attributes which lead one to hell, as being as black as
night.

Every legend, moreover, contains its residuum of truth, and the root function
of language is to control the universe by describing it. It is of quite considerable
significance that black men remain, in the imagination, and in overwhelming
numbers in fact, beyond the disciplines of salvation; and this despite the fact that
the West has been "buying" African natives for centuries. There is, I should hazard, an instantaneous necessity to be divorced from this so visibly unsaved
stranger, in whose heart, moreover, one cannot guess what dreams of vengeance
are being nourished; and, at the same time, there are few things on earth more

---

[2] Master race.

attractive than the idea of the unspeakable liberty which is allowed the unredeemed. When, beneath the black mask, a human being begins to make himself felt one cannot escape a certain awful wonder as to what kind of human being it is. What one's imagination makes of other people is dictated, of course, by the laws of one's own personality and it is one of the ironies of black-white relations that, by means of what the white man imagines the black man to be, the black man is enabled to know who the white man is.

I have said, for example, that I am as much a stranger in this village today as I was the first summer I arrived, but this is not quite true. The villagers wonder less about the texture of my hair than they did then, and wonder rather more about me. And the fact that their wonder now exists on another level is reflected in their attitudes and in their eyes. There are the children who make those delightful, hilarious, sometimes astonishingly grave overtures of friendship in the unpredictable fashion of children; other children, having been taught that the devil is a black man, scream in genuine anguish as I approach. Some of the older women never pass without a friendly greeting, never pass, indeed, if it seems that they will be able to engage me in conversation; other women look down or look away or rather contemptuously smirk. Some of the men drink with me and suggest that I learn how to ski—partly, I gather, because they cannot imagine what I would look like on skis—and want to know if I am married, and ask questions about my *métier*. But some of the men have accused *le sale nègre*[3]—behind my back—of stealing wood and there is already in the eyes of some of them that peculiar, intent, paranoiac malevolence which one sometimes surprises in the eyes of American white men when, out walking with their Sunday girl, they see a Negro male approach.

There is a dreadful abyss between the streets of this village and the streets of the city in which I was born, between the children who shout *Neger!* today and those who shouted *Nigger!* yesterday—the abyss is experience, the American experience. The syllable hurled behind me today expresses, above all, wonder: I am a stranger here. But I am not a stranger in America and the same syllable riding on the American air expresses the war my presence has occasioned in the American soul.

For this village brings home to me this fact: that there was a day, and not really a very distant day, when Americans were scarcely Americans at all but discontented Europeans, facing a great unconquered continent and strolling, say, into a marketplace and seeing black men for the first time. The shock this spectacle afforded is suggested, surely, by the promptness with which they decided that these black men were not really men but cattle. It is true that the necessity on the part of the settlers of the New World of reconciling their moral assumptions with the fact—and the necessity—of slavery enhanced immensely the charm of this idea, and it is also true that this idea expresses, with a truly American bluntness, the attitude which to varying extents all masters have had toward all slaves. 15

---

[3] The dirty Negro.

But between all former slaves and slave-owners and the drama which begins for Americans over three hundred years ago at Jamestown, there are at least two differences to be observed. The American Negro slave could not suppose, for one thing, as slaves in past epochs had supposed and often done, that he would ever be able to wrest the power from his master's hands. This was a supposition which the modern era, which was to bring about such vast changes in the aims and dimensions of power, put to death; it only begins, in unprecedented fashion, and with dreadful implications, to be resurrected today. But even had this supposition persisted with undiminished force, the American Negro slave could not have used it to lend his condition dignity, for the reason that this supposition rests on another: that the slave in exile yet remains related to his past, has some means— if only in memory—of revering and sustaining the forms of his former life, is able, in short, to maintain his identity.

This was not the case with the American Negro slave. He is unique among the black men of the world in that his past was taken from him, almost literally, at one blow. One wonders what on earth the first slave found to say to the first dark child he bore. I am told that there are Haitians able to trace their ancestry back to African kings, but any American Negro wishing to go back so far will find his journey through time abruptly arrested by the signature on the bill of sale which served as the entrance paper for his ancestor. At the time—to say nothing of the circumstances—of the enslavement of the captive black man who was to become the American Negro, there was not the remotest possibility that he would ever take power from his master's hands. There was no reason to suppose that his situation would ever change, nor was there, shortly, anything to indicate that his situation had ever been different. It was his necessity, in the words of E. Franklin Frazier, to find a "motive for living under American culture or die." The identity of the American Negro comes out of this extreme situation, and the evolution of this identity was a source of the most intolerable anxiety in the minds and the lives of his masters.

For the history of the American Negro is unique also in this: that the question of his humanity, and of his rights therefore as a human being, became a burning one for several generations of Americans, so burning a question that it ultimately became one of those used to divide the nation. It is out of this argument that the venom of the epithet *Nigger!* is derived. It is an argument which Europe has never had, and hence Europe quite sincerely fails to understand how or why the argument arose in the first place, why its effects are frequently disastrous and always so unpredictable, why it refuses until today to be entirely settled. Europe's black possessions remained—and do remain—in Europe's colonies, at which remove they represented no threat whatever to European identity. If they posed any problem at all for the European conscience it was a problem which remained comfortingly abstract: in effect, the black man, as a *man* did not exist for Europe. But in America, even as a slave, he was an inescapable part of the general social fabric and no American could escape having an attitude toward him. Americans attempt until today to make an abstraction of the Negro, but the very nature of these abstractions reveals the tremendous effects the presence of the Negro has had on the American character.

When one considers the history of the Negro in America it is of the greatest importance to recognize that the moral beliefs of a person, or a people, are never really as tenuous as life—which is not moral—very often causes them to appear; these create for them a frame of reference and a necessary hope, the hope being that when life has done its worst they will be enabled to rise above themselves and to triumph over life. Life would scarcely be bearable if this hope did not exist. Again, even when the worst has been said, to betray a belief is not by any means to have put oneself beyond its power; the betrayal of a belief is not the same thing as ceasing to believe. If this were not so there would be no moral standards in the world at all. Yet one must also recognize that morality is based on ideas and that all ideas are dangerous—dangerous because ideas can only lead to action and where the action leads no man can say. And dangerous in this respect: that confronted with the impossibility of remaining faithful to one's beliefs, and the equal impossibility of becoming free of them, one can be driven to the most inhuman excesses. The ideas on which American beliefs are based are not, though Americans often seem to think so, ideas which originated in America. They came out of Europe. And the establishment of democracy on the American continent was scarcely as radical a break with the past as was the necessity, which Americans faced, of broadening this concept to include black men.

This was, literally, a hard necessity. It was impossible, for one thing, for   20
Americans to abandon their beliefs, not only because these beliefs alone seemed able to justify the sacrifices they had endured and the blood that they had spilled, but also because these beliefs afforded them their only bulwark against a moral chaos as absolute as the physical chaos of the continent it was their destiny to conquer. But in the situation in which Americans found themselves, these beliefs threatened an idea which, whether or not one likes to think so, is the very warp and woof of the heritage of the West, the idea of white supremacy.

Americans have made themselves notorious by the shrillness and the brutality with which they have insisted on this idea, but they did not invent it; and it has escaped the world's notice that those very excesses of which Americans have been guilty imply a certain, unprecedented uneasiness over the idea's life and power, if not, indeed, the idea's validity. The idea of white supremacy rests simply on the fact that white men are the creators of civilization (the present civilization, which is the only one that matters; all previous civilizations are simply "contributions" to our own) and are therefore civilization's guardians and defenders. Thus it was impossible for Americans to accept the black man as one of themselves, for to do so was to jeopardize their status as white men. But not so to accept him was to deny his human reality, his human weight and complexity, and the strain of denying the overwhelmingly undeniable forced Americans into rationalizations so fantastic that they approached the pathological.

At the root of the American Negro problem is the necessity of the American white man to find a way of living with the Negro in order to be able to live with himself. And the history of this problem can be reduced to the means used by Americans—lynch law and law, segregation and legal acceptance, terrorization and concession—either to come to terms with this necessity, or to find a way around it, or (most usually) to find a way of doing both these things at once. The resulting spectacle, at once foolish and dreadful, led someone to make the quite accurate observation that "the Negro-in-America is a form of insanity which overtakes white men."

In this long battle, a battle by no means finished, the unforeseeable effects of which will be felt by many future generations, the white man's motive was the protection of his identity; the black man was motivated by the need to establish an identity. And despite the terrorization which the Negro in America endured and endures sporadically until today, despite the cruel and totally inescapable ambivalence of his status in his country, the battle for his identity has long ago been won. He is not a visitor to the West, but a citizen there, an American; as American as the Americans who despise him, the Americans who fear him, the Americans who love him—the Americans who became less than themselves, or rose to be greater than themselves by virtue of the fact that the challenge he represented was inescapable. He is perhaps the only black man in the world whose relationship to white men is more terrible, more subtle, and more meaningful than the relationship of bitter possessed to uncertain possessors. His survival depended, and his development depends, on his ability to turn his peculiar status in the Western world to his own advantage and, it may be, to the very great advantage of that world. It remains for him to fashion out of his experience that which will give him sustenance, and a voice.

The cathedral at Chartres, I have said, says something to the people of this village which it cannot say to me; but it is important to understand that this cathedral says something to me which it cannot say to them. Perhaps they are struck by the power of the spires, the glory of the windows; but they have known God, after all, longer than I have known him, and in a different way, and I am terrified by the slippery bottomless well to be found in the crypt, down which heretics were hurled to death, and by the obscene, inescapable gargoyles jutting out of the stone and seeming to say that God and the devil can never be divorced. I doubt that the villagers think of the devil when they face a cathedral because they have never been identified with the devil. But I must accept the status which myth, if nothing else, gives me in the West before I can hope to change the myth.

Yet, if the American Negro has arrived at his identity by virtue of the absolute- 25 ness of his estrangement from his past, American white men still nourish the illusion that there is some means of recovering the European innocence, of returning to a state in which black men do not exist. This is one of the greatest errors Americans can make. The identity they fought so hard to protect has, by virtue of that battle, undergone a change: Americans are as unlike any other white people in the world as it is possible to be. I do not think, for example, that it is too much to suggest that the American vision of the world—which allows so little reality, generally speaking, for any of the darker forces in human life, which tends until today to paint moral issues in glaring black and white—owes a great deal to the battle waged by Americans to maintain between themselves and black men a human separation which could not be bridged. It is only now beginning to be borne in on us—very faintly, it must be admitted, very slowly, and very much against our will—that this vision of the world is dangerously inaccurate, and perfectly useless. For it protects our moral high-mindedness at the terrible expense of weakening our grasp of reality. People who shut their eyes to reality simply invite their own destruction, and anyone who insists on remaining in a state of innocence long after that innocence is dead turns himself into a monster.

The time has come to realize that the interracial drama acted out on the American continent has not only created a new black man, it has created a new white man, too. No road whatever will lead Americans back to the simplicity of this European village where white men still have the luxury of looking on me as a stranger. I am not, really, a stranger any longer for any American alive. One of the things that distinguishes Americans from other people is that no other people has ever been so deeply involved in the lives of black men, and vice versa. This fact faced, with all its implications, it can be seen that the history of the American Negro problem is not merely shameful, it is also something of an achievement. For even when the worst has been said, it must also be added that the perpetual challenge posed by this problem was always, somehow, perpetually met. It is precisely this black-white experience which may prove of indispensable value to us in the world we face today. This world is white no longer, and it will never be white again.

W. E. B. DU BOIS

The "Veil" of Self-Consciousness

This essay, first published in the Atlantic Monthly *(1897), helped introduce the Harvard-educated black sociologist W. E. B. Du Bois (1868–1963) to a national audience and went on to become the opening chapter of his classic* Souls of Black Folk *(1903). Du Bois argued that, given the opportunity to educate themselves, American blacks would emerge from behind what he referred to as their "veil" of self-conscious "differentness."*

Between me and the other world there is ever an unasked question: unasked by some through feelings of delicacy; by others through the difficulty of rightly framing it. All, nevertheless, flutter round it. They approach me in a half-hesitant sort of way, eye me curiously or compassionately, and then, instead of saying directly, How does it feel to be a problem? they say, I know an excellent colored man in my town; or I fought at Mechanicsville; or, Do not these Southern outrages make your blood boil? At these I smile, or am interested, or reduce the boiling to a simmer, as the occasion may require. To the real question, How does it feel to be a problem? I answer seldom a word . . .

After the Egyptian and Indian, the Greek and Roman, the Teuton and Mongolian, the Negro is a sort of seventh son, born with a veil, and gifted with second-sight in this American world,—a world which yields him no self-consciousness, but only lets him see himself through the revelation of the other world. It is a peculiar sensation, this double-consciousness, this sense of always looking at one's self through the eyes of others, of measuring one's soul by the tape of a world that looks on in amused contempt and pity. One ever feels his two-ness,—an American, a Negro; two souls, two thoughts, two unreconciled strivings; two warring ideals in one dark body, whose dogged strength alone keeps it from being torn asunder. The history of the American Negro is the history of this strife,—this longing to attain self-conscious manhood, to merge his double self into a better and truer self. In this merging he wishes neither of the older selves to be lost. He does not wish to Africanize America, for America has too much to teach the world and Africa; he does not wish to bleach his Negro blood in a flood of white Americanism, for he believes—foolishly, perhaps, but fervently—that Negro blood has yet a message for the world. He simply wishes to make it possible for a man to be both a Negro and an American without being cursed and spit upon by his fellows, without losing the opportunity of self-development.

This is the end of his striving: to be a co-worker in the kingdom of culture, to escape both death and isolation, and to husband and use his best powers.

QUESTIONS FOR DISCUSSION AND WRITING

1. "The physical characteristics of the Negro" cause James Baldwin problems in Europe as well as in the United States (paragraph 4), as they did for Du Bois fifty years earlier. What are these problems? Does Baldwin, too, experience a "veil of self-consciousness"? What are the differences between the problems he experiences on either side of the Atlantic? What are some of the similarities? How does Baldwin respond to them?

2. What is Baldwin's attitude toward the villagers' practice of "'buying' African natives for the purpose of converting them to Christianity" (paragraph 6)? What is the villagers' attitude toward it? Does Baldwin understand the villagers' "reason" to feel that way? Do they understand his reason not to? Why or why not?

3. What, according to Baldwin, writing in 1955, is "the root of the American Negro problem" (paragraph 22)? Why does he think so? Has society changed sufficiently in the past fifty years in ways that would cause a different judgment today? Why or why not?

4. Have you ever felt like a stranger or an oddball in an unfamiliar culture? country? region? state? town? neighborhood? school? circle? Write an essay about the nature of estrangement, for better or for worse, using examples and analysis.

ESMERALDA SANTIAGO
Jíbara

*Born in Puerto Rico in 1948, the eldest daughter of a poor laboring family, Es-
meralda Santiago divided her early years between a small village in the rural countryside and a suburb near San Juan. When she was thirteen, her mother left
Santiago's father and moved her daughter and nine other children to Brooklyn, New
York. There Santiago attended public junior high school and later graduated from
the High School of Performing Arts in Manhattan. She attended community college
part-time before transferring to Harvard, where she earned a bachelor's degree in
film production in 1976. Her literary career developed from her work as a writer and
producer of documentary films. Her first book, the memoir* When I Was Puerto
Rican, *was published to critical acclaim in 1993. Santiago followed this in 1996 with
a novel,* America's Dream, *about a Puerto Rican housekeeper who flees an abusive
husband to work in the United States. A second memoir,* Almost a Woman, *appeared in 1998, and a third,* The Turkish Lover, *in 2004.*

 In this opening chapter from When I Was Puerto Rican, *Santiago recalls her
early childhood in rural Puerto Rico, where her family lived like* jíbaros, *or country
people, even though their roots were in the city. Santiago says the book was a reaction
to her sense of displacement upon first returning to Puerto Rico as an adult: "I felt as
Puerto Rican as when I left the island, but to those who had never left, I was contaminated by Americanisms, and, therefore, had become less than Puerto Rican. Yet, in
the United States, my darkness, my accented speech, my frequent lapses into the confused silence between English and Spanish identified me as foreign, non-American.
In writing the book I wanted to get back to that feeling of Puertoricanness I had before I came here."*

 Al jíbaro nunca se le quita la mancha de plátano.
 A jíbaro can never wash away the stain of the plantain.

We came to Macún when I was four, to a rectangle of rippled metal sheets on
stilts hovering in the middle of a circle of red dirt. Our home was a giant version
of the lard cans used to haul water from the public fountain. Its windows and
doors were also metal, and, as we stepped in, I touched the wall and burned my
fingers.

 "That'll teach you," Mami scolded. "Never touch a wall on the sunny side."

 She searched a bundle of clothes and diapers for her jar of Vick's VapoRub
to smear on my fingers. They were red the rest of the day, and I couldn't suck my
thumb that night. "You're too big for that anyway," she said.

 The floor was a patchwork of odd-shaped wooden slats that rose in the middle and dipped toward the front and back doors, where they butted against shiny,
worn thresholds. Papi nailed new boards under Mami's treadle sewing machine,

and under their bed, but the floor still groaned and sagged to the corners, threatening to collapse and bring the house down with it.

"I'll rip the whole thing out," Papi suggested. "We'll have to live with a dirt 5 floor for a while...."

Mami looked at her feet and shuddered. A dirt floor, we'd heard, meant snakes and scorpions could crawl into the house from their holes in the ground. Mami didn't know any better, and I had yet to learn not everything I heard was true, so we reacted in what was to become a pattern for us: what frightened her I became curious about, and what she found exciting terrified me. As Mami pulled her feet onto the rungs of her rocking chair and rubbed the goose bumps from her arms, I imagined a world of fascinating creatures slithering underfoot, drawing squiggly patterns on the dirt.

The day Papi tore up the floor, I followed him holding a can into which he dropped the straight nails, still usable. My fingers itched with a rust-colored powder, and when I licked them, a dry, metallic taste curled the tip of my tongue. Mami stood on the threshold scratching one ankle with the toes of the other foot.

"Negi, come help me gather kindling for the fire."

"I'm working with Papi," I whined, hoping he'd ask me to stay. He didn't turn around but continued on his knees, digging out nails with the hammer's claw, muttering the words to his favorite *chachachá*.

"Do as I say!" Mami ordered. Still, Papi kept his back to us. I plunked the can 10 full of nails down hard, willing him to hear and tell me to stay, but he didn't. I dawdled after Mami down the three steps into the yard. Delsa and Norma, my younger sisters, took turns swinging from a rope Papi had hung under the mango tree.

"Why can't they help with the kindling?" I pouted.

Mami swatted the side of my head. "Don't talk back," she said. "You girls keep away from the house while your father is working," she warned as we walked by my sisters having fun.

She led the way into a thicket behind the latrine. Twigs crackled under my bare feet, stinging the soles. A bananaquit flew to the thorny branch of a lemon tree and looked from side to side. Dots of sun danced on the green walls of the shady grove above low bushes weighted with pigeon peas, the earth screened with twigs, sensitive *morivivi* plants, and french weed studded with tiny blue flowers. Mami hummed softly, the yellow and orange flowers of her dress blending into the greenness: a miraculous garden with legs and arms and a melody. Her hair, choked at the nape with a rubber band, floated thick and black to her waist, and as she bent over to pick up sticks, it rained across her shoulders and down her arms, covering her face and tangling in the twigs she cradled. A red butterfly circled her and flew close to her ear. She gasped and swatted it into a bush.

"It felt like it was going right into my brain," she muttered with an embarrassed smile.

Delsa and Norma toddled through the underbrush. "Mami, come see what I 15 found," Delsa called.

A hen had scratched out a hollow and carpeted its walls and floor with dry grass. She had laid four eggs, smaller and not as white as the ones our neighbor Doña Lola gave us from time to time.

"Can we eat them?" Delsa asked.

"No."

"But if we leave them here a snake will get them," I said, imagining a serpent swallowing each egg whole. Mami shuddered and rubbed her arms where tiny bumps had formed making the fine hairs stand straight up. She gave me a look, half puzzled, half angry, and drew us to her side.

"All right, let's get our sticks together and bring them to the kitchen." As she   20 picked hers up, she looked carefully around.

"One, two, three, four," she chanted. "One, two, three, four."

We marched single file into our yard, where Papi stacked floorboards.

"Come look," he said.

The dirt was orange, striped in places where crumbs had slipped through the cracks when Mami swept. Papi had left a few boards down the center of the room and around his and Mami's bed, to stand on until the ground was swept and flattened. Mami was afraid to come into the house. There were small holes in the dirt, holes where snakes and scorpions hid. She turned around swiftly and threw herself off balance so that she skipped toward the kitchen shed.

"Let's go make supper!" She singsang to make it sound like fun. Delsa and   25 Norma followed her skirt, but I stared at the dirt, where squiggly lines stretched from one wall to the other. Mami waited for me.

"Negi, come help in the kitchen."

I pretended not to hear but felt her eyes bore holes in the back of my head. Papi stepped between us.

"Let her stay. I can use the help."

I peered between his legs and saw her squint and pucker her lips as if she were about to spit. He chuckled, "Heh, heh," and she whirled toward the kitchen shed, where the fire in the *fogón* was almost out.

"Take these boards and lay them on the pile for the cooking fire," Papi said.   30 "Careful with the splinters."

I walked a broad circle around Mami, who looked up from her vegetable chopping whenever I went by. When I passed carrying a wide board, Mami asked to see it. Black bugs, like ants, but bigger and blacker, crawled over it in a frenzy.

"Termites!" she gasped.

I was covered with them. They swarmed inside my shirt and panties, into my hair, under my arms. Until Mami saw them, I hadn't felt them sting. But they bit ridges into my skin that itched and hurt at the same time. Mami ran me to the washtub and dunked me among my father's soaking shirts.

"Pablo!" she called, "Oh, my God! Look at her. She's being eaten alive!"

I screamed, imagining my skin disappearing in chunks into the invisible   35 mouths of hundreds of tiny black specks creeping into parts of my body I couldn't even reach. Mami pulled off my clothes and threw them on the ground. The soap in the washtub burned my skin, and Mami scrubbed me so hard her fingernails dug angry furrows into my arms and legs. She turned me around to wash my back and I almost fell out of the tub.

"Be still," she said. "I have to get them all."

She pushed and shoved and turned me so fast I didn't know what to do with my body, so I flailed, seeming to resist, while in fact I wanted nothing more than to be rid of the creepy crawling things that covered me. Mami wrapped me in a towel and lifted me out of the tub with a groan. Hundreds of black bugs floated between the bubbles.

She carried me to the house pressed against her bosom, fragrant of curdled milk. Delsa and Norma ran after us, but Papi scooped them up, one on each arm, and carried them to the rope swing. Mami balanced on the floorboards to her bed, lay me beside her, held me tight, kissed my forehead, my eyes, and murmured, "It's all right. It's over. It's all right."

I wrapped my legs around her and buried my face under her chin. It felt good to have Mami so close, so warm, swathed by her softness, her smell of wood smoke and oregano. She rubbed circles on my back and caressed the hair from my face. She kissed me, brushed my tears with her fingertips, and dried my nose with the towel, or the hem of her dress.

"You see," she murmured, "what happens when you don't do as I say?"   40

I turned away from her and curled into a tight ball of shame. Mami rolled off the bed and went outside. I lay on her pillow, whimpering, wondering how the termites knew I'd disobeyed my mother.

We children slept in hammocks strung across the room, tied to the beams in sturdy knots that were done and undone daily. A curtain separated our side of the room from the end where my parents slept in a four-poster bed veiled with mosquito netting. On the days he worked, Papi left the house before dawn and sometimes joked that he woke the roosters to sing the *barrio* awake. We wouldn't see him again until dusk, dragging down the dirt road, his wooden toolbox pulling on his arm, making his body list sideways. When he didn't work, he and Mami rustled behind the flowered curtain, creaked the springs under their mattress, their voices a murmur that I strained to hear but couldn't.

I was an early riser but was not allowed out until the sun shot in through the crack near Mami's sewing machine and swept a glistening stripe of gold across the dirt floor.

The next morning, I turned out of the hammock and ran outside as soon as the sun streaked in. Mami and Papi sat by the kitchen shed sipping coffee. My arms and belly were pimpled with red dots. The night before, Mami had bathed me in *alcoholado,* which soothed my skin and cooled the hot itch.

"*Ay bendito,*" Mami said, "here's our spotty early riser. Come here, let me   45 look." She turned me around, rubbing the spots. "Are you itchy?"

"No, it doesn't itch at all."

"Stay out of the sun today so the spots don't scar."

Papi hummed along with the battery-operated radio. He never went any-where without it. When he worked around the house, he propped it on a rock, or the nearest fence post, and tuned it to his favorite station, which played romantic ballads, *chachachás*, and a reading of the news every half hour. He delighted in stories from faraway places like Russia, Madagascar, and Istanbul. Whenever the newscaster mentioned a country with a particularly musical name, he'd repeat it or make a rhyme of it. *"Pakistán. Sacristán. ¿Dónde están?"* he sang as he mixed cement or hammered nails, his voice echoing against the walls.

Early each morning the radio brought us a program called "The Day Breaker's Club," which played the traditional music and poetry of the Puerto Rican country dweller, the *jíbaro*. Although the songs and poems chronicled a life of struggle and hardship, their message was that *jíbaros* were rewarded by a life of independence and contemplation, a closeness to nature coupled with a respect for its intractability, and a deeply rooted and proud nationalism. I wanted to be a *jíbara* more than anything in the world, but Mami said I couldn't because I was born in the city, where *jíbaros* were mocked for their unsophisticated customs and peculiar dialect.

"Don't be a *jíbara*," she scolded, rapping her knuckles on my skull, as if to 50 waken the intelligence she said was there.

I ducked away, my scalp smarting, and scrambled into the oregano bushes. In the fragrant shade, I fretted. If we were not *jíbaros*, why did we live like them? Our house, a box squatting on low stilts, was shaped like a *bohío*, the kind of house *jíbaros* lived in. Our favorite program, "The Day Breaker's Club," played the traditional music of rural Puerto Rico and gave information about crops, husbandry, and the weather. Our neighbor Doña Lola was a *jíbara*, although Mami had warned us never to call her that. Poems and stories about the hard-ships and joys of the Puerto Rican *jíbaro* were required reading at every grade level in school. My own grandparents, whom I was to respect as well as love, were said to be *jíbaros*. But I couldn't be one, nor was I to call anyone a *jíbaro*, lest they be offended. Even at the tender age when I didn't yet know my real name, I was puzzled by the hypocrisy of celebrating a people everyone looked down on. But there was no arguing with Mami, who, in those days, was always right.

On the radio, the newscaster talked about submarines, torpedoes, and a place called Korea, where Puerto Rican men went to die. His voice faded as Papi car-ried him into the house just as Delsa and Norma came out for their oatmeal.

Delsa's black curly hair framed a heart-shaped face with tiny pouty lips and round eyes thick with lashes. Mami called her *Muñequita*, Little Doll. Norma's hair was the color of clay, her yellow eyes slanted at the corners, and her skin glowed the same color as the inside of a yam. Mami called her *La Colorá*, the red girl. I thought I had no nickname until she told me my name wasn't Negi but Esmeralda.

"You're named after your father's sister, who is also your godmother. You know her as Titi Merín."

"Why does everyone call me Negi?"   55

"Because when you were little you were so black, my mother said you were a *negrita*. And we all called you *Negrita*, and it got shortened to Negi."

Delsa was darker than I was, nutty brown, but not as sun ripened as Papi. Norma was lighter, rust colored, and not as pale as Mami, whose skin was pink. Norma's yellow eyes with black pupils looked like sunflowers. Delsa had black eyes. I'd never seen my eyes, because the only mirror in the house was hung up too high for me to reach. I touched my hair, which was not curly like Delsa's, nor *pasita*, raisined, like Papi's. Mami cut it short whenever it grew into my eyes, but I'd seen dark brown wisps by my cheeks and near my temples.

"So *Negi* means I'm black?"

"It's a sweet name because we love you, *Negrita*." She hugged and kissed me.

"Does anyone call Titi Merín Esmeralda?"   60

"Oh, sure. People who don't know her well—the government, her boss. We all have our official names, and then our nicknames, which are like secrets that only the people who love us use."

"How come you don't have a nickname?"

"I do. Everyone calls me Monín. That's my nickname."

"What's your real name?"   65

"Ramona."

"Papi doesn't have a nickname."

"Yes he does. Some people call him Pablito."

It seemed too complicated, as if each one of us were really two people, one who was loved and the official one who, I assumed, was not.

QUESTIONS FOR DISCUSSION AND WRITING

1. How would you characterize Santiago's parents in terms of their relationship both to each other and to their children? How would you characterize Santiago's feelings for her parents?

2. Santiago writes that *jíbaros*, the poor country people of Puerto Rico, are both celebrated for their struggle and independence and mocked for their lack of sophistication. What qualities does this contradiction attribute to Puerto Ricans? What, if any, groups within your culture are likewise celebrated and scorned? Examine some other readings in this book, such as Lynda Barry's cartoon rendering of multicultural poverty (p. 440) and W. E. B. Du Bois's definition of "The 'Veil' of Self-Consciousness" (p. 127), which Sherman Alexie's "What Sacagewea Means to Me" (p. 142) satirically illustrates.

3. Santiago writes at some length about the nicknames her family members had for one another. In what ways might such nicknames, beginning in childhood, have a role in shaping one's identity? Why, as Santiago suggests, might family nicknames create a conflict of identity? You might consider this question in terms of

the language of family and the language of the outside world that Richard Rodriguez writes about in "Aria: A Memoir of a Bilingual Childhood" (p. 298).

4. Part of the charm of this memoir lies in Santiago's description of her and her sisters' mischievous behavior and her mother's response to it. In an essay, narrate some mischievous behavior from your childhood—innocent or not so innocent—that brought the wrath of a parent or other authority figure. To what extent was that angry response justified?

BOBBIE ANN MASON
Being Country

Born (1940) in Mayfield, Kentucky, Bobbie Ann Mason grew up on a dairy farm, and in Clear Springs: A Memoir *(1999), she describes her family's "independence, stability, authenticity" along with their "crippling social isolation." She earned a bachelor's degree at the University of Kentucky (1962), a master's at the State University of New York at Binghamton (1966), and a doctorate at the University of Connecticut (1972). She contributes regularly to* Mother Jones, The Atlantic Monthly, *and* The New Yorker. *Her novel* In Country *(1984) was made into a film in 1989. Other works include* Shiloh and Other Stories *(1983) and* Feather Crowns *(1994). Her themes are often the encroachment of modern life—television, fast food, shopping malls, the Vietnam War—into traditional rural life; her characters, farmers and working-class people, try to cope with change and balance their individual needs with those of their families.*

Mason's writing style, unsentimental and spare, echoes the language of rural, western Kentuckians. She uses names—places, roads, brand names, popular musicians, and TV characters—to portend changes to rural life, changes that have already become commonplace elsewhere. In "Being Country" from Clear Springs, *Mason uses physical images from her youth, the routines and rhythms of farm life, and a constant concern for food, home-grown, home-cooked food, to illustrate rural experience.*

One day Mama and Granny were shelling beans and talking about the proper method of drying apples. I was nearly eleven and still entirely absorbed with the March girls in *Little Women*. Drying apples was not in my dreams. Beth's death was weighing darkly on me at that moment, and I threw a little tantrum—what Mama called a hissy fit.

"Can't y'all talk about anything but food?" I screamed.

There was a shocked silence. "Well, what else is there?" Granny asked.

Granny didn't question a woman's duties, but I did. I didn't want to be hulling beans in a hot kitchen when I was fifty years old. I wanted to *be* somebody, maybe an airline stewardess. Also, I had been listening to the radio. I had notions.

Our lives were haunted by the fear of crop failure. We ate as if we didn't 5 know where our next meal might come from. All my life I have had a recurrent food dream: I face a buffet or cafeteria line, laden with beautiful foods. I spend the entire dream choosing the foods I want. My anticipation is deliciously agonizing. I always wake up just as I've made my selections but before I get to eat.

Working with food was fraught with anxiety and desperation. In truth, no one in memory had missed a meal—except Peyton Washam on the banks of Panther Creek wistfully regarding his seed corn. But the rumble of poor Peyton's belly must have survived to trouble our dreams. We were at the mercy of nature, and it wasn't to be trusted. My mother watched the skies at evening for a portent of the morrow. A cloud that went over and then turned around and came back was an especially bad sign. Our livelihood—even our lives—depended on forces outside our control.

I think this dependence on nature was at the core of my rebellion. I hated the constant sense of helplessness before vast forces, the continuous threat of failure. Farmers didn't take initiative, I began to see; they reacted to whatever presented itself. I especially hated women's part in the dependence.

My mother allowed me to get spoiled. She never even tried to teach me to cook. "You didn't want to learn," she says now. "You were a lady of leisure, and you didn't want to help. You had your nose in a book."

I believed progress meant freedom from the field and the range. That meant moving to town, I thought.

Because we lived on the edge of Mayfield, I was acutely conscious of being 10 country. I felt inferior to people in town because we grew our food and made our clothes, while they bought whatever they needed. Although we were self-sufficient and resourceful and held clear title to our land, we lived in a state of psychological poverty. As I grew older, this acute sense of separation from town affected me more deeply. I began to sense that the fine life in town—celebrated in magazines, on radio, in movies—was denied us. Of course we weren't poor at all. Poor people had too many kids, and they weren't landowners; they rented decrepit little houses with plank floors and trash in the yard. "Poor people are wormy and eat wild onions," Mama said. We weren't poor, but we were country.

We had three wardrobes—everyday clothes, school clothes, and Sunday clothes. We didn't wear our school clothes at home, but we could wear them to town. When we got home from church, we had to change back into everyday clothes before we ate Mama's big Sunday dinner.

"Don't eat in your good clothes!" Mama always cried. "You'll spill something on them."

Mama always preferred outdoor life, but she was a natural cook. At harvest time, after she'd come in from the garden and put out a wash, she would whip out a noontime dinner for the men in the field—my father and grandfather and maybe some neighbors and a couple of hired hands: fried chicken with milk gravy, ham, mashed potatoes, lima beans, field peas, corn, slaw, sliced tomatoes, fried apples, biscuits, and peach pie. This was not considered a banquet, only plain hearty food, fuel for work. All the ingredients except the flour, sugar, and salt came from our farm—the chickens, the hogs, the milk and butter, the Irish potatoes, the beans, peas, corn, cabbage, apples, peaches. Nothing was processed, except by Mama. She was always butchering and plucking and planting and hoeing and shredding and slicing and creaming (scraping cobs for the creamed corn) and pressure-cooking and canning and freezing and thawing and mixing and shaping and baking and frying.

We would eat our pie right on the same plate as our turnip greens so as not to mess up another dish. The peach cobbler oozed all over the turnip-green juice and the pork grease. "It all goes to the same place," Mama said. It was boarding-house reach, no "Pass the peas, please." Conversation detracted from the sensuous pleasure of filling yourself. A meal required meat and vegetables and dessert. The beverages were milk and iced tea ("ice-tea"). We never used napkins or ate tossed salad. Our salads were Jell-O and slaw. We ate "poke salet" and wilted lettuce. Mama picked tender, young pokeweed in the woods in the spring, before it turned poison, and cooked it a good long time to get the bitterness out. We liked it with vinegar and minced boiled eggs. Wilted lettuce was tender new lettuce, shredded, with sliced radishes and green onions, and blasted with hot bacon grease to blanch the rawness. "Too many fresh vegetables in summer gives people the scours," Daddy said.

Food was better in town, we thought. It wasn't plain and everyday. The centers of pleasure were there—the hamburger and barbecue places, the movie shows, all the places to buy things. Woolworth's, with the pneumatic tubes overhead rushing money along a metallic mole tunnel up to a balcony; Lochridge & Ridgway, with an engraved sign on the third-story cornice: STOVES, APPLIANCES, PLOWS. On the mezzanine at that store, I bought my first phonograph records, brittle 78s of big-band music—Woody Herman and Glenn Miller, and Glen Gray and his Casa Loma Orchestra playing "No Name Jive." A circuit of the courthouse square took you past the grand furniture stores, the two dime stores, the shoe stores, the men's stores, the ladies' stores, the banks, the drugstores. You'd walk past the poolroom and an exhaust fan would blow the intoxicating smell of hamburgers in your face. Before she bought a freezer, Mama stored meat in a rented food locker in town, near the ice company. She stored the butchered calf there, and she fetched hunks of him each week to fry. But hamburgers in town were better. They were greasier, and they came in waxed-paper packages.

At the corner drugstore, on the square, Mama and Janice and I sat at filigreed wrought-iron tables on a black-and-white mosaic tile floor, eating peppermint ice cream. It was very cold in there, under the ceiling fans. The ice cream was served elegantly, in paper cones sunk into black plastic holders. We were uptown.

The A&P grocery, a block away, reeked of the rich aroma of ground coffee. Daddy couldn't stand the smell of coffee, but Mama loved it. Daddy retched and

15

scoffed in his exaggerated fashion. "I can't stand that smell!" Granny perked coffee, and Granddaddy told me it would turn a child black. I hated coffee. I wouldn't touch it till I was thirty. We savored store-bought food—coconuts, pineapples, and Vienna sausages and potted meat in little cans that opened with keys. We rarely went to the uptown A&P. We usually traded at a small mom-and-pop grocery, where the proprietors slapped the hands of black children who touched the candy case. I wondered if they were black from coffee.

QUESTIONS FOR DISCUSSION AND WRITING

1. Mason says she "wanted to *be* somebody" (paragraph 4), particularly someone who is not preoccupied with food. Judging by the essay, to what extent does she succeed? What passages support your view?

2. Although town food is touted as more sophisticated and desirable than farm food, is Mason working a subtle irony in the juxtaposition? Homemade "gravy, ham, mashed potatoes" were ordinary, but town hamburgers "were better. They were greasier, and they came in waxed-paper packages" (paragraph 15). If there is an irony here, what is it, and how might Mason have intended for it to work?

3. Mason uses lists to describe Mama's work with food. How do these lists affect you as a reader? What difference would it make if Mason had chosen to break them up into shorter sentences?

4. Compare and contrast Mason's lists with the list that opens Eric Liu's "Notes of a Native Speaker" (p. 112). Write an essay that includes a description of some activity with which you are very familiar, using lists to convey the movements and sensations—sight, sound, smell, touch, taste—that accompany the activity. See if you can make your reader experience the same things you experience.

5. In your upbringing, did you ever yearn, as Mason did, for fundamentally different surroundings? For example, did you ever wish you could live a different sort of life? Explain why you were attracted to a different place or different people—or even different foods. If you eventually got to experience these things, describe what the experience was like and discuss whether it met your expectations.

ART SPIEGELMAN
Mein Kampf (My Struggle)

Art Spiegelman was born in Stockholm, Sweden, in 1948 to Nazi concentration camp survivors, and grew up in Queens, New York. The legacy of Spiegelman's family, his American Jewish identity, and his dedication to sequential art shaped his Pulitzer Prize-winning graphic novel Maus, A Survivor's Tale *(two volumes, 1986 and 1992).* Maus, *which was translated into twenty languages, gave the world new metaphors for the Holocaust, portraying Jews as mice and Nazis as predatory cats, an idea that came to Spiegelman when he noticed parallels between the mice in cat-and-mouse cartoons and racist stereotypes in films. A graduate of New York's famous public High School of Art and Design, Spiegelman attended Harpur College in upstate New York, worked as a commercial artist, and in 1971 joined the countercultural comic book scene in San Francisco, California. He subsequently taught at the School of Visual Arts in New York City, married sequential artist and editor Françoise Mouly, and collaborated with her on the magazine* Raw, *in which episodes of* Maus *were first serialized. More recently, Spiegelman has authored* In the Shadow of No Towers *(2004), which deals with the September 11, 2001, attacks from a New Yorker City dweller's perspective.*

"Mein Kampf" (My Struggle), published in the New York Times Magazine *in 1996, is both a twisted reference to the Holocaust and a study of creative crisis. Spiegelman copies the title of Adolf Hitler's autobiographical political manifesto, but he explores career issues instead of genocidal theories. The piece gives a new meaning to the term "victim of his own success," as the artist is stalked by his own creation.*

I WAS JUST ANOTHER BABY-BOOM BOY...

Fort Tryon Park c.1956

SNAPSHOTS ILLUMINATE MY PAST LIKE FLARES IN THE DARKNESS...

FAMILY ALBUM

ALTHOUGH OFTEN THEY ONLY HELP ME REMEMBER HAVING SEEN THE PHOTOS BEFORE!

MAN, I LOVED MY CISCO KID OUTFIT. I WANTED TO BE A COWBOY BECAUSE I LIKED THE WAY THEY DRESSED.

I WORE IT TILL IT WAS WAY TOO SMALL FOR ME AND I'D WORN IT THROUGH AT THE KNEE.

AND THAT HOWDY DOODY PUPPET— IF I COULDN'T BE A COWBOY I WAS WILLING TO SETTLE FOR PUPPETEER...OR CARTOONIST. MY PARENTS —

PAPA! PAPA!

SHH! NOT RIGHT NOW, DASH! PAPA'S BUSY SOLILOQUIZING.

BUT PAPA! WE WERE WATCHING "KING KONG," AND IT WAS SCARY!...

MY PARENTS DIED BEFORE I HAD ANY KIDS.

IT'S OKAY... IT WAS ONLY A STORY!

SNF...HE WAS CLIMBING ON THE BUILDING AND TH-THEY KILLED HIM!

Dashiell, 1995

I WISH KING KONG JUST ATE THE GIRL...

THEN THERE WOULDN'T BE ANY TROUBLE!

THE KNEE ON DASH'S SUPERMAN PAJAMAS IS RIPPED.

DASH IS FOUR YEARS OLD AND HIS SISTER IS ALMOST NINE. (TWO OF THEIR GRANDPARENTS SURVIVED AUSCHWITZ.)

QUESTIONS FOR DISCUSSION AND WRITING

1. What does Spiegelman mean when he writes, "now I feel like there's a 5,000-pound mouse breathing down my neck!" (panel 4)? What does this mouse, an obvious reference to Spiegelman's graphic novel *Maus*, symbolize? In what ways does Spiegelman intertwine the personal and the political in this autobiographical account? Identify recurrent images, characters, language.

2. Graphic novels are closely allied with comic strips; both can present serious subject manner in an apparently humorous format. In "Mein Kampf" Spiegelman uses humor to address grave issues of genocide, human survival, family relationships, and artistic representations of these, as well as his own creative crisis and his problems with memory. What does the graphic art format accomplish that might be hard to achieve in a poem or a novel? What advantages might poetry or fiction have? (It will be helpful to have a specific work of literature in mind when you answer this.)

3. In the last few panels, the artist's son appears. How does this add to or extend the meaning of "Mein Kampf"? In what way is the ending a satisfactory resolution to the piece? Are any questions or problems left unresolved?

4. Write an analysis of the way "Mein Kampf" tells a story and develops a set of ideas. With a partner or in a team, working through each frame in order, explain what you learn as you move from one frame to the next (in addition to what the dialogue balloons express). What subtle as well as obvious interactions do you see between the words and the images that contribute to the overall message and emotional tone?

5. Compare "Mein Kampf" with Lynda Barry's graphic treatment of "Hate" (p. 438) in their autobiographical approach to issues of ethnic, racial, and cultural stereotypes, prejudices, and hate. Are there positives to counteract the negatives? If you like one better than the other, explain why.

SHERMAN ALEXIE
What Sacagawea Means to Me

For Alexie's biographical information, see page 47. "What Sacagawea Means to Me," originally published in Time *(2002), uses the ultra-American image of the theme park as a springboard for creative cultural analysis. Alexie raises questions about ethnicity, gender, and social class in relation to Sacagawea, a Native American woman who, in 1804, was drafted into Lewis and Clark's expedition and lived out a complex relationship to the conquering race.*

In the future, every U.S. citizen will get to be Sacagawea for fifteen minutes. For the low price of admission, every American, regardless of race, religion, gender, and age, will climb through the portal into Sacagawea's Shoshone Indian brain. In the multicultural theme park called Sacagawea Land, you will be kidnapped as a child by the Hidatsa tribe and sold to Toussaint Charbonneau, the French-Canadian trader who will take you as one of his wives and father two of your children. Your first child, Jean-Baptiste, will be only a few months old as you carry him during your long journey with Lewis and Clark. The two captains will lead the adventure, fighting rivers, animals, weather, and diseases for thousands of miles, and you will march right beside them. But you, the aboriginal multitasker, will also breastfeed. And at the end of your Sacagawea journey, you will be shown the exit and given a souvenir T-shirt that reads, IF THE U.S. IS EDEN, THEN SACAGAWEA IS EVE.

Sacagawea is our mother. She is the first gene pair of the American DNA. In the beginning, she was the word, and the word was possibility. I revel in the wondrous possibilities of Sacagawea. It is good to be joyous in the presence of her spirit, because I hope she had moments of joy in what must have been a grueling life. This much is true: Sacagawea died of some mysterious illness when she was only in her twenties. Most illnesses were mysterious in the nineteenth century, but I suspect that Sacagawea's indigenous immune system was defenseless against an immigrant virus. Perhaps Lewis and Clark infected Sacagawea. If that is true, then certain postcolonial historians would argue that she was murdered not by germs but by colonists who carried those germs. I don't know much about the science of disease and immunities, but I know enough poetry to recognize that individual human beings are invaded and colonized by foreign bodies, just as individual civilizations are invaded and colonized by foreign bodies. In that sense, colonization might be a natural process, tragic and violent to be sure, but predictable and ordinary as well, and possibly necessary for the advance, however constructive and destructive, of all civilizations.

After all, Lewis and Clark's story has never been just the triumphant tale of two white men, no matter what the white historians might need to believe. Sacagawea was not the primary hero of this story either, no matter what the Native American historians and I might want to believe. The story of Lewis and Clark is also the story of the approximately forty-five nameless and faceless first- and second-generation European Americans who joined the journey, then left or completed it, often without monetary or historical compensation. Considering the time and place, I imagine those forty-five were illiterate, low-skilled laborers subject to managerial whims and nineteenth-century downsizing. And it is most certainly the story of the black slave York, who also cast votes during this allegedly democratic adventure. It's even the story of Seaman, the domesticated Newfoundland dog who must have been a welcome and friendly presence and who survived the risk of becoming supper during one lean time or another. The Lewis and Clark Expedition was exactly the kind of multicultural, trigenerational, bigendered, animal-friendly, government-supported, partly French-Canadian project that should rightly be celebrated by liberals and castigated by conservatives.

In the end, I wonder if colonization might somehow be magical. After all, Miles Davis is the direct descendant of slaves and slave owners. Hank Williams is the direct descendant of poor whites and poorer Indians. In 1876 Emily Dickinson was writing her poems in an Amherst attic while Crazy Horse was killing Custer on the banks of the Little Big Horn. I remain stunned by these contradictions, by the successive generations of social, political, and artistic mutations that can be so beautiful and painful. How did we get from there to here? This country somehow gave life to Maria Tallchief and Ted Bundy, to Geronimo and Joe McCarthy, to Nathan Bedford Forrest and Toni Morrison, to the Declaration of Independence and Executive Order No. 1066, to César Chávez and Richard Nixon, to theme parks and national parks, to smallpox and the vaccine for smallpox.

As a Native American, I want to hate this country and its contradictions. I   5
want to believe that Sacagawea hated this country and its contradictions. But this country exists, in whole and in part, because Sacagawea helped Lewis and Clark. In the land that came to be called Idaho, she acted as diplomat between her long-lost brother and the Lewis and Clark party. Why wouldn't she ask her brother and her tribe to take revenge against the men who had enslaved her? Sacagawea is a contradiction. Here in Seattle, I exist, in whole and in part, because a half-white man named James Cox fell in love with a Spokane Indian woman named Etta Adams who gave birth to my mother. I am a contradiction; I am Sacagawea.

QUESTIONS FOR DISCUSSION AND WRITING

1. The opening paragraph of Alexie's essay places the reader in the frame of the story with sentences such as "You will be kidnapped as a child by the Hidatsa tribe and sold to Toussaint Charbonneau." Why does Alexie change the reader's identity? What ideas is he trying to convey, and what connections is he attempting to create? For example, when he writes "you, the aboriginal multitasker, will also breastfeed," how is he trying to affect you as a male or female Indian or non-Indian reader?

2. Alexie states that "Lewis and Clark's story has never been just the triumphant tale of two white men, no matter what the white historians might need to believe" (paragraph 3). Why would white historians "need to believe" a different account from what Alexie offers? In what ways is Alexie's tale *non-triumphant* or *non-white*? Make a list of the ways Alexie attempts to modify, contradict, or update the story told by traditional historians. You could extend this discussion by bringing to class some traditional accounts of the Lewis and Clark Expedition, or write a research paper on contrasting interpretations of the Lewis and Clark Expedition.

3. Although Alexie is a Native American author deeply concerned with the effects of colonization on his ancestors, he also discusses the "forty-five nameless and faceless first- and second-generation European Americans who joined the

journey" (paragraph 3), who are white. Why does he draw attention to this group?

4. In the last two paragraphs of "What Sacagawea Means to Me," Alexie discusses contradictions. Write a paper about one or more of these contradictions in which you explain its meaning or try to resolve it, or both. For example, what should we make of the fact that Emily Dickinson was composing classic American poetry at the same time that Crazy Horse was massacring Custer? Are these activities equivalent? Does one cancel out the other? Do they represent a larger contradiction in American society? How can one nation (the "United" States) embody such differences? Or consider the following question: What does America *stand for* if it can produce both Geronimo and Joe McCarthy, both the Declaration of Independence and Executive Order No. 1066 (which provided for the internment of Japanese Americans during World War II)?

5. Compare Alexie's way of discussing the problems experienced by non-whites in America to that of Zitkala-Sa in the excerpt "from The School Days of an Indian Girl" (p. 292). Which writer's approach to the problem of non-white existence and identity is more effective, in your opinion? Why? By yourself or with a partner write an essay in which you explain which of the two essays is more likely to change readers' perceptions about the experience of being non-white in America.

N. SCOTT MOMADAY
The Way to Rainy Mountain

N. Scott Momaday (b. 1934) in Lawton, Oklahoma, grew up on an Indian reservation in the Southwest, where his Cherokee-Caucasian mother and Kiowa father were both teachers. After earning his doctorate at Stanford University (1963), where he was a student of essayist and novelist Wallace Stegner, Momaday taught English at the University of California at Santa Barbara (1963–1969) and at Berkeley (1969–1972), Stanford (1973–1981), and the University of Arizona (1981–1989). For Momaday, identity is "a moral idea, for it accounts for the way in which [a man] reacts to other men and to the world in general." Primarily a poet (Angle of Geese, 1974; The Gourd Dancer, 1976), Momaday has also written two novels— the Pulitzer Prize–winning House Made of Dawn (1968), which launched a renaissance in Native American writing, and The Ancient Child (1989), as well as The Names: A Memoir (1976). Like his earlier books, Momaday's recent collections— In the Presence of the Sun: Stories and Poems (1992), The Man Made of Words: Essays, Stories, Passages (1997), and In the Bear's House (1999)—combine story, poem, prose poem, dialogue, ethnography, history, and personal history.

Originally published in The Reporter *(1967), "The Way to Rainy Mountain" also appeared as the introduction to Momaday's book of the same title. In it he preserves and validates the Native American oral tradition, retelling Kiowa legends, tracing the history of the Kiowas' migration, lyrically describing the landscape of their journey, and placing himself and his family within that matrix: "Although my grandmother lived out her long life in the shadow of Rainy Mountain, the immense landscape of the continental interior lay like memory in her blood." The Context readings following this essay explore how stories "take place," how a storyteller listens to others' stories and creates several storytelling voices, and how listeners understand a story in terms of other stories they know and create.*

A single knoll rises out of the plain in Oklahoma, north and west of the Wichita Range. For my people, the Kiowas, it is an old landmark, and they gave it the name Rainy Mountain. The hardest weather in the world is there. Winter brings blizzards, hot tornadic winds arise in the spring, and in summer the prairie is an anvil's edge. The grass turns brittle and brown, and it cracks beneath your feet. There are green belts along the rivers and creeks, linear groves of hickory and pecan, willow and witch hazel. At a distance in July or August the steaming foliage seems almost to writhe in fire. Great green and yellow grasshoppers are everywhere in the tall grass, popping up like corn to sting the flesh, and tortoises crawl about on the red earth, going nowhere in the plenty of time. Loneliness is an aspect of the land. All things in the plain are isolate; there is no confusion of objects in the eye, but *one* hill or *one* tree or *one* man. To look upon that landscape in the early morning, with the sun at your back, is to lose the sense of proportion. Your imagination comes to life, and this, you think, is where Creation was begun.

I returned to Rainy Mountain in July. My grandmother had died in the spring, and I wanted to be at her grave. She had lived to be very old and at last infirm. Her only living daughter was with her when she died, and I was told that in death her face was that of a child.

I like to think of her as a child. When she was born, the Kiowas were living the last great moment of their history. For more than a hundred years they had controlled the open range from the Smoky Hill River to the Red, from the headwaters of the Canadian to the fork of the Arkansas and Cimarron. In alliance with the Comanches, they had ruled the whole of the southern Plains. War was their sacred business, and they were among the finest horsemen the world has ever known. But warfare for the Kiowas was preeminently a matter of disposition rather than of survival, and they never understood the grim, unrelenting advance of the U.S. Cavalry. When at last, divided and ill-provisioned, they were driven onto the Staked Plains in the cold rains of autumn, they fell into panic. In Palo Duro Canyon they abandoned their crucial stores to pillage and had nothing then but their lives. In order to save themselves, they surrendered to the soldiers at Fort Sill and were imprisoned in the old stone corral that now stands as a military museum. My grandmother was spared the humiliation of those high gray walls by eight or ten years, but she must have known from birth the affliction of defeat, the dark brooding of old warriors.

Her name was Aho, and she belonged to the last culture to evolve in North America. Her forebears came down from the high country in western Montana nearly three centuries ago. They were a mountain people, a mysterious tribe of hunters whose language has never been positively classified in any major group. In the late seventeenth century they began a long migration to the south and east. It was a journey toward the dawn, and it led to a golden age. Along the way the Kiowas were befriended by the Crows, who gave them the culture and religion of the Plains. They acquired horses, and their ancient nomadic spirit was suddenly free of the ground. They acquired Tai-me, the sacred Sun Dance doll, from that moment the object and symbol of their worship, and so shared in the divinity of the sun. Not least, they acquired the sense of destiny, therefore courage and pride. When they entered upon the southern Plains they had been transformed. No longer were they slaves to the simple necessity of survival; they were a lordly and dangerous society of fighters and thieves, hunters and priests of the sun. According to their origin myth, they entered the world through a hollow log. From one point of view, their migration was the fruit of an old prophecy, for indeed they emerged from a sunless world.

Although my grandmother lived out her long life in the shadow of Rainy 5 Mountain, the immense landscape of the continental interior lay like memory in her blood. She could tell of the Crows, whom she had never seen, and of the Black Hills, where she had never been. I wanted to see in reality what she had seen more perfectly in the mind's eye, and traveled fifteen hundred miles to begin my pilgrimage.

Yellowstone, it seemed to me, was the top of the world, a region of deep lakes and dark timber, canyons and waterfalls. But, beautiful as it is, one might have the sense of confinement there. The skyline in all directions is close at hand, the high wall of the woods and deep cleavages of shade. There is a perfect freedom in the mountains, but it belongs to the eagle and the elk, the badger and the bear. The Kiowas reckoned their stature by the distance they could see, and they were bent and blind in the wilderness.

Descending eastward, the highland meadows are a stairway to the plain. In July the inland slope of the Rockies is luxuriant with flax and buckwheat, stonecrop and larkspur. The earth unfolds and the limit of the land recedes. Clusters of trees, and animals grazing far in the distance, cause the vision to reach away and wonder to build upon the mind. The sun follows a longer course in the day, and the sky is immense beyond all comparison. The great billowing clouds that sail upon it are shadows that move upon the grain like water, dividing light. Farther down, in the land of the Crows and Blackfeet, the plain is yellow. Sweet clover takes hold of the hills and bends upon itself to cover and seal the soil. There the Kiowas paused on their way; they had come to the place where they must change their lives. The sun is at home on the plains. Precisely there does it have the certain character of a god. When the Kiowas came to the land of the

Crows, they could see the dark lees of the hills at dawn across the Bighorn River, the profusion of light on the grain shelves, the oldest deity ranging after the solstices. Not yet would they veer southward to the caldron of the land that lay below; they must wean their blood from the northern winter and hold the mountains a while longer in their view. They bore Tai-me in procession to the east.

A dark mist lay over the Black Hills, and the land was like iron. At the top of a ridge I caught sight of Devil's Tower upthrust against the gray sky as if in the birth of time the core of the earth had broken through its crust and the motion of the world was begun. There are things in nature that engender an awful quiet in the heart of man; Devil's Tower is one of them. Two centuries ago, because they could not do otherwise, the Kiowas made a legend at the base of the rock. My grandmother said:

> Eight children were there at play, seven sisters and their brother. Suddenly the boy was struck dumb; he trembled and began to run upon his hands and feet. His fingers became claws, and his body was covered with fur. Directly there was a bear where the boy had been. The sisters were terrified; they ran, and the bear after them. They came to the stump of a great tree, and the tree spoke to them. It bade them climb upon it, and as they did so it began to rise into the air. The bear came to kill them, but they were just beyond its reach. It reared against the tree and scored the bark all around with its claws. The seven sisters were borne into the sky, and they became the stars of the Big Dipper.

From that moment, and so long as the legend lives, the Kiowas have kinsmen in the night sky. Whatever they were in the mountains, they could be no more. However tenuous their well-being, however much they had suffered and would suffer again, they had found a way out of the wilderness.

My grandmother had a reverence for the sun, a holy regard that now is all but gone out of mankind. There was a wariness in her, and an ancient awe. She was a Christian in her later years, but she had come a long way about, and she never forgot her birthright. As a child she had been to the Sun Dances; she had taken part in those annual rites, and by then she had learned the restoration of her people in the presence of Tai-me. She was about seven when the last Kiowa Sun Dance was held in 1887 on the Washita River above Rainy Mountain Creek. The buffalo were gone. In order to consummate the ancient sacrifice — to impale the head of a buffalo bull upon the medicine tree — a delegation of old men journeyed into Texas, there to beg and barter for an animal from the Goodnight herd. She was ten when the Kiowas came together for the last time as a living Sun Dance culture. They could find no buffalo; they had to hang an old hide from the sacred tree. Before the dance could begin, a company of soldiers rode out from Fort Sill under orders to disperse the tribe. Forbidden without cause the essential act of their faith, having seen the wild herds slaughtered and left to rot upon the ground, the Kiowas backed away forever from the medicine tree. That was July 20, 1890, at the great bend of the Washita. My grandmother was there. Without bitterness, and for as long as she lived, she bore a vision of deicide.

Now that I can have her only in memory, I see my grandmother in the sev- 10 eral postures that were peculiar to her: standing at the wood stove on a winter morning and turning meat in a great iron skillet; sitting at the south window, bent above her beadwork, and afterwards, when her vision failed, looking down for a long time into the fold of her hands; going out upon a cane, very slowly as she did when the weight of age came upon her; praying. I remember her most often at prayer. She made long, rambling prayers out of suffering and hope, having seen many things. I was never sure that I had the right to hear, so exclusive were they of all mere custom and company. The last time I saw her she prayed standing by the side of her bed at night, naked to the waist, the light of a kerosene lamp moving upon her dark skin. Her long, black hair, always drawn and braided in the day, lay upon her shoulders and against her breasts like a shawl. I do not speak Kiowa, and I never understood her prayers, but there was something inherently sad in the sound, some merest hesitation upon the syllables of sorrow. She began in a high and descending pitch, exhausting her breath to silence; then again and again—and always the same intensity of effort, of something that is, and is not, like urgency in the human voice. Transported so in the dancing light among the shadows of her room, she seemed beyond the reach of time. But that was illusion; I think I knew then that I should not see her again.

Houses are like sentinels in the plain, old keepers of the weather watch. There, in a very little while, wood takes on the appearance of great age. All colors wear soon away in the wind and rain, and then the wood is burned gray and the grain appears and the nails turn red with rust. The windowpanes are black and opaque; you imagine there is nothing within, and indeed there are many ghosts, bones given up to the land. They stand here and there against the sky, and you approach them for a longer time than you expect. They belong in the distance; it is their domain.

Once there was a lot of sound in my grandmother's house, a lot of coming and going, feasting and talk. The summers there were full of excitement and reunion. The Kiowas are a summer people; they abide the cold and keep to themselves, but when the season turns and the land becomes warm and vital they cannot hold still; an old love of going returns upon them. The aged visitors who came to my grandmother's house when I was a child were made of lean and leather, and they bore themselves upright. They wore great black hats and bright ample shirts that shook in the wind. They rubbed fat upon their hair and wound their braids with strips of colored cloth. Some of them painted their faces and carried the scars of old and cherished enmities. They were an old council of warlords, come to remind and be reminded of who they were. Their wives and daughters served them well. The women might indulge themselves; gossip was at once the mark and compensation of their servitude. They made loud and elaborate talk among themselves, full of jest and gesture, fright and false alarm. They went abroad in fringed and flowered shawls, bright beadwork and German silver. They were at home in the kitchen, and they prepared meals that were banquets.

There were frequent prayer meetings, and great nocturnal feasts. When I was a child I played with my cousins outside, where the lamplight fell upon the ground and the singing of the old people rose up around us and carried away into the darkness. There were a lot of good things to eat, a lot of laughter and surprise. And afterwards, when the quiet returned, I lay down with my grandmother and could hear the frogs away by the river and feel the motion of the air.

Now there is a funeral silence in the rooms, the endless wake of some final word. The walls have closed in upon my grandmother's house. When I returned to it in mourning, I saw for the first time in my life how small it was. It was late at night, and there was a white moon, nearly full. I sat for a long time on the stone steps by the kitchen door. From there I could see out across the land; I could see the long row of trees by the creek, the low light upon the rolling plains, and the stars of the Big Dipper. Once I looked at the moon and caught sight of a strange thing. A cricket had perched upon the handrail, only a few inches away from me. My line of vision was such that the creature filled the moon like a fossil. It had gone there, I thought, to live and die, for there, of all places, was its small definition made whole and eternal. A warm wind rose up and purled like the longing within me.

The next morning I awoke at dawn and went out on the dirt road to Rainy   15
Mountain. It was already hot, and the grasshoppers began to fill the air. Still, it was early in the morning, and the birds sang out of the shadows. The long yellow grass on the mountain shone in the bright light, and a scissortail hied above the land. There, where it ought to be, at the end of a long and legendary way, was my grandmother's grave. Here and there on the dark stones were ancestral names. Looking back once, I saw the mountain and came away.

CONTEXTS FOR
"THE WAY TO RAINY MOUNTAIN"

Stories often open by establishing a location and its atmosphere. Because his stories are rooted in history and biography, Momaday's choice of location is somewhat limited: The Kiowas actually lived here, *migrated* there. *Nevertheless, he is free to choose the places from which his storyteller tells those events: Of all the places where the Kiowas lived, he chooses Rainy Mountain and its nearby cemetery, and that choice governs what his storyteller can see and tell or not tell.*

"Rainy Mountain. Many of my relatives lie in the cemetery nearby. The grasshoppers are innumerable."

N. SCOTT MOMADAY

East of My Grandmother's House

In section 24 of The Way to Rainy Mountain, *N. Scott Momaday reflects on the way place can inspire imagination.*

East of my grandmother's house the sun rises out of the plain. Once in his life a man ought to concentrate his mind upon the remembered earth, I believe. He ought to give himself up to a particular landscape in his experience, to look at it from as many angles as he can, to wonder about it, to dwell upon it. He ought to imagine that he touches it with his hands at every season and listens to the sounds that are made upon it. He ought to imagine the creatures there and all the faintest motions of the wind. He ought to recollect the glare of noon and all the colors of the dawn and dusk.

N. SCOTT MOMADAY

I Invented History

In one short paragraph of his memoir, The Names *(1976), N. Scott Momaday explains that as the past ("tracks" beneath his feet) and the future (the "infinite promise" of childhood's horizon) bear upon the present moment in a particular place, they gradually shape one's identity.*

I invented history. In April's thin white light, in the white landscape of the Staked Plains, I looked for tracks among the tufts of coarse, brittle grass, amid the stones, beside the tangle of dusty hedges. When I look back upon those days— days of infinite promise and steady adventure and the certain sanctity of child-hood—I see how much was there in the balance. The past and the future were simply the large contingencies of a given moment; they bore upon the present and gave it shape. One does not pass through time, but time enters upon him, in his place. As a child, I knew this surely, as a matter of fact; I am not wise to doubt it now. Notions of the past and future are essentially notions of the present. In the same way an idea of one's ancestry and posterity is really an idea of the self. About this time I was formulating an idea of myself.

From N. Scott Momaday, *The Way to Rainy Mountain* (Albuquerque: University of New Mexico Press, 1969), 83.

From N. Scott Momaday, The Names: A Memoir (New York: Harper, 1976), 101–102.

N. SCOTT MOMADAY

Disturbing the Spirits:
Indian Bones Must Stay in the Ground

In this op-ed piece, occasioned by the discovery of a 9,300-year-old skeleton near the Columbia River in Washington State, N. Scott Momaday explains that "Native American creationism—which holds that the Indians sprang from the spirit world around us"—underlies the historical and spiritual attitudes that prompt Native Americans to oppose scientific research of archaeological sites and exhumed skeletons.

It might appear that the battle between evolutionists and creationists has broken out again in the case of a 9,300-year-old skeleton recently discovered near the Columbia River in Washington State. But because these remains were found on the sacred land of an Indian tribe, the Umatilla in nearby Oregon, it is not quite as simple as that. There is also history to consider and vindication. . . .

Reason, naturally is on the side of science. Indian creationists, like creationists in general, assume unreasonable attitudes. "We did not come from Asia," said a Hopi friend who opposes research on our origins. "We did not come from elsewhere. We were always here."

Even as intelligent a man as Vine Deloria Jr., a prominent Indian historian, dismisses as "scientific folklore" the discovery that Indians arrived in North America by crossing a land bridge across the Bering Strait. Yet there is solid evidence that people migrated that way from Asia to North America some 20,000 years ago.

There is no question that the arguments in favor of scientific inquiry are legitimate. Science has unlocked countless doors, has allowed human beings to see themselves with a clarity not available to our forebears.

The problem is this: Archeologists and anthropologists, especially, have given science a bad name in the Indian world. For hundreds of years, the remains of American Indians have been taken from the earth and deposited in museums. The scientists involved have often acted without respect, much less reverence, toward these remains.

The violation of burial sites and the confiscation of human remains have been shameful and unprofessional. The boxes of human bones stacked in the Smithsonian Institution, often unidentified, virtually forgotten, are a sad reminder of this disrespect.

To many Native Americans, the theft of what is sacred to their community stands as the greatest of all the crimes perpetrated upon them. Wounds to the spirit are considered eminently more serious than wounds to the body. Indians have endured massacres, alcoholism, disease, poverty. The desecration of spiritual life has been no less an assault. Because the scientific scrutiny of human remains once interred in sacred ground is indelibly associated with this painful

From N. Scott Momaday, "Disturbing the Spirits," *New York Times*, 2 November 1996, p. 23.

history, Native Americans will resist. They feel they must. At stake is their identity, their dignity and their spirit.

N. SCOTT MOMADAY
The Native Voice

There are different kinds of stories. The basic story is one that centers upon an event. In American Indian oral tradition stories range from origin myths through trickster and hero tales to prophecy. With the exception of epic matter and certain creation myths, they are generally short. Concentration is a principle of their structure. Stories are formed. The form of the story is particular and perceptible.

Stories are true. They are true to our common experience, actual or imagined; they are statements that concern the human condition. To the extent that the human condition involves moral considerations, stories have moral implications. Beyond that, stories are true in that they are established squarely upon belief. In the oral tradition stories are told not merely to entertain or to instruct; they are told to be believed. Stories are not subject to the imposition of such questions as true or false, fact or fiction. Stories are realities lived and believed. In this sense they are indisputably true.

The storyteller is he who tells the story. To say this is to say that the storyteller is preeminently *entitled* to tell the story. He is original and creative. He creates the storytelling experience and himself and his audience in the process. He exists in the person of the storyteller for the sake of telling the story. When he is otherwise occupied, he is someone other than the storyteller. His telling of the story is a unique performance. The storyteller creates himself in the sense that the mask he wears for the sake of telling the story is of his own making, and it is never the same. He creates his listener in the sense that he determines the listener's existence within, and in relation to, the story, and it is never the same. The storyteller says in effect: "On this occasion I am, for I imagine that I am; and on this occasion you are, for I imagine that you are. And this imagining is the burden of the story, and indeed it is the story."

I have lived with the Kiowa story of the arrowmaker all my life. I have literally no memory that is older than that of hearing my father tell it to me when I was a small child. Such things take precedence in the mind. I set the story down in writing for the first time, and I have expressed my thoughts concerning it. I have told the story many times to many people in many parts of the world, and I believe that I have not yet found out its whole meaning. 5

From N. Scott Momaday, "The Native Voice," in *Columbia Literary History of the United States*, ed. Emory Elliott (New York: Columbia University Press, 1988), 5–15.

N. SCOTT MOMADAY

The Whole Journey and *Three Voices*

The preceding passage from "The Native Voice" helps us understand Momaday's explanation of Rainy Mountain *as a "whole journey," though not in linear form (first this happened, then that. . .). The author braids together three complementary storytelling voices (visually signaled by a different font or typeface): the mythical, the historical, and the immediately personal. In "The Man Made of Words" (1970), Momaday elaborates on the Prologue to* Rainy Mountain: *Every human being, he says, is "made of words" in the sense that language is "the element in which we think and dream and act, in which we live our daily lives." To answer the question, "What is an American Indian?" Momaday retells passages from* Rainy Mountain. *Knowledge passes from one generation to another, he says, through "racial memory" expressed in the workings of imagination: When "imagination is superimposed upon historical event . . . [i]t becomes a story . . . deeply invested with meaning." He describes the "three voices" of* Rainy Mountain *as the voice of myth, the voice of history, and the voice of immediacy.*

THE WHOLE JOURNEY

Three hundred years ago the Kiowa lived in the mountains of what is now western Montana, near the headwaters of the Yellowstone River. Near the end of the 17th century they began a long migration to the south and east. They passed along the present border between Montana and Wyoming to the Black Hills and proceeded southward along the eastern slopes of the Rockies to the Wichita Mountains in the Southern Plains (Southwestern Oklahoma).

I mention this old journey of the Kiowas because it is in a sense definitive of the tribal mind; it is essential to the way in which the Kiowas think of themselves as a people. The migration was carried on over a course of many generations and many hundreds of miles. When it began, the Kiowas were a desperate and divided people, given up wholly to a day-by-day struggle for survival. When it ended, they were a race of centaurs, a lordly society of warriors and buffalo hunters. Along the way they had acquired horses, a knowledge and possession of the open land, and a sense of destiny. In alliance with the Comanches, they ruled the southern plains for a hundred years.

That migration—and the new golden age to which it led—is closely reflected in Kiowa legend and lore. Several years ago I retraced the route of that migration, and when I came to the end, I interviewed a number of Kiowa elders and

From N. Scott Momaday, "The Man Made of Words," in *Indian Voices: The First Convocation of American Indian Scholars*, ed. Rupert Costo et al. (San Francisco: Indian Historian Press, 1970), 49–52, 58–59.

obtained from them a remarkable body of history and learning, fact and fiction—all of it in the oral tradition and all of it valuable in its own right and for its own sake.

THREE VOICES

There are three distinct narrative voices in *The Way to Rainy Mountain*—the mythical, the historical, and the immediate. Each of the translations is followed by two kinds of commentary; the first is documentary and the second is privately reminiscent. Together, they serve, hopefully, to validate the oral tradition to an extent that might not otherwise be possible. The commentaries are meant to provide a context in which the elements of oral tradition might transcend the categorical limits of prehistory, anonymity, and archaeology in the narrow sense.

All of this is to say that I believe there is a way (first) in which the elements 5 of oral tradition can be shown, dramatically, to exist within the framework of a literary continuance, a deeper and more vital context of language and meaning than that which is generally taken into account; and (secondly) in which those elements can be located, with some precision on an evolutionary scale.

The device of the journey is peculiarly appropriate to such a principle of narration as this. And *The Way to Rainy Mountain* is a whole journey, intricate with notion and meaning; and it is made with the whole memory, that experience of the mind which is legendary as well as historical, personal as well as cultural.

PAULA GUNN ALLEN

Voice of the Turtle:
American Indian Literature, 1900–1970

UCLA Professor Paula Gunn Allen rejects the notion that Native American literary history is " 'evolutionary,' a white materialist-determinist notion that has no vital part in the Native Narrative Tradition; it is, rather, an account of how the transitory and the enduring interact." Just as Momaday tells the "whole journey" of the Kiowas by braiding together three storytelling voices, so Allen adopts weaving, rather than linear progress, as her metaphor for literary transformation.

A number of factors contributed to the sudden silencing of Native voices in publishing circles, the most important of these being the Great Depression and World War Two. The very influential work of the American historian Frederick B. Turner played a large role in the redefinition of Native people as forever beyond the pale of "civilized" culture, as did a dramatic rise in xenophobia, cultural

From Paula Gunn Allen, *Voice of the Turtle: American Indian Literature, 1900–1970* (New York: Ballantine, 1994), 4–8.

Portrait of N. Scott Momaday

chauvinism, and white supremacist thought that culminated in the establishment of the Third Reich in Germany but was by no means confined to that unhappy nation.

In the bland and blinding white cocoon of the 1950s, with its Red Scare, Cold War, and suburban fixations, a reawakened consciousness stirred in the United States. As a result, the nation returned to its former self in the 1960s, as though recovering from profound shock. In the ferment of the sixties, via Hippies, Civil Rights, the Peace Movement, Kennedy's Manpower Act, Johnson's War on Poverty, and especially the GI Bill that educated thousands of Native vets from the Second World War and the Korean and Vietnam Wars, Native writers began to publish fiction once again. The signal events of those years were the publication of N. Scott Momaday's *House Made of Dawn* in 1968 and John Milton's anthology, *The American Indian Speaks* which was published in 1969—the year Momaday was awarded the Pulitzer Prize for fiction. In a sense, 1970 marked the end of literary and cultural dispossession. As the last quarter of the century has unfolded, the tiny trickle of fiction begun by Native writers during the first seventy years has become a broad and stately river.

Modern people think of change as progress, and that is the primary organizing principle—motivating force and raison d'être—of modern life. But Native people see change as the fundamental sacred process, as Transformation, as Ritual, as intrinsic to all of existence whenever and wherever, in whatever form or style it takes. Transformation: to change someone or something from one state or condition to another. Magic. What mages, wise ones, shamans do. Also what all peoples, human or otherwise, participate in. The wise are conscious of the process of Ritual Transformation in every facet of life.

Native American fiction in the twentieth century has two sides: the Oral Tradition of the Native Nations, and Western fiction and its antecedents. As does the Bible for the thought and literature of the West, ceremonial texts provide a major source of the symbols, allusions, and philosophical assumptions that inform our world and thus our work. It is a mistake to believe that ceremonial texts are "dated" and thus irrelevant to the work of modern writers. Which of these is inhalation, sine, and which exhalation, cosine, is impossible to say. They interact, as wings of a bird in flight interact. They give shape to our experience. They *signify*.

QUESTIONS FOR DISCUSSION AND WRITING

1. If you were to tell a grandchild or another youngster about a place in your childhood that shaped your character, what place would it be? Make a long list of everything you can remember about the place; then sort your list into clusters of things—maybe the atmosphere, the physical qualities, the personal associations that certain physical qualities evoke, whatever works. Think about what made this place special for you and in what ways its special quality became an important part of who you are.

   Read the "Writing about Places" section of the introduction (p. 24), and then write a sketch—complemented by photographs or drawings if you like—that shows your special place to others in your class.

2. Momaday says "I invented history" (p. 152). His writings in the Context readings address several dimensions of history: natural, personal, social, and cultural. In what ways does the special place you wrote about in question 1 fit into the past and the future? How and to what extent does it connect with various dimensions of history? In what ways do Sherman Alexie's (p. 142) and Gloria Anzaldúa's (p. 159) interpretations corroborate or alter Momaday's views of cultural history?

3. Read the "Narration" section of the introduction (p. 22), and then reflect on a story you were told as a child. What, if any, was the moral of the story? How explicit was it? Write about this story, and share your writing with your classmates, reflecting with them on how your story connects with stories they recall. As Momaday does, write about how that childhood story helps shape a story you now tell about yourself as an adult.

4. Reread Momaday's "The Native Voice" (p. 154); then reflect on a storytelling performance that has significance for you. Who told the story? How would you describe the scene of the storytelling? Try writing down as much of the story as you can in the language you recall. Considering *The Way to Rainy Mountain*'s "three voices"—immediate, historical, and mythic—explain which "voice" your story already embodies, and write companion pieces for it that embody the other two voices.

5. The final section of the Context readings explains how stories evoke other stories in order to persuade people to take action. To whom might you retell your story from question 4, and what action might that person or persons take in response? What other familiar stories do you want them to keep in mind? Rewrite your story, including references to related stories, as a call to a particular audience to take a particular action. On the basis of your story, what should they do?

6. Sherman Alexie says, "I always want to be on the edge of offending somebody." Thus he has criticized the "Mother Earth Father Sky" clichés that he claims are perpetuated by Indian authors such as Momaday. Compare and contrast Alexie's satiric interpretation of an iconic Indian woman, Sacagewea (p. 142) with Momaday's depiction of his grandmother in "The Way to Rainy Mountain" (p. 145). Is Alexie's criticism of Momaday justified? Has Momaday offered any defense of his depiction of his ancestors and their native land in any of the readings in this chapter?

GLORIA ANZALDÚA

From *Beyond Traditional Notions of Identity*

Gloria Anzaldúa, among the first openly lesbian Chicana authors, was born in 1942 in southwest Texas, a borderland between the United States and Mexico that she considers "une herida abierta," an open wound, where "the Third World grates against the First and bleeds." The daughter of a sharecropper and a field worker, she labored in the fields weekends and summers throughout high school and college, before graduating with a bachelor's degree from Pan American University in 1969. She earned a master's degree in English and education from the University of Texas in Austin (1972) and a doctorate from the University of California at Santa Cruz. Her work, such as This Bridge Called My Back: Radical Writings by Women of Color *(co-edited with Cherríe Moraga, 1981) and* Borderlands/La Frontera, The New Mestiza *(1987), powerfully addresses—in two English and six Spanish dialects—issues of poverty, racism, and gender. Anzaldúa died in 2004. "Beyond Traditional Notions of Identity," revisiting "Borderlands" after two decades, was published in the* Chronicle of Higher Education *October 11, 2002.*

More than two decades ago, Cherríe Moraga and I edited a multigenre collection giving voice to radical women of color, *This Bridge Called My Back: Writings by Radical Women of Color*. Every generation that reads *This Bridge Called My Back* rewrites it. Like the trestle bridge, and other things that have reached their zenith, it will decline unless we attach it to new growth or append new growth to it. In a new collection of writings and art, *this bridge we call home: radical visions for transformation*, AnaLouise Keating and I, together with our contributors, attempt to continue the dialogue of the past 21 years, rethink the old ideas, and germinate new theories. We move from focusing on what has been done to us (victimhood) to a more extensive level of agency, one that questions what we're doing to each other, to those in distant countries, and to the earth's environment.

Twenty-one years ago we struggled with the recognition of difference within the context of commonality. Today we grapple with the recognition of commonality within the context of difference. While *This Bridge Called My Back* displaced whiteness, *this bridge we call home* carries that displacement further. It questions the terms *white* and *women of color* by showing that whiteness may not be applied to all whites, because some possess women-of-color consciousness, just as some women of color bear white consciousness. We intend to change notions of identity, viewing it as part of a more complex system covering a larger terrain, and demonstrating that the politics of exclusion based on traditional categories diminishes our humanness.

Today categories of race and gender are more permeable and flexible than they were for those of us growing up before the 1980s. Today we need to move beyond separate and easy identifications, creating bridges that cross race and other classifications among different groups via intergenerational dialogue. Rather than legislating and restricting racial identities, we hope to make them more pliant.

We must learn to incorporate additional underrepresented voices; we must attempt to break the impasse between women of color and other groups. By including women and men of different "races," nationalities, classes, sexualities, genders, and ages in our discussions, we complicate the debates within feminist theory both inside and outside the academy and inside and outside the United States.

Our goal is not to use differences to separate us from others, but neither is   5 it to gloss over those differences. Many of us identify with groups and social positions not limited to our ethnic, racial, religious, class, gender, and national classifications. Though most people self-define by what they exclude, we define who we are by what we include—what I call the new tribalism. I fear that many *mujeres de color* will not want whites or men to join the dialogue. We risk the displeasure of those women. There are no safe spaces. "Home" can be unsafe and dangerous because it bears the likelihood of intimacy and thus thinner boundaries.

QUESTIONS FOR DISCUSSION AND WRITING

1. Anzaldúa explains that two decades earlier her work had "struggled with the recognition of difference within the context of commonality" but that now "we grapple with the recognition of commonality within the context of difference" (paragraph 2). Explain how this perspective applies to Eric Liu's "Notes of a Native Speaker" (p. 112), Sherman Alexie's "What Sacagawea Means to Me" (p. 142), and Richard Rodriguez's "Aria" (p. 298).

2. What does Anzaldúa mean by "Today categories of race and gender are more permeable and flexible than they were for those of us growing up before the 1980s" (paragraph 3)? Consider such essays as those by McCloskey, "Yes, Ma'am" (p. 173), and Yoshino, "The Pressure to Cover" (p. 456), in your answer.

3. "Today," says Anzaldúa, "we need to . . . [create] bridges that cross race and other classifications among different groups via intergenerational dialogue" (paragraph 3). With a partner, preferably one of a racial or ethnic group different from yours and possibly of another generation, write an essay expanding on this idea.

THOMAS JEFFERSON

George Washington

Thomas Jefferson (1743–1826), the third president of the United States, was a patrician and revolutionary who embodied the democratic spirit of the new nation. He excelled as a philosopher, architect, inventor, writer, and, above all, consummate politician. Born in Charlottesville, Virginia, and educated at the College of William and Mary, Jefferson served as a delegate to the Continental Congress in 1775, helped draft the Declaration of Independence (see p. 369), and was governor of the Commonwealth of Virginia. In 1789, after the Revolutionary War and the ratification of the U.S. Constitution, Jefferson became secretary of state in the new government under George Washington, who relied on Jefferson's advice in matters of personal ethics as well as politics. Politics, however, soon put a strain on the relationship as Jefferson opposed Secretary of the Treasury Alexander Hamilton's Federalist program and accused Hamilton of being a monarchist. The rift between them became permanent in 1796, when a letter of Jefferson's containing a bitter criticism of Washington's administration appeared in print.

In 1814 Doctor Walter Jones, who was writing an account of Washington's career, asked Jefferson for a sketch of his long-time acquaintance. In the resulting portrait, Jefferson expresses his reverence for the great leader's character—and provides an unabashed appraisal of Washington's nonphilosophical and unimaginative nature.

I think I knew General Washington intimately and thoroughly; and were I called on to delineate his character, it should be in terms like these.

His mind was great and powerful, without being of the very first order; his penetration strong, though not so acute as that of a Newton, Bacon, or Locke; and as far as he saw, no judgment was ever sounder. It was slow in operation, being little aided by invention or imagination, but sure in conclusion. Hence the common remark of his officers, of the advantage he derived from councils of war, where hearing all suggestions, he selected whatever was best; and certainly no general ever planned his battles more judiciously. But if deranged during the course of the action, if any member of his plan was dislocated by sudden circumstances, he was slow in re-adjustment. The consequence was, that he often failed in the field, and rarely against an enemy in station, as at Boston and York. He was incapable of fear, meeting personal dangers with the calmest unconcern. Perhaps the strongest feature in his character was prudence, never acting until every circumstance, every consideration, was maturely weighed; refraining if he saw a doubt, but, when once decided, going through with his purpose, whatever obstacles opposed. His integrity was most pure, his justice the most inflexible I have ever known, no motives of interest or consanguinity, of friendship or hatred, being able to bias his decision. He was, indeed, in every sense of the words, a wise, a good, and a great man. His temper was naturally irritable and high toned; but reflection and resolution had obtained a firm and habitual ascendency over it. If ever, however, it broke its bonds, he was most tremendous in his wrath. In his expenses he was honorable, but exact; liberal in contributions to whatever promised utility; but frowning and unyielding on all visionary projects, and all unworthy calls on his charity. His heart was not warm in its affections; but he exactly calculated every man's value, and gave him a solid esteem proportioned to it. His person, you know, was fine, his stature exactly what one would wish, his deportment easy, erect and noble; the best horseman of his age, and the most graceful figure that could be seen on horseback. Although in the circle of his friends, where he might be unreserved with safety, he took a free share in conversation, his colloquial talents were not above mediocrity, possessing neither copiousness of ideas, nor fluency of words. In public, when called on for a sudden opinion, he was unready, short and embarrassed. Yet he wrote readily, rather diffusely, in an easy and correct style. This he had acquired by conversation with the world, for his education was merely reading, writing and common arithmetic, to which he added surveying at a later day. His time was employed in action chiefly, reading little, and that only in agriculture and English history. His correspondence became necessarily extensive, and, with journalizing his agricultural proceedings, occupied most of his leisure hours within doors. On the whole, his character was, in its mass, perfect, in nothing bad, in few points indifferent; and it may truly be said, that never did nature and fortune combine more perfectly to make a man great, and to place him in the same constellation with whatever worthies have merited from man an everlasting remembrance. For his was the singular destiny and merit, of leading the armies of his country successfully through an arduous war, for the establishment of its independence; of conducting its councils through the birth of a government, new in its forms and principles, until it had settled down into a quiet and orderly train; and of scrupulously obeying the laws through the whole of his career, civil and military, of which the history of the world furnishes no other example.

I am satisfied, the great body of republicans think of him as I do. We were, indeed, dissatisfied with him on his ratification of the British treaty. But this was short lived. We knew his honesty, the wiles with which he was encompassed, and that age had already begun to relax the firmness of his purposes; and I am convinced he is more deeply seated in the love and gratitude of the republicans, than in the Pharisaical homage of the federal monarchists. For he was no monarchist from preference of his judgment. The soundness of that gave him correct views of the rights of man, and his severe justice devoted him to them. He has often declared to me that he considered our new Constitution as an experiment on the practicability of republican government, and with what dose of liberty man could be trusted for his own good; that he was determined the experiment should have a fair trial, and would lose the last drop of his blood in support of it. And these declarations he repeated to me the oftener and more pointedly, because he knew my suspicions of Colonel Hamilton's views, and probably had heard from him the same declarations which I had, to wit, "that the British constitution, with its unequal representation, corruption and other existing abuses, was the most perfect government which had ever been established on earth, and that a reformation of those abuses would make it an impracticable government." I do believe that General Washington had not a firm confidence in the durability of our government. He was naturally distrustful of men, and inclined to gloomy apprehensions; and I was ever persuaded that a belief that we must at length end in something like a British constitution, had some weight in his adoption of the ceremonies of levees, birthdays, pompous meetings with Congress, and other forms of the same character, calculated to prepare us gradually for a change which he believed possible, and to let it come on with as little shock as might be to the public mind.

These are my opinions of General Washington which I would vouch at the judgment seat of God, having been formed on an acquaintance of thirty years. I served with him in the Virginia legislature from 1769 to the Revolutionary war, and again, a short time in Congress, until he left us to take command of the army. During the war and after it we corresponded occasionally, and in the four years of my continuance in the office of Secretary of State, our intercourse was daily, confidential and cordial. After I retired from that office, great and malignant pains were taken by our federal monarchists, and not entirely without effect, to make him view me as a theorist, holding French principles of government, which would lead infallibly to licentiousness and anarchy. And to this he listened the more easily, from my known disapprobation of the British treaty. I never saw him afterwards, or these malignant insinuations should have been dissipated before his just judgment, as mists before the sun. I felt on his death, with my countrymen, that "verily a great man hath fallen this day in Israel."

QUESTIONS FOR DISCUSSION AND WRITING

1. Before you read Jefferson's portrait of George Washington you must have already had some impression of Washington — as an American revolutionary, a general, a president, or a person. What characteristics about Washington — defects as well as virtues — have you learned from Jefferson? Why do you think Jefferson

chose to include these characteristics? Write a short essay comparing and contrasting your impressions of Washington before and after you read Jefferson's piece.

2. Is Jefferson's portrait of Washington convincing? Does he provide any clue about how Washington developed? If so, what is it?

3. How does Jefferson establish his authority in this portrait of Washington? What is his tone of voice? Is it effective? In what ways?

4. Spend an hour or so in the library or online researching the sociohistorical background of this piece in order to answer these questions: Who was the original audience? In what situation was this piece written? To what purposes? Would Jefferson have written differently had the audience, rhetorical conditions, and purposes been different? Why or why not? What is the significance of Jefferson's commentary for today's readers?

PAUL STAROBIN
Misfit America

International policy expert and journalist Paul Starobin has reported from Russia, Central Asia, the Caucasus, the Middle East, and Western and Eastern Europe. Born in 1958, he grew up in Worcester, Massachusetts, graduated from Wesleyan University in Middletown, Connecticut (B.A., 1979), and earned a degree in International Relations from the London School of Economics and Political Science (M.S., 1981). After working for Congressional Quarterly *in Washington, D.C., and the John F. Kennedy School of Government at Harvard University, he served as a contributing editor of* Columbia Journalism Review. *His international expertise was gained during a stint as Moscow bureau chief for* Business Week *magazine (1999–2003), where he specialized in the former Soviet Union region, including Russia. Currently, he reports on international and domestic issues for* National Journal *and is a contributing editor of* The Atlantic Monthly.*

Although Americans like to analyze and interpret their national character, the international perspective that Starobin provides challenges such self-evaluations. "Misfit America" shows how far our national self-image can deviate from the image other nations have of us. Starobin's conclusions may be surprising, as he argues that our ideas of American uniqueness are often based on outdated assumptions.

Let's try to think of an original American tableau—the sort of scene, not happening elsewhere, that shows just how very different we are from all others. We might point to the wide-bottomed twelve-year-old, fresh from his double cheeseburger with fries, plunging into the neighborhood pool. Or to the pasty-faced workaholic, hunched over his computer in a lonely cubicle late at night. Death row comes to mind (few other countries routinely execute criminals), and so do images of people freely doing things that would land them in jail elsewhere. No other nation is as legally tolerant of Holocaust deniers, flag burners, and users of the N-word—not even our progenitor the United Kingdom.

But in a shrinking world it is getting harder to think of distinctive American scenes without invoking the Grand Canyon or Maine lobster. It is particularly striking how few of the cutting-edge things in American society are uniquely American. Male teenagers the world over ogle the same pornographic images on the Internet. Circles of friends swap digital photos on their mobile phones in London, Moscow, and Hong Kong just as they do in Los Angeles. Worried about our video-game addicts? It was a South Korean who recently dropped dead after playing the battle-simulation game StarCraft for nearly fifty hours straight. Much of what Americans may now think of as culturally or technologically novel has already happened elsewhere: the kind of WiFi system that San Francisco aims to establish in its public places already exists in Tokyo.

As for the things the United States did invent, such as the melting pot and popular democracy, they are being widely (if not always successfully) imitated. Consider, for example, Australia—a fast-growing democracy that has a higher percentage of immigrants than America, and is emerging as an important experiment in multiculturalism. The pro-democracy group Freedom House rates fifty-eight countries as comparable to the United States in political freedom.

If American culture and society are losing their historically distinctive cast, perhaps it is good news—at least for our foreign relations. America has long stood out from the crowd, in ways that seem to have complicated as much as helped our relationships with other states. If a global culture is slowly emerging—if our values have blended with others through some subtle osmosis—we might expect our international relations to become less fractious.

And yet, as a bruised Karen Hughes, undersecretary of state for public di- 5 plomacy, can attest, many foreigners not only view Americans as fundamentally different from themselves but also seem to despise the United States. And even though much of that antipathy stems from unpopular U.S. foreign policies, misgivings about America's culture figure prominently too—even among Europeans.

If American culture is less distinctive than it once was, it nevertheless remains unusual in several fundamental respects. Unfortunately, those unique qualities that have faded were usually attractive to foreigners; and many of those that remain are viewed today with discomfort or even disdain.

American exceptionalism, the idea (and the reality) that America is unique, is rooted in part in the populist values arising from the Jacksonian revolution of the 1820s. Frontiersmen battling both the Cherokee and the Boston banker, in a revolt of the muddy boots, drove the country westward and seemed to permanently dispel the Old World vision of America held by Alexander Hamilton and other Founding Fathers. In a speech extolling the wisdom of the "rich and well-born" in matters of governance Hamilton said, "The people are turbulent and changing; they seldom judge or determine right."

The Jacksonian spirit, the notion that every man is a king, still helps to set America apart. It is evident in the continuing popularity of referenda for settling contentious political issues in a number of states; in many Americans' devotion to gun ownership; and in the particular brand of kick-ass patriotism—sometimes accompanied by Confederate-flag waving—on display in the South, Andrew Jackson's home turf.

But much of the Jacksonian ethos has been lost, especially when it comes to the idea of America as an equal-opportunity society—a basic tenet of this creed and, for that matter, of the ideals set forth in the Declaration of Independence. Economic mobility has been declining for three decades: a study published by the Federal Reserve Bank of Boston in 2002 found that since the 1970s U.S. families have been significantly less likely to move up the income ladder, prompting questions that "go to the heart of our identity as a nation." (Indeed, by some measurements income mobility is now higher in Canada, France, and the United Kingdom.) One reason is that the children of better-off families begin their schooling with huge advantages over everyone else. The melting pot may still dissolve ethnic differences, but it has accommodated itself to class-based divisions.

These divisions are getting harder to overlook. In luxury-box America an afternoon at the ballpark is less often the class mixer it used to be. Jury duty may be the only experience left in which America's starched shirts and blue collars sit and sweat together—and it's mandatory. Just ask the have-not victims of Hurricane Katrina—the ones who were left to fend for themselves in the New Orleans Superdome—about a classless America. The disaster exposed the kind of squalid lives familiar to travelers to Haiti and readers of Graham Greene's harrowing tales of the Third World.

At the same time, Hamilton's ghost has returned in the form of a fixation on status and privilege. Although conspicuous consumption is not new in American life (we've long had our robber barons), it has spread to sectors of society that are supposed to embody an elevated public-spiritedness. Thus the Louis XIV-type behavior of American University's president Benjamin Ladner. At a New Year's dinner to celebrate the engagement of his son, paid for by the university, guests enjoyed truffles and caviar washed down by Cuvée Palmes d'Or champagne. The appalled trustees eventually ousted Ladner, but his actions speak to a larger phenomenon: as the late social critic Christopher Lasch wrote in the mid-1990s, a new and dandified aristocracy of talent has arisen in America. Its members are continuing to remove themselves from common life.

To appreciate the arc we have traveled, just recall the "secular Scripture of the United States," as the critic Harold Bloom has called *Leaves of Grass*. In 1855 Walt Whitman used the first poem in the collection, "Song of Myself," to celebrate America as a Jacksonian jumble of disparate types sharing the same adventure.

Of every hue and caste am I, of every rank and religion,
A farmer, mechanic, artist, gentleman, sailor, quaker,
Prisoner, fancy-man, rowdy, lawyer, physician, priest.
I resist any thing better than my own diversity,
Breathe the air but leave plenty after me,
And am not stuck up, and am in my place.

Whitman's poetry also evokes an innocence that once seemed to brand America as refreshingly different from jaded and war-prone Europe; but with America's climb to global prominence, that, too, has faded. Paradoxically, historians may one day look back on America's achievement of superpower status—on the arrival of the "American Century"—as the beginning of the end of America's claim to distinctiveness. The development of the atomic bomb, the landing of the first man on the moon: these were impressive technological achievements, but not marks of national character.

Power tends to make uniform demands on its aspirants. In America's case the imperatives of power—building the secretive infrastructure of the national-security state, transforming provincial, sleepy Washington into a fortresslike imperial capital, diminishing the role of Congress in war-making decisions—have eaten at the fiber of popular democracy.

For a time the Cold War masked this. The Soviet Union served as a nearly perfect foil for the United States. Stalin's monstrous crimes and the lesser evils of his Bolshevik brethren, not to mention the torpor and sheer inanity of so much of Soviet life, highlighted many of the better and more historically distinctive American qualities, including a commitment to human rights and personal liberty and an aversion to strong state controls. Those ideals may seem less vivid since the fall of the Soviet Union, while the realities of American power unchecked by any rival have been thrown into relief.

Unbridled power tends to breed arrogance and greed no matter who holds it. Perhaps the lesson is that a nation may seek to be either powerful or original, but it is difficult to be both.

So is America still an exceptional country? The answer is yes. Our remaining exceptionalism resides in our culture's striking combination of deep religious faith and nearly libertarian social permissiveness. These qualities don't rub elbows easily, and their twinned presence separates the United States from nearly all other countries, rich or poor.

It is well known that Americans are more deeply religious than the citizens of just about any other affluent post-industrial society. In a typical assessment the Pew Global Attitudes Project found that 59 percent of respondents in America answered the question "How important is religion in your life?" with "Very important," compared with 33 percent in the United Kingdom, 30 percent in Canada, 27 percent in Italy, 21 percent in Germany, 12 percent in Japan, and 11 percent in France. Across the past several decades religiosity has fallen steeply in all these places except America. And although Republicans are more likely than Democrats to say that religion is very important to them, religious belief is still far more intense in the blue states than in the rich, modern patches of ground outside the United States.

Of course, that doesn't mean the United States is unique in its religious character—just that it is unique among rich nations. In this regard America is more like, say, Chile and Turkey. We are also like those countries, and unlike Europe, in our attachment to certain conservative social values that tend to be associated with traditional religious conviction. Thus America, Chile, and Turkey—but generally not the countries of Western Europe—score high in surveys of such values as patriotism and the importance of family. These aspects of our culture are not vestigial; they are active and self-renewing.

Of course, America is culturally quite different from Chile and Turkey in other core respects. Unlike the inhabitants of those relatively poor countries, or of Egypt and Pakistan, most Americans are not preoccupied with economic survival. An emphasis on survival, economic or physical, tends to draw societies inward and make them fearful of outsiders and of change. Cultural conformity is often valued, and duty to family and community preferred over individual pursuits. Survivalist societies also tend to welcome state ownership of industry, and tend not to value educating women or protecting the environment. America has had survivalist periods, but since World War II survivalist values have held little sway. 20

Rather, Americans—like the Swedes, the French, the Australians, and other rich peoples—focus on the infinite variety of leisure and educational activities that our wealth permits us to pursue. The ascendant value in this domain is one that has always been dear to the American character: personal autonomy, the ability to do one's own thing.

Having a foot in both fixed traditionalism and permissive modernism makes us still something of an outlier nation—astride both camps and at home in neither.

Some may argue that the coincidence of interests, not values, is what counts in foreign relations. But values are interests of a kind; shared values might dispose other nations to help achieve America's purposes in the world, and deeply conflicting values might limit trust and cause other nations to ascribe the worst motives to the United States. Whatever "realists" may think, good will is important both in maintaining alliances and in avoiding crises.

In the current climate, marked by widespread ill will over the Iraq War, our unusual combination of values probably works against us: traditional societies tend to see us as more permissive than we actually are, and permissive societies as more traditional than we actually are. And in an age of shared global experiences American values may come to be defined as those that others don't want. The future may therefore look friendless and isolated for superpower America, even after George W. Bush leaves office.

Fortunately, however, things are not quite as bleak as they look. In a less contentious time America's unique blend of qualities might cause some societies to reach out to us. Every nation has at least one important value in common with multifaceted America—and the natural bond between the United States and some other powers, both established and rising, is stronger than one might think. A brief tour of the world, with values in mind, reveals a lot about our likely future relationships.

The Arab and broader Muslim world, the most problematic terrain today, seems a natural place to start. Since 9/11 there has been considerable debate over whether Arab resentment of the United States results from "who we are" or "what we do." Without a doubt, what we do has not always helped our position. In both the Arab world and other Muslim lands America is widely seen as unfaithful to its own founding principle of justice for all, largely because it favors Israel at the expense of Arabs, but also because of its prisoner-abuse scandals, including Abu Ghraib, which have come while the United States presses Egypt and other countries to improve their treatment of prisoners. The American double standard affords a wide opening for hateful tirades by Islamic radicals. Conceivably, America could narrow that opening by living up to the values it claims to cherish.

But changing our behavior would be unlikely to solve our problems in the Middle East; our permissive social values are in fundamental conflict with its traditional ones. This conflict will no doubt persist for a long time, as Edward S. Walker Jr., the president of the Middle East Institute, in Washington, explains. Over the course of four decades Walker has served as ambassador to several Middle Eastern states, including the United Arab Emirates. These are "societies that have just come out of the desert," he told me. "When I graduated from high school, in 1958, it was the first year that the UAE had a high school." This perspective, even more than Islamic culture, shapes their attitude toward American values.

The Arab world, already prone to distrust America as an imperial successor to the British, now tends to focus on—and sometimes fear—the export of American culture. Hollywood portrays Americans as alarmingly expressive and permissive in every corner of their lives, from the bedroom to the classroom. "We are seen as an agent of change—in some sense as attacking tradition," Walker says. This is particularly the case with respect to images of the "liberated" American woman. In Saudi Arabia, remember, women still are not allowed to drive.

As for China, a largely secular yet in many ways traditional, family-oriented society, the operative mode has been ambivalence. "Chinese images of America are positive and negative simultaneously," says David Shambaugh, who directs the China-policy program at George Washington University's Elliott School of International Affairs and wrote a 1991 book, *Beautiful Imperialist: China Perceives America, 1972–1990,* on this theme.

The balance of opinion these days, however, leans negative. In a June 2005 Pew Global Attitudes survey only 42 percent of the Chinese gave America an overall favorable rating, though 70 percent viewed Americans as inventive. They liked America better back in the 1980s.

In part this negative rating represents a communitarian society's opinion of America as distressingly individualistic. "They have had an increasing amount of contact with the United States, and that contact has not increased their admiration," Shambaugh says. "They perceive racism, crime, inequality, neglect of the elderly, and many other negative aspects of American society."

China's disenchantment could have long-term consequences. The Chinese already seem to be shifting their sights away from America and toward Europe as a place worth befriending. Since Europe and China announced their "strategic partnership" to bring about a multipolar world, in 2003, Europe has become China's No. 1 trade partner. And many of the Chinese students who might have flocked to the United States now get their degrees in Europe, where tuition is cheaper and visas are easier to come by. China may adopt elements of our capitalist model, but it is unlikely to come to view itself as our protégé.

America's religiosity, which helps frame our view of the Chinese, is not a major factor in their view of us. Western Europeans, however, are apt to see America's religious values as a defining mark of character—and not a positive one. Respondents to the Pew survey in France, the Netherlands, Great Britain, and Germany think we are too religious. Many Europeans view the United States as a kind of crusader nation, wreaking havoc in the world. That picture is a caricature, and Europeans—whose media have informed them that blue America is nearly as big as red America, and that the war in Iraq has become unpopular in the States—undoubtedly know it. Yet they fixate on their differences with us, and they are faithful, sometimes gleeful, chroniclers of every American deviance from the Jacksonian creed, such as our growing economic inequality and the corruption of our political system by big money.

But such criticism masks the convergence of American and European attitudes on issues of personal autonomy, including abortion, euthanasia, and gay rights. And though desert Arabs may obsess about sexually (and professionally) empowered American women, the modern women's movement is a transatlantic production, as much Simone de Beauvoir as Betty Friedan. Even on the death penalty, a long-standing bone of contention between the United States and Europe, America is moving in a European direction, as the Supreme Court cites European precedent in decisions curtailing capital punishment for juveniles and the mentally retarded. There is still no global region with which America has more in common than Europe.

Europe emphasizes differences over our similarities because its perspective is warped by envy, which has been evident since the reports of the earliest European visitors to America; the calm, clear-eyed Alexis de Tocqueville is a notable exception. Historically, the most envious have been not the French but the English—which should not be surprising, since we emerged from their womb only to defeat and then to surpass them. (Typical in this regard were Frances Trollope and her novelist son, Anthony, who on their visits to the new nation took issue with virtually every aspect of the American "persona," including the demand of the "adult infant" for "fresh ice in his water.")

Europe's envy of America is probably forever, but it isn't and never has been an insurmountable obstacle to amicable relations. America is now in part being punished for the sin of re-electing George W. Bush; presumably there will be some forgiveness if post-Bush America is governed by a less easily cartooned figure.

A variant of the envy distortion can be found in post-Soviet Russia, a humiliated land now gripped by survival values. As a foreign correspondent I was based in Moscow for four years, from 1999 to 2003, and I was surprised at how the Cold War seemed to live on for so many Russians. Rich, powerful America is resented, and perhaps not so much disliked as distrusted. In the Pew survey 52 percent of Russians gave the United States a favorable opinion rating—slightly lower than the British but higher than the Dutch, the Germans, or the Spanish. Yet Russians are wary of U.S. efforts to exploit the Soviet collapse, and of the expansion of NATO to include former Soviet satellites.

If Russia can put the Cold War in the past, the two countries could build a genuine friendship—one based on something more than Russia's oil and America's interest in consuming it. Religious sensibility is returning to Russia; one of the more intriguing trends in post-Soviet Russia is the revival of the Orthodox Church, whose culturally conservative outlook is something like that of America's religious right. The ordinary Russian shares the ordinary American's fear of Islamic terrorism. And the most enterprising Russian businessmen I met were fans of freewheeling American-style capitalism over the more state-regulated European variety.

If Western Europeans and Muslims harp on America's failure to measure up to its ideals, others, rather amazingly, seem to regard us as arguably more innocent and selfless, truer to the best of the Jacksonian spirit, than we actually are. Indeed, the last, heroic view of America is retained in countries that have chafed under other imperialists and apprehend America as different and better. That perspective is especially prevalent in the former Soviet empire—in places such as Lithuania and Georgia. In his speech last May in Tbilisi, Georgia's capital, Bush was raucously cheered by tens of thousands, much as John F. Kennedy was in his iconic "*Ich bin ein Berliner*" address in West Berlin, in June of 1963.

In such countries, I've found, discussion of America's values inevitably starts 40 with a rant against cruel, conniving, supercilious Moscow. Reform-oriented elites can relate to America's founding in a rebellion against a colonial power; they read the U.S. Constitution and the *Federalist Papers* without irony. Indeed, leaders such as Georgia's president, Mikhail Saakashvili—the maker of the country's pro-democracy Rose Revolution in 2003—proudly advertise their connections to Washington insiders. When I visited Saakashvili in Tbilisi before the Rose Revolution, I saw on his wall framed photographs of his meetings with Ted Kennedy and other Washington figures. There is undoubtedly an element of geopolitical calculation in small Georgia's eager alliance with America, but the admiration for U.S. political institutions is genuine.

A romance between the Georgias of the planet and America is nice, but is that the best we can hope for? Are we destined to be disliked, resented, envied, or feared by all the world's larger powers? No. One very large power has values remarkably well aligned with ours: India, a democracy of more than a billion people, an economic titan in the making, a nuclear state. In the Pew survey 71 percent of Indians registered a favorable opinion of both the United States and Americans—highest on both counts among the sixteen foreign publics surveyed. When asked where they would go "to lead a good life," only Indians named America as their top choice. (The Poles picked Great Britain, and the British picked Australia, as did the Canadians, the Dutch, and the Germans.) A survey-high 58 percent of Indians—compared with 35 percent of Chinese—said they regarded Americans as honest.

India was a reliable ally of the Soviet Union in the Cold War. Cynics may say that its heart has warmed toward America merely in response to the influx of dollars from outsourcing arrangements. But as Chinese attitudes indicate, dollars don't necessarily buy affection. So why do Indians like America and Americans? I asked Miriam Rajkumar, an Indian citizen who is a South Asia and Middle East nonproliferation analyst at the Carnegie Endowment for International Peace, in Washington. "The Indian public has always been enchanted with the United States," she said. "Many families have someone out here who has done well" in fields like science and high technology.

Of course, the same can be said of other immigrant groups. But perhaps India also thinks well of America, Rajkumar suggested, because it understands from its own history how important an ideal like freedom of religion is. Indians tend to be highly religious, even more so than Americans—and, like Americans, they live in a multicultural, democratic federal state. Moreover, India has Britain, not America, to blame for its trials under colonialism. And America's post-9/11 rise to the challenge of battling Muslim extremism aligns with the long resistance of India to what it views as a Pakistan-inspired Islamic insurgency.

Another element may be at work as well. In international relations—as sometimes in personal ones—too long an acquaintance can be an irritant. But except for some testy episodes in the 1970s in which America sided with Pakistan, the United States and India have little history to mar the honeymoon atmosphere. Indians, unlike those hectoring Europeans and smoldering Chinese, seem content to take America as it is, without judgment. This is a relief. As much as we want to be liked, we are happiest when we are allowed to be our natural selves. In that we are exactly like everyone else.

QUESTIONS FOR DISCUSSION AND WRITING

1. In the first section of this essay, Starobin contrasts both the "Jacksonian spirit," the notion that "every man is a king" (paragraph 8), and the "equal-opportunity society" (paragraph 9) with current American social realities.

What are the facts that contradict America's Jacksonian identity, according to Starobin?

2. How have "the imperatives of power . . . eaten at the fiber of popular democracy" according to Starobin (paragraph 14)? In what way did the Cold War mask this change?

3. Starobin takes the reader on a "brief tour of the world" beginning halfway through the essay (paragraph 25). Why does he present this international perspective? What does the reader learn on this "tour of the world"? How is the tour meant to reinforce the points made in the previous section of the essay (see questions 1 and 2)?

4. Starobin asks the question, "Are we destined to be disliked, resented, envied, or feared by all the world's larger powers?" (paragraph 41). One of the underlying assumptions of his essay is that Americans should care about what the rest of the world thinks of America. One example he uses to support this idea is his claim that Chinese "disenchantment" with American culture has led China to strengthen its ties with Europe in preference to the United States (paragraph 32). With a classmate, preferably someone whose culture or nationality differs from your own, write an essay explaining why Americans should, or should not, change their behavior in order to attract trade or secure other benefits of international acceptance.

5. Investigate foreign opinions about America's position or behavior on a current issue with international consequences. Choose one or two examples of strong approval or disapproval, as reported in foreign newspapers and, perhaps, the Pew Global Attitudes Survey. Explain who expressed the opinion, why, and whether you believe that the opinion was justified.

DEIRDRE N. McCLOSKEY

Yes, Ma'am

Deirdre N. McCloskey was born Donald McCloskey in 1942, in Ann Arbor, Michigan. As Donald, McCloskey earned undergraduate and graduate degrees in economics at Harvard University and became a professor at the University of Chicago and the University of Iowa as well as a scholar noted for taking a sometimes controversial cross-disciplinary approach that combined economic theory and practice with history, philosophy, and rhetoric. In the mid-1990s, after years of internal struggle, McCloskey—who had been married for three decades and had two children— began the process of a gender change, resulting in complete gender reassignment surgery in 1996 and a new identity as Deirdre N. McCloskey. Now a professor at the University of Illinois at Chicago and at Erasmus Universiteit in the Netherlands, McCloskey has published a second edition of The Rhetoric of Economics *(1998, originally published in 1985),* If You're So Smart: The Narrative of Economic*

Expertise *(1998), and* How to Be Human—*though an* Economist *(2001); continues to co-edit the highly regarded series* The Rhetoric of Inquiry; *and has expanded her scholarly work into the field of gender studies. Her highly personal* Crossing: A Memoir *appeared in 1999 to much critical acclaim.*

Clients contemplating a sex change are generally required by their physicians to live life as a member of the opposite sex for a year or more before gender reassignment surgery, and even after surgery they must continue to adapt physically to their new identity. In the following chapter from Crossing, *McCloskey describes her early attempts to assume a physical identity that strangers would accept as that of a woman. She also considers the gestural differences between women and men and the hostility directed at those perceived to be cross-gendered.*

It's hard to pass. You just try it, Dee would say. I mean really try to pass as the opposite gender, not just put on a joke dress and a lampshade hat for the Lions picnic. You'll be surprised at how many gender clues there are and how easy it is to get them wrong. Scores of them, natural and unnatural, genetic and socially constructed.

No, hundreds. Women stand and sit at angles. Men offer their hands to shake. Women put their hands to their chests when speaking of themselves. Men barge through. Women look frequently at nonspeaking participants in a conversation. Men don't look at each other when talking. Women carry papers and books clutched to their midriffs, men balance things on their hips. Women smile at other women when entering their space. Men never smile at male strangers. Women put their hands on their hips with fingers pointing backward. Men use wide gestures. Women frequently fold their hands together in their laps. Men walk from their shoulders, women from their hips. And on and on.

Dee watched other women in her culture for characteristic gestures and practiced them on the spot. **The way the hands gesture together, as though in a little dance. The way the fingers lie up the arm when the arms are crossed. Standing with feet in a ballet pose. Pulling your hair from under a coat just put on.** (It was some time before her hair was long enough to make that feminine gesture useful.) Years into her transition she could amuse herself in a dull moment in a mall or airport by breaking down other women's gestures and trying them out. Like square dancing: hundreds of calls.

Rest one elbow on the back of the other hand, laid horizontally across your middle, the free hand stretching vertically to frame your face from the bottom, palm out. In touching your face, which you should do frequently, hold the hand in a graceful pose. For situations such as display at the dinner table, learn the hand pose used in ballet—fingers arched and separated, middle finger almost touching the thumb. Pinky up, but not too much, since it's an obvious parody of the ladylike. Overacting evokes the theatrical tradition of drag. Try to create a somewhat splayed effect with the fingers, angled up, instead of masculine cupping. When shaking hands—don't be the first to offer—use no strong grip, and place your hand sideward into the other person's. Check your hair frequently. Play idly with your jewelry. Check your clothing (a set of gestures that women's clothes require more often than men's, or else you stride out of the ladies' room with the back of your skirt up around your behind). Always stand more on one foot than the other. Stand with your legs crossed (a youngish gesture, this). Never stand manlike with feet parallel and legs spread wide. Angle your feet when you stop at the corner before crossing. Rest with hands together, not sprawled all over like a man's. When sitting cross your legs, either knee over knee angled to one side (never lower leg crossed horizontally over the knee, like the Greek boy in the statue removing a splinter) or to one side beneath the chair ankle over ankle. Never slouch when you sit. Stick your rear end solidly into the back of the chair, and never stretch your legs out, crossed at the ankles. Keep your knees together when you sit—"close the gates of hell" used to be the misogynist joke about it—which is easier if your knees are naturally angled inward, as girls' and especially women's are. If your feet are not crossed when sitting, keep your legs together from feet to knees. "Take up less space" is one formula; another is "keep your wrists loose," and still another "keep your elbows close to your body," this one imitating the effect of a female angle in the elbow, a piece of biology. But the formulas are hard to apply, like formal grammatical rules. Imitate, imitate, the way girls learn it. Deirdre was congratulated three years into full time: "Last year your motions were a little abrupt; now they are convincingly feminine." The gesture language is probably imitated with the same ease and at the same age as the spoken language, and like the spoken language it is hard to learn as an adult. Little girls act different from little boys, independent of the slight structural differences in their bodies. By age ten many girls even know the secret smile.

Much of behavior is gendered. A lot of it is culturally specific and variable 5 from person to person. European men cross their legs in a way that in America is coded as feminine. American soldiers in Vietnam would sneer at what they read as femininity in their Vietnamese allies and enemies: "They're all queer, you know." Mediterranean and Middle Eastern women make broader gestures, not the little dance of hands that upper-middle-class women in America use. The gender clues figure in any culture in an abundance that only a gender crosser or Dustin Hoffman preparing for *Tootsie* can grasp.

Of course if you are *aiming* to be funny then you want to be read, even if you are skillful at giving appropriate gender clues. Passing is not at issue. The Australian comedian who has developed the character "Dame Edna" is good at it. Without a leer or a nudge, he simply *is* the absurd Dame and sometimes spends hours in character, yet of course his audience knows. Miss Piggy of the Muppets is similar. She is gloriously who she is, yet everyone knows it's cross-speaking— her voice is always that of a man using falsetto. Getting read is part of the joke.

If you are not trying to be funny, you do not want to get read. Really, you don't. A sincere but detected attempt to jump the gender border from male to female—and no joking about it—creates anxiety in men, to be released by laughter if they can handle it or by a length of steel pipe if they can't. A 1997 survey claimed that 60 percent of cross-gendered people had been assaulted. Deirdre knew a gender crosser who had been beaten by four young men outside a bar even in peaceful Iowa City. The director of Gender PAC noted that "RuPaul is funny so long as she stays in a television studio. But try walking to the subway and she'll be a grease spot on the sidewalk before she makes it home." (If a female-to-male crosser was read by men maybe he would be regarded as cute, or rational: after all, it's rational to prefer to be a man, isn't it? Like the daily prayer by Orthodox Jewish men thanking God for not making them women. On the other hand, Brandon Teena, a pre-op female-to-male thief outed by the Falls City, Nebraska, police department was raped, complained about it to the police, who did nothing, and the next week in 1993 was murdered. Not by women.)

The anxiety is weirdly strong. A standard routine in the movies is that two men are forced to sleep with each other by circumstances (oh, sure), and then one of them dreams that he's sleeping with a woman. The other man, horrified by the amorous advances, rejects them violently, and the awakened dreamer is ashamed. The routine enacts over and over again the male anxiety about being homosexual, much less being a woman, and the violent reaction the anxiety arouses. With this threat of violence in mind, Donald's sister had given him her own pepper spray. The pepper spray, though, wouldn't be much good against a steel pipe.

Women who read a crossdresser are not violent, but frightened and indignant. Who is this guy? What's he up to? Deirdre knew from being a woman on trains late at night in Holland or walking by Dutch cafés in the summertime or living later in the less demonstrative but more dangerous environment of America that women have daily experiences of men in fact being up to something, often something sexual, often enough something dangerous. At first it was flattering, the knocking on windows of the *eetcafé* as she went by, the propositions to come into the jazz club and have a drink. Then it was tedious or frightening. Women experience dangerous men all day long and are on the alert. The alertness is not male bashing, merely prudence in the company of people with greater upper-body strength and the inclination to use it, intoxicated by lethal fantasies about What She Really Wants. Women who read a gender crosser are putting her in this category of dangerous men. To be read by women is utterly demoralizing. After all, the gender crosser is trying to join the women, to pass as one, and instead they are treating her like a man, maybe nuts, probably dangerous, definitely another one of those bloody *men.*

On all counts it is better for a gender crosser to pass rapidly to the other side, and making the crossing rapid ought to be the purpose of medical intervention, such as facial surgery, and social intervention, such as counseling on gender clues. Women acquainted with a gender crosser sometimes think of her interest in facial surgery as vanity. Natural-born women have no problem passing as women. "You're silly to want operations," says a woman out of a face with pointed chin, no browridges, high cheekbones. Deirdre's mother declared that getting electrolysis, which she regarded as merely temporary, was "vain." But a nose job or a facelift or electrolysis that will make a gender crosser passable will also make her less likely to be scorned or raped or killed—at any rate at no more than the shocking rates for genetic women. Deirdre knew a not very passable gender crosser in tolerant Holland who had been raped three times. It is merely prudent to pass.

Some radical feminists object to gender crossing. They complain of the gender crosser that she (when they have the ruth to call her "she") is adopting oppressive stereotypes about women and therefore contributing to society's discrimination. The gender crosser, they claim, is pulling women back to the 1950s, white gloves and pillbox hats, lovely garden parties, and a *Leave It to Beaver* vision of a woman's life.

There is little truth in the stereotype argument. The crossphobe who uses it ordinarily doesn't know any gender crossers. A gender crosser with a job or career outside the home tries to keep it and does not in practice dissolve into a 1950s heaven of full-time cookie baking and teatime gossip. Far from becoming passive and stereotypically feminine, the gender crossers Deirdre knew often retained much of their masculine sides. The crossphobes mix up gender crossers with drag queens or female impersonators, whose shtick is indeed a parody of women—sometimes demeaning and stereotypical, though often enough loving and amusing. In 1958 the sociologist Harold Garfinkel described a gender crosser named Agnes. Latter-day crossphobes attack Agnes as "displaying rigidly traditional ideas of what a woman is" or having "stereotypical views of femininity" or "constructing an extremely narrow and constricted view of womanhood." Agnes was nineteen, a typist, at the height of the feminine mystique. But no allowances: "I don't support you in your effort to have an operation, because you have stereotypical views of what it means to be a woman." Unlike all the other nineteen-year-old typists in 1958. (Agnes had the operation, and was fine, because Garfinkel and a psychiatrist named Stoller did support her.)

A gender crosser trying to be a woman must reproduce enough of the characteristic gestures to escape being read, and often—especially in voice—this is difficult. It becomes second nature, and a comfort to oneself even when alone. But if you fail you are classed with people stereotyping women. Or murdered. The crossphobe radical feminists are allies in hatred with the gay-bashing murderers of Matthew Shephard.

The complaint about stereotyping will be delivered by a genetic woman whose every gesture and syllable is stereotypically feminine. At seminars in which Deirdre was attacked for stereotyping she would reply with the same stereotypically feminine gestures or turns of phrase just used by the crossphobe—who had been practicing them since she was a little girl. This was Garfinkel's point, that gender is something "done," a performance, not an essence springing from genitals or chromosomes. Deirdre would say, "Of course I [putting her hand to her chest in the feminine way of referring to oneself, just used by the crossphobe] would never [doing a deprecating double flap with her hands in the style of American middle-class women] want to damage women by *stereotyping* [raising her voice in the falsetto of emphasis stereotypical of women, for instance the crossphobe attacking the genuineness of gender crossers]."

The passing worked better, slowly, each month, if she dressed carefully and   15
worked at it. Each little acceptance delighted her. The signal was being called
"mevrouw" in Holland, "ma'am" in America, "madame" in France, "madam" in
England. *Yes: call me madam.*

She is getting up to leave a Dutch tram at Oostzeedijk, intent on how to
make the transfer to the subway. *Let's see: across there and down. Remember to
watch for the bicycles.* The tram has almost stopped and she is pressing the exit
button when she hears finally through her English thoughts and the haze of a foreign tongue, *"Mevrouw! Mevrouw!" It's me they're calling,* she thinks. *Oh. I've
left a package.* She smiles in thanks and snatches up the package, slipping out the
door as it closes, still smiling. They see her as "ma'am."

At the grocery store she is accosted by a woman giving out samples of a
Dutch delicacy. It doesn't look very good. The woman babbles at Dee in Dutch,
and Dee catches only the blessed "mevrouw." She smiles and shakes her head no
thank you and pushes the cart toward the canned goods.

In May in Paris with an economist friend, Nancy, who is visiting there for a
year, she walks out of a hat store, wearing the lovely lace floppy number just purchased. An elegant Frenchman goes by and says with a smile, "Un beau chapeau,
madame!" Deirdre's French is poor, and she is still wondering if he could have
said what she thought he had said when he politely repeats it in English over his
shoulder as he walks on, "A beautiful hat, madame!" She would say when telling
the story, "I could have kissed him. If he had proposed, I would have married
him on the spot. Even though he was shorter."

A month later she wears the hat (which can be worn only in Paris or at special events) to a daylong concert of classical music in the park in Rotterdam. Sitting at luncheon on the grass with some members of her women's group, she
feels particularly lovely. A Dutchman passes by and makes in Dutch the same remark the Frenchman had made, "A beautiful hat, mevrouw!"

The women's group meets at a restaurant in Rotterdam. It is a year since   20
she abandoned the male role. The waiter asks the *"dames"* (DAH-mez) what
they want, including Deirdre without notice or comment. *One of the dames. Yes.*

QUESTIONS FOR DISCUSSION AND WRITING

1. In her opening paragraphs, McCloskey observes a number of "gender clues,"
   distinctions between the physical behavior and gestures of women and men. Are
   these distinctions borne out by your own observations?

2. At the end of paragraph 4, McCloskey claims that children early on learn gendered behavior through imitation. In paragraph 5, she makes the further point
   that gender-identified behavior differs from culture to culture. What do these
   ideas suggest about her views on gender?

3. McCloskey writes that both men and women respond negatively when they detect in someone a "sincere . . . attempt to jump the gender border from male to female," but in different ways (paragraphs 7–9). How does she account for these different negative reactions?

4. McCloskey refers to herself throughout this essay in the third person—as "she," "Dee," "Deirdre," and even "Donald" (her pre-crossing name). Why might she have chosen to do this? What is its effect on you as a reader?

5. "Some radical feminists object to gender crossing," McCloskey writes at the beginning of paragraph 11. Starting with McCloskey's elaboration of this point, write an essay in which you explore your views about gendered behavior, as described in paragraphs 4–5, and gender stereotypes such as the female homemakers and garden clubbers and the male breadwinners and sports enthusiasts depicted in popular films and television.

BRIEF TAKES ON CREATIVITY: INTERVIEWS

"How did she think of that?" A spark jumps the gap between this *idea and* that *idea, bringing the two together, leading in a flash to something entirely new. We value creativity in part because it is so hard for us to understand it. These brief interviews with creative people offer insight into that mysterious process. Welty talks about where she writes (as does Mayes) and, like Trillin, she identifies who is and is not fair game to exploit for creative purposes. By telling us about his childhood interest in fooling around with electronics, Wozniak reveals how his contributions to inventing the PC grew out of that early passion. And, although the myth of the genius working alone persists, Al Gore explains how creativity is often a social act, a negotiation among parties.*

ALICE WALKER

Eudora Welty: An Interview

*Alice Walker is a Pulitzer Prize-winning novelist (*The Color Purple, *1982); she also writes poetry and nonfiction. Eudora Welty (1909–2001) was a multiple winner of the O. Henry Award for Short Stories, and received the Pulitzer Prize for* The Optimist's Daughter *(1973) and the National Medal for Literature in 1979.*

AW *[Alice Walker]:* Did you think there was anything *wrong* with Mississippi [in terms of race] in those days, when you were young? Did you see a way in which things might change?

EW *[Eudora Welty]:* Well, I could tell when things were wrong with *people*, and when things happened to individual people, people that we knew or knew of, they were very real to me. It was the same with my parents. I felt their sympathy, I guess it guided mine, when they responded to these things in the same way. And I think this is the way real sympathy *has* to start—from direct feeling for something present and known. People are first and last individuals, and I don't think of them in the mass when I feel for them most.

AW: How does living in Jackson affect your writing?

EW: It's where I live and look around me—it's my piece of the world—it teaches me. Also as a domestic scene it's completely familiar and self-explanatory. It's not everything, though—it's just a piece of everything, that happens to be my sample. It lets me alone to work as I like. It's full of old friends with whom I'm happy to be. And I'm not stuck, either, not compelled to stay here—I'm free to leave when I feel like it, which makes me love it more, I suppose.

AW: What do your friends think of your writing? Do they read it? Do any of them ever creep into your fiction? 5

EW: Oh yes. They do read it. But they don't creep in. I never write about people that I know. I don't want to, and couldn't if I did want to. I work entirely in terms of the imagination — using, of course, bits and pieces of the real world along with the rest.

AW: Do you write every day?

EW: No, I don't write every day — I write only when I'm in actual work on a particular story. I'm not a notebook keeper. Sustained time is what I fight for, would probably sell my soul for — it's so hard to manage that. I'd like to write a story from beginning to end right through without having to stop. Where I write is upstairs in my bedroom.

AW: In bed?   10

EW: Oh no, I write at a desk. I have a long room with six big windows in it, and a desk and typewriter at one end.

AW: What does it overlook? A garden? Trees?

EW: It overlooks the street. I like to be aware of the world going on while I'm working. I think I'd get claustrophobic sitting in front of a blank wall with life cut off from view.

AW: Do you have a "Philosophy of Life"? Some pithy saying that you quote to yourself when you seem inundated with troubles?

EW: No. I have work in place of it, I suppose. My "philosophy" is like the rest of my thinking — it comes out best in the translation of fiction. I put what I think about people and their acts in my stories. Of course back of it all there would have to be honesty.

AW: Many modern writers don't seem overly concerned with it.   15

EW: It's noticeable. Truth doesn't seem to be the thing they're getting at, a good deal of the time.

KENNETH A. BROWN

Steve Wozniak: Inventing the PC

Steve Wozniak is one of the co-founders of Apple, Inc. He is author with Gina Smith of iWoz: From Computer Geek to Cult Icon: How I Invented the Personal Computer, Co-Founded Apple, and Had Fun Doing It *(2006).*

INTERVIEWER: Was there anyone in your background who really encouraged you to become an inventor?

SW: Tom Swift,[1] no question. He made it a good thing to invent and be a scientist. Winning science fairs at an early age or even entering science fairs was

---

[1] "The *Tom Swift, Jr.* books were a series about an inventor that was popular when I was growing up in the 1950s. They were sold alongside *Nancy Drew* and *The Hardy Boys*. I can recall always waiting until a new one I hadn't read yet came out!" — Steve Wozniak

also important. If you enter a science fair and do something well, you get a lot of positive feedback from parents and teachers and the like. In your head, being an inventor becomes a good thing.

My father also gave me some direction because he was an electrical engineer. When the right times came around, he helped me with electronics projects. He would stand at a blackboard for no reason at all and teach me about transistors. He helped me learn things that weren't even taught in school. He also gave me some of the first books on computer programming, even though he didn't program himself. So, he influenced me a lot and gave me direction. I kind of wanted to be an engineer like my father.

INTERVIEWER: What do you consider your first invention? Was it the Apple?

SW: Not really. Whenever you solve a problem, whether it's mathematics in 5 school or an electronics project, in a way you're inventing. Before I worked on the Apple, I worked on some electronics problems that were really kind of inventions. I built an adder-subtracter in the eighth grade, and I solved some circuit problems such as how to build a gate with two diodes. The two diodes wouldn't work, so I had to put transistors in there as well.

While I was in college, I invented my own version of a blue box.[2] In the three years just before the Apple, I totally designed a video terminal and a version of the video game Pong, which influenced some of the people at Atari who wanted to hire me. I also designed a movie system for hotel-room televisions back in 1970. Because I was interested in electronics, I was doing a lot of projects on the side even though I was working at Hewlett-Packard as an engineer on calculators.

INTERVIEWER: Did you see the first Apple computers as filling a need or creating one?

SW: Filling a need. I knew I needed a personal computer. I was lucky. Back in those days, I didn't have to understand a market of several million; nobody had a computer. All I had to understand was one person: myself.

I needed a computer for my work at Hewlett-Packard to calculate a few solutions for designing gates and registers for the calculating chips. I even knew a few programs I wanted to write in BASIC. And, I also wanted to play the type of video games that send text to you and you type text back. It says, "I smell a wumpus. You're getting farther away." You type back, "Go left." That sort of thing. It was hard to visualize those sorts of games until the Apple II.

INTERVIEWER: The early days of Apple have been described as a "ride on a rocket." 10 Were you ever surprised at the way the personal computer market took off when the Apple was introduced?

SW: No, never once. I designed these computers to show off to my friends; I didn't have any plan to start a company. I knew from my electronics background that computers were going to sell at least a million units, even

---

[2] Electronic device that generates tones to "fool" and trigger telephone circuits. The original blue box was built by John Draper, alias Captain Crunch, who served a prison term for using his invention.

when they had sold only twenty thousand. I used to have a ham radio license, and I knew there was a large market for ham radios. And I also knew there were more computer people than ham radio operators.

In the beginning it wasn't a big shock. It happened so gradually that, by the time the market became as big as it is today, we already were very successful and already had a big, successful company. It was then that the personal computer industry went much further than we thought. Instead of being a $2 billion industry it was maybe an $8 billion industry.

I didn't think we would sell as many as we did or that the industry would become as big as it is today. If I had, I would have based all the decisions on building a product that consumers would like and that we could sell. And, we probably would have made the wrong decisions technically and built the wrong product.

DAVID ROBERTS

An Interview with Accidental Movie Star Al Gore

From 1993 to 2001 Al Gore was the forty-first vice president of the United States. He is also known for his work to stop global climate change. His lecture on this topic was made into a movie, An Inconvenient Truth, *in 2006.*

DR: Did you have direct control over the editing of the movie? Or did you leave it in the hands of the creative team?

AG: It was a collaborative process. I want to be careful in answering, because I don't want to step on the creative role that the moviemakers played. It's their vision. It's their movie, particularly Davis Guggenheim's. But at every step he asked me, what about leaving this in or taking this out? We had a mutual agreement on every aspect of that; there was not a single point where we had any serious disagreement at all.

DR: There's a lot of debate right now over the best way to communicate about global warming and get people motivated. Do you scare people or give them hope? What's the right mix?

AG: I think the answer to that depends on where your audience's head is. In the United States of America, unfortunately we still live in a bubble of unreality. And the Category 5 denial is an enormous obstacle to any discussion of solutions. Nobody is interested in solutions if they don't think there's a problem. Given that starting point, I believe it is appropriate to have an overrepresentation of factual presentations on how dangerous it is, as a predicate for opening up the audience to listen to what the solutions are, and how hopeful it is that we are going to solve this crisis.

FRANCES MAYES

Interview: On Writing Under the Tuscan Sun

Frances Mayes is the author of four books about Tuscany, including the best-selling memoir Under the Tuscan Sun *(1996). She has also written six books of poetry.*

Q: You say in your book that when you wrote the last line of *Under the Tuscan Sun*, you wrote the first line of *Bella Tuscany*. What do you mean?

FM: When I finished *Under the Tuscan Sun* I was in the beginning of my life in Italy. When I ended that book, I wanted to continue to write about the place —such a powerful landscape—and I was just falling under its spell. I sensed early that Italy is endless; five years later, I'm still at the beginning.

Q: You often say how you feel more at home in Italy than anywhere else. Why is that?

FM: I thought I was strange to feel this way. Since I've met so many people who read *Under the Tuscan Sun*, I've found out that lots of people feel this way. It's complicated but feels so very easy. The warmth of the people, the human scale of the towns, the robust food, yes, but I've begun to think, too, that it's the natural connection with art, the natural exposure to beauty on a day-to-day basis. This concept is a big focus of *Bella Tuscany*. We all know the Italians have more fun. This makes us feel at home, or rather returned to a sense of play, which we may not have experienced so fully since childhood.

Q: What do you think Americans need to learn from Italians about living?   5

FM: Well, I could write a book on this subject. In fact, I have! A few quick things— work does not have to govern life. So many of us are work-obsessed. I've loved experiencing how Italian friends take the time to enjoy family and friends, how they pursue their interests with so much pleasure, how they enter the community life of the piazza. I'm fascinated by the importance of the table, the central role it plays—and, of course, by the generosity and abundance of what's served forth, with all that is implied by those values. People of all ages mix easily; we separate people according to age too much. It's absurd.

Q: Why does Italy inspire so many comparisons in your mind with the South, where you grew up?

FM: Fitzgerald, Georgia, where I grew up, is a very small place. Everyone knew everyone. In Cortona people say, "Neighbors know what you're going to do even before you do." I rather like that. Everyone is someone, someone special. More mysteriously, I feel an emotional affinity with the gentle green landscape of Tuscany, punctuated by cypress trees and hill towns. And I feel the same affinity with the very different south Georgia landscape of black water swamps, pine forests, big rivers, and palmettos.

Q: How have the people of Cortona reacted to your book?

FM: They seem so pleased! They're immensely proud of Cortona's history, art, and beauty and, I think, are thrilled that an American tried to express a love for the place. I was honored a few years ago to have been made an honorary citizen of the town. They had a formal ceremony with ribbons and swords and music. Uniformed policemen—no uniforms like Italian uniforms!— escorted me up the grand townhall steps. The terror was that I had to give a ten-minute speech in Italian to the gathered citizens, dignitaries, and TV cameras. After I did that, I decided I could do anything.

CALVIN TRILLIN

Writing about Family

American journalist, humorist, and novelist Calvin Trillin is best known for his writings about food and eating.

CT: And again, to do a book on my father as if he were Winston Churchill and I were an eminent historian gathering all the material together—it just wouldn't have worked out. I think the material controls the way you write it.

Q: Do you feel it would be harder to write about your mother?

CT: No. I got along fine with my mother. She just didn't have the same sort of impact on my life as my father did. She obviously went along with this grand plan, but I don't think with a song on her lips. I think she would have been happy to see me close to home, with a decent job and behaving myself. She wasn't as imposing a figure in my life as my father was. Also, she didn't do things like he did—write poetry on the menus, collect curses and stuff. She was a much more conventional person than my father.

A lot of writers make a life's project of writing about their relatives even when the stories aren't that dramatic.

Writers are always desperate to find something to write about, so they'll   5 write about anything they can get away with. I've used my own family in writing—as opposed to what a social scientist would call my family of origin. I've written about them, but they each have a persona—they are not them. Alice really is a more sensible person than I am, as she's presented in the books about eating. But when people meet her, they expect her to be a nutritionist in sensible shoes, hair in a bun. Once I was giving a speech here and I said that, and someone asked, "Is she in the audience?" and I said, "Yes." She asked, "Would she stand?" So Alice stood, and then she held up this $30,000 Italian shoe to show everybody that she did not have sensible shoes. But that's quite different than writing about her, really, and I haven't actually done that.

And my girls, I wrote about them by name until they were about eight, and then I decided they were getting too old; it would be embarrassing. Even though I wasn't obviously writing about any of their problems. I just can't imagine—somebody once sent me some columns to look at, something about his teenage daughter and the various problems she had, kind of making fun of her, and I said, "Jesus, the guy's got to be crazy." I did a couple of pieces in a column where I used initials, "a teenager I know named 'S'." But I had my daughter Sarah read it before I turned it in.

Q: A. A. Milne's son never forgave his father for writing *Winnie the Pooh*.

CT: I know it. I read that obituary of him in the *New York Times* and thought God, what a sad life he had. It's a chancy thing. You really can't do it very much. I think that's one of the reasons Anna Quindlen in the *Times* quit doing a personal column. She had two boys and she wrote about them, and then they got too old and she quit doing it.

Writing about your family is tricky business. I think the rule of thumb is very easy on that: If you have any reason to believe that you are Dostoyevsky, it's OK. But if you don't have any reason to believe you're Dostoyevsky, it isn't OK. And I don't know too many people who have reason to believe they are Dostoyevsky.

Q: You once made a remark about food writers being obsessive and crazy, and I've noticed that, too. Why do you think that is?

CT: Did I say that? For one thing, obviously, people literally become obsessive   10 about eating. There are actual pathologies having to do with eating, as opposed to, say, being a sports writer. There are very few pathologies having to do with being a sports writer. The sports writer is just usually eccentric. Not all food writers, but I think some food writers, for one thing, get into a position where they actually think it's very important whether this restaurant is the second or third best French restaurant in Chicago. And because most of them are intelligent people, they know in the great scheme of things it really isn't important.

Q: Are you sure they know that?

CHAPTER 3

Relationships and Life Choices: Where We Live and What We Live For

HENRY DAVID THOREAU

Where I Lived, and What I Lived For

"The mass of men lead lives of quiet desperation," wrote Henry David Thoreau (1817–1862) in Walden, *a book that taught the civilized world how to live closer to nature and eternal truth, or "reality," as he termed it. A poet, diarist, and essayist, his widely anthologized works are essential statements of American romantic idealism. While Thoreau's mind ranged widely, he spent his entire life in or near his birthplace of Concord, Massachusetts. After graduating from Harvard, he worked intermittently as a teacher, gardener, and surveyor while doing his real work as an original thinker. As a transcendentalist, Thoreau believed that intuitive understanding transcends the limits of human experience and that ideas and the natural world are powerful—and more important than material goods. These views pervade his two major works,* A Week on the Concord and Merrimack Rivers *(1849) and* Walden, or Life in the Woods *(1854), the latter being Thoreau's interpretation of his two years at Concord's Walden Pond. There he lived frugally in the small cabin he built himself, feasting on the wonders of his natural surroundings. Although he often traveled to more civilized surroundings, dining and visiting with friends in Concord, the fact that he could raise his own beans and spend days in the woods alone made him the model of self-reliance, praised by his mentor and neighbor, Ralph Waldo Emerson.*

"Where I Lived, and What I Lived For," from the second chapter of Walden, *gained worldwide renown as a philosophical manifesto and meditation on nature. Here Thoreau, in the guise of a rustic philosopher, spans the universe from earth to heaven, exploring what is essential to a good life well lived, and what is not. His mind having been shaped by classical learning, wide reading, and philosophical so-phistication, he experienced modern life as frenetic, chaotic, and banal. He identifies the various enemies of self-knowledge—a preoccupation with speed (the railroad) and trivia (the latest news). "Our life is frittered away by detail," he boldly claims — then points the way back to genuine experience.*

I went to the woods because I wished to live deliberately, to front only the essential facts of life, and see if I could not learn what it had to teach, and not, when I came to die, discover that I had not lived. I did not wish to live what was not life, living is so dear; nor did I wish to practice resignation, unless it was quite necessary. I wanted to live deep and suck out all the marrow of life, to live so sturdily and Spartan-like as to put to rout all that was not life, to cut a broad swath and shave close, to drive life into a corner, and reduce it to its lowest terms, and, if it proved to be mean, why then to get the whole and genuine meanness of it, and publish its meanness to the world; or if it were sublime, to know it by experience, and be able to give a true account of it in my next excursion. For most men, it appears to me, are in a strange uncertainty about it, whether it is of the devil or of God, and have *somewhat hastily* concluded that it is the chief end of man here to "glorify God and enjoy him forever."

Still we live meanly, like ants; though the fable tells us that we were long ago changed into men; like pygmies we fight with cranes; it is error upon error, and clout upon clout, and our best virtue has for its occasion a superfluous and evitable wretchedness. Our life is frittered away by detail. An honest man has hardly need to count more than his ten fingers, or in extreme cases he may add his ten toes, and lump the rest. Simplicity, simplicity, simplicity! I say, let your affairs be as two or three, and not a hundred or a thousand; instead of a million count half a dozen, and keep your accounts on your thumb-nail. In the midst of this chopping sea of civilized life, such are the clouds and storms and quicksands and thousand-and-one items to be allowed for, that a man has to live, if he would not founder and go to the bottom and not make his port at all, by dead reckoning, and he must be a great calculator indeed who succeeds. Simplify, simplify. Instead of three meals a day, if it be necessary eat but one; instead of a hundred dishes, five; and reduce other things in proportion. Our life is like a German Confederacy, made up of petty states, with its boundary forever fluctuating, so that even a German cannot tell you how it is bounded at any moment. The nation itself, with all its so-called internal improvements, which, by the way are all external and superficial, is just such an unwieldy and overgrown establishment, cluttered with furniture and tripped up by its own traps, ruined by luxury and heedless expense, by want of calculation and a worthy aim, as the million households in the lands; and the only cure for it, as for them, is in a rigid economy, a stern and more than Spartan simplicity of life and elevation of purpose. It lives too fast. Men think that it is essential that the *Nation* have commerce, and export ice, and talk through a telegraph, and ride thirty miles an hour, without a doubt, whether *they* do or not; but whether we should live like baboons or like men, is a little uncertain. If we do not get out sleepers, and forge rails, and devote days and nights to the work, but go to tinkering upon our *lives* to improve *them,* who will build railroads? And if railroads are not built, how shall we get to heaven in season? But if we stay at home and mind our business, who will want railroads? We do not ride on the railroad; it rides upon us. Did you ever think what those sleepers are that underlie the railroad? Each one is a man, an Irishman, or a Yankee man. The rails are laid on them, and they are covered with sand, and the cars run smoothly over them. They are sound sleepers, I assure you. And every few years a new lot is laid down and run over; so that, if some have the pleasure of riding on a rail, others have the misfortune to be ridden upon. And when they run over a man that is walking in his sleep, a supernumerary sleeper in the wrong position, and wake him up, they suddenly stop the cars, and make a hue and cry about it, as if this were an exception. I am glad to know that it takes a gang of men for every five miles to keep the sleepers down and level in their beds as it is, for this is a sign that they may sometimes get up again.

Why should we live with such hurry and waste of life? We are determined to be starved before we are hungry. Men say that a stitch in time saves nine, and so they take a thousand stitches today to save nine to-morrow. As for *work,* we haven't any of any consequence. We have the Saint Vitus' dance, and cannot possibly keep our heads still. If I should only give a few pulls at the parish bell-rope, as for a fire, that is, without setting the bell, there is hardly a man on his farm in the outskirts of Concord, notwithstanding that press of engagements which was his excuse so many times this morning, nor a boy, nor a woman, I might almost say, but would foresake all and follow that sound, not mainly to save property from the flames, but, if we will confess the truth, much more to see it burn, since burn it must, and we, be it known, did not set it on fire,—or to see it put out, and have a hand in it, if that is done as handsomely; yes, even if it were the parish church itself. Hardly a man takes a half-hour's nap after dinner, but when he wakes he holds up his head and asks, "What's the news?" as if the rest of mankind had stood his sentinels. Some give directions to be waked every half-hour, doubtless for no other purpose; and then, to pay for it, they tell what they have dreamed. After a night's sleep the news is as indispensable as the breakfast. "Pray tell me anything new that has happened to a man anywhere on this globe,"—and he reads it over his coffee and rolls, that a man has had his eyes gouged out this morning on the Wachito River; never dreaming the while that he lives in the dark unfathomed mammoth cave of this world, and has but the rudiment of an eye himself.

For my part, I could easily do without the post-office. I think that there are very few important communications made through it. To speak critically, I never received more than one or two letters in my life—I wrote this some years ago—that were worth the postage. The penny-post is, commonly, an institution through which you seriously offer a man that penny for his thoughts which is so often safely offered in jest. And I am sure that I never read any memorable news in a newspaper. If we read of one man robbed, or murdered, or killed by accident, or one house burned, or one vessel wrecked, or one steamboat blown up, or one cow run over on the Western Railroad, or one mad dog killed, or one lot of grasshoppers in the winter,—we never need read of another. One is enough. If you are acquainted with the principle, what do you care for a myriad instances and applications? To a philosopher all *news,* as it is called, is gossip, and they who edit and read it are old women over their tea. Yet not a few are greedy after this gossip. There was such a rush, as I hear, the other day at one of the offices to learn the foreign news by the last arrival, that several large squares of plate glass belonging to the establishment were broken by the pressure,—news which I seriously think a ready wit might write a twelvemonth, or twelve years, beforehand with sufficient accuracy. As for Spain, for instance, if you know how to throw in Don Carlos and the Infanta, and Don Pedro and Seville and Granada, from time to time in the right proportions,—they may have changed the names a little since I saw the papers,—and serve up a bull-fight when other entertainments fail, it will be true to the letter, and give us as good an idea of the exact state or ruin of things in Spain as the most succinct and lucid reports under this head in the newspapers: and as for England, almost the last significant scrap of news from that quarter was the revolution of 1649; and if you have learned the history of her crops for an average year, you never need attend to that thing again, unless your speculations are of a merely pecuniary character. If one may judge who rarely looks into the newspapers, nothing new does ever happen in foreign parts, a French revolution not excepted.

What news! how much more important to know what that is which was never old! "Kieou-he-yu (great dignitary of the state of Wei) sent a man to Khoung-tseu to know his news. Khoung-tseu caused the messenger to be seated near him, and questioned him in these terms: What is your master doing? The messenger answered with respect: My master desires to diminish the number of his faults, but he cannot come to the end of them. The messenger being gone, the philosopher remarked: What a worthy messenger! What a worthy messenger!" The preacher, instead of vexing the ears of drowsy farmers on their day of rest at the end of the week,—for Sunday is the fit conclusion of an ill-spent week, and not the fresh and brave beginning of a new one,—with this one other draggle-tail of a sermon, should shout with thundering voice, "Pause! Avast! Why so seeming fast, but deadly slow?"

Shams and delusions are esteemed for soundest truths, while reality is fabulous. If men would steadily observe realities only, and not allow themselves to be deluded, life, to compare it with such things as we know, would be like a fairy tale and the Arabian Nights Entertainments. If we respected only what is inevitable and has a right to be, music and poetry would resound along the streets. When we are unhurried and wise, we perceive that only great and worthy things have any permanent and absolute existence, that petty fears and petty pleasures are but the shadow of the reality. This is always exhilarating and sublime. By closing the eyes and slumbering, and consenting to be deceived by shows, men establish and confirm their daily life of routine and habit everywhere, which still is built on purely illusory foundations. Children, who play life, discern its true law and relations more clearly than men, who fail to live it worthily, but who think that they are wiser by experience, that is, by failure. I have read in a Hindoo book, that "there was a king's son, who, being expelled in infancy from his native city, was brought up by a forester, and, growing up to maturity in that state, imagined himself to belong to the barbarous race with which he lived. One of his father's

5

ministers having discovered him, revealed to him what he was, and the misconception of his character was removed, and he knew himself to be a prince. "So soul," continues the Hindoo philosopher, "from the circumstances in which it is placed, mistakes its own character, until the truth is revealed to it by some holy teacher, and then it knows itself to be *Brahme.*" I perceive that we inhabitants of New England live this mean life that we do because our vision does not penetrate the surface of things. We think that that *is* which *appears* to be. If a man should walk through this town and see only the reality, where, think you, would the "Mill-dam" go to? If he should give us an account of the realities he beheld there, we should not recognize the place in his description. Look at the meeting-house, or a court-house, or a jail, or a shop, or a dwelling-house, and say what that thing really is before a true gaze, and they would all go to pieces in your account of them. Men esteem truth remote, in the outskirts of the system, behind the farthest star, before Adam and after the last man. In eternity there is indeed something true and sublime. But all these times and places and occasions are now and here. God himself culminates in the present moment, and will never be more divine in the lapse of all the ages. And we are enabled to apprehend at all what is sublime and noble only by the perpetual instilling and drenching of the reality that surrounds us. The universe constantly and obediently answers to our conceptions; whether we travel fast or slow, the track is laid for us. Let us spend our lives in conceiving then. The poet or the artist never yet had so fair and noble a design but some of his posterity at least could accomplish it.

Let us spend one day as deliberately as Nature, and not be thrown off the track by every nutshell and mosquito's wing that falls on the rails. Let us rise early and fast, or breakfast, gently and without perturbation; let company come and let company go, let the bells ring and the children cry,—determined to make a day of it. Why should we knock under and go with the stream? Let us not be upset and overwhelmed in that terrible rapid and whirlpool called a dinner, situated in the meridian shallows. Weather this danger and you are safe, for the rest of the way is down hill. With unrelaxed nerves, with morning vigor, sail by it, looking another way, tied to the mast like Ulysses. If the engine whistles, let it whistle till it is hoarse for its pains. If the bell rings, why should we run? We will consider what kind of music they are like. Let us settle ourselves, and work and wedge our feet downward through the mud and slush of opinion, and prejudice, and tradition, and delusion, and appearance, that alluvion which covers the globe, through Paris and London, through New York and Boston and Concord, through Church and State, through poetry and philosophy and religion, till we come to a hard bottom and rocks in place, which we can call *reality,* and say, This is, and no mistake; and then begin, having a *point d'appui,* below freshet and frost and fire, a place where you might found a wall or a state, or set a lamp-post safely, or perhaps a gauge, not a Nilometer, but a Realometer, that future ages might know how deep a freshet of shams and appearances had gathered from time to time. If you stand right fronting and face to face to a fact, you will see the sun glimmer on both its surfaces, as if it were a cimeter, and feel its sweet edge dividing you through the heart and marrow, and so you will happily conclude your mortal career. Be it life or death, we crave only reality. If we are really dying, let us hear the rattle in our throats and feel cold in the extremities; if we are alive, let us go about our business.

Time is but the stream I go a-fishing in. I drink at it; but while I drink I see the sandy bottom and detect how shallow it is. Its thin current slides away, but eternity remains. I would drink deeper; fish in the sky, whose bottom is pebbly with stars. I cannot count one. I know not the first letter of the alphabet. I have always been regretting that I was not as wise as the day I was born. The intellect is a cleaver; it discerns and rifts its way into the secret of things. I do not wish to be any more busy with my hands than is necessary. My head is hands and feet. I feel all my best faculties concentrated in it. My instinct tells me that my head is an organ for burrowing, as some creatures use their snout and fore paws, and with it I would mine and burrow my way through these hills. I think that the richest vein is somewhere hereabouts; so by the divining-rod and thin rising vapors I judge; and here I will begin to mine.

HENRY DAVID THOREAU

From *Civil Disobedience*

The individualism Thoreau celebrates in "Where I Lived, and What I Lived For" is fundamental to the political beliefs he affirms in "Civil Disobedience," originally given as a lecture at the Concord Lyceum (1848) and published as "Resistance to Civil Government." In this essay, Thoreau argues that the individual is sovereign and may choose to live outside the legal system. Thus, for Thoreau, an individual is justified in performing acts of civil disobedience even if there are democratic processes for enacting change. He also argues that an individual who violates the social contract by breaking laws in order to resist injustice can relinquish the benefits of living in society by isolating himself. The individual, then, actively chooses to obey society's laws and so is not bound to obey unjust laws.

After all, the practical reason why, when the power is once in the hands of the people, a majority are permitted, and for a long period continue, to rule is not because they are most likely to be in the right, nor because this seems fairest to the minority, but because they are physically the strongest. But government in which the majority rule in all cases can not be based on justice, even as far as men understand it. Can there not be a government in which the majorities do not virtually decide right and wrong, but conscience? — in which majorities decide only those questions to which the rule of expediency is applicable? Must the citizen ever for a moment, or in the least degree, resign his conscience to the legislator?

Why has every man a conscience then? I think that we should be men first, and subjects afterward. It is not desirable to cultivate a respect for the law, so much as for the right. The only obligation which I have a right to assume is to do at any time what I think right.

. . .

The mass of men serve the state . . . not as men mainly, but as machines, with their bodies. They are the standing army, and the militia, jailers, constables, posse comitatus, etc. In most cases there is no free exercise whatever of the judgement or of the moral sense; but they put themselves on a level with wood and earth and stones; and wooden men can perhaps be manufactured that will serve the purpose as well. Such command no more respect than men of straw or a lump of dirt. They have the same sort of worth only as horses and dogs. Yet such as these seen are commonly esteemed good citizens. Others—as most legislators, politicians, lawyers, ministers, and office-holders—serve the state chiefly with their heads; and, as [they] rarely make any moral distinctions, they are as likely to serve the devil, without intending it, as God. A very few—as heroes, patriots, martyrs, reformers in the great sense, and men—serve the state with their consciences also, and so necessarily resist it for the most part; and they are commonly treated as enemies by it.

QUESTIONS FOR DISCUSSION AND WRITING

1. In "Where I Lived, and What I Lived For," Thoreau argues that "we are enabled to apprehend at all what is sublime and noble only by the perpetual instilling and drenching of the reality that surrounds us" (paragraph 6). In observing this reality, "we perceive that only great and worthy things have any permanent and absolute existence, that petty fears and petty pleasures are but the shadow of the reality." Do you see a connection between Thoreau's notion of the "very few" who make "moral distinctions" in "Civil Disobedience" with his belief in the possibility of a heightened perception of reality?

2. Thoreau begins "Civil Disobedience" with the Jeffersonian sentiment, "That government is best which governs least" and follows it with the claim that the best government "governs not at all." How does this apparent support of political anarchy coexist with his claim in "Where I Lived, and What I Lived For" that nature can teach "the essential facts of life"? Does his belief that "only great and worthy things have any permanent and absolute existence" suggest that political organization is, as he argues in "Civil Disobedience," "at best but an expedient"?

3. After reading "Where I Lived, and What I Lived For" and "Civil Disobedience" describe how Thoreau envisions the development of individual conscience. Consider Thoreau's challenge to "spend one day as deliberately as Nature, and not be thrown off the track by every nutshell and mosquito's wing that falls on the rails" (paragraph 7). Try doing so, and write a paper explaining and analyzing your experience. Would you ever repeat the experiment?

E. B. WHITE
Once More to the Lake

E. B. (Elwyn Brooks) White (1899–1985) is beloved for his children's books—Stuart Little *(1945),* Charlotte's Web *(1952), and* The Trumpet of the Swan *(1970)— and famous for his distinguished essays. He was the youngest of six children growing up in Mount Vernon, New York, a place of ponds and spacious yards and amateur musicales. Each summer, the family enjoyed the month of August at Great Pond in Belgrade Lake, Maine. In later years, White humorously reflected that his childhood lacked the deprivation and loneliness often thought to be essential to becoming a writer. After graduating from Cornell, where he edited the* Daily Sun, *in 1926 White joined the staff of the country's most sophisticated and politically astute magazine,* The New Yorker. *White wrote the "Talk of the Town" and "Notes and Comment" columns for thirty years. Between 1938 and 1943, he also wrote the "One Man's Meat" column for* Harper's. *The essays from these three columns were collected in* One Man's Meat *(1942) and* The Points of My Compass *(1962). In 1937 White helped his former English professor at Cornell, William Strunk Jr., to revise* The Elements of Style *(originally published in 1918). Now known as "Strunk and White," this classic handbook for writers advocates clarity, precision, and simple elegance.*

In 1957 White and his wife and stepson moved permanently to their saltwater farm in Allen Cove, Maine, where they had periodically stayed for many years. He continued publishing his essays until the late 1970s, and in 1971 he received the National Medal for Literature. The Essays of E. B. White, *his own arrangement of early and more recent essays, appeared in 1977.*

*"Once More to the Lake" (*Harper's, *August 1941) became a staple of the essay canon because of the elegant simplicity of White's style. With sophistication, light irony, and gentle common sense, White examines the humorous and serious sides of ordinary life—most often a life of rural New England that contrasts with Manhattan's literary milieu. To describe a place, a writer needs to convey its own special quality and meaning and suggest why and for whom the description is worth writing.*

One summer, along about 1904, my father rented a camp on a lake in Maine and took us all there for the month of August. We all got ringworm from some kittens and had to rub Pond's Extract on our arms and legs night and morning, and my father rolled over in a canoe with all his clothes on; but outside of that the vacation was a success and from then on none of us ever thought there was any place in the world like that lake in Maine. We returned summer after summer— always on August 1 for one month. I have since become a saltwater man, but sometimes in summer there are days when the restlessness of the tides and the fearful cold of the sea water and the incessant wind that blows across the afternoon and into the evening make me wish for the placidity of a lake in the woods. A few weeks ago this feeling got so strong I bought myself a couple of bass hooks and a spinner and returned to the lake where we used to go, for a week's fishing and to revisit old haunts.

I took along my son, who had never had any fresh water up his nose and who had seen lily pads only from train windows. On the journey over to the lake I began to wonder what it would be like. I wondered how time would have marred this unique, this holy spot—the coves and streams, the hills that the sun set behind, the camps and the paths behind the camps. I was sure that the tarred road would have found it out, and I wondered in what other ways it would be desolated. It is strange how much you can remember about places like that once you allow your mind to return into the grooves that lead back. You remember one thing, and that suddenly reminds you of another thing. I guess I remembered clearest of all the early mornings, when the lake was cool and motionless, remembered how the bedroom smelled of the lumber it was made of and of the wet woods whose scent entered through the screen. The partitions in the camp were thin and did not extend clear to the top of the rooms, and as I was always the first up I would dress softly so as not to wake the others, and sneak out into the sweet outdoors and start out in the canoe, keeping close along the shore in the long shadows of the pines. I remembered being very careful never to rub my paddle against the gunwale for fear of disturbing the stillness of the cathedral.

The lake had never been what you would call a wild lake. There were cottages sprinkled around the shores, and it was in farming country although the shores of the lake were quite heavily wooded. Some of the cottages were owned by nearby farmers, and you would live at the shore and eat your meals at the farmhouse. That's what our family did. But although it wasn't wild, it was a fairly large and undisturbed lake and there were places in it that, to a child at least, seemed infinitely remote and primeval.

I was right about the tar: it led to within half a mile of the shore. But when I got back there, with my boy, and we settled into a camp near a farmhouse and into the kind of summertime I had known, I could tell that it was going to be pretty much the same as it had been before—I knew it, lying in bed the first morning smelling the bedroom and hearing the boy sneak quietly out and go off along the shore in a boat. I began to sustain the illusion that he was I, and therefore, by simple transposition, that I was my father. This sensation persisted, kept cropping up all the time we were there. It was not an entirely new feeling, but in this setting it grew much stronger. I seemed to be living a dual existence. I would be in the middle of some simple act, I would be picking up a bait box or laying down a table fork, or I would be saying something and suddenly it would be not I but my father who was saying the words or making the gesture. It gave me a creepy sensation.

We went fishing the first morning. I felt the same damp moss covering the 5 worms in the bait can, and saw the dragonfly alight on the tip of my rod as it hovered a few inches from the surface of the water. It was the arrival of this fly that convinced me beyond any doubt that everything was as it always had been, that the years were a mirage and that there had been no years. The small waves were the same, chucking the rowboat under the chin as we fished at anchor, and the boat was the same boat, the same color green and the ribs broken in the same places, and under the floorboards the same fresh water leavings and débris—the dead hellgrammite, the wisps of moss, the rusty discarded fishhook, the dried blood from yesterday's catch. We stared silently at the tips of our rods, at the dragonflies that came and went. I lowered the tip of mine into the water, tentatively, pensively dislodging the fly, which darted two feet away, poised, darted two feet back, and came to rest again a little farther up the rod. There had been no years between the ducking of this dragonfly and the other one—the one that was part of memory. I looked at the boy, who was silently watching his fly, and it was my hands that held his rod, my eyes watching. I felt dizzy and didn't know which rod I was at the end of.

We caught two bass, hauling them in briskly as though they were mackerel, pulling them over the side of the boat in a businesslike manner without any landing net, and stunning them with a blow on the back of the head. When we got back for a swim before lunch, the lake was exactly where we had left it, the same number of inches from the dock, and there was only the merest suggestion of a breeze. This seemed an utterly enchanted sea, this lake you could leave to its own devices for a few hours and come back to, and find that it had not stirred, this constant and trustworthy body of water. In the shallows, the dark, water-soaked sticks and twigs, smooth and old, were undulating in clusters on the bottom against the clean ribbed sand, and the track of the mussel was plain. A school of minnows swam by, each minnow with its small individual shadow, doubling the attendance, so clear and sharp in the sunlight. Some of the other campers were in swimming, along the shore, one of them with a cake of soap, and the water felt thin and clear and unsubstantial. Over the years there had been this person with the cake of soap, this cultist, and here he was. There had been no years.

Up to the farmhouse to dinner through the teeming dusty field, the road under our sneakers was only a two-track road. The middle track was missing, the one with the marks of the hooves and the splotches of dried, flaky manure. There had always been three tracks to choose from in choosing which track to walk in; now the choice was narrowed down to two. For a moment I missed terribly the middle alternative. But the way led past the tennis court, and something about the way it lay there in the sun reassured me; the tape had loosened along the backline, the alleys were green with plantains and other weeds, and the net (installed in June and removed in September) sagged in the dry noon, and the whole place steamed with midday heat and hunger and emptiness. There was a choice of pie for dessert, and one was blueberry and one was apple, and the waitresses were the same country girls, there having been no passage of time, only the illusion of it as in a dropped curtain—the waitresses were still fifteen; their hair had been washed, that was the only difference—they had been to the movies and seen the pretty girls with the clean hair.

Summertime, oh, summertime, pattern of life indelible with fade-proof lake, the wood unshatterable, the pasture with the sweetfern and the juniper forever and ever, summer without end; this was the background, and the life along the shore was the design, the cottages with their innocent and tranquil design, their tiny docks with the flagpole and the American flag floating against the white clouds in the blue sky, the little paths over the roots of the trees leading from camp to camp and the paths leading back to the outhouses and the can of lime for sprinkling, and at the souvenir counters at the store the miniature birch-bark canoes and the postcards that showed things looking a little better than they looked. This was the American family at play, escaping the city heat, wondering whether the newcomers in the camp at the head of the cove were "common" or "nice," wondering whether it was true that the people who drove up for Sunday dinner at the farmhouse were turned away because there wasn't enough chicken.

It seemed to me, as I kept remembering all this, that those times and those summers had been infinitely precious and worth saving. There had been jollity and peace and goodness. The arriving (at the beginning of August) had been so big a business in itself, at the railway station the farm wagon drawn up, the first smell of the pine-laden air, the first glimpse of the smiling farmer, and the great importance of the trunks and your father's enormous authority in such matters, and the feel of the wagon under you for the long ten-mile haul, and at the top of the last long hill catching the first view of the lake after eleven months of not see- ing this cherished body of water. The shouts and cries of the other campers when they saw you, and the trunks to be unpacked, to give up their rich burden. (Ar- riving was less exciting nowadays, when you sneaked up in your car and parked it under a tree near the camp and took out the bags and in five minutes it was all over, no fuss, no loud wonderful fuss about trunks.)

Peace and goodness and jollity. The only thing that was wrong now, really, 10 was the sound of the place, an unfamiliar nervous sound of the outboard motors. This was the note that jarred, the one thing that would sometimes break the illu- sion and set the years moving. In those other summertimes all motors were in- board; and when they were at a little distance, the noise they made was a sedative, an ingredient of summer sleep. They were one-cylinder and two-cylinder en- gines, and some were make-and-break and some were jump-spark, but they all made a sleepy sound across the lake. The one-lungers throbbed and fluttered, and the twin-cylinder ones purred and purred, and that was a quiet sound, too. But now the campers all had outboards. In the daytime, in the hot mornings, these motors made a petulant, irritable sound; at night in the still evening when the afterglow lit the water, they whined about one's ears like mosquitoes. My boy loved our rented outboard, and his great desire was to achieve single-handed mastery over it, and authority, and he soon learned the trick of choking it a little (but not too much), and the adjustment of the needle valve. Watching him I would remember the things you could do with the old one-cylinder engine with the heavy flywheel, how you could have it eating out of your hand if you got re- ally close to it spiritually. Motorboats in those days didn't have clutches, and you would make a landing by shutting off the motor at the proper time and coasting in with a dead rudder. But there was a way of reversing them, if you learned the trick, by cutting the switch and putting it on again exactly on the final dying rev- olution of the flywheel, so that it would kick back against compression and begin reversing. Approaching a dock in a strong following breeze, it was difficult to slow up sufficiently by the ordinary coasting method, and if a boy felt he had complete mastery over his motor, he was tempted to keep it running beyond its time and then reverse it a few feet from the dock. It took a cool nerve, because if you threw the switch a twentieth of a second too soon you would catch the fly-wheel when it still had speed enough to go up past center, and the boat would leap ahead, charging bull-fashion at the dock.

We had a good week at the camp. The bass were biting well and the sun shone endlessly, day after day. We would be tired at night and lie down in the ac-cumulated heat of the little bedrooms after the long hot day and the breeze would stir almost imperceptibly outside and the smell of the swamp drift in through the rusty screens. Sleep would come easily and in the morning the red squirrel would be on the roof, tapping out his gay routine. I kept remembering everything, lying in bed in the mornings—the small steamboat that had a long rounded stern like the lip of a Ubangi, and how quietly she ran on the moonlight sails, when the older boys played their mandolins and the girls sang and we ate doughnuts dipped in sugar, and how sweet the music was on the water in the shining night, and what it had felt like to think about girls then. After breakfast we would go up to the store and the things were in the same place—the min-nows in a bottle, the plugs and spinners disarranged and pawed over by the youngsters from the boys' camp, the Fig Newtons and the Beeman's gum. Out-side, the road was tarred and cars stood in front of the store. Inside, all was just as it had always been, except there was more Coca-Cola and not so much Moxie and root beer and birch beer and sarsaparilla. We would walk out with the bottle of pop apiece and sometimes the pop would backfire up our noses and hurt. We explored the streams, quietly, where the turtles slid off the sunny logs and dug their way into the soft bottom; and we lay on the town wharf and fed worms to the tame bass. Everywhere we went I had trouble making out which was I, the one walking at my side, the one walking in my pants.

One afternoon while we were at that lake a thunderstorm came up. It was like the revival of an old melodrama that I had seen long ago with childish awe. The second-act climax of the drama of the electrical disturbance over a lake in America had not changed in any important respect. This was the big scene, still the big scene. The whole thing was so familiar, the first feeling of oppression and heat and a general air around camp of not wanting to go very far away. In mid-afternoon (it was all the same) a curious darkening of the sky, and a lull in every-thing that had made life tick; and then the way the boats suddenly swung the other way at their moorings with the coming of a breeze out of the new quarter, and the premonitory rumble. Then the kettle drum, then the snare, then the bass drum and cymbals, then crackling light against the dark, and the gods grinning and licking their chops in the hills. Afterward the calm, the rain steadily rustling in the calm lake, the return of light and hope and spirits, and the campers run-ning out in joy and relief to go swimming in the rain, their bright cries perpetuat-ing the deathless joke about how they were getting simply drenched, and the children screaming with delight at the new sensation of bathing in the rain, and the joke about getting drenched linking the generations in a strong indestructible chain. And the comedian who waded in carrying an umbrella.

When the others went swimming my son said he was going in, too. He pulled his dripping trunks from the line where they had hung all through the shower and wrung them out. Languidly, and with no thought of going in, I watched him, his hard little body, skinny and bare, saw him wince slightly as he pulled up around his vitals the small, soggy, icy garment. As he buckled the swollen belt, suddenly my groin felt the chill of death.

CONTEXTS FOR "ONCE MORE TO THE LAKE"

E. B. White and brother Stanley paddling a canoe at Belgrade Lake, 1910.

BRIAN DOYLE

From *Joyas Voladoras*

Brian Doyle, editor of Portland Magazine, *has published six collections of essays;* The Wet Engine *(2005), which includes "Joyas Voladoras," is about "the magic & muddle & mangle & miracle & music of hearts."*

So much held in a heart in a lifetime. So much held in a heart in a day, an hour, a moment. We are utterly open with no one, in the end—not mother and father, not wife or husband, not lover, not child, not friend. We open windows to each but we live alone in the house of the heart. Perhaps we must. Perhaps we could not bear to be so naked, for fear of a constantly harrowed heart. When young we think there will come one person who will savor and sustain us always; when we are older we know this is the dream of a child, that all hearts finally are bruised and scarred, scored and torn, repaired by time and will, patched by force of character, yet fragile and rickety forevermore, no matter how ferocious the defense and how many bricks you bring to the wall. You can brick up your heart as stout and tight and hard and cold and impregnable as you possibly can and down it comes in an instant, felled by a woman's second glance, a child's apple breath, the shatter of glass in the road, the words "I have something to tell you," a cat with a broken spine dragging itself into the forest to die, the brush of your mother's papery ancient hand in the thicket of your hair, the memory of your father's voice early in the morning echoing from the kitchen where he is making pancakes for his children.

CHANG-RAE LEE

Coming Home Again

Chang-Rae Lee emigrated to the United States in 1968 from Seoul, South Korea. His novels include Native Speaker *(1995) and* A Gesture Life *(1999); "Coming Home Again," from* The New Yorker *(1996) addresses his characteristic themes of "the plasticity of identity" and the blending of cultures.*

When my mother began using the electronic pump that fed her liquids and medication, we moved her to the family room. The bedroom she shared with my father was upstairs, and it was impossible to carry the machine up and down

From Brian Doyle, "Joyas Voladoras," *American Scholar* 73. 4 (Autumn 2004).

From Chang-Rae Lee, "Coming Home Again" *Manoa* 14. 2:187–195.

all day and night. The pump itself was attached to a metal stand on casters, and she pulled it along wherever she went. From anywhere in the house, you could hear the sound of the wheels clicking out a steady time over the grout lines of the slate-tiled foyer, her main thoroughfare to the bathroom and the kitchen. Sometimes you would hear her halt after only a few steps, to catch her breath or steady her balance, and whatever you were doing was instantly suspended by a pall of silence.

I was usually in the kitchen, preparing lunch or dinner, poised over the butcher block with her favorite chef's knife in my hand and her old yellow apron slung around my neck. I'd be breathless in the sudden quiet, and, having ceased my mincing and chopping, would stare blankly at the brushed sheen of the blade. Eventually, she would clear her throat or call out to say she was fine, then begin to move again, starting her rhythmic *ka-jug*; and only then could I go on with my cooking, the world of our house turning once more, wheeling through the black.

I wasn't cooking for my mother but for the rest of us. When she first moved downstairs she was still eating, though scantily, more just to taste what we were having than from any genuine desire for food. The point was simply to sit to- gether at the kitchen table and array ourselves like a family again. My mother would gently set herself down in her customary chair near the stove. I sat across from her, my father and sister to my left and right, and crammed in the center was all the food I had made—a spicy codfish stew, say, or a casserole of gingery beef, dishes that in my youth she had prepared for us a hundred times.

When I was six or seven years old, I used to watch my mother as she pre- pared our favorite meals. It was one of my daily pleasures. She shooed me away in the beginning, telling me that the kitchen wasn't my place, and adding, in her half-proud, half-deprecating way, that her kind of work would only serve to weaken me. "Go out and play with your friends," she'd snap in Korean, "or bet- ter yet, do your reading and homework." She knew that I had already done both, and that as the evening approached there was no place to go save her small and tidy kitchen, from which the clatter of her mixing bowls and pans would ring through the house.

I would enter the kitchen quietly and stand beside her, my chin lodging 5 upon the point of her hip. Peering through the crook of her arm, I beheld the movements of her hands. For *kalbi*, she would take up a butchered short rib in her narrow hand, the flinty bone shaped like a section of an airplane wing and deeply embedded in gristle and flesh, and with the point of her knife cut so that the bone fell away, though not completely, leaving it connected to the meat by the barest opaque layer of tendon. Then she methodically butterflied the flesh, cutting and unfolding, repeating the action until the meat lay out on her board, glistening and ready for seasoning. She scored it diagonally, then sifted sugar into the crevices with her pinched fingers, gently rubbing in the crystals. The sugar would tenderize as well as sweeten the meat. She did this with each rib, and then set them all aside in a large shallow bowl. She minced a half-dozen cloves of garlic, a stub of gingerroot, sliced up a few scallions, and spread it all over the meat. She wiped her hands and took out a bottle of sesame oil, and, after pausing for a moment, streamed the dark oil in two swift circles around the bowl. After adding a few splashes of soy sauce, she thrust her hands in and kneaded the flesh, careful not to dislodge the bones. I asked her why it mattered that they remain connected. "The meat needs the bone nearby," she said, "to borrow its richness." She wiped her hands clean of the marinade, except for her little finger, which she would flick with her tongue from time to time, because she knew that the flavor of a good dish developed not at once but in stages.

Whenever I cook, I find myself working just as she would, readying the ingredients—a mash of garlic, a julienne of red peppers, fantails of shrimp—and piling them in little mounds about the cutting surface. My mother never left me any recipes, but this is how I learned to make her food, each dish coming not from a list or a card but from the aromatic spread of a board.

I've always thought it was particularly cruel that the cancer was in her stomach, and that for a long time at the end she couldn't eat.

SCOTT RUSSELL SANDERS

The Inheritance of Tools

Scott Russell Sanders, an English professor at Indiana University, has published more than a dozen collections of essays focusing on human and spiritual ties to families, towns, the land, and "the practical problems of living on a small planet." "The Inheritance of Tools" reveals one face of Sanders's father, "Under the Influence" (p. 209) another face; juxtaposed, they present pieces of the intricate mosaic that represents parent–child relationships.

At just about the hour when my father died, soon after dawn one February morning when ice coated the windows like cataracts, I banged my thumb with a hammer. Naturally I swore at the hammer, the reckless thing, and in the moment of swearing I thought of what my father would say: "If you'd try hitting the nail it would go in a whole lot faster. Don't you know your thumb's not as hard as that hammer?" We both were doing carpentry that day, but far apart. He was building cupboards at my brother's place in Oklahoma; I was at home in Indiana, putting up a wall in the basement to make a bedroom for my daughter. By the time my mother called with news of his death—the long distance wires whittling her voice until it seemed too thin to bear the weight of what she had to say—my

From Scott Russell Sanders, *The Paradise of Bombs* (Athens: University of Georgia Press, 1987), 102–110.

thumb was swollen. A week or so later a white scar in the shape of a crescent moon began to show above the cuticle and month by month it rose across the pink sky of my thumbnail. It took the better part of a year for the scar to disappear, and every time I noticed it I thought of my father.

The hammer had belonged to him, and to his father before him. The three of us have used it to build houses and barns and chicken coops, to upholster chairs and crack walnuts, to make doll furniture and bookshelves and jewelry boxes. The head is scratched and pockmarked, like an old plowshare that has been working rocky fields, and it gives off the sort of dull sheen you see on fast creek water in the shade. It is a finishing hammer, about the weight of a bread loaf, too light, really, for framing walls, too heavy for cabinet work, with a curved claw for pulling nails, a rounded head for pounding, a fluted neck for looks, and a hickory handle for strength.

The present handle is my third one, bought from a lumberyard in Tennessee, down the road from where my brother and I were helping my father build his retirement house. I broke the previous one by trying to pull sixteen-penny nails out of floor joists—a foolish thing to do with a finishing hammer, as my father pointed out. "You ever hear of a crowbar?" he said. No telling how many handles he and my grandfather had gone through before me. My grandfather used to cut down hickory trees on his farm, saw them into slabs, cure the planks in his hayloft, and carve handles with a drawknife. The grain in hickory is crooked and knotty, and therefore tough, hard to split, like the grain in the two men who owned this hammer before me.

After proposing marriage to a neighbor girl, my grandfather used this hammer to build a house for his bride on a stretch of river bottom in northern Mississippi. The lumber for the place, like the hickory for the handle, was cut on his own land. By the day of the wedding he had not quite finished the house, and so right after the ceremony he took his wife home and put her to work. My grandmother had worn her Sunday dress for the wedding, with a fringe of lace tacked on around the hem in honor of the occasion. She removed this lace and folded it away before going out to help my grandfather nail siding on the house. "There she was in her good dress," he told me some fifty-odd years after that wedding day, "holding up them long pieces of clapboard while I hammered, and together we got the place covered up before dark." As the family grew to four, six, eight, and eventually thirteen, my grandfather used this hammer to enlarge his house room by room, like a chambered nautilus expanding its shell.

By and by the hammer was passed along to my father. One day he was up on 5 the roof of our pony barn nailing shingles with it, when I stepped out the kitchen door to call him for supper. Before I could yell, something about the sight of him straddling the spine of that roof and swinging the hammer caught my eye and made me hold my tongue. I was five or six years old, and the world's commonplaces were still news to me. He would pull a nail from the pouch at his waist, bring the hammer down, and a moment later the *thunk* of the blow would reach my ears. And that is what had stopped me in my tracks and stilled my tongue, that momentary gap between seeing and hearing the blow. Instead of yelling from the kitchen door, I ran to the barn and climbed two rungs up the ladder—as far as I was allowed to go—and spoke quietly to my father. On our walk to the house he explained that sound takes time to make its way through air. Suddenly the world seemed larger, the air more dense, if sound could be held back like any ordinary traveler.

By the time I started using this hammer, at about the age when I discovered the speed of sound, it already contained houses and mysteries for me. The smooth handle was one my grandfather had made. In those days I needed both hands to swing it. My father would start a nail in a scrap of wood, and I would pound away until I bent it over.

"Looks like you got ahold of some of those rubber nails," he would tell me. "Here, let me see if I can find you some stiff ones." And he would rummage in a drawer until he came up with a fistful of more cooperative nails. "Look at the head," he would tell me. "Don't look at your hands, don't look at the hammer. Just look at the head of that nail and pretty soon you'll learn to hit it square."

Pretty soon I did learn. While he worked in the garage cutting dovetail joints for a drawer or skinning a deer or tuning an engine, I would hammer nails. I made innocent blocks of wood look like porcupines. He did not talk much in the midst of his tools, but he kept up a nearly ceaseless humming, slipping in and out of a dozen tunes in an afternoon, often running back over the same stretch of melody again and again, as if searching for a way out. When the humming did cease, I knew he was faced with a task requiring great delicacy or concentration, and I took care not to distract him.

He kept scraps of wood in a cardboard box—the ends of two-by-fours, slabs of shelving and plywood, odd pieces of molding—and everything in it was fair game. I nailed scraps together to fashion what I called boats or houses, but the results usually bore only faint resemblance to the visions I carried in my head. I would hold up these constructions to show my father, and he would turn them over in his hands admiringly, speculating about what they might be. My cobbled-together guitars might have been alien spaceships, my barns might have been models of Aztec temples, each wooden contraption might have been anything but what I had set out to make.

Now and again I would feel the need to have a chunk of wood shaped or ¹⁰ shortened before I riddled it with nails, and I would clamp it in a vise and scrape at it with a handsaw. My father would let me lacerate the board until my arm gave out, and then he would wrap his hand around mine and help me finish the cut, showing me how to use my thumb to guide the blade, how to pull back on the saw to keep it from binding, how to let my shoulder do the work.

"Don't force it," he would say, "just drag it easy and give the teeth a chance to bite."

As the saw teeth bit down, the wood released its smell, each kind with its own fragrance, oak or walnut or cherry or pine—usually pine because it was the softest, easiest for a child to work. No matter how weathered and gray the board, no matter how warped and cracked, inside there was this smell waiting, as of something freshly baked. I gathered every smidgen of sawdust and stored it away in coffee cans, which I kept in a drawer of the workbench. When I did not feel like hammering nails, I would dump my sawdust on the concrete floor of the garage and landscape it into highways and farms and towns, running miniature cars and trucks along miniature roads. Looming as huge as a colossus, my father worked over and around me, now and again bending down to inspect my work, careful not to trample my creations. It was a landscape that smelled dizzyingly of wood. Even after a bath my skin would carry the smell, and so would my father's hair, when he lifted me for a bedtime hug.

I tell these things not only from memory but also from recent observation, because my own son now turns blocks of wood into nailed porcupines, dumps cans full of sawdust at my feet and sculpts highways on the floor. He learns how to swing a hammer from the elbow instead of the wrist, how to lay his thumb beside the blade to guide a saw, how to tap a chisel with a wooden mallet, how to mark a hole with an awl before starting a drill bit. My daughter did the same before him, and even now, on the brink of teenage aloofness, she will occasionally drag out my box of wood scraps and carpenter something. So I have seen my apprenticeship to wood and tools reenacted in each of my children, as my father saw his own apprenticeship renewed in me.

The saw I use belonged to him, as did my level and both of my squares, and all four tools had belonged to his father. The blade of the saw is the bluish color of gun barrels, and the maple handle, dark from the sweat of hands, is inscribed with curving leaf designs. The level is a shaft of walnut two feet long, edged with brass and pierced by three round windows in which air bubbles float in oil-filled tubes of glass. The middle window serves for testing if a surface is horizontal, the others for testing if a surface is plumb or vertical. My grandfather used to carry this level on the gun rack behind the seat in his pickup, and when I rode with him I would turn around to watch the bubbles dance. The larger of the two squares is called a framing square, a flat steel elbow, so beat up and tarnished you can barely make out the rows of numbers that show how to figure the cuts on rafters. The smaller one is called a try square, for marking right angles, with a blued steel blade for the shank and a brass-faced block of cherry for the head.

I was taught early on that a saw is not to be used apart from a square: "If you're going to cut a piece of wood," my father insisted, "you owe it to the tree to cut it straight." 15

Long before studying geometry, I learned there is a mystical virtue in right angles. There is an unspoken morality in seeking the level and the plumb. A house will stand, a table will bear weight, the sides of a box will hold together, only if the joints are square and the members upright. When the bubble is lined up between two marks etched in the glass tube of a level, you have aligned yourself with the forces that hold the universe together. When you miter the corners of a picture frame each angle must be exactly forty-five degrees, as they are in the perfect triangles of Pythagoras, not a degree more or less. Otherwise the frame will hang crookedly, as if ashamed of itself and of its maker. No matter if the joints you are cutting do not show. Even if you are butting two pieces of wood together inside a cabinet, where no one except a wrecking crew will ever see them, you must take pains to ensure that the ends are square and the studs are plumb.

I took pains over the wall I was building on the day my father died. Not long after that wall was finished—paneled with tongue-and-groove boards of yellow pine, the nail holes filled with putty and the wood all stained and sealed—I came close to wrecking it one afternoon when my daughter ran howling up the stairs to announce that her gerbils had escaped from their cage and were hiding in my brand new wall. She could hear them scratching and squeaking behind her bed. Impossible! I said. How on earth could they get inside my drum-tight wall? Through the heating vent, she answered. I went downstairs, pressed my ear to the honey-colored wood, and heard the *scritch scritch* of tiny feet.

"What can we do?" my daughter wailed. "They'll starve to death, they'll die of thirst, they'll suffocate."

"Hold on," I soothed. "I'll think of something."

While I thought and she fretted, the radio on her bedside table delivered us 20 the headlines: Several thousand people had died in a city in India from a poisonous cloud that had leaked overnight from a chemical plant. A nuclear-powered submarine had been launched. Rioting continued in South Africa. An airplane had been hijacked in the Mediterranean. Authorities calculated that several thousand homeless people slept on the streets within sight of the Washington Monument. I felt my usual helplessness in the face of all these calamities. But here was my daughter, weeping because her gerbils were holed up in a wall. This calamity I could handle.

"Don't worry," I told her. "We'll set food and water by the heating vent and lure them out. And if that doesn't do the trick, I'll tear the wall apart until we find them."

She stopped crying and gazed at me. "You'd really tear it apart? Just for my gerbils? The *wall*?" Astonishment slowed her down only for a second, however, before she ran to the workbench and began tugging at drawers, saying, "Let's see, what'll we need? Crowbar. Hammer. Chisels. I hope we don't have to use them—but just in case."

We didn't need the wrecking tools. I never had to assault my handsome wall, because the gerbils eventually came out to nibble at a dish of popcorn. But for several hours I studied the tongue-and-groove skin I had nailed up on the day of my father's death, considering where to begin prying. There were no gaps in that wall, no crooked joints.

I had botched a great many pieces of wood before I mastered the right angle with a saw, botched even more before I learned to miter a joint. The knowledge of these things resides in my hands and eyes and the webwork of muscles, not in the tools. There are machines for sale—powered miter boxes and radial-arm saws, for instance—that will enable any casual soul to cut proper angles in boards. The skill is invested in the gadget instead of the person who uses it, and this is what distinguishes a machine from a tool. If I had to earn my keep by making furniture or building houses, I suppose I would buy powered saws and pneumatic nailers; the need for speed would drive me to it. But since I carpenter only for my own pleasure or to help neighbors or to remake the house around the ears of my family, I stick with hand tools. Most of the ones I own were given to me by my father, who also taught me how to wield them. The tools in my workbench are a double inheritance, for each hammer and level and saw is wrapped in a cloud of knowing.

All of these tools are a pleasure to look at and to hold. Merchants would   25
never paste NEW NEW NEW! signs on them in stores. Their designs are old because they work, because they serve their purpose well. Like folk songs and aphorisms and the grainy bits of language, these tools have been pared down to essentials. I look at my claw hammer, the distillation of a hundred generations of carpenters, and consider that it holds up well beside those other classics—Greek vases, Gregorian chants, *Don Quixote*, barbed fish hooks, candles, spoons. Knowledge of hammering stretches back to the earliest humans who squatted beside fires, chipping flints. Anthropologists have a lovely name for those unworked rocks that served as the earliest hammers. "Dawn stones," they are called. Their only qualification for the work, aside from hardness, is that they fit the hand. Our ancestors used them for grinding corn, tapping awls, smashing bones. From dawn stones to this claw hammer is a great leap in time, but no great distance in design or imagination.

On that iced-over February morning when I smashed my thumb with the hammer, I was down in the basement framing the wall that my daughter's gerbils would later hide in. I was thinking of my father, as I always did whenever I built anything, thinking how he would have gone about the work, hearing in memory what he would have said about the wisdom of hitting the nail instead of my thumb. I had the studs and plates nailed together all square and trim, and was lifting the wall into place when the phone rang upstairs. My wife answered, and in a moment she came to the basement door and called down softly to me. The stillness in her voice made me drop the framed wall and hurry upstairs. She told me my father was dead. Then I heard the details over the phone from my mother. Building a set of cupboards for my brother in Oklahoma, he had knocked off work early the previous afternoon because of cramps in his stomach. Early this morning, on his way into the kitchen of my brother's trailer, maybe going for a glass of water, so early that no one else was awake, he slumped down on the linoleum and his heart quit.

For several hours I paced around inside my house, upstairs and down, in and out of every room, looking for the right door to open and knowing there was no such door. My wife and children followed me and wrapped me in their arms and backed away again, circling and staring as if I were on fire. Where was the door, the door, the door? I kept wondering. My smashed thumb turned purple and throbbed, making me furious. I wanted to cut it off and rush outside and scrape away at the snow and hack a hole in the frozen earth and bury the shameful thing.

I went down into the basement, opened a drawer in my workbench, and stared at the ranks of chisels and knives. Oiled and sharp, as my father would have kept them, they gleamed at me like teeth. I took up a clasp knife, pried out the longest blade, and tested the edge on the hair of my forearm. A tuft came away cleanly, and I saw my father testing the sharpness of tools on his own skin, the blades of axes and knives and gouges and hoes, saw the red hair shaved off in patches from his arms and the backs of his hands. "That will cut bear," he would say. He never cut a bear with his blades, now my blades, but he cut deer, dirt, wood. I closed the knife and put it away. Then I took up the hammer and went back to work on my daughter's wall, snugging the bottom plate against a chalk line on the floor, shimming the top plate against the joists overhead, plumbing the studs with my level, making sure before I drove the first nail that every line was square and true.

QUESTIONS FOR DISCUSSION AND WRITING

1. Explain Brian Doyle's observation in relation to one or more of these readings. In your own experience, is his an accurate observation of the human condition? Would you accept all of what he says? If not, explain how you would modify this statement: "When young we think there will come one person who will savor and sustain us always; when we are older we know this is the dream of a child, that all hearts finally are bruised and scarred, scored and torn, repaired by time and will, patched by force of character, yet fragile and rickety forevermore, no matter how ferocious the defense and how many bricks you bring to the wall."

2. Although Tolstoy has famously said, "All happy families are alike," each of these writers offers snapshots of happy families, and each is different. What characteristics have they in common? In what ways do they differ? Write a definition of a happy family, based on these readings and your own family (happy or not) and those of others. How does the ideal compare with the reality? Is it consistent over time or often changing?

3. Is there any hint of problems to come in E. B. White's commentary on idyllic three-generation family relationships in "Once More to the Lake"? In what ways does White remind readers of both the presence and passing of time? What is the significance of Chang-Rae Lee's treatment of time in his description of cooking for his dying mother?

4. Children learn from the adults around them, for better and for worse. Identify some of the values, as well as skills, that White's son learned from his father, just as White had learned from his own father. What values and skills did Lee and Sanders learn from their parents? In what ways have the values they learned as

children influenced the adults they have become? Under what circumstances do children learn the truth of Doyle's observations quoted in question 1?

5. After discussion with a classmate, good friend, or relative, write an essay in which you address Doyle's comment: "We are utterly open with no one, in the end—not mother and father, not wife or husband, not lover, not child, not friend. We open windows to each other but we live alone in the house of the heart."

LINKED READINGS: LOST PARENTS

SCOTT RUSSELL SANDERS

Under the Influence: Paying the Price of My Father's Booze

Guilt, shame, rage, and fear, along with the specter of insanity and abandonment, represent the legacy of alcoholism for Scott Russell Sanders, whose father died at the age of sixty-four from drinking. For Sanders, alcohol "turned a key" in his father's head, transforming him into another person—a person who had to be disavowed, hidden from neighbors and relatives, hidden from oneself. In the preceding essay, "The Inheritance of Tools," Sanders portrays his life as the son of a gifted craftsman. Comparing that vision to the personal torment described in the present essay raises the question of multiple lives and multiple selves—for both the father and the son.

Taken from Sanders's essay collection entitled Secrets of the Universe: Scenes from the Journey Home *(1991), "Under the Influence" does not compete with tales of suffering. "Other people have keener sources of grief: poverty, racism, rape, war," writes Sanders. "I am only trying to understand the corrosive mixture of helplessness, responsibility, and shame that I learned to feel as the son of an alcoholic." He depicts this ordeal in clear images that accumulate until reality is unmistakable. Childhood perception, adult realization, biblical analogies, and family ritual combine with bittersweet humor—perhaps the key to survival—to create a disturbing yet compelling human testament.*

My father drank. He drank as a gut-punched boxer gasps for breath, as a starving dog gobbles food—compulsively, secretly, in pain and trembling. I use the past tense not because he ever quit drinking but because he quit living. That is how the story ends for my father, age sixty-four, heart bursting, body cooling, slumped and forsaken on the linoleum of my brother's trailer. The story continues for my brother, my sister, my mother, and me, and will continue as long as memory holds.

In the perennial present of memory, I slip into the garage or barn to see my father tipping back the flat green bottles of wine, the brown cylinders of whiskey, the cans of beer disguised in paper bags. His Adam's apple bobs, the liquid gurgles, he wipes the sandy-haired back of a hand over his lips, and then, his bloodshot gaze bumping into me, he stashes the bottle or can inside his jacket, under the workbench, between two bales of hay, and we both pretend the moment has not occurred.

"What's up, buddy?" he says, thick-tongued and edgy.

"Sky's up," I answer, playing along.

"And don't forget prices," he grumbles. "Prices are always up. And taxes."   5

In memory, his white 1951 Pontiac with the stripes down the hood and the Indian head on the snout lurches to a stop in the driveway; or it is the 1956 Ford station wagon, or the 1963 Rambler shaped like a toad, or the sleek 1969 Bonneville that will do 120 miles per hour on straightaways; or it is the robin's-egg-blue pickup, new in 1980, battered in 1981, the year of his death. He climbs out, grinning dangerously, unsteady on his legs, and we children interrupt our game of catch, our building of snow forts, our picking of plums, to watch in silence as he weaves past us into the house, where he drops into his overstuffed chair and falls asleep. Shaking her head, our mother stubs out a cigarette he has left smoldering in the ashtray. All evening, until our bedtimes, we tiptoe past him, as past a snoring dragon. Then we curl fearfully in our sheets, listening. Eventually he wakes with a grunt, Mother slings accusations at him, he snarls back, she yells, he growls, their voices clashing. Before long, she retreats to their bedroom, sobbing—not from the blows of fists, for he never strikes her, but from the force of his words.

Left alone, our father prowls the house, thumping into furniture, rummaging in the kitchen, slamming doors, turning the pages of the newspaper with a savage crackle, muttering back at the late-night drivel from television. The roof might fly off, the walls might buckle from the pressure of his rage. Whatever my brother and sister and mother may be thinking on their own rumpled pillows, I lie there hating him, loving him, fearing him, knowing I have failed him. I tell myself he drinks to ease the ache that gnaws at his belly, an ache I must have caused by disappointing him somehow, a murderous ache I should be able to relieve by doing all my chores, earning A's in school, winning baseball games, fixing the broken washer and the burst pipes, bringing in the money to fill his empty wallet. He would not hide the green bottles in his toolbox, would not sneak off to the barn with a lump under his coat, would not fall asleep in the daylight, would not roar and fume, would not drink himself to death, if only I were perfect.

I am forty-four, and I know full well now that my father was an alcoholic, a man consumed by disease rather than by disappointment. What had seemed to me a private grief is in fact, of course, a public scourge. In the United States alone, some ten or fifteen million people share his ailment, and behind the doors they slam in fury or disgrace, countless other children tremble. I comfort myself with such knowledge, holding it against the throb of memory like an ice pack against a bruise. Other people have keener sources of grief: poverty, racism, rape, war. I do not wish to compete to determine who has suffered most. I am only trying to understand the corrosive mixture of helplessness, responsibility, and shame that I learned to feel as the son of an alcoholic. I realize now that I did not cause my father's illness, nor could I have cured it. Yet for all this grownup knowledge, I am still ten years old, my own son's age, and as that boy I struggle in guilt and confusion to save my father from pain.

Consider a few of our synonyms for *drunk*: tipsy, tight, pickled, soused, and plowed; stoned and stewed, lubricated and inebriated, juiced and sluiced; three sheets to the wind, in your cups, out of your mind, under the table; lit up, tanked up, wiped out; besotted, blotto, bombed, and buzzed; plastered, polluted, putrefied; loaded or looped, boozy, woozy, fuddled, or smashed; crocked and shit-faced, corked and pissed, snockered and sloshed.

It is a mostly humorous lexicon, as the lore that deals with drunks—in jokes   10 and cartoons, in plays, films and television skits—is largely comic. Aunt Matilda nips elderberry wine from the sideboard and burps politely during supper. Uncle Fred slouches to the table glassy-eyed, wearing a lampshade for a hat and murmuring, "Candy is dandy, but liquor is quicker." Inspired by cocktails, Mrs. Somebody recounts the events of her day in a fuzzy dialect, while Mr. Somebody nibbles her ear and croons a bawdy song. On the sofa with Boyfriend, Daughter Somebody giggles, licking gin from her lips, and loosens the bows in her hair. Junior knocks back some brews with his chums at the Leopard Lounge and stumbles home to the wrong house, wonders foggily why he cannot locate his pajamas, and crawls naked into bed with the ugliest girl in school. The family dog slurps from a neglected martini and wobbles to the nursery, where he vomits in Baby's shoe.

It is all great fun. But if in the audience you notice a few laughing faces turn grim when the drunk lurches onstage, don't be surprised, for these are the children of alcoholics. Over the grinning mask of Dionysus, the leering face of Bacchus, these children cannot help seeing the bloated features of their own parents. Instead of laughing, they wince, they mourn. Instead of celebrating the drunk as one freed from constraints, they pity him as one enslaved. They refuse to believe *in vino veritas*, having seen their befuddled parents skid away from truth toward folly and oblivion. And so these children bite their lips until the lush staggers into the wings.

My father, when drunk, was neither funny nor honest; he was pathetic, frightening, deceitful. There seemed to be a leak in him somewhere, and he poured in booze to keep from draining dry. Like a torture victim who refuses to squeal, he would never admit that he had touched a drop, not even in his last year, when he seemed to be dissolving in alcohol before our very eyes. I never knew him to lie about anything, ever, except about this one ruinous fact. Drowsy, clumsy, unable to fix a bicycle tire, balance a grocery sack, or walk across a room, he was stripped of his true self by drink. In a matter of minutes, the contents of a bottle could transform a brave man into a coward, a buddy into a bully, a gifted athlete and skilled carpenter and shrewd businessman into a bumbler. No dictionary of synonyms for *drunk* would soften the anguish of watching our prince turn into a frog.

Father's drinking became the family secret. While growing up, we children never breathed a word of it beyond the four walls of our house. To this day, my brother and sister rarely mention it, and then only when I press them. I did not confess the ugly, bewildering fact to my wife until his wavering and slurred speech forced me to. Recently, on the seventh anniversary of my father's death, I asked my mother if she ever spoke of his drinking to friends. "No, no, never," she replied hastily. "I couldn't bear for anyone to know."

The secret bores under the skin, gets in the blood, into the bone, and stays there. Long after you have supposedly been cured of malaria, the fever can flare up, the tremors can shake you. So it is with the fevers of shame. You swallow the bitter quinine of knowledge, and you learn to feel pity and compassion toward the drinker. Yet the shame lingers and, because of it, anger.

For a long stretch of my childhood we lived on a military reservation in Ohio, an arsenal where bombs were stored underground in bunkers and vintage airplanes burst into flames and unstable artillery shells boomed nightly at the dump. We had the feeling, as children, that we played within a minefield, where a heedless footfall could trigger an explosion. When Father was drinking, the house, too, became a minefield. The least bump could set off either parent. 15

The more he drank, the more obsessed Mother became with stopping him. She hunted for bottles, counted the cash in his wallet, sniffed at his breath. Without meaning to snoop, we children blundered left and right into damning evidence. On afternoons when he came home from work sober, we flung ourselves at him for hugs and felt against our ribs the telltale lump in his coat. In the barn we tumbled on the hay and heard beneath our sneakers the crunch of broken glass. We tugged open a drawer in his workbench, looking for screwdrivers or crescent wrenches, and spied a gleaming six-pack among the tools. Playing tag, we darted around the house just in time to see him sway on the rear stoop and heave a finished bottle into the woods. In his goodnight kiss we smelled the cloying sweetness of Clorets, the mints he chewed to camouflage his dragon's breath.

I can summon up that kiss right now by recalling Theodore Roethke's lines about his own father:

The whiskey on your breath
Could make a small boy dizzy;
But I hung on like death:
Such waltzing was not easy.

Such waltzing was hard, terribly hard, for with a boy's scrawny arms I was trying to hold my tipsy father upright.

For years, the chief source of those incriminating bottles and cans was a grimy store a mile from us, a cinderblock place called Sly's, with two gas pumps outside and a mangy dog asleep in the window. Inside, on rusty metal shelves or in wheezing coolers, you could find pop and Popsicles, cigarettes, potato chips, canned soup, raunchy postcards, fishing gear, Twinkies, wine, and beer. When Father drove anywhere on errands, Mother would send us along as guards, warning us not to let him out of our sight. And so with one or more of us on board, Father would cruise up to Sly's, pump a dollar's worth of gas or plump the tires with air, and then, telling us to wait in the car, he would head for the doorway.

Dutiful and panicky, we cried, "Let us go with you!"

"No," he answered. "I'll be back in two shakes."   20

"Please!"

"No!" he roared. "Don't you budge or I'll jerk a knot in your tails!"

So we stayed put, kicking the seats, while he ducked inside. Often, when he had parked the car at a careless angle, we gazed in through the window and saw Mr. Sly fetching down from the shelf behind the cash register two green pints of Gallo wine. Father swigged one of them right there at the counter, stuffed the other in his pocket, and then out he came, a bulge in his coat, a flustered look on his reddened face.

Because the mom and pop who ran the dump were neighbors of ours, living just down the tar-blistered road, I hated them all the more for poisoning my father. I wanted to sneak in their store and smash the bottles and set fire to the place. I also hated the Gallo brothers, Ernest and Julio, whose jovial faces beamed from the labels of their wine, labels I would find, torn and curled, when I burned the trash. I noted the Gallo brothers' address in California and studied the road atlas to see how far that was from Ohio, because I meant to go out there and tell Ernest and Julio what they were doing to my father, and then, if they showed no mercy, I would kill them.

While growing up on the back roads and in the country schools and cramped   25
Methodist churches of Ohio and Tennessee, I never heard the word *alcoholic*, never happened across it in books or magazines. In the nearby towns, there were no addiction-treatment programs, no community mental-health centers, no Alcoholics Anonymous chapters, no therapists. Left alone with our grievous secret, we had no way of understanding Father's drinking except as an act of will, a deliberate folly or cruelty, a moral weakness, a sin. He drank because he chose to, pure and simple. Why our father, so playful and competent and kind when sober, would choose to ruin himself and punish his family we could not fathom.

Our neighborhood was high on the Bible, and the Bible was hard on drunkards. "Woe to those who are heroes at drinking wine and valiant men in mixing strong drink," wrote Isaiah. "The priest and the prophet reel with strong drink, they are confused with wine, they err in vision, they stumble in giving judgment. For all tables are full of vomit, no place is without filthiness." We children had seen those fouled tables at the local truck stop where the notorious boozers hung out, our father occasionally among them. "Wine and new wine take away the understanding," declared the prophet Hosea. We had also seen evidence of that in our father, who could multiply seven-digit numbers in his head when sober but when drunk could not help us with fourth-grade math. Proverbs warned: "Do not look at wine when it is red, when it sparkles in the cup and goes down smoothly. At the last it bites like a serpent and stings like an adder. Your eyes will see strange things, and your mind utter perverse things." Woe, woe.

Dismayingly often, these biblical drunkards stirred up trouble for their own kids. Noah made fresh wine after the flood, drank too much of it, fell asleep without any clothes on, and was glimpsed in the buff by his son Ham, whom Noah promptly cursed. In one passage—it was so shocking we had to read it under our blankets with flashlights—the patriarch Lot fell down drunk and slept with his daughters. The sins of the fathers set their children's teeth on edge.

Our ministers were fond of quoting St. Paul's pronouncement that drunkards would not inherit the kingdom of God. These grave preachers assured us that the wine referred to in the Last Supper was in fact grape juice. Bible and sermons and hymns combined to give us the impression that Moses should have brought down from the mountain another stone tablet, bearing the Eleventh Commandment: Thou shalt not drink.

The scariest and most illuminating Bible story apropos of drunkards was the one about the lunatic and the swine. We knew it by heart: When Jesus climbed out of his boat one day, this lunatic came charging up from the graveyard, stark naked and filthy, frothing at the mouth, so violent that he broke the strongest chains. Nobody would go near him. Night and day for years, this madman had been wailing among the tombs and bruising himself with stones. Jesus took one look at him and said, "Come out of the man, you unclean spirits!" for he could see that the lunatic was possessed by demons. Meanwhile, some hogs were conveniently rooting nearby. "If we have to come out," begged the demons, "at least let us go into those swine." Jesus agreed, the unclean spirits entered the hogs, and the hogs raced straight off a cliff and plunged into a lake. Hearing the story in Sunday school, my friends thought mainly of the pigs. (How big a splash did they make? Who paid for the lost pork?) But I thought of the redeemed lunatic, who bathed himself and put on clothes and calmly sat at the feet of Jesus, restored—so the Bible said—to "his right mind."

When drunk, our father was clearly in his wrong mind. He became a   30
stranger, as fearful to us as any graveyard lunatic, not quite frothing at the mouth but fierce enough, quick-tempered, explosive; or else he grew maudlin and weepy, which frightened us nearly as much. In my boyhood despair, I reasoned that maybe he wasn't to blame for turning into an ogre: Maybe, like the lunatic, he was possessed by demons.

If my father was indeed possessed, who would exorcise him? If he was a sinner, who would save him? If he was ill, who would cure him? If he suffered, who would ease his pain? Not ministers or doctors, for we could not bring ourselves to confide in them; not the neighbors, for we pretended they had never seen him drunk; not Mother, who fussed and pleaded but could not budge him; not my brother and sister, who were only kids. That left me. It did not matter that I, too, was only a child, and a bewildered one at that. I could not excuse myself.

On first reading a description of delirium tremens—in a book on alcoholism I smuggled from a university library—I thought immediately of the frothing lunatic and the frenzied swine. When I read stories or watched films about grisly metamorphoses—Dr. Jekyll and Mr. Hyde, the mild husband changing into a werewolf, the kindly neighbor inhabited by a brutal alien—I could not help but see my own father's mutation from sober to drunk. Even today, knowing better, I am attracted by the demonic theory of drink, for when I recall my father's transformation, the emergence of his ugly second self, I find it easy to believe in being possessed by unclean spirits. We never knew which version of Father would come home from work, the true or the tainted, nor could we guess how far down the slope toward cruelty he would slide.

How far a man *could* slide we gauged by observing our back-road neighbors—the out-of-work miners who had dragged their families to our corner of Ohio from the desolate hollows of Appalachia, the tightfisted farmers, the surly mechanics, the balked and broken men. There was, for example, whiskey-soaked Mr. Jenkins, who beat his wife and kids so hard we could hear their screams from the road. There was Mr. Lavo the wino, who fell asleep smoking time and again, until one night his disgusted wife bundled up the children and went outside and left him in his easy chair to burn; he awoke on his own, staggered out coughing into the yard, and pounded her flat while the children looked on and the shack turned to ash. There was the truck driver, Mr. Sampson, who tripped over his son's tricycle one night while drunk and got mad, jumped into his semi, and drove away, shifting through the dozen gears, and never came back. We saw the bruised children of these fathers clump onto our school bus, we saw the abandoned children huddle in the pews at church, we saw the stunned and battered mothers begging for help at our doors.

Our own father never beat us, and I don't think he beat Mother, but he threatened often. The Old Testament Yahweh was not more terrible in His rage. Eyes blazing, voice booming, Father would pull out his belt and swear to give us a whipping, but he never followed through, never needed to, because we could imagine it so vividly. He shoved us, pawed us with the back of his hand, not to injure, just to clear a space. I can see him grabbing Mother by the hair as she cowers on a chair during a nightly quarrel. He twists her neck back until she gapes up at him, and then he lifts over her skull a glass quart bottle of milk, and milk spilling down his forearm, and he yells at her, "Say just one more word, one goddamn word, and I'll shut you up!" I fear she will prick him with her sharp tongue, but she is terrified into silence, and so am I, and the leaking bottle quivers in the air, and milk seeps through the red hair of my father's uplifted arm, and the entire scene is there to this moment, the head jerked back, the club raised.

When the drink made him weepy, Father would pack, kiss each of us chil-   35
dren on the head, and announce from the front door that he was moving out.
"Where to?" we demanded, fearful each time that he would leave for good, as Mr.
Sampson had roared away for good in his diesel truck. "Someplace where I won't
get hounded every minute," Father would answer, his jaw quivering. He stabbed
a look at Mother, who might say, "Don't run into the ditch before you get there,"
or "Good riddance," and then he would slink away. Mother watched him go with
arms crossed over her chest, her face closed like the lid on a box of snakes. We
children bawled. Where could he go? To the truck stop, that den of iniquity? To
one of those dark, ratty flophouses in town? Would he wind up sleeping under a
railroad bridge or on a park bench or in a cardboard box, mummied in rags like
the bums we had seen on our trips to Cleveland and Chicago? We bawled and
bawled, wondering if he would ever come back.

He always did come back, a day or a week later, but each time there was a
sliver less of him.

In Kafka's *Metamorphosis,* which opens famously with Gregor Samsa waking up
from uneasy dreams to find himself transformed into an insect, Gregor's family
keep reassuring themselves that things will be just fine again "when he comes
back to us." Each time alcohol transformed our father we held out the same
hope, that he would really and truly come back to us, our authentic father, the
tender and playful and competent man, and then all things would be fine. We
had grounds for such hope. After his tearful departures and chapfallen returns,
he would sometimes go weeks, even months, without drinking. Those were glad
times. Every day without the furtive glint of bottles, every meal without a fight,
every bedtime without sobs encouraged us to believe that such bliss might go on
forever.

Mother was fooled by such a hope all during the forty-odd years she knew
Greeley Ray Sanders. Soon after she met him in a Chicago delicatessen on the eve
of World War II and fell for his butter-melting Mississippi drawl and his wavy
red hair, she learned that he drank heavily. But then so did a lot of men. She
would soon coax or scold him into breaking the nasty habit. She would point out
to him how ugly and foolish it was, this bleary drinking, and then he would quit.
He refused to quit during their engagement, however, still refused during the first
years of marriage, refused until my older sister came along. The shock of father-
hood sobered him, and he remained sober through my birth at the end of the war
and right on through until we moved in 1951 to the Ohio arsenal. The arsenal
had more than its share of alcoholics, drug addicts, and other varieties of escape
artists. There I turned six and started school and woke into a child's flickering
awareness, just in time to see my father begin sneaking swigs in the garage.

He sobered up again for most of a year at the height of the Korean War, to
celebrate the birth of my brother. But aside from that dry spell, his only breaks
from drinking before I graduated from high school were just long enough to raise
and then dash our hopes. Then during the fall of my senior year — the time of the

Cuban Missile Crisis, when it seemed that the nightly explosions at the munitions dump and the nightly rages in our household might spread to engulf the globe — Father collapsed. His liver, kidneys, and heart all conked out. The doctors saved him, but only by a hair. He stayed in the hospital for weeks, going through a withdrawal so terrible that Mother would not let us visit him. If he wanted to kill himself, the doctors solemnly warned him, all he had to do was hit the bottle again. One binge would finish him.

Father must have believed them, for he stayed dry the next fifteen years. It 40 was an answer to prayer, Mother said, it was a miracle. I believe it was a reflex of fear, which he sustained over the years through courage and pride. He knew a man could die from drink, for his brother Roscoe had. We children never laid eyes on doomed Uncle Roscoe, but in the stories Mother told us he became a fairy-tale figure, like a boy who took the wrong turn in the woods and was gobbled up by the wolf.

The fifteen-year dry spell came to an end with Father's retirement in the spring of 1978. Like many men, he gave up his identity along with his job. One day he was a boss at the factory, with a brass plate on his door and a reputation to uphold; the next day he was a nobody at home. He and Mother were leaving Ontario, the last of the many places to which his job had carried them, and they were moving to a new house in Mississippi, his childhood stomping ground. As a boy in Mississippi, Father sold Coca-Cola during dances while the moonshiners peddled their brew in the parking lot; as a young blade, he fought in bars and in the ring, winning a state Golden Gloves championship; he gambled at poker, hunted pheasant, raced motorcycles and cars, played semiprofessional baseball, and, along with all his buddies — in the Black Cat Saloon, behind the cotton gin, in the woods — he drank hard. It was a perilous youth to dream of recovering.

After his final day of work, Mother drove on ahead with a car full of begonias and violets, while Father stayed behind to oversee the packing. When the van was loaded, the sweaty movers broke open a six-pack and offered him a beer.

"Let's drink to retirement!" they crowed. "Let's drink to freedom! to fishing! hunting! loafing! Let's drink to a guy who's going home!"

At least I imagine some such words, for that is all I can do, imagine, and I see Father's hand trembling in midair as he thinks about the fifteen sober years and about the doctors' warning, and he tells himself, *Goddamnit, I am a free man*, and *Why can't a free man drink one beer after a lifetime of hard work?* and I see his arm reaching, his fingers closing, the can tilting to his lips. I even supply a label for the beer, a swaggering brand that promises on television to deliver the essence of life. I watch the amber liquid pour down his throat, the alcohol steal into his blood, the key turn in his brain.

Soon after my parents moved back to Father's treacherous stomping ground, my 45 wife and I visited them in Mississippi with our four-year-old daughter. Mother had been too distraught to warn me about the return of the demons. So when I climbed out of the car that bright July morning and saw my father napping in the hammock, I felt uneasy, and when he lurched upright and blinked his bloodshot eyes and greeted us in a syrupy voice, I was hurled back into childhood.

"What's the matter with Papaw?" our daughter asked.

"Nothing," I said. "Nothing!"

Like a child again, I pretended not to see him in his stupor, and behind my phony smile I grieved. On that visit and on the few that remained before his death, once again I found bottles in the workbench, bottles in the woods. Again his hands shook too much for him to run a saw, to make his precious miniature furniture, to drive straight down back roads. Again he wound up in the ditch, in the hospital, in jail, in the treatment center. Again he shouted and wept. Again he lied. "I never touched a drop," he swore. "Your mother's making it up."

I no longer fancied I could reason with the men whose names I found on the bottles—Jim Beam, Jack Daniel's—but I was able now to recall the cold statistics about alcoholism: ten million victims, fifteen million, twenty. And yet, in spite of my age, I reacted in the same blind way as I had in childhood, by vainly seeking to erase through my efforts whatever drove him to drink. I worked on their place twelve and sixteen hours a day, in the swelter of Mississippi summers, digging ditches, running electrical wires, planting trees, mowing grass, building sheds, as though what nagged at him was some list of chores, as though by taking his worries upon my shoulders I could redeem him. I was flung back into boyhood, acting as though my father would not drink himself to death if only I were perfect.

I failed of perfection; he succeeded in dying. To the end, he considered himself not sick but sinful. "Do you want to kill yourself?" I asked him. "Why not?" he answered. "Why the hell not? What's there to save?" To the end, he would not speak about his feelings, would not or could not give a name to the beast that was devouring him. 50

In silence, he went rushing off to the cliff. Unlike the biblical swine, however, he left behind a few of the demons to haunt his children. Life with him and the loss of him twisted us into shapes that will be familiar to other sons and daughters of alcoholics. My brother became a rebel, my sister retreated into shyness, I played the stalwart and dutiful son who would hold the family together. If my father was unstable, I would be a rock. If he squandered money on drink, I would pinch every penny. If he wept when drunk—and only when drunk—I would not let myself weep at all. If he roared at the Little League umpire for calling my pitches balls, I would throw nothing but strikes. Watching him flounder and rage, I came to dread the loss of control. I would go through life without making anyone mad. I vowed never to put in my mouth or veins any chemical that would banish my everyday self. I would never make a scene, never lash out at the ones I loved, never hurt a soul. Through hard work, relentless work, I would achieve something dazzling—in the classroom, on the basketball court, in the science lab, in the pages of books—and my achievement would distract the world's eyes from his humiliation. I would become a worthy sacrifice, and the smoke of my burning would please God.

It is far easier to recognize these twists in my character than to undo them. Work has become an addiction for me, as drink was an addiction for my father. Knowing this, my daughter gave me a placard for the wall: WORKAHOLIC. The labor is endless and futile, for I can no more redeem myself through work than I could redeem my father. I still panic in the face of other people's anger, because his drunken temper was so terrible. I shrink from causing sadness or disappointment even to strangers, as though I were still concealing the family shame. I still notice every twitch of emotion in those faces around me, having learned as a child to read the weather in faces, and I blame myself for their least pang of unhappiness or anger. In certain moods I blame myself for everything. Guilt burns like acid in my veins.

I am moved to write these pages now because my own son, at the age of ten, is taking on himself the griefs of the world, and in particular the griefs of his father. He tells me that when I am gripped by sadness, he feels responsible; he feels there must be something he can do to spring me from depression, to fix my life, and that crushing sense of responsibility is exactly what I felt at the age of ten in the face of my father's drinking. My son wonders if I, too, am possessed. I write, therefore, to drag into the light what eats at me—the fear, the guilt, the shame—so that my own children may be spared.

I still shy away from nightclubs, from bars, from parties where the solvent is alcohol. My friends puzzle over this, but it is no more peculiar than for a man to shy away from the lions' den after seeing his father torn apart. I took my own first drink at the age of twenty-one, half a glass of burgundy. I knew the odds of my becoming an alcoholic were four times higher than for the children of nonalcoholic fathers. So I sipped warily.

I still do—once a week, perhaps, a glass of wine, a can of beer, nothing 55 stronger, nothing more. I listen for the turning of a key in my brain.

ANNA QUINDLEN

Anniversary

Anna Quindlen's columns for the New York Times *and* Newsweek *have made her "the unintended voice of the baby boom generation." "Anniversary" (*Newsweek*, 1997) addresses familiar mother–daughter issues that transcend time.*

I needed my mother again the other day. This time it was a fairly serious matter, a question from my doctor about our family medical history. Most of the time what I want is more trivial: the name of the family that lived next to us on Kenwood

Road, the fate of that black wool party dress with the killer neckline, curiosity about whether those tears were real or calculated to keep all five of us in line. "When Mom cried, man," my brother Bob said not long ago. "That's what I really couldn't handle."

I've needed my mother many many times over the last twenty-five years, but she has never been there, except in my mind, where she tells me to buy quality, keep my hair off my face, and give my father the benefit of the doubt. When Bob's wife was dying of cancer several years ago, we made her make video- and audiotapes for her children because our little sister, who was eight when our own mother died, cannot remember what Prudence Marguerite Pantano Quindlen looked or sounded like. I remember. I remember everything. I was nineteen; I was older. I am older now by five years than my mother was when she died. Her death transformed my life.

We're different, those of us whose mothers have gone and left us to fend for ourselves. For that is what we wind up doing, no matter how good our fathers, or family, or friends: On some deep emotional level, we fend for ourselves. The simplest way to say it is also the most true—we are the world's grown-ups. "No girl becomes a woman until her mother dies" goes an old proverb. No matter what others may see, or she herself thinks, we believe down to our bones that our mother's greatest calling was us; with that fulcrum to our lives gone, we become adults overnight.

This makes some of us hard, sometimes, and driven, too. We perform for a theater of empty seats: Look at me, Ma, I did good, I'm okay, I'll get by. It was no surprise to me to discover that Madonna's mother died when she was a child. Rosie O'Donnell used to watch the old talk shows, Mike Douglas, Merv Griffin, with her mom before her mom died when she was a kid. I don't know Rosie O'Donnell, but I know whom she thinks of every time she steps through those curtains and onto that stage and hears the applause. Maybe she hears the sound of two hands clapping, the two that are not there, the only ones that count.

The funny thing is that the loss makes us good and happy people in some   5
ways, too, in love with life because we know how fleeting and how precious it can be. We have our priorities straight.

QUESTIONS FOR DISCUSSION AND WRITING

1. What is the price that Sanders has paid, and is still paying, for his father's drinking problem? What evidence does Sanders provide to demonstrate that alcoholism is a social problem rather than an isolated, individual matter?

2. What was the father like when he was sober? What was he like when drunk? Does he seem to be the same father you encounter in Sanders's other essay, "The Inheritance of Tools" (p. 202)? What examples are the most powerful, the most painful, or the most pleasant in each essay?

3. For what audience is Sanders writing? His mother, siblings, and children? Other alcoholics and their families? People who know little about alcoholism? Himself? What is the relation of alcohol to each of these audiences?

4. Every family has a significant secret. For the Sanders family, it is the father's drinking. Write an essay about one of your family secrets, exploring its effects on various family members, particularly on yourself. If you wish to keep the secret, don't show your essay to anyone. The point of this writing assignment is to help you come to terms with the matter.

5. Define the tone of "Under the Influence." Is Sanders still angry at his father? How can you tell? What is his attitude toward his mother? His siblings? As a victim of his father's alcoholism, how does Sanders avoid self-pity?

6. Parents can powerfully affect their children's values and actions long after the children have grown up and the parents have died. Compare and contrast the influence of Sanders's father, drunk and sober, on his adult son with those of Anna Quindlen's mother on her. [Expand the discussion to include the mothers of Amy Tan (p. 38), Amy Borkowsky (p. 42), and Chang-Rae Lee (p. 200), if you wish.]

7. Is Quindlen's reminder that "the loss [of one's parent] makes us good and happy people in some ways, too, in love with life because we know how fleeting and how precious it can be" (paragraph 5) reflected in her own essay? In either of Sanders's essays? In your own life, if you've lost a parent or grandparent with whom you've had a significant relationship?

DAVID SEDARIS

Old Faithful

David Sedaris's career and fame started, unexpectedly, after he did his first reading for National Public Radio's show "Morning Edition" in December 1992. This brilliant self-satirizing account of his career as Santa's elf during Christmas season, "SantaLand Diaries," was such a hit that he soon had offers of writing jobs and two book contracts. The on-air piece, which dwelled on the backstage seediness of playing Crumpet the elf, was an extract from Sedaris's diaries. He had been writing since his teens but never considered himself a writer. Born in Raleigh, North Carolina, in 1957, Sedaris graduated from the Art Institute of Chicago in 1987. In Chicago he began performing readings from his diaries for audiences. To write "SantaLand Diaries," he recently told Michael Taylor at NPR, "All I did was take things from my diary and arrange them. When they said, 'Do you want to be on again?' I thought, 'Well, what would I talk about?!' At that point I wasn't used to writing nonfiction. By now, I can't remember how to write fiction anymore." Now, six books later, Sedaris is one of America's preeminent humorists. Recently, his biting satirical tone has softened somewhat in stories about living in Paris with his life companion, Hugh, as in Me Talk Pretty One Day *(2000) and about his dysfunctional family, in* Dress Your Family in Corduroy and Denim *(2004).*

"Old Faithful," originally published in The New Yorker *(November 11, 2004), begins with a frequent Sedaris topic, his health, and expands into a witty diatribe on committed monogamy.*

Out of nowhere I developed this lump. I think it was a cyst or a boil, one of those words you associate with trolls, and it was right on my tailbone, like a peach pit. That's what it felt like, anyway. I was afraid to look. At first it was just this insignificant knot, but as it grew larger it started to hurt. Sitting became difficult, and forget about lying on my back or bending over. By day five my tailbone was throbbing and I told myself, just as I had the day before, that if this kept up I was going to see a doctor. "I mean it," I said. I even went so far as to pull out the phone book and turn my back on it, hoping that the boil would know that I meant business and go away on its own. But of course it didn't.

All of this took place in London, which is cruelly, insanely expensive. My boyfriend, Hugh, and I went to the movies one night, and our tickets cost a total of forty dollars, this after spending sixty dollars on pizzas. And these were mini-pizzas, not much bigger than pancakes. Given the price of a simple evening out, I figured that a doctor's visit would cost about the same as a customized van. More than the money, though, I was afraid of the diagnosis. "Lower-back cancer," the doctor would say. "It looks like we'll have to remove your entire bottom."

Actually, this being England, he'd probably have said "bum," a word I have never really cottoned to. The sad thing is that they could remove my ass and most people wouldn't even notice. It's so insubstantial that the boil was actually an improvement, something like a bustle but filled with poison. The only real drawback was the pain.

For the first few days I kept my discomfort to myself, thinking all the while of what a good example I was setting. When Hugh feels bad, you hear about it immediately. A tiny splinter works itself into his palm and he claims to know exactly how Jesus must have felt on the cross. He demands sympathy for insect bites and paper cuts, while I have to lose at least a quart of blood before I get so much as a pat on the hand.

One time in France we were lucky enough to catch an identical stomach 5
virus. It was a twenty-four-hour bug, the kind that completely empties you out and takes away your will to live. You'd get a glass of water, but that would involve standing, and so instead you just sort of stare toward the kitchen, hoping that maybe one of the pipes will burst and the water will come to you. We had the exact same symptoms, yet he insisted that his virus was much more powerful than mine. I suspected the same thing, so there we were, competing over who was the sickest.

"You can at least move your hands," he said.

"No," I told him, "it was the wind that moved them. I have no muscle control whatsoever."

"Liar."

"Well, that's a nice thing to say to someone who'll probably die during the night. Thanks a lot, pal."

At such times you have to wonder how things got to this point. You meet 10
someone and fall in love, then thirteen years later you're lying on the floor in a foreign country, promising, hoping, as a matter of principle, that you'll be dead by sunrise. "I'll show you," I moaned, and then I must have fallen back to sleep.

When Hugh and I bicker over who is in the most pain, I think back to my first boyfriend, whom I met while I was in my late twenties. Something about our combination was rotten, and as a result we competed over everything, no matter how petty. When someone laughed at one of his jokes, I would need to make that person laugh harder. If I found something at a yard sale, he would have to find something better—and so on. My boyfriend's mother was a handful, and every year, just before Christmas, she would schedule a mammogram, knowing she would not get the results until after the holidays. The remote possibility of cancer was something to hang over her children's heads, just out of reach, like mistletoe, and she took great pleasure in arranging it. The family would gather and she'd tear up, saying, "I don't want to spoil your happiness, but this may well be our last Christmas together." Other times, if somebody had something going on—a wedding, a graduation—she'd go in for exploratory surgery, anything to capture and hold attention. By the time I finally met her, she did not have a single organ that had not been touched by human hands. "Oh, my God," I thought, watching her cry on our living room sofa, "my boyfriend's family is more fucked up than my own." I mean, this actually bothered me.

We were together for six years, and when we broke up I felt like a failure, a divorced person. I now had what the self-help books called relationship baggage, which I would carry around for the rest of my life. The trick was to meet someone with similar baggage, and form a matching set, but how would one go about finding such a person? Bars were out; I knew that much. I'd met my first boyfriend at a place called the Man Hole—not the sort of name that suggests fidelity. It was like meeting someone at Fisticuffs and then complaining when he turned out to be violent. To be fair, he had never actually promised to be monogamous. That was my idea, and I tried my hardest to convert him, but the allure of other people was just too great.

Almost all of the gay couples I knew at that time had some sort of an arrangement. Boyfriend A could sleep with someone else as long as he didn't bring him home—or as long as he *did* bring him home. And boyfriend B was free to do the same. It was a good setup for those who enjoyed variety and the thrill of the hunt, but to me it was just scary, and way too much work—like having one job while applying for another. One boyfriend was all I could handle, all I wanted to handle, really, and while I found this to be perfectly natural, my friends saw it as a form of repression and came to view me as something of a puritan. Am I? I wondered. But there were buckles to polish and stones to kneel upon, and so I put the question out of my mind.

I needed a boyfriend as conventional as I was, and luckily I found one—just met him one evening through a mutual friend. I was thirty-three and Hugh had just turned thirty. Like me, he had recently broken up with someone, and had moved to New York to start over. His former boyfriend had been a lot like mine, and we spent our first few weeks comparing notes. "Did he ever say he was going out for a hamburger and then—"

"—up with someone he'd met that afternoon on a bus? Yes!"

15

We had a few practical things in common as well, but what really brought Hugh and me together was our mutual fear of abandonment and group sex. It was a foundation, and we built on it, adding our fears of AIDS and pierced nipples, of commitment ceremonies and the loss of self-control. In dreams sometimes I'll discover a handsome stranger waiting in my hotel room. He's usually someone I've seen earlier that day, on the street or in a television commercial, and now he's naked and beckoning me toward the bed. I look at my key, convinced that I have the wrong room, and when he springs forward and reaches for my zipper I run for the door, which is inevitably made of snakes or hot tar, one of those maddening, hard-to-clean building materials so often used in dreams. The handle moves this way and that, and while struggling to grab it I stammer an explanation as to why I can't go through with this. "I have a boyfriend, see, and, well, the thing is that he'd kill me if he ever found out I'd been, you know, unfaithful or anything."

Really, though, it's not the fear of Hugh's punishment that stops me. I remember once riding in the car with my dad. I was twelve, and it was just the two of us, coming home from the bank. We'd been silent for blocks, when out of nowhere he turned to me and said, "I want you to know that I've never once cheated on your mother."

"Um. OK," I said. And then he turned on the radio and listened to a football game.

Years later, I mentioned this incident to a friend, who speculated that my father had said this specifically because he *had* been unfaithful. "That was a guilty conscience talking," she said, but I knew that she was wrong. More likely my father was having some problem at work and needed to remind himself that he was not completely worthless. It sounds like something you'd read on a movie poster, but sometimes the sins you haven't committed are all you have to hold on to. If you're really desperate, you might find yourself groping, saying, for example, "I've never killed anyone *with a hammer*" or "I've never stolen from anyone *who didn't deserve it.*" But whatever his faults, my dad did not have to stoop quite that low.

I have never cheated on a boyfriend, and, as with my father, it's become part 20 of my idea of myself. In my foiled wet dreams I can glimpse at what my life would be like without my perfect record, of how lost I'd feel without this scrap of integrity, and the fear is enough to wake me up. Once I'm awake, though, I tend to lie there wondering if I've made a terrible mistake.

In books and movies infidelity always looks so compelling, so right. Here are people who defy petty convention and are rewarded with only the tastiest bits of human experience. Never do they grow old or suffer the crippling panic I feel whenever Hugh gets spontaneous and suggests we go to a restaurant.

"A restaurant? But what will we talk about?"

"I don't know," he'll say. "What does it matter?"

Alone together, I enjoy our companionable silence, but it creeps me out to sit in public, propped in our chairs like a pair of mummies. At a nearby table there's always a couple in their late seventies, blinking at their menus from behind thick glasses.

"Soup's a good thing," the wife will say, and the man will nod or grunt or 25 fool with the stem of his wineglass. Eventually he'll look my way, and I'll catch in his eyes a look of grim recognition. "We are your future," he seems to say. "Get used to it."

I'm so afraid that Hugh and I won't have anything to talk about that now, before leaving home, I'll comb the papers and jot down a half dozen topics that might keep a conversation going at least through the entrées. The last time we ate out, I prepared by reading both the *Herald Tribune* and the *Animal Finders' Guide*, a publication devoted to exotic pets and the nuts who keep them. The waiter took our orders, and as he walked away I turned to Hugh, saying, "So, anyway, I hear that monkeys can really become surly once they reach breeding age."

"Well, I could have told you that," he said. "It happened with my own monkey."

I tried to draw him out, but it saddens Hugh to discuss his childhood monkey. "Oh, Maxwell," he'll sigh, and within a minute he'll have started crying.

Next on my list were the five warning signs of depression among captive camels, but I couldn't read my handwriting, and the topic crashed and burned after sign number two: an unwillingness to cush[1]. At a nearby table an elderly woman arranged and rearranged the napkin in her lap. Her husband stared at a potted plant, and I resorted to the *Herald Tribune*. "Did you hear about those three Indian women who were burned as witches?"

"What?"

"Neighbors accused them of casting spells and burned them alive."   30

"Well, that's horrible," he said, slightly accusatory, as if I myself had had a hand in it. "You can't go around burning people alive, not in this day and age."

"I know it, but—"

"It's sick is what it is. I remember once when I was living in Somalia there was this woman . . ."

"Yes!" I whispered, and then I looked over at the elderly couple, thinking, "See, we're talking about witch burnings!" It's work, though, and it's always *my* work. If left up to Hugh, we'd just sit there acting like what we are: two people so familiar with one another they could scream. Sometimes, when I find it hard to sleep, I'll think of when we first met, of the newness of each other's body, and my impatience to know everything about this person. Looking back, I should have taken it more slowly, measured him out over the course of fifty years rather than cramming him in so quickly. By the end of our first month together, he'd been so thoroughly interrogated that all I had left was breaking news—what little had happened in the few hours since I'd last seen him. Were he a cop or an emergency room doctor, there might have been a lot to catch up on, but like me Hugh works alone, so there was never much to report. "I ate some potato chips," he might say, to which I'd reply, "What kind?" or "That's funny, so did I!" More often than not we'd just breathe into our separate receivers.

"Are you still there?"   35

"I'm here."

"Good. Don't hang up."

"I won't."

In New York we slept on a futon. I took the left side and would lie awake at night, looking at the closet door. In Paris we got a real bed in a room just big enough to contain it. Hugh would fall asleep immediately, the way he's always done, and I'd stare at the blank wall, wondering about all the people who had slept in this room before us. The building dated from the seventeenth century, and I envisioned musketeers in tall, soft boots, pleasuring the sorts of women who wouldn't complain when sword tips tore the sheets. I saw gentlemen in top hats and sleeping caps, women in bonnets and berets and beaded headbands, a swarm of phantom copulators all looking down and comparing my life with theirs.

---

[1]Lie down.

After Paris came London, and a bedroom on the sixth floor with windows 40
looking onto neat rows of Edwardian chimney tops. A friend characterized it as
"a Peter Pan view," and now I can't see it any other way. I lie awake thinking of
someone with a hook for a hand, and then, inevitably, of youth and whether I
have wasted it. Twenty-five years ago I was twenty-two, a young man with his
whole sexual life ahead of him. How had 9,125 relatively uneventful days passed
so quickly, and how might I slow the days ahead? In another twenty-five years I'll
be seventy-two, and twenty-five years after that I'll be one of the figures haunting
my Paris bedroom. Is it morally permissible, I wonder, to cheat after death? Is it
even called cheating at that point? What are the rules? Do I have to wait a certain
amount of time, or can I just jump or, as the case may be, seep right in?

During the period that I had my boil, these questions seemed particularly relevant. The pain was always greater after dark, and by the sixth night I was fairly
certain that I was dying. Hugh had gone to sleep hours earlier, and it startled me
to hear his voice. "What do you say we lance that thing?" he said.

It's the sort of question that takes you off guard. "Did you just use the verb
'to lance'?" I asked.

He turned on the lights.

"Since when did you learn to lance boils?"

"I didn't," he said. "But I bet I could teach myself."   45

With anyone else I'd put up a fight, but Hugh can do just about anything he
sets his mind to. This is a person who welded the plumbing pipes at his house in
Normandy, then went into the cellar to make his own cheese. There's no one I
trust more than him, and so I limped to the bathroom, that theater of home
surgery, where I lowered my pajama bottoms and braced myself against the towel
rack, waiting as he sterilized the needle.

"This is hurting me a lot more than it's hurting you," he said. It was his standard line, but I knew that this time he was right. Worse than the boil was the stuff
that came out of it. What got to me, and got to him even worse, was the stench,
which was unbearable and unlike anything I had come across before. It was, I
thought, what evil must smell like—not an evil person but the wicked ideas that
have made him that way. How could a person continue to live with something so
rotten inside? And so much of it! "How are you doing back there?" I asked, but
he was dry-heaving and couldn't answer.

When my boil was empty, he doused it with alcohol and put a bandage on it,
as if it had been a minor injury, a shaving cut, a skinned knee, something normal
he hadn't milked like a dead cow. And this, to me, was worth at least a hundred
of the hundred and twenty nights of Sodom. Back in bed I referred to him as Sir
Lance-a-Lot.

"Once is not a lot," he said.

This was true, but Sir Lance Occasionally lacks a certain ring. "Besides," I   50
said, "I know you'll do it again if I need you to. We're an elderly monogamous
couple, and this is all part of the bargain."

The thought of this kept Hugh awake that night, and still does. We go to bed and he stares toward the window as I sleep soundly beside him, my bandaged boil silently weeping onto the sheets.

QUESTIONS FOR DISCUSSION AND WRITING

1. The author and Hugh are portrayed as a bickering conventional couple with nothing left to talk about (paragraphs 22–34). If fidelity and monogamy are the central topics of Sedaris's essay (paragraph 12), why does he go out of his way to poke fun at and deflate the idea of being faithful?

2. Sedaris shows that his relationship with Hugh is largely built on fear—fear of "abandonment and group sex," of "AIDS and pierced nipples, of commitment ceremonies and the loss of self-control" (paragraph 16). Excitement, adventurousness, and growth seem to be drastically missing from the relationship. To what extent do you sympathize with, or identify with, the idea of a relationship built on fear? Is Sedaris being honest about a fear that everybody should admit to, or is he describing a stunted relationship?

3. Sedaris is seriously funny. He employs a wide range of humor in "Old Faithful," from the scene where he and Hugh are competing about who has the worse case of a stomach virus (paragraph 5) to jokes like the one about looking for someone with similar relationship baggage to "form a matching set" (paragraph 12). What is the purpose of Sedaris's humor? To what extent does it allow him to address certain issues or feelings that might be hard to discuss otherwise?

4. Write an analysis of the relationship between Sedaris and Hugh. Is it a healthy and successful one? What are the strengths and weaknesses of the relationship? Sedaris goes out of his way to portray their "old faithful" liaison as conventional, boring, and driven by fear (see questions 1 and 2 above). How do these factors detract from or add to his relationship's viability?

5. Write an essay about one of your relationships. Provide plenty of information and details about events, thoughts, feelings, and interactions so the reader gets a clear picture of the relationship in all its dimensions.

LINKED READINGS: FAMILIES, TOGETHER AND APART

STEPHANIE COONTZ
Blaming the Family for Economic Decline

Coontz (born in Seattle, 1944) earned a bachelor's degree at the University of California at Berkeley (1966), and a master's degree at the University of Washington (1970). Since 1975 she has taught history and women's studies at Evergreen State College. Her books include Women's Work, Men's Property *(1986) and* The Social Origins of Private Life: A History of American Families *(1988). In* The Way We

Never Were: American Families and the Nostalgia Trap *(1992), Coontz argues that the ideal nuclear family of 1950s sitcoms such as* Ozzie and Harriet *never really existed. Instead, there were sweatshops; child labor; immigrant and black "servant girls" caring for the children of middle-class white homes; and overall government neglect of families. In* The Way We Really Are: Coming to Terms with America's Changing Families *(1997), from which the following selection is taken, Coontz identifies the main cause of child poverty not as divorce or unwed motherhood but as the decline in real wages; many families can't live on a single income, and Coontz proposes social programs to help them.*

The fallback position for those in denial about the socioeconomic transformation we are experiencing is to admit that many families are in economic stress but to blame their plight on divorce and unwed motherhood. Lawrence Mead of New York University argues that economic inequalities stemming from differences in wages and employment patterns "are now trivial in comparison to those stemming from family structure." David Blankenhorn claims that the "primary fault line" dividing privileged and nonprivileged Americans is no longer "race, religion, class, education, or gender" but family structure. Every major newspaper in the country has published editorials and opinion pieces along these lines. This "new consensus" produces a delightfully simple, inexpensive solution to the economic ills of America's families. From Republican Dan Quayle to the Democratic Party's Progressive Policy Institute, we hear the same words: "Marriage is the best anti-poverty program for children."[1]

Now I am as horrified as anyone by irresponsible parents who yield to the temptations of our winner-take-all society and abandon their family obligations. But we are kidding ourselves if we think the solution to the economic difficulties of America's children lies in getting their parents back together. Single-parent families, it is true, are five to six times more likely to be poor than two-parent ones. But correlations are not the same as causes. The association between poverty and single parenthood has several different sources, suggesting that the battle to end child poverty needs to be fought on a number of different fronts.

One reason that single-parent families are more liable to be poor than two-parent families is because falling real wages have made it increasingly difficult for one earner to support a family. More than one-third of all *two-parent* families with children would be poor if both parents didn't work. In this case, the higher poverty rates of one-parent families are not caused by divorce or unwed motherhood per se but by the growing need for more than one income per household. Thus a good part of the gap between two-parent and one-parent families, which is much higher today than it was in the past, is the consequence rather than the cause of economic decline.[2]

Another reason that one-parent families are likely to be poor is because the vast majority of single-parent heads of household are women, who continue to be paid far less than men. One study conducted during the highest period of divorce rates found that if women were paid the same as similarly qualified men, the number of poor families would be cut in half.[3]

Many single-parent families fall into poverty, at least temporarily, because of 5 unfair property divisions or inadequate enforcement of child support after a divorce. Although the figures were exaggerated in past studies, the fact remains that women, especially women with children, usually lose income after a divorce. The most recent data show a 27 percent drop in women's standard of living in the first year after divorce and a 10 percent increase in that of men. In 1995, only 56 percent of custodial mothers were awarded child support, and only half of these received the full amount they were due.[4]

In these examples, the solution to poverty in single-parent families does not lie in getting parents back together again but in raising real wages, equalizing the pay of men and women, and making child support and maintenance provisions more fair. In many cases, though, parents who don't earn enough to support two households *could* adequately support one. In such circumstances, it may be technically correct to say that marriage is the solution to child poverty. But even here, things are not always so simple.

Sometimes, for example, the causal arrow points in the opposite direction. Poor parents are twice as likely to divorce as more affluent ones, and job loss also increases divorce even among nonpoor families. Sociologist Scott South calculates that every time the unemployment rate rises by 1 percent, approximately 10,000 extra divorces occur. Jobless individuals are two to three times less likely to marry in the first place. And regardless of their individual values or personal characteristics, teens who live in areas of high unemployment and inferior schools are five to seven times more likely to become unwed parents than more fortunately situated teens.[5]

In the majority of cases, it is poverty and social deprivation that cause unwed motherhood, not the other way around. The fall in real wages and employment prospects for youth after 1970 *preceded* the rise in teen childbearing, which started after 1975 and accelerated in the 1980s. Indeed, reports researcher Mike Males, "the correlation between childhood poverty and later teenage childbearing is so strong that during the 1969–1993 period, the teen birth rate could be calculated with 90 percent accuracy from the previous decade's child poverty rate." According to a two-year study conducted by the Alan Guttmacher Institute, 38 percent of America's 15- to 19-year-old youths were poor in 1994. But of the one in forty teens who became an unwed parent, 85 percent were poor.[6]

Of course causal relationships seldom flow entirely in one direction. Single parenthood can worsen poverty, educational failure, and low earnings capacity, creating a downward spiral. And I certainly wouldn't deny that values regarding marriage have changed, so that more men and women refuse to get married than in the past. But it's also true, as one poverty researcher has put it, that "almost no one volunteers for roles and duties they cannot fulfill." The fact is that fewer and fewer young men from low-income communities can *afford* to get married, or can be regarded by women as suitable marriage partners.[7]

Today the real wages of a young male high school graduate are lower than 10 those earned by a comparable worker back in 1963. Between 1972 and 1994 the percentage of men aged 25 to 34 with incomes *below* the poverty level for a family of four increased from 14 percent to 32 percent. When you realize that almost a third of all young men do not earn more than $15,141 a year, which is the figure defined as poverty level for a family of four in 1994, it's easier to understand why many young men are not rushing to get married, and why many young women don't bother to pursue them. By 1993, nearly half the African-American and Latino men aged 25 to 34 did not earn enough to support a family of four.[8]

For African-American families in particular, the notion that family structure has replaced class and race as the main cause of poverty is absurd. The head of the U.S. Census Department Bureau of Marriage and Family Statistics estimates that at least one-half to three-fourths—perhaps more—of the black–white differential in childhood poverty would remain even if *all* children in African-American families had two parents present in the home. Nor do other family and cultural variations explain the high rates of African-American poverty: Youth poverty rates for African Americans have grown steadily over a period during which black teenage birth rates have dropped and high school graduation rates and test scores have risen.[9]

The most recent and thorough review of the research on the links between poverty and family structure was issued by the Tufts University Center on Hunger, Poverty and Nutrition in 1995. After reviewing seventy-three separate scholarly studies of the subject, the researchers concluded that "single-parent families are not a primary cause of the overall growth of poverty." Rather, poverty is increasing because of declines in employment, wages, and job training opportunities—"far-reaching changes in the economy . . . which hurt both poor and non-poor Americans." Most poverty, in other words, comes from our changing earnings structure, not our changing family structure.[10]

Obviously, single parenthood and family instability intensify preexisting financial insecurity, throwing some people into economic distress and increasing the magnitude of poverty for those already impoverished. And equally obviously, those exceptional individuals who can construct a stable two-parent family in the absence of a stable community or a stable job will usually benefit from doing so. But marriage will not resolve the crisis of child well-being in our country. According to Donald Hernandez, chief of the U.S. Census Department Bureau of Marriage and Family Statistics, even if we could reunite every child in America with both biological parents—and any look at abuse statistics tells you that's certainly not in the best interest of every child—two-thirds of the children who are poor today would *still* be poor.[11]

NOTES

1. Mead, quoted in George Will, "Stable Families Key to Stable Children," *Olympian*, September 27, 1991; David Blankenhorn, *Fatherless America: Confronting Our Most Urgent Social Problem* (New York: Basic Books, 1995), p. 2; Progressive Policy Institute, *Mandate for Change* (Washington, D.C.: PPI, 1992), p. 157.

2. Coontz, *The Way We Never Were*, pp. 258–270; *Washington Post*, January 17, 1992, p. 14; Gary Gowen, Laura Desimore, and Jennifer McKay, "Poverty and the Single Mother Family: A Macroeconomic Perspective," *Marriage and Family Review* 20 (1995).

3. Holly Sklar, *Chaos or Community? Seeking Solutions, Not Scapegoats, for Bad Economics* (Boston: South End Press, 1995), p. 91.

4. "Key Study on Divorce Debunked," *Olympian*, May 17, 1996; *New York Times*, May 9, 1996, p. A9; Daniel Meyer and Judi Bartfeld, "Compliance with Child Support Orders in Divorce Cases," *Journal of Marriage and the Family* 58 (1996), p. 201.

5. *New York Times*, January 15, 1993, p. A6; Don Burroughs, "Love and Money," *U.S. News & World Report*, October 19, 1992, p. 58; John Billy and David Moore, "A Multilevel Analysis of Marital and Nonmarital Fertility in the U.S.," *Social Forces* 70 (1992), pp. 977–1011; Sara McLanahan and Irwin Garfinkel, "Welfare Is No Incentive," *New York Times*, July 29, 1994, p. A13; *New York Times*, January 15, 1993, p. A6; Elaine McCrate, "Expectations of Adult Wages and Teenage Childbearing," *International Review of Applied Economics* 6 (1992); Ellen Coughlin, "Policy Researchers Shift the Terms of the Debate on Women's Issues," *Chronicle of Higher Education*, May 31, 1989; Marian Wright Edelman, *Families in Peril; An Agenda for Social Change* (Cambridge, Mass.: Harvard University Press, 1987), p. 55; Lawrence Lynn and Michael McGeary, eds., *Inner-City Poverty in the United States* (Washington, D.C.: National Academy Press, 1990), pp. 163–167; Jonathan Crane, "The Epidemic Theory of Ghetto and Neighborhood Effects on Dropping Out and Teenaged Childbearing," *American Journal of Sociology* 96 (1991), pp. 1226–1259; Sara McLanahan and Lynne Casper, "Growing Diversity and Inequality in the American Family," in Reynolds Farley, ed., *State of the Union*, vol. 2 (New York: Russell Sage, 1995), pp. 10–11; Mike Males, "Poverty, Rape, Adult/Teen Sex: Why 'Pregnancy Prevention' Programs Don't Work," *Phi Delta Kappan* (January 1994), p. 409; Mike Males, "In Defense of Teenaged Mothers," *The Progressive* (August 1994), p. 23.

6. Mike Males, *The Scapegoat Generation* (Monroe, Me.: Common Courage Press, 1996) pp. 11, 61.

7. Ramon McLeod, "Why More Families Are without a Father," *San Francisco Chronicle*, April 24, 1995.

8. Bernstein, "Inequality"; Sam Roberts, *Who We Are: A Portrait of America Based on the Latest U.S. Census* (New York: Times Books, 1995), p. 168; Judith Chafel, ed., *Child Poverty and Public Policy* (Washington, D.C.: Urban Institute Press, 1993), pp. 96–97; *Money Income of Households, Families, and Persons in the United States: 1992*, U.S. Bureau of the Census, Current Population Reports, Consumer Income, Series P–60, no. 184 (Washington, D.C.: U.S. Government Printing Office, September 1993); *Kids Count* (Baltimore: The Annie E. Casey Foundation, 1995), pp. 5–6.

9. Donald Hernandez, *America's Children: Resources from Family, Government and the Economy* (New York: Russell Sage, 1993), pp. 325, 311–312; Michael Katz, *The Undeserving Poor: From the War on Poverty to the War on Welfare* (New York: Pantheon Books, 1989), p. 213; Christopher Jencks, *Rethinking Social Policy: Race, Poverty, and the Underclass* (Cambridge, Mass.: Harvard University Press, 1994); Greg Duncan and Willard Rodgers, "Longitudinal Aspects of Childhood Poverty," *Journal of Marriage and the Family* 50 (November 1988), p. 1012; "Black Families Headed by Single Mothers," *Social Work* 33 (July–August 1988), p. 310; "Still Far from the Dream: Recent Developments in Black Income, Employment and Poverty" (Washington, D.C.: Center on Budget and Pol-

icy Priorities, October 1988), p. 12; Mary Jo Bane, "Household Composition and Poverty," in Sheldon Danziger and Daniel Weinberg, eds., *Fighting Poverty: What Works and What Doesn't* (Cambridge, Mass.: Harvard University Press, 1986), pp. 214–216; *Chicago Tribune,* March 2, 1991, p. 9; Pear, "Poverty in U.S. Grew Faster Than Population Last Year," p. A10; Hayward Horton, Melvin Thomas, and Cedric Herring, "Rural–Urban Differences in Black Family Structure: An Analysis of the 1990 Census," *Journal of Family Issues* 16 (1995), pp. 298–313; Grissmer et al., *Student Achievement and the Changing American Family* (RAND, 1994).

10.   "Statement on Key Welfare Reform Issues," p. 20, and foreword (no page number); Daniel T. Lichter and David J. Eggebeen, "The Effect of Parental Employment on Child Poverty," *Journal of Marriage and the Family* 56 (August 1994), p. 637; Steven Holmes, "Children of Working Poor Up Sharply, Study Says," *New York Times,* June 4, 1996, p. C19.

11.   Hernandez, *America's Children,* pp. 290, 325, 311–312.

KATE ZERNIKE

Why Are There So Many Single Americans?

Kate Zernike is a reporter who has worked for the Boston Globe *and currently writes for the* New York Times *on such topics as politics and social issues. The following selection appeared in the* New York Times *on January 21, 2007.*

The news that 51 percent of all women live without a spouse might be enough to make you invest in cat futures.

But consider, too, the flip side: about half of all men find themselves in the same situation. As the number of people marrying has dropped off in the last 45 years, the marriage rate has declined equally for men and for women.

The stereotype has been cemented in the popular culture: the hard-charging career girl who gets her comeuppance, either violently or dying a slow death by late-night memo and Chinese takeout. Think Glenn Close in "Fatal Attraction" and Sigourney Weaver in "Working Girl," two enduring icons. In last year's model, Meryl Streep in "The Devil Wears Prada" ends up single, if still singularly successful.

But when it comes to marriage, the two Americas aren't divided by gender. And it's not the career girls on the losing end. It's their less educated manicurists or housekeepers, women who might arguably be less able to live on their own.

The emerging gulf is instead one of class — what demographers, sociologists and those who study the often depressing statistics about the wedded state call a "marriage gap" between the well-off and the less so. 5

Statistics show that college-educated women are more likely to marry than non-college-educated women—although they marry, on average, two years later. The popular image might have been true even 20 years ago—though generally speaking, most women probably didn't boil the bunny rabbit the way Ms. Close's character did in 1987. In the past, less educated women often "married up." In "Working Girl," Melanie Griffith triumphs. Now, marriage has become more one of equals; when more highly educated men marry, it tends to be more highly educated women. Today, Harrison Ford and Sigourney Weaver would live happily ever after.

Women with more education also are becoming less likely to divorce, or inclined to divorce, than those with less education. They are even less likely to be widowed all in all, less likely to end up alone.

"Educated women used to have a difficult time," said David Popenoe, co-director of the National Marriage Project at Rutgers University. "Now they're the most desired." In Princeton, where he lives, men used to marry "way down the line," Mr. Popenoe said. No more.

The difference extends across race lines: black women are significantly less likely to marry than white women, but among blacks, women with a college education are more likely to marry than those who do not.

Among women ages 25–34, 59 percent of college graduates are married, 10 compared with 51 percent of non-college graduates, according to an analysis of the Census Bureau's June 2006 Current Population Survey by Steven P. Martin, a sociologist at the University of Maryland. The same is true at older age groups: the difference is 75 percent to 62 percent for those ages 35–44, and 50 percent to 41 percent among those 65 and older.

The difference is smaller between men and women. According to the census, 55 percent of men are married, down from 69.3 percent in 1960, and 51.5 percent of women are, down from 65.9 percent in 1960.

The number of women living without a spouse is greater largely because women live longer, leaving them more likely to be widowed. Older men are also more likely to remarry. To control for these variables, consider 35–44 year olds. In 2005, according to the census, 66.2 percent of men in this age group were married, down from 88 percent in 1960; 67.2 percent of women were married, down from 87.4 percent.

The marriage gap exists for men, too. But particularly at younger ages, it is not nearly as wide as it is among women.

Commitment-averse men in their 20's and 30's, it turns out, look the same whether or not they have a college degree. In surveys and focus groups, they fit depressingly well into the old stereotypes: they fear marriage means a loss of liberty; they worry a wife will want to change them. They don't trust women to tell the truth about past relationships, or they are waiting for the soul mate who hasn't appeared. With the rising frequency of cohabitation, they can get sex without marriage, and they might lose their hard-earned money in a divorce, so what's the rush?

As a Marriage Project report concluded, with no biological or sociological   15
clock ticking, "boys can remain boys indefinitely."

But that gap widens among older men. Among men ages 25 to 34, 50 percent
of college graduates are married, compared to 47 percent of those who did not
graduate from college. In older age brackets, there is a difference of 12 percentage
points.

The class gap happens in large part because, as Christopher Jencks, a professor of social policy at Harvard, said, "like marries like."

"If you wanted to predict the characteristics of who I would marry," he said,
"knowing my education, the strongest correlation you could observe is that someone who is educated is more likely to marry someone who is educated, and someone who is not educated is more likely to marry someone who is not educated."

Why have things changed so much for women who don't have the choices
that educated women have? While marriage used to be something you did before
launching a life or career, now it is seen as something you do after you're financially stable — when you can buy a house, say. The same is true for all classes. But
the less educated may not get there.

"Women are saying, 'I'm not ready, I want to work for a while, the guys I   20
hang around with don't make enough money and they don't want a commitment,'" Mr. Jencks said. "It's the same thing a lot of African-American women in
poor neighborhoods are saying. But there's the difference that they're having
children."

Women of all education levels figure their earning power will flatten out
after they have children, he said. "The longer you wait, the higher the level it flat-
tens out at," he said. "That's a good argument to wait. For the less educated,
there isn't a steep increase in salary, so there's less incentive to wait."

Maybe in the past, a man with little education nevertheless had a good-paying
manufacturing job, with a health care and pension plan. He was a catch and represented stability.

Today, it may be hyperbolic to talk about the emasculation of the blue-collar
man. But it is not only liberals concerned with the wealth gap who are watching
these national trends with alarm. Social and religious conservatives have called
on society to do more to address economic strains faced by this class.

"Marriage is more difficult today than it was in the past," Mr. Popenoe said.
"The people who excel in one area probably excel in that area, too. And people
who are high school dropouts probably have a higher propensity to drop out of
marriage."

The last 30 years have seen a huge shift in educated women's attitudes about   25
divorce. Mr. Martin, who has written about women and divorce, said that three
decades ago, about 30 percent of women who had graduated from college said it
should be harder to get a divorce. Now, about 65 percent say so, he said.

But for less educated women and for men, the numbers have not changed;
only 40 percent — a minority — say it should be harder to get a divorce.

"The way we used to look at marriage was that if women were highly educated, they had higher earning power, they were more culturally liberal and people might have predicted less marriage among them," Mr. Martin said. "What's becoming more powerful is the idea that economic resources are conducive to stable marriages. Women who have more money or the potential for more money are married to men who have more stable income."

All this leads to a happiness gap, too. According to the Marriage Project, the percentage of spouses who rate their marriage as "very happy" has dropped among those without a college education, while it has risen or held steady among those better educated.

The better educated husbands and wives tend to share intellectual interests and economic backgrounds, as well as ideas about the division of household roles. They also have more earning power. And as in so many other things, in marriage, money helps ease the way.

DAVID BROOKS

The Elusive Altar

David Brooks graduated from the University of Chicago in 1983 and has worked at The Wall Street Journal *and* The Weekly Standard. *His articles have appeared in* The New Yorker, *the* New York Times Magazine, Forbes, *the* Washington Post, Commentary, The Public Interest, *and many other magazines. He is editor of the anthology* Backward and Upward: The New Conservative Writing *(1996) and is author of* Bobos in Paradise: The New Upper Class and How They Got There *(2000) and* On Paradise Drive: How We Live Now (and Always Have) in the Future Tense *(2004).*

He is currently a commentator on The Newshour with Jim Lehrer *and a columnist for the* New York Times, *where the following piece appeared on January 18, 2007.*

If all the world were south of 96th Street, what a happy place it would be! If all the world were south of 96th Street, then we could greet with unalloyed joy the news that after decades of social change, more American women are living without husbands than with them.

We could revel in the stories of women—from Riverside Drive all the way to TriBeCa!—liberated from constraining marriages and no longer smothered by self-absorbed spouses. We could celebrate with those—the ad executives as well as the law partners!—who now have the time and freedom to go back to school and travel abroad, and who are choosing not to get remarried.

But alas, there are people in this country who do not live within five miles of MoMA, and for them, the fact that many more people are getting divorced or never marrying at all is not such good news.

For voluminous research shows that further down the social scale there are millions of people who long to marry, but who are trapped just beyond the outskirts of matrimony. They have partners. They move in together. Often they have children with the people they love. But they never quite marry, or if they do, the marriage falls apart, with horrible consequences for their children. This is the real force behind the rise of women without men.

The research shows that far from rejecting traditional marriage, many people 5 down the social scale revere it too highly. They put it on a pedestal, or as Andrew Cherlin of Johns Hopkins puts it, they regard marriage not as the foundation of adult life, but as the capstone.

They don't want to marry until they are financially secure and emotionally mature. They don't want to marry until they can afford a big white-dress wedding and have the time to plan it. They don't want to marry until they are absolutely sure they can trust the person they are with.

Having seen the wreckage of divorce, they are risk averse, but this risk aversion keeps them trapped in a no man's land between solitude and marriage. Often they slide into parenthood even though they consider themselves not ready for marriage. The Fragile Families study shows that nearly 90 percent of the people who are living together when their child is born plan to get married someday. But the vast majority never will.

In her essential new book, *Marriage and Caste in America*, Kay Hymowitz describes the often tortuous relations between unskilled, unmarried parents. Both are committed to their child, but in many cases they have ill-defined and conflicting expectations about their roles. The fathers often feel used, Hymowitz writes, "valued only for their not-so-deep pockets." The mothers feel the fathers are unreliable. There are grandparents taking sides. The relationship ends, and the child is left with one parent, not two.

It's as if there are two invisible rivers of knowledge running through society, steering people subtly toward one form of relationship or another. These rivers consist of a million small habits, expectations, tacit understandings about how people should act and map out their lives.

Among those who are well educated and who are rewarded by the information- 10 age economy, the invisible river reinforces the assumption that childbearing is more arduous and more elevated than marriage. One graduates from marriage to childbearing.

But among those who are less educated and less rewarded, there is an invisible river that encourages the anomalous idea that marriage is more arduous and more elevated than childbearing. One graduates from childbearing to matrimony.

The people in the first river are seeing their divorce rates drop and their children ever better prepared to compete. Only 10 percent of students at an elite college like Cornell are from divorced families, according to a study led by Dean Lillard and Jennifer Gerner.

The people in the second river are falling further behind, and their children face bad odds. For them, social facts like the rise of women without men cannot be greeted with equanimity. The main struggle of their lives is not against the patriarchy.

The first step toward a remedy, paradoxically, may be to persuade people in this second river to value marriage less, to see it less as a state of sacred bliss that cannot be approached until all the conditions are perfect, and more as a social machine, which, if accompanied with the right instruction manual, can be useful for achieving practical ends.

JUDITH WALLERSTEIN
The Legacy of Divorce

Judith Wallerstein is a psychologist and researcher who has studied the long-term effects of divorce. Wallerstein began her research in the early 1970s in California with 131 children of divorce. She interviewed both the children and their parents at length and as the children matured into adulthood and started families of their own, she continued periodic interviews. From 1966 to 1992, Wallerstein was Senior Lecturer at the School of Social Welfare, University of California at Berkeley. She is the author of Surviving the Breakup: How Children and Parents Cope with Divorce *(1980),* Second Chances: Men, Women, and Children a Decade after Divorce *(1989), and* The Unexpected Legacy of Divorce *(2000).*

Having spent the last thirty years of my life traveling here and abroad talking to professional, legal, and mental health groups plus working with thousands of parents and children in divorced families, it's clear that we've created a new kind of society never before seen in human culture. Silently and unconsciously, we have created a culture of divorce. It's hard to grasp what it means when we say that first marriages stand a 45 percent chance of breaking up and that second marriages have a 60 percent chance of ending in divorce. What are the consequences for all of us when 25 percent of people today between the ages of eighteen and forty-four have parents who divorced? What does it mean to a society when people wonder aloud if the family is about to disappear? What can we do when we learn that married couples with children represent a mere 26 percent of households in the 1990s and that the most common living arrangement nowadays is a household of unmarried people with no children? These numbers are terrifying. But like all massive social change, what's happening is affecting us in ways that we have yet to understand.

For people like me who work with divorcing families all the time, these abstract numbers have real faces. I can relate to the millions of children and adults who suffer with loneliness and to all the teenagers who say, "I don't want a life like either of my parents." I can empathize with the countless young men and women who despair of ever finding a lasting relationship and who, with a brave toss of the head, say, "Hey, if you don't get married then you can't get divorced." It's only later, or sometimes when they think I'm not listening, that they add softly, "but I don't want to grow old alone." I am especially worried about how our divorce culture has changed childhood itself. A million new children a year are added to our march of marital failure. As they explain so eloquently, they lose the carefree play of childhood as well as the comforting arms and lap of a loving parent who is always rushing off because life in the postdivorce family is so incredibly difficult to manage. We must take very seriously the complaint of children like Karen who declare, "The day my parents divorced is the day my childhood ended."

Many years ago the psychoanalyst Erik Erikson taught us that childhood and society are vitally connected. But we have not yet come to terms with the changes ushered in by our divorce culture. Childhood is different, adolescence is different, and adulthood is different. Without our noticing, we have created a new class of young children who take care of themselves, along with a whole generation of overburdened parents who have no time to enjoy the pleasures of parenting. So much has happened so fast, we cannot hold it all in our minds. It's simply overwhelming.

But we must not forget a very important other side to all these changes. Because of our divorce culture, adults today have a greater sense of freedom. The importance of sex and play in adult life is widely accepted. We are not locked into our early mistakes and forced to stay in wretched, lifelong relationships. The change in women—their very identity and freer role in society—is part of our divorce culture. Indeed, two-thirds of divorces are initiated by women despite the high price they pay in economic and parenting burdens afterward. People want and expect a lot more out of marriage than did earlier generations. Although the divorce rate in second and third marriages is sky-high, many second marriages are much happier than the ones left behind. Children and adults are able to escape violence, abuse, and misery to create a better life. Clearly there is no road back.

The sobering truth is that we have created a new kind of society that offers 5 greater freedom and more opportunities for many adults, but this welcome change carries a serious hidden cost. Many people, adults and children alike, are in fact not better off. We have created new kinds of families in which relationships are fragile and often unreliable. Children today receive far less nurturance, protection, and parenting than was their lot a few decades ago. Long-term marriages come apart at still surprising rates. And many in the older generation who started the divorce revolution find themselves estranged from their adult children. Is this the price we must pay for needed change? Can't we do better? . . .

The life histories of this first generation to grow up in a divorce culture tell us truths we dare not ignore. Their message is poignant, clear, and contrary to what so many want to believe. They have taught me the following:

From the viewpoint of the children, and counter to what happens to their parents, divorce is a cumulative experience. Its impact increases over time and rises to a crescendo in adulthood. At each developmental stage divorce is experienced anew in different ways. In adulthood it affects personality, the ability to trust, expectations about relationships, and ability to cope with change.

The first upheaval occurs at the breakup. Children are frightened and angry, terrified of being abandoned by both parents, and they feel responsible for the divorce. Most children are taken by surprise, few are relieved. As adults, they remember with sorrow and anger how little support they got from their parents when it happened. They recall how they were expected to adjust overnight to a terrifying number of changes that confounded them. Even children who had seen or heard violence at home made no connection between that violence and the decision to divorce. The children concluded early on, silently and sadly, that family relationships are fragile and that the tie between a man and woman can break capriciously without warning. They worried ever after that parent-child relationships are also unreliable and can break at any time. These early experiences colored their later expectations.

As the postdivorce family took shape, their world increasingly resembled what they feared most. Home was a lonely place. The household was in disarray for years. Many children were forced to move, leaving behind familiar schools, close friends, and other supports. What they remember vividly as adults is the loss of the intact family and the safety net it provided, the difficulty of having two parents in two homes, and how going back and forth cut badly into playtime and friendships. Parents were busy with work, preoccupied with rebuilding their social lives. Both moms and dads had a lot less time to spend with their children and were less responsive to their children's needs or wishes. Little children especially felt that they had lost both parents and were unable to care for themselves. Children soon learned that the divorced family has porous walls that include new lovers, live-in partners, and stepparents. Not one of these relationships was easy for anyone. The mother's parenting was often cut into by the very heavy burdens of single parenthood and then by the demands of remarriage and stepchildren.

Relationships with fathers were heavily influenced by live-in lovers or stepmothers in second and third marriages. Some second wives were interested in the children while others wanted no part of them. Some fathers were able to maintain their love and interest in their children but few had time for two or sometimes three families. In some families both parents gradually stabilized their lives within happy remarriages or well-functioning, emotionally gratifying single parenthood. But these people were never a majority in any of my work. . . . 10

But it's in adulthood that children of divorce suffer the most. The impact of divorce hits them most cruelly as they go in search of love, sexual intimacy, and commitment. Their lack of inner images of a man and a woman in a stable relationship and their memories of their parents' failure to sustain the marriage badly hobble their search, leading them to heartbreak and even despair. They cried, "No one taught me." They complain bitterly that they feel unprepared for adult relationships and that they have never seen a "man and woman on the same beam," that they have no good models on which to build their hopes. And indeed they have a very hard time formulating even simple ideas about the kind of person they're looking for. Many end up with unsuitable or very troubled partners in relationships that were doomed from the start.

QUESTIONS FOR DISCUSSION AND WRITING

1. In "Why Are There So Many Single Americans?" (p. 234), Kate Zernike concludes that "better educated husbands and wives tend to share intellectual interests and economic backgrounds, as well as ideas about the division of household roles" (paragraph 29). What is her evidence for this statement? What do expectations concerning sex roles imply for relations between husband and wife? Interview a parent or grandparent about their expectations upon marriage and analyze their answers. Did their marriage play out according to their expectations of sex roles? What were the consequences of these expectations?

2. In "Blaming the Family for Economic Decline" (p. 229), Stephanie Coontz refutes the belief that "[m]arriage is the best anti-poverty program for children" (paragraph 1). How does Zernike's and Brooks's discussion of a "marriage gap" on the basis of class complicate Coontz's emphasis on "falling real wages" (paragraph 3) as the source of poverty among single-parent families and on "equalizing the pay of men and women" as the "solution to child poverty" (paragraph 6)?

3. What, in your view, is likely to be the impact of a woman's higher education on her decision to marry? Zernike draws on statistics that "college-educated women are more likely to marry than non-college-educated women" (paragraph 6), while women "with more education also are becoming less likely to divorce, or inclined to divorce, than those with less education" (paragraph 7). Yet, as a whole, Wallerstein points out, "two-thirds of divorces are initiated by women despite the high price they pay in economic and parenting burdens afterward" (paragraph 4) and attributes "our divorce culture" in part to changes in women's identity and their "freer role in society" (paragraph 4). If, as Tamar Lewin reports in the *New York Times* on July 9, 2006, many more women than men continue to go to college and to perform better academically than men, what are the consequences likely to be for marriage in the immediate and longer term?

4. If you are single now, do you expect to get married? Work out your definition of marriage and write a paper addressing one or more of the following issues. When will you marry? Will this be a marriage of equals—in wage earning and domestic tasks? If so, why? If not, who will do what? Will you have children? If so, who will provide the primary child care? In what ways will your partner be involved with child rearing?

5. If you have experienced divorce, your own or that of your parents or friends or relatives, analyze the impact using the concepts Wallerstein employs in her research. Discuss any stages that children from divorced families go through, such as the "upheaval" at the breakup (paragraph 8). To what extent have you or someone you know experienced the long-term effects of divorce that Wallerstein describes? Write a paper discussing what you would have recommended to save the marriage. Would the salvage have been worth the effort? Or, alternatively, write a paper on the principles and actions you would employ in your own marriage, actual or prospective, to ensure a happy, successful, and long-term marriage.

WALKER EVANS

Ford River Rouge Plant, Michigan, 1947

QUESTIONS FOR DISCUSSION AND WRITING

1. What is the dominant geometric form in this photo? How does it serve the composition of the image? What rhythm do you see in the image? How is it expressed?

2. This plant established a continuous flow of automobile production in 1940s' Michigan, converting iron ore and other raw materials into finished automobiles. Its various components comprised 75 miles of manufacturing and assembly lines. How would you describe the technological achievement shown in this image? In your opinion, do people today think about technology in the same way people did in the 1940s when this photo was taken? Why or why not?

3. Compare the implicit industrial energy in this 1947 photograph, when Detroit's auto industry was robust, catching up on pent-up wartime demand, and the same (or comparable sites) today, when the U.S. auto industry is fighting to survive.

BARBARA EHRENREICH

Serving in Florida

Social commentator and critic Barbara Ehrenreich (b. 1941) has for most of her writing life brought a decidedly liberal viewpoint to many issues of contemporary political and public concern. She grew up in Butte, Montana, in a working-class family of what she has described as "fourth- or fifth-generation atheists," and so she comes by her iconoclasm honestly. After earning a doctorate in biology at Rockefeller University, Ehrenreich pursued an academic career but soon turned her attention to writing for general audiences.

Her books include Fear of Falling: The Inner Life of the Middle Class *(1989),* The Worst Years of Our Lives: Irreverent Notes on a Decade of Greed *(1990), and* Bait and Switch (2005).

Nickel and Dimed: On (Not) Getting by in America (2001) is Ehrenreich's report on the plight of the working poor in the United States. To research the book, she relocated to various parts of the country and tried to live on the income she could make in each place as a relatively unskilled laborer. The following excerpt from the book finds Ehrenreich working as a server in a series of Florida restaurants.

I could drift along like this, in some dreamy proletarian idyll, except for two things. One is management. If I have kept this subject to the margins so far it is because I still flinch to think that I spent all those weeks under the surveillance of men (and later women) whose job it was to monitor my behavior for signs of sloth, theft, drug abuse, or worse. Not that managers and especially "assistant managers" in low-wage settings like this are exactly the class enemy. Mostly, in the restaurant business, they are former cooks still capable of pinch-hitting in the kitchen, just as in hotels they are likely to be former clerks, and paid a salary of only about $400 a week. But everyone knows they have crossed over to the other side, which is, crudely put, corporate as opposed to human. Cooks want to prepare tasty meals, servers want to serve them graciously, but managers are there for only one reason—to make sure that money is made for some theoretical entity, the corporation, which exists far away in Chicago or New York, if a corporation can be said to have a physical existence at all. Reflecting on her career, Gail tells me ruefully that she swore, years ago, never to work for a corporation again. "They don't cut you no slack. You give and you give and they take."

Managers can sit—for hours at a time if they want—but it's their job to see that no one else ever does, even when there's nothing to do, and this is why, for servers, slow times can be as exhausting as rushes. You start dragging out each little chore because if the manager on duty catches you in an idle moment he will give you something far nastier to do. So I wipe, I clean, I consolidate catsup bottles and recheck the cheesecake supply, even tour the tables to make sure the customer evaluation forms are all standing perkily in their places—wondering all the time how many calories I burn in these strictly theatrical exercises. In desperation, I even take the desserts out of their glass display case and freshen them up with whipped cream and bright new maraschino cherries; anything to look busy. When, on a particularly dead afternoon, Stu finds me glancing at a *USA Today* a customer has left behind, he assigns me to vacuum the entire floor with the broken vacuum cleaner, which has a handle only two feet long, and the only way to do that without incurring orthopedic damage is to proceed from spot to spot on your knees.

On my first Friday at Hearthside there is a "mandatory meeting for all restaurant employees," which I attend, eager for insight into our overall marketing strategy and the niche (your basic Ohio cuisine with a tropical twist?) we aim to inhabit. But there is no "we" at this meeting. Phillip, our top manager except for an occasional "consultant" sent out by corporate headquarters, opens it with a sneer: "The break room—it's disgusting. Butts in the ashtrays, newspapers lying around, crumbs." This windowless little room, which also houses the time clock for the entire hotel, is where we stash our bags and civilian clothes and take our half-hour meal breaks. But a break room is not a right, he tells us, it can be taken away. We should also know that the lockers in the break room and whatever is in them can be searched at any time. Then comes gossip; there has been gossip; gossip (which seems to mean employees talking among themselves) must stop. Off-duty employees are henceforth barred from eating at the restaurant, because "other servers gather around them and gossip." When Phillip has exhausted his agenda of rebukes, Joan complains about the condition of the ladies' room and I throw in my two bits about the vacuum cleaner. But I don't see any backup coming from my fellow servers, each of whom has slipped into her own personal funk; Gail, my role model, stares sorrowfully at a point six inches from her nose. The meeting ends when Andy, one of the cooks, gets up, muttering about breaking up his day off for this almighty bullshit.

Just four days later we are suddenly summoned into the kitchen at 3:30 P.M., even though there are live tables on the floor. We all—about ten of us—stand around Phillip, who announces grimly that there has been a report of some "drug activity" on the night shift and that, as a result, we are now to be a "drug-free" workplace, meaning that all new hires will be tested and possibly also current employees on a random basis. I am glad that this part of the kitchen is so dark because I find myself blushing as hard as if I had been caught toking up in the ladies' room myself: I haven't been treated this way—lined up in the corridor, threatened with locker searches, peppered with carelessly aimed accusations— since at least junior high school. Back on the floor, Joan cracks, "Next they'll be telling us we can't have *sex* on the job." When I ask Stu what happened to inspire the crackdown, he just mutters about "management decisions" and takes the opportunity to upbraid Gail and me for being too generous with the rolls. From now on there's to be only one per customer and it goes out with the dinner, not with the salad. He's also been riding the cooks, prompting Andy to come out of the kitchen and observe—with the serenity of a man whose customary implement is a butcher knife—that "Stu has a death wish today."

Later in the evening, the gossip crystallizes around the theory that Stu is   5
himself the drug culprit, that he uses the restaurant phone to order up marijuana and sends one of the late servers out to fetch it for him. The server was caught and she may have ratted out Stu, at least enough to cast some suspicion on him, thus accounting for his pissy behavior. Who knows? Personally, I'm ready to believe anything bad about Stu, who serves no evident function and presumes too much on our common ethnicity, sidling up to me one night to engage in a little nativism directed at the Haitian immigrants: "I feel like I'm the foreigner here. They're taking over the country." Still later that evening, the drug in question escalates to crack. Lionel, the busboy, entertains us for the rest of the shift by standing just behind Stu's back and sucking deliriously on an imaginary joint or maybe a pipe.

The other problem, in addition to the less-than-nurturing management style, is that this job shows no sign of being financially viable. You might imagine, from a comfortable distance, that people who live, year in and year out, on $6 to $10 an hour have discovered some survival stratagems unknown to the middle class. But no. It's not hard to get my coworkers talking about their living situations, because housing, in almost every case, is the principal source of disruption in their lives, the first thing they fill you in on when they arrive for their shifts. After a week, I have compiled the following survey:

Gail is sharing a room in a well-known downtown flophouse for $250 a week. Her roommate, a male friend, has begun hitting on her, driving her nuts, but the rent would be impossible alone.

Claude, the Haitian cook, is desperate to get out of the two-room apartment he shares with his girlfriend and two other, unrelated people. As far as I can determine, the other Haitian men live in similarly crowded situations.

Annette, a twenty-year-old server who is six months pregnant and abandoned by her boyfriend, lives with her mother, a postal clerk.

Marianne, who is a breakfast server, and her boyfriend are paying $170 a week for a one-person trailer.

Billy, who at $10 an hour is the wealthiest of us, lives in the trailer he owns, paying only the $400-a-month lot fee.

The other white cook, Andy, lives on his dry-docked boat, which, as far as I can tell from his loving descriptions, can't be more than twenty feet long. He offers to take me out on it once it's repaired, but the offer comes with inquiries as to my marital status, so I do not follow up on it.

Tina, another server, and her husband are paying $60 a night for a room in the Days Inn. This is because they have no car and the Days Inn is in walking distance of the Hearthside. When Marianne is tossed out of her trailer for subletting (which is against trailer park rules), she leaves her boyfriend and moves in with Tina and her husband.

Joan, who had fooled me with her numerous and tasteful outfits (hostesses wear their own clothes), lives in a van parked behind a shopping center at night and showers in Tina's motel room. The clothes are from thrift shops.[1]

It strikes me, in my middle-class solipsism, that there is gross improvidence in some of these arrangements. When Gail and I are wrapping silverware in napkins—the only task for which we are permitted to sit—she tells me she is thinking of escaping from her roommate by moving into the Days Inn herself. I am astounded: how she can even think of paying $40 to $60 a day? But if I was afraid of sounding like a social worker, I have come out just sounding like a fool. She squints at me in disbelief: "And where am I supposed to get a month's rent and a month's deposit for an apartment?" I'd been feeling pretty smug about my $500 efficiency, but of course it was made possible only by the $1,300 I had allotted myself for start-up costs when I began my low-wage life: $1,000 for the first month's rent and deposit, $100 for initial groceries and cash in my pocket, $200 stuffed away for emergencies. In poverty, as in certain propositions in physics, starting conditions are everything.

There are no secret economies that nourish the poor; on the contrary, there are a host of special costs. If you can't put up the two months' rent you need to secure an apartment, you end up paying through the nose for a room by the week. If you have only a room, with a hot plate at best, you can't save by cooking up huge lentil stews that can be frozen for the week ahead. You eat fast food or

---

[1] I could find no statistics on the number of employed people living in cars or vans, but according to a 1997 report of the National Coalition for the Homeless, "Myths and Facts about Homelessness," nearly one-fifth of all homeless people (in twenty-nine cities across the nation) are employed in full- or part-time jobs.

the hot dogs and Styrofoam cups of soup that can be microwaved in a convenience store. If you have no money for health insurance—and the Hearthside's niggardly plan kicks in only after three months—you go without routine care or prescription drugs and end up paying the price. Gail, for example, was doing fine, healthwise anyway, until she ran out of money for estrogen pills. She is supposed to be on the company health plan by now, but they claim to have lost her application form and to be beginning the paperwork all over again. So she spends $9 a pop for pills to control the migraines she wouldn't have, she insists, if her estrogen supplements were covered. Similarly, Marianne's boyfriend lost his job as a roofer because he missed so much time after getting a cut on his foot for which he couldn't afford the prescribed antibiotic.

My own situation, when I sit down to assess it after two weeks of work, would not be much better if this were my actual life. The seductive thing about waitressing is that you don't have to wait for payday to feel a few bills in your pocket, and my tips usually cover meals and gas, plus something left over to stuff into the kitchen drawer I use as a bank. But as the tourist business slows in the summer heat, I sometimes leave work with only $20 in tips (the gross is higher, but servers share about 15 percent of their tips with the busboys and bartenders). With wages included, this amounts to about the minimum wage of $5.15 an hour. The sum in the drawer is piling up but at the present rate of accumulation will be more than $100 short of my rent when the end of the month comes around. Nor can I see any expenses to cut. True, I haven't gone the lentil stew route yet, but that's because I don't have a large cooking pot, potholders, or a ladle to stir with (which would cost a total of about $30 at Kmart, somewhat less at a thrift store), not to mention onions, carrots, and the indispensable bay leaf. I do make my lunch almost every day—usually some slow-burning, high-protein combo like frozen chicken patties with melted cheese on top and canned pinto beans on the side. Dinner is at the Hearthside, which offers its employees a choice of BLT, fish sandwich, or hamburger for only $2. The burger lasts longest, especially if it's heaped with gut-puckering jalapeños, but by midnight my stomach is growling again.

So unless I want to start using my car as a residence, I have to find a second 10 or an alternative job. I call all the hotels I'd filled out housekeeping applications at weeks ago—the Hyatt, Holiday Inn, Econo Lodge, HoJo's, Best Western, plus a half dozen locally run guest houses. Nothing. Then I start making the rounds again, wasting whole mornings waiting for some assistant manager to show up, even dipping into places so creepy that the front-desk clerk greets you from behind bullet-proof glass and sells pints of liquor over the counter. But either someone has exposed my real-life housekeeping habits—which are, shall we say, mellow—or I am at the wrong end of some infallible ethnic equation: most, but by no means all, of the working housekeepers I see on my job searches are African Americans, Spanish-speaking, or refugees from the Central European post-Communist world, while servers are almost invariably white and monolingually English-speaking. When I finally get a positive response, I have been identified once again as server material. Jerry's—again, not the real name—which is part of a well-known national chain and physically attached here to another bud-get hotel, is ready to use me at once. The prospect is both exciting and terrifying because, with about the same number of tables and counter seats, Jerry's attracts three or four times the volume of customers as the gloomy old Hearthside.

Picture a fat person's hell, and I don't mean a place with no food. Instead there is everything you might eat if eating had no bodily consequences—the cheese fries, the chicken-fried steaks, the fudge-laden desserts—only here every bite must be paid for, one way or another, in human discomfort. The kitchen is a cavern, a stomach leading to the lower intestine that is the garbage and dishwashing area, from which issue bizarre smells combining the edible and the offal: creamy car-rion, pizza barf, and that unique and enigmatic Jerry's scent, citrus fart. The floor is slick with spills, forcing us to walk through the kitchen with tiny steps, like Susan McDougal in leg irons. Sinks everywhere are clogged with scraps of lettuce, decomposing lemon wedges, water-logged toast crusts. Put your hand down on any counter and you risk being stuck to it by the film of ancient syrup spills, and this is unfortunate because hands are utensils here, used for scooping up lettuce onto the salad plates, lifting out pie slices, and even moving hash browns from one plate to another. The regulation poster in the single unisex rest room ad-monishes us to wash our hands thoroughly, and even offers instructions for doing so, but there is always some vital substance missing—soap, paper towels, toilet paper—and I never found all three at once. You learn to stuff your pockets with napkins before going in there, and too bad about the customers, who must eat, although they don't realize it, almost literally out of our hands.

The break room summarizes the whole situation: there is none, because there are no breaks at Jerry's. For six to eight hours in a row, you never sit except to pee. Actually, there are three folding chairs at a table immediately adjacent to the bathroom, but hardly anyone ever sits in this, the very rectum of the gastro-architectural system. Rather, the function of the peri-toilet area is to house the ashtrays in which servers and dishwashers leave their cigarettes burning at all times, like votive candles, so they don't have to waste time lighting up again when they dash back here for a puff. Almost everyone smokes as if their pulmonary well-being depended on it—the multinational mélange of cooks; the dishwash-ers, who are all Czechs here; the servers, who are American natives—creating an atmosphere in which oxygen is only an occasional pollutant. My first morning at Jerry's, when the hypoglycemic shakes set in, I complain to one of my fellow servers that I don't understand how she can go so long without food. "Well, I don't understand how *you* can go so long without a cigarette," she responds in a tone of reproach. Because work is what you do for others; smoking is what you do for yourself. I don't know why the antismoking crusaders have never grasped the element of defiant self-nurturance that makes the habit so endearing to its victims—as if, in the American workplace, the only thing people have to call their own is the tumors they are nourishing and the spare moments they devote to feeding them.

Now, the Industrial Revolution is not an easy transition, especially, in my ex-perience, when you have to zip through it in just a couple of days. I have gone from craft work straight into the factory, from the air-conditioned morgue of the Hearthside directly into the flames. Customers arrive in human waves, some-times disgorged fifty at a time from their tour buses, peckish and whiny. Instead of two "girls" on the floor at once, there can be as many as six of us running around in our brilliant pink-and-orange Hawaiian shirts. Conversations, either with customers or with fellow employees, seldom last more than twenty seconds at a time. On my first day, in fact, I am hurt by my sister servers' coldness. My mentor for the day is a supremely competent, emotionally uninflected twenty-three-year-old, and the others, who gossip a little among themselves about the real reason someone is out sick today and the size of the bail bond someone else has had to pay, ignore me completely. On my second day, I find out why. "Well, it's good to see *you* again," one of them says in greeting. "Hardly anyone comes back after the first day." I feel powerfully vindicated—a survivor—but it would take a long time, probably months, before I could hope to be accepted into this sorority.

I start out with the beautiful, heroic idea of handling the two jobs at once, and for two days I almost do it: working the breakfast/lunch shift at Jerry's from 8:00 till 2:00, arriving at the Hearthside a few minutes late, at 2:10, and attempt-ing to hold out until 10:00. In the few minutes I have between jobs, I pick up a spicy chicken sandwich at the Wendy's drive-through window, gobble it down in the car, and change from khaki slacks to black, from Hawaiian to rust-colored polo. There is a problem, though. When, during the 3:00–4:00 o'clock dead time, I finally sit down to wrap silver, my flesh seems to bond to the seat. I try to refuel with a purloined cup of clam chowder, as I've seen Gail and Joan do dozens of times, but Stu catches me and hisses "No *eating*!" although there's not a customer around to be offended by the sight of food making contact with a server's lips. So I tell Gail I'm going to quit, and she hugs me and says she might just follow me to Jerry's herself.

But the chances of this are minuscule. She has left the flophouse and her an-noying roommate and is back to living in her truck. But, guess what, she reports to me excitedly later that evening, Phillip has given her permission to park overnight in the hotel parking lot, as long as she keeps out of sight, and the park-ing lot should be totally safe since it's patrolled by a hotel security guard! With the Hearthside offering benefits like that, how could anyone think of leaving? This must be Phillip's theory, anyway. He accepts my resignation with a shrug, his main concern being that I return my two polo shirts and aprons. 15

Gail would have triumphed at Jerry's, I'm sure, but for me it's a crash course in exhaustion management. Years ago, the kindly fry cook who trained me to waitress at a Los Angeles truck stop used to say: Never make an unnecessary trip; if you don't have to walk fast, walk slow; if you don't have to walk, stand. But at Jerry's the effort of distinguishing necessary from unnecessary and urgent from whenever would itself be too much of an energy drain. The only thing to do is to treat each shift as a one-time-only emergency: you've got fifty starving people out there, lying scattered on the battlefield, so get out there and feed them! Forget that you will have to do this again tomorrow, forget that you will have to be alert enough to dodge the drunks on the drive home tonight—just burn, burn, burn! Ideally, at some point you enter what servers call a "rhythm" and psychologists term a "flow state," where signals pass from the sense organs directly to the muscles, bypassing the cerebral cortex, and a Zen-like emptiness sets in. I'm on a 2:00–10:00 P.M. shift now, and a male server from the morning shift tells me about the time he "pulled a triple"—three shifts in a row, all the way around the clock—and then got off and had a drink and met this girl, and maybe he shouldn't tell me this, but they had sex right then and there and it was like *beautiful*.

QUESTIONS FOR DISCUSSION AND WRITING

1. Ehrenreich identifies several problems low-wage restaurant workers face, including inadequate housing and health insurance. With a partner or team, identify the factors Ehrenreich implies underlie these conditions. In a paper or oral presentation, suggest ways that working conditions in such a low-wage industry might be improved.

2. In describing the restaurant she designates as "Jerry's," Ehrenreich uses terms like "lower intestine" and "rectum" (paragraphs 11 and 12). How does this metaphor of the restaurant as the entrails of the human body serve as a larger statement about American laborers? Why does Ehrenreich follow her description of the kitchen and rest room with her description of smoking as "defiant self-nurturance" (paragraph 12)?

3. Write an essay about the worst job you've ever held. Did you feel, like Ehrenreich, that you could "drift along" except for "the less-than-nurturing management style" (paragraph 6) and the low pay? Did you ever discuss specific problems with your manager(s) or co-worker(s)? If so, what was the outcome?

MALCOLM GLADWELL

The Physical Genius

Born in 1963 in England of English and Jamaican parents, Malcolm Gladwell grew up in Ontario and attended the University of Toronto (B.A., 1984). For a decade, he was a business and science writer for the Washington Post; *since 1996 he has been a staff writer for* The New Yorker. *His writing often deals with the unexpected implications of social science research for politics, technology, and consumer behavior.* The Tipping Point: How Little Things Can Make a Big Difference *(2000) explains social changes that happen rapidly and unexpectedly.* Blink: The Power of Thinking without Thinking *(2005) is an analysis of intuitive creativity.*

Gladwell's New Yorker *essay "The Physical Genius" (August 1999) emphasizes the human drama of brain surgery through his description of Charlie Wilson — an ace neurosurgeon — and through it, the larger topic: Why do some people excel at disciplines that involve the perfection of physical movement?*

Early one recent morning, while the San Francisco fog was lifting from the surrounding hills, Charlie Wilson performed his two thousand nine hundred and eighty-seventh transsphenoidal resection of a pituitary tumor. The patient was a man in his sixties who had complained of impotence and obscured vision. Diagnostic imaging revealed a growth, eighteen millimeters in diameter, that had enveloped his pituitary gland and was compressing his optic nerve. He was anesthetized and covered in blue surgical drapes, and one of Wilson's neurosurgery residents — a tall, slender woman in her final year of training — "opened" the case, making a small incision in his upper gum, directly underneath his nose. She then tunnelled back through his nasal passages until she reached the pituitary, creating a cavity several inches deep and about one and a half centimetres in diameter.

Wilson entered the operating room quickly, walking stiffly, bent slightly at the waist. He is sixty-nine—a small, wiry man with heavily muscled arms. His hair is cut very close to his scalp, so that, as residents over the years have joked, he might better empathize with the shaved heads of his patients. He is part Cherokee Indian and has high, broad cheekbones and large ears, which stick out at almost forty-five-degree angles. He was wearing Nike cross-trainers, and surgical scrubs marked with the logo of the medical center he has dominated for the past thirty years—Moffitt Hospital, at the University of California, San Francisco. When he was busiest, in the nineteen-eighties, he would routinely do seven or eight brain surgeries in a row, starting at dawn and ending at dusk, lining up patients in adjoining operating rooms and striding from one to the other like a conquering general. On this particular day, he would do five, of which the transsphenoidal was the first, but the rituals would be the same. Wilson believes that neurosurgery is best conducted in silence, with a scrub nurse who can anticipate his every step, and a resident who does not have to be told what to do, only shown. There was no music in the O.R. To guard against unanticipated disturbances, the door was locked. Pagers were set to "buzz," not beep. The phone was put on "Do Not Disturb."

Wilson sat by the patient in what looked like a barber's chair, manipulating a surgical microscope with a foot pedal. In his left hand he wielded a tiny suction tube, which removed excess blood. In his right he held a series of instruments in steady alternation: Cloward elevator, Penfield No. 2, Cloward rongeur, Fulton rongeur, conchatome, Hardy dissector, Kurze scissors, and so on. He worked quickly, with no wasted motion. Through the microscope, the tumor looked like a piece of lobster flesh, white and fibrous. He removed the middle of it, exposing the pituitary underneath. Then he took a ring curette—a long instrument with a circular scalpel perpendicular to the handle—and ran it lightly across the surface of the gland, peeling the tumor away as he did so.

It was, he would say later, like running a squeegee across a windshield, except that in this case the windshield was a surgical field one centimetre in diameter, flanked on either side by the carotid arteries, the principal sources of blood to the brain. If Wilson were to wander too far to the right or to the left and nick either artery, the patient might, in the neurosurgical shorthand, "stroke." If he were to push too far to the rear, he might damage any number of critical nerves. If he were not to probe aggressively, though, he might miss a bit of tumor and defeat the purpose of the procedure entirely. It was a delicate operation, which called for caution and confidence and the ability to distinguish between what was supposed to be there and what wasn't. Wilson never wavered. At one point, there was bleeding from the right side of the pituitary, which signalled to Wilson that a small piece of tumor was still just outside his field of vision, and so he gently slid the ring curette over, feeling with the instrument as if by his fingertips, navigating around the carotid, lifting out the remaining bit of tumor. In the hands of an ordinary neurosurgeon, the operation—down to that last bit of blindfolded acrobatics—might have taken several hours. It took Charlie Wilson twenty-five minutes.

Neurosurgery is generally thought to attract the most gifted and driven of 5 medical-school graduates. Even in that rarefied world, however, there are surgeons who are superstars and surgeons who are merely very good. Charlie Wilson is one of the superstars. Those who have trained with him say that if you showed them a dozen videotapes of different neurosurgeons in action—with the camera focussed just on the hands of the surgeon and the movements of the instruments—they could pick Wilson out in an instant, the same way an old baseball hand could look at a dozen batters in silhouette and tell you which one was Willie Mays. Wilson has a distinctive fluidity and grace.

There are thousands of people who have played in the National Hockey League over the years, but there has been only one Wayne Gretzky. Thousands of cellists play professionally all over the world, but very few will ever earn comparison with Yo-Yo Ma. People like Gretzky or Ma or Charlie Wilson all have an affinity for translating thought into action. They're what we might call physical geniuses. But what makes them so good at what they do?

The temptation is to treat physical genius in the same way that we treat intellectual genius—to think of it as something that can be ascribed to a single factor, a physical version of I.Q. When professional football coaches assess the year's crop of college prospects, they put them through drills designed to measure what they regard as athleticism: How high can you jump? How many pounds can you bench press? How fast can you sprint? The sum of the scores on these tests is considered predictive of athletic performance, and every year some college player's stock shoots up before draft day because it is suddenly discovered that he can run, say, 4.4 seconds in the forty-yard dash as opposed to 4.6 seconds. This much seems like common sense. The puzzling thing about physical genius, however, is that the closer you look at it the less it can be described by such cut-and-dried measures of athleticism.

Consider, for example, Tony Gwynn, who has been one of the best hitters in baseball over the past fifteen years. We would call him extraordinarily coordinated, by which we mean that in the course of several hundred milliseconds he can execute a series of perfectly synchronized muscular actions—the rotation of the shoulder, the movement of the arms, the shift of the hips—and can regulate the outcome of those actions so that his bat hits the ball with exactly the desired degree of force. These are abilities governed by specific neurological mechanisms. Timing, for example, appears to be controlled by the cerebellum. . . .

What sets physical geniuses apart from other people, then, is not merely being able to do something but knowing what to do—their capacity to pick up on subtle patterns that others generally miss. This is what we mean when we say that great athletes have a "feel" for the game, or that they "see" the court or the field or the ice in a special way. Wayne Gretzky, in a 1981 game against the St. Louis Blues, stood behind the St. Louis goal, laid the puck across the blade of his stick, then bounced it off the back of the goalie in front of him and into the net. Gretzky's genius at that moment lay in seeing a scoring possibility where no one had seen one before. "People talk about skating, puck-handling, and shooting," Gretzky told an interviewer some years later, "but the whole sport is angles and caroms, forgetting the straight direction the puck is going, calculating where it will be diverted, factoring in all the interruptions." Neurosurgeons say that when the very best surgeons operate they always know where they are going, and they mean that the Charlie Wilsons of this world possess that same special feel—an ability to calculate the diversions and to factor in the interruptions when faced with a confusing mass of blood and tissue.

When Charlie Wilson came to U.C. San Francisco, in July of 1968, his first   10 case concerned a woman who had just had a pituitary operation. The previous surgeon had done the one thing that surgeons are not supposed to do in pituitary surgery—tear one of the carotid arteries. Wilson was so dismayed by the outcome that he resolved he would teach himself how to do the transsphenoidal, which was then a relatively uncommon procedure. He carefully read the medical literature. He practiced on a few cadavers. He called a friend in Los Angeles who was an expert at the procedure, and had him come to San Francisco and perform two operations while Wilson watched. He flew to Paris to observe Gérard Guiot, who was one of the great transsphenoidal surgeons at the time. Then he flew home. It was the equivalent of someone preparing for a major-league tryout by watching the Yankees on television and hitting balls in an amusement-arcade batting cage. "Charlie went slowly," recalls Ernest Bates, a Bay-area neurosurgeon who scrubbed with Wilson on his first transsphenoidal, "but he knew the anatomy and, boom, he was there. I thought, My God, this was the first? You'd have thought he had done a hundred. Charlie has a skill that the rest of us just don't have."

This is the hard part about understanding physical genius, because the source of that special skill—that "feel"—is still something of a mystery. "Sometimes during the course of an operation, there'll be several possible ways of doing something, and I'll size them up and, without having any conscious reason, I'll just do one of them," Wilson told me. He speaks with a soft, slow drawl, a remnant of Neosho, Missouri, the little town where he grew up, and where his father was a pharmacist, who kept his store open from 7 A.M. to 11 P.M., seven days a week. Wilson has a plainspoken, unpretentious quality. When he talks about his extraordinary success as a surgeon, he gives the impression that he is talking about some abstract trait that he is neither responsible for nor completely able to understand. "It's sort of an invisible hand," he went on. "It begins almost to seem mystical. Sometimes a resident asks, 'Why did you do that?' and I say"—here Wilson gave a little shrug—"'Well, it just seemed like the right thing.'"

There is a neurosurgeon at Columbia Presbyterian Center, in Manhattan, by the name of Don Quest, who served two tours in Vietnam flying A-1s off the *U.S.S. Kitty Hawk*. Quest sounds like the kind of person who bungee jumps on the weekend and has personalized license plates that read "Ace." In fact, he is a thoughtful, dapper man with a carefully trimmed mustache, who plays the trombone in his spare time and quite cheerfully describes himself as compulsive. "When I read the *New York Times*, I don't speed-read it," Quest told me. "I read it carefully. I read everything. It drives my wife crazy." He was wearing a spotless physician's coat and a bow tie. "When I'm reading a novel—and there are so many novels I want to read—even if it's not very good I can't throw it away. I stick with it. It's quite frustrating, because I don't really have time for garbage." Quest talked about what it was like to repair a particularly tricky aneurysm compared to what it was like to land at night in rough seas and a heavy fog when you are running out of fuel and the lights are off on the carrier's landing strip, because the skies are full of enemy aircraft. "I think they are similar," he said, after some thought, and what he meant was that they were both exercises in a certain kind of exhaustive and meticulous preparation. "There is a checklist, before you take off, and this was drilled into us," Quest said. "It's on the dashboard with all the things you need to do. People forget to put the hook down, and you can't land on an aircraft carrier if the hook isn't down. Or they don't put the wheels down. One of my friends, my roommate, landed at night on the aircraft carrier with the wheels up. Thank God, the hook caught, because his engine stopped. He would have gone in the water." Quest did not seem like the kind of person who would forget to put the wheels down. "Some people are much more compulsive than others, and it shows," he went on to say. "It shows in how well they do their landing on the aircraft carrier, how many times they screw up, or are on the wrong radio frequency, or get lost, or their ordinances aren't accurate in terms of dropping a bomb. The ones who are the best are the ones who are always very careful."

Quest isn't saying that fine motor ability is irrelevant. One would expect him to perform extremely well on tests of the sort Ivry and Keele might devise. And, like Tony Gwynn, he's probably an adept and swift decision maker. But these abilities, Quest is saying, are of little use if you don't have the right sort of personality. Charles Bosk, a sociologist at the University of Pennsylvania, once conducted a set of interviews with young doctors who had either resigned or been fired from neurosurgery-training programs, in an effort to figure out what separated the unsuccessful surgeons from their successful counterparts. He concluded that, far more than technical skills or intelligence, what was necessary for success was the sort of attitude that Quest has—a practical-minded obsession with the possibility and the consequences of failure. "When I interviewed the surgeons who were fired, I used to leave the interview shaking," Bosk said. "I would hear these horrible stories about what they did wrong, but the thing was that they didn't *know* that what they did was wrong. In my interviewing, I began to develop what I thought was an indicator of whether someone was going to be a good surgeon or not. It was a couple of simple questions: Have you ever made a mistake? And, if so, what was your worst mistake? The people who said, 'Gee, I haven't really had one,' or, 'I've had a couple of bad outcomes but they were due to things outside my control'—invariably those were the worst candidates. And the residents who said, 'I make mistakes all the time. There was this horrible thing that happened just yesterday and here's what it was.' They were the best. They had the ability to rethink everything that they'd done and imagine how they might have done it differently."

What this attitude drives you to do is practice over and over again, until even the smallest imperfections are ironed out. After doing poorly in a tournament just prior to this year's Wimbledon, Greg Rusedski, who is one of the top tennis players in the world, told reporters that he was going home to hit a thousand practice serves. One of the things that set Rusedski apart from lesser players, in other words, is that he is the kind of person who is willing to stand out in the summer sun, repeating the same physical movement again and again, in single-minded pursuit of some fractional improvement in his performance. Wayne Gretzky was the same way. He would frequently stay behind after practice, long after everyone had left, flipping pucks to a specific spot in the crease, or aiming shot after shot at the crossbar or the goal post.

And Charlie Wilson? In his first few years as a professor at U.C.S.F., he   15
would disappear at the end of the day into a special laboratory to practice his
craft on rats: isolating, cutting, and then sewing up their tiny blood vessels, and
sometimes operating on a single rat two or three times. He would construct an
artificial aneurysm using a vein graft on the side of a rat artery, then manipulate
the aneurysm the same way he would in a human being, toughening its base with
a gentle coagulating current—and return two or three days later to see how
successful his work had been. Wilson sees surgery as akin to a military campaign.
Training with him is like boot camp. He goes to bed somewhere around eleven
at night and rises at 4:30 A.M. For years, he ran upward of eighty miles a week,
competing in marathons and hundred-mile ultra-marathons. He quit only after
he had a hip replacement and two knee surgeries and found himself operating
in a cast. Then he took up rowing. On his days in the operating room, at the
height of his career, Wilson would run his morning ten or twelve miles, conduct
medical rounds, operate steadily until six or seven in the evening, and, in between, see patients, attend meetings, and work on what now totals six hundred
academic articles. . . . [T]o Wilson the perfect operation requires a particular
grace and rhythm. "In every way, it is analogous to the routine of a concert pianist," he says. "If you were going to do a concert and you didn't practice for a
week, someone would notice that, just as I notice if one of my scrub nurses has
been off for a week. There is that fraction-of-a-second difference in the way she
reacts."

"Wilson has a certain way of positioning the arm of the retractor blade"—
an instrument used to hold brain tissue in place—"so that the back end of the
retractor doesn't stick up at all and he won't accidentally bump into it," Michon
Morita told me. "Every once in a while, though, I'd see him when he didn't quite
put it in the position he wanted to, and bumped it, which caused a little bit of
hemorrhage on the brain surface. It wasn't harming the patient, and it was nothing he couldn't handle. But I'd hear 'That was stupid,' and I'd immediately ask
myself, What did I do wrong? Then I'd realize he was chastising himself. Most
people would say that if there was no harm done to the patient it was no big deal.
But he wants to be perfect in everything, and when that perfection is broken he
gets frustrated."

This kind of obsessive preparation does two things. It creates consistency. Practice is what enables Greg Rusedski to hit a serve at a hundred and twenty-five
miles per hour again and again. It's what enables a pianist to play Chopin's
double-thirds Étude at full speed, striking every key with precisely calibrated force.
More important, practice changes the *way* a task is perceived. A chess master, for
example, can look at a game in progress for a few seconds and then perfectly reconstruct that same position on a blank chessboard. That's not because chess
masters have great memories (they don't have the same knack when faced with a
random arrangement of pieces) but because hours and hours of chess playing
have enabled them to do what psychologists call "chunking." Chunking is based

on the fact that we store familiar sequences—like our telephone number or our bank-machine password—in long-term memory as a single unit, or chunk. If I told you a number you'd never heard before, though, you would be able to store it only in short-term memory, one digit at a time, and if I asked you to repeat it back to me you might be able to remember only a few of those digits—maybe the first two or the last three. By contrast, when the chess masters see the board from a real game, they are able to break the board down into a handful of chunks—two or three clusters of pieces in positions that they have encountered before.

In "The Game of Our Lives," a classic account of the 1980–81 season of the Edmonton Oilers hockey team, Peter Gzowski argues that one of the principal explanations for the particular genius of Wayne Gretzky was that he was hockey's greatest chunker. Gretzky, who holds nearly every scoring record in professional hockey, baffled many observers because he seemed to reverse the normal laws of hockey. Most great offensive players prefer to keep the rest of the action on the ice behind them—to try to make the act of scoring be just about themselves and the goalie. Gretzky liked to keep the action in front of him. He would set up by the side of the rink, or behind the opposing team's net, so that the eleven other players on the ice were in full view, and then slide the perfect pass to the perfect spot. He made hockey look easy, even as he was playing in a way that made it more complicated. Gzowski says that Gretzky could do that because, like master chess players, he wasn't seeing all eleven other players individually; he was seeing only chunks. Here is Gzowski's conclusion after talking to Gretzky about a game he once played against the Montreal Canadiens. It could as easily serve as an explanation for Charlie Wilson's twenty-five-minute transsphenoidal resection:

> What Gretzky perceives on a hockey rink is, in a curious way, more simple than what a less accomplished player perceives. He sees not so much a set of moving players as a number of situations. . . . Moving in on the Montreal blueline, as he was able to recall while he watched a videotape of himself, he was aware of the position of all the other players on the ice. The pattern they formed was, to him, one fact, and he reacted to that fact. When he sends a pass to what to the rest of us appears an empty space on the ice, and when a teammate magically appears in that space to collect the puck, he has in reality simply summoned up from his bank account of knowledge the fact that in a particular situation, someone is likely to be in a particular spot, and if he is not there now he will be there presently.

. . . "A good [tennis] player knows where the ball is going," [Charlie] Wilson says. "He anticipates it. He is there. I just wasn't." What Wilson is describing is a failure not of skill or of resolve but of the least understood element of physical genius—imagination. For some reason, he could not make the game come alive in his mind.

When psychologists study people who are expert at motor tasks, they find that almost all of them use their imaginations in a very particular and sophisticated 20 way. Jack Nicklaus, for instance, has said that he has never taken a swing that he didn't first mentally rehearse, frame by frame. Yo-Yo Ma told me that he remembers riding on a bus, at the age of seven, and solving a difficult musical problem by visualizing himself playing the piece on the cello. Robert Spetzler, who trained with Wilson and is widely considered to be the heir to Wilson's mantle, says that when he gets into uncharted territory in an operation he feels himself transferring his mental image of what ought to happen onto the surgical field. Charlie Wilson talks about going running in the morning and reviewing each of the day's operations in his head — visualizing the entire procedure and each potential outcome in advance. "It was a virtual rehearsal," he says, "so when I was actually doing the operation, it was as if I were doing it for the second time." Once, he says, he had finished a case and taken off his gloves and was walking down the hall away from the operating room when he suddenly stopped, because he realized that the tape he had been playing in his head didn't match the operation that had unfolded before his eyes. "I was correlating everything — what I saw, what I expected, what the X-rays said. And I just realized that I had not pursued one particular thing. So I turned around, scrubbed, and went back in, and, sure enough, there was a little remnant of tumor that was just around the corner. It would have been a disaster."

The Harvard University psychologist Stephen Kosslyn has shown that this power to visualize consists of at least four separate abilities, working in combination. The first is the ability to generate an image — to take something out of long-term memory and reconstruct it on demand. The second is what he calls "image inspection," which is the ability to take that mental picture and draw inferences from it. The third is "image maintenance," the ability to hold that picture steady. And the fourth is "image transformation," which is the ability to take that image and manipulate it. If I asked you whether a frog had a tail, for example, you would summon up a picture of a frog from your long-term memory (image generation), hold it steady in your mind (image maintenance), rotate the frog around until you see his backside (image transformation), and then look to see if there was a tail there (image inspection). These four abilities are highly variable. Kosslyn once gave a group of people a list of thirteen tasks, each designed to test a different aspect of visualization, and the results were all over the map. You could be very good at generation and maintenance, for example, without being good at transformation, or you could be good at transformation without necessarily being adept at inspection and maintenance. Some of the correlations, in fact, were negative, meaning that sometimes being good at one of those four things meant that you were likely to be bad at another. Bennett Stein, a former chairman of neurosurgery at Columbia Presbyterian Center, says that one of the reasons some neurosurgery residents fail in their training is that they are incapable of making the transition between the way a particular problem is depicted in an X-ray or an M.R.I., and how the problem looks when they encounter it in real life. These are people whose capacities for mental imaging simply do not match what's required for dealing with the complexities of brain surgery. Perhaps these people can generate an image but are unable to transform it in precisely the way that is necessary to be a great surgeon; or perhaps they can transform the image but they cannot maintain it. . . .

"Certain aneurysms at the base of the brain are surrounded by very important blood vessels and nerves, and the typical neurosurgeon will make that dissection with a set of micro-instruments that are curved, each with a blunt end," Craig Yorke, who trained with Wilson and now practices neurosurgery in Topeka, recalls. "The neurosurgeon will sneak up on them. Charlie would call for a No. 11 blade, which is a thin, very low-profile scalpel, and would just cut down to where the aneurysm was. He would be there in a quarter of the time." The speed and the audacity of Wilson's maneuvers, Yorke said, would sometimes leave him breathless. "Do you know about Gestalt psychology?" he continued. "If I look at a particular field—tumor or aneurysm—I will see the gestalt after I've worked on it for a little while. He would just glance at it and see it. It's a conceptual, a spatial thing. His use of the No. 11 blade depended on his ability to construct a gestalt of the surgical field first. If just anybody had held up the eleven blade in that way it might have been a catastrophe. He could do it because he had the picture of the whole anatomy in his head when he picked up the instrument."

If you think of physical genius as a pyramid, with, at the bottom, the raw components of coordination, and, above that, the practice that perfects those particular movements, then this faculty of imagination is the top layer. This is what separates the physical genius from those who are merely very good. Michael Jordan and Karl Malone, his longtime rival, did not differ so much in their athletic ability or in how obsessively they practiced. The difference between them is that Jordan could always generate a million different scenarios by which his team could win, some of which were chunks stored in long-term memory, others of which were flights of fancy that came to him, figuratively and literally, in midair. Jordan twice won championships in the face of unexpected adversity: once, a case of the flu, and, the second time, a back injury to his teammate Scottie Pippen, and he seemed to thrive on these obstacles, in a way Karl Malone never could.

Yo-Yo Ma says that only once, early in his career, did he try for a technically perfect performance. "I was seventeen," he told me. "I spent a year working on it. I was playing a Brahms sonata at the 92nd Street Y. I remember working really hard at it, and in the middle of the performance I thought, I'm bored. It would have been nothing for me to get up from the stage and walk away. That's when I decided I would always opt for expression over perfection." It isn't that Ma doesn't achieve perfection; it's that he finds striving for perfection to be banal. He says that he sometimes welcomes it when he breaks a string, because that is precisely the kind of thing (like illness or an injury to a teammate) that you cannot prepare for—that you haven't chunked and, like some robot, stored neatly in long-term memory. The most successful performers improvise. They create, in Ma's words, "something living." Ma says he spends ninety per cent of his time "looking at the score, figuring it out—who's saying this, who wrote this and why," letting his mind wander, and only ten per cent on the instrument itself. Like Jordan, his genius originates principally in his imagination. If he spent less time dreaming and more time playing, he would be Karl Malone.

Here is the source of the physical genius's motivation. After all, what is this 25 sensation — this feeling of having what you do fit perfectly into the dimensions of your imagination — but the purest form of pleasure? Tony Gwynn and Wayne Gretzky and Charlie Wilson and all the other physical geniuses are driven to greatness because they have found something so compelling that they cannot put it aside. Perhaps this explains why a great many top neurosurgeons are also highly musical. . . . Wilson . . . is a cellist and, when he was a student in New Orleans, he would play jazz piano at Pat O'Brien's, in the French Quarter. Music is one of the few vocations that offer a kind of sensory and cognitive immersion similar to surgery: the engagement of hand and eye, the challenge of sustained performance, the combination of mind and motion — all of it animated by the full force of the imagination. Once, in an E-mail describing his special training sessions on rats, Wilson wrote that he worked on them for two years and "then trailed off when I finally figured that I was doing it for fun, not for practice." For fun! When someone chooses to end a twelve-hour day alone in a laboratory, inducing aneurysms in the arteries of rats, we might call that behavior obsessive. But that is an uncharitable word. A better explanation is that, for some mysterious and wonderful reason, Wilson finds the act of surgery irresistible, in the way that musicians find pleasure in the sounds they produce on their instruments, or in the way Tony Gwynn gets a thrill every time he strokes a ball cleanly through the infield. Before he was two years old, it is said, Wayne Gretzky watched hockey games on television, enraptured, and slid his stockinged feet on the linoleum in imitation of the players, then cried when the game was over, because he could not understand how something so sublime should have to come to an end. This was long before Gretzky was any good at the game itself, or was skilled in any of its aspects, or could create even the smallest of chunks. But what he had was what the physical genius must have before any of the other layers of expertise fall into place: he had stumbled onto the one thing that, on some profound aesthetic level, made him happy. . . .

PERRI KLASS

The One-in-a-Thousand Illness You Can't Afford to Miss

Perri Klass, born in Trinidad in 1958, is a Harvard-educated pediatrician whose essays about medicine have been collected in A Not Entirely Benign Procedure: Four Years as a Medical Student (1987) *and* Baby Doctor: A Pediatrician's Training (1992). *"The One-in-a-Thousand Illness You Can't Afford to Miss," published in the* New York Times (2006), *illustrates the life-saving significance of intuitive medical knowledge, intellectual understanding in action.*

Evening session at the health center, three of us seeing patients in pediatrics. My colleague asked whether I would take a quick look at a boy with a fever and headache. In the exam room, the overhead light was off because it hurt his eyes. He was lying on the table, but he sat up and answered my questions, and he let me look in his throat, and he moved his head around when I asked him to.

We excused ourselves, my colleague and I, and went out of the room. We conferred. The boy didn't look good. Pronounced photophobia—avoidance of light—and severe headache and fever. And although his neck was not actually stiff, he did indicate some neck pain when we asked him to bend it.

He needs to go to the emergency room, we agreed.

What do you think, my colleague asked, would you send him by ambulance?

"Yes," I said. "I mean, if this is your meningitis, wouldn't you want him in an ambulance?"

She understood what I meant, of course. Sometimes it feels as if you spend your career in primary care pediatrics waiting for your meningitis, your leukemia, your dislocated hip.

The bad things, the things that cross your mind—automatically and usually fleetingly—day after day as you examine children, the diagnoses that statistically will come your way at least once or twice over the course of years and years of walking into one exam room after another.

Every time you examine a little baby's hips—and you always examine a little baby's hips—you are looking for congenital dysplasia of the hip, a hip that doesn't fit properly into its socket. Find it early, fix it early. Don't miss it.

Every time you find unexplained lymphadenopathy, enlarged lymph nodes, in a child, leukemia crosses your mind, at least fleetingly. Children have swollen lymph nodes all the time. But you had better not miss your leukemia.

Or meningitis. In winter especially, lots of children come in with high fevers. Most have flu or other viral illnesses or ear infections. Some look reasonably bright and bouncy, fever and all, and some look sick and miserable.

And as I go from room to room and examine those children and swab their throats for strep or dig the wax out of their ears, I think quickly about meningitis. O.K., the giggling 3-year-old eating crunchy junk food snacks while he runs busily around the exam room may have a temperature of 103, but he does not have meningitis.

But what about the hot-to-the-touch fretful 1-year-old who will not let her mother put her down? Or the feverish, headachy 12-year-old?

Fever, headache, stiff neck, photophobia—these are the clinical hallmarks of meningitis, an infection of the membranes that surround and protect the spine. It can be caused by a variety of viruses and bacteria, and the bacterial form, in particular, can be a virulent fast-moving infection, an infection that can devastate or even kill a child.

It needs to be treated promptly, and to treat it, you need to diagnose it, by doing a spinal tap, and to diagnose it, you need to think about it.

I have seen plenty of children with meningitis. I did my residency in the days before children were routinely vaccinated against Haemophilus influenzae

Type B and Streptococcus pneumoniae, two bacteria with propensities for spinal infections, and I took care of plenty of hospitalized children with meningitis.

I worked in the emergency room and did my share of spinal taps, on the wards, where we took care of some children who ended up deaf or brain damaged, and in the intensive care unit, where the sickest children were on life support.

Nowadays, with children well protected against those two particular bugs, meningitis is less of a worry, but it has not gone away. I know my meningitis will walk in the door in primary care someday, one of those feverish hard-to-console babies or one of those flu-ish unhappy teenagers.

My colleague sent the boy to the emergency room by ambulance. By ambulance, because that way he got there as fast as possible. Because that way we knew he would receive attention immediately. Because that way, if by some chance he was her meningitis and his mental status began to deteriorate or he started to have a seizure—well, at least he would be in an ambulance.

So you worry about it with every sick child, week after week, winter after winter. Hundreds of cases of influenza and other viral illnesses, fevers and headaches and body aches and sore throats and general miseries will come and go.

But at some point, your meningitis will arrive, and it will all come down to 20 whether you recognize it or not.

You stand in the exam room, worrying about this one particular very important child, mindful of the danger and trying to look the threat in the eye and recognize it—even with the lights off.

NANCY C. ANDREASEN

The Creative Mind

Nancy C. Andreasen is author of The Broken Brain *(1984) and* Brave New Brain: Conquering Mental Illness in the Era of the Genome *(2001). She holds a chair in psychiatry at the University of Iowa Hospitals and Clinics and is editor-in-chief for the* Journal of the American Psychiatric Association. *This excerpt is taken from* The Creating Brain: The Neuroscience of Genius *(2005).*

Creative people tend to approach the world in a fresh and original way that is not shaped by preconceptions. The obvious order and rules that are so evident to less creative people, and which give a comfortable structure to life, often are not perceived by the creative individual. . . . This openness to new experience often permits creative people to observe things that others cannot, because they do not wear the blinders of conventionality when they look around them. Openness is accompanied by a tolerance for ambiguity. . . . They enjoy living in a world that is filled with unanswered questions and blurry boundaries.

Creative people enjoy adventure. They like to explore. As they explore, they may push the limits of social conventions. They dislike externally imposed rules, seemingly driven by their own set of rules derived from within. This lack of commonality with the rest of the world may produce feelings of alienation or loneliness. In addition, the lack of evident and obvious standards of perception or information may produce a blurring of the boundaries of identity or self. . . .

Paradoxically, the creative person's indifference to convention is combined with sensitivity. This may take two forms: sensitivity to what others are experiencing, or sensitivity to what the individual himself or herself is experiencing. . . . Inevitably, this combination of pushing the edge and experiencing strong feelings can lead to a sense of injury and pain. Living on "the edge of chaos" may also be psychically dangerous, because approaching too close may even lead to "falling off" occasionally—into mental disorganization or confusion. . . .

Nevertheless, creative people also have traits that make them durable and persistent. . . . Persistence is absolutely fundamental, since creative people typically experience repeated rejection because of their tendency to push the limits and to perceive things in a new way. . . . Creative people also tend to be intensely curious. They like to understand how and why, to take things apart and put them back together again, to move into domains of the mind or spirit that conventional society perceives as hidden or forbidden. Creative people are also often perfectionistic and even obsessional. . . .

These traits tend to be combined with a basic simplicity, defined by a single- 5 ness of vision and dedication to their work. In fact, much of the time, their work is really all that creative people care about.

QUESTIONS FOR DISCUSSION AND WRITING

1. Gladwell emphasizes the physical genius's ability to "pick up on subtle patterns" (paragraph 9) and Andreasen observes that creative people are "durable and persistent" and "intensely curious" (paragraph 4). What do the similarities and differences in Gladwell's and Andreasen's conceptions of gifted people suggest? Might these be differences of emphasis rather than actual qualitative differences?

2. Have you been trained, in classrooms or sports programs or on the job, to use your imagination? If imagination is key to success in various fields, consider what kind of education you have received in using the four visualization skills discussed in paragraph 21 of "The Physical Genius." Does Andreasen's discussion of creativity recognize the importance of these skills?

3. Gladwell focuses on the physical genius's ability to "feel" his or her way through a chosen activity, an intuitive ability that is difficult to explain. Andreasen approaches creativity more as a set of unconventional behaviors. Consider what kinds of activities you associate with intuitive or unconventional approaches. For example, if you play a musical instrument or sing, you might contrast such

an activity with writing or with caring for an animal or working with a mechanical object, such as a car.

4. Find an article or a book that specifically discusses an athlete's use of the imaginative skills Gladwell describes. Write an analysis, emphasizing how the athlete uses his or her imagination in game play or practice routines. Or, find a book on sports training that discusses the roles of imagination and visualization, and compare the ideas there to the ones Gladwell discusses in "The Physical Genius."

5. Research and write about an expert in any field who exhibits the imaginative traits of "physical genius" as Gladwell defines them.

EVAN EISENBERG

Dialogue Boxes You Should Have Read More Carefully

Evan Eisenberg (b. 1955) draws on literature, philosophy, and science in his periodical writings and books that focus on music and technology. The Recording Angel (1987) is a study of the cultural impact of recorded music. The Ecology of Eden (1999) examines the relation of humans to the natural world and presents a model to prevent environmental disaster. "Dialogue Boxes You Should Have Read More Carefully" offers a critique of a familiar product, satirizing its language and underlying mentality.

Dialogue Boxes You Should Have Read More Carefully

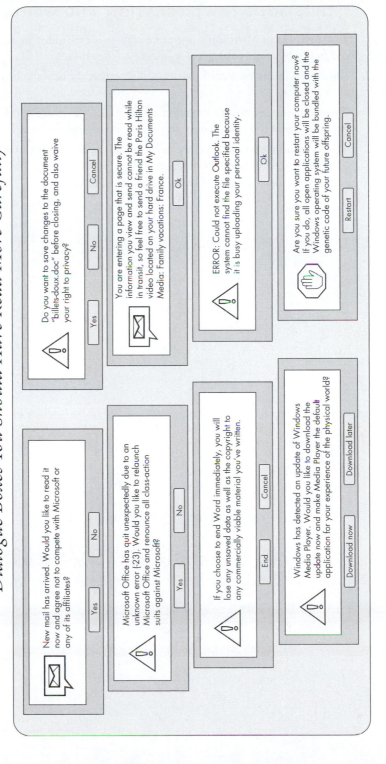

New mail has arrived. Would you like to read it now and agree not to compete with Microsoft or any of its affiliates?

[Yes]   [No]

Microsoft Office has quit unexpectedly due to an unknown error (-23). Would you like to relaunch Microsoft Office and renounce all class-action suits against Microsoft?

[Yes]   [No]

If you choose to end Word immediately, you will lose any unsaved data as well as the copyright to any commercially viable material you've written.

[End]   [Cancel]

Windows has detected an update of Windows Media Player. Would you like to download the update now and make Media Player the default application for your experience of the physical world?

[Download now]   [Download later]

Do you want to save changes to the document "billets-doux.doc" before closing, and also waive your right to privacy?

[Yes]   [No]   [Cancel]

You are entering a page that is secure. The information you view and send cannot be read while in transit, so feel free to send a friend the Paris Hilton video located on your hard drive in My Documents Media: Family vacations: France.

[Ok]

ERROR: Could not execute Outlook. The system cannot find the file specified because it is busy uploading your personal identity.

[Ok]

Are you sure you want to restart your computer now? If you do, all open applications will be closed and the Windows operating system will be bundled with the genetic code of your future offspring.

[Restart]   [Cancel]

QUESTIONS FOR DISCUSSION AND WRITING

1. What criticism of Microsoft's operating system is embedded in each dialogue box? In combination, what larger argument do they make?

2. How can Eisenberg be sure his readers will interpret the boxes as he wants them to?

3. In what ways is Eisenberg's imitation of Microsoft's language and implied reasoning accurate? Is it close enough to provide a recognizable parody?

4. In cartoon format, in one or more panels, make an argument of your own (see Spiegelman, p. 139, and McCloud, p. 62). Or write captions for existing cartoons, such as one in *The New Yorker*'s cartoon bank Web site.

BRIEF TAKES ON TRAVEL: REPORTS FROM OTHER PLACES

Travel throws the world into sharp relief. When we pick up and move we see ourselves in a different light. We adopt new ways of being in the world, if only temporarily. We step outside of ourselves, our daily routines, our familiar environments. It is not always easy. Theroux points out that we're never quite sure what we're getting ourselves in for, since no trip can ever really be duplicated. Twain, Proulx, Kapuscinski, and Morris note that travel to new places is at heart "unnerving," risky, even dangerous. Yet it can also be exciting and earth-changing—there may be no going back.

KYOKO MORI

Date Stamp

A Japanese-American poet, novelist, and nonfiction writer, Kyoko Mori is currently a lecturer in creative writing at Harvard University.

The man picks up the big silver stamp and readjusts the dates, rolling forward the days. I watch him as he stamps my pass: 5/25/90. The ink is dark and perfectly printed without a smear. He pushes the stamped pass toward me without speaking or even smiling. As I nod and turn to go, I realize how different this transaction has been from what I am used to: The man said nothing to me except what strictly pertained to the business at hand; he didn't ask me where I was going, where I was from, what I was doing in Japan. He made no small talk. He didn't even thank me for doing business with his company. For once, I miss what I am mildly irritated by in the American Midwest: people wishing me to have a nice day, perfect strangers engaging in small talk. Here a person could be isolated in polite silence for days.

PAUL THEROUX

Every Trip Is Unique

Paul Theroux is the author of fifteen works of nonfiction, including Riding the Iron Rooster *(1988), and twenty-nine works of fiction, including the novels* The Family Arsenal *(1976),* The Mosquito Coast *(1982),* My Secret History *(1989),* Chicago Loop *(1990),* Hotel Honolulu *(2003), and* The Elephanta Suite *(2007).*

I did not know when I wrote it that every trip is unique. My travel book is about my trip, not yours or anyone else's. Even if someone had come with me and written a book about the trip, it would have been a different book. Another thing I did not know at the time was that every trip has a historical dimension. Not long after I traveled through these countries, they underwent political changes. The shah was exiled and Iran became very dangerous for foreign travelers; Afghanistan went to war with itself, the Soviet Union helping out; India and Pakistan restored their rail link. Laos shut its borders to foreigners and did away with its monarchy. Vietnam repaired its railway, so now it is possible to travel by train from Ho Chi Minh City (Saigon) to Hanoi. Many of the individual trains I rode were taken out of service, most notably the Orient Express. The train that plies the route from London to Venice under that name today is for wealthy, comfort-seeking people who have selfish, sumptuous fantasies about travel bearing no relation to the real thing. However awful my old Orient Express was, at least all sorts of people took it, rich and poor, old and young, rattling back and forth from Europe to Asia. It was cheap and friendly, and like all great trains it was a world on wheels.

When I wrote *Railway Bazaar* I was groping in the dark—although I was careful to disguise this; my self-assurance in the narrative was sheer bravado, a way of whistling to keep my spirits up. I knew that I had taken over a venerable form, the travel book, and was writing it my own way, to suit myself and my peculiar trip and temperament. It was not at all like a novel: fiction required inspiration, intense imagining, and a long period alone in a room. A travel book, I had discovered, was a deliberate act, like the act of travel itself. It took health and strength and confidence, optimism and deep curiosity. When I finished a novel I never knew whether I would be able to write another one. But I knew when I finished this first travel book that I would be able to do it again.

MARK TWAIN

Learning the River

Samuel Langhorne Clemens wrote under the pen name Mark Twain (taken from the cry of a riverboat crew marking depth) and is author of the classic novel Adventures of Huckleberry Finn *(1884).*

The *Paul Jones* was now bound for St. Louis. I planned a siege against my pilot, and at the end of three hard days he surrendered. He agreed to teach me the Mississippi River from New Orleans to St. Louis for five hundred dollars, payable out of the first wages I should receive after graduating. I entered upon the small enterprise of "learning" twelve or thirteen hundred miles of the great Mississippi

River with the easy confidence of my time of life. If I had really known what I was about to require of my faculties, I should not have had the courage to begin. I supposed that all a pilot had to do was to keep his boat in the river, and I did not consider that that could be much of a trick, since it was so wide.

The boat backed out from New Orleans at four in the afternoon, and it was "our watch" until eight. Mr. Bixby, my chief, "straightened her up," plowed her along past the sterns of the other boats that lay at the Levee, and then said, "Here, take her; shave those steamships as close as you'd peel an apple." I took the wheel and my heart went down into my boots; for it seemed to me that we were about to scrape the side off every ship in the line, we were so close. I held my breath and began to claw the boat away from the danger, and I had my own opinion of the pilot who had known no better than to get us into such peril, but I was too wise to express it. In half a minute I had a wide margin of safety intervening between the *Paul Jones* and the ships, and within ten seconds more I was set aside in disgrace and Mr. Bixby was going into danger again and flaying me alive with abuse of my cowardice. I was stung but I was obliged to admire the easy confidence with which my chief loafed from side to side of his wheel and trimmed the ships so closely that disaster seemed ceaselessly imminent. When he had cooled a little he told me that the easy water was close ashore and the current outside, and therefore we must hug the bank up-stream, to get the benefit of the former, and stay well out down-stream, to take advantage of the latter. In my own mind I resolved to be a down-stream pilot and leave the up-streaming to people dead to prudence.

Meantime, the thing that was running in my mind was, "Now, if my ears hear aright, I have not only to get the names of all the towns and islands and bends, and so on by heart, but I must even get up a warm personal acquaintanceship with every old snag and one-limbed cottonwood and obscure wood-pile that ornaments the banks of this river for twelve hundred miles; and more than that, I must actually know where these things are in the dark, unless these guests are gifted with eyes that can pierce through two miles of solid blackness. I wish the piloting business was in Jericho and I had never thought of it."

E. ANNIE PROULX

Travel Is . . . an Unnerving Experience

E. Annie Proulx has published many short stories, including "Brokeback Mountain," which was made into a film in 2005. In 1994 Proulx won, among other awards, the National Book Award and the Pulitzer Prize for Fiction for her novel The Shipping News.

Travel, any kind of travel, is an unnerving experience. Drive and there are the serial killer highways, the chance of running out of gas at midnight in Idaho, sticking in mud wallows, dodging tornadoes or outrunning blizzards, eating cruel food in Mud Butte or Biloxi. Fly, and it is paralysis in boa-constrictor seats, headache from oxygen deprivation, the salmonella sandwich, babble of seatmate who has just started a religious cult and needs followers, ice on the wings, lost luggage. Last spring I got the flu simultaneously with a strep throat, a sinus problem and a double ear infection. I was only half recovered when the book tour began. My ears crackled and echoed. Flying was impossible. It had to be the train. Amtrak.

The trip west was dismal but not perilous. There is nothing like traveling by train; all the socio-industrial crap of North America is visible as in no other form of travel: shacks, trash, tenements, discarded machinery, bus graveyards, ganglia of transmission towers, those pointed gravel storage sheds like enormous brassiere cups, generating stations that turn fog purple, drunk people in the weeds, iridescent wetlands that serve as combination swamp-and-appliance-disposal depots. Yet the trouble came on the return, the so-called Lake Shore Express—the name is a far-fetched conceit—heading east out of Chicago.

I fell asleep a few hours after the train pulled out and enjoyed an unusually restful night. I woke the next morning thinking that Amtrak must have discovered the secret of perfect sleeping-car suspension, and didn't quite take it in when the car attendant said we were still in Toledo, had been in Toledo since eleven o'clock the night before. There's a joke about a Texan trying to impress a New Englander with the size of his state. "Y' know," he says, "you kin boa'd the train in Dallis and twena-foah houas lateh you still in Tixas." It was like that. You board the train in Toledo and ten hours later you're still in Toledo. The car attendant handed me a paper cup of cool coffee and said that a tug was stuck under the railroad bridge over the Maumee River and nothing could get it unstuck, nothing, and that they were waiting for a brace of powerful tugs to come down from Detroit and tear it loose. Hours passed. No one knew anything. An old railroad tradition. Because there was no cellular phone on this train scores of furious passengers got off and went into the station, where they stood in line to use the only pay phone in working order to explain to the boss or spouse that although they should have been in Boston by now they were still—ha ha—in Toledo, home of the Detroit Tiger's minor league team, the Toledo Mud Hens. The ticket seller in the station shrugged and said the same thing had happened in November. More passengers got off to make more phone calls. Suddenly, with a lurch, the train went forward. The bridge was open. Once started the train did not stop, not even for the shouting passengers running down the platform. On the train itself the club car attendant was giving away packets of stale peanuts, Amtrak's solace to enraged passengers. . . .

————————

RYSZARD KAPUSCINSKI
The Truck: Hitchhiking through Hell

Ryszard Kapuscinski was a prize-winning Polish journalist and poet who traveled widely. His books include The Emperor *(1978),* Shah of Shahs *(1982), and* Imperium *(1993).*

I was a pitiful sight—dirty, unshaved, and, above all, wasted by the nightmarish heat of the Saharan summer. An experienced Frenchman had warned me earlier: It will feel as if someone were sticking a knife into you. Into your back. Into your head. At noon, the rays of the sun beat down with the force of a knife.

The driver looked at me and at first said nothing. Then he motioned toward the truck with his hand and called out to me—"*Yallah!*" ("Let's go! We're off!") I climbed into the cab and slammed the door shut. We set off immediately.

I had no sense of where we were going. Sand flashed by in the glow of the headlights, shimmering with different shades, laced with strips of gravel and shards of rock. The wheels reared up on granite ledges or sank down into hollows and stony fissures. In the deep, black night, one could see only two spots of light— two bright, clearly outlined orbs, sliding over the surface of the desert. Nothing else was visible.

Before long, I began to suspect that we were driving blindly, on a shortcut to somewhere, because there were no demarcation points, no signs, posts, or any other traces of a roadway. I tried to question the driver. I gestured at the darkness around us and asked, "Nouakchott?"

He looked at me and laughed. "Nouakchott?" He repeated this dreamily, as 5 if it were the Hanging Gardens of Semiramis that I was asking him about—so beautiful, but for us lowly ones too high to reach. I concluded from this that we were not headed in the direction I desired, but I did not know how to ask him where, in that case, we were going. I desperately wanted to establish some contact with him, to get to know him even a little. "Ryszard," I said, pointing at myself. Then I pointed at him. He understood. "Salim," he said, and laughed again. Silence fell. We must have come upon a smooth stretch of desert, for the Berliet began to roll along more gently and quickly (exactly how fast I don't know, since all the instruments were broken). We drove on for a time without speaking, until finally I fell asleep.

A sudden silence awoke me. The engine had stopped. The truck stood still. Salim was pressing on the gas pedal and turning the key in the ignition. The battery was working—the starter, too—but the engine emitted no sound. It was morning, and already light outside. He began searching around the cab for the lever that opens the hood. This struck me at once as odd and suspicious: a driver who doesn't know how to open the hood? Eventually, he figured out that the latches that needed to be released were on the outside. He then stood on a fender and began to inspect the engine, but he peered at its intricate construction as if he were seeing it for the first time. He would touch something, try to move it, but his gestures were those of an amateur. Every now and then, he would climb into the cab and turn the key in the ignition, but the engine remained dead silent. He located the toolbox, but there wasn't much in it. He pulled out a hammer, several wrenches, screwdrivers. Then he started to take the engine apart.

I stepped down from the cab. All around us was desert. Sand, with dark stones scattered about. Nearby, a large black oval rock. (In the hours following noon, after it had been warmed by the sun, it would radiate heat like a steel-mill oven.) A moonscape, delineated by a level horizon—the earth ends, and then there's nothing but sky and more sky. No hills. No dunes. Not a single leaf. And, of course, no water. Water! It's what instantly comes to mind in such circumstances. In the desert, the first thing a man sees when he opens his eyes in the morning is the face of his enemy—the flaming visage of the sun. The sight elicits in him a reflexive gesture of self-preservation: he reaches for water. Drink! Drink! Only by doing so can he ever so slightly improve his odds in the desert's eternal struggle—the desperate duel with the sun.

I resolved to look around for water, for I had none with me.

MARY MORRIS
My First Night Alone in Mexico

Mary Morris is a fiction writer whose latest novel is The River Queen *(2007).*

In this town of shrieking birds and promenading lovers, I could think of nothing else to do, so I went to church. I walked hesitantly into the large Gothic stone building and down an aisle toward the apse. Slipping into a pew off to the side, I sat beside a campesino family, the woman with a child suckling at her exposed breast, the children in freshly ironed shirts, the father, in a sombrero, keeping a toddler from running away.

I sat down with a blind man and with wide-eyed children, with the toothless, the ancients, the impoverished, the illegitimate mothers, the crippled, the drunk, the miserable, the lost. I prayed with the beggar who had no hands and with the woman whose eyes were empty sockets. I prayed with the contrite and the forlorn, with *los desdichados*—the unlucky, the misfortunate. I prayed until the tears came down my face and I was crying in that church on that Sunday night, my first night alone in Mexico, praying that the reason for this journey would be made clear to me, oblivious of the Mexicans who watched with troubled eyes, moved by my inexplicable grief.

CHAPTER 4

Education and the American Character: Issues of Economics, Politics, and Culture

JONATHAN KOZOL

The Human Cost of an Illiterate Society

Jonathan Kozol (b. 1936) grew up in Newton, Massachusetts, graduated from Harvard (B.A., 1958), and received a Rhodes scholarship but abandoned it to spend four years in Paris writing a novel, The Fume of Poppies *(1958). Moved by the murders of civil rights activists in the South, he returned to the United States to become deeply involved in the civil rights movement and issues of social justice, to which he has devoted the rest of his life as an author, educator, and activist. Kozol's first book,* Death at an Early Age: The Destruction of the Hearts and Minds of Negro Children in the Boston Public Schools *(1967), won the National Book Award in Science, Philosophy, and Religion. Other award-winning books include* Rachel and Her Children: Homeless Families in America *(1988),* Savage Inequalities: Children in America's Schools *(1991), and* Amazing Grace: The Lives of Children and the Conscience of a Nation *(1995). His most recent book is* The Shame of the Nation: The Restoration of Apartheid Schooling in America *(2005).*

"The Human Cost of an Illiterate Society," a chapter from Illiterate America *(1985), shows how illiteracy degrades people's quality of life, makes them vulnerable to others' interpretations of the written word, and prevents their full participation in democratic society.*

PRECAUTIONS. READ BEFORE USING.

Poison: Contains sodium hydroxide (caustic soda-lye).
Corrosive: Causes severe eye and skin damage, may cause blindness.
Harmful or fatal if swallowed.
If swallowed, give large quantities of milk or water.
Do not induce vomiting.

Important: Keep water out of can at all times to prevent contents from violently erupting. . . .

–Warning on a Can of Drāno

We are speaking here no longer of the dangers faced by passengers on Eastern Airlines or the dollar costs incurred by U.S. corporations and taxpayers. We are speaking now of human suffering and of the ethical dilemmas that are faced by a society that looks upon such suffering with qualified concern but does not take those actions which its wealth and ingenuity would seemingly demand.

Questions of literacy, in Socrates' belief, must at length be judged as matters of morality. Socrates could not have had in mind the moral compromise peculiar to a nation like our own. Some of our Founding Fathers did, however, have this question in their minds. One of the wisest of those Founding Fathers (one who may not have been most compassionate but surely was more prescient than some of his peers) recognized the special dangers that illiteracy would pose to basic equity in the political construction that he helped to shape.

"A people who mean to be their own governors," James Madison wrote, "must arm themselves with the power knowledge gives. A popular government without popular information or the means of acquiring it, is but a prologue to a farce or a tragedy, or perhaps both."

Tragedy looms larger than farce in the United States today. Illiterate citizens seldom vote. Those who do are forced to cast a vote of questionable worth. They cannot make informed decisions based on serious print information. Sometimes they can be alerted to their interests by aggressive voter education. More frequently, they vote for a face, a smile, or a style, not for a mind or character or body of beliefs.

The number of illiterate adults exceeds by 16 million the entire vote cast for 5 the winner in the 1980 presidential contest. If even one third of all illiterates could vote, and read enough and do sufficient math to vote in their self-interest, Ronald Reagan would not likely have been chosen president. There is, of course, no way to know for sure. We do know this: Democracy is a mendacious term when used by those who are prepared to countenance the forced exclusion of one third of our electorate. So long as 60 million people are denied significant participation, the government is neither of, nor for, nor by, the people. It is a government, at best, of those two thirds whose wealth, skin color, or parental privilege allows them opportunity to profit from the provocation and instruction of the written word.

The undermining of democracy in the United States is one "expense" that sensitive Americans can easily deplore because it represents a contradiction that endangers citizens of all political positions. The human price is not so obvious at first.

Since I first immersed myself within this work I have often had the following dream: I find that I am in a railroad station or a large department store within a city that is utterly unknown to me and where I cannot understand the printed words. None of the signs or symbols is familiar. Everything looks strange: like mirror writing of some kind. Gradually I understand that I am in the Soviet Union. All the letters on the walls around me are Cyrillic. I look for my pocket dictionary but I find that it has been mislaid. Where have I left it? Then I recall that I forgot to bring it with me when I packed my bags in Boston. I struggle to remember the name of my hotel. I try to ask somebody for directions. One person stops and looks at me in a peculiar way. I lose the nerve to ask. At last I reach into my wallet for an ID card. The card is missing. Have I lost it? Then I remember that my card was confiscated for some reason, many years before. Around this point, I wake up in a panic.

This panic is not so different from the misery that millions of adult illiterates experience each day within the course of their routine existence in the U.S.A.

Illiterates cannot read the menu in a restaurant.

They cannot read the cost of items on the menu in the *window* of the restau-   10
rant before they enter.

Illiterates cannot read the letters that their children bring home from their teachers. They cannot study school department circulars that tell them of the courses that their children must be taking if they hope to pass the SAT exams. They cannot help with homework. They cannot write a letter to the teacher. They are afraid to visit in the classroom. They do not want to humiliate their child or themselves.

Illiterates cannot read instructions on a bottle of prescription medicine. They cannot find out when a medicine is past the year of safe consumption; nor can they read of allergenic risks, warnings to diabetics, or the potential sedative effect of certain kinds of nonprescription pills. They cannot observe preventive health care admonitions. They cannot read about "the seven warning signs of cancer" or the indications of blood-sugar fluctuations or the risks of eating certain foods that aggravate the likelihood of cardiac arrest.

Illiterates live, in more than literal ways, an uninsured existence. They cannot understand the written details on a health insurance form. They cannot read the waivers that they sign preceding surgical procedures. Several women I have known in Boston have entered a slum hospital with the intention of obtaining a tubal ligation and have emerged a few days later after having been subjected to a hysterectomy. Unaware of their rights, incognizant of jargon, intimidated by the unfamiliar air of fear and atmosphere of ether that so many of us find oppressive in the confines even of the most attractive and expensive medical facilities, they have signed their names to documents they could not read and which nobody, in the hectic situation that prevails so often in those overcrowded hospitals that serve the urban poor, had even bothered to explain.

Childbirth might seem to be the last inalienable right of any female citizen within a civilized society. Illiterate mothers, as we shall see, already have been cheated of the power to protect their progeny against the likelihood of demolition in deficient public schools and, as a result, against the verbal servitude within which they themselves exist. Surgical denial of the right to bear that child in the first place represents an ultimate denial, an unspeakable metaphor, a final darkness that denies even the twilight gleamings of our own humanity. What greater violation of our biological, our biblical, our spiritual humanity could possibly exist than that which takes place nightly, perhaps hourly these days, within such overburdened and benighted institutions as the Boston City Hospital? Illiteracy has many costs; few are so irreversible as this.

Even the roof above one's head, the gas or other fuel for heating that protects 15 the residents of northern city slums against the threat of illness in the winter months become uncertain guarantees. Illiterates cannot read the lease that they must sign to live in an apartment which, too often, they cannot afford. They cannot manage check accounts and therefore seldom pay for anything by mail. Hours and entire days of difficult travel (and the cost of bus or other public transit) must be added to the real cost of whatever they consume. Loss of interest on the check accounts they do not have, and could not manage if they did, must be regarded as another of the excess costs paid by the citizen who is excluded from the common instruments of commerce in a numerate society.

"I couldn't understand the bills," a woman in Washington, D.C., reports, "and then I couldn't write the checks to pay them. We signed things we didn't know what they were."

Illiterates cannot read the notices that they receive from welfare offices or from the IRS. They must depend on word-of-mouth instruction from the welfare worker—or from other persons whom they have good reason to mistrust. They do not know what rights they have, what deadlines and requirements they face, what options they might choose to exercise. They are half-citizens. Their rights exist in print but not in fact.

Illiterates cannot look up numbers in a telephone directory. Even if they can find the names of friends, few possess the sorting skills to make use of the yellow pages; categories are bewildering and trade names are beyond decoding capabilities for millions of nonreaders. Even the emergency numbers listed on the first page of the phone book—"Ambulance," "Police," and "Fire"—are too frequently beyond the recognition of nonreaders.

Many illiterates cannot read the admonition on a pack of cigarettes. Neither the Surgeon General's warning nor its reproduction on the package can alert them to the risks. Although most people learn by word of mouth that smoking is related to a number of grave physical disorders, they do not get the chance to read the detailed stories which can document this danger with the vividness that turns concern into determination to resist. They can see the handsome cowboy or the slim Virginia lady lighting up a filter cigarette; they cannot heed the words that tell them that this product is (not "may be") dangerous to their health. Sixty million men and women are condemned to be the unalerted, high-risk candidates for cancer.

Illiterates do not buy "no-name" products in the supermarkets. They must 20 depend on photographs or the familiar logos that are printed on the packages of brand-name groceries. The poorest people, therefore, are denied the benefits of the least costly products.

Illiterates depend almost entirely upon label recognition. Many labels, however, are not easy to distinguish. Dozens of different kinds of Campbell's soup appear identical to the nonreader. The purchaser who cannot read and does not dare to ask for help, out of the fear of being stigmatized (a fear which is unfortunately realistic), frequently comes home with something which she never wanted and her family never tasted.

Illiterates cannot read instructions on a pack of frozen food. Packages sometimes provide an illustration to explain the cooking preparations; but illustrations are of little help to someone who must "boil water, drop the food—*within* its plastic wrapper—in the boiling water, wait for it to simmer, instantly remove."

Even when labels are seemingly clear, they may be easily mistaken. A woman in Detroit brought home a gallon of Crisco for her children's dinner. She thought that she had bought the chicken that was pictured on the label. She had enough Crisco now to last a year—but no more money to go back and buy the food for dinner.

Recipes provided on the packages of certain staples sometimes tempt a semi-literate person to prepare a meal her children have not tasted. The longing to vary the uniform and often starchy content of low-budget meals provided to the family that relies on food stamps commonly leads to ruinous results. Scarce funds have been wasted and the food must be thrown out. The same applies to distribution of food-surplus produce in emergency conditions. Government inducements to poor people to "explore the ways" by which to make a tasty meal from tasteless noodles, surplus cheese, and powdered milk are useless to nonreaders. Intended as benevolent advice, such recommendations mock reality and foster deeper feelings of resentment and of inability to cope. (Those, on the other hand, who cautiously refrain from "innovative" recipes in preparation of their children's meals must suffer the opprobrium of "laziness," "lack of imagination. . . .")

Illiterates cannot travel freely. When they attempt to do so, they encounter 25 risks that few of us can dream of. They cannot read traffic signs and, while they often learn to recognize and to decipher symbols, they cannot manage street names which they haven't seen before. The same is true for bus and subway stops. While ingenuity can sometimes help a man or woman to discern directions from familiar landmarks, buildings, cemeteries, churches, and the like, most illiterates are virtually immobilized. They seldom wander past the streets and neighborhoods they know. Geographical paralysis becomes a bitter metaphor for their entire existence. They are immobilized in almost every sense we can imagine. They can't move up. They can't move out. They cannot see beyond. Illiterates may take an oral test for drivers' permits in most sections of America. It is a questionable concession. Where will they go? How will they get there? How will they get home? Could it be that some of us might like it better if they stayed where they belong?

Travel is only one of many instances of circumscribed existence. Choice, in almost all of its facets, is diminished in the life of an illiterate adult. Even the printed TV schedule, which provides most people with the luxury of preselection, does not belong within the arsenal of options in illiterate existence. One consequence is that the viewer watches only what appears at moments when he happens to have time to turn the switch. Another consequence, a lot more common, is that the TV set remains in operation night and day. Whatever the program offered at the hour when he walks into the room will be the nutriment that he accepts and swallows. Thus, to passivity, is added frequency—indeed, almost uninterrupted continuity. Freedom to select is no more possible here than in the choice of home or surgery or food.

"You don't choose," said one illiterate woman. "You take your wishes from somebody else." Whether in perusal of a menu, selection of highways, purchase of groceries, or determination of affordable enjoyment, illiterate Americans must trust somebody else: a friend, a relative, a stranger on the street, a grocery clerk, a TV copywriter.

"All of our mail we get, it's hard for her to read. Settin' down and writing a letter, she can't do it. Like if we get a bill . . . we take it over to my sister-in-law . . . My sister-in-law reads it."

Billing agencies harass poor people for the payment of the bills for purchases that might have taken place six months before. Utility companies offer an agreement for a staggered payment schedule on a bill past due. "You have to trust them," one man said. Precisely for this reason, you end up by trusting no one and suspecting everyone of possible deceit. A submerged sense of distrust becomes the corollary to a constant need to trust. "They are cheating me . . . I have been tricked . . . I do not know . . ."

Not knowing: This is a familiar theme. Not knowing the right word for the right thing at the right time is one form of subjugation. Not knowing the world that lies concealed behind those words is a more terrifying feeling. The longitude and latitude of one's existence are beyond all easy apprehension. Even the hard, cold stars within the firmament above one's head begin to mock the possibilities for self-location. Where am I? Where did I come from? Where will I go? 30

"I've lost a lot of jobs," one man explains. "Today, even if you're a janitor, there's still reading and writing . . . They leave a note saying, 'Go to room so-and-so . . .' You can't do it. You can't read it. You don't know."

"The hardest thing about it is that I've been places where I didn't know where I was. You don't know where you are . . . You're lost."

"Like I said: I have two kids. What do I do if one of my kids starts choking? I go running to the phone . . . I can't look up the hospital phone number. That's if we're at home. Out on the street, I can't read the sign. I get to a pay phone. 'Okay, tell us where you are. We'll send an ambulance.' I look at the street sign. Right there, I can't tell you what it says. I'd have to spell it out, letter for letter. By that time, one of my kids would be dead . . . These are the kinds of fears you go with, every single day . . ."

"Reading directions, I suffer with. I work with chemicals . . . That's scary to begin with . . ."

"You sit down. They throw the menu in front of you. Where do you go from 35 there? Nine times out of ten you say, 'Go ahead. Pick out something for the both of us.' I've eaten some weird things, let me tell you!"

Menus. Chemicals. A child choking while his mother searches for a word she does not know to find assistance that will come too late. Another mother speaks about the inability to help her kids to read: "I can't read to them. Of course that's leaving them out of something they should have. Oh, it matters. You *believe* it matters! I ordered all these books. The kids belong to a book club. Donny wanted me to read a book to him. I told Donny: 'I can't read.' He said: 'Mommy, you sit down. I'll read it to you.' I tried it one day, reading from the pictures. Donny looked at me. He said, 'Mommy, that's not right.' He's only five. He knew I couldn't read . . ."

A landlord tells a woman that her lease allows him to evict her if her baby cries and causes inconvenience to her neighbors. The consequence of challenging his words conveys a danger which appears, unlikely as it seems, even more alarming than the danger of eviction. Once she admits that she can't read, in the desire to maneuver for the time in which to call a friend, she will have defined herself in terms of an explicit impotence that she cannot endure. Capitulation in this case is preferable to self-humiliation. Resisting the definition of oneself in terms of what one cannot do, what others take for granted, represents a need so great that other imperatives (even one so urgent as the need to keep one's home in winter's cold) evaporate and fall away in face of fear. Even the loss of home and shelter, in this case, is not so terrifying as the loss of self.

"I come out of school. I was sixteen. They had their meetings. The directors meet. They said that I was wasting their school paper. I was wasting pencils . . ."

Another illiterate, looking back, believes she was not worthy of her teacher's time. She believes that it was wrong of her to take up space within her school. She believes that it was right to leave in order that somebody more deserving could receive her place.

Children choke. Their mother chokes another way: on more than chicken bones.   40

People eat what others order, know what others tell them, struggle not to see themselves as they believe the world perceives them. A man in California speaks about his own loss of identity, of self-location, definition:

"I stood at the bottom of the ramp. My car had broke down on the freeway. There was a phone. I asked for the police. They was nice. They said to tell them where I was. I looked up at the signs. There was one that I had seen before. I read it to them: ONE WAY STREET. They thought it was a joke. I told them I couldn't read. There was other signs above the ramp. They told me to try. I looked around for somebody to help. All the cars was going by real fast. I couldn't make them understand that I was lost. The cop was nice. He told me: 'Try once more.' I did my best. I couldn't read. I only knew the sign above my head. The cop was trying to be nice. He knew that I was trapped. 'I can't send out a car to you if you can't tell me where you are.' I felt afraid. I nearly cried. I'm forty-eight years old. I only said: 'I'm on a one-way street . . .'"

Perhaps we might slow down a moment here and look at the realities described above. This is the nation that we live in. This is a society that most of us did not create but which our President and other leaders have been willing to sustain by virtue of malign neglect. Do we possess the character and courage to address a problem which so many nations, poorer than our own, have found it natural to correct?

The answers to these questions represent a reasonable test of our belief in the democracy to which we have been asked in public school to swear allegiance.

QUESTIONS FOR DISCUSSION AND WRITING

1. Quoting Socrates, Kozol argues that questions of literacy are ultimately "matters of morality" (paragraph 2) and that illiteracy is a threat to democracy. How does he support this argument?

2. Kozol opens his chapter on the cost of illiteracy with the warning on a can of Drāno. Why does he include the warning without further explanation about its significance to the chapter? Writing about the human cost of illiteracy, Kozol faces a dilemma that is innate to his subject and medium: One must first be literate to read his book, so those he wants to help have no access to his written message. To what extent does his medium limit the effectiveness of his message?

3. Kozol repeats the same phrase ("Illiterates cannot") to introduce his topic sentences. What is the effect of this repetition? What could be some of the advantages and risks for Kozol in using this rhetorical design? Why does he choose the negative pattern for the repeated opening phrase?

4. Kozol's argument is true for people who have to live in a civilization based on the power of the written word. Yet it is possible to challenge Kozol and perhaps ourselves from a different perspective. Drawing on Henry David Thoreau (p. 187) and especially Leslie Marmon Silko (p. 287), imagine that you are a member of an ancient yet highly advanced oral civilization, and write an essay with a title such as "The Human Cost of a Literate Society."

SHIRLEY BRICE HEATH

Literate Traditions

Shirley Brice Heath (b. 1941) grew up as a foster child in the South and spent her formative years in rural Virginia, working in tobacco fields owned by African Americans—the primary landholders in the area. Beginning her education in a three-room country school, Heath went on to Lynchburg College (B.A., 1962), Ball State University (M.A., 1964), and Columbia University (Ph.D., 1970). One of her first professional assignments was to prepare teachers to work in the newly desegregated southern schools, an experience that led to her highly original study, Ways with Words: Language, Life, and Work in Communities and Classrooms *(1983).* "Literate Traditions," *from* Ways with Words, *examines oral and written language use among working-class and middle-class residents of the Southeast town Heath calls Trackton. Heath was awarded a MacArthur Fellowship in 1984. For two decades as a professor of English and linguistics at Stanford University, Heath studied language socialization—the way people actually read and write at home and in their community, focusing on disadvantaged children and youth around the world—in the United States, Mexico, Guatemala, South Africa, England, Germany, and Sweden. Her publications, reinforced by video and film, range across four major areas: language socialization, organizational learning, youth culture, and language planning. They include collections such as* Writing in the Real World: Making the Transition from School to Work *(1999) and* Multicultural Strategies for Education and Social Change: Carriers of the Torch in the United States and South Africa *(2006). Heath is now at Brown University's Education Department.*

CONCEPTS OF PRINT

Newspapers, car brochures, advertisements, church materials, and homework and official information from school come into Trackton every day. In addition, there are numerous other rather more permanent reading materials in the community: boxes and cans of food products, house numbers, car names and license numbers, calendars and telephone dials, written messages on television, and name brands which are part of refrigerators, stoves, bicycles, and tools. There are few magazines, except those borrowed from the church, no books except school books, the Bible, and Sunday School lesson books, and a photograph album. Just as Trackton parents do not buy special toys for their young children, they do not buy books for them either; adults do not create reading and writing tasks for the young, nor do they consciously model or demonstrate reading and writing behaviors for them. In the home, on the plaza, and in the neighborhood, children are left to find their own reading and writing tasks: distinguishing one television channel from another, knowing the name brands of cars, motorcycles and bicycles, choosing one or another can of soup or cereal, reading price tags at Mr. Dogan's store to be sure they do not pay more than they would at the supermarket. The receipt of mail in Trackton is a big event, and since several houses are residences for transients the postman does not know, the children sometimes take the mail and give it to the appropriate person. Reading names and addresses and return addresses becomes a game-like challenge among all the children, as the school-age try to show the preschoolers how they know "what dat says."

Preschool and school-age children alike frequently ask what something "says," or how it "goes," and adults respond to their queries, making their instructions fit the requirements of the tasks. Sometimes they help with especially hard or unexpected items, and they always correct errors of fact if they hear them. When Lem, Teegie, and other children in Trackton were about two years of age, I initiated the game of reading traffic signs when we were out in the car. Lillie Mae seemed to pay little attention to this game, until one of the children made an error. If Lem termed a "Yield" sign "Stop," she corrected him, saying, "Dat ain't no stop, dat say yield; you have to give the other fellow the right of way." Often the children would read names of fastfood chains as we drove by. Once when one had changed names, and Teegie read the old name, Tony corrected him: "It ain't Chicken Delight no more; it Famous Recipe now." When the children were preparing to go to school, they chose book bags, tee shirts, and stickers for their notebooks which carried messages. Almost all the older boys and girls in the community wore tee shirts with writings scrawled across the front, and the children talked about what these said and vied to have the most original and sometimes the most suggestive.

Reading was a public group affair for almost all members of Trackton from the youngest to the oldest. Miss Lula sometimes read her Bible alone, and Annie Mae would sometimes quietly read magazines she brought home, but to read alone was frowned upon, and individuals who did so were accused of being anti-social. Aunt Berta had a son who as a child used to slip away from the cotton field and read under a tree. He is now a grown man with children, and he has obtained a college degree, but the community still tells tales about his peculiar boyhood habits of wanting to go off and read alone. In general, reading alone, unless one is very old and religious, marks an individual as someone who cannot make it socially.

Jointly or in group affairs, the children of Trackton *read to learn* before they go to school to *learn to read*. The modification of old or broken toys and their incorporation with other items to create a new toy is a common event. One mastermind, usually Tony, announces the idea, and all the children help collect items and contribute ideas. On some of these occasions, such as when one of the boys wants to modify his bicycle for a unique effect, he has to read selectively portions of brochures on bicycles and instructions for tool sets. Reading is almost always set within a context of immediate action: one needs to read a letter's address to prove to the mailman that one should be given the envelope; one must read the price of a bag of coal at Mr. Dogan's store to make the decision to purchase or not. Trackton children are sent to the store almost as soon as they can walk, and since they are told to "watch out for Mr. Dogan's prices," they must learn to read price changes there from week to week for commonly purchased items and remember them for comparisons with prices in the supermarket. As early as age four, Teegie, Lem, Gary, and Gary B. could scan the price tag, which might contain several separate pieces of information, on familiar items and pick out the price. The decimal point and the predictability of the number of numerals which would be included in the price were clues which helped the children search each tag for only those portions meaningful to their decision-making.

Children remember and reassociate the contexts of print. When they see a 5
brand name, particular sets of numbers, or a particular logo, they often recall
when and with whom they first saw it, or they call attention to how the occasion
for this new appearance is not like the previous one. Slight shifts in print styles,
and decorations of mascots used to advertise products, or alterations of written
slogans are noticed by Trackton children. Once they have been in a supermarket
to buy a loaf of bread, they remember on subsequent trips the location of the
bread section and the placement of the kind of "light bread" their family eats.
They seem to remember the scene and staging of print, so that upon recalling
print they visualize the physical context in which it occurred and the reasons for
reading it: that is, what it was they wanted to learn from reading a certain item or
series of items. They are not tutored in these skills by adults of the community,
but they are given numerous graded tasks from a very early age and are provided
with older children who have learned to read to perform the tasks their daily life
requires. Young children watch others read and write for a variety of purposes,
and they have numerous opportunities for practice under the indirect supervision
of older children, so that they come to use print independently and to be able to
model appropriate behaviors for younger children coming up behind them.

The dependence on a strong sense of visual imagery often prevented efficient
transfer of skills learned in one context to another. All of the toddlers knew the
name brands and names of cereals as they appeared on the boxes or in advertisements. Kellogg's was always written in script — the name of the cereal (raisin
bran, etc.) in all capital letters. On Nabisco products, Nabisco was written in
small capitals and the cereal name in capital letters as well. I was curious to know
whether or not the children "read" the names or whether they recognized the
shapes of the boxes and the artwork on the boxes when they correctly identified
the cereals. I cut out the name brands and cereal names and put them on plain
cardboard of different sizes, and asked the children to read the names. After an
initial period of hesitation, most of the children could read the newly placed
names. All of the children could do so by age three. When they were between
three and four, I cut out the printed letters from the cereal names to spell Kellogg's in small capitals and otherwise arranged the information on the plain cardboard as it appeared on the cereal boxes. The children volunteered the name of
the cereal, but did not immediately read Kellogg's now that it was no longer in
the familiar script. When I asked them to read it, they looked puzzled, said it looked
"funny," and they were not sure what it was. When I pointed out to them that the
print small-capital K was another way of writing the script K, they watched with
interest as I did the same for the rest of the letters. They were dubious about the
script e and the print E being "the same," but they became willing to accept that
what configured on the box also configured on the paper, though in some different ways.

Gradually we developed a game of "rewriting" the words they could read,
shifting from script to all capitals, and from all capitals to initial capitals and subsequent small letters for individual words. It was always necessary to do this by

moving from the known mental picture and "reading" of the terms (i.e., the script Kellogg's) to the unknown or unfamiliar (rendering of Kellogg's in small print capitals). Once shown they already "knew" the item, they accepted that they could "know" these items in new contexts and shapes. We continued this type of game with many of the items from their daily life they already knew how to read. When I first wrote house numbers just as they appeared on the house on a piece of notebook paper, the three- and four-year-olds said they could not read it; if I varied slightly the shape of the numerals on the notebook paper, they also did not read the numbers. Once comparisons and differences were pointed out, they recognized that they already "knew" how to read what had seemed like strange information to them on the notebook paper. Using the "real" print and my re-created print in a metaphorical way provided a bridge from the known to the unknown which allowed the children to use their familiar rules for recognition of print. They transferred their own daily operations as successful readers in an interactive way to pencil-and-paper tasks which were not immediately relevant in the community context.

Their strong tendency to visualize how print looked in its surrounding context was revealed when I asked the three- and four-year-old children to "draw" house doors, newspapers, soup cans, and a letter they would write to someone. Figure 1 illustrates how Gary's representation of a newspaper shows that he knew the letters of headlines were bigger than what came below, and that what was below was organized in straight lines. Moreover, the "headline" near the bottom of the page is smaller than that at the top. Mel writes a "letter" which includes the date, salutation, body, closing, and signature. His "letter" is somewhat atypical, but, since Mel's mother, a transient, wrote frequently to her family up-North, he had numerous opportunities to see letters. None of the other preschoolers provided any of the components of a letter other than body and signature. Mel, however, not only indicates several parts, but also scatters some alphabet letters through the body, and signs his name. Mel also "drew" a soup can, making its name brand biggest, and schematically representing the product information and even what I take to be the vertical pricing and inventory information for computerized checking at the bottom of the can. When asked to "read" what they had written, some giggled, others asked older brothers and sisters to do it and some "read" their writing, explaining its context. Mel's reading of his letter was prefaced by "Now I send you dis letter." Then he read "Dear Miz Hea, bring me a truck we go to Hardee's, Mel." Everyone giggled with Mel who enjoyed the joke of having written what he so often said orally to me. His rendering contained only the primary message, not the date or his letter's closing. It is doubtful that Mel knew what went in these slots, since when I asked him if he had read those parts to me, he shrugged his shoulders and said "I dunno." Trackton children had learned before school that they could read to learn, and they had developed expectancies of print. The graphic and everyday life contexts of writing were often critical to their interpretation of the meaning of print, for print to them was not isolated bits and pieces of lines and circles, but messages with varying

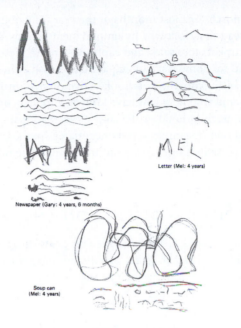

Letter (Mel: 4 years)

Newspaper (Gary: 4 years, 6 months)

Soup can
(Mel: 4 years)

Figure 1. Preschool concepts of print

internal structures, purposes, and uses. For most of these, oral communication surrounded the print.

"TALK IS THE THING"

In almost every situation in Trackton in which a piece of writing is integral to the nature of the participants' interactions and their interpretations of meaning, talk is a necessary component. Knowing which box of cereal is Kellogg's raisin bran does little good without announcing that choice to older brothers and sisters helping pour the cereal. Knowing the kind of bicycle tire and tube on one's old bike is translated into action only at Mr. Green's bicycle shop or with a friend who has an old bike he is not using. Certain types of talk describe, repeat, reinforce, frame, expand, and even contradict written materials, and children in Trackton learn not only how to read print, but also when and how to surround the print in their lives with appropriate talk. For them there are far more occasions in the community which call for appropriate knowledge of forms and uses of talk around or about writing, than there are actual occasions for reading and writing extended connected discourse.

For Trackton adults, reading is a social activity; when something is read in Trackton, it almost always provokes narratives, jokes, side-tracking talk, and active negotiation of the meaning of written texts among the listeners. Authority in the written word does not rest in the words themselves, but in the meanings which are negotiated through the experiences of the group. The evening newspaper is

10

read on the front porch for most months of the year. The obituaries on the back page are usually read first, followed by employment listings, advertisements for grocery and department store sales, and captions beneath pictures and headlines. An obituary is read for some trace of acquaintance with either the deceased, his relatives, place of birth, church, or school; active discussion follows about who the individual was and who he might have known. Circulars or letters to individuals regarding the neighborhood center and its recreational or medical services are read aloud and their meanings jointly negotiated by those who have had experience with such activities or know about the forms to be filled out to be eligible for such services. . . .

QUESTIONS FOR DISCUSSION AND WRITING

1. Many of the literacy tasks that the Trackton residents engage in are learned outside of an academic context. What are the advantages and disadvantages of learning to read and write in this way? At various times, Heath lets the voices of the residents of Trackton be heard. What do their comments and conversations contribute to her study?

2. Discuss Heath's experiments with the learning activities of the residents. For example, when she "cut out the name brands and cereal names and put them on plain cardboard of different sizes, and asked the children to read the names" (paragraph 6), what did she learn?

3. How might Heath's results benefit the residents of Trackton? How could her observations be put to use, for example, by teachers in the Trackton area? What might pupils do in such classrooms, aided now by computers and the Internet?

4. With a partner or writing group, research the types of reading and writing that you see taking place in your academic environment. Consider the full range of reading and writing tasks—academic or nonacademic, solo or collaborative, paper-based or online—that students, teachers, and administrators engage in. Categorize your results and draw some conclusions. Did you discover any unexpected uses of literacy?

LESLIE MARMON SILKO

Language and Literature from a Pueblo Indian Perspective

Of Pueblo, Laguna, Mexican, and white ancestry, Leslie Marmon Silko (b. 1948) grew up on the Laguna Pueblo reservation before earning a bachelor's degree from the University of New Mexico in 1969. Her citation as the 2004 honoree of Women's History Month reads, "The family house sat on the fringe of Laguna Pueblo — not quite excluded, not quite included. It became a metaphor for Silko's life" and work, "anchored to the traditions and stories of Laguna Pueblo on one side with Anglo mainstream on the other." Silko writes fiction (Ceremony, *1977;* Almanac of the Dead, *1991; and* Gardens in the Dunes: A Novel, *1999), poetry (*Laguna Woman: Poems, *1974), and nonfiction (*Yellow Woman and the Beauty of the Spirit, *1997). She has won both the Pushcart Prize for poetry (1977) and a MacArthur "genius" fellowship (1983). Silko's concern for understanding and sharing Pueblo culture on its own terms pervades her work, leading her to examine the interaction between Native American and Western cultures.*

For the Pueblo peoples, geographical, historical, and personal identities are bound up in a web of storytelling that appends tradition to modern reality. In "Language and Literature from a Pueblo Indian Perspective" (in Leslie A. Fiedler and Houston A. Baker, eds., English Literature: Opening Up the Canon, *Baltimore: Johns Hopkins UP, 1979), Silko explains how this oral tradition serves a unifying cultural function: Pueblo Indians learn and rehearse a vast repertoire of oral narratives covering everything from the creation of the world to family stories. Whereas Western anthropologists would create a hierarchy of Pueblo narratives, Silko explains that each Pueblo story — each word, in fact — is a passageway to another story in a seamless unity. The sample narratives included in Silko's essay indeed enmesh the reader in a nonlinear narrative space.*

Where I come from, the words most highly valued are those spoken from the heart, unpremeditated and unrehearsed. Among the Pueblo people, a written speech or statement is highly suspect because the true feelings of the speaker remain hidden as she reads words that are detached from the occasion and the audience. I have intentionally not written a formal paper because I want you to *hear* and to experience English in a structure that follows patterns from the oral tradition. For those of you accustomed to being taken from point A to point B to point C, this presentation may be somewhat difficult to follow. Pueblo expression resembles something like a spider's web — with many little threads radiating from the center, crisscrossing each other. As with the web, the structure emerges as it is made and you must simply listen and trust, as the Pueblo people do, that meaning will be made.

My task is a formidable one: I ask you to set aside a number of basic approaches that you have been using, and probably will continue to use, and instead, to approach language from the Pueblo perspective, one that embraces the whole of creation and the whole of history and time.

What changes would Pueblo writers make to English as a language for literature? I have some examples of stories in English that I will use to address this question. At the same time, I would like to explain the importance of storytelling and how it relates to a Pueblo theory of language.

So, I will begin, appropriately enough, with the Pueblo Creation story, an all-inclusive story of how life began. In this story, Tséitsínako, Thought Woman, by thinking of her sisters, and together with her sisters, thought of everything that is. In this way, the world was created. Everything in this world was a part of the original creation; the people at home understood that far away there were other human beings, also a part of this world. The Creation story even includes a prophecy, which describes the origin of European and African peoples and also refers to Asians.

This story, I think, suggests something about why the Pueblo people are 5 more concerned with story and communication and less concerned with a particular language. There are at least six, possibly seven, distinct languages among the twenty pueblos of the southwestern United States, for example, Zuñi and Hopi. And from mesa to mesa there are subtle differences in language. But the particular language being spoken isn't as important as what a speaker is trying to say, and this emphasis on the story itself stems, I believe, from a view of narrative particular to the Pueblo and other Native American peoples—that is, that language *is* story.

I will try to clarify this statement. At Laguna Pueblo, for example, many individual words have their own stories. So when one is telling a story, and one is using words to tell the story, each word that one is speaking has a story of its own, too. Often the speakers or tellers will go into these word-stories, creating an elaborate structure of stories-within-stories. This structure, which becomes very apparent in the actual telling of a story, informs contemporary Pueblo writing and storytelling as well as the traditional narratives. This perspective on narrative—of story within story, the idea that one story is only the beginning of many stories, and the sense that stories never truly end— represents an important contribution of Native American cultures to the English language.

Many people think of storytelling as something that is done at bedtime, that it is something done for small children. But when I use the term *storytelling*, I'm talking about something much bigger than that. I'm talking about something that comes out of an experience and an understanding of that original view of creation—that we are all part of a whole; we do not differentiate or fragment stories and experiences. In the beginning, Tséitsínako, Thought Woman, thought of all things, and all of these things are held together as one holds many things together in a single thought.

So in the telling (and you will hear a few of the dimensions of this telling) first of all, as mentioned earlier, the storytelling always includes the audience, the listeners. In fact, a great deal of the story is believed to be inside the listener; the storyteller's role is to draw the story out of the listeners. The storytelling continues from generation to generation.

Basically, the origin story constructs our identity—within this story, we know who we are. We are the Lagunas. This is where we come from. We came this way. We came by this place. And so from the time we are very young, we hear these stories, so that when we go out into the world, when one asks who we are, or where we are from, we immediately know: we are the people who came from the north. We are the people of these stories.

In the Creation story, Antelope says that he will help knock a hole in   10
the earth so that the people can come up, out into the next world. Antelope tries and tries; he uses his hooves, but is unable to break through. It is then that Badger says, "Let me help you." And Badger very patiently uses his claws and digs a way through, bringing the people into the world. When the Badger clan people think of themselves, or when the Antelope people think of themselves, it is as people who are of *this* story, and this is *our* place, and we fit into the very beginning when the people first came, before we began our journey south.

Within the clans there are stories that identify the clan. One moves, then, from the idea of one's identity as a tribal person into clan identity, then to one's identity as a member of an extended family. And it is the notion of "extended family" that has produced a kind of story that some distinguish from other Pueblo stories, though Pueblo people do not. Anthropologists and ethnologists have, for a long time, differentiated the types of stories the Pueblos tell. They tended to elevate the old, sacred, and traditional stories and to brush aside family stories, the family's account of itself. But in Pueblo culture, these family stories are given equal recognition. There is no definite, present pattern for the way one will hear the stories of one's own family, but it is a very critical part of one's childhood, and the storytelling continues throughout one's life. One will hear stories of importance to the family—sometimes wonderful stories—stories about the time a maternal uncle got the biggest deer that was ever seen and brought it back from the mountains. And so an individual's identity will extend from the identity constructed around the family—"I am from the family of my uncle who brought in this wonderful deer and it was a wonderful hunt."

Family accounts include negative stories, too; perhaps an uncle did something unacceptable. It is very important that one keep track of all these stories—both positive and not so positive—about one's own family and other families. Because even when there is no way around it—old Uncle Pete *did* do a terrible thing—by knowing the stories that originate in other families, one is able to deal with terrible sorts of things that might happen within one's own family. If a member of the family does something that cannot be excused, one always knows stories about similar inexcusable things done by a member of another family. But this knowledge is not communicated for malicious reasons. It is very important to understand this. Keeping track of all the stories within the community gives us all a certain distance, a useful perspective, that brings incidents down to a level we can deal with. If others have done it before, it cannot be so terrible. If others have endured, so can we.

The stories are always bringing us together, keeping this whole together, keeping this family together, keeping this clan together. "Don't go away, don't isolate yourself, but come here, because we have all had these kinds of experiences." And so there is this constant pulling together to resist the tendency to run or hide or separate oneself during a traumatic emotional experience. This separation not only endangers the group but the individual as well—one does not recover by oneself.

Because storytelling lies at the heart of Pueblo culture, it is absurd to attempt to fix the stories in time. "When did they tell the stories?" or "What time of day does the storytelling take place?"—these questions are nonsensical from a Pueblo perspective, because our storytelling goes on constantly: as some old grandmother puts on the shoes of a child and tells her the story of a little girl who didn't wear her shoes, for instance, or someone comes into the house for coffee to talk with a teenage boy who has just been in a lot of trouble, to reassure him that someone else's son has been in that kind of trouble, too. Storytelling is an ongoing process, working on many different levels.

Here's one story that is often told at a time of individual crisis (and I want   15 to remind you that we make no distinctions between types of story—historical, sacred, plain gossip—because these distinctions are not useful when discussing the Pueblo *experience* of language). There was a young man who, when he came back from the war in Vietnam, had saved up his army pay and bought a beautiful red Volkswagen. He was very proud of it. One night he drove up to a place called the King's Bar right across the reservation line. The bar is notorious for many reasons, particularly for the deep *arroyo* located behind it. The young man ran in to pick up a cold six-pack, but he forgot to put on his emergency brake. And his little red Volkswagen rolled back into the *arroyo* and was all smashed up. He felt very bad about it, but within a few days everybody had come to him with stories about other people who had lost cars and family members to that *arroyo*, for instance, George Day's station wagon, with his mother-in-law and kids inside. So everybody was saying, "Well, at least your mother-in-law and kids weren't in the car when it rolled in," and one can't argue with that kind of story. The story of the young man and his smashed-up Volkswagen was now joined with all the other stories of cars that fell into that *arroyo*. . . .

There are a great many parallels between Pueblo experiences and those of African and Caribbean peoples—one is that we have all had the conqueror's language imposed on us. But our experience with English has been somewhat different in that the Bureau of Indian Affairs schools were not interested in teaching us the canon of Western classics. For instance, we never heard of Shakespeare. We were given Dick and Jane, and I can remember reading that the robins were heading south for the winter. It took me a long time to figure out what was going on. I worried for quite a while about our robins in Laguna because they didn't leave in the winter, until I finally realized that all the big textbook companies are up in Boston and *their* robins do go south in the winter. But in a way, this dreadful formal education freed us by encouraging us to maintain our narratives. Whatever literature we were exposed to at school (which was damn little), at home the storytelling, the special regard for telling and bringing together through the telling, was going on constantly.

And as the old people say, "If you can remember the stories, you will be all right. Just remember the stories." . . .

One of the other advantages that we Pueblos have enjoyed is that we have always been able to stay with the land. Our stories cannot be separated from their geographical locations, from actual physical places on the land. We were not relocated like so many Native American groups who were torn away from their ancestral land. And our stories are so much a part of these places that it is almost impossible for future generations to lose them—there is a story connected with every place, every object in the landscape.

Dennis Brutus has talked about the "yet unborn" as well as "those from the past," and how we are still *all* in *this* place, and language—the storytelling—is our way of passing through or being with them, or being together again. When Aunt Susie told her stories, she would tell a younger child to go open the door so that our esteemed predecessors might bring in their gifts to us. "They are out there," Aunt Susie would say. "Let them come in. They're here, they're here with us *within* the stories."

A few years ago, when Aunt Susie was 106, I paid her a visit, and while I was there she said, "Well, I'll be leaving here soon. I think I'll be leaving here next week, and I will be going over to the Cliff House." She said, "It's going to be real good to get back over there." I was listening, and I was thinking that she must be talking about her house at Paguate Village, just north of Laguna. And she went on, "Well, my mother's sister (and she gave her Indian name) will be there. She has been living there. She will be there and we will be over there, and I will get a chance to write down these stories I've been telling you." Now you must understand, of course, that Aunt Susie's mother's sister, a great storyteller herself, has long since passed over into the land of the dead. But then I realized, too, that Aunt Susie wasn't talking about death the way most of us do. She was talking about "going over" as a journey, a journey that perhaps we can only begin to understand through an appreciation for the boundless capacity of language that, through storytelling, brings us together, despite great distances between cultures, despite great distances in time.

ZITKALA-SA

From *The School Days of an Indian Girl*

Zitkala-Sa (1878–1938) was born on the Pine Ridge Reservation in South Dakota, the daughter of a white father and a Sioux mother. When in 1900 Atlantic Monthly serialized her writings, the public for the first time read an account of American Indian life unmediated by white professional interpreters. "The School Days of an Indian Girl" and "Impressions of an Indian Childhood," among other writings, drew attention to the hardships caused when the whites in power sent Native American children to boarding schools far from home. There, even the most benevolent teachers had a mandate to impose white culture on their displaced pupils.

Zitkala-Sa herself, with great personal misgivings exacerbated by her mother's anguish, left home at the age of eight to attend a Quaker boarding school in Wabash, Indiana. Coming home, for "four strange summers," she found herself "neither a wild Indian nor a tame one" and eventually returned to school, graduating in 1900 from Earlham College, also Quaker, in Richmond, Indiana. She worked as a school teacher, married Sioux Raymond Bonnin, an Indian rights activist, and, in Washington, D.C., lobbied for Indian rights and served as secretary of the Society of American Indians. An integrationist, not a separatist, she founded the National Council of American Indians in 1926, and as its president until her death in 1938 helped to secure the passage of the Indian Citizenship Bill.

The School Days of an Indian Girl describes, in richly descriptive prose, Zitkala-Sa's difficult transition from reservation life to the Quaker school. Her homesickness is intensified by the strangeness of the new environment, the cutting of her hair, and the foreign habits and rituals of the institution, but in the last section, Zitkala-Sa emerges as a girl inhabiting two cultures.

There were eight in our party of bronzed children who were going East with the missionaries. Among us were three young braves, two tall girls, and we three little ones, Judéwin, Thowin, and I.

We had been very impatient to start on our journey to the Red Apple Country, which, we were told, lay a little beyond the great circular horizon of the Western prairie. Under a sky of rosy apples we dreamt of roaming as freely and happily as we had chased the cloud shadows on the Dakota plains. We had anticipated much pleasure from a ride on the iron horse, but the throngs of staring palefaces disturbed and troubled us.

On the train, fair women, with tottering babies on each arm, stopped their haste and scrutinized the children of absent mothers. Large men, with heavy bundles in their hands, halted near by, and riveted their glassy blue eyes upon us. . . .

. . . we rode several days inside of the iron horse, . . .

It was night when we reached the school grounds. . . . My body trembled more from fear than from the snow I trod upon. 5

Entering the house, I stood close against the wall. The strong glaring light in the large whitewashed room dazzled my eyes. The noisy hurrying of hard shoes upon a bare wooden floor increased the whirring in my ears. My only safety seemed to be in keeping next to the wall. As I was wondering in which direction to escape from all this confusion, two warm hands grasped me firmly, and in the same moment I was tossed high in midair. A rosy-cheeked paleface woman caught me in her arms. I was both frightened and insulted by such trifling. I stared into her eyes, wishing her to let me stand on my own feet, but she jumped me up and down with increasing enthusiasm. My mother had never made a plaything of her wee daughter. Remembering this I began to cry aloud. . . .

THE CUTTING OF MY LONG HAIR

The first day in the land of the apples was a bitter-cold one; for the snow still covered the ground, and the trees were bare. A large bell rang for breakfast, its loud metallic voice crashing through the belfry overhead and into our sensitive ears. The annoying clatter of shoes on bare floors gave us no peace. The constant clash of harsh noises, with an undercurrent of many voices murmuring an unknown tongue, made a bedlam within which I was securely tied. And though my spirit tore itself in struggling for its lost freedom, all was useless. . . .

A small bell was tapped, and each of the pupils drew a chair from under the table. Supposing this act meant they were to be seated, I pulled out mine and at

How do you know these girls are Native Americans? What attributes of white middle-class culture are manifest in this photograph? How might the girls be expected to react to these attributes? How might their families be expected to regard the anglicization of their daughters? How would the school personnel—then and now—interpret the girls' clothing, postures, and hairstyles?

once slipped into it from one side. But when I turned my head, I saw that I was the only one seated, and all the rest at our table remained standing. Just as I began to rise, looking shyly around to see how chairs were to be used, a second bell was sounded. All were seated at last, and I had to crawl back into my chair again. I heard a man's voice at one end of the hall, and I looked around to see him. But all the others hung their heads over their plates. As I glanced at the long chain of tables, I caught the eyes of a paleface woman upon me. Immediately I dropped my eyes, wondering why I was so keenly watched by the strange woman. The man ceased his mutterings, and then a third bell was tapped. Every one picked up his knife and fork and began eating. I began crying instead, for by this time I was afraid to venture anything more.

But this eating by formula was not the hardest trial in that first day. Late in the morning, my friend Judéwin gave me a terrible warning. Judéwin knew a few words of English; and she had overheard the paleface woman talk about cutting our long, heavy hair. Our mothers had taught us that only unskilled warriors who were captured had their hair shingled by the enemy. Among our people, short hair was worn by mourners, and shingled hair by cowards!

We discussed our fate some moments, and when Judéwin said, "We have to 10 submit, because they are strong," I rebelled.

"No, I will not submit! I will struggle first!" I answered.

I watched my chance, and when no one noticed I disappeared. I crept up the stairs quietly as I could in my squeaking shoes,—my moccasins had been exchanged for shoes. Along the hall I passed, without knowing whither I was going. Turning aside to an open door, I found a large room with three white beds in it. The windows were covered with dark green curtains, which made the room very dim. Thankful that no one was there, I directed my steps toward the corner farthest from the door. On my hands and knees I crawled under the bed, and cuddled myself in the dark corner.

From my hiding place I peered out, shuddering with fear whenever I heard footsteps near by. Though in the hall loud voices were calling my name, and I knew that even Judéwin was searching for me, I did not open my mouth to answer. Then the steps were quickened and the voices became excited. The sounds came nearer and nearer. Women and girls entered the room. I held my breath, and watched them open closet doors and peep behind large trunks. Some one threw up the curtains, and the room was filled with sudden light. What caused them to stoop and look under the bed I do not know. I remember being dragged out, though I resisted by kicking and scratching wildly. In spite of myself, I was carried downstairs and tied fast in a chair.

I cried aloud, shaking my head all the while until I felt the cold blades of the scissors against my neck, and heard them gnaw off one of my thick braids. Then I lost my spirit. Since the day I was taken from my mother I had suffered extreme indignities. People had stared at me. I had been tossed about in the air like a wooden puppet. And now my long hair was shingled like a coward's! In my anguish I moaned for my mother, but no one came to comfort me. Not a soul reasoned quietly with me, as my own mother used to do: for now I was only one of many little animals driven by a herder. . . .

I asked [my brother] Dawée about something else.   15

"No, my baby sister. I cannot take you with me to the party tonight," he replied. Though I was not far from fifteen, and I felt that before long I should enjoy all the privileges of my tall cousin, Dawée persisted in calling me his baby sister.

That moonlight night, I cried in my mother's presence when I heard the jolly young people pass by our cottage. There were no more young braves in blankets and eagle plumes, nor Indian maids with prettily painted cheeks. They had gone three years to school in the East, and had become civilized. The young men wore the white man's coat and trousers, with bright neckties. The girls wore tight muslin dresses, with ribbons at neck and waist. At these gatherings they talked English. I could speak English almost as well as my brother, but I was not properly dressed to be taken along. I had no hat, no ribbons, and no close-fitting gown. Since my return from school I had thrown away my shoes, and wore again the soft moccasins.

While Dawée was busily preparing to go I controlled my tears. But when I heard him bounding away on his pony, I buried my face in my arms and cried hot tears.

My mother was troubled by my unhappiness. Coming to my side, she offered me the only printed matter we had in our home. It was an Indian Bible, given her some years ago by a missionary. She tried to console me. "Here, my child, are the white man's papers. Read a little from them," she said most piously.

I took it from her hand, for her sake; but my enraged spirit felt more like   20 burning the book, which afforded me no help, and was a perfect delusion to my mother. I did not read it, but laid it unopened on the floor, where I sat on my feet. The dim yellow light of the braided muslin burning in a small vessel of oil flickered and sizzled in the awful silent storm which followed my rejection of the Bible.

Now my wrath against the fates consumed my tears before they reached my eyes. I sat stony, with a bowed head. My mother threw a shawl over her head and shoulders, and stepped out into the night.

After an uncertain solitude, I was suddenly aroused by a loud cry piercing the night. It was my mother's voice wailing among the barren hills which held the bones of buried warriors. She called aloud for her brothers' spirits to support her in her helpless misery. My fingers grew icy cold, as I realized that my unrestrained tears had betrayed my suffering to her, and she was grieving for me.

Before she returned, though I knew she was on her way, for she had ceased her weeping, I extinguished the light, and leaned my head on the window sill.

Many schemes of running away from my surroundings hovered about in my mind. A few more moons of such a turmoil drove me away to the Eastern school. I rode on the white man's iron steed, thinking it would bring me back to my mother in a few winters, when I should be grown tall, and there would be congenial friends awaiting me. . . .

QUESTIONS FOR DISCUSSION AND WRITING

1. Zitkala-Sa emphasizes the disjuncture between Sioux ways and customs in "The Land of the Red Apples," while in "Language and Literature from a Pueblo Perspective" Silko describes the weblike structure of Pueblo storytelling. What images does Zitkala-Sa use that seem to illustrate Silko's distinction between the "basic approaches" of Native American and European-American cultures?

2. Throughout "The School Days of an Indian Girl" the narrative emphasizes the contrast of cultures—Zitkala-Sa's Native American orientation versus the white culture into which she is immersed. What are the main differences between the two cultures? In what ways does the narrative show the two cultures colliding? For example, how do Zitkala-Sa's language use, terminology, and observations show her to have a "dual perspective" in which she inhabits both cultures simultaneously? How does Zitkala-Sa convey her alienation from both school and home? Describe the different stylistic strategies Zitkala-Sa and Silko employ. How does Silko illustrate, through her own storytelling, the nonlinear nature of Pueblo narrative?

3. Silko writes that the Bureau of Indian Affairs (BIA) education "freed us by encouraging us to maintain our narratives" (paragraph 16) and another advantage that the Pueblos have enjoyed "is that we have always been able to stay with the land" (paragraph 18). How does Zitkala-Sa illustrate the impact of losing her sense of place and her connection to her culture's stories? What evidence does Barry Lopez's essay "The American Geographies" (p. 669) present to lend support to Silko's argument about the close connection between Pueblo stories and their land?

4. Write an essay about Zitkala-Sa's identity crisis and/or compare her cultural development with that of Richard Rodriguez in "Aria" (p. 298). Analyze the extent to which these authors, as children and as adults, successfully navigate between the cultural forces confronting them. What difficult choices must they make? Do they attempt to escape from or deny the problems? Do they try to resolve contradictions? How able are they to function and thrive as participants in two very different cultures?

5. Write an essay in which you compare two or more of the writings of Silko, Zitkala-Sa, Rodriguez, Sherman Alexie (p. 47), Eric Liu (p. 112), James Baldwin (p. 118), and Esmerelda Santiago (p. 129) as they reflect on minority experience in America. How do the essays handle issues such as exclusion, prejudice, stereotyping, culture clashes, and dual identity? Explain why one essay succeeds better than the others at educating the reader about groups in America that have been sidelined or repressed during our history.

STEPHANIE MAZE

Literacy in Progress

QUESTIONS FOR DISCUSSION AND WRITING

1. Is the child in this photograph learning to read? To write? Or both? What is his attitude toward the process, literally, at hand? How can you tell?

2. Is the process of becoming literate similar across cultures and nationalities? Compare and contrast the formal and informal aspects of acquiring literacy, as illustrated, for instance, in Shirley Brice Heath's "Literate Traditions" (p. 280). For issues of cultural literacy, see Zitkala-Sa's "The School Days of an Indian Girl" (p. 292) and Richard Rodriguez's "Aria" (p. 298).

RICHARD RODRIGUEZ
Aria: A Memoir of a Bilingual Childhood

Richard Rodriguez, born in San Francisco in 1944, is the author of Days of Obligation: An Argument with My Mexican Father *(1993) and* Brown: An Erotic History of the Americas *(2002). His memoir,* Hunger of Memory: The Education of
Richard Rodriguez *(1982), is a moving and provocative account of growing up
bilingual and bicultural as the son of Mexican immigrants in a largely white neighborhood in Sacramento. The book became a focal point in the 1980s' national debate
about bilingual education, a debate that continues into the twenty-first century with
various "English-only" initiatives.*

*In his memoir's opening chapter, "Aria" (originally titled "Aria: A Memoir of a
Bilingual Childhood" for its publication in the Winter 1980/1981 issue of* The
American Scholar*), Rodriguez reflects on the difficult transition from his private,
Spanish-speaking world to the public, English-speaking one. Although the English-
only classroom brought estrangement from his family and heritage, Rodriguez nevertheless argues in* Hunger of Memory *against both bilingual education and
affirmative action—programs he acknowledges having benefited from as a scholarship student at both Stanford (B.A., 1967) and Columbia (M.A., 1969) and as a
doctoral student in English at the University of California at Berkeley.*

*How does Rodriguez as a memoirist weigh his individuality against the public
dimensions of his experience? How he defines his individual "self" within cultural
traditions, social structures, and political agendas are issues addressed in the Contexts
following "Aria."*

I remember, to start with, that day in Sacramento, in a California now nearly
thirty years past, when I first entered a classroom—able to understand about
fifty stray English words. The third of four children, I had been preceded by my
older brother and sister to a neighborhood Roman Catholic school. But neither
of them had revealed very much about their classroom experiences. They left
each morning and returned each afternoon, always together, speaking Spanish as
they climbed the five steps to the porch. And their mysterious books, wrapped in
brown shopping-bag paper, remained on the table next to the door, closed firmly
behind them.

An accident of geography sent me to a school where all my classmates were
white and many were the children of doctors and lawyers and business executives. On that first day of school, my classmates must certainly have been uneasy
to find themselves apart from their families, in the first institution of their lives.
But I was astonished. I was fated to be the "problem student" in class.

The nun said, in a friendly but oddly impersonal voice: "Boys and girls, this
is Richard Rodriguez." (I heard her sound it out: *Rich-heard Road-ree-guess.*) It
was the first time I had heard anyone say my name in English. "Richard," the nun

repeated more slowly, writing my name down in her book. Quickly I turned to see my mother's face dissolve in a watery blur behind the pebbled-glass door.

Now, many years later, I hear of something called "bilingual education"—a scheme proposed in the late 1960s by Hispanic-American social activists, later endorsed by a congressional vote. It is a program that seeks to permit non-English-speaking children (many from lower-class homes) to use their "family language" as the language of school. Such, at least, is the aim its supporters announce. I hear them, and am forced to say no: It is not possible for a child, any child, ever to use his family's language in school. Not to understand this is to misunderstand the public uses of schooling and to trivialize the nature of intimate life.

Memory teaches me what I know of these matters. The boy reminds the 5 adult. I was a bilingual child, but of a certain kind: "socially disadvantaged," the son of working-class parents, both Mexican immigrants.

In the early years of my boyhood, my parents coped very well in America. My father had steady work. My mother managed at home. They were nobody's victims. When we moved to a house many blocks from the Mexican-American section of town, they were not intimidated by those two or three neighbors who initially tried to make us unwelcome. ("Keep your brats away from my sidewalk!") But despite all they achieved, or perhaps because they had so much to achieve, they lacked any deep feeling of ease, of belonging in public. They regarded the people at work or in crowds as being very distant from us. Those were the others, *los gringos*. That term was interchangeable in their speech with another, even more telling: *los americanos*.

I grew up in a house where the only regular guests were my relations. On a certain day, enormous families of relatives would visit us, and there would be so many people that the noise and the bodies would spill out to the backyard and onto the front porch. Then for weeks no one would come. (If the doorbell rang, it was usually a salesman.) Our house stood apart—gaudy yellow in a row of white bungalows. We were the people with the noisy dog, the people who raised chickens. We were the foreigners on the block. A few neighbors would smile and wave at us. We waved back. But until I was seven years old, I did not know the name of the old couple living next door or the names of the kids living across the street.

In public, my father and mother spoke a hesitant, accented, and not always grammatical English. And then they would have to strain, their bodies tense, to catch the sense of what was rapidly said by *los gringos*. At home, they returned to Spanish. The language of their Mexican past sounded in counterpoint to the English spoken in public. The words would come quickly, with ease. Conveyed through those sounds was the pleasing, soothing, consoling reminder that one was at home.

During those years when I was first learning to speak, my mother and father addressed me only in Spanish; in Spanish I learned to reply. By contrast, English (*inglés*) was the language I came to associate with gringos, rarely heard in the house. I learned my first words of English overhearing my parents speaking to strangers. At six years of age, I knew just enough words for my mother to trust me on errands to stores one block away—but no more.

I was then a listening child, careful to hear the very different sounds of Span- 10
ish and English. Wide-eyed with hearing, I'd listen to sounds more than to
words. First, there were English (*gringo*) sounds. So many words still were unknown to me that when the butcher or the lady at the drugstore said something,
exotic polysyllabic sounds would bloom in the midst of their sentences. Often the
speech of people in public seemed to me very loud, booming with confidence.
The man behind the counter would literally ask, "What can I do for you?" But by
being so firm and clear, the sound of his voice said that he was a gringo; he belonged in public society. There were also the high, nasal notes of middle-class
American speech—which I rarely am conscious of hearing today because I hear
them so often, but could not stop hearing when I was a boy. Crowds at Safeway
or at bus stops were noisy with the birdlike sounds of *los gringos*. I'd move away
from them all—all the chirping chatter above me.

My own sounds I was unable to hear, but I knew that I spoke English poorly.
My words could not extend to form complete thoughts. And the words I did
speak I didn't know well enough to make distinct sounds. (Listeners would usually lower their heads to hear better what I was trying to say.) But it was one thing
for *me* to speak English with difficulty; it was more troubling to hear my parents
speaking in public: their high-whining vowels and guttural consonants; their sentences that got stuck with "eh" and "ah" sounds; the confused syntax; the hesitant
rhythm of sounds so different from the way gringos spoke. I'd notice, moreover,
that my parents' voices were softer than those of gringos we would meet.

I am tempted to say now that none of this mattered. (In adulthood I am embarrassed by childhood fears.) And, in a way, it didn't matter very much that my
parents could not speak English with ease. Their linguistic difficulties had no serious consequences. My mother and father made themselves understood at the
county hospital clinic and at government offices. And yet, in another way, it mattered very much. It was unsettling to hear my parents struggle with English.
Hearing them, I'd grow nervous, and my clutching trust in their protection and
power would be weakened.

There were many times like the night at a brightly lit gasoline station (a blar-
ing white memory) when I stood uneasily hearing my father talk to a teenage attendant. I do not recall what they were saying, but I cannot forget the sounds my
father made as he spoke. At one point his words slid together to form one long
word—sounds as confused as the threads of blue and green oil in the puddle
next to my shoes. His voice rushed through what he had left to say. Toward the
end, he reached falsetto notes, appealing to his listener's understanding. I looked
away at the lights of passing automobiles. I tried not to hear any more. But I
heard only too well the attendant's reply, his calm, easy tones. Shortly afterward,
headed for home, I shivered when my father put his hand on my shoulder. The
very first chance that I got, I evaded his grasp and ran on ahead into the dark,
skipping with feigned boyish exuberance.

But then there was Spanish: *español*, the language rarely heard away from the
house; *español*, the language which seemed to me therefore a private language,

my family's language. To hear its sounds was to feel myself specially recognized as one of the family, apart from *los otros*. A simple remark, an inconsequential comment could convey that assurance. My parents would say something to me and I would feel embraced by the sounds of their words. Those sounds said: *I am speaking with ease in Spanish. I am addressing you in words I never use with los gringos. I recognize you as someone special, close, like no one outside. You belong with us. In the family. Ricardo.*

At the age of six, well past the time when most middle-class children no 15 longer notice the difference between sounds uttered at home and words spoken in public, I had a different experience. I lived in a world compounded of sounds. I was a child longer than most. I lived in a magical world, surrounded by sounds both pleasing and fearful. I shared with my family a language enchantingly private—different from that used in the city around us.

Just opening or closing the screen door behind me was an important experience. I'd rarely leave home all alone or without feeling reluctance. Walking down the sidewalk, under the canopy of tall trees, I'd warily notice the (suddenly) silent neighborhood kids who stood warily watching me. Nervously, I'd arrive at the grocery store to hear there the sounds of the gringo, reminding me that in this so-big world I was a foreigner. But if leaving home was never routine, neither was coming back. Walking toward our house, climbing the steps from the sidewalk, in summer when the front door was open, I'd hear voices beyond the screen door talking in Spanish. For a second or two I'd stay, linger there listening. Smiling, I'd hear my mother call out, saying in Spanish, "Is that you, Richard?" Those were her words, but all the while her sounds would assure me: *You are home now. Come closer inside. With us.* "*Sí*," I'd reply.

Once more inside the house, I would resume my place in the family. The sounds would grow harder to hear. Once more at home, I would grow less conscious of them. It required, however, no more than the blurt of the doorbell to alert me all over again to listen to sounds. The house would turn instantly quiet while my mother went to the door. I'd hear her hard English sounds. I'd wait to hear her voice turn to soft-sounding Spanish, which assured me, as surely as did the clicking tongue of the lock on the door, that the stranger was gone.

Plainly it is not healthy to hear such sounds so often. It is not healthy to distinguish public from private sounds so easily. I remained cloistered by sounds, timid and shy in public, too dependent on the voices at home. And yet I was a very happy child when I was at home. I remember many nights when my father would come back from work, and I'd hear him call out to my mother in Spanish, sounding relieved. In Spanish, his voice would sound the light and free notes that he never could manage in English. Some nights I'd jump up just hearing his voice. My brother and I would come running into the room where he was with our mother. Our laughing (so deep was the pleasure!) became screaming. Like others who feel the pain of public alienation, we transformed the knowledge of our public separateness into a consoling reminder of our intimacy. Excited, our voices joined in a celebration of sounds. *We are speaking now the way we never speak out in public—we are together,* the sounds told me. Some nights no one seemed willing to loosen the hold that sounds had on us. At dinner we invented new words that sounded Spanish, but made sense only to us. We pieced together new words by taking, say, an English verb and giving it Spanish endings. My mother's instructions at bedtime would be lacquered with mock-urgent tones. Or a word like *sí,* sounded in several notes, would convey added measures of feeling. Tongues lingered around the edges of words, especially fat vowels, and we happily sounded that military drum roll, the twirling roar of the Spanish *r.* Family language, my family's sounds: the voices of my parents and sisters and brother. Their voices insisting: *You belong here. We are family members. Related. Special to one another. Listen!* Voices singing and sighing, rising and straining, then surging, teeming with pleasure which burst syllables into fragments of laughter. At times it seemed there was steady quiet only when, from another room, the rustling whispers of my parents faded and I edged closer to sleep.

Supporters of bilingual education imply today that students like me miss a great deal by not being taught in their family's language. What they seem not to recognize is that, as a socially disadvantaged child, I regarded Spanish as a private language. It was a ghetto language that deepened and strengthened my feeling of public separateness. What I needed to learn in school was that I had the right, and the obligation, to speak the public language. The odd truth is that my first-grade classmates could have become bilingual, in the conventional sense of the word, more easily than I. Had they been taught early (as upper-middle-class children often are taught) a "second language" like Spanish or French, they could have regarded it simply as another public language. In my case, such bilingualism could not have been so quickly achieved. What I did not believe was that I could speak a single public language.

Without question, it would have pleased me to have heard my teachers address me in Spanish when I entered the classroom. I would have felt much less afraid. I would have imagined that my instructors were somehow "related" to me; I would indeed have heard their Spanish as my family's language. I would have trusted them and responded with ease. But I would have delayed—postponed for how long?—having to learn the language of public society. I would have evaded—and for how long?—learning the great lesson of school: that I had a public identity. 20

Fortunately, my teachers were unsentimental about their responsibility. What they understood was that I needed to speak public English. So their voices would search me out, asking me questions. Each time I heard them I'd look up in surprise to see a nun's face frowning at me. I'd mumble, not really meaning to answer. The nun would persist. "Richard, stand up. Don't look at the floor. Speak up. Speak to the entire class, not just to me!" But I couldn't believe English could be my language to use. (In part, I did not want to believe it.) I continued to mumble. I resisted the teacher's demands. (Did I somehow suspect that once I learned this public language my family life would be changed?) Silent, waiting for the bell to sound, I remained dazed, diffident, afraid.

Because I wrongly imagined that English was intrinsically a public language and Spanish was intrinsically private, I easily noted the difference between classroom language and the language at home. At school, words were directed to a general audience of listeners. ("Boys and girls . . . ") Words were meaningfully ordered. And the point was not self-expression alone, but to make oneself understood by many others. The teacher quizzed: "Boys and girls, why do we use that word in this sentence? Could we think of a better word to use there? Would the sentence change its meaning if the words were differently arranged? Isn't there a better way of saying much the same thing?" (I couldn't say. I wouldn't try to say.)

Three months passed. Five. A half year. Unsmiling, ever watchful, my teachers noted my silence. They began to connect my behavior with the slow progress my brother and sisters were making. Until, one Saturday morning, three nuns arrived at the house to talk to our parents. Stiffly they sat on the blue living-room sofa. From the doorway of another room, spying on the visitors, I noted the incongruity, the clash of two worlds, the faces and voices of school intruding upon the familiar setting of home. I overheard one voice gently wondering, "Do your children speak only Spanish at home, Mrs. Rodriguez?" While another voice added, "That Richard especially seems so timid and shy."

That Rich-heard!

With great tact, the visitors continued, "Is it possible for you and your husband to encourage your children to practice their English when they are home?" Of course my parents complied. What would they not do for their children's well-being? And how could they question the Church's authority which those women represented? In an instant they agreed to give up the language (the sounds) which had revealed and accentuated our family's closeness. The moment after the visitors left, the change was observed. "*Ahora*, speak to us only *en inglés*," my father and mother told us. 25

At first, it seemed a kind of game. After dinner each night, the family gathered together to practice "our" English. It was still then *inglés*, a language foreign to us, so we felt drawn to it as strangers. Laughing, we would try to define words we could not pronounce. We played with strange English sounds, often over-anglicizing our pronunciations. And we filled the smiling gaps of our sentences with familiar Spanish sounds. But that was cheating, somebody shouted, and everyone laughed.

In school, meanwhile, like my brother and sisters, I was required to attend a daily tutoring session. I needed a full year of this special work. I also needed my teachers to keep my attention from straying in class by calling out, "*Rich-heard*"—their English voices slowly loosening the ties to my other name, with its three notes, *Ri-car-do*. Most of all, I needed to hear my mother and father speak to me in a moment of seriousness in "broken"—suddenly heartbreaking—English. This scene was inevitable. One Saturday morning I entered the kitchen where my parents were talking, but I did not realize that they were talking in Spanish until, the moment they saw me, their voices changed and they began speaking English. The gringo sounds they uttered startled me. Pushed me away. In that moment of trivial misunderstanding and profound insight, I felt my throat twisted by unsounded grief. I simply turned and left the room. But I had no place to escape to where I could grieve in Spanish. My brother and sisters were speaking English in another part of the house.

Again and again in the days following, as I grew increasingly angry, I was obliged to hear my mother and father encouraging me: "Speak to us *en inglés*." Only then did I determine to learn classroom English. Thus, sometime afterward it happened: One day in school, I raised my hand to volunteer an answer to a question. I spoke out in a loud voice and I did not think it remarkable when the entire class understood. That day I moved very far from being the disadvantaged child I had been only days earlier. Taken hold at last was the belief, the calming assurance, that I *belonged* in public.

Shortly after, I stopped hearing the high, troubling sounds of *los gringos*. A more and more confident speaker of English, I didn't listen to how strangers sounded when they talked to me. With so many English-speaking people around me, I no longer heard American accents. Conversations quickened. Listening to persons whose voices sounded eccentrically pitched, I might note their sounds for a few seconds, but then I'd concentrate on what they were saying. Now when I heard someone's tone of voice—angry or questioning or sarcastic or happy or sad—I didn't distinguish it from the words it expressed. Sound and word were thus tightly wedded. At the end of each day I was often bemused, and always relieved, to realize how "soundless," though crowded with words, my day in public had been. An eight-year-old boy, I finally came to accept what had been technically true since my birth: I was an American citizen.

But diminished by then was the special feeling of closeness at home. Gone 30 was the desperate, urgent, intense feeling of being at home among those with whom I felt intimate. Our family remained a loving family, but one greatly changed. We were no longer so close, no longer bound tightly together by the knowledge of our separateness from *los gringos*. Neither my older brother nor my sisters rushed home after school any more. Nor did I. When I arrived home, often there would be neighborhood kids in the house. Or the house would be empty of sounds.

Following the dramatic Americanization of their children, even my parents grew more publicly confident—especially my mother. First she learned the names of all the people on the block. Then she decided we needed to have a telephone in our house. My father, for his part, continued to use the word *gringo*, but it was no longer charged with bitterness or distrust. Stripped of any emotional content, the word simply became a name for those Americans not of Hispanic descent. Hearing him, sometimes, I wasn't sure if he was pronouncing the Spanish word *gringo*, or saying gringo in English.

There was a new silence at home. As we children learned more and more English, we shared fewer and fewer words with our parents. Sentences needed to be spoken slowly when one of us addressed our mother or father. Often the parent wouldn't understand. The child would need to repeat himself. Still the parent misunderstood. The young voice, frustrated, would end up saying, "Never mind"—the subject was closed. Dinners would be noisy with the clinking of knives and forks against dishes. My mother would smile softly between her remarks; my father, at the other end of the table, would chew and chew his food while he stared over the heads of his children.

My mother! My father! After English became my primary language, I no longer knew what words to use in addressing my parents. The old Spanish words (those tender accents of sound) I had earlier used—*mamá* and *papá*—I couldn't use any more. They would have been all-too-painful reminders of how much had changed in my life. On the other hand, the words I heard neighborhood kids call their parents seemed equally unsatisfactory. "Mother" and "father," "ma," "papa," "pa," "dad," "pop" (how I hated the all-American sound of that last word)—all these I felt were unsuitable terms of address for *my* parents. As a result, I never used them at home. Whenever I'd speak to my parents, I would try to get their attention by looking at them. In public conversations, I'd refer to them as my "parents" or my "mother" and "father."

My mother and father, for their part, responded differently, as their children spoke to them less. My mother grew restless, seemed troubled and anxious at the scarceness of words exchanged in the house. She would question me about my day when I came home from school. She smiled at my small talk. She pried at the edges of my sentences to get me to say something more. ("What . . . ?") She'd join conversations she overheard, but her intrusions often stopped her children's talking. By contrast, my father seemed to grow reconciled to the new quiet. Though his English somewhat improved, he tended more and more to retire into silence. At dinner he spoke very little. One night his children and even his wife helplessly giggled at his garbled English pronunciation of the Catholic "Grace Before Meals." Thereafter he made his wife recite the prayer at the start of each meal, even on formal occasions when there were guests in the house.

Hers became the public voice of the family. On official business it was she, not my father, who would usually talk to strangers on the phone or in stores. We children grew so accustomed to his silence that years later we would routinely refer to his "shyness." (My mother often tried to explain: Both of his parents died when he was eight. He was raised by an uncle who treated him as little more than a menial servant. He was never encouraged to speak. He grew up alone—a man of few words.) But I realized my father was not shy whenever I'd watch him speaking Spanish with relatives. Using Spanish, he was quickly effusive. Especially when talking with other men, his voice would spark, flicker, flare alive with varied sounds. In Spanish he expressed ideas and feelings he rarely revealed when speaking English. With firm Spanish sounds he conveyed a confidence and authority that English would never allow him.

The silence at home, however, was not simply the result of fewer words passing between parents and children. More profound for me was the silence created by my inattention to sounds. At about the time I no longer bothered to listen with care to the sounds of English in public, I grew careless about listening to the sounds made by the family when they spoke. Most of the time I would hear someone speaking at home and didn't distinguish his sounds from the words people uttered in public. I didn't even pay much attention to my parents' accented and ungrammatical speech—at least not at home. Only when I was with them in public would I become alert to their accents. But even then their sounds caused me less and less concern. For I was growing increasingly confident of my own public identity.

I would have been happier about my public success had I not recalled, sometimes, what it had been like earlier, when my family conveyed its intimacy through a set of conveniently private sounds. Sometimes in public, hearing a stranger, I'd hark back to my lost past. A Mexican farm worker approached me one day downtown. He wanted directions to some place. "*Hijito*, . . . " he said. And his voice stirred old longings. Another time I was standing beside my mother in the visiting room of a Carmelite convent, before the dense screen which rendered the nuns shadowy figures. I heard several of them speaking Spanish in their busy, singsong, overlapping voices, assuring my mother that, yes, yes, we were remembered, all our family was remembered, in their prayers. Those voices echoed faraway family sounds. Another day a dark-faced old woman touched my shoulder lightly to steady herself as she boarded a bus. She murmured something to me I couldn't quite comprehend. Her Spanish voice came near, like the face of a never-before-seen relative in the instant before I was kissed. That voice, like so many of the Spanish voices I'd hear in public, recalled the golden age of my childhood.

Bilingual educators say today that children lose a degree of "individuality" by becoming assimilated into public society. (Bilingual schooling is a program popularized in the seventies, that decade when middle-class "ethnics" began to resist the process of assimilation—the "American melting pot.") But the bilingualists oversimplify when they scorn the value and necessity of assimilation. They do not seem to realize that a person is individualized in two ways. So they do not realize that, while one suffers a diminished sense of *private* individuality by being assimilated into public society, such assimilation makes possible the achievement of *public* individuality.

Simplistically again, the bilingualists insist that a student should be reminded of his difference from others in mass society, of his "heritage." But they equate mere separateness with individuality. The fact is that only in private—with intimates—is separateness from the crowd a prerequisite for individuality; an intimate "tells" me that I am unique, unlike all others, apart from the crowd. In public, by contrast, full individuality is achieved, paradoxically, by those who are able to consider themselves members of the crowd. Thus it happened for me. Only when I was able to think of myself as an American, no longer an alien in gringo society, could I seek the rights and opportunities necessary for full public individuality. The social and political advantages I enjoy as a man began on the day I came to believe that my name is indeed *Rich-heard Road-ree-guess*. It is true that my public society today is often impersonal; in fact, my public society is usually mass society. But despite the anonymity of the crowd, and despite the fact that the individuality I achieve in public is often tenuous—because it depends on my being one in a crowd—I celebrate the day I acquired my new name. Those middle-class ethnics who scorn assimilation seem to me filled with decadent self-pity, obsessed by the burden of public life. Dangerously, they romanticize public separateness and trivialize the dilemma of those who are truly socially disadvantaged.

If I rehearse here the changes in my private life after my Americanization, it is finally to emphasize a public gain. The loss implies the gain. The house I returned to each afternoon was quiet. Intimate sounds no longer greeted me at the door. Inside there were other noises. The telephone rang. Neighborhood kids ran past the door of the bedroom where I was reading my schoolbooks—covered with brown shopping-bag paper. Once I learned the public language, it would never again be easy for me to hear intimate family voices. More and more of my day was spent hearing words, not sounds. But that may only be a way of saying that on the day I raised my hand in class and spoke loudly to an entire roomful of faces, my childhood started to end.   40

CONTEXTS FOR "ARIA: A MEMOIR OF A BILINGUAL CHILDHOOD"

Richard Rodriguez at age eighteen

Interview Excerpt

In this excerpt from a 1994 interview, Richard Rodriguez briefly reflects on Hunger of Memory *as a youthful work.*

RODRIGUEZ: If you ask me about these individual [minority] students, I think they are required to think of themselves as representing a cause. Their admission is in the name of a larger population for whom they feel responsible, and they do claim to have a kind of communal voice to speak in the name of the people. If you have a different opinion, then you are not of the people.

Multiculturalism, as it is expressed in the platitudes of the American campus, is not multiculturalism. It is an idea about culture that has a specific genesis, a specific history, and a specific politics. What people mean by multiculturalism is different hues of themselves. They don't mean Islamic fundamentalists or skinheads. They mean other brown and black students who share opinions like theirs. It isn't diversity. It's a pretense to diversity. And this is an exposure of it—they can't even tolerate my paltry opinion.

REASON: *Days of Obligation* got a friendlier response than *Hunger of Memory*, partly because it was more Mexican.

RODRIGUEZ: I think of it as more Catholic rather than more Mexican. An older man is writing this book. I thought of my earlier book as a more deeply Protestant book: my objection to the popular ideology of that time; my insistence that *I am this man,* contrary to what you want to make me; my declaration of myself, of my profession—political and personal; my defiance of my mother's wishes in publishing this memoir. It seemed to me very Protestant and very self-assertive—in the best sense. . . .

RICHARD RODRIGUEZ

Slouching towards Los Angeles

To understand what Rodriguez might mean by calling Hunger of Memory *a "Protestant" work, this opinion piece (1993) argues that America was founded on Protestant individualism; ironically, by emphasizing his individuality, Rodriguez places himself in the historically dominant group.*

From Virginia I. Postrel and Nick Gillespie, "The New, New World: Richard Rodriguez on Culture and Assimilation," *Reason: Free Minds and Free Markets*, August/September 1994, 35–41.

From Richard Rodriguez, "Slouching towards Los Angeles," *Los Angeles Times*, 11 April 1993.

I have been traveling recently across America, visiting colleges and making happy-talk appearances on morning television. On airplanes and in classrooms, I have been hearing Americans say what many say in Los Angeles—that America doesn't exist anymore as a unified culture.

So what else is new? Americans have always said that. We Americans have never easily believed in ourselves as a nation. What traditionally we share is the belief that we share nothing in common at all with people on the other side of town. Who is more American, after all, than today's brown and black neo-nationalists in Los Angeles?

America is a Puritan country, Protestant baptized. It was Protestantism that taught Americans to fear the crowd and to believe in individualism. Nineteenth-century nativists feared that Catholics and Jews would undermine the Protestant idea of America. But it was, paradoxically, American Protestantism that allowed for an immigrant nation. Lacking a communal sense, how could Americans resist the coming of strangers? The immigrant country of the nineteenth century became a country of tribes and neighborhoods more truly than a nation of solitary individuals. Then, as today, Americans trusted diversity, not uniformity. Americans trusted the space between us more than we liked any notion of an American melting pot that might turn us into one another.

Our teachers used to be able to tell us this; the schoolmarm used to be subversive of American individuality. Our teachers used to be able to pose the possibility of a national culture—a line connecting Thomas Jefferson, the slave owner, to Malcolm X. Our teachers used to be able to tell us why all of us speak Black English.

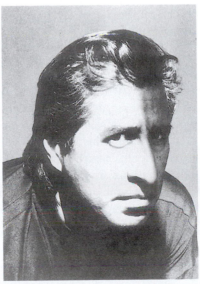

Richard Rodriguez photographed as a Mask.

Or how the Mexican farmworkers in Delano were related to the Yiddish-speaking grandmothers who worked the sweatshops of the Lower East Side. America may not have wanted to listen. But our teachers used to insist that there was something called an American culture, a common history.

All over America, in identical hotels, there are weekend conferences for business executives on multiculturalism. But any immigrant kid could tell you that America exists. There *is* a culture. There is a shared accent, a shared defiance of authority, a shared skepticism about community. There is a stance, a common impatience at the fast-food counter. Moreover, though executives who attend multicultural seminars do not want to hear it, the deepest separation between us derives not from race or ethnicity but from class.

OCTAVIO PAZ

The Labyrinth of Solitude

Mexican diplomat, poet, essayist, translator, and literary and cultural historian Octavio Paz (1914–1998) won the Nobel Prize for literature in 1990. He analyzed the Mexican man's love of silence and privacy in The Labyrinth of Solitude *(1959). The following passage from "Mexican Masks," the second chapter, helps us understand the cultural tradition underlying Rodriguez's father's habitual silence and reticence.*

> *Impassioned heart,*
> *disguise your sorrow . . .*
> *   –Popular song*

The Mexican, whether young or old, *criollo* or *mestizo,*[1] general or laborer or lawyer, seems to me to be a person who shuts himself away to protect himself: his face is a mask and so is his smile. In his harsh solitude, which is both barbed and courteous, everything serves him as a defense: silence and words, politeness and disdain, irony and resignation. He is jealous of his own privacy and that of others, and he is afraid even to glance at his neighbor, because a mere glance can trigger the rage of these electrically charged spirits. He passes through life like a man who has been flayed; everything can hurt him, including words and the very suspicion of words. His language is full of reticences, of metaphors and allusions, of unfinished phrases, while his silence is full of tints, folds, thunderheads, sud-

From Octavio Paz, *The Labyrinth of Solitude*, trans. Lysander Kemp (New York: Grove, 1961), 29–30.

[1]*Criollo*: a person of pure Spanish blood living in the Americas.–*Tr.*
Mestizo: a person of mixed Spanish and Indian blood.–*Tr.*

den rainbows, indecipherable threats. Even in a quarrel he prefers veiled expressions to outright insults: "A word to the wise is sufficient." He builds a wall of indifference and remoteness between reality and himself, a wall that is no less impenetrable for being invisible. The Mexican is always remote, from the world and from other people. And also from himself.

The speech of our people reflects the extent to which we protect ourselves from the outside world: the ideal of manliness is never to "crack," never to back down. Those who "open themselves up" are cowards. Unlike other people, we believe that opening oneself up is a weakness or a betrayal. The Mexican can bend, can bow humbly, can even stoop, but he cannot back down, that is, he cannot allow the outside world to penetrate his privacy. The man who backs down is not to be trusted, is a traitor or a person of doubtful loyalty; he babbles secrets and is incapable of confronting a dangerous situation. Women are inferior beings because, in submitting, they open themselves up. Their inferiority is constitutional and resides in their sex, their submissiveness, which is a wound that never heals.

Hermeticism is one of the several recourses of our suspicion and distrust. It shows that we instinctively regard the world around us to be dangerous. This reaction is justifiable if one considers what our history has been and the kind of society we have created. The harshness and hostility of our environment, and the hidden, indefinable threat that is always afloat in the air, oblige us to close ourselves in, like those plants that survive by storing up liquid within their spiny exteriors. But this attitude, legitimate enough in its origins, has become a mechanism that functions automatically. Our response to sympathy and tenderness is reserve, since we cannot tell whether those feelings are genuine or simulated. In addition, our masculine integrity is as much endangered by kindness as it is by hostility. Any opening in our defenses is a lessening of our manliness.

Our relationships with other men are always tinged with suspicion. Every time a Mexican confides in a friend or acquaintance, every time he opens himself up, it is an abdication. He dreads that the person in whom he has confided will scorn him. Therefore confidences result in dishonor, and they are as dangerous for the person to whom they are made as they are for the person who makes them.

JOSÉ ANTONIO VILLARREAL

Pocho

José Antonio Villarreal's novel Pocho *(1959) was the first to represent the great exodus of Mexicans into Texas after the Mexican Revolution (1910–1917) and the experiences of a second-generation Mexican American during the 1930s. Richard Rubio,*

From José Antonio Villarreal, *Pocho* (New York: Doubleday, 1959), 132–133.

the novel's main character, experiences tensions between languages, cultures, genera-
tions, and social classes—tensions resembling those Rodriguez portrays in Hunger
of Memory.

As the months went by, Richard was quieter, sadder, and, at times, even morose.
He was aware that the family was undergoing a strange metamorphosis. The
heretofore gradual assimilation of this new culture was becoming more pronounced. Along with a new prosperity, the Rubio family was taking on the mores
of the middle class, and he did not like it. It saddened him to see the Mexican tradition begin to disappear. And because human nature is such, he, too, suc-
cumbed, and unconsciously became an active leader in the change.

"Silence!" roared Juan Rubio. "We will not speak the dog language in my
house!" They were at the supper table.

"But this is America, Father," said Richard. "If we live in this country, we
must live like Americans."

"And next you will tell me that those are not tortillas you are eating but
bread, and those are not beans but *hahm an' ecks.*"

"No, but I mean that you must remember that we are not in México. In
México—"   5

"*Hahm an' ecks,*" his father interrupted. "You know, when I was in Los
Angeles for the first time, before your mother found me, all I could say in
the English was *hahm an' ecks*, and I ate all my meals in a restaurant. Remember! What makes you think I have to remember that I am not in México? Why . . ."

"You were in the restaurant, Papá."

"Yes, well. . . . Every morning, when the woman came for my order, I would
say *hahm an' ecks*, at noon *hahm an' ecks*, at night *hahm an' ecks*. I tell you I was
tired, and then, one day, she did not ask, and brought me some soup and some
meat. I do not know whether she felt sorry for me or whether they ran out of
eggs, but I certainly was happy for the change."

RICHARD HOGGART
The Uses of Literacy

Part of Rodriguez's self-definition involves his emergence from working-class life, an
emergence signaled by the title of his prologue to Hunger of Memory: *"Middle-*
Class Pastoral." As the memoir's second chapter explains, Rodriguez read Richard
Hoggart's treatise (published in 1957) on the experience of the working-class stu-

From Richard Hoggart, *The Uses of Literacy: Aspects of Working-Class Life, with Special Reference to
Publications and Entertainments* (London: Chatto, 1957), 239–241.

dent, or "scholarship boy," attending English schools for upper-class and aristocratic boys. A "scholarship boy," writes Hoggart, is "at the friction-point of two cultures," always anxiously adjusting his family's ways—their reading, table manners, vocabulary and pronunciation, conversational topics and gestures, and countless other markers of social class—to those of wealthier boys and their families. Rodriguez read Hoggart's book when he traveled to London's British Museum to research his doctoral dissertation on English Renaissance literature. The book changed his life. Recognizing in himself a Mexican American version of the "scholarship boy," he abandoned his dissertation—and with it his assured career as a university professor—in order to write Hunger of Memory. *The following passage from Hoggart's book is reflected in Rodriguez's "Aria."*

Almost every working-class boy who goes through the process of further education by scholarships finds himself chafing against his environment during adolescence. He is at the friction-point of two cultures; the test of his real education lies in his ability, by about the age of twenty-five, to smile at his father with his whole face and to respect his flighty young sister and his slower brother. I shall be concerned with those for whom the uprooting is particularly troublesome, not because I under-estimate the gains which this kind of selection gives, nor because I wish to stress the more depressing features in contemporary life, but because the difficulties of some people illuminate much in the wider discussion of cultural change. Like transplanted stock, they react to a widespread drought earlier than those who have been left in their original soil.

I am sometimes inclined to think that the problem of self-adjustment is, in general, especially difficult for those working-class boys who are only moderately endowed, who have talent sufficient to separate them from the majority of their working-class contemporaries, but not to go much farther. I am not implying a correlation between intelligence and lack of unease; intellectual people have their own troubles: but this kind of anxiety often seems most to afflict those in the working-classes who have been pulled one stage away from their original culture and yet have not the intellectual equipment which would then cause them to move on to join the "declassed" professionals and experts. In one sense, it is true, no one is ever "declassed"; and it is interesting to see how this occassionally obtrudes (particularly today, when ex-working-class boys move in all the managing areas of society)—in the touch of insecurity, which often appears as an undue concern to establish "presence" in an otherwise quite professorial professor, in the intermittent rough homeliness of an important executive and committee-man, in the tendency to vertigo which betrays a lurking sense of uncertainty in a successful journalist.

But I am chiefly concerned with those who are self-conscious and yet not self-aware in any full sense, who are as a result uncertain, dissatisfied and gnawed by self-doubt. Sometimes they lack will, though they have intelligence, and "it takes will to cross this waste." More often perhaps, though they have as much will as the majority, they have not sufficient to resolve the complex tensions which their uprooting, the peculiar problems of their particular domestic settings, and the uncertainties common to the time create.

As childhood gives way to adolescence and that to manhood, this kind of boy tends to be progressively cut off from the ordinary life of his group. He is marked out early: and here I am thinking not so much of his teachers in the "elementary" school as of fellow-members of his family. "'E's got brains," or " 'E's bright," he hears constantly; and in part the tone is one of pride and admiration. He is in a way cut off by his parents as much as by his talent which urges him to break away from his group. Yet on their side this is not altogether from admiration: "'E's got brains," yes, and he is expected to follow the trail that opens. But there can also be a limiting quality in the tone with which the phrase is used; character counts more. Still, he has brains—a mark of pride and almost a brand; he is heading for a different world, a different sort of job. . . .

PAUL ZWEIG
The Child of Two Cultures

Memoir intrinsically involves its writer in maintaining a balance between private and public selves. By 1994, when Rodriguez insisted "I am this man," he desperately wanted to escape the grasp of political groups who used his name and memoir as mere bumper stickers. In the prologue to Hunger of Memory, *Rodriguez had foreseen this risk:*

> My book is necessarily political, in the conventional sense, for public issues—editorials and ballot stubs, petitions and placards, faceless formulations of greater and lesser good by greater and lesser minds—have bisected my life and changed its course. And, in some broad sense, my writing is political because it concerns my movement away from the company of family and into the city. This was my coming of age: I became a man by becoming a public man.

Paul Zweig places Hunger of Memory *within an American tradition of autobiographical writing that is "as personal as possible so as to be as public as possible." As Zweig points out, if the memoir were entirely individual ("I am this man"), few readers would be interested in it; instead, Rodriguez's achievement is to "identify [the] universal labor of growing up in his own particular experience."* . . .

Advocates of bilingual education are wrong, [Rodriguez] insists, in supposing that the values of home life are embodied in language, not persons. If students at school can learn in their home language, it is claimed, they will be less disori-

---

From Paul Zweig, "The Child of Two Cultures," *New York Times Book Review,* 28 February 1982, 1, 26.

ented, better able to attend to the business of schooling. But the business of schooling is to take children out of the home and thrust upon them a new set of demands. Education, to work, must change children. That is its function, according to Richard Rodriguez. It must teach them a new voice, indeed a new language, less charged with intimate feelings than the old language, less comfortable, but appropriate to the impersonal world in which self-respect, success, money, culture are won. To win is also to lose, yes; but this can't be avoided, shouldn't be avoided.

Here is the political point Mr. Rodriguez wants to drive home. The struggle for social justice begun 20 years ago with the civil rights movement in the South and expanded since to include all "minority" groups—Hispanics, Chicanos, Haitians, but also gays and women—has taken a wrong turn in the matter of education. Affirmative action and bilingual school programs; the demand for ethnic studies in the university, for relevance; the attempt to legitimize black ghetto English—all ignore the essential function of education, which is to change the student, extract him from his intimate circumstance—family, ghetto, minority community—and give him access to the public world, which in the United States is negotiated in standard English, embodied by a set of attitudes, a voice, which is everywhere recognized as a passport to all the larger ambitions the public world makes possible.

The failure of educators and social activists alike to know this, according to Mr. Rodriguez, reflects the larger failure of American education, which rarely succeeds in changing anyone. Its greatest success comes with those children born in closest proximity to the public world, for whom, therefore, the change is smallest: children of the upper middle classes. Mr. Rodriguez offers himself as an example of the long labor of change: its costs, about which he is movingly frank, its loneliness, but also its triumphs.

RICHARD RODRIGUEZ

Interview (1999)

A "self" naturally changes with time, and a tougher, hipper Rodriguez surmises in this 1999 interview excerpt that his former "Bambi" self might now hold little appeal for young Chicano males.

RODRIGUEZ: I must tell you that I am not sure that I would like Richard Rodriguez were I not he. At some very simple level I can tell you that I don't like the voice. I don't even like the tenderness of *Hunger of Memory*; frankly,

From Timothy S. Sedore, "Violating the Boundaries: An Interview with Richard Rodriguez," *Michigan Quarterly Review* (Summer 1999): 425–446.

it's too soft for men. It's not Latino enough, it's a little too feminine, a little too American. He looks like Bambi on the cover. I'm not sure I like this guy. He whimpers too much. He's too soft. He's not what I want.

As a young Mexican American male in the city, I would want something tougher: I would want something more robust. When I think of the Chicano movement in its most wonderful forms I think of my friend Tony who died a few weeks ago. Tony was an artist, and he was a writer. He wasn't a great writer, but he was Chicano in the sense that he was a rebel. He tried to undo society in a wonderfully comic way. He belonged to a group called Culture Clash, and they began a movement about twenty years ago. Tony ultimately became a muralist instead of a performer, but he was always into adolescent forms of rebellion against the gringo society. He was like, "I'm doing the emblems, I'm doing the iconography." He mocked the culture by parodying it. He was constantly playing at the edges of the American culture.

Maybe that's what I would have wanted. I wanted a Rich Rodriguez with more guts, someone who was tougher. I think to myself, if I'm a Chicano and all of my life I've been stuck with losers, then I want somebody who's tough. I want somebody who represents us as a contender. Richard Rodriguez grew up in a little, close, white neighborhood with the Anglos. He's not what I would have in mind as a Chicano. He doesn't have the spirit.

QUESTIONS FOR DISCUSSION AND WRITING

1. In his 1994 interview, Rodriguez examines the "pretense to diversity," an idea he elaborates on in his 1999 interview. What do you think "pretense to diversity" means? Which passages from "Aria" describe qualities that Rodriguez would consider "Chicano" or "non-Chicano"? Make a list of qualities that define each term. Which qualities in each list does he apply to himself? Which describe the qualities of "Bambi," the self-deprecating label he adopts in the 1999 interview? Explain in what ways and to what extent Rodriguez represents Chicanos as a group. What do you think motivates him to reject a Chicano identity? To accept it?

2. In Chapter 2, N. Scott Momaday suggests that we understand a story in terms of other stories we already know (p. 145). Which of the stories that Rodriguez tells in "Aria" seem to you to advocate the individualism he describes in "Slouching towards Los Angeles"? Which seem to challenge that individualism?

3. Which passages in Rodriguez's "Aria" are most closely related to Octavio Paz's account of masks? In each passage, who wears a mask? For what motives? Alternatively, in what ways and to what extent do the Rodriguez family's conversations resemble those re-created by José Antonio Villarreal in the excerpt from *Pocho*? Make a three-column list with the headings "Rubio Family," "Rodriguez

Family Like Rubios," and "Rodriguez Family Unlike Rubios"; then write relevant examples under each heading. What do your findings suggest about diversity among Chicano families?

4. Divide a sheet of paper into four quadrants, labeling the two columns "Richard Hoggart" and "Richard Rodriguez" and the two rows "Similar" and "Different." In each row, write pairs of passages from *The Uses of Literacy* and "Aria." On the basis of your evidence, explain to what extent social class—rather than ethnicity—is the key to the identity of a "scholarship boy." In what ways is Rodriguez a "scholarship boy," and in what ways is he not?

5. Consider Villarreal's representation of Chicano English (*"hahm an' ecks"*) and Hoggart's representation of cockney English ("'E's got brains"). Why might each have chosen these particular representations? Looking closely at the passages in "Aria" where Rodriguez represents differing languages, describe the effects of each representation on you as a reader. What do you think is gained and lost through representations of language variation?

6. One reason that a piece of writing becomes canonical is that various generations of writers find it useful for furthering various political agendas. With a partner, consider the selection on the politics of bilingual education, "The Child of Two Cultures." What do writers try to accomplish by citing Rodriguez's *Hunger of Memory*? In the library or on the Internet, locate some contemporary debates about bilingual and ESL (English as a Second Language) curricula. What differences between these two curricula can you identify? Which passages from "Aria" could be used to support bilingual, ESL, or "English-only" agendas today?

NATALIE BEHRING

The Entrance Exam

QUESTIONS FOR DISCUSSION AND WRITING

1. This photo of an Afghan woman taking a university entrance examination at Kabul's Polytechnic Institute was taken on February 20, 2002. The classroom was destroyed in Afghanistan's civil war. How does the photo portray the contrast between the woman's desire and the material conditions of her education? "Read" the picture to provide specific examples.

2. During the years of rule by the Taliban, women in Afghanistan were forbidden to attend schools or even to learn to read or write. What might the woman in this photograph, and others like her, learn about ways to learn from the essays by Heath (p. 280), Silko (p. 287), Zitkala-Sa (p. 292), Rodriguez (p. 298), and Gardner (p. 322) in this chapter?

PLATO

The Allegory of the Cave

Born in Athens (c. 428–347 B.C.E.), Plato was the most famous pupil of Socrates. To-gether with Aristotle, these three thinkers are the philosophical forebears of Western thought. The dialogues of Plato display the Socratic method of philosophical explo-ration, in which Socrates poses step-by-step questions about concepts of "good," "jus-tice," and "piety." Each question has a simple answer, but cumulatively they reveal contradictions, ambiguities, and other barriers to understanding. For this reason, Plato's The Republic *argues that a just government should be guided by statesmen whose learning—attained through dialogue rather than through the senses—makes them both persuasive and wise.*

"The Allegory of the Cave," from The Republic, *tells of prisoners who under-stand life only through shadows flickering on the wall of their cave. Like all allegories, this story conveys abstract ideas through more concrete representation, in this case, Plato's belief that "ideas," or pure forms, exist only in the spiritual realm. Before birth, we see ideas perfectly, but on earth our memories fade and our senses perceive only unreliable shadows of those ideas. Plato's allegory thus suggests that, like the prisoners, people on earth understand life only through sense perceptions similar to shadows; as a result, they know reality only incompletely.*

Next, said I, here is a parable to illustrate the degrees in which our nature may be enlightened or unenlightened. Imagine the condition of men living is a sort of cavernous chamber underground, with an entrance open to the light and a long passage all down the cave. Here they have been from childhood, chained by the leg and also by the neck, so that they cannot move and can see only what is in front of them, because the chains will not let them turn their heads. At some dis-tance higher up is the light of a fire burning behind them; and between the pris-oners and the fire is a track with a parapet built along it, like the screen at a puppet-show, which hides the performers while they show their puppets over the top.

I see, said he.

Now behind this parapet imagine persons carrying along various artificial objects, including figures of men and animals in wood or stone or other materi-als, which project above the parapet. Naturally, some of these persons will be talking, others silent.

It is a strange picture, he said, and a strange sort of prisoners.

Like ourselves, I replied; for in the first place prisoners so confined would   5 have seen nothing of themselves or of one another, except the shadows thrown by the fire-light on the wall of the Cave facing them, would they?

Not if all their lives they had been prevented from moving their heads.

And they would have seen as little of the objects carried past.

Of course.

Now, if they could talk to one another, would they not suppose that their words referred only to those passing shadows which they saw?

Necessarily.

And suppose their prison had an echo from the wall facing them? When one of the people crossing behind them spoke, they could only suppose that the sound came from the shadow passing before their eyes.

No doubt.

In every way, then, such prisoners would recognize as reality nothing but the shadows of those artificial objects.

Inevitably.

Now consider what would happen if their release from the chains and the healing of their unwisdom should come about in this way. Suppose one of them were set free and forced suddenly to stand up, turn his head, and walk with eyes lifted to the light; all these movements would be painful, and he would be too dazzled to make out the objects whose shadows he had been used to see. What do you think he would say, if someone told him that what he had formerly seen was meaningless illusion, but now, being somewhat nearer to reality and turned towards more real objects, he was getting a truer view? Suppose further that he were shown the various objects being carried by and were made to say, in reply to questions, what each of them was. Would he not be perplexed and believe the objects now shown him to be not so real as what he formerly saw?

Yes, not nearly so real.

And if he were forced to look at the fire-light itself, would not his eyes ache, so that he would try to escape and turn back to the things which he could see distinctly, convinced that they really were clearer than these other objects now being shown to him?

Yes.

And suppose someone were to drag him away forcibly up the steep and rugged ascent and not let him go until he had hauled him out into the sunlight, would he not suffer pain and vexation at such treatment, and, when he had come out into the light, find his eyes so full of its radiance that he could not see a single one of the things that he was now told were real?

Certainly he would not see them all at once.

He would need, then, to grow accustomed before he could see things in that upper world. At first it would be easiest to make out shadows, and then the images of men and things reflected in water, and later on the things themselves. After that, it would be easier to watch the heavenly bodies and the sky itself by night, looking at the light of the moon and stars rather than the Sun and the Sun's light in the day-time.

Yes, surely.

Last of all, he would be able to look at the Sun and contemplate its nature, not as it appears when reflected in water or any alien medium, but as it is in itself in its own domain.

No doubt.

And now he would begin to draw the conclusion that it is the Sun that pro- 25
duces the seasons and the course of the year and controls everything in the visible
world, and moreover is in a way the cause of all that he and his companions used
to see.

Clearly he would come at last to that conclusion.

Then if he called to mind his fellow prisoners and what passed for wisdom in
his former dwelling-place, he would surely think himself happy in the change
and be sorry for them. They may have had a practice of honoring and commend-
ing one another, with prizes for the man who had the keenest eye for the passing
shadows and the best memory for the order in which they followed or accompanied one another, so that he could make a good guess as to which was going to
come next. Would our released prisoner be likely to covet those prizes or to envy
the men exalted to honor and power in the Cave? Would he not feel like Homer's
Achilles, that he would far sooner 'be on earth as a hired servant in the house of a
landless man' or endure anything rather than go back to his old beliefs and live in
the old way?

Yes, he would prefer any fate to such a life.

Now imagine what would happen if he went down again to take his former
seat in the Cave. Coming suddenly out of the sunlight, his eyes would be filled
with darkness. He might be required once more to deliver his opinion on those
shadows, in competition with the prisoners who had never been released, while
his eyesight was still dim and unsteady; and it might take some time to become
used to the darkness. They would laugh at him and say that he had gone up only
to come back with his sight ruined; it was worth no one's while even to attempt
the ascent. If they could lay hands on the man who was trying to set them free
and lead them up, they would kill him.

Yes, they would.   30

Every feature in this parable, my dear Glaucon, is meant to fit our earlier analysis.
The prison dwelling corresponds to the region revealed to us through the sense of
sight, and the fire-light within it to the power of the Sun. The ascent to see the
things in the upper world you may take as standing for the upward journey of the
soul into the region of the intelligible; then you will be in possession of what I
surmise, since that is what you wish to be told. Heaven knows whether it is true;
but this, at any rate, is how it appears to me. In the world of knowledge, the last
thing to be perceived and only with great difficulty is the essential Form of Goodness. Once it is perceived, the conclusion must follow that, for all things, this is
the cause of whatever is right and good; in the visible world it gives birth to light
and to the lord of light, while it is itself sovereign in the intelligible world and the
parent of intelligence and truth. Without having had a vision of this Form no one
can act with wisdom, either in his own life or in matters of state.

QUESTIONS FOR DISCUSSION AND WRITING

1. Visualize Plato's parable by means of an outline or a drawing. How many stages are there in the process through which "our nature may be enlightened or unenlightened" (paragraph 1)? In what sequence are these stages arranged? Why does Plato choose this order?

2. Why does Plato use the prisoners in a cave (almost a dungeon) as a metaphor of people in search of knowledge? What can we learn from this metaphor about Plato's evaluation of knowledge and the human capacity for acquiring knowledge? Can human beings acquire complete and certain knowledge? Why or why not?

3. Describe the characteristics of the Socratic dialogue based on specific details from "The Allegory of the Cave." Who talks most often? Who responds with brief phrases? What problems does the unequal use of language reveal about the form of the Socratic dialogue? What possible truths does this format discourage us from discovering?

4. Why does Plato emphasize the importance of goodness in a dialogue that deals with the process and capability of humans for knowing truth? What is the relationship between the good and the true in Plato's view?

5. Rewrite the dialogue, giving Glaucon more opportunities to speak up or challenge Socrates' theory of knowledge and giving Socrates more of a passive role of brief responses. Would Socrates' argument be equally compelling in your revision? What can you learn about the power, or even the violence, of language? What role does language play in the search for truth?

LINKED READINGS: MEASURING INTELLIGENCE

HOWARD GARDNER
Who Owns Intelligence?

Howard Gardner was born in Scranton, Pennsylvania, in 1943. As a boy, he was a gifted pianist. He attended Harvard University (B.A., 1965; Ph.D., 1971) and, as a Harvard professor, has researched normal and gifted children's creativity. Brain Damage: Gateway to the Mind *(1975) reports on his research with aphasic adults — those unable to process language. Recipient of a 1981 MacArthur "genius" fellowship, Gardner soon turned his attention to the theory of intelligence used in the social sciences and standardized testing. His conclusion — that people possess more than one type of intelligence — inspired his book* Frames of Mind: The Theory of Multiple Intelligences *(1983), in which he categorizes intelligence as "object-related" (math and logic), "object-free" (music and language), and "personal" (our percep-*

tions of ourselves and of others). Other books build on his earlier research: Multiple Intelligences: The Theory in Practice *(1993) and* Intelligence Reframed: Multiple Intelligences for the Twenty-first Century *(1999).* The Disciplined Mind: Beyond Facts and Standardized Tests *(2000) counters E. D. Hirsch Jr.'s emphasis on acquisition of factual knowledge in* Cultural Literacy *(1987) and instead argues for deep understanding of a few traditional disciplines.*

Gardner summarizes current theory and his own beliefs in "Who Owns Intelligence?" (Atlantic 1999). After first reviewing the history of the IQ test, the first measure of intellectual potential to be developed by modern psychology, he surveys current theories of intelligence, arguing that several schools of "experts are competing for the 'ownership' of intelligence in the next century."

Almost a century ago Alfred Binet, a gifted psychologist, was asked by the French Ministry of Education to help determine who would experience difficulty in school. Given the influx of provincials to the capital, along with immigrants of uncertain stock, Parisian officials believed they needed to know who might not advance smoothly through the system. Proceeding in an empirical manner, Binet posed many questions to youngsters of different ages. He ascertained which questions when answered correctly predicted success in school, and which questions when answered incorrectly foretold school difficulties. The items that discriminated most clearly between the two groups became, in effect, the first test of intelligence.

Binet is a hero to many psychologists. He was a keen observer, a careful scholar, an inventive technologist. Perhaps even more important for his followers, he devised the instrument that is often considered psychology's greatest success story. Millions of people who have never heard Binet's name have had aspects of their fate influenced by instrumentation that the French psychologist inspired. And thousands of psychometricians—specialists in the measurement of psychological variables—earn their living courtesy of Binet's invention.

Although it has prevailed over the long run, the psychologists' version of intelligence is now facing its biggest threat. Many scholars and observers—and even some iconoclastic psychologists—feel that intelligence is too important to be left to the psychometricians. Experts are extending the breadth of the concept—proposing many intelligences, including emotional intelligence and moral intelligence. They are experimenting with new methods of ascertaining intelligence, including some that avoid tests altogether in favor of direct measures of brain activity. They are forcing citizens everywhere to confront a number of questions: What is intelligence? How ought it to be assessed? And how do our notions of intelligence fit with what we value about human beings? In short, experts are competing for the "ownership" of intelligence in the next century.

The outline of the psychometricians' success story is well known. Binet's colleagues in England and Germany contributed to the conceptualization and instrumentation of intelligence testing—which soon became known as IQ tests.

(An IQ, or intelligence quotient, designates the ratio between mental age and chronological age. Clearly we'd prefer that a child in our care have an IQ of 120, being smarter than average for his or her years, than an IQ of 80, being older than average for his or her intelligence.) Like other Parisian fashions of the period, the intelligence test migrated easily to the United States. First used to determine who was "feeble-minded," it was soon used to assess "normal" children, to identify the "gifted," and to determine who was fit to serve in the Army. By the 1920s the intelligence test had become a fixture in educational practice in the United States and much of Western Europe.

Early intelligence tests were not without their critics. Many enduring con-   5 cerns were first raised by the influential journalist Walter Lippmann, in a series of published debates with Lewis Terman, of Stanford University, the father of IQ testing in America. Lippmann pointed out the superficiality of the questions, their possible cultural biases, and the risks of trying to determine a person's intellectual potential with a brief oral or paper-and-pencil measure.

Perhaps surprisingly, the conceptualization of intelligence did not advance much in the decades following Binet's and Terman's pioneering contributions. Intelligence tests came to be seen, rightly or wrongly, as primarily a tool for selecting people to fill academic or vocational niches. In one of the most famous—if irritating—remarks about intelligence testing, the influential Harvard psychologist E. G. Boring declared, "Intelligence is what the tests test." So long as these tests did what they were supposed to do (that is, give some indication of school success), it did not seem necessary or prudent to probe too deeply into their meaning or to explore alternative views of the human intellect.

Psychologists who study intelligence have argued chiefly about three questions. The first: Is intelligence singular, or does it consist of various more or less independent intellectual faculties? The purists—ranging from the turn-of-the-century English psychologist Charles Spearman to his latter-day disciples Richard J. Herrnstein and Charles Murray (of *The Bell Curve* fame)—defend the notion of a single overarching "g," or general intelligence. The pluralists—ranging from L. L. Thurstone, of the University of Chicago, who posited seven vectors of the mind, to J. P. Guilford, of the University of Southern California, who discerned 150 factors of the intellect—construe intelligence as composed of some or even many dissociable components. In his much cited *The Mismeasure of Man* (1981) the paleontologist Stephen Jay Gould argued that the conflicting conclusions reached on this issue reflect alternative assumptions about statistical procedures rather than the way the mind is. Still, psychologists continue the debate, with a majority sympathetic to the general-intelligence perspective.

The public is more interested in the second question: Is intelligence (or are intelligences) largely inherited? This is by and large a Western question. In the Confucian societies of East Asia individual differences in endowment are assumed to be modest, and differences in achievement are thought to be due largely to effort. In the West, however, many students of the subject sympathize with the view—defended within psychology by Lewis Terman, among others—

that intelligence is inborn and one can do little to alter one's intellectual birthright.

Studies of identical twins reared apart provide surprisingly strong support for the "heritability" of psychometric intelligence. That is, if one wants to predict someone's score on an intelligence test, the scores of the biological parents (even if the child has not had appreciable contact with them) are more likely to prove relevant than the scores of the adoptive parents. By the same token, the IQs of identical twins are more similar than the IQs of fraternal twins. And, contrary to common sense (and political correctness), the IQs of biologically related people grow closer in the later years of life. Still, because of the intricacies of behavioral genetics and the difficulties of conducting valid experiments with human child-rearing, a few defend the proposition that intelligence is largely environmental rather than heritable, and some believe that we cannot answer the question at all.

Most scholars agree that even if psychometric intelligence is largely inherited, it is not possible to pinpoint the sources of differences in average IQ between groups, such as the fifteen-point difference typically observed between African-American and white populations. That is because in our society the contemporary—let alone the historical—experiences of these two groups cannot be equated. One could ferret out the differences (if any) between black and white populations only in a society that was truly color-blind.   10

One other question has intrigued laypeople and psychologists: Are intelligence tests biased? Cultural assumptions are evident in early intelligence tests. Some class biases are obvious—who except the wealthy could readily answer a question about polo? Others are more subtle. Suppose the question is what one should do with money found on the street. Although ordinarily one might turn it over to the police, what if one had a hungry child? Or what if the police force were known to be hostile to members of one's ethnic group? Only the canonical response to such a question would be scored as correct.

Psychometricians have striven to remove the obviously biased items from such measures. But biases that are built into the test situation itself are far more difficult to deal with. For example, a person's background affects his or her reaction to being placed in an unfamiliar locale, being instructed by someone dressed in a certain way, and having a printed test booklet thrust into his or her hands. And as the psychologist Claude M. Steele has argued . . . , the biases prove even more acute when people know that their academic potential is being measured and that their racial or ethnic group is widely considered to be less intelligent than the dominant social group.

The idea of bias touches on the common assumption that tests in general, and intelligence tests in particular, are inherently conservative instruments— tools of the establishment. It is therefore worth noting that many testing pioneers thought of themselves as progressives in the social sphere. They were devising instruments that could reveal people of talent even if those people came from "remote and apparently inferior backgrounds," to quote from a college catalogue of the 1950s. And occasionally the tests did discover intellectual diamonds in the rough. More often, however, they picked out the privileged. The still unresolved question of the causal relationship between IQ and social privilege has stimulated many a dissertation across the social sciences.

Paradoxically, one of the clearest signs of the success of intelligence tests is that they are no longer widely administered. In the wake of legal cases about the propriety of making consequential decisions about education on the basis of IQ scores, many public school officials have become test-shy. By and large, the testing of IQ in the schools is restricted to cases involving a recognized problem (such as a learning disability) or a selection procedure (determining eligibility for a program that serves gifted children).

Despite this apparent setback, intelligence testing and the line of thinking that underlies it have actually triumphed. Many widely used scholastic measures, chief among them the SAT (renamed the Scholastic Assessment Test a few years ago), are thinly disguised intelligence tests that correlate highly with scores on standard psychometric instruments. Virtually no one raised in the developed world today has gone untouched by Binet's seemingly simple invention of a century ago. 15

MULTIPLE INTELLIGENCES

The concept of intelligence has in recent years undergone its most robust challenge since the days of Walter Lippmann. Some who are informed by psychology but not bound by the assumptions of the psychometricians have invaded this formerly sacrosanct territory. They have put forth their own ideas of what intelligence is, how (and whether) it should be measured, and which values should be invoked in considerations of the human intellect. For the first time in many years the intelligence establishment is clearly on the defensive—and the new century seems likely to usher in quite different ways of thinking about intelligence.

One evident factor in the rethinking of intelligence is the perspective introduced by scholars who are not psychologists. Anthropologists have commented on the parochialism of the Western view of intelligence. Some cultures do not even have a concept called intelligence, and others define intelligence in terms of traits that we in the West might consider odd—obedience, good listening skills, or moral fiber, for example. Neuroscientists are skeptical that the highly differentiated and modular structure of the brain is consistent with a unitary form of intelligence. Computer scientists have devised programs deemed intelligent; these programs often go about problem solving in ways quite different from those embraced by human beings or other animals.

Even within the field of psychology the natives have been getting restless. Probably the most restless is the Yale psychologist Robert J. Sternberg. A prodigious scholar, Sternberg, who is forty-nine, has written dozens of books and hundreds of articles, the majority of them focusing in one or another way on intelligence. Sternberg began with the strategic goal of understanding the actual mental processes mobilized by standard test items, such as the solving of analogies.

But he soon went beyond standard intelligence testing by insisting on two hitherto neglected forms of intelligence: the "practical" ability to adapt to varying contexts (as we all must in these days of divorcing and downsizing), and the capacity to automate familiar activities so that we can deal effectively with novelty and display "creative" intelligence.

Sternberg has gone to greater pains than many other critics of standard intelligence testing to measure these forms of intelligence with the paper-and-pencil laboratory methods favored by the profession. And he has found that a person's ability to adapt to diverse contexts or to deal with novel information can be differentiated from success at standard IQ-test problems. His efforts to create a new intelligence test have not been crowned with easy victory. Most psychometricians are conservative—they like the tests that have been in use for decades, and if new ones are to be marketed, these must correlate well with existing instruments. So much for openness to novelty within psychometrics.

Others in the field seem less bound by its strictures. The psychologist and journalist Daniel Goleman has achieved worldwide success with his book *Emotional Intelligence* (1995). Contending that this new concept (sometimes nicknamed EQ) may matter as much as or more than IQ, Goleman draws attention to such pivotal human abilities as controlling one's emotional reactions and "reading" the signals of others. In the view of the noted psychiatrist Robert Coles, author of *The Moral Intelligence of Children* (1997), among many other books, we should prize character over intellect. He decries the amorality of our families, hence our children; he shows how we might cultivate human beings with a strong sense of right and wrong, who are willing to act on that sense even when it runs counter to self-interest. Other, frankly popular accounts deal with leadership intelligence (LQ), executive intelligence (EQ or ExQ), and even financial intelligence.

Like Coles's and Goleman's efforts, my work on "multiple intelligences" eschews the psychologists' credo of operationalization and test-making. I began by asking two questions: How did the human mind and brain evolve over millions of years? and How can we account for the diversity of skills and capacities that are or have been valued in different communities around the world?

Armed with these questions and a set of eight criteria, I have concluded that all human beings possess at least eight intelligences: linguistic and logical-mathematical (the two most prized in school and the ones central to success on standard intelligence tests), musical, spatial, bodily-kinesthetic, naturalist, interpersonal, and intrapersonal.

I make two complementary claims about intelligence. The first is universal. We all possess these eight intelligences—and possibly more. Indeed, rather than seeing us as "rational animals," I offer a new definition of what it means to be a human being, cognitively speaking: *Homo sapiens sapiens* is the animal that possesses these eight forms of mental representation.

My second claim concerns individual differences. Owing to the accidents of heredity, environment, and their interactions, no two of us exhibit the same intelligences in precisely the same proportions. Our "profiles of intelligence" differ from one another. This fact poses intriguing challenges and opportunities for our education system. We can ignore these differences and pretend that we are all the same; historically, that is what most education systems have done. Or we can fashion an education system that tries to exploit these differences, individualizing instruction and assessment as much as possible.

INTELLIGENCE AND MORALITY

As the century of Binet and his successors draws to a close, we'd be wise to take 25 stock of, and to anticipate, the course of thinking about intelligence. Although my crystal ball is no clearer than anyone else's (the species may lack "future intelligence"), it seems safe to predict that interest in intelligence will not go away.

To begin with, the psychometric community has scarcely laid down its arms. New versions of the standard tests continue to be created, and occasionally new tests surface as well. Researchers in the psychometric tradition churn out fresh evidence of the predictive power of their instruments and the correlations between measured intelligence and one's life chances. And some in the psychometric tradition are searching for the biological basis of intelligence: the gene or complex of genes that may affect intelligence, the neural structures that are crucial for intelligence, or telltale brain-wave patterns that distinguish the bright from the less bright.

Beyond various psychometric twists, interest in intelligence is likely to grow in other ways. It will be fed by the creation of machines that display intelligence and by the specific intelligence or intelligences. Moreover, observers as diverse as Richard Herrnstein and Robert B. Reich, President Clinton's first Secretary of Labor, have agreed that in coming years a large proportion of society's rewards will go to those people who are skilled symbol analysts—who can sit at a computer screen (or its technological successor), manipulate numbers and other kinds of symbols, and use the results of their operations to contrive plans, tactics, and strategies for enterprises ranging from business to science to war games. These people may well color how intelligence is conceived in decades to come—just as the need to provide good middle-level bureaucrats to run an empire served as a primary molder of intelligence tests in the early years of the century.

Surveying the landscape of intelligence, I discern three struggles between opposing forces. The extent to which, and the manner in which, these various struggles are resolved will influence the lives of millions of people. I believe that the three struggles are interrelated; that the first struggle provides the key to the other two; and that the ensemble of struggles can be resolved in an optimal way.

The first struggle concerns the breadth of our definition of intelligence. One camp consists of the purists, who believe in a single form of intelligence—one that basically predicts success in school and in school-like activities. Arrayed against the purists are the progressive pluralists, who believe that many forms of intelligence exist. Some of these pluralists would like to broaden the definition of intelligence considerably, to include the abilities to create, to lead, and to stand out in terms of emotional sensitivity or moral excellence.

The second struggle concerns the assessment of intelligence. Again, one readily encounters a traditional position. Once chiefly concerned with paper-and-pencil tests, the traditionally oriented practitioner is now likely to use computers to provide the same information more quickly and more accurately. But other positions abound. Purists disdain psychological tasks of any complexity, preferring to look instead at reaction time, brain waves, and other physiological measures of intellect. In contrast, simulators favor measures closely resembling the actual abilities that are prized. And skeptics warn against the continued expansion of testing. They emphasize the damage often done to individual life chances and self-esteem by a regimen of psychological testing, and call for less technocratic, more humane methods—ranging from self-assessment to the examination of portfolios of student work to selection in the service of social equity.

The final struggle concerns the relationship between intelligence and the qualities we value in human beings. Although no one would baldly equate intellect and human worth, nuanced positions have emerged on this issue. Some (in the *Bell Curve* mold) see intelligence as closely related to a person's ethics and values; they believe that brighter people are more likely to appreciate moral complexity and to behave judiciously. Some call for a sharp distinction between the realm of intellect on the one hand, and character, morality, or ethics on the other. Society's ambivalence on this issue can be discerned in the figures that become the culture's heroes. For every Albert Einstein or Bobby Fischer who is celebrated for his intellect, there is a Forrest Gump or a Chauncey Gardiner[1] who is celebrated for human—and humane—traits that would never be captured on any kind of intelligence test.

Thanks to the work of the past decade or two, the stranglehold of the psychometricians has at last been broken. This is a beneficent development. Yet now that the psychometricians have been overcome, we risk deciding that anything goes—that emotions, morality, creativity, must all be absorbed into the "new (or even the New Age) intelligence." The challenge is to chart a concept of intelligence that reflects new insights and discoveries and yet can withstand rigorous scrutiny.

An analogy may help. One can think of the scope of intelligence as represented by an elastic band. For many years the definition of intelligence went unchallenged, and the band seemed to have lost its elasticity. Some of the new definitions expand the band, so that it has become taut and resilient; and yet earlier work on intelligence is still germane. Other definitions so expand the band that it is likely finally to snap—and the earlier work on intelligence will no longer be of use.

---

[1]Chauncey Gardiner is the hero of Jerzy Kosinski's novel *Being There*, who begins as Chauncey, an actual gardener, and becomes a U.S. president; understanding nothing, he talks about the only thing he knows—gardening—but is hailed as a genius who uses the garden to describe the world situation. [Editors' note.]

Until now the term "intelligence" has been limited largely to certain kinds of problem-solving involving language and logic—the skills at a premium in the bureaucrat or the law professor. However, human beings are able to deal with numerous kinds of content besides words, numbers, and logical relations—for example, space, music, the psyches of other human beings. Like the elastic band, definitions of intelligence need to be expanded to include human skill in dealing with these diverse contents. And we must not restrict attention to solving problems that have been posed by others; we must consider equally the capacity of individuals to fashion products—scientific experiments, effective organizations— that draw on one or more human intelligences. The elastic band can accommodate such broadening as well.

So long as intelligences are restricted to the processing of contents in the world, we avoid epistemological problems—as we should. "Intelligence" should not be expanded to include personality, motivation, will, attention, character, creativity, and other important and significant human capacities. Such stretching is likely to snap the band.

Let's see what happens when one crosses one of these lines—for example, when one attempts to conflate intelligence and creativity. Beginning with a definition, we extend the descriptor "creative" to those people (or works or institutions) who meet two criteria: they are innovative, and their innovations are eventually accepted by a relevant community.

No one denies that creativity is important—and, indeed, it may prove even more important in the future, when nearly all standard (algorithmic) procedures will be carried out by computers. Yet creativity should not be equated with intelligence. An expert may be intelligent in one or more domains but not necessarily inclined toward, or successful in, innovation. Similarly, although it is clear that the ability to innovate requires a certain degree of intelligence, we don't find a significant correlation between measures of intellect and of creativity. Indeed, creativity seems more dependent on a certain kind of temperament and personality—risk-taking, tough-skinned, persevering, above all having a lust to alter the status quo and leave a mark on society—than on efficiency in processing various kinds of information. By collapsing these categories together we risk missing dimensions that are important but separate; and we may think that we are training (or selecting) one when we are actually training (or selecting) the other.

Next consider what happens when one stretches the idea of intelligence to include attitudes and behaviors—and thus confronts human values within a culture. A few values can be expressed generically enough that they command universal respect: the Golden Rule is one promising candidate. Most values, however, turn out to be specific to certain cultures or subcultures—even such seeming unproblematic ones as the unacceptability of killing or lying. Once one conflates morality and intelligence, one needs to deal with widely divergent views of what is good or bad and why. Moreover, one must confront the fact that people who score high on tests of moral reasoning may act immorally outside the test situation—even as courageous and self-sacrificing people may turn out to be unremarkable on formal tests of moral reasoning or intelligence. It is far preferable to construe intelligence itself as morally neutral and then decide whether a given use of intelligence qualifies as moral, immoral, or amoral in context.

As I see it, no intelligence is moral or immoral in itself. One can be gifted in language and use that gift to write great verse, as did Johann Wolfgang von Goethe, or to foment hatred, as did Joseph Goebbels. Mother Teresa and Lyndon Johnson, Mohandas Gandhi and Niccolò Machiavelli, may have had equivalent degrees of interpersonal intelligence, but they put their skills to widely divergent uses.

Perhaps there is a form of intelligence that determines whether or not a situation harbors moral consideration or consequences. But the term "moral intelligence" carries little force. After all, Adolf Hitler and Joseph Stalin may well have had an exquisite sense of which situations contained moral considerations. However, either they did not care or they embraced their own peculiar morality according to which eliminating Jews was the moral thing to do in quest of a pure Aryan society, or wiping out a generation was necessary in the quest to establish a communist state.

THE BORDERS OF INTELLIGENCE

Writing as a scholar rather than as a layperson, I see two problems with the notion of emotional intelligence. First, unlike language or space, the emotions are not contents to be processed; rather, cognition has evolved so that we can make sense of human beings (self and others) that possess and experience emotions. Emotions are part and parcel of all cognition, though they may well prove more salient at certain times or under certain circumstances: they accompany our interactions with others, our listening to great music, our feelings when we solve—or fail to solve—a difficult mathematical problem. If one calls some intelligences emotional, one suggests that other intelligences are not—and that implication flies in the face of experience and empirical data.

The second problem is the conflation of emotional intelligence and a certain preferred pattern of behavior. This is the trap that Daniel Goleman sometimes falls into in his otherwise admirable *Emotional Intelligence*. Goleman singles out as emotionally intelligent those people who use their understanding of emotions to make others feel better, to solve conflicts, or to cooperate in home or work situations. No one would dispute that such people are wanted. However, people who understand emotion may not necessarily use their skills for the benefit of society.

For this reason I prefer the term "emotional sensitivity"—a term (encompassing my interpersonal and intrapersonal intelligences) that could apply to people who are sensitive to emotions in themselves and in others. Presumably, clinicians and salespeople excel in sensitivity to others, poets and mystics in sensitivity to themselves. And some autistic or psychopathological people seem completely insensitive to the emotional realm. I would insist, however, on a strict distinction between emotional sensitivity and being a "good" or "moral" person.

A person may be sensitive to the emotions of others but use that sensitivity to manipulate or to deceive them, or to create hatred.

I call, then, for a delineation of intelligence that includes the full range of contents to which human beings are sensitive, but at the same time designates as off limits such valued but separate human traits as creativity, morality, and emotional appropriateness. I believe that such a delineation makes scientific and epistemological sense. It reinvigorates the elastic band without stretching it to the breaking point. It helps to resolve the two remaining struggles: how to assess, and what kinds of human beings to admire.

Once we decide to restrict intelligence to human information-processing and product-making capacities, we can make use of the established technology of assessment. That is, we can continue to use paper-and-pencil or computer-adapted testing techniques while looking at a broader range of capacities, such as musical sensitivity and empathy with others. And we can avoid ticklish and possibly unresolvable questions about the assessment of values and morality that may well be restricted to a particular culture and that may well change over time.

Still, even with a limited perspective on intelligence, important questions remain about which assessment path to follow—that of the purist, the simulator, or the skeptic. Here I have strong views. I question the wisdom of searching for a "pure" intelligence—be it general intelligence, musical intelligence, or interpersonal intelligence. I do not believe that such alchemical intellectual essences actually exist; they are a product of our penchant for creating terminology rather than determinable and measurable entities. Moreover, the correlations that have thus far been found between supposedly pure measures and the skills that we actually value in the world are too modest to be useful.

What does exist is the use of intelligences, individually and in concert, to carry out tasks that are valued by a society. Accordingly, we should be assessing the extent to which human beings succeed in carrying out tasks of consequence that presumably involve certain intelligences. To be concrete, we should not test musical intelligence by looking at the ability to discriminate between two tones or timbres; rather, we should be teaching people to sing songs or play instruments or transform melodies and seeing how readily they master such feats. At the same time, we should abjure a search for pure emotional sensitivity—for example, a test that matches facial expressions to galvanic skin response. Rather, we should place (or observe) people in situations that call for them to be sensitive to the aspirations and motives of others. For example, we could see how they handle a situation in which they and colleagues have to break up a fight between two teenagers, or persuade a boss to change a policy of which they do not approve.

Here powerful new simulations can be invoked. We are now in a position to draw on technologies that can deliver realistic situations or problems and also record the success of subjects in dealing with them. A student can be presented with an unfamiliar tune on a computer and asked to learn that tune, transpose it, orchestrate it, and the like. Such exercises would reveal much about the student's intelligence in musical matters.

Turning to the social (or human, if you prefer) realm, subjects can be presented with simulated interactions and asked to judge the shifting motivations of each actor. Or they can be asked to work in an interactive hypermedia production with unfamiliar people who are trying to accomplish some sort of goal, and to respond to their various moves and countermoves. The program can alter responses in light of the moves of the subject. Like a high-stakes poker game, such a measure should reveal much about the interpersonal or emotional sensitivity of a subject.

A significant increase in the breadth—the elasticity—of our concept of intelligence, then, should open the possibility for innovative forms of assessment far more realistic than the classic short-answer examinations. Why settle for an IQ or an SAT test, in which the items are at best remote proxies for the ability to design experiments, write essays, critique musical performances, and so forth? Why not instead ask people actually (or virtually) to carry out such tasks? And yet by not opening up the Pandora's box of values and subjectivity, one can continue to make judicious use of the insights and technologies achieved by those who have devoted decades to perfecting mental measurement.

To be sure, one can create a psychometric instrument for any conceivable human virtue, including morality, creativity, and emotional intelligence in its several senses. Indeed, since the publication of Daniel Goleman's book dozens of efforts have been made to create tests for emotional intelligence. The resulting instruments are not, however, necessarily useful. Such instruments are far more likely to satisfy the test maker's desire for reliability (a subject gets roughly the same score on two separate administrations of the test) than the need for validity (the test measures the trait that it purports to measure).

Such instruments-on-demand prove dubious for two reasons. First, beyond some platitudes, few can agree on what it means to be moral, ethical, a good person: consider the differing values of Jesse Helms and Jesse Jackson, Margaret Thatcher and Margaret Mead. Second, scores on such tests are much more likely to reveal test-taking savvy (skills in language and logic) than fundamental character.

In speaking about character, I turn to a final concern: the relationship between intelligence and what I will call virtue—those qualities that we admire and wish to hold up as examples for our children. No doubt the desire to expand intelligence to encompass ethics and character represents a direct response to the general feeling that our society is lacking in these dimensions; the expansionist view of intelligence reflects the hope that if we transmit the technology of intelligence to these virtues, we might in the end secure a more virtuous population.

I have already indicated my strong reservations about trying to make the word "intelligence" all things to all people—the psychometric equivalent of the true, the beautiful, and the good. Yet the problem remains: how, in a post-Aristotelian, post-Confucian era in which psychometrics looms large, do we think about the virtuous human being?

My analysis suggests one promising approach. We should recognize that intelligences, creativity, and morality—to mention just three desiderata—are separate. Each may require its own form of measurement or assessment, and some will prove far easier to assess objectively than others. Indeed, with respect to creativity and morality, we are more likely to rely on overall judgments by experts than on any putative test battery. At the same time, testing prevents us from looking for people who combine several of these attributes—who have musical and interpersonal intelligence, who are psychometrically intelligent and creative in the arts, who combine emotional sensitivity and a high standard of moral conduct.

Let me introduce another analogy at this point. In college admissions much attention is paid to scholastic performance, as measured by College Board examinations and grades. However, other features are also weighed, and sometimes a person with lower test scores is admitted if he or she proves exemplary in terms of citizenship or athletics or motivation. Admissions officers do not confound these virtues (indeed, they may use different scales and issue different grades), but they recognize the attractiveness of candidates who exemplify two or more desirable traits.

We have left the Eden of classical times, in which various intellectual and ethical values necessarily commingled, and we are unlikely ever to re-create it. We should recognize that these virtues can be separate and will often prove to be remote from one another. When we attempt to aggregate them, through phrases like "emotional intelligence," "creative intelligence," and "moral intelligence," we should realize that we are expressing a wish rather than denoting a necessary or even a likely coupling.

We have an aid in converting this wish to reality: the existence of powerful examples—people who succeed in exemplifying two or more cardinal human virtues. To name names is risky—particularly when one generation's heroes can become the subject of the next generation's pathographies. Even so, I can without apology mention Niels Bohr, George C. Marshall, Rachel Carson, Arthur Ashe, Louis Armstrong, Pablo Casals, Ella Fitzgerald.

In studying the lives of such people, we discover human possibilities. Young human beings learn primarily from the examples of powerful adults around them—those who are admirable and also those who are simply glamorous. Sustained attention to admirable examples may well increase the future incidence of people who actually do yoke capacities that are scientifically and epistemologically separate.

In one of the most evocative phrases of the century the British novelist E. M. 60 Forster counseled us, "Only connect." I believe that some expansionists in the territory of intelligence, though well motivated, have prematurely asserted connections that do not exist. But I also believe that as human beings, we can help to forge connections that may be important for our physical and psychic survival.

Just how the precise borders of intelligence are drawn is a question we can leave to scholars. But the imperative to broaden our definition of intelligence in a responsible way goes well beyond the academy. Who "owns" intelligence promises to be an issue even more critical in the next century than it has been in this era of the IQ test.

SARA IVRY

Entrance Exams, Deconstructed

Sara Ivry is a freelance writer for the New York Times *and* Nextbook.

Which exam did you take? Does this description corroborate your experience?

SAT	ACT	TIP

NUTS AND BOLTS

The new [as of Fall 2004] SAT consists of three parts: math, critical reading (a new name for the old verbal section) and a new writing section. Each will be worth 200 to 800 points, increasing a perfect score to 2400. The whole experience will take 45 more minutes, including 25 minutes to write an essay and an extra stretch break.	Still four sections (English, reading, math and science), the ACT will introduce an optional essay on Feb. 12. Essay writers get 30 extra minutes to complete the task, and they will receive an additional score. The ACT is scored on a scale of 1 to 36.	Thinking of everything, the education publisher Thomson Peterson is offering hints on diet (eat strawberries, for brain power), color (surround yourself with pale apricot, for focus; never red) and scent (sniff spearmint for stress, lavender for energy).

WHICH TEST TO TAKE

Historically, the SAT has been viewed as the test preferred by elite institutions. Admissions officers say that such bias no longer exists, and that the decision whether to take the SAT or ACT has more to do with geography than anything else; students on the coasts tend toward the SAT, and their inland peers prefer the ACT.	Some colleges will require students who choose the ACT to take its writing test. A survey this fall by ACT Inc. shows that 37 percent of four-year colleges and universities—many of them the more elite institutions—will require or recommend that students write the essay. To find out what a particular admissions office has decided, consult the ACT site (act.org/aap/writingpref/index.html).	Counselors advise students to take practice tests to see which test they score better on, and to prepare for only that one exam. The Princeton Review has developed two six-page tests that it says can predict whether a student will do better on the ACT or the SAT, on the new SAT or the old SAT (free through high school guidance counselors or the Review itself).

SAT	ACT	TIP

WRITINGS

This new section includes grammar for the first time — "improving sentences," "improving paragraphs" and "identifying sentence errors" — and the written essay (accounting for 30 percent of the section's score). Scoring on the essay is holistic, assessing overall clarity and reason more than grammar and spelling (though an essay rendered unreadable because of such errors is unlikely to receive a high mark). . . . The essay prompt will ask students to respond to a quotation or an adapted passage.

The ACT has long included a grammar component. For the new essay, writers are instructed to take a side on an issue that is "relatable to students in some sort of universal way," like mandatory dress codes, says Ed Colby, an ACT spokesman. "The writing test specs are based on the writing skills teachers tell us they're teaching in high school."

"Colleges are looking for a level of discourse that shows that a student can deal with college-level writing, but they're not looking for a polished, complete essay," says Brian O'Reilly, executive director of SAT information services at the College Board, the test's owner. Sample essays, with the merits and weaknesses of each, are posted on the College Board's Web site (collegeboard.com).

READING

Analogies, long criticized as irrelevant to what students actually study in school, are no more. Students will continue to find sentence completions and reading passages. Shorter passages have been added.

No changes. Still consists of reading passages and multiple-choice questions. Analogies? Never.

Coaches and administrators agree on a key preparatory tool. "The best way to develop your range of vocabulary is by reading," says Mr. O'Reilly. "If you're a big reader, you're going to tend to be a better writer as well."

MATH

The new test has done away with the mathematical equivalent of analogies — quantitative comparisons. Between 15 and 20 percent of questions will test material that has not before been examined on the SAT, including algebra II, and concepts introduced before the junior year but not previously addressed.

The ACT already tests the spectrum, from plain geometry to precalculus.

The consensus is to take third-year math. Also: brush up on concepts learned in middle and elementary schools; take practice tests and register for the exam at the end of junior year to get the greatest amount of schooling before the test.

AMERICAN INSTITUTES FOR RESEARCH

American College Grads—Barely Literate, and Beyond

American Institutes for Research, an independent, nonprofit organization (est. 1946), draws particularly on the fields of economics, education, psychology, and sociology to study programs and policies in K–college education, including those emanating from federal and state governments.

WASHINGTON, D.C. (Jan. 19, 2006)—Twenty percent of U.S. college students completing 4-year degrees—and 30 percent of students earning 2-year degrees — have only basic quantitative literacy skills, meaning they are unable to estimate if their car has enough gasoline to get to the next gas station or calculate the total cost of ordering office supplies, according to a new national survey by the American Institutes for Research (AIR).

The new study, "The National Survey of America's College Students" (NSACS), is based on a sample of 1,827 graduating students from 80 randomly selected 2-year and 4-year public and private colleges and universities across the United States. By targeting students nearing the end of their degree programs, the study provides a broader and more comprehensive picture of fundamental college literacy skills than ever before.

- More than 75 percent of students at 2-year colleges and more than 50 percent of students at 4-year colleges do not score at the proficient level of literacy. This means that they lack the skills to perform complex literacy tasks, such as comparing credit card offers with different interest rates or summarizing the arguments of newspaper editorials.
- Students in 2- and 4-year colleges have the greatest difficulty with quantitative literacy: approximately 30 percent of students in 2-year institutions and nearly 20 percent of students in 4-year institutions have only *basic* quantitative literacy. *Basic* skills are those necessary to compare ticket prices or calculate the cost of a sandwich and a salad from a menu.
- There are no significant differences in the literacy of students graduating from public and private institutions. Additionally, in assessing literacy levels, there are no differences between part-time and full-time students. No overall relationship exists between literacy and the length of time it takes to earn a degree, or between literacy and an academic major.
- The literacy skills of college students are directly related to the education of their parents: children whose parents graduated college or attended graduate school have higher literacy than students whose parents did not graduate high school or stopped after receiving a high school diploma or GED.

The complete study is available on the AIR Web site, www.air.org.

QUESTIONS FOR DISCUSSION AND WRITING

1. Gardner explains how elements of a test-taking situation can affect an individual's performance. Have you experienced the elements Gardner describes? To what extent does your experience seem different from that of other people being tested? Why? Did you know the information in Ivry's chart before you took the SAT or the ACT? If so, did this strategic knowledge help you? If not, how might it have been useful?

2. Why does Gardner prefer the term "emotional sensitivity" to "emotional intelligence" (paragraph 43)? Why does his own model of eight kinds of intelligence avoid the same problems he finds in "emotional intelligence"?

3. What is "alchemy"? What does Gardner mean by speaking of "pure intelligence" as "alchemical" (paragraph 46)?

4. What are Gardner's reasons for differentiating intelligence from creativity and from morality? Illustrate your answer with examples you have seen in action.

5. Gardner lists several people who exemplify "two or more cardinal human virtues" (paragraph 58). Find out about one of these people or another equally "virtuous" person of your choice. Write an essay explaining how Gardner and one of the other theorists of intelligence he mentions would interpret these people's "intelligence."

6. The American Institutes for Research 2006 study identifies startling percentages of college students (two-year [30%] and four-year [20%]) lacking "basic quantitative literacy skills" and even higher percentages (75% and 50%, respectively) lacking "the skills to perform complex literacy tasks." Since estimating simple costs, comparing credit card offers, and summarizing editorial arguments are necessary for living and working effectively, why wouldn't high school graduates know how to do these things? Should high schools and two- and four-year colleges offer such basic and essential literacy courses? For credit? Should they be mandatory?

BRIEF TAKES ON THE UPRIGHT LIFE: GOOD ADVICE

Advice, given straightforwardly, is in its barest essence a series of pronouncements. Do this, don't do that (see "The Ten Commandments," p. 636). The speaker or author is presumably an expert on the subject at hand; his or her authority is established and respected by the audience. So the speaker can cut to the chase. Sometimes, as with Franklin's classic scheme for "Arriving at Moral Perfection," no reasons accompany the virtues; their merit is self-evident. Listeners who want to argue with a speaker or author such as Franklin, Stein, Roosevelt, Spinner, or Neusner have to prepare their personal rebuttals and deliver them apart from the public context of the advice giving. In the excerpt from David Sedaris's "What I Learned . . . at Princeton," Sedaris spoofs the genre of advice-laden commencement speeches (he never went to Princeton). The anonymous "How Many Virginia University Students Does It Take to Change a Lightbulb?" contains no advice but plays on stereotypes of students at various Virginia colleges. Slot in the state of your choice, Google it, and you'll see that the stereotypes span the nation.

BENJAMIN FRANKLIN

Arriving at Moral Perfection

Benjamin Franklin (1706–1790), America's true Renaissance man, was not only a Founding Father but also a scientist, inventor, statesman, author and publisher, and businessman; his practical advice made Poor Richard's Almanack *a best-seller, and his* Autobiography, *from which this advice is taken, immortal.*

It was about this time I conceived the bold and arduous project of arriving at moral perfection. I wished to live without committing any fault at any time; I would conquer all that either natural inclination, custom, or company might lead me into. As I knew, or thought I knew, what was right and wrong, I did not see why I might not always do the one and avoid the other. But I soon found I had undertaken a task of more difficulty than I had imagined. While my attention was taken up and care employed in guarding against one fault, I was often surprised by another. Habit took the advantage of inattention. Inclination was sometimes too strong for reason. I concluded at length that the mere speculative conviction that it was our interest to be completely virtuous was not sufficient to prevent our slipping, and that the contrary habits must be broken and good ones acquired and established before we can have any dependence on a steady, uniform rectitude of conduct. For this purpose I therefore contrived the following method.

These names of virtues with their precepts were

1. Temperance: Eat not to dullness. Drink not to elevation.
2. Silence: Speak not but what may benefit others or yourself. Avoid trifling conversation.
3. Order: Let all your things have their places. Let each part of your business have its time.
4. Resolution: Resolve to perform what you ought. Perform without fail what you resolve.
5. Frugality: Make no expense but to do good to others or yourself; i.e., waste nothing.
6. Industry: Lose no time. Be always employed in something useful. Cut off all unnecessary actions.
7. Sincerity: Use no hurtful deceit. Think innocently and justly; and, if you speak, speak accordingly.
8. Justice: Wrong none by doing injuries or omitting the benefits that are your duty.
9. Moderation: Avoid extremes. Forbear resenting injuries so much as you think they deserve.
10. Cleanliness: Tolerate no uncleanness in body, clothes or habitation.
11. Tranquillity: Be not disturbed at trifles or at accidents common or unavoidable.
12. Chastity: Rarely use venery but for health or offspring—never to dullness, weakness, or the injury of your own or another's peace or reputation.
13. Humility: Imitate Jesus and Socrates.

I made a little book in which I allotted a page for each of the virtues. I ruled each page with red ink so as to have seven columns, one for each day of the week, marking each column with a letter for the day. I crossed these columns with thirteen red lines, marking the beginning of each line with the first letter of one of the virtues, on which line and in its proper column I might mark by a little black spot every fault I found upon examination to have been committed respecting that virtue upon that day.

I determined to give a week's strict attention to each of the virtues successively. Thus in the first week my great guard was to avoid even the least offence against temperance, leaving the other virtues to their ordinary chance, only marking every evening the faults of the day. Thus if in the first week I could keep my first line marked "T." clear of spots, I supposed the habit of that virtue so much strengthened and its opposite weakened that I might venture extending my attention to include the next, and for the following week keep both lines clear of spots. Proceeding thus to the last, I could go thro' a course complete in thirteen weeks, and four courses in a year.

———

BEN STEIN

Birds and Bees? No, Let's Talk about Dollars and Cents

Stein (b. 1944, Washington, D.C.) is a lawyer, economist, law professor, actor, comedian, and former White House speechwriter. His financial columns appear regularly in the New York Times.

Dear Tommy,

I hope that you are well and especially that your football season is going well. It must be difficult to be injured so close to the beginning of the schedule. I hope you are studying. Eleventh grade is a terribly important year.

I think it may be time for me to send you a few thoughts about money and how to make sure that you continue to have the standard of living you have come to love so much. I'd like to try to explain how you have been able to live so large and what you will have to do to keep it going for the rest of your life and for your children's lives. It has to do with a very important word called "capital."

First of all, my grandfathers on both sides came to this country with virtually nothing. My grandfather on my father's side was an Army cavalry officer for a long time and then a skilled tool-and-die maker at Ford Motor and then at General Electric. He accumulated no capital to speak of, in terms of finance, and too little in terms of education to allow him to make a decent living. He was unemployed for a large part of the Great Depression, and Pop's family was supported largely by his mother's work at a department store. On my mother's father's side, there was a small amount of real estate, but it was largely lost in the Great Depression.

My father was the first Stein in all history, as far as we know, to have accumulated any real capital. He did that by getting a fine education at Williams College and then at the University of Chicago. He was a stone genius, and among his many aspects of genius was that he knew that he must regularly convert his human capital—his intelligence and education and connections—into financial capital: namely, savings. He always lived well below his means and saved the difference. A result was that when he grew older, he could send my sister and me to good colleges; I went to Columbia and Yale Law School; she went to Wellesley. I acquired some skills—law, economics, writing, acting, speaking—that paid a good wage.

I have been very lucky and have worked like a maniac, and the results are   5 that I have earned a decent living for many years. Taking a leaf from my father, I have saved some of it—although much less than my father did. I also took the trouble—starting at about the age of 12—to read about investing and had some extremely good luck in that field (although I have also made some disastrous mistakes, both on the buy and sell side). When my parents died, I inherited money. Although it was not a huge amount, it was enough to make a difference.

Your mother, whose father was a hero in World War II and Vietnam, inherited a modest sum after he died recently. But she worked very hard as a lawyer and made a superb living for many years. We managed to save some of the money she made, as well.

Notice a few threads here, my boy; your forebears first acquired human capital—education, work skills, discipline, connections. Then we converted that into financial capital and, with some notable exceptions, it grew and added to our income stream. At all times, we have had to be cautious to keep from being ripped off in our investments. (The possibilities for being defrauded are endless.) We have been able to do this more readily than some others because we have known a bit about the world of investments and when and where to walk away from the table.

Now, for the first time in the history of the Steins and the Denmans—your mother's family, of course—we have enough capital so that even at today's very low interest rates, we could live without working. That is, we do not have to rely entirely upon selling our labor. Our savings can take care of us, albeit at a level far more modest than what you are used to.

But, Tommy, several elements went into this, and you have to continue them all to keep up this standard of living: acquiring good work habits (this does not include playing computer games); getting an education in a field that pays a living wage (not a field that's fun and trendy but offers no possibility for a job); learning at an early age to save; and, very important, living at a level that does not exhaust your savings. We hope to be able to leave you some money, but it would be possible for you to run through it in no time if you were careless. And, in any event, you don't get any of it until you are 40.

The common denominator of all of these bits of advice is the invaluable 10 capital of self-discipline: the self-discipline to learn good work habits, the self-discipline to acquire education in a field where there is a market for your skills, the self-discipline to make connections and be a good friend, the self-discipline to do a good job at your work, the self-discipline to learn about investments, and the self-discipline to save.

When you have these, you gradually make yourself secure. You do not have to worry about tiny or even large sums of money. You are impervious to economic ups and downs, except for very large downs. You do not wake up at 3 a.m. worrying about money. Most of all, you have capital. That's the magic word. Capital—human and financial—lets you have an aura of safety around yourself and allows you to enjoy yourself and not live in a cage of fear and insecurity. And the first step and the last step toward capital is self-discipline.

My grandfathers did not even remotely have the opportunities you have—the chance to accumulate free education, have connections, have money waiting to be inherited. You are the first member of my family ever to grow up in luxury. But you can lose it all quickly if you don't remember where capital comes from and don't bear in mind that indiscipline with money can leave you back where my grandparents were. Shirtsleeves to shirtsleeves can be avoided only by rolling up your sleeves and going to work on yourself. Capital in this society comes from your own state of mind.

Love, Pop

THEODORE ROOSEVELT
What College Graduates Owe America

In 1894, seven years before he assumed the presidency, Theodore Roosevelt, then a thirty-five-year-old member of the Civil Service Commission and a regular Atlantic *contributor, argued that it is incumbent upon men of means and education to take an active role in public affairs.*

It is proper to demand more from the man with exceptional advantages than from the man without them. A heavy moral obligation rests upon the man of means and upon the man of education to do their full duty by their country. On no class does this obligation rest more heavily than upon the men with a collegiate education, the men who are graduates of our universities. Their education gives them no right to feel the least superiority over any of their fellow-citizens; but it certainly ought to make them feel that they should stand foremost in the honorable effort to serve the whole public by doing their duty as Americans in the body politic . . .

To the great body of men who have had exceptional advantages in the way of educational facilities we have a right, then, to look for good service to the state. The service may be rendered in many different ways. In a reasonable number of cases, the man may himself rise to high political position. That men actually do so rise is shown by the number of graduates of Harvard, Yale, and our other universities who are now taking a prominent part in public life. These cases must necessarily, however, form but a small part of the whole. The enormous majority of our educated men have to make their own living, and are obliged to take up careers in which they must work heart and soul to succeed. Nevertheless, the man of business and the man of science, the doctor of divinity and the doctor of law, the architect, the engineer, and the writer, all alike owe a positive duty to the community, the neglect of which they cannot excuse on any plea of their private affairs. They are bound to follow understandingly the course of public events; they are bound to try to estimate and form judgment upon public men; and they are bound to act intelligently and effectively in support of the principles which they deem to be right and for the best interests of the country . . .

For educated men of weak fiber, there lies a real danger in that species of literary work which appeals to their cultivated senses because of its scholarly and pleasant tone, but which enjoins as the proper attitude to assume in public life one of mere criticism and negation; which teaches the adoption toward public men and public affairs of that sneering tone which so surely denotes a mean and small mind. If a man does not have belief and enthusiasm, the chances are small indeed that he will ever do a man's work in the world. . . .

Again, there is a certain tendency in college life . . . to make educated men shrink from contact with the rough people who do the world's work, and associate only with one another and with those who think as they do. This is a most danger-ous tendency. It is very agreeable to deceive one's self into the belief that one is performing the whole duty of man by sitting at home in ease, doing nothing wrong, and confining one's participation in politics to conversations and meetings with men who have had the same training and look at things in the same way. It is always a temptation to do this, because those who do nothing else often speak as if in some way they deserved credit for their attitude, and as if they stood above their brethren who plough the rough fields.

JACKIE SPINNER

The Only Thing You Should Be Advocating Is the Truth

Jackie Spinner (b. 1970) was Washington Post *bureau chief in Baghdad in 2003 and 2004. She delivered this commencement speech to the Mass Communications majors graduating from her alma mater, Southern Illinois University, in 2005.*

I reported on car bombs and power plant reconstruction, wrote stories about soldiers in battle, soldiers waiting for battle, soldiers dying in battle. I inter-viewed hundreds of Iraqis, sometimes without ever leaving my hotel. I met them instead through the scribbled notes of our Iraqi staff. When they came back from an assignment too dangerous for me to cover myself, we sat together in front of my computer, while I grilled them about what they saw. . . . *Did he re-ally say that? . . . What do you mean he looked anxious? . . . Was he sweating? What were his hands doing while he talked?* I owe everything to these brave Iraqi men and women who act as my eyes and ears in reporting the story of Iraq to our *Washington Post* readers. They are the real heroes. Without them, we could not do our jobs.

The greatest challenge about being a reporter in Baghdad was not being able to report for myself. If we want to travel outside of Baghdad, we do it with the U.S. military. People who go out alone risk being kidnapped. It was not safe for me to identify myself as a foreigner or for our Iraqi staff to be seen with a for-eigner. We did not linger anywhere in public. If I wanted to talk to someone on the street, I sent one of our Iraqi staff members to do the interviews or I ducked into a shop for a few minutes and then ducked back out, not wanting to stay long enough to be identified.

I stopped carrying my American passport when I left the bureau, and learned how to lose my American ways, the smallest things that might betray me as a foreigner. They were little things. My staff advised me to:

Wear lots of lipstick. Iraqi women may hide their hair, but they love flashy
  lips painted in bright reds and oranges.
I traded in my silver jewelry for gold because Iraqis wear gold.
They bought me a purse my grandmother would love and I hung it on the
  crook of my arm just like she would.
And upon the advice of my staff, I stopped smiling when I went into public.
  After all, Iraqis are suffering.

I disappeared into my Iraqi identity, even adopting an Iraqi name that the
translators could use to summon me when we were outside. Our biggest fear was
coming across an illegal insurgent checkpoint. If they found out I was an American, I'd most likely be kidnapped, and my Iraqi traveling companions would be
shot on the spot. It had happened to other foreigners.

Like my father in Vietnam, I had never felt more abandoned by the America   5
that claimed my passport. I was constantly beat up by readers who sent e-mails
accusing me of being for or against the war, for or against the occupation, depending on their own agenda. People made assumptions about me because of my
name, my news organization, where I went to school, other stories I had written.
It was hard not to take it personally, given the tremendous danger we were in. I
started to question why I was there, if the American public didn't believe anything I was telling them anyway.

This will be your battle, too, whether you go to Iraq or to Louisville, Los Angeles, Salt Lake City, New York City or Herrin, Ill. Our ratings, as communica-
tors, are at their lowest levels in history. People don't believe in us anymore, they
don't believe us, and that is largely our fault. Many journalists have abandoned
the pursuit of objectivity, simply chucked this ideal out the window. Journalists
have causes now, agendas. They want to advocate. The only thing you should be
advocating is the truth. Even when the truth is difficult to get at, even if it means
standing up to your editors, even if it means getting passed by or passed over.
The American media are in the position they are in with the public because we
care more about being first and about scoops than we do about being right. Get it
right. . . .

You keep yourself honest by staying on your path. You will be your own best
competition. Sometimes I look around my own newsroom, a place filled with
graduates of the Ivy League, a place with people whose fathers were ambassadors,
people who grew up among the American elite. I am proud of my struggle. Every
day that I walk into the *Washington Post* newsroom, I am grateful to be there.
When you get where you are going, don't forget to look back. In my own rearview
mirror, I can see a road littered with rejection letters, letters that I have saved all of
these years. I keep them in a trunk and occasionally take them out to look at them,
to remind myself that I am still that kid from Illinois with humble Midwestern
roots who got her start at a place called the *Daily Egyptian*. These letters, I'm ready
to let go of them now. So I'm going to give them to you. Keep them as a reminder. Bring one out on occasion, and ask yourself, well, if Jackie Spinner could
do it, WHY can't I? Why NOT ME?

So see you later . . . [*crumples up rejection letters and tosses them to the audience*]
Louisville Courier News
Huntsville Alabama Times
Springfield State Journal Register
Baltimore Sun
Corpus Christi Caller Times
Decatur Herald and Review, my hometown newspaper
The Gannett Newspaper chain, the entire chain
Chicago Sun-Times, twice
Houston Chronicle
Orlando Sentinel
San Francisco Examiner
St. Petersburg Times
Colorado Springs Gazette

I am sure you already have received plenty of career advice, maybe even read a few books about how to get started in whatever field you have chosen. There is plenty of this advice for sale, in books, through seminars and online courses. If you don't have a job lined up, you're probably going to spend the next few months obsessing about it, worrying about it. Perhaps you have an internship at a small newspaper, and you're trying to figure out, how do I get to the top? How long will it take? What can I do to land the big one?

If you remember nothing else from what I've told you today, if years from now you don't even remember my name, remember this:

There is only one way to get where you want to go. And it is really quite simple: Start walking.

10

JACOB NEUSNER
The Speech the Graduates Didn't Hear

Neusner (b. 1932) has written or edited more than 925 books about the Torah and other Jewish theological writings, revolutionizing the study of Judaism and bringing it from the ghetto into the field of mainstream American religious studies.

We the faculty take no pride in our educational achievements with you. We have prepared you for a world that does not exist, indeed, that cannot exist. You have spent four years supposing that failure leaves no record. You have learned at Brown that when your work goes poorly, the painless solution is to drop out. But starting now, in the world to which you go, failure marks you. Confronting difficulty by quitting leaves you changed. Outside Brown, quitters are no heroes.

With us you could argue about why your errors were not errors, why mediocre work really was excellent, why you could take pride in routine and slipshod presentation. Most of you, after all, can look back on honor grades for most of what you have done. So, here grades can have meant little in distinguishing the excellent from the ordinary. But tomorrow, in the world to which you go, you had best not defend errors but learn from them. You will be ill-advised to demand praise for what does not deserve it, and abuse those who do not give it.

For four years we created an altogether forgiving world, in which whatever slight effort you gave was all that was demanded. When you did not keep appointments, we made new ones. When your work came in beyond the deadline, we pretended not to care.

Worse still, when you were boring, we acted as if you were saying something important. When you were garrulous and talked to hear yourself talk, we listened as if it mattered. When you tossed on our desks writing upon which you had not labored, we read it and even responded, as though you earned a response. When you were dull, we pretended you were smart. When you were predictable, unimaginative, and routine, we listened as if to new and wonderful things. When you demanded free lunch, we served it. And all this why?

Despite your fantasies, it was not even that we wanted to be liked by you. It 5 was that we did not want to be bothered, and the easy way out was pretense: smiles and easy Bs.

It is conventional to quote in addresses such as these. Let me quote someone you've never heard of: Professor Carter A. Daniel, Rutgers University (*Chronicle of Higher Education*, May 7, 1979):

> College has spoiled you by reading papers that don't deserve to be read, listening to comments that don't deserve a hearing, paying attention even to the lazy, ill-informed, and rude. We had to do it, for the sake of education. But nobody will ever do it again. College has deprived you of adequate preparation for the last fifty years. It has failed you by being easy, free, forgiving, attentive, comfortable, interesting, unchallenging fun. Good luck tomorrow.

That is why, on this commencement day, we have nothing in which to take much pride.

Oh, yes, there is one more thing. Try not to act toward your co-workers and bosses as you have acted toward us. I mean, when they give you what you want but have not earned, don't abuse them, insult them, act out with them your parlous relationships with your parents. This too we have tolerated. It was, as I said, not to be liked. Few professors actually care whether or not they are liked by peer-paralyzed adolescents, fools so shallow as to imagine professors care not about education but about popularity. It was, again, to be rid of you. So go, unlearn the lies we taught you. To Life!

DAVID SEDARIS

What I Learned/And What I Said at Princeton

Sedaris, in fact, dropped out of Kent State University in 1977, and ten years later graduated from the Art Institute of Chicago. Despite the claims of his baccalaureate address delivered at Princeton and published in The New Yorker *in June 2006, Sedaris did not attend the university of which he speaks so fondly: "This chapel, for instance—I remember when it was just a clearing, cordoned off with sharp sticks. Prayer was compulsory back then, and you couldn't just fake it by moving your lips; you had to know the words, and really mean them. I'm dating myself, but this was before Jesus Christ." For more biographical information, see page 222.*

I had many fine teachers during my years at Princeton, but the one I think of most often was my fortune-telling professor—a complete hag with wild gray hair, warts the size of new potatoes, the whole nine yards. She taught us to forecast the weather up to two weeks in advance, but ask her for anything weightier and you were likely to be disappointed.

The alchemy majors wanted to know how much money they'd be making after graduation. "Just give us an approximate figure," they'd say, and the professor would shake her head and cover her crystal ball with a little cozy given to her by one of her previous classes. When it came to our futures, she drew the line, no matter how hard we begged—and, I mean, we really tried. I was as let down as the next guy, but, in retrospect, I can see that she acted in our best interests. Look at yourself on the day that you graduated from college, then look at yourself today. I did that recently, and it was, like, "What the hell happened?"

The answer, of course, is life. What the hag chose not to foretell—and what we, in our certainty, could not have fathomed—is that stuff comes up. Weird doors open. People fall into things. Maybe the engineering whiz will wind up brewing cider, not because he has to but because he finds it challenging. Who knows? Maybe the athlete will bring peace to all nations, or the class moron will go on to become the President of the United States—though that's more likely to happen at Harvard or Yale, schools that will pretty much let in anybody.

There were those who left Princeton and soared like arrows into the bosoms of power and finance, but I was not one of them. My path was a winding one, with plenty of obstacles along the way. When school was finished, I went back home, an Ivy League graduate with four years' worth of dirty laundry and his whole life ahead of him. "What are you going to do now?" my parents asked.

And I said, "Well, I was thinking of washing some of these underpants."   5

That took six months. Then I moved on to the shirts.

"Now what?" my parents asked.

And, when I told them I didn't know, they lost what little patience they had left. "What kind of a community-college answer is that?" my mother said. "You went to the best school there is—how can you not know something?"

And I said, "I don't know." . . .

ANONYMOUS

How Many Virginia University Students Does It Take to Change a Lightbulb?

This popular Internet compilation plays on stereotypes about students at various colleges. This version focuses on colleges in Virginia but there are many versions oriented to the schools in various states.

How many William and Mary students does it take to change a lightbulb?
Three, one to change the bulb, and two to crack under the pressure.
How many Old Dominion students does it take to change a lightbulb?
Four, two to change the bulb, and two to figure out how to get high off the old one.
How many Mary Washington students does it take to change a lightbulb?
The whole student body, there's nothing better to do on weekends.
How many Georgetown students does it take to change a lightbulb?
Two, one to change the bulb, and one to throw the old bulb at American U students.
How many James Madison University students does it take to change a lightbulb?
None, Harrisonburg doesn't have electricity.
How many Virginia Commonwealth students does it take to change a lightbulb?
None, downtown Richmond looks better in the dark.
How many Eastern Mennonite U students does it take to change a lightbulb?
Two, one to hold the candle, and the other to strike the flint.
How many George Mason University students does it take to change a lightbulb?
Three, if they get lucky and one of them has taken the course at NOVA.
How many Washington and Lee students does it take to change a lightbulb?
Four, one to change a bulb, and three to write up a complaint to the board of directors stating that they could have gone to a better school if they had wanted to.

How many Mary Baldwin students does it take to change a lightbulb?
> Four, one to change the lightbulb, and three to figure out how it will help them meet their future husband.

How many U of Richmond students does it take to change a lightbulb?
> Two, one to mix the martinis and one to call the electrician.

How many Hollins College students does it take to change a lightbulb?
> None, that's what maids are for.

How many Radford University students does it take to change a lightbulb?
> Just one, but it takes six years.

How many Sweet Briar students does it take to change a lightbulb?
> The entire student body, once they hear the word *screw*.

How many Randolph-Macon College students does it take to change a lightbulb?
> One, if she can handle four majors, she sure as hell can handle changing a lightbulb.

CHAPTER 5

History: What Really Happened? How Do We Know or Decide What It Means?

DOROTHEA LANGE

Migrant Mother

QUESTIONS FOR DISCUSSION AND WRITING

1. What do you think of when you imagine the "Great Depression"? How does Dorothea Lange's photograph of this migrant laborer, a pea-picker destitute because the crop failed, humanize this historical event of the 1930s? What do you read in the mother's face? In her posture? In her ragged sleeve?

2. How many children do you see in the picture (the mother, Florence Owens Thompson, 32, had seven)? What is the effect of viewing the baby's face? Why are the older children's faces turned away from the camera? Could these be considered "poster children" for a nation upon hard times? Lange took this photograph in 1936 for the federal Resettlement Administration; for what purposes might the government have used it? (For more information see www.loc.gov/rr/print/list/128_migm.html.)

3. Examine this picture, augmented by the knowledge that the family, as Thompson told Lange, "had been living [in a lean-to tent] on frozen vegetables from the surrounding fields, and birds that the children killed. She had just sold the tires from her car to buy food." Then apply your understanding of this historical phenomenon to contemporary instances of hunger and starvation worldwide, such as that in Darfur or in the United States. What can, what will you do to address this pervasive issue?

ALICE WALKER
In Search of Our Mothers' Gardens

Author of the Pulitzer Prize–winning novel The Color Purple *(1982), Alice Walker is a poet, novelist, essayist, and civil rights activist. She was born (1944) and raised in segregated Eatonton, Georgia, where her parents, Willie Lee and Minnie Walker, were sharecroppers. Walker graduated from Sarah Lawrence (B.A., 1965). During the civil rights movement, she was a voter registration worker in Georgia and a Head Start worker in Mississippi, before teaching at various colleges, including Tougaloo, Wellesley, and her alma mater. Walker addresses the human implications of social issues in her essay collections, including* Living by the Word *(1988) and* Anything We Love Can Be Saved: A Writer's Activism *(1997); short-story collections, such as* In Love and Trouble *(1973) and* You Can't Keep a Good Woman Down *(1981); and novels, including* Meridian *(1976) and* Possessing the Secret of Joy *(1992). Walker's poetry includes* Revolutionary Petunias, and Other Poems *(1973), where "In Search of Our Mothers' Gardens" first appeared under the title "Women"; and* Her Blue Body Everything We Know: Earthling Poems, 1965–1990 *(1991).*

Walker wrote "In Search of Our Mothers' Gardens" for a 1973 Radcliffe symposium on "The Black Woman: Myths and Realities." In 1974 she revised the speech, which was published in Ms. *and later collected in* In Search of Our Mothers'

Gardens: Womanist Prose *(1983), coining* womanist *to denote her philosophical and political commitment to "the survival and wholeness of entire people, male and female." The essay combines historical analysis, literary criticism, and autobiography to explore the "creative spirit" of generations of African American women. Walker urges readers to recognize that many such women expressed their "creative spirit" through quilting, gardening, blues singing, storytelling, and poetry. The Contexts that follow examine Walker's rhetorical relationships with her various audiences.*

I

> *I described her own nature and temperament. Told how they needed a larger life for their expression. . . . I pointed out that in lieu of proper channels, her emotions had overflowed into paths and dissipated them. I talked beautifully I thought, about an art that would be born, an art that would open the way for women the likes of her. I asked her to hope, and build up an inner life against the coming of that day. . . . I sang, with a strange quiver in my voice, a promise song.*
>
> —"AVEY," JEAN TOOMER, CANE

The poet speaking to a prostitute who falls asleep while he's talking—

When the poet Jean Toomer walked through the South in the early twenties, he discovered a curious thing: Black women whose spirituality was so intense, so deep, so *unconscious*, they were themselves unaware of the richness they held. They stumbled blindly through their lives: creatures so abused and mutilated in body, so dimmed and confused by pain, that they considered themselves unworthy even of hope. In the selfless abstractions their bodies became to the men who used them, they became more than "sexual objects," more even than mere women: they became Saints. Instead of being perceived as whole persons, their bodies became shrines; what was thought to be their minds became temples suitable for worship. These crazy "Saints" stared out at the world, wildly, like lunatics—or quietly, like suicides; and the "God" that was in their gate was as mute as a great stone.

Who were these "Saints"? These crazy, loony, pitiful women?

Some of them without a doubt, were our mothers and grandmothers.

In the still heat of the post-Reconstruction South, this is how they seemed to   5
Jean Toomer: exquisite butterflies trapped in an evil honey, toiling away their lives in an era, a century, that did not acknowledge them, except as "the *mule* of the world." They dreamed dreams that no one knew—not even themselves, in any coherent fashion—and saw visions no one could understand. They wandered or sat about the countryside crooning lullabies to ghosts, and drawing the mother of Christ in charcoal on courthouse walls.

They forced their minds to desert their bodies and their striving spirits sought to rise, the frail whirlwinds from the hard red clay. And when those frail whirlwinds fell, in scattered particles, upon the ground, no one mourned. Instead, men lit candles to celebrate the emptiness that remained, as people do who enter a beautiful but vacant space to resurrect a God.

Our mothers and grandmothers, some of them: moving to music not yet written. And they waited.

They waited for a day when the unknown thing that was in them would be made known; but guessed, somehow in their darkness, that on the day of their revelation they would be long dead. Therefore to Toomer they walked, and even ran, in slow motion. For they were going nowhere immediate, and the future was not yet within their grasp. And men took our mothers and grandmothers, "but got no pleasure from it." So complex was their passion and their calm.

To Toomer, they lay vacant and fallow as autumn fields, with harvest time never in sight: and he saw them enter loveless marriages, without joy; and become prostitutes, without resistance; and become mothers of children without fulfillment.

For these grandmothers and mothers of ours were not "Saints," but Artists;   10 driven to a numb and bleeding madness by the springs of creativity in them for which there was no release. They were Creators, who lived lives of spiritual waste, because they were so rich in spirituality—which is the basis of Art—that the strain of enduring their unused and unwanted talent drove them insane. Throwing away this spirituality was their pathetic attempt to lighten the soul to a weight their work-worn, sexually abused bodies could bear.

What did it mean for a Black woman to be an artist in our grandmothers' time? In our great-grandmothers' day? It is a question with an answer cruel enough to stop the blood.

Did you have a genius of a great-great-grandmother who died under some ignorant and depraved white overseer's lash? Or was she required to bake biscuits for a lazy backwater tramp, when she cried out in her soul to paint watercolors of sunsets, or the rain falling on the green and peaceful pasturelands? Or was her body broken and forced to bear children (who were more often than not sold away from her)—eight, ten, fifteen, twenty children—when her one joy was the thought of modeling heroic figures of Rebellion, in stone or clay?

How was the creativity of the Black woman kept alive, year after year and century after century, when for most of the years Black people have been in America, it was a punishable crime for a Black person to read or write? And the freedom to paint, to sculpt, to expand the mind with action, did not exist. Consider, if you can bear to imagine it, what might have been the result if singing, too, had been forbidden by law. Listen to the voices of Bessie Smith, Billie Holiday, Nina Simone, Roberta Flack, and Aretha Franklin, among others, and imagine those voices muzzled for life. Then you may begin to comprehend the lives of our "crazy," "Sainted" mothers and grandmothers. The agony of the lives of women who might have been Poets, Novelists, Essayists, and Short Story Writers (over a period of centuries), who died with their real gifts stifled within them.

And, if this were the end of the story, we would have cause to cry out in my paraphrase of Okot p'Bitek's great poem:

O, my clanswomen
Let us all cry together!
Come,
Let us mourn the death of our mother,
The death of a Queen
The ash that was produced
By a great fire!
O this homestead is utterly dead
Close the gates
With *lacari* thorns,
For our mother
The creator of the Stool is lost!
And all the young women
Have perished in the wilderness.[1]

But this is not the end of the story, for all the young women—our mothers   15
and grandmothers, *ourselves*—have not perished in the wilderness. And if we ask ourselves why, and search for and find the answer, we will know beyond all efforts to erase it from our minds, just exactly who, and of what, we Black American women are.

One example, perhaps the most pathetic, most misunderstood one, can provide a backdrop for our mothers' work: Phillis Wheatley, a slave in the 1700s.

Virginia Woolf, in her book, *A Room of One's Own*, wrote that in order for a woman to write fiction she must have two things, certainly: a room of her own (with a key and lock) and enough money to support herself.

What then are we to make of Phillis Wheatley, a slave, who owned not even herself? This sickly, frail, Black girl who required a servant of her own at times— her health was so precarious—and who, had she been white, would have been easily considered the intellectual superior of all the women and most of the men in the society of her day.

Virginia Woolf wrote further, speaking of course not of our Phillis, that "any woman born with a great gift in the sixteenth century [insert *eighteenth century*, insert *Black woman*, insert *born or made a slave*] would certainly have gone crazed, shot herself, or ended her days in some lonely cottage outside the village, half witch, half wizard [insert *Saint*], feared and mocked at. For it needs little skill and psychology to be sure that a highly gifted girl who had tried to use her gift for poetry would have been so thwarted and hindered by contrary instincts [add *chains, guns, the lash, the ownership of one's body by someone else, submission to an alien religion*] that she must have lost her health and sanity to a certainty."

---

[1]Okot p'Bitek, *Song of Lawino: An Africa Lament* (Nairobi: East African Publishing House, 1966). [Editors' note.]

The key words, as they relate to Phillis, are "contrary instincts." For when we   20
read the poetry of Phillis Wheatley—as when we read the novels of Nella Larsen
or the oddly false-sounding autobiography of that freest of all Black women writers, Zora Hurston—evidence of "contrary instincts" is everywhere. Her loyalties
were completely divided, as was, without question, her mind.

But how could this be otherwise? Captured at seven, a slave of wealthy, dot-
ing whites who instilled in her the "savagery" of the Africa they "rescued" her
from . . . one wonders if she was even able to remember her homeland as she had
known it, or as it really was.

Yet, because she did try to use her gift for poetry in a world that made her a
slave, she was "so thwarted and hindered by . . . contrary instincts that she . . . lost
her health. . . ." In the last years of her brief life, burdened not only with the need
to express her gift but also with a penniless, friendless "freedom" and several
small children for whom she was forced to do strenuous work to feed, she lost
her health, certainly. Suffering from malnutrition and neglect and who knows
what mental agonies, Phillis Wheatley died.

So torn by "contrary instincts" was Black, kidnapped, enslaved Phillis that
her description of "the Goddess"—as she poetically called the Liberty she did
not have—is ironically, cruelly humorous. And, in fact, has held Phillis up to
ridicule for more than a century. It is usually read prior to hanging Phillis's
memory as that of a fool. She wrote:

> The Goddess comes, she moves divinely fair,
> Olive and laurel binds her *golden* hair:
> Wherever shines this native of the skies,
> Unnumber'd charms and recent graces rise.
>
> [Emphasis mine]

It is obvious that Phillis, the slave, combed the "Goddess's" hair every morning; prior, perhaps, to bringing in the milk, or fixing her mistress's lunch. She
took her imagery from the one thing she saw elevated above all others.

With the benefit of hindsight we ask, "How could she?"   25

But at last, Phillis, we understand. No more snickering when your stiff,
struggling, ambivalent lines are forced on us. We know now that you were not an
idiot nor a traitor; only a sickly little Black girl, snatched from your home and
country and made a slave; a woman who still struggled to sing the song that was
your gift, although in a land of barbarians who praised you for your bewildered
tongue. It is not so much what you sang, as that you kept alive, in so many of our
ancestors, the notion of song.

II

Black women are called, in the folklore that so aptly identifies one's status in society, "the *mule* of the world," because we have been handed the burdens that
everyone else—*everyone* else—refused to carry. We have been called "Matriarchs,"

"Superwomen," and "Mean and Evil Bitches." Not to mention "Castrators" and "Sapphire's Mama." When we have pleaded for understanding, our character has been distorted; when we have asked for simple caring, we have been handed empty inspirational appellations, then stuck in the farthest corner. When we have asked for love, we have been given children. In short, even our plainer gifts, our labors of fidelity and love, have been knocked down our throats. To be an Artist and a Black woman, even today, lowers our status in many respects, rather than raises it: and yet, Artists we will be.

Therefore we must fearlessly pull out of ourselves and look at and identify with our lives the living creativity some of our great-grandmothers were not allowed to know. I stress *some* of them because it is well known that the majority of our great-grandmothers knew, even without "knowing" it, the reality of their spirituality, even if they didn't recognize it beyond what happened in the singing at church—and they never had any intention of giving it up.

How they did it: those millions of Black women who were not Phillis Wheatley, or Lucy Terry or Frances Harper or Zora Hurston or Nella Larsen or Bessie Smith—nor Elizabeth Catlett, nor Katherine Dunham, either—brings me to the title of this essay, "In Search of Our Mothers' Gardens," which is a personal account that is yet shared, in its theme and its meaning, by all of us. I found, while thinking about the far-reaching world of the creative Black woman, that often the truest answer to a question that really matters can be found very close.

In the late 1920s my mother ran away from home to marry my father. Marriage, if not running away, was expected of seventeen-year-old girls. By the time she was twenty, she had two children and was pregnant with a third. Five children later, I was born. And this is how I came to know my mother: she seemed a large, soft, loving-eyed woman who was rarely impatient in our home. Her quick, violent temper was on view only a few times a year, when she battled with the white landlord who had the misfortune to suggest to her that her children did not need to go to school. 30

She made all the clothes we wore, even my brothers' overalls. She made all the towels and sheets we used. She spent the summers canning vegetables and fruits. She spent the winter evenings making quilts enough to cover all our beds.

During the "working" day, she labored beside—not behind—my father in the fields. Her day began before sunup, and did not end until late at night. There was never a moment for her to sit down, undisturbed, to unravel her own private thoughts; never a time free from interruption—by work or the noisy inquiries of her many children. And yet, it is to my mother—and all our mothers who were not famous—that I went in search of the secret of what has fed that muzzled and often mutilated, but vibrant, creative spirit that the Black woman has inherited, and that pops out in wild and unlikely places to this day.

But when, you will ask, did my overworked mother have time to know or care about feeding the creative spirit?

The answer is so simple that many of us have spent years discovering it. We have constantly looked high, when we should have looked high—and low.

For example: in the Smithsonian Institution in Washington, D.C., there 35
hangs a quilt unlike any other in the world. In fanciful, inspired, and yet simple
and identifiable figures, it portrays the story of the Crucifixion. It is considered
rare, beyond price. Though it follows no known pattern of quiltmaking, and
though it is made of bits and pieces of worthless rags, it is obviously the work of a
person of powerful imagination and deep spiritual feelings. Below this quilt I saw
a note that says it was made by "an anonymous Black woman in Alabama, a hundred years ago."

If we could locate this "anonymous" Black woman from Alabama, she would
turn out to be one of our grandmothers—an artist who left her mark in the only
materials she could afford, and in the only medium her position in society allowed her to use.

As Virginia Woolf wrote further, in *A Room of One's Own*:

"Yet genius of a sort must have existed among women as it must have existed
among the working class. [Change this to *slaves* and *the wives and daughters of
sharecroppers.*] Now and again an Emily Brontë or a Robert Burns [change this to
a Zora Hurston or a Richard Wright] blazes out and proves its presence. But certainly it never got itself on to paper. When, however, one reads of a witch being
ducked, of a woman possessed by devils [or *Sainthood*], of a wise woman selling
herbs [our rootworkers], or even a very remarkable man who had a mother, then
I think we are on the track of a suppressed poet, of some mute and inglorious
Jane Austen. . . . Indeed, I would venture to guess that Anon, who wrote so many
poems without singing them, was often a woman. . . ."

And so our mothers and grandmothers have, more often than not anony-
mously, handed on the creative spark, the seed of the flower they themselves
never hoped to see: or like a sealed letter they could not plainly read.

And so it is, certainly, with my own mother. Unlike Ma Rainey's songs, 40
which retained their creator's name even while blasting forth from Bessie Smith's
mouth, no song or poem will bear my mother's name. Yet so many of the stories
that I write, that we all write, are my mother's stories. Only recently did I fully realize this: that through years of listening to my mother's stories of her life, I have
absorbed not only the stories themselves, but something of the manner in which
she spoke, something of the urgency that involves the knowledge that her
stories—like her life—must be recorded. It is probably for this reason that so
much of what I have written is about characters whose counterparts in real life
are so much older than I am.

But the telling of these stories, which came from my mother's lips as naturally as breathing, was not the only way my mother showed herself as an artist.
For stories, too, were subject to being distracted, to dying without conclusion.
Dinners must be started, and cotton must be gathered before the big rains. The
artist that was and is my mother showed itself to me only after many years. This
is what I finally noticed:

Like Mem, a character in *The Third Life of Grange Copeland,* my mother
adorned with flowers whatever shabby house we were forced to live in. And not

just your typical straggly country stand of zinnias, either. She planted ambitious gardens—and still does—with over fifty different varieties of plants that bloom profusely from early March until late November. Before she left home for the fields, she watered her flowers, chopped up the grass, and laid out new beds. When she returned from the fields she might divide clumps of bulbs, dig a cold pit, uproot and replant roses, or prune branches from her taller bushes or trees—until night came and it was too dark to see.

Whatever she planted grew as if by magic, and her fame as a grower of flowers spread over three counties. Because of her creativity with her flowers, even my memories of poverty are seen through a screen of blooms—sunflowers, petunias, roses, dahlias, forsythia, spirea, delphiniums, verbena . . . and on and on.

And I remember people coming to my mother's yard to be given cuttings from her flowers; I hear again the praise showered on her because whatever rocky soil she landed on, she turned into a garden. A garden so brilliant with colors, so original in its design, so magnificent with life and creativity, that to this day people drive by our house in Georgia—perfect strangers and imperfect strangers—and ask to stand or walk among my mother's art.

I notice that it is only when my mother is working in her flowers that she is   45 radiant, almost to the point of being invisible—except as Creator: hand and eye. She is involved in work her soul must have. Ordering the universe in the image of her personal conception of Beauty.

Her face, as she prepares the Art that is her gift, is a legacy of respect she leaves to me, for all that illuminates and cherishes life. She had handed down respect for the possibilities—and the will to grasp them.

For her, so hindered and intruded upon in so many ways, being an artist has still been a daily part of her life. This ability to hold on, even in very simple ways, is work Black women have done for a very long time.

This poem is not enough, but it is something, for the woman who literally covered the holes in our walls with sunflowers:

They were women then
My mama's generation
Husky of voice—Stout of
Step
With fists as well as
Hands
How they battered down
Doors
And ironed
Starched white
Shirts
How they led
Armies
Headragged Generals

Across mined
Fields
Booby-trapped
Ditches
To discover books
Desks
A place for us
How they knew what we
Must know
Without knowing a page
Of it
Themselves.

Guided by my heritage of love and beauty and a respect for strength—in search of my mother's garden, I found my own.

And perhaps in Africa over two hundred years ago, there was just such a 50 mother; perhaps she painted vivid and daring decorations in oranges and yellows and greens on the walls of her hut; perhaps she sang—in a voice like Roberta Flack's—*sweetly* over the compounds of her village; perhaps she wove the most stunning mats or told the most ingenious stories of all the village story-tellers. Perhaps she was herself a poet—though only her daughter's name is signed to the poems that we know.

Perhaps Phillis Wheatley's mother was also an artist.

Perhaps in more than Phillis Wheatley's biological life is her mother's signature made clear.

CONTEXTS FOR "IN SEARCH OF OUR MOTHERS' GARDENS"

JAMES BALDWIN

Autobiographical Notes

For biography see p. 118.

I know, in any case, that the most crucial time in my own development came when I was forced to recognize that I was a kind of bastard of the West; when I followed the line of my past I did not find myself in Europe but in Africa. And

From James Baldwin, "Autobiographical Notes," in *Notes of a Native Son* (Boston: Beacon Press, 1955), 6–7.

this meant that in some subtle way, in a really profound way, I brought to Shakespeare, Bach, Rembrandt, to the stones of Paris, to the cathedral at Chartres, and to the Empire State Building, a special attitude. These were not really my creations, they did not contain my history; I might search in them in vain forever for any reflection of myself. I was an interloper; this was not my heritage. At the same time I had no other heritage which I could possibly hope to use—I had certainly been unfitted for the jungle or the tribe. I would have to appropriate these white centuries, I would have to make them mine—I would have to accept my special attitude, my special place in this scheme—otherwise I would have no place in *any* scheme. What was the most difficult was the fact that I was forced to admit something I had always hidden from myself, which the American Negro has had to hide from himself as the price of his public progress; that I hated and feared white people. This did not mean that I loved black people; on the contrary, I despised them, possibly because they failed to produce Rembrandt. In effect, I hated and feared the world. And this meant, not only that I thus gave the world an altogether murderous power over me, but also that in such a self-destroying limbo I could never hope to write.

One writes out of one thing only—one's own experience. Everything depends on how relentlessly one forces from this experience the last drop, sweet or bitter, it can possibly give. This is the only real concern of the artist, to recreate out of the disorder of life that order which is art. The difficulty then, for me, of being a Negro writer was the fact that I was, in effect, prohibited from examining my own experience too closely by the tremendous demands and the very real dangers of my social situation. . . .

AMIRI BARAKA
The Myth of Negro Literature

Poet and playwright Amiri Baraka was born Everett LeRoi Jones in Newark, New Jersey, in 1934. In the 1960s Baraka and other artists sought to define Negritude— that is, the particular artistic quality that expressed the African American experience most authentically. In this excerpt from his address to the American Society of African Culture (1962), Baraka identifies "Negro music" as an authentic expression and insists, since the idea was then controversial, on "calling Negro music Art" with a capital A to emphasize its importance.

From Amiri Baraka, "The Myth of Negro Literature," in *Home, Social Essays* (New York: William Morrow, 1966), 107.

Negro music alone, because it drew its strengths and beauties out of the depth of the black man's soul, and because to a large extent its traditions could be carried on by the lowest classes of Negroes, has been able to survive the constant and willful dilutions of the black middle class. Blues and jazz have been the only consistent exhibitors of "Negritude" in informal American culture simply because the bearers of its tradition maintained their essential identities as Negroes; in no other art (and I will persist in calling Negro music Art) has this been possible.

DANIEL PATRICK MOYNIHAN

The Negro Family: The Case for National Action

Then assistant secretary of labor Daniel Patrick Moynihan issued The Moynihan Report *in 1965, which drew on research by African American sociologists Kenneth Clark and E. Franklin Frazier to trace the economic and social consequences of racial oppression on black families. However, by linking the "black matriarchy" with "social pathology" in the black community, the report, entitled* The Negro Family: The Case for National Action, *from which "The Tangle of Pathology" is excerpted, sparked a searing controversy. Among black leaders, radicals responded with indignation, while conservatives organized "citizenship clinics" and acknowledged Moynihan's record of supporting civil rights.*

THE TANGLE OF PATHOLOGY

That the Negro American has survived at all is extraordinary—a lesser people might simply have died out, as indeed others have. That the Negro community has not only survived, but in this political generation has entered national affairs as a moderate, humane, and constructive national force is the highest testament to the healing powers of the democratic ideal and the creative vitality of the Negro people.

But it may not be supposed that the Negro American community has not paid a fearful price for the incredible mistreatment to which it has been subjected over the past three centuries.

In essence, the Negro community has been forced into a matriarchal structure which, because it is so out of line with the rest of the American society, seriously retards the progress of the group as a whole, and imposes a crushing burden on the Negro male and, in consequence, on a great many Negro women as well. . . .

Ours is a society which presumes male leadership in private and public affairs. The arrangements of society facilitate such leadership and reward it. A subcul-

From Daniel Patrick Moynihan, *The Negro Family: The Case for National Action* (Washington, D.C.: U.S. Department of Labor, 1965).

ture, such as that of the Negro American, in which this is not the pattern, is placed at a distinct disadvantage.

Here an earlier word of caution should be repeated. There is much evidence that a considerable number of Negro families have managed to break out of the tangle of pathology and to establish themselves as stable, effective units, living according to patterns of American society in general. E. Franklin Frazier has suggested that the middle-class Negro American family is, if anything, more patriarchal and protective of its children than the general run of such families. Given equal opportunities, the children of these families will perform as well or better than their white peers. They need no help from anyone, and ask none. . . .

It might be estimated that as much as half of the Negro community falls into the middle class. However, the remaining half is in desperate and deteriorating circumstances. Moreover, because of housing segregation it is immensely difficult for the stable half to escape from the cultural influences of the unstable one. The children of middle-class Negroes often as not must grow up in, or next to the slums, an experience almost unknown to white middle-class children. They are therefore constantly exposed to the pathology of the disturbed group and constantly in danger of being drawn into it. It is for this reason that the propositions put forth in this study may be thought of as having a more or less general application.

Obviously, not every instance of social pathology afflicting the Negro community can be traced to the weakness of family structure. If, for example, organized crime in the Negro community were not largely controlled by whites, there would be more capital accumulation among Negroes, and therefore probably more Negro business enterprises. If it were not for the hostility and fear many whites exhibit towards Negroes, they in turn would be less afflicted by hostility and fear and so on. There is no one Negro community. There is no one Negro problem. There is no one solution. Nonetheless, at the center of the tangle of pathology is the weakness of the family structure. Once or twice removed, it will be found to be the principal source of most of the aberrant, inadequate, or antisocial behavior that did not establish, but now serves to perpetuate the cycle of poverty and deprivation.

It was by destroying the Negro family under slavery that white America broke the will of the Negro people. Although that will has reasserted itself in our time, it is a resurgence doomed to frustration unless the viability of the Negro family is restored.

Matriarchy

A fundamental fact of Negro American family life is the often reversed roles of husband and wife.

Robert O. Blood Jr. and Donald M. Wolfe, in a study of Detroit families, note that "Negro husbands have unusually low power,"[1] and while this is characteristic of all low income families, the pattern pervades the Negro social structure: "the cumulative result of discrimination in jobs . . . , the segregrated housing, and the poor schooling of Negro men."[2] In 44 percent of the Negro families studied, the wife was dominant, as against 20 percent of white wives. "Whereas the majority of white families are equalitarian, the largest percentage of Negro families are dominated by the wife."[3]

The matriarchal pattern of so many Negro families reinforces itself over the generations. This process begins with education. Although the gap appears to be closing at the moment, for a long while, Negro females were better educated than Negro males, and this remains true today for the Negro population as a whole.

NOTES

1. Robert O. Blood Jr., and Donald M. Wolfe, *Husbands and Wives: The Dynamics of Married Living* (Illinois: The Free Press of Glencoe, 1960), p. 34.

2. Ibid., p. 35.

3. Ibid.

ALICE WALKER

Looking to the Side, and Back

In "Looking to the Side, and Back," Walker describes her Radcliffe symposium listeners and their surprisingly conservative reaction to her keynote address. The symposium at which Walker gave her speech aimed to dispel the myth of the "black matriarch," along with other myths identified in the symposium papers: the "simple-minded myths of the black woman [as] a 'castrator,' 'welfare exploiter,' or 'sexual harlot.'" Walker's speech argued that the term "black matriarchy" distorted the characters of black women. Although they apparently accepted her views of African art, they rejected her acknowledgment of divisions within the black community and within black families.

In 1973 I was keynote speaker at a symposium at Radcliffe called "The Black Woman: Myths and Realities." It was to that gathering of the *crème de la crème* of black educated women in America (some two hundred) that I delivered a speech I'd written especially for black women, called "In Search of Our Mothers'

From Alice Walker, "Looking to the Side, and Back" (originally published as "Other Voices, Other Moods" in *Ms.*, February 1979), in *In Search of Our Mothers' Gardens* (San Diego: Harcourt, 1983), 313–319.

Gardens." It is largely about the tenacity of the artistic spirit among us, from a historical perspective. Many women wept, they later told me, as I read it, and they gave me, in the words of the *Radcliffe Quarterly,* which later published the essay, "a tumultuous standing ovation."

Later there was a panel discussion and, still high from my speech, I looked forward to an exchange among all of us that would be more than a sharing of history and survivalist emotion.

June Jordan and I were sitting together in the audience. Four or five women were on stage. One was a psychologist, one a well-known actress, one a Civil Rights lawyer. Every one was *some*thing. I was so excited!

June and I had often talked between ourselves about the plight of young black women who were killing themselves at an alarming (to us) rate. We thought *this* should be brought before our sisters. In fact, the week before, I had visited Sarah Lawrence (where I was at the time a member-of-the-board-of-trustees impersonator) and had been told in grisly detail of the suicide of one young woman. She had been ridiculed by the black men on campus because she dated white guys (meanwhile, these black guys dated white girls and each other). She couldn't take it. She killed herself. That *same* week, a young Oriental girl had jumped to her death from a window at Radcliffe. And from all sides I had been hearing how impossible it was becoming to be a young woman of color. It appeared that any kind of nonconformity was not permitted.

What occurred when June and I brought all this up, however, was nothing 5 short of incredible. There was *no* response whatsoever to the increased suicide rate among young women of color. Instead, we were treated to a lecture on the black woman's responsibilities to the black man. I will never forget my sense of horror and betrayal when one of the panelists said to me (and to the rest of that august body of black women gathered there): "The responsibility of the black woman is to support the black man; *whatever* he does."

It occurred to me that my neck could be at that minute under some man's heel, and this woman would stroll by and say, "Right on."

I burst into the loudest tears I've ever shed. And though I soon dried my face, I didn't stop crying inside for her. Maybe I haven't stopped yet. But that's okay; what I'm crying about is worth it.

But a really fascinating thing happened around my crying: many of the women blamed me for crying! I couldn't believe it. They came over to me, one or two at a time, and said:

"I understand what you are trying to say . . ." (I wasn't *trying,* I muttered through clenched teeth, I *said* it; you just didn't listen.) "but don't let it *get* to you!"

Or: "Why would you let *anyone* make you cry?!"   10

Not *one* of them *ever* said a word about why young women of color were killing themselves. They could take the black woman as invincible, as she was portrayed to some extent in my speech (what they *heard* was the invincible part), but there was no sympathy for struggle that ended in defeat. Which meant there was no sympathy for struggle itself—only for "winning."

In 41 Black colleges today there are thousands of dedicated students who want an education. Some of them may never get it. Their schools are in desperate need of money. Your contributions can help these schools. It's important. **A mind is a terrible thing to waste.**

Give to the United Negro College Fund.
55 E. 52nd St.
New York, N.Y. 10022

"My grandmother takes in washing so I can become a teacher. Now my school is running out of money."

I was reminded of something that had puzzled me about the response of black people to Movement people in the South. During the seven years I lived in Mississippi, I never knew a Movement person (and I include myself) who wasn't damaged in some way from having to put her or his life, principles, children, on the line over long, stressful periods. And this is only natural. But there was a way in which the black community could not look at this. I remember a young boy who was shot through the neck by racist whites, and almost died. When he recovered, he was the same gentle, sweet boy he'd always been, but he hated white people, which at that time didn't fit in with black people's superior notion of themselves as people who could consistently turn the other cheek. Nobody ever really tried to incorporate the new reality of this boy's life. When they spoke of him it was as if his life stopped just before the shot.

I knew a young girl who "desegregated" the local white high school in her small town. No one, except her teachers, spoke to her *for four years*. There was

Courtesy: United Negro College Fund Advertisement from *Ms.* (July 1975, p. 103).

one white guy—whom she spoke of with contempt—who left love notes in her locker. This girl suffered acute anxiety; so that when she dragged herself home from school every day, she went to bed, and stayed there until the next morning, when she walked off, ramrod straight, to school. Even her parents talked only about the bravery, never about the cost.

It was at the Radcliffe symposium that I saw that black women are more loyal to black men than they are to themselves, a dangerous state of affairs that has its logical end in self-destructive behavior.

But I also learned something else: 15

The same panelist who would not address the suicide rate of young women of color also took the opportunity to tell me what she thought my "problem" was. Since I spoke so much of my mother, she said my problem was that I was "trying to 'carry' my mother, and the weight is too heavy."

June, who was sitting beside me, and who was angry but not embarrassed by my tears, put her arms around me and said:

"But why shouldn't you carry your mother; she carried *you*, didn't she?"

That is perfection in a short response.

I had to giggle. And the giggle and the tears and the holding and the sanc- 20
tioning of responsibility to those we love and those who have loved us is what I know will see us through.

ALICE WALKER

Interview (1983)

In this 1983 interview, Walker explains her wish to expand her audience by encouraging reading in the African American community. Twenty years later, Oprah Winfrey's book club was a direct result of efforts like Walker's.

In any case, I think anybody can *only write*. Writing or not writing is not dependent on what the market is—whether your work is going to sell or not. If it were, there is not a black woman who would write. And that includes Phillis Wheatley. Think of *her* antagonistic market! I mean if you really thought about the market, you would probably just take a job canning fish. Even the most successful black women writers don't make a lot of money, compared to what white male and female writers earn just routinely. We live in a society that is racist and white. That is one problem. Another is, we don't have a large black readership; I mean, black people, generally speaking, don't read. That is our *main* problem. Instead of attacking each other, we could try to address that problem by doing whatever we

From Alice Walker, Interview, in *Black Women Writers at Work,* ed. Claudia Tate (New York: Continuum, 1983), 175–187.

can to see that more black works get out into the world . . . and by stimulating an interest in literature among black people. Black women writers seem to be trying to do just that, and that's really commendable.

. . . Black women instinctively feel a need to connect with their reading audience, to be direct, to build a readership for us all, but more than that, to build *independence*. None of us will survive except in very distorted ways if we have to depend on white publishers and white readers forever. And white critics. [. . .]

TONI MORRISON
The Pain of Being Black

Sixteen years after Alice Walker addressed the Radcliffe symposium, the "myths" it aimed to dispel remained. Winner of the 1993 Nobel Prize in Literature and the 1987 Pulitzer Prize for Beloved, *Toni Morrison, in a* Time *magazine interview, rejects* The Moynihan Report's *link between "black matriarchy" and "social pathology."*

Well, neither [unwed teenage pregnancies nor single-parent households] seems to me a debility. I don't think a female running a house is a problem, a broken family. It's perceived as one because of the notion that a head is a man.

Two parents can't raise a child any more than one. You need a whole community—everybody—to raise a child. The notion that the head is the one who brings in the most money is a patriarchal notion, that a woman—and I have raised two children, alone—is somehow lesser than a male head. Or that I am incomplete without the male. This is not true. And the little nuclear family is a paradigm that just doesn't work. It doesn't work for white people or for black people. Why we are hanging onto it, I don't know. It isolates people into little units—people need a larger unit.

QUESTIONS FOR DISCUSSION AND WRITING

1. How do *you* recognize a work of art? What counts as art? What role do institutions such as the Smithsonian play in defining what counts—for others and for you—as a work of art? How can one distinguish "art" from the "Art" Amiri Baraka describes? What passages from Walker's essay support your analysis?

2. In "Autobiographical Notes," Baldwin describes the role of white culture in his development as a black artist. What does he mean by "white culture"? Who

From an interview with Bonnie Angelo, *Time*, 22 May 1989, 120–123.

represents "white culture" in Walker's essay, and what is the role of white culture in Walker's development?

3. What role does gender play in Baldwin's and Walker's definitions of what counts as art? How does Walker redefine art by considering women's production of it?

4. Basing your explanation on the Contexts, who is "the black woman"? What are the various elements of myth, history, and culture that comprise her identity? In what ways—and to what extent—does Walker's mother embody "the black woman"? What passages from the Context readings support your explanation?

5. With particular passages from the Context readings in mind, write a conversation among Morrison, Moynihan, and Walker about the costs and benefits of black women's roles in the family.

6. What definition of *creativity* does Walker provide in "In Search of Our Mothers' Gardens," and how do her examples help you understand its meaning? What is the value of Walker's parenthetical revision of the short passage by Virginia Woolf (paragraph 37)? How does Woolf comment on the nature of imagination?

THOMAS JEFFERSON

The Declaration of Independence

With Benjamin Franklin and John Adams, Thomas Jefferson drafted America's most incendiary document, the Declaration of Independence, in mid-June 1776. Revised by the Continental Congress, it was signed on July 4. The Declaration, often called "an expression of the American mind," reflects Jefferson's belief that democracy is the ideal form of government, a philosophy reinforced by his refusal to sign the U.S. Constitution until the Bill of Rights was added. The Declaration is a deductive argument, based on the premise "We hold these truths to be self-evident," from which the rest of the argument follows. As events were to prove, what the colonists considered an emphatic, plainspoken statement of natural rights, the British considered an inflammatory declaration of war. (For biographical information on Thomas Jefferson, see the headnote to "George Washington," p. 161.)

When in the course of human events, it becomes necessary for one people to dissolve the political bands which have connected them with another, and to assume among the Powers of the earth, the separate and equal station to which the Laws of Nature and of Nature's God entitle them, a decent respect to the opinions of mankind requires that they should declare the causes which impel them to the separation.

We hold these truths to be self-evident, that all men are created equal, that they are endowed by their Creator with certain unalienable Rights, that among these are Life, Liberty and the pursuit of Happiness. That to secure these rights, Governments are instituted among Men deriving their just powers from the consent of the governed. That whenever any Form of Government becomes destructive of these ends, it is the Right of People to alter or to abolish it, and to institute new Government, laying its foundation on such principles and organizing its powers in such form, as to them shall seem most likely to effect their Safety and Happiness. Prudence, indeed, will dictate that Governments long established should not be changed for light and transient causes; and accordingly all experience hath shown, that mankind are more disposed to suffer, while evils are sufferable, than to right themselves by abolishing the forms to which they are accustomed. But when a long train of abuses and usurpations pursuing invariably the same Object evinces a design to reduce them under absolute Despotism, it is their right, it is their duty, to throw off such government, and to provide new Guards for their future security. Such has been the patient sufferance of these Colonies; and such is now the necessity which constrains them to alter their former Systems of Government. The history of the present King of Great Britain is a history of repeated injuries and usurpations, all having in direct object the establishment of an absolute Tyranny over these States. To prove this, let Facts be submitted to a candid world.

He has refused his Assent to Laws, the most wholesome and necessary for the public good.

He had forbidden his Governors to pass Laws of immediate and pressing importance, unless suspended in their operation till his Assent should be obtained; and when so suspended, he has utterly neglected to attend them.

He has refused to pass other Laws for the accommodation of large districts 5 of people, unless those people would relinquish the right of Representation in the Legislature, a right inestimable to them and formidable to tyrants only.

He has called together legislative bodies at places unusual, uncomfortable, and distant from the depository of their Public Records, for the sole purpose of fatiguing them into compliance with his measures.

He has dissolved Representative Houses repeatedly, for opposing with manly firmness his invasions on the rights of the people.

He has refused for a long time, after such dissolutions, to cause others to be elected; whereby the Legislative Powers, incapable of Annihilation, have returned to the People at large for their exercise; the State remaining in the mean time exposed to all the dangers of invasion from without, and convulsions within.

He has endeavoured to prevent the population of these States; for that purpose obstructing the Laws of Naturalization of Foreigners; refusing to pass others to encourage their migration hither, and raising the conditions of new Appropriations of Lands.

He has obstructed the Administration of Justice, by refusing his Assent to 10 Laws for establishing Judiciary Powers.

He has made Judges dependent on his Will alone, for the tenure of their offices, and the amount and payment of their salaries.

He has erected a multitude of New Offices, and sent hither swarms of Officers to harass our People, and eat out their substance.

He has kept among us, in time of peace, Standing Armies without the Consent of our Legislature.

He has affected to render the Military independent of and superior to the Civil Power.

He has combined with others to subject us to jurisdictions foreign to our constitution, and unacknowledged by our laws; giving his Assent to their acts of pretended Legislation:

For quartering large bodies of armed troops among us:

For protecting them, by a mock Trial, from Punishment for any Murders which they should commit on the Inhabitants of these States:

For cutting off our Trade with all parts of the world:

For imposing Taxes on us without our Consent:

For depriving us in many cases, of the benefits of Trial by Jury:

For transporting us beyond Seas to be tried for pretended offenses:

For abolishing the free System of English Laws in a Neighbouring Province, establishing therein an Arbitrary government, and enlarging its boundaries so as to render it at once an example and fit instrument for introducing the same absolute rule into these Colonies:

For taking away our Charters, abolishing our most valuable laws, and altering fundamentally the Forms of our Governments:

For suspending our own Legislatures, and declaring themselves invested with Power to legislate for us in all cases whatsoever.

He has abdicated Government here, by declaring us out of his Protection and waging War against us.

He has plundered our seas, ravaged our Coasts, burnt our towns and destroyed the Lives of our people.

He is at this time transporting large Armies of foreign Mercenaries to compleat works of death, desolation and tyranny, already begun with circumstances of Cruelty & perfidy scarcely paralleled in the most barbarous ages, and totally unworthy the Head of a civilized nation.

He has constrained our fellow Citizens taken Captive on the high Seas to bear Arms against their Country, to become the executioners of their friends and Brethren, or to fall themselves by their Hands.

He has excited domestic insurrections amongst us, and has endeavoured to bring on the inhabitants of our frontiers, the merciless Indian Savages, whose known rule of warfare, is an undistinguished destruction of all ages, sexes and conditions.

In every stage of these Oppressions We Have Petitioned for Redress in the most humble terms: Our repeated petitions have been answered only by repeated injury. A Prince, whose character is thus marked by every act which may define a Tyrant, is unfit to be the ruler of a free People.

Nor have We been wanting in attention to our British brethren. We have warned them from time to time of attempts by their legislature to extend an unwarrantable jurisdiction over us. We have reminded them of the circumstances of our emigration and settlement here. We have appealed to their native justice and magnanimity and we have conjured them by the ties of our common kindred to disavow these usurpations, which would inevitably interrupt our connections and correspondence. They too have been deaf to the voice of justice and of consanguinity. We must, therefore acquiesce in the necessity, which denounces our Separation, and hold them, as we hold the rest of mankind, Enemies in War, in Peace Friends.

We, therefore, the Representatives of the United States of America, in General Congress, Assembled, appealing to the Supreme Judge of the world for the rectitude of our intentions, do, in the Name, and by Authority of the good People of these Colonies, solemnly publish and declare, That these United Colonies are, and of Right ought to be Free and Independent States; that they are Absolved from all Allegiance to the British Crown and that all political connection between them and the State of Great Britain, is and ought to be totally dissolved; and that as Free and Independent States, they have full power to levy War, conclude Peace, contract Alliances, establish Commerce, and to do all other Acts and Things which Independent States may of right do. And for the support of this Declaration, with a firm reliance on the protection of Divine Providence, we mutually pledge to each other our lives, our Fortunes and our sacred Honor.

QUESTIONS FOR DISCUSSION AND WRITING

1. In the first paragraph, Thomas Jefferson establishes the foundation of the American people's "separate and equal station" in the international community by referring to "the Laws of Nature." What are these laws? Why doesn't he specify them?

2. Jefferson is specific yet selective about his fundamental premises, mentioning "Life, Liberty and the pursuit of Happiness" as prime examples of the "unalienable Rights" for all people (paragraph 2). Given Jefferson's historical moment and the task at hand, why do you think he chooses these three examples but not others? Can you think of other rights that are equally essential to a free and just society for all? What could be some of the reasons that Jefferson didn't add those rights to his list of three?

3. In the body of the Declaration, Jefferson offers a long list of grievances (paragraphs 3–31), beginning many of the items with the phrase "He has . . ." Compare Jefferson's use of repetition with that of Jonathan Kozol in "The Human Cost of an Illiterate Society" (p. 273). Are their uses of repetition effective? Why or why not? In what rhetorical situations do they use it? In what situations should we be cautious in, or even avoid, using this well-established technique?

4. Speculate on the effects the Declaration of Independence had on its original audience—the British government in the eighteenth century. Could the British

Crown have read it as a hotheaded manifesto or even a declaration of war? Can a cluster of colonies or any political entity gain independence simply through a declaration?

5. Reread the Declaration of Independence together with Henry David Thoreau's "Civil Disobedience" (p. 192). Then write your own declaration in which you separate yourself from a group whose moral standards (or their absence) and behavior code are no longer acceptable to you.

SOJOURNER TRUTH

Ain't I a Woman?

Born Isabella Van Wagener to a family of slaves in Ulster County, New York, Sojourner Truth (1797–1883) grew up the property of various masters who abused her physically and sexually, until she fled and found refuge in 1827. A religious visionary since childhood, she devoted herself to evangelical work in New York City while raising two children and doing domestic work. In 1843 she heeded a call to "travel up and down the land," changed her name to Sojourner Truth, and embarked on a mission to preach. At a utopian community in Northampton, Massachusetts, she embraced the cause of abolition, eventually taking her message to the Midwest, where her charismatic oratory attracted a large following. In 1850 Truth took on the cause of women's rights and began to fight oppression on two fronts. Her autobiography, The Narrative of Sojourner Truth *(1850)—which she dictated to Olive Gilbert, a sympathetic white woman—sold enough copies to provide a source of income.*

Nell Irvin Painter's Sojourner Truth: A Life, a Symbol *(1996) questions whether Truth's quintessential feminist statement—"Ain't I a Woman?"—is entirely her own creation. She did deliver an effective speech at the 1851 Ohio Women's Rights Convention, but it appears to have been embellished by later biographers. Regardless, this incendiary speech is a model of persuasive oratory.*

Well, children, where there is so much racket there must be something out of kilter. I think that 'twixt the negroes of the South and the women at the North, all talking about rights, the white men will be in a fix pretty soon. But what's all this here talking about?

That man over there says women need to be helped into carriages, and lifted over ditches, and to have the best place everywhere. Nobody ever helps me into carriages, or over mud-puddles, or gives me any best place! And ain't I a woman? Look at me! Look at my arm! I have ploughed and planted, and gathered into barns, and no man could head me! And ain't I a woman? I could work as much and eat as much as a man—when I could get it—and bear the lash as well! And ain't I a woman? I have borne thirteen children, and seen them most all sold off to slavery, and when I cried out with my mother's grief, none but Jesus heard me! And ain't I a woman?

Then they talk about this thing in the head; what's this they call it? [Intellect, someone whispers.] That's it, honey. What's that got to do with women's rights or negro's rights? If my cup won't hold but a pint, and yours holds a quart, wouldn't you be mean not to let me have my little half-measure full?

Then that little man in black there, he says women can't have as much rights as men, 'cause Christ wasn't a woman! Where did your Christ come from? Where did your Christ come from? From God and a woman! Man had nothing to do with Him.

If the first woman God ever made was strong enough to turn the world upside down all alone, these women together ought to be able to turn it back, and get it right side up again! And now they is asking to do it, the men better let them.   5

Obliged to you for hearing me, and now old Sojourner ain't got nothing more to say.

QUESTIONS FOR DISCUSSION AND WRITING

1. How does Sojourner Truth establish her authority to speak on the topic of women's rights? How does she paint a picture of herself that makes the audience sympathetic to her cause?

2. How does the repeated phrase "ain't I a woman?" work in this speech to move the audience and convey Truth's ideas? What would the speech be like if that phrase were absent? What types of rhetorical moves in this piece show that it is a speech and not a written essay?

3. Do you think women have achieved equality in U.S. society since Truth gave her speech? Are there areas in which advances still need to be made? Write a short essay—or perhaps a short speech—designed to convince people of your point of view.

4. How does Truth's self-presentation compare to Alice Walker's description, in "In Search of Our Mothers' Gardens," of the women Jean Toomer met in the 1920s? Does Truth's speech support Moynihan's assertion that "destroying the Negro family under slavery [. . .] broke the will of the Negro people" (paragraph 8)?

ELIZABETH CADY STANTON
Declaration of Sentiments

Elizabeth Cady Stanton (1815–1902) was born in Johnstown, New York. Although she never went to college, she privately studied Greek, Latin, and mathematics and was unusually well-educated for a woman of her time. She was the leading orator and writer of the U.S. women's rights movement that culminated in women's suffrage in 1910. With Lucretia Mott, she called for the Seneca Falls Women's Rights Convention (1848), where she introduced the "Declaration of Sentiments" advocating reforms to establish women's equality. For the next fifty years, Stanton campaigned with Susan B. Anthony for liberalized divorce laws, women's property rights, and women's suffrage. She and Anthony, abolitionists during the Civil War, were bitterly disappointed when voting rights for black men were given precedence over voting rights for women. Stanton was principal author of the "Declaration of Rights for Women" (1876) and author of the federal suffrage amendment, The Woman's Bible *(1895–1898), and an autobiography,* Eighty Years and More *(1898).*

Stanton modeled the "Declaration of Sentiments" on the Declaration of Independence, substituting "men" for "the present King of Great Britain" as the oppressor. The list of charges against patriarchal authority is a blueprint of feminist issues, including the lack of employment opportunities, the inequities of marriage and divorce laws, and disenfranchisement.

When, in the course of human events, it becomes necessary for one portion of the family of man to assume among the people of the earth a position different from that which they have hitherto occupied, but one to which the laws of nature and of nature's God entitle them, a decent respect to the opinions of mankind requires that they should declare the causes that impel them to such a course.

We hold these truths to be self-evident: that all men and women are created equal; that they are endowed by their Creator with certain inalienable rights; that among these are life, liberty, and the pursuit of happiness; that to secure these rights governments are instituted, deriving their just powers from the consent of the governed. Whenever any form of government becomes destructive of these ends, it is the right of those who suffer from it to refuse allegiance to it, and to insist upon the institution of a new government, laying its foundation on such principles, and organizing its powers in such form, as to them shall seem most likely to effect their safety and happiness. Prudence, indeed, will dictate that governments long established should not be changed for light and transient causes; and accordingly all experience hath shown that mankind are more disposed to suffer, while evils are sufferable, than to right themselves by abolishing the forms to which they were accustomed. But when a long train of abuses and usurpations, pursuing invariably the same object evinces a design to reduce them under absolute despotism, it is their duty to throw off such government, and to provide new guards for their future security. Such has been the patient sufferance of the women under this government, and such is now the necessity which constrains them to demand the equal station to which they are entitled.

The history of mankind is a history of repeated injuries and usurpations on the part of man toward woman, having in direct object the establishment of an absolute tyranny over her. To prove this, let facts be submitted to a candid world.

He has never permitted her to exercise her inalienable right to the elective franchise.

He has compelled her to submit to laws, in the formation of which she had 5 no voice.

He has withheld from her rights which are given to the most ignorant and degraded men—both natives and foreigners.

Having deprived her of this first right of a citizen, the elective franchise, thereby leaving her without representation in the halls of legislation, he has oppressed her on all sides.

He has made her, if married, in the eye of the law, civilly dead.

He has taken from her all right in property, even to the wages she earns.

He has made her, morally, an irresponsible being, as she can commit many 10 crimes with impunity, provided they be done in the presence of her husband. In the covenant of marriage, she is compelled to promise obedience to her husband, he becoming, to all intents and purposes, her master—the law giving him power to deprive her of her liberty, and to administer chastisement.

He has so framed the laws of divorce, as to what shall be the proper causes, and in case of separation, to whom the guardianship of the children shall be given, as to be wholly regardless of the happiness of women—the law, in all cases, going upon a false supposition of the supremacy of man, and giving all power into his hands.

After depriving her of all rights as a married woman, if single, and the owner of property, he has taxed her to support a government which recognizes her only when her property can be made profitable to it.

He has monopolized nearly all the profitable employments, and from those she is permitted to follow, she receives but a scanty remuneration. He closes against her all the avenues to wealth and distinction which he considers most honorable to himself. As a teacher of theology, medicine, or law, she is not known.

He has denied her the facilities for obtaining a thorough education, all colleges being closed against her.

He allows her in Church, as well as State, but a subordinate position, claim- 15 ing Apostolic authority for her exclusion from the ministry, and, with some exceptions from any public participation in the affairs of the Church.

He has created a false public sentiment by giving to the world a different code of morals for men and women, by which moral delinquencies which exclude women from society, are not only tolerated, but deemed of little account in man.

He has usurped the prerogative of Jehovah himself, claiming it as his right to assign for her a sphere of action, when that belongs to her conscience and to her God.

He has endeavored, in every way that he could, to destroy her confidence in her own powers, to lessen her self-respect, and to make her willing to lead a dependent and abject life.

Now, in view of this entire disenfranchisement of one-half the people of this country, their social and religious degradation—in view of the unjust laws above mentioned, and because women do feel themselves aggrieved, oppressed, and fraudulently deprived of their most sacred rights, we insist that they have immediate admission to all the rights and privileges which belong to them as citizens of the United States.

In entering upon the great work before us, we anticipate no small amount of   20 misconception, misrepresentation, and ridicule; but we shall use every instrumentality within our power to effect our object. We shall employ agents, circulate tracts, petition the State and National legislatures, and endeavor to enlist the pulpit and the press in our behalf. We hope this Convention will be followed by a series of Conventions embracing every part of the country.

QUESTIONS FOR DISCUSSION AND WRITING

1. In the first two paragraphs, Stanton imitates Jefferson's wording in the Declaration of Independence almost word for word. What is her purpose and what is the effect on the reader?

2. Stanton breaks up the end of the second paragraph of the Declaration of Independence and creates a new one, similar to the original in logic, diction, and sentence pattern, yet different in content. It begins with a sharp, strong statement: "The history of mankind is a history of repeated injuries and usurpations on the part of man toward woman, having in direct object the establishment of an absolute tyranny over her" (paragraph 3). How do you imagine men would have responded to this statement? How do you imagine women would have responded to it?

3. In the next paragraphs (4–18), Stanton provides a long list of evidence. Is it equally convincing, if not more so, as the list offered in the Declaration of Independence against the English Crown? Why or why not?

4. Reviewing Stanton's position as a twenty-first-century reader, modify the list of women's grievances against men.

5. Write a "Bill of Rights for Women and Men" that could serve as the foundation of a constitution that ensures the harmonious coexistence of men and women.

GEORGE ORWELL

Shooting an Elephant

George Orwell (1903–1950) is best known for his anti-totalitarian novels, Animal
Farm *(1945) and* 1984 *(1949). He was born Eric Arthur Blair in Bengal (now
Bihar), India, where his father worked in the colonial civil service. Orwell was edu-
cated at Eton and served with the Indian Imperial Police in Burma, now Myanmar.
Orwell writes of his frustration with racial and social barriers there in his novel*
Burmese Days *(1934) and in his essay "Shooting an Elephant" (1936). In 1928 he
committed himself to a life of hardship among Europe's poor and wrote* Down and
Out in Paris and London *(1933) about his drudgery and near-starvation as a
restaurant kitchen worker and as a tramp. In* The Road to Wigan Pier *(1937), he
describes the harrowing lives of unemployed coal miners in Lancashire; and in*
Homage to Catalonia *(1938), he writes of his fighting in 1936–1937 against the
Communists in the Spanish Civil War. Rejected for military service in World War II,
Orwell worked as a war correspondent for the BBC and the* Observer *until his death
from tuberculosis in 1950. Orwell's political liberalism and his precise language and
ability to tell vivid stories have made his essays the most widely anthologized in the
twentieth-century essay canon.*

*In "Shooting an Elephant," Orwell tells the story of how he, as an Indian Impe-
rial Police officer, killed a rambunctious but not enraged elephant to satisfy the
Burmese crowd daring him to prove himself. Most contemporary historians agree
that the shooting and Orwell's essay were both "overdetermined"—that is, caused
by multiple interacting psychological, ideological, and socioeconomic factors, which
the Context readings sample.*

In Moulmein, in lower Burma, I was hated by large numbers of people—the
only time in my life that I have been important enough for this to happen to me.
I was sub-divisional police officer of the town, and in an aimless, petty kind of
way anti-European feeling was very bitter. No one had the guts to raise a riot, but
if a European woman went through the bazaars alone somebody would probably
spit betel juice over her dress. As a police officer I was an obvious target and was
baited whenever it seemed safe to do so. When a nimble Burman tripped me up
on the football field and the referee (another Burman) looked the other way, the
crowd yelled with hideous laughter. This happened more than once. In the end
the sneering yellow faces of young men that met me everywhere, the insults
hooted after me when I was at a safe distance, got badly on my nerves. The young
Buddhist priests were the worst of all. There were several thousands of them in
the town and none of them seemed to have anything to do except stand on street
corners and jeer at Europeans.

All this was perplexing and upsetting. For at that time I had already made up
my mind that imperialism was an evil thing and the sooner I chucked up my job

and got out of it the better. Theoretically—and secretly, of course—I was all for the Burmese and all against their oppressors, the British. As for the job I was doing, I hated it more bitterly than I can perhaps make clear. In a job like that you see the dirty work of Empire at close quarters. The wretched prisoners huddling in the stinking cages of the lock-ups, the grey, cowed faces of the long-term convicts, the scarred buttocks of the men who had been flogged with bamboos—all these oppressed me with an intolerable sense of guilt. But I could get nothing into perspective. I was young and ill-educated and I had had to think out my problems in the utter silence that is imposed on every Englishman in the East. I did not even know that the British Empire is dying, still less did I know that it is a great deal better than the younger empires that are going to supplant it. All I knew was that I was stuck between my hatred of the empire I served and my rage against the evil-spirited little beasts who tried to make my job impossible. With one part of my mind I thought of the British Raj as an unbreakable tyranny, as something clamped down, *in saecula saeculorum*, upon the will of prostrate peoples: with another part I thought that the greatest joy in the world would be to drive a bayonet into a Buddhist priest's guts. Feelings like these are the normal by-products of imperialism; ask any Anglo-Indian official, if you can catch him off duty.

One day something happened which in a roundabout way was enlightening. It was a tiny incident in itself, but it gave me a better glimpse than I had had before of the real nature of imperialism—the real motives for which despotic governments act. Early one morning the sub-inspector at a police station the other end of the town rang me up on the 'phone and said that an elephant was ravaging the bazaar. Would I please come and do something about it? I did not know what I could do, but I wanted to see what was happening and I got on to a pony and started out. I took my rifle, an old .44 Winchester and much too small to kill an elephant, but I thought the noise might be useful *in terrorem*. Various Burmans stopped me on the way and told me about the elephant's doings. It was not, of course, a wild elephant, but a tame one which had gone "must." It had been chained up, as tame elephants always are when their attack of "must" is due, but on the previous night it had broken its chain and escaped. Its mahout, the only person who could manage it when it was in that state, had set out in pursuit, but had taken the wrong direction and was now twelve hours' journey away, and in the morning the elephant had suddenly reappeared in the town. The Burmese population had no weapons and were quite helpless against it. It had already destroyed somebody's bamboo hut, killed a cow and raided some fruit-stalls and devoured the stock; also it had met the municipal rubbish van and, when the driver jumped out and took to his heels, had turned the van over and inflicted violences upon it.

The Burmese sub-inspector and some Indian constables were waiting for me in the quarter where the elephant had been seen. It was a very poor quarter, a labyrinth of squalid bamboo huts, thatched with palm-leaf, winding all over a steep hillside. I remember that it was a cloudy, stuffy morning at the beginning of the rains. We began questioning the people as to where the elephant had gone and, as usual, failed to get any definite information. That is invariably the case in the East;

a story always sounds clear enough at a distance, but the nearer you get to the scene of events the vaguer it becomes. Some of the people said that the elephant had gone in one direction, some said that he had gone in another, some professed not even to have heard of any elephant. I had almost made up my mind that the whole story was a pack of lies, when we heard yells a little distance away. There was a loud, scandalized cry of "Go away, child! Go away this instant!" and an old woman with a switch in her hand came round the corner of a hut, violently shooing away a crowd of naked children. Some more women followed, clicking their tongues and exclaiming; evidently there was something that the children ought not to have seen. I rounded the hut and saw a man's dead body sprawling in the mud. He was an Indian, a black Dravidian coolie, almost naked, and he could not have been dead many minutes. The people said that the elephant had come suddenly upon him round the corner of the hut, caught him with its trunk, put its foot on his back and ground him into the earth. This was the rainy season and the ground was soft, and his face had scored a trench a foot deep and a couple of yards long. He was lying on his belly with arms crucified and head sharply twisted to one side. His face was coated with mud, the eyes wide open, the teeth bared and grinning with an expression of unendurable agony. (Never tell me, by the way, that the dead look peaceful. Most of the corpses I have seen looked devilish.) The friction of the great beast's foot had stripped the skin from his back as neatly as one skins a rabbit. As soon as I saw the dead man I sent an orderly to a friend's house nearby to borrow an elephant rifle. I had already sent back the pony, not wanting it to go mad with fright and throw me if it smelt the elephant.

The orderly came back in a few minutes with a rifle and five cartridges, and meanwhile some Burmans had arrived and told us that the elephant was in the paddy fields below, only a few hundred yards away. As I started forward practically the whole population of the quarter flocked out of the houses and followed me. They had seen the rifle and were all shouting excitedly that I was going to shoot the elephant. They had not shown much interest in the elephant when he was merely ravaging their homes, but it was different now that he was going to be shot. It was a bit of fun to them, as it would be to an English crowd; besides they wanted the meat. It made me vaguely uneasy. I had no intention of shooting the elephant—I had merely sent for the rifle to defend myself if necessary—and it is always unnerving to have a crowd following you. I marched down the hill, looking and feeling a fool, with the rifle over my shoulder and an ever-growing army of people jostling at my heels. At the bottom, when you got away from the huts, there was a metalled road and beyond that a miry waste of paddy fields a thousand yards across, not yet ploughed but soggy from the first rains and dotted with coarse grass. The elephant was standing eight yards from the road, his left side towards us. He took not the slightest notice of the crowd's approach. He was tearing up bunches of grass, beating them against his knees to clean them and stuffing them into his mouth.

I had halted on the road. As soon as I saw the elephant I knew with perfect certainty that I ought not to shoot him. It is a serious matter to shoot a

5

working elephant—it is comparable to destroying a huge and costly piece of machinery—and obviously one ought not to do it if it can possibly be avoided. And at that distance, peacefully eating, the elephant looked no more dangerous than a cow. I thought then and I think now that his attack of "must" was already passing off; in which case he would merely wander harmlessly about until the mahout came back and caught him. Moreover, I did not in the least want to shoot him. I decided that I would watch him for a little while to make sure that he did not turn savage again, and then go home.

But at that moment I glanced round at the crowd that had followed me. It was an immense crowd, two thousand at the least and growing every minute. It blocked the road for a long distance on either side. I looked at the sea of yellow faces above the garish clothes—faces all happy and excited over this bit of fun, all certain that the elephant was going to be shot. They were watching me as they would watch a conjurer about to perform a trick. They did not like me, but with the magical rifle in my hands I was momentarily worth watching. And suddenly I realized that I should have to shoot the elephant after all. The people expected it of me and I had got to do it; I could feel their two thousand wills pressing me forward, irresistibly. And it was at this moment, as I stood there with the rifle in my hands, that I first grasped the hollowness, the futility of the white man's dominion in the East. Here was I, the white man with his gun, standing in front of the unarmed native crowd—seemingly the leading actor of the piece; but in reality I was only an absurd puppet pushed to and fro by the will of those yellow faces behind. I perceived in this moment that when the white man turns tyrant it is his own freedom that he destroys. He becomes a sort of hollow, posing dummy, the conventionalized figure of a sahib. For it is the condition of his rule that he shall spend his life in trying to impress the "natives," and so in every crisis he has got to do what the "natives" expect of him. He wears a mask, and his face grows to fit it. I had got to shoot the elephant. I had committed myself to doing it when I sent for the rifle. A sahib has got to act like a sahib; he has got to appear resolute, to know his own mind and do definite things. To come all that way, rifle in hand, with two thousand people marching at my heels, and then to trail feebly away, having done nothing—no, that was impossible. The crowd would laugh at me. And my whole life, every white man's life in the East, was one long struggle not to be laughed at.

But I did not want to shoot the elephant. I watched him beating his bunch of grass against his knees, with that preoccupied grandmotherly air that elephants have. It seemed to me that it would be murder to shoot him. At that age I was not squeamish about killing animals, but I had never shot an elephant and never wanted to. (Somehow it always seems worse to kill a *large* animal.) Besides, there was the beast's owner to be considered. Alive, the elephant was worth at least a hundred pounds; dead, he would only be worth the value of his tusks, five pounds, possibly. But I had got to act quickly. I turned to some experienced-looking Burmans who had been there when we arrived, and asked them how the elephant had been behaving. They all said the same thing: he took no notice of you if you left him alone, but he might charge if you went too close to him.

It was perfectly clear to me what I ought to do. I ought to walk up to within, say, twenty-five yards of the elephant and test his behavior. If he charged, I could shoot; if he took no notice of me, it would be safe to leave him until the mahout came back. But also I knew that I was going to do no such thing. I was a poor shot with a rifle and the ground was soft mud into which one would sink at every step. If the elephant charged and I missed him, I should have about as much chance as a toad under a steam-roller. But even then I was not thinking particularly of my own skin, only of the watchful yellow faces behind. For at that moment, with the crowd watching me, I was not afraid in the ordinary sense, as I would have been if I had been alone. A white man mustn't be frightened in front of "natives"; and so, in general, he isn't frightened. The sole thought in my mind was that if anything went wrong those two thousand Burmans would see me pursued, caught, trampled on and reduced to a grinning corpse like that Indian up the hill. And if that happened it was quite probable that some of them would laugh. That would never do. There was only one alternative. I shoved the cartridges into the magazine and lay down on the road to get a better aim.

The crowd grew very still, and a deep, low, happy sigh, as of people who see the theatre curtain go up at last, breathed from innumerable throats. They were going to have their bit of fun after all. The rifle was a beautiful German thing with cross-hair sights. I did not then know that in shooting an elephant one would shoot to cut an imaginary bar running from ear-hole to ear-hole. I ought, therefore, as the elephant was sideways on, to have aimed straight at his ear-hole; actually I aimed several inches in front of this, thinking the brain would be further forward. 10

When I pulled the trigger I did not hear the bang or feel the kick — one never does when a shot goes home — but I heard the devilish roar of glee that went up from the crowd. In that instant, in too short a time, one would have thought, even for the bullet to get there, a mysterious, terrible change had come over the elephant. He neither stirred nor fell, but every line of his body had altered. He looked suddenly stricken, shrunken, immensely old, as though the frightful impact of the bullet had paralyzed him without knocking him down. At last, after what seemed a long time — it might have been five seconds, I dare say — he sagged flabbily to his knees. His mouth slobbered. An enormous senility seemed to have settled upon him. One could have imagined him thousands of years old. I fired again into the same spot. At the second shot he did not collapse but climbed with desperate slowness to his feet and stood weakly upright, with legs sagging and head drooping. I fired a third time. That was the shot that did for him. You could see the agony of it jolt his whole body and knock the last remnant of strength from his legs. But in falling he seemed for a moment to rise, for as his hind legs collapsed beneath him he seemed to tower upward like a huge rock toppling, his trunk reaching skywards like a tree. He trumpeted, for the first and only time. And then down he came, his belly towards me, with a crash that seemed to shake the ground even where I lay.

I got up. The Burmans were already racing past me across the mud. It was obvious that the elephant would never rise again, but he was not dead. He was breathing very rhythmically with long rattling gasps, his great mound of a side painfully rising and falling. His mouth was wide open—I could see far down into caverns of pale pink throat. I waited a long time for him to die, but his breathing did not weaken. Finally I fired my two remaining shots into the spot where I thought his heart must be. The thick blood welled out of him like red velvet, but still he did not die. His body did not even jerk when the shots hit him, the tortured breathing continued without a pause. He was dying, very slowly and in great agony, but in some world remote from me where not even a bullet could damage him further. I felt that I had got to put an end to that dreadful noise. It seemed dreadful to see the great beast lying there, powerless to move and yet powerless to die, and not even to be able to finish him. I sent back for my small rifle and poured shot after shot into his heart and down his throat. They seemed to make no impression. The tortured gasps continued as steadily as the ticking of a clock.

In the end I could not stand it any longer and went away. I heard later that it took him half an hour to die. Burmans were bringing dahs and baskets even before I left, and I was told they had stripped his body almost to the bones by the afternoon.

Afterwards, of course, there were endless discussions about the shooting of the elephant. The owner was furious, but he was only an Indian and could do nothing. Besides, legally I had done the right thing, for a mad elephant has to be killed, like a mad dog, if its owner fails to control it. Among the Europeans opinion was divided. The older men said I was right, the younger men said it was a damn shame to shoot an elephant for killing a coolie, because an elephant was worth more than any damn Coringhee coolie. And afterwards I was very glad that the coolie had been killed; it put me legally in the right and it gave me a sufficient pretext for shooting the elephant. I often wondered whether any of the others grasped that I had done it solely to avoid looking a fool.

CONTEXTS FOR "SHOOTING AN ELEPHANT"

Eric Arthur Blair at Police Training School, Mandalay, 1923. (Blair is standing third from left.)

RUDYARD KIPLING

The White Man's Burden

The ideology—the body of doctrine, myth, and symbol used by a movement, social class, or nation to justify its aims—of British imperialism found its voice in Rudyard Kipling, whose works include Barrack-Room Ballads *(1890, 1892) and the novel* Kim *(1901). Kipling's poem "Mandalay," expressing a retired British soldier's nostalgia for the romance of his days in Burma, was Orwell's favorite. Admitting that "Kipling is a jingo imperialist," Orwell defended the "good bad poet" for his "grip on reality." In the following excerpt from "The White Man's Burden," Kipling voices a complex ambivalence about colonial rule that the narrator of "Shooting an Elephant" shares.*

Take up the White Man's burden—
Send forth the best ye breed—

From Rudyard Kipling, "The White Man's Burden," *McClure's*, 12 February 1899.

Go, bind your sons to exile
        To serve your captives' need;
To wait, in heavy harness,   5
        On fluttered folk and wild—
Your new-caught sullen peoples,
        Half devil and half child.

Take up the White Man's burden—
        In patience to abide,   10
To veil the threat of terror
        And check the show of pride;
By open speech and simple,
        An hundred times made plain,
To seek another's profit
        And work another's gain.   15

JOHN KAYE

History of the Indian Mutiny of 1857–8

John Kaye, a historian of the British Empire, enumerates "differences" in terms of an imperialist ideology that leads him to advocate violent repression of the "other."

In all countries, and under all forms of government, the dangers which threaten the State, starting in the darkness, make headway towards success before they are clearly discerned by the rulers of the land. . . . The peculiarities of our Anglo-Indian Empire converted a probability into a certainty. Differences of race, differences of language, differences of religion, differences of customs, all indeed that could make a great antagonism of sympathies and of interests, severed the rulers and the ruled as with a veil of ignorance and obscurity. We could not see or hear with our own senses what was going on, and there was seldom any one to tell us. When by some accident the truth at last transpired, . . . much time was lost. . . . The great safeguard of sedition was to be found in the slow processes of departmental correspondence. . . . When prompt and effectual action was demanded, Routine called for pens and paper. A letter was written where a blow ought to have been struck.

From John Kaye, *History of the Indian Mutiny of 1857–8*, vol. I, ed. G. B. Malleson (London: 1898), 374.

ALOK RAI
Orwell and the Politics of Despair

Marxist historians explore the economic and political underpinnings of ideology. They ask who owns property, who threatens and who safeguards it, who employs whom, how workers are rewarded and regulated, how economic pressures affect ostensibly nonpolitical groups, and so on. In response to social upheaval and nationalist opposition to British imperialism in Burma, the British put certain reforms into place in 1922. Alok Rai explains how the Burmese monks reacted to those reforms.

By the time Orwell arrived in Burma traditional Burmese society had been crumbling under economic pressure for some time. The commercial cultivation of rice had increased several-fold since the opening of the Suez Canal in 1869, and this, coupled with the exploitation of Burmese oil and mineral resources, released forces which ensured that Burmese society was dangerously in flux. Moreover, apart from the influence of strictly economic processes, the British had antagonized the Buddhist clergy by setting up secular schools, thus depriving the monks of the basis of their traditional secular authority. The monks were, as a consequence, driven increasingly into oppositional, "nationalist" roles—a fact which might, perhaps, account for Orwell's desire, acknowledged in "Shooting an Elephant," to disembowel a Buddhist monk.

The death agony of the wounded elephant is a kind of extended reproach, a sudden and unexpected image of that colonial damage which can neither be undone nor decently, quickly, buried. "He was dying," Orwell notes, "very slowly and in great agony." The sympathetic suffering of the colonial officer is intensified by the fact that, unable as he is to undo the terrible violence which he has inflicted, he is unable also, with that violence which is his sole allotted part, to reach into "some world remote from me" where the elephant is slowly, accusingly, dying but "where not even a bullet could damage him further. . . . In the end I could not stand it any longer and went away."

STEPHEN SPENDER (1950)

His integrity consisted in his going through the worst aspects of everything he wrote about. Whether he was a down-and-out in Paris, or a police officer in Burma, or a volunteer among the anarchists on the Catalan front, or a patient in

---

From Alok Rai, *Orwell and the Politics of Despair* (Cambridge: Cambridge University Press, 1988), 58–59.

From Stephen Spender, "A Measure of Orwell," *New York Times Book Review*, 29 October 1950, 4.

one of the worst hospitals of Paris. The force of his writing is that it contains a maximum of lived experience and a minimum of literary inventiveness. Someone pointed out that he called his last novel *1984* because he knew that no one would accept it as true if he had called it *1948*; but to himself it was, in some grim and secret way, what he had experienced, 1948.

CHRISTOPHER SYKES (1950)

In his review of "Shooting an Elephant," British novelist and critic Christopher Sykes compares Orwell's moral subtlety to that of Shakespeare's character Hamlet, whose famous "To be, or not to be" soliloquy expresses the moral paralysis that results from his seeing too many conflicting sides of the question:

> Thus conscience does make cowards of us all,
> And thus the native hue of resolution
> Is sicklied o'er with the pale cast of thought,
> And enterprises of great pith and moment
> With this regard their currents turn awry,
> And lose the name of action.

Sykes relies on his readers to know these lines, and without quoting them, he writes as follows.

George Orwell's writing and character can be described by a somewhat overworked idea: he was extremely "Hamletish," not in the sense that he was a morbid brooder—he was never that—but in the deeper sense of being able to see both sides of many questions with equal and therefore puzzling sympathy. He was an essentially paradoxical man. He was a person who saw through prejudice, but was never rid of his own. He hated the use of un-thought-out political catchphrases, and yet he could use words such as "Left" and "reactionary" as though they contained precise meaning. He ridiculed the pretensions and affectations of people who regarded themselves as advanced thinkers, "the Pansy-Left" as he sometimes called them, but he never lost an absurd conviction that everyone on the opposite political side was basically mad or wicked. I believe he would rather have been killed than have committed any action in the least treacherous to the rights and liberties of artists, but his understanding of pictures and poetry was negligible. This saintly man regarded sanctity as rubbish.

From Christopher Sykes, "An Enigmatical Genius," *New Republic*, 4 December 1950, 20.

EDMUND WILSON (1951)

American critic Edmund Wilson, in his review of "Shooting an Elephant," says that Orwell is motivated to write as a way of analyzing his motives and their social consequences.

Shooting an Elephant and Other Essays, a posthumous collection of papers by George Orwell, contains miscellaneous pieces relating to various phases of this unconventional writer's life. The first two, "Shooting an Elephant" and "A Hanging," deal, like his novel *Burmese Days*, with Orwell's experience as an officer in the Indian Imperial Police. The first of these tells the story of his reluctantly and probably unwisely killing a runaway work elephant, because he knew that the natives expected it of him and that it was necessary in order to keep up the prestige of the British occupation. It is curious to compare this story with the hunting exploits celebrated by Hemingway. Orwell is interested not in the danger or in the victory over the brute, which he could not bear to watch dying, but in scrutinizing his own motives and deducing their social implications. The third sketch, "How the Poor Die," is an episode in the self-imposed pilgrimage, the submergence in the misery of modern life—described in *The Road to Wigan Pier* and *Down and Out in Paris and London*—by which, having resigned from the police, he attempted to expiate his years as an agent of imperial oppression. The rest of the essays deal mostly with the problems of the radical attitude that he was then compelled to develop and with the reflections to which he was led by the assignments of literary journalism by which he had to make a living.

ROBERT PEARCE

Orwell Now

According to one modern theory of historiography, historians are storytellers who simultaneously weave together three distinct levels of narrative: what certainly did happen, what probably or plausibly happened, and what might have happened. In order to create their stories, historians consult various kinds of historical data: official documents, public records, letters, diaries, autobiographies, and other primary sources. They also seek out connections among such sources. Robert Pearce, a reader in modern history at the University of St. Martin in Lancaster, England, offers three ways in which historians find Orwell's writing useful.

From Edmund Wilson, "Review," *New Yorker*, 13 January 1951, 76.

From Robert Pearce, "Orwell Now," *History Today*, October 1997, 4–6.

[W]hy are historians so interested in Orwell's works? One answer is that Orwell had an uncanny knack of being involved with important events and processes. He was simply *there*. He worked in the Raj, observing and experiencing what he believed to be the insidious corruption of both rulers and ruled inherent in imperialism. He was in the doss houses of Paris and London, and in the Wigan lodgings during the Depression, experiencing the seamy under-side of empire and the unacceptable face of capitalism. He also took up the sword against Fascism in Spain, and thereafter wielded a mighty pen against totalitarian rule in general. . . . Indeed he was a pioneer of the study of popular culture and thus of social history. In short, he was surely one of the most remarkably broad-sighted and acute historical witnesses of our country and our world in the first half of the twentieth century. . . .

There are two further reasons why historians admire Orwell. The first is that, by depicting a nightmare world in which the past is not studied, he showed the vital necessity for research far more convincingly than any historian has ever done. *Nineteen Eighty-Four* shows, above all, that the past must be investigated as fully and as objectively as possible. If it is not, and if we are dependent on our feeble memories, autocrats like Big Brother will dictate history to us to justify the current party line and cement their political domination. "Who controls the past," ran the Party slogan in Oceania, "controls the future: and who controls the present controls the past." It follows that history—the real study of the past—safeguards us against totalitarianism.

The final reason for Orwell's popularity is his "window-pane" writing. After a long apprenticeship of unceasing effort, he made himself into a brilliant prose stylist. He believed that what can be said can be said clearly, and with freshness and elegance as well. He was the man who made political writing into an art, in the process becoming the fiercest opponent of cant, jargon and mystification. To some, he is one of the great intellectual heroes of the twentieth century, a man of scrupulous intellectual honesty who fought a duel against lies. . . .

QUESTIONS FOR DISCUSSION AND WRITING

1. Think about a time when you had to make a tough choice—and act on it — in public. Write a narrative about this incident, revealing the conflicting desires and actions of the people involved and showing your attitude toward those you resisted. Exchange essays with your classmates and make some notes on the word choices through which other writers reveal their conflicting feelings and attitudes.

2. Since the events of September 11, 2001, much thought has been given to ways of identifying terrorists ("them") without compromising the civil liberties of others ("us"), especially people with Middle Eastern backgrounds who practice Islam. Identify from library and Internet sources some of the characteristics that distinguish

"them" (the terrorists) from "us" (peaceful citizens). What parallels can you draw between these people and Blair (Orwell) in Burma? For what reasons could you compare Blair with "them"? With "us"?

3. Considering Kipling's portrayal of the "White Man's Burden," look back at the passages in Orwell's "Shooting an Elephant" that show the narrator as an oppressor and as oppressed. For each passage, write a sentence that answers the question, Who oppresses whom, and why? Explain how you think Orwell's representation of the officer's role relates to Kipling's portrayal.

4. Consider the behavior of Blair (Orwell) in "Shooting an Elephant." Supporting your views with passages from the essay, explain whether, in John Kaye's words, "a blow ought to have been struck." What might have been the outcome had the Imperial Police officer not taken, again in Kaye's words, "prompt and effectual action"?

5. Turn to the excerpt from Alok Rai (p. 386), who (almost a century after John Kaye) suggests that the wounded elephant represents both the personal suffering of the colonial officer and the political death throes of colonial power. Make a three-column list with the headings "Elephant," "Officer," and "Colonialism." Beginning in the "Elephant" column, list the words and phrases Orwell uses to describe the elephant throughout the essay. Your list will be long. Now go back to the beginning of the essay and collect words and phrases describing the officer, placing them beside the "Elephant" terms to which you see either resemblances or differences. In what respects does the elephant/officer comparison work? In what respects does it break down? Finally, go back again to the beginning of the essay and collect words and phrases describing colonial power, writing resemblances and differences in column three. In what respects does the elephant/colonialism metaphor work? Break down?

LINDA SIMON

The Naked Source

Linda Simon (b. 1946) earned a doctorate in English and American literature from Brandeis University in 1983, and is currently associate professor of English at Skidmore College. She has written several biographical studies, including The Biography of Alice B. Toklas *(1977),* Of Virtue Rare: Margaret Beaufort, Matriarch of the House of Tudor *(1982),* Genuine Reality: A Life of William James *(1998), and* Dark Light: Electricity and Anxiety from the Telegraph to the X-Ray *(2004), making her an authority on the interpretation of primary data that underpins biographical and historical writing.*

"The Naked Source," originally published in the Michigan Quarterly Review *(1998), is a manifesto for revamping historical education. Primary sources—naked data—wait for us to interpret them and render them into coherent narratives by*

using our curiosity, imagination, intuition, and perseverance. History is more than stuff to learn for a test—it's a way of making sense of the world.

It is true that my students do not know history. That annals of the American past, as students tell it, are compressed into a compact chronicle: John Kennedy and Martin Luther King flourish just a breath away from FDR and Woodrow Wilson, who themselves come right on the heels of Jefferson and Lincoln. The far and distant past is more obscure still.

Some, because they are bright and inquisitive, have learned names, dates, and the titles of major events. But even these masters of Trivial Pursuit often betray their ignorance of a real sense of the past. Teachers all have favorite oneliners that point to an abyss in historical knowledge. Mine is: Sputnik *who?*

There is no debate here. Students do not know history. Students should learn history. There is less agreement about what they should know, why they should know it, and far less agreement about how they should pursue this study of the past.

When I ask my students why they need to know history, they reply earnestly: We need to learn history because those who do not know history are doomed to repeat the mistakes of the past. They have heard this somewhere, although no one can attribute the remark. And if they are told that George Santayana said it, they know not who Santayana was, although if you care to inform them they will dutifully record his name, dates (1863–1952), and the title of the work (*The Life of Reason*) in which the remark was made.

Is that so? I ask. What will not be repeated?   5

Inevitably they respond emotionally with the example of the Holocaust. Some have watched an episode of a PBS series. Some have seen the film *The Diary of Anne Frank.* Such genocide, they reply, will not be repeated because we know about it. Undaunted by examples of contemporary genocide, they remain firm in their conviction. Genocide, they maintain. And the Great Depression.

The Great Depression has made a big impact on the adolescent imagination. Given any work of literature written at any time during the 1930s, some students will explain it as a direct response to the Great Depression. Wasn't everyone depressed, after all? And aren't most serious works of literature grim, glum, dark, and deep. There you have it.

But now we know about the Great Depression. And so it will not, cannot, happen again.

I am not persuaded that requiring students to read Tacitus or Thucydides, Carl Becker or Francis Parkman, Samuel Eliot Morison or Arnold Toynbee will remedy this situation, although I believe that students, and we, might well benefit from these writers' illumination. What students lack, after all, is a sense of historical-mindedness, a sense that lives were lived in a context, a sense that events (the Battle of Barnet, for example) had consequences (if men were slain on the battlefield, they could not return to the farm), a sense that answers must generate questions, more questions, and still more subtle questions.

As it is, students learning history, especially in the early grades, are asked 10 prescribed questions and are given little opportunity to pursue their own inquiry or satisfy their own curiosity. The following questions are from current high school texts:

> Has the role of the present United Nations proved that the hopes and dreams of Woodrow Wilson were achievable? If so, how? If not, why?

> What were the advantages of an isolationist policy for the United States in the nineteenth century? Were there disadvantages?

Questions such as these perpetuate the idea that history is a body of knowledge on which students will be tested. The first question, in other words, asks students: Did you read the section in the text on the role of the United Nations? Did you read the section on Wilson's aims in proposing the League of Nations? Can you put these two sections together?

The second question asks students: Did you understand the term *isolationist*? Did you read the section on U.S. foreign relations in the nineteenth century? Can you summarize the debate that the authors of the textbook recount?

Questions such as these perpetuate the idea that history can uncover "facts" and "truth," that history is objective, and that students, if only they are diligent, can recover "right answers" about the past. Questions such as these ignore the role of historians. Even those bright students who can recall dates and events rarely can recall the name of a historian, much less any feeling about who this particular man or woman was. For many students, historical facts are things out there, like sea shells or autumn leaves, and it hardly matters who fetches them. The sea shell will look the same whether it is gathered in Charles Beard's pocket or Henri Pirenne's.

What students really need to learn, more than "history," is a sense of the historical method of inquiry. They need to know what it is that historians do and how they do it. They need to understand the role of imagination and intuition in the telling of histories, they need to practice, themselves, confronting sources, making judgments, and defending conclusions.

When I ask my freshmen what they think historians do, they usually offer 15 me some lofty phrases about "influencing the course of future events." But what I mean is: what do historians do after breakfast? That is a question few of my students can answer. And they are surprised when I read them the following passage by British historian A. L. Rowse from his book *The Use of History.*

> You might think that in order to learn history you need a library of books to begin with. Not at all: that only comes at the end. What you need at the beginning is a pair of stout walking shoes, a pencil and a notebook; perhaps I should add a good county guide covering the area you mean to explore . . . and a map of the country . . . that gives you field footpaths and a wealth of things of interest, marks churches and historic buildings and ruins, wayside crosses and holy wells, prehistoric camps and dykes, the sites of battles. When

you can't go for a walk, it is quite a good thing to study the map and plan where you would like to go. I am all in favor of the open-air approach to history; the most delightful and enjoyable, the most imaginative and informative, and—what not everybody understands—the best training.

It is the best training because it gives the would-be historian an encounter with the things that all historians look at and puzzle over: primary sources about the past. Historians look at battlefields and old buildings, read letters and diaries and documents, interview eyewitnesses or participants in events. And they ask questions of these sources. Gradually, after asking increasingly sophisticated questions, they make some sense, for themselves, of what once happened.

What professional historians do, however, is not what most students do when they set out to learn history within the confines of a course. Instead of putting students face to face with primary sources, instructors are more likely to send them to read what other people say about the past. Students begin with a library of books of secondary sources, or they may begin with a text. But that, cautions Rowse, should come "at the end." Instead of allowing students to gain experience in weighing evidence and making inferences, the structures of many courses encourage them to amass information. "I found it!" exclaim enthusiastic students. They need to ask, "But what does it mean?"

They need to ask that question of the kinds of sources that historians actually use. Instead of reading Morison's rendering of Columbus's voyages, for example, students might read Columbus himself: his journal, his letters to the Spanish monarchs. Then they can begin to decide for themselves what sort of man this was and what sort of experience he had. Morison—as excellent a historian as he is—comes later. With some sense of the sources that Morison used, students can begin to evaluate his contribution to history, to understand how he drew conclusions from the material available to him, to see how "facts" are augmented by historical intuition. They can begin to understand, too, that the reconstruction of the past is slow and painstaking work.

Courses that cover several decades or even millennia may give students a false impression of historical inquiry. Historians, like archaeologists or epidemiologists, move slowly through bumpy and perilous terrain. They are used to travelling for miles only to find themselves stranded at a dead end. Once, in the archives of Westminster Abbey, I eagerly awaited reading a fragment of a letter from King Henry VI (after all, that is how it was described in the card catalog), only to lift out of an envelope the corner of a page, about an inch across, with the faintest ink-mark the only evidence that it had, five hundred years before, been a letter at all.

Slowly the historian assembles pieces of the past. A household expense record might be the only artifact proving that a certain medieval woman existed. How much can be known about her? How much can be known by examining someone's checkbook today? Yet historians must make do with just such odd legacies: wills and land deeds, maps and drawings, family portraits or 20 photographs. Can you imagine the excitement over the discovery of a diary or a cache of letters? At last, a text. But the diary may prove a disappointment, a frustration. William James recorded the title of a book he may have been reading or the name of a visitor. Didn't he understand that a historian or biographer would need the deep, reflective ruminations of which we know he was more than capable?

Students have not had these experiences. When they are asked to write, they write *about* history. The research paper or the term paper seems to many of them another form of test—this time a take-home drawn out over weeks. Even if they have learned that "voice" and "audience" are important for a writer, they see history papers as different. They must be objective; they must learn proper footnoting and documentation. They must compile an impressive bibliography. Most important, they must find something out. The research paper produces nothing so much as anxiety, and the student often feels overwhelmed by the project.

They might, instead, be asked to write history as historians do it. They might be introduced to archives—in their college, in their community, in their state capital. They might be encouraged to interview people, and to interview them again and again until they begin to get the kind of information that will enlighten them about a particular time or event. They might be encouraged to read newspapers on microfilm or the bound volumes of old magazines that are yellowing in the basement of their local library. And then they might be asked to write in that most challenging form: the historical narrative.

"I can recall experiencing upon the completing of my first work of history," George Kennan wrote once, ". . . a moment of panic when the question suddenly presented itself to me: What is it that I have done here? Perhaps what I have written is not really history but rather some sort of novel, the product of my own imagination,—an imagination stimulated, inspired and informed, let us hope, by the documents I have been reading, but imagination nevertheless." Most historians share Kennan's reaction.

Students, of course, can never discover the boundary between "fact" and imaginative construction unless they have contact with primary sources. They cannot know where the historian has intervened to analyze the information he or she has discovered. "Most of the facts that you excavate," Morison wrote in "History as a Literary Art," "are dumb things; it is for you to make them speak by proper selection, arrangement, and emphasis." Morison suggested that beginning historians look to such writers as Sherwood Anderson and Henry James for examples of the kind of palpable description and intense characterization that can make literature—historical or fictional—come alive.

Students need to be persuaded that they are writing literature, not taking a 25 test, when they set out to be historians. Their writing needs to be read and evaluated not only for the facts that they have managed to compile, but for the sense of the past that they have conveyed. They need to discover that the past was not only battles and elections, Major Forces and Charismatic Leaders, but ordinary people, growing up, courting, dancing to a different beat, camping by a river that has long since dried up, lighting out for a territory that no longer exists. Except in the imagination of historians, as they confront the naked source, unaided.

QUESTIONS FOR DISCUSSION AND WRITING

1. Do you agree with Simon that "[t]here is no debate here. Students do not know history" (paragraph 3)? Consider your experience with history classes. Have you studied the past in the way that Simon recommends, or have you merely amassed dates and names to repeat back on tests?

2. Simon asserts that well-written history is a type of literature—not merely a compilation of facts. The historian actually interprets the primary data and makes up a plausible story. How does this image of the historian at work match your experience as a reader of history? How does Robert Pearce's interest in George Orwell's writings illustrate Simon's view of the historian at work? Would Simon consider Orwell a historian?

3. Write a historical narrative based on primary sources like those discussed by Simon. Investigate a person or an event from your local history—your family or hometown, for example. Use: diaries, old news reports, town records, archives, or photographs. You might also interview people who know about the subject of your study.

4. Explore an aspect of history that intrigues you by writing a two-part essay sequence. First, write a short essay in which you describe a period, an event, or a person that you would like to learn more about; also explain why this subject interests you. Include a list of questions about your subject that you would like to answer. Next, find several sources of information—history books, encyclopedias, videos, Web sites—and write a second, longer essay about your subject. Explain what you learned, what surprises you encountered, and how closely the historical record matches what you expected to find. Were you able to answer all of your questions? Why or why not? Where could you turn to find the answers?

WILL COUNTS

Central High School, Little Rock, Arkansas, September 4, 1957

QUESTIONS FOR DISCUSSION AND WRITING

1. The Associated Press has designated this photograph, taken by Will Counts in 1957, as one of the top one hundred photographs of the twentieth century. Read the picture as if you were innocent of its historical context or significance. What's going on? Where are these people going? Who is the most conspicuous figure? Can you read her expression? Why are so many of the people so angry? Why are helmeted soldiers present?

2. Now, read the picture again with this information in mind. Elizabeth Eckford (b. 1941) was one of nine black students, "The Little Rock Nine," designated by

the federal courts to desegregate Little Rock's Central High School in September 1957. Her family had no phone, so she didn't learn of a change of meeting place for the nine, and arrived alone at the school. Twice she tried to enter the school, surrounded by an angry mob chanting "Two, four, six, eight, we ain't gonna integrate," and was turned back by Arkansas National Guard troops, ordered by Governor Orval Faubus. Because all Little Rock high schools were closed the following year, Eckford had to complete her high school education by correspondence and night courses. In what ways, if any, does this information alter your understanding of the picture? You may use this as the springboard to a paper on some aspect of school desegregation, if you wish.

3. Time marches on, and history changes. Eckford (with the other eight) was awarded the prestigious Spingarn Medal by the National Association for the Advancement of Colored People in 1958 and the Congressional Gold Medal, presented by President Bill Clinton in 1999. In 1997 Hazel Bryan Massery (the girl immediately behind Eckford, with segregationist mouth wide open — the very picture of "hate assailing grace") apologized to Eckford at a reconciliation rally in Little Rock in 1997, and the two subsequently made speeches together. In what ways does this additional information affect your understanding of the changed racial climate in the United States, as represented by the actions of these two former adversaries, now allies?

LINKED READINGS: DIFFICULT IMAGES

SUSAN SONTAG
Looking at the Unbearable

Sontag (1933–2004) was charismatic, brilliant, and controversial; she was a reigning, glamorous intellectual in the United States, which generally distrusts intellectuals. Reared in Tucson and Los Angeles, she entered the University of Chicago at 16, married professor Philip Rieff at 17, bore a son (who later became his mother's editor at Farrar, Straus), and was divorced after eight years of graduate work at Harvard and Oxford. "Notes on Camp" (1964) presented a startling analysis of taste, something "so bad it's good"; Against Interpretation (1966) secured her international reputation as a literary critic. Sontag examined Illness as Metaphor (1978), derived from her fight against breast and uterine cancer, and revisited the subject in AIDS and Its Metaphors (1988); indeed, her death from leukemia may have been precipitated by the cancer treatment.

Her consistent criticism of American political involvement in Vietnam and Iraq is reflected in her commentary on "Looking at the Unbearable," written for Transforming Vision: Writers on Art (1994). Here she analyzes the "relentless, unforgiving" images of Francisco Goya's (1746–1828) series of 82 prints, the Disasters of

War (1810–1820), a bitter commentary on the atrocities both sides committed in the Spanish War of Independence (1808–1814) and Napoleon's invasion of Spain.

First of all, it's a series—though not a narrative. A sequence (of images, and their captions) to be read. In its original state, something like a book: loose pages, a portfolio. In reproduction, invariably a book.

Easy to imagine more plates. Indeed, to the eighty published in the first edition of 1863, in Madrid by the Royal Academy of San Fernando, later editions invariably include at least two more plates, clearly intended for the series but which were rediscovered after 1863.

Easy to imagine fewer plates, too. How few? How do they kill thee? Let me count the ways.

Would one image be enough? (*The Disaster of War?*) No.

How to look at, how to read, the unbearable?   5

The problem is how not to avert one's glance. How not to give way to the impulse to stop looking.

The problem is despair. For it is not simply that this happened: Zaragoza, Chinchón, Madrid (1808–13). It *is* happening: Vucovar, Mostar, Srebrenica, Stupni Do, Sarajevo (1991–).

What to do with the knowledge communicated, shared by these images. Emerson wrote: "He has seen but half the universe who has never been shown the house of pain." It seems optimistic now to think that the house of pain describes no more than half the universe.

The images are relentless, unforgiving. That is, they do not forgive us—who are merely being shown, but do not live in the house of pain. The images tell us we have no right not to pay attention to the crimes of this order which are taking place right now. And the captions—mingling the voices of the murderers, who think of themselves as warriors, and the lamenting artist-witness—mutter and wail.

Although Goya himself may not have written the captions (anyway, they're   10
not in his hand), it's thought that whoever did them took the phrases from the artist's notes.

They are meant—images and captions—to awaken, shock, rend. No reproduction in a book comes close in sheer unbearableness to the impact these images have in the original 1863 edition. Here in the words of some of the captions is what they show:

> One cannot look at this.
> This is bad.
> This is how it happened.
> This always happens.
> There is no one to help them.
> With or without reason.

He defends himself well.
He deserved it.
Bury them and keep quiet.
There was nothing to be done and he died.
What madness!
This is too much!
Why?
Nobody knows why.
Not in this case either.
This is worse.
Barbarians!
This is the absolute worst!
It will be the same.
All this and more.
The same thing elsewhere.
Perhaps they are of another breed.
I saw it.
And this too.
Truth has died.
This is the truth.

No se puede mirar. / Esto es malo. / Así sucedió. / Siempre sucede. / No hay quien los socorra. / Con razón o sin ella. / Se defiende bien. / Lo merecía. / Enterrar y callar. / Espiró sin remedio. / Que locura! / Fuerte cosa es! / Por qué? / No se puede saber por qué. / Tampoco. / Esto es peor. / Bárbaros! / Esto es lo peor! / Será lo mismo. / Tanto y mas. / Lo mismo en otras partes. / Si son de otro linage. / Yo lo ví. / Y esto también. / Murió la verdad. / Esto es lo verdadero.

FRANCISO GOYA

From The Disasters of War

Francisco Goya, **Qué hay que hacer más? (What more can be done?)**

Francisco Goya, **No hay quién los socorra. (There is no one to help them.)**

QUESTIONS FOR DISCUSSION AND WRITING

1. Sontag distinguishes between "a series" and "a narrative" (paragraph 1) in her discussion of the Goya sequence. How does this distinction lead into her discussion of "enough" images? Does the absence of narrative make the images more unbearable?

2. How does Sontag describe the relationship of the viewer to Goya's images?

3. Sontag employs a number of writing techniques, including repetition, rhetorical questions, incomplete sentences, and allusion. How do these techniques emphasize the "unbearableness" of Goya's images?

4. What does Sontag imply the reader "do with the knowledge communicated, shared by these images" (paragraph 8)?

H. BRUCE FRANKLIN

From Realism to Virtual Reality: Images of America's Wars

Franklin was born (1934) in Brooklyn, educated at Amherst (B.A.) and Stanford (Ph.D. in English). A radical Marxist, he was fired from a professorship at Stanford in 1972 for leading students to occupy the computer center and allegedly inciting violent protests against the bombing of Laos. Currently the John Cotton Dana Professor of English and American Studies at Rutgers University–Newark, Franklin has written and edited eighteen books, including War Stars: The Superweapon and the American Imagination *(1990) and* Vietnam and Other Fantasies *(2000).* Future Perfect: American Science Fiction of the Nineteenth Century *(1966; revised 1995) reflects another aspect of Franklin's pioneering scholarship, as do his studies of prison literature.*

In "From Realism to Virtual Reality," originally published in the Georgia Review *(Spring 1994), Franklin offers a history of the graphic depiction of warfare, beginning with early photographic images of the Civil War dead and culminating with the strict military control of media imagery during the 1990 Gulf War. Franklin argues that as the technology of devastation has grown, so have the means of perfecting images of propaganda.*

The Industrial Revolution was only about one century old when modern technological warfare burst upon the world in the U.S. Civil War. During that century human progress had already been manifested in the continually increasing deadliness and range of weapons, as well as in other potential military benefits of industrial capitalism. But it was the Civil War that actually demonstrated industrialism's ability to produce carnage and devastation on an unprecedented scale, thus foreshadowing a future more and more dominated by what we have come to call *technowar*. For the first time, immense armies had been transported by railroad, coordinated by telegraph, and equipped with an ever-evolving arsenal of mass-produced weapons designed by scientists and engineers. The new machines of war—such as the repeating rifle, the primitive machine gun, the submarine, and the steam-powered, ironclad warship—were being forged by other machines. Industrial organization was essential, therefore, not only in the factories where the technoweapons were manufactured but also on the battlefields and waters where these machines destroyed each other and slaughtered people.

Prior to the Civil War, visual images of America's wars were almost without exception expressions of romanticism and nationalism. Paintings, lithographs, woodcuts, and statues displayed a glorious saga of thrilling American heroism from the Revolution through the Mexican War. Drawing on their imagination, artists could picture action-filled scenes of heroic events, such as Emmanuel Leutze's 1851 painting *Washington Crossing the Delaware*.[1]

Literature, however, was the only art form capable of projecting the action of warfare as temporal flow and movement. Using words as a medium, writers had few limitations on how they chose to paint this action, and their visions had long covered a wide spectrum. One of the Civil War's most distinctively modern images was expressed by Herman Melville in his poem "A Utilitarian View of the Monitor's Fight." Melville sees the triumph of "plain mechanic power" placing war "Where War belongs — / Among the trades and artisans," depriving it of "passion": "all went on by crank, / Pivot, and screw, / And calculations of caloric." Since "warriors / Are now but operatives," he hopes that "War's made / Less grand than Peace."

The most profoundly deglamorizing images of that war, however, were produced not by literature but directly by technology itself. The industrial processes and scientific knowledge that created technowar had also brought forth a new means of perceiving its devastation. Industrial chemicals, manufactured metal plates, lenses, mirrors, bellows, and actuating mechanisms—all were essential to the new art and craft of photography. Thus the Civil War was the first truly modern war—both in how it was fought and in how it was imaged. The romantic images of warfare projected by earlier visual arts were now radically threatened by images of warfare introduced by photography.

Scores of commercial photographers, seeking authenticity and profits, 5 followed the Union armies into battle. Although evidently more than a million photographs of the Civil War were taken, hardly any show actual combat or other exciting action typical of the earlier paintings.[2] The photographers' need to stay close to their cumbersome horse-drawn laboratory wagons usually kept them from the thick of battle, and the collodion wet-plate process, which demanded long exposures, forced them to focus on scenes of stillness rather than action. Among all human subjects, those who stayed most perfectly still for the camera were the dead. Hence Civil War photography, dominated by images of death, inaugurated a grim, profoundly antiromantic realism.

Perhaps the most widely reproduced photo from the war, Timothy O'Sullivan's *A Harvest of Death, Gettysburg*, contains numerous corpses of Confederate soldiers, rotting after lying two days in the rain (see Figure 1). Stripped of their shoes and with their pockets turned inside out, the bodies stretch into the distance beyond the central corpse, whose mouth gapes gruesomely.

---

[1]See especially Alan Trachtenberg, *Reading American Photographs: Images as History, Mathew Brady to Walker Evans* (New York: Hill and Wang, 1989), p. 74; and William A. Frassanito, *Antietam: The Photographic Legacy of America's Bloodiest Day* (New York: Charles Scribner's Sons, 1978), pp. 27–28.

[2]William C. Davis, "Finding the Hidden Images of the Civil War," *Civil War Times Illustrated*, 21 (1982, #2), 9.

Figure 1. *A Harvest of Death, Gettysburg,* 1863, photograph by Timothy O'Sullivan, courtesy of George Eastman House.

The first of such new images of war were displayed for sale to the public by Mathew Brady at his Broadway gallery in October 1862. Brady entitled his show "The Dead of Antietam." *The New York Times* responded in an awed editorial:

> Mr. Brady has done something to bring home to us the terrible reality and earnestness of war. If he has not brought bodies and laid them in our dooryards and along the streets, he has done something very like it. At the door of his gallery hangs a little placard, "The Dead of Antietam." . . . You will see hushed, reverent groups standing around these weird copies of carnage, bending down to look in the pale faces of the dead, chained by the strange spell that dwells in dead men's eyes.[3]

Oliver Wendell Holmes went further in explicating the meaning of the exhibition, which gives "some conception of what a repulsive, brutal, sickening, hideous thing it is, this dashing together of two frantic mobs to which we give the name of armies."[4]

Nevertheless, three decades after the end of the Civil War the surging forces of militarism and imperialism were reimaging the conflict as a glorious episode in America's history. The disgust, shame, guilt, and deep national divisions that had followed this war—just like those a century later that followed the Vietnam

---

[3]"Brady's Photographs: Pictures of the Dead at Antietam," *The New York Times,* 20 October 1862.
[4]Oliver Wendell Holmes's "Doings of the Sunbeam," *Atlantic Monthly* (July 1863), p. 12.

War—were being buried under an avalanche of jingoist culture, the equivalent of contemporary Ramboism, even down to the cult of muscularism promulgated by Teddy Roosevelt. . . .

World War I, of course, generated millions of still photographs, many showing scenes at least as ghastly as the corpse-strewn battlefields of the Civil War, and now there was also authentic documentary film of live action. But for various reasons the most influential photographic images from World War I, though realistic in appearance, displayed not reality but fantasy. Filmmakers who wished to record actual combat were severely restricted by the various governments and military authorities. At the same time, powerful forces were making a historic discovery: the tremendous potential of movies for propaganda and for profits. This was the dawn of twentieth-century image-making.

In the United States the most important photographic images were movies 10 designed to inflame the nation, first to enter the war and then to support it. Probably the most influential was *The Battle Cry of Peace*, a 1915 smash hit that played a crucial role in rousing the public against Germany by showing realistic scenes of the invasion and devastation of America by a rapacious Germanic army. Once the U.S. entered the war, the American public got to view an endless series of feature movies, such as *To Hell with the Kaiser; The Kaiser, the Beast of Berlin*; and *The Claws of the Hun*—each outdoing its predecessors in picturing German bestiality. Erich von Stroheim's career began with his portrayal of the archetypal sadistic German officer in films like *The Unbeliever* and *Heart of Humanity*, where in his lust to rape innocent young women he murders anyone who gets in the way—even the crying baby of one intended victim. This genre is surveyed by Larry Wayne Ward, who describes the 1918 Warner Brothers hit *My Four Years in Germany*, which opens with a title card telling the audience they are seeing "Fact Not Fiction":

> After the brutal conquest of Belgium, German troops are shown slaughtering innocent refugees and tormenting prisoners of war. Near the end of the film one of the German officials boasts that "America Won't Fight," a title which dissolves into newsreel footage of President Wilson and marching American soldiers. Soon American troops are seen fighting their way across the European battlefields. As he bayonets another German soldier, a young American doughboy turns to his companions and says, "I promised Dad I'd get six."[5]

Before the end of World War I, the motion picture had already proved to be a more effective vehicle for romanticizing and popularizing war than the antebellum school of heroic painting that had been partly debunked by Civil War photography. Indeed, the audiences that thronged to *My Four Years in Germany* frequently burned effigies of the kaiser outside the theaters and in some cases turned into angry mobs that had to be dispersed by police.

---

[5]Larry Wayne Ward, *The Motion Picture Goes to War: The U.S. Government Film Effort during World War I* (Ann Arbor: UMI Research Press, 1985), pp. 55–56.

To restore the glamour of preindustrial war, however, it would take more than glorifying the men fighting on the ground or even the aviators supposedly dueling like medieval knights high above the battlefield. What was necessary to reverse Melville's "utilitarian" view of industrial warfare was the romanticizing of machines of war themselves.

The airplane was potentially an ideal vehicle for this romance. But photographic technology had to develop a bit further to bring home the thrills generated by destruction from the sky, because it needed to be seen *from* the sky, not from the ground where its reality was anything but glamorous. The central figure in America's romance with warplanes (as I have discussed at length elsewhere)[6] was Billy Mitchell, who also showed America and the world how to integrate media imagery with technowar.

In 1921, Mitchell staged a historic event by using bombers to sink captured German warships and turning the action into a media bonanza. His goal was to hit the American public with immediate, nationwide images of the airplane's triumph over the warship. The audacity of this enterprise in 1921 was remarkable. There were no satellites to relay images, and no television; in fact, the first experimental radio broadcast station had begun operation only in November 1920.

Back in 1919, Mitchell had given the young photographer George Goddard   15 his own laboratory where, with assistance from Eastman Kodak, Goddard developed high-resolution aerial photography. As soon as Mitchell won the opportunity to bomb the German ships, he put Goddard in command of a key unit: a team of aerial photographers provided with eighteen airplanes and a dirigible. Mitchell's instructions were unambiguous: "I want newsreels of those sinking ships in every theater in the country, just as soon as we can get 'em there." This demanded more than mere picture taking. With his flair for public relations, Mitchell explained to Goddard: "Most of all I need you to handle the newsreel and movie people. They're temperamental, and we've got to get all we can out of them."[7] Goddard had to solve unprecedented logistical problems, flying the film first to Langley Field and thence to Bolling Field for pickup by the newsreel people who would take it to New York for development and national distribution. The sinking of each ship, artfully filmed by relays of Goddard's planes, was screened the very next day in big-city theaters across the country.

This spectacular media coup implanted potent images of the warplane in the public mind, and Mitchell himself became an overnight national hero as millions watched the death of great warships on newsreel screens. Mitchell was a prophet. The battleship was doomed. The airplane would rule the world.

America was now much closer to the 1990 media conception of the Gulf War than to Melville's "Utilitarian View of the Monitor's Fight." Melville's vision of technowar as lacking "passion" was becoming antiquated, for what could be

---

[6]H. Bruce Franklin, *War Stars: The Superweapon and the American Imagination* (New York: Oxford University Press, 1988), chapter 15.

[7]Burke Davis, *The Billy Mitchell Affair* (New York: Random House, 1967), p. 16.

more thrilling—even erotic—than aerial war machines? The evidence is strewn throughout modern America: the warplane models assembled by millions of boys and young men during World War II; the thousands of warplane magazines and books filled with glossy photographs that some find as stimulating as those in "men's" magazines; and Hollywood's own warplane romances, such as *Top Gun*—one of the most popular movies of the 1980s—or *Strategic Air Command*, in which Jimmy Stewart's response to his first sight of a B-47 nuclear bomber is, "She's the most beautiful thing I've ever seen in my life."

One of the warplane's great advantages as a vehicle of romance is its distance from its victims. From the aircraft's perspective, even the most grotesque slaughter it inflicts is sufficiently removed so that it can be imaged aesthetically. The aesthetics of aerial bombing in World War II were prefigured in 1937 by Mussolini's son Vittorio, whose ecstasy about his own experience bombing undefended Ethiopian villages was expressed in his image of his victims "bursting out like a rose after I had landed a bomb in the middle of them."[8] These aesthetics were consummated at the end of World War II by the mushroom clouds that rose over Hiroshima and Nagasaki. . . .

Pictures of bomb patterns were not, of course, the most influential American photographic image-making in World War II. The still photos published in *Life* [magazine] alone could be the subject of several dissertations, and World War II feature movies about strategic bombing have been discussed at length by myself and many others. Indeed, in 1945 one might have wondered how the camera could possibly play a more important role in war.

The answer came in Vietnam, the first war to be televised directly into tens of millions of homes.[9] Television's glimpses of the war's reality were so horrendous and so influential that these images have been scapegoated as one of the main causes of the United States' defeat. Indeed, the Civil War still photographs of corpses seem innocuous when compared to the Vietnam War's on-screen killings, as well as live-action footage of the bulldozing of human carcasses into mass graves, the napalming of children, and the ravaging of villages by American soldiers. . . .

One of the most influential and enduring single images from the Vietnam War—certainly the most contested—exploded into the consciousness of millions of Americans in February 1968 when they actually watched, within the comfort of their own homes, as the chief of the Saigon national police executed a manacled NLF[10] prisoner. In a perfectly framed sequence, the notorious General Nguyen Ngoc Loan unholsters a snub-nosed revolver and places its muzzle to the

20

---

[8]*Voli sulle ambe* (Florence, 1937), a book Vittorio Mussolini wrote to convince Italian boys they should all try war, "the most beautiful and complete of all sports." Quoted by Denis Mack Smith, *Mussolini's Roman Empire* (New York: Viking, 1976), p. 75.

[9]When the Korean War began in mid-1950, there were fewer than ten million television sets in the United States. Americans' principal visual images of that war came from newsreels shown before feature films in movie theaters and from still photos in magazines.

[10]The National Liberation Front opposed the government of South Vietnam because it was allied with the North Vietnamese. [Editors' note.]

Figure 2. General Nguyen Ngoc Loan, head of South Vietnam's police and intelligence, executing a prisoner: 1968 photograph by Eddie Adams—AP/Wide World Photos.

prisoner's right temple. The prisoner's head jolts, a sudden spurt of blood gushes straight out of his right temple, and he collapses in death. The next morning, newspaper readers were confronted with AP [Associated Press] photographer Eddie Adams' potent stills of the execution (see Figure 2). The grim ironies of the scene were accentuated by the cultural significance of the weapon itself: a revolver, a somewhat archaic handgun, symbolic of the American West.

Precisely one decade later this image, with the roles now reversed, was transformed into the dominant metaphor of a Hollywood production presenting a new version of the Vietnam War: *The Deer Hunter*. This lavishly financed movie, which the New York Film Critics' Circle designated the best English-language film of 1978 and which received four Academy Awards, including Best Picture of 1978, succeeded not only in radically reimaging the war but in transforming prisoners of war (POWs) into central symbols of American manhood for the 1980s and 1990s.

The manipulation of familiar images—some already accruing symbolic power—was blatant, though most critics at the time seemed oblivious to it. The basic technique was to take images of the war that had become deeply embedded in America's consciousness and transform them into their opposites. For example, in the film's first scene in Vietnam, a uniformed soldier throws a grenade into an underground village shelter harboring women and children, and then with his automatic rifle mows down a woman and her baby. Although the scene resembles the familiar TV sequence of GIs in Vietnamese villages (as well as *Life*'s photographs of the My Lai massacre), the soldier turns out to be not American but North Vietnamese. In turn he is killed by a lone guerrilla—who is not a Viet

Figure 3. In *The Deer Hunter* (1978), General Loan's revolver metamorphoses into a North Vietnamese revolver,
and his NLF prisoner is replaced by South Vietnamese and
U.S. prisoners forced to play Russian roulette.

Cong but our Special Forces hero, played by Robert DeNiro. Later, when two
men plummet from a helicopter, the images replicate a familiar telephotographic
sequence showing an NLF prisoner being pushed from a helicopter to make
other prisoners talk;[11] but the falling men in the movie are American POWs attempting to escape from their murderous North Vietnamese captors.

The structuring metaphor of the film is the Russian roulette that the sadistic
Asian Communists force their prisoners to play. The crucial torture scene consists of sequence after sequence of images replicating and replacing the infamous
killing of the NLF prisoner by General Nguyen Ngoc Loan. Prisoner after prisoner is hauled out of the tiger cages (which also serve as a substitute image for the
tiger cages of the Saigon government) and then forced by the demonic North
Vietnamese officer in charge (who always stands to the prisoner's right, our left)
to place a revolver to his own right temple. Then the image is framed to eliminate
the connection between the prisoner's body and the arm holding the revolver,
thus bringing the image closer to the famous execution image (see Figure 3). One
sequence even replicates the blood spurting out of the victim's right temple. . . .

Toward the end of the 1980s, however, the infamous execution got manipu-   25
lated incredibly further, actually shifting the role of the most heartless shooter
(originally a South Vietnamese official) from the Vietnamese Communists to the
photographers themselves! For example, the cover story of the November 1988
issue of the popular comic book *The 'Nam* portrays the photojournalists, both
still photographers and TV cameramen, as the real enemies because they had

[11]"How Helicopter Dumped a Viet Captive to Death," *Chicago Sun-Times*, 29 November 1969;
"Death of a Prisoner," *San Francisco Chronicle*, 29 November 1969.

Figure 4. Cover story of the November 1988 issue of
The 'Nam, glorifying General Nguyen Ngoc Loan
and making the photographer into the villain.

placed the image on the "front page of every newspaper in the states!" The cover
literally reverses the original image by showing the execution scene from a position behind the participants (Figure 4). This offers a frontal view of the photographer, whose deadly camera conceals his face and occupies the exact center of
the picture. The prisoner appears merely as an arm, shoulder, and sliver of a body
on the left. The only face shown belongs to the chief of the security police, who
displays the righteous—even heroic—indignation that has led him to carry out
this justifiable revenge against the treacherous actions of the "Viet Cong" pictured in the story. The climactic image (Figure 5) is a full page in which the execution scene appears as a reflection in the gigantic lens of the camera above the
leering mouth of the photographer, from which comes a bubble with his greedy
words, "Keep shooting! Just keep shooting!" "Shooting" a picture here has become
synonymous with murder and treason. In the next panel, two GIs register their
shock—not at the execution, but at a TV cameraman focusing on the dead body:

"Front page of every newspaper in the states!"
"Geez . . ."

Figure 5. *The 'Nam* images the photographer as the shooter—and the camera as the most destructive weapon.

One can hardly imagine a more complete reversal of the acclaim accorded to Civil War photographers for bringing the reality of war and death home to the American people.

The logic of this comic-book militarism, put into practice for each of America's wars since Vietnam, is inescapable: photographers must be allowed to image for the public only what the military deems suitable. Nonmilitary photographers and all journalists were simply banished from the entire war zone during the 1983 invasion of Grenada. Partly as a result of this treatment, the major media accepted a pool system for the 1989 invasion of Panama—and meekly went along with the military's keeping even these selected journalists confined to a U.S. base throughout most of the conflict. (A European reporter who attempted to report directly from the scene was actually shot to death when the military unit sent to arrest him became involved in "friendly fire" with another group of U.S. soldiers.)

The almost complete absence of photographic images was quite convenient for the Grenada and Panama invasions, which were carried out so swiftly and with such minimal military risk that they required no Congressional or public endorsement. And for the first several days after U.S. troops had been dispatched to confront Iraq in August 1990, Secretary of Defense Dick Cheney refused to allow journalists to accompany them. The Pentagon seemed to be operating under the belief that photographic and televised images had helped bring about the U.S. defeat in Vietnam. But for the Gulf War, with its long buildup, its potential for significant casualties, and its intended international and domestic political purposes, *some* effective images proved to be essential.

To control these images, the U.S. government set up pools of selected reporters and photographers, confined them to certain locations, required them to have military escorts when gathering news, established stringent guidelines limiting what could be reported or photographed, and subjected all written copy, photographs, and videotape to strict censorship.[12] Most of those admitted to the pools, it is interesting to note, represented the very newspapers and TV networks that were simultaneously mounting a major campaign to build support for the war. Journalists were forced to depend on military briefings, where they were often fed deliberately falsified information. Immediately after the ground offensive began, all press briefings and pool reports were indefinitely suspended. In a most revealing negation of the achievement of Civil War photography, with its shocking disclosure of the reality of death, the Pentagon banned the press entirely from Dover Air Force Base during the arrival of the bodies of those killed in the war. Responding to an ACLU legal argument that it was attempting to shield the public from disturbing images, the Pentagon replied that it was merely protecting the privacy of grieving relatives.[13]

Although the media were largely denied access to the battlefields, the Gulf War nevertheless gained the reputation of the first "real-time" television war, and the images projected into American homes helped to incite the most passionate war fever since World War II. These screened images ranged from the most traditional to the most innovative modes of picturing America's wars. Even the antiquated icon of the heroic commanding general, missing for about forty years, was given new life. Although hardly as striking a figure as the commander in Leutze's *Washington Crossing the Delaware* or the posed picture of General Douglas MacArthur returning to the Philippines during World War II, a public idol took shape in the corpulent form of General Norman Schwarzkopf in his fatigues, boots, and jaunty cap.

But perhaps the most potent images combined techniques pioneered by Billy   30
Mitchell with General Peckem's quest for aerial photos of perfect bomb patterns, the medium of television, and the technological capabilities of the weapons themselves. After all, since one of the main goals of the warmakers was to create the impression of a "clean" technowar—almost devoid of human suffering and death, conducted with surgical precision by wondrous mechanisms—why not project the war from the point of view of the weapons? And so the most thrilling images were transmitted directly by the laser-guidance systems of missiles and by those brilliant creations, "smart" bombs. Fascinated and excited, tens of millions of Americans stared at their

---

[12]Everette E. Dennis et al., *The Media at War: The Press and the Persian Gulf Conflict* (New York: Gannett Foundation, 1991), pp. 17–18.

[13]Dennis, pp. 21–22.

Figure 6. Technowar triumphs in TV sequence of a smart bomb destroying an Iraqi building.

screens, sharing the experience of these missiles and bombs unerringly guided by the wonders of American technology to a target identified by a narrator as an important military installation. The generation raised in video arcades and on Nintendo could hardly be more satisfied. The target got closer and closer, larger and larger (Figure 6). And then everything ended with the explosion. There were no bloated human bodies, as in the photographs of the battlefields of Antietam and Gettysburg—and none of the agony of the burned and wounded glimpsed on television relays from Vietnam. There was just nothing at all. In this magnificent triumph of technowar, America's images of its wars had seemingly reached perfection.

QUESTIONS FOR DISCUSSION AND WRITING

1. Franklin writes that "the Civil War was the first truly modern war—both in how it was fought and in how it was imaged" (paragraph 4). How does this opening point provide the basis for his subsequent discussion?

2. How does Franklin characterize the images of war produced during the two world wars? What part does this discussion play in his overall argument?

3. What seems to be Franklin's attitude toward the images of the Vietnam War that were broadcast on television in the 1960s? In what ways were these images later manipulated, according to Franklin, and how does he characterize these manipulations?

4. Franklin implicitly argues that the photographs taken during the Civil War possessed a reality that was absent from the media images of the Gulf War. How does Franklin develop this argument? Does he convince you of his views? Apply his analysis to contemporary war photography of Afghanistan, Iraq, Lebanon, and elsewhere.

BRIEF TAKES ON WAR AND PEACE: DIARIES AND MEMOIRS

The diary excerpts from Walt Whitman, Mary Chesnut, and Anne Frank, along with Art Spiegelman's graphic depiction of the same scene Frank describes, represent some of the materials historians use to interpret events of the past. Such accounts humanize official reports, statistics, records of births and deaths, newspaper stories, and authorized histories. Every account is an interpretation, first by the author and then by those who edit and read the authors' published diaries. As you read these and other historical documents, you will have your own interpretation—just as historians do—formed by a mixture of knowledge, inference, and analogy with what you understand about comparable events, and perhaps by ideology, political agenda, and wishful thinking.

WALT WHITMAN

A Night Battle

Whitman (1819–1892), nineteenth-century America's premier poet, celebrated the common people in Leaves of Grass *(1855) and "Song of Myself" (1881). Whitman served as a volunteer nurse in the Civil War, tending both Northern and Southern troops in hospitals in Washington, D.C., during which time he kept notes, including "A Night Battle."*

But it was the tug of Saturday evening, and through the night and Sunday morning, I wanted to make a special note of. It was largely in the woods, and quite a general engagement. The night was very pleasant, at times the moon shining out full and clear, all Nature so calm in itself, the early summer grass so rich, and foliage of the trees—yet there the battle raging, and many good fellows lying helpless, with new accessions to them, and every minute amid the rattle of muskets and crash of cannon (for there was an artillery contest too) the red life-blood oozing out from heads or trunks or limbs upon that green and dew-cool grass. Patches of the woods take fire, and several of the wounded, unable to move, are consumed—quite large spaces are swept over, burning the dead also—some of the men have their hair and beards singed—some, burns on their faces and hands—others holes burnt in their clothing. The flashes of fire from the cannon, the quick flaring flames and smoke, and the immense roar—the musketry so general, the light nearly bright enough for each side to see the other—the crashing, tramping of men—the yelling—close quarters—we hear the secesh yells—our men cheer loudly back, especially if Hooker is in sight—hand-to-hand conflicts, each side stands up to it, brave, determined as demons, they often charge upon us—a thousand deeds are done, worth to write newer greater poems on—

and still the woods on fire—still many are not only scorched—too many, unable to move, are burned to death.

Then the camps of the wounded—O heavens, what scene is this?—is this indeed *humanity*—these butchers' shambles? There are several of them. There they lie, in the largest, in an open space in the woods, from 200 to 300 poor fellows—the groans and screams—the odor of blood, mixed with the fresh scent of the night, the grass, the trees—that slaughterhouse! O well is it their mothers, their sisters cannot see them—cannot conceive, and never conceived, these things. One man is shot by a shell, both in the arm and leg—both are amputated—there lie the rejected members. Some have their legs blown off—some bullets through the breast—some indescribably horrid wounds in the face or head, all mutilated, sickening, torn, gouged out—some in the abdomen—some mere boys—many rebels, badly hurt—they take their regular turns with the rest, just the same as any—the surgeons use them just the same. Such is the camp of the wounded—such a fragment, a reflection afar off of the bloody scene—while over all the clear, large moon comes out at times softly, quietly shining. Amid the woods, that scene of flitting souls—amid the crack and crash and yelling sounds—the impalpable perfume of the woods—and yet the pungent, stifling smoke—the radiance of the moon, looking from heaven at intervals so placid—the sky so heavenly—the clear-obscure up there, those buoyant upper oceans—a few large placid stars beyond, coming silently and languidly out, and then disappearing—the melancholy, draperied night above, around.

MARY CHESNUT

Slavery a Curse to Any Land

"There is no slave after all like a wife," wrote Chesnut, wife of U.S. senator and plantation owner James Chesnut. Her mammoth, novelistic diary, Mary Chesnut's Civil War *(1981), provides an intimate, passionate account of the impact, devastating yet democratizing, of the Civil War on families, slaves, soldiers, farmers, and the Southern aristocracy.*

MARCH 18, 1861

I wonder if it be a sin to think slavery a curse to any land. Sumner said not one word of this hated institution which is not true. Men and women are punished when their masters and mistresses are brutes and not when they do wrong—and then we live surrounded by prostitutes. An abandoned woman is sent out of any decent house elsewhere. Who thinks any worse of a negro or mulatto woman for being a thing we can't name? God forgive us, but ours is a *monstrous* system and wrong and iniquity. Perhaps the rest of the world is as bad—this *only* I see. Like the patriarchs of old our men live all in one house with their wives and their concubines, and the mulattoes one sees in every family exactly resemble the white children—and every lady tells you who is the father of all the mulatto children in everybody's household, but those in her own she seems to think drop from the clouds, or pretends so to think. Good women we have, *but* they talk of all *nastiness*—tho' they never do wrong, they talk day and night of [*erasures illegible save for the words* "all unconsciousness"] my disgust sometimes is boiling over— but they are, I believe, in conduct the purest women God ever made. Thank God for my countrywomen—alas for the men! No worse than men everywhere, but the lower their mistresses, the more degraded they must be.

My mother-in-law told me when I was first married not to send my female servants in the street on errands. Then they were tempted, led astray. . . .

ANNE FRANK

We Live in a Paradise Compared to the Jews Who Aren't in Hiding

"I want to go on living after my death. And therefore I am grateful to God for giving me this gift . . . of expressing all that is in me," wrote Anne Frank (1929–1945), the Holocaust's most distinguished diarist. Her family's hiding place in the secret annex above her father's pharmaceutical office in Amsterdam sheltered them from July 1942 through August 1944, when they were betrayed and sent to Auschwitz, then to Bergen-Belsen concentration camp; there the entire family, except Anne's father, perished.

SUNDAY, MAY 2, 1943

When I think about our lives here, I usually come to the conclusion that we live in a paradise compared to the Jews who aren't in hiding. All the same, later on, when everything has returned to normal, I'll probably wonder how we, who always lived in such comfortable circumstances, could have "sunk" so low. With respect to manner, I mean. For example, the same oilcloth has covered the dining table ever since we've been here. After so much use, it's hardly what you'd call spotless. I do my best to clean it, but since the dishcloth was also purchased before we went into hiding and consists of more holes than cloth, it's a thankless task. The van Daans have been sleeping all winter long on the same flannel sheet, which can't be washed because detergent is rationed and in short supply. Besides, it's of such poor quality that it's practically useless. Father is walking around in frayed trousers, and his tie is also showing signs of wear and tear. Mama's corset snapped today and is beyond repair, while Margot is wearing a bra that's two sizes too small. Mother and Margot have shared the same three undershirts the entire winter, and mine are so small they don't even cover my stomach. These are all things that can be overcome, but I sometimes wonder: how can we, whose every possession, from my underpants to Father's shaving brush, is so old and worn, ever hope to regain the position we had before the war?

SUNDAY, MAY 2, 1943

Mr. van Daan. In the opinion of us all, this revered gentleman has great insight into politics. Nevertheless, he predicts we'll have to stay here until the end of '43. That's a very long time, and yet it's possible to hold out until then. But who can assure us that this war, which has caused nothing but pain and sorrow, will then be over? And that nothing will have happened to us and our helpers long before that time? No one! That's why each and every day is filled with tension. Expectation and hope generate tension, as does fear—for example, when we hear a noise inside or outside the house, when the guns go off or when we read new "proclamations" in the paper, since we're afraid our helpers might be forced to go into hiding themselves sometime. These days everyone is talking about having to hide. We don't know how many people are actually in hiding; of course, the number is relatively small compared to the general population, but later on we'll no doubt be astonished at how many good people in Holland were willing to take Jews and Christians, with or without money, into their homes. There're also an unbelievable number of people with false identity papers.

ART SPIEGELMAN

From Maus

For biography, see p. 139.

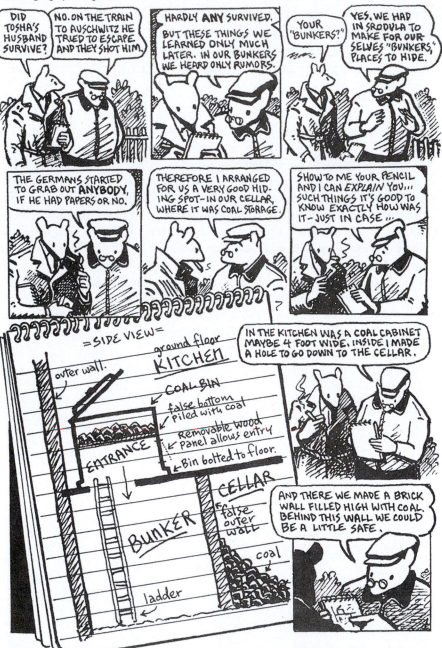

CHAPTER 6

Society and Politics:
Human Rights, Social Class

MAXINE HONG KINGSTON
No Name Woman

Maxine Hong Kingston (b. 1940) attended the University of California at Berkeley (B.A., 1962) and then taught school in Hawaii as she pursued her writing career. Her alma mater designated her a Chancellor's Distinguished Professor (1990), and the state of Hawaii named her a National Treasure. Her first book, The Woman Warrior: Memoir of a Girlhood among Ghosts *(1976), received the National Book Critics Circle Award and became instantly popular and widely taught. Kingston's other works include* China Men *(1980), the novel* Tripmaster Monkey: His Fake Book *(1989), and* The Fifth Book of Peace *(2003). In these works she mixes autobiography and fiction, history and fantasy. She explores the influence of cultural stories, both from China, where her father was a scholar and her mother was a doctor, and from Stockton, California, where her immigrant parents ran a laundry business.*

"No Name Woman" is the opening chapter of The Woman Warrior. *It was originally published as "The Death of Precious Only Daughter: All about Adultery and the Fate of Girl Babies in China" in* Viva *(January 1975). Kingston tells of No Name Aunt, who commited suicide in 1924 in China, after her village neighbors destroyed her house and beat her for becoming pregnant out of wedlock. Kingston's mother forbids her to tell this horrifying and (to her family) shameful story, but Kingston views her own silence as participation in her aunt's punishment. Her storytelling thus becomes a way both to atone to her aunt and to reinterpret a legacy of disgrace as a tale of bravery. It also becomes a means of understanding the author and her culture.*

"You must not tell anyone," my mother said, "what I am about to tell you. In China your father had a sister who killed herself. She jumped into the family well. We say that your father has all brothers because it is as if she had never been born.

"In 1924 just a few days after our village celebrated seventeen hurry-up weddings—to make sure that every young man who went 'out on the road' would responsibly come home—your father and his brothers and your grandfather and his brothers and your aunt's new husband sailed for America, the Gold Mountain. It was your grandfather's last trip. Those lucky enough to get contracts waved goodbye from the decks. They fed and guarded the stowaways and helped them off in Cuba, New York, Bali, Hawaii. 'We'll meet in California next year,' they said. All of them sent money home.

"I remember looking at your aunt one day when she and I were dressing; I had not noticed before that she had such a protruding melon of a stomach. But I did not think, 'She's pregnant,' until she began to look like other pregnant women, her shirt pulling and the white tops of her black pants showing. She could not have been pregnant, you see, because her husband had been gone for years. No one said anything. We did not discuss it. In early summer she was ready to have the child, long after the time when it could have been possible.

"The village had also been counting. On the night the baby was to be born the villagers raided our house. Some were crying. Like a great saw, teeth strung with lights, files of people walked zigzag across our land, tearing the rice. Their lanterns doubled in the disturbed black water, which drained away through the broken bunds. As the villagers closed in, we could see that some of them, probably men and women we knew well, wore white masks. The people with long hair hung it over their faces. Women with short hair made it stand up on end. Some had tied white bands around their foreheads, arms, and legs.

"At first they threw mud and rocks at the house. Then they threw eggs and   5
began slaughtering our stock. We could hear the animals scream their deaths—the roosters, the pigs, a last great roar from the ox. Familiar wild heads flared in our night windows; the villagers encircled us. Some of the faces stopped to peer at us, their eyes rushing like searchlights. The hands flattened against the panes, framed heads, and left red prints.

"The villagers broke in the front and the back doors at the same time, even though we had not locked the doors against them. Their knives dripped with the blood of our animals. They smeared blood on the doors and walls. One woman swung a chicken, whose throat she had slit, splattering blood in red arcs about her. We stood together in the middle of our house, in the family hall with the pictures and tables of the ancestors around us, and looked straight ahead.

"At that time the house had only two wings. When the men came back, we would build two more to enclose our courtyard and a third one to begin a second courtyard. The villagers pushed through both wings, even your grandparents' rooms, to find your aunt's, which was also mine until the men returned. From this room a new wing for one of the younger families would grow. They ripped up her clothes and shoes and broke her combs, grinding them underfoot. They tore her work from the loom. They scattered the cooking fire and rolled the new weaving in it. We could hear them in the kitchen breaking our bowls and banging the pots. They overturned the great waist-high earthenware jugs; duck eggs, pickled fruits, vegetables burst out and mixed in acrid torrents. The old woman from the next field swept a broom through the air and loosed the spirits-of-the-broom over our heads. 'Pig.' 'Ghost.' 'Pig,' they sobbed and scolded while they ruined our house.

"When they left, they took sugar and oranges to bless themselves. They cut pieces from the dead animals. Some of them took bowls that were not broken and clothes that were not torn. Afterward we swept up the rice and sewed it back up into sacks. But the smells from the spilled preserves lasted. Your aunt gave birth in the pigsty that night. The next morning when I went for the water, I found her and the baby plugging up the family well.

"Don't let your father know that I told you. He denies her. Now that you have started to menstruate, what happened to her could happen to you. Don't humiliate us. You wouldn't like to be forgotten as if you had never been born. The villagers are watchful."

Whenever she had to warn us about life, my mother told stories that ran like 10 this one, a story to grow up on. She tested our strength to establish realities. Those in the emigrant generations who could not reassert brute survival died young and far from home. Those of us in the first American generations have had to figure out how the invisible world the emigrants built around our childhoods fits in solid America.

The emigrants confused the gods by diverting their curses, misleading them with crooked streets and false names. They must try to confuse their offspring as well, who, I suppose, threaten them in similar ways—always trying to get things straight, always trying to name the unspeakable. The Chinese I know hide their names; sojourners take new names when their lives change and guard their real names with silence.

Chinese-Americans, when you try to understand what things in you are Chinese, how do you separate what is peculiar to childhood, to poverty, insanities, one family, your mother who marked your growing with stories, from what is Chinese? What is Chinese tradition and what is the movies?

If I want to learn what clothes my aunt wore, whether flashy or ordinary, I would have to begin, "Remember Father's drowned-in-the-well sister?" I cannot ask that. My mother has told me once and for all the useful parts. She will add nothing unless powered by Necessity, a riverbank that guides her life. She plants vegetable gardens rather than lawns; she carries the odd-shaped tomatoes home from the fields and eats food left for the gods.

Whenever we did frivolous things, we used up energy; we flew high kites. We children came up off the ground over the melting cones our parents brought home from work and the American movie on New Year's Day—*Oh, You Beautiful Doll* with Betty Grable one year, and *She Wore a Yellow Ribbon* with John Wayne another year. After the one carnival ride each, we paid in guilt; our tired father counted his change on the dark walk home.

Adultery is extravagance. Could people who hatch their own chicks and eat 15 the embryos and the heads for delicacies and boil the feet in vinegar for party food, leaving only the gravel, eating even the gizzard lining—could such people engender a prodigal aunt? To be a woman, to have a daughter in starvation time was a waste enough. My aunt could not have been the lone romantic who gave up everything for sex. Women in the old China did not choose. Some man had commanded her to lie with him and be his secret evil. I wonder whether he masked himself when he joined the raid on her family.

Perhaps she had encountered him in the fields or on the mountain where the daughters-in-law collected fuel. Or perhaps he first noticed her in the market-place. He was not a stranger because the village housed no strangers. She had to have dealings with him other than sex. Perhaps he worked an adjoining field, or he sold her the cloth for the dress she sewed and wore. His demand must have surprised, then terrified her. She obeyed him; she always did as she was told.

When the family found a young man in the next village to be her husband, she had stood tractably beside the best rooster, his proxy, and promised before they met that she would be his forever. She was lucky that he was her age and she would be the first wife, an advantage secure now. The night she first saw him, he had sex with her. Then he left for America. She had almost forgotten what he looked like. When she tried to envision him, she only saw the black and white face in the group photograph the men had had taken before leaving.

The other man was not, after all, much different from her husband. They both gave orders: she followed. "If you tell your family, I'll beat you. I'll kill you. Be here again next week." No one talked sex, ever. And she might have separated the rapes from the rest of living if only she did not have to buy her oil from him or gather wood in the same forest. I want her fear to have lasted just as long as rape lasted so that the fear could have been contained. No drawn-out fear. But women at sex hazarded birth and hence lifetimes. The fear did not stop but per-meated everywhere. She told the man, "I think I'm pregnant." He organized the raid against her.

On nights when my mother and father talked about their life back home, sometimes they mentioned an "outcast table" whose business they still seemed to be settling, their voices tight. In a commensal tradition, where food is precious, the powerful older people made wrongdoers eat alone. Instead of letting them start separate new lives like the Japanese, who could become samurais and geishas, the Chinese family, faces averted but eyes glowering sideways, hung on to the offenders and fed them leftovers. My aunt must have lived in the same house as my parents and eaten at an outcast table. My mother spoke about the raid as if she had seen it, when she and my aunt, a daughter-in-law to a different household, should not have been living together at all. Daughters-in-law lived with their husbands' parents, not their own; a synonym for marriage in Chinese is "taking a daughter-in-law." Her husband's parents could have sold her, mort-gaged her, stoned her. But they had sent her back to her own mother and father, a mysterious act hinting at disgraces not told me. Perhaps they had thrown her out to deflect the avengers.

She was the only daughter; her four brothers went with her father, husband, and uncles "out on the road" and for some years became western men. When the goods were divided among the family, three of the brothers took land, and the youngest, my father, chose an education. After my grandparents gave their daughter away to her husband's family, they had dispensed all the adventure and all the property. They expected her alone to keep the traditional ways, which her brothers, now among the barbarians, could fumble without detection. The heavy, deep-rooted women were to maintain the past against the flood, safe for returning. But the rare urge west had fixed upon our family, and so my aunt crossed boundaries not delineated in space.

The work of preservation demands that the feelings playing about in one's guts not be turned into action. Just watch their passing like cherry blossoms. But perhaps my aunt, my forerunner, caught in a slow life, let dreams grow and fade and after some months or years went toward what persisted. Fear at the enormities of the forbidden kept her desires delicate, wire and bone. She looked at a man because she liked the way the hair was tucked behind his ears, or she liked the question-mark line of a long torso curving at the shoulder and straight at the hip. For warm eyes or a soft voice or a slow walk—that's all—a few hairs, a line, a brightness, a sound, a pace, she gave up family. She offered us up for a charm that vanished with tiredness, a pigtail that didn't toss when the wind died. Why, the wrong lighting could erase the dearest thing about him.

It could very well have been, however, that my aunt did not take subtle enjoyment of her friend, but, a wild woman, kept rollicking company. Imagining her free with sex doesn't fit, though. I don't know any women like that, or men either. Unless I see her life branching into mine, she gives me no ancestral help.

To sustain her being in love, she often worked at herself in the mirror, guessing at the colors and shapes that would interest him, changing them frequently in order to hit on the right combination. She wanted him to look back.

On a farm near the sea, a woman who tended her appearance reaped a reputation for eccentricity. All the married women blunt-cut their hair in flaps about their ears or pulled it back in tight buns. No nonsense. Neither style blew easily into heart-catching tangles. And at their weddings they displayed themselves in their long hair for the last time. "It brushed the backs of my knees," my mother tells me. "It was braided, and even so, it brushed the backs of my knees."

At the mirror my aunt combed individuality into her bob. A bun could have 25 been contrived to escape into black streamers blowing in the wind or in quiet wisps about her face, but only the older women in our picture album wear buns. She brushed her hair back from her forehead, tucking the flaps behind her ears. She looped a piece of thread, knotted into a circle between her index fingers and thumbs, and ran the double strand across her forehead. When she closed her fingers as if she were making a pair of shadow geese bite, the string twisted together catching the little hairs. Then she pulled the thread away from her skin, ripping the hairs out neatly, her eyes watering from the needles of pain. Opening her fingers, she cleaned the thread, then rolled it along her hairline and the tops of her eyebrows. My mother did the same to me and my sisters and herself. I used to believe that the expression "caught by the short hairs" meant a captive held with a depilatory string. It especially hurt at the temples, but my mother said we were lucky we didn't have to have our feet bound when we were seven. Sisters used to sit on their beds and cry together, she said, as their mothers or their slaves re-moved the bandages for a few minutes each night and let the blood gush back into their veins. I hope that the man my aunt loved appreciated a smooth brow, that he wasn't just a tits-and-ass man.

Once my aunt found a freckle on her chin, at a spot that the almanac said predestined her for unhappiness. She dug it out with a hot needle and washed the wound with peroxide.

More attention to her looks than these pullings of hairs and pickings at spots would have caused gossip among the villagers. They owned work clothes and good clothes, and they wore good clothes for feasting the new seasons. But since a woman combing her hair hexes beginnings, my aunt rarely found an occasion to look her best. Women looked like great sea snails—the corded wood, babies, and laundry they carried were the whorls on their backs. The Chinese did not ad-mire a bent back; goddesses and warriors stood straight. Still there must have been a marvelous freeing of beauty when a worker laid down her burden and stretched and arched.

Such commonplace loveliness, however, was not enough for my aunt. She dreamed of a lover for the fifteen days of New Year's, the time for families to ex-change visits, money, and food. She plied her secret comb. And sure enough she cursed the year, the family, the village, and herself.

Even as her hair lured her imminent lover, many other men looked at her. Uncles, cousins, nephews, brothers would have looked, too, had they been home between journeys. Perhaps they had already been restraining their curiosity, and they left, fearful that their glances, like a field of nesting birds, might be startled and caught. Poverty hurt, and that was their first reason for leaving. But another, final reason for leaving the crowded house was the never-said.

She may have been unusually beloved, the precious only daughter, spoiled 30 and mirror gazing because of the affection the family lavished on her. When her husband left, they welcomed the chance to take her back from the in-laws; she could live like the little daughter for just a while longer. There are stories that my grandfather was different from other people, "crazy ever since the little Jap bayo-neted him in the head." He used to put his naked penis on the dinner table, laughing. And one day he brought home a baby girl, wrapped up inside his brown western-style greatcoat. He had traded one of his sons, probably my fa-ther, the youngest, for her. My grandmother made him trade back. When he fi-nally got a daughter of his own, he doted on her. They must have all loved her, except perhaps my father, the only brother who never went back to China, hav-ing once been traded for a girl.

Brothers and sisters, newly men and women, had to efface their sexual color and present plain miens. Disturbing hair and eyes, a smile like no other, threatened the ideal of five generations living under one roof. To focus blurs, people shouted face to face and yelled from room to room. The immigrants I know have loud voices, unmodulated to American tones even after years away from the village where they called their friendships out across the fields. I have not been able to stop my mother's screams in public libraries or over telephones. Walking erect (knees straight, toes pointed forward, not pigeon-toed, which is Chinese-feminine) and speaking in an inaudible voice, I have tried to turn myself American-feminine. Chinese communication was loud, public. Only sick people had to whisper. But at the dinner table, where the family members came nearest one another, no one could talk, not the outcasts nor any eaters. Every word that falls from the mouth is a coin lost. Silently they gave and accepted food with both hands. A preoccupied child who took his bowl with one hand got a sideways glare. A complete moment of total attention is due everyone alike. Children and lovers have no singularity here, but my aunt used a secret voice, a separate attentiveness.

She kept the man's name to herself throughout her labor and dying; she did not accuse him that he be punished with her. To save her inseminator's name she gave silent birth.

He may have been somebody in her own household, but intercourse with a man outside the family would have been no less abhorrent. All the village were kinsmen, and the titles shouted in loud country voices never let kinship be forgotten. Any man within visiting distance would have been neutralized as a lover—"brother," "younger brother," "older brother"—one hundred and fifteen relationship titles. Parents researched birth charts probably not so much to assure good fortune as to circumvent incest in a population that has but one hundred surnames. Everybody has eight million relatives. How useless then sexual mannerisms, how dangerous.

As if it came from an atavism deeper than fear, I used to add "brother" silently to boys' names. It hexed the boys, who would or would not ask me to dance, and made them less scary and as familiar and deserving of benevolence as girls.

But, of course, I hexed myself also—no dates. I should have stood up, both 35 arms waving, and shouted out across libraries, "Hey, you! Love me back." I had no idea, though, how to make attraction selective, how to control its direction and magnitude. If I made myself American-pretty so that the five or six Chinese boys in the class fell in love with me, everyone else—the Caucasian, Negro, and Japanese boys—would too. Sisterliness, dignified and honorable, made much more sense.

Attraction eludes control so stubbornly that whole societies designed to organize relationships among people cannot keep order, not even when they bind people to one another from childhood and raise them together. Among the very poor and the wealthy, brothers married their adopted sisters, like doves. Our family allowed some romance, paying adult brides' prices and providing dowries so that their sons and daughters could marry strangers. Marriage promises to turn strangers into friendly relatives—a nation of siblings.

In the village structure, spirits shimmered among the live creatures, balanced and held in equilibrium by time and land. But one human being flaring up into violence could open up a black hole, a maelstrom that pulled in the sky. The frightened villagers, who depended on one another to maintain the real, went to my aunt to show her a personal, physical representation of the break she had made in the "roundness." Misallying couples snapped off the future, which was to be embodied in true offspring. The villagers punished her for acting as if she could have a private life, secret and apart from them.

If my aunt had betrayed the family at a time of large grain yields and peace, when many boys were born, and wings were being built on many houses, perhaps she might have escaped such severe punishment. But the men—hungry, greedy, tired of planting in dry soil—had been forced to leave the village in order to send food-money home. There were ghost plagues, bandit plagues, wars with the Japanese, floods. My Chinese brother and sister had died of an unknown sickness. Adultery, perhaps only a mistake during good times, became a crime when the village needed food.

The round moon cakes and round doorways, the round tables of graduated sizes that fit one roundness inside another, round windows and rice bowls— these talismans had lost their power to warn this family of the law: a family must be whole, faithfully keeping the descent line by having sons to feed the old and the dead, who in turn look after the family. The villagers came to show my aunt and her lover-in-hiding a broken house. The villagers were speeding up the circling of events because she was too shortsighted to see that her infidelity had already harmed the village, that waves of consequences would return unpredictably, sometimes in disguise, as now, to hurt her. This roundness had to be made coin-sized so that she would see its circumference: punish her at the birth of her baby. Awaken her to the inexorable. People who refused fatalism because they could invent small resources insisted on culpability. Deny accidents and wrest fault from the stars.

After the villagers left, their lanterns now scattering in various directions toward home, the family broke their silence and cursed her. "Aiaa, we're going to die. Death is coming. Death is coming. Look what you've done. You've killed us. Ghost! Dead ghost! Ghost! You've never been born." She ran out into the fields, far enough from the house so that she could no longer hear their voices, and pressed herself against the earth, her own land no more. When she felt the birth coming, she thought that she had been hurt. Her body seized together. "They've hurt me too much," she thought. "This is gall, and it will kill me." With forehead and knees against the earth, her body convulsed and then relaxed. She turned on her back, lay on the ground. The black well of sky and stars went out and out and out forever; her body and her complexity seemed to disappear. She was one of the stars, a bright dot in blackness, without home, without a companion, in eternal cold and silence. An agoraphobia rose in her, speeding higher and higher, bigger and bigger; she would not be able to contain it; there would be no end to fear.

Flayed, unprotected against space, she felt pain return, focusing her body. This pain chilled her—a cold, steady kind of surface pain. Inside, spasmodically, the other pain, the pain of the child, heated her. For hours she lay on the ground, alternately body and space. Sometimes a vision of normal comfort obliterated

40

reality: she saw the family in the evening gambling at the dinner table, the young people massaging their elders' backs. She saw them congratulating one another, high joy on the mornings the rice shoots came up. When these pictures burst, the stars drew yet further apart. Black space opened.

She got to her feet to fight better and remembered that old-fashioned women gave birth in their pigsties to fool the jealous, pain-dealing gods, who do not snatch piglets. Before the next spasms could stop her, she ran to the pigsty, each step a rushing out into emptiness. She climbed over the fence and knelt in the dirt. It was good to have a fence enclosing her, a tribal person alone.

Laboring, this woman who had carried her child as a foreign growth that sickened her every day, expelled it at last. She reached down to touch the hot, wet, moving mass, surely smaller than anything human, and could feel that it was human after all—fingers, toes, nails, nose. She pulled it up on to her belly, and it lay curled there, butt in the air, feet precisely tucked one under the other. She opened her loose shirt and buttoned the child inside. After resting, it squirmed and thrashed and she pushed it up to her breast. It turned its head this way and that until it found her nipple. There, it made little snuffling noises. She clenched her teeth at its preciousness, lovely as a young calf, a piglet, a little dog.

She may have gone to the pigsty as a last act of responsibility: she would protect this child as she had protected its father. It would look after her soul, leaving supplies on her grave. But how would this tiny child without family find her grave when there would be no marker for her anywhere, neither in the earth nor the family hall? No one would give her a family hall name. She had taken the child with her into the wastes. At its birth the two of them had felt the same raw pain of separation, a wound that only the family pressing tight could close. A child with no descent line would not soften her life but only trail after her, ghost-like, begging her to give it purpose. At dawn the villagers on their way to the fields would stand around the fence and look.

Full of milk, the little ghost slept. When it awoke, she hardened her breasts 45 against the milk that crying loosens. Toward morning she picked up the baby and walked to the well.

Carrying the baby to the well shows loving. Otherwise abandon it. Turn its face into the mud. Mothers who love their children take them along. It was probably a girl; there is some hope of forgiveness for boys.

"Don't tell anyone you had an aunt. Your father does not want to hear her name. She has never been born." I have believed that sex was unspeakable and words so strong and fathers so frail that "aunt" would do my father mysterious harm. I have thought that my family, having settled among immigrants who had also been their neighbors in the ancestral land, needed to clean their name, and a wrong word would incite the kinspeople even here. But there is more to this silence: they want me to participate in her punishment. And I have.

In the twenty years since I heard this story I have not asked for details nor said my aunt's name; I do not know it. People who can comfort the dead can also chase after them to hurt them further—a reverse ancestor worship. The real punishment was not the raid swiftly inflicted by the villagers, but the family's deliberately forgetting her. Her betrayal so maddened them, they saw to it that she would suffer forever, even after death. Always hungry, always needing, she would have to beg food from other ghosts, snatch and steal it from those whose living descendants give them gifts. She would have to fight the ghosts massed at crossroads for the buns a few thoughtful citizens leave to decoy her away from village and home so that the ancestral spirits could feast unharassed. At peace, they could act like gods, not ghosts, their descent lines providing them with paper suits and dresses, spirit money, paper houses, paper automobiles, chicken, meat, and rice into eternity—essences delivered up in smoke and flames, steam and incense rising from each rice bowl. In an attempt to make the Chinese care for people outside the family, Chairman Mao encourages us now to give our paper replicas to the spirits of outstanding soldiers and workers, no matter whose ancestors they may be. My aunt remains forever hungry. Goods are not distributed evenly among the dead.

My aunt haunts me—her ghost drawn to me because now, after fifty years of neglect, I alone devote pages of paper to her, though not origamied into houses and clothes. I do not think she always means me well. I am telling on her, and she was a spite suicide, drowning herself in the drinking water. The Chinese are always very frightened of the drowned one, whose weeping ghost, wet hair hanging and skin bloated, waits silently by the water to pull down a substitute.

CONTEXTS FOR "NO NAME WOMAN"

MAXINE HONG KINGSTON

Interview (1982)

"The Death of Precious Only Daughter: All about Adultery and the Fate of Girl Babies in China," the article Kingston later revised and retitled as "No Name Woman," first appeared in 1975 in Viva, *an erotic magazine. In the 1975 publication, the editors' misleading lead-in, "She knew little about love and desire, but she knew that her life would be nothing without them," was accompanied by a drawing of Japanese women in kimonos.*

In the following 1982 interview, Kingston discusses the cliché "All Asians look alike."

From Maxine Hong Kingston, "Cultural Mis-readings by American Reviewers" (Interview), in *Asian and Western Writers in Dialogue: New Cultural Identities,* ed. Guy Amirthanayagam (London: Macmillan Ltd., 1982).

Sometimes you just have to laugh because there really is no malice, and they are trying their best. *Viva* magazine published the "No Name Woman" chapter with a full-page color illustration of Japanese maidens at the window; they wear kimonos, lacquered hair-dos, and through the window is lovely, snow-capped Mt. Fuji. Surprise, Asian brothers and sisters! We may as well think of ourselves as Asian Americans because we are all alike anyway. I did not feel angry until I pointed out the Japanese picture to some Caucasians who said, "It doesn't matter." (And yet, if an Asian American movement that includes Chinese, Japanese, Filipinos is possible, then solidarity with Caucasian Americans is possible. I for one was raised with vivid stories about Japanese killing ten million Chinese, including my relatives, and was terrified of Japanese, especially AJAs, the only ones I had met.)

It appears that when the critics looked at my book, they heard a jingle in their heads, "East is east and west is west. . . ." Yes, there were lazy literary critics who actually used that stupid Kipling British-colonial cliché to get a handle on my writing. . . .

I do not want the critics to decide whether the twain shall or shall not meet. I want them to be sensitive enough to know that they are not to judge Chinese American writing through the viewpoint of nineteenth-century British-colonial writing.

Maxine Hong Kingston

SARA BLACKBURN

Review of The Woman Warrior

An erotic magazine like Viva *and a feminist magazine like* Ms. *might seem worlds apart, but each has promulgated stereotypes. Offering her own rendition of* Viva's *"all Asians look alike" cliché, Sara Blackburn assumes that all women are alike, "class, age, race, or ethnicity be damned."*

In this searing, beautiful memoir of growing up as the first-generation American daughter of Chinese immigrant parents, Maxine Hong Kingston illuminates the experience of everyone who has ever felt the terror of being an emotional outsider. It seems to me that the best records of the immigrant experience and the bittersweet legacy it bestows upon the next generation fascinate us because of the insights they provide into the life of the family, that mystified arena where we first learn, truly or falsely, our own identities. It should therefore not be very startling—as it was to me—that this dazzling mixture of pre-revolutionary Chinese village life and myth, set against its almost unbearable contradictions in contemporary American life, could unfold as almost a psychic transcript of every woman I know—class, age, race, or ethnicity be damned. Here is the real meaning of America as melting pot.

A tragic dynamic gets played out here. Taught that our own needs are illegitimate, too many of us repress them and spend our lives serving what we perceive to be the more legitimate needs of others. It is in this way that Kingston's ambivalent responses to growing up in this family and culture evoke the history of women around the world.

MAXINE HONG KINGSTON

Interview (1998)

In the 1970s, the slogan "Sisterhood Is Powerful" aimed to promote political goals, but it did so at the cost of erasing differences among white-, pink-, blue-, and no-collar workers, between heterosexuals and lesbians, and so on.

In this 1998 interview with Laura E. Skandera-Trombley, Kingston acknowledges her ambivalence about categories that ignore differences: While the 1970s' activism on

From Sara Blackburn, "Notes of a Chinese Daughter," *Ms.*, January 1977, 39.

From Laura E. Skandera-Trombley, "A Conversation with Maxine Hong Kingston," in *Critical Essays on Maxine Hong Kingston*, ed. Laura Skandera-Trombley (New York: G. K. Hall, 1998), 33–35.

behalf of women and various minorities helped make The Woman Warrior *canonical, its categories also obscured the authenticity of its characters' experiences and the originality of its artistic genre.*

LST: How does it feel to be canonized and yet, it seems to me, under attack for the changes that you have created? *Woman Warrior* is so widely taught and anthologized, but it seems to me that there is a real backlash going on right now to the broadening of the canon, and you seem to be in the middle of this in a certain sense.

MHK: I have all kinds of ambivalent feelings. I feel honored, and I feel honored appropriately, when I see that my work is in English and American literature classes and I feel that I've been, well, canonized. But I am also caught in all these, I don't know what they are, they're wars. Ethnic wars. Because there's actually disagreement between the disciplines and some people are very personal, and ethnic-studies people have an idea about one being appropriated or assimilated, which they don't consider a good thing. It is very shocking to me when students come in—students have come in from ethnic-studies classes during office hours—and they ask me, "Are you an assimilationist writer?" Then where do I begin looking at the assumption behind that question and talk about what literature is? It bothers me when books are read for political messages and with an absence of looking at the aesthetic reason. . . . I was very concerned when *The Woman Warrior* came out right at the height of the feminist movement, and everyone saw my work as being the epitome of a feminist book. I felt really mad about that because that's not all that it is. . . .
You know, what I wish that people could appreciate, they could see that what I'm doing is riding that border between fiction and nonfiction. You know, we have a land of fiction and there is a land of nonfiction; there's a border in the middle. Well, what I'm doing is making that border very wide, and I am taking into consideration I am writing about real people and these real people have powerful imaginations. They have minds that make up fictions constantly, and so if I was going to write a true biography or an autobiography I would have to take into consideration the stories that people tell. . . .

"WHAT IS CHINESE TRADITION AND WHAT IS THE MOVIES?"

One of the most often quoted sentences of "No Name Woman" is "What is Chinese tradition and what is the movies?" It appears at the end of paragraph 12, one of five new paragraphs that Kingston added when she revised the original article written for *Viva*. (The others are paragraphs 14, 22, 34, and 35.) Kingston brings to the foreground the question of which similarities count as Chinese and as Chinese American. Many reviewers ignored the question and instead reviewed *The Woman Warrior* in the very terms Kingston had challenged: "exotic, inscrutable, mysterious, oriental." However, one group of readers led by dramatist and editor Frank Chin berated Kingston for reinforcing stereotypes and misrepresenting Chinese traditions. This section moves from a glimpse of the reviews that played up stereotypes to a focus on the debate Chin initiated.

MAXINE HONG KINGSTON

Interview (1982)

Now, of course, I expected *The Woman Warrior* to be read from the women's lib angle and the Third World angle, the *Roots* angle; but it is up to the writer to transcend trendy categories. What I did not foresee was the critics measuring the book and me against the stereotype of the exotic, inscrutable, mysterious oriental. About two-thirds of the reviews did this. In some cases, I must admit, it was only a line or a marring word that made my stomach turn, the rest of the review being fairly sensible. You might say I am being too thin-skinned; but a year ago I had really believed that the days of gross stereotyping were over, that the 1960s, the Civil Rights movement, and the end of the war in Vietnam had enlightened America, if not in deeds at least in manners. Pridefully enough, I believed that I had written with such power that the reality and humanity of my characters would bust through any stereotypes of them. Simple-mindedly, I wore a sweat-shirt for the dust-jacket photo, to deny the exotic. I had not calculated how blinding stereotyping is, how stupefying. The critics who said how the book was good because it was, or was not, like the oriental fantasy in their heads might as well have said how weak it was, since it in fact did not break through that fantasy.

Here are some examples of exotic-inscrutable-mysterious-oriental reviewing:

Margaret Manning in *The Boston Globe*: "Mythic forces flood the book. Echoes of the Old Testament, fairy tales, the *Golden Bough* are here, but they have their own strange and brooding atmosphere inscrutably foreign, oriental."

Barbara Burdick in the *Peninsula Herald:* "No other people have remained so mysterious to Westerners as the inscrutable Chinese. Even the word China brings to mind ancient rituals, exotic teas, superstitions, silks and fire-breathing dragons."

Helen Davenport of the Chattanooga *News-Free Press:* "At her most obscure,   5 though, as when telling about her dream of becoming a fabled 'woman warrior' the author becomes as inscrutable as the East always seems to the West. In fact, this book seems to reinforce the feeling that 'East is East and West is West and never the twain shall meet,' or at any rate it will probably take more than one generation away from China."

From Maxine Hong Kingston, "Cultural Mis-readings by American Reviewers" (Interview), in *Asian and Western Writers in Dialogue: New Cultural Identities*, ed. Guy Amirthanayagam (London: Macmillan Ltd., 1982).

Alan McMahan in the Fort Wayne *Journal-Gazette*: "The term 'inscrutable' still applies to the rank and file of Chinese living in their native land." (I do not understand. Does he mean Chinese Americans? What native land? Does he mean America? My native land is America.) . . .

How dare they call their ignorance our inscrutability!

FRANK CHIN

Come All Ye Asian American Writers of the Real and the Fake

In 1991 Chin charged Kingston with misrepresenting a classic Chinese poem by turning its protagonist, Fa Mulan, into a feminist. Chin contrasts the original with Kingston's adaptation.

What if all the whites were to vanish from the American hemisphere, right now? No more whites to push us around, or to be afraid of, or to try to impress, or to prove ourselves to. What do we Asian Americans, Chinese Americans, Japanese Americans, Indo-Chinese, and Korean Americans have to hold us together? What is "Asian America," "Chinese America," and "Japanese America"? For, no matter how white we dress, speak, and behave, we will never be white. No matter how well we speak Spanish, or sing, dance, and play flamenco, we will never be Spanish gypsies.

What seems to hold Asian American literature together is the popularity among whites of Maxine Hong Kingston's *Woman Warrior* (450,000 copies sold since 1976 [up to 1990]); David Henry Hwang's *F.O.B.* (Obie, best off-Broadway play) and *M. Butterfly* (Tony, best Broadway play); and Amy Tan's *The Joy Luck Club*. These works are held up before us as icons of our pride, symbols of our freedom from the icky-gooey evil of a Chinese culture where the written word for "woman" and "slave" are the same word (Kingston) and Chinese brutally tattoo messages on the backs of women (Kingston and Hwang).

In *The Woman Warrior*, Kingston takes a childhood chant, "The Ballad of Mulan," which is as popular today as "London Bridge Is Falling Down," and rewrites the heroine, Fa Mulan, to the specs of the stereotype of the Chinese woman as a pathological white supremacist victimized and trapped in a hideous Chinese civilization. The tattoos Kingston gives Fa Mulan, to dramatize cruelty to women, actually belong to the hero Yue Fei, a man whose tomb is now a

---

From Frank Chin, "Come All Ye Asian American Writers of the Real and the Fake," in *The Big Aiiieeee! An Anthology of Chinese American and Japanese American Literature* (New York: Meridian, 1991), 2–3, 26–27.

tourist attraction at West Lake, in Hanzhou city. Fake work breeds fake work. David Henry Hwang repeats Kingston's revision of Fa Mulan and Yue Fei, and goes on to impoverish and slaughter Fa Mulan's family to further dramatize the cruelty of the Chinese.

Kingston, Hwang, and Tan are the first writers of any race, and certainly the first writers of Asian ancestry, to so boldly fake the best-known works from the most universally known body of Asian literature and lore in history. And, to legitimize their faking, they have to fake all of Asian American history and literature, and argue that the immigrants who settled and established Chinese America lost touch with Chinese culture, and that a faulty memory combined with new experience produced new versions of these traditional stories. This version of history is their contribution to the stereotype.

The lie of their version of history is easily proven by one simple fact: Chinese 5 America was never illiterate. Losing touch with China did not result in Chinese Americans losing touch with "The Ballad of Mulan." It was and is still chanted by children in Chinatowns around the Western hemisphere. Losing touch with England did not result in English whites losing touch with the texts of the Magna Carta or Shakespeare.

Their elaboration of this version of history, in both autobiography and autobiographical fiction, is simply a device for destroying history and literature. . . .

Misogyny is the only unifying moral imperative in this Christian vision of Chinese civilization. All women are victims. America and Christianity represent freedom from Chinese civilization. In the Christian yin/yang of the dual personality/ identity crisis, Chinese evil and perversity is male. And the Americanized honorary white Chinese American is female.

MAXINE HONG KINGSTON
Imagined Life

In a lecture presented to students and faculty of the University of Michigan's creative writing program, Kingston gives writers the following advice based on her own method of approaching complex truths.

All right. To make your mother and your scandalous friends read about themselves and still like you, you have to be very cunning, very crafty. Don't commit yourself. Don't be pinned down. Give many versions of events. Tell the most flattering motives. Say: "Of course, it couldn't have been money that she was after."

From Maxine Hong Kingston, "Imagined Life," Hopwood Lecture. *Michigan Quarterly Review* 22.4 (Fall 1983): 561–570.

In *The Woman Warrior,* my mother-book, the No Name Woman might have been raped; she might have had a love affair; she might have been "a wild woman, and kept rollicking company. Imagining her free with sex. . . ." Imagining many lives for her made me feel free. I have so much freedom in telling about her, I'm almost free even from writing itself, and therefore obeying my mother, who said, "Don't tell."

PAULA RABINOWITZ

Eccentric Memories: A Conversation with Maxine Hong Kingston

PR: Yes. I wanted to ask, now that you have been to China, what happened?

MHK: I was very afraid to go because it's really there. What if China invalidated every-thing that I was thinking and writing? So, one of the great thrills was to see how well I had imagined it. Many of the colors, and the smells, the people, the faces, the incidents, were much as I imagined. Many people said to me, "Welcome home." I did feel that I was going back to a place that I had never been.

    Actually, it was a new adventure, too, but there were just small things that I wish hadn't happened, in a way. There were some things that I wish I had seen before I had written my books. The tight quarters of the rooms and of the villages. If I had been in those rooms earlier, I would have un-derstood even better the sense of a village and how each person's drama re-verberates throughout the village. I would have seen that people did not have to walk as far as I said to go from one place to another. At my father's village, the well where the aunt drowned herself was right next to the Hong family temple. My mother said that the guys used to hang around on the steps of the temple and make remarks at the girls to try to get them to drop and break their water jars. That is so real to everyone, of all cultures. You know, guys whistling at girls, and, also, it's so sexy. I wish I had had it in the book. I saw small things like that that I wished I had had earlier, but noth-ing large that invalidated the whole work.

PR: So then the idea that you are speaking out of a cultural community is crucial?

MHK: I don't see how I would live without a community, family, friends. But I   5
am always very interested in how one can be an individual and be part of a collective people and a collective memory. Of course, that's very American

From Paula Rabinowitz, "Eccentric Memories: A Conversation with Maxine Hong Kingston," *Michi-gan Quarterly Review* 26.1 (Winter 1987): 177–187.

too, because Americans strive to stand alone. I am always figuring out how the lone person forms a community.

PR: Well, it seems that memory does that for you in a way. It becomes the translation between an individual narrator and the family, whose stories have been narrated, and the history in which that family has lived its stories.

MHK: Yes, and then that brings us to the tribal memory, the family memory, the cultural memory. Well, I guess I contain them all in my own individual memory, but some of the stories that I write began with memories that we all have. Those collective memories are the myths. For example, immigration stories about how you got through Angel Island—having four or five versions of your immigration—that's not just the way my head works, that's the way narration and memory and stories work in our culture. So, that's a gift given to me by our culture, and not something that I imagined on my own. I invented new literary structures to contain multiversions and to tell the true lives of non-fiction people who are storytellers.

PR: Your books are categorized as autobiography or cultural history and as fiction and I am wondering what you see as the relationship between fact and fiction?

MHK: It doesn't bother me very much; it bothers other people more than me. It has caused problems. When the British reviewed my work, they could not get past the question, "Is this fiction or non-fiction?" There have been articles that just addressed that, and never got to what I am talking about. . . .

QUESTIONS FOR DISCUSSION AND WRITING

1. What stereotypes of Chinese women and Chinese society does "No Name Woman" attempt to dispel? The second section of the Contexts focuses on differences between what is stereotypically "the movies" and what is authentically Chinese and Chinese American. Look back at paragraphs 12, 14, 22, 34, and 35 of "No Name Woman," the paragraphs Kingston added to the original version published in *Viva*. In what ways and to what extent does each addition change the original essay and its intended readers? For example, how does paragraph 22 correct a misreading by the editors of *Viva*?

2. What are Frank Chin's reasons for objecting to *The Woman Warrior*? What passages could you bring forward from "No Name Woman" and from Kingston's two interviews in the final section of the Contexts to address Chin's objections?

3. Chin objects to contemporary alterations of a familiar Chinese tale by a Chinese American woman. Yet myths, Bible stories, fairy tales, and other familiar narratives survive centuries of cultural change because they are infinitely adaptable. Using "No Name Woman" (or, if you've read it, the "White Tigers" section of *Woman Warrior*, which transforms the male Fa Mulan myth into a woman warrior), buttressed by your knowledge of familiar fairy tales, defend Kingston's (or any storyteller's) right to do this.

If you have seen the Disney version, *Mulan* (1998), in which Eddie Murphy provided the dragon's voice, compare Disney's version with Kingston's and argue for or against the appropriateness of this film, made by an American film-maker for a Western audience.

4. In your opinion, how should people read "No Name Woman"? Is this a caution-ary tale, a warning to girls on the verge of sexual maturity to behave according to community standards? Is it a feminist re-interpretation of a familiar tale, allow-ing more independence of mind and agency of action to a young woman ex-pected to be submissive? Is it a tale of love? Of lust? rape? vengeance? murder? Some or all of the above? With a partner of the opposite sex, write a paper that will form the basis of a debate in class. Use the Contexts readings that reinforce your points.

LYNDA BARRY

Hate

Lynda Barry (b. 1956), daughter of a Filipino mother and an American father, grew up in an interracial Seattle neighborhood whose cultural mixture of languages, cus-toms, wrong-side-of-the-tracks marginality, prejudices, shifting friendships, and an-tagonisms forms the matrix of many of the comics for which she is known. The life she depicts is harsh, tenuous, but with redeeming features and sparks of hope and love that shine, incandescent, through the dark. By the time she graduated from Evergreen State College (1978), she realized that her cartoons could make her friends laugh, and "Ernie Pook's Comeek"—now a widely syndicated strip—was born. She teaches a course called "Writing the Unthinkable," perhaps a reflection of her second novel, Cruddy *(1998).*

One! Hundred! Demons!, her autobiography in graphic form, was published in 2003. "Hate" is one chapter; there is no chapter on "Love," perhaps because Barry regards love as "an exploding cigar we willingly smoke."

BUT IF HATE WAS NOT DETESTING OR LOATHING OR COMPARING SOMEONE TO PIG BARF, WHAT <u>WAS</u> IT? EVEN THE DICTIONARY COULDN'T HELP EXPLAIN IT.

AT THE LIBRARY...

WHAT ARE YOU LOOKING UP, LITTLE GIRL?

UM... "FLOWERS"

HOW NICE.

IT'S THE SAME WORDS. DETEST. INTENSE DISLIKE. TO LOATHE, TO ABHOR, TO EXECRATE.

LIKE A LOT OF KIDS, I LEARNED HOW TO LIE ABOUT HOW I FELT. HATING PEOPLE SE-CRETLY WAS BETTER THAN GETTING LECTURES.

(FEELING HOLY?)

WE MAY DISLIKE, WE MAY EVEN <u>LOATHE</u> OR DETEST. BUT HATE? OH NO, DEAR CHILDREN.

OK, WE PROMISE NEVER TO HATE. CAN WE PLAY NOW?

MAN, I HATE HER RIGHT NOW.

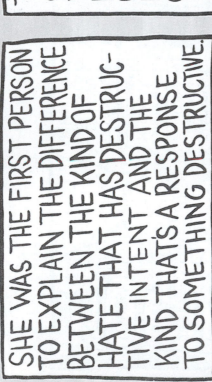

QUESTIONS FOR DISCUSSION AND WRITING

1. What definitions of *hate* does Barry offer? Why does she use hearts to flank "hate" in the introductory panel? Why is it a "main rule of life" that "you can never hate your own parents. No matter what"—with the exception of stepparents (panel 8)? Are readers to believe this? How can her mother say someone "is pig vomit and should be eaten by snakes," and yet claim that she doesn't hate her (panel 10)? Why is hate defined throughout with relation to love?

2. What is the significance of distinguishing "between the kind of hate that has destructive intent and the kind that's a response to something destructive," as explained in panel 17? Why does the recognition of this distinction prompt the Lynda character to tell the substitute teacher "I. Love. You." (panel 18)? With a partner, arrive at a definition of hate and its antithesis, and write a paper arguing for your definition in comparison with alternative definitions, such as that offered by Art Spiegelman in "Mein Kampf" (p. 139).

3. What does graphic art enable Barry to accomplish that she couldn't do with words alone? How can her fairly unattractive (some might say ugly) characters be appealing?

4. Present a definition of an abstract concept (such as love, your own version of hate, fear, pleasure, rejection, acceptance) through a combination of words and drawings. If you're not an artist, team up with a classmate who is, or use existing cartoons, drawings, or other pictures and substitute your own captions.

5. By yourself or with a partner write a paper in which you analyze and explain Barry's "Hate" in comparison with Spiegelman's "Mein Kampf" (p. 139) or one of Gary Trudeau's comic strips.

HARRIET JACOBS
The Slaves' New Year's Day

Harriet Jacobs (1813–1897) was born into slavery in Edenton, North Carolina. After her mother's death, Jacobs was raised from the age of six in the house of her white mistress, who taught her to read and write. When that mistress died in 1825, Jacobs was willed to another white family; after resisting the sexual advances of her new master, she was forced to work as a field hand. At twenty-two, Jacobs escaped her captors and hid for almost seven years in a crawl space at the home of her grandmother, a freed former slave. There she was exposed, in season, to freezing and sweltering temperatures and was always in danger of detection. In 1842 she fled to New York City, where she worked for the family of a noted abolitionist who eventually purchased and freed her. Incidents in the Life of a Slave Girl *was published pseudonymously in 1861 and reissued in 1987 to great acclaim, when scholar Jean Fagin Yellin authenticated Jacobs's authorship.*

In the introduction to Incidents in the Life of a Slave Girl, *Jacobs explains her intentions in writing about her life:*

> *I have not written my experiences in order to attract attention to myself; on the contrary, it would have been more pleasant to me to have been silent about my own history. Neither do I care to excite sympathy for my own sufferings. But I do earnestly desire to arouse the women of the North to a realizing sense of the condition of two millions of women in the South, still in bondage, suffering what I suffered, and most of them far worse. I want to add my testimony to that of abler pens to convince the people of the Free States what Slavery really is. Only by experience can any one realize how deep, and dark, and foul is that pit of abominations.*

"The Slaves' New Year's Day" is an excerpt from her book.

Dr. Flint owned a fine residence in town, several farms, and about fifty slaves, besides hiring a number by the year.

Hiring-day at the south takes place on the 1st of January. On the 2d, the slaves are expected to go to their new masters. On a farm, they work until the corn and cotton are laid. They then have two holidays. Some masters give them a good dinner under the trees. This over, they work until Christmas eve. If no heavy charges are meantime brought against them, they are given four or five holidays, whichever the master or overseer may think proper. Then comes New Year's eve; and they gather together their little alls, or more properly speaking, their little nothings, and wait anxiously for the dawning of day. At the appointed hour the grounds are thronged with men, women, and children, waiting, like criminals, to hear their doom pronounced. The slave is sure to know who is the most humane, or cruel master, within forty miles of him.

It is easy to find out, on that day, who clothes and feeds his slaves well; for he is surrounded by a crowd, begging, "Please, massa, hire me this year. I will work *very* hard, massa."

If a slave is unwilling to go with his new master, he is whipped, or locked up in jail, until he consents to go, and promises not to run away during the year. Should he chance to change his mind, thinking it justifiable to violate an extorted promise, woe unto him if he is caught! The whip is used till the blood flows at his feet; and his stiffened limbs are put in chains, to be dragged in the field for days and days!

If he lives until the next year, perhaps the same man will hire him again, 5 without even giving him an opportunity of going to the hiring-ground. After those for hire are disposed of, those for sale are called up.

O, you happy free women, contrast *your* New Year's day with that of the poor bond-woman! With you it is a pleasant season, and the light of the day is blessed. Friendly wishes meet you every where, and gifts are showered upon you. Even hearts that have been estranged from you soften at this season, and lips that have been silent echo back, "I wish you a happy New Year." Children bring their little offerings, and raise their rosy lips for a caress. They are your own, and no hand but that of death can take them from you.

But to the slave mother New Year's day comes laden with peculiar sorrows. She sits on her cold cabin floor, watching the children who may all be torn from her the next morning; and often does she wish that she and they might die before the day dawns. She may be an ignorant creature, degraded by the system that has brutalized her from childhood; but she has a mother's instincts, and is capable of feeling a mother's agonies.

On one of these sale days, I saw a mother lead seven children to the auction-block. She knew that *some* of them would be taken from her; but they took *all.* The children were sold to a slave-trader, and their mother was bought by a man in her own town. Before night her children were all far away. She begged the trader to tell her where he intended to take them; this he refused to do. How *could* he, when he knew he would sell them, one by one, wherever he could command the highest price? I met that mother in the street, and her wild, haggard face lives to-day in my mind. She wrung her hands in anguish, and exclaimed, "Gone! All gone! Why *don't* God kill me?" I had no words wherewith to comfort her. Instances of this kind are of daily, yea, of hourly occurrence.

Slaveholders have a method, peculiar to their institution, of getting rid of *old* slaves, whose lives have been worn out in their service. I knew an old woman, who for seventy years faithfully served her master. She had become almost helpless, from hard labor and disease. Her owners moved to Alabama, and the old black woman was left to be sold to any body who would give twenty dollars for her.

QUESTIONS FOR DISCUSSION AND WRITING

1. Considering Jacobs's audience, "the women of the North," how does her use of the cycles of days, seasons, and years make her message more effective?

2. How might Jacobs's narrative function, like Maxine Hong Kingston's "No Name Woman" (p. 420), "to reinterpret a legacy of disgrace as a tale of bravery"? Whose bravery does Jacobs allude to?

3. Do you think that either Jacobs or Kingston intended to appeal particularly to women readers? On what evidence do you base your answer?

4. How does Jacobs's purpose differ from that of Frederick Douglass in "Resurrection" (p. 452)? How does it differ from that of Sojourner Truth in her speech "Ain't I a Woman?" (p. 373)? What role does gender play in each reading?

FREDERICK DOUGLASS

Resurrection

Frederick Douglass (1817–1895) grew up as a slave in Baltimore, where his owner's wife taught him to read—a subversive and dangerous act. Douglass quickly learned that whatever his white overseers forbade was a prize to pursue. He became attracted to the art of speechmaking via the popular text The Columbian Orator *and discovered abolitionist writing in the* Baltimore American. *After escaping to the North in 1838, he spent the next twenty-five years touring the country as the abolitionist movement's most visible and forceful proponent. His powerful speech delivery was enhanced by his impressive physical strength, magnificent bearing, and charming manner. He wrote for William Lloyd Garrison's antislavery newspaper and his own,* The North Star *(1847–1860), and authored a novella,* The Heroic Slave *(1853). His autobiography,* Narrative of the Life of Frederick Douglass, an American Slave *(1845), with its direct language and multidimensional portraits of whites as well as blacks, was popular and influential in its time and has since become an American classic.*

Although the autobiography omits much detail about Douglass's youth (in part to better portray a typical African American life and in part to protect those who helped him escape), in the following excerpt he narrates how at sixteen he was sent to labor on an Eastern Shore plantation, where he fought back against a harsh overseer, Covey, whose vicious whippings were designed to break both his body and his spirit.

I have already intimated that my condition was much worse, during the first six months of my stay at Mr. Covey's, than in the last six. The circumstances leading to the change in Mr. Covey's course toward me form an epoch in my humble history. You have seen how a man was made a slave; you shall see how a slave was made a man. On one of the hottest days of the month of August, 1833, Bill Smith, William Hughes, a slave named Eli, and myself, were engaged in fanning wheat. Hughes was clearing the fanned wheat from before the fan. Eli was turning, Smith was feeding, and I was carrying wheat to the fan. The work was simple, requiring strength rather than intellect; yet, to one entirely unused to such work, it came very hard. About three o'clock of that day, I broke down; my strength failed me; I was seized with a violent aching of the head, attended with extreme dizziness; I trembled in every limb. Finding what was coming, I nerved myself up, feeling it would never do to stop work. I stood as long as I could stagger to the hopper with grain. When I could stand no longer, I fell, and felt as if held down by an immense weight. The fan of course stopped; every one had his own work to do; and no one could do the work of the other, and have his own go on at the same time.

Mr. Covey was at the house, about one hundred yards from the treading-yard where we were fanning. On hearing the fan stop, he left immediately, and came to the spot where we were. He hastily inquired what the matter was. Bill answered that I was sick, and there was no one to bring wheat to the fan. I had by this time crawled away under the side of the post-and-rail fence by which the yard was enclosed, hoping to find relief by getting out of the sun. He then asked where I was. He was told by one of the hands. He came to the spot, and, after looking at me awhile, asked me what was the matter. I told him as well as I could, for I scarce had strength to speak. He then gave me a savage kick in the side, and told me to get up. I tried to do so, but fell back in the attempt. He gave me another kick, and again told me to rise. I again tried, and succeeded in gaining my feet; but, stooping to get the tub with which I was feeding the fan, I again staggered and fell. While down in this situation, Mr. Covey took up the hickory slat with which Hughes had been striking off the half-bushel measure, and with it gave me a heavy blow upon the head, making a large wound, and the blood ran freely; and with this again told me to get up. I made no effort to comply, having now made up my mind to let him do his worst. In a short time after receiving this blow, my head grew better. Mr. Covey had now left me to my fate. At this moment I resolved, for the first time, to go to my master, enter a complaint, and ask his protection. In order to do this, I must that afternoon walk seven miles; and this, under the circumstances, was truly a severe undertaking. I was exceedingly feeble; made so as much by the kicks and blows which I received, as by the severe fit of sickness to which I had been subjected. I, however, watched my chance, while Covey was looking in an opposite direction, and started for St. Michael's: I succeeded in getting a considerable distance on my way to the woods, when Covey discovered me, and called after me to come back, threatening what he would do if I did not come. I disregarded both his calls and his threats, and made my way to the woods as fast as my feeble state would allow; and thinking I might be overhauled by him if I kept to the road, I walked through the woods, keeping far enough from the road to avoid detection, and near enough to prevent losing my way. I had not gone far before my little strength again failed me. I could go no farther. I fell down, and lay for a considerable time. The blood was yet oozing from the wound on my head. For a time I thought I should bleed to death; and think now that I should have done so, but that the blood so matted my hair as to stop the wound. After lying there about three quarters of an hour, I nerved myself up again, and started on my way, through bogs and briers, barefooted and bareheaded, tearing my feet sometimes at nearly every step; and after a journey of about seven miles, occupying some five hours to perform it, I arrived at master's store. I then presented an appearance enough to affect any but a heart of iron. From the crown of my head to my feet, I was covered with blood. My hair was all clotted with dust and blood; my shirt was stiff with blood. My legs and feet were torn in sundry places with briers and thorns, and were also covered in blood. I suppose I looked like a man who had escaped a den of wild beasts, and barely escaped them. In this state I appeared before my master, humbly entreating him to interpose his authority for my protection. I told him all the circumstances as well as I could, and it seemed, as I spoke, at times to affect him. He would then walk the floor, and seek to justify Covey by saying he expected I deserved it. He asked me what I wanted. I told him, to let me get a new home; that as sure as I lived with Mr. Covey again, I should live with but to die with him; that Covey would surely kill me; he was in a fair way for it. Master Thomas ridiculed the idea that there was any danger of Mr. Covey's killing me, and said that he knew Mr. Covey, that he was a good man, and that he could not think of taking me from him; that, should he do so, he would lose the whole year's wages; that I belonged to Mr. Covey for one year, and that I must go back to him, come what might; and that I must not trouble him with any more stories, or that he would himself *get hold of me.* After threatening me thus, he gave me a very large dose of salts, telling me that I might remain in St. Michael's that night, (it being quite late,) but that I must be off back to Mr. Covey's early in the morning; and that if I did not, he would *get hold of me,* which meant that he would whip me. I remained all night, and, according to his orders, I started off to Covey's in the morning, (Saturday morning,) wearied in body and broken in spirit. I got no supper that night, or breakfast that morning. I reached Covey's about nine o'clock; and just as I was getting over the fence that divided Mrs. Kemp's fields from ours, out ran Covey with his cowskin, to give me another whipping. Before he could reach me, I succeeded in getting to the cornfield; and as the corn was very high, it afforded me the means of hiding. He seemed very angry, and searched for me a long time. My behavior was altogether unaccountable. He finally gave up the chase, thinking, I suppose, that I must come home for something to eat; he would give himself no further trouble in looking for me. I spent that day mostly in the woods, having the alternative before me—to go home and be whipped to death, or stay in the woods and be starved to death. That night, I fell in with Sandy Jenkins, a slave with whom I was somewhat acquainted. Sandy had a free wife who lived about four miles from Mr. Covey's; and it being Saturday, he was on his way to see her. I told him my circumstances, and he very kindly invited me to go home with him. I went home with him, and talked this whole matter over, and got his advice as to what course it was best for me to pursue. I found Sandy an old adviser. He told me, with great solemnity, I must go back to Covey; but that before I went, I must go with him into another part of the woods, where there was a certain *root,* which, if I would take some of it with me, carrying it *always on my right side,* would render it impossible for Mr. Covey, or any other white man, to whip me. He said he had carried it for years; and since he had done so, he had never received a blow, and never expected to while he carried it. I at first rejected the idea, that the simple carrying of a root in my pocket would have any such effect as he had said, and was not disposed to take it; but Sandy impressed the necessity with much earnestness, telling me it could do no harm, if it did no good. To please him, I at length took the root, and, according to his direction, carried it upon my right side. This was Sunday morning. I immediately started for home; and upon entering the yard gate, out came Mr. Covey on his way to meeting. He spoke to me very kindly, bade me drive the pigs from a lot near by, and passed on towards the church. Now, this singular conduct of Mr. Covey really made me begin to think that there was something in the *root* which Sandy had given me; and had it been on any other day than Sunday, I could have attributed the conduct to no other cause than the influence of that root; and as it was, I was half inclined to think the *root* to be something more than I at first had taken it to be. All went well till Monday morning. On this morning, the virtue of the *root* was fully tested. Long before daylight, I was called to go and rub, curry, and feed, the horses. I obeyed, and was glad to obey. But whilst thus engaged, whilst in the act of throwing down some blades from the loft, Mr. Covey entered the stable with a long rope; and just as I was half out of the loft, he caught hold of my legs, and was about tying me. As soon as I found what he was up to, I gave a sudden spring, and as I did so, he holding to my legs, I was brought sprawling on the stable floor. Mr. Covey seemed now to think he had me, and could do what he pleased; but at this moment—from whence came the spirit I don't know—I resolved to fight; and, suiting my action to the resolution, I seized Covey hard by the throat; and as I did so, I rose. He held on to me, and I to him. My resistance was so entirely unexpected, that Covey seemed taken all aback. He trembled like a leaf. This gave me assurance, and I held him uneasy, causing the blood to run where I touched him with the ends of my fingers. Mr. Covey soon called out to Hughes for help. Hughes came, and while Covey held me, attempted to tie my right hand. While he was in the act of doing so, I watched my chance, and gave him a heavy kick close under the ribs. This kick fairly sickened Hughes, so that he left me in the hands of Mr. Covey. This kick had the effect of not only weakening Hughes, but Covey also. When he saw Hughes bending over with pain, his courage quailed. He asked me if I meant to persist in my resistance. I told him I did, come what might; that he had used me like a brute for six months, and that I was determined to be used so no longer. With that, he strove to drag me to a stick that was lying just out of the stable door. He meant to knock me down. But just as he was leaning over to get the stick, I seized him with both hands by his collar, and brought him by a sudden snatch to the ground. By this time, Bill came. Covey called upon him for assistance. Bill wanted to know what he could do. Covey said, "Take hold of him, take hold of him!" Bill said his master hired him out to work, and not to help whip me; so he left Covey and myself to fight our own battle out. We were at it for nearly two hours. Covey at length let me go, puffing and blowing at a great rate, saying that if I had not resisted, he would not have whipped me half so much. The truth was, that he had not whipped me at all. I considered him as getting entirely the worst end of the bargain; for he had drawn no blood from me, but I had from him. The whole six months afterwards, that I spent with Mr. Covey, he never laid the weight of his finger upon me in anger. He would occasionally say, he didn't want to get hold of me again. "No," thought I, "you need not; for you will come off worse than you did before."

This battle with Mr. Covey was the turning-point in my career as a slave. It rekindled the few expiring embers of freedom, and revived within me a sense of my own manhood. It recalled the departed self-confidence, and inspired me again with a determination to be free. The gratification afforded by the triumph was a full compensation for whatever else might follow, even death itself. He only can understand the deep satisfaction which I experienced, who has himself repelled by force the bloody arm of slavery. I felt as I never felt before. It was a glorious resurrection, from the tomb of slavery, to the heaven of freedom. My long-crushed spirit rose, cowardice departed, bold defiance took its place; and I now resolved that, however long I might remain a slave in form, the day had passed forever when I could be a slave in fact. I did not hesitate to let it be known of me, that the white man who expected to succeed in whipping, must also succeed in killing me.

QUESTIONS FOR DISCUSSION AND WRITING

1. Douglass narrates his defiance of Covey, "the turning point in my career as a slave" (paragraph 3), twelve years after the event actually took place. What seems to be the effect of the passage of time in Douglass's understanding of the significance of the event?

2. Who would be the most likely audience for Douglass's narrative? Taking into consideration the constraints on Douglass as a writer and his purpose in writing, consider how slave owners might have responded to his autobiography.

3. How might Douglass respond to the Declaration of Independence (p. 369)? How might he have responded to Elizabeth Cady Stanton's version, the "Declaration of Sentiments" (p. 375)?

4. Douglass uses biblical language when, for example, he writes that "from the crown of my head to my feet, I was covered in blood" and "I looked like a man who had escaped a den of wild beasts" (paragraph 2). What is the effect of this language? How does it reinforce his message that to resist "the bloody arm of slavery" is key to his "glorious resurrection" (paragraph 3)?

5. Write a narrative about an event that has changed your life, your sense of identity, or your status in the eyes of friends and neighbors. To what extent were you aware of the significance of the turning-point experience when you were actually living through it? When did you fully realize the change it brought to your life? How do you evaluate it now?

KENJI YOSHINO

The Pressure to Cover

Kenji Yoshino was a Harvard graduate (B.A., 1991), and a Rhodes Scholar (Oxford M.Sc., 1993), before entering Yale Law School, from which he earned his law degree (J.D.) in 1996. He is now professor and deputy dean for intellectual life at his alma mater, specializing in constitutional law, antidiscrimination law, law and literature, and Japanese law and society. He identifies himself as a "homosexual professional rather than a professional homosexual."

"Everyone covers," begins the jacket copy of his book, Covering: The Hidden Assault on Our Civil Rights *(2006).* Covering *is not the same as* passing, *the attempt to render a stigmatized trait invisible (as when a light-skinned black person passes as white); rather, it downplays an acknowledged but "disfavored trait so as to blend into the mainstream. Because many of us possess stigmatized attributes" (such as race, sex, sexual orientation, religion, or disability), "we all encounter pressure to cover in our daily lives. . . . Racial minorities are pressed to 'act white' by changing their names, languages, or cultural practices. Women are told to 'play like men' at work. . . . The devout are instructed to minimize expressions of faith. . . ." While discrimination is largely outlawed, the pressure to cover is pervasive and potentially destructive of one's civil liberties. Rejecting identity politics, Yoshino urges readers to "make common cause around a new civil rights paradigm based on our desire for authenticity—a desire that brings us together rather than driving us apart."*

"The Pressure to Cover," adapted from the book and published in the New York Times Magazine *(January 15, 2006), is a concise version of his argument. Here he explains how he came to take his stand against forced assimilation, and his vision of authentic personal identity in America.*

When I began teaching at Yale Law School in 1998, a friend spoke to me frankly. "You'll have a better chance at tenure," he said, "if you're a homosexual professional than if you're a professional homosexual." Out of the closet for six years at the time, I knew what he meant. To be a "homosexual professional" was to be a professor of constitutional law who "happened" to be gay. To be a "professional homosexual" was to be a gay professor who made gay rights his work. Others echoed the sentiment in less elegant formulations. Be gay, my world seemed to say. Be openly gay, if you want. But don't flaunt.

I didn't experience the advice as antigay. The law school is a vigorously tolerant place, embedded in a university famous for its gay student population. (As the undergraduate jingle goes: "One in four, maybe more / One in three, maybe me / One, in two, maybe you.") I took my colleague's words as generic counsel to leave my personal life at home. I could see that research related to one's identity—referred to in the academy as "mesearch"—could raise legitimate questions about scholarly objectivity.

I also saw others playing down their outsider identities to blend into the mainstream. Female colleagues confided that they would avoid references to their children at work, lest they be seen as mothers first and scholars second. Conservative students asked for advice about how open they could be about their politics without suffering repercussions at some imagined future confirmation hearing. A religious student said he feared coming out as a believer, as he thought his intellect would be placed on a 25 percent discount. Many of us, it seemed, had to work our identities as well as our jobs.

It wasn't long before I found myself resisting the demand to conform. What bothered me was not that I had to engage in straight-acting behavior, much of which felt natural to me. What bothered me was the felt need to mute my passion for gay subjects, people, culture. At a time when the law was transforming gay rights, it seemed ludicrous not to suit up and get in the game.

"Mesearch" being what it is, I soon turned my scholarly attention to the pres- 5 sure to conform. What puzzled me was that I felt that pressure so long after my emergence from the closet. When I stopped passing, I exulted that I could stop thinking about my sexuality. This proved naïve. Long after I came out, I still experienced the need to assimilate to straight norms. But I didn't have a word for this demand to tone down my known gayness.

Then I found my word, in the sociologist Erving Goffman's book "Stigma." Written in 1963, the book describes how various groups—including the disabled, the elderly and the obese—manage their "spoiled" identities. After discussing passing, Goffman observes that "persons who are ready to admit possession of a stigma . . . may nonetheless make a great effort to keep the stigma from looming large." He calls this behavior covering. He distinguishes passing from covering by noting that passing pertains to the *visibility* of a characteristic, while covering pertains to its *obtrusiveness.* He relates how F.D.R. stationed himself behind a desk before his advisers came in for meetings. Roosevelt was not passing, since everyone knew he used a wheelchair. He was covering, playing down his disability so people would focus on his more conventionally presidential qualities.

As is often the case when you learn a new idea, I began to perceive covering everywhere. Leafing through a magazine, I read that Helen Keller replaced her natural eyes (one of which protruded) with brilliant blue glass ones. On the radio, I heard that Margaret Thatcher went to a voice coach to lower the pitch of her voice. Friends began to send me e-mail. Did I know that Martin Sheen was Ramon Estevez on his birth certificate, that Ben Kingsley was Krishna Bhanji, that Kirk Douglas was Issur Danielovitch Demsky and that Jon Stewart was Jonathan Leibowitz?

In those days, spotting instances of covering felt like a parlor game. It's hard to get worked up about how celebrities and politicians have to manage their public images. Jon Stewart joked that he changed his name because Leibowitz was "too Hollywood," and that seemed to get it exactly right. My own experience with covering was also not particularly difficult—once I had the courage to write from my passions, I was immediately embraced.

It was only when I looked for instances of covering in the law that I saw how lucky I had been. Civil rights case law is peopled with plaintiffs who were severely punished for daring to be openly different. Workers were fired for lapsing into Spanish in English-only workplaces, women were fired for behaving in stereotypically "feminine" ways and gay parents lost custody of their children for engaging in displays of same-sex affection. These cases revealed that far from being a parlor game, covering was the civil rights issue of our time.

THE NEW DISCRIMINATION

In recent decades, discrimination in America has undergone a generational shift.   10
Discrimination was once aimed at entire groups, resulting in the exclusion of all
racial minorities, women, gays, religious minorities and people with disabilities.
A battery of civil rights laws—like the Civil Rights Act of 1964 and the Americans with Disabilities Act of 1990—sought to combat these forms of discrimination. The triumph of American civil rights is that such categorical exclusions by
the state or employers are now relatively rare.

Now a subtler form of discrimination has risen to take its place. This discrimination does not aim at groups as a whole. Rather, it aims at the subset of the group
that refuses to cover, that is, to assimilate to dominant norms. And for the most
part, existing civil rights laws do not protect individuals against such covering demands. The question of our time is whether we should understand this new discrimination to be a harm and, if so, whether the remedy is legal or social in nature.

Consider the following cases:

- Renee Rogers, an African-American employee at American Airlines, wore
  cornrows to work. American had a grooming policy that prevented employees
  from wearing an all-braided hairstyle. When American sought to enforce this
  policy against Rogers, she filed suit, alleging race discrimination. In 1981, a
  federal district court rejected her argument. It first observed that cornrows
  were not distinctively associated with African-Americans, noting that Rogers
  had only adopted the hairstyle after it "had been popularized by a white actress
  in the film '10.'" As if recognizing the unpersuasiveness of what we might call
  the Bo Derek defense, the court further alleged that because hairstyle, unlike
  skin color, was a mutable characteristic, discrimination on the basis of grooming was not discrimination on the basis of race. Renee Rogers lost her case.
- Lydia Mikus and Ismael Gonzalez were called for jury service in a case involving a defendant who was Latino. When the prosecutor asked them whether
  they could speak Spanish, they answered in the affirmative. The prosecutor
  struck them, and the defense attorney then brought suit on their behalf, claiming national-origin discrimination. The prosecutor responded that he had not
  removed the potential jurors for their ethnicity but for their ability to speak
  Spanish. His stated concern was that they would not defer to the court translator in listening to Spanish-language testimony. In 1991, the Supreme Court
  credited this argument. Lydia Mikus and Ismael Gonzalez lost their case.
- Diana Piantanida had a child and took a maternity leave from her job at the
  Wyman Center, a charitable organization in Missouri. During her leave, she
  was demoted, supposedly for previously having handed in work late. The man
  who was then the Wyman Center's executive director, however, justified her
  demotion by saying the new position would be easier "for a new mom to handle." As it turned out, the new position had less responsibility and half the pay
  of the original one. But when Piantanida turned this position down, her successor was paid Piantanida's old salary. Piantanida brought suit, claiming she

had been discharged as a "new mom." In 1997, a federal appellate court refused to analyze her claim as a sex-discrimination case, which would have led to comparing the treatment she received to the treatment of "new dads." Instead, it found that Piantanida's (admittedly vague) pleadings raised claims only under the Pregnancy Discrimination Act, which it correctly interpreted to protect women only while they are pregnant. Diana Piantanida lost her case.

- Robin Shahar was a lesbian attorney who received a job offer from the Georgia Department of Law, where she had worked as a law student. The summer before she started her new job, Shahar had a religious same-sex commitment ceremony with her partner. She asked a supervisor for a late starting date because she was getting married and wanted to go on a celebratory trip to Greece. Believing Shahar was marrying a man, the supervisor offered his congratulations. Senior officials in the office soon learned, however, that Shahar's partner was a woman. This news caused a stir, reports of which reached Michael Bowers, the attorney general of Georgia who had successfully defended his state's prohibition of sodomy before the United States Supreme Court. After deliberating with his lawyers, Bowers rescinded her job offer. The staff member who informed her read from a script, concluding, "Thanks again for coming in, and have a nice day." Shahar brought suit, claiming discrimination on the basis of sexual orientation. In court, Bowers testified that he knew Shahar was gay when he hired her, and would never have terminated her for that reason. In 1997, a federal appellate court accepted that defense, maintaining that Bowers had terminated Shahar on the basis of her conduct, not her status. Robin Shahar lost her case.

- Simcha Goldman, an Air Force officer who was also an ordained rabbi, wore a yarmulke at all times. Wearing a yarmulke is part of the Orthodox tradition of covering one's head out of deference to an omnipresent god. Goldman's religious observance ran afoul of an Air Force regulation that prohibited wearing headgear while indoors. When he refused his commanding officer's order to remove his yarmulke, Goldman was threatened with a court martial. He brought a First Amendment claim, alleging discrimination on the basis of religion. In 1986, the Supreme Court rejected his claim. It stated that the Air Force had drawn a reasonable line between "religious apparel that is visible and that which is not." Simcha Goldman lost his case.

These five cases represent only a fraction of those in which courts have refused to protect plaintiffs from covering demands. In such cases, the courts routinely distinguish between immutable and mutable traits, between being a member of a legally protected group and behavior associated with that group. Under this rule, African-Americans cannot be fired for their skin color, but they could be fired for wearing cornrows. Potential jurors cannot be struck for their ethnicity but can be struck for speaking (or even for admitting proficiency in) a foreign language. Women cannot be discharged for having two X chromosomes but can be penalized (in some jurisdictions) for becoming mothers. Although the weaker protections for sexual orientation mean gays can sometimes be fired for their status alone, they will be much more vulnerable if they are perceived to "flaunt" their sexuality. Jews cannot be separated from the military for being Jewish but can be discharged for wearing yarmulkes.

This distinction between being and doing reflects a bias toward assimilation. Courts will protect traits like skin color or chromosomes because such traits cannot be changed. In contrast, the courts will not protect mutable traits, because individuals can alter them to fade into the mainstream, thereby escaping discrimination. If individuals choose not to engage in that form of self-help, they must suffer the consequences.

The judicial bias toward assimilation will seem correct and just to many Americans. Assimilation, after all, is a precondition of civilization—wearing clothes, having manners and obeying the law are all acts of assimilation. Moreover, the tie between assimilation and *American* civilization may be particularly strong. At least since Hector St. John de Crèvecoeur's 1782 "Letters from an American Farmer," this country has promoted assimilation as the way Americans of different backgrounds would be "melted into a new race of men." By the time Israel Zangwill's play "The Melting Pot" made its debut in 1908, the term had acquired the burnish of an American ideal. Theodore Roosevelt, who believed hyphenations like "Polish-American" were a "moral treason," is reputed to have yelled, "That's a great play!" from his box when it was performed in Washington. (He was wrong—it's no accident the title has had a longer run than the play.) And notwithstanding challenges beginning in the 1960s to move "beyond the melting pot" and to "celebrate diversity," assimilation has never lost its grip on the American imagination.

If anything, recent years have seen a revival of the melting-pot ideal. We are currently experiencing a pluralism explosion in the United States. Patterns of immigration since the late 1960s have made the United States the most religiously various country in the history of the world. Even when the demographics of a group—like the number of individuals with disabilities—are presumably constant, the number of individuals claiming membership in that group may grow exponentially. In 1970, there were 9 disability-related associations listed in the Encyclopedia of Associations; in 1980, there were 16; in 1990, there were 211; and in 2000, there were 799. The boom in identity politics has led many thoughtful commentators to worry that we are losing our common culture as Americans. Fearful that we are breaking apart into balkanized fiefs, even liberal lions like Arthur Schlesinger have called for a recommitment to the ethic of assimilation.

Beyond keeping pace with the culture, the judiciary has institutional reasons for encouraging assimilation. In the yarmulke case, the government argued that ruling in favor of the rabbi's yarmulke would immediately invite suits concerning the Sikh's turban, the yogi's saffron robes and the Rastafarian's dreadlocks. Because the courts must articulate principled grounds for their decisions, they are particularly ill equipped to protect some groups but not others in an increasingly diverse society. Seeking to avoid judgments about the relative worth of groups, the judiciary has decided instead to rely on the relatively uncontroversial principle of protecting immutable traits.

Viewed in this light, the judiciary's failure to protect individuals against covering demands seems eminently reasonable. Unfortunately, it also represents an abdication of its responsibility to protect civil rights.

THE CASE AGAINST ASSIMILATION

The flaw in the judiciary's analysis is that it casts assimilation as an unadulterated good. Assimilation is implicitly characterized as the way in which groups can evade discrimination by fading into the mainstream—after all, the logic goes, if a bigot cannot discriminate between two individuals, he cannot discriminate against one of them. But sometimes assimilation is not an escape from discrimination, but precisely its effect. When a Jew is forced to convert to Protestantism, for instance, we do not celebrate that as an evasion of anti-Semitism. We should not blind ourselves to the dark underbelly of the American melting pot.

Take the cornrows case. Initially, this case appears to be an easy one for the employer, as hairstyle seems like such a trivial thing. But if hair is so trivial, we might ask why American Airlines made it a condition of Renee Rogers's employment. What's frustrating about the employment discrimination jurisprudence is that courts often don't force employers to answer the critical question of why they are requiring employees to cover. If we look to other sources, the answers can be troubling.

John T. Molloy's perennially popular self-help manual "New Dress for Success" also tells racial minorities to cover. Molloy advises African-Americans to avoid "Afro hairstyles" and to wear "conservative pin-stripe suits, preferably with vests, accompanied by all the establishment symbols, including the Ivy League tie." He urges Latinos to "avoid pencil-line mustaches," "any hair tonic that tends to give a greasy or shiny look to the hair," "any articles of clothing that have Hispanic associations" and "anything that is very sharp or precise."

Molloy is equally frank about why covering is required. The "model of success," he says, is "white, Anglo-Saxon and Protestant." Those who do not possess these traits "will elicit a negative response to some degree, regardless of whether that response is conscious or subconscious." Indeed, Molloy says racial minorities must go "somewhat overboard" to compensate for immutable differences from the white mainstream. After conducting research on African-American corporate grooming, Molloy reports that "blacks had not only to dress more conservatively but also more expensively than their white counterparts if they wanted to have an equal impact."

Molloy's basic point is supported by social-science research. The economists Marianne Bertrand and Sendhil Mullainathan recently conducted a study in which they sent out résumés that were essentially identical except for the names at the top. They discovered that résumés with white-sounding names like Emily Walsh or Greg Baker drew 50 percent more callbacks than those with African-

American-sounding names like Lakisha Washington or Jamal Jones. So it seems that even when Americans have collectively set our faces against racism, we still react negatively to cultural traits—like hairstyles, clothes or names—that we associate with historically disfavored races.

We can see a similar dynamic in the termination of Robin Shahar. Michael Bowers, the state attorney general, disavowed engaging in first-generation discrimination when he said he had no problem with gay employees. This raises the question of why he fired Shahar for having a religious same-sex commitment ceremony. Unlike American Airlines, Bowers provided some answers. He argued that retaining Shahar would compromise the department's ability to deny same-sex couples marriage licenses and to enforce sodomy statutes.

Neither argument survives scrutiny. At no point did Shahar seek to marry 25 her partner legally, nor did she agitate for the legalization of same-sex marriage. The Georgia citizenry could not fairly have assumed that Shahar's religious ceremony would entitle the couple to a civil license. Bowers's claim that Shahar's wedding would compromise her ability to enforce sodomy statutes is also off the mark. Georgia's sodomy statute (which has since been struck down) punished cross-sex as well as same-sex sodomy, meaning that any heterosexual in the department who had ever had oral sex was as compromised as Shahar.

Stripped of these rationales, Bowers's termination of Shahar looks more sinister. When she told a supervisor she was getting married, he congratulated her. When he discovered she was marrying a woman, it wasn't long before she no longer had a job. Shahar's religious ceremony was not in itself indiscreet; cross-sex couples engage in such ceremonies all the time. If Shahar was flaunting anything, it was her belief in her own equality: her belief that she, and not the state, should determine what personal bonds are worthy of celebration.

The demand to cover is anything but trivial. It is the symbolic heartland of inequality—what reassures one group of its superiority to another. When dominant groups ask subordinated groups to cover, they are asking them to be small in the world, to forgo prerogatives that the dominant group has and therefore to forgo equality. If courts make critical goods like employment dependent on covering, they are legitimizing second-class citizenship for the subordinated group. In doing so, they are failing to vindicate the promise of civil rights.

So the covering demand presents a conundrum. The courts are right to be leery of intervening in too brusque a manner here, as they cannot risk playing favorites among groups. Yet they also cannot ignore the fact that the covering demand is where many forms of inequality continue to have life. We need a paradigm that gives both these concerns their due, adapting the aspirations of the civil rights movement to an increasingly pluralistic society.

THE NEW CIVIL RIGHTS

The new civil rights begins with the observation that everyone covers. When I lecture on covering, I often encounter what I think of as the "angry straight white man" reaction. A member of the audience, almost invariably a white man, almost invariably angry, denies that covering is a civil rights issue. Why shouldn't racial minorities or women or gays have to cover? These groups should receive legal protection against discrimination for things they cannot help. But why should they receive protection for behaviors within their control—wearing cornrows, acting "feminine" or flaunting their sexuality? After all, the questioner says, I have to cover all the time. I have to mute my depression, or my obesity, or my alcoholism, or my shyness, or my working-class background or my nameless anomie. I, too, am one of the mass of men leading lives of quiet desperation. Why should legally protected groups have a right to self-expression I do not? Why should my struggle for an authentic self matter less?

I surprise these individuals when I agree. Contemporary civil rights has erred 30 in focusing solely on traditional civil rights groups—racial minorities, women, gays, religious minorities and people with disabilities. This assumes those in the so-called mainstream—those straight white men—do not also cover. They are understood only as obstacles, as people who prevent others from expressing themselves, rather than as individuals who are themselves struggling for self-definition. No wonder they often respond to civil rights advocates with hostility. They experience us as asking for an entitlement they themselves have been refused—an expression of their full humanity.

Civil rights must rise into a new, more inclusive register. That ascent makes use of the recognition that the mainstream is a myth. With respect to any particular identity, the word "mainstream" makes sense, as in the statement that straights are more mainstream than gays. Used generically, however, the word loses meaning. Because human beings hold many identities, the mainstream is a shifting coalition, and none of us are entirely within it. It is not normal to be completely normal.

This does not mean discrimination against racial minorities is the same as discrimination against poets. American civil rights law has correctly directed its concern toward certain groups and not others. But the aspiration of civil rights— the aspiration that we be free to develop our human capacities without the impediment of witless conformity—is an aspiration that extends beyond traditional civil rights groups.

To fulfill that aspiration, we must think differently both within the law and outside it. With respect to legal remedies, we must shift away from claims that demand equality for particular groups toward claims that demand liberty for us all. This is not an exhortation that we strip protections from currently recognized groups. Rather, it is a prediction that future courts will be unable to sustain a group-based vision of civil rights when faced with the broad and irreversible trend toward demographic pluralism. In an increasingly diverse society, the courts must look to what draws us together as citizens rather than to what drives us apart.

As if in recognition of that fact, the Supreme Court has moved in recent years away from extending protections on the basis of group membership and toward doing so on the basis of liberties we all possess. In 2003, the Court struck down a

Texas statute that prohibited same-sex sodomy. It did not, however, frame the case as one concerning the equality rights of gays. Instead, it cast the case as one concerning the interest we all—straight, gay or otherwise—have in controlling our intimate lives. Similarly, in 2004, the Court held that a state could be required by a Congressional statute to make its courthouses wheelchair accessible. Again, the Court ruled in favor of the minority group without framing its analysis in group-based equality rhetoric. Rather, it held that all people—disabled or otherwise—have a "right of access to the courts," which had been denied in that instance.

In these cases, the Court implicitly acknowledged the national exhaustion with group-based identity politics and quieted the anxiety about pluralism that is driving us back toward the assimilative ideal. By emphasizing the interest all individuals have in our own liberty, the Court focused on what unites us rather than on what divides us. While preserving the distinction between being and doing, the Court decided to protect doing in its own right.

If the Supreme Court protects individuals against covering demands in the future, I believe it will do so by invoking the universal rights of people. I predict that if the Court ever recognizes the right to speak a native language, it will protect that right as a liberty to which we are all entitled, rather than as a remedial concession granted to a particular national-origin group. If the Court recognizes rights to grooming, like the right to wear cornrows, I believe it will do so under something akin to the German Constitution's right to personality rather than as a right attached to racial minorities. And I hope that if the Court protects the right of gays to marry, it will do so by framing it as the right we all have to marry the person we love, rather than defending "gay marriage" as if it were a separate institution. 35

A liberty-based approach to civil rights, of course, brings its own complications, beginning with the question of where my liberty ends and yours begins. But the ability of liberty analysis to illuminate our common humanity should not be underestimated. This virtue persuaded both Martin Luther King Jr. and Malcolm X to argue for the transition from civil rights to human rights at the ends of their lives. It is time for American law to follow suit.

While I have great hopes for this new legal paradigm, I also believe law will play a relatively small part in the new civil rights. A doctor friend told me that in his first year of medical school, his dean described how doctors were powerless to cure the vast majority of human ills. People would get better, or they would not, but it would not be doctors who would cure them. Part of becoming a doctor, the dean said, was to surrender a layperson's awe for medical authority. I wished then that someone would give an analogous lecture to law students and to Americans at large. My education in law has been in no small part an education in its limitations.

As an initial matter, many covering demands are made by actors the law does not—and in my view should not—hold accountable, like friends, family, neighbors, the "culture" or individuals themselves. When I think of the covering demands I have experienced, I can trace many of them only to my own censorious consciousness. And while I am often tempted to sue myself, I recognize this is not my healthiest impulse.

Law is also an incomplete solution to coerced assimilation because it has yet to recognize the myriad groups that are subjected to covering demands even though these groups cannot be defined by traditional classifications like race, sex, orientation, religion and disability. Whenever I speak about covering, I receive new instances of identities that can be covered. The law may someday move to protect some of these identities. But it will never protect them all.

For these and other reasons, I am troubled that Americans seem increasingly 40 inclined to turn toward the law to do the work of civil rights precisely when they should be turning away from it. The primary solution lies in all of us as citizens, not in the tiny subset of us who are lawyers. People confronted with demands to cover should feel emboldened to seek a reason for that demand, even if the law does not reach the actors making the demand or recognize the group burdened by it. These reason-forcing conversations should happen outside courtrooms— in public squares and prayer circles, in workplaces and on playgrounds. They should occur informally and intimately, in the everyday places where tolerance is made and unmade.

What will constitute a good-enough reason to justify assimilation will obviously be controversial. We have come to some consensus that certain reasons are illegitimate—like racism, sexism or religious intolerance. Beyond that, we should expect conversations rather than foreordained results—what reasons count, and for what purposes, will be for us all to decide by facing one another as citizens. My personal inclination is always to privilege the claims of the individual against countervailing interests like "neatness" or "workplace harmony." But we should have that conversation.

Such conversations are the best—and perhaps the only—way to give both assimilation and authenticity their due. They will help us alleviate conservative, alarmists' fears of a balkanized America and radical multiculturalists' fears of a monocultural America. The aspiration of civil rights has always been to permit people to pursue their human flourishing without limitations based on bias. Focusing on law prevents us from seeing the revolutionary breadth of that aspiration. It is only when we leave the law that civil rights suddenly stops being about particular agents of oppression, and particular victimized groups and starts to become a project of human flourishing in which we all have a stake.

I don't teach classes on gay rights any more. I suspect many of my students now experience me as a homosexual professional rather than as a professional homosexual, if they think of me in such terms at all. But I don't experience myself as covering. I've just moved on to other interests, in the way scholars do. So the same behavior—not teaching gay rights—has changed in meaning over time.

This just brings home to me that the only right I have wanted with any consistency is the freedom to be who I am. I'll be the first to admit that I owe much of that freedom to group-based equality movements, like the gay rights movement. But it is now time for us as a nation to shift the emphasis away from equality and toward liberty in our debates about identity politics. Only through such freedom can we live our lives as works in progress, which is to say, as the complex, changeful and contradictory creatures that we are.

QUESTIONS FOR DISCUSSION AND WRITING

1. Yoshino writes that "The demand to cover is anything but trivial. It is the symbolic heartland of inequality—what reassures one group of its superiority to another." What is the demand to cover? How does it "legitimize second-class citizenship" for a subordinated group (paragraph 27)? How does this relate to the five cases Yoshino presents in paragraph 12? Why are legal remedies less effective than "reason-forcing conversations" in combating the pressure to cover (paragraphs 38–42)?

2. What does Kenji Yoshino mean when he claims that "America has undergone a generational shift" in its fight against discrimination (paragraph 10)? If the first generation of the struggle fought against discrimination aimed at entire groups, how does this differ from the fight of the "liberty-based" approach against "covering demands" (paragraphs 11, 13–15)? To what extent does Yoshino's anecdote about the "angry straight white man" (paragraphs 29–30) help you understand why Yoshino advocates the liberty-based approach?

3. Research a case of "covering pressure" in history or in current events. This should be a case of discrimination against "doing" rather than "being" (paragraphs 14–15). In what ways was the wronged party pressured to assimilate into the mainstream? How could Yoshino's ideas help that person fight the requirement to assimilate? What kind of "reason-forcing" conversation could that person have with the authorities who pressured him or her to cover? (See paragraphs 40–42 for Yoshino's description of a reason-forcing conversation.) You could discuss a case involving a dress code, a code of conduct, or restrictions on speech, for example.

4. Have you ever felt the pressure to cover? Write an essay about your experience using Kenji Yoshino's theory of covering to explain what happened to you and what you did in response. (Alternatively, interview someone about their experience of being pressured to assimilate into the norm.) You might want to write this paper in the form of a "reason-forcing" memo to the person who pressured you to cover, inviting them to have a conversation about why you should change your behavior or appearance. Demand a rational explanation. Are they simply asking you to conform to dominant norms? Question reasons like "neatness" and "workplace harmony." Explain why their demands inhibit your right to "flourish" as an authentic human being.

BOB DAEMMRICH

Nobody Knows I'm Gay

QUESTIONS FOR DISCUSSION AND WRITING

1. "Meaning in context"—is there any other kind? How do you "read" the message on the T-shirt? Though amusing, is it serious? Is the wearer blowing his "cover"? Is Yoshino (p. 456), who is "out" but "covering," appearing in the equivalent of an unmarked shirt? What messages on the subject is he sending to his readers?

2. Suppose the wearer is actually not gay. Are there any clues in the picture about the sexual orientations of this man or his two companions? Does your interpretation change if you know that this photograph was taken on October 11, 2003, National Coming Out Day, at a gay rights rally at the University of Texas at Austin?

3. Suppose the T-shirt were plain white. How would that affect your interpretation of the people in the photograph? Would you even remember it? By analogy, how could such a photograph, with and without messages on the T-shirt, illustrate Richard Rodriguez's "Family Values" (p. 492)?

JONATHAN SWIFT

A Modest Proposal

Jonathan Swift (1667–1745) was born of English parents in Dublin and attended Trinity College; he immigrated to England during the revolution of 1688. In London Swift found his literary voice as a satirist, decided on a career in the church, and worked as a political journalist. In 1713 his reward for service to the Tory party was the deanship of St. Patrick's (Anglican) Cathedral in Dublin. There he wrote his best-known and greatest work, Gulliver's Travels *(1726)—a satire on "the vanity of human wishes," politics, scientific excesses, and other human follies.*

Although Swift adhered firmly to Anglicanism, he sympathized with the Roman Catholic Irish subjects among whom he lived. This is perhaps nowhere so clear as in "A Modest Proposal" (1729). Written after three years of drought and crop failures in Ireland, and the starvation and homelessness of thirty-five thousand Irish share-croppers, "A Modest Proposal" uses impeccable logic to advocate infanticide and cannibalism—namely, that the English eat Irish children. As a satirist, Swift relies on his readers to pass moral judgment on the indifference of the English to Irish suffering.

It is a melancholy object to those who walk through this great town or travel in the country, when they see the streets, the roads, and cabin doors, crowded with beggars of the female sex, followed by three, four, or six children, all in rags and importuning every passenger for an alms. These mothers, instead of being able to work for their honest livelihood, are forced to employ all their time in strolling to beg sustenance for their helpless infants: who as they grow up either turn thieves for want of work, or leave their dear native country to fight for the pretender in Spain, or sell themselves to the Barbadoes.

I think it is agreed by all parties that this prodigious number of children in the arms, or on the backs, or at the heels of their mothers, and frequently of their fathers, is in the present deplorable state of the kingdom a very great additional grievance; and, therefore, whoever could find out a fair, cheap, and easy method of making these children sound, useful members of the commonwealth, would deserve so well of the public as to have his statue set up for a preserver of the nation.

But my intention is very far from being confined to provide only for the children of professed beggars; it is of a much greater extent, and shall take in the whole number of infants at a certain age who are born of parents in effect as little able to support them as those who demand our charity in the streets.

As to my own part, having turned my thoughts for many years upon this important subject, and maturely weighed the several schemes of our projectors, I have always found them grossly mistaken in their computation. It is true, a child just dropped from its dam may be supported by her milk for a solar year, with little other nourishment; at most not above the value of two shillings, which the mother may certainly get, or the value in scraps, by her lawful occupation of beg-ging; and it is exactly at one year old that I propose to provide for them in such a manner as instead of being a charge upon their parents or the parish, or wanting food and raiment for the rest of their lives, they shall on the contrary contribute to the feeding, and partly to the clothing, of many thousands.

There is likewise another great advantage in my scheme, that it will prevent those voluntary abortions, and that horrid practice of women murdering their bastard children, alas! too frequent among us! sacrificing the poor innocent babes I doubt more to avoid the expense than the shame, which would move tears and pity in the most savage and inhuman breast.

The number of souls in this kingdom being usually reckoned one million and half, of these I calculate there may be about two hundred thousand couple whose wives are breeders; from which number I subtract thirty thousand couple who are able to maintain their own children (although I apprehend there cannot be so many, under the present distress of the kingdom); but this being granted, there will remain an hundred and seventy thousand breeders. I again subtract fifty thousand for those women who miscarry, or whose children die by accident or disease within the year. There only remain an hundred and twenty thousand children of poor parents annually born. The question therefore is, how this num-ber shall be reared and provided for? which, as I have already said, under the present situation of affairs, is utterly impossible by all the methods hitherto pro-posed. For we can neither employ them in handicraft or agriculture; we neither build houses (I mean in the country) nor cultivate land; they can very seldom pick up a livelihood by stealing, till they arrive at six years old, except where they are of towardly parts; although I confess they learn the rudiments much earlier; during which time they can, however, be properly looked upon only as proba-tioners; as I have been informed by a principal gentleman in the county of Cavan, who protested to me that he never knew above one or two instances under the age of six, even in a part of the kingdom so renowned for the quickest proficiency in that art.

I am assured by our merchants, that a boy or a girl before twelve years old is no saleable commodity; and even when they come to this age they will not yield above three pounds, or three pounds and a half a crown at most on the Ex-change; which cannot turn to account either to the parents or kingdom, the charge of nutriment and rags having been at least four times that value.

I shall now therefore humbly propose my own thoughts, which I hope will not be liable to the least objection.

I have been assured by a very knowing American of my acquaintance in Lon-don, that a young healthy child well nursed is at a year old the most delicious, nourishing, and wholesome food, whether stewed, roasted, baked, or broiled; and I make no doubt that it will equally serve in a fricassee or a ragout.

I do therefore humbly offer it to public consideration that of the hundred and twenty thousand children already computed, twenty thousand may be re-served for breed, whereof only one fourth part to be males; which is more than we allow to sheep, black cattle, or swine; and my reason is, that these children are seldom the fruits of marriage, a circumstance not much regarded by our savages; therefore, one male will be sufficient to serve four females. That the remaining hundred thousand may, at a year old, be offered in sale to the persons of quality and fortune through the kingdom; always advising the mother to let them suck plentifully in the last month, so as to render them plump and fat for a good table. A child will make two dishes at an entertainment for friends; and when the family dines alone, the fore or hind quarter will make a reasonable dish, and seasoned with a little pepper or salt will be very good boiled on the fourth day, especially in winter.

I have reckoned upon a medium that a child just born will weigh twelve pounds, and in a solar year, if tolerably nursed, will increase to twenty-eight pounds.

I grant this food will be somewhat dear, and therefore very proper for landlords, who, as they have already devoured most of the parents, seem to have the best title to the children.

Infant's flesh will be in season throughout the year, but more plentiful in March, and a little before and after: for we are told by a grave author, an eminent French physician, that fish being a prolific diet, there are more children born in Roman Catholic countries about nine months after Lent than at any other season; therefore, reckoning a year after Lent, the markets will be more glutted than usual, because the number of popish infants is at least three to one in this kingdom: and therefore it will have one other collateral advantage, by lessening the number of papists among us.

I have already computed the charge of nursing a beggar's child (in which list I reckon all cottagers, laborers, and four-fifths of the farmers) to be about two shillings per annum, rags included; and I believe no gentleman would repine to give ten shillings for the carcass of a good fat child, which, as I have said, will make four dishes of excellent nutritive meat, when he has only some particular friend or his own family to dine with him. Thus the squire will learn to be a good landlord, and grow popular among the tenants; the mother will have eight shillings net profit, and be fit for work till she produces another child.

Those who are more thrifty (as I must confess the times require) may flay the carcass; the skin of which artificially dressed will make admirable gloves for ladies, and summer boots for fine gentlemen.

As to our city of Dublin, shambles may be appointed for this purpose in the most convenient parts of it, and butchers we may be assured will not be wanting: although I rather recommend buying the children alive, and dressing them hot from the knife as we do roasting pigs.

A very worthy person, a true lover of his country, and whose virtues I highly esteem, was lately pleased in discoursing on this matter to offer a refinement upon my scheme. He said that many gentlemen of this kingdom, having of late destroyed their deer, he conceived that the want of venison might be well supplied by the bodies of young lads and maidens, not exceeding fourteen years of age nor under twelve; so great a number of both sexes in every country being now ready to starve for want of work and service; and these to be disposed of by their parents, if alive, or otherwise by their nearest relations. But with due deference to so excellent a friend and so deserving a patriot, I cannot be altogether in his sentiments; for as to the males, my American acquaintance assured me from frequent experience that their flesh was generally tough and lean, like that of our schoolboys by continual exercise, and their taste disagreeable; and to fatten them would not answer the charge. Then as to the females, it would, I think, with humble submission be a loss to the public, because they soon would become breeders themselves: and besides, it is not improbable that some scrupulous people might be apt to censure such a practice (although indeed very unjustly), as a little bordering upon cruelty; which, I confess, has always been with me the strongest objection against any project, how well soever intended.

But in order to justify my friend, he confessed that this expedient was put into his head by the famous Psalmanazar, a native of the island Formosa, who came from thence to London about twenty years ago: and in conversation told my friend, that in his country when any young person happened to be put to death, the executioner sold the carcass to persons of quality as a prime dainty; and that in his time the body of a plump girl of fifteen, who was crucified for an attempt to poison the emperor, was sold to his imperial majesty's prime minister of state, and other great mandarins of the court, in joints from the gibbet, at four hundred crowns. Neither indeed can I deny, that if the same use were made of several plump young girls in this town, who without one single groat to their fortunes cannot stir abroad without a chair, and appear at the playhouse and assemblies in foreign fineries which they never will pay for, the kingdom would not be the worse.

Some persons of a desponding spirit are in great concern about that vast number of poor people, who are aged, diseased, or maimed, and I have been desired to employ my thoughts what course may be taken to ease the nation of so grievous an encumbrance. But I am not in the least pain upon that matter, because it is very well known that they are every day dying and rotting by cold and famine, and filth and vermin, as fast as can be reasonably expected. And as to the young laborers, they are now in as hopeful a condition: they cannot get work, and consequently pine away for want of nourishment, to a degree that if at any time they are accidentally hired to common labor, they have not strength to perform it; and thus the country and themselves are happily delivered from the evils to come.

I have too long digressed, and therefore shall return to my subject. I think 20 the advantages by the proposal which I have made are obvious and many, as well as of the highest importance.

For first, as I have already observed, it would greatly lessen the number of papists, with whom we are yearly overrun, being the principal breeders of the nation as well as our most dangerous enemies; and who stay at home on purpose to deliver the kingdom to the Pretender, hoping to take their advantage by the absence of so many good Protestants, who have chosen rather to leave their country than stay at home and pay tithes against their conscience to an Episcopal curate.

Secondly, The poor tenants will have something valuable of their own, which by law may be made liable to distress and help to pay their landlord's rent, their corn and cattle being already seized, and money a thing unknown.

Thirdly, Whereas the maintenance of a hundred thousand children from two years old and upward, cannot be computed at less than ten shillings a piece per annum, the nation's stock will be thereby increased fifty thousand pounds per annum, beside the profit of a new dish introduced to the tables of all gentlemen of fortune in the kingdom who have any refinement in taste. And the money will circulate among ourselves, the goods being entirely of our own growth and manufacture.

Fourthly, The constant breeders beside the gain of eight shillings sterling per annum by the sale of their children, will be rid of the charge of maintaining them after the first year.

Fifthly, This food would likewise bring great custom to taverns, where the 25 vintners will certainly be so prudent as to procure the best receipts for dressing it to perfection, and consequently have their houses frequented by all the fine gentlemen, who justly value themselves upon their knowledge in good eating; and a skillful cook who understands how to oblige his guests, will contrive to make it as expensive as they please.

Sixthly, This would be a great inducement to marriage, which all wise nations have either encouraged by rewards or enforced by laws and penalties. It would increase the care and tenderness of mothers toward their children, when they were sure of a settlement for life to the poor babes, provided in some sort by the public, to their annual profit instead of expense. We should see an honest emulation among the married women, which of them would bring the fattest child to the market. Men would become as fond of their wives during the time of their pregnancy as they are now of their mares in foal, their cows in calf, their sows when they are ready to farrow; nor offer to beat or kick them (as is too frequent a practice) for fear of a miscarriage.

Many other advantages might be enumerated. For instance, the addition of some thousand carcasses in our exportation of barreled beef, the propagation of swine's flesh, and improvement in the art of making good bacon, so much wanted among us by the great destruction of pigs, too frequent at our table; which are no way comparable in taste or magnificence to a well-grown, fat, yearling child, which roasted whole will make a considerable figure at a lord mayor's feast or any other public entertainment. But this and many others I omit, being studious of brevity.

Supposing that one thousand families in this city would be constant customers for infants' flesh, besides others who might have it at merry-meetings, particularly at weddings and christenings, I compute that Dublin would take off annually about twenty thousand carcasses; and the rest of the kingdom (where probably they will be sold somewhat cheaper) the remaining eighty thousand.

I can think of no one objection that will possibly be raised against this proposal, unless it should be urged that the number of people will be thereby much lessened in the kingdom. This I freely own, and it was indeed one principal de-sign in offering it to the world. I desire the reader will observe, that I calculate my remedy for this one individual kingdom of Ireland and for no other that ever was, is, or I think ever can be upon earth. Therefore let no man talk to me of other expedients; of taxing our absentees at five shillings a pound: of using nei-ther clothes nor household furniture except what is of our own growth and man-ufacture: of utterly rejecting the materials and instruments that promote foreign luxury: of curing the expensiveness of pride, vanity, idleness, and gaming in our women: of introducing a vein of parsimony, prudence, and temperance: of learn-ing to love our country, in the want of which we differ even from Laplanders and the inhabitants of Topinamboo: of quitting our animosities and factions, nor act-ing any longer like the Jews, who were murdering one another at the very mo-ment their city was taken: of being a little cautious not to sell our country and conscience for nothing: of teaching landlords to have at least one degree of mercy toward their tenants; lastly, of putting a spirit of honesty, industry, and skill into our shopkeepers; who, if a resolution could now be taken to buy only our native goods, would immediately unite to cheat and exact upon us in the price, the mea-sure, and the goodness, nor could ever yet be brought to make one fair proposal of just dealing, though often and earnestly invited to it.

Therefore I repeat, let no man talk to me of these and the like expedients, till 30 he has at least some glimpse of hope that there will be ever some hearty and sin-cere attempts to put them in practice.

But as to myself, having been wearied out for many years with offering vain, idle, visionary thoughts, and at length utterly despairing of success, I fortunately fell upon this proposal; which, as it is wholly new, so it has something solid and real, of no expense and little trouble, full in our own power, and whereby we can incur no danger in disobliging England. For this kind of commodity will not bear exportation, the flesh being of too tender a consistence to admit a long continu-ance in salt, although perhaps I could name a country which would be glad to eat up our whole nation without it.

After all, I am not so violently bent upon my own opinion as to reject any offer proposed by wise men, which shall be found equally innocent, cheap, easy, and ef-fectual. But before something of that kind shall be advanced in contradiction to my scheme, and offering a better, I desire the author or authors will be pleased ma-turely to consider two points. First, as things now stand, how they will be able to find food and raiment for a hundred thousand useless mouths and backs. And sec-ondly, there being a round million of creatures in human figure throughout this kingdom, whose subsistence put into a common stock would leave them in debt two millions of pounds sterling, adding those who are beggars by profession to the bulk of farmers, cottagers, and laborers, with the wives and children who are beg-gars in effect; I desire those politicians who dislike my overture, and may perhaps be so bold as to attempt an answer, that they will first ask the parents of these mor-tals, whether they would not at this day think it a great happiness to have been sold for food at a year old in the manner I prescribe, and thereby have avoided such a perpetual scene of misfortunes as they have since gone through by the oppression of landlords, the impossibility of paying rent without money or trade, the want of common sustenance, with neither house nor clothes to cover them from the inclemencies of the weather, and the most inevitable prospect of entailing the like or greater miseries upon their breed for ever.

I profess, in the sincerity of my heart, that I have not the least personal interest in endeavoring to promote this necessary work, having no other motive than the public good of my country, by advancing our trade, providing for infants, relieving the poor, and giving some pleasure to the rich. I have no children by which I can propose to get a single penny; the youngest being nine years old, and my wife past child-bearing.

QUESTIONS FOR DISCUSSION AND WRITING

1. Do you believe that Swift really wanted his countrymen to eat poverty-stricken Irish babies, as his overt thesis suggests? You might find some research on the definitions of *irony, satire,* and *parody* helpful.

2. What is the prevailing tone of Swift's essay? How does this tone undermine the narrator's overt argument? How does it reinforce Swift's implied thesis?

3. Why do you think the narrator uses so much mathematical calculation throughout the essay? What kind of personality comes through? Does the math support the economic argument? Why or why not?

4. Why do you think Swift refers to the Irish people in general categories — as parents, babies, mothers, "beggars of the female sex"—but does not give any personal names? Why is Maxine Hong Kingston's aunt a "No Name Woman" (p. 420)? Why does Harriet Jacobs omit her name in her book's title (p. 450), while Frederick Douglass includes his name in his *Narrative* (p. 452)? What exactly *is* in a name?

WOLE SOYINKA
Every Dictator's Nightmare

Playwright, poet, novelist, and essayist Wole Soyinka (pronounced Wo-leh Shaw-yin-ka) was born in 1934 in Isara, Nigeria. He grew up in the village of Ake, where his grandfather taught him Yoruba tribal culture. In contrast, his father served as headmaster in a British colonial school, and his mother (a Christian) organized a tax revolt leading to Nigerian independence. Soyinka earned a bachelor's degree (1959) from the University of Leeds. He chaired the theater arts departments at the universities of Ibadan and Ife while also founding and directing several theater groups. Soyinka was imprisoned in 1965 and 1967–1969 on charges of opposing the

Nigerian government's abuses of power; in solitary confinement he wrote a diary,
The Man Died *(1972). In 1986 Soyinka was awarded the Nobel Prize in Literature
for his poetic dramas. His postwar plays express despair and rage at abuses of power,
dramatized in explicit scenes of corruption, tyranny, torture, and slaughter. His recent political writings include* The Open Sore of a Continent: A Personal Narrative
of the Nigerian Crisis *(1996) and* The Burden of Memory, the Muse of Forgiveness *(1998).*

*Soyinka's commitment to the concept of fundamental human rights animates
his essay "Every Dictator's Nightmare," originally published in the* New York Times
Magazine *(April 1999). The idea that all people belong to the human race—as opposed to specific races, creeds, and ideologies—is a foil to the hopes of dictators and
other rapacious powermongers who would create divisions between ethnic and social
groups. This seems particularly relevant in light of contemporary wars and political
oppression worldwide.*

With the blood-soaked banner of religious fanaticism billowing across the skies as
one prominent legacy of this millennium, Martin Luther's famous theses against
religious absolutism struck me early as a strong candidate for the best idea of the
last thousand years. By progressive association, so did the microprocessor and its
implications—the liberalization of access to knowledge, and a quantum boost for
the transmission of ideas. There is, however, a nobler idea that has spread by its
own power in this millennium and that has now begun to flourish: the idea that
certain fundamental rights are inherent to all humanity.

Humankind has always struggled to assert certain values in their own
right, values that the individual intuitively felt belonged to each person as part
of natural existence. It is difficult to imagine a period when such values were
not pursued in spasmodic acts of dissent from norms that appeared to govern
society even in its most rudimentary form. Even after years of conformity to
hallowed precedents, a few dissidents always arise, and they obtain their primary impulse in crucial instances from the individual's seizure of his or her
subjective worth.

In the devolution of authority to one individual as the head of a collective, a
system of checks on arbitrary authority is prevalent. Take, for instance, monar-
chical rule among the Yoruba, the people now concentrated in western Nigeria.
At the apex is a quasi-deified personage, endowed with supreme authority over
his subjects. To preserve the mystic aura of such a ruler, he is never seen to eat or
drink. In earlier times, he was not permitted to speak directly to his people but
had to employ an intermediary voice, a spokesman. For the highest-ranked kings
in the Yoruban world, the *ekeji orisa* (companions to the deities), it was forbidden even to see their faces. Despite the social and psychological distance between
the leader and his subjects, the monarch was pledged to rule within a strict contract of authority. Transgression of a taboo, say, or failure to fulfill ceremonial
duties on time, resulted in fines, rituals of appeasement or a period of ostracism.

The major crime, however, was abuse of power, excessive authoritarianism and a trampling on the rights of the citizenry. For this category of crimes, there was only one response: the king, on being found guilty, was given a covered calabash and invited to retreat to his inner chambers. He understood the sentence: he must never again be seen among the living.

Sometimes, of course, an individual manages to convert collective authority into a personal monopoly. In these instances, society is characterized by tensions, palpable or hidden, between the suppressed rights of the people and the power rapacity of one individual. But where does society ground its claims, its resistant will, in such circumstances? We know that rebellion may be triggered by recollections of more equitable relationships, by material expropriation or by a cultural transgression that affects the spiritual well-being of the community or individual. Such rebellion finds its authority in the belief, in one citizen after another, that the ruler has violated a fundamental condition of human existence.

The *droit du seigneur*, the "right" that confers on the lord the pleasure of de-   5 flowering, on her marriage night, the bride of any of his vassals—on what does the ritually cuckolded groom finally ground his rebellion other than a subjective sense of self-worth? What of the Yoruban monarch who, even today in certain parts of my world, tries to exercise his "right" to *gbese le*—that is, to place his royal slipper, symbolically, on any woman who catches his fancy, and thus assign her to his harem? The manor lord's entitlement to compulsory labor from his peasants, the ownership of another being as a slave, the new age of enslavement of womanhood in countries like Afghanistan—the challenges to these and other so-called rights surely commence with the interrogation of self-worth, expanding progressively toward an examination of the common worth of the human entity as a unit of irreducible properties and rights.

It took centuries for societies to influence one another to the critical extent needed to incite the philosophic mind to address the concept of the human race in general, and not simply as members of a specific race or occupants of a geographical space. In its rudimentary beginnings, each society remained limited by a process that codified its own now-recognizable collective interests against all others, like the Magna Carta and the Bill of Rights. Such oaths of fealty by petty chieftains imposed duties on the suzerain but also entrenched their own equally arbitrary mechanisms of authority and coercion over the next level of society. This sometimes resulted in the bizarre alliance of the monarch with his lowest vassals against his overreaching barons and chieftains.

Like race and citizenship, religion was not far behind in the exclusionist philosophy of rights, formulating codes to protect the rights of the faithful but denying the same to others—the Cross against the Crescent, Buddhist versus Hindu, the believer against the infidel. Or simply religion versus secularism. Ground into powder beneath the hooves of the contending behemoths of religion, ideology and race, each social unit ponders, at least periodically, how he or she differs from cattle or sheep, from the horses that pull the carriages of majesty, even when such choices are the mere expressions of the collective will. If order alone, ornamentation, social

organization, technology, bonding and even productive structures were all that defined the human species, then what significant properties marked out Homo sapiens as distinct from the rest of the living species?

Polarizations within various micro-worlds—us versus the inferior them—
have long been armed with industrious rationalizations. Christian and Islamic
theologians throughout history have quarried their scriptures for passages that
stress the incontestable primacy of an unseen and unknowable Supreme Deity
who has conferred authority on them. And to what end? Largely to divide the
world into us and the rest. The great philosophical minds of Europe, like Hume,
Hegel and Kant, bent their prodigious talents to separating the species into those
with rights and those with none, founded on the convenient theory that some
people were human and others less so. The Encyclopedists of France, products of
the so-called Age of Reason, remain the most prolific codifiers of the human
(and other) species on an ambitiously comprehensive scale, and their scholarly
industry conferred a scientific benediction on a purely commercial project that
saw millions of souls dragged across the ocean to serve as beasts of burden. Religion and commerce—far older professions than the one that is sometimes
granted that distinction, but of an often-identical temperament—were reinforced by the authority of new scientific theories to divide humanity into
higher and lower manifestations of the species. The dichotomy of the world
was complete.

It took the near triumph of fascism to bring the world to its senses. The horror of the Holocaust finally took the rulers of the world back to the original question: what is the true value of humanity? It is to be doubted if the victorious three
meeting in Yalta actually went into any profound philosophical niceties in the
discussions that resulted in the United Nations, that partial attempt to reverse the
dichotomizing course of humanity. That course, taken to its ultimate conclusion,
had just resulted in an attempted purification of the species, the systematic elimination of millions in gas chambers and a war that mired the potential of Europe
in the blood of its youth. After all, the concept of the master race was not new,
but it was never before so obsessively articulated and systematically pursued. It
was time to rethink the entire fate of humanity. The conversations at Yalta, conversations that led to the birth of the United Nations, were a partial answer to
that question.

The first stage was to render the new thinking in concrete terms, to enshrine   10
in a charter of rights the product of the bruising lessons of the immediate past:
the United Nations and the Universal Declaration of Human Rights. The informing recognition is that long-suppressed extract of the intuition that humanity had
guarded through evolution, one that had been proposed, compromised,
amended, vitiated, subverted but never abandoned: that, for all human beings,
there do exist certain fundamental rights.

The idea already exists in the Bible, in the Koran, in the Bhagavad-Gita, in
the Upanishads, but always in curtailed form, relativist, patriarchal, always subject to the invisible divine realms whose interpreters are mortals with distinct,

secular agendas, usually allied to the very arbitrary controls that are a contradiction to such ideas. Quiet, restrained, ignored by but also blissfully indifferent to the so-called world religions, Ifa, the corpus of Yoruban spiritual precepts and secular philosophy, its origins lost in antiquity but preserved and applied till today, annunciates identical ideas through Orunmila, the god of divination:

> *Dandan enia l'ayan ko mu ire lo s'aye . . . Ipo rere naa ni aye-amotan ohung-bogbo, ayo nnigbagbogbo, igbesi laisi ominu tabi iberu ota.*

> Certainly, it is the human being that was elected to bring values to the world . . . and his place of good is the knowledge of all things, joy at all times, freedom from anxiety and freedom from fear of the enemy. [Irosu Wori]

Humanity has been straining to seize the fullness of this doctrine, the right to knowledge, the freedom from anxiety, the right to security of existence as inherent to the species. It is only the process of promulgating its pertinence to all mankind that has been long and costly. The kernel of the idea, therefore, is both timeless and new. Its resurrection—the concrete seizure of the idea within this millennium, answering the exigencies of politics, religion and power and securing it within the bedrock of universality—was a destiny that would first be embraced by France.

There, alas, the events that gave new life to this idea did not encourage its adoption on a universal scale, indeed not even durably within France itself. The restoration of slavery by Napoleon was surely the most blatant contradiction of the idea, but this did not much trouble the Emperor.

Still, the idea had taken hold, the idea of the rights of man as a universal principle. It certainly motored the passion of the genuine idealists in the abolition of the slave trade, who must always be distinguished from those to whom abolition was simply a shrewd commercial calculation. The idea of the American Declaration of Independence—an idea that still lacks full realization—that "all men are created equal, that they are endowed by their Creator with certain unalienable Rights" is an adumbration of that original idea from which the French Revolution obtained its inspiration, one that has continued to convulse the unjust order of the world wherever it has been grasped: the fundamental rights of man.

It is an idea whose suppression is the main occupation of dictatorships— 15 be these military or civilian, of the right or the left, secular or theocratic. It is, however, their nightmare, their single province of terror, one that they cannot exorcise, not even through the most unconscionable pogroms, scorched-earth campaigns and crimes against humanity. It is an idea that has transformed the lives of billions and remains poised to liberate billions more, since it is an idea that will not settle for tokenism or for relativism—it implicitly links the liberation of one to the liberation of all. Its gospel of universalism is anchored in the most affective impulse that cynics attribute to the choices made by humanity, self-love, but one that now translates humanity as one's own self.

QUESTIONS FOR DISCUSSION AND WRITING

1. What are fundamental human rights, in Soyinka's view? Why do these form the basis of "every dictator's nightmare"?

2. How do human rights conflict with the *droit du signeur* (paragraph 5), any arrogations of power that the ruler wishes to assume?

3. What forms do a dictator's major crimes —"abuse of power, excessive authoritarianism and a trampling of rights of the citizenry" (paragraph 3)—take in the various societies Soyinka examines throughout his essay? How can people recognize their rights? What can they do to protect them? Compare Soyinka's perspective on human rights with Posner's conservative discussion of "Security versus Civil Liberties" (below) and Elaine Scarry's liberal analysis in "Acts of Resistance" (p. 484).

4. Soyinka provides a historical examination of religion, commerce, and science's divisions of "humanity into higher and lower manifestations of the species" (paragraph 8 on). Why do dictators and various totalitarian groups (including some fundamentalists) depend on such divisions to assume and sustain their power? Identify such a group in power (or contested power) somewhere in the world today, and with a partner, analyze in an essay the situation and the abuses, then present a feasible solution to the problem.

5. Drawing on the essays by Soyinka, Posner, Scarry, and Swift in this chapter and "The Declaration of Independence" (p. 369), with a partner or a team, write your own "Declaration of Human Rights."

RICHARD A. POSNER
Security versus Civil Liberties

Richard A. Posner is a federal appellate court judge for the Seventh Circuit in Chicago, a lecturer at the University of Chicago Law School, and an author who presents a complex conservative point of view in hundreds of articles in law journals and the popular press. Born (1939) in New York City, Posner earned a bachelor's degree at Yale (1959) and a law degree at Harvard (1962). Although he initially shared his family's liberal views, he became disenchanted with what he considered excesses of leftist politics in the 1960s. Growing more conservative, in the 1970s Posner helped found the "law-and-economics movement," using traditional supply-and-demand theory to predict the economic effects of legal rulings, and was appointed to the Seventh Circuit Court in 1981 during the Reagan administration. Nevertheless, Posner differs from many conservatives in that his moral views are pragmatic and relative rather than absolute. Several of his judicial opinions, for instance, are sympathetic to abortion rights.

Author of more than thirty books on economics and the law, age and aging, sex and sexuality, and other topics, Posner has recently weighed in on national security with Catastrophe: Risk and Response *(2004) and* Uncertain Shield: The U.S. Intelligence System in the Throes of Reform *(2006). "Security versus Civil Liberties" debates the balance between protecting individual freedoms, such as freedom of the press and protection of privacy, and protecting the nation from attack.*

In the wake of the September 11 terrorist attacks have come many proposals for tightening security; some measures to that end have already been taken. Civil libertarians are troubled. They fear that concerns about national security will lead to an erosion of civil liberties. They offer historical examples of supposed overreactions to threats to national security. They treat our existing civil liberties—freedom of the press, protections of privacy and of the rights of criminal suspects, and the rest—as sacrosanct, insisting that the battle against international terrorism accommodate itself to them.

I consider this a profoundly mistaken approach to the question of balancing liberty and security. The basic mistake is the prioritizing of liberty. It is a mistake about law and a mistake about history. Let me begin with law. What we take to be our civil liberties—for example, immunity from arrest except upon probable cause to believe we've committed a crime and from prosecution for violating a criminal statute enacted after we committed the act that violates it—were made legal rights by the Constitution and other enactments. The other enactments can be changed relatively easily, by amendatory legislation. Amending the Constitution is much more difficult. In recognition of this the Framers left most of the constitutional provisions that confer rights pretty vague. The courts have made them definite.

Concretely, the scope of these rights has been determined, through an interaction of constitutional text and subsequent judicial interpretation, by a weighing of competing interests. I'll call them the public-safety interest and the liberty interest. Neither, in my view, has priority. They are both important, and their relative importance changes from time to time and from situation to situation. The safer the nation feels, the more weight judges will be willing to give to the liberty interest. The greater the threat that an activity poses to the nation's safety, the stronger will the grounds seem for seeking to repress that activity, even at some cost to liberty. This fluid approach is only common sense.

Supreme Court Justice Robert Jackson gave it vivid expression many years ago when he said, in dissenting from a free-speech decision he thought doctrinaire, that the Bill of Rights should not be made into a suicide pact. It was not intended to be such, and the present contours of the rights that it confers, having been shaped far more by judicial interpretation than by the literal text (which doesn't define such critical terms as "due process of law" and "unreasonable" arrests and searches) are alterable in response to changing threats to national security.

If it is true, therefore, as it appears to be at this writing, that the events of   5
September 11 have revealed the United States to be in much greater jeopardy from international terrorism than had previously been believed—have revealed it to

be threatened by a diffuse, shadowy enemy that must be fought with police measures as well as military force—it stands to reason that our civil liberties will be curtailed. They *should* be curtailed, to the extent that the benefits in greater security outweigh the costs in reduced liberty. All that can reasonably be asked of the responsible legislative and judicial officials is that they weigh the costs as carefully as the benefits.

It will be argued that the lesson of history is that officials habitually exaggerate dangers to the nation's security. But the lesson of history is the opposite. It is because officials have repeatedly and disastrously underestimated these dangers that our history is as violent as it is. Consider such underestimated dangers as that of secession, which led to the Civil War, of a Japanese attack on the United States, which led to the disaster at Pearl Harbor, of Soviet espionage in the 1940s, which accelerated the Soviet Union's acquisition of nuclear weapons and emboldened Stalin to encourage North Korea's invasion of South Korea; of the installation of Soviet missiles in Cuba, which precipitated the Cuban missile crisis; of political assassinations and outbreaks of urban violence in the 1960s; of the Tet Offensive of 1968; of the Iranian revolution of 1979 and the subsequent taking of American diplomats as hostages; and, for that matter, of the events of September 11.

It is true that when we are surprised and hurt, we tend to overreact—but only with the benefit of hindsight can a reaction be separated into its proper and excess layers. In hindsight we know that interning Japanese Americans did not shorten World War II. But was this known at the time? If not, shouldn't the Army have erred on the side of caution, as it did? Even today we cannot say with any assurance that Abraham Lincoln was wrong to suspend habeas corpus during the Civil War, as he did on several occasions, even though the Constitution is clear that only Congress can suspend this right. (Another of Lincoln's wartime measures, the Emancipation Proclamation, may also have been unconstitutional.) But Lincoln would have been wrong to cancel the 1864 presidential election, as some urged: by November of 1864 the North was close to victory, and canceling the election would have created a more dangerous precedent than the wartime suspension of habeas corpus. This last example shows that civil liberties remain part of the balance even in the most dangerous of times, and even though their relative weight must then be less.

Lincoln's unconstitutional acts during the Civil War show that even legality must sometimes be sacrificed for other values. We are a nation under law, but first, we are a nation. I want to emphasize something else, however: the malleability of law, its pragmatic rather than dogmatic character. The law is not absolute, and the slogan "*Fiat iustitia ruat caelum*" ("Let justice be done though the heavens fall") is dangerous nonsense. The law is a human creation rather than a divine gift, a tool of government rather than a mandarin mystery. It is an instrument for promoting social welfare, and as the conditions essential to that welfare change, so must it change.

Civil libertarians today are missing something else—the opportunity to challenge other public-safety concerns that impair civil liberties. I have particularly in mind the war on drugs. The sale of illegal drugs is a "victimless" crime in the special but important sense that it is a consensual activity. Usually there is no complaining witness, so in order to bring the criminals to justice the police have to rely heavily on paid informants (often highly paid and often highly unsavory), undercover agents, wiretaps and other forms of electronic surveillance, elaborate sting operations, the infiltration of suspect organizations, random searches, and monitoring of airports and highways, the "profiling" of likely suspects on the basis of ethnic or racial identity or national origin, compulsory drug tests, and other intrusive methods that put pressure on civil liberties. The war on drugs has been a big flop; moreover, in light of what September 11 has taught us about the gravity of the terrorist threat to the United States, it becomes hard to take entirely seriously the threat to the nation that drug use is said to pose. Perhaps it is time to redirect law-enforcement resources from the investigation and apprehension of drug dealers to the investigation and apprehension of international terrorists. By doing so we may be able to minimize the net decrease in our civil liberties that the events of September 11 have made inevitable.

QUESTIONS FOR DISCUSSION AND WRITING

1. Posner asserts that the "public-safety interest" currently needs to be stressed more and the "liberty interest" less. What does he mean by this, and what reasons does he give to back up his claim? (paragraph 3).

2. To what extent do you agree with Posner that liberties such as freedom of the press, protections of privacy, and some rights of criminal suspects (paragraph 1) should be curtailed as necessary for national security reasons? Posner gives the example of Abraham Lincoln's suspension of habeas corpus during the Civil War (paragraph 7). Why would you, or why would you not, be in favor of our president acting unconstitutionally to provide more security at this present time? If so, why? If not, are there any circumstances under which you would approve of this?

3. To what extent do you agree that "the war on drugs has been a big flop" (paragraph 9) and we should redirect resources away from that effort and toward "the investigation and apprehension of international terrorists"? What would be the effect on our society if we followed Posner's advice in this matter? Would the eventual outcome be generally positive or negative? Why? Debate the issue with a classmate and collaborate on a paper discussing this (see question 4). Take the essays of Soyinka (p. 475) and Scarry (p. 484) into account, as well.

4. Use question 2 or 3 (above) as the topic of an argumentative, thesis-driven essay. If you like, write it in the form of a letter to Richard A. Posner, in which you agree or disagree with his proposals, or to your congressperson or to the president. Give reasons and detailed evidence to back up your claims.

ELAINE SCARRY

Acts of Resistance

Elaine Scarry was born in Summit, New Jersey (1946), attended Chatham College in Pittsburgh (B.A., 1968), and earned advanced degrees at the University of Connecticut (Ph.D., 1974). She held a professorship at the University of Pennsylvania before moving to Harvard University's English department (1988), where she is Walter M. Cabot Professor of Aesthetics and the General Theory of Value. Her book The Body in Pain: The Making and Unmaking of the World *(1985) brought her to national prominence as a cross-disciplinary thinker with concerns about justice and the widespread use of torture. Arguing that torturers use pain to exploit human vulnerability and display power, Scarry claimed that the opposite of torture is the creative human imagination. Torture was an issue for many socially conscious writers in the 1980s, as brutal dictatorships in Central and South America attempted to suppress democratic reforms. Scarry continued to explore the human imagination in* Dreaming by the Book *(1999), where she discussed the way readers transform literature into mental imagery.*

In "Acts of Resistance" Scarry questions the constitutionality of the U.S. Patriot Act, passed by Congress in the fall of 2001 and partially reauthorized in 2006. This legislation was intended to thwart terrorist attacks against the United States, but many American communities have passed resolutions against it. Scarry explains some of the most common objections, which center on the way the act decreases the rights of individual persons, while making law-enforcement agencies "invisible" to individuals, something the drafters of the Constitution wished to avoid.

When the U.S.A. Patriot Act arrived in our midst in the fall of 2001, its very title seemed to deliver an injury: "Uniting and Strengthening America by Providing Appropriate Tools Required to Intercept and Obstruct Terrorism." One might have thought that "United States of America" would be a sufficient referent for the letters "U.S.A." and that no one would presume to bestow a new meaning on the word "patriot," with its heavy freight of history (Paul Revere, Patrick Henry, Emma Lazarus) and its always fresh aspiration ("O beautiful for patriot dream").

In the two and a half years since it was passed, the U.S.A. Patriot Act has become the locus of resistance against the unceasing injuries of the Bush-Rumsfeld-Ashcroft triumvirate, as first one community, then two, then eleven, then twenty-seven, and now 272 have passed resolutions against it, as have four state legislatures. The letters "U.S.A." and the word "patriot" are gradually reacquiring their earlier solidity and sufficiency as local and state governments reanimate the practice of self-rule by opposing the Patriot Act's assault on the personal privacy, free flow of information, and freedom of association that lie at the heart of democracy. Each of the resolutions affirms the town's obligation to uphold the constitutional rights of all persons who live there, and many of them explicitly direct police and other residents to refrain from carrying out the provisions of the Act, even when instructed to do so by a federal officer.

When the resistance was first beginning, in the winter of 2001–2002, it took five months for the first five resolutions to come into being; by the winter of 2003–2004, a new resolution was being drafted almost every day. The resolutions come from towns ranging from small villages—Wendell, Massachusetts (986), Riverside, Washington (348), Gaston, Oregon (620)—to huge cities—Philadelphia (1,517,550), Baltimore (651,000), Chicago (2,896,000), Detroit (951,000), Austin (656,300), San Francisco (777,000). Approximately a third of the resolutions come from towns and cities with populations between 20,000 and 200,000.

The fact that the Patriot Act has engendered such resistance may at first seem puzzling. True, its legislative history is sordid: it was rushed through Congress in several days; no hearings were held; it went largely unread; only a few of its many egregious provisions were modified. But at least it was passed by Congress: many other blows to civil liberties have been delivered as unmodified executive edicts, such as the formation of military tribunals and the nullification of attorney-client privilege. True, the Patriot Act severed words from their meanings (beginning with the letters "U.S.A."), but executive statements associating Iraq with nuclear weapons and with Al Qaeda severed words from their basis in material fact, at the very great cost of a war that continues to be materially and mortally destructive. True, the Patriot Act has degraded the legal stature of the United States by permitting the executive branch to bypass constitutional law, but our legal degradation outside the Patriot Act has gone even further: Evidence indicates that the Bush Administration has created offshore torture centers in Bagram, Afghanistan, and on the British island of Diego Garcia, and has sent prisoners to interrogation centers in countries with documented histories of torture such as Egypt, Jordan, Saudi Arabia, and Syria.

The executive edicts, the war against Iraq, and the alleged use of torture have all elicited protest, but what differentiates the opposition to the Patriot Act is the fact that it has enabled the population to move beyond vocalizing dissent to retarding, and potentially reversing, the executive's inclination to carry out actions divorced from the will of the people.

If many members of Congress failed to read the Patriot Act during its swift passage, it is in part because it is almost unreadable. The Patriot Act is written as an extended sequence of additions to and deletions from previously existing statutes, instructing the bewildered reader to insert three words into paragraph X of statute Y without ever providing the altered sentence in either its original or its amended form. Only someone who had scores of earlier statutes open to the relevant pages could step painstakingly through the revisions. Reading the Patriot Act is like standing outside the public library trying to infer the sentences in the books inside by listening to hundreds of mice chewing away on the pages.

The act does, however, have a coherent and unitary purpose: to increase the power of the Justice Department and to decrease the rights of individual persons.

The constitutional rights abridged by the Patriot Act are enumerated in the town resolutions, which most often specify violations of the First Amendment guarantee of free speech and assembly, the Fourth Amendment guarantee against search and seizure, the Fifth and Fourteenth Amendment guarantees of due process, and the Sixth and Eighth Amendment guarantees of a speedy and public trial and of protection against cruel and unusual punishment.

The objective of the Patriot Act becomes even clearer if it is understood concretely as making the population *visible* and the Justice Department *invisible*. The act inverts the constitutional requirement that people's lives be private and the work of government officials be public; it instead crafts a set of conditions that make our inner lives transparent and the workings of the government opaque. Either one of these outcomes would imperil democracy; together they not only injure the country but also cut off the avenues of repair.

When we say democracy requires that the people's privacy be ensured, we mean that we ourselves should control the degree to which, and the people to whom, our lives are revealed. Under the Patriot Act, the inner lives of people are made involuntarily transparent by provisions that increase the ability of federal officers to enter and search a person's house, to survey private medical records, business records, library records, and educational records, and to monitor telephone, email, and Internet use. The Fourth Amendment states: "The right of the people to be secure in their persons, houses, papers, and effects, against unreasonable searches and seizures, shall not be violated, and no Warrants shall issue, *but upon probable cause, supported by Oath or affirmation, and particularly describing the place to be searched, and the persons or things to be seized*" (emphasis added). The Patriot Act both explicitly lowers the "probable cause" requirement, thereby diminishing judicial review, and eliminates the specificity clause—"particularly describing the place to be searched, and the persons or things to be seized"—which, like "probable cause," puts severe restraints on the scope and duration of the search. The act is a sweeping license to search and seize, everywhere and anywhere, guided not by court-validated standards of evidence but by Justice Department hunches and racially inflected intuitions.

As necessary to democracy as the nontransparency of persons is the transparency of government actions, and indeed the Constitution pauses again and again to insist upon open records: "Each house [of Congress] shall keep a Journal of its Proceedings, and from time to time publish the same" with "the Yeas and Nays of the Members . . . entered on the Journal"; "a regular Statement and Account of the Receipts and Expenditures of all public Money shall be published from time to time"; presidential objections to a piece of legislation must be forwarded to the house in which the legislation originated and published in its journal; the counting of the Electoral College votes must take place in the presence of the full Congress; treason proceedings will take place in "open Court" and criminal prosecutions in a "public trial," etc.

The obligation of each branch to make its actions public—to make them visible both to the people and to the other branches—is often construed as a right belonging to the populace, the right of "freedom of information." Indeed, it is hard to disagree with the argument that democratic deliberation is impossible without this access to information. Secrecy, the legal theorist Cass Sunstein writes, "is inconsistent with the principle of self-rule." He identifies citizen deliberation as the primary benefit of open government, but there are other benefits, including checks and balances (one branch cannot check the other if it does not know what the other is doing), and "sunlight as a disinfectant" (if deliberations are carried out in secret, "participants may be less careful to ensure that their behavior is unaffected by illegitimate or irrelevant considerations").

Because both the privacy of individual action and the publication of government action are necessary to democratic self-rule, the major complaint of the local resolutions has been the damage done to the liberties of persons and to the integrity of our laws. The most forceful formulation of this worry comes at the conclusion of the Blount County, Tennessee, resolution, which calls upon all residents "to study the Bill of Rights so that they can recognize and resist attempts to undermine our Constitutional Republic . . . and declare null and void all future attempts to establish Martial Law, [or] Declared States of Emergency." Although most of the other resolutions are more measured in their language, they consistently register the view that both the people and the laws of this country are endangered.

The resolutions have a second, closely related focus. Although the Patriot Act enables the federal government to detain and investigate both citizens and noncitizens, and to carry out surveillance of both citizens and noncitizens, its blows fall most heavily on those who are not U.S. citizens.

Consider section 412. As summarized by the city of Ann Arbor, Michigan, it permits the incarceration of noncitizens for seven days without charge and "for six month periods indefinitely, without access to counsel" if the attorney general "determines release would endanger the security of the country or of a specific person." Before it was modified by Congress, the bill authorized the unlimited detention of immigrants, but the revision is less of an improvement than it seems, since various loopholes release the executive branch from the seven-day constraint.

The resolutions collectively work to prevent this imperilment of all residents 15 of the United States. Almost without exception, the 272 resolutions celebrate their commitment to law and liberty for all "persons" or "residents," not only "citizens." This is expressed in part as a matter of constitutional conviction: The very first clause of the very first resolution (Ann Arbor) begins by echoing the 2001 Supreme Court decision *Zadvydas* v. *Davis*: "The due process and equal protection clauses of the Fifth and Fourteenth Amendments to the United States Constitution guarantee certain due process and equal protection rights to all residents of the United States regardless of citizenship or immigration status . . . " Other resolutions remind all residents that discrimination based on "citizenship status" is no more permissible than discrimination based on race or gender. They complain that the Patriot Act tries "to drive a wedge" between citizens and noncitizens, or between police and foreign nationals, a situation held to be intolerable because the town depends on the diversity of its population for its "vitality" and its "economy, culture, and civic character."

Almost the only time when "citizens" are singled out is when the documents place on them the burden of acting to ensure that all "persons" or "residents" enjoy the benefits of due process, protection from unwarranted search and seizure, freedom of speech, freedom of assembly, and privacy. If, in other words, citizens are unique, it is because they are the guardians of rights belonging to citizens and noncitizens alike, not the exclusive holders of those rights.

In addition to aiming blows at our legal framework of self-governance, the Patriot Act licenses the executive branch to harm other institutions—among them financial markets and universities—and once again its blows appear to be structural.

Take, for example, the provisions that require bankers, broker-dealers, and trading advisers to file "suspicious activity reports" (SARs) when they notice their clients carrying out unusual transfers greater than $5,000. Failure to file is punishable by criminal and civil charges, with fines reaching $10,000. Furthermore, they are prohibited from telling their client about the SAR, which not only taints the client relationship but eliminates at the outset the possibility of determining whether the transfer has some sensible explanation that, if they only knew it, would convince them that the filing was preposterous.

Universities, too, are among the institutions the Patriot Act seeks to change, and the situation may be swiftly assessed by looking at the most widely discussed aspect of the act, section 215, which applies to both college and public libraries (and, in many cases, bookstores). When approached by an FBI or CIA agent, librarians must turn over a record of the books a specified patron has taken out, and, like the bankers, they are prohibited from telling anyone of the intelligence gathering in which they have just participated.

In his fall 2003 tour of thirty cities to defend the Patriot Act, Attorney General John Ashcroft dismissed the idea that the Justice Department could conceivably care about librarians or library records. A University of Illinois study found, however, that by February 2002 (four months after the Patriot Act was passed) 4 percent of all U.S. libraries and 11 percent of libraries in communities of more than 50,000 people had already been visited by FBI agents requesting information about their patrons' reading habits. Ashcroft insisted that not-yet-released FBI records would demonstrate the indifference of the Justice Department to the libraries, but the Justice Department has in fact refused to release these very same records, despite Freedom of Information Act petitions filed by the American Civil Liberties Union and other organizations.

In distilled form, the logic of the Patriot Act and its defense involves four steps: Maximize the power of the Justice Department; erase the public record of Justice Department actions; respond with indignation if anyone protests that the Justice Department might actually be using its newly expanded powers; point out that the protesters are speaking without any hard evidence or facts without mentioning that the executive branch has withheld those very facts from the public.

From the founding of this country the phrase "a government of laws and not of men" has meant that the country cannot pass open-ended laws that will be good if the governors happen to be good and bad if the governors happen to be bad. The goal has always been to pass laws that will protect everyone regardless of the temperament and moral character of the individual governors. The country, as Justice Davis famously observed in the nineteenth century, "has no right to expect that it will always have wise and humane rulers." That's why it is crucial to pass good laws. And crucial, also, to repeal bad ones.

Despite impediments to resistance, 272 towns, cities, and counties have created a firewall against executive trespass in their communities. The resolutions direct residents to decline to assist the federal government in any act that violates the Constitution: local police should abstain from assisting federal officers in house searches that violate the Fourth Amendment, and librarians should abstain from giving out private library records that violate the First and Fourth Amendments.

Here we have the key to why the Patriot Act—rather than the executive edicts—has become the focus of so much resistance. Since military tribunals do not require the assistance of the population, what we think about the military tribunals is a matter of indifference to the executive. Since the country has a standing army rather than a draft, the war against Iraq was neither ours to assist nor ours to decline to assist. If, without the population's assistance, 5,000 foreign nationals can be detained without charges (only three of whom were ever charged with terrorism-related acts), then the population's disapproval of this detention is like smoke rings in the wind. But since the aspirations encoded in the Patriot Act cannot come about without the help of police, bankers, and librarians, the refusal to assist provides a concrete brake on the actions of the federal government.

Although the Justice Department has tried to portray resistance to the Patriot Act as a liberal complaint, the resisters repeatedly assert that they occupy positions across the political spectrum. And, so far, both Congress and the courts appear to be listening. Various congressmen and senators have initiated bills to nullify or limit specific provisions of the Patriot Act. In July 2003 the House passed an amendment to the 2004 Appropriations Bill that withholds all federal funding from section 213—the provision that allows the Justice Department to search a house without notifying the resident. The courts, too, share the concerns of the local resolutions. In January a federal court in Los Angeles ruled one section of the Patriot Act unconstitutional; the judge objected to the provision making it a crime to provide "expert advice or assistance" to terrorists on the grounds that the phrasing is so vague as to license the Justice Department to interfere with First Amendment speech guarantees. In December two federal courts issued rulings declaring acts of detention carried out by the Bush Administration unlawful on grounds similar to those mentioned in the town resolutions.

Sorting out the legal status of the Patriot Act may take some time. The United States Constitution prohibits acts that the Patriot Act licenses, and, although constitutional provisions take legal precedence over contradictory legislation, for the time being the act appears to empower the federal government not only to call upon the country's residents for assistance but also to impose criminal and civil penalties on those who fail to assist.

Whether the resistance to the Patriot Act gains momentum or is ultimately derailed, the town resolutions remind us that the power of enforcement lies not just with local police but with all those who reside in cities, towns, villages, isolated byways, and country lanes. Law—whether local, state, federal, or constitutional—is only real if, as Patrick Henry said, the rest of us will put our hands to it, put our hearts to it, stand behind it.

QUESTIONS FOR DISCUSSION AND WRITING

1. In what way does the Constitution protect democracy, according to Scarry? Consider her points about privacy, freedom of association, search and seizure, due process, speedy public trials, and protection against cruel and unusual punishment, for example (paragraphs 2, 7). Do you agree with Scarry that some, or all, of these constitutionally protected rights are endangered by the U.S.A. Patriot Act? With a partner whose view opposes your own, find evidence from reliable sources in print and via the Internet to support each position and construct a well-reasoned debate, either orally or in writing.

2. According to the American Civil Liberties Union, by 2006 more than 400 communities had passed resolutions seeking reforms of the Patriot Act, as compared to the 272 when Scarry wrote this article. Some of these resolutions "direct police and other residents to refrain from carrying out the provisions of the act, even when instructed to do so by a federal officer" (paragraph 2). What are some of the provisions of the act that have raised objections? (See paragraphs 7, 9, 18–20.) To what extent do you object to these provisions? Would you urge your home community to vote for a resolution against the act? Why? Why not?

3. Find a provision of the U.S.A. Patriot Act that you either agree or disagree with and write a paper defending your stance. Consult library materials or reliable Internet sources such as the ACLU and the White House official site to clarify the exact meaning of the provision. Explain your agreement or objection in terms of the constitutional rights of American citizens or probable outcomes of the legislation. Construct two or three scenarios of what would happen if the provision were enforced.

4. Richard A. Posner, in "Security versus Civil Liberties" (p. 480), discusses issues similar to Scarry's—unconstitutional government action and national security—but Posner argues that Americans need to be prepared to give up some of their liberties for the sake of national security. With a partner who holds the opposite viewpoint, write a paper explaining whose ideas on liberty versus security you sympathize with more, comparing and contrasting Scarry's and Posner's arguments and justifying your support of one or the other. Use Wole Soyinka's "Every Dictator's Nightmare" (p. 475) to provide a historical and international frame of reference.

MARY ELLEN MARK

The Damm Family in Their Car, Los Angeles, 1987

QUESTIONS FOR DISCUSSION AND WRITING

1. Analyze this photograph of a homeless family in their car. What do you under-stand from each element of the photograph: the figures? their expressions, pos-tures, apparent nutrition level, clothing? the condition of the car? the road and the rest of the background? If you hadn't been told that this family was homeless, would you have known from the details?

2. "Read" the people in this picture. What stories does this picture tell? Would each family member tell the same story? To whom? Why do you think the Damm fam-ily would have allowed Mark, a professional photographer, to take their picture?

3. What message(s) does this picture send? To whom? Is there any expectation of hope? Or change? What are viewers supposed to think or to do as a consequence of seeing this picture?

BRIEF TAKES FROM INSIDERS:
CODES, CONVERSATIONS, CONVENTIONS

The pieces in this section offer various perspectives on what it means to be an insider, to share behavior such as laughter (Cathy Davidson), spirituality (Robert Coles), coded language (Henry Louis Gates Jr.), values (Richard Rodriguez, Beth Kephart), principles (Alice Walker)—and in all cases, a sense of community.

RICHARD RODRIGUEZ
Family Values

For biographical information on Rodriguez, see p. 298.

I am sitting alone in my car, in front of my parents' house—a middle-aged man with a boy's secret to tell. What words will I use to tell them? I hate the word *gay*, find its little affirming sparkle more pathetic than assertive. I am happier with the less polite *queer*. But to my parents I would say *homosexual*, avoid the Mexican slang *joto* (I had always heard it said in our house with hints of condescension), though *joto* is less mocking than the sissy-boy *maricon*.

The buzz on everyone's lips now: Family values. The other night on TV, the vice president of the United States, his arm around his wife, smiled into the camera and described homosexuality as "mostly a choice." But how would he know? Homosexuality never felt like a choice to me. . . .

My parents live on a gray, treeless street in San Francisco not far from the ocean. Probably more than half of the neighborhood is immigrant. India lives next door to Greece, who lives next door to Russia. I wonder what the Chinese lady next door to my parents makes of the politicians' phrase *family values*.

What immigrants know, what my parents certainly know, is that when you come to this country, you risk losing your children. The assurance of family—continuity, inevitably—is precisely what America encourages its children to overturn. *Become your own man*. We who are native to this country know this too, of course, though we are likely to deny it. Only a society so guilty about its betrayal of family would tolerate the pieties of politicians regarding family values.

On the same summer day that Republicans were swarming in Houston 5 (buzzing about family values), a friend of mine who escaped family values awhile back and who now wears earrings resembling intrauterine devices, was complaining to me over coffee about the Chinese. The Chinese will never take over San Francisco, my friend said, because the Chinese do not want to take over San Francisco. The Chinese do not even see San Francisco! All they care about is their damn families. All they care about is double-parking smack in front of the restaurant on Clement Street and pulling granny out of the car—and damn anyone who happens to be in the car behind them or the next or the next.

Politicians would be horrified by such as American opinion, of course. But then what do politicians, Republicans or Democrats, really know of our family life? Or what are they willing to admit? Even in that area where they could reasonably be expected to have something to say—regarding the relationship of family life to our economic system—the politicians say nothing. Republicans celebrate American economic freedom, but Republicans don't seem to connect that economic freedom to the social breakdown they find appalling. Democrats, on the other hand, if more tolerant of the drift from familial tradition, are suspicious of the very capitalism that creates social freedom.

CATHY DAVIDSON

Laughing in English

Cathy Davidson is professor of English and vice provost for interdisciplinary studies at Duke University and author of groundbreaking research in American literature and women's studies.

The students were now all laughing, but in polite Japanese-girl fashion, a hand covering the mouth.

"*Wait!*" I shouted in my sternest voice. "This is Oral English class!"

The laughter stopped. They looked ashamed.

"No, no. In this class, you must *laugh* in English. Think about it. You've all seen American movies. How do you laugh in English?"

I could see a gleam in Miss Shimura's eye, and I called on her: "Would an 5 American woman ever put her hand over her mouth when she laughed, Miss Shimura?"

"No, *sensei*—I mean, teacher."

"Show me. Laugh like an American movie star."

Miss Shimura kept her hands plastered at her side. She threw back her head. She opened her mouth as far as it would go. She made a deep, staccato sound at the back of her throat. *Hanh. Hanh. Hanh.*

We all laughed hysterically.

"Hands down!" I shouted again. "This is Oral English!"   10

They put their hands at their sides and imitated Miss Shimura's American head-back, open-mouth plosive laugh.

"What about the body?" I asked.

I parodied a Japanese laugh, pulling my arms in to my sides, bowing my head and shoulders forward, putting a hand coyly to my mouth.

Again they laughed. This time it was American-style.

"Oral English is about bodies too, not just words." I smiled.   15

S
R
L

Miss Kato raised her hand.

"*Hai?*" (Yes?).

"Americans also laugh like this." She put her head back, opened her mouth, and rocked her upper body from side to side, her shoulders heaving and dodging, like Santa Claus.

There were gleeful shouts of "Yes! Yes!" and again a roomful of American-style laughter. It would start to die down, then someone would catch her friend doing the funny American laugh, and she'd break into hysterics again, the hand going to her mouth, me pointing, her correcting herself with the Santa Claus laughter. I continued to laugh Japanese-style, which made them laugh even louder, bouncier. We were off and running, laughing in each other's languages.

HENRY LOUIS GATES JR.
Signifying

Henry Louis Gates Jr. has combined a distinguished academic appointment as W. E. B. Du Bois Professor of Humanities at Harvard with a career as an American public intellectual and cultural critic—witty, learned, and accessible.

> *And they asked me right at Christmas*
> *If my blackness, would it rub off?*
> *I said, ask your Mama.*
> —LANGSTON HUGHES

The Black concept of *signifying* incorporates essentially a folk notion that dictionary entries for words are not always sufficient for interpreting meanings or messages, or that meaning goes beyond such interpretations. Complimentary remarks may be delivered in a left-handed fashion. A particular utterance may be an insult in one context and not another. What pretends to be informative may intend to be persuasive. The hearer is thus constrained to attend to all potential meaning carrying symbolic systems in speech events—the total universe of discourse.[1]

----

[1]Claudia Mitchell-Kernan, *Language Behavior in a Black Urban Community.* Monographs of the Language-Behavior Laboratory, University of California, Berkeley, No. 2 (Feb. 1971), exp. pp. 87–129; rpt. in *Mother Wit from the Laughing Barrel: Readings in the Interpretation of Afro-American Folklore,* ed. Alan Dundes (Englewood Cliffs, N.J.: Prentice-Hall, 1973). Subsequent quotations from Mitchell-Kernan are from pp. 314–321.

Signifyin(g), in other words, is the figurative difference between the literal and the metaphorical, between surface and latent meaning. Mitchell-Kernan calls this feature of discourse an "implicit content or function, which is potentially obscured by the surface content or function." Finally, Signifyin(g) presupposes an "encoded" intention to say one thing but to mean quite another.

Mitchell-Kernan presents several examples of Signifyin(g), as she is defining it. Her first example is a conversation among three women about the meal to be served at dinner. One woman asks the other two to join her for dinner, that is, if they are willing to eat "chit'lins." She ends her invitation with a pointed rhetorical question: "Or are you one of those Negroes who don't eat chit'lins?" The third person, the woman not addressed, responds with a long defense of why she prefers "prime rib and T-bone" to "chit'lins," ending with a traditional ultimate appeal to special pleading, a call to unity within the ranks to defeat white racism. Then she leaves. After she has gone, the initial speaker replies to her original addressee in this fashion: "Well, I wasn't signifying at her, but like I always say, if the shoe fits wear it." Mitchell-Kernan concludes that while the manifest subject of this exchange was dinner, the latent subject was the political orientation of two black people vis-à-vis cultural assimilation or cultural nationalism, since many middle-class blacks refuse to eat this item from the traditional black cuisine. Mitchell-Kernan labels this form of Signifyin(g) "allegory," because "the significance or meaning of the words must be derived from known symbolic values."

This mode of Signifyin(g) is commonly practiced by Afro-American adults. It is functionally equivalent to one of its embedded tropes, often called louding or loud-talking, which as we might expect connotes exactly the opposite of that which it denotes: one successfully loud-talks by speaking to a second person remarks in fact directed to a third person, at a level just audible to the third person. A sign of the success of this practice is an indignant "What?" from the third person, to which the speaker responds, "I wasn't talking to you." Of course, the speaker was, yet simultaneously was not. Loud-talking is related to Mitchell-Kernan's second figure of Signification, which she calls "obscuring the addressee" and which I shall call naming. Her example is one commonly used in the tradition, in which "the remark is, on the surface, directed toward no one in particular":

> I saw a woman the other day in a pair of stretch pants, she must have weighed 300 pounds. If she knew how she looked she would burn those things.

If a member of the speaker's audience is overweight and frequently wears stretch pants, then this message could well be intended for her. If she protests, the speaker is free to maintain that she was speaking about someone else and to ask why her auditor is so paranoid. Alternatively, the speaker can say, "if the shoe fits. . . ."

BETH KEPHART
Playing for Keeps

Beth Kephart is an award-winning novelist, autobiographer, and essayist.

> *Hopes and fears of a soccer mom*
> —B.C.

. . . The red team was our team, the Cosmos; they had not been winning much. The littlest kid was our ten-year-old son, still learning soccer, playing for keeps. The community was the kind of community that is formed when perfect little strangers don identical synthetic shirts, and their parents, every Saturday, do a ragged sideline dance. *Come on, Cosmos,* we were screaming, stamping our feet. *Take it down the side!* Exhorting. *Center it.* Pleading. *Come on and shoot! Cosmos, shoot! Ahh.* Despair. *Next time.* Hope. *Next time, guys. Nice try.* The wind blowing our voices back over our own hunched shoulders, the kids way far out there, on their own. "Jeremy's in as striker," I told my husband what he already knew. Bill nodded, quietly. A gust came up, and so we blew inconsequentially on our hands. . . .

ROBERT COLES
Two Languages, One Soul

Robert Coles is a distinguished child psychiatrist, Harvard-based, world-renowned for his sensitive studies of children from many backgrounds, many cultures.

"But this priest of ours gives no one the benefit of the doubt. I have no right to find fault with him; I know that. Who am I to do so? I am simply an old lady, and I had better watch out: the Lord no doubt punishes those who disagree with His priests. But our old priest who died last year was so much finer, so much better to hear on a warm Sunday morning. Every once in a while he would even lead us outside to the courtyard and talk with us there, give us a second sermon. I felt so much better for listening to him. He was not in love with the sound of his own voice, as this new priest is. He did not stop and listen to the echo of his words. He did not brush away dust from his coat, or worry if the wind went through his hair. He was not always looking for a paper towel to wipe his shoes. My husband says he will buy this priest a dozen handkerchiefs and tell him they are to be used for his shoes only. Here when we get rain we are grateful, and it is not too high a price to pay, a little mud to walk through. Better mud that sticks than dust that blows away.

"Well, I should not go on so long about a vain man. We all like to catch ourselves in the mirror and find ourselves good to look at. Here I am, speaking ill of him, yet I won't let my family celebrate my birthdays any more; and when I look at myself in the mirror a feeling of sadness comes over me. I pull at my skin and try to erase the lines, but no luck. I think back: all those years when my husband and I were young, and never worried about our health, our strength, our appearance. I don't say we always do now; but there are times when we look like ghosts of ourselves. I will see my husband noticing how weak and tired I have become, how hunched over. I pretend not to see, but once the eyes have caught something, one cannot shake the picture off. And I look at him, too; he will straighten up when he feels my glance strike him, and I quickly move away. Too late, though; he has been told by me, without a word spoken, that he is old, and I am old, and that is our fate, to live through these last years.

"But it is not only pity we feel for ourselves. A few drops of rain and I feel grateful; the air is so fresh afterwards. I love to sit in the sun. We have the sun so often here, a regular visitor, a friend one can expect to see often and trust. I like to make tea for my husband and me. At midday we take our tea outside and sit on our bench, our backs against the wall of the house. Neither of us wants pillows; I tell my daughters and sons that they are soft—those beach chairs of theirs. Imagine beach chairs here in New Mexico, so far from any ocean! The bench feels strong to us, not uncomfortable. The tea warms us inside, the sun on the outside. I joke with my husband; I say we are part of the house: the adobe gets baked, and so do we. For the most part we say nothing, though. It is enough to sit and be part of God's world. We hear the birds talking to each other, and are grateful they come as close to us as they do; all the more reason to keep our tongues still and hold ourselves in one place. We listen to cars going by and wonder who is rushing off. A car to us is a mystery. The young understand a car. They cannot imagine themselves not driving. They have not the interest we had in horses. Who is to compare one lifetime with another, but a horse is alive and one loves a horse and is loved by a horse. Cars come and go so fast. One year they command all eyes. The next year they are a cause for shame. The third year they must be thrown away without the slightest regret. I may exaggerate, but not much!

CHAPTER 7

Science and Technology: Discovery, Invention, and Controversy

ELLEN GOODMAN

Cure or Quest for Perfection?

Ellen Goodman (b. 1941) graduated from Radcliffe in 1963 and began her career in journalism as a researcher for Newsweek, *then as a reporter at the* Detroit Free Press. *Now a columnist at the* Boston Globe, *she received a Pulitzer Prize for Distinguished Commentary in 1980. Among her five volumes of collected columns are* Close to Home *(1979),* Making Sense *(1989), and* Value Judgments *(1993). Turning Points (1979) addresses the contemporary roles of women; Goodman and Patricia O'Brien have collaborated on* I Know Just What You Mean: The Power of Friendship in Women's Lives *(2000). Although "Cure or Quest for Perfection" was originally published in the* Boston Globe *in January 2002, it remains particularly relevant in light of President George W. Bush's veto of the stem cell research bill in July 2006—the first veto of his presidency.*

As someone who scraped through the college science requirement with a physics-for-poets course, I should be pleased that the President's Council on Bioethics opened its first session on a literary note.

The required reading for the panel assembled to grapple with 21st-century problems was a 19th-century short story. "The Birthmark," written by Nathaniel Hawthorne in 1843, is a tale of a young scientist who emerged from his grimy lab, "washed the stain of acids from his fingers and persuaded a beautiful woman to become his wife."

No sooner were they wed than he became obsessed with her one small flaw, a tiny hand-shaped birthmark on her pale cheek. Eventually, the scientist created a potion to remove the birthmark. Alas, it also removed his wife.

There are several ways to interpret this story. (Is there a marriage counselor in the room?) But Leon Kass, the assigning professor and chair of the president's panel, meant it as a cautionary moral tale about scientific hubris. The tale, he said, "allows us to reflect deeply on the human aspiration to eliminate all defects, the aspiration for perfection."

The aspiration for perfection? Did this critic stack the literary and public policy deck?

The first bioethics debate before the council and the country is human cloning. The House of Representatives has already passed a total ban. Soon the issue will come before the Senate in two forms. One bill backs the total ban supported by the president. The other would ban cloning to make genetic replicas of people but allow cloning to treat disease. This is the distinction supported by the National Academy of Sciences.

Today, no responsible scientist or public policy maker is in favor of reproductive cloning. There's no compelling reason that justifies the risks or the results. But therapeutic cloning—creating very early human embryos in the quest to cure diseases—is another story. A story that doesn't fit Hawthorne's plot or Kass's lit-crit.

Just imagine what parents of a child born with a devastating disease such as Fanconi anemia would make of having it compared to this "birthmark." Cystic fibrosis, for that matter, is not a little blemish on a perfect cheek. And curing Parkinson's disease is not the hubristic pursuit of perfection.

There are indeed some serious moral arguments about what is a "defect." But is anyone ready to argue that Alzheimer's disease should be protected from the mad hand of a scientist?

As Dartmouth bioethicist Ron Green says: "The people who are trying to develop the new tools of genetic science and cell research are not seeking perfection. They are, like scientists and physicians for the past 200 years, seeking to reduce the burden of human suffering."

The plot thickens because this promising line of research entails early-stage embryos. Every scientific inquiry and bioethical conversation about cloning runs into the propeller of religion and prolife politics.

The fundamental question is not about the moral status of the scientist but the moral status of the embryo. Is an embryo an "unborn child"? Does this cluster of cells have equal or greater moral weight than a suffering adult? Says Green, "I believe that the cloning issue is being used as a pretext to impose a radical right-to-life agenda on scientific research."

Last summer [2001] President Bush signed on to a political compromise that allowed government funding of research for some existing stem cells. But he opposes cloning on the grounds that life begins at conception. And on Tuesday, the 29th anniversary of *Roe v. Wade*, the president again declared that "unborn children should be welcomed in life and protected in law." But what are the implications of that for, say, in vitro fertilization? And what will happen now that Britain allows therapeutic cloning? Can we ban importing cures based on cloning?

Philip Kitcher, who argues forcefully for democratic checks on science in "Science, Truth, and Democracy," nevertheless says, "When religion enters the public sphere, then all of a sudden claims held very firmly go unchallenged and we reach a stalemate."

In the bioethics debate that goes on inside our own heads, most Americans 15 sense that the embryo is neither a child nor a mere piece of tissue. We should be wary watchdogs over scientists or manufacturers who would deal with embryos as commodities. But using these clusters of cells to cure suffering of existing humans passes the moral threshold test.

As for aspiring to perfection? If Hawthorne's scientist had simply cured his wife's birthmark, I imagine he would have found fault with her cooking. In my own required reading, I keep a jaundiced eye on progress, but somehow I'm glad medicine didn't stop "aspiring" in 1843.

QUESTIONS FOR DISCUSSION AND WRITING

1. Goodman employs several rhetorical questions, for example, in her title and in the text, to suggest a counterargument. To what other purposes does she employ such questions? Do you find this tactic effective? Why or why not?

2. Explain what Goodman means by "the moral threshold test" (paragraph 15). Does Hawthorne's story suggest a threshold? What are Goodman's objections to "The Birthmark" as a metaphor for the bioethics issues she raises?

3. Goodman positions herself as a mainstream American when she writes that "most Americans sense that an embryo is neither a child nor a mere piece of tissue" (paragraph 15). Identify other ways in which she garners the reader's support for her stance. On what basis does she argue that political radicalism in the bioethics debate is inappropriate?

BILL McKIBBEN

Designer Genes

Born in Palo Alto, California, in 1960, McKibben earned a bachelor's degree from Harvard (1982) and soon began his writing career as a staff writer and editor for the New Yorker. *His work for the past two decades has been mainly about environmental issues, from a serious yet hopeful perspective.* The End of Nature *(1989) concerns the impact of human behavior on the planet.* Hope, Human and Wild: True Stories of Living Lightly on the Earth *(1995), focuses on some recent positive outcomes of environmentalism. In* Maybe One: A Case for Smaller Families *(1998), McKibben offers a father's perspective on overpopulation. While not insisting on one-child families, he argues that an only child often has many advantages over a child with siblings. Moreover, the world's current population growth rate will lead to species extinction, soil erosion, and food shortages.*

Bioethics—making informed choices about the impact of science on human life—is the topic of McKibben's Staying Human in an Engineered Age *(2003). "Designer Genes," which originally appeared in* Orion, *ponders the consequences of enhancing children's genes. Advances in genetic engineering may soon offer parents ways to increase their offspring's intelligence and physical strength, but, as McKibben points out, we should consider the unintended—and undesirable—outcomes.*

I grew up in a household where we were very suspicious of dented cans. Dented cans were, according to my mother, a well-established gateway to botulism, and botulism was a bad thing, worse than swimming immediately after lunch. It was one of those bad things measured in extinctions, as in "three tablespoons of botulism toxin could theoretically kill every human on Earth." Or something like that.

So I refused to believe the early reports, a few years back, that socialites had begun injecting dilute strains of the toxin into their brows in an effort to temporarily remove the vertical furrow that appears between one's eyes as one ages. It sounded like a Monty Python routine, some clinic where they daubed your soles with plague germs to combat athlete's foot. But I was wrong to doubt. As the world now knows, Botox has become, in a few short years, a staple weapon in the cosmetic arsenal—so prevalent that, in the words of one writer, "it is now rare in certain social enclaves to see a woman over the age of thirty-five with the ability to look angry." With their facial muscles essentially paralyzed, actresses are having trouble acting; since the treatment requires periodic booster shots, doctors "warn that you could marry a woman (or a man) with a flawlessly even face and wind up with someone who four months later looks like a Shar-Pei." But never mind—now you can get Botoxed in strip mall storefronts and at cocktail parties.

People, in other words, will do fairly far out things for less than pressing causes. And more so all the time: public approval of "aesthetic surgery" has grown 50 percent in the United States in the last decade. But why stop there? Once you accept the idea that our bodies are essentially plastic and that it's okay to manipulate that plastic, there's no reason to think that consumers would balk because "genes" were involved instead of, say, "toxins." Especially since genetic engineering would not promote your own vanity, but instead be sold as a boon to your child.

The vision of genetic engineers is to do to humans what we have already done to salmon and wheat, pine trees and tomatoes. That is, to make them *better* in some way; to delete, modify, or add genes in developing embryos so that the cells of the resulting person will produce proteins that make them taller and more muscular, or smarter and less aggressive, maybe handsome and possibly straight. Even happy. As early as 1993, a March of Dimes poll found that 43 percent of Americans would engage in genetic engineering "simply to enhance their children's looks or intelligence."

Ethical guidelines promulgated by the scientific oversight boards so far prohibit actual attempts at human genetic engineering, but researchers have walked   5 right to the line, maybe even stuck their toes a trifle over. In the spring of 2001, for instance, a fertility clinic in New Jersey impregnated fifteen women with embryos fashioned from their own eggs, their partner's sperm, and a small portion of an egg donated by a second woman. The procedure was designed to work around defects in the would-be mother's egg—but in at least two of the cases, tests showed the resulting babies carried genetic material from all three "parents."

And so the genetic modification of humans is not only possible, it's coming fast; a mix of technical progress and shifting mood means it could easily happen in the next few years. Consider what happened with plants. A decade ago, university research farms were growing small plots of genetically modified grain and vegetables. Sometimes activists who didn't like what they were doing would come and rip the plants up, one by one. Then, all of a sudden in the mid-1990s, before anyone had paid any real attention, farmers had planted half the corn and soybean fields in America with transgenic seed.

Every time you turn your back this technology creeps a little closer. Gallops, actually, growing and spreading as fast as the internet. One moment you've sort of heard of it; the next moment it's everywhere. But we haven't done it yet. For the moment we remain, if barely, a fully human species. And so we have time yet to consider, to decide, to act. This is arguably the biggest decision humans will ever make.

Right up until this decade, the genes that humans carried in their bodies were exclusively the result of chance—of how the genes of the sperm and the egg, the father and the mother, combined. The only way you could intervene in the process was by choosing who you would mate with—and that was as much wishful thinking as anything else, as generation upon generation of surprised parents have discovered.

But that is changing. We now know two different methods to change human genes. The first, and less controversial, is called somatic gene therapy. Somatic gene therapy begins with an existing individual—someone with, say, cystic fibrosis. Researchers try to deliver new, modified genes to some of her cells, usually by putting the genes aboard viruses they inject into the patient, hoping that the viruses will infect the cells and thereby transmit the genes. Somatic gene therapy is, in other words, much like medicine. You take an existing patient with an existing condition, and you in essence try and convince her cells to manufacture the medicine she needs.

Germline genetic engineering, on the other hand, is something very novel indeed. "Germ" here refers not to microbes, but to the egg and sperm cells, the germ cells of the human being. Scientists intent on genetic engineering would probably start with a fertilized embryo a week or so old. They would tease apart the cells of that embryo, and then, selecting one, they would add to, delete, or modify some of its genes. They could also insert artificial chromosomes containing predesigned genes. They would then take the cell, place it inside an egg whose nucleus had been removed, and implant the resulting new embryo inside a woman. The em-   10 bryo would, if all went according to plan, grow into a genetically engineered child. His genes would be pushing out proteins to meet the particular choices made by his parents and by the companies and clinicians they were buying the genes from. Instead of coming solely from the combination of his parents, and thus the combination of their parents, and so on back through time, those genes could come from any other person, or any other plant or animal, or out of the thin blue sky. And once implanted, they will pass to his children and on into time.

But all this work will require one large change in our current way of doing business. Instead of making babies by making love, we will have to move conception to the laboratory. You need to have the embryo out there where you can work on it—to make the necessary copies, try to add or delete genes, and then implant the one that seems likely to turn out best. Gregory Stock, a researcher at the University of California and an apostle of the new genetic technologies, says that "the union of egg and sperm from two individuals . . . would be too unpredictable with intercourse." And once you've got the embryo out on the lab bench, gravity disappears altogether. "Ultimately," says Michael West, CEO of Advanced Cell Technology, the firm furthest out on the cutting edge of these technologies, "the dream of biologists is to have the sequence of DNA, the programming code of life, and to be able to edit it the way you can a document on a word processor."

Does it sound far-fetched? We began doing it with animals (mice) in 1978, and we've managed the trick with most of the obvious mammals, except one. Some of the first germline interventions might be semi-medical. You might, say some advocates, start by improving "visual and auditory acuity," first to eliminate nearsightedness or prevent deafness, then to "improve artistic potential." But why stop there? "If something has evolved elsewhere, then it is possible for us to determine its genetic basis and transfer it into the human genome," says Princeton geneticist Lee Silver—just as we have stuck flounder genes into strawberries to keep them from freezing, and jellyfish genes into rabbits and monkeys to make them glow in the dark.

But would we actually do this? Is there any real need to raise these questions as more than curiosities, or will the schemes simply fade away on their own, ignored by the parents who are their necessary consumers?

Anyone who has entered a baby supply store in the last few years knows that even the soberest parents can be counted on to spend virtually unlimited sums in pursuit of successful offspring. What if the "Baby Einstein" video series, which immerses "learning-enabled" babies in English, Spanish, Japanese, Hebrew, German, Russian, and French, could be bolstered with a little gene tweaking to improve memory? What if the Wombsongs prenatal music system, piping in Brahms to your waiting fetus, could be supplemented with an auditory upgrade? One sociologist told the New York Times we'd crossed the line from parenting to "product development," and even if that remark is truer in Manhattan than elsewhere, it's not hard to imagine what such attitudes will mean across the affluent world.

Here's one small example. In the 1980s, two drug companies were awarded   15
patents to market human growth hormone to the few thousand American children suffering from dwarfism. The PDA thought the market would be very small,
so HGH was given "orphan drug status," a series of special market advantages
designed to reward the manufacturers for taking on such an unattractive business. But within a few years, HGH had become one of the largest selling drugs in
the country, with half a billion dollars in sales. This was not because there'd been
a sharp increase in the number of dwarves, but because there'd been a sharp increase in the number of parents who wanted to make their slightly short children
taller. Before long the drug companies were arguing that the children in the bottom 5 percent of their normal height range were in fact in need of three to five
shots a week of HGH. Take eleven-year-old Marco Oriti. At four foot one, he was
about four inches shorter than average, and projected to eventually top out at
five foot four. This was enough to convince his parents to start on a six-day-a-
week HGH regimen, which will cost them $150,000 over the next four years.
"You want to give your child the edge no matter what," said his mother.

A few of the would-be parents out on the current cutting edge of the reproduction revolution—those who need to obtain sperm or eggs for in vitro fertilization
—exhibit similar zeal. Ads started appearing in Ivy League college newspapers a
few years ago: couples were willing to pay $50,000 for an egg, provided the donor
was at least five feet, ten inches tall, white, and had scored 1400 on her SATs.
There is, in other words, a market just waiting for the first clinic with a catalogue
of germline modifications, a market that two California artists proved when they
opened a small boutique, Gene Genies Worldwide, in a trendy part of Pasadena.
Tran Kim-Trang and Karl Mihail wanted to get people thinking more deeply
about these emerging technologies, so they outfitted their store with petri dishes
and models of the double helix and printed up brochures highlighting traits with
genetic links: creativity, extroversion, thrill-seeking criminality. When they opened
the doors, they found people ready to shell out for designer families (one man insisted he wanted the survival ability of a cockroach). The "store" was meant to be
ironic, but the irony was lost on a culture so deeply consumeristic that this land
of manipulation seems like the obvious next step. "Generally, people refused to
believe this store was an art project," says Tran. And why not? The next store in
the mall could easily have been a Botox salon.

But say you're not ready. Say you're perfectly happy with the prospect of a
child who shares the unmodified genes of you and your partner. Say you think
that manipulating the DNA of your child might be dangerous, or presumptuous,
or icky. How long will you be able to hold that line if the procedure begins to
spread among your neighbors? Maybe not so long as you think. If germline manipulation actually does begin, it seems likely to set off a kind of biological arms
race. "Suppose parents could add thirty points to their child's IQ?" asks MIT
economist Lester Thurow. "Wouldn't you want to do it? And if you don't, your
child will be the stupidest in the neighborhood." That's precisely what it might
feel like to be the parent facing the choice. Individual competition more or less

defines the society we've built, and in that context love can almost be defined as giving your kids what they need to make their way in the world. Deciding not to soup them up . . . well, it could come to seem like child abuse.

Of course, the problem about arms races is that you never really get anywhere. If everyone's adding thirty IQ points, then having an IQ of one hundred fifty won't get you any closer to Stanford than you were at the outset. The very first athlete engineered to use twice as much oxygen as the next guy will be unbeatable in the Tour de France—but in no time he'll merely be the new standard. You'll have to do what he did to be in the race, but your upgrades won't put you ahead, merely back on a level playing field. You might be able to argue that society as a whole was helped, because there was more total brainpower at work, but your kid won't be any closer to the top of the pack. All you'll be able to do is guarantee she won't be left hopelessly far behind.

In fact, the arms race problem has an extra ironic twist when it comes to genetic manipulation. The United States and the Soviet Union could, and did, keep adding new weapons to their arsenals over the decades. But with germline manipulation, you get only one shot; the extra chromosome you stick in your kid when he's born is the one he carries throughout his life. So let's say baby Sophie has a state-of-the-art gene job: her parents paid for the proteins discovered by, say, 2005 that on average yield ten extra IQ points. By the time Sophie is five, though, scientists will doubtless have discovered ten more genes linked to intelligence. Now anyone with a platinum card can get twenty IQ points, not to mention a memory boost and a permanent wrinkle-free brow. So by the time Sophie is twenty-five and in the job market, she's already more or less obsolete—the kids coming out of college plainly just have better hardware.

"For all his billions, Bill Gates could not have purchased a single genetic enhancement for his son Rory John," writes Gregory Stock at the University of California. "And you can bet that any enhancements a billion dollars can buy Rory's child in 2030 will seem crude alongside those available for modest sums in 2060." It's not, he adds, "so different from upgraded software. You'll want the new release." 20

The vision of one's child as a nearly useless copy of Windows 95 should make parents fight like hell to make sure we never get started down this path. But the vision gets lost easily in the gushing excitement about "improving" the opportunities for our kids.

Beginning the hour my daughter came home from the hospital, I spent part of every day with her in the woods out back, showing her trees and ferns and chipmunks and frogs. One of her very first words was "birch," and you couldn't have asked for a prouder papa. She got her middle name from the mountain we see out the window; for her fifth birthday she got her own child-sized canoe; her school wardrobe may not be relentlessly up-to-date, but she's never lacked for hiking boots. As I write these words, she's spending her first summer at sleep-away camp, one we chose because the kids sleep in tents and spend days in the mountains. All of which is to say that I have done everything in my power to try to mold her into a lover of the natural world. That is where my deepest satisfactions lie, and I want the same for her. It seems benign enough, but it has its drawbacks; it means less time and money and energy for trips to the city and music lessons and so forth. As time goes on and she develops stronger opinions of her own, I yield more and more, but I keep trying to stack the deck, to nudge her in the direction that's meant something to me. On a Saturday morning, when the question comes up of what to do, the very first words out of my mouth always involve yet another hike. I can't help myself.

In other words, we already "engineer" our offspring in some sense of the word: we do our best, and often our worst, to steer them in particular directions. And our worst can be pretty bad. We all know people whose lives were blighted trying to meet the expectations of their parents. We've all seen the crazed devotion to getting kids into the right schools, the right professions, the right income brackets. Parents try to pass down their prejudices, their politics, their attitude toward the world ("we've got to toughen that kid up—he's going to get walked all over"). There are fathers who start teaching the curveball at the age of four, and sons made to feel worthless if they don't make the Little League traveling team. People move house so that their kids can grow up with the right band of schoolmates. They threaten to disown them for marrying African Americans, or for not marrying African Americans. No dictator anywhere has ever tried to rule his subjects with as much attention to detail as the average modern parent.

Why not take this just one small step further? Why not engineer children to up the odds that all that nudging will stick? In the words of Lee Silver, a Princeton geneticist, "Why not seize this power? Why not control what has been left to chance in the past? Indeed, we control all other aspects of our children's lives and identities through powerful social and environmental influences. . . . On what basis can we reject positive genetic influences on a person's essence when we accept the rights of parents to benefit their children in every other way?" If you can buy your kid three years at Deerfield, four at Harvard, and three more at Harvard Law, why shouldn't you be able to turbocharge his IQ a bit?

But most likely the answer has already occurred to you as well. Because you know plenty of people who managed to rebel successfully against whatever agenda their parents laid out for them, or who took that agenda and bent it to fit their own particular personality. In our society that's often what growing up is all about—the sometimes excruciatingly difficult, frequently liberating break with the expectations of your parents. The decision to join the Peace Corps (or, the decision to leave the commune where you grew up and go to business school). The discovery that you were happiest davening in an Orthodox shul three hours a day, much to the consternation of your good suburban parents who almost always made it to Yom Kippur services; the decision that, much as you respected the Southern Baptist piety of your parents, the Bible won't be your watchword.

Without the grounding offered by tradition, the search for the "authentic you" can be hard; our generations contain the first people who routinely shop religions, for instance. But the sometimes poignant difficulty of finding yourself merely underscores how essential it is. Silver says the costs of germline engineering and a college education might be roughly comparable; in both cases, he goes on, the point is to "increase the chances the child will become wiser in some way, and better able to achieve success and happiness." But that's half the story, at best. College is where you go to be exposed to a thousand new influences, ideas that should be able to take you in almost any direction. It's where you go to get out from under your parents' thumb, to find out that you actually don't have to go to law school if you don't want to. As often as not, the harder parents try to wrench their kids in one direction, the harder those kids eventually fight to determine their own destiny. I am as prepared as I can be for the possibility—the probability—that Sophie will decide she wants to live her life in the concrete heart of Manhattan. It's her life (and perhaps her kids will have a secret desire to come wander in the woods with me).

We try to shape the lives of our kids—to "improve" their lives, as we would measure improvement—but our gravity is usually weak enough that kids can break out of it if and when they need to. (When it isn't, when parents manage to bend their children to the point of breaking, we think of them as monstrous.) "Many of the most creative and valuable human lives are the result of particularly difficult struggles" against expectation and influence, writes the legal scholar Martha Nussbaum.

That's not how a genetic engineer thinks of his product. He works to ensure absolute success. Last spring an Israeli researcher announced that he had managed to produce a featherless chicken. This constituted an improvement, to his mind, because "it will be cheaper to produce since its lack of feathers means there is no need to pluck it before it hits the shelves." Also, poultry farmers would no longer have to ventilate their vast barns to keep their birds from overheating. "Feathers are a waste," the scientist explained. "The chickens are using feed to produce something that has to be dumped, and the farmers have to waste electricity to overcome that fact." Now, that engineer was not trying to influence his chickens to shed their feathers because they'd be happier and the farmer would be happier and everyone would be happier. He was inserting a gene that created a protein that made good and certain they would not be producing feathers. Just substitute, say, an even temperament for feathers, and you'll know what the human engineers envision.

"With reprogenetics," writes Lee Silver, "parents can gain *complete control* [emphasis mine] over their destiny, with the ability to guide and enhance the characteristics of their children, and their children's children as well." Such parents would not be calling their children on the phone at annoying frequent intervals to suggest that it's time to get a real job; instead, just like the chicken guy, they would be inserting genes that produced proteins that would make their child behave in certain ways throughout his life. You cannot rebel against the production of that protein. Perhaps you can still do everything in your power to defeat the wishes of your parents, but that protein will nonetheless be pumped out relentlessly into your system, defining who you are. You won't grow feathers, no matter how much you want them. And maybe they can engineer your mood enough that your lack of plumage won't even cross your mind.

Such children will, in effect, be assigned a goal by their programmers: "intelli- 30 gence," "even temper," "athleticism." (As with chickens, the market will doubtless lean in the direction of efficiency. It may be hard to find genes for, say, dreaminess.) Now two possibilities arise. Perhaps the programming doesn't work very well, and your lad spells poorly, or turns moody, or can't hit the inside fastball. In the present world, you just tell yourself that that's who he is. But in the coming world, he'll be, in essence, a defective product. Do you still accept *him* unconditionally? Why? If your new Jetta got thirty miles to the gallon instead of the forty it was designed to get, you'd take it back. You'd call it a lemon. If necessary, you'd sue.

Or what if the engineering worked pretty well, but you decided, too late, that you'd picked the wrong package, hadn't gotten the best features? Would you feel buyer's remorse if the kid next door had a better ear, a stronger arm?

Say the gene work went a little awry and left you with a kid who had some serious problems; what kind of guilt would that leave you with? Remember, this is not a child created by the random interaction of your genes with those of your partner, this is a child created with specific intent. Does *Consumer Reports* start rating the various biotech offerings?

What if you had a second child five years after the first, and by that time the upgrades were undeniably improved: how would you feel about the first kid? How would he feel about his new brother, the latest model?

The other outcome—that the genetic engineering works just as you had hoped—seems at least as bad. Now your child is a product. You can take precisely as much pride in her achievements as you take in the achievements of your dishwashing detergent. It was designed to produce streak-free glassware, and she was designed to be sweet-tempered, social, and smart. And what can she take pride in? Her good grades? She may have worked hard, but she'll always know that she was spec'ed for good grades. Her kindness to others? Well, yes, it's good to be kind— but perhaps it's not much of an accomplishment once the various genes with some link to sociability have been catalogued and manipulated. I have no doubt that these qualms would be one of the powerful psychological afflictions of the future—at least until someone figures out a fix that keeps the next generations from having such bad thoughts.

Britain's chief rabbi, Jonathan Sacks, was asked a few years ago about the an- 35 nouncement that Italian doctors were trying to clone humans. "If there is a mystery at the heart of human condition, it is otherness: the otherness of man and woman, parent and child. It is the space we make for otherness that makes love something other than narcissism." I remember so well the feeling of walking into the maternity ward with Sue, and walking out with Sue and Sophie: where there had been two there were now, somehow, three, each of us our own person, but now commanded to make a family, a place where we all could thrive. She was so mysterious, that Sophie, and in many ways she still is. There are times when, like every parent, I see myself reflected in her, and times when I wonder if she's even related. She's ours to nurture and protect, but she is who *she is*. That's the mystery and the glory of any child.

Mystery, however, is not one of the words that thrills engineers. They try to deliver solid bridges, unyielding dams, reliable cars. We wouldn't want it any other way. The only question is if their product line should be expanded to include children.

Right now both the genes, and the limits that they set on us, connect us with every human that came before. Human beings can look at rock art carved into African cliffs and French caves thirty thousand years ago and feel an electric, immediate kinship. We've gone from digging sticks to combines, and from drum circles to symphony orchestras (and back again to drum circles), but we still hear in the same range and see in the same spectrum, still produce adrenaline and dopamine in the same ways, still think in many of the same patterns. We are, by and large, the same people, more closely genetically related to one another than we may be to our engineered grandchildren.

These new technologies show us that human meaning dangles by a far thinner thread than we had thought. If germline genetic engineering ever starts, it will accelerate endlessly and unstoppably into the future, as individuals make the calculation that they have no choice but to equip their kids for the world that's being made. The first child whose genes come in part from some corporate lab, the first child who has been "enhanced" from what came before — that's the first child who will glance back over his shoulder and see a gap between himself and human history.

These would be mere consumer decisions — but that also means that they would benefit the rich far more than the poor. They would take the gap in power, wealth, and education that currently divides both our society and the world at large, and write that division into our very biology. A sixth of the American population lacks health insurance of any kind — they can't afford to go to the doctor for a *check-up*. And much of the rest of the world is far worse off. If we can't afford the fifty cents per person it would take to buy bed nets to protect most of Africa from malaria, it is unlikely we will extend to anyone but the top tax bracket these latest forms of genetic technology. The injustice is so obvious that even the strongest proponents of genetic engineering make little attempt to deny it. "Anyone who accepts the right of affluent parents to provide their children with an expensive private school education cannot use 'unfairness' as a reason for rejecting the use of reprogenetic technologies," says Lee Silver.

These new technologies, however, are not yet inevitable. Unlike global warming, this genie is not yet out of the bottle. But if germline genetic engineering is going to be stopped, it will have to happen now, before it's quite begun. It will have to be a political choice, that is — one we make not as parents but as citizens, not as individuals but as a whole, thinking not only about our own offspring but about everyone.

So far the discussion has been confined to a few scientists, a few philosophers, a few ideologues. It needs to spread widely, and quickly, and loudly. The stakes are absurdly high, nothing less than the meaning of being human. And given the seductions that we've seen—the intuitively and culturally delicious prospect of a *better* child—the arguments against must be not only powerful but also deep. They'll need to resonate on the same intuitive and cultural level. We'll need to feel in our gut the reasons why, this time, we should tell Prometheus thanks, but no thanks.

QUESTIONS FOR DISCUSSION AND WRITING

1. "Individual competition more or less defines the society we've built," argues McKibben, discussing a potential "arms race" resulting from the genetic enhancement of children (paragraphs 17–18). What evidence does McKibben give that parents already are in a race to enhance their children? Consider his points about baby supply stores, HGH, and egg donations (paragraphs 14–16). To what extent do you agree with McKibben's predictions about a competition in genetic child enhancement?

2. Do you agree with McKibben that, in our society, growing up is often "the sometimes excruciatingly difficult, frequently liberating break with the expectations of your parents" (paragraph 25)? In what ways would germline genetic engineering of children interfere with maturation (paragraphs 26–29)? How important is it for an individual's maturation to have to make one's own decisions and to be independent?

3. Write a paper on McKibben's concerns about economic inequality and genetic engineering. Consider the consequences of genetically engineering children, given the fact that wealth would determine whose children received the most enhancements (paragraphs 38–39). What would happen to the world of sports, for example, if the offspring of rich children had the best genetic modifications of their strength and stamina genes? How would the world of academia change if wealthy children were engineered for intelligence, while poorer children were not? Would these changes be essentially positive or negative for America?

HENRY GROSKINSKY

Replaceable You

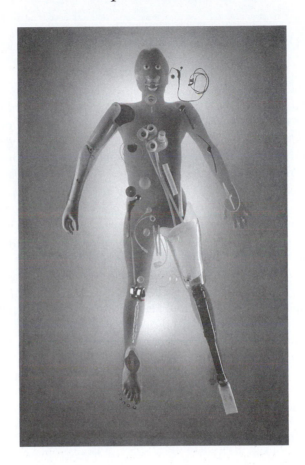

QUESTIONS FOR DISCUSSION AND WRITING

1. The twenty-six artificial body parts are glass eye, cheek implant, teeth, ear, chin, voice box, heart, pacemaker, shoulder, elbow, wrist, finger joints, insulin dispenser, hip, blood vessels, arm and hand, experimental hand, bladder, sphincter, testicle (nonfunctional), penile implant, tendon, knee, ligament, leg and foot, foot and toe joints. What does this image say about the impact of technology on our lives? How close could, or should, someone come to being bionic?

2. This image was constructed in 1989. What replacement body parts are now available to humans that were unavailable fifteen years ago? Can you think of any negative consequences to the individual or to society? Consider, for

instance, the potential total cost of such replacements. Or are there only positive benefits? What are some of these?

STEPHEN JAY GOULD

Evolution as Fact and Theory

Stephen Jay Gould (1941–2002) was born in New York City, attended Antioch College (B.A., 1963) and Columbia University (Ph.D., 1967), and taught zoology at Harvard for thirty-five years. A MacArthur "genius" Fellow (1981–1986), his wide-ranging knowledge of the liberal arts enabled him to bridge scientific and humanistic learning and thus to make complex scientific concepts understandable to nonscientists. Gould's witty "This View of Life" columns in Natural History *are brimmed with literary, musical, and historical learning. Collections of these columns include* The Panda's Thumb *(1980), winner of the National Book Award;* The Flamingo's Smile *(1985); and* Bully for Brontosaurus *(1991). Among his other award-winning books are* The Mismeasure of Man *(1981) on fallacies and abuses of intelligence testing;* Time's Arrow, Time's Cycle *(1987) on the discovery of geological time; and* Wonderful Life: The Burgess Shale and the Nature of History *(1989). In* Full House: The Spread of Excellence from Plato to Darwin *(1996), he wrote that the "suppression of human arrogance [is] the common achievement of great scientific revolutions." An example of that arrogance, Gould often argues, is the belief that human beings are superior to all other creatures.*

"Evolution as Fact and Theory" first appeared in Discover *(May 1981). The* Contexts *following "Evolution as Fact and Theory" explore how scientists form definitions and how definitions can function politically, especially in the debate about creationism.*

Kirtley Mather, who died last year at age 89, was a pillar of both science and the Christian religion in America and one of my dearest friends. The difference of half a century in our ages evaporated before our common interests. The most curious thing we shared was a battle we each fought at the same age. For Kirtley had gone to Tennessee with Clarence Darrow to testify for evolution at the Scopes trial of 1925. When I think that we are enmeshed again in the same struggle for one of the best documented, most compelling and exciting concepts in all of science, I don't know whether to laugh or cry.

According to idealized principles of scientific discourse, the arousal of dormant issues should reflect fresh data that give renewed life to abandoned notions. Those outside the current debate may therefore be excused for suspecting that creationists have come up with something new, or that evolutionists have generated some serious internal trouble. But nothing has changed; the creationists

have not a single new fact or argument. Darrow and Bryan were at least more entertaining than we lesser antagonists today. The rise of creationism is politics,
pure and simple; it represents one issue (and by no means the major concern) of
the resurgent evangelical right. Arguments that seemed kooky just a decade ago
have re-entered the mainstream.

CREATIONISM IS NOT SCIENCE

The basic attack of the creationists falls apart on two general counts before we even
reach the supposed factual details of their complaints against evolution. First, they
play upon a vernacular misunderstanding of the word "theory" to convey the false
impression that we evolutionists are covering up the rotten core of our edifice. Second, they misuse a popular philosophy of science to argue that they are behaving
scientifically in attacking evolution. Yet the same philosophy demonstrates that
their own belief is not science, and that "scientific creationism" is therefore meaningless and self-contradictory, a superb example of what Orwell called "newspeak."

In the American vernacular, "theory" often means "imperfect fact"—part of
a hierarchy of confidence running downhill from fact to theory to hypothesis to
guess. Thus the power of the creationist argument: evolution is "only" a theory,
and intense debate now rages about many aspects of the theory. If evolution is
less than a fact, and scientists can't even make up their minds about the theory,
then what confidence can we have in it? Indeed, President Reagan echoed this argument before an evangelical group in Dallas when he said (in what I devoutly
hope was campaign rhetoric): "Well, it is a theory. It is a scientific theory only,
and it has in recent years been challenged in the world of science—that is, not
believed in the scientific community to be as infallible as it once was."

Well, evolution *is* a theory. It is also a fact. And facts and theories are different   5
things, not rungs in a hierarchy of increasing certainty. Facts are the world's data.
Theories are structures of ideas that explain and interpret facts. Facts do not go
away when scientists debate rival theories to explain them. Einstein's theory of gravitation replaced Newton's, but apples did not suspend themselves in mid-air pending the outcome. And human beings evolved from apelike ancestors whether they
did so by Darwin's proposed mechanism or by some other, yet to be discovered.

Moreover, "fact" does not mean "absolute certainty." The final proofs of
logic and mathematics flow deductively from stated premises and achieve certainty only because they are *not* about the empirical world. Evolutionists make
no claim for perpetual truth, though creationists often do (and then attack us for
a style of argument that they themselves favor). In science, "fact" can only mean
"confirmed to such a degree that it would be perverse to withhold provisional assent." I suppose that apples might start to rise tomorrow, but the possibility does
not merit equal time in physics classrooms.

Evolutionists have been clear about this distinction between fact and theory
from the very beginning, if only because we have always acknowledged how
far we are from completely understanding the mechanisms (theory) by which

evolution (fact) occurred. Darwin continually emphasized the difference between his two great and separate accomplishments: establishing the fact of evolution, and proposing a theory—natural selection—to explain the mechanism of evolution. He wrote in *The Descent of Man*: "I had two distinct objects in view; firstly, to show that species had not been separately created, and secondly, that natural selection had been the chief agent of change. . . . Hence if I have erred in . . . having exaggerated its [natural selection's] power . . . I have at least, as I hope, done good service in aiding to overthrow the dogma of separate creations."

Thus Darwin acknowledged the provisional nature of natural selection while affirming the fact of evolution. The fruitful theoretical debate that Darwin initiated has never ceased. From the 1940s through the 1960s, Darwin's own theory of natural selection did achieve a temporary hegemony that it never enjoyed in his lifetime. But renewed debate characterizes our decade, and, while no biologist questions the importance of natural selection, many now doubt its ubiquity. In particular, many evolutionists argue that substantial amounts of genetic change may not be subject to natural selection and may spread through populations at random. Others are challenging Darwin's linking of natural selection with gradual, imperceptible change through all intermediary degrees; they are arguing that most evolutionary events may occur far more rapidly than Darwin envisioned.

Scientists regard debates on fundamental issues of theory as a sign of intellectual health and a source of excitement. Science is—and how else can I say it?—most fun when it plays with interesting ideas, examines their implications, and recognizes that old information may be explained in surprisingly new ways. Evolutionary theory is now enjoying this uncommon vigor. Yet amidst all this turmoil no biologist has been led to doubt the fact that evolution occurred; we are debating *how* it happened. We are all trying to explain the same thing: the tree of evolutionary descent linking all organisms by ties of genealogy. Creationists pervert and caricature this debate by conveniently neglecting the common conviction that underlies it, and by falsely suggesting that we now doubt the very phenomenon we are struggling to understand.

Using another invalid argument, creationists claim that "the dogma of separate creations," as Darwin characterized it a century ago, is a scientific theory meriting equal time with evolution in high school biology curricula. But a prevailing viewpoint among philosophers of science belies this creationist argument. Philosopher Karl Popper has argued for decades that the primary criterion of science is the falsifiability of its theories. We can never prove absolutely, but we can falsify. A set of ideas that cannot, in principle, be falsified is not science.

The entire creationist argument involves little more than a rhetorical attempt to falsify evolution by presenting supposed contradictions among its supporters. Their brand of creationism, they claim, is "scientific" because it follows the Popperian model in trying to demolish evolution. Yet Popper's argument must apply in both directions. One does not become a scientist by the simple act of trying to falsify another scientific system; one has to present an alternative system that also meets Popper's criterion—it too must be falsifiable in principle.

"Scientific creationism" is a self-contradictory, nonsense phrase precisely because it cannot be falsified. I can envision observations and experiments that would disprove any evolutionary theory I know, but I cannot imagine what potential data could lead creationists to abandon their beliefs. Unbeatable systems are dogma, not science. Lest I seem harsh or rhetorical, I quote creationism's leading intellectual, Duane Gish, Ph.D., from his recent (1978) book *Evolution? The Fossils Say No!* "By creation we mean the bringing into being by a supernatural Creator of the basic kinds of plants and animals by the process of sudden, or fiat, creation. We do not know how the Creator created, what processes He used, *for He used processes which are not now operating anywhere in the natural universe* [Gish's italics]. This is why we refer to creation as special creation. We cannot discover by scientific investigations anything about the creative processes used by the Creator." Pray tell, Dr. Gish, in the light of your last sentence, what then is "scientific" creationism?

THE FACT OF EVOLUTION

Our confidence that evolution occurred centers upon three general arguments. First, we have abundant, direct, observational evidence of evolution in action, from both the field and the laboratory. It ranges from countless experiments on change in nearly everything about fruit flies subjected to artificial selection in the laboratory to the famous British moths that turned black when industrial soot darkened the trees upon which they rest. (The moths gain protection from sharp-sighted bird predators by blending into the background.) Creationists do not deny these observations; how could they? Creationists have tightened their act. They now argue that God only created "basic kinds," and allowed for limited evolutionary meandering within them. Thus toy poodles and Great Danes come from the dog kind and moths can change color, but nature cannot convert a dog to a cat or a monkey to a man.

The second and third arguments for evolution—the case for major changes—do not involve direct observation of evolution in action. They rest upon inference, but are no less secure for that reason. Major evolutionary change requires too much time for direct observation on the scale of recorded human history. All historical sciences rest upon inference, and evolution is no different from geology, cosmology, or human history in this respect. In principle, we cannot observe processes that operated in the past. We must infer them from results that still survive: living and fossil organisms for evolution, documents and artifacts for human history, strata and topography for geology.

The second argument—that the imperfection of nature reveals evolution— 15 strikes many people as ironic, for they feel that evolution should be most elegantly displayed in the nearly perfect adaptation expressed by some organisms— the chamber of a gull's wing, or butterflies that cannot be seen in ground litter because they mimic leaves so precisely. But perfection could be imposed by a wise creator or evolved by natural selection. Perfection covers the tracks of past history. And past history—the evidence of descent—is our mark of evolution.

Evolution lies exposed in the *imperfections* that record a history of descent. Why should a rat run, a bat fly, a porpoise swim, and I type this essay with structures built of the same bones unless we all inherited them from a common ancestor? An engineer, starting from scratch, could design better limbs in each case. Why should all the large native mammals of Australia be marsupials, unless they descended from a common ancestor isolated on this island continent? Marsupials are not "better," or ideally suited for Australia; many have been wiped out by placental mammals imported by man from other continents. This principle of imperfection extends to all historical sciences. When we recognize the etymology of September, October, November, and December (seventh, eighth, ninth, and tenth, from the Latin), we know that two additional items (January and February) must have been added to an original calendar of ten months.

The third argument is more direct: transitions are often found in the fossil record. Preserved transitions are not common—and should not be, according to our understanding of evolution (see next section)—but they are not entirely wanting, as creationists often claim. The lower jaw of reptiles contains several bones, that of mammals only one. The non-mammalian jawbones are reduced, step by step, in mammalian ancestors until they become tiny nubbins located at the back of the jaw. The "hammer" and "anvil" bones of the mammalian ear are descendants of these nubbins. How could such a transition be accomplished? the creationists ask. Surely a bone is either entirely in the jaw or in the ear. Yet paleontologists have discovered two transitional lineages or therapsids (the so-called mammal-like reptiles) with a double jaw joint—one composed of the old quadrate and articular bones (soon to become the hammer and anvil), the other of the squamosal and dentary bones (as in modern mammals). For that matter, what better transitional form could we desire than the oldest human, *Australopithecus afarensis*, with its apelike palate, its human upright stance, and a cranial capacity larger than any ape's of the same body size but a full 1,000 cubic centimeters below ours? If God made each of the half dozen human species discovered in ancient rocks, why did he create in an unbroken temporal sequence of progressively more modern features—increasing cranial capacity, reduced face and teeth, larger body size? Did he create to mimic evolution and test our faith thereby?

AN EXAMPLE OF CREATIONIST ARGUMENT

Faced with these facts of evolution and the philosophical bankruptcy of their own position, creationists rely upon distortion and innuendo to buttress their rhetorical claim. If I should sound sharp or bitter, indeed I am—for I have become a major target of these practices.

I count myself among the evolutionists who argue for a jerky, or episodic, rather than a smoothly gradual, pace of change. In 1972 my colleague Niles Eldredge and I developed the theory of punctuated equilibrium. We argued that two outstanding facts of the fossil record—geologically "sudden" origin of new species and failure to change thereafter (stasis)—reflect the predictions of evolutionary theory, not the imperfections of the fossil record. In most theories, small isolated populations are the source of new species, and the process of speciation takes thousands or tens of thousands of years. This amount of time, so long when measured against our lives, is a geological microsecond. It represents much less than 1 percent of the average life span for a fossil invertebrate species—more than 10 million years. Large, widespread, and well-established species, on the other hand, are not expected to change very much. We believe that the inertia of large populations explains the stasis of most fossil species over millions of years.

We proposed the theory of punctuated equilibrium largely to provide a differ- 20 ent explanation for pervasive trends in the fossil record. Trends, we argued, cannot be attributed to gradual transformation within lineages, but must arise from the differential success of certain kinds of species. A trend, we argued, is more like climbing a flight of stairs (punctuations and stasis) than rolling up an inclined plane.

Since we proposed punctuated equilibria to explain trends, it is infuriating to be quoted again and again by creationists—whether through design or stupidity, I do not know—as admitting that the fossil record includes no transitional forms. Transitional forms are generally lacking at the species level, but are abundant between larger groups. The evolution from reptiles to mammals, as mentioned earlier, is well documented. Yet a pamphlet entitled "Harvard Scientists Agree Evolution Is a Hoax" states: "The facts of punctuated equilibrium which Gould and Eldredge . . . are forcing Darwinists to swallow fit the picture that Bryan insisted on, and which God has revealed to us in the Bible."

Continuing the distortion, several creationists have equated the theory of punctuated equilibrium with a caricature of the beliefs of Richard Goldschmidt, a great early geneticist. Goldschmidt argued, in a famous book published in 1940, that new groups can arise all at once through major mutations. He referred to these suddenly transformed creatures as "hopeful monsters." (I am attracted to some aspects of the non-caricatured version, but Goldschmidt's theory still has nothing to do with punctuated equilibrium.) Creationist Luther Sunderland talks of the "punctuated equilibrium hopeful monster theory" and tells his hopeful readers that "it amounts to tacit admission that anti-evolutionists are correct in asserting there is no fossil evidence supporting the theory that all life is connected to a common ancestor." Duane Gish writes, "According to Goldschmidt, and now apparently according to Gould, a reptile laid an egg from which the first bird, feathers and all, was produced." Any evolutionist who believed such nonsense would rightly be laughed off the intellectual stage; yet the only theory that could ever envision such a scenario for the evolution of birds is creationism—God acts in the egg.

CONCLUSION

I am both angry at and amused by the creationists; but mostly I am deeply sad. Sad for many reasons. Sad because so many people who respond to creationist appeals are troubled for the right reason, but venting their anger at the wrong target. It is true that scientists have often been dogmatic and elitist. It is true that we have often allowed the white-coated, advertising image to represent us— "Scientists say that Brand X cures bunions ten times faster than . . ." We have not fought it adequately because we derive benefits from appearing as a new priest-hood. It is also true that faceless bureaucratic state power intrudes more and more into our lives and removes choices that should belong to individuals and communities. I can understand that requiring that evolution be taught in schools might be seen as one more insult on all these grounds. But the culprit is not, and cannot be, evolution or any other fact of the natural world. Identify and fight your legitimate enemies by all means, but we are not among them.

I am sad because the practical result of this brouhaha will not be expanded coverage to include creationism (that would also make me sad), but the reduc-tion or excision of evolution from high school curricula. Evolution is one of the half dozen "great ideas" developed by science. It speaks to the profound issues of genealogy that fascinate all of us—the "roots" phenomenon writ large. Where did we come from? Where did life arise? How did it develop? How are organisms related? It forces us to think, ponder, and wonder. Shall we deprive millions of this knowledge and once again teach biology as a set of dull and unconnected facts, without the thread that weaves diverse material into a supple unity?

But most of all I am saddened by a trend I am just beginning to discern 25 among my colleagues. I sense that some now wish to mute the healthy debate about theory that has brought new life to evolutionary biology. It provides grist for creationist mills, they say, even if only by distortion. Perhaps we should lie low and rally round the flag of strict Darwinism, at least for the moment—a kind of old-time religion on our part.

But we should borrow another metaphor and recognize that we too have to tread a straight and narrow path, surrounded by roads to perdition. For if we ever begin to suppress our search to understand nature, to quench our own intel-lectual excitement in a misguided effort to present a united front where it does not and should not exist, then we are truly lost.

CONTEXTS FOR "EVOLUTION AS FACT AND THEORY"

THOMAS HENRY HUXLEY

Evolution and Ethics

. . . Man, the animal, in fact, has worked his way to the headship of the sentient world, and has become the superb animal which he is, in virtue of his success in the struggle for existence. The conditions having been of a certain order, man's

From Thomas Henry Huxley, "Evolution and Ethics," in *Evolution and Ethics and Other Essays* (New York: Appleton, 1893), 50–52.

organization has adjusted itself to them better than that of his competitors in the cosmic strife. In the case of mankind, the self-assertion, the unscrupulous seizing upon all that can be grasped, the tenacious holding of all that can be kept, which constitute the essence of the struggle for existence, have answered. For his successful progress, throughout the savage state, man has been largely indebted to those qualities which he shares with the ape and the tiger; his exceptional physical organization; his cunning, his sociability, his curiosity, and his imitativeness; his ruthless and ferocious destructiveness when his anger is roused by opposition.

But, in proportion as men have passed from anarchy to social organization, and in proportion as civilization has grown in worth, these deeply ingrained serviceable qualities have become defects. After the manner of successful persons, civilized man would gladly kick down the ladder by which he has climbed. He would be only too pleased to see "the ape and tiger die." But they decline to suit his convenience; and the unwelcome intrusion of these boon companions of his hot youth into the ranged existence of civil life adds pains and griefs, innumerable and immeasurably great, to those which the cosmic process necessarily brings on the mere animal. In fact, civilized man brands all these ape and tiger promptings with the name of sins; he punishes many of the acts which flow from them as crimes; and, in extreme cases, he does his best to put an end to the survival of the fittest of former days by axe and rope.

DEFINING "THEORY"

As Gould explains in paragraphs 10 and 11 of "Evolution as Fact and Theory," the feature that differentiates scientific theory from theory in other fields is its "falsifiability." In the sixteenth century, Sir Francis Bacon argued that a scientific theory is confirmed by accumulated empirical evidence in its favor. This positive empirical evidence is only half the story, however, as the twentieth-century philosopher Karl Popper argues in *The Logic of Scientific Discovery* (1959), a translation of *Logik der Forschung* (1935). The other half is counterevidence, which scientists must also seek in order to discover where a theory breaks down. This counterevidence may consist of newly available empirical evidence, anomalies newly detected in the old evidence, or changes in what scientists agree "counts" as evidence. A scientific revolution begins when an old theory is increasingly questioned and a new theory gradually gains scientists' acceptance. The new agreement is what Thomas Kuhn, in his well-known 1962 article "The Historical Structure of Scientific Discovery," calls a "paradigm shift." Thus, what we consider scientific knowledge is only a set of beliefs that we have not yet been able to break or "falsify." What counts as scientific knowledge, then, does go through changes, and evolution is no exception.

Paleontologists acknowledge that there are "gaps" in the physical evidence for the evolution of certain species—that is, not all of the fossil remains that demonstrate a steady change in a species have been found. Thus, paleontologists must infer the existence of certain structures at various stages of a species' development, as Gould notes in "Evolution and the Triumph of Homology" (1986), where he further explains that Darwin's scientific methodology was also historical (in the sense that, in the absence of a full documentary record, historians infer connections from one event to another). The "gaps" in the fossil record are not, however, to be confused with the "gaps" or flaws in scientific reasoning.

Theories in fields other than science are not "falsifiable" in the same sense. Positive evidence may be found to support them, and counterevidence may break them. But that evidence is not entirely empirical. For example, historians may explain events through Marxist theory (which rests only in part on "hard" economic data) or "great man" theory, but evidence for either theory does not "break" the other. The two theories can coexist. The social sciences (anthropology, economics, psychology, and sociology), as their name implies, may be more or less scientific, depending on the falsifiability of particular claims. However, cultural elements prevent the social sciences from being as scientific, or as "falsifiable," as the natural sciences. Religious belief rests on sacred texts such as Genesis, which some believers take to be literally the word of God. There may be positive empirical evidence for some passages in sacred texts, but the belief that they are the word of the divine is just that: belief, not empirically falsifiable fact. Gould calls these entirely separate yet authoritative teachings "Nonoverlapping Magisteria" (1997). (A *magisterium* is an authoritative teaching.) Neither teaching "breaks" the other, yet one is empirical and the other is moral.

PHILLIP E. JOHNSON

The Unraveling of Scientific Materialism

Creationist Phillip E. Johnson, professor of law at the University of California at Berkeley, argues in this essay that paleontologists lack proof of evolution because the fossil record is incomplete, a fact paleontologists readily acknowledge. Johnson does not, however, dispute the positive evidence through which paleontologists infer developmental stages from the fossil records that are available. Rather, Johnson rejects Gould's argument in "Nonoverlapping Magisteria" because, he writes, Gould denies religion's "power to determine the facts" or to "make an independent judgment about the evidence that supports the 'facts.'"

. . . Not even the strictest biblical literalists deny the bred varieties of dogs, the variation of finch beaks, and similar instances within types. The more controversial claims of large-scale evolution are what arouse skepticism. Scientists may think they have good reasons for believing that living organisms evolved natu-

From Philip E. Johnson, "The Unraveling of Scientific Materialism," *First Things: A Monthly Journal of Religion and Public Life* 77 (November 1997): 22–25.

rally from nonliving chemicals, or that complex organs evolved by the accumulation of micromutations through natural selection, but having reasons is not the same as having proof. I have seen people, previously inclined to believe whatever "science says," become skeptical when they realize that the scientists actually do seem to think that variations in finch beaks or peppered moths, or the mere existence of fossils, proves all the vast claims of "evolution." It is as though the scientists, so confident in their answers, simply do not understand the question.

The reason for opposition to scientific accounts of our origins, according to [Richard C.] Lewontin, is not that people are ignorant of facts, but that they have not learned to think from the right starting point. In his words, "The primary problem is not to provide the public with the knowledge of how far it is to the nearest star and what genes are made of. . . . Rather, the problem is to get them to reject irrational and supernatural explanations of the world, the demons that exist only in their imaginations, and to accept a social and intellectual apparatus, Science, as the only begetter of truth." What the public needs to learn is that, like it or not, "We exist as material beings in a material world, all of whose phenomena are the consequences of material relations among material entities." In a word, the public needs to accept materialism, which means that they must put God (whom Lewontin calls the "Supreme Extraterrestrial") in the trash can of history where such myths belong.

Although Lewontin wants the public to accept science as the only source of truth, he freely admits that mainstream science itself is not free of the hokum that Sagan so often found in fringe science. . . .

Lewontin laments that even scientists frequently cannot judge the reliability of scientific claims outside their fields of speciality, and have to take the word of recognized authorities on faith. . . .

Lewontin is brilliantly insightful, but too crankily honest to be as good a manipulator as his Harvard colleague Stephen Jay Gould. Gould displays both his talent and his unscrupulousness in an essay in the March 1997 issue of *Natural History*, entitled "Nonoverlapping Magisteria" and subtitled "Science and religion are not in conflict, for their teachings occupy distinctly different domains." With a subtitle like that, you can be sure that Gould is out to reassure the public that evolution leads to no alarming conclusions. True to form, Gould insists that the only dissenters from evolution are "Protestant fundamentalists who believe that every word of the Bible must be literally true." Gould also insists that evolution (he never defines the word) is "both true and entirely compatible with Christian belief." Gould is familiar with nonliteralist opposition to evolutionary naturalism, but he blandly denies that any such phenomenon exists. . . .

The centerpiece of Gould's essay is an analysis of the complete text of Pope John Paul's statement of October 22, 1996, to the Pontifical Academy of Sciences endorsing evolution as "more than a hypothesis." He fails to quote the Pope's crucial qualification that "theories of evolution which, in accordance with the philosophies inspiring them, consider the spirit as emerging from the forces of living matter or as a mere epiphenomenon of this matter, are incompatible with the truth about man." Of course, a theory based on materialism assumes by definition that there is no "spirit" active in this world that is independent of matter. Gould knows this perfectly well, and he also knows, just as Richard Lewontin does, that the evidence doesn't support the claims for the creative power of natural selection made by writers such as Richard Dawkins. That is why the philosophy that really supports the theory has to be protected from critical scrutiny.

Gould's essay is a tissue of half-truths aimed at putting the religious people to sleep, or luring them into a "dialogue" on terms set by the materialists. Thus Gould graciously allows religion to participate in discussions of morality or the meaning of life, because science does not claim authority over such questions of value, and because "Religion is too important to too many people for any dismissal or denigration of the comfort still sought by many folks from theology." Gould insists, however, that all such discussion must cede to science the power to determine the *facts*, and one of the facts is an evolutionary process that is every bit as materialistic and purposeless for Gould as it is for Lewontin or Dawkins. If religion wants to accept a dialogue on those terms, that's fine with Gould—but don't let those religious people think they get to make an independent judgment about the evidence that supposedly supports the "facts." And if the religious people are gullible enough to accept materialism as one of the facts, they won't be capable of causing much trouble.

POLITICAL DIMENSIONS OF DEFINITION

The term *newspeak* (which Gould mentions in paragraph 3 of "Evolution as Fact and Theory") was coined by George Orwell in his novel *Nineteen Eighty-Four* (1949) to contrast with oldspeak (or Standard English). Orwell defined it, in part, as the practice of stripping words of certain meanings that do not serve the particular political beliefs of Ingsoc, or "English Socialism":

> The purpose of Newspeak was not only to provide a medium of expression for the world view and mental habits proper to the devotees of Ingsoc, but to make all other modes of thought impossible. It was intended that when Newspeak had been adopted once and for all and Oldspeak forgotten, a heretical thought—that is, a thought diverged from the principles of Ingsoc—should be literally unthinkable . . .

Gould calls "scientific creationism" an example of newspeak. Creationism's argument that evolution is "just a theory" involves stripping two essential meanings—empirically grounded and falsifiable—from the scientific definition of theory. Hence, *scientific creationism* is a contradiction in terms. Similarly, creationism's argument that a gap in the fossil record constitutes a gap in the theory of evolution blurs two distinct definitions: absence and logical flaw.

JAMES GLEICK

Stephen Jay Gould: Breaking Tradition with Darwin

A decade ago, [Gould] and Niles Eldredge, a fellow paleontologist at the American Museum of Natural History in New York, broke with orthodox Darwinism by proposing a new model for the pace of evolutionary change. The traditional view was, and is, that big changes are made gradually, by the accumulation of many tiny changes over eons. Gould and Eldredge, joined now by many other American and British paleontologists, argue for a theory of fits and starts. Most important change, they believe, takes place in the geological instant when a new species is born—a long instant, to be sure, lasting perhaps 5,000 to 50,000 years, but virtually no time at all compared to the millions of years most species survive. After that first burst of change comes a long period of stability.

The fits-and-starts theory—known as punctuated equilibrium, or, familiarly, as "punk eke"—addresses one of the great nuisances of evolutionary theory, the fossil record. As creationists love to point out, the evidence preserved in the earth's rocks shows many species virtually unchanged throughout their histories, with precious few transitional stages between them. Darwin and his successors have had to argue that the fossil record is incomplete by its very nature, preserving only a tiny fraction of organisms and preserving them at unreliable intervals. Gould and Eldredge ask whether the rocks might not after all be telling a true story. Perhaps transitional stages rarely appear because their existence really was brief.

This initial break with Neo-Darwinism, now accepted by many in the field, gave the modern debates their shape, but its implications have remained poorly understood except by specialists.

One piece of evolutionary theory that has firmly established itself in the way we think about human origins is the idea that we descended from our primate ancestors by continuously improving features such as brain size. Gould and Eldredge challenge that, suggesting that the important history of human ancestors is not a matter of gradual improvement, but of new humanlike species splitting off from the old. Our evolutionary history is more like a copiously branching bush than a ladder toward perfection. The new species probably formed quickly in small, geographically isolated populations and from then on, Gould and Eldredge argue, they remained more or less static.

"So that at any one time," Eldredge suggests, "you might have two or three species of various brain sizes, and the long-term winners of their competition would be the bigger-brained species. It's an analogue of natural selection at the species level."

A major area of contention to flow from punctuated equilibrium is just this suggestion—that individuals are not the only players on the evolutionary stage.

5

From James Gleick, "Stephen Jay Gould: Breaking Tradition with Darwin," *New York Times Magazine,* November 20, 1983, 54–56.

Perhaps species or local populations or even genes can be targets of natural selection. That is the basis of the hierarchical model of evolution that Gould and others are building—a model meant to explain the great events, the birth and death of species and the reshaping of ecosystems.

Whether natural selection is sorting individuals or species, it is still a process of adaptation—and the traditional view remains that what we are, what we have made ourselves, arises from usefulness in survival and reproduction. Gould challenges that as well.

"I don't doubt for a moment that there was a conventional selective reason for our large brain," he said. "That reason's probably complex—there are a whole host of interrelated advantages of large brains. What I do want to say very strongly is that most of what our brains do—most of what is essential to our considering of ourselves as being human—is not directly selected for, is not a product of natural selection, but arises as a nonadaptive structural consequence of building a computer so powerful as the human brain.

"To give just one example: The most terrible fact that the evolution of the large brain allowed us to learn is the fact of our personal mortality. Think of how much of the architecture of human culture and cultural traditions, how much of human religion, for example, arises and attempts to deal with that terrible fact, which we have come to learn as a result of the complex structure of our brain. You can't argue the brain became large *so that* we would learn the fact of our coming personal mortality."

QUESTIONS FOR DISCUSSION AND WRITING

1. In "Evolution as Fact and Theory," Gould distinguishes between "the mechanisms (theory) by which evolution (fact) occurred" (paragraph 7). How does this definition serve Gould's purpose?

2. In "Knight Takes Bishop?" Gould quotes Huxley on "the practical value of the art of public speaking" (paragraph 4). After reading these selections, write an essay on the media's role in the development of science. How does Gould view scientific endeavor and the public role of the scientist? How does public debate shape scientific disagreement and consensus? (For additional perspective, how does Norimitsu Onishi's "In a Country That Craved Respect, Stem Cell Scientist Rode a Wave of Korean Pride" (p. 548) describe the media's role in Dr. Hwang Woo Suk's scientific fraud?)

3. Huxley writes in "Evolution and Ethics" that "civilized man brands all these ape and tiger promptings with the name of sins" (paragraph 2). How might Huxley and Gould define sin? What might each argue are the social purposes of his definition of sin?

4. Edward O. Wilson explains that "success by organisms can ultimately be disastrous for their species" ("Microbes 3, Humans 2," p. 531, paragraph 3). In view

of Gould's theory of "punctuated equilibrium" (see Gleick's "Stephen Jay Gould: Breaking Tradition with Darwin"), what implications might Gould draw from the observation that an organism's success can jeopardize the survival of its species?

5. Gould writes in "Evolution as Fact and Theory" that science is "most fun when it plays with interesting ideas [and] examines their implications" (paragraph 9). On what basis, then, does Gould exclude creationism from this set of "interesting ideas"?

6. After reading the selections in this chapter, write an essay on the process through which "facts" become accepted as such.

7. In *Darwin Loves You: Natural Selection and the Re-enchantment of the World* (2006), George Levine claims that through his literary style Darwin expressed "almost mystical awe at the sheer existence of life in the universe; Darwin disenchanted believers in Heaven, but he reënchanted lovers of Earth" (Adam Gopnik, "Rewriting Nature," *New Yorker*, October 23, 2006, p. 59). Do you discern any of this enchantment in the essays by Gould and Darwin included here?

CHARLES DARWIN

Understanding Natural Selection

Charles Darwin (1809–1882) was the first to establish the concept of evolution by natural selection, the biological process through which species change and adapt over time. Born in Shrewsbury, England, Darwin was always more interested in direct observation and specimen collecting than in his formal studies, whether in medical school at the University of Edinburgh or divinity school at Cambridge University (B.A., 1831). In 1831 to 1836, he voyaged to South America and the South Pacific aboard the HMS Beagle, *recording in his journal his meticulous observations of flora and fauna, from trees to insects. Published in 1839, this journal remains a classic of natural history. After taking careful notes and collecting specimens, Darwin began to work privately on his hypothesis that within species "favorable variations would tend to be preserved, and unfavorable ones to be destroyed," leading to the gradual formation of new species. His theory, published as* On the Origin of Species by Means of Natural Selection *(1859), is the source of the following excerpt.*

In "Understanding Natural Selection," Darwin explains that variations within a species endure if those variations aid in survival or enhance reproduction. Through genetic mutation, some members of a species will be more likely to produce offspring who will increase in number compared to those of less well-adapted members, and a new species may arise.

Although natural selection can act only through and for the good of each being, yet characters and structures, which we are apt to consider as of very trifling importance, may thus be acted on. When we see leaf-eating insects green, and bark-feeders mottled-grey; the alpine ptarmigan white in winter, the red-grouse the color of heather, and the black-grouse that of peaty earth, we must believe that these tints are of service to these birds and insects in preserving them from danger. Grouse, if not destroyed at some period of their lives, would increase in countless numbers; they are known to suffer largely from birds of prey; and hawks are guided by eyesight to their prey—so much so, that on parts of the Continent persons are warned not to keep white pigeons, as being the most liable to destruction. Hence I can see no reason to doubt that natural selection might be most effective in giving the proper color to each kind of grouse, and in keeping that color, when once acquired, true and constant. Nor ought we to think that the occasional destruction of an animal of any particular color would produce little effect: we should remember how essential it is in a flock of white sheep to destroy every lamb with the faintest trace of black. In plants the down on the fruit and the color of the flesh are considered by botanists as characters of the most trifling importance: yet we hear from an excellent horticulturist, Downing, that in the United States smooth-skinned fruits suffer far more from a beetle, a curculio, than those with down; that purple plums suffer far more from a certain disease than yellow plums; whereas another disease attacks yellow-fleshed peaches far more than those with other colored flesh. If, with all the aids of art, these slight differences make a great difference in cultivating the several varieties, assuredly, in a state of nature, where the trees would have to struggle with other trees and with a host of enemies, such differences would effectually settle which variety, whether a smooth or downy, a yellow or purple fleshed fruit, should succeed.

In looking at many small points of difference between species, which, as far as our ignorance permits us to judge, seem to be quite unimportant, we must not forget that climate, food, and so on probably produce some slight and direct effect. It is, however, far more necessary to bear in mind that there are many unknown laws of correlation to growth, which, when one part of the organization is modified through variation, and the modifications are accumulated by natural selection for the good of the being, will cause other modifications, often of the most unexpected nature.

As we see that those variations which under domestication appear at any particular period of life, tend to reappear in the offspring of the same period; for instance, in the seeds of the many varieties of our culinary and agricultural plants; in the caterpillar and cocoon stages of the varieties of the silkworm; in the eggs of poultry, and in the color of the down of their chickens; in the horns of our sheep and cattle when nearly adult; so in a state of nature, natural selection will be enabled to act on and modify organic beings at any age, by the accumulation of profitable variations at that age, and by their inheritance at a corresponding age. If it profit a plant to have its seeds more and more widely disseminated by the wind, I can see no greater difficulty in this being effected through natural selection, than in the cotton-planter increasing and improving by selection the down in the pods on his cotton-trees. Natural selection may modify and adapt the larva of an insect to a score of contingencies, wholly different from those which concern the mature insect. These modifications will no doubt affect, through the laws of correlation, the structure of the adult; and probably in the case of those insects which live only for a few hours, and which never feed, a large part of their structure is merely the correlated result of successive changes in the structure of their larvae. So, conversely, modifications in the adult will probably often affect the structure of the larva; but in all cases natural selection will ensure that modifications consequent on other modifications at a different period of life, shall not be in the least degree injurious: for if they became so, they would cause the extinction of the species.

Natural selection will modify the structure of the young in relation to the parent, and of the parent in relation to the young. In social animals it will adapt the structure of each individual for the benefit of the community; if each in consequence profits by the selected change. What natural selection cannot do, is to modify the structure of one species, without giving it any advantage, for the good of another species; and though statements to this effect may be found in works of natural history, I cannot find one case which will bear investigation. A structure used only once in an animal's whole life, if of high importance to it, might be modified to any extent by natural selection; for instance, the great jaws possessed by certain insects, and used exclusively for opening the cocoon — or the hard tip to the beak of nestling birds, used for breaking the egg. It has been asserted, that of the best short-beaked tumbler pigeons more perish in the egg than are able to get out of it; so that fanciers assist in the act of hatching. Now, if nature had to make the beak of a full-grown pigeon very short for the bird's own advantage, the process of modification would be very slow, and there would be simultaneously the most rigorous selection of the young birds within the egg, which had the most powerful and hardest beaks, for all with weak beaks would inevitably perish: or, more delicate and more easily broken shells might be selected, the thickness of the shell being known to vary like every other structure.

SEXUAL SELECTION

Inasmuch as peculiarities often appear under domestication in one sex and become   5
hereditarily attached to that sex, the same fact probably occurs under nature, and if so, natural selection will be able to modify one sex in its functional relations to the other sex, or in relation to wholly different habits of life in the two sexes, as is sometimes the case with insects. And this leads me to say a few words on what I call sexual selection. This depends, not on a struggle for existence, but on a struggle between the males for possession of the females; the result is not death to the unsuccessful competitor, but few or no offspring. Sexual selection is, therefore, less rigorous than natural selection. Generally, the most vigorous males, those which are best fitted for their places in nature, will leave most progeny. But in many cases,

victory will depend not on general vigor, but on having special weapons, confined to the male sex. A hornless stag or spurless cock would have a poor chance of leaving offspring. Sexual selection by always allowing the victor to breed might surely give indomitable courage, length to the spur, and strength to the wing to strike in the spurred leg, as well as the brutal cock-fighter, who knows well that he can improve his breed by careful selection of the best cocks. How low in the scale of nature this law of battle descends, I know not; male alligators have been described as fighting, bellowing, and whirling round, like Indians in a war dance, for the possession of the females; male salmons have been seen fighting all day long; male stag-beetles often bear wounds from the huge mandibles of other males. The war is, perhaps, severest between the males of polygamous animals, and these seem oftenest provided with special weapons. The males of carnivorous animals are already well armed; though to them and to others, special means of defence may be given through means of sexual selection, as the mane to the lion, the shoulder-pad to the boar, and the hooked jaw to the male salmon, for the shield may be as important for victory, as the sword or spear.

Amongst birds, the contest is often of a more peaceful character. All those who have attended to the subject, believe that there is the severest rivalry between the males of many species to attract by singing the females. The rock-thrush of Guiana, birds of Paradise, and some others, congregate; and successive males display their gorgeous plumage and perform strange antics before the females, which standing by as spectators, as last choose the most attractive partner. Those who have closely attended to birds in confinement well know that they often take individual preferences and dislikes: thus Sir R. Heron has described how one pied peacock was eminently attractive to all his hen birds. It may appear childish to attribute any effect to such apparently weak means: I cannot here enter on the details necessary to support this view; but if man can in a short time give elegant carriage and beauty to his bantams, according to his standard of beauty, I can see no good reason to doubt that female birds, by selecting, during thousands of generations, the most melodious or beautiful males, according to their standard of beauty, might produce a marked effect. I strongly suspect that some well-known laws with respect to the plumage of male and female birds, in comparison with the plumage of the young, can be explained on the view of plumage having been chiefly modified by sexual selection, acting when the birds have come to the breeding age or during the breeding season; the modifications thus produced being inherited at corresponding ages or seasons, either by the males alone, or by the males and females; but I have not space here to enter on this subject.

Thus it is, as I believe, that when the males and females of any animal have the same general habits of life, but differ in structure, color, or ornament, such differences have been mainly caused by sexual selection; that is, individual males have had, in successive generations, some slight advantage over other males, in their weapons, means of defence, or charms; and have transmitted these advantages to their male offspring. Yet, I would not wish to attribute all such sexual differences to this agency: for we see peculiarities arising and becoming attached to the male sex in our domestic animals (as the wattle in male carriers, horn-like protuberances in the cocks of certain fowls, and so on), which we cannot believe to be either useful to the males in battle, or attractive to the females. We see analogous cases under nature, for instance, the tuft of hair on the breast of the turkey-cock, which can hardly be either useful or ornamental to this bird; indeed, had the tuft appeared under domestication, it would have been called a monstrosity.

ILLUSTRATION OF THE ACTION OF NATURAL SELECTION

. . . Let us take the case of a wolf, which preys on various animals, securing some by craft, some by strength, and some by fleetness; and let us suppose that the fleetest prey, a deer for instance, had from any change in the country increased in numbers, or that other prey had decreased in numbers, during that season of the year when the wolf is hardest pressed for food. I can under such circumstances see no reason to doubt that the swiftest and slimmest wolves would have the best chance of surviving, and so be preserved or selected—provided always that they retain strength to master their prey at this or at some other period of the year, when they might be compelled to prey on other animals. I can see no more reason to doubt this, than that man can improve the fleetness of his greyhounds by careful and methodical selection, or by that unconscious selection which results from each man trying to keep the best dogs without any thought of modifying the breed.

Even without any change in the proportional numbers of the animals on which our wolf preyed, a cub might be born with an innate tendency to pursue certain kinds of prey. Nor can this be thought very improbable; for we often observe great differences in the natural tendencies of our domestic animals; one cat, for instance, taking to catch rats, another mice; one cat . . . bringing home winged game, another hares or rabbits, and another hunting on marshy ground and almost nightly catching woodcocks or snipes. The tendency to catch rats rather than mice is known to be inherited. Now, if any slight innate change of habit or of structure benefited an individual wolf, it would have the best chance of surviving and of leaving offspring. Some of its young would probably inherit the same habits or structure, and by the repetition of this process, a new variety might be formed which would either supplant or coexist with the parent-form of wolf. Or, again, the wolves inhabiting a mountainous district, and those frequenting the lowlands, would naturally be forced to hunt different prey; and from the continued preservation of the individuals best fitted for the two sites, two varieties might slowly be formed. . . .

QUESTIONS FOR DISCUSSION AND WRITING

1. What is "natural selection"? Why, according to Darwin, is it difficult for people to see natural selection at work?

2. What is the effect of subtle variations within a species, according to Darwin?

3. What does Darwin mean by "sexual selection" (paragraph 5)? How does it help explain variations among males and among females of a species? How does sexual selection differ from natural selection?

4. What examples does Darwin use to support his argument for natural selection? Do you find some examples more persuasive than others? If so, which ones? Read Stephen Jay Gould's "Evolution as Fact and Theory" (p. 512) for a fuller understanding of this subject. How does Gould help you understand Darwin's argument?

5. Did you find any of Darwin's writing difficult to follow? If so, what parts? What might account for their difficulty?

EDWARD O. WILSON
Microbes 3, Humans 2

Edward O. Wilson (b. 1929) is famed as an expert on insect societies and as a pioneer in sociobiological research (the biological bases of behavior). Many critics see Wilson's controversial Sociobiology: The New Synthesis *(1975), which argues that behavior—even altruism—is motivated by individuals' selfish need to propagate their own genes, as potentially arguing on behalf of racism and eugenics.*

As his autobiography Naturalist *(1994) relates, Wilson's boyhood interest in observing nature turned into a systematic study of insects. Educated at the University of Alabama (B.S., 1949; M.S., 1950) and at Harvard (Ph.D., 1955), he has taught zoology at Harvard since 1956. He was awarded the National Medal of Science for his work and has written two Pulitzer Prize–winning books,* On Human Nature *(1979) and* The Ants *(1990, coauthored with myrmecologist Bert Hölldobler). In Consilience (1998), he argues that all fields of knowledge—the sciences, humanities, and arts—are in search of fundamental order in the world;* The Future of Life *(2002) makes a plea for environmental sanity.*

"Microbes 3, Humans 2," originally published in the New York Times Magazine *(April 1999), focuses on the question of which species are the most successful. Wilson approaches this highly complex issue by highlighting the various types of success, such as "most abundant," "most social," and "most intelligent."*

Let us mince words. When we say "best," we mean some kind of success, implying the existence of goals, which in turn are the exclusive property of organisms and not of species. Where the goal of a runner in a track meet is to break the tape, where a dragonfly succeeds when it snatches a fly from the air for dinner, where even a colon bacterium reverses the spin of its flagella, causing it to tumble and depart in a new direction that leads to dissolved sugar, it takes an organism to have a best.

As a result of natural selection, species—or more precisely, the organisms composing species—generally perform brilliantly in the niche to which they are specialized. There are probably 10 million or more species alive on earth. Which are the best at filling their niches? All are, I guess. Consider this Zenlike question: Can a bird fly better than a fish can swim? Live species are by definition all successes, because the losers are extinct, having fallen victim to nature's equivalent of the Foreign Legion command, March or die.

Of course, success by organisms can ultimately be disastrous for their species. Browsing animals, like the American white-tailed deer, can be superlatively efficient and as a result wipe out the plants on which they depend, whereupon the species and the organisms it comprises plunge toward extinction. Or take the same principle in reverse: the most successful parasites are those that least harm their host. The champion human parasites may be the Demodex mites, microscopic spiderlike creatures that live unnoticed on the eyelashes and eyebrows of a large percentage of the human population.

That said, I am unwilling to give up entirely the quest for successful species. So let me use subjective, human-oriented criteria to pin some gold medals on members of the world's fauna and flora.

Most abundant. Bacterial species win this one easily. There are more *E. coli* 5
and other intestinal bacteria in your colon at this moment than there are human beings who have ever lived.

Longest lived. All living species are in a dead heat, since all have descended from early forms of life that originated more than 3.5 billion years ago. When biologists speak of ancient forms and living fossils, they really mean certain combinations of traits that have persisted for relatively long periods of time in certain lines of descent, like modern horseshoe crabs and coelacanth fish. But the direct ancestry of human beings goes back just as far as these living fossils, the only difference being that the traits that distinguish *Homo sapiens* as a species are less than one-hundredth as old.

Most likely to survive. Without doubt, bacteria and allied organisms known as archaea win again, especially the species that use photosynthesis or inorganic chemicals to grow and reproduce. If every kind of plant and animal on earth were destroyed, these hardy organisms would carry on. Even if the earth's surface were blasted to a cinder, the inorganic-energy extractors and petroleum feeders would continue their lives many kilometers below the surface of the earth. Given a few billion years, they might give rise to new higher life forms on the surface.

Most social. As an entomologist, I will be accused of insect chauvinism, but I say ants, termites and honeybees win hands down. That is, they win if we use the following criteria: altruism, the complexity of anatomy, instincts devoted to social life and the tightness of the bonds that turn colonies into virtual superorganisms.

Most intelligent. At last, a gold medal for humanity.

Most powerful. Human beings win again. Peering into the future and under- 10
standing how the world works, we have acquired the power of life and death over

all other higher life forms. Whether we choose life for them and ultimately for ourselves is surely a valid criterion of success. To achieve that goal, however, requires wise management of the environment, an enterprise for which we have so far shown little dedication or talent.

QUESTIONS FOR DISCUSSION AND WRITING

1. In paragraph 1, Wilson inverts the familiar saying, "Let us not mince words." What might be his purpose in opening the essay this way?

2. Wilson's list of "gold medal" winners gives only two awards to humans; we aren't even the most social species, according to him. Why would Wilson want to demonstrate that humans aren't the best at everything?

3. Wilson explains that "success by organisms can ultimately be disastrous for their species" (paragraph 3). Why is abundance a "gold medal" for *E. coli* but not for white-tailed deer? In what ways could each of Wilson's "gold medals" turn into disasters for various species?

4. Considering that humans are not at the top of the animal kingdom in all categories (according to Wilson's analysis), write about the relative importance of the human race. How important is our species compared to other species, if we are not the most successful at everything? Where would Wilson stand in the debate between Stephen Jay Gould and creationists?

5. Wilson makes the paradoxical observation that an organism's success can jeopardize the survival of its species (see question 3). Are the success and intelligence of the human race similarly jeopardizing human survival? Write an essay using Wilson's model of perilous success, along with the ideas of Rachel Carson in "The Obligation to Endure" (p. 663), to discuss whether our impact on the environment (through pollution, war, and overdevelopment, for example) could render us extinct.

STANLEY FISH

Academic Cross-Dressing: How Intelligent Design Gets Its Arguments from the Left

Fish's prominence as a literary and cultural critic is intertwined with his reputation as an academic mover, shaker, and gadfly—as seen in such works as Is There a Text in this Class? *(1986), "The Unbearable Ugliness of Volvos" (1994), and* There's No Such Thing as Free Speech: And It's a Good Thing, Too *(1994). Born in 1939 in Providence, Rhode Island, Fish earned a doctorate in English from Yale (1962) and taught at the University of California at Berkeley, Johns Hopkins, and Duke, where he was also executive director of Duke University Press. After six years as dean of the College of Liberal Arts and Sciences at the University of Illinois at Chicago, he became a law professor at Florida International University. Fish's work often focuses on "interpretive communities"—how and why readers accept a common set of foundational assumptions as the basis for interpreting what they read and think. This reader-response view undergirds his books on Milton,* Surprised by Sin *(1967) and* How Milton Works *(2001), as well as his interpretation of the way people lock themselves into doctrinaire positions, in "Academic Cross-Dressing: How Intelligent Design Gets Its Arguments from the Left," originally published in* Harper's Magazine *(December 2005).*

When George W. Bush said recently that evolution and Intelligent Design should be taught side by side, so that students "can understand what the debate is about," he probably didn't know that he was subscribing to the wisdom of Gerald Graff, a professor of English at the University of Illinois, Chicago, and a founder of Teachers for a Democratic Culture, an organization dedicated to "combating conservative misrepresentations" of what goes on in college classrooms. Graff and Intelligent Design are now a couple on the Internet; a Google search for both together will turn up more than 100,000 pages, even though Graff had never written a word on the subject until he wrote in protest against his having been "hijacked by the Christian Right." What the Christian Right took from him (without acknowledgment) was the idea that college instructors should "teach the conflicts" around academic issues so that students will learn that knowledge is neither inertly given nor merely a matter of personal opinion but is established in the crucible of controversy. What is ironic is that although Graff made his case for teaching the controversies in a book entitled *Beyond the Culture Wars*, the culture wars have now appropriated his thesis and made it into a weapon. In the Intelligent Design army, from Bush on down to every foot soldier, "teach the controversy" is the battle cry.

It is an effective one, for it takes the focus away from the scientific credibility of Intelligent Design—away from the question, "Why should it be taught in a biology class?"—and puts it instead on the more abstract issues of freedom and open inquiry. Rather than saying we're right, the other guys are wrong, and here are the scientific reasons why, Intelligent Design polemicists say that every idea should at least get a hearing; that unpopular or minority views should always be represented; that questions of right and wrong should be left open; that what currently counts as knowledge should always be suspect, because it will typically reflect the interests and preferences of those in power. These ideas have been appropriated wholesale from the rhetoric of multiculturalism—a school of thought, emerging from the 1960s left, that proceeds from the unimpeachable observation that there are many different standards of judgment in the world to the unwarranted conclusion that judgment should therefore be dethroned entirely. Multiculturalism's goal was to gain acceptance for practices ruled out of bounds by established authority; its strategy was not to put new forms of authority in place of the old ones (which would have required the constructing of arguments) but instead to render all authority illegitimate, by explaining it away as the accidental ascendancy of one tradition over its equally worthy rivals. Why should we accept a canon of literature put in place by dead white males? Why should we stigmatize homosexual behavior just because it is condemned by a few church fathers? Once questions like these are posed and the expected answer — there is no reason, just prejudice and custom — has been given, the way is open for any constituency to play the same game. If multiculturalists can defend gay marriage by challenging the right of a church or a state to define what marriage is, why can't Intelligent Design proponents demand equal time in the classroom by challenging the right of Ivy League professors to say what science is?

One needn't believe in this line of argument in order to employ it; it is purely a matter of tactics. Phillip E. Johnson, a leading Intelligent Design advocate, is quite forthright about this. "I'm no postmodernist," he declares in a 1996 interview with the sociologist Amy Binder, but "I've learned a lot" from reading them. What he's learned, he reports, is how to talk about "hidden assumptions" and "power relationships," and how to use those concepts to cast doubt on the authority of "science educators" and other purveyors of the reigning orthodoxy. His views, he says, "are considered outlandish in the academic world," but the strategy he borrows from the postmodernists — the strategy of claiming to have been marginalized by the powers that be — is, he boasts, "dead-bang mainstream academia these days."

This is nothing if not clever. In an academy where talk of "marginalization" and "hegemonic exclusion" is routine, Johnson and his friends can use that talk — in which they have no real stake — to gain a hearing for ideas that have failed to make their way in the usual give-and-take of the academic debates Graff celebrates. In Graff's book, "teach the controversy" is a serious answer to a serious question: namely, how can we make students aware of the underlying issues that structure academic discourse? In the work of Johnson and other Intelligent Design proponents, "teach the controversy" is the answer to no question. Instead it is a wedge for prying open the doors of a world to which they have been denied access by gatekeepers — individual scientists, departments of biology, professional associations, editors of learned journals — who have found what they say unpersuasive. In their hands, the idea of teaching the controversies ceases to be an academic proposal directed at teachers and students and becomes a political proposal directed at legislators, school boards, and the general public.* They say "teach the controversy," but what they mean is that biology, having rejected Intelligent Design on scientific grounds, should nevertheless be forced to include it on the larger grounds of fairness.

The sleight of hand here is to deflect attention from the specific merits of one's claims by attaching them to some general truth or value that can then be

---

* This is why they regard as evidence the fact that, according to a recent poll, 65 percent of the American population wants the creation account found in Genesis to be taught side by side with Darwinism; the scientific response to that — or any other — number is, "So what?"

piously affirmed. This is why Intelligent Design advocates so often urge a long view of history. Isn't it the case, they ask, that it was once evolutionary theory that was kept out of some classrooms in this country? That proved to be an error; isn't it possible that, someday, refusing to teach Intelligent Design in science classes will be thought to have been an error, too? After all, haven't many once-discredited theories been accepted by a later generation of scholars? And doesn't history show us that apparently settled wisdom is often kept in place by those whose careers are invested in it? Although the answer to all these questions is undeniably yes, the mistake—and it is one made by some postmodern thinkers and seized upon by conservative polemicists—is to turn the fact of past error into a reason for distrusting any and all conclusions reached in the present. The judgment of experts is not discredited generally because it has occasionally turned out to be wrong; one has to go with the evidence one has, even if that evidence may be overtaken in the long run. It is no method at all to say that given our uncertainty as to what might turn up in the distant future, we therefore should systematically distrust what now appears to us to be sound and true.

Unfortunately (or fortunately for the Intelligent Design agenda), this is precisely what is said by multiculturalists and some postmodernists; and in saying it they have merely drawn out the implications of one strain of liberalism, the strain that finds its source in John Stuart Mill. In *On Liberty*, Mill insists that knowledge not meeting the test of repeated challenge is not really knowledge; indeed, he goes so far as to recommend that when a settled conclusion seems to have no challengers, some must be invented, for in his view the process of debate and controversy is more important than any conclusions it might deliver. This is also the prevailing view of First Amendment doctrine, as articulated by *New York Times* v. *Sullivan* (1964), a case in which the values of truth and accuracy are subordinated to the supposedly greater value of "uninhibited, robust, and wide-open" discussion. In its opinion the Court blurs the distinction between true and false statements by recharacterizing the latter (in a footnote that cites Mill) as a "valuable contribution to the public debate," thus paving the way for those who, like the advocates of Intelligent Design, assert that their views deserve to be considered (and taught), even when—especially when—the vast majority of authorities in the field have declared them to be without scientific merit. It is an assertion that liberals by and large resist when the message is racist or sexist, but it is a logical consequence of liberalism's privileging of tolerance over judgment.

Liberalism privileges tolerance because it is committed to fallibilism, the idea that our opinions about the world, derived as they are from the local, limited perspectives in which we necessarily live, are likely to be in error even when—again, especially when—we are wholly committed to them. If God or God's representative is removed as the guarantor of right judgment, all that remains is the judgment of fallible men and women who will be pretending to divinity whenever they confuse what seems to them to be true for what is really true. Because this mistake is natural to us, because the beliefs we acquire always seem to us to be perspicuous and indubitable, it is necessary, liberalism tells us, to put obstacles in the way of our assenting too easily to what are finally only our opinions. One way to do this is to institutionalize Mill's advice and to require, as a matter of principle, a diversity of views with respect to any question. The *New York Times* v. *Sullivan* decision quotes with approval Judge Learned Hand's declaration that in essence the First Amendment "presupposes that right conclusions are more likely to be gathered out of a multitude of tongues, than through any kind of authoritative selection." Typically, those who make pronouncements like this assume (without saying so) that the tongues making up the multitude will belong to persons who are committed to the protocols of rational inquiry; frivolous persons, persons who exploit those protocols or play with them to gain political ends, are not imagined. (When Graff counsels "teach the controversy," he means teach the real controversies, not the manufactured ones.) But nothing in a statement like Hand's rules them out, and once "authoritative selection" has been discounted and even rendered suspect because of its necessarily fallible origins, there is no reason at all for excluding any voice no matter how outlandish its assertions. After all, who's to say?

Intelligent Designers are not the first denizens of the right to borrow arguments and strategies from the liberal and postmodern left. In the early 1990s the Holocaust denier Bradley Smith was able to place an ad — actually an essay — in college student newspapers in part because he presented his ideas under the heading "The Holocaust Controversy: The Case for Open Debate." Not the case for why there was no campaign to exterminate the Jews, or for why the Nazis were innocent of genocidal thoughts, or for why Holocaust-promoting Jews are just trying to drum tip "financial support for Jewish causes" — though all these things were asserted in the body of the ad — but the case for open debate, and how could anyone, especially an academic, be against that? Ours is not a "radical point of view," Smith asserts. We are just acting on premises that "were worked out some time ago during a little something called the Enlightenment." In short, we are the true liberals, and it is the scholars who have become "Thought Police" either by actively working to exclude us or by sitting "dumbly by, allowing campus totalitarians to determine what can be said and what can be read on their campus."

Proponents of Intelligent Design are rightly outraged when their efforts are linked to the efforts of Holocaust deniers, for there is no moral equivalence between the two projects. One, after all, is in the business of whitewashing genocide, whereas the other wishes only to give God the credit for having created the wonders of the physical world. (I know that Intelligent Design literature stays away from the word "God," but no one, in or out of the movement, gives any other answer to the question, "Designed by whom?") There is, however, an equivalence of strategy that makes linking the two inevitable: in both cases, issues that have been settled in the relevant academic departments — history and biology, respectively — are reopened by reframing them as abstract questions about the value of debate as a moral good. When John West of the Discovery Institute (the Intelligent Design think tank) declares that "All Americans who cherish free speech" should reject any effort to exclude Intelligent Design from the classroom and invokes "the free marketplace of ideas" to clinch his case, his words could be incorporated wholesale into Bradley Smith's ad. Intelligent Designers and Holocaust deniers, despite the great differences between them, play the same shell game; they both say: Look here, in the highest reaches of speculation about inquiry in general, and not there, in the places where the particular, nitty-gritty work of inquiry is actually being done. They appeal to a higher value—the value of controversy as a good no matter what its content or who its participants—and thereby avoid questions about the qualifications necessary to be legitimate competitors in the competition. In the guise of upping the stakes, Intelligent Designers lower them, moving immediately to a perspective so broad and inclusive that all claims are valued not because they have proven out in the contest of ideas but simply because they are claims. When any claim has a right to be heard and taught just because it is one, judgment falls by the wayside and is replaced by the imperative to let a hundred (or a million) flowers bloom.

There's a word for this, and it's *relativism*. Polemicists on the right regularly   10 lambaste intellectuals on the left for promoting relativism and its attendant bad practices—relaxing or abandoning standards, opening the curriculum to any idea with a constituency attached to it, dismissing received wisdom by impugning the motives of those who have established it; disregarding inconvenient evidence and replacing it with grand theories supported by nothing but the partisan beliefs and desires of the theorizers. Whether or not this has ever been true of the right's targets, it is now demonstrably true of the right itself, whose members now recite the mantras of "teach the controversy" or "keep the debate open" whenever they find it convenient. They do so not out of a commitment to scrupulous scholarship (although that will be what is asserted) but in an effort to accomplish through misdirection and displacement what they cannot accomplish through evidence and argument.

QUESTIONS FOR DISCUSSION AND WRITING

1. Fish analyzes "the rhetoric of multiculturalism" to show how it proceeds from correctly observing "that there are many different standards of judgment in the world" to the "unwarranted conclusion" that renders "all authority illegitimate, by explaining it away as the accidental ascendancy of one tradition over its equally worthy rivals" (paragraph 2). Does Fish convince you that the claim that all arguments are equal is wrong? Do all arguments have to be fair, even if to be fair perpetuates falsehood?

2. Examine the analogy that Fish uses to explain the argument from Intelligent Design: "If multiculturalists can defend gay marriage by challenging the right of a state to define what marriage is, why can't Intelligent Design proponents demand equal time in the classroom by challenging the right of Ivy League professors to say what science is?" (paragraph 2). Is this a "manufactured controversy"? What's wrong with this analogy? What's wrong with arguing by analogy?

3. What do Intelligent Design proponents claim about evolution and the creation of the universe? How do they evade the argument by saying "Teach the controversy" (paragraph 4)? If evolutionists don't believe there is a controversy, are they being co-opted into presenting the Intelligent Design argument by this exhortation? Must every claim on every subject be accompanied by information about alternative points of view even if they remain speculative or are largely discredited?

4. What parallels are there between the argumentative strategies of the Holocaust deniers and Intelligent Design proponents (paragraph 8)? If they argue in similar ways, must both be right? Or both be wrong?

5. Fish observes, Intelligent Designers and Holocaust deniers "play the same shell game. . . . They appeal to a higher value—the value of controversy as a good no matter what its content or who its participants—and thereby avoid questions about the qualifications necessary to be legitimate competitors in the competition" (paragraph 9). With a partner, evaluate the merits of Fish's analysis throughout the essay. Yes, he opposes the argumentative strategy of the Intelligent Designers. He offers detailed reasons. Must he give a rebuttal equal time?

NATALIE ANGIER

Men, Women, Sex and Darwin

"It's bad luck to be born either sex" is Natalie Angier's favorite quotation (from biologist Sarah Hrdy). Angier was born in 1958 and grew up in the Bronx, New York. She earned a bachelor's degree from Barnard College (1978). She has worked as a reporter for Time *and the* Atlantic. *Her books include* Natural Obsessions *(1988), on the world of cancer research, and* The Beauty of the Beastly *(1995), on invertebrates. In 1991 Angier received the Pulitzer Prize for her science writing in the* New York Times. *More recently, Angier's attention has turned to female genetics, anatomy, physiology, and endocrinology from the fetus to menopause in* Woman: An Intimate Geography *(1999), which argues that males and females are less distinct than is often supposed and that androgynous features are not rare. In the ongoing debate over whether the behavior of men and women is determined more by genetics or culture, Angier favors "nurture" over "nature." In "Men, Women, Sex and Darwin," originally published in the* New York Times Magazine *(February 1999), she argues against evolutionary psychologists who claim that sexual stereotypes have evolved over millions of years and are programed into human genes.*

Life is short but jingles are forever. None more so, it seems, than the familiar ditty, variously attributed to William James, Ogden Nash and Dorothy Parker: "Hoggamus, higgamus, / Men are polygamous, / Higgamus, hoggamus, / Women monogamous."

Lately the pith of that jingle has found new fodder and new fans, through the explosive growth of a field known as evolutionary psychology. Evolutionary psychology professes to have discovered the fundamental modules of human nature, most notably the essential nature of man and of woman. It makes sense to be curious about the evolutionary roots of human behavior. It's reasonable to try to understand our impulses and actions by applying Darwinian logic to the problem. We're animals. We're not above the rude little prods and jests of natural and sexual selection. But evolutionary psychology as it has been disseminated across mainstream consciousness is a cranky and despotic Cyclops, its single eye glaring through an overwhelmingly masculinist lens. I say "masculinist" rather than "male" because the view of male behavior promulgated by hard-core evolutionary psychologists is as narrow and inflexible as their view of womanhood is.

I'm not interested in explaining to men what they really want or how they should behave. If a fellow chooses to tell himself that his yen for the fetching young assistant in his office and his concomitant disgruntlement with his aging wife make perfect Darwinian sense, who am I to argue with him? I'm only proposing here that the hard-core evolutionary psychologists have got a lot about women wrong—about some of us, anyway—and that women want more and deserve better than the cartoon *Olive Oyl* handed down for popular consumption.

The cardinal premises of evolutionary psychology of interest to this discussion are as follows: 1. Men are more promiscuous and less sexually reserved than women are. 2. Women are inherently more interested in a stable relationship than men are. 3. Women are naturally attracted to high-status men with resources. 4. Men are naturally attracted to youth and beauty. 5. Humankind's core preferences and desires were hammered out long, long ago, a hundred thousand years or more, in the legendary Environment of Evolutionary Adaptation, or E.E.A., also known as the ancestral environment, also known as the Stone Age, and they have not changed appreciably since then, nor are they likely to change in the future.

In sum: Higgamus, hoggamus, Pygmalionus, *Playboy* magazine, *eternitas*.   5 Amen.

Hard-core evolutionary psychology types go to extremes to argue in favor of the yawning chasm that separates the innate desires of women and men. They declare ringing confirmation for their theories even in the face of feeble and amusingly contradictory data. For example: Among the cardinal principles of the evo-psycho set is that men are by nature more polygamous than women are, and much more accepting of casual, even anonymous, sex. Men can't help themselves, they say: they are always hungry for sex, bodies, novelty and nubility. Granted, men needn't act on such desires, but the drive to sow seed is there nonetheless, satyric and relentless, and women cannot fully understand its force. David Buss, a professor of psychology at the University of Texas at Austin and one of the most outspoken of the evolutionary psychologists, says that asking a man not to lust after a pretty young woman is like telling a carnivore not to like meat.

At the same time, they recognize that the overwhelming majority of men and women get married, and so their theories must extend to different innate mate preferences among men and women. Men look for the hallmarks of youth, like smooth skin, full lips and perky breasts; they want a mate who has a long child-bearing career ahead of her. Men also want women who are virginal and who seem as though they'll be faithful and not make cuckolds of them. The sexy, vampy types are fine for a Saturday romp, but when it comes to choosing a marital partner, men want modesty and fidelity.

Women want a provider, the theory goes. They want a man who seems rich, stable and ambitious. They want to know that they and their children will be cared for. They want a man who can take charge, maybe dominate them just a little, enough to reassure them that the man is genotypically, phenotypically, eternally, a king. Women's innate preference for a well-to-do man continues to this day, the evolutionary psychologists insist, even among financially independent and professionally successful women who don't need a man as a provider. It was adaptive in the past to look for the most resourceful man, they say, and adaptations can't be willed away in a generation or two of putative cultural change.

And what is the evidence for these male-female verities? For the difference in promiscuity quotas, the hard-cores love to raise the example of the differences between gay men and lesbians. Homosexuals are seen as a revealing population because they supposedly can behave according to the innermost impulses of their sex, untempered by the need to adjust to the demands and wishes of the opposite sex, as heterosexuals theoretically are. What do we see in this ideal study group? Just look at how gay men carry on! They are perfectly happy to have hundreds, thousands, of sexual partners, to have sex in bathhouses, in bathrooms, in Central Park. By contrast, lesbians are sexually sedate. They don't cruise sex clubs. They couple up and stay coupled, and they like cuddling and hugging more than they do serious, genitally based sex.

In the hard-core rendering of inherent male-female discrepancies in promis-   10
cuity, gay men are offered up as true men, real men, men set free to be men, while lesbians are real women, ultra-women, acting out every woman's fantasy of love and commitment. Interestingly, though, in many neurobiology studies gay men are said to have somewhat feminized brains, with hypothalamic nuclei that are closer in size to a woman's than to a straight man's, and spatial-reasoning skills that are modest and ladylike rather than manfully robust. For their part, lesbians are posited to have somewhat masculinized brains and skills—to be sportier, more mechanically inclined, less likely to have played with dolls or tea sets when young—all as an ostensible result of exposure to prenatal androgens. And so gay men are sissy boys in some contexts and Stone Age manly men in others, while lesbians are battering rams one day and flower into the softest and most sexually divested girlish girls the next.

On the question of mate preferences, evo-psychos rely on surveys, most of them compiled by David Buss. His surveys are celebrated by some, derided by others, but in any event they are ambitious—performed in 37 countries, he says, on six continents. His surveys, and others emulating them, consistently find that men rate youth and beauty as important traits in a mate, while women give comparatively greater weight to ambition and financial success. Surveys show that surveys never lie. Lest you think that women's mate preferences change with their own mounting economic clout, surveys assure us that they do not. Surveys of female medical students, according to John Marshall Townsend, of Syracuse University, indicate that they hope to marry men with an earning power and social status at least equal to and preferably greater than their own.

Perhaps all this means is that men can earn a living wage better, even now, than women can. Men make up about half the world's population, but they still own the vast majority of the world's wealth—the currency, the minerals, the timber, the gold, the stocks, the amber fields of grain. In her superb book *Why So Slow?* Virginia Valian, a professor of psychology at Hunter College, lays out the extent of lingering economic discrepancies between men and women in the United States. In 1978 there were two women heading Fortune 1000 companies; in 1994, there were still two; in 1996, the number had jumped all the way to four. In 1985, 2 percent of the Fortune 1000's senior-level executives were women; by 1992, that number had hardly budged, to 3 percent. A 1990 salary and compensation survey of 799 major companies showed that of the highest-paid officers and directors, less than one-half of 1 percent were women. Ask, and he shall receive. In the United States the possession of a bachelor's degree adds $28,000 to a man's salary but only $9,000 to a woman's. A degree from a high-prestige school contributes $11,500 to a man's income but *subtracts* $2,400 from a woman's. If women continue to worry that they need a man's money, because the playing field remains about as level as the surface of Mars, then we can't conclude anything about innate preferences. If women continue to suffer from bag-lady syndrome even as they become properous, if they still see their wealth as provisional and capsizable, and if they still hope to find a man with a dependable income to supplement their own, then we can credit women with intelligence and acumen, for inequities abound.

There's another reason that smart, professional women might respond on surveys that they'd like a mate of their socioeconomic status or better. Smart, professional women are smart enough to know that men can be tender of ego—is it genetic?—and that it hurts a man to earn less money than his wife, and that resentment is a noxious chemical in a marriage and best avoided at any price. "A woman who is more successful than her mate threatens his position in the male hierarchy," Elizabeth Cashdan, of the University of Utah, has written. If women could be persuaded that men didn't mind their being high achievers, were in fact pleased and proud to be affiliated with them, we might predict that the women would stop caring about the particulars of their mates' income. The anthropologist Sara Blaffer Hrdy writes that "when female status and access to resources do not depend on her mate's status, women will likely use a range of criteria, not primarily or even necessarily prestige and wealth, for mate selection." She cites a 1996 *New York Times* story about women from a wide range of professions—bankers, judges, teachers, journalists—who marry male convicts. The allure of such men is not their income, for you can't earn much when you make license plates for a living. Instead, it is the men's gratitude that proves irresistible. The women also like the fact that their husbands' fidelity is guaranteed. "Peculiar as it is," Hrdy writes, "this vignette of sex-reversed claustration makes a serious point about just how little we know about female choice in breeding systems where male interests are not paramount and patrilines are not making the rules."

Do women love older men? Do women find gray hair and wrinkles attractive on men—as attractive, that is, as a fine, full head of pigmented hair and a vigorous, firm complexion? The evolutionary psychologists suggest yes. They believe that women look for the signs of maturity in men because a mature man is likely to be a comparatively wealthy and resourceful man. That should logically include baldness, which generally comes with age and the higher status that it often confers. Yet, as Desmond Morris points out, a thinning hairline is not considered a particularly attractive state.

Assuming that women find older men attractive, is it the men's alpha status? 15 Or could it be something less complimentary to the male, something like the following—that an older man is appealing not because he is powerful but because in his maturity he has lost some of his power, has become less marketable and desirable and potentially more grateful and gracious, more likely to make a younger woman feel that there is a balance of power in the relationship? The rude little calculation is simple: He is male, I am female—advantage, man. He is older, I am younger—advantage, woman. By the same token, a woman may place little value on a man's appearance because she values something else far more: room to breathe. Who can breathe in the presence of a handsome young man, whose ego, if expressed as a vapor, would fill Biosphere II? Not even, I'm afraid, a beautiful young woman.

In the end, what is important to question, and to hold to the fire of alternative interpretation, is the immutability and adaptive logic of the discrepancy, its basis in our genome rather than in the ecological circumstances in which a genome manages to express itself. Evolutionary psychologists insist on the essential discordance between the strength of the sex drive in males and females. They admit that many nonhuman female primates gallivant about rather more than we might have predicted before primatologists began observing their behavior in the field—more, far more, than is necessary for the sake of reproduction. Nonetheless, the credo of the coy female persists. It is garlanded with qualifications and is admitted to be an imperfect portrayal of female mating strategies, but then, that little matter of etiquette attended to, the credo is stated once again.

"Amid the great variety of social structure in these species, the basic theme . . . stands out, at least in minimal form: males seem very eager for sex and work hard to find it; females work less hard," Robert Wright says in *The Moral Animal*. "This isn't to say the females don't like sex. They love it, and may initiate it. And, intriguingly, the females of the species most closely related to humans—chimpanzees and bonobos—seem particularly amenable to a wild sex life, including a variety of partners. Still, female apes don't do what male apes do: search high and low, risking life and limb, to find sex, and to find as much of it, with as many different partners, as possible; it has a way of finding them." In fact female chimpanzees do search high and low and take great risks to find sex with partners other than the partners who have a way of finding them. DNA studies of chimpanzees in West Africa show that half the offspring in a group of closely scrutinized chimpanzees turned out not to be the offspring of the resident males. The females of the group didn't rely on sex "finding" its way to them; they proactively left the local environs, under such conditions of secrecy that not even their vigilant human observers knew they had gone, and became impregnated by outside males. They did so even at the risk of life and limb—their own and those of their offspring. Male chimpanzees try to control the movements of fertile females. They'll scream at them and hit them if they think the females aren't listening. They may even kill an infant they think is not their own. We don't know why the females take such risks to philander, but they do, and to say that female chimpanzees "work less hard" than males do at finding sex does not appear to be supported by the data.

Evo-psychos pull us back and forth until we might want to sue for whiplash. On the one hand we are told that women have a lower sex drive than men do. On the other hand we are told that the madonna-whore dichotomy is a universal stereotype. In every culture, there is a tendency among both men and women to adjudge women as either chaste or trampy. The chaste ones are accorded esteem. The trampy ones are consigned to the basement, a notch or two below goats in social status. A woman can't sleep around without risking terrible retribution, to her reputation, to her prospects, to her life. "Can anyone find a single culture in which women with unrestrained sexual appetites *aren't* viewed as more aberrant than comparably libidinous men?" Wright asks rhetorically.

Women are said to have lower sex drives than men, yet they are universally punished if they display evidence to the contrary—if they disobey their "natural" inclination toward a stifled libido. Women supposedly have a lower sex drive than men do, yet it is not low enough. There is still just enough of a lingering female infidelity impulse that cultures everywhere have had to gird against it by articulating a rigid dichotomy with menacing implications for those who fall on the wrong side of it. There is still enough lingering female infidelity to justify infibulation, purdah, claustration. Men have the naturally higher sex drive, yet all the laws, customs, punishments, shame, strictures, mystiques and antimystiques are aimed with full hominid fury at that tepid, sleepy, hypoactive creature, the female libido.

"It seems premature . . . to attribute the relative lack of female interest in 20 sexual variety to women's biological nature alone in the face of overwhelming evidence that women are consistently beaten for promiscuity and adultery," the primatologist Barbara Smuts has written. "If female sexuality is muted compared to that of men, then why must men the world over go to extreme lengths to control and contain it?"

Why indeed? Consider a brief evolutionary apologia for President Clinton's adulteries written by Steven Pinker, of the Massachusetts Institute of Technology. "Most human drives have ancient Darwinian rationales," he wrote. "A prehistoric man who slept with fifty women could have sired fifty children, and would have been more likely to have descendants who inherited his tastes. A woman who slept with fifty men would have no more descendants than a woman who slept with one. Thus, men should seek quantity in sexual partners; women, quality." And isn't it so, he says, everywhere and always so? "In our society," he continues, "most young men tell researchers that they would like eight sexual partners in the next two years; most women say that they would like one." Yet would a man find the prospect of a string of partners so appealing if the following rules were applied: that no matter how much he may like a particular woman and be pleased by her performance and want to sleep with her again, he will have no say in the matter and will be dependent on her mood and good graces for all future contact; that each act of casual sex will cheapen his status and make him increasingly less attractive to other women; and that society will not wink at his randiness but rather sneer at him and think him pathetic, sullied, smaller than life? Until men are subjected to the same severe standards and threat of censure as women are, and until they are given the lower hand in a so-called casual encounter from the start, it is hard to insist with such self-satisfaction that, hey, it's natural, men like a lot of sex with a lot of people and women don't.

Reflect for a moment on Pinker's philandering caveman who slept with 50 women. Just how good a reproductive strategy is this chronic, random shooting of the gun? A woman is fertile only five or six days a month. Her ovulation is concealed. The man doesn't know when she's fertile. She might be in the early stages of pregnancy when he gets to her; she might still be lactating and thus not ovulating. Moreover, even if our hypothetical Don Juan hits a day on which a woman is ovulating, the chances are around 65 percent that his sperm will fail to fertilize her egg; human reproduction is complicated, and most eggs and sperm are not up to the demands of proper fusion. Even if conception occurs, the resulting embryo has about a 30 percent chance of miscarrying at some point in gestation. In sum, each episode of fleeting sex has a remarkably small probability of yielding a baby—no more than 1 or 2 percent at best.

And because the man is trysting and running, he isn't able to prevent any of his casual contacts from turning around and mating with other men. The poor fellow. He has to mate with many scores of women for his wham-bam strategy to pay off. And where are all these women to be found, anyway? Population densities during that purportedly all-powerful psyche shaper the "ancestral environment" were quite low, and long-distance travel was dangerous and difficult.

There are alternatives to wantonness, as a number of theorists have emphasized. If, for example, a man were to spend more time with one woman rather than dashing breathlessly from sheet to sheet, if he were to feel compelled to engage in what animal behaviorists call mate guarding, he might be better off, reproductively speaking, than the wild Lothario, both because the odds of impregnating the woman would increase and because he'd be monopolizing her energy and keeping her from the advances of other sperm bearers. It takes the average couple three to four months of regular sexual intercourse to become pregnant. That number of days is approximately equal to the number of partners our hypothetical libertine needs to sleep with to have one encounter result in a "fertility unit," that is, a baby. The two strategies, then, shake out about the same. A man can sleep with a lot of women — the quantitative approach — or he can sleep with one woman for months at a time, and be madly in love with her — the qualitative tactic.

It's possible that these two reproductive strategies are distributed in discrete   25 packets among the male population, with a result that some men are born phi-landerers and can never attach, while others are born romantics and perpetually in love with love; but it's also possible that men teeter back and forth from one impulse to the other, suffering an internal struggle between the desire to bond and the desire to retreat, with the circuits of attachment ever there to be toyed with, and their needs and desires difficult to understand, paradoxical, fickle, treacherous and glorious. It is possible, then, and for perfectly good Darwinian reason, that casual sex for men is rarely as casual as it is billed.

It needn't be argued that men and women are exactly the same, or that hu-mans are meta-evolutionary beings, removed from nature and slaves to culture, to reject the perpetually regurgitated model of the coy female and the ardent male. Conflicts of interest are always among us, and the outcomes of those con-flicts are interesting, more interesting by far than what the ultra-evolutionary psychology line has handed us. Patricia Gowaty, of the University of Georgia, sees conflict between males and females as inevitable and pervasive. She calls it sexual dialectics. Her thesis is that females and males vie for control over the means of reproduction. Those means are the female body, for there is as yet no such beast as the parthenogenetic man.

Women are under selective pressure to maintain control over their repro-duction, to choose with whom they will mate and with whom they will not — to exercise female choice. Men are under selective pressure to make sure they're chosen or, barring that, to subvert female choice and coerce the female to mate against her will. "But once you have this basic dialectic set in motion, it's going to be a constant push-me, pull-you," Gowaty says. "That dynamism cannot possibly result in a unitary response, the caricatured coy woman and ardent man. Instead there are going to be some coy, reluctantly mating males and some ardent fe-males, and any number of variations in between.

"A female will choose to mate with a male whom she believes, consciously or otherwise, will confer some advantage on her and her offspring. If that's the case, then her decision is contingent on what she brings to the equation." For example, she says, "the 'good genes' model leads to oversimplified notions that there is a 'best male' out there, a top-of-the-line hunk whom all females would prefer to mate with if they had the wherewithal. But in the viability model, a female brings her own genetic complement to the equation, with the result that what looks good genetically to one woman might be a clash of colors for another."

Maybe the man's immune system doesn't complement her own, for example, Gowaty proposes. There's evidence that the search for immune variation is one of the subtle factors driving mate selection, which may be why we care about how our lovers smell; immune molecules may be volatilized and released in sweat, hair, the oil on our skin. We are each of us a chemistry set, and each of us has a distinctive mix of reagents. "What pleases me might not please somebody else," Gowaty says. "There is no one-brand great male out there. We're not all programmed to look for the alpha male and only willing to mate with the little guy or the less aggressive guy because we can't do any better. But the propaganda gives us a picture of the right man and the ideal woman, and the effect of the propaganda is insidious. It becomes self-reinforcing. People who don't fit the model think, I'm weird, I'll have to change my behavior." It is this danger, that the ostensible "discoveries" of evolutionary psychology will be used as propaganda, that makes the enterprise so disturbing.

Variation and flexibility are the key themes that get set aside in the breathless 30 dissemination of evolutionary psychology. "The variation is tremendous, and is rooted in biology," Barbara Smuts said to me. "Flexibility itself is the adaptation." Smuts has studied olive baboons, and she has seen males pursuing all sorts of mating strategies. "There are some whose primary strategy is dominating other males, and being able to gain access to more females because of their fighting ability," she says. "Then there is the type of male who avoids competition and cultivates long-term relationships with females and their infants. These are the nice, affiliative guys. There's a third type, who focuses on sexual relationships. He's the consorter. . . . And as far as we can tell, no one reproductive strategy has advantages over the others."

Women are said to need an investing male. We think we know the reason. Human babies are difficult and time consuming to raise. Stone Age mothers needed husbands to bring home the bison. Yet the age-old assumption that male parental investment lies at the heart of human evolution is now open to serious question. Men in traditional foraging cultures do not necessarily invest resources in their offspring. Among the Hadza of Africa, for example, the men hunt, but they share the bounty of that hunting widely, politically, strategically. They don't deliver it straight to the mouths of their progeny. Women rely on their senior female kin to help feed their children. The women and their children in a gathering-hunting society clearly benefit from the meat that hunters bring back to the group. But they benefit as a group, not as a collection of nuclear family units, each beholden to the father's personal pound of wildeburger.

This is a startling revelation, which upends many of our presumptions about the origins of marriage and what women want from men and men from women. If the environment of evolutionary adaptation is not defined primarily by male parental investment, the bedrock of so much of evolutionary psychology's theories, then we can throw the door wide open and ask new questions, rather than endlessly repeating ditties and calling the female coy long after she has run her petticoats through the Presidential paper shredder.

For example: Nicholas Blurton Jones, of the University of California at Los Angeles, and others have proposed that marriage developed as an extension of men's efforts at mate guarding. If the cost of philandering becomes ludicrously high, the man might be better off trying to claim rights to one woman at a time. Regular sex with a fertile woman is at least likely to yield offspring at comparatively little risk to his life, particularly if sexual access to the woman is formalized through a public ceremony—a wedding. Looked at from this perspective, one must wonder why an ancestral woman bothered to get married, particularly if she and her female relatives did most of the work of keeping the family fed from year to year. Perhaps, Blurton Jones suggests, to limit the degree to which she was harassed. The cost of chronic male harassment may be too high to bear. Better to agree to a ritualized bond with a male and to benefit from whatever hands-off policy that marriage may bring, than to spend all of her time locked in one sexual dialectic or another.

Thus marriage may have arisen as a multifaceted social pact: between man and woman, between male and male and between the couple and the tribe. It is a reasonable solution to a series of cultural challenges that arose in concert with the expansion of the human neocortex. But its roots may not be what we think they are, nor may our contemporary mating behaviors stem from the pressures of an ancestral environment as it is commonly portrayed, in which a woman needed a mate to help feed and clothe her young. Instead, our "deep" feelings about marriage may be more pragmatic, more contextual and, dare I say it, more egalitarian than we give them credit for being.

If marriage is a social compact, a mutual bid between man and woman to contrive a reasonably stable and agreeable microhabitat in a community of shrewd and well-armed members, then we can understand why, despite rhetoric to the contrary, men are as eager to marry as women are. A raft of epidemiological studies have shown that marriage adds more years to the life of a man than it does to that of a woman. Why should that be, if men are so "naturally" ill suited to matrimony?   35

What do women want? None of us can speak for all women, or for more than one woman, really, but we can hazard a mad guess that a desire for emotional parity is widespread and profound. It doesn't go away, although it often hibernates under duress, and it may be perverted by the restrictions of habitat or culture into something that looks like its opposite. The impulse for liberty is congenital. It is the ultimate manifestation of selfishness, which is why we can count on its endurance.

QUESTIONS FOR DISCUSSION AND WRITING

1. Throughout much of her article, Angier uses humorous words ("wildeburger") and phrases ("trysting and running") as well as informal words ("guy") and

expressions ("hey"). With your classmates, gather other examples of such features. What kind of reader does Angier seem to be addressing? How do these expressions affect you as a reader? In what passages does she *avoid* using such expressions? Speculate on why she varies her style.

2. Angier writes that the "impulse for liberty is congenital" (paragraph 36). How do evolutionary psychologists explain the manifestations of this impulse? How does Angier explain them?

3. Which of the various stereotypical behaviors of men and women that Angier mentions have you seen or heard discussed in the press, in the media, or in conversation? What causes these behaviors, in your opinion — nature or culture?

4. What do primate studies reveal about the relative sexual activity of males and females? What implications for human beings are drawn by evolutionary psychologists and by Angier? Write an essay explaining why you find Angier's approach more or less persuasive than that of the evolutionary psychologists.

5. Write an essay comparing and contrasting the ways in which evolutionary psychologists and Angier view the notion that females choose males who can best care for them and their infants.

LINKED READINGS: BAD SCIENCE

NORIMITSU ONISHI

In a Country That Craved Respect, Stem Cell Scientist Rode a Wave of Korean Pride

Onishi is an experienced reporter of international news for the New York Times, *in which this article appeared on January 22, 2006.*

After first gaining attention in South Korea for cloning a cow in 1999, Dr. Hwang Woo Suk, the fallen stem cell scientist, promised to clone next an animal with deeper meaning to Koreans: a tiger.

A holy animal according to Korean lore, tigers once populated the peninsula but were hunted to virtual extinction during Japanese colonial rule. They are believed to exist today, if they exist at all, in North Korea's Mount Paektu, which Koreans consider their ancestral origin.

"I'll spread the Korean people's spirit by cloning the Mount Paektu tiger," Dr. Hwang said at the time.

From his promise to clone a tiger half a decade ago to his apology for disgracing his country last week, Dr. Hwang never shied away from the strong appeals to nationalism that helped turn him into a hero.

The scientist's spectacular rise and fall, as well as one of the biggest scientific ⁵ frauds in recent history, took place in the crucible of a country whose deep-rooted insecurities had been tempered by a newfound confidence and yearning for international recognition.

"Dr. Hwang was going to give South Korea the momentum to leap ahead in its position in the world," said Won Suk Min, 26, an electrical engineering student at Korea University here. "A lot of people around me feel empty now. They feel that there is nothing to look forward to."

Last week, an investigative panel appointed by Seoul National University, where Dr. Hwang was a professor, concluded that he had faked the evidence for landmark papers on stem cell and embryonic research in 2004 and 2005.

The conclusion was a psychological blow to South Koreans, for whom Dr. Hwang's success had appeared to confirm their country's new place in the world. In the past half decade, South Korea had surged forward on different levels, as companies like Samsung overtook Sony, the "Korean Wave" of pop culture spread throughout Asia and the country became the world's most wired nation.

By contrast, in 1999, recapturing South Korea's spirit resonated powerfully in a country that was still reeling from the Asian financial crisis of 1997.

"It was a beacon of light in the dark," said Kim Ki Jung, a political scientist at ¹⁰ Yonsei University here.

"Hwang triggered Korean sentiments of nationalistic pride," Mr. Kim said, adding that the sentiments eventually led to a national mood of "blind patriotism" toward the scientist.

Dr. Hwang began drawing the country's adulation when, in February 2004, he became an international celebrity for writing in the leading scientific journal, *Science*, that he had cloned human embryos. In June 2005, he published a paper, again in *Science*, to the effect that he had developed a technique to extract embryonic stem cells from fewer human eggs than previous methods required. This further raised the hopes for therapeutic cloning and the possibility of converting a patient's own cells into new tissues to treat various diseases.

The papers transformed Dr. Hwang into a national hero: a handsome 53-year-old scientist who had risen from humble origins to lead South Korea to places it and the rest of the world had not seen. Web sites went up in his honor, women volunteered to donate eggs, Korean Air volunteered to fly him anywhere free.

The government of President Roh Moo Hyun, who had embraced and promoted him aggressively, gave him millions of dollars in research money, made him the country's top scientist and assigned him bodyguards. It issued a postage stamp that engraved Dr. Hwang's promise to make paralyzed people walk through images of a man in a wheelchair who stands up, dances and embraces a woman. The government also extolled his exploits in government school textbooks, describing him in a sixth-grade textbook as a challenger for the Nobel Prize.

"He was going to change our country's image and make South Korea No. 1 ¹⁵ in the world in this sector," said Huh Hyun, 37, who was shopping on a recent day at the Carafe megastore with her husband. "We don't have someone to represent us to the world. South Africa, for example, has Mandela."

South Koreans also spoke of Dr. Hwang in terms of national interests.

"Because we are a homogenous people, we identified ourselves with this one individual and overlooked his faults," said Cheon Jeong Seok, 34, another shopper.

Mr. Cheon said the worship of Dr. Hwang was also rooted in the fierce nationalism fostered during the decades of military dictatorship, until the late 1980s. "We were taught constantly about national interests and that the ends justified the means," Mr. Cheon said.

In this atmosphere, Dr. Hwang became untouchable.

"Many of us didn't trust him," Kim Jae Sup, professor of developmental biology at the Korea Advanced Institute of Science and Technology, said of Korean scientists. "But the pressure from the public and government to support him actually inhibited our criticism. We couldn't say anything. That's why scientists posted evidence against him on Web sites. It was anonymous."   20

A whistleblower scientist also contacted "PD Notebook," an investigative program at the television network MBC, which exposed Dr. Hwang. The producer of the program later said that, in response, "'PD Notebook' was treated like a Judas who sold off Jesus Christ."

Huge protests and boycotts were aimed at the program.

After Japanese researchers published a paper on dog stem cells, the *Chosun Ilbo*, the largest South Korean daily newspaper, contended that Dr. Hwang had been preparing such a paper before he was "pestered by 'PD Notebook.'"

The newspaper touched upon one of the undercurrents in the wave supporting Dr. Hwang: South Korea's sense of rivalry with Japan, its former colonial power, and its fixation with elevating its position in the world.

That goal was manifested in what some call the country's "Nobel Prize disease" or its obsession with winning its first Nobel Prize in the sciences. (South Korea's only Nobel laureate, Kim Dae Jung, the former president, won a Nobel Peace Prize.) With Dr. Hwang, the prize had seemed within easy grasp; now there were other worries.   25

"I hear that this is being reported around the world, in the United States and in Japan," said Park Soon Yeh, a woman in her 60's who sells handbags and suitcases at the Nam-daemun Market here. "I'm worried that when young Korean scientists go abroad now, foreigners will not have confidence in them."

As his research imploded in recent weeks, Dr. Hwang grasped at the same kind of nationalistic sentiments that had propelled him to stardom. He said he would keep "fighting in a white robe," a reference to Yi Sun Shin, the naval commander who repelled a Japanese invasion in the 16th century and saved Korea.

Last Thursday, after the government announced that it would discontinue the stamps in his honor and edit out references to him in textbooks, Dr. Hwang insisted that he still had the technology to extract stem cells from human embryos, saying, "This is the Republic of Korea's technology."

He apologized for the fraudulent data in his work, blaming a research partner.

"I was crazy with work," Dr. Hwang said. "I could see nothing in front of 30 me. I only saw one thing and that is how this country called the Republic of Korea could stand straight in the center of the world."

Like many other South Koreans interviewed, Lee Yong Koo, 50, who also sells clothes at the market, said that even if he no longer trusted Dr. Hwang, he was willing to give him another chance. He was not pegging the country's future on him anymore, though.

"I don't expect him to bring foreign money into South Korea or make this country rich," Mr. Lee said. "We have Samsung and other companies to do that."

South Korean children, beside a picture of Dr. Hwang Woo Suk, the disgraced stem cell researcher, attended a rally for him in Seoul.

ROBERT L. PARK

The Seven Warning Signs of Bogus Science

From the unverifiable claims of cold fusion experiments to plans for building a livable atmosphere on Mars, misleading, fallacious, and economically impractical ideas abound, masquerading as science, according to Robert L. Park. Labeling these claims "voodoo science," Park has devoted himself to informing and educating the public about scientific accuracy. Far from berating readers for being uninformed, however, his main target is bad information promulgated by government and media sources. Park's background is one of practical experience and theoretical depth. After serving as an electronics officer in the United States Air Force (1951–1956), he studied physics at the University of Texas (B.S., 1958; M.A., 1960) and Brown University (Ph.D., 1964). He worked at Sandia Laboratories for a decade until becoming a physics professor at the University of Maryland at College Park, where he continues to teach.

Park's writing in Voodoo Science: The Road from Foolishness to Fraud *(2000), ten essays for a lay audience, has been praised in* Science *as "an articulate and skeptical voice of reason about science," using "pathological science as a starting point for far-reaching discussions of science and society." "The Seven Warning Signs of Bogus Science," originally published in the* Chronicle of Higher Education *(January 31, 2003) offers policy makers and the general public a skeptic's guide to suspicious scientific claims.*

The National Aeronautics and Space Administration is investing close to a million dollars in an obscure Russian scientist's antigravity machine, although it has failed every test and would violate the most fundamental laws of nature. The Patent and Trademark Office recently issued Patent 6,362,718 for a physically impossible motionless electromagnetic generator, which is supposed to snatch free energy from a vacuum. And major power companies have sunk tens of millions of dollars into a scheme to produce energy by putting hydrogen atoms into a state below their ground state, a feat equivalent to mounting an expedition to explore the region south of the South Pole.

There is, alas, no scientific claim so preposterous that a scientist cannot be found to vouch for it. And many such claims end up in a court of law after they have cost some gullible person or corporation a lot of money. How are juries to evaluate them?

Before 1993, court cases that hinged on the validity of scientific claims were usually decided simply by which expert witness the jury found more credible. Expert testimony often consisted of tortured theoretical speculation with little or no supporting evidence. Jurors were bamboozled by technical gibberish they could not hope to follow, delivered by experts whose credentials they could not evaluate.

In 1993, however, with the Supreme Court's landmark decision in *Daubert* v. *Merrell Dow Pharmaceuticals, Inc.* the situation began to change. The case involved Bendectin, the only morning-sickness medication ever approved by the Food and Drug Administration. It had been used by millions of women, and more than 30 published studies had found no evidence that it caused birth defects. Yet eight so-called experts were willing to testify, in exchange for a fee from the Daubert family, that Bendectin might indeed cause birth defects.

In ruling that such testimony was not credible because of lack of supporting 5 evidence, the court instructed federal judges to serve as "gatekeepers," screening juries from testimony based on scientific nonsense. Recognizing that judges are not scientists, the court invited judges to experiment with ways to fulfill their gate-keeper responsibility.

Justice Stephen G. Breyer encouraged trial judges to appoint independent experts to help them. He noted that courts can turn to scientific organizations, like the National Academy of Sciences and the American Association for the Advancement of Science, to identify neutral experts who could preview questionable scientific testimony and advise a judge on whether a jury should be exposed to it. Judges are still concerned about meeting their responsibilities under the *Daubert* decision, and a group of them asked me how to recognize questionable scientific claims. What are the warning signs?

I have identified seven indicators that a scientific claim lies well outside the bounds of rational scientific discourse. Of course, they are only warning signs— even a claim with several of the signs could be legitimate.

1. **The discoverer pitches the claim directly to the media.** The integrity of science rests on the willingness of scientists to expose new ideas and findings to the scrutiny of other scientists. Thus, scientists expect their colleagues to reveal new findings to them initially. An attempt to bypass peer review by taking a new result directly to the media, and thence to the public, suggests that the work is unlikely to stand up to close examination by other scientists.

   One notorious example is the claim made in 1989 by two chemists from the University of Utah, B. Stanley Pons and Martin Fleischmann, that they had discovered cold fusion—a way to produce nuclear fusion without expensive equipment. Scientists did not learn of the claim until they read reports of a news conference. Moreover, the announcement dealt largely with the economic potential of the discovery and was devoid of the sort of details that might have enabled other scientists to judge the strength of the claim or to repeat the experiment. (Ian Wilmut's announcement that he had successfully cloned a sheep was just as public as Pons and Fleischmann's claim, but in the case of cloning, abundant scientific details allowed scientists to judge the work's validity.)

   Some scientific claims avoid even the scrutiny of reporters by appearing in paid commercial advertisements. A health-food company marketed a dietary supplement called Vitamin O in full-page newspaper ads. Vitamin O turned out to be ordinary saltwater.

2. **The discoverer says that a powerful establishment is trying to suppress his or her work.** The idea is that the establishment will presumably stop at nothing to suppress discoveries that might shift the balance of wealth and power in society. Often, the discoverer describes mainstream science as part of a larger conspiracy that includes industry and government. Claims that the oil companies are frustrating the invention of an automobile that runs on water, for instance, are a sure sign that the idea of such a car is baloney. In the case of cold fusion, Pons and Fleischmann blamed their cold reception on physicists who were protecting their own research in hot fusion. 10

3. **The scientific effect involved is always at the very limit of detection.** Alas, there is never a clear photograph of a flying saucer, or the Loch Ness monster. All scientific measurements must contend with some level of background noise or statistical fluctuation. But if the signal-to-noise ratio cannot be improved, even in principle, the effect is probably not real and the work is not science.

Thousands of published papers in parapsychology, for example, claim to report verified instances of telepathy, psychokinesis, or precognition. But those effects show up only in tortured analyses of statistics. The researchers can find no way to boost the signal, which suggests that it isn't really there.

4. **Evidence for a discovery is anecdotal.** If modern science has learned anything in the past century, it is to distrust anecdotal evidence. Because anecdotes have a very strong emotional impact, they serve to keep superstitious beliefs alive in an age of science. The most important discovery of modern medicine is not vaccines or antibiotics, it is the randomized double-blind test, by means of which we know what works and what doesn't. Contrary to the saying, "data" is not the plural of "anecdote."

5. **The discoverer says a belief is credible because it has endured for centuries.** There is a persistent myth that hundreds or even thousands of years ago, long before anyone knew that blood circulates throughout the body, or that germs cause disease, our ancestors possessed miraculous remedies that modern science cannot understand. Much of what is termed "alternative medicine" is part of that myth.

Ancient folk wisdom, rediscovered or repackaged, is unlikely to match the   15
output of modern scientific laboratories.

6. **The discoverer has worked in isolation.** The image of a lone genius who struggles in secrecy in an attic laboratory and ends up making a revolutionary breakthrough is a staple of Hollywood's science-fiction films, but it is hard to find examples in real life. Scientific breakthroughs nowadays are almost always syntheses of the work of many scientists.

7. **The discoverer must propose new laws of nature to explain an observation.** A new law of nature, invoked to explain some extraordinary result, must not conflict with what is already known. If we must change existing laws of nature or propose new laws to account for an observation, it is almost certainly wrong.

I began this list of warning signs to help federal judges detect scientific nonsense. But as I finished the list, I realized that in our increasingly technological society, spotting voodoo science is a skill that every citizen should develop.

QUESTIONS FOR DISCUSSION AND WRITING

1. Is "spotting voodoo science" a necessary survival skill for twenty-first-century citizens (paragraph 18)? Why or why not? What are some bogus scientific claims, questionable "expert testimony," or problems with scientific accuracy that have

caught your attention? How would Park's seven warning signs help in dealing with this problem? How could such an analysis have brought suspicion on Dr. Hwang Woo Suk's fraudulent stem cell claims for, say, a decade before they were discredited in the scientific community (see p. 548)?

2. To what extent could any of Park's seven warning signs be applied to fields besides science? Discuss questionable claims and "facts" from your experience or reading in nonscientific fields such as history, business, health, and Internet fraud. For example, what are some things that are accepted based mainly on anecdotal evidence? (warning sign 4). Have you encountered any questionable beliefs that are touted as true merely because they have endured for centuries? (warning sign 5). How would you reason with someone who holds these beliefs?

3. How might you test claims of folk medicine, miracle treatments and "cures," ESP, or other phenomena that depend on a person's willingness to believe? Pick something a person you know swears by. Interview the person (Why do you believe in this? What evidence do you have that it works? Always? How can its failures, if any, be explained?) and consult a library and the Internet for claims and counterclaims. Write up your results.

4. Write a case study of a piece of bogus science, using Park's warning signs to analyze how the claim was made and why it was ultimately rejected. Using library and Internet research, find the earliest newspaper or magazine reports of the claim, before it was debunked. Show how the warning sign appears in these reports. Then show how the fallacious claim was discredited.

DAVID DOBBS

Trial and Error

Science writer David Dobbs explains that science journalism can extend beyond science to provide a cultural critique: "[L]ooking at science and medicine and how they are done and received can show us as much about our culture as can critiquing books movies, music, or art." The author of three books and a prolific contributor to magazines such as Scientific American, Mind, Slate, *and the* New York Times Magazine, *Dobbs was born in 1958 in Houston, Texas, and earned a bachelor's degree from Oberlin College. His first book, written with Richard Ober,* The Northern Forest *(1995), was about both historical and current threats to the vast forest of the northeastern United States brought on by development and over-harvesting. In* The Great Gulf: Fishermen, Scientists, and the Struggle to Revive the World's Greatest Fishery *(2000), Dobbs investigated the calamitous decline of the New England cod fishery, honoring the views of fishermen as well as government scientists. Dobbs's third book,* Reef Madness: Charles Darwin, Alexander Agassiz, and the Meaning of Coral *(2005), looked at a key nineteenth-century controversy between oceanographer Alexander*

Agassiz and Charles Darwin over the formation of coral reefs. Then, as now, the culture was deeply split over idealism and empiricism, God and evolution.

"Trial and Error," which appeared in the New York Times Magazine *(January 15, 2006), looks at another foundational question of modern science. Here Dobbs investigates the practice of peer review, asking whether it ultimately helps or hinders the progress of scientific research and presenting some intriguing alternatives.*

Many of us consider science the most reliable, accountable way of explaining how the world works. We trust it. Should we? John Ioannidis, an epidemiologist, recently concluded that most articles published by biomedical journals are flat-out wrong. The sources of error, he found, are numerous: the small size of many studies, for instance, often leads to mistakes, as does the fact that emerging disciplines, which lately abound, may employ standards and methods that are still evolving. Finally, there is bias, which Ioannidis says he believes to be ubiquitous. Bias can take the form of a broadly held but dubious assumption, a partisan position in a long-standing debate (e.g., whether depression is mostly biological or environmental) or (especially slippery) a belief in a hypothesis that can blind a scientist to evidence contradicting it. These factors, Ioannidis argues, weigh especially heavily these days and together make it less than likely that any given published finding is true.

Ioannidis's argument induces skepticism about science . . . and a certain awe. Even getting half its findings wrong, science in the long run gets most things right —or, as Paul Grobstein, a biologist, puts it, "progressively less wrong." Falsities pose no great problem. Science will out them and move on.

Yet not all falsities are equal. This shows plainly in the current outrage over the revelation that the South Korean researcher Hwang Woo Suk faked the existence of the stem-cell colonies he claimed to have cloned. When Hwang published his results last June in *Science*, they promised to open the way to revolutionary therapies—and perhaps fetch Hwang a Nobel Prize. The news that he had cooked the whole thing dismayed scientists everywhere and refueled an angst-filled debate: how can the scientific community prevent fraud and serious error from entering journals and thereby becoming part of the scientific record?

Journal editors say they can't prevent fraud. In an absolute sense, they're right. But they could make fraud harder to commit. Some critics, including some journal editors, argue that it would help to open up the typically closed peer-review system, in which anonymous scientists review a submitted paper and suggest revisions. Developed after World War II, closed peer review was meant to ensure candid evaluations and elevate merit over personal connections. But its anonymity allows reviewers to do sloppy work, steal ideas or delay competitors' publication by asking for elaborate revisions (it happens) without fearing exposure. And it catches error and fraud no better than good editors do. "The evidence against peer review keeps getting stronger," says Richard Smith, former editor of the *British Medical Journal*, "while the evidence on the upside is weak." Yet peer review has become a sacred cow, largely because passing peer review confers great prestige—and often tenure.

Lately a couple of alternatives have emerged. In open peer review, reviewers 5 are known and thus accountable to both author and public; the journal might also publish the reviewers' critiques as well as reader comments. A more radical alternative amounts to open-source reviewing. Here the journal posts a submitted paper online and allows not just assigned reviewers but anyone to critique it. After a few weeks, the author revises, the editors accept or reject and the journal posts all, including the editors' rationale.

Some worry that such changes will invite a cacophony of contentious discussion. Yet the few journals using these methods find them an orderly way to produce good papers. The prestigious *British Medical Journal* switched to nonanonymous reviewing in 1999 and publishes reader responses at each paper's end. "We do get a few bores" among the reader responses, says Tony Delamothe, the deputy editor, but no chaos, and the journal, he says, is richer for the exchange: "Dialogue is much better than monologue." *Atmospheric Chemistry and Physics* goes a step further, using an open-source model in which any scientist who registers at the Web site can critique the submitted paper. The papers' review-and-response sections make fascinating reading—science being made—and the papers more informative.

The public, meanwhile, has its own, even more radical open-source review experiment under way at the online encyclopedia Wikipedia, where anyone can edit any entry. Wikipedia has lately suffered some embarrassing errors and a taste of fraud. But last month *Nature* found Wikipedia's science entries to be almost as accurate as the *Encyclopaedia Brittanica*'s.

Open, collaborative review may seem a scary departure. But scientists might find it salutary. It stands to maintain rigor, turn review processes into productive forums and make publication less a proprietary claim to knowledge than the spark of a fruitful exchange. And if collaborative review can't prevent fraud, it seems certain to discourage it, since shady scientists would have to tell their stretchers in public. Hwang's fabrications, as it happens, were first uncovered in Web exchanges among scientists who found his data suspicious. Might that have happened faster if such examination were built into the publishing process? "Never underestimate competitors," Delamothe says, for they are motivated. *Science*— and science—might have dodged quite a headache by opening Hwang's work to wider prepublication scrutiny.

In any case, collaborative review, by forcing scientists to read their reviews every time they publish, would surely encourage humility—a tonic, you have to suspect, for a venture that gets things right only half the time.

QUESTIONS FOR DISCUSSION AND WRITING

1. What is the purpose of peer review? What are its problems and limitations, according to David Dobbs? What alternatives are scientific publishers considering? (paragraphs 4–6).

2. Although peer reviewers are cautioned to report conflicts of interest, Dobbs claims that they may "steal ideas or delay competitors' publication"—putting their personal interests ahead of scientific progress (paragraph 4). Read some official pronouncements on peer review, such as the National Institutes of Health's Office of Extramural Research Web site on Peer Review Policies and Issues. What arguments do these agencies use in support of peer review? What conflicts of interest must reviewers report? (See http://grants2.nih.gov/grants/peer/ and http://grants2.nih.gov/grants/peer/COI_Information.doc, for example.)

3. To test the effectiveness of open, collaborative review (paragraph 8), review a paper or two written by your classmates. Circulate the paper in the class, and have each reader attach comments and suggestions for revision of substance and style. Then submit these to the writer. After the writer has revised, have a round-table discussion about the process. In what ways does the writer feel that the collaborative review helped him or her revise the paper? What, if any, drawbacks are there to this process? Identify some significant differences between amateur and professional peer reviews.

4. As a writing project, study a case in which the peer-review process went awry, such as South Korean scientist Dr. Hwang Woo Suk's fraudulent stem cell research. See Norimitsu Onishi's article "In a Country That Craved Respect" (p. 548). Where did the peer-review process break down in that case? What should have been done to make the peer review work? Explain how future abuses of peer review could be prevented, supporting your argument with information from Dobbs's article or other articles about Dr. Hwang.

BRIEF TAKES ON TECHNOLOGY:
WRITING HUMOR

*Writers, if not actual technophobes, often take humorous opposition to techno-
logical innovation and change. They usually present themselves as preferring
the old, unable to understand directions or otherwise cope with new inventions
and mechanical devices, which are themselves the source of mystery, threats,
and terror—nameless but persistent. The writers presented here never learn,
but they have the last laugh, nonetheless.*

JAMES THURBER

The Wild-Eyed Edison's Dangerous Experiments

James Thurber (1894–1961) was The New Yorker's *premier comic writer for forty
years, known for his sublimely ridiculous fiction, essays, fables, and cartoons.*

My mother, for instance, thought—or, rather, knew—that it was dangerous to
drive an automobile without gasoline: it fried the valves, or something. "Now
don't you dare drive all over town without gasoline!" she would say to us when
we started off. Gasoline, oil, and water were much the same to her, a fact that
made her life both confusing and perilous. Her greatest dread, however, was the
Victrola—we had a very early one, back in the "Come Josephine in My Flying
Machine" days. She had an idea that the Victrola might blow up. It alarmed her,
rather than reassured her, to explain that the phonograph was run neither by
gasoline nor by electricity. She could only suppose that it was propelled by some
newfangled and untested apparatus which was likely to let go at any minute,
making us all the victims and martyrs of the wild-eyed Edison's dangerous experiments. The telephone she was comparatively at peace with, except, of course,
during storms, when for some reason or other she always took the receiver off the
hook and let it hang. She came naturally by her confused and groundless fears,
for her own mother lived the latter years of her life in the horrible suspicion that
electricity was dripping invisibly all over the house. It leaked, she contended, out
of empty sockets if the wall switch had been left on. She would go around screw-
ing in bulbs, and if they lighted up she would hastily and fearfully turn off the
wall switch and go back to her *Pearson's* or *Everybody's*, happy in the satisfaction
that she had stopped not only a costly but a dangerous leakage. Nothing could
ever clear this up for her.

ERMA BOMBECK

Technology's Coming . . . Technology's Coming

Erma Bombeck (1927–1996) wrote a syndicated column, At Wit's End, *from the perspective of a harried, domestically challenged housewife.*

"The clock on the oven says it's 11," [said our son].

"That's wrong," said my husband. "Your mother can't see what she's twirling half the time without her glasses and sometimes when she sets the timer, she resets the clock."

"And the one on the VCR?" he asked.

". . . is always 12 and blinking," I said, "because your father screwed up between steps two and five when the power went out."

"God, Mom, you and Dad are out of it. It's like the *Twilight Zone*. How do   5
you two function around here? I'd be lost without technology. This little beeper," he said, patting his shirt pocket, "keeps me in touch with the world."

"He's right, Mom," said our daughter, "you oughta have one of those signals attached to your car keys and your glasses. Think of the time you could save."

It was a subject I hated.

Slowly but steadily I was replaced by beeps, switches, flashing lights, electronic devices, and monotone voices.

In the beginning, I taught my children how to tie their shoes and button and zip their clothing. Then along came Velcro tabs on their shoes and on their clothes where buttons and zippers used to be.

I used to tell them how to place an emergency call to Grandma if they   10
needed her. Now it was a matter of pushing a button on a memory phone and it was done for them.

I used to enlighten them about the stove. I showed them how to turn it on and off so they wouldn't get burned. They don't have stoves anymore. They have microwave ovens that have little buttons to push and are cool to the touch.

At one time I pulled them on my lap and together we traced our fingers across the printed page as I read to them. I don't read anymore. All they have to do is insert book cassettes into their stereos and hear them read by professionals.

I have been replaced by ouchless adhesive bandages, typewriters that correct their spelling, color-coded wardrobes, and computers that praise them when they get the right answers. The future is here.

The kids are wrong. It isn't that we don't give technology a chance. We use the VCR. True, it was in our home for a full six months before we turned it on.

From time to time my husband would leaf through the manual with an in-   15
tensity usually reserved for a nervous flier reading about the evacuation procedures on an aircraft. Then one day he said, "Since we are going out to dinner, I am going to tape *Dallas* so we can watch it later."

I put my hand over his. "I want you to know that whatever happens, I think you're the bravest man I have ever met."

BAILEY WHITE
Flying Saucer

Bailey White (b. 1950) is a first-grade teacher whose low-key humorous commentary on NPR's All Things Considered *has been collected in books such as* Sleeping at the Starlite Motel *(1995).*

My mother is old, but she doesn't make up stories that aren't true, and she doesn't see things that aren't there. That's why we didn't doubt her for a minute when she told us she had seen a flying saucer go over the house early one spring morning.

She was lying in her bed on the screen porch when she saw it coming down. She unlatched the door and went out into the yard for a better look. It was round, flat, silent, and surrounded by yellow flames. It hovered over the garden for a minute. Then, without a sound, it was gone. Our dog, who is not the excitable type, barked wildly and ran around and around.

Mama called the young man down the road, who is crazed on the subject of extraterrestrial life. Within an hour the yard was swarming with UFO enthusiasts. One of them set to work with calipers to measure the little cone-shaped holes the armadillos had dug all over the yard during the night. Another took samples of grass, leaves, and dirt and put them into carefully labeled plastic bags.

Our wild-eyed neighbor, Darrell, interviewed Mama. His bristly red hair was standing on end. "Exactly when. . . ? How long. . . ? What color? What shape? How big?" He eyed our dog. "Does your dog always sleep that much?"

"Well, he's old. He sleeps a lot." Mama said defensively.   5

But Darrell explained that sometimes after an encounter of this kind, pets will exhibit strange behaviors. "And yourself," he continued, "did you notice any unusual depression, dullness of mind, or euphoria after the sighting?"

"No," said Mama, "I'm pretty steady, for a person my age."

"And these red spots on your arm?"

"Ant bites."

"Did you lose any time?" He told us that sometimes these spaceships take   10
humans on board. They keep them for a few hours, performing fiendish experiments on them, taking tissue samples, and probing all their orifices with nimble fingers. Then they return the humans home. Because of the strange hypnotic

state induced by the spacemen, the people have no recollection of the experience. Only their clocks tell them that hours have passed. It's called "lost time."

"Nope, no lost time," Mama told him. "My coffee was still hot."

"How about this brown area, right under where the saucer descended? The grass everywhere else is green."

"That's our cover crop this year—brown-topped millet."

The UFO people sighed. . . . Mama felt that she had disappointed them. They got into their cars and drove away.

FRAN LEIBOWITZ

The Sound of Music: Enough Already

Fran Leibowitz (b. 1951) published Metropolitan Life *(1978), a collection of her satiric columns in* Mademoiselle *and* Interview *magazines.*

First off, I want to say that as far as I am concerned, in instances where I have not personally and deliberately sought it out, the only difference between music and Muzak is the spelling. Pablo Casals practicing across the hall with the door open—being trapped in an elevator, the ceiling of which is broadcasting "Parsley, Sage, Rosemary, and Thyme"—it's all the same to me. Harsh words? Perhaps. But then again these are not gentle times we live in. And they are being made no more gentle by this incessant melody that was once real life.

There was a time when music knew its place. No longer. Possibly this is not music's fault. It may be that music fell in with a bad crowd and lost its sense of common decency. I am willing to consider this. I am willing even to try and help. I would like to do my bit to set music straight in order that it might shape up and leave the mainstream of society. The first thing that music must understand is that there are two kinds of music—good music and bad music. Good music is music that I want to hear. Bad music is music that I don't want to hear.

So that music might more clearly see the error of its ways I offer the following. If you are music and you recognize yourself on this list, you are bad music.

1. MUSIC IN OTHER PEOPLE'S CLOCK RADIOS

There are times when I find myself spending the night in the home of another. Frequently the other is in a more reasonable line of work than I and must arise at a specific hour. Ofttimes the other, unbeknownst to me, manipulates an appliance in such a way that I am awakened by Stevie Wonder. On such occasions I announce that if I wished to be awakened by Stevie Wonder I would sleep with Stevie Wonder. I do not, however, wish to be awakened by Stevie Wonder and that is why God invented alarm clocks. Sometimes the other realizes that I am right. Sometimes the other does not. And that is why God invented *many* others.

2. MUSIC RESIDING IN THE HOLD BUTTONS OF OTHER PEOPLE'S BUSINESS TELEPHONES

I do not under any circumstances enjoy hold buttons. But I am a woman of rea- 5
son. I can accept reality. I can face the facts. What I cannot face is the music. Just as there are two kinds of music — good and bad — so there are two kinds of hold buttons — good and bad. Good hold buttons are hold buttons that hold one silently. Bad hold buttons are hold buttons that hold one musically. When I hold I want to hold silently. That is the way it was meant to be, for that is what God was talking about when he said, "Forever hold your peace." He would have added, "and quiet," but he thought you were smarter.

UMBERTO ECO

Ideal Operating Instructions

Umberto Eco (b. 1932), a professor of semiotics at the University of Bologna, is a notable wit, as well as a novelist, his first being The Name of the Rose *(1980).*

A . . . very desirable job is that of writing the instructions included in, or printed on, the packaging of domestic appliances and electronic instruments. Above all, these instructions must prevent installation. The ideal model is not that of the thick manuals supplied with computers; these also achieve this aim, but at great cost to the manufacturer. The proper model is rather the folded slip of paper accompanying pharmaceuticals, products with the extra feature of having names that, while apparently scientific, have actually been devised to make obvious the nature of the product as if to ensure that its purchase embarrasses the purchaser (Prostatan, Menopausin, Crabex). The instructions enclosed in the box, in contrast, succeed with a minimum of words in making incomprehensible the warnings on which our lives depend: "No counterindication, except in cases of unforeseen lethal reaction to product."

For domestic appliances et similia the instructions must expound at length things so self-evident that you are tempted to skip them, thus missing the one truly essential bit of information:

In order to install the PZ40 it is necessary to unwrap the packaging and remove the appliance from the box. The PZ40 can be extracted from its container only after the latter is opened. The container is opened by lifting, in opposite directions, the two flaps of the upper side of the box (see diagram below). Take care, during the process of opening, to keep the container in a vertical position, with the lid facing up, otherwise the PZ40 may fall out during the operation and suffer damage. The lid to be opened is clearly marked with the words THIS SIDE UP. In the event that the lid does not open at the first attempt, the consumer is advised to try a second time. Once the lid is opened, it is advisable to tear off the red strip before removing the inner, aluminum lid; otherwise the container will explode. WARNING: after the PZ40 has been removed, the container can be discarded.

CHAPTER 8

Ethics:
Principles and Actions

MARTIN LUTHER KING JR.

Letter from Birmingham Jail

Martin Luther King Jr. (1929–1968) grew up listening to his father's and grandfather's sermons at Ebenezer Baptist Church in Atlanta. He earned a bachelor's degree in sociology at Morehouse College in 1948, a degree with honors at Crozer Theological Seminary in 1951, and a doctorate in theology at Boston University in 1955. When in December 1955 Rosa Parks refused to give up a "white" seat on a segregated bus, King became the eloquent and forceful leader of the subsequent Montgomery bus boycott. In 1957 he founded the Southern Christian Leadership Conference (SCLC) to challenge racial segregation in schools and public accommodations nationwide. King taught civil rights protesters how to practice the Gandhian doctrine of passive resistance in support of civil disobedience, a means of nonviolently breaking an unjust law in order to enact social change. King also reminded civil rights workers to protest with dignity and steady purpose in the face of segregationists' intimidation and violence.

In a letter published in the Birmingham Post-Herald, *eight white clergymen admonished King, the SCLC, and civil rights workers to wait peacefully for better conditions rather than persist in defying unjust laws. On April 12, 1963, Public Safety Commissioner Eugene "Bull" Connor arrested Dr. King for the thirteenth time, this time for "parading without a permit." From his jail cell, King wrote his "Letter from Birmingham Jail," ostensibly replying to the* Post-Herald *letter but actually addressing a national audience.*

"Letter from Birmingham Jail," revised and reprinted in King's Why We Can't Wait *(1964), entered the essay canon as a manifesto. King's "Letter" is now taught not only for its ideas but also for its moving sermonic style, its sentence rhythms recalling those of Cicero and Donne, and its allusions to ideas gleaned from many cultures—thirty years before the 1990s "invented" multiculturalism. The Contexts section that follows King's "Letter" focuses on how the terms* law, justice, *and* extremism *were variously defined during the civil rights movement.*

April 16, 1963[1]

My Dear Fellow Clergymen:

While confined here in the Birmingham city jail, I came across your recent statement calling my present activities "unwise and untimely." Seldom do I pause to answer criticism of my work and ideas. If I sought to answer all the criticisms that cross my desk, my secretaries would have little time for anything other than such correspondence in the course of the day, and I would have no time for constructive work. But since I feel that you are men of genuine good will and that your criticisms are sincerely set forth, I want to try to answer your statement in what I hope will be patient and reasonable terms.

I think I should indicate why I am here in Birmingham, since you have been influenced by the view which argues against "outsiders coming in." I have the honor of serving as president of the Southern Christian Leadership Conference, an organization operating in every southern state, with headquarters in Atlanta, Georgia. We have some eighty-five affiliated organizations across the South, and one of them is the Alabama Christian Movement for Human Rights. Frequently we share staff, educational and financial resources with our affiliates. Several months ago the affiliate here in Birmingham asked us to be on call to engage in a nonviolent direct-action program if such were deemed necessary. We readily consented, and when the hour came we lived up to our promise. So I, along with several members of my staff, am here because I was invited here. I am here because I have organizational ties here.

But more basically, I am in Birmingham because injustice is here. Just as the prophets of the eighth century B.C. left their villages and carried their "thus saith the Lord" far beyond the boundaries of their home towns, and, just as the Apostle Paul left his village of Tarsus and carried the gospel of Jesus Christ to the far corners of the Greco-Roman world, so am I compelled to carry the gospel of freedom beyond my own home town. Like Paul, I must constantly respond to the Macedonian call for aid.

Moreover, I am cognizant of the interrelatedness of all communities and states. I cannot sit idly by in Atlanta and not be concerned about what happens in Birmingham. Injustice anywhere is a threat to justice everywhere. We are caught in an inescapable network of mutuality, tied in a single garment of destiny. Whatever affects one directly, affects all indirectly. Never again can we afford to live with the narrow, provincial "outside agitator" idea. Anyone who lives inside the United States can never be considered an outsider anywhere within its bounds.

---

[1] This response to a published statement by eight fellow clergymen from Alabama (Bishop C. C. J. Carpenter, Bishop Joseph A. Durick, Rabbi Hilton L. Grafman, Bishop Paul Hardin, Bishop Holan B. Harmon, the Reverend George M. Murray, the Reverend Edward V. Ramage, and the Reverend Earl Stallings) was composed under somewhat constricting circumstances. Begun on the margins of the newspaper in which the statement appeared while I was in jail, the letter was continued on scraps of writing paper supplied by a friendly Negro trusty, and concluded on a pad my attorneys were eventually permitted to leave me. Although the text remains in substance unaltered, I have indulged in the author's prerogative of polishing it for publication.

You deplore the demonstrations taking place in Birmingham. But your 5 statement, I am sorry to say, fails to express a similar concern for the conditions that brought about the demonstrations. I am sure that none of you would want to rest content with the superficial kind of social analysis that deals merely with effects and does not grapple with underlying causes. It is unfortunate that demonstrations are taking place in Birmingham, but it is even more unfortunate that the city's white power structure left the Negro community with no alternative.

In any nonviolent campaign there are four basic steps: collection of the facts to determine whether injustices exist; negotiation; self-purification; and direct action. We have gone through all these steps in Birmingham. There can be no gainsaying the fact that racial injustice engulfs this community. Birmingham is probably the most thoroughly segregated city in the United States. An ugly record of brutality is widely known. Negroes have experienced grossly unjust treatment in the courts. There have been more unsolved bombings of Negro homes and churches in Birmingham than in any other city in the nation. These are the hard brutal facts of the case. On the basis of these conditions, Negro leaders sought to negotiate with the city fathers. But the latter consistently refused to engage in good-faith negotiation.

Then, last September, came the opportunity to talk with leaders of Birmingham's economic community. In the course of the negotiations, certain promises were made by the merchants—for example, to remove the stores' humiliating racial signs. On the basis of these promises, the Reverend Fred Shuttlesworth and the leaders of the Alabama Christian Movement for Human Rights agreed to a moratorium on all demonstrations. As the weeks and months went by, we realized that we were the victims of a broken promise. A few signs, briefly removed, returned; the others remained.

As in so many past experiences, our hopes had been blasted, and the shadow of deep disappointment settled upon us. We had no alternative except to prepare for direct action, whereby we would present our very bodies as a means of laying our case before the conscience of the local and the national community. Mindful of the difficulties involved, we decided to undertake a process of self-purification. We began a series of workshops on nonviolence, and we repeatedly asked ourselves: "Are you able to accept blows without retaliating?" "Are you able to endure the ordeal of jail?" We decided to schedule our direct-action program for the Easter season, realizing that except for Christmas, this is the main shopping period of the year. Knowing that a strong economic-withdrawal program would be the by-product of direct action, we felt that this would be the best time to bring pressure to bear on the merchants for the needed change.

Then it occurred to us that Birmingham's mayoral election was coming up in March, and we speedily decided to postpone action until after election day. When we discovered that the Commissioner of Public Safety, Eugene "Bull" Connor, had piled up enough votes to be in the run-off, we decided again to postpone action until the day after the run-off so that the demonstrations could not be used to cloud the issues. Like many others, we waited to see Mr. Connor defeated, and to this end we endured postponement after postponement. Having aided in this community need, we felt that our direct-action program could be delayed no longer.

You may well ask: "Why direct action? Why sit-ins, marches and so forth? Isn't negotiation a better path?" You are quite right in calling for negotiation. Indeed this is the very purpose of direct action. Nonviolent direct action seeks to create such a crisis and foster such a tension that a community which has constantly refused to negotiate is forced to confront the issue. It seeks so to dramatize the issue that it can no longer be ignored. My citing the creation of tension as part of the work of the nonviolent-resister may sound rather shocking. But I must confess that I am not afraid of the word "tension." I have earnestly opposed violent tension, but there is a type of nonviolent tension which is necessary for growth. Just as Socrates felt that it was necessary to create a tension in the mind so that individuals could rise from the bondage of myths and half-truths to the unfettered realm of creative analysis and objective appraisal, so must we see the need for nonviolent gadflies to create the kind of tension in society that will help men rise from the dark depths of prejudice and racism to the majestic heights of understanding and brotherhood.

The purpose of our direct-action program is to create a situation so crisis-packed that it will inevitably open the door to negotiation. I therefore concur with you in your call for negotiation. Too long has our beloved Southland been bogged down in a tragic effort to live in monologue rather than dialogue.

One of the basic points in your statement is that the action that I and my associates have taken in Birmingham is untimely. Some have asked: "Why didn't you give the new city administration time to act?" The only answer that I can give to this query is that the new Birmingham administration must be prodded about as much as the outgoing one, before it will act. We are sadly mistaken if we feel that the election of Albert Boutwell as mayor will bring the millennium to Birmingham. While Mr. Boutwell is a much more gentle person than Mr. Connor, they are both segregationists, dedicated to maintenance of the status quo. I have hope that Mr. Boutwell will be reasonable enough to see the futility of massive resistance to desegregation. But he will not see this without pressure from devotees of civil rights. My friends, I must say to you that we have not made a single gain in civil rights without determined legal and nonviolent pressure. Lamentably, it is an historical fact that privileged groups seldom give up their privileges voluntarily. Individuals may see the moral light and voluntarily give up their unjust posture; but, as Reinhold Niebuhr has reminded us, groups tend to be more immoral than individuals.

We know through painful experience that freedom is never voluntarily given by the oppressor; it must be demanded by the oppressed. Frankly, I have yet to engage in a direct-action campaign that was "well-timed" in the view of those who have not suffered unduly from the disease of segregation. For years now I have heard the word "Wait!" It rings in the ear of every Negro with piercing familiarity. This "Wait" has almost always meant "Never." We must come to see, with one of our distinguished jurists, that "justice too long delayed is justice denied."

We have waited for more than 340 years for our constitutional and God-given rights. The nations of Asia and Africa are moving with jetlike speed toward gaining political independence, but we still creep at horse-and-buggy pace toward gaining a cup of coffee at a lunch counter. Perhaps it is easy for those who have never felt the stinging darts of segregation to say, "Wait." But when you have seen vicious mobs lynch your mothers and fathers at will and drown your sisters and brothers at whim; when you have seen hate-filled policemen curse, kick, and even kill your black brothers and sisters; when you see the vast majority of your twenty million Negro brothers smothering in an airtight cage of poverty in the midst of an affluent society; when you suddenly find your tongue twisted and your speech stammering as you seek to explain to your six-year-old daughter why she can't go to the public amusement park that has just been advertised on television, and see tears welling up in her eyes when she is told that Funtown is closed to colored children, and see ominous clouds of inferiority beginning to form in her little mental sky, and see her beginning to distort her personality by developing an unconscious bitterness toward white people; when you have to concoct an answer for a five-year-old son who is asking: "Daddy, why do white people treat colored people so mean?"; when you take a cross-country drive and find it necessary to sleep night after night in the uncomfortable corners of your automobile because no motel will accept you; when you are humiliated day in and day out by nagging signs reading "white" and "colored"; when your first name becomes "nigger," your middle name becomes "boy" (however old you are), and your last name becomes "John," and your wife and mother are never given the respected title "Mrs."; when you are harried by day and haunted by night by the fact that you are a Negro, living constantly at tiptoe stance, never quite knowing what to expect next, and are plagued with inner fears and outer resentments; when you are forever fighting a degenerating sense of "nobodiness"—then you will understand why we find it difficult to wait. There comes a time when the cup of endurance runs over, and men are no longer willing to be plunged into the abyss of despair. I hope, sirs, you can understand our legitimate and unavoidable impatience.

You express a great deal of anxiety over our willingness to break laws. This is   15
certainly a legitimate concern. Since we so diligently urge people to obey the Supreme Court's decision of 1954 outlawing segregation in the public schools, at first glance it may seem rather paradoxical for us consciously to break laws. One may well ask: "How can you advocate breaking some laws and obeying others?" The answer lies in the fact that there are two types of laws: just and unjust. I would be the first to advocate obeying just laws. One has not only a legal but a moral responsibility to obey just laws. Conversely, one has a moral responsibility to disobey unjust laws. I would agree with St. Augustine that "an unjust law is no law at all."

Now, what is the difference between the two? How does one determine whether a law is just or unjust? A just law is a man-made code that squares with the moral law or the law of God. An unjust law is a code that is out of harmony with the moral law. To put it in the terms of St. Thomas Aquinas: An unjust law is a human law that is not rooted in eternal law and natural law. Any law that up-lifts human personality is just. Any law that degrades human personality is un-just. All segregation statutes are unjust because segregation distorts the soul and damages the personality. It gives the segregator a false sense of superiority and the segregated a false sense of inferiority. Segregation, to use the terminology of the Jewish philosopher Martin Buber, substitutes an "I-it" relationship for an "I-thou" relationship and ends up relegating persons to the status of things. Hence segregation is not only politically, economically, and sociologically unsound, it is morally wrong and sinful. Paul Tillich has said that sin is separation. Is not segre-gation an existential expression of man's tragic separation, his awful estrange-ment, his terrible sinfulness? Thus it is that I can urge men to obey the 1954 decision of the Supreme Court, for it is morally right; and I can urge them to dis-obey segregation ordinances, for they are morally wrong.

Let us consider a more concrete example of just and unjust laws. An unjust law is a code that a numerical or power majority group compels a minority group to obey but does not make binding on itself. This is *difference* made legal. By the same token, a just law is a code that a majority compels a minority to follow and that it is willing to follow itself. This is *sameness* made legal.

Let me give another explanation. A law is unjust if it is inflicted on a minor-ity that, as a result of being denied the right to vote, had no part in enacting or devising the law. Who can say that the legislature of Alabama which set up that state's segregation laws was democratically elected? Throughout Alabama all sorts of devious methods are used to prevent Negroes from becoming registered voters, and there are some counties in which even though Negroes constitute a majority of the population, not a single Negro is registered. Can any law enacted under such circumstances be considered democratically structured?

Sometimes a law is just on its face and unjust in its application. For instance, I have been arrested on a charge of parading without a permit. Now, there is nothing wrong in having an ordinance which requires a permit for a parade. But such an ordinance becomes unjust when it is used to maintain segregation and to deny citizens the First-Amendment privilege of peaceful assembly and protest.

I hope you are able to see the distinction I am trying to point out. In no 20 sense do I advocate evading or defying the law, as would the rabid segregationist. That would lead to anarchy. One who breaks an unjust law must do so openly, lovingly, and with a willingness to accept the penalty. I submit that an individual who breaks a law that conscience tells him is unjust, and who willingly accepts the penalty of imprisonment in order to arouse the conscience of the community over its injustice, is in reality expressing the highest respect for the law.

Of course, there is nothing new about this kind of civil disobedience. It was evidenced sublimely in the refusal of Shadrach, Meshach, and Abednego to obey the laws of Nebuchadnezzar, on the ground that a higher moral law was at stake. It was practiced superbly by the early Christians, who were willing to face hungry lions and the excruciating pain of chopping blocks rather than submit to certain unjust laws of the Roman Empire. To a degree, academic freedom is a reality today because Socrates practiced civil disobedience. In our own nation, the Boston Tea Party represented a massive act of civil disobedience.

We should never forget that everything Adolf Hitler did in Germany was "legal" and everything the Hungarian freedom fighters did in Hungary was "illegal." It was "illegal" to aid and comfort a Jew in Hitler's Germany. Even so, I am sure that, had I lived in Germany at the time, I would have aided and comforted my Jewish brothers. If today I lived in a Communist country where certain principles dear to the Christian faith are suppressed, I would openly advocate disobeying that country's anti-religious laws.

I must make two honest confessions to you, my Christian and Jewish brothers. First, I must confess that over the past few years I have been gravely disappointed with the white moderate. I have almost reached the regrettable conclusion that the Negro's great stumbling block in his stride toward freedom is not the White Citizen's Counciler or the Ku Klux Klanner, but the white moderate, who is more devoted to "order" than to justice; who prefers a negative peace which is the absence of tension to a positive peace which is the presence of justice; who constantly says: "I agree with you in the goal you seek, but I cannot agree with your methods of direct action"; who paternalistically believes he can set the timetable for another man's freedom; who lives by a mythical concept of time and who constantly advises the Negro to wait for a "more convenient season." Shallow understanding from people of good will is more frustrating than absolute misunderstanding from people of ill will. Lukewarm acceptance is much more bewildering than outright rejection.

I had hoped that the white moderate would understand that law and order exist for the purpose of establishing justice and that when they fail in this purpose they become the dangerously structured dams that block the flow of social progress. I had hoped that the white moderate would understand that the present tension in the South is a necessary phase of the transition from an obnoxious negative peace, in which the Negro passively accepted his unjust plight, to a substantive and positive peace, in which all men will respect the dignity and worth of human personality. Actually, we who engage in nonviolent direct action are not the creators of tension. We merely bring to the surface the hidden tension that is already alive. We bring it out in the open, where it can be seen and dealt with. Like a boil that can never be cured so long as it is covered up but must be opened with all its ugliness to the natural medicines of air and light, injustice must be exposed, with all the tension its exposure creates, to the light of human conscience and the air of national opinion before it can be cured.

In your statement you assert that our actions, even though peaceful, must be 25 condemned because they precipitate violence. But is this a logical assertion? Isn't this like condemning a robbed man because his possession of money precipitated the evil act of robbery? Isn't this like condemning Socrates because his unswerving commitment to truth and his philosophical inquiries precipitated the act by the misguided populace in which they made him drink hemlock? Isn't this like condemning Jesus because his unique God-consciousness and never-ceasing devotion to God's will precipitated the evil act of crucifixion? We must come to see that, as the federal courts have consistently affirmed, it is wrong to urge an individual to cease his efforts to gain his basic constitutional rights because the quest may precipitate violence. Society must protect the robbed and punish the robber.

I had also hoped that the white moderate would reject the myth concerning time in relation to the struggle for freedom. I have just received a letter from a white brother in Texas. He writes: "All Christians know that the colored people will receive equal rights eventually, but it is possible that you are in too great a religious hurry. It has taken Christianity almost two thousand years to accomplish what it has. The teachings of Christ take time to come to earth." Such an attitude stems from a tragic misconception of time, from the strangely irrational notion that there is something in the very flow of time that will inevitably cure all ills. Actually, time itself is neutral; it can be used either destructively or constructively. More and more I feel that the people of ill will have used time much more effectively than have the people of good will. We will have to repent in this generation not merely for the hateful words and actions of the bad people but for the appalling silence of the good people. Human progress never rolls in on wheels of inevitability; it comes through the tireless efforts of men willing to be co-workers with God, and without this hard work, time itself becomes an ally of the forces of social stagnation. We must use time creatively, in the knowledge that the time is always ripe to do right. Now is the time to make real the promise of democracy and transform our pending national elegy into a creative psalm of brotherhood. Now is the time to lift our national policy from the quicksand of racial injustice to the solid rock of human dignity.

You speak of our activity in Birmingham as extreme. At first I was rather disappointed that fellow clergymen would see my nonviolent efforts as those of an extremist. I began thinking about the fact that I stand in the middle of two opposing forces in the Negro community. One is a force of complacency, made up in part of Negroes who, as a result of long years of oppression, are so drained of self-respect and a sense of "somebodiness" that they have adjusted to segregation; and in part of a few middle-class Negroes who, because of a degree of academic and economic security and because in some ways they profit by segregation, have become insensitive to the problems of the masses. The other force is one of bitterness and hatred, and it comes perilously close to advocating violence. It is expressed in the various black nationalist groups that are springing up across the nation, the largest and best-known being Elijah Muhammad's Muslim movement. Nourished by the Negro's frustration over the continued existence of racial discrimination, this movement is made up of people who have lost faith in America, who have absolutely repudiated Christianity, and who have concluded that the white man is an incorrigible "devil."

I have tried to stand between these two forces, saying that we need emulate neither the "do-nothingism" of the complacent nor the hatred and despair of the black nationalist. For there is the more excellent way of love and nonviolent protest. I am grateful to God that, through the influence of the Negro church, the way of nonviolence became an integral part of our struggle.

If this philosophy had not emerged, by now many streets of the South would, I am convinced, be flowing with blood. And I am further convinced that if our white brothers dismiss as "rabble-rousers" and "outside agitators" those of us who employ nonviolent direct action, and if they refuse to support our nonviolent efforts, millions of Negroes will, out of frustration and despair, seek solace and security in black-nationalist ideologies—a development that would inevitably lead to a frightening racial nightmare.

Oppressed people cannot remain oppressed forever. The yearning for freedom eventually manifests itself, and that is what has happened to the American Negro. Something within has reminded him of his birthright of freedom, and something without has reminded him that it can be gained. Consciously or unconsciously, he has been caught up by the *Zeitgeist*, and with his black brothers of Africa and his brown and yellow brothers of Asia, South America, and the Caribbean, the United States Negro is moving with a sense of great urgency toward the promised land of racial justice. If one recognizes this vital urge that has engulfed the Negro community, one should readily understand why public demonstrations are taking place. The Negro has many pent-up resentments and latent frustrations, and he must release them. So let him march; let him make prayer pilgrimages to the city hall; let him go on freedom rides—and try to understand why he must do so. If his repressed emotions are not released in nonviolent ways, they will seek expression through violence; this is not a threat but a fact of history. So I have not said to my people: "Get rid of your discontent." Rather, I have tried to say that this normal and healthy discontent can be channeled into the creative outlet of nonviolent direct action. And now this approach is being termed extremist.

But though I was initially disappointed at being categorized as an extremist, as I continued to think about the matter I gradually gained a measure of satisfaction from the label. Was not Jesus an extremist for love: "Love your enemies, bless them that curse you, do good to them that hate you, and pray for them which despitefully use you, and persecute you." Was not Amos an extremist for justice: "Let justice roll down like waters and righteousness like an ever-flowing stream." Was not Paul an extremist for the Christian gospel: "I bear in my body the marks of the Lord Jesus." Was not Martin Luther an extremist: "Here I stand; I cannot do otherwise, so help me God." And John Bunyan: "I will stay in jail to the end of my days before I make a butchery of my conscience." And Abraham Lincoln: "This nation cannot survive half slave and half free." And Thomas Jefferson: "We hold these truths to be self-evident, that all men are created equal. . . ." So the question is not whether we will be extremists, but what kind of extremists we will be. Will we be extremists for hate or for love? Will we be extremists for the preservation of injustice or for the extension of justice? In that dramatic scene on Calvary's hill three men were crucified. We must never forget that all three were crucified for the same crime—the crime of extremism. Two were extremists for immorality, and thus fell below their environment. The other, Jesus Christ, was an extremist for love, truth, and goodness, and thereby rose above his environment. Perhaps the South, the nation, and the world are in dire need of creative extremists.

I had hoped that the white moderate would see this need. Perhaps I was too optimistic; perhaps I expected too much. I suppose I should have realized that few members of the oppressor race can understand the deep groans and passionate yearnings of the oppressed race, and still fewer have the vision to see that injustice must be rooted out by strong, persistent, and determined action. I am thankful, however, that some of our white brothers in the South have grasped the meaning of this social revolution and committed themselves to it. They are still all too few in quantity, but they are big in quality. Some—such as Ralph McGill, Lillian Smith, Harry Golden, James McBride Dabbs, Ann Braden, and Sarah Patton Boyle—have written about our struggle in eloquent and prophetic terms. Others have marched with us down nameless streets of the South. They have languished in filthy, roach-infested jails, suffering the abuse and brutality of policemen who view them as "dirty nigger-lovers." Unlike so many of their moderate brothers and sisters, they have recognized the urgency of the moment and sensed the need for powerful "action" antidotes to combat the disease of segregation.

Let me take note of my other major disappointment. I have been so greatly disappointed with the white church and its leadership. Of course, there are some notable exceptions. I am not unmindful of the fact that each of you has taken some significant stands on this issue. I commend you, Reverend Stallings, for your Christian stand on this past Sunday, in welcoming Negroes to your worship service on a nonsegregated basis. I commend the Catholic leaders of this state for integrating Spring Hill College several years ago.

But despite these notable exceptions, I must honestly reiterate that I have been disappointed with the church. I do not say this as one of those negative critics who can always find something wrong with the church. I say this as a minister of the gospel, who loves the church; who was nurtured in its bosom; who has been sustained by its spiritual blessings and who will remain true to it as long as the cord of life shall lengthen.

When I was suddenly catapulted into the leadership of the bus protest in 35 Montgomery, Alabama, a few years ago, I felt we would be supported by the white church. I felt that the white ministers, priests, and rabbis of the South would be among our strongest allies. Instead, some have been outright opponents, refusing to understand the freedom movement and misrepresenting its leaders; all too many others have been more cautious than courageous and have remained silent behind the anesthetizing security of stained-glass windows.

In spite of my shattered dreams, I came to Birmingham with the hope that the white religious leadership of this community would see the justice of our cause and, with deep moral concern, would serve as the channel through which our just grievances could reach the power structure. I had hoped that each of you would understand. But again I have been disappointed.

I have heard numerous southern religious leaders admonish their worshipers to comply with a desegregation decision because it is the law, but I have longed to hear white ministers declare: "Follow this decree because integration is morally right and because the Negro is your brother." In the midst of blatant injustices inflicted upon the Negro, I have watched white churchmen stand on the sideline and mouth pious irrelevancies and sanctimonious trivialities. In the midst of a mighty struggle to rid our nation of racial and economic injustice, I have heard many ministers say: "Those are social issues, with which the gospel has no real concern." And I have watched many churches commit themselves to a completely other-worldly religion which makes a strange, un-Biblical distinction between body and soul, between the sacred and the secular.

I have traveled the length and breadth of Alabama, Mississippi, and all the other southern states. On sweltering summer days and crisp autumn mornings I have looked at the South's beautiful churches with their lofty spires pointing heavenward. I have beheld the impressive outlines of her massive religious-education buildings. Over and over I have found myself asking: "What kind of people worship here? Who is their God? Where were their voices when the lips of Governor Barnett dripped with words of interposition and nullification? Where were they when Governor Wallace gave a clarion call for defiance and hatred? Where were their voices of support when bruised and weary Negro men and women decided to rise from the dark dungeons of complacency to the bright hills of creative protest?"

Yes, these questions are still in my mind. In deep disappointment I have wept over the laxity of the church. But be assured that my tears have been tears of love. There can be no deep disappointment where there is not deep love. Yes, I love the church. How could I do otherwise? I am in the rather unique position of being the son, the grandson, and the great-grandson of preachers. Yes, I see the church as the body of Christ. But, oh! How we have blemished and scarred that body through social neglect and through fear of being nonconformists.

There was a time when the church was very powerful—in the time when the 40 early Christians rejoiced at being deemed worthy to suffer for what they believed. In those days the church was not merely a thermometer that recorded the ideas and principles of popular opinion; it was a thermostat that transformed the mores of society. Whenever the early Christians entered a town, the people in power became disturbed and immediately sought to convict the Christians for being "disturbers of the peace" and "outside agitators." But the Christians pressed on, in the conviction that they were "a colony of heaven," called to obey God rather than man. Small in number, they were big in commitment. They were too God-intoxicated to be "astronomically intimidated." By their effort and example they brought an end to such ancient evils as infanticide and gladiatorial contests.

Things are different now. So often the contemporary church is a weak, ineffectual voice with an uncertain sound. So often it is an archdefender of the status quo. Far from being disturbed by the presence of the church, the power structure of the average community is consoled by the church's silent—and often even vocal—sanction of things as they are.

But the judgment of God is upon the church as never before. If today's church does not recapture the sacrificial spirit of the early church, it will lose its authenticity, forfeit the loyalty of millions, and be dismissed as an irrelevant social club with no meaning for the twentieth century. Every day I meet young people whose disappointment with the church has turned into outright disgust.

Perhaps I have once again been too optimistic. Is organized religion too inextricably bound to the status quo to save our nation and the world? Perhaps I must turn my faith to the inner spiritual church, the church within the church, as the true *ekklesia* and the hope of the world. But again I am thankful to God that some noble souls from the ranks of organized religion have broken loose from the paralyzing chains of conformity and joined us as active partners in the struggle for freedom. They have left their secure congregations and walked the streets of Albany, Georgia, with us. They have gone down the highways of the South on tortuous rides for freedom. Yes, they have gone to jail with us. Some have been dismissed from their churches, have lost the support of their bishops and fellow ministers. But they have acted in the faith that right defeated is stronger than evil triumphant. Their witness has been the spiritual salt that has preserved the true meaning of the gospel in these troubled times. They have carved a tunnel of hope through the dark mountain of disappointment.

I hope the church as a whole will meet the challenge of this decisive hour. But even if the church does not come to the aid of justice, I have no despair about the future. I have no fear about the outcome of our struggle in Birmingham, even if our motives are at present misunderstood. We will reach the goal of freedom in Birmingham and all over the nation, because the goal of America is freedom. Abused and scorned though we may be, our destiny is tied up with America's destiny. Before the pilgrims landed at Plymouth, we were here. Before the pen of Jefferson etched the majestic words of the Declaration of Independence across the pages of history, we were here. For more than two centuries our forebears labored in this country without wages; they made cotton king; they built the homes of their masters while suffering gross injustice and shameful humiliation—and yet out of a bottomless vitality they continued to thrive and develop. If the inexpressible cruelties of slavery could not stop us, the opposition we now face will surely fail. We will win our freedom because the sacred heritage of our nation and the eternal will of God are embodied in our echoing demands.

Before closing I feel impelled to mention one other point in your statement 45 that has troubled me profoundly. You warmly commended the Birmingham police force for keeping "order" and "preventing violence." I doubt that you would have so warmly commended the police force if you had seen its dogs sinking their teeth into unarmed, nonviolent Negroes. I doubt that you would so quickly commend the policemen if you were to observe their ugly and inhumane treatment of Negroes here in the city jail; if you were to watch them push and curse old Negro women and young Negro girls; if you were to see them slap and kick old Negro men and young boys; if you were to observe them as they did on two occasions, refuse to give us food because we wanted to sing our grace together. I cannot join you in your praise of the Birmingham police department.

It is true that the police have exercised a degree of discipline in handling the demonstrators. In this sense they have conducted themselves rather "nonviolently" in public. But for what purpose? To preserve the evil system of segregation. Over the past few years I have consistently preached that nonviolence demands that the means we use must be as pure as the ends we seek. I have tried to make clear that it is wrong to use immoral means to attain moral ends. But now I must affirm that it is just as wrong, or perhaps even more so, to use moral means to preserve immoral ends. Perhaps Mr. Connor and his policemen have been rather nonviolent in public, as was Chief Pritchett in Albany, Georgia, but they have used the moral means of nonviolence to maintain the immoral end of racial injustice. As T. S. Eliot has said: "The last temptation is the greatest treason: To do the right deed for the wrong reason."

I wish you had commended the Negro sit-inners and demonstrators of Birmingham for their sublime courage, their willingness to suffer, and their amazing discipline in the midst of great provocation. One day the South will recognize its real heroes. They will be the James Merediths, with the noble sense of purpose that enables them to face jeering and hostile mobs, and with the agonizing loneliness that characterizes the life of the pioneer. They will be old, oppressed, battered Negro women, symbolized in a seventy-two-year-old woman in Montgomery, Alabama, who rose up with a sense of dignity and with her people decided not to ride segregated buses, and who responded with ungrammatical profundity to one who inquired about her weariness: "My feet is tired, but my soul is at rest." They will be the young high school and college students, the young ministers of the gospel and a host of their elders, courageously and nonviolently sitting in at lunch counters and willingly going to jail for conscience' sake. One day the South will know that when these disinherited children of God sat down at lunch counters, they were in reality standing up for what is best in the American dream and for the most sacred values in our Judaeo-Christian heritage, thereby bringing our nation back to those great wells of democracy which were dug deep by the founding fathers in their formulation of the Constitution and the Declaration of Independence.

Never before have I written so long a letter. I'm afraid it is much too long to take your precious time. I can assure you that it would have been much shorter if I had been writing from a comfortable desk, but what else can one do when he is alone in a narrow jail cell, other than write long letters, think long thoughts, and pray long prayers?

If I have said anything in this letter that overstates the truth and indicates an unreasonable impatience, I beg you to forgive me. If I have said anything that understates the truth and indicates my having a patience that allows me to settle for anything less than brotherhood, I beg God to forgive me.

I hope this letter finds you strong in faith. I also hope that circumstances will 50
soon make it possible for me to meet each of you, not as an integrationist or a
civil-rights leader but as a fellow clergyman and a Christian brother. Let us all
hope that the dark clouds of racial prejudice will soon pass away and the deep fog
of misunderstanding will be lifted from our fear-drenched communities, and in
some not too distant tomorrow the radiant stars of love and brotherhood will
shine over our great nation with all their scintillating beauty.

> Yours for the cause of Peace and Brotherhood,
> *Martin Luther King Jr.*

CONTEXTS FOR "LETTER FROM BIRMINGHAM JAIL"

DEFINITION AND ARGUMENT IN ETHICS

Forming a definition involves two basic steps: identifying the kind of things to
which a term belongs (its *genus*) and then differentiating that term from other terms
in that group. Biologists identify an organism's genus and species according to empirically verifiable characteristics, just as they define other terms by proceeding in-
ductively from observable, measurable physical data. In religion and ethics, also
called "moral philosophy," ethicists define such terms as *virtue, happiness, charity,*
and *justice* by comparing the moral precepts found in authoritative religious and
philosophical texts with people's experiences. This experiential element is much
less precisely measurable and verifiable than scientists' empirical data; as anyone
who has heard several witnesses describe an event can tell, the "same" event often
means different things to different participants and observers. Moreover, ethicists
interpret an experience in light of what various authorities have said about it.

History and contemporary society are replete with tragically unjust laws:
laws authorizing slavery; laws restricting suffrage; laws excluding various groups
from schools and occupations (such as the Nazis' Nürnberg laws). "Letter from
Birmingham Jail" begins by presenting a situation that King argues is both illegal
and unjust: long after the U.S. Supreme Court ruled that "separate but equal"
was unconstitutional, local laws persisted in requiring separate accommodations
for whites and Negroes.

At its heart, King's letter differentiates between "just and unjust laws" (paragraphs 15–22), and between the "moderate" who prolongs injustice (paragraphs 23–26) and the "extremist" who combats it (paragraphs 27–32). Just as the
long "when . . . , when . . . , then . . ." sentence accumulates examples of injustice
(paragraph 14), the redefinition of *extremist* builds up examples—Amos, Jesus,

Luther, Lincoln, and others—of people who have engaged in extreme action on behalf of justice (paragraph 31). King's reciprocal movement between a moral term and experiences of it, between deduction and induction, results in a refined understanding of what that term means to him.

BROOKS HAYS

A Southern Moderate Speaks

The Supreme Court decision of May 17, 1954, is too well known to need extensive quotation. The Court swept aside completely the doctrine of "separate but equal" schools for Negro children, first enunciated in the *Plessy* v. *Ferguson* decision of 1896, with the words, "We conclude that in the field of public education the doctrine of 'separate but equal' has no place. Separate educational facilities are inherently unequal." Less well known, except for the phrase "with all deliberate speed," are the provisions to implement the Supreme Court's decision spelled out the following year. . . .

> [T]he courts will require that the defendants make a prompt and reasonable start toward full compliance with our May 17, 1954, ruling. Once such a start has been made, the courts may find that additional time is necessary to carry out the ruling in an effective manner. The burden rests upon the defendants to establish that such time is necessary in the public interest and is consistent with good faith compliance at the earliest practicable date. To that end, the courts may consider problems related to administration, rising from the physical condition of the school plant, the school transportation system, personnel, revision of school districts and attendance areas into compact units to achieve a system of determining admission to the public schools on a nonracial basis, and revision of local laws and regulations which may be necessary in solving the foregoing problems. They will also consider the adequacy of any plans the defendants may propose to meet these problems and to effectuate a transition to a racially nondiscriminatory school system. During this period of transition, the courts will retain jurisdiction of these cases.

The calm that initially prevailed in the South was eventually broken by the establishment of White Citizens Councils and the increased activity of the NAACP. . . . It was in this setting that the great majority of Southern congressmen and senators came together to issue the now-famous Declaration of Constitutional Principles or the so-called "Southern Manifesto." The declaration stated the views of over 100 members of the delegations of eleven Southern states as follows:

From Brooks Hays, *A Southern Moderate Speaks* (Chapel Hill: University of North Carolina Press, 1959), 86–91, 189.

In the case of *Plessy* v. *Ferguson* in 1896, the Supreme Court expressly declared that under the Fourteenth Amendment no person was denied any of his rights if the States provided separate but equal public facilities. This decision has been followed in many other cases. It is notable that the Supreme Court, speaking through Chief Justice Taft, a former President of the United States, unanimously declared in 1927 in *Lum* v. *Rice* that the "separate but equal principle is . . . within the discretion of the State in regulating its public schools and does not conflict with the Fourteenth Amendment."

This interpretation, restated time and again, became a part of the life of the people of many of the States and confirmed their habits, customs, traditions, and way of life. It is founded on elemental humanity and common sense, for parents should not be deprived by government of the right to direct the lives and education of their own children. . . .

We pledge ourselves to use all lawful means to bring about a reversal of this decision which is contrary to the Constitution and to prevent the use of force in its implementation.

I signed this declaration as a proper statement of the South's objections to the overthrow of the *Plessy* v. *Ferguson* decision and violation of the *stare decisis* principle in Constitutional law. While it contained items which to me would have been better omitted and expressed some sentiments in language not to my liking, I believed the declaration was an honest reaction to the injury the South believed had been done to its way of life. I joined with a number of other members of Congress who refused to sign the document unless it removed all mention of the doctrines of nullification and interposition. In this way, the Southern moderates hoped to preserve the Constitutional guarantee of the right to dissent without advocating measures which might do violence to the Constitution. . . .

Eight Clergymen's Statement

King and his lieutenant, the Reverend Ralph Abernathy, led a series of demonstrations in Birmingham in April 1963. King was arrested on April 12 and while he was in jail he read the following statement in the Birmingham Post-Herald. *King then began his "Letter from Birmingham Jail," modeling it on thirteen biblical letters from Jesus's apostle Paul to the Corinthians, Ephesians, and others.*

We the undersigned clergymen are among those who, in January, issued "An Appeal for Law and Order and Common Sense," in dealing with racial problems in Alabama. We expressed understanding that honest convictions in racial matters

From the Birmingham *Post-Herald*, 13 April 1963, p. 10; reprinted in Martin Luther King Jr., *Why We Can't Wait* (New York: Harper, 1964).

King and Abernathy under arrest

could properly be pursued in the courts, but urged that decisions of those courts should in the meantime be peacefully obeyed.

Since that time there had been some evidence of increased forbearance and a willingness to face facts. Responsible citizens have undertaken to work on various problems which cause racial friction and unrest. In Birmingham, recent public events have given indication that we all have opportunity for a new constructive and realistic approach to racial problems.

However, we are now confronted by a series of demonstrations by some of our Negro citizens, directed and led in part by outsiders. We recognize the natural impatience of people who feel that their hopes are slow in being realized. But we are convinced that these demonstrations are unwise and untimely.

We agree with certain local Negro leadership which has called for honest and open negotiations of racial issues in our area. And we believe this kind of facing of issues can best be accomplished by citizens of our town metropolitan area, white and Negro, meeting with their knowledge and experience of the local situation. All of us need to face that responsibility and find proper channels for its accomplishment.

Just as we formerly pointed out that "hatred and violence have no sanction in our religious and political traditions," we also point out that such actions as incite to hatred and violence, however technically peaceful actions may be, have not contributed to the resolution of our local problems. We do not believe that these days of new hope are days when extreme measures are justified in Birmingham.

We commend the community as a whole, and the local news media and law enforcement officials in particular, on the calm manner in which these demonstrations have been handled. We urge the public to continue to show restraint should the

Negro Leaders King (*left*) and Abernathy: bad news in Birmingham

demonstrations continue, and the law enforcement officials to remain calm and continue to protect our city from violence.

We further strongly urge our own Negro community to withdraw support from these demonstrations, and to unite locally in working peacefully for a better Birmingham. When rights are consistently denied, a cause should be pressed in the courts and in negotiations among local leaders, and not in the streets. We appeal to both our white and Negro citizenry to observe the principles of law and order and common sense.

Two Christians' Responses to King's Views

Immediately following the reprinting of King's "Letter" in a June 1963 issue of the Christian Century, T. Olin Binkley responded by advocating "[t]he exercise of truly responsible freedom in the pulpit and the classroom," but he stopped short of mentioning desegregation or civil rights.

Will Herberg rebutted Dr. King's differentiation of just from unjust laws and rejected the notion that individual conscience is a basis for civil disobedience. By basing his argument on a quotation from Paul's Epistle to the Romans, Herberg calls King's scholarly authority into question. Herberg restricts his definition of "authorities" to those who enforce local regulations against demonstrations; he omits mention of the U.S. Supreme Court's authority. He also defines justifiable disobedience as refusal to participate, not as the actions of civil disobedience such as demonstrations.

T. OLIN BINKLEY

Southern Baptist Seminaries

The exercise of truly responsible freedom in the pulpit and in the classroom is justified by the Christian doctrine of the Holy Spirit. The New Testament draws attention to three ways in which the Holy Spirit may be mistreated: he may be resisted, grieved, quenched. If Southern Baptists grieve and quench the Holy Spirit in their seminaries, the springs of Christian scholarship in those schools will dry up and the quality of Baptist witness and work will be diluted and seriously damaged. Such a course would be educationally inexcusable and spiritually disastrous. If, on the other hand, Southern Baptists submit themselves humbly and gratefully to correction and instruction by the Holy Spirit, he will lead them into a deeper knowledge of the mind of Christ; he will draw them together in a fellowship of faith and learning that will prove as strong as steel and as indestructible as truth; he will teach them to order their lives and their schools by what is "good, acceptable and perfect" in the sight of God. . . .

In all that we do in the churches and in the seminaries we are dependent on God who has committed to us the word and the ministry of reconciliation. The teachers and the graduates of Southern Baptist seminaries have their share of distractions and disappointments, but they understand the nature of the Christian ministry and the source of power for its fulfillment. On the most difficult assignments they are able to say with Paul, "Our sufficiency is from God, who has qualified us to be ministers of a new covenant."

WILL HERBERG

A Religious "Right" to Violate the Law?

It is . . . of considerable interest to inquire a little more closely into Dr. King's notions of political responsibility and social order, particularly into his central contention that Christian principles permit, perhaps even require, the violation of laws the individual conscience may hold to be "unjust." . . .

But how does this position square with well-established Christian teaching on government, law, and civil obedience?

ST. PAUL'S TEACHING

The essential Christian teaching on government, law, and civil obedience is grounded on that celebrated Chapter XIII of Paul's Epistle to the Romans, which

---

From T. Olin Binkley, "Southern Baptist Seminaries," *Christian Century*, 12 June 1963, 774–775.

From Will Herberg, "A Religious 'Right' to Violate the Law?" *National Review* 16 (July 1964): 579–580.

itself reflects earlier Jewish teaching. "Let every one be subject to the governing authorities," the Apostle enjoins. "For there is no authority except from God, and the existing authorities have been ordained by God. Therefore, he who resists the authorities resists what God has appointed, and those who resist will incur judgment. . . ." This is balanced in the New Testament by the conviction of Peter and the Apostles, "We must obey God rather than man" (Acts 5:29).

When does loyalty to God come into conflict with obedience to earthly rulers? When earthly rulers are insensate enough (as totalitarian states invariably are) to demand for themselves what is owing only to God — worship and ultimate allegiance. The classical Christian teaching emerges most profoundly perhaps in the writings of St. Augustine, whose position Professor Deane thus summarizes:

> When Augustine says that God's command overrules [human] laws and customs, it seems clear that he is referring to those commands of God that have been directly revealed to men in the Scriptures, such as the prohibition against idol-worship. . . . He does *not* say that if the ruler is unwise or evil, and fails to take the eternal law into account when he frames temporal laws, these laws have no validity, and the subjects have no obligation to obey them; nor does he say that the subjects have a right to determine for themselves, by reference to the natural or eternal law, whether or not such a temporal law is valid and is to be obeyed. (Herbert A. Deane, *The Political and Social Ideas of St. Augustine*, Columbia U.P., 1963, pp. 147, 89, 90; Dr. Deane is professor of government at Columbia)

This, in substance, early became the normative Christian doctrine, stated 5 and restated by Thomas Aquinas, Martin Luther, John Calvin, and every other great moralist and theologian of the Church. It is the standard by which the position advanced by Dr. King and U.S. Representative Adam Clayton Powell *as Christian* must be judged; and, judged by that standard, their position permitting the violation of any law disapproved of by the individual conscience as "unjust," must be judged as not Christian at all, but seriously deviant and heretical.

NO EARLY CHRISTIAN SIT-INS

The early Christians, under the teaching of the apostles, were enjoined to obey the laws of the state, a pagan state, mind you, whether they held these laws to be just or unjust — just so long as the state (the Emperor) did not claim for itself the worship and allegiance owing only to God. At that point, they knew how to draw the line. But even at that point, where they were compelled to disobey, their disobedience was limited to *refusal to participate* in the pagan abominations. The Christian refused, at the risk of life, to take part in the pagan cult, or to sacrifice to the Emperor; he did not set up mass picketing of the temples, or organize sit-ins in the public buildings in which the "blasphemies" (Tertullian) were being performed. . . .

STRANGE DOCTRINE

Would it not be well for Dr. King, as a responsible community leader honored with a Doctor of Laws by Yale University, to consider the consequences of his strange doctrine? Every man has his conscience; and if the individual conscience is absolutized (that is, divinized), and made the final judge of laws to be obeyed or disobeyed, nothing but anarchy and the dissolution of the very fabric of government would result. Thousands and thousands of Americans, eminent, respectable, and responsible, are convinced in their conscience that the new Civil Rights Act is utterly wrong, unjust, and unconstitutional; are they therefore entitled to disobey it, and to organize civil disobedience campaigns to impede its effectuation? Grant this "right" and there would be no law at all, nothing but a clash of "consciences" that could not hope to escape becoming a clash of raw power.[1] . . .

NOTES

1. One important exception must be noted. Under the American system of judicial review, the constitutionality, and therefore the legality, of a law, when challenged, cannot be finally determined until it comes to court; and, very frequently, it cannot come to court until it is somehow violated. Such technical violation for the sake of a *test case* is to be fundamentally distinguished from the mass civil disobedience advocated by Dr. King.

DEBATING "JUSTICE" AND INVOKING THE POWER OF BALLOTS AND BOYCOTTS

Perhaps realizing that ethical and religious debates defining *law* and *justice* could go on indefinitely, leaders of the civil rights movement soon augmented moral persuasion and civil disobedience with political and economic strategies, such as Negro voter registration, boycotts, entrepreneurship, and advocacy for public housing and school desegregation. . . .

While emphasizing the economic power of boycotts, King also expressed confidence that the white church and white community would support the civil rights bill (which President Lyndon Johnson signed into law on July 2, 1964) and that legislation would suppress racist behavior if not also racist attitudes.

Social movements often redefine old terms and coin new ones. Young civil rights leaders redefined *Negro* and *black* throughout the mid-1960s. *Negroes* had connoted respect but now began to mean conservative, even obsequious "Uncle Toms," who would await justice indefinitely. *Blacks* had connoted disrespect but now began to mean people ready to demonstrate, exert economic and political power, wear African dress and natural "Afro" hairstyles, and proclaim that "black is beautiful!" By 1967, King himself became a spokesman for "black power," a term he defined in an article for the *New York Times Magazine* in June of that year.

MARTIN LUTHER KING JR.
Boycotts Will Be Used

Q. Have you seen evidence that white resistance to demands of Negroes is stiffening—taking the form of bloc voting by whites?

A. I think some of this is inevitable in a period of social transition. Many people in the North have come to realize that they probably had much more deep-seated prejudices than they had been conscious of. It took the big push by the Negro community and the allies of the Negro in the white community to bring this whole issue to the surface in 1963.

I'm not at all discouraged. I think that this whole issue is out in the open now in a way that it has never been before. It's something like a boil, which, if kept covered up, will never be cured. It's only when you open it to air and light that it can be cured, even though it's ugly for the moment.

I think that we are bringing to the surface an issue that has been in the background all too long. We have tried to hide it. Now, it is out in the open, and this is the only way that it will be cured. . . .

Q. Why do Negro leaders place such heavy stress on the civil-rights bill? Do 5 **you feel that laws can solve the major problems that Negroes face?**

A. I think laws are very important in getting to the major problems.

I'm not saying that the ultimate problem in human relations can be solved through legislation. You can't make a man, through legal strictures and judicial decrees or executive orders, love somebody else. But we aren't trying to legislate love. We are trying to legislate issues that regulate behavior.

Even though morality cannot be legislated, behavior can be regulated. While the law cannot change the heart, it can certainly restrain the heartless.

MARTIN LUTHER KING JR.
Martin Luther King Defines "Black Power"

The nettlesome task of Negroes today is to discover how to organize our strength into compelling power so that government cannot elude our demands. We must develop, from strength, a situation in which the Government finds it wise and

---

From Martin Luther King Jr., "Boycotts Will Be Used," *U.S. News and World Report*, 24 February 1964, 56–61.

From Martin Luther King Jr., "Martin Luther King Defines 'Black Power,'" *New York Times Magazine*, 11 June 1967, 26–27, 93–95.

prudent to collaborate with us. It would be the height of naïveté to wait passively until the Administration had somehow been infused with such blessings of good-will that it implored us for our programs. . . .

The *economic* highway to power has few entry lanes for Negroes. Nothing so vividly reveals the crushing impact of discrimination and the heritage of exclusion as the limited dimensions of Negro business in the most powerful economy in the world. America's industrial production is half of the world's total, and within it the production of Negro business is so small that it can scarcely be measured on any definable scale.

Yet in relation to the Negro community the value of Negro business should not be underestimated. In the internal life of the Negro society it provides a degree of stability. Despite formidable obstacles it has developed a corps of men of competence and organizational discipline who constitute a talented leadership reserve, who furnish inspiration and who are a resource for the development of programs and planning. They are a strength among the weak though they are weak among the mighty.

There exist two other areas, however, where Negroes can exert substantial influence on the broader economy. As employees and consumers, Negro numbers and their strategic disposition endow them with a certain bargaining strength.

Within the ranks of organized labor there are nearly two million Negroes,   5
and they are concentrated in key industries. In the truck transportation, steel, auto and food industries, which are the backbone of the nation's economic life, Negroes make up nearly 20 per cent of the organized work force, although they are only 10 per cent of the general population. This potential strength is magnified further by the fact of their unity with millions of white workers in these occupations. As co-workers there is a basic community of interest that transcends many of the ugly divisive elements of traditional prejudice. There are undeniably points of friction, for example, in certain housing and education questions. But the severity of the abrasions is minimized by the more commanding need for cohesion in union organizations.

The union record in relation to Negro workers is exceedingly uneven, but potential for influencing union decisions still exists. In many of the larger unions the white leadership contains some men of ideals and many more who are pragmatists. Both groups find they are benefited by a constructive relationship to their Negro membership. For those compelling reasons, Negroes, who are almost wholly a working people, cannot be casual toward the union movement. This is true even though some unions remain incontestably hostile.

In days to come, organized labor will increase its importance in the destinies of Negroes. Negroes pressed into the proliferating service occupations—traditionally unorganized and with low wages and long hours—need union protection, and the union movement needs their membership to maintain its relative strength in the whole society. On this new frontier Negroes may well become the pioneers that they were in the early organizing days of the thirties. . . .

The other economic lever available to the Negro is as a consumer. The Southern Christian Leadership Council has pioneered in developing mass boycott movements in a frontal attack on discrimination. In Birmingham it was not the marching alone that brought about integration of public facilities in 1963. The downtown business establishments suffered for weeks under our almost unbelievably effective boycott. The significant percentage of their sales that vanished, the 98 per cent of their Negro customers who stayed home, educated them forcefully to the dignity of the Negro as a consumer. . . .

The final major area of untapped power for the Negro is in the *political* arena. Higher Negro birth rates and increasing Negro migration, along with the exodus of the white population to the suburbs, are producing fast-gathering Negro majorities in the large cities. This changing composition of the cities has political significance. Particularly in the North, the large cities substantially determine the political destiny of the state. These states, in turn, hold the dominating electoral votes in Presidential contests. . . .

QUESTIONS FOR DISCUSSION AND WRITING

1. In paragraphs 27 through 32 of "Letter from Birmingham Jail," King answers charges that his actions are "extreme." What does *extreme* mean for King in the context of civil rights demonstrations? Consider various contemporary connotations of "extreme," as in extreme risk, extreme strength, extreme sports, extreme brutality. Is there a common core of the meaning of *extreme* in these contexts? Are there significant differences? In what ways do these definitions resemble or differ from Dr. King's usage?

2. Brooks Hays and the eight clergymen from Birmingham advocate moderation. What do their definitions of moderation have in common, and what differences can you identify?

3. On what grounds does King defend extremism (paragraphs 27–31), and how extreme does he think he actually is? Who is more radical than King, and in what ways? Locate and read the whole of Henry David Thoreau's "Civil Disobedience," a portion of which is reprinted on p. 192, and explain how it lays the groundwork for King's defense of extremism, passive resistance, and demonstrations employed in the civil rights movement.

4. What ethical and social values do the two photographs from *Time* and *Newsweek* (pp. 581–582) seem to represent? What do the photographs seem to be saying about the relative merits of moderation and extremism?

5. What are the hallmarks of "Christian morality" as T. Olin Binkley and Will Herberg understand it, and how does their version differ from King's?

6. The rhythm of King's sentences is often traced to the preaching style used to address many African American congregations. Read aloud John Donne's "Meditation" (p. 590), listening for the rhythm of the sentences. What features of Donne's

sentences produce the rhythm? Which sentences in King's "Letter from Birmingham Jail" sound similar to Donne's, and which features produce the similarities?

LEONARD FREED

Martin Luther King Jr. after Receiving the Nobel Peace Prize, Baltimore, 1963

QUESTIONS FOR DISCUSSION AND WRITING

1. What is the central focus of this image? That is, where is your eye drawn as you look at it? What is the overall mood?

2. King is at the left of the photo, rather than at the center. What effect does his position have on this image? What do the expressions and body language of the people shown contribute to the overall effect?

3. Speculate on why Freed cropped the slightly blurry face at the right of the frame.

4. Based on your reading of "Letter from Birmingham Jail" and the Contexts that follow it, why do you think King received the Nobel Peace Prize? Amplify your answer with reference to the Nobel Peace Prize acceptance speeches of Rigoberta Menchú (p. 694) and the fourteenth Dalai Lama (p. 697).

JOHN DONNE

Meditation

Poet and clergyman John Donne (1572–1631), like several famous poets of the English Renaissance, did not consider literature to be a career. Although he hoped for a place at the royal court, as a Catholic, however, his career prospects were limited; Protestant England had been at war with Catholic Spain, and anti-Catholic sentiment was high. At Cambridge and Oxford Universities, Donne studied languages and science voraciously but never earned a degree because matriculation would have required him to convert to Protestantism. After abandoning Catholicism, studying law, and serving as a soldier, he won a promising appointment as secretary to a high government official, but his political hopes were dashed when he secretly married Ann More, his employer's seventeen-year-old niece. Ann's father saw to it that Donne was imprisoned briefly, and the couple lived in poverty. Only becoming an Anglican priest (1615) enabled him to win fame for his erudite, witty, and eloquent sermons and to become Dean of St. Paul's Cathedral (1621–1631). His poetry, on topics ranging from love to religion, displays brilliant metaphorical structure and verbal wit, but fell out of fashion until T. S. Eliot and other twentieth-century critics embraced Donne's fusion of emotion and intellect.

Donne wrote the following passage in response to Ann More's death in 1617 and his recovery from serious illness in 1623. It forms "Meditation 17" of Devotions upon Emergent Occasions *(1624), the most enduring of Donne's prose works because of its blend of private feeling and theological insight. Through a series of linked metaphors, Donne affirms each individual's integral place in the social community: "No man is an island."*

> Now, this bell tolling softly
> for another, says to me,
> Thou must die.

Perchance he for whom this bell tolls, may be so ill, as that he knows not it tolls for him; and perchance I may think myself so much better than I am, as that they who are about me, and see my state, may have caused it to toll for me, and I know not that. The Church is Catholic, universal, so are all her actions; all that she does belongs to all. When she baptizes a child, that action concerns me; for that child is thereby connected to that Head which is my Head too, and engrafted into that body, whereof I am a member. And when she buries a man, that action concerns me: all mankind is of one Author, and is one volume; when one man dies, one chapter is not torn out of the book, but translated into a better language; and every chapter must be so translated; God employs several translators; some pieces are translated by age, some by sickness, some by war, some by justice; but God's hand is in every translation; and his hand shall bind up all our scattered leaves again, for that Library where every book shall lie open to one another: As therefore the bell that rings to a sermon, calls not upon the preacher only, but upon the congregation to come; so this bell calls us all: but how much more me, who am brought so near the door by this sickness. There was a contention as far as a suit (in which both piety and dignity, religion and estimation, were mingled), which of the religious orders should ring to prayers first in the morning; and it was determined, that they should ring first that rose earliest. If we understand aright the dignity of this bell that tolls for our evening prayer, we would be glad to make it ours, by rising early, in that application, that it might be ours, as well as his, whose indeed it is. The bell doth toll for him that thinks it doth; and though it intermit again, yet from that minute, that that occasion wrought upon him, he is united to God. Who casts not up his eye to the sun when it rises? but who takes off his eye from a comet when that breaks out? Who bends not his ear to any bell, which upon any occasion rings? but who can remove it from that bell, which is passing a piece of himself out of this world? No man is an island, entire of itself; every man is a piece of the continent, a part of the main; if a clod be washed away by the sea, Europe is the less, as well as if a promontory were, as well as if a manor of thy friends or of thine own were; any man's death diminishes me, because I am involved in mankind; and therefore never send to know for whom the bell tolls; it tolls for thee. Neither can we call this a begging of misery or a borrowing of misery, as though we were not miserable enough of ourselves, but must fetch in more from the next house, in taking upon us the misery of our neighbors. Truly it were an excusable covetousness if we did; for affliction is a treasure, and scarce any man hath enough of it. No man hath affliction enough that is not matured, and ripened by it, and made fit for God by that affliction. If a man carry treasure in bullion, or in a wedge of gold, and have none coined into current monies, his treasure will not defray him as he travels. Tribulation is treasure in the nature of it, but it is not current money in the use of it, except we get nearer and nearer our home, Heaven, by it. Another man may be sick too, and sick to death, and this affliction may lie in his bowels, as gold in a mine, and be of no use to him; but this bell, that tells me of his affliction, digs out, and applies that gold to me; if by this consideration of another's danger I take mine own into contemplation, and so secure myself by making my recourse to my God, who is our only security.

QUESTIONS FOR DISCUSSION AND WRITING

1. How would this "bell tolling softly / for another" person affect you? Why?

2. Donne organizes the first half of his devotional meditation around a series of textual metaphors (author, volume, chapter, book, translation). Do these metaphors enhance his postulation that people are closely related? How so? What does he mean when he argues that death is merely a "translation"?

3. The second half of the meditation is held together by geographical metaphors (island, continent, main, promontory). How do they support his theme of universal connection? Are they consistent with the textual metaphors preceding them? Why or why not?

4. The first law of ecology is that everything is connected to everything else. Compare and contrast Donne's seventeenth-century religious vision of connectedness with the twenty-first-century environmental visions of it.

JEFFREY WATTLES

The Golden Rule—One or Many, Gold or Glitter?

Jeffrey Wattles (b. 1945) received his bachelor's degree from Stanford University and his master's degree and doctorate from Northwestern. He is a professor of philosophy at Kent State University, where his research and teaching focus on ethics, comparative religious thought, and ways of integrating science, philosophy, and religion. He has written extensively about the golden rule in such journal articles as "Levels of Meaning in the Golden Rule" and "Plato's Brush with the Golden Rule" as well as in a book, The Golden Rule *(1996), a detailed examination of the history, cultural variations, and interpretations of the classic moral dictum "Do to others as you want others to do to you."*

The following selection is from the opening chapter of The Golden Rule. *Here Wattles summarizes the themes of his book, particularly his response to critics who argue that the golden rule fails to acknowledge differences among human beings, that it establishes a relatively low standard of morality, and that it encourages a simplistic moral outlook.*

Children are taught to respect parents and other authority figures. Adolescents are urged to control their impulses. Adults are told to conduct themselves in accord with certain moral and ethical standards. Morality, then, may seem to be just an affair of imposition, a cultural voice that says "no" in various ways to our desires. To be sure, there are times when the word "no" must be spoken and enforced. But, time and again, people have discovered something more to morality, something rooted in life itself. The "no" is but one word in the voice of life, a voice that has other words, including the golden rule: Do to others as you want others to do to you. This book is about the life in that principle.

THE UNITY OF THE RULE

What could be easier to grasp intuitively than the golden rule? It has such an immediate intelligibility that it serves as a ladder that anyone can step onto without a great stretch. I know how I like to be treated; and that is how I am to treat others. The rule asks me to be considerate of others rather than indulging in self-centeredness. The study of the rule, however, leads beyond conventional interpretation, and the practice of the rule leads beyond conventional morality.

The rule is widely regarded as obvious and self-evident. Nearly everyone is familiar with it in some formulation or other. An angry parent uses it as a weapon: "Is that how you want others to treat you?" A defense attorney invites the members of the jury to put themselves in the shoes of his or her client. Noting that particular rules and interpretations do not cover every situation, a manual of professional ethics exhorts members to treat other professionals with the same consideration and respect that they would wish for themselves. Formulated in one way or another, the rule finds its way into countless speeches, sermons, documents, and books on the assumption that it has a single, clear sense that the listener or reader grasps and approves of. In an age where differences so often occasion violence, here, it seems, is something that everyone can agree on.

Promoting the notion that the golden rule is "taught by all the world's religions," advocates have collected maxims from various traditions, producing lists with entries like the following: "Hinduism: 'Let no man do to another that which would be repugnant to himself.'" "Islam: 'None of you [truly] believes until he wishes for his brother what he wishes for himself.'" The point of these lists is self-evident. Despite the differences in phrasing, all religions acknowledge the same basic, universal moral teaching. Moreover, this principle may be accepted as common ground by secular ethics as well.

Under the microscope of analysis, however, things are not so simple. Different formulations have different implications, and differences in context raise the question of whether the same concept is at work in passages where the wording is nearly identical. Is the meaning of the rule constant whenever one of these phrases is mentioned? There is a persistent debate, for example, about the relative merit of the positive formulation versus the negative one, "Do not do to others what you do not want others to do to you." Nor can the full meaning of a sentence be grasped in isolation. For example, to point to "the golden rule in Confucianism" by quoting a fifteen-word sentence from the *Analects* of Confucius does not convey the historical dynamism of the rule's evolving social, ethical, and spiritual connotations. What do the words mean in their original context? How prominent is the rule within that particular tradition? Finally, how does the rule function in a given interaction between the speaker or writer and the listener or reader? The rule may function as an authoritative reproach, a pious rehearsal of tradition, a specimen for analytic dissection, or a confession of personal commitment. Is the rule one or many? Can we even properly speak of *the* golden rule at all? Some Hindus interpret the injunction to treat others as oneself as an invitation to identify with the divine spirit within each person. Some Muslims take the golden rule to apply primarily to the brotherhood of Islam. Some Christians regard the rule as a shorthand summary of the morality of Jesus's religion. And countless people think of the rule without any religious associations at all.

Raising the question about the meanings of the golden rule in different contexts is not intended to reduce similarities to dust and ashes merely by appealing to the imponderable weight of cultural differences. Context is not the last word on meaning; the sentence expressing the golden rule contributes meaning of its own to its context. Meaning does involve context, but the fact that contexts differ does not prove that there is no commonality of meaning. Language and culture, moreover, are not reliable clues for identifying conceptual similarity and difference, since conceptual harmony is experienced across these boundaries.

The golden rule, happily, has more than a single sense. It is not a static, one-dimensional proposition with a single meaning to be accepted or rejected, defended or refuted. Nor is its multiplicity chaotic. There is enough continuity of meaning in its varied uses to justify speaking of *the* golden rule. My own thesis is that the rule's unity is best comprehended not in terms of a single meaning but as a symbol of a process of growth on emotional, intellectual, and spiritual levels.

THE QUALITY OF THE RULE

"Gold is where you find it" runs a proverb coined by miners who found what they were seeking in unexpected places. So what sort of ore or alloy or sculpture is the teaching that, since the seventeenth century, has been called "the golden rule"? Is it gold or glitter? Certain appreciative remarks on the golden rule seem to bear witness to a discovery. "Eureka!" they seem to say. "There is a supreme principle of living! It *can* be expressed in a single statement!"

By contrast, theologian Paul Tillich found the rule an inferior principle. For him, the biblical commandment to love and the assurance that God *is* love "infinitely transcend" the golden rule. The problem with the rule is that it "does not tell us what we *should* wish."

Is the rule *golden*? In other words, is it worthy to be cherished as a rule of living or even as *the* rule of living? The values of the rule are as much in dispute as its meanings. Most people, it seems, intuitively regard the golden rule as a good principle, and some have spoken as though there is within the rule a special kind of agency with the power to transform humankind. 10

It is understandable that the golden rule has been regarded as *the* supreme moral principle. I do not want to be murdered; therefore I should not murder another. I do not want my spouse to commit adultery, my property to be stolen, and so forth; therefore I should treat others with comparable consideration. Others have comparable interests, and the rule calls me to treat the other as someone akin to myself. Moreover, I realize that I sometimes have desires to be treated in ways that do not represent my considered best judgment, and this reflection makes it obvious that reason is required for the proper application of the golden rule. Finally, in personal relationships, I want to be loved, and, in consequence, the rule directs me to be loving. From the perspective of someone simply interested in living right rather than in the construction and critique of theories, the rule has much to recommend it.

Some writers have put the rule on a pedestal, giving the impression that the rule is *sufficient* for ethics in the sense that no one could ever go wrong by adhering to it or in the sense that all duties may be inferred from it. Others have claimed that the rule is a *necessary* criterion for right action; in other words, an action must be able to pass the test of the golden rule if it is to be validated as right, and any action that fails the test is wrong. Some philosophers have hoped for an ethical theory that would be self-sufficient (depending on no controversial axioms), perfectly good (invulnerable to counterexamples), and all-powerful (enabling the derivation of every correct moral judgment, given appropriate data about the situation). They have dreamed of sculpting ethics into an independent, rational, deductive system, on the model of geometry, with a single normative axiom. However much reason may hanker for such a system, once the golden rule is taken as a candidate for such an axiom, a minor flexing of the analytic bicep is enough to humiliate it. A single counterexample suffices to defeat a pretender to this throne.

Many scholars today regard the rule as an acceptable principle for popular use but as embarrassing if taken with philosophic seriousness. Most professional ethicists rely instead on other principles, since the rule seems vulnerable to counterexamples, such as the current favorite, "What if a sadomasochist goes forth to treat others as he wants to be treated?"

Technically, the golden rule can defend itself from objections, since it contains within itself the seed of its own self-correction. Any easily abused interpretation may be challenged: "Would you want to be treated according to a rule construed in this way?" The recursive use of the rule—applying it to the results of its own earlier application—is a lever that extricates it from many tangles. Close examination of the counterexample of the sadomasochist . . . shows that to use the rule properly requires a certain degree of maturity. The counterexample does not refute the golden rule, properly understood; rather, it serves to clarify the interpretation of the rule—that the golden rule functions appropriately in a *growing* personality; indeed, the practice of the rule itself promotes the required growth. Since the rule is such a compressed statement of morality, it takes for granted at least a minimum sincerity that refuses to manipulate the rule sophistically to "justify" patently immoral conduct. Where that prerequisite cannot be assumed, problems multiply.

The objections that have been raised against the rule are useful to illustrate 15 misinterpretations of the rule and to make clear assumptions that must be satisfied for the rule to function in moral theory.

It has been objected that the golden rule assumes that human beings are basically alike and thereby fails to do justice to the differences between people. In particular, the rule allegedly implies that what we want is what others want. As George Bernard Shaw quipped, "Don't do to others as you want them to do unto you. Their tastes may be different." The golden rule may also seem to imply that what we want for ourselves is good for ourselves and that what is good for ourselves is good for others. The positive formulation, in particular, is accused of harboring the potential for presumption; thus, the rule is suited for immediate application only among those whose beliefs and needs are similar. In fact, however, the rule calls for due consideration for any relevant difference between persons—just as the agent would want such consideration from others.

Another criticism is that the golden rule sets too low a standard because it makes ordinary wants and desires the criterion of morality. On one interpretation, the rule asks individuals to do whatever they imagine they might wish to have done to them in a given situation; thus a judge would be obliged by the golden rule to sentence a convicted criminal with extreme leniency. As a mere principle of sympathy, therefore, it is argued, the rule is incapable of guiding judgment in cases where the necessary action is unwelcome to its immediate recipient.

A related problem is that the rule, taken merely as a policy of sympathy, amounts to the advice "Treat others as they want you to treat them," as in a puzzle from the opening chapter of Herman Melville's *Moby-Dick*, where Ishmael is invited by his new friend, Queequeg, to join in pagan worship. Ishmael pauses to think it over:

> But what is worship?—to do the will of God—*that* is worship. And what is the will of God?—to do to my fellow man what I would have my fellow man to do to me—*that* is the will of God. Now, Queequeg is my fellow man. And what do I wish that this Queequeg would do to me? Why, unite with me in my particular Presbyterian form of worship. Consequently, I must then unite with him in his; ergo, I must turn idolator.

If the golden rule is taken to require the agent to identify with the other in a simplistic and uncritical way, the result is a loss of the higher perspective toward which the rule moves the thoughtful practitioner.

The next clusters of objections have a depth that a quick, initial reply would betray, so I defer my response until later. If the rule is not to be interpreted as setting up the agent's idiosyncratic desires—or those of the recipient—as a supreme standard of goodness, then problems arise because the rule does not specify what the agent ought to desire. The rule merely requires consistency of moral judgment: one must apply the same standards to one's treatment of others that one applies to others' treatment of oneself. The lack of specificity in the rule, its merely formal or merely procedural character, allegedly renders its guidance insubstantial.

The rule seems to exhibit the limitations of any general moral principle: it does [20] not carry sufficiently rich substantive implications to be helpful in the thicket of life's problems. Even though most people live with some allegiance to integrating principles, action guides, mottoes, proverbs, or commandments that serve to unify the mind, the deficiency of any principle is that it is merely a principle, merely a beginning; only the full exposition of a system of ethics can validate the place of an asserted principle. An appeal to a general principle, moreover, can function as a retreat and a refusal to think through issues in their concreteness.

There is also criticism of a practice widely associated with the rule—imagining oneself in the other person's situation. The charge is that this practice is an abstract, derivative, artificial, male, manipulative device, which can never compensate for the lack of human understanding and spontaneous goodness.

The rule has been criticized as a naïvely idealistic standard, unsuited to a world of rugged competition. The rule may seem to require that, if I am trustworthy and want to be trusted, I must treat everyone as being equally trustworthy. Furthermore, the broad humanitarianism of the golden rule allegedly makes unrealistic psychological demands; it is unfair to family and friends to embrace the universal concerns of the golden rule.

Last, some religious issues. The golden rule has been criticized for being a teaching that misleadingly lets people avoid confronting the higher teachings of religious ethics, for example, Jesus's commandment, "Love one another as I have loved you." Some find the rule of only intermediate usefulness, proposing that spiritual living moves beyond the standpoint of rules. Others have criticized the golden rule's traditional links to religion, arguing that moral intuition and moral reason can operate without reference to any religious foundation.

For responding to all these objections, there are three possible strategies: abandon the rule, reformulate it, or retain it as commonly worded, while taking advantage of objections to clarify its proper interpretation. I take the third way.

QUESTIONS FOR DISCUSSION AND WRITING

1. In paragraphs 4 and 5, Wattles offers variations on the golden rule, from Hinduism and Islam as well as the rule in its negative formulation. Do these variations state essentially the same moral precept, or are there subtle differences among them? Why do you think so?

2. Wattles writes that it is "obvious that reason is required for the proper application of the golden rule" (paragraph 11). What does he mean? How does this idea fit in with his point that the rule "takes for granted at least a minimum sincerity that refuses to manipulate the rule sophistically to 'justify' patently immoral conduct" (paragraph 14)?

3. Wattles raises objections that have been made regarding the usefulness of the golden rule, some of which he briefly responds to. His point, however, is that considering these various objections is "useful to illustrate misinterpretations of the rule and to make clear assumptions that must be satisfied for the rule to function in moral theory" (paragraph 15). Might this kind of thinking tend to make what is essentially a straightforward statement of moral principle into something too complicated to put into practice? Given the objections Wattles mentions, how would you go about interpreting the golden rule?

4. In an essay, consider the principles that you live by and explain whether they help you "in the thicket of life's problems." Do you ever use them "as a retreat and a refusal to think through issues in their concreteness" (paragraph 20)? Do any of the principles in "The Analects" (p. 634), "The Ten Commandments" (p. 636), or "Fundamentals of Islam" (p. 636) seem vulnerable to "the limitations of any general moral principle" (paragraph 20)?

ANNA QUINDLEN

Uncle Sam and Aunt Samantha

Published in Newsweek *less than two months after the 2001 World Trade Center and Pentagon attacks, "Uncle Sam and Aunt Samantha" takes on a topic that eludes most discussions of America's new military situation. Pulitzer Prize–winning journalist Anna Quindlen asks why men are subject to the military draft whereas women are not. Born in Philadelphia (1953), Quindlen graduated from Barnard (B.A., 1974) and became a reporter for the* New York Times, *eventually writing regular columns of which "Public and Private" earned her a Pulitzer (1992). In 1994 Quindlen left the* Times *to devote herself to fiction writing.* Object Lessons *(1991) is a novel about the "dislocations of growing up";* One True Thing *(1995) concerns a person's right to die; and* Black and Blue *(1998) explores the theme of domestic violence. She turns her attention to quality-of-life issues in such nonfiction works as* How Reading Changed My Life *(1998) and* A Short Guide to a Happy Life *(2000).*

A devoted liberal feminist and mother of three children, Quindlen points out, "Neither the left nor the right has been particularly inclined to consider this issue judiciously"; making the draft gender-blind would remove one of the last legal barriers to equality, but the question remains a political "hot potato."

One out of every five new recruits in the United States military is female.

The Marines gave the Combat Action Ribbon for service in the Persian Gulf to 23 women.

Two female soldiers were killed in the bombing of the USS *Cole.*

The Selective Service registers for the draft all male citizens between the ages of 18 and 25.

What's wrong with this picture?   5

As Americans read and realize that the lives of most women in this country are as different from those of Afghan women as a Cunard cruise is from maximum-security lockdown, there has nonetheless been little attention paid to one persistent gender inequity in U.S. public policy. An astonishing anachronism, really: while women are represented today in virtually all fields, including the armed forces, only men are required to register for the military draft that would be used in the event of a national-security crisis.

Since the nation is as close to such a crisis as it has been in more than 60 years, it's a good moment to consider how the draft wound up in this particular time warp. It's not the time warp of the Taliban, certainly, stuck in the worst part of the 13th century, forbidding women to attend school or hold jobs or even reveal their arms, forcing them into sex and marriage. Our own time warp is several decades old. The last time the draft was considered seriously was 20 years ago, when registration with the Selective Service was restored by Jimmy Carter after the Soviet invasion of, yep, Afghanistan. The president, as well as the Army chief of staff, asked at the time for the registration of women as well as men.

Amid a welter of arguments—women interfere with esprit de corps, women don't have the physical strength, women prisoners could be sexually assaulted, women soldiers would distract male soldiers from their mission—Congress shot down the notion of gender-blind registration. So did the Supreme Court, ruling that since women were forbidden to serve in combat positions and the purpose of the draft was to create a combat-ready force, it made sense not to register them.

But that was then, and this is now. Women have indeed served in combat positions, in the Balkans and the Middle East. More than 40,000 managed to serve in the Persian Gulf without destroying unit cohesion or failing because of upper-body strength. Some are even now taking out targets in Afghanistan from fighter jets, and apparently without any male soldier's falling prey to some predicted excess of chivalry or lust.

Talk about cognitive dissonance. All these military personnel, male and fe-   10
male alike, have come of age at a time when a significant level of parity was taken for granted. Yet they are supposed to accept that only males will be required to defend their country in a time of national emergency. This is insulting to men. And it is insulting to women. Caroline Forell, an expert on women's legal rights and a professor at the University of Oregon School of Law, puts it bluntly: "Failing to require this of women makes us lesser citizens."

Neither the left nor the right has been particularly inclined to consider this issue judiciously. Many feminists came from the antiwar movement and have let their distaste for the military in general and the draft in particular mute their response. In 1980 NOW released a resolution that buried support for the registration of women beneath opposition to the draft, despite the fact that the draft had been redesigned to eliminate the vexing inequities of Vietnam, when the sons of the working class served and the sons of the Ivy League did not. Conservatives, meanwhile, used an equal-opportunity draft as the linchpin of opposition to the Equal Rights Amendment, along with the terrifying specter of unisex bathrooms. (I have seen the urinal, and it is benign.) The legislative director of the right-wing group Concerned Women for America once defended the existing regulations by saying that most women "don't want to be included in the draft." All those young men who went to Canada during Vietnam and those who today register with fear and trembling in the face of the World Trade Center devastation might be amazed to discover that lack of desire is an affirmative defense.

Parents face a series of unique new challenges in this more egalitarian world, not the least of which would be sending a daughter off to war. But parents all over this country are doing that right now, with daughters who enlisted; some have even expressed surprise that young women, in this day and age, are not required to register alongside their brothers and friends. While all involved in this debate over the years have invoked the assumed opposition of the people, even 10 years ago more than half of all Americans polled believed women should be made eligible for the draft. Besides, this is not about comfort but about fairness. My son has to register with the Selective Service this year, and if his sister does not when she turns 18, it makes a mockery not only of the standards of this household but of the standards of this nation.

It is possible in Afghanistan for women to be treated like little more than fecund pack animals precisely because gender fear and ignorance and hatred have been codified and permitted to hold sway. In this country, largely because of the concerted efforts of those allied with the women's movement over a century of struggle, much of that bigotry has been beaten back, even buried. Yet in improbable places the creaky old ways surface, the ways suggesting that we women were made of finer stuff. The finer stuff was usually porcelain, decorative and on the shelf, suitable for meals and show. Happily, the finer stuff has been transmuted into the right stuff. But with rights come responsibilities, as teachers like to tell their students. This is a responsibility that should fall equally upon all, male and female alike. If the empirical evidence is considered rationally, if the decision is divested of outmoded stereotypes, that's the only possible conclusion to be reached.

QUESTIONS FOR DISCUSSION AND WRITING

1. List all the reasons Quindlen mentions for the existence of a male-only draft law in the United States during an era of sexual equality. What arguments have been made to justify the continuation of this law?

2. Quindlen notes in paragraph 11 that "[c]onservatives . . . used an equal-opportunity draft as the linchpin of opposition to the Equal Rights Amendment." The Equal Rights Amendment (ERA) was an attempt to write gender equality into law. Research the history of this amendment and report to your class about how conservatives could use the concept of a gender-blind draft to organize opposition to the ERA.

3. Quindlen asserts in paragraph 13 that given our belief in equality and the record of women's recent service in the military, we must conclude that the draft law should be made gender-blind. Write an essay explaining why you agree or disagree with her conclusion.

4. Besides making draft registration mandatory for women as well as men, another way to end the debate would be to eliminate the draft law. Do you think it is eth-

ical for the state to require a citizen to perform military service? Write an argumentative essay on this topic.

PETER SINGER

The Singer Solution to World Poverty

When Princeton University appointed Peter Singer to a new chair in bioethics in 1998, a New Yorker *profile hailed him as "the most influential living philosopher," and the* New York Times *as "perhaps the world's most controversial ethicist." Born in Melbourne, Australia (1946), Singer attended the University of Melbourne (B.A., 1967; M.A., 1969) and Oxford (B. Phil., 1971). After teaching at Oxford and at New York University, he led the Centre for Human Bioethics at Monash University in Australia (1983–1998). A vegetarian since college, Singer has devoted his career to protecting animals from human "speciesism"—the valuing of human rights above those of other species. In* Animal Liberation: A New Ethics for Our Treatment of Animals *(1975), he argues against redundant experimentation, advocates humane food production, and recommends that we consume more vegetable protein and less meat. Singer's work as coauthor and editor includes* Making Babies: The New Science and Ethics of Conception *(1985), about ethical issues in human conception such as in vitro fertilization and surrogate motherhood;* Should the Baby Live? The Problem of Handicapped Infants *(1985); and* Rethinking Life and Death *(1995), about the quality-of-life issues raised by modern technology.*

In "The Singer Solution to World Poverty," originally published in the New York Times Magazine *(September 1999), Singer interrogates the ethics of affluence, arguing that because it is just as immoral to ignore the plight of sick and starving children overseas as it is to allow a child to be killed, we should willingly donate to charity the portion of our income not spent on necessities.*

In the Brazilian film *Central Station*, Dora is a retired schoolteacher who makes ends meet by sitting at the station writing letters for illiterate people. Suddenly she has an opportunity to pocket $1,000. All she has to do is persuade a homeless 9-year-old boy to follow her to an address she has been given. (She is told he will be adopted by wealthy foreigners.) She delivers the boy, gets the money, spends some of it on a television set and settles down to enjoy her new acquisition. Her neighbor spoils the fun, however, by telling her that the boy was too old to be adopted—he will be killed and his organs sold for transplantation. Perhaps Dora knew this all along, but after her neighbor's plain speaking, she spends a troubled night. In the morning Dora resolves to take the boy back.

Suppose Dora had told her neighbor that it is a tough world, other people have nice new TV's too, and if selling the kid is the only way she can get one, well, he was only a street kid. She would then have become, in the eyes of the audience, a monster. She redeems herself only by being prepared to bear considerable risks to save the boy.

At the end of the movie, in cinemas in the affluent nations of the world, people who would have been quick to condemn Dora if she had not rescued the boy go home to places far more comfortable than her apartment. In fact, the average family in the United States spends almost one-third of its income on things that are no more necessary to them than Dora's new TV was to her. Going out to nice restaurants, buying new clothes because the old ones are no longer stylish, vacationing at beach resorts—so much of our income is spent on things not essential to the preservation of our lives and health. Donated to one of a number of charitable agencies, that money could mean the difference between life and death for children in need.

All of which raises a question: In the end, what is the ethical distinction between a Brazilian who sells a homeless child to organ peddlers and an American who already has a TV and upgrades to a better one—knowing that the money could be donated to an organization that would use it to save the lives of kids in need?

Of course, there are several differences between the two situations that could   5 support different moral judgments about them. For one thing, to be able to consign a child to death when he is standing right in front of you takes a chilling kind of heartlessness; it is much easier to ignore an appeal for money to help children you will never meet. Yet for a utilitarian philosopher like myself—that is, one who judges whether acts are right or wrong by their consequences—if the upshot of the American's failure to donate the money is that one more kid dies on the streets of a Brazilian city, then it is, in some sense, just as bad as selling the kid to the organ peddlers. But one doesn't need to embrace my utilitarian ethic to see that, at the very least, there is a troubling incongruity in being so quick to condemn Dora for taking the child to the organ peddlers while, at the same time, not regarding the American consumer's behavior as raising a serious moral issue.

In his 1996 book, *Living High and Letting Die*, the New York University philosopher Peter Unger presented an ingenious series of imaginary examples designed to probe our intuitions about whether it is wrong to live well without giving substantial amounts of money to help people who are hungry, malnourished or dying from easily treatable illnesses like diarrhea. Here's my paraphrase of one of these examples:

Bob is close to retirement. He has invested most of his savings in a very rare and valuable old car, a Bugatti, which he has not been able to insure. The Bugatti is his pride and joy. In addition to the pleasure he gets from driving and caring for his car, Bob knows that its rising market value means that he will always be able to sell it and live comfortably after retirement. One day when Bob is out for a drive, he parks the Bugatti near the end of a railway siding and goes for a walk up the track. As he does so, he sees that a runaway train, with no one aboard, is running down the railway track. Looking farther down the track, he sees the small figure of a child very likely to be killed by the runaway train. He can't stop the train and the child is too far away to warn of the danger, but he can throw a switch that will divert the train down the siding where his Bugatti is parked. Then nobody will be killed—but the train will destroy his Bugatti. Thinking of his joy in owning the car and the financial security it represents, Bob decides not to throw the switch. The child is killed. For many years to come, Bob enjoys owning his Bugatti and the financial security it represents.

Bob's conduct, most of us will immediately respond, was gravely wrong. Unger agrees. But then he reminds us that we, too, have opportunities to save the lives of children. We can give to organizations like UNICEF or Oxfam America. How much would we have to give one of these organizations to have a high probability of saving the life of a child threatened by easily preventable diseases? (I do not believe that children are more worth saving than adults, but since no one can argue that children have brought their poverty on themselves, focusing on them simplifies the issues.) Unger called up some experts and used the information they provided to offer some plausible estimates that include the cost of raising money, administrative expenses and the cost of delivering aid where it is most needed. By his calculation, $200 in donations would help a sickly 2-year-old transform into a healthy 6-year-old—offering safe passage through childhood's most dangerous years. To show how practical philosophical argument can be, Unger even tells his readers that they can easily donate funds by using their credit card and calling one of these toll-free numbers: (800) 367-5437 for UNICEF; (800) 693-2687 for Oxfam America.

Now you, too, have the information you need to save a child's life. How should you judge yourself if you don't do it? Think again about Bob and his Bugatti. Unlike Dora, Bob did not have to look into the eyes of the child he was sacrificing for his own material comfort. The child was a complete stranger to him and too far away to relate to in an intimate, personal way. Unlike Dora, too, he did not mislead the child or initiate the chain of events imperiling him. In all these respects, Bob's situation resembles that of people able but unwilling to donate to overseas aid and differs from Dora's situation.

If you still think that it was very wrong of Bob not to throw the switch that 10 would have diverted the train and saved the child's life, then it is hard to see how you could deny that it is also very wrong not to send money to one of the organizations listed above. Unless, that is, there is some morally important difference between the two situations that I have overlooked.

Is it the practical uncertainties about whether aid will really reach the people who need it? Nobody who knows the world of overseas aid can doubt that such uncertainties exist. But Unger's figure of $200 to save a child's life was reached after he had made conservative assumptions about the proportion of the money donated that will actually reach its target.

One genuine difference between Bob and those who can afford to donate to overseas aid organizations but don't is that only Bob can save the child on the tracks, whereas there are hundreds of millions of people who can give $200 to overseas aid organizations. The problem is that most of them aren't doing it. Does this mean that it is all right for you not to do it?

Suppose that there were more owners of priceless vintage cars—Carol, Dave, Emma, Fred and so on, down to Ziggy—all in exactly the same situation as Bob, with their own siding and their own switch, all sacrificing the child in order to preserve their own cherished car. Would that make it all right for Bob to do the same? To answer this question affirmatively is to endorse follow-the-crowd ethics—the kind of ethics that led many Germans to look away when the Nazi atrocities were being committed. We do not excuse them because others were behaving no better.

We seem to lack a sound basis for drawing a clear moral line between Bob's situation and that of any reader of this article with $200 to spare who does not donate it to an overseas aid agency. These readers seem to be acting at least as badly as Bob was acting when he chose to let the runaway train hurtle toward the unsuspecting child. In the light of this conclusion, I trust that many readers will reach for the phone and donate that $200. Perhaps you should do it before reading further.

Now that you have distinguished yourself morally from people who put their vintage cars ahead of a child's life, how about treating yourself and your partner to dinner at your favorite restaurant? But wait. The money you will spend at the restaurant could also help save the lives of children overseas! True, you weren't planning to blow $200 tonight, but if you were to give up dining out just for one month, you would easily save that amount. And what is one month's dining out, compared to a child's life? There's the rub. Since there are a lot of desperately needy children in the world, there will always be another child whose life you could save for another $200. Are you therefore obliged to keep giving until you have nothing left? At what point can you stop? 15

Hypothetical examples can easily become farcical. Consider Bob. How far past losing the Bugatti should he go? Imagine that Bob had got his foot stuck in the track of the siding, and if he diverted the train, then before it rammed the car it would also amputate his big toe. Should he still throw the switch? What if it would amputate his foot? His entire leg?

As absurd as the Bugatti scenario gets when pushed to extremes, the point it raises is a serious one: only when the sacrifices become very significant indeed would most people be prepared to say that Bob does nothing wrong when he decides not to throw the switch. Of course, most people could be wrong; we can't decide moral issues by taking opinion polls. But consider for yourself the level of sacrifice that you would demand of Bob, and then think about how much money you would have to give away in order to make a sacrifice that is roughly equal to that. It's almost certainly much, much more than $200. For most middle-class Americans, it could easily be more like $200,000.

Isn't it counterproductive to ask people to do so much? Don't we run the risk that many will shrug their shoulders and say that morality, so conceived, is fine for saints but not for them? I accept that we are unlikely to see, in the near or even medium-term future, a world in which it is normal for wealthy Americans to give the bulk of their wealth to strangers. When it comes to praising or blaming people for what they do, we tend to use a standard that is relative to some conception of normal behavior. Comfortably off Americans who give, say, 10 percent of their income to overseas aid organizations are so far ahead of most of their equally comfortable fellow citizens that I wouldn't go out of my way to chastise them for not doing more. Nevertheless, they should be doing much more, and they are in no position to criticize Bob for failing to make the much greater sacrifice of his Bugatti.

At this point various objections may crop up. Someone may say: "If every citizen living in the affluent nations contributed his or her share I wouldn't have to make such a drastic sacrifice, because long before such levels were reached, the resources would have been there to save the lives of all those children dying from lack of food or medical care. So why should I give more than my fair share?" Another, related, objection is that the Government ought to increase its overseas aid allocations, since that would spread the burden more equitably across all taxpayers.

Yet the question of how much we ought to give is a matter to be decided in 20 the real world—and that, sadly, is a world in which we know that most people do not, and in the immediate future will not, give substantial amounts to overseas aid agencies. We know, too, that at least in the next year, the United States Government is not going to meet even the very modest United Nations–recommended target of 0.7 percent of gross national product; at the moment it lags far below that, at 0.09 percent, not even half of Japan's 0.22 percent or a tenth of Denmark's 0.97 percent. Thus, we know that the money we can give beyond that theoretical "fair share" is still going to save lives that would otherwise be lost. While the idea that no one need do more than his or her fair share is a powerful one, should it prevail if we know that others are not doing their fair share and that children will die preventable deaths unless we do more than our fair share? That would be taking fairness too far.

Thus, this ground for limiting how much we ought to give also fails. In the world as it is now, I can see no escape from the conclusion that each one of us with wealth surplus to his or her essential needs should be giving most of it to help people suffering from poverty so dire as to be life-threatening. That's right: I'm saying that you shouldn't buy that new car, take that cruise, redecorate the house or get that pricey new suit. After all, a $1,000 suit could save five children's lives.

So how does my philosophy break down in dollars and cents? An American household with an income of $50,000 spends around $30,000 annually on necessities, according to the Conference Board, a nonprofit economic research organization. Therefore, for a household bringing in $50,000 a year, donations to help the world's poor should be as close as possible to $20,000. The $30,000 required for necessities holds for higher incomes as well. So a household making $100,000 could cut a yearly check for $70,000. Again, the formula is simple: whatever money you're spending on luxuries, not necessities, should be given away.

Now, evolutionary psychologists tell us that human nature just isn't sufficiently altruistic to make it plausible that many people will sacrifice so much for strangers. On the facts of human nature, they might be right, but they would be wrong to draw a moral conclusion from those facts. If it is the case that we ought to do things that, predictably, most of us won't do, then let's face that fact head-on. Then, if we value the life of a child more than going to fancy restaurants, the next time we dine out we will know that we could have done something better with our money. If that makes living a morally decent life extremely arduous, well, then that is the way things are. If we don't do it, then we should at least know that we are failing to live a morally decent life—not because it is good to wallow in guilt but because knowing where we should be going is the first step toward heading in that direction.

When Bob first grasped the dilemma that faced him as he stood by that railway switch, he must have thought how extraordinarily unlucky he was to be placed in a situation in which he must choose between the life of an innocent child and the sacrifice of most of his savings. But he was not unlucky at all. We are all in that situation.

QUESTIONS FOR DISCUSSION AND WRITING

1. What types of charitable donations do you or people you know make? What are the reasons for supporting these particular causes? How do they stack up against Singer's cause?

2. Singer's article opens with reference to the film *Central Station*. Later he advocates that we avoid spending money on luxuries in order to donate it to save children's lives. Is going to the movies a luxury? To what extent is Singer being morally or logically inconsistent?

3. Singer considers some of the reasons people might give to justify their not reducing their consumption of "luxuries" in order to save poor children's lives. What are those reasons? What other reasons might you or people you know offer? Speculate on why Singer does not consider them. How does his neglect of those other reasons affect his ability to persuade you as a reader?

4. One critic, Peter Berkowitz, argues (in the *New Republic*, January 2000) that Singer's example of Bob is oversimplified through *either/or* reasoning (either Bob threw the switch or he did not), through "focusing on a single moral intuition" rather than "the clash between competing moral intuitions," and through neglecting such competing values as that of "perfecting [one's] own talents," which takes time and money. Write an essay that supports Berkowitz's charges or that defends Singer from them.

5. Learn about efforts to "save children's lives" in a particular situation abroad, such as in Darfur, Ethiopia, Somalia, or Bangladesh. In the situation you analyze, what are the meanings of the word *save*? Write an essay describing the relief

agencies' goals and accomplishments as well as the factors that inhibit the agencies' effectiveness.

6. To what extent do the moral principles in "The Analects" (p. 634), "The Ten Commandments" (p. 636) and "Fundamentals of Islam" (p. 636) provide guidance to the questions Singer presents?

GEORGE F. WILL

Life and Death at Princeton

Will was born in Champaign, Illinois (1941), and educated at Trinity College (B.A., 1962), Oxford (1962–1964), and Princeton (Ph.D., 1967). For more than thirty years, he has been a columnist for the Washington Post *and a contributing editor at* Newsweek. *In 1977 he won the Pulitzer Prize for Distinguished Commentary. Will's collections of essays include* The Morning After: American Successes and Excesses, 1981–1986 *(1986). His books of political analysis include* Restoration: Congress, Term Limits, and the Recovery of Deliberative Democracy *(1992), in which he argues that congressional term limits would reduce politicians' self-aggrandizement while restoring the genuine deliberation of ideas. His political philosophy resembles that of Edmund Burke, John Henry Newman, and other nineteenth-century thinkers who placed the community's claims above those of individuals. With equal moral seriousness, Will's books on baseball,* Men at Work *(1990) and* Bunts *(1998), portray the professional ethics of sports as a microcosm of the good society's ways of negotiating power, reward, and survival.*

Contrary to Peter Singer, Will believes that human choice must be based on considerations beyond utilitarianism. In "Life and Death at Princeton," originally published in Newsweek *(September 1999), he criticizes Singer's stance on such issues as abortion, infanticide for severely handicapped infants, and terminal illness.*

The university's motto, "*dei sub numine viget*," does not say, as some Princetonians insist, "God went to Princeton." It says, "Under God's Power She Flourishes." As the academic year commences, Peter Singer comes to campus to teach that truly ethical behavior will not flourish until humanity abandons the fallacy, as he sees it, of "the sanctity of life."

He comes trailing clouds of controversy because he argues, without recourse to euphemism or other semantic sleights-of-hand, the moral justification of some homicides, including infanticide and euthanasia. He rejects "the particular moral order" which supposes that human beings are extraordinarily precious because God made them so. He also rejects secular philosophies that depict human beings as possessing a unique and exalted dignity that sharply distinguishes them from, and justifies their "tyranny" over, other species of animals.

The appointment of the 53-year-old Australian philosopher to a tenured professorship of bioethics was unanimously recommended by a Princeton search committee and was approved by President Harold Shapiro, who chairs the National Bioethics Advisory Commission.

Princeton's position is that Singer's copious publications are serious scholarship; that he has helped to shape debates, worldwide, concerning animal rights and the ethical dilemmas posed by new medical technologies that blur the boundaries between life and death; that universities do not endorse views by permitting the teaching of them; that Singer's views can be rationally defended; that intellectual diversity is a good thing and (in Shapiro's words) he "challenges long-established ways of thinking."

Critics of the appointment argue that 150 years ago slavery was defended no   5
less rationally, given certain premises, than Singer defends his views, and the slavery proponents had premises not more repellent than Singer's. Critics note that a university's passion for intellectual diversity is today much more apt to encompass advocacy of infanticide than of protection for the unborn. They argue that a great university exists not only to provoke students to think about difficult matters, which Singer certainly will do, but also to transmit, down the generations, sustaining precepts of our civilization, some of which Singer wishes to extirpate. And they argue that the derivative prestige that Singer's views will gain from his Princeton connection will weaken respect for life and for the rights of the severely handicapped.

The critics are mostly correct. However, their worries about Singer's potential influence on students and public policy are excessive. He will be, on balance, a useful stimulant at Princeton. And he will be particularly useful to his most adamant critics. He appalls the right-to-life movement but actually he is the abortion-rights movement's worst nightmare. The logic of moral reasoning often is that he who says A must say B. Singer and other pro-choice people say A. But he then says: A entails B, and B includes infanticide.

Singer subscribes to utilitarianism, which holds that there is a single goal for human conduct — satisfaction of preferences and avoidance of suffering. Hence the foundation of morals is the obligation to maximize the satisfaction of preferences and minimize the thwarting of them. Like Jeremy Bentham (1748–1832), the founding father of utilitarianism, Singer believes that "pushpin is as good as poetry" — that one pleasure is as good as another. And Singer, the principal progenitor of the animal-rights movement, says the pleasures and sufferings of other species are not necessarily of a moral significance inferior to those of humans. To say otherwise, he says, is "speciesism."

Regarding humans, he says that assigning intrinsic moral significance to birth is arbitrary and logically indefensible. Birth is morally insignificant because a newborn, like a fetus, is incapable of regarding itself as "a distinct entity with a life of its own to lead." Because there are, he says, degrees of personhood, the intrinsic moral significance of the taking of the life of an individual gradually increases, like the physical being of the individual, from near nothingness in infancy.

With muscular candor, Singer faces biological facts: he does not deny that killing a fetus or a baby involves killing a human being. He has contempt for mincing, flinching language. (In an example of that, Kate Michelman, the abortion-rights advocate, has spoken of an aborted fetus "undergoing demise.") Singer says infanticide is not necessarily more morally important than abortion, which is morally negligible. In fact, some infanticide is not even as important as, say, killing a happy cat. (A cat can be self-conscious, and thus has a degree of personhood. Hence his use of the political category, "tyranny," to describe *Homo sapiens'* treatment of animals.) Killing an infant is never killing a person and is morally permissible in at least two kinds of situations.

One is when a handicapped baby faces a life in which suffering will predominate. Singer has cited Down's syndrome and spina bifida babies. However, he, like most people, is not well-informed about Down's syndrome citizens, some of whom are taxpayers who read the sports pages on the way to work. And spina bifida can involve a wide range of affliction. Singer's response to these facts is that sparing a Down or spina-bifida baby's life should be based on a utilitarian calculation with reference to the baby's projected quality of life, and the impact of the baby's life on others, all of which will depend on the severity of the disability. 10

Another situation when infanticide is justified is when parents with a handicapped baby—Singer's example is a hemophiliac—will, if relieved of the burden of the baby, have another baby which will be happier than the handicapped baby would be, and will bring the parents more happiness. By one form of utilitarian calculation, concerning which Singer is agnostic, the arithmetic is easy: the "total amount" of happiness would be increased.

Actually, the logic of his position is that until a baby is capable of self-awareness, there is no controlling reason not to kill it to serve any preference of the parents. Indeed, he has proposed (but is rethinking) a one-month postnatal period for legal discretionary infanticide. During the Senate debate on partial-birth abortion—in which procedure all of a baby except the top of the skull is delivered from the birth canal, then the skull is collapsed—two pro-choice senators were asked: Suppose the baby slips all the way out before the doctor can kill it. *Then* does it have a right to life? Both senators said no, it was still the mother's choice. Told of what the senators said, Singer says briskly: "They're right."

Singer's vocation is the important one of thinking about various choices forced upon us by modern medicine. What care is owed to anencephalic babies (born, essentially, without brains but with some brain-stem functions) or to persons in a persistent vegetative state? What is the moral importance of the distinction between "allowing nature to take its course" with the terminally ill and intervening to accelerate the course of nature?

But proximity, even familial attachment—these are moral irrelevancies in Singer's analysis of one's obligations to others. Should one spend a sum to ease the suffering of a family member or send the same sum to ease the sufferings of 10 Sudanese? Singer is consistent: In the Sudan the money will better serve the world's total amount of happiness. To his credit, he does not practice what he preaches.

He told a *New Yorker* magazine interviewer that money he spends on nursing care for his mother, who has Alzheimer's disease, at least "does provide employment for a number of people who find something worthwhile in what they're doing."

Thus were debutante parties rationalized during the Depression. *The New Yorker*'s interviewer calls Singer's rationalization "a noble sentiment." However, utilitarianism has no place for nobility, which presupposes the upward pull of a thoughtfulness that is higher than the low, common calculations of pain and pleasure, or of satisfying preferences and avoiding suffering.

Singer may fancy himself the advance guard of the future, but the trend of intellectual life is away from him. Medicine's multiplying capacities for therapeutic intervention in utero is changing how people think about the moral claims of fetal life. And there is a growing recoil from philosophies that misdescribe human beings as utterly autonomous individuals, "unencumbered" selves living in splendid self-sufficiency. There is heightened receptivity to philosophies that recognize that dependency on others is a universal and permanent fact of every life, throughout life. Dependency varies in kind and degree as people pass from birth to death, but can never of itself be a reason for denying personhood.

Singer's defenders say that some of his most arresting statements have been stripped of nuance by being taken out of context. There is some truth to that. However, while utilitarianism has interesting permutations, nuance is never its strong suit. Which is why Singer probably will not be a powerful shaper of Princeton students or public discourse.

Powerful teachers are unfinished products, combining certainties with a capacity for uncertainty and revision. Singer enjoys the intricacy of applying his utilitarian calculus to thorny practical problems. But on matters more fundamental than applications of his calculus, his thinking is as fixed and lifeless as a fly in amber. Although he says startling things en route to shocking conclusions, his work lacks the real drama of the life of the mind. He seems to be a strangely unreflective—almost unphilosophic—philosopher. He does not really worry about the deep questions of meaning and value that are behind the questions of life and death. For utilitarians, there can be no truly deep questions because human beings are no deeper than Bentham's depiction of them as under the sovereignty of pains and pleasures.

Given utilitarianism's unnaturally tidy conclusions about the human condition, utilitarian thinking serves a simple, even simpleminded, imperative—adding pleasures and subtracting pains in this or that situation. The result often resembles mere logic-chopping, without the risks of more wide-ranging reasoning about the deeper ambiguities surrounding life's possibilities. When moral reasoning is reduced to arithmetic—quantification involving categories as crude as pain and pleasure—moral reasoning is no more complex or interesting than the grinding of an adding machine.

A thoroughgoing utilitarian has the unlovely security and unenviable serenity of an inmate in what Chesterton called "the clean, well-lit prison of one idea." Singer's utilitarianism is so dry and desiccated that it drains the drama from philosophy. Gone is the juice of life that human beings seek in poetry or religion or the poetry of religion. Students may, at first, experience a flush of fascination with Singer's rigor in applying his rules to recalcitrant reality.

Still, Singer, three of whose grandparents died in the Holocaust, brings to his vocation the earnestness of one who knows that ideas have consequences. He is engaging, accessible and, unlike most contemporary philosophers, he is determined to bring philosophy to bear on urgent practical questions. He will do more to stimulate serious reflection—and more to stimulate opposition to his (literally) homicidal ideas—than he will to make his ideas acceptable.

Which is to say, Princeton can justify his appointment by utilitarian arithmetic. Such arithmetic has its uses, but not Singer's uses.

QUESTIONS FOR DISCUSSION AND WRITING

1. A *euphemism* is a mild or roundabout term that is substituted for a more blunt or painful one. Read Peter Singer's "The Singer Solution to World Poverty" (p. 601), keeping an eye out for phrases written with what Will calls "muscular candor." Then work with your classmates to translate some of Singer's tough or offensive language into euphemisms.

2. Will portrays the university as a place where serious scholarship takes place, where ideas can be taught without censorship, and where intellectual diversity should prevail. To what extent does his portrayal agree with your impression of university life? Discuss some controversial issues or speakers or evidence of diverse thinking in your academic and extracurricular experience.

3. According to Will, Singer advocates infanticide for infants born with Down's syndrome, spina bifida, hemophilia, and anencephaly. What arguments does Will say Singer uses to support his views? What are Will's objections to these arguments? Which do you find more convincing? Write an essay in which you take a stand on this issue, presenting both Singer's and Will's sides of the question and giving your reasoned opinion on the controversy.

WENDY SIMONDS

Talking with Strangers: A Researcher's Tale

Wendy Simonds received her bachelor's degree in environmental studies from the University of Pennsylvania in 1984 and a doctorate from the City University of New York in 1990. She is currently a sociology professor at Georgia State University, focusing on the sociology of procreative experiences. She is the author of Women and Self-Help Culture: Reading between the Lines *(1992) and* Abortion at Work: Ideology and Practice in a Feminist Clinic *(1996). In the following essay, originally published in the* Chronicle of Higher Education *(November 2001), Simonds considers the ethics of interviewing and ethnography in social science research, wondering if such research is "inherently exploitative" of its subjects.*

I became a sociologist largely because I wanted to overcome my fear of talking to strangers. That impetus for my professional life was not always apparent to me; in fact, only recently, when I was putting together my tenure dossier, did I come to understand my own motives. Originally, I thought I had pursued a scholarly life because I would be able to sleep late and would get paid to read and write books (which is how one of my college mentors had advertised academe).

I really had no idea what sociology was when I took it up; now, what I like about it is that it remains comfortably amorphous and nonrestrictive—undisciplined—as a discipline. But what I do, in terms of my research, has always been the same, even if how I think about doing it has changed. I talk to strangers, and then I write about what they tell me. And it still frightens me.

I had no formal training in interviewing or ethnography. In graduate school, I took one run-of-the-mill methods course, in which we spent the bulk of the time playing with a large statistical data set on computers, and very little time on anything else. In the handful of readings on interacting with live people, I perceived the general disciplinary view to be that research participants were troublesome, unreliable, and untrustworthy. They had to be carefully manipulated into participating, and then they could not be relied upon to tell the truth—because they were too stupid to know what the truth was, or because they would try to give us the answers they thought we wanted. Thus, our questions should be devised to trick them into not concealing the truth. (None of the readings actually used the words "trick" or "stupid," but that was the impression I came away with.)

A sense of entitlement pervaded the literature, as if research participants (usually referred to as subjects) were unhappily both the obstacle and the key to our ability to produce valuable social science. We briefly discussed building rapport with participants, but I can't remember anything substantive from that tiny snippet of the course.

I don't think that if I had been better educated about qualitative research I 5 would have done much of anything differently. My experience writing for my college newspaper (also undertaken because I wanted to conquer my fear of talking to strangers) was probably more useful than any course could have been. I had a general sense of how to ask coherent questions and how to listen actively, mainly by making sincerely enthusiastic and encouraging faces while people talked.

During my first big research project—my dissertation, a study of women who read self-help books—I wondered why the women had agreed to talk to me, a stranger. If I were to listen now to the tapes I made of those interviews, I know I would be embarrassed by my awkward attempts to cover bewilderment with "mm-hmm's" and by my clumsy questions, which I asked in all the wrong places.

Some of the women opened up their lives to me, sharing their thoughts with apparent ease, while others seemed awkward, closed, or superficial. At first, I thought the variable success of the interviews was because of my own inadequacies: I could usually feel the mood of the participant, but I felt relatively powerless to change someone reticent into a loquacious talker, or to restrict a talker from wandering into areas that seemed inappropriately personal, and that I feared she might later regret talking about to me. I felt that if I were a better interviewer, I should have been able to make anyone feel comfortable and willing to tell me what I wanted to know. But the more I thought about it, the more I wondered who the hell I was to expect people to expose themselves to me.

Many researchers have written about the ethics of interviewing and ethnography, of striving for the fair representation of research participants, of practicing non-exploitative interviewing strategies so that participants will feel that the experience has been beneficial to them in some way. But how does one guarantee a nonexploitative, beneficial experience? As Judith Stacey, a sociologist at the University of Southern California, has framed the question, Can there be a feminist ethnography? That issue remains surprisingly slippery. Stacey believes that because research is an intervention into subjects' lives, despite the researcher's best intentions, intimacy with subjects can be dangerous.

Consider this example of the unexpected ways in which intimate methods can be interpreted: I did research at an abortion clinic in the early 1990s. When my book *Abortion at Work: Ideology and Practice in a Feminist Clinic* (Rutgers University Press, 1996) came out, I gave a copy to the director of the clinic, who had not been there during my research. She called me the next morning, sounding frantic and anxious. She said she had been up all night. She told me she felt exposed by my book—though in it, I never named the clinic or its location, and I used pseudonyms for all the workers who had participated in my research. Nonetheless, she was afraid that everyone in the small world of abortion providers would know the clinic in the book was hers. She was worried that everyone would think it was a racist clinic, because I had discussed the workers' perceptions of race and racism there.

She appeared most distraught about how anti-abortionist campaigners 10 might use the book, because it describes in depth the ways that clinic workers do, and think about doing, second-trimester abortions. The book was honest and accurate, she told me, but clearly she felt threatened by it.

A few weeks later, I learned from a board member that the director had called up all the members of the board to tell them she was upset about the book. She also told them, untruthfully, that many staff members had not been aware that I was planning to use what they said in a book. Yet everyone I cited in the book had agreed that I could cite them; and everyone who worked in the clinic knew what I was doing there. They didn't know exactly what my book would say; neither did I at the time.

Is that sort of research inherently exploitative? Exposure may feel exploitative, obviously. Is it the researcher's responsibility to prepare participants for exposure, or to protect them from it? If so, how? I had not anticipated the director's response. Frankly, I had anticipated only excitement and praise, so proud was I of my work. I considered the women who took part in my book to be engaged in a heroic feminist struggle, and I thought that I had done a great job of representing the complexity of their work.

Because of my experience with the clinic director, I now work harder to anticipate the consequences of my research. But every project has unintended consequences. Must the researcher bear the responsibility for those?

Mitchell Duneier, the author of *Sidewalk* (Farrar, Straus and Giroux, 1999), an ethnographic account—complete with photographs taken by Ovie Carter— of the lives of street vendors in Greenwich Village, attempted to read each participant his completed manuscript. "Ultimately, I believe I should never publish anything about an identifiable person which I cannot look him or her in the eye and read," he notes in the book. His identification of participants by their real names and his participatory strategies—like reading his work to his subjects before publication and sharing his profits with participants—opened my eyes to ways of conducting research I had never considered. So far, though, I have continued to use pseudonyms for my subjects, because of time and energy constraints, and because I want to shield myself and them from the inevitable failures in, and unintended consequences of, my eventual representations of them.

I saw a documentary recently about the photographer Spencer Tunick, who   15 traveled throughout the United States to take photographs of people naked in public settings in all 50 states (the result was the widely acclaimed exhibit "Naked States"). In the documentary, Tunick stands on one street corner after another, passing out leaflets and talking to people, trying to persuade them to participate. I was impressed with his ability to engage people in conversation and to explain—over and over—his goals as an artist. But I was also disturbed by his unflagging annoyance at the difficulty of recruiting and controlling participants.

I was struck by how similar his quest was to mine: I too want to capture people in certain poses—in which they are, at least metaphorically, uncovered. Yet I do not want to control my participants.

I continually struggle with the research process and feel uncomfortable in my roles as interrogator and observer. Am I more than an intruder, a voyeur, a manipulator? I hope I am. What difference will the revelations that I seek from strangers make to the world? I don't think what I do is justified by so-called scientific curiosity—although, based on what I learned in my methods class, many scholars feel that way about their work. Yet I have a nebulous ideal of some greater good that my research will serve, some step toward a more socially just world that I can encourage society to take. Talking to people who understand that vague hope is my favorite kind of research.

Throughout the research process—from formulating questions to writing up my results—I attempt to imagine the range of responses and regrets that participants might feel in retrospect. I always keep in mind that I must be sensitive to my effects on the people who make my work possible. I believe their fear of talking to strangers is justified. After all, I share it.

QUESTIONS FOR DISCUSSION AND WRITING

1. In paragraph 8, Simonds refers to "the ethics of interviewing and ethnography." Does she believe that a "nonexploitative, beneficial experience" is possible for the human subjects of sociological research? Is, for example, the Confucian principle of reciprocity applicable to sociological research? Can a researcher ever put herself in the position of research participant?

2. Simonds suggests that researchers often feel the need to control their subjects. Why does this feeling prevail? What is Simonds's response?

3. If you were to participate in the kind of research project Simonds describes — allowing a researcher to observe and question you in your workplace or some private setting—what would you expect from the researcher? To what extent and for what reasons would you respond candidly to questions or feel the need to control what the researcher learned about you?

4. What does Simonds find valuable in the kind of research she does? What value, if any, do you find in such research? Shirley Brice Heath's "Literate Traditions" (p. 280) is based on the sort of ethnographic research that Simonds is writing about here. In what ways might these two research writers respond to each other?

KELLY RITTER

The Economics of Authorship: Online Paper Mills, Student Writers, and First-Year Composition

Kelly Ritter is an English professor and coordinator of first-year composition at Southern Connecticut State University. "The Economics of Authorship" was published in College Composition and Communication *(2005), a journal for teachers of college writing. The abstract of the article explains: "Using sample student analyses of online paper mill Web sites, student survey responses, and existing scholarship on plagiarism, authorship, and intellectual property, this article examines how the consumerist rhetoric of the online paper mills construes academic writing as a commodity for sale, and why such rhetoric appeals to students in first-year composition, whose cultural disconnect from the academic system of authorship increasingly leads them to patronize these sites" (p. 601).*

The question of what constitutes plagiarism, let alone how to address its many permutations in this age of electronic cut-and-paste, has characterized much of the recent research into academic dishonesty both inside and outside composition studies. This scholarship promotes the notion that one egregious type of plagiarism—the patronage of online term-paper mills—is a willfully deceptive act that needs no further study against the less wholesale, more "complicated" forms that merit examination. Purchasing a term paper is engaging in "the plagiarism that approaches fraud"[1] and is the academic sin that we most dread our students' committing. I propose that online paper mills have thus been allowed to prosper in the absence of true critical reflection on their persuasive power, especially in composition studies, where definitions of authorship are the most contested and where student understanding of authorial agency is the most tenuous. There are compelling reasons that an examination of the consumer-driven discourse of online paper mills should be integrated into our research on student authorship, in the context of how it competes for, and often wins, our students' attention.

First-year composition students today carefully weigh interconnected economic, academic, and personal needs when choosing whether to do their own college writing and research or purchase it elsewhere. Instead of employing the World Wide Web to piece together a paper of their own, these students often are seeking out already-finished, available-for-purchase papers by nameless and faceless authors, so as to meet their academic ends more quickly and with more certainty of success (i.e., a finished paper is a better bet than a pieced-together product of unknown resulting quality). Without these students—who do not believe that they can or should be authors of their own academic work, but do believe that they can *and should* co-opt the accomplished authorship of others when necessary—the anonymous and powerful online paper-mill industry could not exist. First-year composition students are the most likely group to fall victim to this industry, as they are not only unfamiliar with the university and its discourse but also enrolled in a required course that emphasizes the development of intellectual identity through writing. Anxious about the course and sometimes even angry that a new form of writing is being foisted upon them, one that often contradicts or complicates what the time and space of their high school English curriculum allowed them to learn, first-year composition students may quite literally buy into the paper mills' rhetoric. In the process, they shape their lifelong perceptions of what authorship in academia really means.

---

[1]Rebecca Moore Howard, *Standing in the Shadow of Giants: Plagiarists, Authors, Collaborators.* Stamford, CT: Ablex, 1999.

These students patronize online paper mills not because of any desire to outwit the academic system of authorship, but because of their cultural and ideological disconnection from the system itself. The rhetoric present in online paper mills and in our students' support of them challenges our comfortable and traditional definition of plagiarism, which is predicated upon academia's intrinsic defense of authorship as an intellectual, creative activity. The paper-mill Web sites, in order to rationalize their existence, negate the academic value of authorship in their easy online commerce with our students, instantly changing that innocent eighteen-year-old in one's composition class from an author to a plagiarist, or, in the rhetoric of the paper-mill sites, from a student to a *consumer*. In order to truly understand how and why students continue to engage in dishonest practices in the composition classroom, we thus must seek to understand how and when students see themselves as authors; how students see themselves as *consumers*, not just in the purchase of a college education, but also in a society defined by anonymity, convenience, and privacy; and how students reconcile the warring concepts of author and consumer in the space of their own writing.

The composition-studies community has yet to tackle two important questions underlying these students' absent notions of authorship. First, what is the complicated relationship already in place between *student* authors and consumer culture that dictates the role that writing plays in one's college career? Second, how might this relationship explain why the online paper mills consistently, even exponentially, profit from our students' patronage? Since first-year students do not, and perhaps *cannot*, always share faculty definitions of authorship and intellectual property, they cannot always reconcile their personal and academic needs with our course standards, which reinforce the idea that authorship is valuable, and that academic work itself is more than an economic means to an end. Addressing these questions thus begins a necessary inquiry into how and why our students frequently see college writing—their own, their friends', that which is provided by the paper mills—as an economic rather than an intellectual act.

When considering whether, when, and how often to purchase an academic paper from an online paper-mill site, first-year composition students therefore work with two factors that I wish to investigate here in pursuit of answering the questions posed above: the negligible desire to do one's own writing, or to be an author, with all that entails in this era of faceless authorship vis-à-vis the Internet; and the ever-shifting concept of "integrity," or responsibility when purchasing work, particularly in the anonymous arena of online consumerism. This latter concept is contingent upon the lure of a good academic/economic bargain—the purchased paper that might raise or solidify one's academic standing in the form of a "good" grade. To investigate these factors from a student standpoint, I will contextualize scholarly approaches to the notions of authorship, textual production, and academic dishonesty with not just samples of the discourse found on the paper mill Web sites, but also select responses from both a coursewide student survey completed by 247 students enrolled in English 101 (research-based first-year

5

composition) during one semester at my institution, and responses from an English 101 essay assignment, in which my own students (who have given me permission to cite their work here using pseudonyms) visited select paper-mill Web sites and analyzed the arguments put forth persuading students to buy their products. By privileging student responses in my study of the online paper mills and their antiacademic (and proeconomic) discourse, I hope to emphasize the important role that students themselves might play in our scholarship on this and allied subjects, as the responses articulate a compelling range of multilayered (and often internally competing) student perceptions of academic dishonesty and authorship. . . .

CONCLUSION: ASK THE AUTHOR(S)

Ed White, in "Student Plagiarism as an Institutional and Social Issue," warns:

> The response to theft cannot be merely individual [. . .]. Indeed, we should all expect that much plagiarism will naturally occur unless we help students understand what all the fuss is about; many students simply are clueless about the issue and many faculty think the issue is simpler than it is. Taking moral high ground is important and necessary, but, as with other moral issues, too many of the statements from that ground are hypocritical and not cognizant of the complex motives behind student actions. (207)[2]

White makes it clear that we must combat plagiarism from two sides, "prevention through education as well as punishment for violations" (p. 206). He believes that things will never change unless we help to change them by *educating* the "violators," our students. Like White, I am not against punishment, nor do I believe that it alone will stop plagiarism, or that punishment, for some, teaches any long-term lessons. Those who do not *want* to learn how authorship builds and validates a writer's identity will find ways *not* to listen. Thus, while I agree with Woodmansee's astute observation that "authorship does not exist to innocent eyes; they see only writing and texts" (p. 1), I also recognize that some students — including a few of my own — will remain willfully "innocent" unless, until, and sometimes in spite of having been proven "guilty."

Ultimately, I believe that what we have been doing thus far, particularly where online paper mills are concerned, is *not working*. We *do* have to take note of the now-slippery state of authorship vis-à-vis the expanding Internet, and be diligent about teaching our students that plagiarism is wrong and that academic ethics mean something. But let us not use the exponential — and seemingly unstoppable — growth power of online paper mills as an excuse to give up on the idea of *singular student authorship* altogether; let us instead take this opportunity to revisit theories of authorship with our students and reinforce the value of the

---

[2]Edward M. White, "Student Plagiarism as an Institutional and Social Issue." *Perspectives on Plagiarism and Intellectual Property in a Postmodern World.* Ed. Lise Buranen and Alice Roy (Albany: SUNY Press, 1999), 205–210.

writer-author. While cheating may arise from a complicated notion of personal worth and academic (in)ability, the purchase of essays from online companies strikes an even more basic chord in our students: the power to purchase this worth and ability, and by extension a new academic identity.

We should continue, in our battle against plagiarism, to see the composition classroom as a site for "responsible writing and learning" (White 210) on the part of teachers and students alike. Instead of further sublimating the author ourselves, we should work to solidify our students' ideas of authorship, and their identities as writers, so that if—or when—they visit an online paper mill, they will not be persuaded to erase their writing identity in favor of a good academic bargain. Students and teachers should work to find a way, together, to shape how the ethics of the writing classroom, and the larger university, should operate: not like a business, and not in the service of economics.

APPENDIX: SURVEY OF STUDENT OPINIONS ON ACADEMIC DISHONESTY IN ENGLISH 101

Please answer the following questions honestly. Your answers will become part of a study focusing on how students conceive of academic honesty and how these conceptions affect college professors who teach research-based writing.

Please circle *as many answers as are applicable* to your response for each question. Please use "*other*" if available to provide an answer that is not listed below. *Do not put your name on this survey*, as all survey responses will be kept anonymous.

1. When I hear the word "cheating" I think of:

   a. Copying answers from another student during an exam or in-class work (238; 96 percent)

   b. Copying lecture notes from another student when I have missed class, then using those notes in a paper or on an exam (27; 11 percent)

   c. Getting help outside of class from another student when writing a paper or take-home exam (30; 12 percent)

   d. Asking another student or a friend to write a paper for me (194; 79 percent)

   e. Buying a paper from an outside source, either a company or an individual (204; 83 percent)

   f. Taking source material from the Internet and using it as my own in a paper or take-home exam (175; 71 percent)

   g. Taking source material from books, magazines, or journals and using it as my own in a paper or take-home exam (169; 68 percent)

   h. Using a professor's lecture material as my own in a paper or take-home exam without naming my professor as a source (131; 53 percent)

   i. Bringing notes to a closed-book, in-class examination (180; 73 percent)

   j. Other (please specify): _____ (12; 5 percent)

2. In my experience, students I have known who have cheated in school have:

   a. Always been caught and punished by the teacher or professor (8; 3 percent)
   b. Always been caught and punished by someone outside the school (such as a parent) (4; 2 percent)
   c. Sometimes been caught and punished by the teacher or professor (97; 39 percent)
   d. Sometimes been caught and punished by someone outside the school (31; 13 percent)
   e. Seldom been caught or punished by the teacher or professor (126; 51 percent)
   f. Seldom been caught or punished by someone outside the school (38; 15 percent)
   g. Never been caught or punished by the teacher or professor (54; 22 percent)
   h. Never been caught or punished by anyone outside of school (55; 22 percent)
   i. I have never known anyone who has cheated in school (10; 4 percent)

3. The typical punishment for students I have known who have cheated has been:

   a. Failure of the paper or exam for which the cheating was done (206; 83 percent)
   b. Failure in the course in which the cheating was done (44; 18 percent)
   c. Higher disciplinary action (such as academic probation) or expulsion from school (34; 14 percent)
   d. No punishment, but the student has dropped the class or has dropped out of school (6; 2 percent)
   e. No punishment at all; no consequences for the student (31; 13 percent)

4. In my opinion, it is acceptable for me to cheat in school if:

   a. I am short on time and the assignment is due; if I don't cheat, I won't finish the work (24; 10 percent)
   b. I am under other personal stresses (such as relationship or family problems) that keep me from doing the work on my own (27; 11 percent)
   c. I am confused about the subject and can't do the work well on my own (32; 13 percent)
   d. I am uninterested in the subject and don't care if I do the work well, or if I do it myself (18; 7 percent)
   e. I will be punished by my parents or other authority if I do this work poorly (16; 6 percent)
   f. It is never acceptable for me to cheat (180; 73 percent)
   g. Other (please specify): _____ (10; 4 percent)

5. To me, being an "author" means:

   a. Writing a book or academic article (157; 64 percent)
   b. Writing anything, whether it is "academic" or not, that is then published (150; 61 percent)
   c. Writing anything, whether it is "academic" or not, and whether it is published or not (144; 58 percent)
   d. Writing material for the Internet (either a personal or business Web site) (96; 39 percent)

e. Writing a paper or a project for a college course (86; 35 percent)
f. Writing something for which one may become famous or well-known (112; 45 percent)
g. Co-writing a project of any kind with another person or persons (87; 35 percent)
h. Gathering different sources and pasting them together as a collection of writing, then putting your name on that collection (16; 6 percent)
i. Other (please specify): _____ (8; 3 percent)

6. Most of the papers I have written for college courses could best be defined as:

a. Material that has no use outside the particular course or area of study (82; 33 percent)
b. Material that may be used in other situations, such as a job or professional applications (63; 26 percent)
c. Material that represents who I am as a writer (110; 45 percent)
d. Material that in no way represents who I am as a writer (28; 11 percent)
e. Material that has required extensive research (84; 34 percent)
f. Material that has required moderate research (146; 59 percent)
g. Material that has required little to no research (45; 18 percent)

7. I would define "research" done for college papers as:

a. Going to the library and finding books and journal articles to use in my paper (214; 87 percent)
b. Going to a resource of some kind and learning more about a subject for my paper (172; 70 percent)
c. Going to the Internet and downloading any and all information that I can use in a paper (158; 64 percent)
d. Going to friends, family, or other persons and getting ideas or suggestions to use in my paper (129; 52 percent)
e. Other (please specify): _____ (9; 4 percent)

8. My opinion about the overall function or use of the Internet in college research is:

a. It is a very necessary and beneficial component of my research for college writing projects (132; 53 percent)
b. It is a somewhat necessary and beneficial component of my research for college writing projects (64; 26 percent)
c. It is an option for research in college writing projects; sometimes I use the Internet, sometimes I don't (109; 44 percent)
d. It is not an option for me, either because I don't have Internet access or don't like using the Internet (18; 7 percent)
e. Other (please specify): _____ (11; 4 percent)

Tallied results = (number of responses; percentage of total)
Total number of students surveyed = 247

QUESTIONS FOR DISCUSSION AND WRITING

1. What steps do you take to write a paper, and in what order?

2. When a paper is assigned, how far in advance of the due date do you begin to write it? How much time do you allow for investigating the subject? For writing a first draft? Do you consult outside sources? If so, how do you decide which ones to consult? Do you allow time to rethink your paper and to revise it before you turn it in?

3. How do you define "research" (see question 7 in the survey, p. 621)? In what ways is the Internet helpful in doing the type of research you need to do? Are there other equally or more useful ways to do research? Because the type of research depends, in part, on the problem at hand, you can identify a specific topic or issue to help you answer this question.

4. With a partner, answer survey question 1, including its subparts (p. 619): "When I hear the word 'cheating' I think of:" Or you could ask the same question to ten other students in different classes. Write a definition of "cheating" based on your survey results.

5. Answer survey question 4 (p. 620), "In my opinion, it is acceptable for me to cheat in school if:" and its subparts. Compare your answers with a partner's and write a code of ethics for student authors (for models, see "The Ten Commandments," p. 636, and "Society of Professional Journalists," p. 638).

G. ANTHONY GORRY

Steal This MP3 File: What Is Theft?

G. Anthony Gorry is a preeminent authority on the way technology and information processing affects our institutions, culture, and values. At Rice University, Professor Gorry directs the W. M. Keck Center for Computational Biology and the Center for Technology in Teaching and Learning. A graduate of Yale (B.A., 1962), he did graduate work at the University of California at Berkeley (M.S., 1963) and MIT (Ph.D., 1967). In addition to applying artificial intelligence—sophisticated computer algorithms that can mimic human decision processes—to the practice of medicine and management, Gorry has written extensively on other issues in applied computation in organizations and educational settings.

In "Steal This MP3 File," originally published in the Chronicle of Higher Education *(2003), Gorry addresses the moral consequences of new technologies, specifically the ways in which advances in computing can change people's ethical standards, focusing on students' pervasive practice of ripping, burning, and sharing music files.*

Sometimes when my students don't see life the way I do, I recall the complaint from *Bye Bye Birdie*, "What's the matter with kids today?" Then I remember that the "kids" in my class are children of the information age. In large part, technology has made them what they are, shaping their world and what they know. For my students, the advance of technology is expected, but for me, it remains both remarkable and somewhat unsettling.

In one course I teach, the students and I explore the effects of information technology on society. Our different perspectives on technology lead to engaging and challenging discussions that reveal some of the ways in which technology is shaping the attitudes of young people. An example is our discussion of intellectual property in the information age, of crucial importance to the entertainment business.

In recent years, many users of the Internet have launched an assault on the music business. Armed with tools for "ripping" music from compact discs and setting it "free" in cyberspace, they can disseminate online countless copies of a digitally encoded song. Music companies, along with some artists, have tried to stop this perceived pillaging of intellectual property by legal and technical means. The industry has had some success with legal actions against companies that provide the infrastructure for file sharing, but enthusiasm for sharing music is growing, and new file-sharing services continue to appear.

The Recording Industry Association of America recently filed lawsuits against four college students, seeking huge damages for "an emporium of music piracy" run on campus networks. However, the industry settled those lawsuits less than a week after a federal judge in California ruled against the association in another case, affirming that two of the Internet's most popular music-swapping services are not responsible for copyright infringements by their users. (In the settlement, the students admitted no wrongdoing but agreed to pay amounts ranging from $12,000 to $17,500 in annual installments over several years and to shut down their file-sharing systems.)

With so many Internet users currently sharing music, legal maneuvers alone 5 seem unlikely to protect the industry's way of doing business. Therefore, the music industry has turned to the technology itself, seeking to create media that cannot be copied or can be copied only in prescribed circumstances. Finding the right technology for such a defense, however, is not easy. Defensive technology must not prevent legitimate uses of the media by customers, yet it must somehow ward off attacks by those seeking to "liberate" the content to the Internet. And each announcement of a defensive technology spurs development of means to circumvent it.

In apparent frustration, some companies have introduced defective copies of their music into the file-sharing environment of the Internet, hoping to discourage widespread downloading of music. But so far, the industry's multifaceted defense has failed. Sales of CDs continue to decline. And now video ripping and sharing is emerging on the Internet, threatening to upset another industry in the same way.

Music companies might have more success if they focused on the users instead of the courts and technology. When they characterize file sharing as theft, they overlook the interplay of technology and behavior that has altered the very idea of theft, at least among young people. I got a clear demonstration of that change in a class discussion that began with the matter of a stolen book.

During the '60s, I was a graduate student at a university where student activism had raised tensions on and around the campus. In the midst of debates, demonstrations, and protests, a football player was caught leaving the campus store with a book he had not bought. Because he was well known, his misadventure made the school newspaper. What seemed to be a simple case of theft, however, took on greater significance. A number of groups with little connection to athletics rose to his defense, claiming that he had been entrapped: The university required that he have the book, the publisher charged an unfairly high price, and the bookstore put the book right in front of him, tempting him to steal it. So who could blame him?

Well, my students could. They thought it was clear that he had stolen the book. But an MP3 file played from my laptop evoked a different response. Had I stolen the song? Not really, because a student had given me the file as a gift. Well, was that file stolen property? Was it like the book stolen from the campus bookstore so many years ago? No again, because it was a copy, nct the original, which presumably was with the student. But then what should we make of the typical admonition on compact-disc covers that unauthorized duplication is illegal? Surely the MP3 file was a duplication of the original. To what extent is copying stealing?

The readings for the class amply demonstrated the complexity of the legal, technical, and economic issues surrounding intellectual property in the information age and gave the students much to talk about. Some students argued that existing regulations are simply inadequate at a time when all information "wants to be free" and when liberating technology is at hand. Others pointed to differences in the economics of the music and book businesses. In the end, the students who saw theft in the removal of the book back in the '60s did not see stealing in the unauthorized copying of music. For me, that was the most memorable aspect of the class because it illustrates how technology affects what we take to be moral behavior.

The technology of copying is closely related to the idea of theft. For example, my students would not take books from a store, but they do not consider photocopying a few pages of a book to be theft. They would not copy an entire book, however, perhaps because they vaguely acknowledge intellectual-property rights but probably more because copying would be cumbersome and time-consuming. They would buy the book instead. In that case, the very awkwardness of the copying aligns their actions with moral guidelines and legal standards.

But in the case of digital music, where the material is disconnected from the physical moorings of conventional stores and copying is so easy, many of my students see matters differently. They freely copy and share music. And they copy and share software, even though such copying is often illegal. If their books were digital and thus could be copied with comparable ease, they most likely would copy and share them.

Of course, the Digital Millennium Copyright Act, along with other laws, prohibits such copying. So we could just say that theft is theft, and complain with the song, "Why can't they be like we were, perfect in every way? . . . Oh, what's the matter with kids today?" But had we had the same digital technology when we were young, we probably would have engaged in the same copying and sharing of software, digital music, and video that are so common among students today. We should not confuse lack of tools with righteousness.

The music industry would be foolish to put its faith in new protective schemes and devices alone. Protective technology cannot undo the changes that previous technology has caused. Should the industry aggressively pursue legal defenses like the suits against the four college students? Such highly publicized actions may be legally sound and may even slow music sharing in certain settings, but they cannot stop the transformation of the music business. The technology of sharing is too widespread, and my students (and their younger siblings) no longer agree with the music companies about right and wrong. Even some of the companies with big stakes in recorded music seem to have recognized that lawsuits and technical defenses won't work. Sony, for example, sells computers with "ripping and burning" capabilities, MP3 players, and other devices that gain much of their appeal from music sharing. And the AOL part of AOL Time Warner is promoting its new broadband service for faster downloads, which many people will use to share music sold by the Warner part of the company.

The lesson from my classroom is that digital technology has unalterably 15 changed the way a growing number of customers think about recorded music. If the music industry is to prosper, it must change, too—perhaps offering repositories of digital music for downloading (like Apple's newly announced iTunes Music Store), gaining revenue from the scope and quality of its holdings, and from a variety of new products and relationships, as yet largely undefined. Such a transformation will be excruciating for the industry, requiring the abandonment of previously profitable business practices with no certain prospect of success. So it is not surprising that the industry has responded aggressively, with strong legal actions, to the spread of file sharing. But by that response, the industry is risking its relationship with a vital segment of its market. Treating customers like thieves is a certain recipe for failure.

QUESTIONS FOR DISCUSSION AND WRITING

1. Gorry claims that "technology affects what we take to be moral behavior" (paragraph 10). To what extent do you agree that ease of copying changes the way people feel about copying music files versus copying textbooks? (paragraph 11).

2. The music file on Gorry's laptop should not be considered stolen because it was a copy, according to his students (paragraph 9). By this criterion, copying is ethically permissible but stealing is not. If copying is ethical, however, why is copying a classmate's final exam answer forbidden in academia?

3. If you make copies of MP3 files or share them with friends, write an essay explaining why this infraction of the copyright law is permissible or why you feel justified in not paying the musicians for their work. It might help to research the U.S. copyright laws concerning music files to lend more authority to your argument. Or write the essay with a partner who disagrees with you; each of you will need to justify and support your respective point of view.

4. Write about a change in technology that has impacted ethical decision making. For example, to what extent has the use of birth control methods affected people's sexual behavior? What moral issues in professional or amateur sports have been raised by the availability of steroid drugs? Where do you stand on these issues? Support your claims with evidence and detailed arguments.

MICHAEL J. BUGEJA

Facing the Facebook

Poet, professor, ethicist, and academic administrator Michael J. Bugeja (pronounced "boo-shay-ah") was born (1952) in Hackensack, New Jersey, and attended St. Peter's College, New Jersey (B.A., 1974). After graduate study at South Dakota State University (M.S., 1976) and Oklahoma State University (Ph.D., 1985), he worked for United Press International before becoming a journalism professor. Bugeja is currently director of the Greenlee School of Journalism and Communication at Iowa State University. An author of several books of poetry and a regular contributor to literary magazines, Bugeja is also a prolific nonfiction writer. Culture's Sleeping Beauty: Essays on Poetry, Prejudice, and Belief *(1992) is about literature and spirituality, while* Academic Socialism: Merit and Moral in Higher Education *(1994) and* Living Ethics: Developing Values in Mass Communication *(1996) are concerned with value systems and institutions. His recent study,* Interpersonal Divide: The Search for Community in a Technological Age *(2005), deals with the interpersonal dimensions of our computerized society.*

"Facing the Facebook," first published in the Chronicle of Higher Education *(January 2006), surveys one of the most popular online student identity networks. This virtual subculture absorbs thousands of student-hours, yet many professors are unaware of its existence. Bugeja argues that the ethical and educational consequences of the time students spend online need more attention. Colleges like to invest in technology, but technology could be undermining their educational goal, which is "to inspire critical thinking in learners rather than multitasking."*

Information technology in the classroom was supposed to bridge digital divides and enhance student research. Increasingly, however, our networks are being used to entertain members of "the Facebook Generation" who text-message during class, talk on their cell phones during labs, and listen to iPods rather than guest speakers in the wireless lecture hall.

That is true at my institution, Iowa State University. With a total enrollment of 25,741, Iowa State logs 20,247 registered users on *Facebook*, which bills itself as "an online directory that connects people through social networks at schools." While I'd venture to say that most of the students on any campus are regular visitors to Facebook.com, many professors and administrators have yet to hear about Facebook, let alone evaluate its impact.

On many levels, Facebook is fascinating—an interactive, image-laden directory featuring groups that share lifestyles or attitudes. Many students find it addictive, as evidenced by discussion groups with names like "Addicted to the Facebook," which boasts 330 members at Iowa State. Nationwide, Facebook tallies 250 million hits every day and ranks ninth in overall traffic on the Internet.

That kind of social networking affects all levels of academe:

- Institutions seeking to build enrollment learn that "technology" rates higher than "rigor" or "reputation" in high-school focus groups. That may pressure provosts and deans to continue investing in technology rather than in tenure-track positions.
- Professors and librarians encounter improper use of technology by students, and some of those cases go to judiciary officials enforcing the student code.
- Career and academic advisers must deal with employers and parents who have screened Facebook and discovered what users have been up to in residence halls.
- Finally, academics assessing learning outcomes often discover that technology is as much a distraction in the classroom as a tool.

To be sure, classroom distractions have plagued teachers in less technological times. In my era, there was the ubiquitous comic book hidden in a boring text. A comic book cannot compare with a computer, of course. Neither did it require university money at the expense of faculty jobs.

John W. Curtis, research director at the American Association of University Professors, believes that investment in technology is one of several factors responsible for the well-documented loss of tenured positions in the past decade. "We often hear the assertion that rising faculty salaries drive the cost of tuition," he says, but data over 25 years show that is not the case. "One of the several sources behind rising tuition rates is investment in technology."

Facebook is not the sole source for those woes. However, it is a Janus-faced symbol of the online habits of students and the traditional objectives of higher education, one of which is to inspire critical thinking in learners rather than multitasking. The situation will only get worse as freshmen enter our institutions weaned on high-school versions of the Facebook and equipped with gaming devices, cell phones, iPods, and other portable technologies.

Michael Tracey, a journalism professor at the University of Colorado, recounts a class discussion during which he asked how many people had seen the previous night's *NewsHour* on PBS or read that day's *New York Times*. "A couple of hands went up out of about 140 students who were present," he recalls. "One student chirped: 'Ask them how many use Facebook.' I did. Every hand in the room went up. She then said: 'Ask them how many used it today.' I did. Every hand in the room went up. I was amazed."

Christine Rosen, a fellow at the Ethics and Public Policy Center in Washington, believes experiences like that are an example of what she calls "egocasting, the thoroughly personalized and extremly narrow pursuit of one's personal taste."

"Facebook is an interesting example of the egocasting phenomenon," she   10
says, "because it encourages egocasting even though it claims to further 'social networking' and build communities." Unlike real communities, however, most interactions in online groups do not take place face-to-face. "It would be more accurate to call it 'Imagebook' rather than 'Facebook,'" Rosen says, "because users first see an image of a face, not the face itself, and identities are constructed and easily manipulated (and often not truthful)." It's no surprise, she says, that "people who use networks like Facebook have a tendency to describe themselves like products."

To test that, I registered on the Iowa State Facebook and noticed that the discussion groups looked a lot like direct mailing lists. Some, in fact, are the same or barely distinguishable from mailing lists compiled in *The Lifestyle Market Analyst*, a reference book that looks at potential audiences for advertisers. For instance, "Baseball Addicts" and "Kick Ass Conservatives" are Facebook groups while "Baseball Fanatics" and "Iowa Conservatives" are the names of commercial mailing lists. You can find "PC Gamers," "Outdoor Enthusiasts," and advocates for and against gun control on both Facebook and in marketing directories. Several Facebook groups resemble advertisements for products or lifestyles such as "Apple Macintosh Users," "Avid Sweatpants Users," or "Brunettes Having More Fun."

"It is ironic," Rosen said, "that the technologies we embrace and praise for the degree of control they give us individually also give marketers and advertisers the most direct window into our psyche and buying habits they've ever had."

Online networks like Facebook allow high levels of surveillance, she adds, and not just for marketers. "College administrators are known to troll the profiles on Facebook for evidence of illegal behavior by students," she said. "Students might think they are merely crafting and surfing a vast network of peers, but because their Facebook profile is, in essence, a public diary, there is nothing to stop anyone else—from marketers, to parents, to college officials—from reading it as well."

Her comments bear out. For instance, a panel at the University of Missouri at Columbia has been formed to educate students on Facebook content that may violate student-conduct policies or local laws. A Duquesne University student was asked to write a paper because the Facebook group he created was deemed homophobic. Students at Northern Kentucky University were charged with code violations when a keg was seen in a dorm-room picture online, and a University of Oklahoma student was visited by the Secret Service because of assassination references in comments regarding President Bush.

My concerns are mostly ethical. In my field, I know of students who show- 15 case inappropriate pictures of partners or use stereotypes to describe themselves and others on Facebook. What does that mean in terms of taste, sensitivity, and bias?

I know of online disclosures of substance abuse that have come back to haunt students under investigation for related offenses. I know of fictitious Facebook personae that masquerade as administrators, including college presidents. Such inventions mirror the fabricated sources and situations used by Stephen Glass in articles for *The New Republic* and other publications before his deceptions were exposed in 1998.

Facebook forbids such fabrications. According to Chris Hughes, a spokesman, misrepresentation is against the "Terms of Service." "In other words," he says, "you can't create a profile for Tom Cruise using your account. When users report a profile, we take a look and decide if the content seems authentic. If not, we'll remove the user from the network."

Shortly after interviewing Hughes, I heard from Michael Tracey, the Colorado journalism professor, who learned that an account had been opened in his name on MySpace, another networking site, "with photos and all kinds of weird details." He suspects one of the students from the course he spoke with me about is behind the ruse.

Unless we reassess our high-tech priorities, issues associated with insensitivity, indiscretion, bias, and fabrication will consume us in higher education. Potential solutions will challenge core beliefs concerning digital divides, pedagogies, budget allocations, and, above all, our duty to instill critical thinking in multitaskers.

Christine Rosen believes that "those who run institutions of higher learn- 20 ing have embraced technology as a means of furthering education. But they have failed to realize that the younger generation views technology largely as a means of delivering entertainment—be it music, video games, Internet access, or television—and secondarily, as a means of communicating."

"Technology," she adds, "also provides new and unusual ways to isolate oneself from opinions or ideas that make us uncomfortable, from people who we would rather not have to know, from those often-awkward social interactions with strangers in public spaces. In the college context this is more worrisome since part of the purpose of a liberal education is to expose students to ideas that challenge them to think in new ways and expose them to things that they hadn't known about before."

What can we do in the short term about the misuse of technology, especially in wireless locales? The Facebook's spokesman, Hughes, is not overly concerned. He notes that students who use computers in classrooms and labs routinely perform "a host of activities online while listening to lectures," like checking their e-mail, sending instant messages, or reading the news. "Usage of Facebook during class," he says, "doesn't strike me as being that different than usage of any of those other tools. If professors don't want their students to have access to the Internet during class," Hughes adds, "they can remove wireless installations or ask their students not to bring computers to class."

Some less-drastic measures include clauses in syllabi warning against using Facebook or other nonassigned Internet sites during class. Some professors punish students who violate such rules and reward those who visit the library. Still others have stopped using technology in the classroom, forcing students to listen, debate, and otherwise hone their interpersonal skills.

A few institutions are assessing how to respond to Facebook and similar digital distractions. Last fall the University of New Mexico blocked access to Facebook because of security concerns. My preference is not to block content but to instill in students what I call "interpersonal intelligence," or the ability to discern when, where, and for what purpose technology may be appropriate or inappropriate.

That, alas, requires critical thinking and suggests that we have reached a point   25
where we must make hard decisions about our investment in technology and our tradition of high standards. Because the students already have.

QUESTIONS FOR DISCUSSION AND WRITING

1. Although colleges spend millions of dollars on computer technology for their students' use, many professors are unaware of the amount of time students spend on networks such as Facebook, argues Michael J. Bugeja. What problems does he attribute to the use of this online community? What does Facebook have to do with ethical questions such as surveillance, illegal behavior, insensitivity, and homophobia?

2. University administrators are obviously patrolling the Facebook community in some colleges—students have been disciplined for posting content that violates conduct policies, as in the case where a keg appeared in a dorm-room picture online. To what extent do administrators have the right to use Facebook as a surveillance tool? Are students' rights being violated in such cases? Why or why not?

3. Ask two people—a professor or college administrator and yourself or another student—the following questions and write a paper on your findings, addressing the role of Facebook or comparable phenomena in college culture. Do you think that Internet services such as Facebook have a predominantly positive or negative effect on our culture? What is the predominant type of information exchanged or learned via these networks? What would change, in your life or in college culture in general, if Facebook and MySpace became unavailable? Would these changes be for the better or for worse? Is there any consensus among those polled? On what do your respondents agree? Disagree? Explain why.

4. As a class project, write a collaborative paper on Facebook, explaining this social and technological phenomenon to the uninitiated. Include an explanation of what Facebook is and what it does, why students use it, what typical ways it is used, and any important issues or problems connected with Facebook activities. You might want to interview students in or outside the class, using a question-naire to gather quantitative data (e.g., hours spent using Facebook, types of use, number of Facebook "friends" listed). You could also structure this project around a particular issue, such as Internet addiction or whether Facebook is a community-building technology.

FRANK GANNON

Pre-approved for Platinum

Gannon's satires, parodies, and essays appear frequently in The New Yorker, GQ, *and a variety of other magazines including* Harper's, Atlantic Monthly, *and the* New York Times Magazine. *Gannon (b. 1952), who was educated at the University of Georgia (B.A., 1974; M.A., 1977) and lives in Georgia, has published an acerbic memoir,* Midlife Irish: Discovering My Family and Myself *(2003); and* Vanna Karenina and Other Reflections *(1988), a collection of his* New Yorker *writings. His humorous, self-deprecating commentary is characteristic: "I guess that my books . . . are about my hopeless inability to have values, thoughts, and beliefs like other writers. I had a very happy childhood, and I've had a very nice life, so I can't really blame anybody. But, given enough time, I probably will."*

"Pre-approved for Platinum," first published in The New Yorker *(2005), satirizes the credit card industry's insidious, insincere sales pitch in tone, language, and attitude. Would you, "a breed apart," ever fall for such a pitch?*

Dear Occupant:

You've been pre-approved! What does that mean? Let us tell you.

Just the other day, we were sitting around asking ourselves, "Where are we going to find exactly the kind of person we need?" This was a hard question, because our standards and specifications are stringent. We spent weeks asking ourselves this question. We got sick of looking at one another because we were meeting so often with the same people and asking the same question over and over. One of us started to ridicule another one of us for his slight Midwestern "twang." Another one of us broke down sobbing. It was a trying period. There were some pretty heated confrontations in there, let me tell you! Some of us didn't make it.

But, finally, after countless cups of coffee and cigarettes and frantic phone calls and consultations and trips to the bathroom and looking things up in the dictionary and the thesaurus and just throwing our hands up in despair, we came up with somebody. And that somebody just happened to be someone you know—you!

We know you. You are a person who appreciates life. You know how to savor the little things. You know how a good bowl of chicken soup is supposed to taste, and you're not settling for crap. *What is this? Take it away and bring me some real soup. I don't drink dishwater. Now go!* You've said that more than once.

You appreciate the opposite sex. You like them as people, and you hate it 5 when they are treated as one-dimensional objects. They're not playthings. You hate the way they can bump into a "glass ceiling" sometimes. You hate unfairness. You've hated it since you were a child. Life is too short for a playing field that is not precisely level. It makes you upset if anyone even alludes to it. Because you know that a member of the opposite sex is a three-dimensional being whose features are composed in a pleasant way. A way that you find exciting. And you're not ashamed of that.

We know what kinds of actions you like to take. We don't have to spell things out for you. We don't think that you are the sort of person who wants everything explained. Because you already know a whole lot. You couldn't even get everything you know into a book. Forget about books—you couldn't get everything you know into a room. Unless the room is really pretty big, like a garage.

We're not limiting you. Limits aren't for you. Even the sky isn't your limit. That's why we know you're going to take advantage of our one-time offer to consolidate all of your credit-card debt into one account with one easy-to-remember card. And your wallet is going to have that "sleek" look that the wallets owned by so many of the truly knowledgeable people have.

That look isn't for everyone. Most people have huge bulgy wallets with stuff sticking out. They can't even take their wallets out of their pockets without a bunch of lint and gum wrappers coming out with them. They look like such idiots when they do that. They look, truth be told, like they have brain damage. Like they need someone to go with them and open the door for them and remind them to pay for things before they walk out with a bunch of stuff and get arrested. Frankly, that's what they deserve. Some hard prison time. Maybe that will straighten them out. It can't hurt.

They just can't own up to it, though. They say their mother never taught them the right way to act. Then they go and blame it on her. That is pathetic.

You're not like that, and I and the other people here would just like to say 10 that we appreciate people like you. You're a breed apart. You're going to be enjoying zero-per-cent interest for the first six months. Then you will have a truly great variable rate of 9.4 per cent. But those bulgy-wallet people won't. May they rot in Hell. We hate to use language like that, but sometimes it just fits. This really couldn't happen to a better person. God didn't make many of you. We mean that.

QUESTIONS FOR DISCUSSION AND WRITING

1. In what ways does the salutation "Dear Occupant" undercut the writer's claims that the recipient is unique and special, "a breed apart"?

2. How could the writer know all of these alleged "facts" about "Occupant"? Why is this sales pitch written in the plural?

3. What evidence does the writer present to show how discriminating "Occupant" is? Is it likely that "Occupant" would say, of inferior chicken soup, *Take it away and bring me some real soup. I don't drink dishwater. Now go!"* (paragraph 4)?

4. Paragraphs 5, 6, and 7 are full of clichés. Why use so many in writing to "Occupant," who is allegedly superior to such trite language?

5. Write a satiric sales-pitch letter to an anonymous recipient, appealing to his or her vanity, and designed to extract something from the victim (money, purchases, action) that he or she would ordinarily resist.

BRIEF TAKES ON ETHICAL CODES: PRESCRIPTIONS FOR THE GOOD LIFE

The first three of the following moral and ethical principles represent major philosophical and religious traditions: Confucianism, Judeo-Christianity, and Islam. The Analects, *or sayings, of Confucius (551–479 B.C.E.) were collected by his followers posthumously.* The Ten Commandments *are said to have been handed down by God to Moses on Mount Sinai about 1445 B.C.E. Fundamentals of Islam are excerpted from* Sahih Bukhari, *a collection of the Prophet Muhammad's (570–632 C.E.) sayings and deeds.*

The excerpts from The Analects *presented here focus on the ethical and moral philosophy of Confucius, which stresses self-restraint and compassion for others to enable the individual to live in harmony with nature and the cosmos.* The Ten Commandments *form a moral code of behavior guiding individuals' relations with God and with one another; they play a prominent role in Judaism, Islam, and Christianity.* Fundamentals of Islam *also form a code of ethical behavior. These excerpts illustrate some differences in the three philosophical traditions: Confucianism emphasizes individual physical and mental self-discipline and Islamic and Judeo-Christian traditions stipulate the practices of religious observance as well as specify prohibitions relevant to private and public life. The Society of Professional Journalists, like many other professional societies, has established its code of ethics, continually revised, to ensure appropriate professional behavior and maintain public trust.*

Three of these codes are centuries old, the fourth is a contemporary set of ethical principles for journalists. As you read and compare them, consider reasons that the first three endure. What do they offer for today's citizens—American or throughout the world? Do they need updating or modifications to be relevant? Which, if any, of these principles does the Society of Professional Journalists incorporate? Individually or with a group, perhaps professional or preprofessional, develop a code of ethics, say ten or a dozen principles, for your personal guidance (see also Benjamin Franklin, "Arriving at Moral Perfection," p. 339). Will your code always be operative? Are there exceptions? If so, what are they and under what circumstances would they be overridden?

CONFUCIUS

The Analects

FROM BOOK I, XUE ER

The virtuous man does not seek to gratify his appetite in foods, nor does he seek the appliances of ease in his dwelling place; earnest in action and careful in speech, he seeks the company of men of moral principle so that he may be rectified.—chap. 14

FROM BOOK II, WEI ZHENG

To know that you know what you know, and to know that you do not know what you do not know, that is true knowledge. — chap. 17

FROM BOOK IV, LI REN

All men desire wealth and honor, but the virtuous man does not seek them through inappropriate ways; all men dislike poverty and humiliation, but the virtuous man does not avoid them through inappropriate ways. — chap. 5

I am not concerned that I have no honorable social status; I am concerned how I may fit myself for one. I am not concerned that I am not famous; I seek to be worthy of being known. — chap. 14

Upon seeing an honorable man, emulate him; upon seeing a man of questionable character, turn inward and examine yourself. — chap. 17

FROM BOOK VII, SHU ER

Eating coarse foods, drinking plain water, and using my bent arm for a pillow, I still find happiness in such a lifestyle. Wealth and status acquired by unrighteous ways are to me as ephemeral as a floating cloud. — chap. 16

FROM BOOK XV, LORD WEILING

For the virtuous man righteousness is essential in everything: he performs it with propriety, he utters it in humility, and he completes it in honesty. Such a virtuous man! — chap. 18

[When asked by one of his disciples whether there was one word that may serve as a rule of practice for all one's life,] Confucius responded, "Is not reciprocity such a word? What you do not want to be done to yourself, do not do to others." — chap. 24

The uncorrected error is the real error. — chap. 30

Teach them and never mind what classes they are from. — chap. 39

The Ten Commandments

And God spoke all these words, saying,

"I am the LORD your God, who brought you out of the land of Egypt, out of the house of bondage.

"You shall have no other gods before me.

"You shall not make for yourself a graven image, or any likeness of anything that is in heaven above, or that is in the earth beneath, or that is in the water under the earth; you shall not bow down to them or serve them; for I the LORD your God am a jealous God, visiting the iniquity of the fathers upon the children to the third and the fourth generation of those who hate me, but showing steadfast love to thousands of those who love me and keep my commandments.

"You shall not take the name of the LORD your God in vain; for the LORD will   5 not hold him guiltless who takes his name in vain.

"Remember the sabbath day, to keep it holy. Six days you shall labor, and do all your work; but the seventh day is a sabbath to the LORD your God; in it you shall not do any work, you, or your son, or your daughter, your manservant, or your maidservant, or your cattle, or the sojourner who is within your gates; for in six days the LORD made heaven and earth, the sea, and all that is in them, and rested the seventh day; therefore the LORD blessed the sabbath day and hallowed it.

"Honor your father and your mother, that your days may be long in the land which the LORD your God gives you.

"You shall not kill.

"You shall not commit adultery.

"You shall not steal.   10

"You shall not bear false witness against your neighbor.

"You shall not covet your neighbor's house; you shall not covet your neighbor's wife, or his manservant, or his maidservant, or his ox, or his ass, or anything that is your neighbor's."

Now when all the people perceived the thunderings and the lightnings and the sound of the trumpet and the mountain smoking, the people were afraid and trembled; and they stood afar off, and said to Moses, "You speak to us, and we will hear; but let not God speak to us, lest we die." And Moses said to the people, "Do not fear; for God has come to prove you, and that the fear of him may be before your eyes, that you may not sin."

Fundamentals of Islam

Narrated Ibn 'Umar:

Allah's Apostle said: Islam is based on (the following) five (principles):

1. To testify that none has the right to be worshipped but Allah and Muhammad is Allah's Apostle.

2. To offer the (compulsory congregational) prayers dutifully and perfectly.
3. To pay Zakat (i.e., obligatory charity).
4. To perform Hajj (i.e., Pilgrimage to Mecca).
5. To observe fast during the month of Ramadan. (*Volume 1, Book 2, Number 7*). . . .

Narrated 'Ubada bin As-Samit:

1. Not to join anything in worship along with Allah.
2. Not to steal.
3. Not to commit illegal sexual intercourse.
4. Not to kill your children.
5. Not to accuse an innocent person (to spread such an accusation among people).
6. Not to be disobedient (when ordered) to do [a] good deed.

The Prophet added: "Whoever among you fulfills his pledge will be rewarded by Allah. And whoever indulges in any one of them (except the ascription of partners to Allah) and gets the punishment in this world, that punishment will be an expiation for that sin. And if one indulges in any of them, and Allah conceals his sin, it is up to Him to forgive or punish him (in the Hereafter)." (*Volume 1, Book 2, Number 17*). . . .

Narrated Abu Jamra:
The Prophet ordered them to do four things and forbade them from four things. He ordered them to believe in Allah Alone and asked them, "Do you know what is meant by believing in Allah Alone?" They replied, "Allah and His Apostle know better." Thereupon the Prophet said, "It means:

1. To testify that none has the right to be worshipped but Allah and Muhammad is Allah's Apostle.
2. To offer prayers perfectly.
3. To pay the Zakat (obligatory charity).
4. To observe fast during the month of Ramadan.
5. And to pay Al-Khumus (one fifth of the booty to be given in Allah's Cause).

Then he forbade them four things, namely, Hantam, Dubba', Naqir Ann Muzaffat or Muqaiyar. (These were the names of pots in which alcoholic drinks were prepared. The Prophet mentioned the container of wine and he meant the wine itself.) The Prophet further said (to them): "Memorize them (these instructions) and convey them to the people whom you have left behind." (*Volume 1, Book 2, Number 50*)

SOCIETY OF PROFESSIONAL JOURNALISTS
Code of Ethics

PREAMBLE

Members of the Society of Professional Journalists believe that public enlightenment is the forerunner of justice and the foundation of democracy. The duty of the journalist is to further those ends by seeking truth and providing a fair and comprehensive account of events and issues. Conscientious journalists from all media and specialties strive to serve the public with thoroughness and honesty. Professional integrity is the cornerstone of a journalist's credibility. Members of the Society share a dedication to ethical behavior and adopt this code to declare the Society's principles and standards of practice.

SEEK TRUTH AND REPORT IT

Journalists should be honest, fair and courageous in gathering, reporting and interpreting information.

Journalists should:

- Test the accuracy of information from all sources and exercise care to avoid inadvertent error. Deliberate distortion is never permissible.
- Diligently seek out subjects of news stories to give them the opportunity to respond to allegations of wrongdoing.
- Identify sources whenever feasible. The public is entitled to as much information as possible on sources' reliability.
- Always question sources' motives before promising anonymity. Clarify conditions attached to any promise made in exchange for information. Keep promises.
- Make certain that headlines, news teases and promotional material, photos, video, audio, graphics, sound bites and quotations do not misrepresent. They should not oversimplify or highlight incidents out of context.
- Never distort the content of news photos or video. Image enhancement for technical clarity is always permissible. Label montages and photo illustrations.
- Avoid misleading re-enactments or staged news events. If re-enactment is necessary to tell a story, label it.
- Avoid undercover or other surreptitious methods of gathering information except when traditional open methods will not yield information vital to the public. Use of such methods should be explained as part of the story.
- Never plagiarize.
- Tell the story of the diversity and magnitude of the human experience boldly, even when it is unpopular to do so.
- Examine their own cultural values and avoid imposing those values on others.

- Avoid stereotyping by race, gender, age, religion, ethnicity, geography, sexual orientation, disability, physical appearance or social status.
- Support the open exchange of views, even views they find repugnant.
- Give voice to the voiceless; official and unofficial sources of information can be equally valid.
- Distinguish between advocacy and news reporting. Analysis and commentary should be labeled and not misrepresent fact or context.
- Distinguish news from advertising and shun hybrids that blur the lines between the two.
- Recognize a special obligation to ensure that the public's business is conducted in the open and that government records are open to inspection.

MINIMIZE HARM

Ethical journalists treat sources, subjects and colleagues as human beings deserving of respect.

Journalists should:

- Show compassion for those who may be affected adversely by news coverage. Use special sensitivity when dealing with children and inexperienced sources or subjects.
- Be sensitive when seeking or using interviews or photographs of those affected by tragedy or grief.
- Recognize that gathering and reporting information may cause harm or discomfort. Pursuit of the news is not a license for arrogance.
- Recognize that private people have a greater right to control information about themselves than do public officials and others who seek power, influence or attention. Only an overriding public need can justify intrusion into anyone's privacy.
- Show good taste. Avoid pandering to lurid curiosity.
- Be cautious about identifying juvenile suspects or victims of sex crimes.
- Be judicious about naming criminal suspects before the formal filing of charges.
- Balance a criminal suspect's fair trial rights with the public's right to be informed.

ACT INDEPENDENTLY

Journalists should be free of obligation to any interest other than the public's right to know.

Journalists should:

- Avoid conflicts of interest, real or perceived.
- Remain free of associations and activities that may compromise integrity or damage credibility.

- Refuse gifts, favors, fees, free travel and special treatment, and shun secondary employment, political involvement, public office and service in community organizations if they compromise journalistic integrity.
- Disclose unavoidable conflicts.
- Be vigilant and courageous about holding those with power accountable.
- Deny favored treatment to advertisers and special interests and resist their pressure to influence news coverage.
- Be wary of sources offering information for favors or money; avoid bidding for news.

BE ACCOUNTABLE

Journalists are accountable to their readers, listeners, viewers and each other.
Journalists should:

- Clarify and explain news coverage and invite dialogue with the public over journalistic conduct.
- Encourage the public to voice grievances against the news media.
- Admit mistakes and correct them promptly.
- Expose unethical practices of journalists and the news media.
- Abide by the same high standards to which they hold others.

CHAPTER 9

The Twenty-First-Century World: Issues of Ecology, War and Peace, Spirituality

ANNIE DILLARD

Heaven and Earth in Jest

Dillard was born (1945) and raised in Pittsburgh, where indulgent parents encouraged her interests in the natural world and art. In An American Childhood *(1987) she portrays herself as a curious, imaginative risk-taker, and ultimately a teenage rebel against her church (Presbyterian) but inspired by life's possibilities: "Why not . . . write an epic, become a medical missionary to the Amazon?" She studied creative writing at Hollins College (B.A., 1967; M.A., 1968) and soon became a literary superstar, with the publication of Pulitzer Prize-winning* Pilgrim at Tinker Creek *(1974). In all of her works, whether poetry (*Tickets for a Prayer Wheel, *1974), commentary on writing (*The Writing Life, *1989), or fiction (*The Living, *1992), Dillard, sometimes labeled an* eco-theologist, *maintains her eclectic, impassioned, eloquent contemplation of God's presence—or absence.*

In her most popular book, Pilgrim at Tinker Creek, *from which the following selection is excerpted, Dillard's work is play. For a year in her cabin beside Tinker Creek, she plays Thoreau at Walden Pond (see p. 649). She takes on his character as a self-reliant, spiritually oriented naturalist who finds transcendental meaning in animals and plants—indeed in all aspects of the natural world. She closely observes details: exactly how a giant water bug consumes a frog, how a frog consumes dragonflies. A stalker of animals, she also stalks and consumes ideas from the Koran to writings by Blaise Pascal and Nikos Kazantzakis. She stalks readers as well, embellishing her precisely detailed observations with both analyses and verbal cartoons: a panicked frog she startles emits "a froggy 'Yike!'" and splashes into the water. Indeed, the commentary following "Heaven and Earth in Jest" examines the workings of figurative language, such as metaphor and allusions to people, events, and other authors' works—ways of enriching the natural history, the theology.*

I used to have a cat, an old fighting tom, who would jump through the open window by my bed in the middle of the night and land on my chest. I'd half-awaken. He'd stick his skull under my nose and purr, stinking of urine and blood. Some nights he kneaded my bare chest with his front paws, powerfully, arching his back, as if sharpening his claws, or pummeling a mother for milk. And some mornings I'd wake in daylight to find my body covered with paw prints in blood; I looked as though I'd been painted with roses.

It was hot, so hot the mirror felt warm. I washed before the mirror in a daze, my twisted summer sleep still hung about me like sea kelp. What blood was this, and what roses? It could have been the rose of union, the blood of murder, or the rose of beauty bare and the blood of some unspeakable sacrifice or birth. The sign on my body could have been an emblem or a stain, the keys to the kingdom or the mark of Cain. I never knew. I never knew as I washed, and the blood streaked, faded, and finally disappeared, whether I'd purified myself or ruined the blood sign of the passover. We wake, if we ever wake at all, to mystery, rumors of death, beauty, violence. . . . "Seem like we're just set down here," a woman said to me recently, "and don't nobody know why."

These are morning matters, pictures you dream as the final wave heaves you up on the sand to the bright light and drying air. You remember pressure, and a curved sleep you rested against, soft, like a scallop in its shell. But the air hardens your skin; you stand; you leave the lighted shore to explore some dim headland, and soon you're lost in the leafy interior, intent, remembering nothing.

I still think of that old tomcat, mornings, when I wake. Things are tamer now; I sleep with the window shut. The cat and our rites are gone and my life is changed, but the memory remains of something powerful playing over me. I wake expectant, hoping to see a new thing. If I'm lucky I might be jogged awake by a strange birdcall. I dress in a hurry, imagining the yard flapping with auks, or flamingos. This morning it was a wood duck, down at the creek. It flew away.

I live by a creek, Tinker Creek, in a valley in Virginia's Blue Ridge. An anchorite's hermitage is called an anchor-hold; some anchor-holds were simple sheds clamped to the side of a church like a barnacle to a rock. I think of this house clamped to the side of Tinker Creek as an anchor-hold. It holds me at anchor to the rock bottom of the creek itself and it keeps me steadied in the current, as a sea anchor does, facing the stream of light pouring down. It's a good place to live; there's a lot to think about. The creeks—Tinker and Carvin's—are an active mystery, fresh every minute. Theirs is the mystery of the continuous creation and all that providence implies: the uncertainty of vision, the horror of the fixed, the dissolution of the present, the intricacy of beauty, the pressure of fecundity, the elusiveness of the free, and the flawed nature of perfection. The mountains— Tinker and Brushy, McAfee's Knob and Dead Man—are a passive mystery, the oldest of all. Theirs is the one simple mystery of creation from nothing, of matter itself, anything at all, the given. Mountains are giant, restful, absorbent. You can heave your spirit into a mountain and the mountain will keep it, folded, and not throw it back as some creeks will. The creeks are the world with all its stimulus and beauty; I live there. But the mountains are home.

The wood duck flew away. I caught only a glimpse of something like a bright torpedo that blasted the leaves where it flew. Back at the house I ate a bowl of oatmeal; much later in the day came the long slant of light that means good walking.

If the day is fine, any walk will do; it all looks good. Water in particular looks its best, reflecting blue sky in the flat, and chopping it into graveled shallows and white chute and foam in the riffles. On a dark day, or a hazy one, everything's washed-out and lackluster but the water. It carries its own lights. I set out for the railroad tracks, for the hill the flocks fly over, for the woods where the white mare lives. But I go to the water.

Today is one of those excellent January partly cloudies in which light chooses an unexpected part of the landscape to trick out in gilt, and then shadow sweeps it away. You know you're alive. You take huge steps, trying to feel the planet's roundness arc between your feet. Kazantzakis says that when he was young he had a canary and a globe. When he freed the canary, it would perch on the globe and sing. All his life, wandering the earth, he felt as though he had a canary on top of his mind, singing.

West of the house, Tinker Creek makes a sharp loop, so that the creek is both in back of the house, south of me, and also on the other side of the road, north of me. I like to go north. There the afternoon sun hits the creek just right, deepening the reflected blue and lighting the sides of trees on the banks. Steers from the pasture across the creek come down to drink; I always flush a rabbit or two there; I sit on a fallen trunk in the shade and watch the squirrels in the sun. There are two separated wooden fences suspended from cables that cross the creek just upstream from my tree-trunk bench. They keep the steers from escaping up or down the creek when they come to drink. Squirrels, the neighborhood children, and I use the downstream fence as a swaying bridge across the creek. But the steers are there today.

I sit on the downed tree and watch the black steers slip on the creek bottom. 10
They are all bred beef: beef heart, beef hide, beef hocks. They're a human product like rayon. They're like a field of shoes. They have cast-iron shanks and tongues like foam insoles. You can't see through to their brains as you can with other animals; they have beef fat behind their eyes, beef stew.

I cross the fence six feet above the water, walking my hands down the rusty cable and tightroping my feet along the narrow edge of the planks. When I hit the other bank and terra firma, some steers are bunched in a knot between me and the barbed-wire fence I want to cross. So I suddenly rush at them in an enthusiastic sprint, flailing my arms and hollering, "Lightning! Copperhead! Swedish meatballs!" They flee, still in a knot, stumbling across the flat pasture. I stand with the wind on my face.

When I slide under a barbed-wire fence, cross a field, and run over a sycamore trunk felled across the water, I'm on a little island shaped like a tear in the middle of Tinker Creek. On one side of the creek is a steep forested bank; the water is swift and deep on that side of the island. On the other side is the level field I walked through next to the steers' pasture; the water between the field and the island is shallow and sluggish. In summer's low water, flags and bulrushes grow along a series of shallow pools cooled by the lazy current. Water striders patrol the surface film, crayfish hump along the silt bottom eating filth, frogs shout and glare, and shiners and small bream hide among roots from the sulky green heron's eye. I come to this island every month of the year. I walk around it, stopping and staring, or I straddle the sycamore log over the creek, curling my legs out of the water in winter, trying to read. Today I sit on dry grass at the end of the island by the slower side of the creek. I'm drawn to this spot. I come to it as to an oracle; I return to it as a man years later will seek out the battlefield where he lost a leg or an arm.

A couple of summers ago I was walking along the edge of the island to see what I could see in the water, and mainly to scare frogs. Frogs have an inelegant way of taking off from invisible positions on the bank just ahead of your feet, in dire panic, emitting a froggy "Yike!" and splashing into the water. Incredibly, this amused me, and, incredibly, it amuses me still. As I walked along the grassy edge of the island, I got better and better at seeing frogs both in and out of the water. I learned to recognize, slowing down, the difference in texture of the light reflected from mudbank, water, grass, or frog. Frogs were flying all around me. At the end of the island I noticed a small green frog. He was exactly half in and half out of the water, looking like a schematic diagram of an amphibian, and he didn't jump.

He didn't jump; I crept closer. At last I knelt on the island's winterkilled grass, lost, dumbstruck, staring at the frog in the creek just four feet away. He was a very small frog with wide, dull eyes. And just as I looked at him, he slowly crumpled and began to sag. The spirit vanished from his eyes as if snuffed. His skin emptied and drooped; his very skull seemed to collapse and settle like a kicked tent. He was shrinking before my eyes like a deflating football. I watched the taut, glistening skin on his shoulders ruck, and rumple, and fall. Soon, part of his skin, formless as a pricked balloon, lay in floating folds like bright scum on top of the water: it was a monstrous and terrifying thing. I gaped bewildered, appalled. An oval shadow hung in the water behind the drained frog; then the shadow glided away. The frog skin bag started to sink.

I had read about the giant water bug, but never seen one. "Giant water bug"   15
is really the name of the creature, which is an enormous, heavy-bodied brown bug. It eats insects, tadpoles, fish, and frogs. Its grasping forelegs are mighty and hooked inward. It seizes a victim with these legs, hugs it tight, and paralyzes it with enzymes injected during a vicious bite. That one bite is the only bite it ever takes. Through the puncture shoot the poisons that dissolve the victim's muscles and bones and organs—all but the skin—and through it the giant water bug

sucks out the victim's body, reduced to a juice. This event is quite common in warm fresh water. The frog I saw was being sucked by a giant water bug. I had been kneeling on the island grass; when the unrecognizable flap of frog skin settled on the creek bottom, swaying, I stood up and brushed the knees of my pants. I couldn't catch my breath.

Of course, many carnivorous animals devour their prey alive. The usual method seems to be to subdue the victim by downing or grasping it so it can't flee, then eating it whole or in a series of bloody bites. Frogs eat everything whole, stuffing prey into their mouths with their thumbs. People have seen frogs with their wide jaws so full of live dragonflies they couldn't close them. Ants don't even have to catch their prey: in the spring they swarm over newly hatched, featherless birds in the nest and eat them tiny bite by bite.

That it's rough out there and chancy is no surprise. Every live thing is a survivor on a kind of extended emergency bivouac. But at the same time we are also created. In the Koran, Allah asks, "The heaven and the earth and all in between, thinkest thou I made them *in jest*?" It's a good question. What do we think of the created universe, spanning an unthinkable void with an unthinkable profusion of forms? Or what do we think of nothingness, those sickening reaches of time in either direction? If the giant water bug was not made in jest, was it then made in earnest? Pascal uses a nice term to describe the notion of the creator's, once having called forth the universe, turning his back to it: *Deus Absconditus*. Is this what we think happened? Was the sense of it there, and God absconded with it, ate it, like a wolf who disappears round the edge of the house with the Thanksgiving turkey? "God is subtle," Einstein said, "but not malicious." Again, Einstein said that "nature conceals her mystery by means of her essential grandeur, not by her cunning." It could be that God has not absconded but spread, as our vision and understanding of the universe have spread, to a fabric of spirit and sense so grand and subtle, so powerful in a new way, that we can only feel blindly of its hem. In making the thick darkness a swaddling band for the sea, God "set bars and doors" and said, "Hitherto shalt thou come, but no further." But have we come even that far? Have we rowed out to the thick darkness, or are we all playing pinochle in the bottom of the boat?

Cruelty is a mystery, and the waste of pain. But if we describe a world to compass these things, a world that is a long, brute game, then we bump against another mystery: the inrush of power and light, the canary that sings on the skull. Unless all ages and races of men have been deluded by the same mass hypnotist (who?), there seems to be such a thing as beauty, a grace wholly gratuitous. About five years ago I saw a mockingbird make a straight vertical descent from the roof gutter of a four-story building. It was an act as careless and spontaneous as the curl of a stem or the kindling of a star.

The mockingbird took a single step into the air and dropped. His wings were still folded against his sides as though he were singing from a limb and not falling, accelerating thirty-two feet per second per second, through empty air. Just a breath before he would have been dashed to the ground, he unfurled his wings with exact, deliberate care, revealing the broad bars of white, spread his elegant, white-banded tail, and so floated onto the grass. I had just rounded a corner when his insouciant step caught my eye; there was no one else in sight. The fact of his free fall was like the old philosophical conundrum about the tree that falls in the forest. The answer must be, I think, that beauty and grace are performed whether or not we will or sense them. The least we can do is try to be there.

Another time I saw another wonder: sharks off the Atlantic coast of Florida.   20 There is a way a wave rises above the ocean horizon, a triangular wedge against the sky. If you stand where the ocean breaks on a shallow beach, you see the raised water in a wave is translucent, shot with lights. One late afternoon at low tide a hundred big sharks passed the beach near the mouth of a tidal river in a feeding frenzy. As each green wave rose from the churning water, it illuminated within itself the six- or eight-foot-long bodies of twisting sharks. The sharks disappeared as each wave rolled toward me; then a new wave would swell above the horizon, containing in it, like scorpions in amber, sharks that roiled and heaved. The sight held awesome wonders: power and beauty, grace tangled in a rapture with violence.

We don't know what's going on here. If these tremendous events are random combinations of matter run amok, the yield of millions of monkeys at millions of typewriters, then what is it in us, hammered out of those same typewriters, that they ignite? We don't know. Our life is a faint tracing on the surface of mystery, like the idle, curved tunnels of leaf miners on the face of a leaf. We must somehow take a wider view, look at the whole landscape, really see it, and describe what's going on here. Then we can at least wail the right question into the swaddling band of darkness, or, if it comes to that, choir the proper praise.

At the time of Lewis and Clark, setting the prairies on fire was a well-known signal that meant, "Come down to the water." It was an extravagant gesture, but we can't do less. If the landscape reveals one certainty, it is that the extravagant gesture is the very stuff of creation. After the one extravagant gesture of creation in the first place, the universe has continued to deal exclusively in extravagances, flinging intricacies and colossi down aeons of emptiness, heaping profusions on profligacies with ever-fresh vigor. The whole show has been on fire from the word go. I come down to the water to cool my eyes. But everywhere I look I see fire; that which isn't flint is tinder, and the whole world sparks and flames.

I have come to the grassy island late in the day. The creek is up; icy water sweeps under the sycamore log bridge. The frog skin, of course, is utterly gone. I have stared at that one spot on the creek bottom for so long, focusing past the rush of water, that when I stand, the opposite bank seems to stretch before my eyes and flow grassily upstream. When the bank settles down I cross the sycamore log and enter again the big plowed field next to the steers' pasture.

The wind is terrific out of the west; the sun comes and goes. I can see the shadow on the field before me deepen uniformly and spread like a plague. Everything seems so dull I am amazed I can even distinguish objects. And suddenly the light runs across the land like a comber, and up the trees, and goes again in a wink: I think I've gone blind or died. When it comes again, the light, you hold your breath, and if it stays you forget about it until it goes again.

It's the most beautiful day of the year. At four o'clock the eastern sky is a dead stratus black flecked with low white clouds. The sun in the west illuminates the ground, the mountains, and especially the bare branches of trees, so that everywhere silver trees cut into the black sky like a photographer's negative of a landscape. The air and the ground are dry; the mountains are going on and off like neon signs. Clouds slide east as if pulled from the horizon, like a tablecloth whipped off a table. The hemlocks by the barbed-wire fence are flinging themselves east as though their backs would break. Purple shadows are racing east; the wind makes me face east, and again I feel the dizzying, drawn sensation I felt when the creek bank reeled.

At four-thirty the sky in the east is clear; how could that big blackness be blown? Fifteen minutes later another darkness is coming overhead from the northwest; and it's here. Everything is drained of its light as if sucked. Only at the horizon do inky black mountains give way to distant, lighted mountains—lighted not by direct illumination but rather paled by glowing sheets of mist hung before them. Now the blackness is in the east; everything is half in shadow, half in sun, every clod, tree, mountain, and hedge. I can't see Tinker Mountain through the line of hemlock, till it comes on like a streetlight, ping, *ex nihilo*. Its sandstone cliffs pink and swell. Suddenly the light goes; the cliffs recede as if pushed. The sun hits a clump of sycamores between me and the mountains; the sycamore arms light up, and *I can't see the cliffs*. They're gone. The pale network of sycamore arms, which a second ago was transparent as a screen, is suddenly opaque, glowing with light. Now the sycamore arms snuff out, the mountains come on, and there are the cliffs again.

I walk home. By five-thirty the show has pulled out. Nothing is left but an unreal blue and a few banked clouds low in the north. Some sort of carnival magician has been here, some fast-talking worker of wonders who has the act backwards. "Something in this hand," he says, "something in this hand, something up my sleeve, something behind my back . . ." and abracadabra, he snaps his fingers, and it's all gone. Only the bland, blank-faced magician remains, in his unruffled coat, barehanded, acknowledging a smattering of baffled applause. When you look again the whole show has pulled up stakes and moved on down the road. It never stops. New shows roll in from over the mountains and the magician reappears unannounced from a fold in the curtain you never dreamed was an opening. Scarves of clouds, rabbits in plain view, disappear into the black hat forever. Presto chango. The audience, if there is an audience at all, is dizzy from head-turning, dazed.

Like the bear who went over the mountain, I went out to see what I could see. And, I might as well warn you, like the bear, all that I could see was the other side

of the mountain: more of same. On a good day I might catch a glimpse of another wooded ridge rolling under the sun like water, another bivouac. I propose
to keep here what Thoreau called "a meteorological journal of the mind," telling
some tales and describing some of the sights of this rather tamed valley, and exploring, in fear and trembling, some of the unmapped dim reaches and unholy
fastnesses to which those tales and sights so dizzyingly lead.

I am no scientist. I explore the neighborhood. An infant who has just learned
to hold his head up has a frank and forthright way of gazing about him in bewilderment. He hasn't the faintest clue where he is, and he aims to learn. In a couple
of years, what he will have learned instead is how to fake it: he'll have the cock-
sure air of a squatter who has come to feel he owns the place. Some unwonted,
taught pride diverts us from our original intent, which is to explore the neighborhood, view the landscape, to discover at least *where* it is that we have been so star-
tlingly set down, if we can't learn why.

So I think about the valley. It is my leisure as well as my work, a game. It is a   30
fierce game I have joined because it is being played anyway, a game of both skill
and chance, played against an unseen adversary—the conditions of time—in
which the payoffs, which may suddenly arrive in a blast of light at any moment,
might as well come to me as anyone else. I stake the time I'm grateful to have, the
energies I'm glad to direct. I risk getting stuck on the board, so to speak, unable
to move in any direction, which happens enough, God knows; and I risk the searing, exhausting nightmares that plunder rest and force me face down all night
long in some muddy ditch seething with hatching insects and crustaceans.

But if I can bear the nights, the days are a pleasure. I walk out; I see something, some event that would otherwise have been utterly missed and lost; or
something sees me, some enormous power brushes me with its clean wing, and I
resound like a beaten bell.

I am an explorer, then, and I am also a stalker, or the instrument of the hunt
itself. Certain Indians used to carve long grooves along the wooden shafts of their
arrows. They called the grooves "lightning marks," because they resembled the
curved fissure lightning slices down the trunks of trees. The function of lightning
marks is this: if the arrow fails to kill the game, blood from a deep wound will
channel along the lightning mark, streak down the arrow shaft, and spatter to the
ground, laying a trail dripped on broadleaves, on stones, that the barefoot and
trembling archer can follow into whatever deep or rare wilderness it leads. I am
the arrow shaft, carved along my length by unexpected lights and gashes from the
very sky, and this book is the straying trail of blood.

Something pummels us, something barely sheathed. Power broods and
lights. We're played on like a pipe; our breath is not our own. James Houston describes two young Eskimo girls sitting cross-legged on the ground, mouth on
mouth, blowing by turns each other's throat cords, making a low, unearthly
music. When I cross again the bridge that is really the steers' fence, the wind has
thinned to the delicate air of twilight; it crumples the water's skin. I watch the
running sheets of light raised on the creek's surface. The sight has the appeal of

the purely passive, like the racing of light under clouds on a field, the beautiful dream at the moment of being dreamed. The breeze is the merest puff, but you yourself sail headlong and breathless under the gale force of the spirit.

Annie Dillard in early 1974

CONTEXTS FOR "HEAVEN AND EARTH IN JEST"

HENRY DAVID THOREAU
From *Journal*

(For biography, see p. 187.) In the following journal entry for August 19, 1851, Thoreau wrote the passage that Dillard mentions in paragraph 28, where she defines

From Henry David Thoreau, *The Writings of Henry D. Thoreau: Journal*, vol. 3, *1848–1851*, ed. John C. Broderick, Robert Satelmeyer, Mark R. Patterson, and William Rossi (Princeton: Princeton University Press, 1990), 377.

the goal of her writing at Tinker Creek as keeping a "'meteorological journal of the mind.'"

As travellers go round the world and report natural objects and phenomena — so faithfully let another stay at home and report the phenomena of his own life. Catalogue stars — those thoughts whose orbits are as rarely calculated as comets. It matters not whether they visit my mind or yours — whether the meteor falls in my field or in yours — only that it came from heaven. (I am not concerned to express that kind of truth which nature has expressed. Who knows but I may suggest some things to her. Time was when she was indebted to such suggestions from another quarter — as her present advancement shows. I deal with the truths that recommend themselves to me — please me — not those merely which any system has voted to accept.) A meteorological journal of the mind — You shall observe what occurs in your latitude, I in mine.

METAPHOR

A writer's deepest work is often play with metaphor, the assertion of identity between two different things. Metaphor is stronger than simile. Simile asserts mere likeness, *a ~ b:* the dying frog collapses "like a kicked tent . . . like a deflating football" (paragraph 14). Metaphor asserts identity between two different things. It equates, *a = b:* "I am the arrow shaft, . . . and this book is the straying trail of blood" (32). As the poet Robert Frost observes, "all metaphor breaks down somewhere," because its two elements *are* different. Everybody knows that Dillard is not, literally, an arrow shaft. The playful work, then, is to figure out the ways in which Dillard and the arrow shaft *are* identical. Each way joins Dillard and the arrow shaft through a third term *with respect to* which they are identical: Dillard is the arrow shaft *with respect to* being an "instrument of the hunt" (for meaning in the natural world?), *with respect to* being "carved . . . by unexpected lights" (visions? intuitions?), *with respect to* bearing the gashes through which the game (meaning?) bleeds, leaving a trail (clues observable in language?) for the archer (a seeker after meaning? a reader?) to follow, and so on. When one metaphor leads into others (an archer is a reader *with respect to* . . . and *with respect to* . . . and so on), we call it an extended metaphor, an ancient figure of speech prominent in sacred writings and epic poetry. But our everyday language teems with metaphors, including those implied by concrete verbs: we *cover* a subject, *buttress* our arguments, *dig deeper* into our research, *stake out* our territory, and on and on. Playful work, workful play.

ALLUSION

An allusion is a casual reference to a well-known historical or literary text, figure, or event. The reference invites readers to compare and contrast the text, figure, or event alluded to with whatever subject the writer is addressing. It also invites readers to compare and contrast themselves with the writer. A writer alludes to something that the readers she has in mind are likely to understand with little or no explanation. Dillard's allusions help construct her persona: She is a person who reads the Koran, the *Pensées* of French mathematician Blaise Pascal (1623–1662), Thoreau's *Walden*, and so on. Allusions also help construct a writer's imagined readers and establish solidarity with them: "Dear Reader, you and I get this, but others don't." "Oh," we reply, "Pascal, of course." The catch, however, is that some readers reply, "Pascal, who?" The allusion then separates them from the writer, making the writer seem more learned or cosmopolitan than they. Even more subtle allusions withhold names and titles, relying on readers' attuned ears to catch echoes of other texts, as Dillard does in paraphrasing the British poet Gerard Manley Hopkins and her fellow American naturalist writer, Wendell Berry.

From *The Koran*

The divine reveals itself in and through its works: heaven and earth, or creation. The Koran often enjoins believers to recognize creation as a communication and a sign from Allah, and warns them not to take Allah's signs "in jest." The Bible similarly teaches Jews and Christians to see creation as evidence of God's existence and divinity, a view that many evolutionary biologists question (see Stephen Jay Gould's "Evolution as Fact and Theory" and its Contexts in Chapter 7). Dillard's allusion to the Koran in paragraph 17 may create solidarity with her Muslim readers, with those of other faiths who admire her as a reader of sacred texts, and with secular readers who admire a learned mind.

23. AL-MU'MENOON ("THE BELIEVERS"): VERSES 112–116

He will say: "What number of years did ye stay on earth?"

They will say: "We stayed a day or part of a day: but ask those who keep account."

He will say: "Ye stayed not but a little,—if ye had only known!

"Did ye then think that We had created you in jest, and that ye would not be brought back to Us (for account)?"

Therefore exalted be God, the King, the Reality: there is no god but He, the Lord   5
of the Throne of Honor!

BLAISE PASCAL

Pensées

Blaise Pascal (1623–1662), a devout Roman Catholic, was a precocious mathematician, a physicist, and a religious philosopher whose Pensées—*a collection of notes and manuscript fragments—presents his thoughts on Christian theology. In the passage that Dillard alludes to in paragraph 17, Pascal argues that if Christianity says that God is unknowable, then any deity whom Christians profess to know and understand cannot be God. By alluding to the Koran and to Pascal in almost the same breath, Dillard suggests that she is a learned reader of religious texts. Their seriousness notwithstanding, however, she playfully, breezily, and some might say blasphemously modernizes Pascal's Latin term* Deus absconditus: *Whereas Pascal's God has hidden* from *our knowledge, Dillard's has hidden* away with *the meaning of the universe—like a wolf stealing away with a turkey.*

194. . . . . Let them at least learn what is the religion they attack, before attacking it. If this religion boasted of having a clear view of God, and of possessing it open and unveiled, it would be attacking it to say that we see nothing in the world which shows it with this clearness. But since, on the contrary, it says that men are in darkness and estranged from God, that He has hidden Himself from their knowledge, that this is in fact the name which He gives Himself in the Scriptures, *Deus absconditus*;* and finally, if it endeavors equally to establish these two things: that God has set up in the Church visible signs to make Himself known to those who should seek Him sincerely, and that He has nevertheless so disguised them that He will only be perceived by those who seek Him with all their heart; what advantage can they obtain, when, in the negligence with which they make profession of being in search of the truth, they cry out that nothing reveals it to them; and since that darkness in which they are, and with which they upbraid the Church, establishes only one of the things which she affirms, without touching the other, and, very far from destroying, proves her doctrine?

NIKOS KAZANTZAKIS

Report to Greco

Dillard alludes in paragraph 8 to Greek poet, novelist, playwright, and travel writer Nikos Kazantzakis (1885–1957), who wrote in his posthumously published autobiography, Report to Greco *(1961), about his ability to see the world from seemingly*

---

*"Thou art a God that hidest thyself."

From Blaise Pascal, *Pensées*, section 3, "The Necessity of the Wager," http://www.mala.bc.ca/~mcneil/PEN03.htm.

From Nikos Kazantzakis, *Report to Greco* (1961), trans. P. B. Bien (New York: Simon, 1965), 44.

contradictory perspectives: the materialist and the spiritual. Like Kazantzakis, ever intent on discovering reciprocal illumination in the material and spiritual worlds, Dillard paraphrases his story of the gift that—metaphysically and metaphorically— shaped his life.

I must have been four years old. On New Year's Day my father gave me a canary and a revolving globe as a handsel, "a good hand," as we say in Crete. Closing the doors and windows of my room, I used to open the cage and let the canary go free. It had developed the habit of sitting at the very top of the globe and singing for hours and hours, while I held my breath and listened.

This extremely simple event, I believe, influenced my life more than all the books and all the people I came to know afterwards. Wandering insatiably over the earth for years, greeting and taking leave of everything, I felt that my head was the globe and that a canary sat perched on the top of my mind, singing.

WENDELL BERRY

A Secular Pilgrimage

Berry (b. 1934), an American essayist and naturalist, published "A Secular Pilgrimage" in 1970 (collected in A Continuous Harmony, *1975). Both Berry's and Dillard's titles convey the concept of secular pilgrimage, and Berry's analysis of nature poets— exemplified by Wordsworth and Hopkins—applies equally well to Dillard's point of view, and to her ecstatic, poetic prose.*

Gerard Manley Hopkins, more conventionally religious than Wordsworth, had the same eagerness to thrust through appearances toward a realization of the divine. With Hopkins, this was not the anonymous Presence of Wordsworth's poems, but God, Jehovah, who broods over his creation in which his glory is manifest. But Hopkins was nevertheless a keener observer than Wordsworth; he loved the physical facts of nature, and took pains to capture their look and feel and movement. In the accuracy of his observation, and in the onomatopoeia of his diction and rhythms, he is clearly a forebear of the contemporary nature poets. "God's Grandeur" gives not only a sense of his technique but also of his critical values with respect to nature and civilization:

From Wendell Berry, "A Secular Pilgrimage" (1970), in *A Continuous Harmony: Essays Cultural and Agricultural* (New York: Harcourt, 1975), 3–35.

The world is charged with the grandeur of God.
　It will flame out, like shining from shook foil;
　It gathers to a greatness like the ooze of oil
Crushed. Why do men then now not reck his rod?
Generations have trod, have trod, have trod;
　And all is seared with trade; bleared, smeared with toil;
　And wears man's smudge and shares man's smell: the soil
Is bare now, nor can foot feel, being shod. . . .

QUESTIONS FOR DISCUSSION AND WRITING

1. Dillard borrows the simile of poet as astronomer from Thoreau. In what ways does the simile help explain her work at Tinker Creek? How are Thoreau's and Dillard's works alike? In the longer excerpt from Thoreau's *Walden* in Chapter 3 ("Where I Lived, and What I Lived For," p. 187), what similes can you identify, how does each one affect you as a reader, and in what ways (if any) could they illuminate further aspects of Dillard's sojourn on Tinker Creek?

2. Read about allusion—in the "Reading in Context" section of the Introduction (p. 650)—as a way of defining one's intended reading audience and oneself. What kind of person do Dillard's allusions seem to add up to, and what type of audience does she seem to be writing to?

3. Dillard's "Heaven and Earth in Jest," like the writings of Thoreau, her model and source of inspiration (see "Where I Lived and What I Lived For," p. 187), conveys the impression that the author is an isolated individual, communing with the many facets of the natural world. Yet the author is hardly alone. What human, natural, and divine elements does her universe consist of? Why does it seem so full, so abundant?

4. The Tinker Creek environment is an energetic place; ducks fly, frogs jump, "the whole world sparks and flames" (paragraph 22). Identify the main manifestations of activity and energy—Dillard's own and those of animals and the environment, compounded by a spiritual energy. Why does she include all these?

5. The Tinker Creek environment is also a beautiful place, experienced on "the most beautiful day of the year" (paragraph 25). What makes it so beautiful?

6. Keep a daily journal about your environment for a week, and use it as the basis for an essay that is both descriptive and analytic of the place's characteristic energy and atmosphere. If it's beautiful, show why; if not, explain why not. Was it once beautiful but is no longer so? To what extent is this beauty in the eye of the beholder?

KEITH CARTER

Fireflies

QUESTIONS FOR DISCUSSION AND WRITING

1. What is going on in this photo? What is the effect of the blurry images? Of the figures in silhouette?

2. How might this edenic photograph illustrate Dillard's "Heaven and Earth in Jest" (p. 641)? What are some possible relations of this photograph to the readings that follow by Williams, "The Clan of One-Breasted Women" (p. 656); Carson, "The Obligation to Endure" (p. 663); Lopez, "The American Geographies"

(p. 669); Rees, "Life in the Lap of Luxury as Ecosystems Collapse" (p. 678); and/or Postel, "Troubled Waters" (p. 675)?

3. Write a short story, either true or fictional, that includes and interprets this scene. Will you write it from a child's point of view? An adult's? God's? In what time and place will you set this scene?

TERRY TEMPEST WILLIAMS
The Clan of One-Breasted Women

When the U.S. government decided to test atomic weapons in a "virtually unin-habited" section of Utah in the 1950s, environmentalist Terry Tempest Williams's family was among the "virtual uninhabitants," as she puts it. In one of the most troubling episodes in U.S. history, Williams (b. 1955) and other Utah residents were being exposed to fallout while the federal government assured them that they were safe; thousands died of radiation-related diseases. As she watched the women in her family die of cancer, and as the government refused to acknowledge the claims of the test victims, she came to realize that "tolerating blind obedience in the name of patri-otism or religion ultimately takes our lives." Williams earned degrees in English (B.S., 1979) and environmental education (M.S., 1984) at the University of Utah. All of her books—including The Secret Language of Snow *(1984), a children's book;* Pieces of White Shell: A Journey to Navajo Land *(1984); and* Leap *(2000)—reflect her belief in the vital link among human beings, animals, and the earth. These themes prevail in her best-known work,* Refuge: An Unnatural History of Family and Place *(1992). In "The Clan of One-Breasted Women" (1991), the epilogue to* Refuge, *Williams tells the story of her family's history with cancer. Her analysis be-comes an emotional and ethical protest against the federal government's routine de-nial that anyone was harmed by the radioactive fallout.*

I belong to a Clan of One-Breasted Women. My mother, my grandmothers, and six aunts have all had mastectomies. Seven are dead. The two who survive have just completed rounds of chemotherapy and radiation.

I've had my own problems: two biopsies for breast cancer and a small tumor between my ribs diagnosed as a "borderline malignancy."

This is my family history.

Most statistics tell us breast cancer is genetic, hereditary, with rising percent-ages attached to fatty diets, childlessness, or becoming pregnant after thirty. What they don't say is living in Utah may be the greatest hazard of all.

We are a Mormon family with roots in Utah since 1847. The "word of wis-   5
dom" in my family aligned us with good foods—no coffee, no tea, tobacco, or alcohol. For the most part, our women were finished having their babies by the

time they were thirty. And only one faced breast cancer prior to 1960. Traditionally, as a group of people, Mormons have a low rate of cancer.

Is our family a cultural anomaly? The truth is, we didn't think about it. Those who did, usually the men, simply said, "bad genes." The women's attitude was stoic. Cancer was part of life. On February 16, 1971, the eve of my mother's surgery, I accidentally picked up the telephone and overheard her ask my grandmother what she could expect.

"Diane, it is one of the most spiritual experiences you will ever encounter."

I quietly put down the receiver.

Two days later, my father took my brothers and me to the hospital to visit her. She met us in the lobby in a wheelchair. No bandages were visible. I'll never forget her radiance, the way she held herself in a purple velvet robe, and how she gathered us around her.

"Children, I am fine. I want you to know I felt the arms of God around me." 10

We believed her. My father cried. Our mother, his wife, was thirty-eight years old.

A little over a year after Mother's death, Dad and I were having dinner together. He had just returned from St. George, where the Tempest Company was completing the gas lines that would service southern Utah. He spoke of his love for the country, the sandstoned landscape, bare-boned and beautiful. He had just finished hiking the Kolob trail in Zion National Park. We got caught up in reminiscing, recalling with fondness our walk up Angel's Landing on his fiftieth birthday and the years our family had vacationed there.

Over dessert, I shared a recurring dream of mine. I told my father that for years, as long as I could remember, I saw this flash of light in the night in the desert—that this image had so permeated my being that I could not venture south without seeing it again, on the horizon, illuminating buttes and mesas.

"You did see it," he said.

"Saw what?" 15

"The bomb. The cloud. We were driving home from Riverside, California. You were sitting on Diane's lap. She was pregnant. In fact, I remember the day, September 7, 1957. We had just gotten out of the Service. We were driving north, past Las Vegas. It was an hour or so before dawn, when this explosion went off. We not only heard it, but felt it. I thought the oil tanker in front of us had blown up. We pulled over and suddenly, rising from the desert floor, we saw it, clearly, this golden-stemmed cloud, the mushroom. The sky seemed to vibrate with an eerie pink glow. Within a few minutes, a light ash was raining on the car."

I stared at my father.

"I thought you knew that," he said. "It was a common occurrence in the fifties."

It was at this moment that I realized the deceit I had been living under. Children growing up in the American Southwest, drinking contaminated milk from contaminated cows, even from the contaminated breasts of their mothers, my mother—members, years later, of the Clan of One-Breasted Women.

It is a well-known story in the Desert West, "The Day We Bombed Utah," or 20
more accurately, the years we bombed Utah: above ground atomic testing in
Nevada took place from January 27, 1951 through July 11, 1962. Not only were
the winds blowing north covering "low-use segments of the population" with
fallout and leaving sheep dead in their tracks, but the climate was right. The
United States of the 1950s was red, white, and blue. The Korean War was raging.
McCarthyism was rampant. Ike was it, and the cold war was hot. If you were
against nuclear testing, you were for a communist regime.

Much has been written about this "American nuclear tragedy." Public health
was secondary to national security. The Atomic Energy Commissioner, Thomas
Murray, said, "Gentlemen, we must not let anything interfere with this series of
tests, nothing."

Again and again, the American public was told by its government, in spite of
burns, blisters, and nausea, "It has been found that the tests may be conducted
with adequate assurance of safety under conditions prevailing at the bombing
reservations." Assuaging public fears was simply a matter of public relations.
"Your best action," an Atomic Energy Commission booklet read, "is not to be
worried about fallout." A news release typical of the times stated, "We find no
basis for concluding that harm to any individual has resulted from radioactive
fallout."

On August 30, 1979, during Jimmy Carter's presidency, a suit was filed, *Irene
Allen* v. *The United States of America*. Mrs. Allen's case was the first on an alphabetical list of twenty-four test cases, representative of nearly twelve hundred
plaintiffs seeking compensation from the United States government for cancers
caused by nuclear testing in Nevada.

Irene Allen lived in Hurricane, Utah. She was the mother of five children
and had been widowed twice. Her first husband, with their two oldest boys, had
watched the tests from the roof of the local high school. He died of leukemia in
1956. Her second husband died of pancreatic cancer in 1978.

In a town meeting conducted by Utah Senator Orrin Hatch, shortly before 25
the suit was filed, Mrs. Allen said, "I am not blaming the government, I want you
to know that, Senator Hatch. But I thought if my testimony could help in any way
so this wouldn't happen again to any of the generations coming up after us . . . I
am happy to be here this day to bear testimony of this."

God-fearing people. This is just one story in an anthology of thousands.

On May 10, 1984, Judge Bruce S. Jenkins handed down his opinion. Ten
of the plaintiffs were awarded damages. It was the first time a federal court had
determined that nuclear tests had been the cause of cancers. For the remaining
fourteen test cases, the proof of causation was not sufficient. In spite of the
split decision, it was considered a landmark ruling. It was not to remain so for
long.

In April 1987, the Tenth Circuit Court of Appeals overturned Judge Jenkins's
ruling on the ground that the United States was protected from suit by the legal

doctrine of sovereign immunity, a centuries-old idea from England in the days of absolute monarchs.

In January 1988, the Supreme Court refused to review the Appeals Court decision. To our court system it does not matter whether the United States government was irresponsible, whether it lied to its citizens, or even that citizens died from the fallout of nuclear testing. What matters is that our government is immune: "The King can do no wrong."

In Mormon culture, authority is respected, obedience is revered, and independent thinking is not. I was taught as a young girl not to "make waves" or "rock the boat." 30

"Just let it go," Mother would say. "You know how you feel, that's what counts."

For many years, I have done just that—listened, observed, and quietly formed my own opinions, in a culture that rarely asks questions because it has all the answers. But one by one, I have watched the women in my family die common, heroic deaths. We sat in waiting rooms hoping for good news, but always receiving the bad. I cared for them, bathed their scarred bodies, and kept their secrets. I watched beautiful women become bald as Cytoxan, cisplatin, and Adriamycin were injected into their veins. I held their foreheads as they vomited green-black bile, and I shot them with morphine when the pain became inhuman. In the end, I witnessed their last peaceful breaths, becoming a midwife to the rebirth of their souls.

The price of obedience has become too high.

The fear and inability to question authority that ultimately killed rural communities in Utah during atmospheric testing of atomic weapons is the same fear I saw in my mother's body. Sheep. Dead sheep. The evidence is buried.

I cannot prove that my mother, Diane Dixon Tempest, or my grandmothers, 35 Lettie Romney Dixon and Kathryn Blackett Tempest, along with my aunts developed cancer from nuclear fallout in Utah. But I can't prove they didn't.

My father's memory was correct. The September blast we drove through in 1957 was part of Operation Plumbbob, one of the most intensive series of bomb tests to be initiated. The flash of light in the night in the desert, which I had always thought was a dream, developed into a family nightmare. It took fourteen years, from 1957 to 1971, for cancer to manifest in my mother—the same time, Howard L. Andrews, an authority in radioactive fallout at the National Institutes of Health, says radiation cancer requires to become evident. The more I learn about what it means to be a "downwinder," the more questions I drown in.

What I do know, however, is that as a Mormon woman of the fifth generation of Latter-day Saints, I must question everything, even if it means losing my faith, even if it means becoming a member of a border tribe among my own people. Tolerating blind obedience in the name of patriotism or religion ultimately takes our lives.

When the Atomic Energy Commission described the country north of the Nevada Test Site as "virtually uninhabited desert terrain," my family and the birds at Great Salt Lake were some of the "virtual uninhabitants."

One night, I dreamed women from all over the world circled a blazing fire in the desert. They spoke of change, how they hold the moon in their bellies and wax and wane with its phases. They mocked the presumption of even-tempered beings and made promises that they would never fear the witch inside themselves. The women danced wildly as sparks broke away from the flames and entered the night sky as stars.

And they sang a song given to them by Shoshone grandmothers: 40

Ah ne nah, nah	Consider the rabbits
nin nah nah—	How gently they walk on the earth—
ah ne nah, nah	Consider the rabbits
nin nah nah—	How gently they walk on the earth—
Nyaga mutzi	We remember them
oh ne nay—	We can walk gently also—
Nyaga mutzi	We remember them
oh ne nay—	We can walk gently also—

The women danced and drummed and sang for weeks, preparing themselves for what was to come. They would reclaim the desert for the sake of their children, for the sake of the land.

A few miles downwind from the fire circle, bombs were being tested. Rabbits felt the tremors. Their soft leather pads on paws and feet recognized the shaking sands, while the roots of mesquite and sage were smoldering. Rocks were hot from the inside out and dust devils hummed unnaturally. And each time there was another nuclear test, ravens watched the desert heave. Stretch marks appeared. The land was losing its muscle.

The women couldn't bear it any longer. They were mothers. They had suffered labor pains but always under the promise of birth. The red hot pains beneath the desert promised death only, as each bomb became a stillborn. A contract had been made and broken between human beings and the land. A new contract was being drawn by the women, who understood the fate of the earth as their own.

Under the cover of darkness, ten women slipped under a barbed-wire fence and entered the contaminated country. They were trespassing. They walked toward the town of Mercury, in moonlight, taking their cues from coyote, kit fox, antelope squirrel, and quail. They moved quietly and deliberately through the maze of Joshua trees. When a hint of daylight appeared they rested, drinking tea and sharing their rations of food. The women closed their eyes. The time had come to protest with the heart, that to deny one's genealogy with the earth was to commit treason against one's soul.

At dawn, the women draped themselves in mylar, wrapping long streamers of silver plastic around their arms to blow in the breeze. They wore clear masks that became the faces of humanity. And when they arrived at the edge of Mercury, they carried all the butterflies of a summer day in their wombs. They paused to allow their courage to settle.

The town that forbids pregnant women and children to enter because of 45 radiation risks was asleep. The women moved through the streets as winged messengers, twirling around each other in slow motion, peeking inside homes and watching the easy sleep of men and women. They were astonished by such stillness and periodically would utter a shrill note or low cry just to verify life.

The residents finally awoke to these strange apparitions. Some simply stared. Others called authorities, and in time, the women were apprehended by wary soldiers dressed in desert fatigues. They were taken to a white, square building on the other edge of Mercury. When asked who they were and why they were there, the women replied, "We are mothers and we have come to reclaim the desert for our children."

The soldiers arrested them. As the ten women were blindfolded and hand-cuffed, they began singing:

> You can't forbid us everything
> You can't forbid us to think—
> You can't forbid our tears to flow
> And you can't stop the songs that we sing.

The women continued to sing louder and louder, until they heard the voices of their sisters moving across the mesa:

> Ah ne nah, nah
> nin nah nah—
> Ah ne nah, nah
> nin nah nah—
> Nyaga mutzi
> oh ne nay—
> Nyaga mutzi
> oh ne nay—

"Call for reinforcements," one soldier said.

"We have," interrupted one woman, "we have—and you have no idea of our numbers."

I crossed the line at the Nevada Test Site and was arrested with nine other Utahns for trespassing on military lands. They are still conducting nuclear tests in the desert. Ours was an act of civil disobedience. But as I walked toward the town of

Mercury, it was more than a gesture of peace. It was a gesture on behalf of the Clan of One-Breasted Women.

As one officer cinched the handcuffs around my wrists, another frisked my 50 body. She found a pen and a pad of paper tucked inside my left boot.

"And these?" she asked sternly.

"Weapons," I replied.

Our eyes met. I smiled. She pulled the leg of my trousers back over my boot.

"Step forward, please," she said as she took my arm.

We were booked under an afternoon sun and bused to Tonopah, Nevada. It 55 was a two-hour ride. This was familiar country. The Joshua trees standing their ground had been named by my ancestors, who believed they looked like prophets pointing west to the Promised Land. These were the same trees that bloomed each spring, flowers appearing like white flames in the Mojave. And I recalled a full moon in May, when Mother and I had walked among them, flushing out mourning doves and owls.

The bus stopped short of town. We were released.

The officials thought it was a cruel joke to leave us stranded in the desert with no way to get home. What they didn't realize was that we were home, soul-centered and strong, women who recognized the sweet smell of sage as fuel for our spirits.

QUESTIONS FOR DISCUSSION AND WRITING

1. Terry Tempest Williams's family is prominent in Utah; her father was a member of the Stake High Council of the regional Mormon Church. Why does Williams define her "family history" (paragraph 3) in terms of women with breast cancer rather than men of power?

2. "The Clan of One-Breasted Women" is the ten-page epilogue to Williams's book *Refuge*. How many sections is the epilogue divided into? Why is it important to notice the demarcation of these sections? What is the significance — structurally and thematically — of the two "dreams" she describes (paragraphs 13 and 39)?

3. As a little girl, Williams was taught by her Mormon culture "not to 'make waves.'" As an adult woman, especially as a conscientious writer, she changed her behavior pattern: "[A]s a Mormon woman of the fifth generation of Latter-day Saints, I must question everything . . ." (paragraph 37). What is the significance of this change to her intellectual and spiritual growth?

4. According to Williams, the Atomic Energy Commission, which is made up of mostly male members declared the "desert terrain" to be "virtually uninhabited" (paragraph 38). What factors (socioeconomic, geographic, political, psychological, cultural) might prompt continued disregard for the inhabitants? How does the existence of new, heavily populated desert communities in Arizona and Nevada (not to mention Middle Eastern countries) affect your answer?

5. What are the differences, for Terry Tempest Williams, between writing as a form of advocacy and the act of civil disobedience she describes in "The Clan of One-Breasted Women"? Consider in your response Martin Luther King Jr.'s advocacy of a "direct-action campaign" in support of civil rights and the role his "Letter from Birmingham Jail" (p. 565) played in influencing protesters' behavior.

6. Using Terry Tempest Williams, Henry David Thoreau (p. 187), and Annie Dillard (p. 641) as examples, write an essay in which you argue for or against the precept that where we live determines what we live for. Or argue the converse, that what we live for determines where and how we live, to whom we belong, and indeed, who we are.

RACHEL CARSON

The Obligation to Endure

Before environmentalism was a movement—or even a common word—biologist Rachel Carson alerted us to the potentially fatal consequences of modern industrial pollution. Born in Pennsylvania in 1907, Carson attended Johns Hopkins University (M.A., 1932) and worked for the U.S. Fish and Wildlife Service as an aquatic biologist and publications editor-in-chief. Her works include Under the Sea-Wind *(1941);* The Sea around Us *(1951), a National Book Award winner and the basis for an Oscar-winning documentary;* The Edge of the Sea *(1955); and* The Sense of Wonder *(published posthumously in 1965). Carson died of cancer in 1964.*

"The Obligation to Endure" is the second chapter from Silent Spring *(1962), Carson's passionate and thoroughly researched demonstration that agricultural pesticides poison the environment, a radical argument for its time.*

The history of life on earth has been a history of interaction between living things and their surroundings. To a large extent, the physical form and the habits of the earth's vegetation and its animal life have been molded by the environment. Considering the whole span of earthly time, the opposite effect, in which life actually modifies its surroundings, has been relatively slight. Only within the moment of time represented by the present century has one species—man—acquired significant power to alter the nature of his world.

During the past quarter century this power has not only increased to one of disturbing magnitude but it has changed in character. The most alarming of all man's assaults upon the environment is the contamination of air, earth, rivers, and sea with dangerous and even lethal materials. This pollution is for the most part irrecoverable; the chain of evil it initiates not only in the world that must support life but in living tissues is for the most part irreversible. In this now universal contamination of the environment, chemicals are the sinister and little-recognized partners of radiation in changing the very nature of the world—the very nature of its life. Strontium 90, released through nuclear explosions into the air, comes to earth in rain or drifts down as fallout, lodges in soil, enters into the grass or corn or wheat grown there, and in time takes up its abode in the bones of a human being, there to remain until his death. Similarly, chemicals sprayed on croplands or forests or gardens lie long in soil, entering into living organisms, passing from one to another in a chain of poisoning and death. Or they pass mysteriously by underground streams until they emerge and, through the alchemy of air and sunlight, combine into new forms that kill vegetation, sicken cattle, and work unknown harm on those who drink from once pure wells. As Albert Schweitzer has said, "Man can hardly even recognize the devils of his own creation."

It took hundreds of millions of years to produce the life that now inhabits the earth—eons of time in which that developing and evolving and diversifying life reached a state of adjustment and balance with its surroundings. The environment, rigorously shaping and directing the life it supported, contained elements that were hostile as well as supporting. Certain rocks gave out dangerous radiation; even within the light of the sun, from which all life draws its energy, there were short-wave radiations with power to injure. Given time—time not in years but in millennia—life adjusts, and a balance has been reached. For time is the essential ingredient; but in the modern world there is no time.

The rapidity of change and the speed with which new situations are created follow the impetuous and heedless pace of man rather than the deliberate pace of nature. Radiation is no longer merely the background radiation of rocks, the bombardment of cosmic rays, the ultraviolet of the sun that have existed before there was any life on earth; radiation is now the unnatural creation of man's tampering with the atom. The chemicals to which life is asked to make its adjustment are no longer merely the calcium and silica and copper and all the rest of the minerals washed out of the rocks and carried in rivers to the sea; they are the synthetic creations of man's inventive mind, brewed in his laboratories, and having no counterparts in nature.

To adjust to these chemicals would require time on the scale that is nature's; it would require not merely the years of a man's life but the life of generations. And even this, were it by some miracle possible, would be futile, for the new chemicals come from our laboratories in an endless stream; almost five hundred annually find their way into actual use in the United States alone. The figure is staggering and its implications are not easily grasped—500 new chemicals to which the bodies of men and animals are required somehow to adapt each year, chemicals totally outside the limits of biologic experience.

Among them are many that are used in man's war against nature. Since the mid-1940s over 200 basic chemicals have been created for use in killing insects, weeds, rodents, and other organisms described in the modern vernacular as "pests"; and they are sold under several thousand different brand names.

These sprays, dusts, and aerosols are now applied almost universally to farms, gardens, forests, and homes—nonselective chemicals that have the power to kill every insect, the "good" and the "bad," to still the song of birds and the leaping of fish in the streams, to coat the leaves with a deadly film, and to linger on in soil—all this though the intended target may be only a few weeds or insects. Can anyone believe it is possible to lay down such a barrage of poisons on the surface of the earth without making it unfit for all life? They should not be called "insecticides," but "biocides."

The whole process of spraying seems caught up in an endless spiral. Since DDT was released for civilian use, a process of escalation has been going on in which ever more toxic materials must be found. This has happened because insects, in a triumphant vindication of Darwin's principle of the survival of the fittest, have evolved super races immune to the particular insecticide used, hence a deadlier one has always to be developed—and then a deadlier one than that. It has happened also because, for reasons to be described later, destructive insects often undergo a "flareback," or resurgence, after spraying, in numbers greater than before. Thus the chemical war is never won, and all life is caught in its violent crossfire.

Along with the possibility of the extinction of mankind by nuclear war, the central problem of our age has therefore become the contamination of man's total environment with such substances of incredible potential for harm—substances that accumulate in the tissues of plants and animals and even penetrate the germ cells to shatter or alter the very material of heredity upon which the shape of the future depends.

Some would-be architects of our future look toward a time when it will be possible to alter the human germ plasm by design. But we may easily be doing so now by inadvertence, for many chemicals, like radiation, bring about gene mutations. It is ironic to think that man might determine his own future by something so seemingly trivial as the choice of an insect spray.

All this has been risked—for what? Future historians may well be amazed by our distorted sense of proportion. How could intelligent beings seek to control a few unwanted species by a method that contaminated the entire environment and brought the threat of disease and death even to their own kind? Yet this is precisely what we have done. We have done it, moreover, for reasons that collapse the moment we examine them. We are told that the enormous and expanding use of pesticides is necessary to maintain farm production. Yet is our real problem not one of *overproduction*? Our farms, despite measures to remove acreages from production and to pay farmers *not* to produce, have yielded such a staggering excess of crops that the American taxpayer in 1962 is paying out more than one billion dollars a year as the total carrying cost of the surplus-food storage program. And is the situation helped when one branch of the Agriculture Department tries to reduce production while another states, as it did in 1958, "It is believed generally that reduction of crop acreages under provisions of the Soil

Bank will stimulate interest in use of chemicals to obtain maximum production on the land retained in crops."

All this is not to say there is no insect problem and no need of control. I am saying, rather, that control must be geared to realities, not to mythical situations, and that the methods employed must be such that they do not destroy us along with the insects.

The problem whose attempted solution has brought such a train of disaster in its wake is an accompaniment of our modern way of life. Long before the age of man, insects inhabited the earth—a group of extraordinarily varied and adaptable beings. Over the course of time since man's advent, a small percentage of the more than half a million species of insects have come into conflict with human welfare in two principal ways: as competitors for the food supply and as carriers of human disease.

Disease-carrying insects become important where human beings are crowded together, especially under conditions where sanitation is poor, as in time of natural disaster or war or in situations of extreme poverty and deprivation. Then control of some sort becomes necessary. It is a sobering fact, however, as we shall presently see, that the method of massive chemical control has had only limited success, and also threatens to worsen the very conditions it is intended to curb.

Under primitive agricultural conditions the farmer had few insect problems.   15
These arose with the intensification of agriculture—the devotion of immense acreages to a single crop. Such a system set the stage for explosive increases in specific insect populations. Single-crop farming does not take advantage of the principles by which nature works; it is agriculture as an engineer might conceive it to be. Nature has introduced great variety into the landscape, but man has displayed a passion for simplifying it. Thus he undoes the built-in checks and balances by which nature holds the species within bounds. One important natural check is a limit on the amount of suitable habitat for each species. Obviously then, an insect that lives on wheat can build up its population to much higher levels on a farm devoted to wheat than on one in which wheat is intermingled with other crops to which the insect is not adapted.

The same thing happens in other situations. A generation or more ago, the towns of large areas of the United States lined their streets with the noble elm tree. Now the beauty they hopefully created is threatened with complete destruction as disease sweeps through the elms, carried by a beetle that would have only limited chance to build up large populations and to spread from tree to tree if the elms were only occasional trees in a richly diversified planting.

Another factor in the modern insect problem is one that must be viewed against a background of geologic and human history: the spreading of thousands of different kinds of organisms from their native homes to invade new territories. This worldwide migration has been studied and graphically described by the British ecologist Charles Elton in his recent book *The Ecology of Invasions*. During the Cretaceous Period, some hundred million years ago, flooding seas cut many land bridges between continents and living things found themselves confined in what Elton calls "colossal separate nature reserves." There, isolated from others of their kind, they developed many new species. When some of the land masses were joined again, about 15 million years ago, these species began to move out into new territories—a movement that is not only still in progress but is now receiving considerable assistance from man.

The importation of plants is the primary agent in the modern spread of species, for animals have almost invariably gone along with the plants, quarantine being a comparatively recent and not completely effective innovation. The United States Office of Plant Introduction alone has introduced almost 200,000 species and varieties of plants from all over the world. Nearly half of the 180 or so major insect enemies of plants in the United States are accidental imports from abroad, and most of them have come as hitchhikers on plants.

In new territory, out of reach of the restraining hand of the natural enemies that kept down its numbers in its native land, an invading plant or animal is able to become enormously abundant. Thus it is no accident that our most troublesome insects are introduced species.

These invasions, both the naturally occurring and those dependent on 20 human assistance, are likely to continue indefinitely. Quarantine and massive chemical campaigns are only extremely expensive ways of buying time. We are faced, according to Dr. Elton, "with a life-and-death need not just to find new technological means of suppressing this plant or that animal"; instead we need the basic knowledge of animal populations and their relations to their surroundings that will "promote an even balance and damp down the explosive power of outbreaks and new invasions."

Much of the necessary knowledge is now available but we do not use it. We train ecologists in our universities and even employ them in our governmental agencies but we seldom take their advice. We allow the chemical death rain to fall as though there were no alternative, whereas in fact there are many, and our ingenuity could soon discover many more if given opportunity.

Have we fallen into a mesmerized state that makes us accept as inevitable that which is inferior or detrimental, as though having lost the will or the vision to demand that which is good? Such thinking, in the words of the ecologist Paul Shepard, "idealizes life with only its head out of water, inches above the limits of toleration of the corruption of its own environment. . . . Why should we tolerate a diet of weak poisons, a home in insipid surroundings, a circle of acquaintances who are not quite our enemies, the noise of motors with just enough relief to prevent insanity? Who would want to live in a world which is just not quite fatal?"

Yet such a world is pressed upon us. The crusade to create a chemically sterile, insect-free world seems to have engendered a fanatic zeal on the part of many specialists and most of the so-called control agencies. On every hand there is evidence that those engaged in spraying operations exercise a ruthless power. "The regulatory entomologists . . . function as prosecutor, judge and jury, tax assessor and collector and sheriff to enforce their own orders," said Connecticut entomologist Neely Turner. The most flagrant abuses go unchecked in both state and federal agencies.

It is not my contention that chemical insecticides must never be used. I do contend that we have put poisonous and biologically potent chemicals indiscriminately into the hands of persons largely or wholly ignorant of their potentials for harm. We have subjected enormous numbers of people to contact with these poisons, without their consent and often without their knowledge. If the Bill of Rights contains no guarantee that a citizen shall be secure against lethal poisons distributed either by private individuals or by public officials, it is surely only because our forefathers, despite their considerable wisdom and foresight, could conceive of no such problem.

I contend, furthermore, that we have allowed these chemicals to be used   25 with little or no advance investigation of their effect on soil, water, wildlife, and man himself. Future generations are unlikely to condone our lack of prudent concern for the integrity of the natural world that supports all life.

There is still very limited awareness of the nature of the threat. This is an era of specialists, each of whom sees his own problem and is unaware of or intolerant of the larger frame into which it fits. It is also an era dominated by industry, in which the right to make a dollar at whatever cost is seldom challenged. When the public protests, confronted with some obvious evidence of damaging results of pesticide applications, it is fed little tranquilizing pills of half truth. We urgently need an end to these false assurances, to the sugar coating of unpalatable facts. It is the public that is being asked to assume the risks that the insect controllers calculate. The public must decide whether it wishes to continue on the present road, and it can do so only when in full possession of the facts. In the words of Jean Rostand, "The obligation to endure gives us the right to know."

QUESTIONS FOR DISCUSSION AND WRITING

1. Why does Carson open her chapter with the disturbing claim that within a couple of decades in the mid-twentieth century, humans suddenly "acquired significant power" to disrupt the subtle balance "between living things and their surroundings" (paragraph 1)? What evidence does she cite? What has happened since then to corroborate her argument?

2. Thoreau asks in "Where I Lived and What I Lived For" (p. 187), "Why should we live with such hurry and waste of life?" Similarly, Carson urges us to follow "the deliberate pace of nature," not "the impetuous and heedless pace of man" (paragraph 4). How might both Thoreau and Carson be considered ecological prophets? Karen Armstrong writes, in "Does God Have a Future?" (p. 702), that "people have always created new symbols to act as a focus for spirituality . . . , to cultivate their sense of the wonder and ineffable significance of life" (para-

graph 20). Might Thoreau's and Carson's passion for nature represent, in part, an alternative to religious faith?

3. Compare Carson's notion of "little tranquilizing pills of half truth" (paragraph 26) with Williams's analysis in "Clan of the One-Breasted Women" of the federal government's deceitful assurance during the decade of above-ground nuclear testing in Utah and Nevada, "'It has been found that the tests may be conducted with adequate assurance of safety'" (paragraph 22ff.). What hierarchy of values appears to govern the dissemination of scientific information to the general public by government and industry? How can the public influence or change that hierarchy of values?

LINKED READINGS: GEOGRAPHY AND ECOLOGY

BARRY LOPEZ
The American Geographies

Born in Port Chester, New York (1945), Barry Lopez attended Notre Dame (B.A., 1966; M.A.T., 1968). His study of folklore at the University of Oregon led to his collection of Native American stories, Desert Notes *(1976). In his nature essays, Lopez uses the natural world to elucidate human nature. In* Of Wolves and Men *(1978), he rejects the image of wolves as ruthless killers and reveals human beings' tendency to project aspects of their own personalities onto animals.* Arctic Dreams *(1986), which won the National Book Award, examines Eskimo life, the contentious history of northern explorations, and natural history, analyzing such phenomena as light, ice, geology, and animals — including birds, bears, and seals.*

In "The American Geographies," taken from About This Life: Journeys on the Threshold of Memory *(1998), Lopez argues that America has become, for many, a generalized fantasy landscape in which people experience the land through television commercials and theme-park hype. Yet geography is actually a collection of specific sites where land, vegetation, and animal life exist in a complex harmony. On exploratory journeys with local experts and through regional literature, Lopez explains the need to protect our astonishingly diverse geographies from destruction.*

It has become commonplace to observe that Americans know little of the geography of their country, that they are innocent of it as a landscape of rivers, mountains, and towns. They do not know, supposedly, the location of the Delaware Water Gap, the Olympic Mountains, or the Piedmont Plateau; and, the indictment continues, they have little conception of the way the individual components of this landscape are imperiled, from a human perspective, by modern farming practices or industrial pollution.

I do not know how true this is, but it is easy to believe that it is truer than most of us would wish. A recent Gallup Organization and National Geographic Society survey found Americans woefully ignorant of world geography. Three out of four couldn't locate the Persian Gulf. The implication was that we knew no more about our own homeland, and that this ignorance undermined the integrity of our political processes and the efficiency of our business enterprises.

As Americans, we profess a sincere and fierce love for the American landscape, for our rolling prairies, free-flowing rivers, and "purple mountains' majesty"; but it is hard to imagine, actually, where this particular landscape is. It is not just that a nostalgic landscape has passed away—Mark Twain's Mississippi is now dammed from Illinois to Louisiana and the prairies have all been sold and fenced. It is that it's always been a romantic's landscape. In the attenuated form in which it is presented on television today, in magazine articles and in calendar photographs, the essential wildness of the American landscape is reduced to attractive scenery. We look out on a familiar, memorized landscape that portends adventure and promises enrichment. There are no distracting people in it and few artifacts of human life. The animals are all beautiful, diligent, one might even say well behaved. Nature's unruliness, the power of rivers and skies to intimidate, and any evidence of disastrous human land management practices are all but invisible. It is, in short, a magnificent garden, a colonial vision of paradise imposed on a real place that is, at best, only selectively known.

The real American landscape is a face of almost incomprehensible depth and complexity. If one were to sit for a few days, for example, among the ponderosa pine forests and black lava fields of the Cascade Mountains in western Oregon, inhaling the pines' sweet balm on an evening breeze from some point on the barren rock, and then were to step off to the Olympic Peninsula in Washington, to those rain forests with sphagnum moss floors soft as fleece underfoot and Douglas firs too big around for five people to hug, and then head south to walk the ephemeral creeks and sun-blistered playas of the Mojave Desert in southern California, one would be reeling under the sensations. The contrast is not only one of plants and soils, a different array, say, of brilliantly colored beetles. The shock to the senses comes from a different shape to the silence, a difference in the very quality of light, in the weight of the air. And this relatively short journey down the West Coast would still leave the traveler with all that lay to the east to explore— the anomalous sand hills of Nebraska, the heat and frog voices of Okefenokee Swamp, the fetch of Chesapeake Bay, the hardwood copses and black bears of the Ozark Mountains.

No one of these places, of course, can be entirely fathomed, biologically or aesthetically. They are mysteries upon which we impose names. Enchantments. We tick the names off glibly but lovingly. We mean no disrespect. Our genuine desire, though we may be skeptical about the time it would take and uncertain of its practical value to us, is to actually know these places. As deeply ingrained in the American psyche as the desire to conquer and control the land is the desire to sojourn in it, to sail up and down Pamlico Sound, to paddle a canoe through Minnesota's boundary waters, to walk on the desert of the Great Salt Lake, to camp in the stony hardwood valleys of Vermont.

To do this well, to really come to an understanding of a specific American geography, requires not only time but a kind of local expertise, an intimacy with place few of us ever develop. There is no way around the former requirement: if you want to know you must take the time. It is not in books. A specific geographical understanding, however, can be sought out and borrowed. It resides with men and women more or less sworn to a place, who abide there, who have a feel for the soil and history, for the turn of leaves and night sounds. Often they are glad to take the outlander in tow.

These local geniuses of American landscape, in my experience, are people in whom geography thrives. They are the antithesis of geographical ignorance. Rarely known outside their own communities, they often seem, at the first encounter, unremarkable and anonymous. They may not be able to recall the name of a particular wildflower—or they may have given it a name known only to them. They might have forgotten the precise circumstances of a local historical event. Or they can't say for certain when the last of the Canada geese passed through in the fall, or can't differentiate between two kinds of trout in the same creek. Like all of us, they have fallen prey to the fallacies of memory and are burdened with ignorance; but they are nearly flawless in the respect they bear these places they love. Their knowledge is intimate rather than encyclopedic, human but not necessarily scholarly. It rings with the concrete details of experience.

America, I believe, teems with such people. The paradox here, between a faulty grasp of geographical knowledge for which Americans are indicted and the intimate, apparently contradictory familiarity of a group of largely anonymous people, is not solely a matter of confused scale. (The local landscape is easier to know than a national landscape—and many local geographers, of course, are relatively ignorant of a national geography.)

And it is not simply ironic. The paradox is dark. To be succinct: the politics and advertising that seek a national audience must project a national geography; to be broadly useful that geography must, inevitably, be generalized and it is often romantic. It is therefore frequently misleading and imprecise. The same holds true with the entertainment industry, but here the problem might be clearer. The same films, magazines, and television features that honor an imaginary American landscape also tout the worth of the anonymous men and women who interpret it. Their affinity for the land is lauded, their local allegiance admired. But the rigor of their local geographies, taken as a whole, contradicts a patriotic, national vision of unspoiled, untroubled land. These men and women are ultimately forgotten, along with the details of the landscapes they speak for, in the face of more pressing national matters. It is the chilling nature of modern society to find an ignorance of geography, local or national, as excusable as an ignorance of hand tools; and to find the commitment of people to their home places only momentarily entertaining. And finally naïve.

In forty thousand years of human history, it has only been in the last few hun- 10
dred years or so that a people could afford to ignore their local geographies as
completely as we do and still survive. Technological innovations from refriger-
ated trucks to artificial fertilizers, from sophisticated cost accounting to mass air
transportation, have utterly changed concepts of season, distance, soil productiv-
ity, and the real cost of drawing sustenance from the land. It is now possible for a
resident of Kansas City to bite into a fresh mango in the dead of winter; for
someone in San Francisco to travel to Atlanta in a few hours with no worry of
how formidable might be crossings of the Great Basin Desert or the Mississippi
River; for an absentee farmer to gain a tax advantage from a farm that leaches
poisons into its water table and on which crops are left to rot. . . . Year by year,
the number of people with firsthand experience in the land dwindles. Rural populations continue to shift to the cities. The family farm is in a state of demise, and
government and industry continue to apply pressure on the native peoples of
North America to sever their ties with the land. In the wake of this loss of personal and local knowledge, the knowledge from which a real geography is derived, the knowledge on which a country must ultimately stand, has come
something hard to define but I think sinister and unsettling—the packaging and
marketing of land as a form of entertainment. An incipient industry, capitalizing
on the nostalgia Americans feel for the imagined virgin landscapes of their ancestors, and on a desire for adventure, now offers people a convenient though sometimes incomplete or even spurious geography as an inducement to purchase a
unique experience. But the line between authentic experience and a superficial
exposure to the elements of experience is blurred. And the real landscape, in all
its complexity, is distorted even further in the public imagination. No longer in-
nately mysterious and dignified, a ground from which experience grows, it becomes a curiously generic backdrop on which experience is imposed.

In theme parks the profound, subtle, and protracted experience of running a
river is reduced to a loud, quick, safe equivalence, a pleasant distraction. People
only able to venture into the countryside on annual vacations are, increasingly,
schooled in the belief that wild land will, and should, provide thrills and exceptional scenery on a timely basis. If it does not, something is wrong, either with
the land itself or possibly with the company outfitting the trip.

People in America, then, face a convoluted situation. The land itself, vast
and differentiated, defies the notion of a national geography. If applied at all it
must be applied lightly, and it must grow out of the concrete detail of local geographies. Yet Americans are daily presented with, and have become accustomed
to talking about, a homogenized national geography, one that seems to operate
independently of the land, a collection of objects rather than a continuous bolt of
fabric. It appears in advertisements, as a background in movies, and in patriotic
calendars. The suggestion is that there *can* be a national geography because the
constituent parts are interchangeable and can be treated as commodities. In day-
to-day affairs, in other words, one place serves as well as another to convey one's
point. On reflection, this is an appalling condescension and a terrible impreci-

sion, the very antithesis of knowledge. The idea that either the Green River in Utah or the Salmon River in Idaho will do, or that the valleys of Kentucky and West Virginia are virtually interchangeable, is not just misleading. For people still dependent on the soil for their sustenance, or for people whose memories tie them to those places, it betrays a numbing casualness, a utilitarian, expedient, and commercial frame of mind. It heralds a society in which it is no longer necessary for human beings to know where they live, except as those places are described and fixed by numbers. The truly difficult and lifelong task of discovering where one lives is finally disdained.

If a society forgets or no longer cares where it lives, then anyone with the political power and the will to do so can manipulate the landscape to conform to certain social ideals or nostalgic visions. People may hardly notice that anything has happened, or assume that whatever happens—a mountain stripped of timber and eroding into its creeks—is for the common good. The more superficial a society's knowledge of the real dimensions of the land it occupies becomes, the more vulnerable the land is to exploitation, to manipulation for short-term gain. The land, virtually powerless before political and commercial entities, finds itself finally with no defenders. It finds itself bereft of intimates with indispensable, concrete knowledge. (Oddly, or perhaps not oddly, while American society continues to value local knowledge as a quaint part of its heritage, it continues to cut such people off from any real political power. This is as true for small farmers and illiterate cowboys as it is for American Indians, native Hawaiians, and Eskimos.)

The intense pressure of imagery in America, and the manipulation of images necessary to a society with specific goals, means the land will inevitably be treated like a commodity; and voices that tend to contradict the proffered image will, one way or another, be silenced or discredited by those in power. This is not new to America; the promulgation in America of a false or imposed geography has been the case from the beginning. All local geographies, as they were defined by hundreds of separate, independent native traditions, were denied in the beginning in favor of an imported and unifying vision of America's natural history. The country, the landscape itself, was eventually defined according to dictates of Progress like Manifest Destiny, and laws like the Homestead Act which reflected a poor understanding of the physical lay of the land. . . .

The promulgation of false geographies, which threaten the fundamental notion of what it means to live somewhere, is a current with a stable and perhaps growing countercurrent. People living in New York City are familiar with the stone basements, the cratonic geology, of that island and have a feeling for birds migrating through in the fall, their sequence and number. They do not find the city alien but human, its attenuated natural history merely different from that of rural Georgia or Wisconsin. I find the countermeasure, too, among Eskimos who cannot read but who might engage you for days on the subtleties of sea-ice topography. And among men and women who, though they have followed in the footsteps of their parents, have come to the conclusion that they cannot farm or fish or log in the way their ancestors did; the finite boundaries to this sort of wealth have appeared in their lifetime. Or among young men and women who have taken several decades of book-learned agronomy, zoology, silviculture and horticulture, ecology, ethnobotany, and fluvial geomorphology and turned it into a new kind of local knowledge, who have taken up residence in a place and sought, both because of and in spite of their education, to develop a deep intimacy with it. Or they have gone to work, idealistically, for the National Park Service or the fish and wildlife services or for a private institution like the Nature Conservancy. They are people to whom the land is more than politics or economics. These are people for whom the land is alive. It feeds them, directly, and that is how and why they learn its geography.

In the end, then, if you begin among the blue crabs of Chesapeake Bay and wander for several years, down through the Smoky Mountains and back to the bluegrass hills, along the drainages of the Ohio and into the hill country of Missouri, where in summer a chorus of cicadas might drown out human conversation, then up the Missouri itself, reading on the way the entries of Meriwether Lewis and William Clark and musing on the demise of the plains grizzly and the sturgeon, cross west into the drainage of the Platte. . . . [y]ou would have seen so much, breathtaking, startling, and outsize, that you might not be able for a long time to break the spell, the sense, especially finishing your journey in the West, that the land had not been as rearranged or quite as compromised as you had first imagined.

After you had slept some nights on the beach, however, with that finite line of the ocean before you and the land stretching out behind you, the wind first battering then cradling you, you would be compelled by memory, obligated by your own involvement, to speak of what left you troubled. To find the rivers dammed and shrunken, the soil washed away, the land fenced, a tracery of pipes and wires and roads laid down everywhere, blocking and channeling the movement of water and animals, cutting the eye off repeatedly and confining it—you had expected this. It troubles you no more than your despair over the ruthlessness, the insensitivity, the impetuousness of modern life. What underlies this obvious change, however, is a less noticeable pattern of disruption: acidic lakes, skies empty of birds, fouled beaches, the poisonous slags of industry, the sun burning like a molten coin in ruined air.

It is a tenet of certain ideologies that man is responsible for all that is ugly, that everything nature creates is beautiful. Nature's darkness goes partly unreported, of course, and human brilliance is often perversely ignored. What is true is that man has a power, literally beyond his comprehension, to destroy. The lethality of some of what he manufactures, the incompetence with which he stores it or seeks to dispose of it, the cavalier way in which he employs in his daily living substances that threaten his health, the leniency of the courts in these matters (as though products as well as people enjoyed the protection of the Fifth Amendment), and the treatment of open land, rivers, and the atmosphere as if, in some medieval way, they could still be regarded as disposal sinks of infinite capacity, would make you wonder, standing face to in the wind at Cape Mendocino, if we weren't bent on an errand of madness.

The geographies of North America, the myriad small landscapes that make up the national fabric, are threatened—by ignorance of what makes them unique, by utilitarian attitudes, by failure to include them in the moral universe, and by brutal disregard. A testament of minor voices can clear away an ignorance of any place, can inform us of its special qualities; but no voice, by merely telling a story, can cause the poisonous wastes that saturate some parts of the land to decompose, to evaporate. This responsibility falls ultimately to the national community, a vague and fragile entity to be sure, but one that, in America, can be ferocious in exerting its will.

Geography, the formal way in which we grapple with this areal mystery, is fi- 20 nally knowledge that calls up something in the land we recognize and respond to. It gives us a sense of place and a sense of community. Both are indispensable to a state of well-being, an individual's and a country's.

SANDRA POSTEL

Troubled Waters

Sandra Postel, former vice president for research at the Worldwatch Institute, a Washington, D.C.–based environmental policy organization, is currently director of the Global Water Policy Project in Amherst, Massachusetts, where her research focuses on international water issues and strategies. She is also a visiting lecturer in environmental studies at Mount Holyoke College.

The following commentary is from an essay in Science *in 2000.*

In June 1991, after a leisurely lunch in the fashionable Washington, D.C., neighborhood of Dupont Circle, Alexei Yablokov, then a Soviet parliamentarian, told me something shocking. Some years back he had had a map hanging on his office wall depicting Soviet central Asia without the vast Aral Sea. Cartographers had drawn it in the 1960s, when the Aral was still the world's fourth-largest inland body of water.

I felt for a moment like a cold war spy to whom a critical secret had just been revealed. The Aral Sea, as I knew well, was drying up. The existence of such a map implied that its ongoing destruction was no accident. Moscow's central planners had decided to sacrifice the sea, judging that the two rivers feeding it could be put to more valuable use irrigating cotton in the central Asian desert. Such a planned elimination of an ecosystem nearly the size of Ireland was surely one of humanity's more arrogant acts.

Four years later, when I traveled to the Aral Sea region, the Soviet Union was no more; the central Asian republics were now independent. But the legacy of

Moscow's policies lived on: thirty-five years of siphoning the region's rivers had decreased the Aral's volume by nearly two thirds and its surface area by half. I stood on what had once been a seaside bluff outside the former port town of Muynak, but I could see no water. The sea was twenty-five miles away. A graveyard of ships lay before me, rotting and rusting in the dried-up seabed. Sixty thousand fishing jobs had vanished, and thousands of people had left the area. Many of those who remained suffered from a variety of cancers, respiratory ailments, and other diseases. Winds ripping across the desert were lifting tens of millions of tons of a toxic salt-dust chemical residue from the exposed seabed each year and dumping it on surrounding croplands and villages. Dust storms and polluted rivers made it hazardous to breathe the air and drink the water.

The tragedy of the Aral Sea is by no means unique. Around the world countless rivers, lakes, and wetlands are succumbing to dams, river diversions, rampant pollution, and other pressures. Collectively they underscore what is rapidly emerging as one of the greatest challenges facing humanity in the decades to come: how to satisfy the thirst of a world population pushing nine billion by the year 2050, while protecting the health of the aquatic environment that sustains all terrestrial life.

The problem, though daunting, is not insurmountable. A number of technologies and management practices are available that could substantially reduce the amount of water used by agriculture, industry, and households. But the sad reality is that the rules and policies that drive water-related decisions have not adequately promoted them. We have the ability to provide both people and ecosystems with the water they need for good health, but those goals need to be elevated on the political agenda.

KIM WARP

Rising Sea Levels—An Alternative Theory

Rising Sea Levels — An Alternative Theory

QUESTIONS FOR DISCUSSION AND WRITING

1. What does Lopez suggest can and should be done about the contradiction between Americans' avowed love of the land and actual ignorance of it?

2. Identify the important features of what Lopez calls a "national geography." In what ways has this essay changed your thinking about a "national geography"? In what ways will you be more critical of the sweeping glorification of our country that provides few details of specific places?

3. List the important characteristics of Lopez's concept of "local geographies" and explain why he uses the plural. Write an essay about the personal significance of a particular local geography (or geographies). To gather details and information, you may want to follow Thoreau's example and go to the woods or some other spot where you can "live deliberately, to front only the essential facts of life" (p. 188). Or roam the terrain and examine what you see with great care, as Dillard does in "Heaven and Earth in Jest" (p. 641).

4. What is "the tragedy of the Aral Sea" (Postel, paragraph 4)? In what ways is this representative of the larger problem of worldwide water consumption and

governmental water policies? Relate the disappearance of the Aral Sea to the environmental problems Lopez alludes to, as well as to those Terry Tempest Williams discusses in "Clan of the One-Breasted Women" (p. 656).

WILLIAM E. REES

Life in the Lap of Luxury as Ecosystems Collapse

William E. Rees received his doctorate in bioecology from the University of Toronto. Since 1969, he has been a professor at the University of British Columbia, where for many years he directed the School of Community and Regional Planning, a program that focuses on issues of environmentally sound global development. A founding member of Pollution Probe and a former president of the Canadian Society for Ecological Economics, Rees has focused much of his research and writing on sustainable socioeconomic development and on the public policy and planning implications of global environmental trends. He is the coauthor of Our Ecological Footprint: Reducing Human Impact on the Earth *(1995), which considers ways to measure area-based indicators of worldwide environmental sustainability. Rees has also argued extensively for limits on and alternatives to the industrial nations' use of dwindling reserves of fossil fuel and other resources. In the following essay from the* Chronicle of Higher Education *(July 30, 1999), Rees warns that growing urban centers increasingly drain worldwide ecological capacity, which could soon lead to environmental and political disaster.*

Have you ever asked yourself how much of the earth's surface is required to support you in the style to which you are accustomed? Every free-range dairy farmer knows, within a few square meters, how much pasture of a given quality is needed to support each of his cattle, and just how many head he can safely graze on the back forty. Similar questions, however, seldom come up in relation to people.

The Cartesian dualism that underpins Western philosophy and science has been so successful in psychologically separating humans from nature that we simply don't conceive of ourselves as ecological beings, as creatures of the land. Ignoring our dependence on our environment is a serious mistake.

In recent decades, the world has experienced an event of profound significance: the massive migration of people from the countryside to the city. In 1950, New York was the only city on the planet with 10 million or more inhabitants; by 2015, as many as 27 cities—most of them in the developing world—will be that large. In the 1990s alone, the population of the world's cities will increase by 50 per cent, to 3 billion people. The United Nations projects that an additional 2.1 billion people—which was roughly the population of the entire globe in the early 1930s—will be living in cities by 2025.

We usually think of urbanization mainly as a demographic or economic transition. Hardly anyone acknowledges it as a potential ecological problem. On the contrary, many observers interpret urbanization as further evidence of humanity's increasing technical prowess and independence from the land. Such technological hubris is an illusion. Separating billions of people from the land that sustains them is a giddy leap of faith with serious implications for ecological security.

For proof, let's explore the fundamental ecological question posed above. We can analyze an average person's ecological footprint to estimate how much land people actually use. The analysis involves identifying and quantifying all significant categories of materials and energy appropriated from nature to support the consumption patterns of a defined group of people. We can then calculate the area of land and water required to supply the materials and energy. For example, about 25 square meters of former tropical forest are needed just to produce the coffee beans for the average java drinker in an industrialized country. We can also estimate the ecosystem area needed to absorb certain critical wastes. Heavy users of fossil fuels need 2 to 3 hectares (4.9 to 7.4 acres) of forest somewhere on the planet to absorb their carbon-dioxide emissions alone.

In summary, the ecological footprint of a population is the total area of land and water required to produce the resources that the population consumes, and to assimilate the wastes that the population generates, wherever on earth that land is located.

As Mathis Wackernagel and I have shown in *Our Ecological Footprint* (New Society, 1995), the residents of high-income countries typically need 4 to 9 hectares (10 to 22 acres) per capita to support their consumer life styles. That area seems large. However, since our calculations assume that all the land involved is being managed sustainably (which is rarely the case), our results actually underestimate the total demand. Thus, it is easy to see that cities typically impose an ecological footprint on the earth several hundred times larger than their political or geographic areas.

Most people think of cities as centers of culture and learning, and as the productive engines of economic growth. All that is true, but they also are sites of intense consumption of material and production of waste. As the well-known U.S. ecologist Eugene P. Odum recognized in *Fundamentals of Ecology*, "Great cities are planned and grow without any regard for the fact that they are parasites on the countryside which must somehow supply food, water, and air, and degrade huge quantities of waste." In short, far from signaling humanity's final separation from nature, urbanization merely removes people both spatially and psychologically from the land that sustains them.

In that light, consider the following additional dimensions of urban human ecology:

- The principal material effect of technology has been to extend the spatial scale and intensity of humans' capacity to exploit nature. Contrary to conventional views, our ecological footprint is expanding, not decreasing, with increasing wealth and technological advances.

- Many croplands and forests are being used more intensively than ever to sustain the world's burgeoning urban populations. In that sense, the great plains of North America are an essential component of the urban ecosystem.
- While the citizens of urban industrial societies use up to 9 hectares of productive land and water, the earth contains only about 2 hectares of such ecosystems per capita. The consumer life styles of rich countries cannot be extended sustainably to the entire human population, using current technologies.
- In a world of rapid change, no city can be truly sustainable unless the lands in its footprint are secure from ecological change and international hostilities.

Cities have been part of the human cultural landscape for thousands of years, but only in recent decades has it become possible for the majority of people to live in cities. For better or worse, however, this phase of our development may be relatively short-lived. The recent explosive growth of the human population, our intensely material culture, and urbanization itself are all products of what the sociologist William R. Catton has called the "age of exuberance." In *Overshoot*, Catton explained that the heady optimism of twentieth-century North America, for example, has been sustained by a sense of unlimited abundance as we have exploited the continent's stocks of natural resources, particularly fossil fuels. But Catton recognized that that exuberance "had to be temporary, for [it leads] inexorably to a change in the environmental conditions that made [it] possible." 10

In short, we have been consuming resources in this century that will therefore not be available in the next. Global grain production per capita has been falling for more than a decade, the production of the world's fisheries peaked in the late 1980s, water supplies are stretched to the limit in many parts of the world, and global oil production will probably peak in the next decade. (The United States has been producing less and less oil for the past 30 years and now imports most of its petroleum.)

Although the world's wealthy nations have been protected so far from the consequences of such trends by their purchasing power in global markets, it is questionable whether that isolation can be maintained for long, in the face of growing demand and collapsing ecosystems. The political scientists Thomas Homer-Dixon, Jeffrey H. Boutwell, and George W. Rathjens directed a project on environmental change and acute conflict, sponsored by the University of Toronto and the American Academy of Arts and Sciences. In a 1993 article in *Scientific American*, they wrote that "in many parts of the world, environmental degradation seems to have passed a threshold of irreversibility" and that "renewable resource scarcities of the next 50 years will probably occur with a speed, complexity, and magnitude unprecedented in history." The authors made the case that the widespread loss of ecological stability—including the collapse of fisheries, deforestation, and chronic drought—is likely to lead to greater geopolitical strife and even war in the coming decades.

In an era of global change and increasing political uncertainty, should we not be developing strategies to insure the viability and sustainability of our cities? More fundamentally, should we encourage or resist further urbanization? In *Cities and Sustainable Development*, Diana Mitlin and David Satterthwaite stress that high urban-population densities produce the economies of scale needed for energy-saving strategies such as recycling and mass transit. However, their analysis implicitly assumes that the city enjoys a stable and predictable relationship with its hinterland. But can any city be viable, let alone sustainable, if its distant sources of supply are threatened by ecological change or international hostilities?

The perspectives and skills of many disciplines are required to assess the vulnerability of urban populations in the twenty-first century and to determine the measures needed to enhance their security. Perhaps most important, we must develop a holistic concept of the city-as-system. Urban planning should include as much as possible of the city's ecological footprint.

That would shift the focus of planning from mere growth management to mechanisms to reduce the city's dependence on distant parts of the planet. I am not advocating self-sufficiency: Clearly, trade will continue to be important— and, despite global warming, it will be some time before we can grow coffee in the suburbs of Chicago. However, major cities should have secure access to food and other staples, preferably close at hand, and learn to recycle their wastes locally. Even this simpler goal is a daunting one at current levels of resource consumption and waste production. The ecological footprint of London, for example, is larger than the entire United Kingdom.

The time has come for us to take seriously the idea that each of us lives in a bioregion—a geographic area defined by both biophysical characteristics, including watershed boundaries, and patterns of occupancy by humans and other species—and that our urban ecological footprints should be contained as much as possible within our local bioregions. Ecologists and economists should work together to determine criteria for delineating bioregions. Geographers and urban planners might study such issues as the optimal pattern of human population distribution within various bioregions, and the appropriate size for cities. Political scientists should consider which powers federal and state or provincial governments might devolve to the local level, and which they should keep, to facilitate the planning that long-term urban sustainability will require.

In the long run, the most secure and sustainable cities may be those that succeed in reintegrating the geography of living and employment, of production and consumption, of city and hinterland. As Sim Van der Ryn and Peter Calthorpe wrote in *Sustainable Communities,* such a transformed city, "rather than being merely the site of consumption, might, through its very design, produce some of its own food and energy, as well as become the locus of work for its residents."

If we followed such ecological design principles, urban regions could gradually become not only more self-reliant, but also more socially rewarding and ecologically benign. Through greater dependence on local ecosystems, city dwellers would become more aware of their connectedness to nature. As they became more conscientious stewards of the environment, their lives would become less materialistic; in turn, that change would reduce both cities' ecological footprints and the political tensions they would otherwise foster.

To the upwardly mobile beneficiaries of the age of exuberance, all that may sound surreal, even ridiculous. We are accustomed to expecting a future of more and bigger, of freewheeling technological mastery over the natural world. But that road leads inevitably to a dead end. Accelerating global change has shown that the earth cannot keep an infinitely expanding population in the lap of luxury. Scholars should start looking for a new route now.

QUESTIONS FOR DISCUSSION AND WRITING

1. Why, according to Rees, do urban areas and high-income countries create a disproportionate drain on worldwide environmental resources? Why is it so easy to overlook this fact?

2. In your own words, what is the "ecological footprint" of a population? In what ways is this concept central to Rees's argument here? Does Rees succeed in convincing you of the urgency of the problem he describes? Why or why not?

3. Based on Rees's argument here, what are some things that you could do to reduce your consumption of dwindling natural resources? With a partner, write a position paper offering advice to your peers, and perhaps to community planners, on how to shrink one's individual footprint.

MARGARET MEAD

Warfare Is Only an Invention — Not a Biological Necessity

Margaret Mead's life (1901–1978) and career as an anthropologist were dominated by her imaginative curiosity about how people negotiated life's major issues. She devoted her energy, ingenuity, and creativity to research — particularly of women and children — through total immersion in the tribal societies ("natural laboratories") she studied in Bali, Samoa, and New Guinea. Her doctoral research at Columbia University (Ph.D., 1929) was significantly influenced by her mentor, Franz Boas. Instead of the dry statistical analyses that had prevailed in anthropology before World War I, Mead learned the tribal languages and kept elaborate notes on the culture, customs, and artifacts, which she wrote up in a descriptive, colorful style. This, coupled with her accessible style of public speaking, made her books such as Coming of Age in Samoa *(1928),* Growing Up in New Guinea *(1930), and* Sex and Temperament in Three Primitive Societies *(1935) wildly popular, as was her autobiography,* Blackberry Winter *(1972). In "Warfare Is Only an Invention— Not a Biological Necessity," originally published in* Asia *magazine (1940), Mead employs her typical means of argument by using numerous comparable examples from various societies.*

Is war a biological necessity, a sociological inevitability or just a bad invention? Those who argue for the first view endow man with such pugnacious instincts that some outlet in aggressive behavior is necessary if man is to reach full human stature. It was this point of view which lay back of William James's famous essay, "The Moral Equivalent of War," in which he tried to retain the warlike virtues and channel them in new directions. A similar point of view has lain back of the Soviet Union's attempt to make competition between groups rather than between individuals. A basic, competitive, aggressive, warring human nature is assumed, and those who wish to outlaw war or outlaw competitiveness merely try to find new and less socially destructive ways in which these biologically given aspects of man's nature can find expression. Then there are those who take the second view: warfare is the inevitable concomitant of the development of the state, the struggle for land and natural resources of class societies springing, not from the nature of man, but from the nature of history. War is nevertheless inevitable unless we change our social system and outlaw classes, the struggle for power, and possessions; and in the event of our success warfare would disappear, as a symptom vanishes when the disease is cured.

One may hold a sort of compromise position between these two extremes; one may claim that all aggression springs from the frustration of man's biologically determined drives and that, since all forms of culture are frustrating, it is certain each new generation will be aggressive and the aggression will find its natural and inevitable expression in race war, class war, nationalistic war, and so on. All three of these positions are very popular today among those who think seriously about the problems of war and its possible prevention, but I wish to urge another point of view, less defeatist perhaps than the first and third, and more accurate than the second: that is, that warfare, by which I mean recognized conflict between two groups *as groups,* in which each group puts an army (even if the army is only fifteen pygmies) into the field to fight and kill, if possible, some of the members of the army of the other group—that warfare of this sort is an invention like any other of the inventions in terms of which we order our lives, such as writing, marriage, cooking our food instead of eating it raw, trial by jury or burial of the dead, and so on. Some of this list anyone will grant are inventions: trial by jury is confined to very limited portions of the globe; we know that there are tribes that do not bury their dead but instead expose or cremate them; and we know that only part of the human race has had the knowledge of writing as its cultural inheritance. But, whenever a way of doing things is found universally, such as the use of fire or the practice of some form of marriage, we tend to think at once that it is not an invention at all but an attribute of humanity itself. And yet even such universals as marriage and the use of fire are inventions like the rest, very basic ones, inventions which were perhaps necessary if human history was to take the turn that it has taken, but nevertheless inventions. At some point in his social development man was undoubtedly without the institution of marriage or the knowledge of the use of fire.

The case for warfare is much clearer because there are peoples even today who have no warfare. Of these the Eskimos are perhaps the most conspicuous examples, but the Lepchas of Sikkim described by Geoffrey Gorer in *Himalayan Village* are as good. Neither of these peoples understands war, not even defensive warfare. The idea of warfare is lacking, and this idea is as essential to really carrying on war as an alphabet, or a syllabary is to writing. But whereas the Lepchas are a gentle, unquarrelsome people, and the advocates of other points of view might argue that they are not full human beings or that they had never been frustrated and so had no aggression to expand in warfare, the Eskimo case gives no such possibility of interpretation. The Eskimo are not a mild and meek people; many of them are turbulent and troublesome. Fights, theft of wives, murder, cannibalism, occur among them—all outbursts of passionate men goaded by desire or intolerable circumstance. Here are men faced with hunger, men faced with loss of their wives, men faced with the threat of extermination by other men, and here are orphan children, growing up miserably with no one to care for them, mocked and neglected by those about them. The personality necessary for war, the circumstances necessary to goad men to desperation are present, but there is no war. When a traveling Eskimo entered a settlement he might have to fight the strongest man in the settlement to establish his position among them, but this was a test of strength and bravery, not war. The idea of warfare, of one *group* organizing against another *group* to maim and wound and kill them was absent. And without that idea passions might rage but there was no war.

But, it may be argued, isn't this because the Eskimo have such a low and undeveloped form of social organization? They own no land, they move from place to place, camping, it is true, season after season on the same site, but this is not something to fight for as the modern nations of the world fight for land and raw materials. They have no permanent possessions that can be looted, no towns that can be burned. They have no social classes to produce stress and strains within the society which might force it to go to war outside. Doesn't the absence of war among the Eskimo, while disproving the biological necessity of war, just go to confirm the point that it is the state of development of the society which accounts for war, and nothing else?

We find the answer among the pygmy peoples of the Andaman Islands in the Bay of Bengal. The Andamans also represent an exceedingly low level of society; they are a hunting and food-gathering people; they live in tiny hordes without any class stratification; their houses are simpler than the snow houses of the Eskimo. But they knew about warfare. The army might contain only fifteen determined pygmies marching in a straight line, but it was the real thing nonetheless. Tiny army met tiny army in open battle, blows were exchanged, casualties suffered, and the state of warfare could only be concluded by a peacemaking ceremony.

Similarly, among the Australian aborigines, who built no permanent dwellings but wandered from water hole to water hole over their almost desert country, warfare—and rules of "international law"—were highly developed. The student of social evolution will seek in vain for his obvious causes of war, struggle for lands, struggle for power of one group over another, expansion of population, need to divert the minds of a populace restive under tyranny, or even the ambition of a successful leader to enhance his own prestige. All are absent, but warfare as a practice remained, and men engaged in it and killed one another in the course of a war because killing is what is done in wars.

From instances like these it becomes apparent that an inquiry into the cause of war misses the fundamental point as completely as does an insistence upon the biological necessity of war. If people have an idea of going to war and the idea that war is the way in which certain situations, defined within their society, are to be handled, they will sometimes go to war. If they are a mild and unaggressive people, like the Pueblo Indians, they may limit themselves to defensive warfare; but they will be forced to think in terms of war because there are peoples near them who have warfare as a pattern, and offensive, raiding, pillaging warfare at that. When the pattern of warfare is known, people like the Pueblo Indians will defend themselves, taking advantage of their natural defenses, the *mesa* village site, and people like the Lepchas, having no natural defenses and no idea of warfare, will merely submit to the invader. But the essential point remains the same. There is a way of behaving which is known to a given people and labeled as an appropriate form of behavior; a bold and warlike people like the Sioux or the Maori may label warfare as desirable as well as possible; a mild people like the Pueblo Indians may label warfare as undesirable; but to the minds of both peoples the possibility of warfare is present. Their thoughts, their hopes, their plans are oriented about this idea, that warfare may be selected as the way to meet some situation.

So simple peoples and civilized peoples, mild peoples and violent, assertive peoples, will all go to war if they have the invention, just as those peoples who have the custom of dueling will have duels and peoples who have the pattern of vendetta will indulge in vendetta. And, conversely, peoples who do not know of dueling will not fight duels, even though their wives are seduced and their daughters ravished; they may on occasion commit murder but they will not fight duels. Cultures which lack the idea of the vendetta will not meet every quarrel in this way. A people can use only the forms it has. So the Balinese have their special way of dealing with a quarrel between two individuals: if the two feel that the causes of quarrel are heavy they may go and register their quarrel in the temple before the gods, and, making offerings, they may swear never to have anything to do with each other again. Today they register such mutual "not-speaking" with the Dutch government officials. But in other societies, although individuals might feel as full of animosity and as unwilling to have any further contact as do the Balinese, they cannot register their quarrel with the gods and go on quietly about their business because registering quarrels with the gods is not an invention of which they know.

Yet, if it be granted that warfare is after all an invention, it may nevertheless be an invention that lends itself to certain types of personality, to the exigent needs of autocrats, to the expansionist desires of crowded peoples, to the desire for plunder and rape and loot which is engendered by a dull and frustrating life. What, then, can we say of this congruence between warfare and its uses? If it is a form which fits so well, is not this congruence the essential point? But even here the primitive material causes us to wonder, because there are tribes who go to war merely for glory, having no quarrel with the enemy, suffering from no tyrant within their boundaries, anxious neither for land nor loot nor women, but merely anxious to win prestige which within that tribe has been declared obtainable only by war and without which no young man can hope to win his sweetheart's smile of approval. But if, as was the case with the Bush Negroes of Dutch Guiana, it is artistic ability which is necessary to win a girl's approval, the same young man would have to be carving rather than going out on a war party.

In many parts of the world, war is a game in which the individual can win   10
counters—counters which bring him prestige in the eyes of his own sex or of the opposite sex; he plays for these counters as he might, in our society, strive for a tennis championship. Warfare is a frame for such prestige-seeking merely because it calls for the display of certain skills and certain virtues; all of these skills—riding straight, shooting straight, dodging the missiles of the enemy, and sending one's own straight to the mark—can be equally well exercised in some other framework, and, equally, the virtues—endurance, bravery, loyalty, steadfastness—can be displayed in other contexts. The tie-up between proving oneself a man and proving this by a success in organized killing is due to a definition which many societies have made of manliness. And often, even in those societies which counted success in warfare a proof of human worth, strange turns were given to the idea, as when the Plains Indians gave their highest awards to the man who touched a live enemy rather than to the man who brought in a scalp—from a dead enemy—because the latter was less risky. Warfare is just an invention known to the majority of human societies by which they permit their young men either to accumulate prestige or avenge their honor or acquire loot or wives or slaves or sago lands or cattle or appease the blood lust of their gods or the restless souls of the recently dead. It is just an invention, older and more widespread than the jury system, but nonetheless an invention.

But, once we have said this, have we said anything at all? Despite a few instances, dear to the hearts of controversialists, of the loss of the useful arts, once an invention is made which proves congruent with human needs or social forms, it tends to persist. Grant that war is an invention, that it is not a biological necessity nor the outcome of certain special types of social forms, still, once the invention is made, what are we to do about it? The Indian who had been subsisting on the buffalo for generations because with his primitive weapons he could slaughter only a limited number of buffalo did not return to his primitive weapons when he saw that the white man's more efficient weapons were exterminating the buffalo. A desire for the white man's cloth may mortgage the South Sea Islander to the white man's plantation, but he does not return to making bark cloth, which would have left him free. Once an invention is known and accepted, men do not easily relinquish it. The skilled workers may smash the first steam looms which they feel are to be their undoing, but they accept them in the end, and no movement which has insisted upon the mere abandonment of usable inventions has ever had much success. Warfare is here, as part of our thought; the deeds of warriors are immortalized in the words of our poets; the toys of our children are modeled upon the weapons of the soldier; the frame of reference within which our statesmen and our diplomats work always contains war. If we know that it is not inevitable, that it is due to historical accident that warfare is one of the ways in which we think of behaving, are we given any hope by that? What hope is there of persuading nations to abandon war, nations so thoroughly imbued with the idea that resort to war is, if not actually desirable and noble, at least inevitable whenever certain defined circumstances arise?

In answer to this question I think we might turn to the history of other social inventions, and inventions which must once have seemed as firmly entrenched as warfare. Take the methods of trial which preceded the jury system: ordeal and trial by combat. Unfair, capricious, alien as they are to our feeling today, they were once the only methods open to individuals accused of some offense. The invention of trial by jury gradually replaced these methods until only witches, and finally not even witches, had to resort to the ordeal. And for a long time the jury system seemed the one best and finest method of settling legal disputes, but today new inventions, trial before judges only or before commissions, are replacing the jury system. In each case the old method was replaced by a new social invention; the ordeal did not go out because people thought it unjust or wrong, it went out because a method more congruent with the institutions and feelings of the period was invented. And, if we despair over the way in which war seems such an ingrained habit of most of the human race, we can take comfort from the fact that a poor invention will usually give place to a better invention.

For this, two conditions at least are necessary. The people must recognize the defects of the old invention, and someone must make a new one. Propaganda against warfare, documentation of its terrible cost in human suffering and social waste, these prepare the ground by teaching people to feel that warfare is a defective social institution. There is further needed a belief that social invention is possible and the invention of new methods which will render warfare as out-of-date as the tractor is making the plow, or the motor car the horse and buggy. A form of behavior becomes out-of-date only when something else takes its place, and in order to invent forms of behavior which will make war obsolete, it is a first requirement to believe that an invention is possible.

QUESTIONS FOR DISCUSSION AND WRITING

1. Margaret Mead outlines three possible explanations for the occurrence of warfare: It may be a "biological necessity, a sociological inevitability, or just a bad invention" (paragraph 1). Which of these possibilities seems most believable? Why? What evidence does Mead use to refute the idea that war is a universal biological necessity? How does this evidence show that warfare is not caused by urges innate to all people? What evidence does she use to refute the idea that warfare is caused by the development of nation-states, the struggle for natural resources, social class systems, or for other sociological reasons? How does this evidence show that warfare is not caused by social tensions or problems?

2. Mead argues that warfare was created by humans and that it could be outlawed or become obsolete just like certain other human inventions. A synonym for "an invention," in this case, might be "a social practice" or "a custom." The duel is one invention that Mead mentions that is no longer used in Western culture (paragraph 8). What others does she specify? Can you think of other social inventions—violent or not—that once were used but have been abandoned? Why have these inventions fallen into disuse? What has replaced them? Examples to consider might include child labor, corporal punishment of schoolchildren, and execution by decapitation.

3. Mead asserts that for people to rid themselves of any invention, they must "recognize the defects of the old invention, and someone must make a new one" (paragraph 13). What invention could be created to replace warfare, in your opinion? To answer this question in depth, you will need to explain the types of problems that warfare is typically meant to solve—whether or not it actually does so. Then you will need to show, in some detail, how your proposed alternative invention could address these problems and convince your readers that your solution would be an improvement over warfare.

4. Take an example of a war from history or current events, analyze its causes, and show how an alternative to warfare could have been used to solve the problems that the war was meant to address. What were the causes of the war? What problems was the war meant to solve? Was the war effective in resolving these problems or even in diminishing them? What alternative methods of solving these problems, involving less—or no—bloodshed, could have been used instead of war?

JIM MacMILLAN

Family and Soldiers in Iraq

QUESTIONS FOR DISCUSSION AND WRITING

1. This photo juxtaposes a woman and child with armed American soldiers. How does the arrangement of the figures contribute to the meaning of the photograph? What emotions or reactions does this composition solicit? Describe the facial expressions of the soldier in the foreground and of the woman. Does this image tell you anything about the relationship of U.S. forces and Iraqi civilians?

2. Does the information that the photo was taken during a search for insurgent weapons influence your reaction to the photograph? Does the information that U.S. soldiers took responsibility for securing the area while Iraqi troops conducted the search change that reaction?

ABRAHAM LINCOLN

The Gettysburg Address

The self-taught, self-made son of Kentucky pioneers, Abraham Lincoln (1809–1865) served four terms in the Illinois state legislature before being elected to Congress in 1847. As the sixteenth president of the United States (1861–1865), Lincoln exerted supreme efforts to secure the passage of the Thirteenth Amendment that would forever outlaw slavery, while preserving the Union amid the bloody Civil War that claimed over six hundred thousand American lives and threatened to destroy the economy and the government itself. Lincoln was a gifted writer of speeches at a time when public officials still wrote their own; his first and second inaugural addresses join the Gettysburg Address as American classics. Trained in formal rhetoric and versed in early modern models such as Shakespeare, Francis Bacon, and the King James Bible, Lincoln was anxious to speak at Gettysburg, even though another outstanding speaker, Edward Everett of Harvard, had also been invited. At the dedication of the battlefield at Gettysburg as a memorial to the Civil War dead, Lincoln's delivery did not match his magnificent words; he was incubating smallpox ("At last I have something I can give to everybody," he joked) when he delivered the address "in a thin, high voice" that left his audience—accustomed to a booming oratory—unimpressed. Some journalists were quite negative, describing the "silly remarks" and "ludicrous" sallies of the president. However, later reviewers would recognize the speech as a classic. Its words—rich with biblical similes, birth metaphors, antitheses (oppositions and contrasts), and tricolons (the division of an idea into three harmonious parts as in "government of the people, by the people, for the people")—still resonate today, simultaneously plainspoken and majestic.

Four score and seven years ago our fathers brought forth on this continent, a new nation, conceived in liberty, and dedicated to the proposition that all men are created equal.

Now we are engaged in a great civil war, testing whether that nation, or any nation so conceived and so dedicated, can long endure. We are met on a great battlefield of that war. We have come to dedicate a portion of that field, as a final resting place for those who here gave their lives that the nation might live. It is altogether fitting and proper that we should do this.

But, in a larger sense, we cannot dedicate—we cannot consecrate—we cannot hallow—this ground. The brave men, living and dead, who struggled here, have consecrated it, far above our poor power to add or detract. The world will little note, nor long remember what we say here, but it can never forget what they did here. It is for us the living, rather, to be dedicated here to the unfinished work which they who fought here have thus far so nobly advanced. It is rather for us to be here dedicated to the great task remaining before us—that from these honored dead we take increased devotion—that we here highly resolve that these dead shall not have died in vain—that this nation, under God, shall have a new birth of freedom—and that the government of the people, by the people, for the people, shall not perish from the earth.

QUESTIONS FOR DISCUSSION AND WRITING

1. In the Declaration of Independence (p. 369), Jefferson identifies the fundamental premises as "Life, Liberty, and the Pursuit of Happiness." Lincoln establishes the moral principles for his speech as liberty and equality (paragraph 1). What factors in their different historical situations and rhetorical occasions caused Jefferson and Lincoln to select these particular founding principles for their respective texts?

2. Why did Lincoln, knowing that his audience expected lengthy orations, choose to make his speech so short?

3. Why do you think Lincoln opens and closes his speech with conspicuously biblical language and phrasing ("Four score and seven years ago" rather than "eighty-seven years ago")? Identify other rhetorical patterns in his speech, such as parallelism, antithesis, alliteration, and repetition of key words.

4. Write a dignified speech, preferably short, for a solemn occasion (real or imaginary). Lend majesty to your language through conspicuous rhetorical patterns.

POPE JOHN XXIII

Disarmament

Angelo Giuseppe Roncalli was born in 1881 into a sharecropper's large family at Sotto il Monte (Bergamo), Italy. He was educated in a seminary in Bergamo (beginning at the age of twelve) and at the Apollinaris in Rome. After time out for military service, he completed his doctorate in theology and was ordained in 1904. He served as a military chaplain, then as secretary to the bishop of Bergamo, focusing on working-class problems. Eventually he became Apostolic Visitator to Bulgaria (1925) and later served a comparable role in Turkey and Greece.

A religious activist, during World War II Angelo Roncalli established an apostolic office in Istanbul to help find prisoners of war. From 1944 to 1952, as papal nuncio to Paris, he aided in postwar relief work; later he was appointed the first permanent observer of the Holy See at UNESCO. In 1958 the 76-year-old Roncalli's election as pope, whereupon he took the name John XXIII, marked—as the Vatican acknowledged—"a turning point in history and a new age for the Church." His dramatic modernizations of the Roman Catholic Church, accomplished by means of the Second Vatican Council, included enlarging the College of Cardinals from 70 to 87, greatly expanding its international membership, and a major revision of the Code of Canon Law. John XXIII was considered an exceptionally warm humanitarian; the world's testimony at his death in 1963 was epitomized in a newspaper drawing of the earth, shrouded in mourning, captioned "A Death in the Family."

Pacem in terris (Peace on Earth), encyclical letter of Pope John XXIII, of which "Disarmament" is a section, was published in 1963. In scope, stature, and significance it is analogous to Beethoven's Ninth Symphony (the peace symphony) and has been praised worldwide as "one of the strongest and most eloquent papal statements on peace ever made." "Peace among all peoples requires," said John XXIII, "truth as its foundation, justice as its rule, love as its driving force, liberty as its atmosphere." Its central idea is "direct and clear," says commentator Peter Riga in Peace on Earth *(1964), "the freedom, dignity, rights, and responsibilities of each human person are the only valid foundation upon which any national or international organization can be built. Universal peace is primarily a question of law, and this law, properly understood, must embody in concrete and operative structures the inalienable rights possessed by every human being." Pope John XXIII's broad, ecumenical approach theoretically ended the Catholic ghetto mentality prevalent since the Reformation. Summarizes Riga, "The concept of the Church as an armed fortress fighting off the onslaughts of the enemy is a thing of the past. The pope tells Catholics that they must become involved in the modern world, with all of its particular problems."*

109. On the other hand, it is with deep sorrow that We note the enormous stocks of armaments that have been and still are being made in more economically developed countries, with a vast outlay of intellectual economic resources. And so it happens that, while the people of these countries are loaded with heavy burdens, other countries as a result are deprived of the collaboration they need in order to make economic and social progress.

110. The production of arms is allegedly justified on the grounds that in present-day conditions peace cannot be preserved without an equal balance of armaments. And so, if one country increases its armaments, others feel the need to do the same; and if one country is equipped with nuclear weapons, other countries must produce their own, equally destructive.

111. Consequently, people live in constant fear lest the storm that every moment threatens should break upon them with dreadful violence. And with good reason, for the arms of war are ready at hand. Even though it is difficult to believe that anyone would deliberately take the responsibility for the appalling destruction and sorrow that war would bring in its train, it cannot be denied that the conflagration may be set off by some unexpected and obscure event. And one must bear in mind that, even though the monstrous power of modern weapons acts as a deterrent, it is to be feared that the mere continuance of nuclear tests, undertaken with war in mind, will prove a serious hazard for life on earth.

112. Justice, then, right reason and humanity urgently demand that the arms race should cease; that the stockpiles which exist in various countries should be reduced equally and simultaneously by the parties concerned; that nuclear weapons

should be banned; and that a general agreement should eventually be reached about progressive disarmament and an effective method of control. In the words of Pius XII, Our Predecessor of happy memory: *The calamity of a world war, with the economic and social ruin and the moral excesses and dissolution that accompany it, must not be permitted to envelop the human race for a third time.*[1]

113. All must realize that there is no hope of putting an end to the building up of armaments, nor of reducing the present stocks, nor, still less, of abolishing them altogether, unless the process is complete and thorough and unless it proceeds from inner conviction: unless, that is, everyone sincerely co-operates to banish the fear and anxious expectation of war with which men are oppressed. If this is to come about, the fundamental principle on which our present peace depends must be replaced by another, which declares that the true and solid peace of nations consists not in equality of arms but in mutual trust alone. We believe that this can be brought to pass, and We consider that it is something which reason requires, that it is eminently desirable in itself and that it will prove to be the source of many benefits.

114. In the first place, it is an objective demanded by reason. There can be, or at least there should be, no doubt that relations between States, as between individuals, should be regulated not by the force of arms but by the light of reason, by the rule, that is, of truth, of justice and of active and sincere co-operation.

115. Secondly, We say that it is an objective earnestly to be desired in itself. Is there anyone who does not ardently yearn to see war banished, to see peace preserved and daily more firmly established?

116. And finally, it is an objective which will be a fruitful source of many benefits, for its advantages will be felt everywhere, by individuals, by families, by nations, by the whole human family. The warning of Pius XII still rings in our ears: *Nothing is lost by peace; everything may be lost by war.*[2]

117. Since this is so, We, the Vicar on earth of Jesus Christ, Savior of the World and Author of Peace, and as interpreter of the very profound longing of the entire human family, following the impulse of Our heart, seized by anxiety for the good of all, We feel it Our duty to beseech men, especially those who have the responsibility of public affairs, to spare no labor in order to ensure that world events follow a reasonable and humane course.

118. In the highest and most authoritative assemblies, let men give serious thought to the problem of a peaceful adjustment of relations between political communities on a world level: an adjustment founded on mutual trust, on sincerity in negotiations, on faithful fulfillment of obligations assumed. Let them study the problem until they find that point of agreement from which it will be possible to commence to go forward towards accords that will be sincere, lasting and fruitful.

---

[1]Cf. Pius XII's *Radio Broadcast*, Christmas Eve, 1941, *A.A.S.*, XXXIV (1942), p. 17; and Benedict XV's *Adhortatio* to the rulers of peoples at war, August 1, 1917, *A.A.S.*, IX (1917), p. 418.
[2]Cf. Pius XII's broadcast message, August 24, 1939, *A.A.S.*, XXXI (1939) 334.

119. We, for Our part, will not cease to pray God to bless these labors so that they may lead to fruitful results.

QUESTIONS FOR DISCUSSION AND WRITING

1. Examine America's national expenditures on its military endeavors—ongoing operations, current wars, debt for past wars, veterans' benefits and bonuses. After ascertaining some totals, compare these with amounts allocated to other governmental programs—health care, hurricane relief, education, space exploration, scientific research, the judicial system. What can you conclude about the relation between costs and benefits, both obtained and forgone?

2. According to Pope John XXIII, competition among nations to acquire armaments leads to a more dangerous world. What is the likely upshot of an arms race, with conventional or unconventional weapons? To keep the peace, is it necessary to prepare for war? Answer this question with reference to a specific current or recent war in Africa, the Middle East, Europe, or to international terrorism—threatened and executed.

3. Is it in the world's best interests to prevent the building and stockpiling of nuclear weapons? Rockets and missiles? Is the equilateral and simultaneous reduction of weapons worldwide possible to attain? Or is this an unworkable solution to the problem "Disarmament" identifies? Why or why not?

4. "Is there anyone who does not ardently yearn to see war banished, to see peace preserved and daily more firmly established?" asks Pope John XXIII in section 115. Whose interests are best served by war? By peace? If peace generally provides the most benefits for the most people, why are there so many wars? What keeps universal peace from breaking out?

5. Write a paper in which you update Pope John XXIII's frame of reference. Has the nature of war changed so dramatically, as demonstrated by the events of 9/11 in which airplanes were used as missiles, that stockpiling makes no sense? If commonplace objects such as box cutters can be used as weapons, what should be "disarmed"? Who will determine the disarming, and who will perform the disarmament?

LINKED READINGS: NOBEL PEACE PRIZE ACCEPTANCE SPEECHES

RIGOBERTA MENCHÚ

Five Hundred Years of Major Oppression

Nearly all Nobel Peace Prizes are awarded for humanitarian activities as a response to war or other forms of human oppression, and Rigoberta Menchú's receipt of the Nobel Peace Prize in 1992 is no exception. Guatemala, typical of many South and

Central American countries, was in the 1970s and 1980s the site of enormous tension
between the descendants of European immigrants and the native Indian population,
which was brutally suppressed and persecuted. As a prominent advocate of native
rights, Menchú (born in 1959 to a poor Mayan peasant family in Guatemala) be-
came an iconic figure whose family history represented poverty, persecution, resis-
tance, and activism for social reform. Menchú devoted her efforts in the 1980s to
organizing farm laborers to improve their working conditions and to resist torture
and murder by the military, first through the Committee of the Peasant Union, later
through the "United Representation of the Guatemalan Opposition (RUOG)." She
told her family's life story—involving arrest, imprisonment, rape, torture, and mur-
der—to an anthropologist, Elizabeth Burgos-Debray; the resulting book, I, Rigoberta
Menchú *(1983), was translated into a dozen languages and became an international*
rallying point for opposition to atrocities committed against peasants by the
Guatemalan army during the civil war.

This award, like many Nobel Peace Prizes, was contentious, particularly after
David Stoll published a corrective to Menchú's autobiography, Rigoberta Menchú
and the Story of All Poor Guatemalans *(1999), identifying major misrepresenta-*
tions even when Menchú speaks as an eyewitness. Although Stoll acknowledges the
justice of the Nobel Prize award, he claims that "by inaccurately portraying the
events in her own village as representative of what happened in all such indigenous
villages in Guatemala," Menchú misrepresents the Mayan peasants' involvement in
the revolution. Despite calls to revoke the prize, the Nobel committee stood by its de-
cision. Arturo Arias edited The Rigoberta Menchú Controversy *(2002), an excel-*
lent collection of primary documents and scholars' interpretations of the debate's
historical, cultural, and political significance.

Please allow me, ladies and gentlemen, to say some words about my country and
the Civilization of the Mayas. The Maya people developed and spread geographically through some 300,000 square km; they occupied parts of the South of
Mexico, Belize, Guatemala, as well as Honduras and El Salvador; they developed a very rich civilization in the area of political organization, as well as in social and economic fields; they were great scientists in the fields of mathematics,
astronomy, agriculture, architecture and engineering; they were great artists in the
fields of sculpture, painting, weaving and carving. . . .

Who can predict what other great scientific conquests and developments
these people could have achieved, if they had not been conquered in blood and
fire, and subjected to an ethnocide that affected nearly 50 million people in the
course of 500 years.

I would describe the meaning of this Nobel Prize, in the first place as a tribute to the indian people who have been sacrificed and have disappeared because
they aimed at a more dignified and just life with fraternity and understanding
among the human beings. To those who are no longer alive to keep up the hope
for a change in the situation in respect of poverty and marginalization of the

indians, of those who have been banished, of the helpless in Guatemala as well as in the entire American Continent.

This growing concern is comforting, even though it comes 500 years later, to the suffering, the discrimination, the oppression and the exploitation that our people have been exposed to, but who, thanks to their own cosmovision—and concept of life—have managed to withstand and finally see some promising prospects. How those roots, that were to be eradicated, now begin to grow with strength, hopes and visions for the future!

It also represents a sign of the growing international interest for, and under- 5 standing of the original Rights of the People, of the future of more than 60 million indians that live in our America, and their uproar because of the 500 years of oppression that they have endured. For the genocides beyond comparison that they have had to suffer all this time, and from which other countries and the elite of the Americas have profited and taken advantage.

Let there be freedom for the indians, wherever they may be in the American Continent or else in the world, because while they are alive, a glow of hope will be alive as well as the real concept of life.

The expressions of great happiness by the Indian Organizations in the entire Continent and the worldwide congratulations received for the award of the Nobel Peace Prize, clearly indicate the great importance of this decision. It is the recognition of the European debt to the American indigenous people; it is an appeal to the conscience of Humanity so that those conditions of marginalization that condemned them to colonialism and exploitation may be eradicated; it is a cry for life, peace, justice, equality and fraternity between human beings.

The peculiarities of the vision of the indian people are expressed according to the way in which they relate. First of all, between human being[s], through communication. Second, with the earth, as with our mother, because she gives us our lives and is not a mere merchandise. Third, with nature, because we are integral parts of it, and not its owners.

To us mother earth is not only a source of economic riches that give us the maize, which is our life, but she also provides so many other things that the privileged ones of today strive after. The earth is the root and the source of our culture. She keeps our memories, she receives our ancestors and she therefore demands that we honor her and return to her, with tenderness and respect, those goods that she gives us. We have to take care of her and look after mother earth so that our children and grandchildren may continue to benefit from her. If the world does not learn now to show respect to nature, what kind of future will the new generations have?

From these basic features derive behavior, rights and obligations in the 10 American Continent, for indians as well as for non-indians, whether they be racially mixed, blacks, whites or Asian. The whole society has the obligation to show mutual respect, to learn from each other and to share material and scientific achievements, in the most convenient way. The indians have never had, and they do not have, the place that they should have occupied in the progress and benefits of science and technology, although they have represented an important basis.

If the indian civilizations and the European civilizations could have made exchanges in a peaceful and harmonious manner, without destruction, exploitation, discrimination and poverty, they could, no doubt, have achieved greater and more valuable conquests for Humanity.

Let us not forget that when the Europeans came to America, there were flourishing and strong civilizations there. One cannot talk about a discovery of America, because one discovers that which one does not know about, or that which is hidden. But America and its native civilizations had discovered themselves long before the fall of the Roman Empire and the Medieval Europe. The significance of its cultures form part of the heritage of humanity and continue to astonish the learned ones. . . .

We the indians are willing to combine tradition with modernism, but not at all costs. We will not tolerate nor permit that our future be planned as possible guardians of ethno-touristic projects at continental level.

At a time when the commemoration of the Fifth Centenary of the arrival of Columbus in America has repercussions all over the world, the revival of hopes for the indian people claims that we reassert to the world our existence and the value of our cultural identity. It demands that we endeavor to actively participate in the decisions that concern our destiny, in the building-up of our countries/nations. Should we, in spite of all, not be taken into consideration, there are factors that guarantee our future: struggle and endurance; courage; the decision to maintain our traditions that have been exposed to so many perils and sufferings; solidarity towards our struggle on the part of numerous countries, governments, organizations and citizens of the world.

That is why I dream of the day when the relationship between the indige- 15 nous people and other people is strengthened; when they can join their potentialities and their capabilities and contribute to make life on this planet less unequal.

THE DALAI LAMA (TENZIN GYATSO)

Inner Peace and Human Rights

Unlike his predecessors, Tenzin Gyatso, the fourteenth Dalai Lama, has led the Tibetan government throughout much of his reign from a position of exile, in Dharamsala, in India. Also in contrast to previous lamas, instead of leading a life secluded in Lhasa's immense Potala Palace, as a public citizen he travels the world. His diplomatic quest seeks international support to maintain the political integrity of Tibet and to sustain its cultural heritage in the course of sixty years of Chinese encroachment. More than a sixth of Tibet's population of six million died during the thirty years of Chinese occupation; heritage buildings—temples, monasteries, and historic sites—

were destroyed; the surviving citizens were "deprived of the right to life, movement, speech, worship." Thousands of ethnic Chinese have since been "resettled" in Tibet, further adulterating the culture. When the Dalai Lama accepted the Nobel Peace Prize in 1989, a quarter of a million Chinese troops were stationed in this small country.

Born to a peasant family in 1935, at two years old Tenzin Gyatso was identified as the reincarnation of the thirteenth Dalai Lama; all lamas are manifestations of the Bodhisattva of Compassion, designated to reincarnate to serve their people. His monastic education, which began at six, was completed with a Doctorate of Buddhist Philosophy twenty-one years later. He became head of state in 1950, only to see his petitions for independence ignored by Mao Tse-Tung and Chou En-Lai; he was forced into exile in 1959. At the Congressional Human Rights Caucus in 1987 he proposed a Five-Point Peace Plan that would (1) designate Tibet as a zone of peace, (2) end the massive transfer of ethnic Chinese into Tibet, (3) restore fundamental human rights, (4) abandon China's use of Tibet to produce nuclear weapons and dump nuclear waste, (5) create a self-governing Tibet, in conjunction with the People's Republic of China, in which the Tibetans would be "the ultimate deciding authority." To date, despite international recognition of the Dalai Lama's efforts from individual support-ers as well as the award of the Nobel Peace Prize, none of these points has been ef-fected; indeed, Tibet becomes more and more Chinese every year.

Peace, in the sense of the absence of war, is of little value to someone who is dying of hunger or cold. It will not remove the pain of torture inflicted on a pris-oner of conscience. It does not comfort those who have lost their loved ones in floods caused by senseless deforestation in a neighboring country. Peace can only last where human rights are respected, where the people are fed, and where indi-viduals and nations are free. True peace with oneself and with the world around us can only be achieved through the development of mental peace. The other phenomena mentioned above are similarly interrelated. Thus, for example, we see that a clean environment, wealth or democracy mean little in the face of war, especially nuclear war, and that material development is not sufficient to ensure human happiness.

Material progress is of course important for human advancement. In Tibet, we paid much too little attention to technological and economic development, and today we realize that this was a mistake. At the same time, material develop-ment without spiritual development can also cause serious problems. In some countries too much attention is paid to external things and very little importance is given to inner development. I believe both are important and must be devel-oped side by side so as to achieve a good balance between them. Tibetans are al-ways described by foreign visitors as being a happy, jovial people. This is part of our national character, formed by cultural and religious values that stress the im-portance of mental peace through the generation of love and kindness to all other living sentient beings, both human and animal. Inner peace is the key: if you have inner peace, the external problems do not affect your deep sense of peace and tranquility. In that state of mind you can deal with situations with calmness and reason, while keeping your inner happiness. That is very important. Without this inner peace, no matter how comfortable your life is materially, you may still be worried, disturbed or unhappy because of circumstances.

Clearly, it is of great importance, therefore, to understand the interrelationship among these and other phenomena, and to approach and attempt to solve problems in a balanced way that takes these different aspects into consideration. Of course it is not easy. But it is of little benefit to try to solve one problem if doing so creates an equally serious new one. So really we have no alternative: we must develop a sense of universal responsibility not only in the geographic sense, but also in respect to the different issues that confront our planet.

Responsibility does not only lie with the leaders of our countries or with those who have been appointed or elected to do a particular job. It lies with each one of us individually. Peace, for example, starts with each one of us. When we have inner peace, we can be at peace with those around us. When our community is in a state of peace, it can share that peace with neighboring communities, and so on. When we feel love and kindness towards others, it not only makes others feel loved and cared for, but it helps us also to develop inner happiness and peace. And there are ways in which we can consciously work to develop feelings of love and kindness. For some of us, the most effective way to do so is through religious practice. For others it may be nonreligious practices. What is important is that we each make a sincere effort to take our responsibility for each other and for the natural environment we live in seriously.

I am very encouraged by the developments which are taking place around 5 us. After the young people of many countries, particularly in northern Europe, have repeatedly called for an end to the dangerous destruction of the environment which was being conducted in the name of economic development, the world's political leaders are now starting to take meaningful steps to address this problem. The report to the United Nations Secretary-General by the World Commission on the Environment and Development (the Brundtland Report) was an important step in educating governments on the urgency of the issue. Serious efforts to bring peace to war-torn zones and to implement the right to self-determination of some people have resulted in the withdrawal of Soviet troops from Afghanistan and the establishment of independent Namibia. Through persistent nonviolent popular efforts dramatic changes, bringing many countries closer to real democracy, have occurred in many places, from Manila in the Philippines to Berlin in East Germany. With the Cold War era apparently drawing to a close, people everywhere live with renewed hope. Sadly, the courageous efforts of the Chinese people to bring similar change to their country was brutally crushed last June. But their efforts too are a source of hope. The military might has not extinguished the desire for freedom and the determination of the Chinese people to achieve it. I particularly admire the fact that these young people who have been taught that "power grows from the barrel of the gun," chose, instead, to use nonviolence as their weapon.

What these positive changes indicate is that reason, courage, determination, and the inextinguishable desire for freedom can ultimately win. In the struggle between forces of war, violence and oppression on the one hand, and peace, reason and freedom on the other, the latter are gaining the upper hand. This realization fills us Tibetans with hope that some day we too will once again be free.

The awarding of the Nobel Prize to me, a simple monk from faraway Tibet, here in Norway, also fills us Tibetans with hope. It means, despite the fact that we have not drawn attention to our plight by means of violence, we have not been forgotten. It also means that the values we cherish, in particular our respect for all forms of life and the belief in the power of truth, are today recognized and encouraged. It is also a tribute to my mentor, Mahatma Gandhi, whose example is an inspiration to so many of us. This year's award is an indication that this sense of universal responsibility is developing. I am deeply touched by the sincere concern shown by so many people in this part of the world for the suffering of the people of Tibet. That is a source of hope not only for us Tibetans, but for all oppressed people.

As you know, Tibet has, for forty years, been under foreign occupation. Today, more than a quarter of a million Chinese troops are stationed in Tibet. Some sources estimate the occupation army to be twice this strength. During this time, Tibetans have been deprived of their most basic human rights, including the right to life, movement, speech, worship, only to mention a few. More than one sixth of Tibet's population of six million died as a direct result of the Chinese invasion and occupation. Even before the Cultural Revolution started, many of Tibet's monasteries, temples and historic buildings were destroyed. Almost everything that remained was destroyed during the Cultural Revolution. I do not wish to dwell on this point, which is well documented. What is important to realize, however, is that despite the limited freedom granted after 1979, to rebuild parts of some monasteries and other such tokens of liberalization, the fundamental human rights of the Tibetan people are still today being systematically violated. In recent months this bad situation has become even worse.

If it were not for our community in exile, so generously sheltered and supported by the government and people of India and helped by organizations and individuals from many parts of the world, our nation would today be little more than a shattered remnant of a people. Our culture, religion and national identity would have been effectively eliminated. As it is, we have built schools and monasteries in exile and have created democratic institutions to serve our people and preserve the seeds of our civilization. With this experience, we intend to implement full democracy in a future free Tibet. Thus, as we develop our community in exile on modern lines, we also cherish and preserve our own identity and culture and bring hope to millions of our countrymen and -women in Tibet.

The issue of most urgent concern at this time is the massive influx of Chinese settlers into Tibet. Although in the first decades of occupation a considerable number of Chinese were transferred into the eastern parts of Tibet—in the Tibetan provinces of Amdo (Chinghai) and Kham (most of which has been annexed by neighboring Chinese provinces)—since 1983 an unprecedented number of Chinese have been encouraged by their government to migrate to all parts of Tibet, including central and western Tibet (which the People's Republic of China refers to as the so-called Tibet Autonomous Region). Tibetans are rapidly being reduced to an insignificant minority in their own country. This development, which threatens the very survival of the Tibetan nation, its culture and spiritual heritage, can still be stopped and reversed. But this must be done now, before it is too late.

QUESTIONS FOR DISCUSSION AND WRITING

1. Menchú's description of the "concept of life" of those native to the Americas (paragraph 4) emphasizes the Indians' relationship to "mother earth," which is "not only a source of economic riches," but is also "the root and source of our culture" (paragraph 9). Describe the relationship Menchú sees between the Native American view of nature and the "rights and obligations" (paragraph 10) she would like all ethnic groups in society to recognize. How does the basis on which she defines human rights differ from the Dalai Lama's philosophy? Do they share a similar vision of a democratic society?

2. Both Menchú and the Dalai Lama express concern about the survival of their cultures. Compare the conflict Menchú sees between Native American traditions and "modernism" (paragraph 3) with the problem of "the massive influx of Chinese settlers into Tibet" (paragraph 10). Does Menchú's vision of "mutual respect" among coexisting ethnic groups (paragraph 10) seem possible in view of the "500 years of oppression" that indigenous Americans have endured (paragraph 5)? Why does the Dalai Lama, in his Five-Point Peace Plan, insist on Tibetan autonomy and an end to Chinese immigration into Tibet? How does each situation differ and how do these differences suggest distinct political problems and solutions?

3. What do you suppose Menchú means when she says that "other countries and the elite of the Americas have profited and taken advantage" (paragraph 5) of the genocides of Native Americans? What do Menchú and the Dalai Lama suggest is the basis of genocidal policies?

4. Do doubts about the authenticity of Menchú's story alter your perception of her work? Why do you suppose the Nobel Prize committee refused to revoke the prize? How do the Dalai Lama's personal history and diplomatic efforts endow him with the authority to speak for the Tibetan people?

KAREN ARMSTRONG

Does God Have a Future?

Karen Armstrong, a comparative theologian, arrived at her current ecumenical philo-
sophical perspective through the fire of pain, suffering, and near-suicide. Born near
Birmingham, England, in 1945, at the age of seventeen she entered a Roman Catholic
convent but left for a more secular life after seven years, epileptic and anorexic. Through
the Narrow Gate *(1981), a critical account of her life in the convent, still draws hate*
mail. After earning a bachelor's degree in literature from St. Anne's College, Oxford
University, she taught modern literature at the University of London and at a private
girls' school before becoming a freelance writer and broadcaster on religious subjects in
1982. The Spiral Staircase: My Climb Out of Darkness *(2004) is a hopeful, inspiring*
account of her transformation from personal despair into the ecstasy and transcen-
dence derived from her illuminating study of world religions.

Armstrong is a faculty member at the Leo Baeck School for the Study of Judaism
and the Training of Rabbis and Teachers, as well as an honorary member of the Associ-
ation of Muslim Social Sciences, her status earned through numerous writings on Islam,
including Muhammed: A Biography of the Prophet *(1992), the first biography of*
Muhammad, the Islamic prophet, written for a Western audience. Islam: A Short History *(2000) presented the added challenge of writing an "impossibly brief history of*
Islam" in 222 compact, accessible pages. Armstrong's most recent book is The Great
Transformation: The Beginning of Our Religious Traditions *(2006). Particularly*
since 9/11, she has been trying to prevent people from "falling back on old patterns of
bigotry," for these acts of violence are "totally unrepresentative of the Islamic tradition."

Her most widely read book is A History of God: The 400-Year Quest of Judaism, Christianity, and Islam *(1993), in which "Does God Have a Future?" appears.*
This work brought international attention and controversy with its thesis that God
has been invented and reinvented through the centuries by the three monotheistic,
Abrahamic religions of Christianity, Judaism, and Islam. "All religions change and
develop," she writes. "If they do not, they will become obsolete." Consequently, "each
generation has to create its own imaginative conception of God."

As we approach the end of the second millennium, it seems likely that the world
we know is passing away. For decades we have lived with the knowledge that we
have created weapons that could wipe out human life on the planet. The Cold
War may have ended, but the new world order seems no less frightening than the
old. We are facing the possibility of ecological disaster. The AIDS virus threatens
to bring a plague of unmanageable proportions. Within two or three generations,
the population will become too great for the planet to support. Thousands are
dying of famine and drought. Generations before our own have felt that the end
of the world is nigh, yet it does seem that we are facing a future that is unimagin-
able. How will the idea of God survive in the years to come? For 4,000 years it has

constantly adapted to meet the demands of the present, but in our own century, more and more people have found that it no longer works for them, and when religious ideas cease to be effective they fade away. Maybe God really is an idea of the past. The American scholar Peter Berger notes that we often have a double standard when we compare the past with our own time. Where the past is analyzed and made relative, the present is rendered immune to this process and our current position becomes an absolute: thus "the New Testament writers are seen as afflicted with a false consciousness rooted in *their* time, but the analyst takes the consciousness of *his* time as an unmixed intellectual blessing."[1] Secularists of the nineteenth and early twentieth centuries saw atheism as the irreversible condition of humanity in the scientific age.

There is much to support this view. In Europe, the churches are emptying; atheism is no longer the painfully acquired ideology of a few intellectual pioneers but a prevailing mood. In the past it was always produced by a particular idea of God, but now it seems to have lost its inbuilt relationship to theism and become an automatic response to the experience of living in a secularized society. Like the crowd of amused people surrounding Nietzsche's madman, many are unmoved by the prospect of life without God. Others find his absence a positive relief. Those of us who have had a difficult time with religion in the past find it liberating to be rid of the God who terrorized our childhood. It is wonderful not to have to cower before a vengeful deity, who threatens us with eternal damnation if we do not abide by his rules. We have a new intellectual freedom and can boldly follow up our own ideas without pussyfooting around difficult articles of faith, feeling all the while a sinking loss of integrity. We imagine that the hideous deity we have experienced is the authentic God of Jews, Christians and Muslims and do not always realize that it is merely an unfortunate aberration.

There is also desolation. Jean-Paul Sartre (1905–1980) spoke of the God-shaped hole in the human consciousness, where God had always been. Nevertheless, he insisted that even if God existed, it was still necessary to reject him, since the idea of God negates our freedom. Traditional religion tells us that we must conform to God's idea of humanity to become fully human. Instead, we must see human beings as liberty incarnate. Sartre's atheism was not a consoling creed, but other existentialists saw the absence of God as a positive liberation. Maurice Merleau-Ponty (1908–1961) argued that instead of increasing our sense of wonder, God actually negates it. Because God represents absolute perfection, there is nothing left for us to do or achieve. Albert Camus (1913–1960) preached a heroic atheism. People should reject God defiantly in order to pour out all their loving solicitude upon mankind. As always, the atheists have a point. God had indeed been used in the past to stunt creativity; if he is made a blanket answer to every possible problem and contingency, he can indeed stifle our sense of wonder or achievement. A passionate and committed atheism can be more religious than a weary or inadequate theism. . . .

The fact that people who have no conventional religious beliefs should keep returning to central themes that we have discovered in the history of God indicates that the idea is not as alien as many of us assume. Yet during the second half of the twentieth century, there has been a move away from the idea of a personal God who behaves like a larger version of us. There is nothing new about this. As we have seen, the Jewish scriptures, which Christians call their "Old" Testament, show a similar process; the Koran saw al-Lah in less personal terms than the Judeo-Christian tradition from the very beginning. Doctrines such as the Trinity and the mythology and symbolism of the mystical systems all strove to suggest that God was beyond personality. Yet this does not seem to have been made clear to many of the faithful. When John Robinson, Bishop of Woolwich, published *Honest to God* in 1963, stating that he could no longer subscribe to the old personal God "out there," there was uproar in Britain. A similar furor has greeted various remarks by David Jenkins, Bishop of Durham, even though these ideas are commonplace in academic circles. Don Cupitt, Dean of Emmanuel College, Cambridge, has also been dubbed "the atheist priest": he finds the traditional realistic God of theism unacceptable and proposes a form of Christian Buddhism, which puts religious experience before theology. Like Robinson, Cupitt has arrived intellectually at an insight that mystics in all three faiths have reached by a more intuitive route. Yet the idea that God does not really exist and that there is Nothing out there is far from new.

There is a growing intolerance of inadequate images of the Absolute. This is a healthy iconoclasm, since the idea of God has been used in the past to disastrous effect. One of the most characteristic new developments since the 1970s has been the rise of a type of religiosity that we usually call "fundamentalism" in most of the major world religions, including the three religions of God. A highly political spirituality, it is literal and intolerant in its vision. In the United States, which has always been prone to extremist and apocalyptic enthusiasm, Christian fundamentalism has attached itself to the New Right. Fundamentalists campaign for the abolition of legal abortion and for a hard line on moral and social decency. Jerry Falwell's Moral Majority achieved astonishing political power during the Reagan years. Other evangelists such as Maurice Cerullo, taking Jesus's remarks literally, believe that miracles are an essential hallmark of true faith. God will give the believer anything that he asks for in prayer. In Britain, fundamentalists such as Colin Urquhart have made the same claim. Christian fundamentalists seem to have little regard for the loving compassion of Christ. They are swift to condemn the people they see as the "enemies of God." Most would consider Jews and Muslims destined for hellfire, and Urquhart has argued that all oriental religions are inspired by the devil.

There have been similar developments in the Muslim world, which have been much publicized in the West. Muslim fundamentalists have toppled governments and either assassinated or threatened the enemies of Islam with the death penalty. Similarly, Jewish fundamentalists have settled in the Occupied Territories of the West Bank and the Gaza Strip with the avowed intention of driving out the Arab inhabitants, using force if necessary. Thus they believe that they are paving a way for the advent of the Messiah, which is at hand. In all its forms, fundamentalism is a fiercely reductive faith. Thus Rabbi Meir Kahane, the most extreme member of Israel's Far Right until his assassination in New York in 1990:

> There are not several messages in Judaism. There is only one. And this message is to do what God wants. Sometimes God wants us to go to war, sometimes he wants us to live in peace. . . . But there is only one message: God wanted us to come to this country to create a Jewish state.[2]

This wipes out centuries of Jewish development, returning to the Deuteronomist perspective of the Book of Joshua. It is not surprising that people who hear this kind of profanity, which makes "God" deny other people's human rights, think that the sooner we relinquish him the better.

Yet . . . , this type of religiosity is actually a retreat from God. To make such human, historical phenomena as Christian "Family Values," "Islam" or "the Holy Land" the focus of religious devotion is a new form of idolatry. This type of belligerent righteousness has been a constant temptation to monotheists throughout the long history of God. It must be rejected as inauthentic. The God of Jews, Christians and Muslims got off to an unfortunate start, since the tribal deity Yahweh was murderously partial to his own people. Latter-day crusaders who return to this primitive ethos are elevating the values of the tribe to an unacceptably high status and substituting man-made ideals for the transcendent reality which should challenge our prejudices. They are also denying a crucial monotheistic theme. Ever since the prophets of Israel reformed the old pagan cult of Yahweh, the God of monotheists has promoted the ideal of compassion.

. . . Compassion was a characteristic of most of the ideologies that were created during the Axial Age. The compassionate ideal even impelled Buddhists to make a major change in their religious orientation when they introduced devotion (*bhakti*) to the Buddha and *bodhisattvas*. The prophets insisted that cult and worship were useless unless society as a whole adopted a more just and compassionate ethos. These insights were developed by Jesus, Paul and the Rabbis, who all shared the same Jewish ideals and suggested major changes in Judaism in order to implement them. The Koran made the creation of a compassionate and just society the essence of the reformed religion of al-Lah. Compassion is a particularly difficult virtue. It demands that we go beyond the limitations of our egotism, insecurity and inherited prejudice. Not surprisingly, there have been times when all three of the God-religions have failed to achieve these high standards. During the eighteenth century, deists rejected traditional Western Christianity largely because it had become so conspicuously cruel and intolerant. The same will hold good today. All too often, conventional believers, who are not fundamentalists, share their aggressive righteousness. They use "God" to prop up their own loves and hates, which they attribute to God himself. But Jews, Christians and Muslims who punctiliously attend divine services yet denigrate people who belong to different ethnic and ideological camps deny one of the basic truths of their religion. It is equally inappropriate for people who call themselves Jews, Christians and Muslims to condone an inequitable social system. The God of historical monotheism demands mercy not sacrifice, compassion rather than decorous liturgy.

There has often been a distinction between people who practice a cultic form of religion and those who have cultivated a sense of the God of compassion. The prophets fulminated against their contemporaries who thought that temple worship was sufficient. Jesus and St. Paul both made it clear that external observance was useless if it was not accompanied by charity: it was little better than sounding brass or a tinkling cymbal. Muhammad came into conflict with those Arabs who wanted to worship the pagan goddesses alongside al-Lah in the ancient rites, without implementing the compassionate ethos that God demanded as a condition of all true religion. There had been a similar divide in the pagan world of Rome: the old cultic religion celebrated the status quo, while the philosophers preached a message that they believed would change the world. It may be that the compassionate religion of the One God has only been observed by a minority; most have found it difficult to face the extremity of the God-experience with its uncompromising ethical demands. Ever since Moses brought the tablets of the Law from Mount Sinai, the majority have preferred the worship of a Golden Calf, a traditional, unthreatening image of a deity they have constructed for themselves, with its consoling, time-honored rituals. Aaron, the high priest, presided over the manufacture of the golden effigy. The religious establishment itself is often deaf to the inspiration of prophets and mystics who bring news of a much more demanding God.

God can also be used as an unworthy panacea, as an alternative to mundane   10
life and as the object of indulgent fantasy. The idea of God has frequently been used as the opium of the people. This is a particular danger when he is conceived as an-other Being—just like us, only bigger and better—in his own heaven, which is itself conceived as a paradise of earthly delights. Yet originally, "God" was used to help people to concentrate on this world and to face up to unpleasant reality. Even the pagan cult of Yahweh, for all its manifest faults, stressed his involvement in current events in profane time, as opposed to the sacred time of rite and myth. The prophets of Israel forced their people to confront their own social culpability and impending political catastrophe in the name of the God who revealed himself in these historical occurrences. The Christian doctrine of Incarnation stressed the divine immanence in the world of flesh and blood. Concern for the here and now was especially marked in Islam: nobody could have been more of a realist than Muhammad, who was a political as well as a spiritual genius. As we have seen, later generations of Muslims have shared his concern to incarnate the divine will in human history by establishing a just and decent society. From the very beginning, God was experienced as an imperative to action. From the moment when—as either El or Yahweh—God called Abraham away from his family in Haran, the cult entailed concrete action in this world and often a painful abandonment of the old sanctities.

This dislocation also involved great strain. The Holy God, who was wholly other, was experienced as a profound shock by the prophets. He demanded a similar holiness and separation on the part of his people. When he spoke to Moses on Sinai, the Israelites were not allowed to approach the foot of the mountain. An entirely new gulf suddenly yawned between humanity and the divine, rupturing the holistic vision of paganism. There was, therefore, a potential for alienation from the world, which reflected a dawning consciousness of the inalienable autonomy of the individual. It is no accident that monotheism finally took root during the exile to Babylon, when the Israelites also developed the ideal of personal responsibility, which has been crucial in both Judaism and Islam.[3] . . . The Rabbis used the idea of an immanent God to help Jews to cultivate a sense of the sacred rights of the human personality. Yet alienation has continued to be a danger in all three faiths: in the West the experience of God was continually accompanied by guilt and by a pessimistic anthropology. In Judaism and Islam there is no doubt that the observance of Torah and Shariah has sometimes been seen as a heteronymous compliance with an external law, even though we have seen that nothing could have been further from the intention of the men who compiled these legal codes.

Those atheists who preached emancipation from a God who demands such servile obedience were protesting against an inadequate but unfortunately familiar image of God. Again, this was based on a conception of the divine that was too personalistic. It interpreted the scriptural image of God's judgment too literally and assumed that God was a sort of Big Brother in the sky. This image of the divine Tyrant imposing an alien law on his unwilling human servants has to go. Terrorizing the populace into civic obedience with threats is no longer acceptable or even practicable, as the downfall of communist regimes demonstrated so dramatically in the autumn of 1989. The anthropomorphic idea of God as Law-giver and Ruler is not adequate to the temper of post-modernity. Yet the atheists who complained that the idea of God was unnatural were not entirely correct. . . . Jews, Christians and Muslims have developed remarkably similar ideas of God, which also resemble other conceptions of the Absolute. When people try to find an ultimate meaning and value in human life, their minds seem to go in a certain direction. They have not been coerced to do this; it is something that seems natural to humanity.

Yet if feelings are not to degenerate into indulgent, aggressive or unhealthy emotionalism, they need to be informed by the critical intelligence. The experience of God must keep abreast of other current enthusiasms, including those of the mind. The experiment of Falsafah was an attempt to relate faith in God with the new cult of rationalism among Muslims, Jews and, later, Western Christians. Eventually Muslims and Jews retreated from philosophy. Rationalism, they decided, had its uses, especially in such empirical studies as science, medicine and mathematics, but it was not entirely appropriate in the discussion of a God who lay beyond concepts. The Greeks had already sensed this and developed an early distrust of their native metaphysics. One of the drawbacks of the philosophic method of discussing God was that it could make it sound as though the Supreme Deity were simply another Being, the highest of all the things that exist, instead of a reality of an entirely different order. Yet the venture of Falsafah was important, since it showed an appreciation of the necessity of relating God to other experiences—if only to define the extent to which this was possible. To push God into intellectual isolation in a holy ghetto of his own is unhealthy and unnatural. It can encourage people to think that it is not necessary to apply normal standards of decency and rationality to behavior supposedly inspired by "God."

From the first, Falsafah had been associated with science. It was their initial enthusiasm for medicine, astronomy and mathematics which had led the first Muslim Faylasufs to discuss al-Lah in metaphysical terms. Science had effected a major change in their outlook, and they found that they could not think of God in the same way as their fellow Muslims. The philosophic conception of God was markedly different from the Koranic vision, but Faylasufs did recover some insights that were in danger of being lost in the *ummah* at that time. Thus the Koran had an extremely positive attitude to other religious traditions: Muhammad had not believed that he was founding a new, exclusive religion and considered that all rightly guided faith came from the One God. By the ninth century, however, the *ulema* were beginning to lose sight of this and were promoting the cult of Islam as the one true religion. The Faylasufs reverted to the older universalist approach, even though they reached it by a different route. We have a similar opportunity today. In our scientific age, we cannot think about God in the same way as our forebears, but the challenge of science could help us to appreciate some old truths.

. . . Albert Einstein had an appreciation of mystical religion. Despite his famous remarks about God not playing dice, he did not believe that his theory of relativity should affect the conception of God. During a visit to England in 1921, Einstein was asked by the Archbishop of Canterbury what were its implications for theology. He replied: "None. Relativity is a purely scientific matter and has nothing to do with religion."[4] When Christians are dismayed by such scientists as Stephen Hawking, who can find no room for God in his cosmology, they are perhaps still thinking of God in anthropomorphic terms as a Being who created the world in the same way as we would. Yet creation was not originally conceived in such a literal manner. Interest in Yahweh as Creator did not enter Judaism until the exile to Babylon. It was a conception that was alien to the Greek world: creation *ex nihilo* was not an official doctrine of Christianity until the Council of Nicaea in 341. Creation is a central teaching of the Koran, but, like all its utterances about God, this is said to be a "parable" or a "sign" (*aya*) of an ineffable truth. Jewish and Muslim rationalists found it a difficult and problematic doctrine, and many rejected it. Sufis and Kabbalists all preferred the Greek metaphor of emanation. In any case, cosmology was not a scientific description of the origins of the world but was originally a symbolic expression of a spiritual and psychological truth. There is consequently little agitation about the new science in the Muslim world: . . . the events of recent history have been more of a threat than has science to the traditional conception of God. In the West, however, a more literal understanding of scripture has long prevailed. When some Western Christians feel their faith in God undermined by the new science, they are probably imagining God as Newton's great Mechanick, a personalistic notion of God which should, perhaps, be rejected on religious as well as on scientific grounds. The challenge of science might shock the churches into a fresh appreciation of the symbolic nature of scriptural narrative.

The idea of a personal God seems increasingly unacceptable at the present time for all kinds of reasons: moral, intellectual, scientific and spiritual. Feminists are also repelled by a personal deity who, because of "his" gender, has been male since his tribal, pagan days. Yet to talk about "she"—other than in a dialectical way—can be just as limiting, since it confines the illimitable God to a purely human category. The old metaphysical notion of God as the Supreme Being, which has long been popular in the West, is also felt to be unsatisfactory. The God of the philosophers is the product of a now outdated rationalism, so the traditional "proofs" of his existence no longer work. The widespread acceptance of the God of the philosophers by the deists of the Enlightenment can be seen as the first step to the current atheism. Like the old Sky God, this deity is so remote from humanity and the mundane world that he easily becomes *Deus Otiosus* and fades from our consciousness.

The God of the mystics might seem to present a possible alternative. The mystics have long insisted that God is not an-Other Being; they have claimed that he does not really exist and that it is better to call him Nothing. This God is in tune with the atheistic mood of our secular society, with its distrust of inadequate images of the Absolute. Instead of seeing God as an objective fact, which can be demonstrated by means of scientific proof, mystics have claimed that he is a subjective experience, mysteriously experienced in the ground of being. This God is to be approached through the imagination and can be seen as a kind of art form, akin to the other great artistic symbols that have expressed the ineffable mystery, beauty and value of life. Mystics have used music, dancing, poetry, fiction, stories, painting, sculpture and architecture to express this Reality that goes beyond concepts. Like all art, however, mysticism requires intelligence, discipline and self-criticism as a safeguard against indulgent emotionalism and projection. The God of the mystics could even satisfy the feminists, since both Sufis and Kabbalists have long tried to introduce a female element into the divine.

There are drawbacks, however. Mysticism has been regarded with some suspicion by many Jews and Muslims since the Shabbetai Zevi fiasco and the decline of latter-day Sufism. In the West, mysticism has never been a mainstream religious enthusiasm. The Protestant and Catholic Reformers either outlawed or marginalized it, and the scientific Age of Reason did not encourage this mode of perception. Since the 1960s, there has been a fresh interest in mysticism, expressed in the enthusiasm for Yoga, meditation and Buddhism, but it is not an approach that easily consorts with our objective, empirical mentality. The God of the mystics is not easy to apprehend. It requires long training with an expert and a considerable investment of time. The mystic has to work hard to acquire this sense of the reality known as God (which many have refused to name). Mystics often insist that human beings must deliberately create this sense of God for themselves, with the same degree of care and attention that others devote to artistic creation. It is not something that is likely to appeal to people in a society which has become used to speedy gratification, fast food and instant communication. The God of the mystics does not arrive readymade and prepackaged. He cannot be experienced as quickly as the instant ecstasy created by a revivalist preacher, who quickly has a whole congregation clapping its hands and speaking in tongues.

It is possible to acquire some of the mystical attitudes. Even if we are incapable of the higher states of consciousness achieved by a mystic, we can learn that God does not exist in any simplistic sense, for example, or that the very word "God" is only a symbol of a reality that ineffably transcends it. The mystical agnosticism could help us to acquire a restraint that stops us rushing into these complex matters with dogmatic assurance. But if these notions are not felt upon the pulse and personally appropriated, they are likely to seem meaningless abstractions. Secondhand mysticism could prove to be as unsatisfactory as reading the explanation of a poem by a literary critic instead of the original. . . . Mysticism was often seen as an esoteric discipline, not because the mystics wanted to exclude the vulgar herd but because these truths could only be perceived by the intuitive part of the mind after special training. They mean something different when they are approached by this particular route, which is not accessible to the logical, rationalist faculty.

Ever since the prophets of Israel started to ascribe their own feelings and experiences to God, monotheists have in some sense created a God for themselves. God has rarely been seen as a self-evident fact that can be encountered like any other objective existent. Today many people seem to have lost the will to make this imaginative effort. This need not be a catastrophe. When religious ideas have lost their validity, they have usually faded away painlessly: if the human idea of God no longer works for us in the empirical age, it will be discarded. Yet in the past people have always created new symbols to act as a focus for spirituality. Human beings have always created a faith for themselves, to cultivate their sense of the wonder and ineffable significance of life. The aimlessness, alienation, anomie and violence that characterize so much of modern life seem to indicate that now that they are not deliberately creating a faith in "God" or anything else—it matters little what—many people are falling into despair.

In the United States, . . . ninety-nine percent of the population claim to believe in God, yet the prevalence of fundamentalism, apocalypticism and "instant" charismatic forms of religiosity in America is not reassuring. The escalating crime rate, drug addiction and the revival of the death penalty are not signs of a spiritually healthy society. In Europe there is a growing blankness where God once existed in the human consciousness. One of the first people to express this dry desolation—quite different from the heroic atheism of Nietzsche—was Thomas Hardy. In "The Darkling Thrush," written on December 30, 1900, at the turn of the twentieth century, he expressed the death of spirit that was no longer able to create a faith in life's meaning:

> I leant upon a coppice gate
> When Frost was spectre-grey
> And Winter's dregs made desolate
> The weakening eye of day.
> The tangled bine-stems scored the sky
> Like strings of broken lyres,
> And all mankind that haunted nigh
> Had sought their household fires.
>
> The land's sharp features seemed to be
> The Century's corpse outleant,
> His crypt the cloudy canopy,
> The wind his death-lament.
> The ancient pulse of germ and birth
> Was shrunken hard and dry,
> And every spirit upon earth
> Seemed fervourless as I.
>
> At once a voice arose among
> The bleak twigs overhead
> In a full-hearted evensong
> Of joy illimited;
> An aged thrush, frail, gaunt, and small,
> In blast-beruffled plume,
> Had chosen thus to fling his soul
> Upon the growing gloom.
>
> So little cause for carolings
> Of such ecstatic sound
> Was written on terrestrial things
> Afar or nigh around,
> That I could think there trembled through
> His happy good-night air
> Some blessed Hope, whereof he knew
> And I was unaware.

Human beings cannot endure emptiness and desolation; they will fill the vacuum by creating a new focus of meaning. The idols of fundamentalism are not good substitutes for God; if we are to create a vibrant new faith for the twenty-first century, we should, perhaps, ponder the history of God for some lessons and warnings.

NOTES

1. Peter Berger, *A Rumour of Angels* (London, 1970), p. 58.

2. Quoted in Raphael Mergui and Philippa Simmonot, *Israel's Ayatollahs; Meir Kahane and the Far Right in Israel* (London, 1987), p. 43.

3. Personal responsibility is also important in Christianity, of course, but Judaism and Islam have stressed it by their lack of a mediating priesthood, a perspective that was recovered by the Protestant Reformers.

4. Philipp Frank, *Einstein: His Life and Times* (New York, 1947), pp. 189–190.

QUESTIONS FOR DISCUSSION AND WRITING

1. At the heart of Karen Armstrong's argument is a theory about how the concept of God evolved over the course of history. As with many evolutionary theorists, Armstrong describes several stages or "ages" of development, but contrary to many Western discussions of religious history, she discusses Islam along with Christianity and other faiths. How many stages of development does Armstrong describe, and what are the characteristics of God at each stage? For example, what is the difference between the tribal God Yahweh (paragraph 7) and the God of the "Axial Age" (paragraph 8)? How do these differences affect the way people, at each stage, worship their deity and view members of other religions?

2. Fundamentalism in its Christian, Jewish, and Islamic versions is a central concern for Armstrong. She describes how violence (paragraph 6) and "belligerent righteousness" (paragraph 7) often accompany fundamentalist beliefs. What other characteristics of fundamentalism does Armstrong mention? How are these characteristics related to fundamentalism's view of God—for example, "the tribal deity Yahweh" (paragraph 7)?

3. Armstrong raises the question of why "Jews, Christians, and Muslims have developed remarkably similar ideas of God" that also resemble concepts of the Absolute in other religious traditions (paragraph 12). She goes on to conclude that people think alike when they "try to find an ultimate meaning and value in human life" (paragraph 12). What ultimate meaning and value do you see in human life? How closely is this meaning tied to an idea of God or the Absolute? To what extent do the media you watch, the books you read, and the courses you take raise questions about the meaning and value of life? How much meaning and value does the quest for money, things, status, and leisure time give to human life?

4. Answer question 3 in a personal essay. You may want to expand the topic to discuss meaning, value, and God (or the Absolute) in your generation versus another generation or in your cultural and ethnic background versus others.

5. As a research project, read more of Karen Armstrong's book, *A History of God*, along with other relevant texts to explore question 2 or 3 in more depth. For example, you could analyze two or more stages in the development of the idea of God, showing the major similarities and differences between the stages, and how

this explains people's attitude toward religion in our time. Or, you could use Armstrong's ideas to analyze a fundamentalist movement active in the world today, explaining how its view of God influences its view of morality or politics.

DAVID OWEN
Your Three Wishes: F.A.Q.

David Owen (b. 1955), Harvard graduate and former Lampoon *editor, has been a* New Yorker *staff writer since 1991. He writes a monthly humor column for* Golf Digest *and has contributed articles and satires to magazines such as* Harper's, *the* Atlantic, *and* Esquire. *He often writes about how to do things, and how things — machines, organizations, systems — work. His most recent book,* Sheetrock & Shellac *(2006), is a characteristically amusing examination of his attempts to renovate his two-hundred-year-old farmhouse in Washington, Connecticut, in which, for instance, constructing a bookcase expands into building his entire office.* Copies in Seconds *(2004) is a biography of Chester F. Carlson, inventor of the Xerox machine and its dramatic influence on sharing knowledge, which Owen likens to Gutenberg's printing press. With Marilyn Doerr, he wrote* None of the Above: The Truth behind the SATs *(1999), a serious exposé of college testing.*

*"Your Three Wishes: F.A.Q." (*New Yorker, *2006) parodies the format and language of frequently asked questions and answers, attributing cosmic significance to the familiar fairy-tale plot. If you had three wishes to be granted, what would they be? And what would be the consequences, expected and unexpected? Be careful what you wish for.*

You have been granted three wishes — congratulations. If you wish wisely, your wishes may bring you great happiness. Before wishing, please take a moment to read the following frequently asked questions.

1. *Do my wishes have an expiration date?*
   No. Your wishes are good until used. Once you have made a wish, however, you cannot revoke it, except by using another wish, should any remain.

2. *May I wish for absolutely anything?*
   A wish, if it is to be granted, must not violate the physical laws of the universe. You may wish for a particular co-worker to be fired (for example), or for Mt. Everest to collapse into a heap of rubble; you may not wish to live literally forever, or for the speed of light to be lowered to five miles an hour.

3. *May I use one of my wishes to wish for more wishes?*
   No. You have been granted exactly three wishes. You cannot increase that number by wishing.

4. *What happens if I merely think a wish?*   5

   No wish will be executed until you speak it out loud, so "wishful thinking" does not count. Note: If you inadvertently use one of your wishes to render yourself permanently speechless—by turning yourself into a pig, for example, or by wishing that you were dead—you will be unable to use your remaining wishes, if any are left, to correct the error.

5. *How specific do I have to be? If I wish for "world peace," will you know what I'm talking about?*

   As a practical matter, no one ever wishes for "world peace." But it is always best to be specific. "I wish for my penis, when erect, to measure eighteen inches in length and six inches in diameter" is clear and concise—and it counts as one wish only, because length and diameter are two dimensions of the same object. "I wish for my penis, when erect, to measure eighteen inches in length and six inches in diameter, and I want it to be erect all the time" is two wishes. "I wish to be a global celebrity, but not Michael Jackson or Tom Cruise" is three.

6. *If I wish for money, how much may I wish for?*

   There is no preset limit. However, you should keep in mind that money has value only in a functioning economic system. If you wish for "all the money in the world," you may have no opportunity to spend your fortune. It is best to be both realistic and unambiguous. If you wish merely for "great wealth" or "untold riches," you could end up with (for example) attractive grandchildren, stimulating hobbies, or a clean bill of health.

7. *How come people who get three wishes always seem to wish for something that they regret, big-time—like that woodcutter and the sausages?*

   The grantor of your wishes does not take ironic pleasure in human folly. Nevertheless, you alone are responsible for the outcome of your wishing. Hint: Avoid phrases that are open to catastrophic interpretation, such as "for the rest of my life." Also, keep in mind that the media tends to focus on wishes that turn out badly. "Man gets three wishes and lives happily ever after" is not considered news.

8. *Can I use one of my three wishes to guarantee that neither of my other wishes will have negative consequences that I failed to foresee?*

   Hmm, I'm going to say no.

QUESTIONS FOR DISCUSSION AND WRITING

1. Owen uses a number of strategies in this piece to ratchet up the humor. Comment on the effectiveness of the following:

   a. Absurd questions, deadpan (and sometimes startling—see answer 5) answers.

b. The questioner's stylized language. Would a questioner really say, for example, "Do my wishes have an expiration date?"

c. The respondent's equally stylized language, formal and authoritative: "No wish will be executed until you speak it out loud."

2. By yourself or with a partner, write your own F.A.Q. parody. Tee hee!

Acknowledgments

Marjorie Agosín. "Always Living in Spanish." Translated by Celeste Kostopulos-Cooperman. Copyright © Marjorie Agosín. Reprinted with permission of the author.

Sherman Alexie. "The Joy of Reading and Writing: Superman and Me." First published in *The Most Wonderful Books*. Copyright © 1997 by Sherman Alexie. Reprinted with permission of Nancy Stauffer Associates as agent for the author.
"What Sacagawea Means to Me." From *Time*, July 8, 2002. www.time.com. Copyright © 2002 by Time, Inc. Reprinted with permission. Time is a registered trademark of Time, Inc. All rights reserved.

Paula Gunn Allen. From *Voice of the Turtle: American Indian Literature 1900–1970* by Paula Gunn Allen. Copyright © 1994 by Paula Gunn Allen. Reprinted by permission of the Beth Vesel Literary Agency for the author.

Brian J. Alters. Excerpt from interview with Stephen Jay Gould. National Association of Biology Teachers. From *The American Biology Teacher* 60.4 (April 1998): 272–75. © 1998. Reprinted by permission.

American Institutes for Research. "American College Grads—Barely Literate, and Beyond." From *New Study of the Literacy of College Students Finds Some Are Graduating with Only Basic Skills*, by The American Institute for Research, January 19, 2006. www.air.org. Reprinted with permission.

Nancy Andreasen. "The Creative Mind." From *The Creating Brain: The Neuroscience of Genius* by Nancy Andreasen. Copyright © 2006 by Nancy C. Andreasen. Published by Dana Press. Reprinted with permission.

Natalie Angier. "Men, Women, Sex and Darwin." From *Woman: An Intimate Geography* by Natalie Angier. Copyright © 1999 by Natalie Angier. Adapted by permission of Houghton Mifflin Company. All rights reserved.

Gloria Anzaldúa. "Beyond Traditional Notions of Identity." From *Chronicle of Higher Education* B11–13. A different version of this essay was originally published as "(Un)natural bridges, (Un)safe spaces" in *this bridge we call home: radical visions for transformation*, ed. by Gloria E. Anzaldúa and Analouise Keating. Reprinted by permission of the Gloria E. Anzaldúa Literary Trust.

Karen Armstrong. "Does God Have a Future?" From *A History of God: The 400-Year Quest of Judaism, Christianity, and Islam* by Karen Armstrong. Copyright © 1993 by Karen Armstrong. Used by permission of Alfred A. Knopf, a division of Random House, Inc.

James Baldwin. "Stranger in the Village" and "Autobiographical Notes." From *Notes of a Native Son* by James Baldwin. Copyright © 1955, renewed 1983 by James Baldwin. Reprinted by permission of Beacon Press, Boston.

Dennis Baron. "The New Technologies of the Word." From 2002 talk given to the *International Association of World Englishes* by Dennis Baron. Copyright © 2002 by Dennis Baron. Reprinted by permission of the author.

T. Olin Binkley. "Southern Baptist Seminaries." From *The Christian Century*, June 12, 1963. Copyright © 1963 Christian Century. Reprinted with permission.

The Birmingham Post-Herald. "Eight Clergymen's Statement." From *The Birmingham Post-Herald*, April 13, 1963, p. 10. Copyright © 1963 by Martin Luther King Jr. Copyright renewed 1991 Coretta Scott King. Reprinted by arrangement with The Heirs to the Estate of Martin Luther King Jr., c/o Writers House as agent for the proprietor New York, NY.

Wendy Bishop. "Revision is a Recursive Process." Excerpt from *Working Words: The Process of Creative Writing*. Copyright © 1992. Reprinted by permission of The McGraw-Hill Companies.

Erma Bombeck. "Technology's Coming … Technology's Coming." From *At Wit's End* by Erma Bombeck. Copyright © 2007 Erma Bombeck. Reprinted with permission of the Aaron Priest Literary Agency.

Amy Borkowsky. "Amy's Answering Machine." Taken from transcript of Bob Edwards interview with Amy Borkowsky, May 10, 2002. © 2007 National Public Radio, Inc. Excerpts from pp. 92 & 14 (with slight changes), 17, and 69, as used in Bob Edwards interview with Amy Borkowsky on National Public Radio. Reprinted with the permission of Atria Books, a Division of Simon & Schuster, Inc., from *Amy's Answering Machine: Messages from Mom* by Amy Borkowsky. Copyright © 2001 by Amy Borkowsky.

David Brooks. "The Elusive Altar." Originally published in *The New York Times*, January 18, 2007. Copyright © 2007 by David Brooks. Reprinted by permission of the author.

Kenneth A. Brown. "Steve Wozniak: Inventing the PC." From *Inventors at Work: Interviews with 16 Notable American Inventors*. Copyright © 1988 by Tempus Books of Microsoft Press. Reprinted with permission of the publisher.

Rita Mae Brown. "Kissing Off Ma Bell." From *Starting from Scratch: A Different Kind of Writer* by Rita Mae Brown. Copyright © 1988 by Speakeasy Productions, Inc. Used by permission of Bantam Books, a division of Random House, Inc.

Michael J. Bugeja. "Facing the Facebook." Originally published in *The Chronicle of Higher Education*, January 27, 2006, C1, 4. Copyright © 2006 by Michael J. Bugeja. Reprinted by permission of the author.

Rachel Carson. "The Obligation to Endure." From *Silent Spring* by Rachel Carson. Copyright © 1962 by Rachel L. Carson. Renewed 1990 by Roger Christie. Reprinted with permission of Houghton Mifflin Company. All rights reserved.

Frank Chin. "Come All Ye Asian American Writers of the Real and the Fake." From *The Big Aiiieeeee!* By Jeffrey Paul Chan, Frank Chin, Lawson Fusao Inada, and Shawn Wong. Copyright © 1991 by Jeffrey Paul Chan, Frank Chin, Lawson Fusao Inada, and Shawn Wong. Used with permission of Dutton Signet, a division of Penguin Putnam, Inc.

Robert Coles. "Two Languages, One Soul." From *The Old Ones of New Mexico* by Robert Coles. Copyright © 1973 by Robert Coles. Reprinted with permission of the University of New Mexico Press.

Stephanie Coontz. "Blaming the Family for Economic Decline." From *The Way We Really Are: Coming to Terms with America's Changing Families* by Stephanie Coontz. Copyright © 1997 by Stephanie Coontz. Copyright © 1997 by Basic Books, a Division of HarperCollins Publishers, Inc. Reprinted by permission of Basic Books, a member of Perseus Books, LLC.

The 14th Dalai Lama (Tenzin Gyatso). "Inner Peace and Human Rights (1989)." Reprinted with permission of The Office of His Holiness the Dalai Lama.

Cathy N. Davidson. "Laughing in English." From *36 Views of Mount Fuji* by Cathy N. Davidson. Copyright © 1933 by Cathy N. Davidson. Used with permission of Elaine Markson Literary Agency.

Joan Didion. "On Keeping a Notebook." From *Slouching Toward Bethlehem* by Joan Didion. © 1966, 1968 and renewed 1996 by Joan Didion. Reprinted with permission of Farrar, Straus and Giroux, LLC.
"Why I Write." Originally published in the *New York Times Book Review* by Joan Didion. Copyright © 1976 by Joan Didion. Reprinted with permission of the author. "Last Words." Originally published in *The New Yorker*, November 9, 1998, 74–80. Copyright © 1998 by Joan Didion. Reprinted with permission of Jankow & Nesbit, agents for the author.

Annie Dillard. "Heaven and Earth in Jest." From *Pilgrim at Tinker Creek* by Annie Dillard. Copyright © 1964 by Annie Dillard. Reprinted by permission of HarperCollins Publishers, Inc.

David Dobbs. "Trial and Error: The scientific-publishing system does little to prevent scientific fraud. Is there a better way?" From *The New York Times Magazine*, January 15, 2006. Copyright © 2006 by The New York Times Company, Inc. Reprinted with permission.

Brian Doyle. Excerpt from "Joyas Voladoras." Reprinted from *The American Scholar*, Autumn 2004, Vol. 73, 84. Copyright © 2004 by Brian Doyle. Reprinted by permission of The American Scholar.

Umberto Eco. "Operating Instructions." From "How to Choose a Remunerative Profession." In *How to Travel with a Salmon & Other Essays* by Umberto Eco. Copyright © Gruppo Editoriale Fabbri, Bompiani, Sonzogno, Etas S.p.A. English translation by William Weaver. Copyright © 1994 by Harcourt, Inc. Reprinted by permission of Harcourt, Inc.

Barbara Ehrenreich. "Serving in Florida." From *Nickel and Dimed: On (Not) Getting By in America* by Barbara Ehrenreich. Copyright © 2001 by Barbara Ehrenreich. Reprinted with permission of Henry Holt & Company, LLC.

Peter Elbow. "Freewriting." Excerpt from *Writing Without Teachers* by Peter Elbow. Copyright © 1973, 1998 by Peter Elbow. Used by permission of Oxford University Press.

Anne Fadiman. "Marrying Libraries." From *Ex Libris: Confessions of a Common Reader* by Anne Fadiman. Copyright © 1998 by Anne Fadiman. Reprinted by permission of Farrar, Strauss & Giroux, LLC.

Ryszard Kapuscinski. "The Truck: Hitchhiking through Hell." From *Shadow of the Sun* by Ryszard Kapuscinski. Translation copyright © 2001 by Klara Glowczewska. Used by permission of Alfred A. Knopf, a division of Random House, Inc.

Garrison Keillor. "The Anthem: If famous poets had written 'The Star-Spangled Banner.'" From *The Atlantic Monthly*, January–February 2006. Copyright © 2006. Reprinted with permission of National Public Radio.

Martin Luther King Jr. "Letter from Birmingham Jail." From *Why We Can't Wait*. Copyright © 1963 by Dr. Martin Luther King Jr. Copyright renewed 1991 by Coretta Scott King.

"Defines Black Power." Originally published in *The New York Times*, June 11, 1967. Copyright © 1967 by Martin Luther King Jr. Copyright renewed 1995 by Coretta Scott King. Reprinted by arrangement with the Estate of Martin Luther King Jr., c/o Writer's House as agent for the proprietor, New York, NY.

"Boycotts Will Be Used." From interview with Martin Luther King, Jr. in *U.S. News & World Report*, Febuary 24, 1964, pp. 59–61. Copyright © 1961 U.S. News & World Report. Reprinted with permission.

Stephen King. "Write or Die." From *A Memoir of the Craft* by Stephen King. Copyright © Stephen King. Reprinted with permisson. All rights reserved.

Maxine Hong Kingston. "No Name Woman." From *The Woman Warrior* by Maxine Hong Kingston. Copyright © 1975, 1976 by Maxine Hong Kingston. Used by permission of Alfred A. Knopf, a division of Random House, Inc.

"Interview" (1998). From "A Conversation with Maxine Hong Kingston," From pp. 33–35 in *Critical Essays on Maxine Hong Kingston*, edited by Laura Skandera-Trombley, 1998. Reprinted with permission of Thomson Learning www.thomsonrights.com.

"Interview" (1982) by Guy Amirthanayagam. From "Cultural Mis-readings by American Reviewers." Published in *Asian and Western Writers in Dialogue: New Cultural Identities*, edited by Guy Amirthanayagam. Copyright © 1982. Reprinted with permission of Macmillan Oxford and Maxine Hong Kingston.

"Imagined Life." From *Michigan Quarterly Review*, 22.4 (Fall 1983): 561–570. Copyright © 1983. Reprinted with permission of the Michigan Quarterly Review. Excerpt (1 page) from "Eccentric Memories: A Conversation with Maxine Hong Kingston" by Paula Rabinowitz. Originally published in the Michigan *Quarterly Review* 26 (1987). Reprinted with permission of the author.

Perri Klass. "The One-in-a-Thousand Illness You Can't Afford to Miss." From *The New York Times*, January 24, 2006. Copyright © 2006 by The New York Times Company, Inc. Reprinted with permission.

Georgina Kleege. "Close Reading." From *Sight Unseen* by Georgina Kleege. Copyright © 1999 by Georgina Kleege. Reprinted with permission of Mildred Marmur Associates on behalf of the author.

Jonathan Kozol. "The Human Cost of An Illiterate Society." From *Illiterate in America* by Jonathan Kozol. Copyright © 1985 by Jonathan Kozol. Used by permission of Doubleday, a division of Random House, Inc.

Chang Rae Lee. Excerpt from *Coming Home Again*. Originally published in *The New Yorker*. Copyright © 1995 by Chang Rae Lee. Reprinted by permission of International Creative Management, Inc.

Fran Lebowitz. "The Sound of Music—Enough Already." From *Metropolitan Life* by Fran Lebowitz. Copyright © 1978 by Vintage. Reprinted with permission of Janklow & Nesbit, agents for the author.

Eric Liu. "Notes of a Native Speaker." From *The Accidental Asian: Notes of a Native Speaker* by Eric Liu. Copyright © 1998 by Eric Liu. Used by permission of Random House, Inc.

Barry Lopez. "The American Geographies." From *About This Life* by Barry Lopez. Copyright © 1998 by Barry Holstun Lopez. Used by permission of Alfred A. Knopf, a division of Random House, Inc. and SLL/Sterling Lord Literistic, Inc.

Bobbie Ann Mason. "Being Country." From *Clear Springs* by Bobbie Ann Mason. Copyright © 1999 by Bobbie Ann Mason. Used by permission of Random House, Inc.

Frances Mayes. "Interview: Frances Mayes on Writing Under the Tuscan Sun." *Online Interview with Frances Mayes*. Taken from www.randomhouse.com. Used by permission of Random House, Inc.

Deirdre N. McCloskey. "Yes, Ma'am." From *Crossing: A Memoir* by Deirdre N. McCloskey. Copyright © 1999 by Deirdre N. McCloskey. Reprinted by permission of The University of Chicago Press and the author. All rights reserved.

Bill McKibben. "Designer Genes." From *Enough: Staying Human in an Engineering Age* by Bill McKibben. Copyright © 2003 Bill McKibben. Reprinted by permission of Henry Holt & Company, NYC.

Margaret Mead. "Warfare Is Only an Invention—Not a Biological Necessity." First published in *Asia*, Volume 40, No. 8, August, pp. 402–5. Copyright © 1940 by Margaret Mead. Reprinted with permission of the Institute for Intercultural Studies.

N. Scott Momaday. "Introduction," pp. 5–12, "East of My Grandmother's House," p. 83, from *The Way to Rainy Mountain*. Copyright © 1969 by N. Scott Momaday. Reprinted with permission of the University of New Mexico Press.

"Disturbing the Spirits: Indian Bones Must Stay in the Ground," from *The New York Times*, November 2, 1996, p. 25. Copyright © 1996 by The New York Times Company, Inc. Reprinted with permission.

"The Native Voice," originally published in the *Columbia Literary History of the United States*, edited by Emory Elliott. © 1998 Columbia University Press. Reprinted with permission of the publisher.

"The Whole Journey," originally published in "The Man Made of Words" and "Three Voices" from *Indian Voices: The First Convocation of American Indian Scholars*, edited by Rupert Costo et al. Copyright © 1970. Published by Indian Historian Press. Reprinted with permission.

"I Invented History," p. 97. From *The Names: A Memoir*. Copyright © 1976 by N. Scott Momaday. Reprinted with permission of the author.

Kyoto Mori. "Date Stamp." Excerpt from *The Dream of Water: A Memoir* by Kyoto Mori. Copyright © 1995 by Kyoto Mori. Reprinted by permission of Henry Holt & Company.

Mary Morris. "My First Night Alone in Mexico." From *Nothing to Declare* by Mary Morris. Copyright © 1988 Mary Morris. Reprinted with permission of Houghton Mifflin Company. All rights reserved.

Toni Morrison. "The Pain of Being Black: Interview with Bonnie Angelo." First published in *Time*, 1989. Copyright © 1989 by Toni Morrison. Reprinted by permission of International Creative Management, Inc.

Gloria Naylor. "The Love of Books." From *The Writing Life*, 1995. Copyright © 1986 by Gloria Naylor. Reprinted with permission of Sterling Lord Literary Agency.

Jacob Neusner. "The Speech the Graduates Didn't Hear." Originally published in *Brown University Daily Herald*, June 12, 1983. Copyright © 1983 Jacob Neusner. Reprinted by permission of the author.

Norimitsu Onishi. "In a Country that Craved Respect, Stem Cell Scientist Rode a Wave of Korean Pride." From *The New York Times*, January 22, 2006. Copyright © 2006 by The New York Times Company, Inc. Reprinted with permission.

George Orwell. "Shooting an Elephant." From *Shooting an Elephant and Other Essays* by George Orwell. Copyright © 1950 by Sonia Brownell Orwell and renewed 1978 by Sonia Pitt-Rivers. Reprinted with permission of Harcourt, Inc.

David Owen. "Your Three Wishes: F.A.Q." Originally published in *The New Yorker*, January 16, 2006, p. 37, 1p. Copyright © 2006 by David Owen. Reprinted with permission of the author.

Robert L. Park. "The Seven Warning Signs of Bogus Science." Originally published in *The Chronicle of Higher Education*, January 31, 2003. Copyright © 2003 by Robert Park. Reprinted with permission of the author.

Octavio Paz. Excerpt from pp. 29–30 in *The Labyrinth of Solitude* by Octavio Paz. Translated by Lysander Kemp, 1961. Copyright © 1985 by Grove Press, Inc. Used by permission of Grove/Atlantic, Inc.

Okot P'Bitek. "Song of Lawino: An African Lament." Published by East African Publishing House, 1966. Reprinted by permission of the publisher. www.fountainpublishers.co.ug.

Robert Pearce. "Orwell Now." Excerpt from *History Today*, October 1997. Copyright © 1997 by *History Today*. Reprinted with permission of the publisher.

Pope John Paul XXIII. "Disarmament." From *Pacem in Terris*. © Libreria Editrice Vaticana. Reproduced by permission.

Katherine Anne Porter. "You Do Not Create a Style. You Work...." First published in *The Paris Review*. Copyright © 1963 by The Paris Review. Copyright renewed 1991 by The Paris Review. Reprinted with permission of The Wylie Agency.

Richard A. Posner. "Security versus Civil Liberties." First published in *The Atlantic Monthly*, December 2001, volume 288, no. 5, pp. 141–43. Copyright ©2001 Richard A. Posner. Reprinted with permission of the author.

Sandra Postel. "Troubled Waters." From *The Sciences*, March/April 2000 issue. Copyright © 2000 The Sciences. Reprinted by permission of the New York Academy of Sciences.

Virginia I. Postrel and Nick Gillespie. "The New, New World: Richard Rodriguez on Culture and Assimilation." Interview from *Reason* magazine, August/September 1994. Copyright 2002 by Reason Foundation, 3415 S. Sepulveda Blvd., Suite 400, Los Angeles, CA 90034. www.reason.com. Reprinted with permission of the publisher.

Annie Proulx. "Travel Is … an Unnerving Experience." Excerpt from "The Book Tour" in *Without a Guide: Contemporary Women's Travel Adventures* edited by Katherine Govier. Copyright © 1996, Hungry Mind Press. Reprinted with permission of Darhansoff, Verrill Feldman Literary Agents.

Anna Quindlen. "Anniversary." From *Loud and Clear*. Copyright © 2004 by Anna Quindlen. "Uncle Sam and Samantha." First appeared in *Newsweek*, November 2001. Copyright © 2001 by Anna Quindlen. Reprinted with permission of International Creative Management, Inc.

Alok Rai. Excerpt of pp. 58–59 from *Orwell and the Politics of Despair* by Alok Rai. Copyright © 1988. Reprinted with the permission of Cambridge University Press.

William E. Rees. "Life in the Lap of Luxury as Ecosytems Collapse." Originally published in the *Chronicle of Higher Education*, July 30, 1999. Copyright © 1999 by William E. Rees. Reprinted with permission of the author.

Kelly Ritter. "The Economics of Authorship: Online Paper Mills, Student Writers, and First-Year Composition." Published in *College Composition and Communication* 56.4 (June 2005): 601–31. Copyright © 2005 by the National Council of Teachers of English. Reprinted with permission.

David Roberts. "An Interview with Accidental Movie Star Al Gore." From www.grist.org. Reprinted by permission of the publisher.

Richard Rodriguez. "Slouching Towards Los Angeles." Originally published in the *Los Angeles Times*, April 11, 1993. Copyright © 1993 by Richard Rodriguez. Used by permission of Georges Borchardt, Inc., on behalf of Richard Rodriguez.

"Aria." From *A Memoir of a Bilingual Childhood: The Education of Richard Rodriguez* by Richard Rodriguez. Pp. 11–28. Copyright © 1982 by Richard Rodriguez. Reprinted by permission of David R. Godine, Publisher, Inc.

Roger Rosenblatt. Excerpt from "Rules of Aging." From *Modern Maturity*, September/October 1999. Copyright © 1999 AARP. Reprinted with permission from *Modern Maturity* and the author.

Scott Russell Sanders. "Under the Influence." First appeared in *Harper's* from *Secrets of the Universe* by Scott Russell Sanders. Copyright © 1989 by Scott Russell Sanders.

"The Inheritance of Tools." First appeared in *The North American Review*. Later published in *The Paradise of Bombs* by Scott Russell Sanders. Copyright © 1986 by Scott Russell Sanders. Reprinted by permission of the author and the author's agents, the Virginia Kidd Agency, Inc.

Esmeralda Santiago. "Jíbara." From *When I Was a Puerto Rican* by Esmeralda Santiago. Copyright © 1993 by Esmeralda Santiago. Used with permission of Perseus Books, LLC.

Elaine Scarry. "Acts of Resistance." First published in *The Boston Review*, February/March 2004. Copyright © 2004 by Elaine Scarry. Reprinted with permission of the author.

David Sedaris. "What I Learned/And What I Said at Princeton." Excerpt from "What I Learned at Princeton." Originally published in *The New Yorker*, June 26, 2006. Copyright © 2006 by David Sedaris.

"Old Faithful." Originally published in *The New Yorker*, November 29, 2004. Copyright © 2004 by David Sedaris. Reprinted by permission of Don Congdon Associates.

Timothy S. Sedore. "Violating the Boundaries: An Interview with Richard Rodriguez." Originally published in the *Michigan Quarterly Review*, Summer 1999, one page excerpt from pp. 425–46. Reprinted by permission of the author.

Leslie Marmon Silko. "We Are All Part of Our Stories." From *English Literature: Opening Up the Canon: Selected Papers from the English Institute*, edited by Leslie A. Fiedler and Houston A. Baker. Copyright © 1979, 1981. Reprinted with permission of The Johns Hopkins University Press.

Linda Simon. "The Naked Source." First published in *Michigan Quarterly Review*. Copyright © 1998 by Linda Simon. Reprinted by permission of the author.

Wendy Simonds. "Talking with Strangers: A Researcher's Tale." Originally published in *The Chronicle of Higher Education*, November 30, 2001. Copyright © 2001 by Wendy Simonds. Reprinted by permission of the author.

Peter Singer. "The Singer Solution to World Poverty." Originally published in *The New York Times Magazine*, September 5, 1999. Copyright © 1999 by Peter Singer. Reprinted by permission of the author.

Society of Professional Journalists. "Code of Ethics." From Society of Professional Journalists. www .spj.org. Copyright © 2006 by Society of Professional Journalists. Reprinted with permission.

Susan Sontag. "Looking at the Unbearable." From *Transforming Vision Writers on Art* by Susan Sontag. Copyright © 1994 by Susan Sontag. Reprinted by permission of The Wylie Agency.

Wole Soyinka. "Every Dictator's Nightmare." First appeared in *The New York Times Magazine*. Copyright © 1999 by Wole Soyinka. Reprinted with permission of Melanie Jackson Agency, LLC.

Stephen Spender. Excerpt from *A Measure of Orwell*. First published in *The New York Times Review*, October 29, 1950. Copyright © 1950 by Stephen Spender. Reprinted by permission of Ed Victor, Ltd., as agents for the Estate of Stephen Spender.

Jackie Spinner. "The Only Thing You Should Be Advocating Is the Truth." Commencement address to 2005 Graduating Class, May 14, 2005. College of Mass Communication & Media Arts, Southern Illinois University, Carbondale, IL. Reprinted by permission of the Melanie Jackson Literary Agency, on behalf of the author.

Paul Starobin. "Misfit America." First published in *The Atlantic Monthly*, January/February 2006. Copyright © 2006 by Paul Starobin. Reprinted by permission of the author.

Ben Stein. "Birds and Bees? No, Let's Talk About Dollars and Cents." From *The New York Times*, October 10, 2004. Copyright © 2004 by The New York Times Company, Inc. Reprinted with permission.

Amy Tan. "Mother Tongue." First appeared in *The Threepenny Review*. Copyright © 1990 by Amy Tan. Reprinted by permission of the author and the Sandra Dijkstra Literary Agency.

Paul Theroux. "Every Trip Is Unique." From *Fresh Air Fiend: Travel Writings* by Paul Theroux. Copyright © 2000 by Paul Theroux. Reprinted with permission of Houghton Mifflin Company. All rights reserved.

James Thurber. "Telling Stories." From *The Paris Review*, 1963. Copyright © 1963 by The Paris Review. Copyright renewed 1991 by The Paris Review. Reprinted with permission of The Wylie Agency as agents for The Paris Review.

Calvin Trillin. "On Writing About Family." (Our title). Excerpt from *Interview with Calvin Trillin* By Laura Miller. "Calvin Trillin, The Food Writer and Humorist Gets Serious About Fathers and Sons." Posted on *Salon.com*, www.salon.com. Reprinted by permission of Salon.com.

Rigoberta Menchú Tum. "Five Hundred Years of Mayan Oppression." From *Nobel Lectures, Peace 1991–1995*, Editor Irwin Abrams, World Scientific Publishing Co., Singapore (1999). Copyright © 1992 The Nobel Foundation. Reprinted with permission.

José Antonio Villareal. Excerpt from *Pocho* by José Antonio Villareal. Copyright © 1959 José Antonio Villareal. Used by permission of Doubleday, a division of Random House, Inc.

Alice Walker. "In Search of Our Mother's Gardens" and "Looking to the Side and Back." From *In Search of Our Mother's Gardens: Womanist Prose* by Alice Walker. Copyright © 1974, 1979 by Alice Walker. Reprinted with permission of Harcourt, Inc.
"Eudora Welty: An Interview." From *The Harvard Advocate*, 106 (Winter 1973): 68–72. Copyright © 1973. Reprinted with permission of the publisher.

Judith Wallerstein. "The Divorce Revolution." From *The Unexpected Legacy of Divorce* by Judith Wallerstein, Julia Lewis, and Sandra Blakeslee. Copyright © 2000 Judith Wallerstein, Julia Lewis, and Sandra Blakeslee. Reprinted with permission of Hyperion. All rights reserved.

Jeffrey Wattles. "The Golden Rule—One or Many, Gold or Glitter?" From *The Golden Rule* by Jeffrey Wattles. Copyright © 1996 by Jeffrey Wattles. Used by permission of Oxford University Press, Inc.

Eudora Welty. "Listening." From *One Writer's Beginnings* by Eudora Welty. Copyright © 1983, 1984 by Eudora Welty. Reprinted by permission of Harvard University Press.

Bailey White. "Flying Saucer." From *Mama Makes Up Her Mind: and Other Dangers of Southern Living* by Bailey White. Copyright © 1993 by Bailey White. Reprinted with permission of Vintage Books, an imprint of Random House, Inc.

E. B. White. "Once More to the Lake." From *One Man's Meat* by E. B. White. Copyright © 1941 by E. B. White. Copyright renewed. Reprinted by permission of Tilbury House, Publishers, Gardiner, Maine.

George F. Will. "Life and Death at Princeton." First published in *Newsweek Magazine*, September 13, 1999. Copyright © 1999 by George F. Will. Reprinted with permission of the author.

Terry Tempest Williams. "The Clan of One-Breasted Women." From *Refugee: An Unnatural History of Family and Place* by Terry Tempest Williams. Copyright © 1991 by Terry Tempest Williams. Used by permission of Pantheon Books, a division of Random House, Inc.

Edward O. Wilson. "Microbes 3, Humans 2." First published in *The New York Times Magazine*, April 18, 1999. Copyright © 1999 by Edward O. Wilson. Reprinted with permission of the author. "Review" from *The New Yorker*, January 13, 1951, p. 76. Copyright © 1951. Reprinted by permission.

Richard Wright. "Fighting Words." From *Black Boy* by Richard Wright. Copyright © 1937, 1942, 1944, 1945 by Richard Wright. Renewed © 1973 by Ellen Wright. Reprinted with permission of HarperCollins Publishers.

Kenji Yoshino. "The Pressure to Cover." From *Covering* by Kenji Yoshino. Copyright © 2006 by Kenji Yoshino. Used by permission of Random House, Inc.

Kate Zernike. "Why Are There So Many Single Americans?" From *The New York Times*, January 21, 2007. Copyright © 2007 by The New York Times Company, Inc. Reprinted with permission.

Paul Zweig. "The Child of Two Cultures." Originally appeared in *The New York Times Book Review*, February 28, 1982. Copyright © 1982 by Paul Zweig. Reprinted with permission of Georges Borchardt, Inc., on behalf of the author.

Picture Credits

Chapter 1:
Page 27: "The Work of Writing." David Hanover/Getty Images. Used by permission.
Page 62: "Reading the Comics." Pages 67 and 68 from UNDERSTANDING COMICS by SCOTT MCCLOUD. Copyright © 1993, 1994 by Scott McCloud. Reprinted by permission of HarperCollins Publishers.
Page 102: "The I.M.s of Romeo and Juliet." © The New Yorker Collection 2002. Roz Chast from cartoonbank. com. All Rights Reserved.

Chapter 2:
Page 110: "An Authentic Indian." Neg. Transparency no. 11608, courtesy the Library, American Museum of Natural History.
Page 111: "College Graduates." © John Henley/ CORBIS.
Pages 140–141: "Mein Kampf." First published in The New York Times Magazine, May 12, 1996. © 1996 by Art Spiegelman, permission of The Wylie Agency.
Page 151: "Rainy Mountain." N. Scott Momaday.
Page 157: "N. Scott Momaday." © Nancy Crampton.

Chapter 3:
Page 199: "E. B. White and brother on Belgrade Lake." Permission granted by the E. B. White Estate.
Page 242: "Ford River Rouge Plant." Ford River Rouge Plant, Dearborn, Michigan, 1946. Copyright Walker Evans Archive. All rights reserved. The Metropolitan Museum of Art.
Page 265: "Dialogue Boxes You Should Have Read More Carefully." Evan Eisenberg.

Rhetorical Index

Analogy

Sherman Alexie, *What Sacagawea Means to Me*, 142
John Donne, *Meditation*, 590
W. E. B. Du Bois, *The "Veil" of Self-Consciousness*, 127
Plato, *The Allegory of the Cave*, 319
Anna Quindlen, *Uncle Sam and Aunt Samantha*, 598
William E. Rees, *Life in the Lap of Luxury as Ecosystems Collapse*, 678
Art Spiegelman, from *Maus*, 418
Jeffrey Wattles, *The Golden Rule—One or Many, Gold or Glitter?*, 592

Analysis

Paula Gunn Allen, *Voice of the Turtle*, 156
American Institutes for Research, *American College Grads—Barely Literate, and Beyond*, 337
Natalie Angier, *Men, Women, Sex, and Darwin*, 538
Gloria Anzaldúa, *Beyond Traditional Notions of Identity*, 159
Karen Armstrong, *Does God Have a Future?*, 702
James Baldwin, *Stranger in the Village*, 118
Dennis Baron, *The New Technologies of the Word*, 92
Michael J. Bugeja, *Facing the Facebook*, 626
Rachel Carson, *The Obligation to Endure*, 663
Stephanie Coontz, *Blaming the Family for Economic Decline*, 228
The Fourteenth Dalai Lama (Tenzin Gyatso), *Inner Peace and Human Rights*, 697
David Dobbs, *Trial and Error*, 557
Barbara Ehrenreich, *Serving in Florida*, 243
Stanley Fish, *Academic Cross-Dressing: How Intelligent Design Gets Its Arguments from the Left*, 532
Deborah Franklin, *"Informed Consent"—What Information? What Consent?*, 64
H. Bruce Franklin, *From Realism to Virtual Reality: Images of American Wars*, 403
Henry Louis Gates Jr., *Signifying*, 494
G. Anthony Gorry, *Steal This MP3 File: What Is Theft?*, 622
Shirley Brice Heath, *Literate Traditions*, 280
Harriet Jacobs, *The Slaves' New Year's Day*, 449
Perri Klass, *The One-in-a-Thousand Illness You Can't Afford to Miss*, 260
Eric Liu, *Notes of a Native Speaker*, 112

Barry Lopez, *The American Geographies*, 669

Bill McKibben, *Designer Genes*, 500

Margaret Mead, *Warfare Is Only an Invention—Not a Biological Necessity*, 682

Rigoberta Menchú, *Five Hundred Years of Mayan Oppression*, 694

N. Scott Momaday, *Three Voices*, 119

Jacob Neusner, *The Speech the Graduates Didn't Hear*, 346

Robert L. Park, *The Seven Warning Signs of Bogus Science*, 551

Octavio Paz, *The Labyrinth of Solitude*, 309

Richard A. Posner, *Security versus Civil Liberties*, 480

William E. Rees, *Life in the Lap of Luxury as Ecosystems Collapse*, 678

Kelly Ritter, *The Economics of Authorship: Online Paper Mills, Student Writers, and First-Year Composition*, 615

Theodore Roosevelt, *What College Graduates Owe America*, 343

Elaine Scarry, *Acts of Resistance*, 484

Susan Sontag, *Looking at the Unbearable*, 397

Wole Soyinka, *Every Dictator's Nightmare*, 475

Elizabeth Cady Stanton, *Declaration of Sentiments*, 375

Paul Starobin, *Misfit America*, 164

Ben Stein, *Birds and Bees? No, Let's Talk About Dollars and Cents*, 341

Henry David Thoreau
   Civil Disobedience, 192
   Where I Lived, and What I Lived For, 187

Alice Walker, *Looking to the Side, and Back*, 364

Judith Wallerstein, *The Legacy of Divorce*, 238

Jeffrey Wattles, *The Golden Rule—One or Many, Gold or Glitter?*, 592

Kenji Yoshino, *The Pressure to Cover*, 456

Argument and Persuasion

Natalie Angier, *Men, Women, Sex, and Darwin*, 538

Gloria Anzaldúa, *Beyond Traditional Notions of Identity*, 159

Karen Armstrong, *Does God Have a Future?*, 702

James Baldwin, *Stranger in the Village*, 118

Dennis Baron, *The New Technologies of the Word*, 92

Michael J. Bugeja, *Facing the Facebook*, 626

Rachel Carson, *The Obligation to Endure*, 663

The Fourteenth Dalai Lama (Tenzin Gyatso), *Inner Peace and Human Rights*, 697

David Dobbs, *Trial and Error*, 555

W. E. B. Du Bois, *The "Veil" of Self-Consciousness*, 127

Stanley Fish, *Academic Cross-Dressing: How Intelligent Design Gets Its Arguments from the Left*, 532

Howard Gardner, *Who Owns Intelligence?*, 322

G. Anthony Gorry, *Steal This MP3 File: What Is Theft?*, 622

Stephen Jay Gould, *Evolution as Fact and Theory*, 512

Thomas Jefferson, *The Declaration of Independence*, 370

Martin Luther King Jr., *Letter from Birmingham Jail*, 565

Jonathan Kozol, *The Human Cost of an Illiterate Society*, 273

Barry Lopez, *The American Geographies*, 669

Bill McKibben, *Designer Genes*, 500

Margaret Mead, *Warfare Is Only an Invention—Not a Biological Necessity*, 682

Rigoberta Menchú, *Five Hundred Years of Mayan Oppression*, 694

N. Scott Momaday, *Disturbing the Spirits*, 153

New York Times, Ending the Bilingual Double-Talk, 276

Jacob Neusner, *The Speech the Graduates Didn't Hear*, 346

Pope John XXIII, *Disarmament*, 691

Richard A. Posner, *Security versus Civil Liberties*, 480

Anna Quindlen, *Uncle Sam and Aunt Samantha*, 598

William E. Rees, *Life in the Lap of Luxury as Ecosystems Collapse*, 678

Theodore Roosevelt, *What College Graduates Owe America*, 343

Elaine Scarry, *Acts of Resistance*, 484

Peter Singer, *The Singer Solution to World Poverty*, 601

Wole Soyinka, *Every Dictator's Nightmare*, 475

Jackie Spinner, *The Only Thing You Should Be Advocating Is the Truth*, 344

Elizabeth Cady Stanton, *Declaration of Sentiments*, 375

Paul Starobin, *Misfit America*, 164

Ben Stein, *Birds and Bees? No, Let's Talk About Dollars and Cents*, 341

Henry David Thoreau
   Civil Disobedience, 192
    Where I Lived, and What I Lived For, 187

Judith Wallerstein, *The Legacy of Divorce*, 238

Terry Tempest Williams, *The Clan of One-Breasted Women*, 656

Kenji Yoshino, *The Pressure to Cover*, 456

Autobiography

Sherman Alexie, *The Joy of Reading and Writing: Superman and Me*, 47

Joan Didion, *Why I Write*, 79

Frederick Douglass, *Resurrection*, 452

Eric Liu, *Notes of a Native Speaker*, 112

Bobbie Ann Mason, *Being Country*, 135

Gloria Naylor, *The Love of Books*, 69

Anna Quindlen, *Anniversary*, 219

Richard Rodriguez, *Aria: A Memoir of a Bilingual Childhood*, 298

Esmeralda Santiago, *Jíbara*, 129

David Sedaris, *Old Faithful*, 222

Art Spiegelman, *Mein Kampf (My Struggle)*, 139

Jackie Spinner, *The Only Thing You Should Be Advocating Is the Truth*, 344

Ben Stein, *Birds and Bees? No, Let's Talk About Dollars and Cents*, 341

Eudora Welty, *Listening*, 33

Cause and Effect

Karen Armstrong, *Does God Have a Future?*, 702
Dennis Baron, *The New Technologies of the Word*, 92
Rachel Carson, *The Obligation to Endure*, 663
The Fourteenth Dalai Lama (Tenzin Gyatso), *Inner Peace and Human Rights*, 697
Charles Darwin, *Understanding Natural Selection*, 525
Howard Gardner, *Who Owns Intelligence?*, 322
Shirley Brice Heath, *Literate Traditions*, 280
John Kennedy, *The Purpose of Poetry*, 30
Maxine Hong Kingston, *No Name Woman*, 420
Abraham Lincoln, *The Gettysburg Address*, 690
Bill McKibben, *Designer Genes*, 500
Rigoberta Menchú, *Five Hundred Years of Mayan Oppression*, 694
Gloria Naylor, *The Love of Books*, 69
Norimitsu Onishi, *In a Country That Craved Respect, Stem Cell Scientist Rode a
     Wave of Korean Pride*, 548
Plato, *The Allegory of the Cave*, 319
William E. Rees, *Life in the Lap of Luxury as Ecosystems Collapse*, 678
Scott Russell Sanders, *Under the Influence*, 209
Ben Stein, *Birds and Bees? No, Let's Talk About Dollars and Cents*, 341
Jonathan Swift, *A Modest Proposal*, 469
Henry David Thoreau, *Civil Disobedience*, 192
Alice Walker, *In Search of Our Mothers' Gardens*, 352
Judith Wallerstein, *The Legacy of Divorce*, 238
Terry Tempest Williams, *The Clan of One-Breasted Women*, 656

Classification and Division

Natalie Angier, *Men, Women, Sex, and Darwin*, 538
Judy Brady, *I Want a Wife*, 176
Stephanie Coontz, *Blaming the Family for Economic Decline*, 228
Howard Gardner, *Who Owns Intelligence?*, 322
Richard Hoggart, *The Uses of Literacy*, 312
Perri Klass, *The One-in-a-Thousand Illness You Can't Afford to Miss*, 260
Deirdre N. McCloskey, *Yes, Ma'am*, 173
Peter Singer, *The Singer Solution to World Poverty*, 601

Comparison/Contrast

Marjorie Agosín, *Always Living in Spanish*, 44
Paula Gunn Allen, *Voice of the Turtle*, 156
American Institutes for Research, *American College Grads—Barely Literate, and
     Beyond*, 337
Natalie Angier, *Men, Women, Sex, and Darwin*, 538
Anonymous, *How Many Virginia University Students Does It Take to Change a
     Lightbulb?*, 349

James Baldwin, *Stranger in the Village*, 118

Judy Brady, *I Want a Wife*, 176

Rachel Carson, *The Obligation to Endure*, 663

Stephanie Coontz, *Blaming the Family for Economic Decline*, 228

Charles Darwin, *Understanding Natural Selection*, 525

Cathy Davidson, *Laughing in English*, 493

David Dobbs, *Trial and Error*, 555

Frederick Douglass, *Resurrection*, 452

Stephen Jay Gould, *Evolution as Fact and Theory*, 512

Sara Ivry, *Entrance Exams, Deconstructed*, 335

Martin Luther King Jr., *Letter from Birmingham Jail*, 565

Maxine Hong Kingston, *No Name Woman*, 420

Eric Liu, *Notes of a Native Speaker*, 112

Barry Lopez, *The American Geographies*, 669

Bobbie Ann Mason, *Being Country*, 135

Deirdre N. McCloskey, *Yes, Ma'am*, 173

Bill McKibben, *Designer Genes*, 500

Margaret Mead, *Warfare Is Only an Invention—Not a Biological Necessity*, 682

Plato, *The Allegory of the Cave*, 319

William E. Rees, *Life in the Lap of Luxury as Ecosystems Collapse*, 678

Richard Rodriguez, *Aria: A Memoir of a Bilingual Childhood*, 298

Scott Russell Sanders, *Under the Influence*, 209

Paul Starobin, *Misfit America*, 164

Amy Tan, *Mother Tongue*, 38

Henry David Thoreau, *Where I Lived, and What I Lived For*, 187

Sojourner Truth, *Ain't I a Woman?*, 373

E. B. White, *Once More to the Lake*, 194

Kenji Yoshino, *The Pressure to Cover*, 456

Definition

Paula Gunn Allen, *Voice of the Turtle*, 156

Nancy Andreasen, *The Creative Mind*, 263

Lynda Barry, *Hate*, 438

Judy Brady, *I Want a Wife*, 176

Stephanie Coontz, *Blaming the Family for Economic Decline*, 228

Charles Darwin, *Understanding Natural Selection*, 525

Joan Didion

   On Keeping a Notebook, 73

   Why I Write, 79

Frederick Douglass, *Resurrection*, 452

Brian Doyle, from *Joyas Voladoras*, 200

Stanley Fish, *Academic Cross-Dressing: How Intelligent Design Gets Its Arguments from the Left*, 532

Howard Gardner, *Who Owns Intelligence?*, 322

G. Anthony Gorry, *Steal This MP3 File: What Is Theft?*, 622

Richard Hoggart, *The Uses of Literacy*, 312

Thomas Jefferson, *The Declaration of Independence*, 369

John Kennedy, *The Purpose of Poetry*, 30

Martin Luther King Jr.
  Letter from Birmingham Jail, 565
  Martin Luther King Defines "Black Power," 586

Maxine Hong Kingston, *No Name Woman*, 420

Jonathan Kozol, *The Human Cost of an Illiterate Society*, 273

Abraham Lincoln, *The Gettysburg Address*, 690

Kenneth Lincoln, *Word Senders: Black Elk and N. Scott Momaday*, 123

Eric Liu, *Notes of a Native Speaker*, 112

Bobbie Ann Mason, *Being Country*, 135

Deirdre N. McCloskey, *Yes, Ma'am*, 173

Bill McKibben, *Designer Genes*, 500

Scott McCloud, *Understanding Comics*, 62

Margaret Mead, *Warfare Is Only an Invention—Not a Biological Necessity*, 682

N. Scott Momaday
  The Native Voice, 154
  The Way to Rainy Mountain, 145

Robert L. Park, *The Seven Warning Signs of Bogus Science*, 551

Octavio Paz, *The Labyrinth of Solitude*, 309

Pope John XXIII, *Disarmament*, 691

William E. Rees, *Life in the Lap of Luxury as Ecosystems Collapse*, 678

Richard Rodriguez
  Aria: A Memoir of a Bilingual Childhood, 298
  Family Values, 492

Scott Russell Sanders, *Under the Influence*, 209

Linda Simon, *The Naked Source*, 390

Wole Soyinka, *Every Dictator's Nightmare*, 475

Henry David Thoreau, *Civil Disobedience*, 192

Sojourner Truth, *Ain't I a Woman?*, 373

Alice Walker, *In Search of Our Mothers' Gardens*, 352

Eudora Welty, *Listening*, 33

Tom Wolfe, *The New Journalism*, 81

Kenji Yoshino, *The Pressure to Cover*, 456

Description

Stephen Jay Gould, *Evolution as Fact and Theory*, 512

Shirley Brice Heath, *Literate Traditions*, 280

Barry Lopez, *The American Geographies*, 669

N. Scott Momaday, *The Way to Rainy Mountain*, 145

Esmeralda Santiago, *Jíbara*, 129

Eudora Welty, *Listening*, 33

Dialogue

Amy Borkowsky, *Amy's Answering Machine*, 42
David Sedaris, *Old Faithful*, 222
Richard Wright, *Fighting Words*, 57

Editorial, Column, and Op-Ed

Michael J. Bugeja, *Facing the Facebook*, 626
David Dobbs, *Trial and Error*, 555
Stanley Fish, *Academic Cross-Dressing: How Intelligent Design Gets Its Arguments from the Left*, 532
G. Anthony Gorry, *Steal This MP3 File: What Is Theft?*, 622
New York Times, *Ending the Bilingual Double-Talk*, 276
N. Scott Momaday, *Disturbing the Spirits*, 153
Anna Quindlen, *Uncle Sam and Aunt Samantha*, 598
Ben Stein, *Birds and Bees? No, Let's Talk About Dollars and Cents*, 341

Graphic essay

Lynda Barry, *Hate*, 438
Scott McCloud, *Understanding Comics*, 62
Art Spiegelman
    from *Maus*, 418
    Mein Kampf (My Struggle), 139

Humor and Satire

Sherman Alexie, *What Sacagawea Means to Me*, 142
Anonymous, *How Many Virginia University Students Does it Take to Change a Lightbulb?*, 349
Amy Borkowsky, *Amy's Answering Machine*, 42
Roz Chast, *The I.M.s of Romeo and Juliet*, 102
Evan Eisenberg, *Dialogue Boxes You Should Have Read More Carefully*, 264
Frank Gannon, *Pre-Approved for Platinum*, 631
Garrison Keillor, *The Anthem: If Famous Poets Had Written "The Star-Spangled Banner,"* 88
Jacob Neusner, *The Speech the Graduates Didn't Hear*, 346
David Owen, *Your Three Wishes: F.A.Q.*, 713
David Sedaris, *Old Faithful*, 222

Illustration

Marjorie Agosín, *Always Living in Spanish*, 44
Sherman Alexie, *The Joy of Reading and Writing: Superman and Me*, 47
Karen Armstrong, *Does God Have a Future?*, 702
James Baldwin, *Stranger in the Village*, 118
Dennis Baron, *The New Technologies of the Word*, 92
Michael J. Bugeja, *Facing the Facebook*, 626

Cathy Davidson, *Laughing in English*, 493

Joan Didion, *On Keeping a Notebook*, 73

Barbara Ehrenreich, *Serving in Florida*, 243

Deborah Franklin, *"Informed Consent"—What Information? What Consent?*, 64

H. Bruce Franklin, *From Realism to Virtual Reality: Images of American Wars*, 402

Henry Louis Gates Jr., *Signifying*, 494

G. Anthony Gorry, *Steal This MP3 File: What Is Theft?*, 622

Stephen Jay Gould, *Evolution as Fact and Theory*, 512

Shirley Brice Heath, *Literate Traditions*, 280

Thomas Jefferson, *The Declaration of Independence*, 369

Beth Kephart, *Playing for Keeps*, 496

Martin Luther King Jr., *Letter from Birmingham Jail*, 565

Maxine Hong Kingston, *No Name Woman*, 420

Perri Klass, *The One-in-a-Thousand Illness You Can't Afford to Miss*, 260

Jonathan Kozol, *The Human Cost of an Illiterate Society*, 273

Eric Liu, *Notes of a Native Speaker*, 112

Barry Lopez, *The American Geographies*, 669

Bobbie Ann Mason, *Being Country*, 135

Scott McCloud, *Understanding Comics*, 62

Margaret Mead, *Warfare Is Only an Invention—Not a Biological Necessity*, 682

Gloria Naylor, *The Love of Books*, 69

George Orwell, *Shooting an Elephant*, 378

Plato, *The Allegory of the Cave*, 319

Anna Quindlen, *Anniversary*, 219

Richard Rodriguez, *Family Values*, 492

Elaine Scarry, *Acts of Resistance*, 484

David Sedaris, *Old Faithful*, 222

Linda Simon, *The Naked Source*, 390

Peter Singer, *The Singer Solution to World Poverty*, 601

Paul Starobin, *Misfit America*, 164

Henry David Thoreau
  Civil Disobedience, 192
  Where I Lived and What I Lived For, 187

Sojourner Truth, *Ain't I a Woman?*, 373

Alice Walker, *In Search of Our Mothers' Gardens*, 352

E. B. White, *Once More to the Lake*, 194

Terry Tempest Williams, *The Clan of One-Breasted Women*, 656

Kenji Yoshino, *The Pressure to Cover*, 456

Implied Argument

Sherman Alexie
  What Sacagawea Means to Me, 142
  The Joy of Reading and Writing: Superman and Me, 47

American Institutes for Research, *American College Grads—Barely Literate, and Beyond*, 337

Lynda Barry, *Hate*, 438

Roz Chast, *The I.M.s of Romeo and Juliet*, 102

Barbara Ehrenreich, *Serving in Florida*, 243

Evan Eisenberg, *Dialogue Boxes You Should Have Read More Carefully*, 264

Harriet Jacobs, *The Slaves' New Year's Day*, 449

Maxine Hong Kingston, *No Name Woman*, 420

George Orwell, *Shooting an Elephant*, 378

Richard Rodriguez, *Aria: A Memoir of a Bilingual Childhood*, 298

Zitkala-Sa, from *The School Days of an Indian Girl*, 292

Scott Russell Sanders, *Under the Influence*, 209

Art Spiegelman, from *Maus*, 418

Jonathan Swift, *A Modest Proposal*, 469

Interview

Amy Borkowsky, *Amy's Answering Machine*, 42

Robert Coles, *Two Languages, One Soul*, 496

Katherine Anne Porter, *You Do Not Create a Style. You Work . . .* , 86

Richard Rodriguez, *Interview (1994)*, 266

Alice Walker, *Eudora Welty: An Interview*, 180

List

Anonymous, *How Many Virginia University Students Does it Take to Change a Lightbulb?*, 349

Wendy Bishop, *Revision Is a Recursive Process*, 100

Confucius, from *The Analects*, 634

Benjamin Franklin, *Arriving at Moral Perfection*, 339

Thomas Jefferson, *The Declaration of Independence*, 369

John Kennedy, *The Purpose of Poetry*, 30

Eric Liu, *Notes of a Native Speaker*, 112

Bobbie Ann Mason, *Being Country*, 135

Deirdre N. McCloskey, *Yes, Ma'am*, 173

Robert L. Park, *The Seven Warning Signs of Bogus Science*, 551

Society of Professional Journalists, *Code of Ethics*, 638

Elizabeth Cady Stanton, *Declaration of Sentiments*, 375

Edward O. Wilson, *Microbes 3, Humans 2*, 530

Tom Wolfe, *The New Journalism*, 81

Metaphor

Judy Brady, *I Want a Wife*, 176

John Donne, *Meditation*, 590

W. E. B. Du Bois, *The "Veil" of Self-Consciousness*, 127

Barbara Ehrenreich, *Serving in Florida*, 243

H. Bruce Franklin, *From Realism to Virtual Reality: Images of American Wars*, 402

Henry Louis Gates Jr., *Signifying*, 494

N. Scott Momaday, *The Way to Rainy Mountain*, 145

Plato, *The Allegory of the Cave*, 319

Henry David Thoreau, *Where I Lived, and What I Lived For*, 187

Narration

Marjorie Agosín, *Always Living in Spanish*, 44

Sherman Alexie, *The Joy of Reading and Writing: Superman and Me*, 47

James Baldwin, *Stranger in the Village*, 118

Lynda Barry, *Hate*, 438

Frederick Douglass, *Resurrection*, 452

Harriet Jacobs, *The Slaves' New Year's Day*, 449

Stephen King, *Write or Die*, 28

Maxine Hong Kingston, *No Name Woman*, 420

Jonathan Kozol, *The Human Cost of an Illiterate Society*, 273

Eric Liu, *Notes of a Native Speaker*, 112

Bobbie Ann Mason, *Being Country*, 135

N. Scott Momaday, *The Way to Rainy Mountain*, 145

Gloria Naylor, *The Love of Books*, 69

George Orwell, *Shooting an Elephant*, 378

Plato, *The Allegory of the Cave*, 319

Anna Quindlen, *Anniversary*, 219

Richard Rodriguez, *Aria: A Memoir of a Bilingual Childhood*, 298

Zitkala-Sa, from *The School Days of an Indian Girl*, 292

Scott Russell Sanders, *Under the Influence*, 209

Esmeralda Santiago, *Jíbara*, 129

David Sedaris, *Old Faithful*, 222

Art Spiegelman
   from *Maus*, 418
   Mein Kampf (My Struggle), 139

Amy Tan, *Mother Tongue*, 38

Henry David Thoreau, *Where I Lived, and What I Lived For*, 187

José Antonio Villarreal, *Pocho*, 311

Eudora Welty, *Listening*, 33

E. B. White, *Once More to the Lake*, 194

Richard Wright, *Fighting Words*, 57

Parody

Garrison Keillor, *The Anthem: If Famous Poets Had Written "The Star-Spangled Banner,"* 88

David Sedaris, *What I Learned/And what I said at Princeton*, 348

Portrait

Scott Russell Sanders, *Under the Influence*, 209

Amy Tan, *Mother Tongue*, 38

Process Analysis

Sherman Alexie, *The Joy of Reading and Writing: Superman and Me*, 47

Wendy Bishop, *Revision Is a Recursive Process*, 100

Robert Coles, *Two Languages, One Soul*, 496

Joan Didion, *Why I Write*, 79

H. Bruce Franklin, *From Realism to Virtual Reality: Images of American Wars*, 402

Stephen King, *Write or Die*, 28

Eric Liu, *Notes of a Native Speaker*, 112

Deirdre N. McCloskey, *Yes, Ma'am*, 173

Bill McKibben, *Designer Genes*, 500

N. Scott Momaday, *The Native Voice*, 154

Gloria Naylor, *The Love of Books*, 69

George Orwell, *Shooting an Elephant*, 378

Robert L. Park, *The Seven Warning Signs of Bogus Science*, 551

Katherine Anne Porter, *You Do Not Create a Style. You Work . . .* , 86

Scott Russell Sanders, *Under the Influence*, 209

Linda Simon, *The Naked Source*, 390

Jonathan Swift, *A Modest Proposal*, 469

Speech

The Fourteenth Dalai Lama (Tenzin Gyatso), *Inner Peace and Human Rights*, 697

John F. Kennedy, *The Purpose of Poetry*, 30

Rigoberta Menchú, *Five Hundred Years of Mayan Oppression*, 694

David Sedaris, *What I Learned/And what I said at Princeton*, 348

Jackie Spinner, *The Only Thing You Should Be Advocating Is the Truth*, 344

Index of Titles and Authors

Academic Cross-Dressing: How Intelligent Design Gets Its Arguments from the Left (Fish), 532

Acts of Resistance (Scarry), 484

Agosín, Marjorie, *Always Living in Spanish*, 44

Ain't I a Woman? (Truth), 373

Alexie, Sherman

    The Joy of Reading and Writing: Superman and Me, 47

    What Sacagawea Means to Me, 145

Allegory of the Cave, The (Plato), 319

Allen, Paula Gunn, *Voice of the Turtle: American Indian Literature, 1900–1970*, 156

Always Living in Spanish (Agosín), 44

American College Grads — Barely Literate, and Beyond (American Institutes for Research), 337

American Geographies, The (Lopez), 669

American Institutes for Research, *American College Grads — Barely Literate, and Beyond*, 337

Amy's Answering Machine (Borkowsky), 42

Analects, The (Confucius), 634

Andreasen, Nancy, *The Creative Mind*, 262

Angier, Natalie, *Men, Women, Sex, and Darwin*, 538

Anniversary (Quindlen), 219

Anonymous, *How Many Virginia University Students Does It Take to Change a Lightbulb?*, 349

Anthem: If Famous Poets Had Written "The Star-Spangled Banner," The (Keillor), 88

Anzaldúa, Gloria, *Beyond Traditional Notions of Identity*, 159

Aria: Memoir of a Bilingual Childhood (Rodriguez), 298

Armstrong, Karen, *Does God Have a Future?*, 702

Arriving at Moral Perfection (Franklin), 339

Authentic Indian, An (Boaz and Hunt), 110

Autobiographical Notes (Baldwin), 360

Baldwin, James

    Autobiographical Notes, 360

    Stranger in the Village, 118

Baraka, Amiri, *The Myth of Negro Literature*, 361

Baron, Dennis, *The New Technologies of the Word*, 92

Barry, Lynda, *Hate* [graphic essay], 438

Behring, Natalie, *The Entrance Exam* [photograph], 318

Being Country (Mason), 135

Berry, Wendell, *A Secular Pilgrimage*, 653

Beyond Traditional Notions of Identity (Anzaldúa), 159

Binkley, T. Olin, *Southern Baptist Seminaries*, 583

Birds and Bees? No, Let's Talk About Dollars and Cents (Stein), 341

Bishop, Wendy, *Revision Is a Recursive Process*, 85

Blackburn, Sara, *Review of* The Woman Warrior, 431

Blaming the Family for Economic Decline (Coontz), 228

Boas, Franz and George Hunt, *An Authentic Indian* [photograph], 110

Bombeck, Erma, *Technology's Coming . . . Technology's Coming*, 560

Borkowsky, Amy, *Amy's Answering Machine*, 42

Boycotts Will Be Used (King), 586

Brooks, David, *The Elusive Altar*, 236

Brown, Kenneth A., *Steve Wozniak: Inventing the PC*, 181

Brown, Rita Mae, *Kissing Off Ma Bell*, 105

Buceja, Michael J., *Facing the Facebook*, 626

Carson, Rachel, *The Obligation to Endure*, 663

Carter, Keith, *Fireflies* [photograph], 655

Central High School, Little Rock, Arkansas, September 4, 1957 [photograph] (Counts), 396

Chast, Roz, *The I.M.s of Romeo and Juliet* [cartoon], 102

Chesnut, Mary, *Slavery a Curse to Any Land*, 415

Child of Two Cultures, The (Zweig), 314

Chin, Frank, *Come All Ye Asian American Writers of the Real and Fake*, 434

Civil Disobedience (Thoreau), 192

Clan of One-Breasted Women, The (Williams), 656

Coles, Robert, *Two Languages, One Soul*, 496

Come All Ye Asian American Writers of the Real and Fake (Chin), 434

Coming Home Again (Lee), 200

Confucius, *The Analects*, 634

Coontz, Stephanie, *Blaming the Family for Economic Decline*, 228

Counts, Will, *Central High School, Little Rock, Arkansas, September 4, 1957* [photograph], 396

Creating a Design (Murray), 108

Creative Mind, The (Andreasen), 262

Cure or Quest for Perfection? (Goodman), 498

Daemmrich, Bob, *Nobody Knows I'm Gay* [photograph], 468

Dalai Lama (Tenzin Gyatso), *Inner Peace and Human Rights*, 697

Damm Family in Their Car, Los Angeles, 1987, The [photograph] (Mark), 491

Darwin, Charles, *Understanding Natural Selection*, 525

Date Stamp (Mori), 267

Davidson, Cathy, *Laughing in English*, 493

Declaration of Independence, The (Jefferson), 369

Declaration of Sentiments (Stanton), 375

Designer Genes (McKibben), 500

Dialogue Boxes You Should Have Read More Carefully [graphic essay] (Eisenberg), 264

Didion, Joan
  On Keeping a Notebook, 73
  Why I Write, 79
  Last Words, 83
  Interview (1999), 84

Dillard, Annie, *Heaven and Earth in Jest*, 641

Disarmament (Pope John XXIII), 691

Disasters of War, The [paintings] (Goya), 400

Disturbing the Spirits (Momaday), 153

Dobbs, David, *Trial and Error*, 555

Does God Have a Future? (Armstrong), 702

Donne, John, *Meditation*, 590

Douglass, Frederick, *Resurrection*, 452

Doyle, Brian, *Joyas Voladoras*, 200

Du Bois, W. E. B., *The "Veil" of Self-Consciousness*, 127

East of My Grandmother's House (Momaday), 152

Eccentric Memories: A Conversation with Maxine Hong Kingston (Rabinowitz), 436

Eco, Umberto, *Ideal Operating Instructions*, 563

Economics of Authorship: Online Paper Mills, Student Writers, and First-Year Composition, The (Ritter), 615

Ehrenreich, Barbara, *Serving in Florida*, 243

Eight Clergymen's Statement, 580

Eisenberg, Evan, *Dialogue Boxes You Should Have Read More Carefully* [graphic essay], 264

Elbow, Peter, *Freewriting*, 106

Elusive Altar, The (Brooks), 236

Entrance Exam, The (Behring), 319

Entrance Exams, Deconstructed (Ivry), 335

Eudora Welty: An Interview (Walker), 180

Evans, Walker, *Ford River Rouge Plant, Michigan, 1947* [photograph], 242

Every Dictator's Nightmare (Soyinka), 475

Every Trip Is Unique (Theroux), 267

Evolution as Fact and Theory (Gould), 512

Evolution and Ethics (Huxley), 518

Facing the Facebook (Buceja), 626

Fadiman, Anne, *Marrying Libraries*, 60

Family and Soldiers in Iraq [photograph] (MacMillan), 689

Family Values (Rodriguez), 492

Fighting Words (Wright), 57

Fireflies [photograph] (Carter), 655

Fish, Stanley, *Academic Cross-Dressing: How Intelligent Design Gets Its Arguments from the Left*, 532

Five Hundred Years of Mayan Oppression (Menchú), 694

Flying Saucer (White), 561

Ford River Rouge Plant, Michigan, 1947 [photograph] (Evans), 242

Frank, Anne, *We Live in a Paradise Compared to the Jews Who Aren't in Hiding*, 416

Franklin, Benjamin, *Arriving at Moral Perfection*, 339

Franklin, Deborah, *"Informed Consent" — What Information? What Consent?*, 64

Franklin, H. Bruce, *From Realism to Virtual Reality: Images of American War*, 402

Freed, Leonard, *Martin Luther King Jr. after Receiving the Nobel Peace Prize, Baltimore, 1963* [photograph], 589

Freewriting (Elbow), 106

From Realism to Virtual Reality: Images of American War (Franklin), 402

Fundamentals of Islam, 636

Gannon, Frank, *Pre-Approved for Platinum*, 631

Gardner, Howard, *Who Owns Intelligence?*, 322

Gates, Henry Louis, Jr., *Signifying*, 494

George Washington (Jefferson), 164
Getting Started (Lamott), 107
Gettysburg Address, The (Lincoln), 690
Gladwell, Malcolm, *The Physical Genius*, 251
Gleick, James, *Stephen Jay Gould, Breaking Tradition with Darwin*, 523
Golden Rule—One or Many, Gold or Glitter?, The (Wattles), 592
Goodman, Ellen, *Cure or Quest for Perfection?*, 498
Gorry, G. Anthony, *Steal This MP3 File: What Is Theft?*, 622
Gould, Stephen Jay, *Evolution as Fact and Theory*, 512
Goya, Francisco, *The Disasters of War* [paintings], 400
Graduates, The (Henley), 111
Groskinsky, Henry, *Replaceable You* [photograph], 511

Hanover, David, *The Work of Writing* [photograph], 27
Hate [graphic essay] (Barry), 438
Have Good Sentences in Your Ears (Kenyon), 108
Hays, Brooks, *A Southern Moderate Speaks*, 579
Heath, Shirley Brice, *Literate Traditions*, 280
Heaven and Earth in Jest (Dillard), 641
Hemingway, Ernest, *Write Every Morning*, 105
Henley, John, *The Graduates*, 111
Herberg, Will, *A Religious "Right" to Violate the Law?*, 585
History of the Indian Mutiny 1857–8 (Kaye), 385
Hoggart, Richard, *The Uses of Literacy*, 312
How Many Virginia University Students Does It Take to Change a Lightbulb? (Anonymous), 349
Human Cost of an Illiterate Society, The (Kozol), 273
Hunt, George and Franz Boaz, *An Authentic Indian*, 110
Huxley, Thomas Henry, *Evolution and Ethics*, 518

Ideal Operating Instructions (Eco), 563
I Invented History (Momaday), 152
Imagined Life (Kingston), 435
I.M.s of Romeo and Juliet, The [cartoon] (Chast), 102
In a Country That Craved Respect, Stem Cell Scientist Rode a Wave of Korean Pride (Onishi), 548
"Informed Consent"—What Information? What Consent? (Franklin), 64
Inheritance of Tools, The (Sanders), 202
Inner Peace and Human Rights (Dalai Lama), 697

In Search of Our Mothers' Gardens (Walker), 352
Interview (1999) (Didion), 84
Interview with Accidental Movie Star Al Gore, An (Roberts), 183
Ivry, Sara, *Entrance Exams, Deconstructed*, 335

Jacobs, Harriet, *The Slaves' New Year's Day*, 449
Jíbara (Santiago), 129
Jefferson, Thomas
    The Declaration of Independence, 369
    George Washington, 164
Johnson, Phillip E., *The Unraveling of Scientific Materialism*, 520
Journal (Thoreau), 649
Joyas Voladoras (Doyle), 200
Joy of Reading and Writing: Superman and Me, The (Alexie), 47

Kapuscinski, Ryszard, *The Truck: Hitchhiking through Hell*, 271
Kaye, John, *History of the Indian Mutiny of 1857–8*, 385
Kazantzakis, Nikos, *Report to Greco*, 652
Keillor, Garrison, *The Anthem: If Famous Poets Had Written "The Star-Spangled Banner,"* 88
Kennedy, John, *The Purpose of Poetry*, 30
Kenyon, Jane, *Have Good Sentences in Your Ears*, 108
Kephart, Beth, *Playing for Keeps*, 496
King, Martin Luther, Jr.
    Boycotts Will Be Used, 586
    Letter from Birmingham Jail, 565
    Martin Luther King Jr. Defends "Black Power," 586
King, Stephen, *Write or Die*, 28
King and Abernathy [photograph], 582
King and Abernathy Under Arrest [photograph], 581
Kingston, Maxine Hong
    Imagined Life, 435
    Interview (1982), 429, 433
    Interview (1998), 431
    No Name Woman, 420
Kipling, Rudyard, *The White Man's Burden*, 384
Kissing Off Ma Bell (Brown), 105
Klass, Perri, *The One-in-a-Thousand Illness You Can't Afford to Miss*, 260
Kleege, Georgina, *Up Close, In Touch*, 65
Koran, Al-Mu' Menoon ("The Believers"), 651
Kozol, Jonathan, *The Human Cost of an Illiterate Society*, 273

Labyrinth of Solitude, The (Paz), 309
Lamott, Anne, *Getting Started*, 107

Lange, Dorothea, *Migrant Mother* [photograph], 351

Language and Literature from a Pueblo Indian Perspective (Silko), 287

Last Words (Didion), 83

Laughing in English (Davidson), 493

Learning the River (Twain), 268

Lee, Chang-Rae, *Coming Home Again*, 200

Legacy of Divorce, The (Wallerstein), 238

Lebowitz, Fran, *The Sound of Music: Enough Already*, 562

Letter from Birmingham Jail (King), 565

Life and Death at Princeton (Will), 607

Life in the Lap of Luxury as Ecosystems Collapse (Rees), 678

Lincoln, Abraham, *The Gettysburg Address*, 690

Listening (Welty), 33

Literacy in Progress [photograph] (Maze), 297

Literate Traditions (Heath), 280

Liu, Eric, *Notes of a Native Speaker*, 112

Looking at the Unbearable (Sontag), 397

Looking to the Side, and Back (Walker), 364

Lopez, Barry, *The American Geographies*, 669

Love of Books, The (Naylor), 51

MacMillan, Jim, *Family and Soldiers in Iraq* [photograph], 689

Mark, Mary Ellen, *The Damm Family in Their Car, Los Angeles, 1987* [photograph], 491

Marrying Libraries (Fadiman), 60

Martin Luther King Jr. after Receiving the Nobel Peace Prize, Baltimore, 1963 [photograph] (Freed), 589

Martin Luther King Jr. Defends "Black Power" (King), 587

Mason, Bobbie Ann, *Being Country*, 135

Maus [graphic essay] (Spiegelman), 418

Mayes, Frances, *On Writing* Under the Tuscan Sun, 184

Maze, Stephanie, *Literacy in Progress* [photograph], 297

McCloskey, Deirdre N., *Yes, Ma'am*, 173

McCloud, Scott, *Reading the Comics* [graphic essay], 62

McKibben, Bill, *Designer Genes*, 500

Mead, Margaret, *Warfare Is Only an Invention — Not a Biological Necessity*, 682

Meditation (Donne), 590

Mein Kampf (My Struggle) [graphic essay] (Spiegelman), 139

Menchú, Rigoberta, *Five Hundred Years of Mayan Oppression*, 694

Men, Women, Sex, and Darwin (Angier), 538

Microbes 3, Humans 2 (Wilson), 530

Migrant Mother [photograph] (Lange), 351

Misfit America (Starobin), 164

Modest Proposal, A (Swift), 469

Momaday, N. Scott
  Disturbing the Spirits, 153
  East of My Grandmother's House, 152
  I Invented History, 152
  Native Voice, The, 154
  Three Voices, 155
  The Way to Rainy Mountain, 145
  The Whole Journey, 155

Mori, Kyoko, *Date Stamp*, 267

Morris, Mary, *My First Night Alone in Mexico*, 272

Morrison, Toni, *The Pain of Being Black*, 368

Mother Tongue (Tan), 38

Moynihan, Daniel Patrick, *The Negro Family: The Case for National Action*, 362

Murray, Donald M., *Creating a Design*, 108

My First Night Alone in Mexico (Morris), 272

Myth of Negro Literature, The (Baraka), 361

Naked Source, The (Simon), 390

Native Voice, The (Momaday), 154

Naylor, Gloria, *The Love of Books*, 51

Negro Family: The Case for National Action, The (Moynihan), 362

Neusner, Jacob, *The Speech the Graduates Didn't Hear*, 346

Never Correct Anybody's English (Rosenblatt), 104

New Journalism, The (Wolfe), 81

New Technologies of the Word, The (Baron), 92

Night Battle, A (Whitman), 414

Nobody Knows I'm Gay [photograph] (Daemmrich), 468

No Name Woman (Kingston), 420

Notes of a Native Speaker (Liu), 112

Obligation to Endure, The (Carson), 663

Old Faithful (Sedaris), 222

Once More to the Lake (White), 194

One-in-a-Thousand Illness You Can't Afford to Miss, The (Klass), 260

Onishi, Norimitsu, *In a Country That Craved Respect, Stem Cell Scientist Rode a Wave of Korean Pride*, 548

On Keeping a Notebook (Didion), 73

Only Thing You Should Be Advocating Is the Truth, The (Spinner), 344

On Writing Under the Tuscan Sun (Mayes), 184

Orwell, George, *Shooting an Elephant*, 378

Orwell and the Politics of Despair (Rai), 386

Orwell Now (Pearce), 388

Owen, David, *Your Three Wishes: F.A.Q.*, 713

Pain of Being Black, The (Morrison), 368

Park, Robert L., *The Seven Warning Signs of Bogus Science*, 551

Pascal, Blaise, *Pensées*, 652

Paz, Octavio, *The Labyrinth of Solitude*, 309

Pearce, Robert, *Orwell Now*, 388

Pensées (Pascal), 652

Physical Genius, The (Gladwell), 251

Plato, *The Allegory of the Cave*, 319

Playing for Keeps (Kephart), 496

Pocho (Villareal), 311

Pope John XXIII, *Disarmament*, 691

Porter, Katherine Anne, *You Do Not Create a Style. You Work. . . .*, 86

Posner, Richard A., *Security versus Civil Liberties*, 480

Postel, Sandra, *Troubled Waters*, 675

Pre-Approved for Platinum (Gannon), 631

Pressure to Cover, The (Yoshino), 456

Proulx, Annie, *Travel Is . . . An Unnerving Experience*, 269

Purpose of Poetry, The (Kennedy), 30

Quindlen, Anna
 Anniversary, 219
 Uncle Sam and Aunt Samantha, 598

Rabinowitz, Paul, *Eccentric Memories: A Conversation with Maxine Hong Kingston*, 436

Rai, Alok, *Orwell and the Politics of Despair*, 386

Reading the Comics [graphic essay] (McCloud), 62

Rees, William E., *Life in the Lap of Luxury as Ecosystems Collapse*, 678

Religious "Right" to Violate the Law?, A (Herberg), 583

Replaceable You [photograph] (Groskinsky), 511

Report to Greco (Kazantzakis), 652

Resurrection (Douglass), 452

Review of The Woman Warrior (Blackburn), 431

Revision Is a Recursive Process (Bishop), 85

Rising Sea Levels—An Alternative Theory (Warp), 677

Ritter, Kelly, *The Economics of Authorship: Online Paper Mills, Student Writers, and First-Year Composition*, 615

Roberts, Dave, *An Interview with Accidental Movie Star Al Gore*, 183

Rodriguez, Richard
 Aria: Memoir of a Bilingual Childhood, 298
 Family Values, 492
 Interview (1999), 315

Interview Excerpt, 308

Slouching Towards Los Angeles, 308

Roosevelt, Theodore, *What College Graduates Owe America*, 343

Rosenblatt, Roger, *Never Correct Anybody's English*, 104

Sanders, Scott Russell
 The Inheritance of Tools, 202
 Under the Influence: Paying the Price of My Father's Booze, 209

Santiago, Esmeralda, *Jíbara*, 129

Scarry, Elaine, *Acts of Resistance*, 484

School Days of an Indian Girl, The (Zitkala-Sa), 292

Sedaris, David
 Old Faithful, 222
 What I Learned/And what I Said at Princeton, 348

Secular Pilgrimage, A (Berry), 653

Security versus Civil Liberties (Posner), 480

Serving in Florida (Ehrenreich), 243

Seven Warning Signs of Bogus Science, The (Park), 551

Shooting an Elephant (Orwell), 378

Signifying (Gates), 494

Silko, Leslie Marmon, *Language and Literature from a Pueblo Indian Perspective*, 287

Simon, Linda, *The Naked Source*, 390

Simonds, Wendy, *Talking with Strangers: A Researcher's Tale*, 611

Singer, Peter, *The Singer Solution to World Poverty*, 601

Singer Solution to World Poverty, The (Singer), 601

Slavery a Curse to Any Land (Chesnut), 415

Slaves' New Year's Day, The (Jacobs), 449

Slouching Towards Los Angeles (Rodriguez), 308

Society of Professional Journalists Code of Ethics, 638

Sontag, Susan, *Looking at the Unbearable*, 397

Sound of Music: Enough Already, The (Lebowitz), 562

Southern Baptist Seminaries (Binkley), 583

Southern Moderate Speaks, A (Hays), 579

Soyinka, Wole, *Every Dictator's Nightmare*, 475

Speech the Graduates Didn't Hear, The (Neusner), 346

Spiegelman, Art
 Maus [graphic essay], 418
 Mein Kampf (My Struggle) [graphic essay], 142

Spinner, Jackie, *The Only Thing You Should Be Advocating Is the Truth*, 344

Stanton, Elizabeth Cady, *Declaration of Sentiments*, 375

Starobin, Paul, *Misfit America*, 164

Steal This MP3 File: What Is Theft? (Gorry), 622

Stein, Ben, *Birds and Bees? No, Let's Talk About Dollars and Cents*, 341

Stephen Jay Gould, *Breaking Tradition with Darwin* (Gleick), 523

Steve Wozniak, *Inventing the PC* (Brown), 181

Stranger in the Village (Baldwin), 118

Swift, Jonathan, *A Modest Proposal*, 469

Talking with Strangers: A Researcher's Tale (Simonds), 611

Tan, Amy, *Mother Tongue*, 38

Technology's Coming . . . Technology's Coming (Bombeck), 560

Telling Stories (Thurber), 104

Ten Commandents, The, 636

Theroux, Paul, *Every Trip Is Unique*, 267

Thoreau, Henry David
    Civil Disobedience, 192
    Journal, 649
    Where I Lived and What I Lived For, 187

Three Voices (Momaday), 155

Thurber, James
    Telling Stories, 104
    The Wild-Eyed Edison's Dangerous Experiments, 559

Travel Is . . . an Unnerving Experience (Proulx), 269

Trial and Error (Dobbs), 555

Trillin, Calvin, *Writing about Family*, 185

Troubled Waters (Postel), 675

Truck: Hitchhiking through Hell, The (Kapuscinski), 271

Truth, Sojourner, *Ain't I a Woman?*, 373

Twain, Mark, *Learning the River*, 268

Two Languages, One Soul (Coles), 496

Uncle Sam and Aunt Samantha (Quindlen), 600

Understanding Natural Selection (Darwin), 525

Unraveling of Scientific Materialism, The (Johnson), 520

Up Close, In Touch (Kleege), 65

Uses of Literacy, The (Hoggart), 312

"Veil" of Self-Consciousness, The (Du Bois), 127

Villareal, José Antonio, *Pocho*, 311

Voice of the Turtle: American Indian Literature, 1900–1970, The (Allen), 156

Walker, Alice
    Eudora Welty: An Interview, 180

In Search of Our Mothers' Gardens, 352
    Interview (1983), 367
    Looking to the Side, and Back, 364

Wallerstein, Judith, *The Legacy of Divorce*, 238

Warfare Is Only an Invention—Not a Biological Necessity (Mead), 682

Warp, Kim, *Rising Sea Levels—An Alternative Theory* [cartoon], 677

Wattles, Jeffrey, *The Golden Rule—One or Many, Gold or Glitter?*, 592

Way to Rainy Mountain (Momaday), 145

We Live in a Paradise Compared to the Jews Who Aren't in Hiding (Frank), 416

Welty, Eudora, *Listening*, 33

What College Graduates Owe America (Roosevelt), 343

What I Learned/And What I Said at Princeton (Sedaris), 348

What Sacagawea Means to Me (Alexie), 142

Where I Lived and What I Lived For (Thoreau), 187

White, Bailey, *Flying Saucer*, 561

White, E. B., *Once More to the Lake*, 194

White Man's Burden, The (Kipling), 384

Whitman, Walt, *A Night Battle*, 414

Whole Journey, The (Momaday), 155

Who Owns Intelligence? (Gardner), 322

Why Are There So Many Single Americans? (Zernike), 233

Why I Write (Didion), 79

Wild-Eyed Edison's Dangerous Experiments, The (Thurber), 559

Will, George, *Life and Death at Princeton*, 607

Williams, Terry Tempest, *The Clan of One-Breasted Women*, 656

Wilson, Edward O., *Microbes 3, Humans 2*, 530

Wolfe, Tom, *The New Journalism*, 81

Work of Writing, The [photograph] (Hanover), 27

Wright, Richard, *Fighting Words*, 57

Write Every Morning (Hemingway), 105

Write or Die (King), 28

Writing about Family (Trillin), 185

Yes, Ma'am (McCloskey), 173

Yoshino, Kenji, *The Pressure to Cover*, 456

You Do Not Create a Style. You Work . . . (Porter), 86

Your Three Wishes: F.A.Q. (Owen), 713

Zernike, Kate, *Why Are There So Many Single Americans?*, 233

Zitkala-Sa, *The School Days of an Indian Girl*, 292

Zweig, Paul, *The Child of Two Cultures*, 314

Need more help with writing and research?
Visit Bedford/St. Martin's Re:Writing.

Re:Writing is designed to help with important writing concerns. You'll find advice from experts, models you can rely on, and exercises that will tell you right away how you're doing. And it's all free and available any hour of the day. All of these can be accessed at bedfordstmartins.com/rewriting.

Need help with grammar problems?

Exercise Central (bedfordstmartins.com/exercisecentral)

Want to see what papers for your other courses look like?

Model Documents Gallery (bedfordstmartins.com/modeldocs)

Stuck somewhere in the research process? (Maybe at the beginning?)

The Bedford Research Room (bedfordstmartins.com/researchroom)

Wondering whether a Web site is good enough to use in your paper?

Tutorial for Evaluating Online Sources
(bedfordstmartins.com/onlinesourcestutorial)

Having trouble figuring out how to cite a source?

Research and Documentation Online (bedfordstmartins.com/resdoc)

Confused about plagiarism?

The St. Martin's Tutorial on Avoiding Plagiarism
(bedfordstmartins.com/plagiarismtutorial)

Want to get more out of your word processor?

Using Your Word Processor
(bedfordstmartins.com/wordprocessor)

Trying to improve the look of your paper?

Using Your Word Processor to Design Documents
(bedfordstmartins.com/docdesigntutorial)

Need to create slides for a presentation?

Preparing Presentation Slides Tutorial
(bedfordstmartins.com/presentationslidetutorial)

Interested in creating a Web site?

Web Design Tutorial (bedfordstmartins.com/webdesigntutorial)